Mastering™
Visual Basic® .NET

Evangelos Petroutsos

SYBEX® San Francisco   London

Associate Publisher: Richard Mills

Acquisitions Editor: Denise Santoro Lincoln

Developmental Editor: Tom Cirtin

Editors: Pete Gaughan, Linda Recktenwald

Production Editor: Kylie Johnston

Technical Editors: Jesse Patterson, Greg Guntle

Book Designer: Maureen Forys, Happenstance Type-O-Rama

Graphic Illustrator: Tony Jonick

Electronic Publishing Specialist: Maureen Forys, Happenstance Type-O-Rama

Proofreaders: Nanette Duffy, Amey Garber, Dave Nash, Laurie O'Connell, Yariv Rabinovitch, Nancy Riddiough

Indexer: Ted Laux

CD Coordinator: Christine Detlefs

CD Technician: Keith McNeil

Cover Designer: Design Site

Cover Illustrator/Photographer: Sergie Loobkoff

Library of Congress Card Number: 2001094602

ISBN: 0-7821-2877-7

To my family

Acknowledgments

MANY PEOPLE CONTRIBUTED to this book, and I would like to thank them all. I guess I should start with the programmers at Microsoft, for their commitment to Visual Basic. Visual Basic has evolved from a small, limited programming environment to a first-class development tool.

Special thanks to the talented people at Sybex—to all of them and to each one individually. I'll start with editor Pete Gaughan, who has taken this book personally and improved it in numerous ways. Thanks, Pete. Thank you to developmental editor Tom Cirtin, who has followed the progress of the book, its ups and downs, and managed to coordinate the entire team. To technical editors Jesse Patterson and Greg Guntle for scrutinizing every paragraph and every line of code. To production editor Kylie Johnston, who has done more than I can guess to keep this project in order and on schedule. To designer and compositor Maureen Forys, and everyone else who added their expertise and talent. Thank you all!

I'd like to thank and recognize Matt Tagliaferri for contributing Chapter 17, on exception handling.

I would also like to thank Alvaro Antunes and Harry Heijkoop for their helpful remarks while they were translating earlier versions of *Mastering Visual Basic* into Portuguese and Dutch, respectively.

Contents at a Glance

Contents

Introduction

WELCOME TO .NET AND VISUAL BASIC .NET. As you already know, .NET is a name for a new strategy: a blueprint for building applications for the next decade. It's actually even more than that. It's Microsoft's commitment to remain at the top of a rapidly changing world and give us the tools to address the needs of tomorrow's computing. Visual Basic .NET is a language for creating .NET applications, like many others. It also happens that Visual Basic is the easiest to learn, most productive language (but you already know that).

Visual Basic .NET is released shortly after the tenth anniversary of the first version of VB. The original language that changed the landscape of computing has lasted for 10 years and has enabled more programmers to write Windows application than any other language. Programmers who invested in Visual Basic 10 years ago are in demand today. In the world of computing, however, things change very fast, including languages. At some point, they either die, or they evolve into something new. Visual Basic was a language designed primarily for developing Windows applications. It was a simple language, because it managed to hide many of the low-level details of the operating system. Those who wanted to do more with Visual Basic had to resort to Windows API. In a way, earlier versions of Visual Basic were 'sandboxed' to protect developers from scary details.

Microsoft had to redesign Visual Basic. The old language just didn't belong in the .NET picture (at least, it wouldn't integrate very well into the picture). Visual Basic .NET is not VB7; it's a drastic departure from VB6, but a necessary departure. Visual Basic .NET was designed to take us through the next decade of computing, and if you want to stay ahead, you will have to invest the time and effort to learn it.

The most fundamental component of the .NET initiative is the .NET Framework, or simply the Framework. You can think of the Framework as an enormous collection of functions for just about any programming task. All drawing methods, for example, are part of the System.Drawing class. To draw a rectangle, you call the DrawRectangle method, passing the appropriate arguments. To create a new folder, you call the CreateDirectory method of the Directory class; to retrieve the files in a folder, you call the GetFiles method of the same object. The Framework contains all the functionality of the operating system and makes it available to your application through numerous methods.

VB was such a success because it was a very simple language. You didn't have to learn a lot before you could start using the language. Being able to access the Framework's objects means that you're no longer limited by the language. The new version of the language unlocks the full potential of .NET; now there's hardly anything you can do with another language but can't do with Visual Basic. This makes the language as powerful as any other language, but it also makes the learning curve steeper. The good news is that, if you get started today, you'll get a head start, which may well last for another decade.

Who Should Read This Book?

You don't need to know Visual Basic to read *Mastering Visual Basic .NET*, but you do need a basic understanding of programming. You need to know the meaning of variables and functions and how an If…Then structure works. This book is addressed to the typical programmer who wants to get the most out of Visual Basic. It covers the topics I feel are of use to most VB programmers, and it does so in depth. Visual Basic .NET is an extremely rich programming environment, and I've had to choose between superficial coverage of many topics and in-depth coverage of fewer topics. To make room for more topics, I have avoided including a lot of reference material and lengthy listings. For example, you won't find complete project listings or Form descriptions. I assume you can draw a few controls on a Form and set their properties, and you don't need long descriptions of the properties of the control. I'm also assuming that you don't want to read the trivial segments of each application. Instead, the listings concentrate on the "meaty" part of the code: the procedures that explain the topic at hand. If you want to see the complete listing, it's all on the CD.

The topics covered in this book were chosen to provide a solid understanding of the principles and techniques for developing applications with Visual Basic. Programming isn't about new keywords and functions. I chose the topics I felt every programmer should learn in order to master the language. I was also motivated by my desire to present useful, practical examples. You will not find all topics equally interesting or important. My hope is that everyone will find something interesting and something of value to their daily work—whether it's an application that maps the folders and files of a drive to a TreeView control, an application that prints tabular data, or an application that saves a collection of objects to a file.

Many books offer their readers long, numbered sequences of steps to accomplish something. Following instructions simplifies certain tasks, but programming isn't about following instructions. It's about being creative; it's about understanding principles and being able to apply the same techniques in several practical situations. And the way to creatively exploit the power of a language such as Visual Basic .NET is to understand its principles and its programming model.

In many cases, I provide a detailed, step-by-step procedure that will help you accomplish a task, such as designing a menu. But not all tasks are as simple as designing menus. I explain why things must be done in a certain way, and I present alternatives and try to connect new topics to those explained earlier in the book. In several chapters, I expand on applications developed in earlier chapters. Associating new knowledge to something you have already mastered provides positive feedback and a deeper understanding of the language.

This book isn't about the hottest features of the language; it's about solid programming techniques and practical examples. For example, I'm not going to show you how to write multithreaded applications. The real challenge with multithreaded applications is their debugging, which requires substantial experience. Once you master the basics of programming Windows applications with Visual Basic .NET and you feel comfortable with the more advanced examples of the book, you will find it easy to catch up with the topics that aren't discussed.

How About the Advanced Topics?

Some of the topics discussed in this book are non-trivial, and quite a few topics can be considered advanced. The TreeView control, for example, is not a trivial control, like the Button or TextBox control, but it's ideal for displaying hierarchical information (this is the control that displays the hierarchy of folders in Windows Explorer). If you want to build an elaborate user interface, you should be able to program controls like the TreeView control, which is discussed in Chapter 16. (But you need not read that chapter before you decide to use this control in a project.)

You may also find some examples to be more difficult than you expected. I have tried to make the text and the examples easy to read and understand, but not unrealistically simple. In Chapter 13, you'll find information about the File and Directory objects. You can use these objects to access and manipulate the file system from within your application, but this chapter wouldn't be nearly as useful without an application that shows you how to scan a folder recursively (scan the folder's files and then its subfolders, to any depth). To make each chapter as useful as I could, I've included complex examples, which will provide a better understanding of the topics. In addition, many of these examples can be easily incorporated into your applications.

You can do a lot with the TreeView control with very little programming, but in order to make the most out of this control, you must be ready for some advanced programming. Nothing terribly complicated, but some things just aren't simple. Programming most of the operations of the TreeView control, for instance, is straightforward, but if your application calls for populating a TreeView with an arbitrary number of branches (such as mapping a directory structure to a TreeView), the code can get involved.

The reason I've included the more advanced examples is that the corresponding chapters would be incomplete without them. If you find some material to be over your head at first reading, you can skip it and come back to it after you have mastered other aspects of the language. But don't let a few advanced examples intimidate you. Most of the techniques are well within the reach of an average VB programmer. The few advanced topics were included for the readers who are willing to take that extra step and build elaborate interfaces using the latest tools and techniques.

There's another good reason for including advanced topics. Explaining a simple topic, like how to populate a collection with items, is very simple. But what good is it to populate a collection if you don't know how to save it to disk and read back its items in a later session? Likewise, what good is it to learn how to print simple text files? In a business environment, you will most likely be asked to print a tabular report, which is substantially more complicated than printing text. In Chapter 15 you will learn how to print business reports with headers, footers, and page numbers, and even how to draw grids around the rows and columns of the report. One of my goals in writing this book was to exhaust the topics I've chosen to discuss and to present all the information you need to do something practical.

The Structure of the Book

Mastering Visual Basic .NET isn't meant to be read from cover to cover, and I know that most people don't read computer books this way. Each chapter is independent of the others, although all chapters contain references to other chapters. Each topic is covered in depth; however, I make no assumptions about the reader's knowledge on the topic. As a result, you may find the introductory sections of a chapter too simple. The topics become progressively more advanced, and even experienced programmers will find some new information in each chapter. Even if you are familiar with the topics in a chapter, take a look at the examples. I have tried to simplify many of the advanced topics and demonstrate them with clear, practical examples.

VB6 ➠ VB.NET

Experienced Visual Basic programmers should pay attention to these special sidebars with the "VB6 to VB.NET" icon, which calls your attention to changes in the language. These sections usually describe new features in VB.NET or enhancements of VB6 features, but also VB6 features that are no longer supported by VB.NET.

This book tries to teach through examples. Isolated topics are demonstrated with short examples, and at the end of many chapters, you'll build a large, practical, real-world app that "puts together" the topics and techniques discussed throughout the chapter. You may find some of the more advanced applications a bit more difficult to understand, but you shouldn't give up. Simpler applications would have made my job easier, but the book wouldn't deserve the *Mastering* title and your knowledge of Visual Basic wouldn't be as complete.

In the first part of the book, we'll go through the fundamentals of Visual Basic .NET. You'll learn how to design visual interfaces with point-and-click operations, and how to program a few simple events, like the click of the mouse on a button. After reading the first two chapters, you'll understand the structure of a Windows application. Then we'll explore the elements of the visual interface (the basic Windows controls) and how to program them.

The second part of the book is about building and using objects. Visual Basic .NET is a truly object-oriented language, and objects are the recurring theme in every chapter. Part II is a formal and more systematic treatment of objects. You will learn how to build custom classes and controls, which will help you understand object-oriented programming a little better.

In the third part of the book, we'll discuss some of the most common classes of the Framework. The Framework is the core of .NET. It's your gateway to the functionality of the operating system itself, and it's going to be incorporated into the next version of Windows. In Part III we'll examine collections (like ArrayLists and HashTables), the objects for manipulating files and folders, the StringBuilder object that manipulates text, and a few more.

The fourth part of the book is a collection of intermediate to advanced topics. It includes chapters on graphics and printing, an overview of the debugging tools, and a chapter on recursive programming—a very powerful programming technique. You will also find a chapter on building Multiple Document Interfaces—an interface that hosts multiple windows, each one displaying a different document.

The fifth part of the book is an overview of the data access tools. The emphasis is on the visual tools, and you will learn how to query databases and present data to the user. You will also find information on programming the basic objects of ADO.NET.

Part VI is about Web applications. Here you will learn the basics of ASP .NET, how to develop Web applications, and how to write Web services. Web applications are written Visual Basic .NET, but they deploy a user interface that consists of HTML pages and interact with the user through the browser. Web services are functions that can be called from anywhere, and they're one of the most promising features of the .NET Platform.

Mastering Visual Basic .NET does not cover all the topics you can think of. I hope I've chosen the topics you'll encounter most often in your daily tasks and I've covered them in enough detail, to help you understand the basics and be able to look up more specific topics in the product documentation.

How to Reach the Author

Despite our best efforts, a book this size is bound to contain errors. Although a printed medium isn't as easy to update as a Web site, I will spare no effort to fix every problem you report (or I discover). The revised applications, along with any other material I think will be of use to the readers of this book, will be posted on the Sybex Web site. If you have any problems with the text or the applications in this book, you can contact me directly at pevangelos@yahoo.com.

Although I can't promise a response to every question, I will fix any problems in the examples and provide updated versions. I would also like to hear any comments you may have on the book, about the topics you liked or did not like, and how useful the examples are. Your comments will be taken into consideration in future editions.

Part I

The Fundamentals

Chapter 1

Getting Started with VB.NET

WELCOME TO THE ENTERPRISE Edition of Visual Basic .NET. I'm assuming you have installed Visual Studio .NET, Enterprise Edition. You may have even already explored the new environment on your own, but this book doesn't require any knowledge of Visual Basic 6. It doesn't require anything more than a familiarity with programming. As you already know, Visual Basic .NET is just one of the languages you can use to build applications with Visual Studio .NET. I happen to be convinced that it is also the simplest, most convenient language, but this isn't really the issue. What you should keep in mind is that Visual Studio .NET is an integrated environment for building, testing, and debugging a variety of applications: Windows applications, Web applications, classes and custom controls, even console applications. It provides numerous tools for automating the development process, visual tools to perform many common design and programming tasks, and more features than any author would hope to cover.

The first thing you must learn is the environment you'll be working in from now on. In the first chapter of this book, you'll familiarize yourself with the integrated development environment (IDE) and how its tools allow you to quickly design the user interface of your application, as well as how to program the application.

It will be a while before you explore all the items of the IDE. Visual Studio is an environment for developing all types of applications, from a simple Windows application to a complete Web app involving databases and XML files. I will explain the various items as needed in the course of the book. In this chapter, we'll look at the basic components of the IDE needed to build simple Windows applications.

The Integrated Development Environment

Visual Studio .NET is an environment for developing Windows and Web applications. Visual Basic .NET is just one of the languages you can use to program your applications. Actually, Visual Studio .NET was designed to host any language, and many companies are working on languages that will be integrated in Visual Studio .NET. Some people will develop Windows applications in Visual Studio .NET with COBOL, or FORTRAN.

So, what's the distinction between Visual Studio .NET and the language? Visual Studio .NET is the environment that provides all the necessary tools for developing applications. The language is only one aspect of a Windows application. The visual interface of the application isn't tied to a specific language, and the same tools you'll use to develop your application's interface will also be used by all programmers, regardless of the language they'll use to code the application.

The tools you'll use to access databases are also independent of the language. Visual Studio provides tools that allow you to connect to a database, inspect its objects, retrieve the information you're interested in, and even store it in objects that can be accessed from within any language.

There are many visual tools in the IDE, like the Menu Designer. This tool allows you to visually design menus and to set their names and basic properties (such as checking, enabling, or disabling certain options). Designing a menu doesn't involve any code, and it's carried out with point-and-click operations. Of course, you will have to insert some code behind the commands of your menus, and (again) you can use any language to program them.

To simplify the process of application development, Visual Studio .NET provides an environment that's common to all languages, which is known as *integrated development environment (IDE)*. The purpose of the IDE is to enable the developer to do as much as possible with visual tools, before writing code. The IDE provides tools for designing, executing, and debugging your applications. It's your second desktop, and you'll be spending most of your productive hours in this environment.

The Start Page

When you run Visual Studio for the first time, you will see the window shown in Figure 1.1. On the My Profile tab, you will set your personal preferences by specifying your language. Select Visual Basic Developer in the Profile box, and the other two boxes will be filled automatically. You can leave the other fields to their default values. The ComboBox control at the bottom of the page, the At Startup control, is where you define what you want Visual Studio .NET to do when it starts. The choices are the following:

Show Start Page   Every time you start Visual Studio .NET, this page will appear.

Load Last Loaded Solution   Once you start working on a real project (a project that will take you from a few days to a few months to complete), select this option so that the project will be loaded automatically every time you start Visual Studio .NET.

Show Open Project Dialog Box   Every time you start Visual Studio .NET, the Open Project dialog box will appear, where you can select a project to open.

Show New Project Dialog Box   Every time you start Visual Studio .NET, the New Project dialog box will appear, where you can specify the name of a new project—a setting to avoid.

Show Empty Environment   This option instructs Visual Studio .NET to start a new empty solution, and you're responsible for adding new or existing projects to the solution and new or existing items to a project.

The actions are self-explanatory, and the most common setting is to show the Start Page. The Start Page displays the four most recently opened projects, as well as the New Project and Open Project buttons. To see the Start Page, select the Get Started option.

FIGURE 1.1

This is what you'll
see when you start
Visual Studio for
the first time.

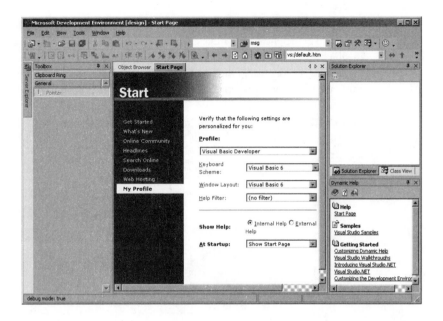

The remaining options lead to Visual Studio sites with up-to-date information about the product, such as news articles, updated documents, and service packs or patches. At the very least, you should switch to the Downloads option from time to time to check for updates. The installation of the updates should be automatic—after you confirm your intention to download and update any new component, of course.

The Web Hosting option leads to a page with information about ISPs that support ASP.NET. You will need the services of these ISPs to post an actual Web application or Web services to the Internet. Web applications and Web services are two types of projects you can develop with Visual Studio (they're discussed in the last part of the book). These projects aren't distributed to users; instead, they run on a Web server; users must connect to the URL of the Web server and run the application in their browser.

NOTE *The official names of the products are Visual Studio .NET and Visual Basic .NET. Throughout the book I will refer to the language as VB.NET and mostly as VB. When referring to the previous version of the language, I will use VB6.*

STARTING A NEW PROJECT

At this point, you can create a new project and start working with Visual Basic .NET. To best explain the various items of the IDE, we are going to build a simple form—it's not even an application. The form is the window of your application—what users will see on their desktop when they run your application.

Open the File menu and select New ➤ Project. In the New Project dialog box (Figure 1.2), you will see a list of project types you can create with Visual Studio. Select the Windows Application template, and Visual Studio will suggest the name WindowsApplication1 as the project name. Change it to MyTestApplication. Under the project's name is another box, named Location. This is the folder in which the new project will be created (every project is stored in its own folder). Visual Studio will create a new folder under the one specified in the Location box and will name it after the project. You can leave the default project folder and click the OK button.

FIGURE 1.2

The New Project dialog box

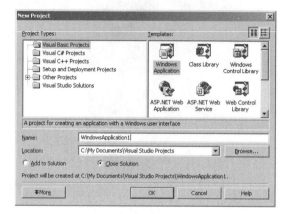

VB6 ➠ VB.NET

Unlike previous versions of Visual Basic, Visual Basic .NET creates a new folder for the project and saves the project's files there, even before you edit them. The IDE saves the changes to the project's files by default every time you run the project. To change this behavior, use the Tools ➢ Options dialog box, which is described later in this book.

What you see now is the Visual Studio IDE displaying the Form Designer for a new project (Figure 1.3). The main window is the Form Designer, and the gray surface on it is the window of your new application in design mode. Using the Form Designer, you'll be able to design the visible interface of the application (place various components of the Windows interface on the form) and then program the application.

The default environment is rather crowded, so let's hide a few of the toolbars we're not going to use in the projects of the first few chapters. You can always show any of the toolbars at any time. Open the View menu and select Toolbars. You will see a submenu with 28 commands, which are toggles. Each command corresponds to a toolbar, and you can turn the corresponding toolbar on or off by clicking one of the commands in the Toolbar submenu. Turn off all the toolbars except for the Layout and Standard toolbars.

The last item in the Toolbars submenu is the Customize command, which leads to a dialog box where you can specify which of the toolbars and which of the commands you want to see.

FIGURE 1.3

The integrated development environment of Visual Studio .NET

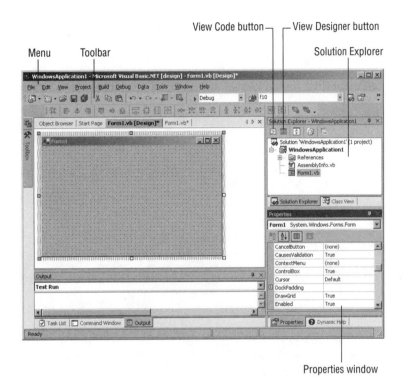

Menu · Toolbar · View Code button · View Designer button · Solution Explorer · Properties window

USING THE WINDOWS FORM DESIGNER

To design the form, you must place on it all the controls you want to display to the user at runtime. The controls are the components of the Windows interface (buttons, radio buttons, lists, and so on). Open the Toolbox by moving the pointer over the Toolbox tab at the far left; the Toolbox will pull out, as shown in Figure 1.4. This toolbox contains an icon for each control you can use on your form.

The controls are organized into tabs, each tab containing controls you can use with a specific type of project. In the first part of the book, we'll create simple Windows applications and we'll use the controls on the Windows Forms tab. When you develop a Web application, the icons of the controls on the Windows Forms tab will become disabled and you will be allowed to place only Web controls on the form (which will be a Web form, as opposed the Windows form you're building in this project). If you click the Web Forms tab now, all the icons on it will be disabled.

To place a control on the form, you can double-click the icon of the control. A new instance with a default size will be placed on the form. Then you can position and resize it with the mouse. Or you can select the control with the mouse, then move the mouse over the form and draw the outline of the control. A new instance of the control will be placed on the form, and it will fill the rectangle you specified with the mouse. Place a TextBox control on the form by double-clicking the TextBox icon on the Toolbox.

FIGURE 1.4

The Windows
Forms Toolbox
of the Visual
Studio IDE

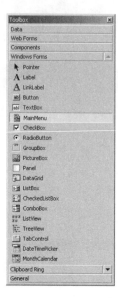

The control's properties will be displayed in the Properties window (Figure 1.5). This window, at the far left edge of the IDE, displays the properties of the selected control on the form. If the Properties window is not visible, select View ➢ Properties Window, or press F4. If no control is selected, the properties of the selected item in the Solution Explorer will be displayed. Place another TextBox control on the form. The new control will be placed almost on top of the previous one. Reposition the two controls on the form with the mouse. Then right-click one of them and, from the context menu, select Properties.

FIGURE 1.5

The properties of a
TextBox control

In the Properties window, also known as the Property Browser, you see the properties that determine the appearance of the control, and in some cases, its function. Locate the TextBox control's Text property and set it to "My TextBox Control" by entering the string (without the quotes) into the box next to property name. Select the current setting, which is TextBox1, and type a new string. The control's Text property is the string that appears in the control.

Then locate its BackColor property and select it with the mouse. A button with an arrow will appear next to the current setting of the property. Click this button and you will see a dialog box with three tabs (Custom, Web, and System), as shown in Figure 1.6. On this dialog box, you can select the color, from any of the three tabs, that will fill the control's background. Set the control's background color to yellow and notice that the control's appearance will change on the form.

FIGURE 1.6

Setting a color property in the Properties dialog box

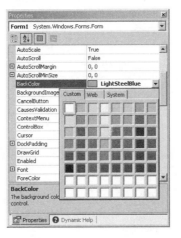

Then locate the control's Font property. You can click the plus sign in front of the property name and set the individual properties of the font, or you can click the button with the ellipsis to invoke the Font dialog box. On this dialog box, you can set the font and its attributes and then click OK to close the dialog box. Set the TextBox control's Font property to Verdana, 14 points, bold. As soon as you close the Font dialog box, the control on the form will be adjusted to the new setting.

There's a good chance that the string you assigned to the control's Text property won't fit in the control's width when rendered in the new font. Select the control on the form with the mouse, and you will see eight handles along its perimeter. Rest the pointer over any of these handles, and it will assume a shape indicating the direction in which you can resize the control. Make the control long enough to fit the entire string. If you have to, resize the form as well. Click somewhere on the form and when the handles along its perimeter appear, resize it with the mouse.

If you attempt to make the control tall enough to accommodate a few lines of text, you'll realize that you can't change the control's height. By default, the TextBox control accepts a single line of text. So far you've manipulated properties that determine the appearance of the control. Now you'll change a property that determines not only the appearance, but the function of the control as well. Locate the Multiline property. Its current setting is False. Expand the list of available settings and change it to True. (You can also change it by double-clicking the name of the property. This action toggles the True/False settings.) Then switch to the form, select the TextBox control, and make it taller.

The Multiline property determines whether the TextBox control can accept one (if Multiline = False) or more (if Multiline = True) lines of text. Set this property to True, go back to the Text property, and this time set it to a long string and press Enter. The control will break the long text into multiple lines. If you resize the control, the lines will change, but the entire string will fit across the control. That's because the control's WordWrap property is True. Set it to False to see how the string will be rendered on the control.

Multiline TextBox controls usually have a vertical scrollbar, so that users can quickly locate the section of the text they're interested in. Locate the control's ScrollBars property and expand the list of possible settings by clicking the button with the arrow. This property's settings are None, Vertical, Horizontal, and Both. Set it to vertical, assign a very long string to its Text property, and watch how the control handles the text. At design time, you can't scroll the text on the control. If you attempt to move the scrollbar, the entire control will be moved. To examine the control's behavior at runtime, press F5. The application will be compiled, and a few moments later, the form with the two TextBox controls will appear on the desktop (like the ones in Figure 1.7). This is what the users of your application would see (if this were an application worth distributing, of course).

FIGURE 1.7

The appearance of a TextBox control displaying multiple text lines

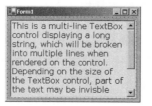
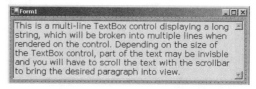

Enter some text at runtime, select text on the control, and copy it to the Clipboard by pressing Ctrl+C. You can also copy text in any other Windows application and paste it on the TextBox control. When you're done, open the Debug menu and select Stop Debugging. This will terminate your application's execution, and you'll be returned to the IDE.

One of the properties of the TextBox control that determines its function, rather than its appearance, is the CharacterCasing property, whose settings are Normal, Upper, and Lower. In normal mode, the characters appear as typed. In Lower mode, the characters are automatically converted to lowercase before they are displayed on the control. The default setting of this property is Normal. Set it to Upper or Lower, run the application again, and see how this property's setting affects the function of the control. Enter some lowercase text on the control, and the control itself will convert it to uppercase (or vice versa).

The design of a new application starts with the design of the application's form. The design of the form determines the functionality of the application. In effect, the controls on the form determine how the application will interact with the user. The form itself is a prototype, and you can demonstrate it to a customer before even adding a single line of code. As you understand, by placing controls on the form and setting their properties you're implementing a lot of functionality before coding the application. The TextBox control with the settings discussed in this section is a functional text editor.

Project Types

Before moving on, let me mention briefly all the types of projects you can build with Visual Studio in addition to Windows applications. All the project types supported by Visual Studio are displayed on the New Project dialog box, and they're the following:

Class library   A class library is a basic code-building component, which has no visible interface and adds specific functionality to your project. Simply put, a class is a collection of functions that will be used in other projects beyond the current one. With classes, however, you don't have to distribute source code. Class libraries are equivalent to ActiveX DLL and ActiveX EXE project types of VB6.

Windows control library   A Windows control (or simply *control*), such as a TextBox or Button, is a basic element of the user interface. If the controls that come with Visual Basic (the ones that appear in the Toolbox by default) don't provide the functionality you need, you can build your own custom controls. People design their own custom controls for very specific operations to simplify the development of large applications in a team environment. If you have a good idea for a custom control, you can market it—the pages of the computer trade magazines are full of ads for advanced custom controls that complement the existing ones.

Console application   A Console application is an application with a very limited user interface. This type of application displays its output on a Command Prompt window and receives input from the same window. You'll see an example of a simple Console application later in this chapter, and that will be the last Console application in this book. The purpose of this book is to show you how to build Windows and Web applications with rich interfaces, not DOS-like applications. However, the product's documentation uses Console applications to demonstrate specific topics, and this is why I've included a short section on Console applications in this chapter.

Windows service   A Windows service is a new name for the old NT services, and they're long-running applications that don't have a visible interface. These services can be started automatically when the computer is turned on, paused, and restarted. An application that monitors and reacts to changes in the file system is a prime candidate for implementing as a Windows service. When users upload files to a specific folder, the Windows service might initiate some processing (copy the file, read its contents and update a database, and so on). We will not discuss Windows services in this book.

ASP.NET Web application   Web applications are among the most exciting new features of Visual Studio. A Web application is an app that resides on a Web server and services requests made through a browser. An online bookstore, for example, is a Web application. The application that runs on the Web server must accept requests made by a client (a remote computer with a browser) and return its responses to the requests in the form of HTML pages. Web applications are not new, but ASP.NET hides many of details of building Web applications and makes the process surprisingly similar to the process of building Windows applications. Web applications and Web services are discussed in detail in the last part of the book.

ASP.NET Web service   A Web service is not the equivalent of a Windows service. A Web service is a program that resides on a Web server and services requests, just like a Web application, but it doesn't return an HTML page. Instead, it returns the result of a calculation or a database lookup. Requests to Web services are usually made by another server, which is responsible for processing the data. A *Web application* that accepts a query for all VB books published by Sybex will return a page with the results. A *Web service* that accepts the same query will return an XML file with the results. The file will be used by the application that made the request to prepare a new page and send it to the client, or to populate a Windows form.

Web control library   Just as you can build custom Windows controls to use with your Windows forms, you can create custom Web controls to use with your Web pages. Web controls are not discussed in this book, but once you've understood how ASP applications work and how Web applications interact with clients, you'll be able to follow the examples in the documentation.

The other three templates in the New Project dialog box—Empty Project, Empty Web Project, and New Project In Existing Folder—are not project types, just a way to organize the new project yourself. When you create a new project of any of the previous types, Visual Studio creates a new folder named after the project and populates it with a few files that are necessary for the specific application type. A Windows application, for example, has a form, and the appropriate file is created automatically in the project's folder when a new Windows application is created. With the last three types of projects, you're responsible for creating and adding all the required items yourself.

Your First VB Application

In this section, we'll develop a very simple application to demonstrate not only the design of the interface, but also how to code the application. We'll build an application that allows the user to enter the name of their favorite programming language, and then we evaluate the choice. Objectively, VB is a step ahead of all other languages and it will receive the best evaluation. All other languages will get the same grade—good, but not VB.

TIP   The project you will build in this section is called WindowsApplication1, and you can find it in this chapter's folder on the CD. Copy the WindowsApplication1 folder from the CD to your hard disk, then clear the Read-Only attribute of the files in the folder. All the files you copy from the CD are read-only. To change this attribute (so that you can save the changes), select all the files in a project's folder, right-click them, and select Properties. In the dialog box that appears, clear the box Read-Only.

You can open the project on the CD and examine it, but I suggest you follow the steps outlined in this paragraph to build the project from scratch. Start a new project, use the default name Windows-Application1, and place a TextBox and a Button control on the form. Use the mouse to position and resize the controls on the form, as shown in Figure 1.8.

FIGURE 1.8

A simple application that processes a user-supplied string

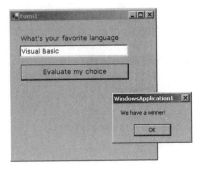

Now we must insert some code to evaluate the user's favorite language. Windows applications are made up of small code segments, called *event handlers,* which react to specific actions. In the case of our example, we want to program the action of clicking the button. When the user clicks the button, we want to execute some code that will display a message.

To insert some code behind the Button control, double-click the control and you'll see the code window of the application, which is shown in Figure 1.9. The line "Private ..." is too long to fit on the printed page, so I've inserted a *line-continuation character* (an underscore) to break it into two lines. When a line is too long, you can break it into two lines by inserting the line continuation character. Alternatively, you can turn on the word wrap feature of the editor (you'll see shortly how to adjust the editor's properties). Notice that I've also inserted quite a bit of space before the second half of the first code line. It's customary to indent continued lines so that they can be easily distinguished from the other lines.

FIGURE 1.9

The outline of a subroutine that handles the Click event of a Button control

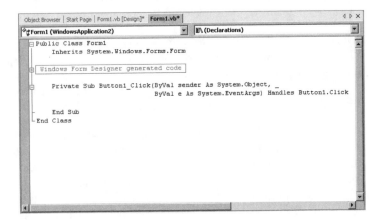

The editor opened a subroutine, which is delimited by the following statements:

```
Private Sub Button1_Click(ByVal sender As System.Object, _
          ByVal e As System.EventArgs) Handles Button1.Click
End Sub
```

At the top of the main pane of the Designer, you will see two tabs named after the form: in Figure 1.9, they're the Form1.vb [Design] tab and the Form1.vb tab. The first tab is the Windows Form Designer (where you build the interface of the application with visual tools) and the second is the code editor, where you insert the code behind the interface. At the top of the code editor, which is what you see in Figure 1.9, are two ComboBoxes. The one on the left contains the names of the controls on the form. The other one contains the names of events each control recognizes. When you select a control (or an object, in general) in the left list, the other list's contents are adjusted accordingly. To program a specific event of a specific control, select the name of the control in the first list (the Objects list) and the name of the event in the right list (the Events list).

The Click event happens to be the default event of the Button control, so when you double-click a Button on the form, you're taken to the Button1_Click subroutine. This subroutine is an event handler. An event handler is invoked automatically every time an event takes place. The event is the Click event of the Button1 control. Every time the Button1 control on the form is clicked, the Button1_Click subroutine is activated. To react to the Click event of the button, you must insert the appropriate code in this subroutine.

The name of the subroutine is made up of the name of the control, followed by an underscore and the name of the event. This is just the default name, and you can change it to anything you like (such as EvaluateLanguage, for this example, or StartCalculations). What makes this subroutine an event handler is the keyword *Handles* at the end of the statement. The Handles keyword tells the compiler what event this subroutine is supposed to handle. `Button1.Click` is the Click event of the Button1 control. If there were another button on the form, the Button2 control, you'd have to write code for a subroutine that would handle the `Button2.Click` event. Each control recognizes many events; for each control and event combination, you can provide a different event handler. Of course, we never program every possible event for every control.

NOTE   *As you will soon realize, the controls have a default behavior and handle the basic events on their own. The TextBox control knows how to handle keystrokes. The CheckBox control (a small square with a check mark) changes state by hiding or displaying the checkmark every time it's clicked. The ScrollBar control moves its indicator (the button in the middle of the control) every time you click one of the arrows at the two ends. Because of this default behavior of the controls, you need not supply any code for the events of most controls on the form.*

Rename Button1_Click subroutine to EvaluateLanguage. However, you shouldn't change the name of the event this subroutine handles. If you change the name of the control after you have inserted some code in an event handler, the name of the event handled by the subroutine will be automatically changed. The name of the subroutine, however, won't change.

Let's add some code to the Click event handler of the Button1 control. When this button is clicked, we want to examine the text on the control and, if it's "Visual Basic", display a message; if not, we'll display a different message. Insert the lines of Listing 1.1 between the `Private Sub` and `End Sub` statements. (I'm showing the entire listing here, but there's no reason to retype the first and last statements.)

LISTING 1.1: PROCESSING A USER-SUPPLIED STRING

```
Private Sub EvaluateLanguage_Click(ByVal sender As System.Object, _
               ByVal e As System.EventArgs) Handles Button1.Click
    Dim language As String
    language = TextBox1.Text
    If language = "Visual Basic" Then
        MsgBox("We have a winner!")
    Else
        MsgBox(language & " is not a bad language.")
    End If
End Sub
```

Here's what this code does. First, it assigns the value of the TextBox1 control to the variable *language*. A variable is a named location in memory, where a value is stored. This memory location can be read later in the code or set to a different value. Variables are where we store the intermediate results of our calculation when we write code. Then the program compares the value of the *language* variable to the literal "Visual Basic", and depending on the outcome of the comparison, it displays one of two messages. The MsgBox() function displays the specified message in a small window with the OK button. Users can view the message and then click the OK button to close the message box.

Even if you're not familiar with the syntax of the language, you should be able to understand what this code does. Visual Basic is the simplest .NET language, and we will discuss the various aspects of the language in detail in the following chapters. In the meantime, you should try to understand the process of developing a Windows application: how to build the visible interface of the application, and how to program the events to which you want your application to react.

Making the Application More Robust

The code of our first application isn't very robust. If the user doesn't enter the string with the exact spelling shown in the listing, the comparison will fail. We can convert the string to uppercase and then compare it to "VISUAL BASIC" to eliminate differences in case. To convert a string to uppercase, use the ToUpper method of the string class. The following expression returns the string stored in the *language* variable, converted to uppercase:

```
language.ToUpper
```

We should also assume that the user may enter "VB" or "VB.NET", so let's modify our code as shown in Listing 1.2.

LISTING 1.2: A MORE ROBUST STRING COMPARISON TECHNIQUE

```
Private Sub EvaluateLanguage_Click(ByVal sender As System.Object, _
               ByVal e As System.EventArgs) Handles Button1.Click
    Dim language As String
    language = TextBox1.Text
```

```
    language = language.ToUpper
    If language = "VISUAL BASIC" Or _
        language = "VB" Or _
        language = "VB.NET" Then
        MsgBox("We have a winner!")
    Else
        MsgBox(language & " is not a bad language")
    End If
End Sub
```

The If statement is a long one, and for clarity I've inserted the underscore character to break it into multiple text lines. As you enter the code, you will either enter an underscore character and then press Enter to move to the following line, or ignore the underscore character and continue typing on the same line. You will see later how you can instruct the code editor to automatically wrap long lines of code.

Run the application, enter the name of your favorite language, and then click the Button to evaluate your choice. It's an extremely simple project, but this is how you write Windows applications: you design the interface and then enter code behind selected events.

In the following section, we'll improve our application. You never know what users may throw at your application, so whenever possible we try to limit their response to the number of available choices. In our case, we can display the names of certain languages (the ones we're interested in) and force the user to select one of them. One way to display a limited number of choices is to use a ComboBox control. In the following section, we'll revise our sample application so that the user won't have to enter the name of the language. The user will be forced to select his or her favorite language from a list, so that we won't have to validate the string supplied by the user.

Making the Application More User-Friendly

Start a new project, the WindowsApplication2 project. If there's already a project by that name in your VB projects folder, name it differently or specify a different location. Click the Browse button on the New Project dialog box and select a new folder. You can also create a new folder like "MyProjects" or "VB.NET Samples" and select this as the default folder for your next few projects. Every time you create a new project, this folder will be suggested by default. When you're ready for your own projects, specify a different location with the Browse button.

When the form of the project appears in the IDE, set the form's Font property. Locate the Font item in the Properties window and click the button with the ellipsis (three dots). The usual Font dialog box will appear, and you can set the form's font. This time, set it to Comic Sans MS, 11 points. All the controls you'll place on the form from will inherit this font.

Open the Toolbox and double-click the icon of the ComboBox tool. A ComboBox control will be placed on your form. Now place a Button control on the form and position it so that your form looks like the one shown in Figure 1.10. To see the properties of a specific control in the Properties window, you must select the appropriate control on the form. Then set the button's Text property to "Evaluate my choice" (just enter this string without the quotes in the box of the Text property in the control's Properties window).

FIGURE 1.10

Displaying options
on a ComboBox
control

We must now populate the ComboBox control with the choices. Select the ComboBox control on the form by clicking it with the mouse and locate its Items property in the Properties window. The setting of this property is "Collection," which means that the Items property doesn't have a single value; it's a collection of items (strings, in our case). Click the ellipsis button and you'll see the String Collection Editor dialog box, as shown in Figure 1.11.

FIGURE 1.11

Click the ellipsis
button next to the
Items property of a
ComboBox to see
the String Collection
Editor dialog box.

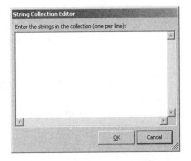

The main pane on the dialog box is a TextBox, where you can enter the items you want to appear in the ComboBox control at runtime. Enter the following strings, one per row and in the order shown here:

C++

C#

Java

Visual Basic

Cobol

Then click the OK button to close the dialog box. The items will not appear on the control at design time, but you will see them when you run the project. Before running the project, set one more property. Locate the ComboBox control's Text property and set it to "Select your favorite language." This is not an item of the list; it's the string that will initially appear on the control.

You can run the project now and see how the ComboBox control behaves. Press F5 and wait for a few seconds. The project will be compiled, and you'll see its form on your desktop, on top of the Visual Studio window. This is the same form we've been designing so far, but in runtime (in effect, what the users of the application will see if you decide to distribute it).

I'm sure you know how this control behaves in a typical Windows application, and our sample application is no exception. You can select an item on the control either with the mouse or with the keyboard. Click the button with the arrow to expand the list, and then select an item with the mouse. Or press the arrow down and arrow up keys to scroll through the list of items. The control isn't expanded, but each time you click an arrow button, the next or previous item in the list appears on the control.

We haven't told the application what to do when the button is clicked, so let's go back and add some code to the project. Stop the application by clicking the Stop button on the toolbar (the solid black square) or by selecting Debug ➤ Stop Debugging from the main menu. When the form appears in design mode, double-click the button and the code window will open, displaying an empty Click event handler. Insert the statements shown in Listing 1.3 between the `Private Sub` and `End Sub` statements.

LISTING 1.3: THE REVISED APPLICATION

```
Private Sub EvaluateLanguage_Click(ByVal sender As System.Object, _
             ByVal e As System.EventArgs) Handles Button1.Click
    Dim language As String
    language = ComboBox1.Text
    If language = "Visual Basic" Then
       MsgBox("We have a winner!")
    Else
       MsgBox(language & " is not a bad language.")
    End If
End Sub
```

When the form is first displayed, a string that doesn't correspond to a language is displayed in the ComboBox control. We must select one of the items from within our code when the form is first loaded. When a form is loaded, the Load event of the Form object is raised. Double-click somewhere on the form, and the editor will open the form's Load event handler:

```
Private Sub Form1_Load(ByVal sender As System.Object, _
             ByVal e As System.EventArgs) Handles MyBase.Load

End Sub
```

Enter the following code to select the item "Visual Basic" when the form is loaded:

```
Private Sub Form1_Load(ByVal sender As System.Object, _
             ByVal e As System.EventArgs) Handles MyBase.Load
    ComboBox1.SelectedIndex = 3
End Sub
```

Now that we select an item from within our code, you can reset the ComboBox's Text property to an empty string.

As you realize, the controls on the Toolbox are more than nice pictures. They encapsulate a lot of functionality, and they expose properties that allow you to adjust their appearance and their functionality. Most properties are usually set at design time.

The IDE Components

The IDE of Visual Studio.NET contains numerous components, and it will take you a while to explore them. It's practically impossible to explain what each tool, each window, and each menu does. We'll discuss specific tools as we go along and as the topics we discuss get more and more advanced. In this section, I will go through the basic items of the IDE, the ones we'll use in the following few chapters to build simple Windows applications.

The IDE Menu

The IDE main menu provides the following commands, which lead to submenus. Notice that most menus can also be displayed as toolbars. Also, not all options are available at all times. The options that cannot possibly apply to the current state of the IDE are either invisible or disabled. The Edit menu is a typical example. It's quite short when you're designing the form and quite lengthy when you edit code. The Data menu disappears altogether when you switch to the code editor—you can't use the options of this menu while editing code.

FILE MENU

The File menu contains commands for opening and saving projects, or project items, as well as the commands for adding new or existing items to the current project.

EDIT MENU

The Edit menu contains the usual editing commands. Among the commands of the Edit menu are the Advanced command and the IntelliSense command.

Advanced Submenu

The more interesting options of the Edit ➢ Advanced submenu are the following. Notice that the Advanced submenu is invisible while you design a form visually and appears when you switch to the code editor.

View White Space   Space characters (necessary to indent lines of code and make it easy to read) are replaced by periods.

Word Wrap   When a code line's length exceeds the length of the code window, it's automatically wrapped.

Comment Selection/Uncomment Selection   Comments are lines you insert between your code's statements to document your application. Sometimes, we want to disable a few lines from our code, but not delete them (because we want to be able to restore them). A simple technique to disable a line of code is to "comment it out" (insert the comment symbol in front of the line). This command allows you to comment (or uncomment) large segments of code in a single move.

IntelliSense Submenu

The Edit ➤ IntelliSense menu item leads to a submenu with four options, which are described next. IntelliSense is a feature of the editor (and of other Microsoft applications) that displays as much information as possible, whenever possible. When you type the name of a function and the opening parenthesis, for example, IntelliSense will display the syntax of the function—its arguments. The IntelliSense submenu includes the following options.

List Members   When this option is on, the editor lists all the members (properties, methods, events, and argument list) in a drop-down list. This list will appear when you enter the name of an object or control followed by a period. Then you can select the desired member from the list with the mouse or with the keyboard. Let's say your form contains a control named TextBox1 and you're writing code for this form. When you enter the following string:

```
TextBox1.
```

a list with the members of the TextBox control will appear (as seen in Figure 1.12). Select the Text property and then type the equal sign, followed by a string in quotes like the following:

```
TextBox1.Text = "Your User Name"
```

FIGURE 1.12

Viewing the members of a control in an IntelliSense drop-down list

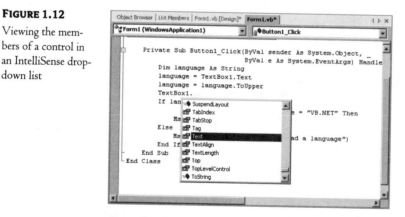

If you select a property that can accept a limited number of settings, you will see the names of the appropriate constants in a drop-down list. If you enter the following statement:

```
TextBox1.TextAlign =
```

you will see the constants you can assign to the property (as shown in Figure 1.13, they are the values HorizontalAlignment.Center, HorizontalAlignment.Right, and HorizontalAlignment.Left). Again, you can select the desired value with the mouse or the arrow keys.

The drop-down list with the members of a control or object (the Members List) remains open until you type a terminator key (the Escape or End key) or switch to another window.

Parameter Info   While editing code, you can move the pointer over a variable, method, or property and see its declaration in a yellow tooltip.

FIGURE 1.13

Viewing the possible settings of a property in an IntelliSense drop-down list

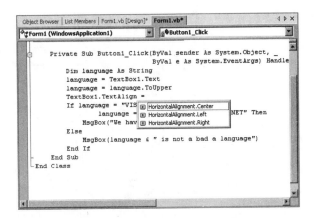

Quick Info   This is another IntelliSense feature that displays information about commands and functions. When you type the opening parenthesis following the name of a function, for example, the function's arguments will be displayed in a tooltip box (a yellow horizontal box). The first argument appears in bold font; after entering a value for this argument, the next one will appear in bold. If an argument accepts a fixed number of settings, these values will appear in a drop-down list, as explained previously.

Figure 1.14 shows the syntax of the DateDiff() function. This function calculates the difference between two dates in a specified time interval. The first argument is the time interval, and its value can be one of the constants shown in the list. The following two arguments are the two dates. The remaining arguments are optional, and they specify options like the first day of the week and the first day of the year. This function returns a Long value (an integer that represents the number of the intervals between the two dates).

Complete Word   The Complete Word feature enables you to complete the current word by pressing Ctrl+spacebar. For example, if you type "TextB" and then press Ctrl+spacebar, you will see a list of words that you're most likely to type (TextBox, TextBox1, and so on).

VIEW MENU

This menu contains commands to display any toolbar or window of the IDE. You have already seen the Toolbars menu (earlier, under "Starting a New Project"). The Other Windows command leads to submenu with the names of some standard windows, including the Output and Command windows. The Output window is the console of the application. The compiler's messages, for example, are displayed in the Output window. The Command window allows you to enter and execute statements. When you debug an application, you can stop it and enter VB statements in the Command window.

PROJECT MENU

This menu contains commands for adding items to the current project (an item can be a form, a file, a component, even another project). The last option in this menu is the Set As StartUp Project command, which lets you specify which of the projects in a multiproject solution is the startup project (the one that will run when you press F5). The Add Reference and Add Web Reference commands

FIGURE 1.14

Viewing the arguments of a function in an IntelliSense box

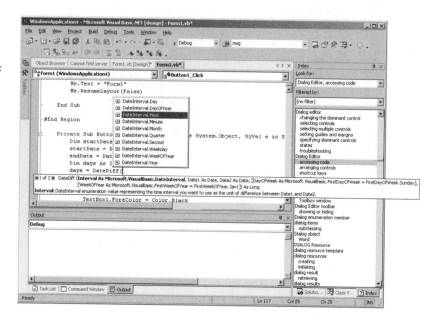

allow you to add references to .NET (or COM) components and Web components respectively. We'll use both commands in later chapters.

BUILD MENU

The Build menu contains commands for building (compiling) your project. The two basic commands in this menu are the Build and Rebuild All commands. The Build command compiles (builds the executable) of the entire solution, but it doesn't compile any components of the project that haven't changed since the last build. The Rebuild All command does the same, but it clears any existing files and builds the solution from scratch.

DEBUG MENU

This menu contains commands to start or end an application, as well as the basic debugging tools (which are discussed in Chapter 17).

DATA MENU

This menu contains commands you will use with projects that access data. You'll see how to use this short menu's commands in sections that describe the visual database tools in Chapters 21 and 22 in Part V of the book.

FORMAT MENU

The Format menu, which is visible only while you design a Windows or Web form, contains commands for aligning the controls on the form. The commands of this menu will be discussed briefly later in this chapter and in more detail in the following chapter.

Tools Menu

This menu contains a list of tools, and most of them apply to C++. The Macros command of the Tools menu leads to a submenu with commands for creating macros. Just as you can create macros in an Office application to simplify many tasks, you can create macros to automate many of the repetitive tasks you perform in the IDE. I'm not going to discuss macros in this book, but once you familiarize yourself with the environment, you should look up the topic of writing macros in the documentation.

Window Menu

This is the typical Window menu of any Windows application. In addition to the list of open windows, it also contains the Hide command, which hides all Toolboxes and devotes the entire window of the IDE to the code editor or the Form Designer. The Toolboxes don't disappear completely. They're all retracted, and you can see their tabs on the left and right edges of the IDE window. To expand a Toolbox, just hover the mouse pointer over the corresponding tab.

Help Menu

This menu contains the various help options. The Dynamic Help command opens the Dynamic Help window, which is populated with topics that apply to the current operation. The Index command opens the Index window, where you can enter a topic and get help on the specific topic.

The Toolbox Window

Here you will find all the controls you can use to build your application's interface. The Toolbox window is usually retracted, and you must move the pointer over it to view the Toolbox. This window contains these tabs:

Crystal Reports

Data

XML Schema

Dialog Editor

Web Forms

Components

Windows Forms

HTML

Clipboard Ring

General

The Windows Forms tab contains the icons of the controls you can place on a Windows form, and we'll work exclusively with this tab in the course of the next few chapters. Likewise, the Web Forms and HTML tabs contain the icons of the controls you can place on a Web form. The controls on these tabs are examined in Part VI of the book.

The Data tab contains the icons of the objects you will use to build data-driven applications, and they're explored in Part V of the book. The items on the Data tab are objects with no visible interface. The XML Schema tab contains the tools you'll need to work with schema XML files. We'll touch this topic in Part V of the book, but you don't really need to understand XML to use it. You'll see how to create XML files with visual tools.

The Solution Explorer

This window contains a list of the items in the current solution. A solution may contain multiple projects, and each project may contain multiple items. The Solution Explorer displays a hierarchical list of all the components, organized by project. You can right-click any component of the project and select Properties in the context menu to see the selected component's properties in the Properties window. If you select a project, you will see the Project Properties dialog box. You will find more information on project properties in the following chapter.

If a project contains multiple forms, you can right-click the form you want to become the startup form and select Set As StartUp Object. If the solution contains multiple projects, you can right-click the project you want to become the startup form and select Set As StartUp Project. You can also add items to a project with the Add Item command of the context menu, or remove a component from the project with the Exclude From Project command. This command removes the selected component from the project, but doesn't affect the component's file on the disk. The Remove command removes the selected component from the project and also deletes the component's file from the disk.

The Properties Window

This window (also known as the Property Browser) displays all the properties of the selected component and their settings. Every time you place a control on a form, you switch to this window to adjust the appearance of the control on the form, and you have already seen how to manipulate the properties of a control through the Properties window.

Many properties are set to a single value, like a number or a string. If the possible settings of a property are relatively few, they're displayed as meaningful constants in a drop-down list. Other properties are set through a more elaborate interface. Color properties, for example, are set from within a Color dialog box that's displayed right in the Properties window. Font properties are set through the usual Font dialog box. Collections are set in a Collection Editor dialog box, where you can enter one string for each item of the collection.

If the Properties window is hidden or you have closed it, you can either select the View ➤ Properties Window command or right-click a control on the form and select Properties. Or you can simply press F4 to bring up this window. There will be occasions where a control may totally overlap another control, and you won't be able to select the hidden control and view its properties. In this case, you can select the desired control in the ComboBox part of the Properties window. This box contains the names of all the controls on the form, and you can select a control on the form by selecting its name on this box. Use this technique to set the properties of a control that's covered by another control.

The Output Window

The Output window is where many of the tools, including the compiler, send their output. Every time you start an application, a series of messages is displayed on the Output window. These messages are generated by the compiler, and you need not understand them at this point. If the Output window is not visible, select the View ➢ Other Windows ➢ Output command from the menu.

You can also send output to this window from within your code with the `Console.WriteLine` method. Actually, this is a widely used debugging technique—to print the values of certain variables before entering a problematic area of the code. As you will learn in Chapter 17, there are more elaborate tools to help you debug your application, but printing a few values to the Output window is a time-honored practice in programming with VB to test a function or display the results of intermediate calculations.

In many of the examples of this book, especially in the first few chapters, I use the `Console.WriteLine` statement to print something to the Output window. To demonstrate the use of the DateDiff() function, for example, I'll use a statement like the following:

```
Console.WriteLine(DateDiff(DateInterval.Day, #3/9/2001#, #5/15/2001#))
```

When this statement is executed, the value 67 will appear in the Output Window. This statement demonstrates the syntax of the DateDiff() function, which returns the difference between the two dates in days.

The Command Window

While testing a program, you can interrupt its execution by inserting a *breakpoint.* When the breakpoint is reached, the program's execution is suspended and you can execute a statement in the Command window. Any statement that can appear in your VB code can also be executed in the Command window.

The Task List Window

This window is usually populated by the compiler with error messages, if the code can't be successfully compiled. You can double-click an error message in this window, and the IDE will take you to the line with the statement in error—which you should fix.

You can also add your own tasks to this window. Just click the first empty line and start typing. A task can be anything, from comments and reminders, to URLs to interesting sites. If you add tasks to the list, you're responsible for removing them. Errors are removed automatically as soon as you fix the statement that caused them.

Environment Options

The Visual Studio IDE is highly customizable. I will not discuss all the customization options here, but I will show you how to change the default settings of the IDE. Open the Tools menu and select Options (the last item in the menu). The Options dialog box will appear, where you can set all the options regarding the environment. Figure 1.15 shows the options for the font of the various items of the IDE. Here you can set the font for various categories of items, like the Text Editor, the dialogs and toolboxes, and so on. Select an item in the Show Settings For list and then set the font for this item in the box below.

FIGURE 1.15

The Fonts and Col-
ors options

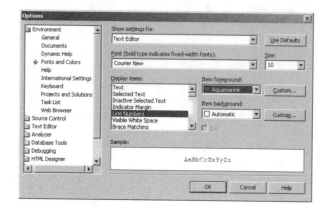

FIGURE 1.15

The Fonts and Col-
ors options

Figure 1.16 shows the Projects and Solutions options. The top box is the default location for new projects. The three radio buttons in the lower half of the dialog box determine when the changes to the project are saved. By default, changes are saved when you run a project. If you activate the last option, then you must save your project from time to time with the File ➢ Save All command.

FIGURE 1.16

The Projects and
Solutions options

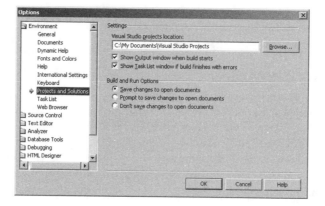

Most of the tabs on the Options dialog box are straightforward, and you should take a look at them. If you don't like some of the default aspects of the IDE, this is the place to change them.

A Few Common Properties

In the next few sections, I will go through some of the properties, methods, and events that are common to many controls, so that I will not have to repeat them with every control in the following chapters. These are very simple members you'll be using in every application from now on.

To manipulate a control you use its properties, either on the Property Browser at design time, or though your code at runtime. To program a control, supply a handler for the appropriate events.

Controls expose methods, too, which act on the control. The Hide method, for example, makes the control invisible. Properties, methods, and events constitute the programmatic interface of the control and are collectively known as the control's *members*.

All controls have a multitude of properties, which are displayed in the Properties window, and you can easily set their values. Different controls expose different properties, but here are some that are common to most:

Name   The control's name. This name appears at the top of the Properties window when a control is selected on the form and is also used in programming the control. To set the text on a TextBox control from within your code, you will use a statement like the following:

```
TextBox1.Text = "My TextBox Control"
```

You will see how to program the controls shortly.

Font   A Font object that determines how the text of the control will be rendered at both design and runtime.

Enabled   By default, all controls are enabled. To disable a control, set its Enabled property to False. When a control is disabled, it appears in gray color and users can't interact with it. Disabling a control isn't as rare as you may think, because many controls are not functional at all times. If the user hasn't entered a value in all required fields on the form, clicking the Process button isn't going to do anything. After all fields have been set to a valid value, you can enable the control, indicating to the user that the button can now be clicked.

Size   Sets, or returns, the control's size. The Size property is a Size object, which exposes two properties, the Width and Height properties. You can set the Size property to a string like "320, 80" or expand the Size property in the Properties window and set the Width and Height properties individually.

Tag   Holds some data you want to associate with a specific control. For example, you can set the Tag property to the control's default value, so that you can restore the control's default value if the user supplies invalid data (a string in a TextBox control that expects a numeric value, or a date).

Text   The text (a string) that appears on the control. The Label control's caption can be set (or read) through the Text property. A control that displays multiple items, like the ListBox or the ComboBox control, returns the currently selected item in the Text property.

TabStop   As you know, only one control at a time can have the focus on a form. To move the focus from one control to the other on the same form, you press the Tab key (and Shift+Tab to move the focus in reverse order). The TabStop property determines whether the control belongs to the so-called tab order. If True (which is the default value), you can move the focus to the control with the Tab key. If False, the control will be skipped in the tab order.

TabIndex   A numeric value that determines the position of the control in the Tab order. The control with the smallest TabIndex value is the one that has the focus when the form is first loaded. If you press Tab once, the focus will be moved to the control with the next larger TabIndex value.

Visible   Sometimes we want to make a control invisible. We do so by setting its Visible property to False (the default value of the property is True).

A Few Common Events

As you have already seen, and will also see in the coming chapters, much of the code of a Windows application manipulates the properties of the various controls on the form. The code of the application resides in selected event handlers. Each control recognizes several events, but we rarely program more than one event per control. In most cases, most of the controls on the form don't have any code behind them. The events that are most frequently used in programming Windows applications are shown next.

Click   This is the most common event in Windows programming, and it's fired when a control is clicked.

DoubleClick   Fired when the control is double-clicked.

Enter   Fired when the control received the focus.

Leave   Fired when the control loses the focus. We usually insert code to validate the control's content in this event's handler.

MouseEnter   Fired when the mouse pointer enters the area of the control. This event is fired once. If you want to monitor the movement of the mouse over a control, use the MouseMove event.

MouseLeave   This is the counterpart of the MouseEnter event, and it's fired when the mouse pointer moves out of the area of the control.

XXXChanged   Some events are fired when a property changes value. These events include BackColorChanged, FontChanged, VisibleChanged, and many more. The control's properties can also change through code, and it's very common to do so. To set the text on a TextBox control from within your code, you can execute a statement like the following:

```
TextBox1.Text = "a new caption"
```

You may wish to change the background color of a TextBox control if the numeric value displayed on it is negative:

```
If Val(TextBox.Text) < 0 Then
    TextBox1.BackColor = Color.Red
End If
```

A Few Common Methods

In addition to properties, controls also expose methods. A method acts upon the control by performing a specific task. Windows controls don't provide many methods, but the objects we'll explore in the following chapters provide many more methods. You have already seen the ToUpper method, which converts a string to uppercase and returns it as a new string. In VB.NET, a string is more than a series of characters: it's an object, and so is just about everything in .NET. Even a number is an object and exposes a few properties and methods of its own.

A String variable exposes the methods Length (it returns the string length), ToUpper (it converts the characters in the string to uppercase and returns a new string), and ToLower (it converts the characters in the string to lowercase and returns a new string). To see these methods in action, create a new application, place a Button control on the form and enter the following statements in its Click event handler:

```
Console.WriteLine("Visual Basic".Length)
Console.WriteLine("Visual Basic".ToUpper)
Console.WriteLine("Visual Basic".ToLower)
```

Then press F5 to run the application, and you will see the following in the Output window (this is where the Console.WriteLine statement sends its output):

```
12
VISUAL BASIC
visual basic
```

NOTE *If the Output window is hidden, select View ➤ Other Windows ➤ Output.*

Here are a few methods that are common to most controls. In later chapters, where we'll explore the Windows controls in detail, you'll learn about the methods that are unique to individual controls. The following methods apply to most of the Windows controls.

Focus This method moves the focus to the control to which the method applies, regardless of the control that has the focus at the time. Your validation routine could move the focus to the control with an erroneous entry with the following statement:

```
TextBox1.Focus
```

It's also possible to "trap" the focus to a specific TextBox control until the user enters a valid value, by calling the Focus method from within the Leave event. The following code segment doesn't allow users to move the focus to another control while TextBox1 doesn't contain a valid numeric value:

```
Private Sub TextBox1_Leave(ByVal sender As Object, _
                ByVal e As System.EventArgs) Handles TextBox1.Leave
    If Not IsNumeric(TextBox1.Text) Then TextBox1.Focus()
End Sub
```

The function IsNumeric() returns True if its argument (the value in parentheses following the function's name) is a numeric value, like 35 or 244.01.

Clear Many controls provide a method to clear their contents, and this is the Clear method. When you call the Clear method on a TextBox control, the control's Text property is set to an empty string.

Hide/Show The Hide and Show methods reveal or conceal the control. The two methods are equivalent to setting the Visible property to True and False respectively.

PerformClick It's rather common to invoke the Click event of a button from within our code. To do so, call the PerformClick method of the Button control. There are no equivalent methods for other events.

Scale This method scales the control by a value specified as argument. The following statement scales the TextBox1 control down to 75 percent of its current size:

```
TextBox1.Scale(0.75)
```

Building a Console Application

One of the new features of Visual Basic .NET is that you can write applications that run in a Command Prompt window. The Command Prompt window isn't really a DOS window, even though it looks like one. It's a text window, and the only way to interact with an application is to enter lines of text and read the output generated by the application, which is displayed on this text window, one line at a time. This type of application is called a Console application, and we're going to demonstrate Console applications with a single example. We will not return to this type of application later in the book, because it's not what you're supposed to do as a Windows developer.

The Console application you'll build in this section, ConsoleApplication1, prompts the user to enter the name of his or her favorite language, and then it prints the appropriate message on a new line, as shown in Figure 1.17.

FIGURE 1.17

A Console application uses the Command Prompt window to interact with the user.

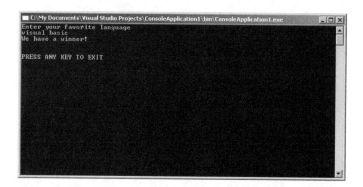

Start a new project and, in the New Project dialog box, select the template Console Application. You can also change its default name from ConsoleApplication1 to a more descriptive name. For the example of this section, don't change the application's name.

A Console application doesn't have a user interface, so the first thing you'll see is the code editor's window with the following statements:

```
Module Module1

    Sub Main()

    End Sub

End Module
```

Unlike a Windows application, which is a class, a Console application is a module. Main() is the name of a subroutine that's executed automatically when you run a Console application. The code you want to execute must be placed between the statements Sub Main() and End Sub. Insert the statements shown in Listing 1.4 in the application's Main() subroutine.

```
Module Module1
    Sub Main()
        Console.WriteLine("Enter your favorite language")
        Dim language As String
        language = Console.ReadLine()
        language = language.ToUpper
        If language = "VISUAL BASIC" Or language = "VB" Or language = "VB.NET" Then
            Console.WriteLine("We have a winner!")
        Else
            Console.WriteLine(language & " is not a bad language.")
        End If
        Console.WriteLine()
        Console.WriteLine()
        Console.WriteLine("PRESS ANY KEY TO EXIT")
        Console.ReadLine()
    End Sub
End Module
```

This code is quite similar to the code of the equivalent Windows applications we developed earlier, except that it uses the `Console.WriteLine` statement to send its output to the Command Prompt window instead of a message box.

A Console application doesn't react to events, because it has no visible interface. However, it's easy to add elements of the Windows interface to a Console application. If you change the `Console.WriteLine` method calls into the MsgBox() function, the message will be displayed on a message box.

The reason to build a Console application is to test a specific feature of the language without having to build a user interface. Many of the examples in the documentation are Console applications; they demonstrate the topic at hand and nothing more. If you want to test the DateDiff() function, for example, you can create a new Console application and enter the lines of Listing 1.5 in its Main() subroutine.

```
Sub Main()
    Console.WriteLine(DateDiff(DateInterval.Day, #3/9/2000#, #5/15/2004#))
    Console.WriteLine("PRESS ANY KEY TO EXIT")
    Console.ReadLine()
End Sub
```

The last two lines will be the same in every Console application you write. Without them, the Command Prompt window will close as soon as the End Sub statement is reached, and you won't have a chance to see the result.

Console applications are convenient for testing short code segments, but Windows programming is synonymous with designing functional user interfaces and you won't find any more Console applications in this book.

Summary

This chapter was a quick introduction to the environment you'll be using to design your applications. It's a very rich environment, and it will take you a while to become quite comfortable with it. Keep in mind that you won't need most of the menus and toolbars in building simple Windows applications.

What you must get accustomed to is how we design Windows applications. We start with the application's visual interface, which is designed with visual tools. This is done with the Windows Form Designer. After completing the design of the interface, you must add some code to the application. Windows applications are event driven. The user interacts with your application through the mouse and keyboard. Every time the user does something with an element of the interface, an event is raised. As a programmer, you must decide what events your application should react to and insert the appropriate code in the handlers of these events.

In the following chapter, you're going to build more simple applications and drill into the concepts of event-driven programming, which is at the core of programming with Visual Studio .NET and Visual Basic .NET.

Chapter 2

Visual Basic Projects

THE PREVIOUS CHAPTER INTRODUCED Visual Studio's IDE, the Toolbox, and the principles of event-driven programming. In this chapter, we expand on that introduction to the language by building some "real" applications. Among other topics, we'll look at how to write applications that validate user input and how to write error-handling routines. We'll also look at several techniques you'll need as you work through the applications we develop in the rest of the book. In the last part of the chapter, you'll learn how to distribute your application with a proper Windows installer (a program that installs your application to the target machine).

The bulk of the chapter demonstrates very basic programming techniques, such as building user interfaces, event programming, validating user input, and handling errors. The goal is to show you how to write simple applications using the most basic elements of the language. This chapter will explain the methodology for building applications. While the code of the applications will be rather simple, it will demonstrate the basics of validating data and trapping errors.

If you're a beginner, you may be thinking, "All I want now is to write a simple application that works—I'll worry about data validation later." It's never too early to start thinking about validating your code's data and error trapping. As you'll see, making sure that your application doesn't crash may require more code than the actual operations it performs! If this isn't quite what you expected, welcome to the club. A well-behaved application must catch and handle every error gracefully, including user errors.

Building a Loan Calculator

One easy-to-implement, practical application is a program that calculates loan parameters. Visual Basic provides built-in functions for performing many types of financial calculations, and you only need a single line of code to calculate the monthly payment given the loan amount, its duration, and the interest rate. Designing the user interface, however, takes much more effort.

Regardless of the language you use, you must go through the following process to develop an application:

1. Decide what the application will do and how it will interact with the user.

2. Design the application's user interface according to the requirements of Step 1.

3. Write the actual code behind the events you want to handle.

How the Loan Application Works

Following the first step of the process outlined above, you decide that the user should be able to specify the amount of the loan, the interest rate, and the duration of the loan in months. You must, therefore, provide three text boxes where the user can enter these values.

Another parameter affecting the monthly payment is whether payments are made at the beginning or at the end of each month, so you must also provide a way for the user to specify whether the payments will be early (first day of the month) or late (last day of the month). The most appropriate type of control for entering Yes/No or True/False type of information is the CheckBox control. This control is a toggle: If it's checked, you can clear it by clicking it. If it's cleared, you can check it by clicking again. The user doesn't enter any data in this control (which means you need not anticipate user errors with this control), and it's the simplest method for specifying values with two possible states. Figure 2.1 shows a user interface that matches our design specifications. This is the main form of the LoanCalculator project, which you will find in this chapter's folder on the CD.

FIGURE 2.1

LoanCalculator is a simple financial application.

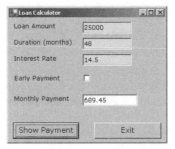

After the user enters all the information on the form, they can click the Show Payment button to calculate the monthly payment. The program will calculate the monthly payment and display it in the lower TextBox control. All the action takes place in the button's Click subroutine. The function for calculating monthly payments is called Pmt() and must be called as follows:

```
MonthlyPayment = Pmt(InterestRate, Periods, Amount, FutureValue, Due)
```

The interest rate (argument *InterestRate*) is specified as a monthly rate. If the interest rate is 16.5%, the value entered by the user in the Interest Rate box should be 16.5, and the monthly rate will be 0.165 / 12. The duration of the loan (*Periods*) is specified in number of months, and *Amount* is the loan's amount. The *FutureValue* of a loan is zero (it would be a positive value for an investment), and the last parameter, *Due*, specifies when payments are due.

The value of *Due* can be one of the constants DueDate.BegOfPeriod and DueDate.EndOfPeriod. These two constants are built into the language, and you can use them without knowing their exact value. In effect, this is the essence of using named constants: you type a self-descriptive name and leave it to VB to convert it to a numeric value. As you will see, .NET uses numerous constants, all of which are categorized in groups called *enumerations*. The constants that apply to the *Due* argument of the Pmt() function belong to the DueDate enumeration, which has two members, the `BegOfPeriod` and `EndOfPeriod` members.

The present value of the loan is the amount of the loan with a negative sign. It's negative because you don't have the money now. You're borrowing it; it's money you owe to the bank. Future value represents the value of something at a stated time—in this case, what the loan will be worth when it's paid off. This is what one side owes the other at the end of the specified period. So the future value of a loan is zero.

Pmt() is a built-in function that uses the five values in the parentheses to calculate the monthly payment. The values passed to the function are called *arguments*. Arguments are the values needed by a function (or subroutine) to carry out an action or calculation. By passing different values to the function, the user can specify the parameters of any loan and calculate its monthly payment. The Pmt() function and other financial functions of Visual Basic are described in the reference "VB.NET Functions and Statements" on the CD that accompanies this book.

You don't need to know how the Pmt() function calculates the monthly payment. The Pmt() function does the calculations and returns the result. To calculate the monthly payment on a loan of $25,000 with an interest rate of 14.5%, payable over 48 months, and due the last day of the payment period (which in our case is a month), you'd call the Pmt() function as follows:

```
Console.WriteLine(Pmt(0.145 / 12, 48, -25000, 0, DueDate.EndOfPeriod))
```

The value 689.448821287218 will be displayed in the Output window (you'll see later how you can limit the digits after the decimal point to two, since this is all the accuracy you need for dollar amounts). Notice the negative sign in front of the *Amount* argument in the statement. If you specify a positive amount, the result will be a negative payment. The payment and the loan's amount have different signs because they represent different cash flows. The loan's amount is money you *owe* to the bank, while the payment is money you *pay* to the bank.

The last two arguments of the Pmt() function are optional. If you omit them, Visual Basic uses their default values, which are 0 for the *FutureValue* argument and `DueDate.BegOfPeriod` for the *Due* argument. You can entirely omit these arguments and call the Pmt() function like this:

```
Console.WriteLine(Pmt(0.145 / 12, 48, -25000))
```

Calculating the amount of the monthly payment given the loan parameters is quite simple. What you need to know or understand are the parameters of a loan and how to pass them to the Pmt() function. You must also know how the interest rate is specified, to avoid invalid values. What you don't need to know is how the payment is calculated—Visual Basic does it for you. This is the essence of functions: they are "black boxes" that perform complicated calculations on their arguments and return the result. You don't have to know how they work, just how to supply the values required for the calculations.

Designing the User Interface

Now that you know how to calculate the monthly payment, you can design the user interface. To do so, start a new project, name it LoanCalculator, and rename its form to LoanForm. The form and the project files can be found in this chapter's folder on the CD.

Your first task is to decide the font and size of the text you'll use for most controls on the form. Although we aren't going to display anything on the form directly, all the controls we place on it will have, by default, the same font as the form. The form is the container of the controls, and they inherit some of the form's properties, such as the Font. You can change the font later during the design, but it's a good idea to start with the right font. At any rate, don't try to align the controls if you're planning to change their fonts. This will, most likely, throw off your alignment efforts.

TIP *Try not to mix fonts on a form. A form, or a printed page for that matter, that includes type in several fonts looks like it has been created haphazardly and is difficult to read. However, you can use different sizes for some of the controls on the form.*

The loan application you'll find on the CD uses the 10-point Verdana font. To change it, select the form with the mouse, double-click the name of the Font property in the Properties window to open the Font dialog box, and select the desired font and attributes. When the form is selected, its name appears in the ComboBox at the top of the window, as shown in Figure 2.2.

FIGURE 2.2

Setting the form's
Font property

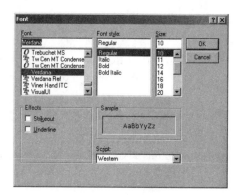

To design the form shown previously in Figure 2.1, follow these steps:

1. Place four labels on the form and assign the following captions to them:

Label	Caption
Label1	Loan Amount
Label2	Duration (months)
Label3	Interest Rate
Label4	Monthly Payment

   The labels should be large enough to fit their captions. You don't need to change the default names of the four Label controls on the form because their captions are all we need. You aren't going to program them.

2. Place a TextBox control next to each label. Set their Name and Text properties to the following values. These initial values correspond to a loan of $25,000 with an interest rate of 14.5% and a payoff period of 48 months.

TextBox	Name	Text
TextBox1	txtAmount	25,000
TextBox2	txtDuration	48
TextBox3	txtRate	14.5
TextBox4	txtPayment	

3. The fourth TextBox control is where the monthly payment will appear. The user isn't supposed to enter any data in this box, so you must set its ReadOnly property to True. You'll be able to change its value from within your code, but users won't be able to type anything in it. (We could have used a Label control instead, but the uniform look of TextBoxes on a form is usually preferred.)

4. Next, place a CheckBox control on the form. By default, the control's caption is Check1, and it appears to the right of the check box. Because we want the titles to be to the left of the corresponding controls, we'll change this default appearance.

5. Select the check box with the mouse (if it's not already selected), and in the Properties window, locate the CheckAlign property. Its value is `MiddleLeft`. If you expand the drop-down list by clicking the arrow button, you'll see that this property has many different settings and each setting is shown as a square. Select the square in the middle row, the right column. The string `MiddleRight` will appear in the property's box when you click the appropriate button. The first component of the CheckAlign property's value indicates the vertical alignment of the check box, and the second component of the value indicates the horizontal alignment. `MiddleRight` means that the check box should be centered vertically and right-aligned horizontally.

6. With the check box selected, locate the Name property in the Properties window, and set it to chkPayEarly.

7. Change the CheckBox's caption by entering the string Early Payment in its Text property field.

8. Place a Button control in the bottom-left corner of the form. Name it bttnShowPayment, and set its caption to Show Payment.

9. Finally, place another Button control on the form, name it bttnExit, and set its Text property to Exit.

ALIGNING THE CONTROLS

Your next step is to align the controls on the form. First, be sure that the captions on the labels are visible. Our labels contain lengthy captions, and if you don't make the labels long enough, the captions may wrap to a second line and become invisible.

TIP   Be sure to make your labels long enough to hold their captions, especially if you're using a nonstandard font. A user's computer may substitute another font for your nonstandard font, and the corresponding captions may increase in length.

The IDE provides commands to align the controls on the form, all of which can be accessed through the Format menu. To align the controls that are already on the LoanForm, follow these steps:

1. Select the four labels on the form with the mouse and left-align them by choosing Format ➤ Align ➤ Lefts. The handles of all selected controls will be white, except for one control whose handles will be black. All controls will be left-aligned with this control. To specify the control that will be used as reference point for aligning the other controls, click it after making the selection. (You can select multiple controls either by drawing a rectangle that encloses them with the mouse, or by clicking each control while holding down the Ctrl button.)

2. With the four text boxes selected, choose Format ➤ Align ➤ Lefts. Don't include the check box in this selection.

TIP   When you select multiple controls to align together, use the control with black handles as a guide for aligning the other controls.

3. With all four text boxes still selected, use the mouse to align them above and below the box of the CheckBox control.

Your form should now look like the one in Figure 2.1. Take a good look at it and check to see if any of your controls are misaligned. In the interface design process, you tend to overlook small problems such as a slightly misaligned control. The user of the application, however, instantly spots such mistakes. It doesn't make any difference how nicely the rest of the controls are arranged on the form; if one of them is misaligned, it will attract the user's attention.

Programming the Loan Application

Now run the application and see how it behaves. Enter a few values in the text boxes, change the state of the check box, and test the functionality already built into the application. Clicking the

Show Payment button won't have any effect because we have not yet added any code. If you're happy with the user interface, stop the application, open the form, and double-click the Show Payment Button control. Visual Basic opens the code window and displays the definition of the Show-Payment_Click event:

```
Private Sub bttnShowPayment_Click(ByVal sender As System.Object, _
            ByVal e As System.EventArgs) Handles bttnShowPayment.Click

End Sub
```

NOTE   *I've broken the first line with an underline character, because it wouldn't fit on the page. The underscore character is the line-continuation character, which allows you to break a long code line into multiple text lines.*

This is the declaration of the Button's Click event handler. This subroutine will be invoked when the user clicks the Show Payment button. Above the definition of the event handler, you will see the following two statements:

```
Public Class LoanForm
    Inherits System.Windows.Forms.Form
```

The first statement creates a new class for the project's form; the second inherits the functionality of the Form object. These statements are placed there by the IDE, and you shouldn't change them. When you learn more about classes and inheritance in the second part of the book, you'll be able to better understand the role of these statements.

Place the pointer between the lines Private Sub and End Sub, and enter the rest of the lines of Listing 2.1 (you don't have to reenter the first and last lines that declare the event handler).

LISTING 2.1: THE SHOW PAYMENT BUTTON

```
Private Sub bttnShowPayment_Click(ByVal sender As System.Object, _
            ByVal e As System.EventArgs) Handles bttnShowPayment.Click
    Dim Payment As Single
    Dim payEarly As DueDate
    If chkPayEarly.Checked Then
        payEarly = DueDate.BegOfPeriod
    Else
        payEarly = DueDate.EndOfPeriod
    End If
    Payment = Pmt(0.01 * txtRate.Text / 12, txtDuration.Text, _
                -txtAmount.Text, 0, payEarly)
    txtPayment.Text = Payment.ToString("#.00")
End Sub
```

The code window should now look like the one shown in Figure 2.3. Notice the underscore character at the end of the first part of the long line. The underscore lets you break long lines so that they will fit nicely in the code window. I'm using this convention in this book a lot to fit long lines on the printed page. The same statement you see as multiple lines in the book may appear in a single, long line in the project.

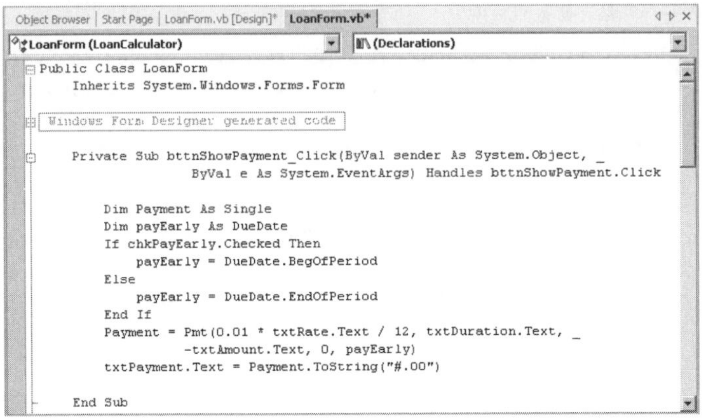

FIGURE 2.3

The Show Payment button's Click event subroutine

```
Object Browser | Start Page | LoanForm.vb [Design]* | LoanForm.vb*          ◁ ▷ ×
LoanForm (LoanCalculator)              ▼   (Declarations)                      ▼
Public Class LoanForm
      Inherits System.Windows.Forms.Form

  Windows Form Designer generated code

      Private Sub bttnShowPayment_Click(ByVal sender As System.Object, _
                    ByVal e As System.EventArgs) Handles bttnShowPayment.Click

          Dim Payment As Single
          Dim payEarly As DueDate
          If chkPayEarly.Checked Then
              payEarly = DueDate.BegOfPeriod
          Else
              payEarly = DueDate.EndOfPeriod
          End If
          Payment = Pmt(0.01 * txtRate.Text / 12, txtDuration.Text, _
                    -txtAmount.Text, 0, payEarly)
          txtPayment.Text = Payment.ToString("#.00")

      End Sub
```

You don't have to break long lines manually as you enter code in the editor's window. Open the Edit menu and select Advanced ➢ Word Wrap. The editor will wrap long lines automatically at a word boundary. While the word wrap feature is on, a check mark appears in front of the Edit ➢ Advanced ➢ Word Wrap command. To turn off word wrapping, select the same command again.

In Listing 2.1, the first line of code within the subroutine declares a variable. It lets the application know that *Payment* is a placeholder for storing a *floating-point number* (a number with a decimal part)—the Single data type. The second line declares a variable of the DueDate type. This is the type of the argument that determines whether the payment takes place at the beginning or the end of the month. The last argument of the Pmt() function must be a variable of this type, so we declare a variable of the DueDate type. As mentioned earlier in this chapter, DueDate is an enumeration with two members: `BegOfPeriod` and `EndOfPeriod`. In short, the last argument of the Pmt() function can be one of the following values:

```
DueDate.BegOfPeriod
DueDate.EndOfPeriod
```

The first really executable line in the subroutine is the If statement that examines the value of the chkPayEarly CheckBox control. If the control is checked, the code sets the *payEarly* variable to `DueDate.BegOfPeriod`. If not, the code sets the same variable to `DueDate.EndOfPeriod`. The Combo-Box control's Checked property returns True if the control is checked at the time, False otherwise. After setting the value of the *payEarly* variable, the code calls the Pmt() function, passing the values of the controls as arguments:

◆ The first argument is the interest rate. The value entered by the user in the txtRate TextBox is multiplied by 0.01 so that the value 14.5 (which corresponds to 14.5%) is passed to the Pmt() function as 0.145. Although we humans prefer to specify interest rates as integers (8%) or floating-point numbers larger than 1 (8.24%), the Pmt() function expects to read a number less than 1. The value 1 corresponds to 100%. Therefore, the value 0.1 corresponds to 10%. This value is also divided by 12 to yield the monthly interest rate.

♦ The second argument is the duration of the loan in months (the value entered in the txtDuration TextBox).

♦ The third argument is the loan's amount (the value entered in the txtAmount TextBox).

♦ The fourth argument (the loan's future value) is 0 by definition.

♦ The last argument is the *payEarly* variable, which is set according to the status of the chkPayEarly control.

The following two statements convert the numeric value returned by the Pmt() function to a string and display this string in the fourth TextBox control. The result is formatted appropriately with the following expression:

```
Payment.ToString("#.00")
```

The *Payment* variable is numeric, and all numeric variables provide the method ToString, which formats the numeric value and converts it to a string. The character # stands for the integer part of the variable. The period separates the integer from the fractional part, which is rounded to two decimal digits. Because the Pmt() function returns a precise number, such as 372.22235687646345, you must round and format it nicely before displaying it. Since the bank can't charge you anything less than a penny, you don't need extreme accuracy. Two fractional digits are sufficient. For more information on formatting numeric (and other) values, see the section "Formatting Numbers" in Chapter 3.

To display the result returned by the Pmt() function directly on the *txtPayment* TextBox control, use the following statement:

```
txtPayment.Text = Pmt(0.01 * txtRate.Text / 12, txtDuration.Text, _
                      -txtAmount.Text, 0, payEarly)
```

This statement assigns the value returned by the Pmt() function directly to the Text property of the control. The monthly payment will be displayed with four decimal digits, but this isn't a proper dollar amount.

TIP *You almost always use the ToString method (or the Format() function) when you want to display the results of numeric calculations, because most of the time you don't need Visual Basic's extreme accuracy. A few fractional digits are all you need. In addition to numbers, the ToString method can format dates and time. The ToString method's formatting capabilities are discussed in Chapter 12, and the Format() function is described in the reference "VB.NET Functions and Statements" on the CD.*

The code of the LoanCalculator project on the CD is different and considerably longer than what I have presented here. The statements discussed in the preceding text are the bare minimum for calculating a loan payment. The user may enter any values on the form and cause the program to crash. In the next section, we'll see how you can validate the data entered by the user, catch errors, and handle them gracefully (that is, give the user a chance to correct the data and proceed), as opposed to terminating the application with a runtime error.

Validating the Data

If you enter a nonnumeric value in one of the fields, the program will crash and display an error message. For example, if you enter **twenty** in the Duration text box, the program will display the error message shown in Figure 2.4. A simple typing error can crash the program. This isn't the way Windows applications should work. Your applications must be able to handle most user errors, provide helpful messages, and in general, guide the user in running the application efficiently. If a user error goes unnoticed, your application will either end abruptly or will produce incorrect results without an indication.

FIGURE 2.4

The Cast Exception message means that you supplied a string where a numeric value was expected.

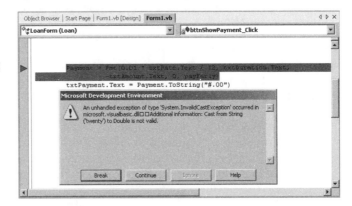

Click the Break button, and Visual Basic will take you back to the application's code window, where the statements that caused the error will be highlighted in green. Obviously, we must do something about user errors. One way to take care of typing errors is to examine each control's contents; if they don't contain valid numeric values, display your own descriptive message and give the user another chance. Listing 2.2 is the revised Click event handler that examines the value of each text box before attempting to use it in any calculations.

LISTING 2.2: THE REVISED SHOW PAYMENT BUTTON

```
Private Sub bttnShowPayment_Click(ByVal sender As System.Object, _
            ByVal e As System.EventArgs) Handles bttnShowPayment.Click
    Dim Payment As Single
    Dim LoanIRate As Single
    Dim LoanDuration As Integer
    Dim LoanAmount As Integer
' Validate amount
    If IsNumeric(txtAmount.Text) Then
        LoanAmount = txtAmount.Text
    Else
        MsgBox("Please enter a valid amount")
        Exit Sub
    End If
' Validate interest rate
    If IsNumeric(txtRate.Text) Then
        LoanIRate = 0.01 * txtRate.Text / 12
    Else
        MsgBox("Invalid interest rate, please re-enter")
```

```
        Exit Sub
    End If
' Validate loan's duration
    If IsNumeric(txtDuration.Text) Then
        LoanDuration = txtDuration.Text
    Else
        MsgBox("Please specify the loan's duration as a number of months")
        Exit Sub
    End If
' If all data were validated, proceed with calculations
    Dim payEarly As DueDate
    If chkPayEarly.Checked Then
        payEarly = DueDate.BegOfPeriod
    Else
        payEarly = DueDate.EndOfPeriod
    End If
    Payment = Pmt(LoanIRate, LoanDuration, -LoanAmount, 0, payEarly)
    txtPayment.Text = Payment.ToString("#.00")
End Sub
```

First, we declare three variables in which the loan's parameters will be stored: *LoanAmount, LoanI-Rate,* and *LoanDuration.* These values will be passed to the Pmt() function as arguments. Each text box's value is examined with an If structure. If the corresponding text box holds a valid number, its value is assigned to the numeric variable. If not, the program displays a warning and exits the subroutine without attempting to calculate the monthly payment. The user can then fix the incorrect value and click the ShowPayment button again. IsNumeric() is another built-in function that accepts a variable and returns True if the variable is a number, False otherwise.

If the Amount text box holds a numeric value, such as 21,000 or 21.50, the function IsNumeric (txtAmount.Text) returns True, and the statement following it is executed. That following statement assigns the value entered in the *Amount* TextBox to the *LoanAmount* variable. If not, the Else clause of the statement is executed, which displays a warning in a message box and then exits the subroutine. The Exit Sub statement tells Visual Basic to stop executing the subroutine immediately, as if the End Sub line were encountered.

You can run the revised application and test it by entering invalid values in the fields. Notice that you can't specify an invalid value for the last argument; the CheckBox control won't let you enter a value. You can only check or clear it and both options are valid. The LoanCalculator application you'll find on the CD contains this last version with the error-trapping code.

The actual calculation of the monthly payment takes a single line of Visual Basic code. Displaying it requires another line of code. Adding the code to validate the data entered by the user, however, is an entire program. And that's the way things are.

NOTE *The applications in this book don't contain much data-validation code because it would obscure the "useful" code that applies to the topic at hand. Instead, they demonstrate specific techniques. You can use parts of the examples in your applications, but you should provide your own data-validation code (and error-handling code, as you'll see in the following section).*

WRITING WELL-BEHAVED APPLICATIONS

A well-behaved application must contain data-validation code. If an application such as LoanCalculator crashes because of a typing mistake, nothing really bad will happen. The user will try again or else give up on your application and look for a more professional one. However, if the user has been entering data for hours, the situation is far more serious. It's your responsibility as a programmer to make sure that only valid data are used by the application and that the application keeps working, no matter how the user misuses or abuses it.

Now run the application one last time and enter an enormous loan amount. Try to find out what it would take to pay off the national debt with a reasonable interest rate in, say, 72 months. The program will crash again (as if you didn't know). This time the program will go down with a different error message. Visual Basic will complain about an "overflow." The exact message is shown in Figure 2.5 and the program will stop at the line that assigns the contents of the *txtAmount* TextBox to the *LoanAmount* variable. Press the Break button and the offending statement in the code will be highlighted.

FIGURE 2.5

Very large values can cause the application to crash with this error message.

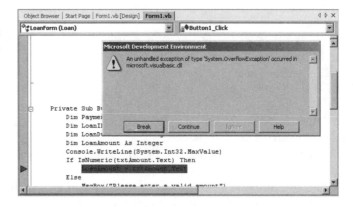

TIP   An overflow is a numeric value too large for the program to handle. This error is usually produced when you divide a number by a very small value. When you attempt to assign a very large value to an Integer variable, you'll also get an overflow exception.

Actually, in the LoanCalculator application, any amount greater than 2,147,483,647 will cause an overflow condition. This is largest value you can assign to an Integer variable; it's plenty for our banking needs, but not nearly adequate for handling government budgets. As you'll see in the next chapter, Visual Basic provides other types of variables, which can store enormous values (making the national debt look really small). In the meantime, if you want to use the loan calculator, change the declaration of the *LoanAmount* variable to:

```
Dim LoanAmount As Single
```

The Single data type can hold much larger values. Besides, the Single data type can also hold non-integer values. I'm assuming you won't ask for a loan of $25,000 and some cents, but if you want to calculate the precise monthly payment for a debt you have accumulated, then you should be able to specify a non-integer amount. In short, we should have declared the *LoanAmount* variable with the Single data type in the first place (but then I wouldn't have been able to demonstrate the overflow exception).

An overflow error can't be caught with data-validation code. There's always a chance your calculations will produce overflows or other types of math errors. Data validation isn't going to help here; you just don't know the result before you carry out the calculations. We need something called *error handling*, or *error trapping*. This is additional code than can handle errors after they occur. In effect, you're telling VB that it shouldn't stop with an error message. This would be embarrassing for you and wouldn't help the user one bit. Instead, VB should detect the error and execute the proper statements that will handle the error. Obviously, you must supply these statements, and you'll see examples of handling errors at runtime in the following section.

Building a Math Calculator

Our next application is more advanced, but not as advanced as it looks. It's a math calculator with a typical visual interface that demonstrates how Visual Basic can simplify the programming of fairly advanced operations. If you haven't tried it, you may think that writing an application such as this one is way too complicated, but it isn't. The MathCalculator application is shown in Figure 2.6, and you'll find it in this chapter's folder on the CD. The application emulates the operation of a hand-held calculator and implements the basic arithmetic operations. It has the structure of a math calculator, and you can easily expand it by adding more features. In fact, adding features like cosines and logarithms is actually simpler than performing the basic arithmetic operations.

FIGURE 2.6

The Calculator application window

Designing the User Interface

The application's interface is straightforward, but it takes quite a bit of effort. You must align buttons on the form and make the calculator look as much like a hand-held calculator as possible. Start a new project, the MathCalculator project, and name its main form CalculatorForm.

Designing the interface of the application isn't trivial, because it's made up of many buttons, all perfectly aligned on the form. To simplify the design, follow these steps:

1. Select a font that you like for the form. All the Command buttons you'll place on the form will inherit this font. The MathCalculator application on the CD uses 10-point Verdana font.

2. Add the Label control, which will become the calculator's display. Set its BorderStyle property to Fixed 3D so that it will have a 3-D look, as shown in Figure 2.6. Change its Fore-Color and BackColor properties too, if you want it to look different than the rest of the form. The project you will find on the CD uses colors that emulate the—now extinct—green CRT monitors.

3. Draw a Button control on the form, change its caption (Text property) to 1, and name it bttn1. Size the button carefully so that its caption is centered on the control. The other buttons on the form will be copies of this one, so make sure you've designed the first button as best as you can, before you start making copies of it.

4. Place the button in its final position on the form. At this point you're ready to create the other buttons for the calculator's digits. Right-click the button and select Copy. The Button control is copied to the Clipboard, and now you can paste it on the form (which is much faster than designing an identical button).

5. Right-click somewhere on the form and select Paste to create a copy of the button you copied earlier. The button you copied to the Clipboard will be pasted on the form, on top of the original button. The copy will have the same caption as the button it was copied from, and its name will be Button1.

6. Now set the button's Name to bttn2 and its Text property to 2. This button is the digit 2. Place the new button to the right of the previous button. You don't have to align the two buttons perfectly now; later we'll use the Format menu to align the buttons on the form.

7. Repeat Steps 5 and 6 eight more times, once for each numeric digit. Each time a new Button control is pasted on the form, Visual Basic names it Button1 and sets its caption to 1; you must change the Name and Text properties. You can name the buttons anything you like; their Click event will be handled by the same subroutine, which will read the button's Text property to find out which digit was clicked.

8. When the buttons of the numeric digits are all on the form, place two more buttons, one for the C (Clear) operation and one for the Period button. Name them bttnClear and bttnPeriod, and set their captions accordingly. Use a larger font size for the Period button to make its caption easier to read.

9. When all the digit buttons of the first group are on the form and in their approximate positions, align them with the commands of the Format menu.

   A. First, align the buttons of the top row. Start by aligning the 1 button with the left side of the lblDisplay Label. Then select all the buttons of the top row and make their horizontal spacing equal (select Format ➤ Horizontal Spacing ➤ Make Equal). Then do the same with the buttons in the first column, and this time, make sure their vertical distances are equal (Format ➤ Vertical Spacing ➤ Make Equal).

   B. Now you can align the buttons in each row and each column separately. Use one of the buttons you aligned in the last step as the guide for the rest of them. The buttons can be aligned in many ways, so don't worry if somewhere in the process you ruin the alignment. You can always use the Undo command in the Edit menu. Select the three buttons on the second row and align their Tops using the first button as reference. Do the same for the third and fourth rows of buttons. Then do the same for the four columns of buttons.

Now, place the buttons for the arithmetic operations on the form—addition (+), subtraction (-), multiplication (*), and division (/). Use the commands on the Format menu to align these buttons as shown earlier in Figure 2.6. The control with the black handles can be used as a reference for aligning the other controls into rows and columns. The form shown in Figure 2.6 has a few more buttons, which you can align using the same techniques you used to align the numeric buttons.

The Equals button at the bottom is called bttnEquals, and you must make it wide enough to cover the space of the three buttons above it.

Programming the MathCalculator App

Now you're ready to add some code to the application. Double-click one of the digit buttons on the form, and you'll see the following in the code window:

```
Private Sub bttn1_Click(ByVal sender As System.Object, _
            ByVal e As System.EventArgs) Handles bttn1.Click

End Sub
```

This is the Click event's handler for a single digit button. Your first attempt is to program the Click event handler of each digit button, but repeating the same code 10 times isn't very productive. We're going to use the same event handler for all buttons that represent digits. All you have to do is append the names of the events to be handled by the same subroutine after the Handles keyword. You should also change the name of the event handler to something that indicates its role. Since this subroutine handles the Click event for all the digit buttons, let's call it Digit_Click(). Here's the revised declaration of a subroutine that can handle all the digit buttons:

```
Private Sub Digit_Click(ByVal sender As System.Object, _
            ByVal e As System.EventArgs) Handles bttn1.Click, bttn2.Click, _
            bttn3.Click, bttn4.Click, bttn5.Click, bttn6.Click, _
            bttn7.Click, bttn8.Click, bttn9.Click, bttn0.Click
End Sub
```

When you press a digit button on a hand-held calculator, the corresponding digit is appended to the display. To emulate this behavior, insert the following line in the Click event handler:

```
lblDisplay.Text = lblDisplay.Text + sender.Text
```

This line appends the digit clicked to the calculator's display. The *sender* argument of the Click event represents the control that was clicked (the control that fired the event). The Text property of this control is the digit of the button that was clicked. For example, if you have already entered the value 345, clicking the digit 0 displays the value 3450 on the Label control that acts as the calculator's display.

The expression sender.Text is not the best method of accessing the Text property of the button that was clicked, but it will work as long as the Strict option is off. We'll return to this topic later in the book, but for now let me briefly explain that you should convert the *sender* object to a TextBox object and then access its Text property with the following statement:

```
CType(sender, TextBox).Text
```

The CType() function is discussed in the following chapter. For now, keep in mind that it converts an object to an object of a different type. You will also notice that after typing the period following the closing parenthesis, all the members of the TextBox control will appear in a list, as if you had entered the name of a TextBox control followed by a period.

The code behind the digit buttons needs a few more lines. After certain actions, the display should be cleared. After pressing one of the buttons that correspond to math operations, the display should be cleared in anticipation of the second operand. Actually, the display must be cleared as soon as the first digit of the second operand is pressed. Revise the Digit_Click event handler as shown in Listing 2.3.

LISTING 2.3: THE DIGIT_CLICK EVENT

```
Private Sub Digit_Click(ByVal sender As System.Object, _
            ByVal e As System.EventArgs) Handles bttn1.Click, bttn2.Click, _
            bttn3.Click, bttn4.Click, bttn5.Click, bttn6.Click, _
            bttn7.Click, bttn8.Click, bttn9.Click, bttn0.Click
    If clearDisplay Then
        lblDisplay.Text = ""
        clearDisplay = False
    End If
    lblDisplay.Text = lblDisplay.Text + sender.text
End Sub
```

The *clearDisplay* variable is declared as Boolean, which means it can take a True or False value. Suppose the user has performed an operation and the result is on the calculator's display. The user now starts typing another number. Without the If clause, the program would continue to append digits to the number already on the display. This is not how calculators work. When a new number is entered, the display must clear. And our program uses the *clearDisplay* variable to know when to clear the display.

The Equals button sets the *clearDisplay* variable to True to indicate that the display contains the result of an operation. The Digit_Click() subroutine examines the value of this variable each time a new digit button is pressed. If the value is True, Digit_Click() clears the display and then prints the new digit on it. The subroutine also sets *clearDisplay* to False so that when the next digit is pressed, the program won't clear the display again.

What if the user makes a mistake and wants to undo an entry? The typical hand-held calculator has no backspace key. The Clear key erases the current number on the display. Let's implement this feature. Double-click the C button and enter the code of Listing 2.4 in its Click event.

```
Private Sub bttnClear_Click(ByVal sender As System.Object, _
            ByVal e As System.EventArgs) Handles bttnClear.Click
    lblDisplay.Text = ""
End Sub
```

Now we can look at the Period button. A calculator, no matter how simple, should be able to handle fractional numbers. The Period button works just like the digit buttons, with one exception. A digit can appear any number of times in a numeric value, but the period can appear only once. A number like 99.991 is valid, but you must make sure that the user can't enter numbers such as 23.456.55. Once a period is entered, this button mustn't insert another one. The code in Listing 2.5 accounts for this.

```
Private Sub bttnPeriod_Click(ByVal sender As System.Object, _
            ByVal e As System.EventArgs) Handles bttnPeriod.Click
    If lblDisplay.Text.IndexOf(".") > 0 Then
        Exit Sub
    Else
        lblDisplay.Text = lblDisplay.Text & "."
    End If
End Sub
```

IndexOf is a method that can be applied to any string. The expression lblDisplay.Text is a string (the text on the Label control), so we can call its IndexOf method. The code IndexOf(".") returns the location of the first instance of the period in the caption of the Label control. If this number is positive, the number entered contains a period already, and another can't be entered. In this case, the program exits the subroutine. If the method returns 0, the period is appended to the number entered so far, just like a regular digit.

Check out the operation of the application. We have already created a functional user interface that emulates a hand-held calculator with data-entry capabilities. It doesn't perform any operations yet, but we have already created a functional user interface with only a small number of statements.

MATH OPERATIONS

Now we can move to the interesting part of the application: considering how a calculator works. Let's start by defining three variables:

Operand1	The first number in the operation
Operator	The desired operation
Operand2	The second number in the operation

When the user clicks one of the math symbols, the value on the display is stored in the variable *Operand1*. If the user then clicks the Plus button, the program must make a note to itself that the current operation is an addition and then clear the display so that the user can enter another value. The symbol of the operation is stored in the *Operator* variable. The user enters another value and then clicks the Equals button to see the result. At this point, our program must do the following:

1. Read the *Operand2* value on the display.

2. Add that value to *Operand1*.

3. Display the result.

The Equals button must perform the following operation:
```
Operand1 Operator Operand2
```
Suppose the number on the display when the user clicks the Plus button is 3342. The user then enters the value 23 and clicks the Equals button. The program must carry out the addition:
```
3342 + 23
```
If the user clicked the Division button, the operation is:
```
3342 / 23
```
In both cases, when Equals is clicked, the result is displayed (and it may become the first operand for the next operation).

Variables are local in the subroutines where they are declared. Other subroutines have no access to them and can't read or set their values. Sometimes, however, variables must be accessed from many places in a program. If the *Operand1*, *Operand2*, and *Operator* variables in this application must be accessed from within more than one subroutine, they must be declared outside any subroutine. The same is true for the *clearDisplay* variable. Their declarations, therefore, must appear outside any procedure, and they usually appear at the beginning of the code with the following statements:
```
Dim clearDisplay As Boolean
Dim Operand1 As Double
Dim Operand2 As Double
Dim Operator As String
```

Let's see how the program uses the *Operator* variable. When the user clicks the Plus button, the program must store the value "+" in the *Operator* variable. This takes place from within the Plus button's Click event. But later, the Equals button must have access to the value of the *Operator* variable in order to carry out the operation (in other words, it must know what type of operation the user specified). Because these variables must be manipulated from within more than a single subroutine, they were declared outside any subroutine.

The keyword Double is new to you. It tells VB to create a numeric variable with the greatest possible precision for storing the values of the operators. (Numeric variables and their types are discussed in detail in the next chapter.) The Boolean type takes two values, True and False. You have already seen how the *clearDisplay* variable is used.

The variables *Operand1*, *Operand2*, and *Operator* are called *Form-wide*, or simply *Form*, variables, because they are visible from within any subroutine on the form. If our application had another form, these variables wouldn't be visible from within the other form(s). In other words, any subroutine on a form on which the variables are declared can read or set the values of the variables, but no subroutine outside that form can do so.

With the variable declarations out of the way, we can now implement the Operator buttons. Double-click the Plus button and, in the Click event's handler, enter the lines shown in Listing 2.6.

LISTING 2.6: THE PLUS BUTTON

```
Private Sub bttnPlus_Click(ByVal sender As System.Object, _
                ByVal e As System.EventArgs) Handles bttnPlus.Click
    Operand1 = Val(lblDisplay.Text)
    Operator = "+"
    clearDisplay = True
End Sub
```

The variable *Operand1* is assigned the value currently on the display. The Val() function returns the numeric value of its argument. The Text property of the Label control is a string. For example, you can assign the value "My Label" to a label's Text property. The actual value stored in the Text property is not a number. It's a string such as "428", which is different from the numeric value 428. That's why we use the Val() function to convert the value of the Label's caption to a numeric value. The remaining buttons do the same, and I won't show their listings here.

So far, we have implemented the following functionality in our application: When an operator button is clicked, the program stores the value on the display in the *Operand1* variable and the operator in the *Operator* variable. It then clears the display so that the user can enter the second operand. After the second operand is entered, the user can click the Equals button to calculate the result. When this happens, the code of Listing 2.7 is executed.

LISTING 2.7: THE EQUALS BUTTON

```
Private Sub bttnEquals_Click(ByVal sender As System.Object, _
                ByVal e As System.EventArgs) Handles bttnEquals.Click
    Dim result As Double
    Operand2 = Val(lblDisplay.Text)
    Select Case Operator
        Case "+"
            result = Operand1 + Operand2
        Case "-"
            result = Operand1 - Operand2
        Case "*"
            result = Operand1 * Operand2
        Case "/"
            If Operand2 <> "0" Then result = Operand1 / Operand2
    End Select
    lblDisplay.Text = result
    clearDisplay = True
End Sub
```

The *result* variable is declared as Double so that the result of the operation will be stored with maximum precision. The code extracts the value displayed in the Label control and stores it in the variable *Operand2*. It then performs the operation with a `Select Case` statement. This statement compares the value of the *Operator* variable to the values listed after each Case statement. If the value of the *Operator* variable matches one of the Case values, the following statement is executed.

- If the operator is "+", the *result* variable is set to the sum of the two operands.

- If the operator is "-", the *result* variable is set to the difference of the first operand minus the second.

- If the operator is "*", the *result* variable is set to the product of the two operands.

- If the operator is "/", the *result* variable is set to the quotient of the first operand divided by the second operand, provided that the divisor is not zero.

NOTE *Division takes into consideration the value of the second operand because if it's zero, the division can't be carried out. The last If statement carries out the division only if the divisor is not zero. If* Operand2 *happens to be zero, nothing happens.*

Now run the application and check it out. It works just like a hand-held calculator, and you can't crash it by specifying invalid data. We didn't have to use any data-validation code in this example because the user doesn't get a chance to type invalid data. The data-entry mechanism is foolproof. The user can enter only numeric values because there are only numeric digits on the calculator. The only possible error is to divide by zero, and that's handled in the Equals button.

DEBUGGING TOOLS

Our application works nicely and is quite easy to test—and to fix, if you discover something wrong with it. But that's only because it's a very simple application. As you write code, you'll soon discover that something doesn't work as expected, and you should be able to find out why and repair it. The process of eliminating errors is called *debugging*, and Visual Studio provides the tools to simplify the process of debugging. These tools are discussed in Chapter 17. There are a few simple operations you should know, though, even as you work with simple projects like this one.

Open the MathCalculator project in the code editor and place the cursor in the line that calculates the difference between the two operands. Let's pretend there's a problem with this line and we want to follow the execution of the program closely, to find out what's going wrong with the application. Press F9 and the line will be highlighted in brown. This line has become a *breakpoint:* as soon as it is reached, the program will stop.

Press F5 to run the application and perform a subtraction. Enter a number, then click the minus button, then another number, and finally the Equals button. The application will stop, and the code editor will open. The breakpoint will be highlighted in yellow. Hover the pointer over the *Operand1* and *Operand2* variables in the code editor's window. The value of the corresponding variable will appear in a small box or tooltip. Move the pointer over any variable in the current event handler to see its value. These are the values of the variables just prior to the execution of the highlighted statement.

The *result* variable will most likely be zero, because the statement hasn't been executed yet. If the variables involved in this statement have their proper values (if not, you know that the problem is prior to this statement, and perhaps in another event handler), then you can execute this statement by pressing F10. By pressing F10, you're executing the highlighted statement only. The program will stop at the next line. The next statement to be executed is the `End Select` statement.

Find an instance of the *result* variable in the current event handler, rest the mouse over it, and you will see the value of the variable after it has been assigned a value. Now you can press F10 to execute another statement or F5 to return to normal execution mode.

You can also evaluate expressions involving any of the variables in the current event handler by entering the appropriate statement in the Command window. The Command window appears at the bottom of the IDE. If it's not visible, then from the main menu, select View ➤ Other Windows ➤ Command Window. The current line in the Output window is prefixed with the greater than symbol (reminiscent of the DOS days). Place the cursor next to it and enter the following statement:

```
? Operand1 / Operand2
```

The quotient of the two values will appear in the following line. The question mark is just a shorthand notation for the Print command. If you want to know the current value on the calculator's display, enter the following statement:

```
? lblDisplay.Text
```

This statement requests the value of a property of a control on the form. The current value of the Label control's Text property will appear in the following line. You can also evaluate math expressions with statements like the following:

```
? Math.Log(3/4)
```

Log() is the logarithm function, and it's a method of the Math class. To create a random value between 0 and 1, enter the statement:

```
? Rnd()
```

With time, you'll discover that the Command window is a very handy tool in debugging applications. If you have a statement with a complicated expression, you can request the values of the individual components of the expression and thereby make sure they can be evaluated.

Now move the pointer off the breakpoint and press F9 again. This will toggle the breakpoint status, and the execution of the program won't halt the next time this statement is executed.

If the execution of the program doesn't stop at a breakpoint, it means that the statement was never reached. In this case, you must search for the bug in statements that are executed before the breakpoint. If you didn't assign the proper value to the *Operator* variable, the `Case "-"` statement will never be reached. You should place the breakpoint at the first executable statement of the Equals button's Click event handler to examine the values of all variables the moment this subroutine starts its execution. If all variables had the expected values, you will continue testing the code forward. If not, you'd have to test the statements that lead to this statement—the statements in the event handlers of the various buttons.

Another simple technique for debugging applications is the Output window. Although this isn't a debugging tool, it's very common among VB programmers (and very practical, may I add). Many programmers print the values of selected variables after the execution of some complicated statements. To do so, use the statement:

```
Console.WriteLine
```

followed by the name of the variable you want to print, or an expression:

```
Console.WriteLine(Operand1)
```

This statement sends its output to the Output window, which is displayed next to the Command window—click the Output tab at the bottom of the IDE to view this window. Alternatively, you can select the command View ➤ Other Windows ➤ Output. This is a very simple technique, but it works. You can also use it to test a function or method call. If you're not sure about the syntax of a function, pass an expression that contains the specific function to the `Console.WriteLine` statement as argument. If the expected value appears in the Output window, you can go ahead and use it in your code.

Let's consider the DateDiff() function, which contains the difference between two dates. The simplest syntax of this function is

```
DateDiff(interval, date1, date2)
```

I never know whether it subtracts *date1* from *date2* or the other way around—if you don't get it right the first time, then every time you want to use this function, there's always a doubt in your mind. Before using the function in my code, I insert a statement like

```
Console.WriteLine(DateDiff(DateInterval.Day, #1/1/2000#, #1/2/2000#))
```

The value printed on the Output window is 1, by the way, indicating that the first date is subtracted from the second.

You will find more information on debugging in Chapter 17. I've just shown you a few simple techniques that will help you take advantage of the simpler debugging tools of Visual Studio as you write your first applications.

Adding More Features

Now that we have implemented the basic functionality of a hand-held calculator, we can add more features to our application. Let's add two more useful buttons:

- ◆ The +/-, or Negate, button, which inverts the sign of the number on the display
- ◆ The 1/x, or Inverse, button, which inverts the display number itself

Open the code window for each of the Command buttons and enter the code from Listing 2.8 in the corresponding Click event handlers. For the +/- button, enter the event handler named bttnNegate_Click, and for the 1/x button, enter the one named bttnInverse_Click.

LISTING 2.8: THE NEGATE AND INVERSE BUTTONS

```
Private Sub bttnNegate_Click(ByVal sender As System.Object, _
            ByVal e As System.EventArgs) Handles bttnNegate.Click
    lblDisplay.Text = -Val(lblDisplay.Text)
```

```
        clearDisplay = True
    End Sub
    Private Sub bttnInverse_Click(ByVal sender As System.Object, _
                    ByVal e As System.EventArgs) Handles bttnInverse.Click
        If Val(lblDisplay.Text) <> 0 Then lblDisplay.Text = 1 / Val(lblDisplay.Text)
        clearDisplay = True
    End Sub
```

As with the Division button, we don't attempt to invert a zero value. The operation $(1 / 0)$ is undefined and causes a runtime error. Notice also that I use the value displayed on the Label control directly in the code. I could have stored the lblDisplay.Text value to a variable and used the variable instead:

```
TempValue = Val(lblDisplay.Text)
If TempValue <> 0 Then lblDisplay.Text = 1 / TempValue
```

This is also better coding, but in short code segments, we all tend to minimize the number of statements.

You can easily expand the Math application by adding Function buttons to it. For example, you can add buttons to calculate common functions, such as Cos, Sin, and Log. The Cos button calculates the cosine of the number on the display. The code behind this button's Click event is a one-liner:

```
lblDisplay.Text = Math.Cos(Val(lblDisplay.Text))
```

It doesn't require a second operand, and it doesn't keep track of the operation. You can implement all math functions with a single line of code.

Of course, you should add some error trapping, and in some cases, you can use data-validation techniques. For example, the Sqrt() function, which calculates the square root of a number, expects a positive argument. If the number on the display is negative, you can issue a warning:

```
If lblDisplay.Text < 0 Then
    MsgBox("Can't calculate the square root of a negative number")
Else
    lblDisplay.Text = Math.Sqrt(Val(lblDisplay.Text))
End If
```

All math functions are part of the Math class; that's why they're prefixed by the name of the class. You can also import the Math class to the project with the following statement and thus avoid prefixing the math functions:

```
Imports System.Math
```

The Log() function can calculate the logarithms of positive numbers only. If you add a button to calculate logarithms and attempt to calculate the logarithm of a negative number, the result will be the string "NaN." This value is similar to infinity, and it says that the result is not a valid number (NaN stands for *not a number* and is discussed in detail in the following chapter). Of course, displaying a value like NaN on the calculator's display isn't the most user-friendly method of handling math errors. I would validate the data and pop up a message box with the appropriate description, as shown in Listing 2.9.

LISTING 2.9: CALCULATING THE LOGARITHM OF A NUMBER

```
Private Sub bttnLog_Click(ByVal sender As System.Object, _
            ByVal e As System.EventArgs) Handles bttnLog.Click
    If Val(lblDisplay.Text) < 0 Then
        MsgBox("Can't calculate the logarithm of a negative number")
    Else
        lblDisplay.Text = Math.Log(lblDisplay.Text)
    End If
    clearDisplay = True
End Sub
```

One more feature you could add to the calculator is a limit to the number of digits on the display. Most calculators can only display a limited number of digits. To add this feature to the Math application (if you consider this a "feature"), use the Len() function to find out the number of digits on the display and ignore any digits entered after the number has reached the maximum number of allowed digits.

Exception Handling

Crashing this application won't be as easy as crashing the Loan application. If you start multiplying very large numbers, you won't get an overflow exception. Enter a very large number by typing repeatedly the digit 9, then multiply this value with another, equally large value. When the result appears, click the multiplication symbol and enter another very large value. Keep multiplying the result with very large numbers, until you exhaust the value range of the Double data type (that is, until the result is so large that it can't be stored to a variable of the Double type). When this happens, the string "infinity" will appear in the display.

Our code doesn't include statements to capture overflows, so where did the string "infinity" come from? As you will learn in the following chapter, it is possible for numeric calculations to return the string "infinity." It's Visual Basic's way of telling you that it can't handle very large numbers. This isn't a limitation of VB; it's the way computers store numeric values: they provide a limited number of bytes for this. You will find out more about oddities such as infinity in the following chapter.

You can't create an overflow exception by dividing a number with zero either, because the code will not even attempt to carry out this calculation. In short, the Calculator application is pretty robust. However, we can't be sure that users won't cause the application to generate an exception, so we must provide some code to handle all types of errors.

Errors are now called *exceptions*. You can think of them as exceptions to the normal (or intended) flow of execution. If an exception occurs, the program must execute special statements to handle the exception—statements that wouldn't be executed normally. I think they're called exceptions because "error" is a word none of us likes, and most people can't admit they wrote code that contains errors. The term *exception* can be vague. What would you rather tell your customers: that the application you wrote has errors, or that your code has raised an exception? You may not have noticed it, but the term *bug* is not used as frequently any more; bugs are now called "known issues." The term *debugging*, however, hasn't changed yet.

VB6 programmers used the term *error* to describe something wrong in their code, and they used to write error-trapping code. With VB.NET, your code is error-free—it just raises exceptions every now and then. Both the error-trapping code of VB6 and the exception-handling features of VB.NET are supported. The error-trapping code of VB6 could get messy, so Microsoft added what they call *structured exception handling*. It's a more organized method to handle runtime errors—or exceptions. The basic premise is that when an exception occurs, the program doesn't crash with an error message. Instead, it executes a segment of code that you, the developer, provide.

TIP   *By the way, if you have a hard time admitting it's a bug in your code, use the expression "mea culpa." It's Latin, and it sounds so sophisticated, most people won't even ask what it means.*

How do you prevent an exception raised by a calculation? Data validation isn't going to help. You just can't predict the result of an operation without actually performing the operation. And if the operation causes an overflow, you can't prevent it. The answer is to add a structured exception handler. Most of the application's code is straightforward, and you can't generate an exception. The only place that an exception may occur is the handler of the Equals button, where the calculations take place. This is where we must add an exception handler. The outline of the error structure is the following:

```
Try
    { statements block }
Catch Exception
    { handler block }
Finally
    { clean-up statements block }
End Try
```

The program will attempt to perform the calculations, which are coded in the `statements block`. If it succeeds, it continues with the `clean-up statements`. These statements are mostly clean-up code, and the Finally section of the statement is optional. If missing, the program execution continues with the statement following the `End Try` statement. If an error occurs in the first block of statements, then the `Catch Exception` section is activated and the statements in the `handler` block are executed.

The Catch block is where you handle the error. There's not much you can do about errors that result from calculations. All you can do is display a warning and give the user a chance to change the values. There are other types of errors, however, which can be handled much more gracefully. If your program can't read a file from a CD drive, you can give the user a chance to insert the CD and retry. In other situations, you can prompt the user for a missing value and continue. In general, there's no unique method to handle all exceptions. You must consider all types of exceptions your application may cause and handle them on an individual basis.

The error handler for the Math application must inform the user that an error occurred and abort the calculations—not even attempt to display a result. If you open the Equals button's Click event handler, you will find the statements detailed in Listing 2.10.

LISTING 2.10: THE REVISED EQUALS BUTTON

```
Private Sub bttnEquals_Click(ByVal sender As System.Object, _
            ByVal e As System.EventArgs) Handles bttnEquals.Click
    Dim result As Double
    Operand2 = Val(lblDisplay.Text)
    Try
        Select Case Operator
            Case "+"
                result = Operand1 + Operand2
            Case "-"
                result = Operand1 - Operand2
            Case "*"
                result = Operand1 * Operand2
            Case "/"
                If Operand2 <> "0" Then result = Operand1 / Operand2
        End Select
        lblDisplay.Text = result
    Catch exc As Exception
        MsgBox(exc.Message)
        lblDisplay.Text= "ERROR"
    Finally
        clearDisplay = True
    End Try
End Sub
```

Most of the time, the error handler remains inactive and doesn't interfere with the operation of the program. If an error occurs, which most likely will be an overflow error, the error-handling section of the Try…Catch…End Try statement will be executed. This code displays a message box with the description of the error, and it also displays the string "ERROR" on the display. The Finally section is executed regardless of whether an exception occurred or not. In this example, the Finally section sets the *clearDisplay* variable to True so that when another digit button is clicked, a new number will appear on the display.

NOTE *The exc variable represents an exception; it exposes a few properties in addition to the Message property, which is the description of the exception. For more information on the members of the Exception class and how to handle exceptions, see Chapter 17.*

Taking the LoanCalculator to the Web

In this section, we're going to build a new project that is a loan calculator just like the one we built earlier. This time, though, the application will run on the browser, and any user who can connect to your server will be able to use it without having to install it on their computer. As you can understand, you're about to convert the LoanCalculator from a Windows application to a Web application. It's a little early in the book to discuss Web applications, but I wanted to show you that building a Web application is quite similar to building a Windows app.

Web applications are discussed in detail in the last part of the book, but since they're among the hot new features of the .NET platform, let me demonstrate why they are so hot. In a sentence, Visual Studio.NET is the first attempt to make the development of Web applications as easy as VB applications. You will see shortly that you can create the interface of a Web form (an HTML page with controls that interact with the user) just as you create a Windows form. As for the application's code, it's just like writing VB code to handle the events of a Windows form.

To write and test Web applications, you must have Internet Information Server (IIS) installed and running on your computer. IIS is distributed with Windows 2000, and you must make sure it's running. Open the Start menu and select Settings ➤ Control Panel. Double-click the Administrative Tools, then double-click the icon of the Internet Services Manager tool. When the Internet Services Manager window appears, expand the node of your computer, right-click the Default Web Site item, and from the context menu, select Start. This will start the Web server.

Start a new project and, on the New Project dialog box, click the ASP.NET Web Application icon. Then enter the name of the application in the Name box—call it WebLoanCalculator. When you close the New Project dialog box, you will see a window with a grid as usual, which represents the Web page, or Web form. This document is called `WebForm1.aspx` (the default name of the Web form). The Web form is equivalent to the Windows form, but it's displayed as HTML on a browser such as Internet Explorer, as you see in Figure 2.7.

FIGURE 2.7

The WebLoan-Calculator Web application

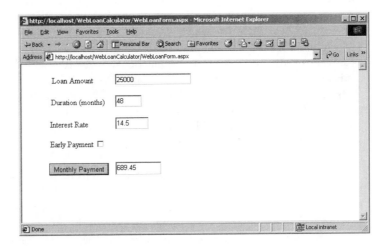

A new Windows project is stored in its own folder under the folder specified in the Location field on the New Project dialog box. Web applications are also stored in their own folder, but this folder is created under the Web server's root folder (usually the `C:\Inetpub\wwwroot` folder).

Opening a Web project is not as simple as double-clicking the icon of a Solution file. I suggest you follow the steps described in this chapter to create the project. If you want to open the WebLoanCalculator project on the CD, copy the entire WebLoanCalculator folder into the Web Server's root folder. Then start Visual Studio.NET and open the WebLoanCalculator solution file.

The text describes how to create the project from scratch. The application's main form is called `WebLoanForm.aspx` (it's equivalent to a Windows form). You can open the application by starting Internet Explorer and enter the following URL in its Address box:

`http://localhost/WebLoanCalculator/WebLoanForm.aspx`

Let me describe the process of building the Web application from scratch. Change the name of WebForm1 to WebLoanForm. Open the Toolbox, and you see that the Web Forms tab is activated, instead of the Windows Forms tab. The Web Forms tab contains the icons of the controls you can place on a Web form, which are similar to the Windows controls but not as elaborate or as rich in functionality. As you already know, Web pages use a much simpler user-interaction model. The viewer can enter text on certain controls, check or clear a few options, and click a button to submit the form to the server. The server reads the values on the controls, processes them, and returns a new page with the results. In the future, you can expect that applications running over the Internet will become more and more elaborate, but for now no one questions the HTML model used so far. As long as the browser can only handle HTML files, the Web application's front end is confined to HTML pages.

There's another tab on the Toolbox, the HTML tab. These are the standard HTML controls you can use on any Web page. The Web Forms tab contains the so-called Web controls, and there are quite a few Web controls, as opposed to the rather limited number of HTML controls. Some of the Web controls are also quite advanced compared to the really limited capabilities of the HTML controls. Does this mean that a page that contains Web controls can't be displayed on a browser other than Internet Explorer? Not at all. Web controls are translated automatically into standard HTML code that can be rendered on any browser. For example, on the Web Forms tab you'll find some very elaborate controls, such as the TreeView control. HTML doesn't provide any controls that come even near the functionality of TreeView. Yet a Web TreeView control can be rendered on any browser. The Web Forms Designer will insert the appropriate HTML tags to create something that looks and behaves like the TreeView control—but it's not a TreeView control. There's a lot to be said about Web controls, but you'll have to wait until the last part of the book. For now, we'll build a simple application that uses Web controls to prompt the user for the parameters of a loan and that will display the monthly payment on the same page, just like a Windows application.

Start by placing four Label controls on the Web form. (Double-click the Label control's icon on the Toolbox four times, and four labels be placed on the Web form for you.) Change their placement on the form by arranging them with the mouse, just as you would do with the controls on a Windows form. You don't have to align them perfectly now; you'll use the commands of the Format menu to align the controls on the form. Just place them roughly at positions shown in Figure 2.7. Then select each Label with the mouse and, in the Properties window, locate the Text property of the control.

As you can see, most of the basic properties of the Web controls have the same name as the Windows controls. Change the captions of the four labels to "Loan Amount," "Duration (months)," "Interest," and 'Monthly Payment." Notice that the Label Web control is resized automatically to accommodate the string you assign to its Text property.

Now place four TextBox controls on the Web form, each next to one of the Labels. By default, all TextBox controls are empty (they have no initial content). Change their size with the mouse and align them roughly to the Label controls they correspond to. Then select them one at a time and change their ID property to txtAmount, txtDuration, txtRate, and txtPayment, respectively. The ID property of a Web control is the unique identifier of the control, similar to the Name property of a Windows control. You'll use the ID property to access the control's members from within your code.

Then place a CheckBox control, set its Text property to Early Payment, and name it chkPay-Early. Set its TextAlign property to Left, so that its check box will be placed to the right of the text. The check box will be drawn immediately after the text, so you have to append a few spaces to the control's caption to clearly separate it from the check box.

The last control to place on the form is the Button control, whose Text property will be "Monthly Payment" and Name property will be bttnShowPayment. This button will submit the loan parameters entered on the form to the server, where the appropriate code will calculate the monthly payment and return it to the client. This is a good point to align the controls on the Web form. Select the Label controls and align them left with the Format ➤ Align ➤ Lefts command. While the labels are selected, use Format ➤ Vertical Spacing ➤ Make Equal to space them equally from one another. Once the labels are in place, you can align each text box to the corresponding label, with the Format ➤ Align ➤ Middles command. Select a pair of a Label and a TextBox control at a time and align them. Just make sure that the Label control is used as the reference control for the alignment.

At this point, you're done designing the interface of the application. The interface is quite similar to the interface of the equivalent Windows application, only this one was designed on a Web form with Web controls. Other than that, the process was the same; even the tools for aligning the controls on the Web form are the same as those for the Windows form. Our next task is to program the application.

Double-click the button on the Web form, and the editor window will open. The Web Form Designer has selected the Click event of the button and inserted its definition. All you have to do is insert the same code we used in the LoanCalculator application. You can switch to the Windows application and copy the code (which was shown back in Listing 2.2). Just paste the code behind the Show Payment button of the LoanCalculator Windows application in the Click event handler of the Monthly payment button of the Web application, and there won't be a single error. You can reuse the code as is!

Press F5 to run the application. It will be several seconds before the Internet Explorer window will pop up, displaying the page you've designed. Enter the parameters of a loan and then click the Monthly Payment button. A few seconds later, the monthly payment will appear on the form. As you will notice, a totally new page will arrive in the browser; this page contains the parameters of the loan (the values you've entered on the form) and the result of the calculations.

If you look at the source code of the document shown on Internet Explorer, you will see straight HTML code. The interface of the WebLoanCalculator application looks fine, but not quite like a Web page. There's none of the color or graphics we're so accustomed to seeing on Web pages. Our Web form contains only controls, but it's an HTML page and you can add any element that could appear on a Web page. In other words, the Web form can be edited as an HTML document. Not only that, but the IDE allows you to edit your page either visually or in HTML mode. Let's add a colored caption and change the page's background color.

Select the Web form by clicking somewhere on the form. In the Properties window, locate the property pageLayout. Its setting is `GridLayout`, which explains why you were able to place the controls anywhere on the page and align them in all possible ways. Those of you familiar with HTML know that aligning controls on a Web form is anything but trivial. Change the pageLayout property from `GridLayout` to `FlowLayout`. Now you're in normal HTML editing mode. Place the cursor at the top of the page and start typing. Enter the string **Easy Loan Calculator** and then select it with the mouse. You will notice that the text-formatting buttons on the toolbar have been enabled. Set the text's size to 6 and set its foreground and background colors. To set these properties, use the two buttons next to the Bold/Italic/Underline group of buttons. The string is flush left on the form, so enter a few spaces in front of the string to center it above the controls.

NOTE   *A quick comment for readers familiar with HTML: Browsers ignore multiple spaces, but the editor silently converts the spaces you enter into* ` ` *codes, which are the HTML equivalent of "hard"—that is, nonbreaking—spaces.*

You can also change the color of the page. Locate the page's bgColor property in the Properties window and set it to a light color. When the Color Picker dialog box appears on the form, you will see the tab with the Web colors. These are the colors than can be displayed by all browsers, the so-called *safe colors*. The form now looks like Figure 2.8 when viewed in a browser.

FIGURE 2.8

The WebLoan-Calculator as a Web page

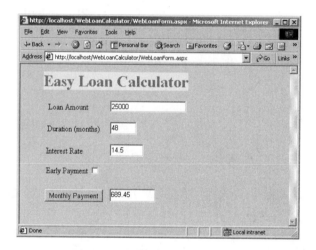

To see how the Web Form Designer handles the HTML elements of the page, click the HTML button at the bottom of the Designer. The Web form can be viewed and designed either in Design view (which is the default view) or in HTML view. The Web Form Designer inserted the following statement in the HTML document to generate the header of the page:

```
<FONT style="BACKGROUND-COLOR: #ffff66" color="#996666" size="6">
<STRONG>Easy Loan Calculator</STRONG></FONT>
```

This is straight HTML code that could appear in any Web page, and it doesn't use any Web controls. Select the <FONT> tag and delete it. Then switch to the Design view to see that the header has disappeared. Switch back to the HTML view and insert the following statement right after the <body> tag and before the <form> tag, as shown in Figure 2.9:

```
<h1>Easy Loan Calculator</h1>
```

FIGURE 2.9

Editing the Web
form's HTML code

Click F5 to run the application. When Internet Explorer appears, enter some values in the text boxes and check out the application. The Web application is functionally equivalent to the Windows loan application you developed at the beginning of this chapter. Yet its user interface runs in the browser, but the calculations take place on the server (the machine to which the clients connect to request the `WebLoanForm.aspx` Web page). Every time you click the Monthly Payment button on the page, the page is *posted* to the server. The browser transmits the values on the various controls back to the server. The server processes these values (actually, it executes the event handler you wrote) and creates a new page, which is sent to the client. This page includes the value of the monthly payment. Web applications are discussed in detail later in this book; with this example I wanted to demonstrate the similarities between Windows forms and Web forms and how the same code works with both types of applications.

Working with Multiple Forms

Let's return to Windows applications. Few applications are built on a single form. Most applications use two, three, or more forms, which correspond to separate sections of the application. In this section, we are going to build an application that uses three forms and lets the user switch among them at will. You'll see how to write an application that opens multiple windows on the Desktop. In Chapter 4, we'll explore in depth the topic of building Windows applications with multiple forms. In this chapter, we'll build a simple example of a multiform application by combining the math and financial calculators we built earlier in the chapter.

The way to combine the two applications is to create a new form, which will become the switching point for the two calculators. The user will be able to invoke either of the two calculators by clicking a button on the new form. Let's design an application that combines the forms of the two projects.

Start a new project and call it Calculators. The project's form will become the switching point between the other two forms, and it's shown in Figure 2.10. Start by renaming the new form from Form1 to CalculatorsForm. To design it, add two Button controls and name them bttnMath and bttnLoan. Then set their Text properties to Simple Math and Simple Loan, respectively. As you can guess, all you have to do now is add the code to invoke each of the existing forms from within each button's Click event handler. Add a third button on the form, call it bttnGame, and later you can add an action game to the Calculators project.

FIGURE 2.10

The main form of the Calculators application

At this point, we must add the forms of the MathCalculator and LoanCalculator projects into the new project. Right-click the name of the project, and from the context menu, select Add Existing Item. In the dialog box that appears, select the item `MathForm.vb` in the MathCalculator project's folder. Do the same for the LoanForm of the LoanCalculator project. The Calculators project now contains three forms.

If you run the project now, you will see the Calculators form, but clicking its button won't bring up the appropriate form. Obviously, you must add a few lines of code in the Click event handler of each button to invoke the corresponding form. To display one form from within another form's code, you must create an object that represents the second form and then call its Show method. The code behind the Simple Math button is shown in Listing 2.11.

LISTING 2.11: INVOKING THE MATH CALCULATOR

```
Private Sub bttnMath_Click(ByVal sender As System.Object, _
            ByVal e As System.EventArgs) Handles bttnMath.Click
    Dim calcForm As New CalculatorForm
    calcForm.Show()
End Sub
```

The *calcForm* variable is an object variable that represents the CalculatorForm form of the Calculators application. The name of the form is actually used as a data type, and this requires some explanation. The form is implemented as a Class and therefore you create objects of this type.

The Dim statement creates a new instance of the form, and the Show method loads and displays the form. If you run the project now, you'll see the main form, and if you click the first button, the math calculator's form will appear. If you click the same button again, another instance of the form will appear. What can we do to prevent this? We would like to display the CalculatorForm initially and then simply show it, but not load another instance of the form. The answer is to move the declaration of the *calcForm* variable outside the event handler, into the Form's declaration section. The variable is declared once, and all the procedures in the form can access its members. Variables declared in an event handler take effect only in the event handler in which they were declared, and that's why at this point, every time you click a button, a new instance of the corresponding form is created and displayed. If the variable *calcForm* points to a single instance of the CalculatorForm, then the form will be displayed every time we click the Simple Math button, but no new instance of it will be created. You'll find out more about the scope of variables in the following chapter.

When one of the two calculators is displayed, it doesn't automatically become the active form. The active form is the one that has the focus, and this is the main form of the application. To work with a calculator, you must click the appropriate form to make it active. To activate the most recently displayed form from within another form's code, we'll use the Activate method of the Form object. Rewrite the Click event handlers of the two buttons on the form as shown in Listing 2.12 (the listing shows the entire code of the form, so that you can see the declarations of the two variables that represent the forms of the application).

LISTING 2.12: THE CALCULATORS PROJECT

```
Public Class CalculatorsForm
    Inherits System.Windows.Forms.Form
    Dim calcForm As New CalculatorForm()
    Dim loanForm As New loanForm()
    Private Sub bttnMath_Click(ByVal sender As System.Object, _
                ByVal e As System.EventArgs) Handles bttnMath.Click
        calcForm.Show()
        calcForm.Activate()
    End Sub
    Private Sub bttnLoan_Click(ByVal sender As System.Object, _
                ByVal e As System.EventArgs) Handles bttnLoan.Click
        loanForm.Show()
        loanForm.Activate()
    End Sub
End Class
```

Notice the statement that declares the *loanForm* variable: the variable has the same name as the data type, but this is no problem. It goes without saying that the name of the variable can be anything. Our next task is to specify which form will be displayed when we start the application. Right-click the Calculators project name and, in the context menu, select Properties. On the Calculators Property Pages dialog box (Figure 2.11) is a ComboBox named StartUp Object. Expand it and you will see the names of all the forms in the project. Select the name of form you want to appear when the program starts, which is the CalculatorsForm.

The code behind the Play A Game button should also call the Show method of another form, but it doesn't. I regret not developing a game for your enjoyment, but I did implement a fun feature. When you click this button, it jumps to another place on the form. The button's Click event handler is shown next:

```
Private Sub bttnGame_Click(ByVal sender As System.Object, _
                ByVal e As System.EventArgs) Handles bttnGame.Click
    bttnGame.Left = Rnd() * Me.Width * 0.8
    bttnGame.Top = Rnd() * Me.Height * 0.8
End Sub
```

FIGURE 2.11

Open the Project Properties dialog box to specify the startup object.

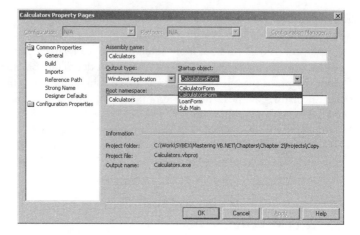

This subroutine manipulates the Left and Top properties of the control to move the button to a different position. The Rnd() function returns a random value between 0 and 1. To calculate the horizontal position, the code multiplies the random value by the width of the form (actually, 80 percent of the width). The vertical position is calculated in a similar manner.

Each Visual Basic project is made up of files that are all listed in the Solution Explorer window. Each project contains quite a few files in addition to the Form files, and they're all stored in a single folder, which is named after the project. If you open the Calculators folder (Figure 2.12), you will see that it contains the CalculatorForm and LoanForm forms. These are copies of the original forms of their corresponding applications. When you add an existing item to a project, VB makes a copy of this item in the project's folder.

FIGURE 2.12

The components of the Calculators project

To move a project to another location, just move the project's folder there. To create a copy of the project, just copy the project's folder to a different location.

Working with Multiple Projects

As you have noticed, every new project you create with VB is a so-called *solution*. Each solution contains a project, which in turn contains one or more files, references to .NET or custom components, and other types of items, which will be discussed in the following chapters. Both solutions and projects are containers—they contain other items. A solution may contain multiple projects. Each project in a solution is independent of the other projects, and you can distribute the projects in a solution separately. So, why create a solution? Let's say you're working on several related projects, which are likely to use common components. Instead of creating a different solution for each project, you can create a single solution to contain all the related projects.

Let's build a solution with two related projects. The two related projects are the two calculators we built earlier in this chapter. The two projects don't share any common components, but they're good enough for a demonstration, and you will see how VB handles the components of a solution.

VB.NET AT WORK: THE CALCULATORS SOLUTION

Create an Empty Project and name it Calculators by selecting File ➢ New ➢ Blank Solution. In the Solution Explorer window, you will see the name of the project and nothing else, not even the list of references that are present in any other project type. To add a project to the solution, choose File ➢ Add Project ➢ Existing Project. (You can also right-click the solution's name in the Solution Explorer, select Add Existing Item ➢ Project, and, in the dialog box that pops up, select the Calculator project.) Do the same for the LoanCalculator project. When the Add Existing Project dialog box appears, navigate to the folders with the corresponding projects and select the project's file.

You now have a solution, called Calculators, that contains two projects. If you attempt to run the project, the IDE doesn't know which of the two projects to execute and will generate an error message. We must decide how to start the new project (that is, which form to display when the user runs the Calculators application). When a solution contains more than a single project, you must specify the startup project. Right-click the name of one of the projects and, from the context menu, select Set As StartUp Project. To test a different project, set a different StartUp project. Normally, you will work for a while with the same project, so switching from one project to another isn't really a problem. It is also possible that different developers will work on different projects belonging to the same solution.

Let's say you're going to design a documentation file for both projects. A good choice for a short documentation file is an HTML file. To add an HTML file to the solution, right-click the solution's name and select Add New Item. In the dialog box, select the HTML Page template, and then enter a name for the new item. An HTML page will be added to the project, and an empty page will appear in the Designer. This is the newly added HTML page, and you must add some content to it.

Place the cursor on the design surface and start typing. Figure 2.13 shows a very simple HTML page with an introduction to the application. To format the text, use the buttons on the toolbar. These buttons embed the appropriate tags in the text, while you see the page as it would appear in the browser. This is the Design view of the document. You can switch to the HTML view and edit the document manually, if you're familiar with HTML. The HTML page can be used by either project—at the very least, you can distribute it with the application.

FIGURE 2.13

Adding an HTML
Document to a
solution

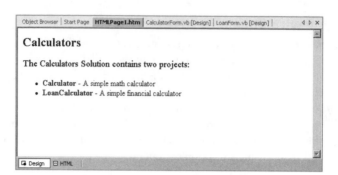

If you open the folder created for the project, you'll find that it contains an unusually small number of files. The projects reside in their respective folders. Make a change to one of the project's files. You can change the background color of the three TextBox controls on the LoanForm to a light shade, like Bisque. Then open the LoanCalculator project, and you will see that the changes have taken effect. VB doesn't create new copies of the forms (or any other component) added to the Calculators solution. It uses the existing files and modifies them, if needed, in their original locations. Of course, you can create a solution from scratch and place all the items in the same folder. Each project is a separate entity, and you can create executables for each project and distribute them.

To create the executables, open the Build menu and select Build Solution or Rebuild Solution. The Build Solution command compiles the files that have been changed since the last build; Rebuild Solution compiles all the files in the project. The executables will be created in the `Bin` folder under each project's folder. The file `Loan.exe` will be created under the `\Loan\Bin` folder and the `Calculator.exe` file under the `\Calculator\Bin` folder.

The solution is a convenience for the programmer. When you work on a large project that involves several related applications, you can put them all in a solution and work with one project at a time. Other developers may be working with other projects belonging to the same solution. A designer may create graphics for the applications, you can include them in the solution, and they'll be available to all the projects belonging to the solution.

The Calculators project we built earlier contains copies of the forms we added to the project. The Calculators solution contains references to external projects.

Executable Files

So far, you have been executing applications within Visual Basic's environment. However, you can't expect the users of your application to have Visual Studio installed on their systems. If you develop an interesting application, you won't feel like giving away the code of the application (the *source code*, as it's called). Applications are distributed as executable files, along with their support files. The users of the application can't see your source code, and your application can't be modified or made to look like someone else's application (that doesn't mean it can't be copied, of course).

NOTE *An executable file is a binary file that contains instructions only the machine can understand and execute. The commands stored in the executable file are known as* machine language.

Applications designed for the Windows environment can't fit in a single file. It just wouldn't make sense. Along with the executable files, your application requires *support files,* and these files may already exist on many of the machines on which your application will be installed. That's why it doesn't make sense to distribute huge files. Each user should install the main application and only the support files that aren't already installed on their computer.

The executable will run on the system on which it was developed, because the support files are there. Under the project's file, you will find two folders named `Bin` and `Obj`. Open the `Obj` folder, and you will see that it contains a subfolder named `Debug`. This is where you will find the executable, which is named after the project and has the extension `.exe`. Make sure that no instance of VS is running on your computer and then double-click the icon of the `MathCalculator.exe` or `LoanCalculator.exe` file. The corresponding application will start outside the Visual Studio IDE, and you can use it like any other application on your PC. You can create desktop shortcuts to the two applications.

The folder `Debug` contains the Debug version of the executable. Normally, after you're done debugging the application, you should change the default configuration of the project from Debug to Release. To change the project's configuration, select Build ➤ Configuration Manager. The Configuration Manager dialog box will pop up, as shown in Figure 2.14.

FIGURE 2.14

The Configuration Manager window

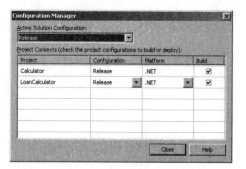

The default configuration for all projects is Debug. This configuration generates code optimized for debugging. The other possible setting for the configuration is Release. Change the configuration to Release and close the dialog box. If you build the project or the solution again, a `Release` folder will be created under the `Obj` folder and will contain the new executable. The difference between the two versions of the executable files is that Debug files contain symbolic debug information. The Release configuration executes faster because it doesn't contain any debugging information.

Distributing an Application

Distributing just an EXE file isn't going to be any good, because the executable requires support files. If these files aren't installed on the target system (the computer on which your application will be installed), then the EXE file isn't going to work. The file will be executed only on a system that has Visual Studio.NET on it. Distributing a large number of files and installing them on the target computer is quite a task. You must create an installation program that (almost) automatically installs your application and the required support files on the target computer. If some of those files are already installed, they will not be installed again.

NOTE *Eventually, all the support files will become part of the operating system, and then you'll be able to distribute a single EXE file (or a small number of files). This hasn't happened with Windows 2000 or Windows XP and won't for some time. Until it does, you must provide your own installer.*

A Setup project creates a Windows installer file (a file with extension .msi), which contains the executable(s) of the application and auxiliary files that are necessary for the application, Registry entries (if the application interacts with the Registry), installation instructions, and so on. The resulting MSI file is usually quite long, and this is the file you distribute to end users. They must double-click the icon of the MSI file to install the application on their computer. If they run the same file again, the application will be removed. Moreover, if something goes wrong during the installation, the installation will be rolled back and any components that were installed in the process will be removed.

The topic of creating and customizing Windows installers is huge, and there are already a couple of books on this topic alone—for example, *VB/VBA Developer's Guide to the Windows Installer* by Mike Gunderloy (Sybex, 2000). As you can understand, in this chapter we'll only scratch the surface. I will show you how to create a simple Setup project for installing the Calculators project on another machine. Your main priority right now is to learn to write .NET applications and master the language. You should be able to distribute even small applications, so the topic of creating Setup projects shouldn't be missing from this book. Yet you aren't going to use the more advanced features for a while—not before you can write elaborate applications that require a customized installation procedure. In this section, I'll show you how to create a Setup project for the Calculators project. It's a simple project that demonstrates the basic steps of creating a Windows installer using the default options, and you'll be able to use this application to install the Calculators application to a target computer.

VB.NET at Work: Creating a Windows Installer

To create a Windows installer, you must add a Setup project to your solution. The Setup project will create an installation program for the projects in the current solution. Open the Calculators solution and add a new project (File ➤ Add Project ➤ New Project). In the dialog box that appears (Figure 2.15), click the Setup and Deployment Projects item. In the Templates pane, you will see five different types of Setup and Deployment projects. The simplest type of Setup project is the Setup Wizard. This wizard takes you through the steps of creating a Setup project, which is another wizard that takes the *user* through the steps of installing the application on the target computer. Select this template and then enter the project's name in the Name box: name the project Simple-Calculators. Click OK, and the first screen of the wizard will appear. This is a welcome screen, and you can click the Next button to skip it.

On the next screen, you'll be prompted to choose a project type. You can create a project that installs an application or one that adds components to an existing installation. We want to create a project that installs an application for the first time, and we have two options: to create a setup for a Windows application or for a Web application. Select the first option, as shown in Figure 2.16, and click Next to move to the next screen of the wizard.

FIGURE 2.15

Adding a Setup and
Deployment project
to your solution

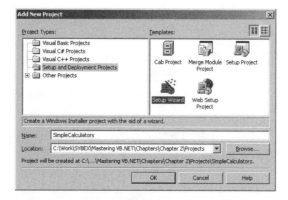

FIGURE 2.16

The Project Type
screen of the wizard

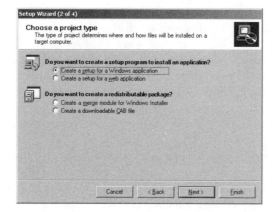

On the next screen, you'll be prompted to select any files you want to add to the installation program. Here you must click the items checked in Figure 2.17. The Primary Output is the executable file, and the Content Files include things like the HTML file we added to the project. In the release version of the program, you don't usually want to include debug symbols or source files (well, perhaps the debug symbols for large projects that are also tested at the client's side). If your application includes localized resource files, you should check the second option. Localized resources allow you to write applications that adjust their text to the end user's culture. It's a special topic that's not covered in this book.

The Setup project we're creating here is part of a solution with the project you want to install on the target machine. I've included the Setup project in the same solution for convenience only. You can also create a Setup project and specify any executable file you want to install. The Setup project takes a while to compile, so you should add it to the solution only after you have debugged the application. Or remove the Setup project from the solution after you have created the setup file.

FIGURE 2.17

Specifying the items
you want to install

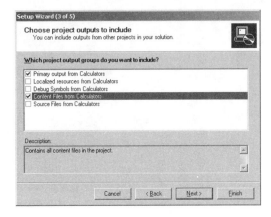

Click Next again to see another screen, where you can specify additional files that are not part of the project. You can add text files with installation instructions, compatibility data, registration information, and so on. Click Next again, and the last screen of the wizard displays a summary of the project you specified. Click Finish to close the wizard and create the Setup project.

The wizard adds the Setup project to your solution. Select the new project with the mouse and open the Properties window to see the properties of the new project. The Solution Explorer and the new project's Properties window should look like the ones shown in Figure 2.18. The good news is that you don't have to write any code for this project. All you have to do is set a few properties and you're done.

The AddRemoveProgramsIcon property lets you specify the icon of the installation and removal programs—yes, VB will also create a program to uninstall the application. You can specify whether the Setup project will detect newer versions of the application and won't overwrite them with an older version. The DetectNewerInstalledVersion property is True by default. You can also specify your company's name and URL, support line, the title of the installation windows, and so on.

FIGURE 2.18

The Setup project's
Properties

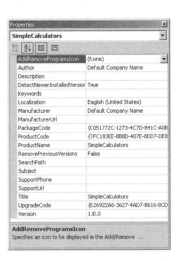

The Manufacturer property will become the name of the folder in which the installation will take place. By default, this folder will be created in the user's `Program Files` folder. Assign a name that reflects either your company or the project type—a string like "The Math Experts" for the Calculators example. The Author property is where your name should appear. The ProductName property is by default the name of the Setup project; change it to "The EasyCalc Project". The Title property is the title of the installer (what users see on the installation wizard's title bar while the application is being installed).

THE SOLUTION EXPLORER BUTTONS

You will notice that the usual buttons on the Solution Explorer have been replaced by six new buttons, which are described in the following sections.

File System Editor Button

Click this button and you will see the four sections of the target machine's file system your setup program can affect. Decide whether your application's action should appear on the user's Desktop or in the Programs menu. Right-click either item and you will see a context menu that contains the commands Add and Create Shortcut. The Add command leads to a submenu with four objects you can automatically create from within your Setup program: Folder, Project Output, File, Assembly. For typical applications you can add a folder (in which you can later place the project's output), or the project output. The less intruding option is to place a shortcut in the user's Programs menu.

To make the project a little more interesting, we'll install not only the Calculators application, but the two individual applications: the Calculator and LoanCalculator projects. We're going to add three new commands to the user's Programs menu, so let's add a folder to this menu and then the names of the applications in this folder. Right-click the item User's Programs Menu and select Add Folder. A new folder will be added under the User's Programs Menu item. Change its name to `Demo Calculators`, as shown in Figure 2.19. Select the new folder and look up its properties. The AlwaysCreate property should be True—if not, the wizard will not add the folder to the user's Programs menu.

Then right-click the newly added folder and select Add ➤ File. A dialog box will pop up where you can select the executables that must appear in the `Demo Calculators` folder on the Programs menu. Browse your disk and locate the Calculators, Calculator, and LoanCalculator executables in the `\Obj\Release` folder under the corresponding project's folder (all three files have the extension EXE).

After adding the items you want to appear in the `Demo Calculators` folder of the Programs menu, the File System Editor should like the one in Figure 2.19.

FIGURE 2.19

Specifying how the installation program will affect the user's File System

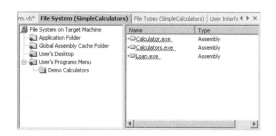

Registry Editor Button

Click this button to add new keys to the user's Registry. You don't *have* to add anything to the user's Registry, especially for this project. But you can place special strings in the Registry, like an encoded date to find out when a demo version of your application may expire. You must first familiarize yourself with the Registry and how to program it with Visual Basic, before you attempt to use it with your applications.

File Types Editor Button

If your application uses its own file type, you can associate that type with your application, so that when the user double-clicks a file of this type your application starts automatically. This is a sure way to ruin the user's file associations. If your application can handle GIF images or HTML files, don't even think of taking over these files. Use this option *only* with files that are unique to your application.

To add a new file type on the user's machine, click the File Types Editor button on the Properties window. On the Designer's surface, you will see a single item: File Types On Target Machine. Right-click the item and select Add File Type. This command will add a new file type and the verb **&Open** under it. Click the new file type and you will see its properties in the Properties window. You can assign a description to the new file type, its extension, and the command that will be used to open the files of this type (the name of your application's EXE file).

User Interface Editor Button

Click this button and you will see the steps of the installation on the Designer's surface, as shown in Figure 2.20. Each phase of the installation process has one or more steps, and a different dialog box is displayed at each step. Some of the dialog boxes contain messages, like a short description of the application or a copyright message. These strings are exposed as properties of the corresponding dialog box, and you can change them. Just click a dialog box in the User Interface Editor and then look up its properties in the Properties window.

FIGURE 2.20

The outline of the installation process

The wizard inserts all the necessary dialog boxes, but you can add custom dialog boxes. If you do, you must also provide some code to process the user's selections on the custom dialog box. For our simple example, we don't need any customized dialog boxes. I will repeat here that the topic of creating a customized Windows installer is one of the major aspects of Visual Studio.NET, and when you're ready to build an installer for a large application, you will have to consult the documentation extensively.

Custom Actions and System Requirements Buttons

The last two buttons on the Properties window allow you to specify custom actions and requirements for the target machine. For example, you may specify that the application be installed only on systems on which a specific component has already been installed. You can ignore these buttons for a simple installation project.

Finishing the Windows Installer

OK, we're almost there. Select Build ➢ Build Solution, and VB will create the installation program. First, it will create a new project folder, the `SimpleCalculators` folder. This is where the Setup project's files will be stored and where the executable file of the installation program will be created. The process of building the executables and creating the Setup program will take several minutes. The output of the build process is the `SimpleCalculators.msi` file. This is an executable file (known as Windows Installer Package), and it will be created in the `\SimpleCalculators\Release` folder. Its size will be approximately 15 MB. If you're wondering what's in this file, take a look at the Output window of the IDE and you will see a large list of components added to the package.

Running the Windows Installer

Now you're ready to install the Calculators project to your computer. If you have access to another computer that doesn't have Visual Studio installed, you should copy the `SimpleCalculators.msi` file there and install the application there. The components required for your application to run properly are already installed on the development machine, and you can test the Setup project better on another machine.

Go to the folder `\SimpleCalculators\Release` and double-click the icon of the Windows Installer Package (or the folder to which you have copied this file on another machine). The MSI file is represented by the typical installation icon (a computer and a CD). The following figures show the installation steps. Please notice where the captions you specified in the Setup project's properties appear in the screens of the installation wizard. Consult these figures as you build a Setup application to make sure the proper messages are displayed during the installation on the target computer.

1. This dialog appears while the Windows installer starts.

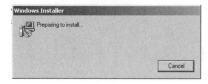

2. The welcome screen of the wizard that will guide the user through the installation procedure. The messages on this screen are the properties CopyrightWarning and WelcomeText of the Welcome dialog box in the User Interface Editor.

3. This screen lets the user change the default path of the application to be installed. Notice how the default path is formed. You can control the default installation path by setting the appropriate properties of the Setup project. The installer will create a folder, under the Pro-gram Files folder, named after the Manufacturer and ProductName properties of the Setup project.

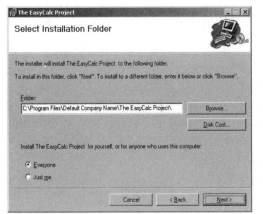
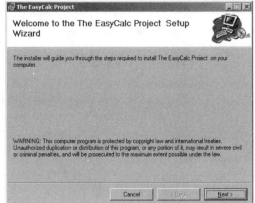

4. This screen asks the user to confirm the installation—which can be cancelled later as well.

5. The application is being installed, and this screen displays a progress indicator. The user can terminate the installation by clicking the Cancel button.

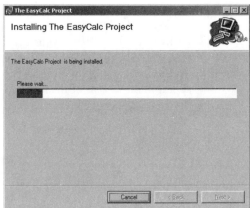

6. The last screen of the installer confirms the successful installation of the application. Click Close to end the program. If there was a problem installing the application, a description of the problem will be displayed on this last screen. In this case, all the components installed in the process will be automatically removed as well.

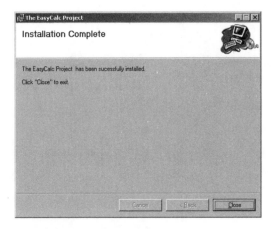

Verifying the Installation

You already know the kind of changes made to your system by an installation program. If you open the Programs menu (Start ➢ Programs), you will see that a new item was added, the Demo Calculators item. If you select it with the mouse, a submenu will open, as shown in Figure 2.21. You can select any of the three commands (Calculators, Calculator, or LoanCalculator) to start the corresponding application.

TIP *All three items in the Demo Calculators submenu have the default application icon. You should change the default icons of your applications for a more professional look.*

FIGURE 2.21

The new items added to the Programs menu by the Windows installer

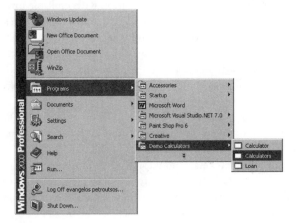

The Windows installer has created and installed a program for uninstalling the application from the target computer. Open Control Panel and double-click the Add/Remove Programs icon. The dialog box that appears contains an item for each program you can remove from your computer. The newly installed application is the item The EasyCalc Project, as shown in Figure 2.22. Click its Remove button to uninstall the application or the Change button to repair an existing installation.

FIGURE 2.22

Use the Add/ Remove Programs utility to remove or repair an application installed by the Windows installer.

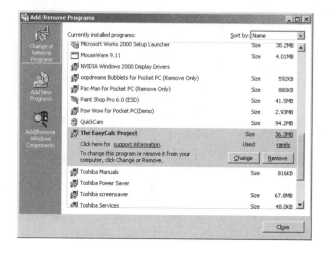

As for the location of the executables and their support files, they're in the `EasyCalc Project` folder under `\Program Files\CompanyName` folder. If the same customer installs another of your applications—say, the ProCalc Project—it will also be installed in its own folder under `\Program Files\CompanyName`. Just make sure all the Setup projects have the same value for the Manufacturer property, and the support files won't be installed in multiple folders.

Summary

This chapter introduced you to the concept of *solutions* and *projects*. You learned how to build a simple solution with a single project, as well as a solution with multiple projects. Use solutions to combine multiple related projects into a single unit, so that your projects can share components. Each project in a solution maintains its individuality, and you can either edit one from within the solution or open it as a project and edit independently of the other projects in the solution.

You also learned how to develop Web applications. With VB.NET, developing Web applications is as easy as developing Windows applications. In a few short years, you should be able to design a single interface that can be used by both types of projects (even if this means that there will be nothing but Web applications). The user interface of Web and Windows applications may be different, but the code behind both types of projects is straight Visual Basic.

After you have developed an application, you will have to distribute it. Distributing Windows application isn't a trivial process, but building a Setup program for your application with VB.NET is. All you have to do is add a Setup project to a solution that contains the project or projects that you want to distribute. The simplest type of Setup program doesn't require any code, and you can create a Windows installer by just setting a few properties. The output of the Setup program is a file with the extension .msi, which you can copy to another computer. Once executed on the target computer, the MSI file will install the application, create a shortcut to the application in the user's Programs menu, and even create an entry in Add/Remove Programs for repairing or uninstalling the application.

By now, you have a good idea about the environment and how Windows applications are built. In the following two chapters, you'll read about the language itself.

Chapter 3

Visual Basic: The Language

THIS CHAPTER AND THE next discuss the fundamentals of any programming language: variables, flow-control statements, and procedures. A *variable* stores data, and a *procedure* is code that manipulates variables. To do any serious programming with Visual Basic, you must be familiar with these concepts. To write efficient applications, you need a basic understanding of some fundamental topics, such as the data types (the kind of data you can store in a variable), the scope and lifetime of variables, and how to write procedures and pass arguments to them.

As you have seen in the first two chapters, most of the code in a Visual Basic application deals with manipulating control properties and variables. This chapter explores in greater depth how variables store data and how programs process variables. If you're familiar with Visual Basic, you might want to simply scan the following pages and make sure you're acquainted with the topics and the sample code discussed in this chapter. I would, however, advise you to read this chapter even if you're an experienced VB programmer.

VB6 ➠ VB.NET

Experienced Visual Basic programmers should pay attention to these special sidebars with the "VB6 to VB.NET" icon, which calls your attention to changes in the language. These sections usually describe new features in VB.NET or enhancements of VB6 features, but also VB6 features that are no longer supported by VB.NET.

If you're new to Visual Basic, you may find that some material in this chapter less than exciting. It covers basic concepts and definitions—in general, tedious, but necessary, material. Think of this chapter as a prerequisite for the following ones. If you need information on core features of the language as you go through the examples in the rest of the book, you'll probably find it here.

Variables

In Visual Basic, as in any other programming language, variables store values during a program's execution. Let's say you're writing a program that converts amounts between different currencies. Instead of prompting the user for the exchange rates all the time—or even worse, editing your code to change the currency rates every day—you can store the exchange rates into variables and use these variables to perform the conversions. If the current exchange rate between the U.S. dollar and the euro is 0.9682, you can store this value to a variable called *USD2Euro*. If you change the value of this variable once in your code, all the conversions will be calculated based on the new rate. Or you can prompt the users for the exchange rate when they start the program, store the rate to the *USD2Euro* variable, and then use it in your code.

A variable has a name and a value. The variable *UserName*, for example, can have the value "Joe," and the variable *Discount* can have the value 0.35. *UserName* and *Discount* are variable names, and "Joe" and 0.35 are their values. "Joe" is a *string* (that is, text or an alphanumeric value), and 0.35 is a numeric value. When a variable's value is a string, it must be enclosed in double quotes. In your code, you can refer to the value of a variable by the variable's name. For example, the following statements calculate and display the discounted price for the amount of $24,500:

```
Dim Amount As Single
Dim Discount As Single
Dim DiscAmount As Single
Amount = 24500
Discount = 0.35
DiscAmount = Amount * (1 - Discount)
MsgBox("Your price is $" & DiscAmount)
```

Single is a numeric data type; it can store both integer and non-integer values. There are other types of numeric variables, which are discussed in the following sections. I've used the Single data type because it's the most commonly used data type for simple calculations that don't require extreme accuracy.

The message that this expression displays depends on the values of the *Discount* and *Amount* variables. If you decide to offer a better discount, all you have to do is change the value of the *Discount* variable. If you didn't use the *Discount* variable, you'd have to make many changes in your code. In other words, if you coded the line that calculated the discounted amount as follows:

```
DiscAmount = 24500 * (1 - 0.35)
```

you'd have to look for every line in your code that calculates discounts and change the discount from 0.35 to another value. By changing the value of the *Discount* variable in a single place in your code, the entire program is updated.

VB6 ➧ VB.NET

In VB6, amounts of money were usually stored in Currency variables. The Currency data type turned out to be insufficient for monetary calculations and was dropped from the language. Use the Decimal data type, discussed later in this chapter, to represent money amounts.

Variables in VB.NET are more than just names, or placeholders, for values. They're intelligent entities that can not only store but also process a value. I don't mean to scare you, but I think you should be told: VB.NET variables are objects. And here's why:

A variable that holds dates must be declared as such with the following statement:

```
Dim expiration As Date
```

Then you can assign a date to the *expiration* variable, with a statement like this:

```
expiration = #1/1/2003#
```

So far, nothing out of the ordinary. This is how you use variables with any other language. In addition to holding a date, however, the *expiration* variable can process it. The expression

```
expiration.AddYears(3)
```

will return a new date that's three years ahead of the date stored in the expiration variable. The new date can be assigned to another Date variable:

```
Dim newExpiration As Date
newExpiration = expiration.AddYears(3)
```

The keywords following the period after the variable's name are called *methods* and *properties*, just like the properties and methods of the controls you place on a form to create your application's visual interface. The methods and properties (or the *members*) of a variable expose the functionality that's built into the class that represents the variable itself. Without this built-in functionality, you'd have to write some serious code to extract the month from a Date variable, to figure out whether a character is a letter, a digit, or a punctuation symbol, and so on. Much of the functionality you'll need in an application that manipulates dates, numbers, or text has already been built into the variables themselves, and you will see examples of other properties and methods exposed by the various data types later in this chapter.

Don't let the terminology scare you. Think of variables as placeholders for values and access their functionality with expressions like the ones shown earlier. Start using variables to store values and, if you need to process them, enter a variable's name followed by a period to see a list of the members it exposes. In most cases, you'll be able to figure out what these members do by just reading their names. I'll come back to the concept of variables as objects, but I wanted to hit it right off the bat. A more detailed discussion of the notion of variables as object can be found later in this chapter.

Since this book isn't for computer scientists, I can simplify the text in the following sections by treating variables as locations in memory where you store values. Later in this chapter, and after discussing the data types of the Common Language Runtime (CLR), I will treat them as objects.

Declaring Variables

In most programming languages, variables must be declared in advance. Historically, the reason for doing this has been to help the compiler. Every time a compiled application runs into a new variable, it has to create it. Doing so doesn't take a lot of statements, but it does produce a delay that could be avoided. If the compiler knows all the variables and their types that are going to be used in the application ahead of time, it can produce the most compact and efficient, or optimized, code. For example, when you tell the compiler that the variable *Discount* will hold a number, the compiler sets aside a certain number of bytes for the *Discount* variable to use.

One of the most popular, yet intensely criticized, features of BASIC was that it didn't force the programmer to declare all variables. As you will see, there are more compelling reasons than speed and efficiency for declaring variables. For example, if the compiler knows the types of the variables, it will catch many errors at design or compile time—errors that otherwise would surface at runtime. When you declare a variable as Date, the compiler won't let you assign an integer value to it. It also won't let you request the Month property of an Integer variable (Month is a property that applies only to Date variables). Because the type of the variable is known at compile time, similar errors will be caught as you enter code and therefore won't cause runtime errors. Later in the chapter, in the section "Why Declare Variables?", you'll see how variable declarations can simplify coding too.

When programming in VB.NET, you should declare your variables, because this is the default mode and Microsoft recommends this practice strongly. They've been recommending it with previous versions of VB, but up to VB6 the language was accepting undeclared variables by default. If you attempt to use an undeclared variable in your code, VB.NET will throw an exception. It will actually catch the error as soon as you complete the line that uses the undeclared variable, underlining it with a wiggly red line. It is possible to change the default behavior and use undeclared variables the way most people did with earlier versions of VB (you'll see how this is done in the section "The Strict and Explicit Options," later in this chapter), but nearly all the examples of the book declare their variables. In any case, you're strongly encouraged to declare your variables.

VB6 ⮕ VB.NET

Although not an absolute requirement, VB.NET encourages the declaration of variables. By default, every variable must be declared. Moreover, when you declare a variable, you must also specify its type. One of the new terms in the VB.NET documentation is *strictly typed*, which simply means that a variable has a specific type and you can't store a value of a different type to the variable. See the discussion of Option Explicit and Option Strict statements later in this chapter for more information on using variables without declaring them, or declaring them without a specific type.

VB.NET recognizes the type identifier characters. A variable name like *note$* implies a String variable, and you need not supply a data type when you declare the variable. The Defxxx statements (DefInt, DefDbl, and so on), however, are not supported by VB.NET. The Defxxx statements were already obsolete, and they were rarely used even with older versions of Visual Basic.

In VB.NET you can declare multiple variables of the same type without having to repeat each variable's type. The following statement, for instance, will create three Integer variables:

```
Dim width, depth, height As Integer
```

The following statement will create three Integer and two Double variables:

```
Dim width, depth, height As Integer, area, volume As Double
```

Another convenient shortcut introduced with VB.NET is that now you can initialize variables along with their declaration. Not only can you declare a variable with the Dim statement, you can also initialize it by assigning a value of the proper type to it:

```
Dim width As Integer = 9
Dim distance As Integer = 100, time As Single = 9.09
```

When you declare variables in your code, you're actually telling the compiler the type of data you intend to store in each variable. This way, the compiler can generate code that handles the variables most efficiently. A variable that holds characters is different from a variable that holds numbers. If the compiler knows in advance the type of data you're going to store in each variable, it can not only optimize the executable it will produce, it can also catch many mistakes as you type (an attempt to store a word to a numeric variable, for instance).

To declare a variable, use the Dim statement followed by the variable's name, the As keyword, and its type, as follows:

```
Dim meters As Integer
Dim greetings As String
```

We'll look at the various data types in detail in the next section. In the meantime, you should know that a variable declared As Integer can store only integer numbers, and a variable declared As String can only store text (strings of characters, or simply strings).

The first variable, *meters*, will store integers, such as 3 or 1,002, and the second variable, *greetings*, will store text, such as "Thank you for using Fabulous Software". You can declare multiple variables of the same or different type in the same line, as follows:

```
Dim Qty As Integer, Amount As Decimal, CardNum As String
```

When Visual Basic finds a Dim statement, it creates one or more new variables, as specified in the statement. That is, it creates a structure in the memory where it can store a value of the specified type and assigns a name to it. Each time this name is used in subsequent commands, Visual Basic accesses this structure to read or set its value. For instance, when you use the statement

```
meters = 23
```

Visual Basic places the value 23 in the structure reserved for the *meters* variable. When the program asks for the value of this variable, Visual Basic reads it from the same structure.

To use the *meters* variable in a calculation, reference it by name in a statement in your code. The statement

```
inches = meters * 39.37
```

multiplies the value stored in the *meters* variable and assigns the result to the *inches* variable. The equal sign is the assignment operator: it assigns the value of the expression that appears to its right, to the variable listed to its left. Only the variable to the left of the equal sign changes value.

The following statement displays the value of the same variable on a message box:

```
MsgBox(meters)
```

It causes Visual Basic to retrieve the value 23 from the area of memory named *meters*.

It's also possible for a single statement to both read and set the value of a variable. The following statement increases the value of the *meters* variable:

```
meters = meters + 1
```

Visual Basic reads the value (here, 23), adds 1 to it, and then stores the new value (24) in the original location.

One good reason for declaring variables is so that Visual Basic knows the type of information the variable must store and can validate the variable's value. Attempting to assign a value of the wrong type to a declared variable generates an error. For example, if you attempt to assign the value "Welcome" to the *meters* variable, Visual Basic won't compile the statement because this assignment violates the variable's declaration. The *meters* variable was declared as Integer, and you're attempting to store a string in it. It will actually underline the statement in the editor with a red wiggly line, which indicates an error. If you hover the pointer over the statement in error, a box with an explanation of the error will appear.

You can use other keywords in declaring variables, such as Private, Public, and Static. These keywords are called *access modifiers*, because they determine what sections of your code can access the specific variables and what sections can't. We'll look at these keywords in later sections of this chapter. In the meantime, bear in mind that all variables declared with the Dim statement exist in the module in which they were declared. If the variable *Count* is declared in a subroutine (an event handler, for example), it exists only in that subroutine. You can't access it from outside the subroutine. Actually, you can have a *Count* variable in multiple procedures. Each variable is stored locally, and they don't interfere with one another.

VARIABLE-NAMING CONVENTIONS

When declaring variables, you should be aware of a few naming conventions. A variable's name:

- ◆ Must begin with a letter.

- ◆ Can't contain embedded periods. Except for certain characters used as data type identifiers (which are described later in this chapter), the only special character that can appear in a variable's name is the underscore character.

- ◆ Mustn't exceed 255 characters.

- ◆ Must be unique within its scope. This means that you can't have two identically named variables in the same subroutine, but you can have a variable named *counter* in many different subroutines.

Variable names in VB.NET are case-insensitive: The variable names *myAge*, *myage*, and *MYAGE* all refer to the same variable in your code. Conversely, you can't use the names *myage* and *MYAGE* to declare two different variables.

TIP   *In fact, as you enter variable names, the editor converts their casing so that they match their declaration.*

VARIABLE INITIALIZATION

You can also initialize variables in the same line that declares them. The following line declares an Integer variable and initializes it to 3,045:

```
Dim distance As Integer = 3045
```

This statement is equivalent to the following statements:

```
Dim distance As Integer
distance = 3045
```

It is also possible to declare and initialize multiple variables, of the same or different type, on the same line:

```
Dim quantity As Integer = 1, discount As Single = 0.25
```

If you want to declare multiple variables of the same type, you need not repeat the type. Just separate all the variables of the same type with commas and set the type of the last variable:

```
Dim length, width, height As Integer, volume, area As Double
```

This statement declares three Integer variables and two Double variables. Double variables hold fractional values (or *floating-point* values, as they're usually called) similar to the Single data type, only they can represent non-integer values with greater accuracy. Declaring and initializing variables in a single step was a common feature among programming languages, but missing from previous versions of Visual Basic.

You can even initialize variables that represent objects on the same line that declares them. In Chapter 14, you will learn about pens and brushes, which are the two "instruments" for drawing. Before you can draw a shape on your form, you must create a Pen or a Brush object and then use it to draw something with. The simplest method of creating a new Pen is to specify its color. The following statement declares a Pen object that will draw in a blue-green color:

```
Dim myPen As Pen = New Pen(Color.AquaMarine)
```

This New keyword is used with object variables and tells VB to create a new instance of the Pen object (in effect, to create a new Pen). Color is another object that lets you manipulate the color of pens, backgrounds, and so on. Among other properties, the Color object exposes the names of colors it recognizes, and `Color.AquaMarine` is one of them.

You can also create variables of type Color. The following statement creates two variables that represent a different color each (one will be used as the background and the other as the drawing color):

```
Dim bgColor As Color = Color.LightYellow, fgColor As Color = Color.Blue
```

VB6 ⟹ VB.NET

Another interesting new feature introduced with VB.NET is the shorthand notation of common operations, such as the addition of a value to a variable. The statement

```
counter = counter + 1
```

can now be written as

```
counter += 1
```

The symbols += form a new VB operator (there's no space between the plus and the equal sign), which adds the value on its left to the value on its right and assigns the result to the initial variable. Only a variable may appear to the left of this operator, while on the right you can type either a variable or a value. The statement

```
totalCount = totalCount + count
```

is equivalent to

```
totalCount += count
```

The same notation applies to other operators, like subtraction (-=), multiplication (*=), division (/=), integer division (\=), and concatenation (&=). All these operators are new to VB.NET. I will not overuse this notation in the book for the sake of current VB programmers; most of them consider this notation one of the trademarks of the C language.

Types of Variables

Visual Basic recognizes the following five categories of variables:

- Numeric
- String
- Boolean
- Date
- Object

The two major variable categories are numeric and string. *Numeric variables* store numbers, and *string variables* store text. *Object variables* can store any type of data. Why bother to specify the type if one type suits all? On the surface, using object variables may seem like a good idea, but they have their disadvantages. Integer variables are optimized for storing integers, and date variables are optimized for storing dates. Before VB can use an object variable, it must determine its type and perform the necessary conversions, if any. If an object variable holds an integer value, VB must convert it to a string before concatenating it with another string. This introduces some overhead, which can be avoided by using typed variables.

We begin our discussion of variable types with numeric variables. Text is stored in string variables, but numbers can be stored in many formats, depending on the size of the number and its precision. That's why there are many types of numeric variables.

NUMERIC VARIABLES

You'd expect that programming languages would use a single data type for numbers. After all, a number is a number. But this couldn't be farther from the truth. All programming languages provide a variety of numeric data types, including the following:

- Integers (there are several integer data types)
- Decimals
- Single, or floating-point numbers with limited precision
- Double, or floating-point numbers with extreme precision

NOTE *Decimal, Single, and Double are the three basic data types for storing floating-point numbers. The Double type can represent these numbers more accurately than the Single type, and it's used almost exclusively in scientific calculations. The integer data types store whole numbers.*

The data type of your variable can make a difference in the results of the calculations. The proper variable types are determined by the nature of the values they represent, and the choice of data type is frequently a trade-off between precision and speed of execution (less-precise data types are manipulated faster). Visual Basic supports the numeric data types shown in Table 3.1.

TABLE 3.1: VISUAL BASIC NUMERIC DATA TYPES

DATA TYPE	MEMORY REPRESENTATION	STORES
Short (Int16)	2 bytes	Integer values in the range −32,768 to 32,767.
Integer (Int32)	4 bytes	Integer values in the range −2,147,483,648 to 2,147,483,647.
Long (Int64)	8 bytes	Very large integer values.
Single	4 bytes	Single-precision floating-point numbers. It can represent negative numbers in the range −3.402823E38 to −1.401298E−45 and positive numbers in the range 1.401298E−45 to 3.402823E38. The value 0 can't be represented precisely (it's a very, very small number, but not exactly 0).
Double	8 bytes	Double-precision floating-point numbers. It can represent negative numbers in the range −1.79769313486232E308 to −4.94065645841247E−324 and positive numbers in the range 4.94065645841247E−324 to 1.79769313486232E308.
Decimal	16 bytes	Integer and floating-point numbers scaled by a factor in the range from 0 to 28. See the description of the Decimal data type for the range of values you can store in it.

VB6 ⟹ VB.NET

The Short data type is the same as the Integer data type of VB6. The new Integer data type is the same as the Long data type of VB6; the VB.NET Long data type is new and can represent extremely large integer values. The Decimal data type is new to VB.NET, and you use it when you want to control the accuracy of your calculations in terms of number of decimal digits.

Integer Variables

There are three different types of variables for storing integers, and the only difference is the range of numbers you can represent with each type. As you understand, the more bytes a type takes, the larger values it can hold. The type of integer variable you'll use depends on the task at hand. You should choose the type that can represent the largest values you anticipate will come up in your calculations. You can go for the Long type, to be safe, but Long variables are four times as large as Short variables, and it takes the computer longer to process them.

The statements in Listing 3.1 will help you understand when to use the various integer data types. Each numeric data type exposes the MinValue and MaxValue properties, which return the minimum and maximum values that can be represented by the corresponding data type. I have included comments after each statement to explain the errors produced by some of the statements.

LISTING 3.1: EXPERIMENTING WITH THE RANGES OF NUMERIC VARIABLES

```
Dim shortInt As Int16
Dim Int As Int32
Dim longInt As Int64
Console.WriteLine(shortInt.MinValue)
Console.WriteLine(shortInt.MaxValue)
Console.WriteLine(Int.MinValue)
Console.WriteLine(Int.MaxValue)
Console.WriteLine(longInt.MinValue)
Console.WriteLine(longInt.MaxValue)
shortInt = shortInt.MaxValue + 1
'   ERROR, exceeds the maximum value of the Short data type
Int = shortInt.MaxValue + 1
'   OK, is within the range of the Integer data type
Int = Int.MaxValue + 1
'   ERROR, exceeds the maximum value of the Integer data type
Int = Int.MinValue - 1
'   ERROR, exceeds the minimum value of the Integer data type
longInt = Int.MaxValue + 1
'   OK, is within the range of the Long data type
longInt = longInt.MaxValue + 1
'   ERROR, exceeds the range of all integer data types
```

The six WriteLine statements will print the minimum and maximum values you can represent with the integer data types. The following statement attempts to assign to a Short integer variable a value that exceeds the largest possible value you can represent with the Short data type, and it will generate an error. If you attempt to store the same value to an Integer variable, there will be no problem, because this value is well within the range of the Integer data type.

The next two statements attempt to store to an Integer variable two values that are also outside the range that an Integer can represent. The first value exceeds the range of positive values, and the second exceeds the range of the negative values.

If you attempt to store these values to a Long variable, there will be no problem. If you exceed the range of values that can be represented by the Long data type, you're out of luck. This value can't be represented as an integer, and you must store it in one of the variable types discussed in the next sections.

Single- and Double-Precision Numbers

The names Single and Double come from single-precision and double-precision numbers. Double-precision numbers are stored internally with greater accuracy than single-precision numbers. In scientific calculations, you need all the precision you can get; in those cases, you should use the Double data type.

The result of the operation 1 / 3 is 0.333333… (an infinite number of digits "3"). You could fill 64 MB of RAM with "3" digits, and the result would still be truncated. Here's a simple, but illuminating, example:

In a button's Click event handler, declare two variables as follows:

```
Dim a As Single, b As Double
```

Then enter the following statements:

```
a = 1 / 3
Console.WriteLine(a)
```

Run the application and you should get the following result in the Output window:

```
.3333333
```

There are seven digits to the right of the decimal point. Break the application by pressing Ctrl+Break and append the following lines to the end of the previous code segment:

```
a = a * 100000
Console.WriteLine(a)
```

This time the following value will be printed in the Output window:

```
33333.34
```

The result is not as accurate as you might have expected initially—it isn't even rounded properly. If you divide *a* by 100,000, the result will be:

```
0.3333334
```

which is different from the number we started with (0.3333333). This is an important point in numeric calculations, and it's called *error propagation*. In long sequences of numeric calculations, errors propagate. Even if you can tolerate the error introduced by the Single data type in a single operation, the cumulative errors may be significant.

Let's perform the same operations with double-precision numbers, this time using the variable *b*. Add these lines to the button's Click event handler:

```
b = 1 / 3
Console.WriteLine(b)
b = b * 100000
Console.WriteLine(b)
```

This time, the following numbers are displayed in the Output window:

```
0.333333333333333
33333.3333333333
```

The results produced by the double-precision variables are more accurate.

NOTE *Smaller-precision numbers are stored in fewer bytes, and larger-precision numbers are stored in more bytes. The actual format of the floating-point numeric types is complicated and won't be discussed in this book. Just keep in mind that fractional values can't be always represented precisely in the computer's memory; they produce more accurate results, but using more precision requires more memory.*

Why are such errors introduced in our calculations? The reason is that computers store numbers internally with two digits: zero and one. This is very convenient for computers, because electronics understand two states: on and off. As a matter of fact, all the statements are translated into bits (zeros and ones) before the computer can understand and execute them. The binary numbering system used by computers is not much different than the decimal system we, humans, use; computers just use fewer digits. We humans use 10 different digits to represent any number, whole or fractional, because we have 10 fingers. Just as with the decimal numbering system some numbers can't be represented precisely, there are numbers that can't be represented precisely in the binary system. Let me give you a more illuminating example.

Create a single-precision variable, *a*, and a double-precision variable, *b*, and assign the same value to them:

```
Dim a As Single, b As Double
a = 0.03007
b = 0.03007
```

Then print their difference:

```
Console.WriteLine(a-b)
```

If you execute these lines, the result won't be zero! It will be -6.03199004634014E-10. This is a very small number that can also be written as 0.000000000603199004634014. Because different numeric types are stored differently in memory, they don't quite match. What this means to you is that all variables in a calculation should be of the same type. In addition, don't make comparisons like:

```
If a = b Then { do something }
```

Use a threshold instead. If the difference is smaller than a threshold, then the two values can be considered equal (depending on the nature of your calculations, of course):

```
If (a - b) < 0.000001 Then { do something }
```

If your applications involve heavy math, always follow the values of the intermediate results to see where truncation errors were introduced.

Eventually, computers will understand mathematical notation and will not convert all numeric expressions into values, as they do today. If you multiply the expression $1/3$ by 3, the result should be 1. Computers, however, must convert the expression $1/3$ into a value before they can multiply it with 3. Since $1/3$ can't be represented precisely, the result of the $(1/3) \times 3$ will not always be 1. If the variables *a* and *b* are declared as Single or Double, the following statements will print 1:

```
a = 3
b = 1 / a
Console.WriteLine(b * a)
```

If the two variables are declared as Decimal, however, the result will be a number very close to 1, but not exactly 1 (it will be 0.9999999999999999999999999999—there are 28 digits after the decimal period).

The Decimal Data Type

Variables of the last numeric data type, Decimal, are stored internally as integers in 16 bytes and are scaled by a power of 10. The scaling power determines the number of decimal digits to the right of the floating point, and it's an integer value from 0 to 28. When the scaling power is 0, the value is multiplied by 10^0, or 1, and it's represented without decimal digits. When the scaling power is 28, the value is divided by 10^{28} (which is 1 followed by 28 zeros—an enormous value), and it's represented with 28 decimal digits.

The largest possible value you can represent with a Decimal value is an integer: 79,228,162,514,264,337,593,543,950,335. The smallest number you can represent with a Decimal variable is the negative of the same value. These values use a scaling factor of 0.

VB6 ➟ VB.NET

The Decimal data type is new to VB.NET and has replaced the Currency data type of previous versions of VB. The Currency type was introduced to handle monetary calculations and had a precision of four decimal digits. It was dropped from the language because it didn't provide enough accuracy for the types of calculations it was designed for. Most programmers wanted to be able to control the accuracy of their calculations, so a new, more flexible type was introduced, the Decimal type.

When the scaling factor is 28, the largest value you can represent with a Decimal variable is quite small, actually. It's 7.9228162514264337593543950335 (and the largest negative value is the same with the minus sign). The number zero can't be represented precisely with a Decimal variable scaled by a factor of 28. The smallest positive value you can represent with the same scaling factor is 0.00...01 (there are 27 zeros between the decimal period and the digit 1)—an extremely small value, but still not quite zero.

NOTE *The more accuracy you want to achieve with a Decimal variable, the smaller the range of available values you have at your disposal—just as with the other numeric types, or just like about everything else in life.*

When using Decimal numbers, VB keeps track of the decimal digits (the digits following the decimal point) and treats all values as integers. The value 235.85 is represented as the integer 23585, but VB knows that it must scale the value by 100 when it's done using it. Scaling by 100 (that is, 10^2) corresponds to shifting the decimal point by two places. First, VB multiplies this value by 100 to make it an integer. Then, it divides it by 100 to restore the original value. Let's say you want to multiply the following values:

```
328.558 * 12.4051
```

First, you must turn them into integers. You must remember that the first number has three decimal digits and the second number has four decimal digits. The result of the multiplication will have seven decimal digits. So you can multiply the following integer values:

```
328558 * 124051
```

and then treat the last seven digits of the result as decimals. Use the Windows Calculator (in the Scientific view) to calculate the previous product. The result is 40,757,948,458. The actual value after taking into consideration the decimal digits is 4,075.7948458. This is how VB works with the

Decimal data type. If you perform the same calculations with Decimals in VB, you will get the exact same result. Insert the following lines in a button's Click event handler and execute the program:

```
Dim a As Decimal = 328.558
Dim b As Decimal = 12.4051
Dim c As Decimal
c = a * b
Console.WriteLine(c)
```

If you perform the same calculations with Single variables, the result will be truncated (and rounded) to 3 decimal digits: 4,075.795. Notice that the Decimal data type didn't introduce any rounding errors. It's capable of representing the result with the exact number of decimal digits. This is the real advantage of decimals, which makes them ideal for financial applications. For scientific calculations, you must still use Doubles. Decimal numbers are the best choice for calculations that require a specific precision (like four or eight decimal digits).

Numeric-calculation errors due to truncation are not unique to VB, or even to Pentium processors. This how computers and programming languages are designed, and you can't avoid them. People who write scientific applications have come up with techniques to minimize the effect of the truncations. For other types of applications, the truncation errors are practically negligible. If you write financial applications, use the Decimal data type and round the amounts to two decimal digits at the end.

INFINITY AND OTHER ODDITIES

VB.NET can represent two very special values, which may not be numeric values themselves but are produced by numeric calculations: NaN (not a number) and Infinity. If your calculations produce NaN or Infinity, you should confirm the data and repeat the calculations, or give up. For all practical purposes, neither NaN nor Infinity can be used in everyday business calculations.

VB6 ⟹ VB.NET

VB.NET introduces the concepts of an undefined number (NaN) and infinity to Visual Basic. In the past, any calculations that produced an abnormal result (i.e., a number that couldn't be represented with the existing data types) generated runtime errors. VB.NET can handle abnormal situations much more gracefully. NaN and Infinity aren't the type of result you'd expect from meaningful numeric calculations, but at least they don't produce run-errors.

Some calculations produce undefined results, like infinity. Mathematically, the result of dividing any number by zero is infinity. Unfortunately, computers can't represent infinity, so they produce an error when you request a division by zero. VB.NET will report a special value, which isn't a number: the Infinity value. If you call the ToString method of this value, however, it will return the string "Infinity". Let's generate an Infinity value. Start by declaring a Double variable, *dblVar*:

```
Dim dblVar As Double = 999
```

Then divide this value by zero:

```
Dim infVar as Double
infVar = dblVar / 0
```

and display the variable's value:

```
MsgBox(infVar)
```

The string "Infinity" will appear on a message box. This string is just a description; it tells you that the result is not a valid number (it's a very large number that exceeds the range of numeric values that can be represented in the computer's memory).

Another calculation that will yield a non-number is when you divide a very large number by a very small number. If the result exceeds the largest value that can be represented with the Double data type, the result is Infinity. Declare three variables as follows:

```
Dim largeVar As Double = 1E299
Dim smallVar As Double = 1E-299
Dim result As Double
```

NOTE *The notation* 1E299 *means* 10 *raised to the power of 299, which is an extremely large number. Likewise,* 1E-299 *means* 10 *raised to the power of* −299, *which is equivalent to dividing* 10 *by a number as large as* 1E299.

Then divide the large variable by the small variable and display the result:

```
result = largeVar / smallVar
MsgBox(result)
```

The result will be Infinity. If you reverse the operands (that is, you divide the very small by the very large variable), the result will be zero. It's not exactly zero, but the Double data type can't accurately represent numeric values that are very, very close to zero.

NOT A NUMBER (NAN)

NaN is not new. Packages like Mathematica and Excel have been using it for years. The value NaN indicates that the result of an operation can't be defined: it's not a regular number, not zero, and not Infinity. NaN is more of a mathematical concept, rather than a value you can use in your calculations. The Log() function, for example, calculates the logarithm of positive values. By default, you can't calculate the logarithm of a negative value. If the argument you pass to the Log() function is a negative value, the function will return the value NaN to indicate that the calculations produced an invalid result.

The result of the division 0 / 0, for example, is not a numeric value. If you attempt to enter the statement "0 / 0" in your code, however, VB will catch it even as you type and you'll get the error message "Division by zero occurs in evaluating this expression".

To divide zero by zero, set up two variables as follows:

```
Dim var1, var2 As Double
Dim result As Double
var1 = 0
var2 = 0
result = var1 / var2
MsgBox(result)
```

If you execute these statements, the result will be a NaN. Any calculations that involve the *result* variable (a NaN value) will yield NaN as a result. The statements:

```
result = result + result
result = 10 / result
result = result + 1E299
MsgBox(result)
```

will all yield NaN.

If you make *var2* a very small number, like 1E-299, the result will be zero. If you make *var1* a very small number, then the result will be Infinity.

For most practical purposes, Infinity is handled just like NaN. They're both numbers that shouldn't occur in business applications, and when they do, it means you must double-check your code or your data. They are much more likely to surface in scientific calculations, and they must be handled with the statements described in the next section.

Testing for Infinity and NaN

To find out whether the result of an operation is a NaN or Infinity, use the IsNaN and IsInfinity methods of the Single and Double data type. The Integer data type doesn't support these methods, even though it's possible to generate Infinity and NaN results with Integers. If the IsInfinity method returns True, you can further examine the sign of the Infinity value with the IsNegativeInfinity and IsPositiveInfinity methods.

In most situations, you'll display a warning and terminate the calculations. The statements of Listing 3.2 do just that. Place these statements in a Button's Click event handler and run the application.

LISTING 3.2: HANDLING NaN AND INFINITY VALUES

```
Dim var1, var2 As Double
Dim result As Double
var1 = 0
var2 = 0
result = var1 / var2
If result.IsInfinity(result) Then
    If result.IsPositiveInfinity(result) Then
        MsgBox("Encountered a very large number. Can't continue")
    Else
        MsgBox("Encountered a very small number. Can't continue")
    End If
Else
    If result.IsNaN(result) Then
        MsgBox("Unexpected error in calculations")
    Else
        MsgBox("The result is " & result.ToString)
    End If
End If
```

This listing will generate a NaN value. Change the value of the *var1* variable to 1 to generate a positive infinity value, or to –1 to generate a negative infinity value. As you can see, the IsInfinity, IsPositiveInfinity, IsNegativeInfinity, and IsNaN methods require that the variable be passed as argument, even though these methods apply to the same variable. An alternate, and easier to read, notation is the following:

```
System.Double.IsInfinity(result)
```

This statement is easier to understand, because it makes it clear that the IsInfinity method is a member of the `System.Double` class. (As if variables that expose methods and properties weren't enough, a class has now surfaced! The class is the "factory" that produces the object. The code that implements the various methods and properties of the variable is stored in the class. You will learn the relationship between objects and classes as you move along.)

This odd notation is something you will have to get used to. Some methods don't apply to the object they refer to, and they're called *shared* methods. They act on the value passed as argument and not the object to which you apply them. You'll read more on shared methods (and their counterparts, the *reference* methods) in Chapter 8.

If you change the values of the *var1* and *var2* variables to the following and execute the application, you'll get the message "Encountered a very large number":

```
var1 = 1E+299
var2 = 1E-299
```

If you reverse the values, you'll get the message "Encountered a very small number." In any case, the program will terminate gracefully and let you know the type of problem that prevents further calculations.

The Byte Data Type

None of the previous numeric types is stored in a single byte. In some situations, however, data is stored as bytes, and you must be able to access individual bytes. The Byte type holds an integer in the range 0 to 255. Bytes are frequently used to access binary files, image and sound files, and so on. Note that you no longer use bytes to access individual characters. Unicode characters are stored in two bytes.

To declare a variable as a Byte, use the following statement:

```
Dim n As Byte
```

The variable *n* can be used in numeric calculations too, but you must be careful not to assign the result to another Byte variable if its value may exceed the range of the Byte type. If the variables *A* and *B* are initialized as follows:

```
Dim A As Byte, B As Byte
A = 233
B = 50
```

the following statement will produce an overflow exception:

```
Console.WriteLine(A + B)
```

The same will happen if you attempt to assign this value to a Byte variable with the following statement:

```
B = A + B
```

The result (283) can't be stored in a single byte. Visual Basic generates the correct answer, but it can't store it into a Byte variable. If you do calculations with Byte variables and the result may exceed the range of the Byte data type, you must convert them to integers, with a statement like the following:

```
Console.WriteLine((CInt(A) + CInt(B)))
```

The CInt() function converts its argument to an Integer value. You will find more information on converting variable types later in this chapter, in the section "Converting Variable Types." Of course, you can start with integer variables and avoid all the conversions between types. In rare occasions, however, you may have to work with bytes and insert the appropriate code to avoid overflows.

TIP   *The operators that won't cause overflows are the Boolean operators AND, OR, NOT, and XOR, which are frequently used with Byte variables. These aren't logical operators that return True or False. They combine the matching bits in the two operands and return another byte. If you combine the numbers 199 and 200 with the AND operator, the result is 192. The two values in binary format are 11000111 and 11001000. If you perform a bitwise AND operation on these two values, the result is 11000000, which is the decimal value 192.*

In addition to the Byte data type, VB.NET provides a Signed Byte data type, which can represent signed values in the range from –128 to 127.

BOOLEAN VARIABLES

The Boolean data type stores True/False values. Boolean variables are, in essence, integers that take the value –1 (for True) and 0 (for False). Actually, any non-zero value is considered True. Boolean variables are declared as:

```
Dim failure As Boolean
```

and they are initialized to False.

Boolean variables are used in testing conditions, such as the following:

```
If failure Then MsgBox("Couldn't complete the operation")
```

They are also combined with the logical operators AND, OR, NOT, and XOR. The NOT operator toggles the value of a Boolean variable. The following statement is a toggle:

```
running = Not running
```

If the variable *running* is True, it's reset to False, and vice versa. This statement is a shorter way of coding the following:

```
Dim running As Boolean
If running = True Then
    running = False
Else
    running = True
End If
```

Boolean operators operate on Boolean variables and return another Boolean as their result. The following statements will display a message if one (or both) of the variables *ReadOnly* and *Hidden* are True (presumably these variables represent the corresponding attributes of a file):

```
If ReadOnly Or Hidden Then
    MsgBox("Couldn't open the file")
Else
    { statements to open and process file }
End If
```

You can reverse the logic and process the file if none of these variables are set to True:

```
If Not (ReadOnly Or Hidden) Then
    { statements to process the file }
Else
    MsgBox("Couldn't open the file")
End If
```

The condition of the If statement combines the two Boolean values with the Or operator. If both, or one, of them are True, the parenthesized expression is True. This value is negated with the Not operator, and the If clause is executed only if the result of the negation is True. If *ReadOnly* is True and *Hidden* is False, the expression is evaluated as:

```
If Not (True Or False)
```

(True Or False) is True, which reduces the expression to

```
If Not True
```

which, in turn, is False.

STRING VARIABLES

The String data type stores only text, and string variables are declared with the String type:

```
Dim someText As String
```

You can assign any text to the variable *someText*. You can store nearly 2 GB of text in a string variable (that's 2 billion characters and is much more text than you care to read on a computer screen). The following assignments are all valid:

```
Dim aString As String
aString = "Now is the time for all good men to come to the aid of their country"
aString = ""
aString = "There are approximately 29,000 words in this chapter"
aString = "25,000"
```

The second assignment creates an empty string, and the last one creates a string that just happens to contain numeric digits, which are also characters. The difference between these two variables

```
Dim aNumber As Integer = 25000
Dim aString As String = "25,000"
```

is that they hold different values. The *aString* variable holds the characters "2", "5", ",", "0", "0", and "0", and *aNumber* holds a single numeric value. However, you can use the variable *aString* in numeric calculations and the variable *aNumber* in string operations. VB will perform the necessary conversions, as long as the Strict option is off (its default value).

VB6 ⟹ VB.NET

Another feature not supported by VB.NET is the fixed-length string. With earlier versions of VB, you could declare variables of fixed length with a statement like the following, to speed up string operations:

```
Dm shortText As String * 100
```

This is no longer needed, as the Framework supports two powerful classes for manipulating strings: the String class and the StringBuilder class. They're both described in Chapter 11.

CHARACTER VARIABLES

Character variables store a single Unicode character in two bytes. In effect, characters are unsigned short integers (UInt16); you can use the CChar() function to convert integers to characters, and the CInt() function to convert characters to their equivalent integer values.

VB6 ⟹ VB.NET

Character variables are new to VB.NET, and they correspond to the String * 1 type so often used with previous versions of VB.

To declare a character variable, use the Char keyword:

```
Dim char1, char2 As Char
```

You can initialize a character variable by assigning either a character or a string to it. In the latter case, only the first character of the string is assigned to the variable. The following statements will print the characters "a" and "A" to the Output window:

```
Dim char1 As Char = "a", char2 As Char = "ABC"
Console.WriteLine(char1)
Console.WriteLine(char2)
```

The integer values corresponding to the English characters are the ANSI codes of the equivalent characters. The statement:

```
Console.WriteLine(CInt("a"))
```

will print the value 65.

If you convert the Greek character alpha (α) to an integer, its value is 945. The Unicode value of the famous character π is 960.

Character variables are used in conjunction with strings. You'll rarely save real data as characters. However, you may have to process the individual characters in a string, one at a time. Because the

Char data type exposes interesting methods (like IsLetter, IsDigit, IsPunctuation, and so on), you can use these methods in your code. Let's say the string variable *password* holds a user's new password, and you require that passwords contain at least one special symbol. The code segment of Listing 3.3 scans the password and rejects if it contains letter and digits only.

LISTING 3.3: PROCESSING INDIVIDUAL CHARACTERS

```
Dim password As String, ch As Char
Dim i As Integer
Dim valid As Boolean = False
While Not valid
    password = InputBox("Please enter your password")
    For i = 0 To password.Length - 1
        ch = password.Chars(i)
        If Not System.Char.IsLetterOrDigit(ch) Then
            valid = True
            Exit For
        End If
    Next
    If valid Then
        MsgBox("You new password will be activated immediately!")
    Else
        MsgBox("Your password must contain at least one special symbol!")
    End If
End While
```

NOTE   If you are not familiar with the If...Then, For...Next, *or* While...End While *structures, you can read their description in the "Flow-Control Statements" section of this chapter and then return to check out this example.*

The code prompts the user with an input box to enter a password. (Later in the book, you'll find out how to create a form that accepts the characters typed but displays asterisks in their place, so that the password isn't echoed on the screen.) The *valid* variable is Boolean, and it's initialized to False (you don't have to initialize a Boolean variable to False, because this is its default initial value, but it makes the code easier to read). It's set to True from within the body of the loop, only if the password contains a character that is not a letter or a digit. We set it to False initially, so that the While...End While loop will be executed at least once. This loop will keep prompting the user until a valid password is entered.

The loop scans the string variable *password*, one letter at a time. At each iteration, the next letter is copied into the *ch* variable. The Chars property of the String data type is an array that holds the individual characters in the string (another example of the functionality built into the data types).

Then the program examines the current character. The IsLetterOrDigit method of the Char data type returns True if a character is either a letter or a digit. If the current character is a symbol, the program sets the *valid* variable to True, so that the outer loop won't be executed again, and it exits the For...Next loop. Finally, it prints the appropriate message and either prompts for another password or quits.

You could write more compact code by using the IsLetterOrDigit method directly on the individual characters of the password, instead of storing them first in a Char variable. Listing 3.4 is another way to code the same program. (I've omitted the variable declarations at the beginning of the code; they're the same as before.)

LISTING 3.4: REQUESTING A PASSWORD WITH ONE SPECIAL CHARACTER

```
While True
    password = InputBox("Please enter your password")
    For i = 0 To password.Length - 1
        If Not System.Char.Chars(i).IsLetterOrDigit(password.Chars(i)) Then
            MsgBox("Your new password will be activated immediately!")
            Exit Sub
        End If
    Next
    MsgBox("Your password must contain at least one special symbol!")
End While
```

It's shorter and certainly much more real code. There's nothing wrong with the first implementation, but the second one is "programmer's code" as opposed to "beginner's code." Don't worry if you don't quite understand how it works; you can come back and explore it after you finish this chapter.

TIP   Notice that neither implementation would be possible without the methods exposed by the Char function. Although the second implementation doesn't use a variable of Char type, it relies on the functionality exposed by the Char data type. The expression **password.Chars(i)** *is actually a character, and that's why we can apply to it the members of the Char data type.*

DATE VARIABLES

Date and time values are stored internally in a special format, but you don't need to know the exact format. They are double-precision numbers: the integer part represents the date and the fractional part represents the time. A variable declared as Date can store both date and time values with a statement like the following:

```
Dim expiration As Date
```

The following are all valid assignments:

```
expiration = #01/01/2004#
expiration = #8/27/2001 6:29:11 PM#
expiration = "July 2, 2002"
expiration = Now()
```

(The Now() function returns the current date and time). The pound sign tells Visual Basic to store a date value to the *expiration* variable, just as the quotes tell Visual Basic that the value is a string. You can store a date as string to a Date variable, but it will be converted to the appropriate format.

If the Strict option is on, you can't specify dates using the long date format (as in the third statement of this example).

TIP   The date format is determined by the Regional Settings (found in Control Panel). In the United States, it's mm/dd/yy (in other countries, the format is dd/mm/yy). If you assign an invalid date to a date variable, like 23/04/2002, Visual Basic will automatically swap the month and day values to produce a valid date as you type. If the date is invalid even after the swapping of the month and day values, then an error message will appear in the Task List window. The description of the error is "Expected expression."

The Date data type is extremely flexible; Visual Basic knows how to handle date and time values, so that you won't have to write complicated code to perform the necessary conversions. To manipulate dates and times, use the members of the Date type, which are discussed in detail in Chapter 12, or the Date and Time functions, which are described in the reference "VB.NET Functions and Statements" on the book's companion CD. The difference between two dates is calculated by the function DateDiff(). This function accepts as argument a constant that determines the units in which the difference will be expressed (days, hours, and so on) as well as two dates, and it returns the difference between them in the specified increments. The following statement returns the number of days in the current millennium:

```
Dim days As Long
days = DateDiff(DateInterval.Day, #12/31/2000#, Now())
```

You can also call the Subtract method of the Date class, which accepts a date as argument and subtracts it from a Date variable. The difference between the two dates is returned as a TimeSpan object, which includes number of days, hours, minutes, and so on. For more information on the members of the Date class, see Chapter 12.

VB6 ⟹ VB.NET

Previous versions of VB allowed direct numeric calculations with date variables. For example, you used to be able to calculate the difference between two dates in days with by subtracting two date variables directly:

```
days = date1 - date2    ' DOESN'T WORK IN VB.NET
```

VB.NET doesn't allow the use of date variables with the arithmetic operators, even if the Strict option has been turned off.

DATA TYPE IDENTIFIERS

Finally, you can omit the As clause of the Dim statement, yet create typed variables, with the variable declaration characters, or *data type identifiers*. These characters are special symbols, which you append to the variable name to denote the variable's type. To create a string variable, you can use the statement:

```
Dim myText$
```

The dollar sign signifies a string variable. Notice that the name of the variable includes the dollar sign—it's *myText$*, not *myText*. To create a variable of a particular type, use one of the data declaration characters in Table 3.2 (not all data types have their own identifier).

TABLE 3.2: DATA TYPE DEFINITION CHARACTERS

SYMBOL	DATA TYPE	EXAMPLE
$	String	*A$, messageText$*
%	Integer (Int32)	*counter%, var%*
&	Long (Int64)	*population&, colorValue&*
!	Single	*distance!*
#	Double	*ExactDistance#*
@	Decimal	*Balance@*

Using type identifiers doesn't help in producing the cleanest and easiest to read code. If you haven't used them in the past, there's no really good reason to start using them now.

THE STRICT AND EXPLICIT OPTIONS

Previous versions of Visual Basic didn't require that variables be declared before they were used. VB.NET doesn't *require* that you declare your variables either, but the default behavior is to throw an exception if you attempt to use a variable that hasn't been previously declared. If an undeclared variable's name appears in your code, the editor will underline the variable's name with a wiggly red line, indicating that it caught an error. Rest the pointer over the segment of the statement in question to see the description of the error.

To change the default behavior, you must insert the following statement at the beginning of the file, above the Imports statements:

```
Option Explicit Off
```

The Option Explicit statement must appear at the very beginning of the file. This setting affects the code in the current module, not in all files of your project or solution.

The sample code in this section assumes that the Option Explicit has been set to Off. For all other examples in the book, I will assume that this option is set to On. Not only that, but in the first few chapters I include the declarations of the variables I use in short code samples that demonstrate an object property or the syntax of a function.

You can also specify the settings of the Strict and Explicit options from the Property Pages dialog box of the current project, as shown in Figure 3.1. To open this dialog box, right-click the name of the project in the Solution Explorer and, from the context menu, select Properties. The settings you specify here take effect for all the components of the current project.

FIGURE 3.1

Setting the Strict
and Explicit options
on the project's
Property Pages

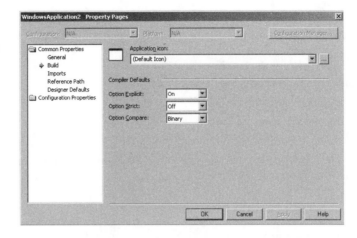

The default value of the `Option Explicit` statement is On. This is also the recommended value, and you should not make a habit of changing this setting. Most programmers familiar with previous versions of VB will not like having to declare their variables, but using variants for all types of variables has never been a good idea. In the later section "Why Declare Variables?", you will see an example of the pitfalls you'll avoid by declaring your variables. (The truth is that all VB programmers will miss variants, but this is a very small price to pay for the new features added to the language.)

By setting the Explicit option to Off, you're telling VB that you intend to use variables without declaring them. As a consequence, VB can't make any assumption as to the variable's type, so it uses a generic type of variable that can hold any type of information. These variables are called Object variables, and they're equivalent to the old variants.

As you work with the `Option Explicit` set to Off, you can use variables as needed, without declaring them first. When Visual Basic meets an undeclared variable name, it creates a new variable on the spot and uses it. The new variable's type is Object, the generic data type that can accommodate all other data types. Using a new variable in your code is equivalent to declaring it without type. Visual Basic adjusts its type according to the value you assign to it. Create two variables, *var1* and *var2*, by referencing them in your code with statements like the following ones:

```
var1 = "Thank you for using Fabulous Software"
var2 = 49.99
```

The *var1* variable is a string variable, and *var2* is a numeric one. You can verify this with the Get-Type method, which returns a variable's type. The following statements print the types shown below each statement, in bold:

```
Console.WriteLine("Variable var1 is " & var1.GetType().ToString)
```
Variable var1 is System.String
```
Console.WriteLine("Variable var2 is " & var2.GetType().ToString)
```
Variable var2 is System.Double

Later in the same program you can reverse the assignments:

```
var1 = 49.99
var2 = "Thank you for using Fabulous Software"
```

If you execute the previous Print statements again, you'll see that the types of the variables have changed. The *var1* variable is now a double, and *var2* is a string.

Another related option is the Strict option, which is Off by default. The Strict option tells the compiler whether the variables should be *strictly typed*. A strictly typed variable can accept values of the same type as the type it was declared with. With the Strict option set to Off, you can use a string variable that holds a number in a numeric calculation:

```
Dim a As String = "25000"
Console.WriteLine(a / 2)
```

The last statement will print the value 12500 on the Output window. Likewise, you can use numeric variables in string calculations:

```
Dim a As Double = 31.03
a = a + "1"
```

If you turn the Strict option on by inserting the following statement at the beginning of the file, you won't be able to mix and match variable types:

```
Option Strict On
```

If you attempt to execute any of the last two code segments while the Strict option is On, the compiler will underline a segment of the statement to indicate an error. If you rest the pointer over the underlined segment of the code, the following error message will appear in a tip box:

```
Option strict disallows implicit conversions from String to Double
```

(or whatever type of conversion is implied by the statement).

When the Strict option is set to On, the compiler doesn't disallow *all* implicit conversions between data types. For example, it will allow you to assign the value of an Integer to a Long, but not the opposite. The Long value may exceed the range of values that can be represented by an Integer variable. You will find more information on implicit conversions in the section "Widening and Narrowing Conversions," later in this chapter.

Moreover, with `Option Strict On`, you can't late-bind an expression. *Late binding* means to call a method or a property of an object, but not be able to resolve this call at design time.

When you declare an object, like a Pen or a Color object, and then you call one of its properties, the compiler can verify that the member you call exists. Take a look at the following lines:

```
Dim myPen As Pen
myPen = New Pen(Color.Red)
myPen.Width = 2
```

These three statements declare a Pen object and initialize it to red color and a width of two pixels. All the shapes you'll draw with this pen will be rendered in red, and their outlines will be two pixels wide. This is *early binding*, because as soon as the variable is declared, the compiler can verify that the Pen object has a Width and a Red property.

Now let's use an Object variable to store our Pen object:

```
Dim objPen As Object
objPen = New Pen(Color.Red)
objPen.Width = 2
```

This is called late binding, and it will work only if the Strict option is turned off. The *objPen* variable is an Object variable and can store anything. The compiler has no way of knowing what type of object you've stored to the variable, and therefore it can't verify that the *objPen* variable exposes a Width property. In this short segment, it's pretty obvious that the *objPen* variable holds a Pen object, but in a larger application the *objPen* variable may be set by any statement.

Early binding seems pretty restricting, but you should always use it. You should keep the default value only when absolutely necessary (which is rare). Notice that you don't have to turn on the Strict option to use early binding—just declare your variables with a specific type. Early-bound variables display their members in a drop-down list when you enter their name, followed by a period. If you enter *myPen* and the following period in the editor's window, you will see a list of all the methods supported by the Pen object. However, if you enter *objPen* and the following period, you will see a list with just four members—the members of any Object variable.

OBJECT VARIABLES

Variants—variables without a fixed data type—were the bread and butter of VB programmers up to version 6.0. VB.NET supports variants only for compatibility reasons, and you shouldn't be surprised if they're dropped altogether from the language in a future version. Variants are the opposite of strictly typed variables: they can store all types of values, from a single character to an object. If you're starting with VB.NET, you should use strictly typed variables. However, variants are a major part of the history of VB, and most applications out there (the ones you may be called to maintain) make use of them. So I will discuss variants briefly in this chapter and show you what was so good (and bad) about them.

VB6 ⫸ VB.NET

By default, you can't use variants with VB.NET. In order for variables to handle any value you assign to them, you can either declare them as Object type or turn off the Strict option. The keyword Variant has disappeared from the language.

Variants were the most flexible data type because they could accommodate all other types. A variable declared as Object (or a variable that hasn't been declared at all) is handled by Visual Basic according to the variable's current contents. If you assign an integer value to an Object variable, Visual Basic treats it as an integer. If you assign a string to an Object variable, Visual Basic treats it as a string. Variants can also hold different data types in the course of the same program. Visual Basic performs the necessary conversions for you.

To declare a variant, you can turn off the Strict option and use the Dim statement without specifying a type, as follows:

```
Dim myVar
```

If you don't want to turn off the Strict option (which isn't recommended anyway), you can declare the variable with the Object data type:

```
Dim myVar As Object
```

Every time your code references a new variable, Visual Basic will create an Object variable. For example, if the variable *validKey* hasn't been declared, when Visual Basic runs into the following line:

```
validKey = "002-6abbgd"
```

it will create a new Object variable and assign the value "002-6abbgd" to it.

You can use Object variables in both numeric and string calculations. Suppose the variable *modemSpeed* has been declared as Object with one of the following statements:

```
Dim modemSpeed                  ' Option Strict = Off
Dim modemSpeed As Object        ' Option Strict = On
```

and later in your code you assign the following value to it:

```
modemSpeed = "28.8"
```

The *modemSpeed* variable is a string variable that you can use in statements such as the following:

```
MsgBox "We suggest a " & modemSpeed & " modem."
```

This statement displays the following message:

```
We suggest a 28.8 modem.
```

You can also treat the *modemSpeed* variable as a numeric value with the following statement:

```
Console.WriteLine "A " & modemSpeed & " modem can transfer " & modemSpeed * _
        1000 / 8 & " bytes per second."
```

This statement displays the following message:

```
A 28.8 modem can transfer 3600 bytes per second.
```

The first instance of the *modemSpeed* variable in the above statement is treated as a string, because this is the variant's type according to the assignment statement (we assigned a string to it). The second instance, however, is treated as a number (a single-precision number). Visual Basic converts it to a numeric value because it's used in a numeric calculation.

Another example of this behavior of variants can be seen in the following statements:

```
Dim I As Integer, S As String
I = 10
S = "11"
Console.WriteLine(I + S)
Console.WriteLine(I & S)
```

The first WriteLine statement will display the numeric value 21, while the second statement will print the string "1011". The plus operator (+) tells VB to add two values. In doing so, VB must convert the two strings into numeric values, then add them. The concatenation operator (&) tells VB to concatenate the two strings.

Visual Basic knows how to handle variables in a way that makes sense. The result may not be what you had in mind, but it certainly is dictated by common sense. If you really want to concatenate the strings "10" and "11", you should use the & operator, which would tell Visual Basic exactly what to do. Quite impressive, but for many programmers this is a strange behavior that can lead to subtle errors, and they avoid it. It's up to you to decide whether to use variants and how far you will go with them. Sure, you can perform tricks with variants, but you shouldn't overuse them to the point that others can't read your code.

You can also store dates and times in an Object variable. To assign a date or time value to a variant, surround the value with pound signs, as follows:

```
date1 = #03/06/1999#
```

All operations that you can perform on date variables (discussed in the section "Date Variables") you can also perform with variants, which hold date and time values.

Converting Variable Types

In some situations, you will need to convert variables from one type into another. Table 3.3 shows the Visual Basic functions that perform data-type conversions. Actually, you will have to convert between data types quite often now that VB doesn't do it for you.

TABLE 3.3: DATA-TYPE CONVERSION FUNCTIONS

FUNCTION	CONVERTS ITS ARGUMENT TO
CBool	Boolean
CByte	Byte
CChar	Unicode character
CDate	Date
CDbl	Double
CDec	Decimal
CInt	Integer (4-byte integer, Int32)
CLng	Long (8-byte integer, Int64)
CObj	Object
CShort	Short (2-byte integer, Int16)
CSng	Single
CStr	String

To convert the variable initialized as

```
Dim A As Integer
```

to a Double, use the function:

```
Dim B As Double
B = CDbl(A)
```

Suppose you have declared two integers, as follows:

```
Dim A As Integer, B As Integer
A = 23
B = 7
```

The result of the operation A / B will be a double value. The following statement:

```
Console.Write(A / B)
```

displays the value 3.28571428571429. The result is a double, which provides the greatest possible accuracy. If you attempt to assign the result to a variable that hasn't been declared as Double, and the Strict option is On, then VB.NET will generate an error message. No other data type can accept this value without loss of accuracy.

As a reminder, the Short data type is equivalent to the old Integer type, and the CShort() function converts its argument to an Int16 value. The Integer data type is represented by 4 bytes (32 bits), and to convert a value to Int32 type, use the CInt() function. Finally, the CLng() function converts its argument to an Int64 value.

You can also use the CType() function to convert a variable or expression from one type to another. Let's say the variable A has been declared as String and holds the value "34.56". The following statement converts the value of the A variable to a Decimal value and uses it in a calculation:

```
Dim A As String = "34.56"
Dim B As Double
B = CType(A, Double) / 1.14
```

The conversion is necessary only if the Strict option is On, but it's a good practice to perform your conversions explicitly. The following section explains what may happen if your code relies to implicit conversions.

WIDENING AND NARROWING CONVERSIONS

In some situations, VB.NET will convert data types automatically, but not always. Let's say you have declared and initialized two variables, an integer and a double, with the following statements:

```
Dim count As Integer = 99
Dim pi As Double = 3.1415926535897931
```

If the Strict option is On and you attempt to assign the value of the *pi* variable to the *count* variable, the compiler will generate an error message to the effect that you can't convert a double to an integer. The exact message is:

```
Option Strict disallows implicit conversions from Double to Integer
```

VB6 ⟹ VB.NET

You will probably see this message many times, especially if you're a VB6 programmer. In the past, VB would store the value 3 to the *count* variable and proceed. If you weren't careful, you'd lose significant decimal digits and might not even know it. This implicit conversion results in loss of accuracy, and VB.NET doesn't perform it by default. This is a typical example of the pitfalls of turning off the Strict option.

When the Strict option is On, VB.NET will perform conversions that do not result in loss of accuracy (precision) or magnitude. These conversions are called *widening* conversions, as opposed to the *narrowing* conversions. When you assign an Integer value to a Double variable, no accuracy or magnitude is lost. On the other hand, when you assign a double value to an integer variable, then some accuracy is lost (the decimal digits must be truncated). Since you, the programmer, are in control, you may wish to give up the accuracy—presumably, it's no longer needed. When the Strict option is on, VB.NET doesn't assume that you're willing to sacrifice the accuracy, even if this is your intention. Instead, it forces you to convert the data type explicitly with one of the data type conversion functions. Normally, you must convert the Double value to an Integer value and then assign it to an Integer variable:

```
count = CInt(pi)
```

This is a narrowing conversion (from a value with greater accuracy or magnitude to a value with smaller accuracy or magnitude), and it's not performed automatically by VB.NET. Table 3.4 summarizes the widening conversions VB.NET will perform for you automatically.

TABLE 3.4: VB.NET WIDENING CONVERSIONS

ORIGINAL DATA TYPE	WIDER DATA TYPE
Any type	Object
Byte	Short, Integer, Long, Decimal, Single, Double
Short	Integer, Long, Decimal, Single, Double
Integer	Long, Decimal, Single, Double
Long	Decimal, Single, Double
Decimal	Single, Double
Single	Double
Double	none
Char	String

In the first beta version of Visual Studio .NET, the Strict option was on by default. It seems that pressure from VB6 programmers forced the designers of Visual Studio to change the default setting of this option. I expect that the default settings of the Strict option will be turned on again in the future, and eventually you won't be able to turn it off.

If the Strict option is off (the default value), the compiler will allow you to assign a Long variable to an Integer variable. Should the Long variable contain a value that exceeds the range of values of the Integer data type, then you'll end up with a runtime error. Of course, you can avoid the runtime error with the appropriate error-handling code. If the Strict option is on, the compiler will point out all the statements that may cause similar runtime errors, and you can re-evaluate your choice of variable types. You can also turn on the Strict option temporarily to see the compiler's warnings, then turn it off again.

User-Defined Data Types

In the previous sections, we assumed that applications create variables to store individual values. As a matter of fact, most programs store sets of data of different types. For example, a program for balancing your checkbook must store several pieces of information for each check: the check's number, amount, date, and so on. All these pieces of information are necessary to process the checks, and ideally, they should be stored together.

A structure for storing multiple values (of the same or different type) is called a *record*. For example, each check in a checkbook-balancing application is stored in a separate record, as shown in Figure 3.2. When you recall a given check, you need all the information stored in the record.

FIGURE 3.2

Pictorial representation of a record

Record Structure

Check Number	Check Date	Check Amount	Check Paid To

Array Of Records

275	04/12/01	104.25	Gas Co.
276	04/12/01	48.76	Books
277	04/14/01	200.00	VISA
278	04/21/01	430.00	Rent

To define a record in VB.NET, use the Structure statement, which has the following syntax:

```
Structure structureName
    Dim variable1 As varType
    Dim variable2 As varType
    ...
    Dim variablen As varType
End Structure
```

varType can be any of the data types supported by the framework. The Dim statement can be replaced by the Private or Public access modifiers. For structures, Dim is equivalent to Public.

After this declaration, you have in essence created a new data type that you can use in your application. *structureName* can be used anywhere you'd use any of the base types (integers, doubles, and so on). You can declare variables of this type and manipulate them as you manipulate all other variables (with a little extra typing). The declaration for the record structure shown in Figure 3.2 is

```
Structure CheckRecord
    Dim CheckNumber As Integer
    Dim CheckDate As Date
    Dim CheckAmount As Single
    Dim CheckPaidTo As String
End Structure
```

This declaration must appear outside any procedure; you can't declare a Structure in a subroutine or function. The CheckRecord structure is a new data type for your application. Depending on where the structure was declared, it may not be visible from the entire code, but it's up to you to give your structure the proper scope (see the section "A Variable's Scope," later in this chapter for more information on variable scoping).

To declare variables of this new type, use a statement such as this one:

```
Dim check1 As CheckRecord, check2 As CheckRecord
```

To assign a value to one of these variables, you must separately assign a value to each one of its components (they are called *fields*), which can be accessed by combining the name of the variable and the name of a field separated by a period, as follows:

```
check1.CheckNumber = 275
```

Actually, as soon as you type the period following the variable's name, a list of all members to the CheckRecord structure will appear, as shown in Figure 3.3. Notice that the structure supports a few members on its own. You didn't write any code for the Equals, GetType, and ToString members, but they're standard members of any Structure object and you can use them in your code. Both the GetType and ToString methods will return a string like "ProjectName.FormName+CheckRecord".

FIGURE 3.3

Variables of custom types expose their members as properties.

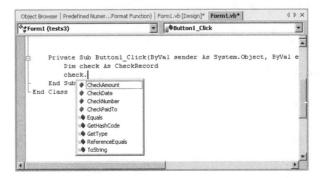

You can think of the record as an object and its fields as properties. Here are the assignment statements for a check:

```
check2.CheckNumber = 275
check2.CheckDate = #09/12/2001#
check2.CheckAmount = 104.25
check2.CheckPaidTo = "Gas Co."
```

You can also create *arrays of records* with a statement such as the following (arrays are discussed later in this chapter):

```
Dim Checks(100) As CheckRecord
```

Each element in this array is a CheckRecord record and holds all the fields of a given check. To access the fields of the third element of the array, use the following notation:

```
Checks(2).CheckNumber = 275
Checks(2).CheckDate = #09/12/2001#
Checks(2).CheckAmount = 104.25
Checks(2).CheckPaidTo = "Gas Co."
```

All data types expose the Equals method, which compares an instance of a data type (a integer variable, for example) to another instance of the same type. This is a trivial operation for simple data types, as you can compare the two variables directly. The Equals method can also compare two Structure variables and return True if all of their fields match. If a single field differs, the two objects represented by the variables are not identical. Use this method to compare variables declared as custom structures to avoid comparing all their members. Let's say you have created two variables of the CheckRecord type:

```
Dim c1, c2 As CheckRecord
{ assign values to the c1 and c2 variables }
If c1.Equals(c2) Then
    MsgBox "Same"
Else
    MsgBox "Different"
End If
```

You can also use arrays as Structure members. The following structure uses an array to store multiple e-mail addresses for the same person:

```
Structure Person
    Dim First As String
    Dim Last As String
    Dim Address As String
    Dim Phone As String
    Dim EMail(10) As String
End Structure
```

Using this structure, you can store up to 10 e-mail addresses per person. To use the Person structure in your code, declare a variable of this type:

```
Dim aPerson As Person
```

To access the first element of the *EMail* member, use the following notation:

```
aPerson.EMail(0) = "JDoe@tex.com"
```

You can also declare an array of Person structures, with the following statement:

```
Dim allPeople(1000) As Person
```

This array can hold contact information for 1,000 persons, and each person is identified by an index. That is, you must know the index corresponding to each person, or you must search the array to locate the person you're interested in. In Chapter 11, you'll learn how to index and search arrays with meaningful keys, like names, rather than indices.

To access an element of the *EMail* array, use two indices, one for the array of structures and another one for the array member: `allPeople(3).EMail(0)`, `allPeople(3).EMail(1)`, and so on.

THE NOTHING VALUE

The Nothing value is used with Object variables and indicates a variable that has not been initialized. If you want to disassociate an Object variable from the object it represents, set it to Nothing. The following statements create an Object variable that references a Brush, use it, and then release it:

```
Dim brush As System.Drawing.Brush
brush = New System.Drawing.Brush(bmap)
```

```
{ use brush object to draw with }
brush = Nothing
```

The first statement declares a Brush variable. At this point, the *brush* variable is Nothing. The second statement initializes the *brush* variable with the appropriate constructor. After the execution of the second statement, the brush variable actually represents an object you can draw with. After using it to draw something, you can release it by setting it to Nothing.

VB6 ⟹ VB.NET

The Set statement is obsolete in VB.NET. You can initialize Object variables just like any other type of variable, with the assignment operator.

If you want to find out whether an object variable has been initialized, use the Is keyword, as shown in the following example:

```
Dim myPen As Pen
{ more statements here }
If myPen Is Nothing Then
    myPen  = New Pen(Color.Red)
End If
```

The variable *myPen* is initialized with the New constructor only if it hasn't been initialized already. If you want to release the *myPen* variable later in your code, you can set it to Nothing with the assignment operator.

Examining Variable Types

Besides setting the types of variables and the functions for converting between types, Visual Basic provides two methods that let you examine the type of a variable. They are the GetType() and Get-TypeCode() methods. The GetType() method returns a string with the variable's type ("Int32", "Decimal", and so on). The GetTypeCode() method returns a value that identifies the variable's type. The code for the Double data type is 14. The values returned by the GetType() and GetType-Code() methods for all data types are shown in Table 3.5.

TABLE 3.5: VARIABLE TYPES AND TYPE CODES

GETTYPE()	GETTYPECODE()	DESCRIPTION
Boolean	3	Boolean value
Byte	6	Byte value (0 to 255)
Char	4	Character
DateTime	16	Date/time value
Decimal	15	Decimal

Continued on next page

TABLE 3.5: VARIABLE TYPES AND TYPE CODES *(continued)*

GETTYPE()	GETTYPECODE()	DESCRIPTION
Double	14	Double-precision floating-point number
Int16	7	2-byte integer (Short)
Int32	9	4-byte integer (Integer)
Int64	11	8-byte integer (Long)
Object		Object (a non-value variable)
SByte	5	Signed byte (−127 to 128)
Single	13	Single-precision floating-point number
String	8	String
UInt16	8	2-byte unsigned integer
UInt32	10	4-byte unsigned integer
UInt64	12	8-byte unsigned integer

Any variable exposes these methods automatically, and you can call them like this:

```
Dim var As Double
Console.WriteLine("The variable's type is " & var.GetType)
```

These functions are used mostly in If structures, like the following one:

```
If var.GetType() Is GetType(System.Double) Then
    { code to handle a Double value }
End If
```

Notice that the code doesn't reference data type names directly. Instead, it uses the value returned by the GetType() function to retrieve the type of the class `System.Double` and then compares this value to the variable's type with the Is keyword.

IS IT A NUMBER OR A STRING?

Another set of Visual Basic functions returns variables' data types, but not the exact type. They return a broader type, such as "numeric" for all numeric data types. This is the type you usually need in your code. The following functions are used to validate user input, as well as data stored in files, before you process them.

IsNumeric()   Returns True if its argument is a number (Short, Integer, Long, Single, Double, Decimal). Use this function to determine whether a variable holds a numeric value before passing it to a procedure that expects a numeric value or process it as a number. You can also use this function to test a value entered by a user when a numeric value is expected. The following statements keep prompting the user with an InputBox for a numeric value. The user must enter a numeric value, or click the Cancel button to exit. As long as the user enters nonnumeric values, the InputBox pops up and prompts for a numeric value:

```
Dim strAge as String = "$"
Dim Age As Integer
While Not IsNumeric(strAge)
    strAge = InputBox("Please enter your age")
End While
```

The variable *strAge* is initialized to a nonnumeric value so that the While…End While loop will be executed at least once. You can use any value in the place of the dollar sign, as long as it's not a valid numeric value.

IsDate()   Returns True if its argument is a valid date (or time). The following expressions return True, because they all represent valid dates:

```
IsDate(#10/12/2010#)
IsDate("10/12/2010")
IsDate("October 12, 2010")
```

If the date expression includes the day name, as in the following expression, the IsDate() function will return False:

```
IsDate("Sat. October 12, 2010")        ' FALSE
```

IsArray()   Returns True if its argument is an array.

IsDBNull()   Detects whether an object variable has been initialized or is a DBNull value. This function is equivalent to the IsNull() function of VB6.

IsReference()   Returns True if its argument is an object. This function is equivalent to the IsObject() function of VB6.

TIP   *All these functions are described in the bonus reference "VB.NET Functions and Statements," on the CD.*

Why Declare Variables?

All previous versions of Visual Basic didn't enforce variable declaration, which was a good thing for the beginner programmer. When you want to slap together a "quick and dirty" program, the last thing you need is someone telling you to decide which variables you're going to use and to declare them before using them.

But most programmers accustomed to the free format of Visual Basic also carry their habits of quick-and-dirty coding to large projects. When writing large applications, you will probably find that variable declaration is a good thing. It will help you write clean code and simplify debugging. Variable declaration eliminates the source of the most common and pesky bugs.

Let's examine the side effects of using undeclared variables in your application. To be able to get by without declaring your variables, you must set the Explicit option to Off. Let's assume you're using the following statements to convert German marks to U.S. dollars:

```
DM2USD = 1.562
USDollars = amount * DM2USD
```

The first time your code refers to the *DM2USD* variable name, Visual Basic creates a new variable and then uses it as if it was declared.

Suppose the variable *DM2USD* appears in many places in your application. If in one of these places you type *DM2UDS* instead of *DM2USD* and the program doesn't enforce variable declaration, the compiler will create a new variable, assign it the value zero, and then use it. Any amount converted with the *DM2UDS* variable will be zero! If the application enforces variable declaration, the compiler will complain (the *DM2UDS* variable hasn't been declared), and you will catch the error.

Many programmers, though, feel restricted by having to declare variables. Others live by it. Depending on your experiences with Visual Basic, you can decide for yourself. For a small application, you don't have to declare variables; just insert the statement `Option Explicit Off` at the top of your files. Be warned, though, that the river won't go backward; VB.NET encourages the explicit declaration of variables, but a future version of VB is quite likely to *enforce* variable declaration—in the spirit of the other two languages of Visual Studio.

A Variable's Scope

In addition to its type, a variable also has a scope. The *scope* (or *visibility*) of a variable is the section of the application that can see and manipulate the variable. If a variable is declared within a procedure, only the code in the specific procedure has access to that variable. This variable doesn't exist for the rest of the application. When the variable's scope is limited to a procedure, it's called *local*.

Suppose you're coding the Click event of a Button to calculate the sum of all even numbers in the range 0 to 100. One possible implementation is shown in Listing 3.5.

LISTING 3.5: SUMMING EVEN NUMBERS

```
Private Sub Button1_Click(ByVal sender As Object, _
                ByVal e As System.EventArgs) Handles Button1.Click
    Dim i As Integer
    Dim Sum As Integer
    For i = 0 to 100 Step 2
        Sum = Sum + i
    Next
    MsgBox "The sum is " & Sum
End Sub
```

The variables *i* and *Sum* are local to the Button1_Click() procedure. If you attempt to set the value of the *Sum* variable from within another procedure, Visual Basic will complain that the variable hasn't been declared. (Or, if you have turned off the Explicit option, it will create another *Sum* variable, initialize it to zero, and then use it. But this won't affect the variable *Sum* in the Button1_Click() subroutine.) The *Sum* variable is said to have *procedure-level* scope. It's visible within the procedure and invisible outside the procedure.

Sometimes, however, you'll need to use a variable with a broader scope, such as one whose value is available to all procedures within the same file. In principle, you could declare all variables outside the procedures that use them, but this would lead to problems. Every procedure in the file would have access to the variable, and you would need to be extremely careful not to change the value of a variable without good reason. Variables that are needed by a single procedure (such as loop counters) should be declared in that procedure.

A new type of scope was introduced with VB.NET: the *block-level* scope. Variables introduced in a block of code, such as an If statement or a loop, are local to the block but invisible outside the block. Let's revise the previous code segment, so that it calculates the sum of squares. To carry out the calculation, we first compute the square of each value and then sum the squares. The square of each value is stored to a variable that won't be used outside the loop, so we can define the *sqrValue* variable in the loop's block and make it local to this specific loop, as shown in Listing 3.6.

LISTING 3.6: A VARIABLE SCOPED IN ITS OWN BLOCK

```
Private Sub Button1_Click(ByVal sender As Object, _
                ByVal e As System.EventArgs) Handles Button1.Click
    Dim i, Sum As Integer
    For i = 0 to 100 Step 2
        Dim sqrValue As Integer
        sqrValue = i * i
        Sum = Sum + sqrValue
    Next
    MsgBox "The sum of the squares is " & Sum
End Sub
```

The *sqrValue* variable is not visible outside the block of the **For…Next** loop. If you attempt to use it before the For statement, or after the Next statement, VB will throw an exception. Insert the statement

```
Console.WriteLine(sqrValue)
```

after the call to the MsgBox function to see what will happen: the *sqrValue* variable maintains its value between iterations. If you insert the WriteLine statement after the line that declares the variable, you will see that it's not initialized at each iteration, even though there's a Dim statement in the loop. The values printed by this statement will keep getting larger, and they're not reset to zero. Of course, if you re-enter the block in which a variable is declared, you must initialize the variable to avoid side effects. Even though the variable's scope is the block in which it was declared, it exists while the subroutine is executing.

Another type of scope is the *module-level* scope. Variables declared outside any procedure in a module are visible from within all procedures in the same module, but they're invisible outside the module. Variables with a module-level scope can be set from within any procedure, so you should try to minimize the number of such variables. Setting many variables from within many procedures can seriously complicate the debugging of the application. Beginners have a tendency to overuse module-level scope, because they simplify the exchange of data among procedures. You can write procedures that don't accept any arguments—they simply act on module-level variables. Even though they may simplify small projects, too many variables with module-level scope reduce the maintainability and readability of large projects.

Let's say you're writing a text-editing application that provides the usual Save and Save As commands. The Save As command prompts the user for the filename in which the text will be stored.

The Save command, however, must remember the name of the file used with the most recent Save As command, so that it can save the text to the same file. It must also remember the name of the file that was read most recently, so that it can save the text back to the same file. The path of the file is needed from within three separate procedures, so it must be saved in a variable with module-level scope: the Open procedure should be able to set this variable, the Save As procedure should be able to either read or set it, and the Save procedure should be able to read it. This is a typical example of a variable with module-level scope.

Finally, in some situations the entire application must access a certain variable. In this case, the variable must be declared as Public. Public variables have a *global* scope: they are visible from any part of the application. To declare a public variable, use the Public statement in place of the Dim statement. Moreover, you can't declare public variables in a procedure. If you have multiple forms in your application and you want the code in one form to see a certain variable in another form, you can use the Public modifier. You can also make a control on a form visible outside its own form, by setting its Modifier property to Public. Setting this property causes VB to insert the Public keyword in the declaration of the control.

NOTE   *You will learn how to access variables declared in one form from within another form's code, in Chapter 5.*

The Public keyword makes the variable available not only to the entire project, but also to all projects that reference the current project. If you want your variables to be public within a project (in other words, available to all procedures in any module in the project) but invisible to referencing projects, use the Friend keyword in the declaration of the module. Variables that you want to use throughout your project, but not have available to other projects that reference the current one, should be declared as Friend. There is no way to make some of the public variables available to the referencing projects.

So, why do we need so many different types of scope? You'll develop a better understanding of scope and which type of scope to use for each variable as you get involved in larger projects. In general, you should try to limit the scope of your variables as much as possible. If all variables were declared within procedures, then you could use the same name for storing a temporary value in each procedure and be sure that one procedure's variables don't interfere with those of another procedure, even if you use the same name. Not that you can run out of variable names, but names like *tempString*, *amount*, *total*, and so on are quite common. All loop counters should also be local to the procedure that uses them. The variable *counter* in the following loop should never be declared outside the procedure:

```
For counter = 1 To 100
    { statements }
Next
```

This statement repeats the block of statements 100 times. There's absolutely no reason to declare the *counter* variable outside the procedure. Most programmers tend to use the same counter names in all of their loops, so they have to use local variables.

Procedure-level variables are necessary, but you should try to minimize their use. If a variable looks like a good candidate for procedure-level scope, see if you can implement the code with two or more local-level scope variables. Many procedure-level variables can be reduced to local-level variables if they're used by a couple of functions only. You can pass their values from one function to the other and avoid the creation of a new procedure-level variable.

The Lifetime of a Variable

In addition to type and scope, variables have a *lifetime*, which is the period for which they retain their value. Variables declared as Public exist for the lifetime of the application. Local variables, declared within procedures with the Dim or Private statement, live as long as the procedure. When the procedure finishes, the local variables cease to exist and the allocated memory is returned to the system. Of course, the same procedure can be called again. In this case, the local variables are recreated and initialized again. If a procedure calls another, its local variables retain their values while the called procedure is running.

You also can force a local variable to preserve its value between procedure calls with the Static keyword. Suppose the user of your application can enter numeric values at any time. One of the tasks performed by the application is to track the average of the numeric values. Instead of adding all the values each time the user adds a new value and dividing by the count, you can keep a running total with the function RunningAvg(), which is shown in Listing 3.7.

LISTING 3.7: CALCULATIONS WITH GLOBAL VARIABLES

```
Function RunningAvg(ByVal newValue As Double) As Double
    CurrentTotal = CurrentTotal + newValue
    TotalItems = TotalItems + 1
    RunningAvg = CurrentTotal / TotalItems
End Function
```

You must declare the variables *CurrentTotal* and *TotalItems* outside the function so that their values are preserved between calls. Alternatively, you can declare them in the function with the Static keyword, as in Listing 3.8.

LISTING 3.8: CALCULATIONS WITH LOCAL STATIC VARIABLES

```
Function RunningAvg(ByVal newValue As Double) As Double
    Static CurrentTotal As Double
    Static TotalItems As Integer
    CurrentTotal = CurrentTotal + newValue
    TotalItems = TotalItems + 1
    RunningAvg = CurrentTotal / TotalItems
End Function
```

The advantage of using static variables is that they help you minimize the number of total variables in the application. All you need is the running average, which the RunningAvg() function provides without making its variables visible to the rest of the application. Therefore, you don't risk changing the variables' values from within other procedures.

VB6 ➡ VB.NET

In VB6 you could declare all the variables in a procedure as static by prefixing the procedure definition with the keyword Static. This option is no longer available with VB.NET: the Static modifier is not a valid modifier for procedures.

Variables declared in a module outside any procedure take effect when the form is loaded and cease to exist when the form is unloaded. If the form is loaded again, its variables are initialized, as if it's being loaded for the first time.

Variables are initialized when they're declared, according to their type. Numeric variables are initialized to zero, string variables are initialized to a blank string, and Object variables are initialized to Nothing. Of course, if the variable is declared with an initializer (as in `Dim last As Integer = 99`), it is initialized to the specified value.

Constants

Some variables don't change value during the execution of a program. These are *constants* that appear many times in your code. For instance, if your program does math calculations, the value of pi (3.14159…) may appear many times. Instead of typing the value 3.14159 over and over again, you can define a constant, name it *pi*, and use the name of the constant in your code. The statement

```
circumference = 2 * pi * radius
```

is much easier to understand than the equivalent

```
circumference = 2 * 3.14159 * radius
```

You could declare *pi* as a variable, but constants are preferred for two reasons:

Constants don't change value. This is a safety feature. Once a constant has been declared, you can't change its value in subsequent statements, so you can be sure that the value specified in the constant's declaration will take effect in the entire program.

Constants are processed faster than variables. When the program is running, the values of constants don't have to be looked up. The compiler substitutes constant names with their values, and the program executes faster.

The manner in which you declare constants is similar to the manner in which you declare variables, except that in addition to supplying the constant's name, you must also supply a value, as follows:

```
Const constantname As type = value
```

Constants also have a scope and can be Public or Private. The constant *pi*, for instance, is usually declared in a module as Public so that every procedure can access it:

```
Public Const pi As Double = 3.14159265358979
```

The name of the constant follows the same rules as variable names. The constant's value is a literal value or a simple expression composed of numeric or string constants and operators. You can't use functions in declaring constants. The best way to define the value of the *pi* variable is to use the pi member of the Math class:

```
pi = Math.pi
```

However, you can't use this assignment *in the constant declaration*. You must supply the actual value.

Constants can be strings, too, like these:
```
Const ExpDate = #31/12/1997#
Const ValidKey = "A567dfe"
```

Visual Basic uses constants extensively to define method arguments and control properties. The value of a CheckBox control, for instance, can be `CheckState.Checked` or `CheckState.UnChecked`. If the CheckBox control's ThreeState property is True, it can have yet another value, which is `Check-State.Intederminate`. These constants correspond to integer values, but you don't need to know what these values are. You see only the names of the constants in the Properties window. If you type the expression

```
CheckBox1.CheckState =
```

a list of all possible values of the CheckState property will appear as soon as you type the equal sign, and you can select one from the list.

VB.NET recognizes numerous constants, which are grouped according to the property they apply to. Each property's possible values form an *enumeration*, and the editor knows which enumeration applies to each property as you type. As a result, you don't have to memorize any of the constant names or look up their names. They're right there as you type, and their names make them self-explanatory. Notice that the name of the constant is prefixed by the name of the enumeration it belongs to.

NOTE *Enumerations are often named after the property they apply to, but not always. The set of possible values of the BorderStyle property for all controls is named BorderStyle enumeration. The value set for the alignment of the text on a control, however, is the HorizontalAlignment enumeration. But you always see the proper enumeration in the Properties window, and the editor knows which one to display and when.*

Constant declarations may include other constants. In math calculations, the value 2 × pi is almost as common as the value pi. You can declare these two values as constants:

```
Public Const pi As Double = 3.14159265358979
Public Const pi2 As Double = 2 * pi
```

TIP *When defining constants in terms of other constants, especially if they reside in different modules, be sure to avoid circular definitions. Try to place all your constant declarations in the same module. If you have modules you use with several applications, try to include the module's name in the constant names to avoid conflicts and duplicate definitions.*

Arrays

A standard structure for storing data in any programming language is the array. Whereas individual variables can hold single entities, such as one number, one date, or one string, *arrays* can hold sets of data of the same type (a set of numbers, a series of dates, and so on). An array has a name, as does a variable, and the values stored in it can be accessed by an index.

For example, you could use the variable *Salary* to store a person's salary:

```
Salary = 34000
```

But what if you wanted to store the salaries of 16 employees? You could either declare 16 variables—*Salary1, Salary2*, up to *Salary16*—or you could declare an array with 16 elements. An array is similar to a variable: it has a name and multiple values. Each value is identified by an index (an integer value) that follows the array's name in parentheses. Each different value is an *element* of the array. If the array *Salaries* holds the salaries of 16 employees, the element `Salaries(0)` holds the salary of the first employee, the element `Salaries(1)` holds the salary of the second employee, and so on up the element `Salaries(15)`.

VB6 ⫸ VB.NET

The indexing of arrays in VB.NET starts at zero, and you can't change this behavior, because the `Option Base` statement, which allowed you to specify whether the indexing of the array would start at 0 or 1, is no longer supported by VB.NET. Whether you like it or not, your arrays must start at index zero. If you don't feel comfortable with the notion of zero being the first element, you can increase the dimensions of your arrays by one and ignore the zeroth element.

In VB6 you could specify not only the dimensions of an array but also the index of the very first element, with a declaration like

```
Dim myArray(101 To 999) As Integer
```

This notation is not valid in VB.NET.

Declaring Arrays

Unlike simple variables, arrays must be declared with the Dim (or Public, or Private) statement followed by the name of the array and the index of the last element in the array in parentheses—for example,

```
Dim Salaries(15) As Integer
```

NOTE Actually, there are occasions when you need not specify the exact dimensions of an array, as you'll see shortly.

As I said before, *Salaries* is the name of an array that holds 16 values (the salaries of the 16 employees), with indices ranging from 0 to 15. `Salaries(0)` is the first person's salary, `Salaries(1)` the second person's salary, and so on. All you have to do is remember who corresponds to each salary, but even this data can be handled by another array. To do this, you'd declare another array of 16 elements as follows:

```
Dim Names(15) As String
```

and then assign values to the elements of both arrays:

```
Names(0) = "Joe Doe"
Salaries(0) = 34000
Names(1) = "Beth York"
Salaries(1) = 62000
...
Names(15) = "Peter Smack"
Salaries(15) = 10300
```

This structure is more compact and more convenient than having to hard-code the names of employees and their salaries in variables.

All elements in an array have the same data type. Of course, when the data type is Object, the individual elements can contain different kinds of data (objects, strings, numbers, and so on).

Arrays, like variables, are not limited to the basic data types. You can declare arrays that hold any type of data, including objects. The following array holds colors, which can be used later in the code as arguments to the various functions that draw shapes:

```
Dim colors(2) As Color
colors(0) = Color.BurlyWood
colors(1) = Color.AliceBlue
colors(2) = Color.Sienna
```

The Color object represents colors, and among the properties it exposes are the names of the colors it recognizes. The Color object recognizes 128 color names (as opposed to the 16 color names of VB6).

As a better technique to store names and salaries together in an array, create a Structure and then declare an array of this type. The following structure holds names and salaries:

```
Structure Employee
    Dim Name As String
    Dim Salary As Single
End Structure
```

Insert this declaration in a form's code file, outside any procedure. Then create an array of the Employee type:

```
Dim Emps(15) As Employee
```

Each elements in the *Emps* array exposes two fields, and you can assign values to them with statements like the following ones:

```
Emps(2).Name = "Beth York"
Emps(2).Salary = 62000
```

The advantage of storing related pieces of information to a structure is that you can access all the items with a single index. The code is more compact, and you need not maintain multiple arrays. In Chapter 11, you'll see how to store structures and other objects to collections like ArrayLists and HashTables.

Initializing Arrays

Just as you can initialize variables in the same line where you declare them, you can initialize arrays, too, with the following constructor:

```
Dim arrayname() As type = {entry0, entry1, … entryN}
```

Here's an example that initializes an array of strings:

```
Dim names() As String = {"Joe Doe", "Peter Smack"}
```

This statement is equivalent to the following statements, which declare an array with two elements and then set their values:

```
Dim names(1) As String
names(0) = "Joe Doe"
names(1) = "Peter Smack"
```

The number of elements in the curly brackets following the array's declaration determines the dimensions of the array, and you can't add new elements to the array without resizing it. If you need to resize the array in your code dynamically, you must use the ReDim statement, as described in the section "Dynamic Arrays," later in this chapter. However, you can change the *value* of the existing elements at will, as you would with any other array. The following declaration initializes an array of Color objects in a single statement:

```
Dim Colors() As Color = {Color.BurlyWood, Color.AliceBlue, Color.Sienna, _
                         Color.Azure, Color.Fuchsia, Color.White}
```

Array Limits

The first element of an array has index 0. The number that appears in parentheses in the Dim statement is one less than the array's total capacity and is the array's upper limit (or upper bound).

The index of the last element of an array (its upper bound) is given by the function UBound(), which accepts as argument the array's name. For the array

```
Dim myArray(19) As Integer
```

its upper bound is 19, and its capacity is 20 elements. The function UBound() is also exposed as a method of the Array object, and it's the GetUpperBound method. It returns the same value as the UBound() function. The GetLowerBound method returns the index of the array's first element, which is always zero anyway. As you will see, arrays can have multiple dimensions, so these two methods require that you specify the dimensions whose limits you want to read as arguments. For one-dimensional arrays, like the ones discussed in this section, this argument is zero. Multidimensional arrays are discussed later in this chapter.

Let's say you need an array to store 20 names. Declare it with the following statement:

```
Dim names(19) As String
```

The first element is names(0), and the last is names(19). If you execute the following statements, the values in bold will appear in the Output window:

```
Console.WriteLine(names.GetLowerBound(0))
0
Console.WriteLine(names.GetUpperBound(0))
19
```

To assign a value to the first and last element of the *names* array, use the following statements:

```
names(0) = "First entry"
names(19) = "Last entry"
```

If you want to iterate through the array's elements, use a loop like the following one:

```
Dim i As Integer, myArray(19) As Integer
For i = 0 To myArray.GetUpperBound(0)
    myArray(i) = i * 1000
Next
```

The actual number of elements in an array is given by the expression myArray.GetUpperBound(0) + 1. You can also use the array's Length property to retrieve the count of elements. The following statement will print the number of elements in the array *myArray* on the Output window:

```
Console.WriteLine(myArray.Length)
```

Still confused with the zero indexing scheme, the count of elements, and the index of the last element in the array? It's safe to make the array a little larger than it need be and ignore the first element. Just make sure you never use the zeroth elements in your code—don't store a value in the element Array(0), and you can then ignore this element. To get 20 elements, declare an array with 21 elements as Dim myArray(20) As type and then ignore the first element.

Arrays are one of the most improved areas of VB.NET. For years, programmers invested endless hours to write routines for sorting and searching arrays. It took Microsoft years to get arrays right, but with VB.NET you can manipulate arrays with several methods and properties available through the Array class, which is described in detail in Chapter 11. In this chapter, you'll learn the basics of declaring, populating, and accessing array elements, which is all you need to start using arrays in your code. The Array class will help you manipulate arrays in more elaborate ways.

Multidimensional Arrays

One-dimensional arrays, such as those presented so far, are good for storing long sequences of one-dimensional data (such as names or temperatures). But how would you store a list of cities *and* their average temperatures in an array? Or names and scores, years and profits, or data with more than two dimensions, such as products, prices, and units in stock? In some situations you will want to store sequences of multidimensional data. You can store the same data more conveniently in an array of as many dimensions as needed. Figure 3.4 shows two one-dimensional arrays—one of them with city names, the other with temperatures. The name of the third city would be City(2), and its temperature would be Temperature(2).

FIGURE 3.4

A two-dimensional array and the two equivalent one-dimensional arrays

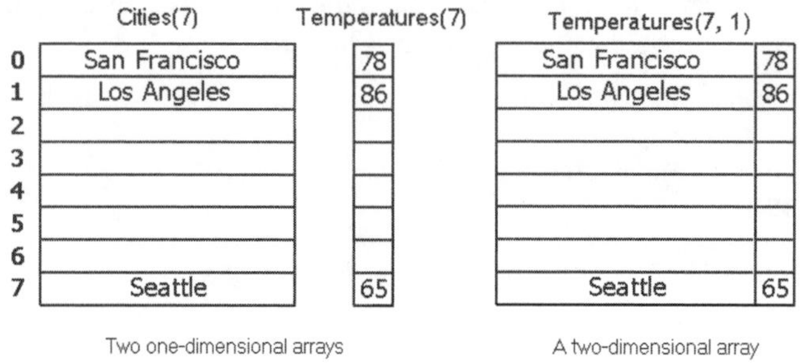

A two-dimensional array has two indices. The first identifies the row (the order of the city in the array), and the second identifies the column (city or temperature). To access the name and temperature of the third city in the two-dimensional array, use the following indices:

```
Temperatures(2, 0)     ' the third city's name
Temperatures(2, 1)     ' the third city's average temperature
```

The benefit of using multidimensional arrays is that they're conceptually easier to manage. Suppose you're writing a game and want to track the positions of certain pieces on a board. Each square on the board is identified by two numbers, its horizontal and vertical coordinates. The obvious structure for tracking the board's squares is a two-dimensional array, in which the first index corresponds to the row number and the second corresponds to the column number. The array could be declared as follows:

```
Dim Board(9, 9) As Integer
```

When a piece is moved from the square on the first row and first column to the square on the third row and fifth column, you assign the value 0 to the element that corresponds to the initial position:

```
Board(0, 0) = 0
```

and you assign 1 to the square to which it was moved, to indicate the new state of the board:

```
Board(2, 4) = 1
```

To find out if a piece is on the top-left square, you'd use the following statement:

```
If Board(0, 0) = 1 Then
   { piece found }
Else
   { empty square }
End If
```

This notation can be extended to more than two dimensions. The following statement creates an array with 1,000 elements (10 by 10 by 10):

```
Dim Matrix(9, 9, 9)
```

You can think of a three-dimensional array as a cube made up of overlaid two-dimensional arrays, such as the one shown in Figure 3.5.

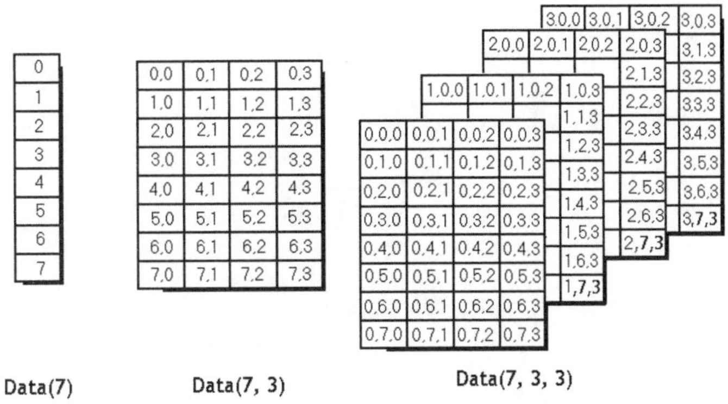

FIGURE 3.5

Pictorial representations of one-, two-, and three-dimensional arrays

Data(7)   Data(7, 3)   Data(7, 3, 3)

It is possible to initialize a multidimensional array with a single statement, just as you do with a one-dimensional array. You must insert enough commas in the parentheses following the array name to indicate the array's rank (the number of commas is one less than the actual dimensions). The following statements initialize a two-dimensional array and then print a couple of its elements:

```
Dim a(,) As Integer = {{10, 20, 30}, {11, 21, 31}, {12, 22, 32}}
Console.WriteLine(a(0, 1))          ' will print 20
Console.WriteLine(a(2, 2))          ' will print 32
```

You should break the line that initializes the dimensions of the array into multiple lines to make your code easier to read. Just insert the line-continuation character at the end of each continued line:

```
Dim a(,) As Integer = {{10, 20, 30}, _
                       {11, 21, 31}, _
                       {12, 22, 32}}
```

If the array has more than one dimension, you can find out the number of dimensions with the `Array.Rank` property. Let's say you have declared an array for storing names as salaries with the following statements:

```
Dim Salaries(1,99) As Object
```

To find out the number of dimensions, use the statement:

```
Salaries.Rank
```

When using the Length property to find out the number of elements in a multidimensional array, you will get back the total number of elements in the array—2 × 100, for our example. To find out the number of elements in a specific dimension use the GetLength method, passing as argument a specific dimension. The following expression will return the number of elements in the first dimension of the array:

```
Console.WriteLine(Salaries.GetLength(0))
```

Since the index of the first array element is zero, the index of the last element is the length of the array minus 1. Let's say you have declared an array with the following statement to store player statistics for 15 players, and there are 5 values per player:

```
Dim Statistics(14, 4) As Integer
```

The following statements will return the values shown beneath them, in bold:

```
Console.WriteLine(Statistics.Rank)
2                            ' dimensions in array
Console.WriteLine(Statistics.Length)
75                           ' total elements in array
Console.WriteLine(Statistics.GetLength(0))
15                           ' elements in first dimension
Console.WriteLine(Statistics.GetLength(1))
5                            ' elements in second dimension
Console.WriteLine(Statistics.GetUpperBound(0))
14                           ' last index in the first dimension
Console.WriteLine(Statistics.GetUpperBound(1))
4                            ' last index in the second dimension
```

Dynamic Arrays

Sometimes you may not know how large to make an array. Instead of making it large enough to hold the (anticipated) maximum number of data (which means that, on the average, most of the array may be empty), you can declare a *dynamic array*. The size of a dynamic array can vary during the course of the program. Or you might need an array until the user has entered a bunch of data and the application has processed it and displayed the results. Why keep all the data in memory when it is no longer needed? With a dynamic array, you can discard the data and return the resources it occupied to the system.

To create a dynamic array, declare it as usual with the Dim statement (or Public or Private) but don't specify its dimensions:

```
Dim DynArray() As Integer
```

Later in the program, when you know how many elements you want to store in the array, use the ReDim statement to redimension the array, this time to its actual size. In the following example, *UserCount* is a user-entered value:

```
ReDim DynArray(UserCount)
```

The ReDim statement can appear only in a procedure. Unlike the Dim statement, ReDim is executable—it forces the application to carry out an action at runtime. Dim statements aren't executable, and they can appear outside procedures.

A dynamic array also can be redimensioned to multiple dimensions. Declare it with the Dim statement outside any procedure as follows:

```
Dim Matrix() As Double
```

and then use the ReDim statement in a procedure to declare a three-dimensional array:

```
ReDim Matrix(9, 9, 9)
```

Note that the ReDim statement can't change the type of the array—that's why the As clause is missing from the ReDim statement. Moreover, subsequent ReDim statements can change the bounds of the array *Matrix* but not the number of its dimensions. For example, you can't use the statement ReDim Matrix(99, 99) later in your code. Once an array has been redimensioned once, its number of dimensions can't change. In the preceding example, the *Matrix* array will remain three-dimensional through the course of the application.

NOTE *The ReDim statement can be issued only from within a procedure. In addition, the array to be redimensioned must be visible from within the procedure that calls the ReDim statement.*

THE PRESERVE KEYWORD

Each time you execute the ReDim statement, all the values currently stored in the array are lost. Visual Basic resets the values of the elements as if they were just declared. (It resets numeric elements to zero and String elements to empty strings.)

In most situations, when you resize an array, you no longer care about the data in it. You can, however, change the size of the array without losing its data. The ReDim statement recognizes the Preserve keyword, which forces it to resize the array without discarding the existing data. For example, you can enlarge an array by one element without losing the values of the existing elements by using the UBound() function as follows:

```
ReDim Preserve DynamicArray(UBound(DynArray) + 1)
```

If the array *DynamicArray* held 12 elements, this statement would add one element to the array, the element DynamicArray(12). The values of the elements with indices 0 through 11 wouldn't change. The UBound() function returns the largest available index (the number of elements) in a one-dimensional array. Similarly, the LBound() function returns the smallest index. If an array was declared with the statement

```
Dim Grades(49) As Integer
```

then the functions LBound(Grades) and UBound(Grades) would return the values 0 and 49. For more information on the functions LBound() and UBound(), see the reference "VB.NET Functions and Statements" on the CD. Obviously, the LBound() function is of no practical value in VB.NET, since the indexing of all arrays must start at 0.

Arrays of Arrays

Arrays are a major part of the language. In the section "User-Defined Data Types," earlier in this chapter, you saw how to create arrays of structures. It is possible to create even more complicated structures for storing data, such as arrays of arrays. If an array is declared as Object, you can assign other types to its elements, including arrays.

NOTE *The technique described in this section will work only when the Strict option is Off. If it is On, VB will generate an error to the effect that the Strict option does not allow late binding.*

Suppose you have declared and populated two arrays, one with integers and another with strings. You can then declare an Object array with two elements and populate it with the two arrays, as shown in Listing 3.9.

LISTING 3.9: POPULATING AN ARRAY OF ARRAYS

```
Dim IntArray(9) As Integer
Dim StrArray(99) As String
Dim BigArray(1) As Object
Dim i As Integer
' populate array IntArray
For i = 0 To 9
   IntArray(i) = i
Next
' populate array StrArray
For i = 0 To 99
   StrArray(i) = "ITEM " & i.ToString("0000")
Next
BigArray(0) = IntArray
BigArray(1) = StrArray
Console.WriteLine(BigArray(0)(7))
Console.WriteLine(BigArray(1)(16))
```

The last two statements will print the following values on the Output window:

```
7
ITEM 0016
```

BigArray was declared as a one-dimensional array, but because each of its elements is an array, you must use two indices to access it. To access the third element of *IntArray* in *BigArray*, use the indices 0 and 2. Likewise, the tenth element of the *StrArray* in *BigArray* is `BigArray(1)(9)`. The notation is quite unusual, but the indices of the *BigArray* must be entered in separate parentheses. In most cases, you'll be able to use Structures and avoid arrays of arrays, so you won't have to bother with this notation.

Variables as Objects

As you have understood by now, variables are objects. This shouldn't come as a surprise, but it's an odd concept for programmers with no experience in object-oriented programming. We haven't covered objects and classes formally yet, but you have a good idea of what an object is. It's an entity that exposes some functionality by means of properties and methods. The TextBox control is an object, and it exposes the Text property, which allows you to read, or set, the text on the control. Any name followed by a period and another name signifies an object. The "other name" is a property or method of the object.

At this point, I'll ask you to take a leap forward. Things will become quite clear when you learn more about objects later in the book, but I couldn't postpone this discussion; you need a good understanding of variables to move on. If you want, you can come back and re-read this section. In the meantime, I'll attempt to explain through examples how VB.NET handles variables. It's a simplified view of objects and, at points, I won't even use proper terminology.

So, What's an Object?

An *object* is a collection of data and code. You don't see the code, and you'll never have to change it—unless you've written it, of course. An integer variable, *intVar*, is an object because it has a value and some properties and methods. Properties and methods are implemented as functions. The method `intVar.ToString` for instance, returns the numeric value held in the variable as a string, so that you can use it in string operations. In other words, an Integer variable is an object that knows about itself. It knows that it holds a whole number; it knows how to convert itself to a string; it knows the minimum and maximum values it can store (properties MinValue and MaxValue); and so on. In the past, a variable was just a named location in the memory. Now, it's a far more complex structure with its own "intelligence." This intelligence consists of code that implements some of the most common actions you're expected to perform on its value. The same is true for strings, even characters. Actually, the Char data type exposes a lot of very useful properties. In the past, programmers wrote their own functions to determine whether a character is a numeric digit or a letter, whether it's in upper- or lowercase, and so forth. With the Char data type, all this functionality comes for free. The IsDigit and IsLetter methods return True if the character is a digit or a letter, respectively, False otherwise. The Date data type even has a property called IsLeapYear.

As I mentioned, in the past programmers had to write their own functions to perform all these operations that are now built into the variables themselves. Since VB1, Microsoft has included many functions to manipulate strings. Without these functions, VB programmers wouldn't be able to do much with String variables. These functions were enhanced with subsequent versions of VB. They did the same with date-manipulation functions, and VB.NET has inherited a large number of functions from VB6. Instead of bloating the language, the designers of VB.NET decided to move all this functionality into the classes that implement the various data types. The old functions are still there, because there are innumerable applications out there that use them. Applications written in VB.NET from scratch should use the newer methods and properties, but old VB programmers are so accustomed to using the equivalent VB functions that it will take them some time to switch to the new way of coding.

The main advantage of exposing so much functionality through the data types, instead of individual functions, is that you don't have to learn the names of all these functions. Now, you can type the period following a variable's name and see the list of members it exposes. The alternative would be to look up the documentation and try to locate a function that provides the desired functionality.

Another good reason for attaching so much functionality to the data types is that the specific functions are meaningless with other data types. Since the IsLeapYear method is so specific to dates, we better contain it in the world of the Date data type.

The real reason Microsoft is trying to eliminate the old functions is that all this functionality will eventually become part of the operating system. As a result, the number of support runtime libraries that are distributed with an EXE today will be greatly reduced.

 The old VB functions that have been replaced by methods and properties are explained in the reference "VB.NET Functions and Statements" on the CD. These functions are still part of the language, and you can't ignore them, because of the applications that already use them. I suspect programmers will mix both functions and methods with VB.NET, and it will be a while before the old functions are abandoned. So, whether you're a VB6 programmer (in which case you're very familiar with the string- and date-manipulation functions of VB) or you're new to VB.NET (in which case you should be able to read and understand existing code), you can't ignore these functions, neither can you ignore the members that expose the same functionality.

How about the code that implements all the functionality built into the variable? The code resides in a *class*. A class is the code that implements the properties and methods of a variable. The class that implements the Date type is the `System.Date` class, and it exposes the same functionality as a Date variable. A Date variable is nothing more than an instance of the `System.Date` class. Here's an example. The Date class exposes the IsLeapYear method, which returns True if a specific year is leap. The expression:

```
System.Date.IsLeapYear(2001)
```

will return False, because 2001 is not a leap year.

If you declare a variable of the Date type, it carries with it all the functionality of the `System.Date` class. The IsLeapYear method can be applied to a Date variable as well:

```
Dim d1 As Date = #3/4/2001#
MsgBox(d1.IsLeapYear(2001))
```

If you execute these statements, a message box will pop up displaying the string "False." But shouldn't the IsLeapYear method be applied to the *d1* variable? The answer is no, because IsLeapYear is a shared method: it requires an argument. You can use the `System.Date` class to call the IsLeapYear method:

```
Console.WriteLine(System.Date.IsLeapYear(2001))
```

It is even possible to use expressions like the following:

```
Console.WriteLine(#3/4/2001#.IsLeapYear(2001))
```

This expression will return False. Change the year to 2004, and it will return True. The date, even though it's a value, it's represented by an instance of the `System.Date` class. The compiler figures out that the expression between the pound signs is a date and loads an instance of the `System.Date` class automatically to represent the value. As an expression, I think it's rather ridiculous, but it's a valid expression nevertheless. (An even more perplexing expression is `#1/1/1900#.IsLeapYear(2020)`, but it's also valid).

NOTE *I've shown you how to create custom data types with the Structure keyword. A Structure doesn't expose any properties or methods, just values. So, can we build custom data types with added functionality, like the functionality found in the base data types? The answer is yes, but you must provide your own class. You'll learn how to build custom data types that provide properties and method, but you must first learn how to build your own classes, in Chapter 8.*

Formatting Numbers

The ToString method, exposed by all data types except the String data type, converts a value to the equivalent string and formats it at the same time. You can call the ToString method without any arguments, as we have done so far, to convert any value to a string. The ToString method, however, accepts an argument, which determines how the value will be formatted as a string. For example, you can format a number as currency by prefixing it with the appropriate sign (e.g., the dollar symbol) and displaying it to two decimal digits.

Notice that ToString is a method, not a property. It returns a value, which you can assign to another variable or pass as arguments to a function like MsgBox(), but the original value is not affected. The ToString method can also format a value if called with the format argument:

```
ToString(formatString)
```

The *formatString* argument is a format specifier (a string that specifies the exact format to be applied to the variable) This argument can be a specific character that corresponds to a predetermined format (*standard numeric format string*, as it's called) or a string of characters that have special meaning in formatting numeric values (a *picture numeric format string*). Use standard format strings for the most common operations and picture strings to specify unusual formatting requirements. To format the value 9959.95 as a dollar amount, you can use the following standard currency format string:

```
Dim int As Single = 9959.95
Dim strInt As String
strInt = int.ToString("C")
```

or the following picture numeric format string:

```
strInt = int.ToString("$###,###.00")
```

Both statements will format the value as "$9,959.95". The "C" argument in the first example means currency and formats the numeric value as currency. If you're using a non-U.S. version of Windows, the currency symbol will change accordingly. Depending on your culture, the currency symbol may also appear after the amount. The picture format string is made up of literals and characters that have special meaning in formatting. The dollar sign has no special meaning and will appear as is. The # symbol is a digit placeholder. All # symbols will be replaced by numeric digits, starting from the right. If the number has fewer digits than specified in the string, the extra symbols to the left will be ignored. The comma tells the Format function to insert a comma between thousands. The period is the decimal point, which is followed by two more digit placeholders. Unlike the # sign, the 0 is a special placeholder: if there are not enough digits in the number for all the zeros you've specified, a 0 will appear in the place of the missing digits. If the original value had been 9959.9, for example, the last statement would have formatted it as $9,959.90. If you used the # placeholder instead, then the string returned by the Format method would have a single decimal digit.

STANDARD NUMERIC FORMAT STRINGS

VB.NET recognizes the standard numeric format strings shown in Table 3.6.

TABLE 3.6: STANDARD NUMERIC FORMAT STRINGS

FORMAT CHARACTER	DESCRIPTION	EXAMPLE
C or c	Currency	12345.67.ToString("C") returns $12,345.67
E or e	Scientific format	12345.67.ToString("E") returns 1.234567E+004
F or f	Fixed-point format	12345.67.ToString("F") returns 12345.67
G or g	General format	Return a value either in fixed-point or scientific format
N or n	Number format	12345.67.ToString("N") returns 12,345.67
X or x	Hexadecimal format	250.ToString("X") returns FA

The format character can be followed by an integer. If present, the integer value specifies the number of decimal places that are displayed. The default accuracy is two decimal digits.

The "C" format string causes the ToString method to return a string representing the number as a currency value. An integer following the "C" determines the number of decimal places that are displayed. If no number is provided, two digits are shown after the decimal separator. The expression `5596.ToString("c")` will return the string "$5,596.00", and the expression `5596.4499.ToString("c3")` will return the string "$5,596.450".

The fixed-point format returns a number with one or more decimal digits. The expression `(134.5).ToString("f3")` will return the value 134.500. I've used the optional parentheses around the value here to make clear that the number has a decimal point. VB doesn't require that you supply these parentheses.

NOTE *Notice that not all format strings apply to all data types. For example, only integer values can be converted to hexadecimal format.*

PICTURE NUMERIC FORMAT STRINGS

If the format characters listed in Table 3.6 are not adequate for the control you need over the appearance of numeric values, you can provide your own picture format strings. Picture format strings contain special characters that allow you to format your values exactly as you like. Table 3.7 lists the picture formatting characters.

TABLE 3.7: PICTURE NUMERIC FORMAT STRINGS

FORMAT CHARACTER	DESCRIPTION	EFFECT
0	Display zero placeholder	Results in a non-significant zero if a number has fewer digits than there are zeros in the format.
#	Display digit placeholder	Replaces the "#" symbol with only significant digits.
.	Decimal point	Displays a "." character.
,	Group separator	Separates number groups; for example, "1,000".
%	Percent notation	Displays a "%" character.
E+0, E-0, e+0, e-0	Exponent notation	Formats the output of exponent notation.
\	Literal character	Used with traditional formatting sequences like "\n" (newline).
" "	Literal string	Displays any string within quotes or apostrophes literally.
;	Section separator	Specifies different output if the numeric value to be formatted is positive, negative, or zero.

Formatting Dates

To format dates, use the format characters shown in Table 3.8.

TABLE 3.8: DATE FORMATTING STRINGS

FORMAT CHARACTER	DESCRIPTION	FORMAT
d	Short date format	MM/dd/yyyy
D	Long date format	dddd, MMMM dd, yyyy
f	Long date followed by short time	dddd, MMMM dd, yyyy HH:mm
F	Long date followed by long time	dddd, MMMM dd, yyyy HH:mm:ss
g	(General) Short date followed by short time	MM/dd/yyyy HH:mm
G	(General) Short date followed by long time	MM/dd/yyyy HH:mm:ss
m or M	Month/day format	MMMM dd
r or R	RFC1123 pattern	ddd, dd MMM yyyy HH:mm:ssGMT
s	Sortable date/time format	yyyy-MM-dd HH:mm:ss
t	Short time format	HH:mm
T	Long time format	HH:mm:ss
u	Universal date/time	yyyy-MM-dd HH:mm:ss
U	Universal sortable date/time format	dddd, MMMM dd, yyyy HH:mm:ss
Y or y	Year month format	MMMM, yyyy

If the variable *birthDate* contains the value #1/1/2000#, the following expressions return the values shown below them, in bold:

```
Console.WriteLine(birthDate.ToString("d"))
1/1/2000
Console.WriteLine(birthDate.ToString("D"))
Saturday, January 01, 2000
Console.WriteLine(birthDate.ToString("f"))
Saturday, January 01, 2000 12:00 AM
Console.WriteLine(birthDate.ToString("s"))
2000-01-01T00:00:00
Console.WriteLine(birthDate.ToString("U"))
Saturday, January 01, 2000 12:00:00 AM
```

Flow-Control Statements

What makes programming languages flexible—capable of handling every situation and programming challenge with a relatively small set of commands—is the capability to examine external conditions and act accordingly. Programs aren't monolithic sets of commands that carry out the same calculations every time they are executed. Instead, they adjust their behavior depending on the data supplied; on external conditions, such as a mouse click or the existence of a peripheral; or even on abnormal conditions generated by the program itself. For example, a program that calculates averages may work time and again until the user forgets to supply any data. In this case, the program attempts to divide by zero, and it must detect this condition and act accordingly. In effect, the statements discussed in the section are what programs are all about. Without the capability to control the flow of the program, computers would just be bulky calculators. To write programs that react to external events and produce the desired results under all circumstances, you'll have to use the following statements.

Test Structures

An application needs a built-in capability to test conditions and take a different course of action depending on the outcome of the test. Visual Basic provides three such decision structures:

- ◆ If...Then
- ◆ If...Then...Else
- ◆ Select Case

IF...THEN

The If...Then statement tests the condition specified; if it's True, the program executes the statement(s) that follow. The If structure can have a single-line or a multiple-line syntax. To execute one statement conditionally, use the single-line syntax as follows:

```
If condition Then statement
```

Visual Basic evaluates the *condition*, and if it's True, executes the statement that follows. If the condition is False, the application continues with the statement following the If statement.

You can also execute multiple statements by separating them with colons:

```
If condition Then statement: statement: statement
```

Here's an example of a single-line If statement:

```
If Month(expDate) > 12 Then expYear = expYear + 1: expMonth = 1
```

You can break this statement into multiple lines by using End If, as shown here:

```
If expDate.Month > 12 Then
    expYear = expYear + 1
    expMonth = 1
End If
```

The Month property of the Date type returns the month of the date to which it's applied as a numeric value. Some programmers prefer the multiple-line syntax of the If...Then statement, even if it contains a single statement, because the code is easier to read. The block of statements between the Then and End If keywords form the body of the conditional statement, and you can have as many statements in the body as needed.

IF...THEN...ELSE

A variation of the If...Then statement is the If...Then...Else statement, which executes one block of statements if the condition is True and another block of statements if the condition is False. The syntax of the If...Then...Else statement is as follows:

```
If condition Then
    statementblock1
Else
    statementblock2
End If
```

Visual Basic evaluates the *condition;* if it's True, VB executes the first block of statements and then jumps to the statement following the End If statement. If the condition is False, Visual Basic ignores the first block of statements and executes the block following the Else keyword.

Another variation of the If...Then...Else statement uses several conditions, with the ElseIf keyword:

```
If condition1 Then
    statementblock1
ElseIf condition2 Then
    statementblock2
ElseIf condition3 Then
    statementblock3
Else
    statementblock4
End If
```

You can have any number of ElseIf clauses. The conditions are evaluated from the top, and if one of them is True, the corresponding block of statements is executed. The Else clause will be executed if none of the previous expressions are True. Listing 3.10 is an example of an If statement with ElseIf clauses.

LISTING 3.10: MULTIPLE ELSEIF STATEMENTS

```
score = InputBox("Enter score")
If score < 50 Then
    Result = "Failed"
ElseIf score < 75 Then
    Result = "Pass"
ElseIf score < 90 Then
    Result = "Very Good"
Else
    Result = "Excellent"
End If
MsgBox Result
```

MULTIPLE IF...THEN STRUCTURES VS. ELSEIF

Notice that once a True condition is found, Visual Basic executes the associated statements and skips the remaining clauses. It continues executing the program with the statement immediately after End If. All following ElseIf clauses are skipped, and the code runs a bit faster. That's why you should prefer the complicated structure with ElseIf statements used in Listing 3.10 to this equivalent series of simple If statements:

```
If score < 50 Then
    Result = "Failed"
End If
If score < 75 And score >= 50 Then
    Result = "Pass"
End If
If score < 90 And score > =75 Then
    Result = "Very Good"
End If
If score >= 90 Then
    Result = "Excellent"
End If
```

Visual Basic will evaluate the conditions of all the If statements, even if the score is less than 50.

You may have noticed that the order of the comparisons is vital in an If...Then structure that uses ElseIf statements. Had you written the previous code segment with the first two conditions switched, like this:

```
If score < 75 Then
    Result = "Pass"
ElseIf score < 50 Then
    Result = "Failed"
ElseIf score < 90 Then
    Result = "Very Good"
Else
    Result = "Excellent"
End If
```

the results would be quite unexpected. Let's assume that *score* is 49. The code would compare the *score* variable to the value 75. Since 49 is less than 75, it would assign the value "Pass" to the variable *Result*, and then it would skip the remaining clauses. Thus, a student who made 49 would have passed the test! So be extremely careful and test your code thoroughly if it uses multiple ElseIf clauses.

SELECT CASE

An alternative to the efficient, but difficult-to-read, code of the multiple-ElseIf structure is the Select Case structure, which compares one expression to different values. The advantage of the Select Case statement over multiple If...Then...Else/ElseIf statements is that it makes the code easier to read and maintain.

The Select Case structure tests a single expression, which is evaluated once at the top of the structure. The result of the test is then compared with several values, and if it matches one of them, the corresponding block of statements is executed. Here's the syntax of the Select Case statement:

```
Select Case expression
    Case value1
        statementblock1
    Case value2
        statementblock2
        .
        .
        .
    Case Else
        statementblockN
End Select
```

A practical example based on the Select Case statement is Listing 3.11.

LISTING 3.11: USING THE SELECT CASE STATEMENT

```
Dim message As String
Select Case Now.DayOfWeek
    Case DayOfWeek.Monday
        message = "Have a nice week"
    Case DayOfWeek.Friday
        message = "Have a nice weekend"
    Case Else
        message = "Welcome back!"
End Select
MsgBox(message)
```

In the listing, the *expression* variable, which is evaluated at the beginning of the statement, is the weekday, as reported by the DayOfWeek property of the Date type. It's a numeric value, but its possible settings are the members of the DayOfWeek enumeration, and you can use the names of these members in your code to make it easier to read. The value of this expression is compared with the values that follow each Case keyword. If they match, the block of statements up to the next Case keyword is executed, and then the program skips to the statement following the End Select statement. The block of the Case Else statement is optional and is executed if none of the previous Case values match the expression. The first two Case statements take care of Fridays and Mondays, and the Case Else statement takes care of the weekdays.

Some Case statements can be followed by multiple values, which are separated by commas. Listing 3.12 is a revised version of the previous example.

LISTING 3.12: A SELECT CASE STATEMENT WITH MULTIPLE CASES PER CLAUSE

```
Select Case Now.DayOfWeek
   Case DayOfWeek.Monday
      message = "Have a nice week"
   Case DayOfWeek.Tuesday, DayOfWeek.Wednesday, _
        DayOfWeek.Thursday, DayOfWeek.Friday
      message = "Welcome back!"
   Case DayOfWeek.Friday, DayOfWeek.Saturday, DayOfWeek.Sunday
      message = "Have a nice weekend!"
End Select
MsgBox(message)
```

Monday, Friday (and weekends), and the remaining weekdays are handled separately by three Case statements. The second Case statement handles multiple values (all weekdays, except for Monday and Friday). Monday is handled by a separate Case statement. This structure doesn't contain a Case Else statement because all possible values are examined in the Case statements. The DayOfWeek method can't return another value.

TIP   *If more than one Case value matches the expression, only the statement block associated with the first matching Case executes.*

For comparison, Listing 3.13 contains the equivalent If...Then...Else statements that would implement the example of Listing 3.12.

LISTING 3.13: LISTING 3.12 IMPLEMENTED WITH NESTED IF STATEMENTS

```
If Now.DayOfWeek = DayOfWeek.Monday Then
   message = "Have a nice week"
Else
   If Now.DayOfWeek >= DayOfWeek.Tuesday And _
      Now.DayOfWeek <= DayOfWeek.Friday Then
      message = "Welcome back!"
   Else
      message = "Have a nice weekend!"
   End If
End If
MsgBox(message)
```

To say the least, this coding is verbose. If you attempt to implement a more elaborate Select Case statement with If...Then...Else statements, the code becomes even more difficult to read.

Of course, the Select Case statement can't always substitute for an If...Then structure. The Select Case structure only evaluates the expression at the beginning. By contrast, the If...Then...Else structure can evaluate a different expression for each ElseIf statement, not to mention that you can use more complicated expressions with the If clause.

Loop Structures

Loop structures allow you to execute one or more lines of code repetitively. Many tasks consist of trivial operations that must be repeated over and over again, and looping structures are an important part of any programming language. Visual Basic supports the following loop structures:

◆ For...Next

◆ Do...Loop

◆ While...End While

FOR...NEXT

The For...Next loop is one of the oldest loop structures in programming languages. Unlike the other two loops, the For...Next loop requires that you know how many times the statements in the loop will be executed. The For...Next loop uses a variable (it's called the loop's *counter*) that increases or decreases in value during each repetition of the loop. The For...Next loop has the following syntax:

```
For counter = start To end [Step increment]
    statements
Next [counter]
```

The keywords in the square brackets are optional. The arguments *counter*, *start*, *end*, and *increment* are all numeric. The loop is executed as many times as required for the *counter* to reach (or exceed) the *end* value.

In executing a For...Next loop, Visual Basic completes the following steps:

1. Sets *counter* equal to *start*

2. Tests to see if *counter* is greater than *end*. If so, it exits the loop. If *increment* is negative, Visual Basic tests to see if *counter* is less than *end*. If it is, it exits the loop.

3. Executes the statements in the block

4. Increments *counter* by the amount specified with the *increment* argument. If the *increment* argument isn't specified, *counter* is incremented by 1.

5. Repeats the statements

The For...Next loop in Listing 3.14 scans all the elements of the numeric array *data* and calculates their average.

LISTING 3.14: ITERATING AN ARRAY WITH A FOR...NEXT LOOP

```
Dim i As Integer, total As Double
For i = 0 To data.GetUpperBound(0)
    total = total + data(i)
Next i
Console.WriteLine (total / data.Length)
```

The single most important thing to keep in mind when working with **For…Next** loops is that the loop's *counter* is set at the beginning of the loop. Changing the value of the *end* variable in the loop's body won't have any effect. For example, the following loop will be executed 10 times, not 100 times:

```
endValue = 10
For i = 0 To endValue
    endValue = 100
    { more statements }
Next i
```

You can, however, adjust the value of the *counter* from within the loop. The following is an example of an endless (or infinite) loop:

```
For i = 0 To 10
    Console.WriteLine(i)
    i = i - 1
Next i
```

This loop never ends because the loop's *counter*, in effect, is never increased. (If you try this, press Ctrl+Break to interrupt the endless loop.)

WARNING *Manipulating the* counter *of a* **For…Next** *loop is strongly discouraged. This practice will most likely lead to bugs such as infinite loops, overflows, and so on. If the number of repetitions of a loop isn't known in advance, use a* **Do…Loop** *or a* **While…End While** *structure (discussed in the following section).*

The *increment* argument can be either positive or negative. If *start* is greater than *end*, the value of increment must be negative. If not, the loop's body won't be executed, not even once.

Finally, the *counter* variable need not be listed after the Next statement, but it makes the code easier to read, especially when **For…Next** loops are nested within each other (nested loops are discussed in the section "Nested Control Structures" later in the chapter).

DO…LOOP

The **Do…Loop** executes a block of statements for as long as a condition is True. Visual Basic evaluates an expression, and if it's True, the statements are executed. When the end of block is reached, the expression is evaluated again and, if it's True, the statements are repeated. If the expression is False, the program continues and the statement following the loop is executed.

There are two variations of the **Do…Loop** statement; both use the same basic model. A loop can be executed either while the condition is True or until the condition becomes True. These two variations use the keywords While and Until to specify how long the statements are executed. To execute a block of statements while a condition is True, use the following syntax:

```
Do While condition
    statement-block
Loop
```

To execute a block of statements until the condition becomes True, use the following syntax:

```
Do Until condition
    statement-block
Loop
```

When Visual Basic executes these loops, it first evaluates *condition*. If *condition* is False, a Do...While loop is skipped (the statements aren't even executed once) but a Do...Until loop is executed. When the Loop statement is reached, Visual Basic evaluates the expression again and repeats the statement block of the Do...While loop if the expression is True, or repeats the statements of the Do...Until loop if the expression is False.

In short, the Do While loop is executed when the condition is True, and the Do Until loop is executed when the condition is False.

The Do...Loop can execute any number of times as long as *condition* is True or False, as appropriate (zero or nonzero if the condition evaluates to a number). Moreover, the number of iterations need not be known before the loops starts. In fact, the statements may never execute if *condition* is initially False for While or True for Until.

Here's a typical example of using a Do...Loop. Suppose the string *MyText* holds a piece of text (perhaps the Text property of a TextBox control), and you want to count the words in the text. (We'll assume that there are no multiple spaces in the text and that the space character separates successive words.) To locate an instance of a character in a string, use the InStr() function, which accepts three arguments:

- ◆ The starting location of the search

- ◆ The text to be searched

- ◆ The character being searched

The following loop repeats for as long as there are spaces in the text. Each time the InStr() function finds another space in the text, it returns the location (a positive number) of the space. When there are no more spaces in the text, the InStr() function returns zero, which signals the end of the loop, as shown:

```
Dim MyText As String = "The quick brown fox jumped over the lazy dog"
Dim position, words As Integer
position = 1
Do While position > 0
    position = InStr(position + 1, MyText, " ")
    words = words + 1
Loop
Console.WriteLine "There are " & words & " words in the text"
```

The Do...Loop is executed while the InStr() function returns a positive number, which happens for as long as there are more words in the text. The variable *position* holds the location of each successive space character in the text. The search for the next space starts at the location of the current space plus 1 (so that the program won't keep finding the same space). For each space found, the program increments the value of the *words* variable, which holds the total number of words when the loop ends.

NOTE *There are simpler methods of breaking a string into its constituent words, like the Split method of the String class. This is just an example of the* Do While *loop.*

You may notice a problem with the previous code segment. It assumes that the text contains at least one word and starts by setting the *position* variable to 1. If the *MyText* variable contains an empty string, the program reports that it contains one word. To fix this problem, you must specify the condition, as shown:

```
Do While InStr(position + 1, MyText, " ")
    position = InStr(position + 1, MyText, " ")
    words = words + 1
Loop
Console.WriteLine("There are " & words & " words in the text")
```

This code segment counts the number of words correctly, even if the *MyText* variable contains an empty string. If the *MyText* String variable doesn't contain any spaces, the function InStr(position + 1, MyText, " ") returns 0, which corresponds to False, and the Do loop isn't executed.

You can code the same routine with the Until keyword. In this case, you must continue to search for spaces until *position* becomes zero. Here's the same code with a different loop (the InStr() function returns 0 if the string it searches for doesn't exist in the longer string):

```
position = 1
Do Until position = 0
    position = InStr(position + 1, MyText, " ")
    words = words + 1
Loop
Console.WriteLine("There are " & words & " words in the text")
```

Another variation of the Do loop executes the statements first and evaluates the *condition* after each execution. This Do loop has the following syntax:

```
Do
    statements
Loop While condition
```

or

```
Do
    statements
Loop Until condition
```

The statements in this type of loop execute at least once, since the condition is examined at the end of the loop.

Could we have implemented the previous example with one of the last two types of loops? The fact that we had to do something special about zero-length strings suggests that this problem shouldn't be coded with a loop that tests the condition at the end. Since the loop's body will be executed once, the *words* variable is never going to be zero.

As you can see, you can code loops in several ways with the Do…Loop statement, and the way you use it depends on the problem at hand and your programming style.

WHILE...END WHILE

The `While...End While` loop executes a block of statements as long as a condition is True. The While loop has the following syntax:

```
While condition
    statement-block
End While
```

VB6 ➡ VB.NET

The `End While` statement replaces the `Wend` statement of VB6.

If *condition* is True, all statements are executed and, when the `End While` statement is reached, control is returned to the While statement, which evaluates *condition* again. If *condition* is still True, the process is repeated. If *condition* is False, the program resumes with the statement following `End While`.

The loop in Listing 3.15 prompts the user for numeric data. The user can type a negative value to indicate that all values are entered.

LISTING 3.15: READING AN UNKNOWN NUMBER OF VALUES

```
Dim number, total As Double
number = 0
While number => 0
    total = total + number
    number = InputBox("Please enter another value")
End While
```

You assign the value 0 to the *number* variable before the loop starts because this value can't affect the total. Another technique is to precede the While statement with an InputBox function to get the first number from the user.

Sometimes, the condition that determines when the loop will terminate is so complicated that it can't be expressed with a single statement. In these cases, we declare a Boolean value and set it to True or False from within the loop's body. Here's the outline of such a loop:

```
Dim repeatLoop As Boolean
repeatLoop = True
While repeatLoop
    { statements }
    If condition Then
        repeatLoop = True
    Else
        repeattLoop = False
    End If
End While
```

You may also see an odd loop statement like the following one:

```
While True
    { statements }
End While
```

This seemingly endless loop must be terminated from within its own body with an Exit statement, which is called when a condition becomes True or False. The following loop terminates when a condition is met in the loop's body:

```
While True
    { statements }
    If condition Then Exit While
    { more statements }
End While
```

Nested Control Structures

You can place, or *nest*, control structures inside other control structures (such as an If...Then block within a For...Next loop). Control structures in Visual Basic can be nested in as many levels as you want. It's common practice to indent the bodies of nested decision and loop structures to make the program easier to read.

When you nest control structures, you must make sure that they open and close within the same structure. In other words, you can't start a For...Next loop in an If statement and close the loop after the corresponding End If. The following pseudocode demonstrates how to nest several flow-control statements:

```
For a = 1 To 100
    { statements }
    If a = 99 Then
        { statements }
    End If
    While b < a
        { statements }
        If total <= 0 Then
            { statements }
        End If
    End While
    For c = 1 to a
        { statements }
    Next
Next
```

I'm not showing the names of the count variables after the Next statement, because it's not necessary. To find the matching closing statement (Next, End If, or End While), move down from the opening statement until you hit a line that starts at the same column. This is the matching closing statement. Notice that you don't have to align the nested structures yourself. The editor reformats the code automatically as you edit. It also inserts the matching closing statement—the End If statement is inserted automatically as soon as you enter an If statement, for example.

Listing 3.16 shows the structure of a nested For…Next loop that scans all the elements of a two-dimensional array.

LISTING 3.16: ITERATING THROUGH A TWO-DIMENSIONAL ARRAY

```
Dim Array2D(6, 4) As Integer
Dim iRow, iCol As Integer
For iRow = 0 To Array2D.GetUpperBound(0)
    For iCol = 0 To Array2D.GetUpperBound(1)
        Array2D(iRow, iCol) = iRow * 100 + iCol
        Console.Write(iRow & ", " & iCol & " = " & Array2D(iRow, iCol) & "      ")
    Next iCol
    Console.WriteLine()
Next iRow
```

The outer loop (with the *iRow* counter) scans each row of the array, and the inner loop scans each column in the current row. At each iteration, the inner loop scans all the elements in the row specified by the counter of the outer loop (*iRow*). After the inner loop completes, the counter of the outer loop is increased by one and the inner loop is executed again, this time to scan the elements of the next row. The loop's body consists of two statements that assign a value to the current array element and then print it in the Output window. The current element at each iteration is Array2D(iRow, iCol).

Part of the output produced by this code segment is shown here. The pair of values separated by a comma are the indices of an element, and its value follows the equal sign:

```
0, 0 = 0     0, 1 = 1     0, 2 = 2     0, 3 = 3     0, 4 = 4
1, 0 = 100   1, 1 = 101   1, 2 = 102   1, 3 = 103   1, 4 = 104
2, 0 = 200   2, 1 = 201   2, 2 = 202   2, 3 = 203   2, 4 = 204
3, 0 = 300   3, 1 = 301   3, 2 = 302   3, 3 = 303   3, 4 = 304
4, 0 = 400   4, 1 = 401   4, 2 = 402   4, 3 = 403   4, 4 = 404
5, 0 = 500   5, 1 = 501   5, 2 = 502   5, 3 = 503   5, 4 = 504
6, 0 = 600   6, 1 = 601   6, 2 = 602   6, 3 = 603   6, 4 = 604
```

TIP   *The presence of the counter names iCol and iRow aren't really required after the Next statement. Actually, if you supply them in the wrong order, Visual Basic will catch the error. In practice, few programmers specify counter values after a Next statement because Visual Basic matches each Next statement to the corresponding For statement. If the loop's body is lengthy, you can improve the program's readability by specifying the corresponding counter name after each Next statement.*

You can also nest multiple If statements. The structure shown in Listing 3.17 tests a user-supplied value to determine whether it's positive and, if so, determines whether the value exceeds a certain limit.

LISTING 3.17: SIMPLE NESTED IF STATEMENTS

```
Income = InputBox("Enter your income")
If Income > 0 Then
    If Income > 10000 Then
        MsgBox "You will pay taxes this year"
    Else
        MsgBox "You won't pay any taxes this year"
    End If
Else
    MsgBox "Bummer"
End If
```

The *Income* variable is first compared with zero. If it's negative, the Else clause of the If…Then statement is executed. If it's positive, it's compared with the value 10,000, and depending on the outcome, a different message is displayed.

The Exit Statement

The Exit statement allows you to exit prematurely from a block of statements in a control structure, from a loop, or even from a procedure. Suppose you have a For…Next loop that calculates the square root of a series of numbers. Because the square root of negative numbers can't be calculated (the Sqrt() function will generate a runtime error), you might want to halt the operation if the array contains an invalid value. To exit the loop prematurely, use the Exit For statement as follows:

```
For i = 0 To UBound(nArray)
    If nArray(i) < 0 Then Exit For
    nArray(i) = Math.Sqrt(nArray(i))
Next
```

If a negative element is found in this loop, the program exits the loop and continues with the statement following the Next statement.

There are similar Exit statements for the Do loop (Exit Do) and the While loop (Exit While), as well as for functions and subroutines (Exit Function and Exit Sub). If the previous loop was part of a function, you might want to display an error and exit not only the loop, but the function itself:

```
For i = 0 To nArray.GetUpperBound()
    If nArray(i) < 0 Then
        MsgBox "Negative value found, terminating calculations"
        Exit Function
    End If
    nArray(i) = Sqr(nArray(i))
Next
```

If this code is part of a subroutine procedure, you use the Exit Sub statement. The Exit statements for loops are Exit For, Exit While, and Exit Do. There is no way (or compelling reason) to exit prematurely from an If or Case statement.

Summary

It's been a long chapter, but we wouldn't be able to go far without the information presented here. You have learned the base data types supported by Visual Basic, how to declare variables, and when to use them. Actually, the base data types aren't supplied by Visual Basic; they're part of the Common Language Runtime (CLR) and are the same for all languages. At this point, it doesn't really make much difference what part of .NET supplies each feature (the CLR, the Framework, or Visual Basic itself).

You've also learned how to store sets of values to an array, which is a great convenience. Arrays have always been a prime tool for programmers, and they've gotten so much better in .NET. You will read more about arrays in Chapter 11.

The base types supported by CLR are just too basic for the needs of a real application. To store more complicated information (like customers, accounts and so on), you can create your own custom structures. After defining the structure of the information, you can declare variables with the same structure. These variables behave like objects (even though they're not technically objects), because they expose the fields of the structure as properties.

The most interesting information presented in this chapter is the notion of variables as objects. That will all make much more sense in Chapter 8, where we'll discuss classes formally and you'll learn how to build your own classes and declared variables that represent them. Until then, think of variables as entities that expose some functionality through properties and methods. Properties and methods are just names following the name of a variable.

Chapter 4

Writing and Using Procedures

THE ONE THING YOU should have learned about programming in Visual Basic so far is that an *application* is made up of small, self-contained segments. The code you write isn't a monolithic listing; it's made up of small segments called *procedures,* and you work on one procedure at a time.

For example, when you write code for a control's Click event, you concentrate on the event at hand—namely, how the program should react to the Click event. What happens when the control is double-clicked, or when another control is clicked, is something you will worry about later, in another control's event handler. This "divide and conquer" approach isn't unique to programming events. It permeates the Visual Basic language, and even the longest applications are written by breaking them into small, well-defined tasks. Each task is performed by a separate procedure that is written and tested separately from the others.

Procedures are also used for implementing repeated tasks, such as frequently used calculations. Suppose you're writing an application that, at some point, must convert temperatures between different scales or calculate the smaller of two numbers. You can always do the calculations inline and repeat them in your code wherever they are needed, or you can write a procedure that performs the calculations and call this procedure. The benefit of the second approach is that code is cleaner and easier to understand and maintain. If you discover a more efficient way to implement the same calculations, you need change the code in only one place. If the same code is repeated in several places throughout the application, you will have to change every instance.

The two types of procedures supported by Visual Basic are the topics we'll explore in this chapter: *subroutines* and *functions*—the building blocks of your applications. We'll discuss them in detail, how to call them with arguments and how to retrieve the results returned by the functions. You may find that some of the topics discussed in this chapter are rather advanced, but I wanted to exhaust the topic in a single chapter, rather than having to interrupt the discussion of other topics to explain an advanced, procedure-related technique. You can skip the sections you find difficult at first reading and come back to these sections later, or look up the technique as needed.

Modular Coding

The idea of breaking a large application into smaller, more manageable sections is not new to computing. Few tasks, programming or otherwise, can be managed as a whole. The event handlers are just one example of breaking a large application into smaller tasks. Some event handlers may require a lot of code. A button that calculates the average purchase or sale price of a specific product must scan all the purchase orders or invoices, find the ones that include the specific product, take into consideration all units purchased or sold and the corresponding prices, and then calculate the average price. You could calculate the net profit with the following statements, which will most likely appear behind a button's event handler:

```
RetrievePOLines(productID)
Sum1 = SumQtyPrice()
Qty1 = SumQuantities()
RetrieveInvoiceLines(productID)
Sum2 = SumQtyPrice()
Net = (Sum2 - Sum1) / Qty1
```

The task is broken into smaller units, and each unit is implemented by a function or subroutine. (I'll define the difference between the two shortly.) The name of the procedure indicates the operation it performs. First, the RetrievePOLines() subroutine retrieves quantities and purchase prices of a specific product—the *productID* argument—from a database. The SumQtyPrice() function multiplies the quantities by prices at which they were sold and sums the results to get the total value paid for the purchase of a specific product. This result is stored in the *Sum1* variable. The SumQuantities() function sums the unit quantities into the *Qty1* variable.

The RetrieveInvoiceLines() subroutine gets similar data from the invoices in the database, so that the SumQtyPrice() function can calculate the total income generated by the same product. The value returned by the SumQtyPrice() function is stored in the *Sum2* variable.

The *Qty1* variable holds the total number of items purchased. We don't take into consideration any units in stock, but we'll assume a very small, or zero, stock. In the last statement, the expression (Sum2 - Sum1) is the total profit, and, dividing by the quantity of units sold, we calculate the average profit made by the specific product.

Even if you have no idea how to retrieve invoices from a database, you can understand what this code segment does. You don't know yet how it does it, but the functions themselves are also broken into small, easy-to-understand parts. Besides, not all programmers in a team need to understand all aspects of the application. Programmers who are responsible for producing charts don't have to understand how the data are actually retrieved from the database. As long as they have the proper data, they can produce the required graphs.

Functions and subroutines are segments of code that perform well-defined tasks and can be called from various parts of an application to perform the same operation, usually on different data. The difference is that functions return a value, while subroutines don't. This explains why function names are assigned to a variable—we save the value returned by a function and reuse it later.

As you can see, the divide-and-conquer approach in software is nothing less than a requirement in large applications. It's so common in programming, that there's a name for it: *modular programming*. Ideally, every program should be broken down into really simple tasks, and the code should read almost like English. You can write your application at a high level, and then start coding the low-level procedures.

The best thing about modular programming is that it allows programmers with different skills to focus on different parts of the application. A database programmer could write the RetrievePOLines() and RetrieveInvoiceLines() procedures, while another programmer could use these procedures as black boxes to build applications, just like the functions that come with the language. Imagine if you had to write code to calculate the number of days between two dates without the advantage of the DateDiff() function!

If you need a procedure to perform certain actions, such as changing the background color of a control or displaying the fields of a record on the form, you can implement it either as a function or subroutine. The choice of the procedure type isn't going to affect the code. The same statements can be used with either type of procedure. However, if your procedure doesn't return a value, then it should be implemented as a subroutine. If it returns a value, then it *must* be implemented as a function. The only difference between subroutines and functions is that functions return a value, while subroutines don't.

Both subroutines and functions can accept *arguments*, which are values you pass to the procedure when you call it. Arguments and the related keywords are discussed in detail in the section "Arguments," later in this chapter.

Subroutines

A *subroutine* is a block of statements that carries out a well-defined task. The block of statements is placed within a set of Sub...End Sub statements and can be invoked by name. The following subroutine displays the current date in a message box and can be called by its name, ShowDate():

```
Sub ShowDate()
    MsgBox(Now())
End Sub
```

Normally, the task a subroutine performs is more complicated than this; nevertheless, even this is a block of code isolated from the rest of the application. All the event handlers in Visual Basic, for example, are coded as subroutines. The actions that must be performed each time a button is clicked are coded in the button's Click procedure.

The statements in a subroutine are executed, and when the End Sub statement is reached, control returns to the calling program. It's possible to exit a subroutine prematurely, with the Exit Sub statement. For example, some condition may stop the subroutine from successfully completing its task.

All variables declared within a subroutine are local to that subroutine. When the subroutine exits, all variables declared in it cease to exist.

Most procedures also accept and act upon *arguments*. The ShowDate() subroutine displays the current date on a message box. If you want to display any other date, you'd have to pass an argument to the subroutine telling it to act on a different value, like this:

```
Sub ShowDate(ByVal birthDate As Date)
    MsgBox(birthDate)
End Sub
```

birthDate is a variable that holds the date to be displayed; its type is Date. (The ByVal keyword means that the subroutine sees a copy of the variable, not the variable itself. What this means practically is that the subroutine can't change the value of the *birthDate* variable.)

To display the current date on a message box, you must call the ShowDate subroutine as follows from within your program:

```
ShowDate()
```

To display another date with the second implementation of the subroutine, use a statement like the following:

```
Dim myBirthDate = #2/9/1960#
ShowDate(myBirthDate)
```

Or, you can pass the value to be displayed directly without the use of an intermediate variable:

```
ShowDate(#2/9/1960#)
```

SUBROUTINES AND EVENT HANDLERS

In the first couple of chapters, you learned to develop applications by placing code in event handlers. An *event handler* is a segment of code that is executed each time an external (or internal to your application) condition triggers the event. When the user clicks a control, the control's Click event handler executes. This handler is nothing more than a subroutine that performs all the actions you want to perform when the control is clicked. It is separate from the rest of the code and doesn't have to know what would happen if another control was clicked, or if the same control was double-clicked. It's a self-contained piece of code that's executed when needed.

Every application is made up of event handlers, which contain code to react to user actions. Event handlers need not return any results, and they're implemented as subroutines. For example, to react to the click of the mouse on the Button1 control, your application must provide a subroutine that handles the `Button1.Click` event. The code in this subroutine is executed independently of any other event handler, and it doesn't return a result because there is no main program to accept it. The code of a Visual Basic application consists of event handlers, which may call other subroutines and functions but aren't called by a main program. They are automatically activated by VB in response to external events.

Functions

A *function* is similar to a subroutine, but a function returns a result. Subroutines perform a task and don't report anything to the calling program; functions commonly carry out calculations and report the result. Because they return values, functions—like variables—have types. The value you pass back to the calling program from a function is called the *return value*, and its type must match the type of the function. Functions accept arguments, just like subroutines. The statements that make up a function are placed in a set of Function…End Function statements, as shown here:

```
Function NextDay() As Date
    Dim theNextDay As Date
    theNextDay = DateAdd(DateInterval.Day, 1, Now())
    Return(theNextDay)
End Function
```

DateAdd() is a built-in function that adds a number of intervals to a date. The interval is specified by the first argument (here, it's days), the number of intervals is the second argument (one day), and the third argument is the date to which the number of intervals is added (today). So the Next-Day() function returns tomorrow's date by adding one day to the current date. (The DateAdd() function is described in the reference "VB.NET Functions and Statements" on the CD.) NextDay() is a custom function, which calls the built-in DateAdd() function to complete its calculations. Another custom function might call NextDay() for its own purposes.

The result of a function is returned to the calling program with the Return statement. In our example, the Return statement happens to be the last statement in the function, but it could appear anywhere; it could even appear several times in the function's code. The first time a Return statement is executed, the function terminates and control is returned to the calling program.

You can also return a value to the calling routine by assigning the result to the name of the function. The following is an alternate method of coding the NextDay() function:

```
Function NextDay() As Date
    NextDay = DateAdd(DateInterval.Day, 1, Now())
End Function
```

Notice that this time I've assigned the result of the calculation to the function's name directly and didn't use a variable.

Similar to variables, a custom function has a name, which must be unique in its scope. If you declare a function in a form, the function name must be unique in the form. If you declare a function as Public or Friend, its name must be unique in the project. Functions have the same scope rules as variables and can be prefixed by many of the same keywords. In effect, you can modify the default scope of a function with the keywords Public, Private, Protected, Friend, and Protected Friend.

BUILT-IN FUNCTIONS

Let's look at a couple of functions, starting with one of the built-in functions, the Abs() function. This function returns the absolute value of its argument. If the argument is positive, the function returns it as is; if it's negative, the function inverts its sign. The Abs() function could be implemented as follows:

```
Function Abs(X As Double) As Double
    If X >= 0 Then
        Return(X)
    Else
        Return(-X)
    End If
End Function
```

This is a trivial procedure, yet it's built into Visual Basic because it's used frequently in math and science calculations. Developers can call a single function rather than supplying their own Abs() functions. Visual Basic and all other programming languages provide many built-in functions to implement the tasks needed most frequently by developers. But each developer has special needs, and you can't expect to find all the procedures you may ever need in a programming language. Sooner or later, you will have to supply your own.

The .NET Framework provides a large number of functions that implement common or complicated tasks. There are functions for the common math operations, functions to perform calculations with dates (these are complicated operations), financial functions, and many more. When you use the built-in functions, you don't have to know how they work internally.

The Pmt() function, for example, calculates the monthly payments on a loan. All you have to know is the arguments you must pass to the function and retrieve the result. The syntax of the Pmt() function is

```
MPay = Pmt(Rate, NPer, PV, FV, Due)
```

where *MPay* is the monthly payment, *Rate* is the monthly interest rate, *NPer* is the number of payments (the duration of the loan in months), and *PV* is the present value of the loan (the amount you took from the bank). *Due* is an optional argument that specifies when the payments are due (the beginning or the end of the month), and *FV* is another optional argument that specifies the future value of an amount; this isn't needed in the case of a loan, but it can help you calculate how much money you should deposit each month to accumulate a target amount over a given time. (The amount returned by the Pmt() function is negative, because it's a negative cash flow—it's money you owe—so pay attention to the sign of your values.)

To calculate the monthly payment for a $20,000 loan paid off over a period of 6 years at a fixed interest rate of 7.25%, you call the Pmt() function as follows:

```
Dim mPay As Double
Dim Duration As Integer = 6 * 12
Dim Rate As Single = (7.25 / 100) / 12
Dim Amount As Single = 20000
mPay = Pmt(Rate, Duration, Amount)
MsgBox("Your monthly payment will be $" & -mPay & vbCrLf & _
       "You will pay back a total of $" & -mPay * duration)
```

Notice that the interest (7.25%) is divided by 12, because the function requires the monthly interest. The value returned by the function is the monthly payment for the loan specified with the *Duration*, *Amount*, and *Rate* variables. If you place the preceding lines in the Click event handler of a Button, run the project, and then click the button, the following message will appear on a message box:

```
Your monthly payment will be $343.3861
You will pay back a total of $24723.8
```

To calculate the monthly deposit amount, you must call the Pmt() function passing 0 as the present value and the target amount as the future value. Replace the statements in the Click event handler with the following and run the project:

```
Dim mPay As Double
Dim Duration As Integer = 15 * 12
```

```
Dim Rate As Single = (4 / 100) / 12
Dim Amount As Single = -40000
mPay = Pmt(Rate, Duration, 0, Amount)
MsgBox("A monthly deposit of $" & mPay & vbCrLf & _
       "every month will yield $40,000 in 15 years")
```

It turns out that if you want to accumulate $40,000 over the next 15 years to send your kid to college, assuming a constant interest rate of 4%, you must deposit $162.55 every month.

Pmt() is one of the simpler financial functions provided by the Framework, but most of us would find it really difficult to write the code for this function. Since financial calculations are quite common in business programming, many of the functions you may need already exist, and all you need to know is how to call them. The financial functions, along with all other built-in functions you can use in your applications, are described in the reference "VB.NET Functions and Statements" (found on the companion CD).

CUSTOM FUNCTIONS

The built-in functions, however, aren't nearly enough for all types of applications. Most of the code we write is in the form of custom functions, which are called from several places in the application. Let's look at an example of a more advanced function that does something really useful.

Every book has a unique International Standard Book Number (ISBN). Every application that manages books—and there are many bookstores on the Internet—needs a function to verify the ISBN, which is made up of nine digits followed by a check digit. To calculate the check digit, you multiply each of the nine digits by a constant; the first digit is multiplied by 10, the second digit is multiplied by 9, and so on. The sum of these multiplications is then divided by 11, and we take the remainder. The check digit is the remainder subtracted from 11. Because the remainder is a digit from 0 to 10, when it turns out to be 10, the check digit is set to "X." This is the only valid character that may appear in an ISBN, and it can only be the check digit. To calculate the check digit for the ISBN 078212283, compute the sum of the following products:

```
0 * 10 + 7 * 9 + 8 * 8 + 2 * 7 + 1 * 6 + 2 * 5 + 2 * 4 + 8 * 3 + 3 * 2
```

The sum is 195, and when you divide that by 11, the remainder is 8. The check digit is $11 - 8$, or 3, and the book's complete ISBN is 0782122833. The ISBNCheckDigit() function, shown in Listing 4.1, accepts the nine digits of the ISBN as argument and returns the appropriate check digit.

LISTING 4.1: THE ISBNCHECKDIGIT() CUSTOM FUNCTION

```
Function ISBNCheckDigit(ByVal ISBN As String) As String
   Dim i As Integer, chksum, chkDigit As Integer
   For i = 0 To 8
      chkSum = chkSum + (10 - i) * ISBN.Substring(i, 1)
   Next
   chkDigit = 11 - (chkSum Mod 11)
   If chkDigit = 10 Then
      Return ("X")
   Else
```

```
        Return (chkDigit.ToString)
      End If
End Function
```

The ISBNCheckDigit() function returns a string value, because the check digit can be either a digit or "X." It also accepts a string, because the complete ISBN (nine digits plus the check digit) is a string, not a number (leading zeros are important in an ISBN but totally meaningless in a numeric value). The Substring method of a String object extracts a number of characters from the string it's applied to. The first argument is the starting location in the string, and the second is the number of characters to be extracted.

The expression ISBN.Substring(i, 1) extracts one character at a time from the *ISBN* string variable. During the first iteration of the loop, it extracts the first character; during the second iteration, it extracts the second character, and so on.

The character extracted is a numeric digit, which is multiplied by the value $(10 - i)$ and the result is added to the *chkSum* variable. This variable is the checksum of the ISBN. After it has been calculated, we divide it by 11 and take its remainder, which we subtract from 11. This is the ISBN's check digit and the function's return value.

VB6 ➡ VB.NET

There's something odd about the way the .NET Framework handles strings. The index of the first character in a string is 0, not 1. That's why the loop that scans the first nine digits of the ISBN goes from 0 to 8. Because the variable *i* is one less than the position of the digit in the ISBN, we subtract it from 10 and not from 11. Up to the last version of Visual Basic, the indexing of strings started at 1, but .NET changed all that, and this is something you must get used to.

You can use this function in an application that maintains a book database, to make sure that all books are entered with a valid ISBN. You can also use it with a Web application that allows viewers to request books by their ISBN. The same code will work with two different applications, even when passed to other developers. Developers using your function don't have to know how the check digit is calculated, just how to call the function and retrieve its result.

 To test the ISBNCheckDigit() function, start a new project, place a button on the form, and enter the following statements in its Click event handler (or open the ISBN project in this chapter's folder on the CD):

```
Private Sub Button1_Click(ByVal sender As System.Object, _
              ByVal e As System.EventArgs) Handles Button1.Click
    Console.WriteLine("The check Digit is " & ISBNCheckDigit("078212283"))
End Sub
```

After inserting the code of the ISBNCheckDigit() function and the code that calls the function, your code editor should look like Figure 4.1. You can place a TextBox control on the Form and pass the Text property of the control to the ISBNCheckDigit() function to calculate the check digit.

FIGURE 4.1

Calling the
ISBNCheckDigit()
function

```
Object Browser | Start Page | Form1.vb [Design]* | Form1.vb*
Form1 (ch04tests)                                              Button1_Click
Public Class Form1
     Inherits System.Windows.Forms.Form

     Windows Form Designer generated code

     Private Sub Button1_Click(ByVal sender As System.Object, ByVal e As System.EventArgs) Handles Button1.Click
         Console.WriteLine("The check Digit is " & ISBNCheckDigit("432598435"))
     End Sub

     Function ISBNCheckDigit(ByVal ISBN As String) As String
         Dim i As Integer, chksum, chkDigit As Integer
         For i = 1 To 9
             chksum = chksum + (11 - i) * Mid(ISBN, i, 1)
         Next
         chkDigit = 11 - (chksum Mod 11)
         If chksum = 11 Then
             Return ("X")
         Else
             Return (chkDigit.ToString)
         End If
     End Function
End Class
```

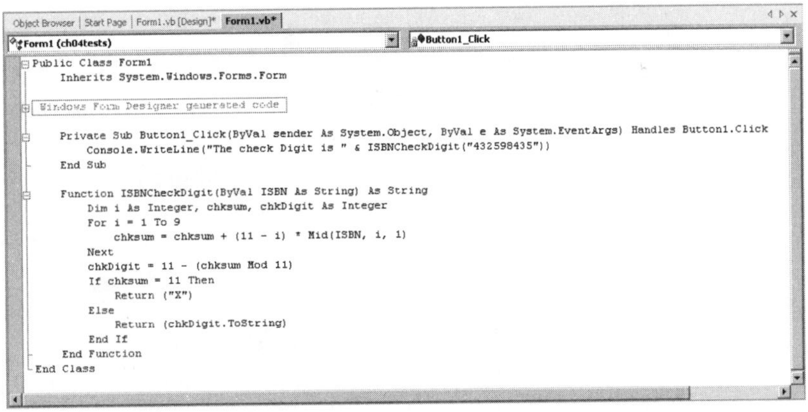

Calling Functions and Subroutines

When you call a procedure, you must supply values for all the arguments specified in the procedure's definition and in the same order. To call a procedure, you simply enter its name, followed by its arguments in parentheses:

```
Dim chDigit As String
chDigit = ISBNCheckDigit("078212283")
```

The values of the arguments must match their declared type. If a procedure expects an integer value, you shouldn't supply a date value or a string. If the procedure is a function, you must assign its return value to a variable so you can use it from within your code. The following statement creates the complete ISBN by calling the ISBNCheckDigit() function:

```
Dim ISBN As String = "078212283"
MsgBox("The complete ISBN is " & ISBN & ISBNCheckDigit(ISBN))
```

The argument of the MsgBox() function needs a some explanation. It calls the ISBNCheckDigit() function, passing the ISBN as argument. Then it appends the check digit (which is the value returned by the function) to the ISBN value and prints it. It is equivalent to the following statements, which are simpler to read, but not nearly as common:

```
Dim wholeISBN As String
wholeISBN = ISBN & ISBNCheckDigit(ISBN)
MsgBox("The complete ISBN is " & wholeISBN)
```

Functions are called by name, and a list of arguments follows the name in parentheses as shown:

```
Degrees = Fahrenheit(Temperature)
```

In this example, the Fahrenheit() function converts the *Temperature* argument (which presumably is the temperature in degrees Celsius) to degrees Fahrenheit, and the result is assigned to the *Degrees* variable.

Functions can be called from within expressions, as the following statement shows:

```
MsgBox("40 degrees Celsius are " & Fahrenheit(40).ToString & _
       " degrees Fahrenheit")
```

Notice that the ToString method applies to the numeric value returned by the function, and you need not implement it as part of your function. All numeric types provide the ToString method, which converts the numeric value to a string.

Suppose the function CountWords() counts the number of words and the function CountChars() counts the number of characters in a string. The average length of a word could be calculated as follows:

```
Dim longString As String, avgLen As Double
longString = TextBox1.Text
avgLen = CountChars(longString) / CountWords(longString)
```

The first executable statement gets the text of a TextBox control and assigns it to a variable, which is then used as an argument to the two functions. When the second statement executes, Visual Basic first calls the functions CountChars() and CountWords() with the specified arguments and then divides the results they return.

You can call functions in the same way that you call subroutines, but the result won't be stored anywhere. For example, the function Convert() may convert the text in a textbox to uppercase and return the number of characters it converts. Normally, you'd call this function as follows:

```
nChars = Convert()
```

If you don't care about the return value—you only want to update the text on a TextBox control—you would call the Convert() function with the following statement.

```
Convert()
```

VB6 ⟹ VB.NET

The Call statement of VB6 has disappeared. Also, the parentheses around the argument list are mandatory, even if the subroutine or function doesn't accept any arguments. You can no longer call a subroutine with a statement like

```
ConvertText myText
```

You must enclose the arguments in a pair of parentheses:

```
ConvertText(myText)
```

Arguments

Subroutines and functions aren't entirely isolated from the rest of the application. Most procedures accept arguments from the calling program. Recall that an *argument* is a value you pass to the procedure and on which the procedure usually acts. This is how subroutines and functions communicate with the rest of the application.

Functions also accept arguments—in many cases, more than one. The function Min(), for instance, accepts two numbers and returns the smaller one:

```
Function Min(ByVal a As Single, ByVal b As Single) As Single
    Min = IIf(a < b, a, b)
End Function
```

IIf() is a built-in function that evaluates the first argument, which is a logical expression. If the expression is True, the IIf() function returns the second argument. If the expression is False, the function returns the third argument.

To call this function use a few statements like the following:
```
Dim val1 As Single = 33.001
Dim val2 As Single = 33.0011
Dim smallerVal as Single
smallerVal = Min(val1, val2)
Console.Write("The smaller value is " & smallerVal)
```

If you execute these statements (place them in a button's Click event handler), you will see the following on the Output window:

```
The smaller value is 33.001
```

If you attempt to call the same function with two double values, as in a statement like the following:

```
Console.WriteLine(Min(3.33000000111, 3.33000000222))
```

you will see the value 3.33 in the Output window. The compiler converted the two values from Double to Single data type and returned one of them. Which one is it? It doesn't make a difference, because when converted to Single, both values are the same.

Interesting things will happen if you attempt to use the Min() function with the Strict option turned on. Insert the statement `Option Strict On` at the very beginning of the file. First, the editor will underline the statement that implements the Min() function—the IIf() function. The IIf() function accepts two Object variables as arguments, and you can't call it with Single or Double values. The Strict option prevents the compiler from converting numeric values to objects. To use the IIf() function with the Strict option, you must change its implementation as follows:

```
Function Min(ByVal a As Object, ByVal b As Object) As Object
    Min = IIf(Val(a) < Val(b), a, b)
End Function
```

Argument-Passing Mechanisms

One of the most important issues in writing procedures is the mechanism used to pass arguments. The examples so far have used the default mechanism: passing arguments by value. The other mechanism is passing them by reference. Although most programmers use the default mechanism, it's important to know the difference between the two mechanisms and when to use each.

PASSING ARGUMENTS BY VALUE

When you pass an argument by value, the procedure sees only a copy of the argument. Even if the procedure changes it, the changes aren't permanent. The benefit of passing arguments by value is that the argument values are isolated from the procedure, and only the code segment in which they are declared can change their values. This is the default argument-passing mechanism in VB.NET.

To specify the arguments that will be passed by value, use the ByVal keyword in front of the argument's name. If you omit the ByVal keyword, the editor will insert it automatically, since it's the default option. To declare that the Degrees() function's arguments are passed by value, use the ByVal keyword in the argument's declaration as follows:

```
Function Degrees(ByVal Celsius as Single) As Single
    Degrees = (9 / 5) * Celsius + 32
End Function
```

To see what the ByVal keyword does, add a line that changes the value of the argument in the function:

```
Function Degrees(ByVal Celsius as Single) As Single
    Degrees = (9 / 5) * Celsius + 32
    Celsius = 0
End Function
```

Now call the function as follows:

```
CTemp = InputBox("Enter temperature in degrees Celsius")
MsgBox(CTemp.ToString & " degrees Celsius are " & Degrees((CTemp)) & _
        " degrees Fahrenheit")
```

If the value entered in the InputBox is 32, the following message is displayed:

```
32 degrees Celsius are 89.6 degrees Fahrenheit
```

Replace the ByVal keyword with the ByRef keyword in the function's definition and call the function as follows:

```
Celsius = 32.0
FTemp = Degrees(Celsius)
MsgBox(Celsius.ToString & " degrees Celsius are " & FTemp & _
        " degrees Fahrenheit")
```

This time the program displays the following message:

```
0 degrees Celsius are 89.6 degrees Fahrenheit
```

When the *Celsius* argument was passed to the Degrees() function, its value was 32. But the function changed its value, and upon return it was 0. Because the argument was passed by reference, any changes made by the procedure affected the variable permanently. When the calling program attempted to use it, the variable had a different value than expected.

NOTE   *When you pass arguments to a procedure by reference, you're actually passing the variable itself. Any changes made to the argument by the procedure will be permanent. When you pass arguments by value, the procedure gets a copy of the variable, which is discarded when the procedure ends. Any changes made to the argument by the procedure won't affect the variable of the calling program.*

NOTE   *When you pass an array as argument to a procedure, the array is always passed by reference—even if you specify the ByVal keyword. The reason for this is that it would take the machine some time to create a copy of the array. Since the copy of the array must also live in memory, passing too many arrays back and forth by value would deplete your system's memory.*

PASSING ARGUMENTS BY REFERENCE

Passing arguments by reference gives the procedure access to the actual variable. The calling procedure passes the address of the variable in memory so that the procedure can change its value permanently. With VB6, this was the default argument-passing mechanism, but this is no longer the case.

Start a new Visual Basic project and enter the following function definition in the form's code window:

```
Function Add(ByRef num1 As Integer, ByRef num2 As Integer) As Integer
    Add = num1 + num2
    num1 = 0
    num2 = 0
End Function
```

This simple function adds two numbers and then sets them to zero.

Next, place a Command button on the form and enter the following code in the button's Click event:

```
Dim A As Integer, B As Integer
A = 10
B = 2
Dim Sum As Integer
Sum = Add(A, B)
Console.WriteLine(A)
Console.WriteLine(B)
Console.WriteLine(Sum)
```

This code displays the following results in the Output window:

```
0
0
12
```

The changes made to the function's arguments take effect even after the function has ended. The values of the variables *A* and *B* have changed value permanently.

Now change the definition of the function by inserting the keyword ByVal before the names of the arguments, as follows:

```
Function Add(ByVal num1 As Integer, ByVal num2 As Integer) As Integer
```

With this change, Visual Basic passes copies of the arguments to the function. The rest of the program remains the same. Run the application, click the button, and the following values display in the Output window:

```
10
2
12
```

The function has changed the values of the arguments, but these changes remain in effect only in the function. The variables *A* and *B* in the Button1_Click event handler haven't been affected.

As you type the names of the arguments in the declaration of a subroutine or function, the editor inserts automatically the ByVal keyword if you omit it (unless, of course, you specify the ByRef keyword). In general, you pass arguments by reference only if the procedure has reason to change its value. If the values of the arguments are required later in the program, you run the risk of changing their values in the procedure.

Returning Multiple Values

If you want to write a function that returns more than a single result, you will most likely pass additional arguments by reference and set their values from within the function's code. The following function calculates the basic statistics of a data set. The values of the data set are stored in an array, which is passed to the function by reference.

The Stats() function must return two values, the average and standard deviation of the data set. In a real-world application, a function like Stats() should calculate more statistics than this, but this is just an example to demonstrate how to return multiple values through the function's arguments. Here's the declaration of the Stats() function:

```
Function Stats(ByRef Data() As Double, ByRef Avg As Double, _
            ByRef StDev As Double) As Integer
```

The function returns an integer, which is the number of values in the data set. The two important values calculated by the function are returned in the *Avg* and *StDev* arguments.

```
Function Stats(ByRef Data() As Double, ByRef Avg As Double, _
            ByRef StDev As Double) As Integer
    Dim i As Integer, sum As Double, sumSqr As Double, points As Integer
    points = Data.Length
    For i = 0 To points - 1
        sum = sum + Data(i)
        sumSqr = sumSqr + Data(i) ^ 2
    Next
    Avg = sum / points
    StDev = System.Math.Sqrt(sumSqr / points - Avg ^ 2)
    Return(points)
End Function
```

To call the Stats() function from within your code, set up an array of doubles and declare two variables that will hold the average and standard deviation of the data set:

```
Dim Values(100) As Double
' Statements to populate the data set
Dim average, deviation As Double
Dim points As Integer
points = Stats(Values, average, deviation)
Console.WriteLine points & " values processed."
Console.WriteLine "The average is " & average & " and"
Console.WriteLine "the standard deviation is " & deviation
```

Using ByRef arguments is the simplest method for a function to return multiple values. However, the definition of your functions may become cluttered, especially if you want to return more than a few values. Another problem with this technique is that it's not clear whether an argument must be set before calling the function or not. As you will see shortly, it is possible for a function to return an array, or a custom structure with fields for any number of values.

Passing Objects as Arguments

When you pass objects as arguments, they're passed by reference, even if you have specified the ByVal keyword. The procedure can access and modify the members of the object passed as argument, and the new value will be visible in the procedure that made the call.

The following code segment demonstrates this. The object is an ArrayList, which is an enhanced form of an array. The ArrayList is discussed in detail later in the book, but to follow this example all you need to know is that the Add method adds new items to the ArrayList, and you can access individual items with an index value, similar to an array's elements. The Click event handler of a Button control creates a new instance of the ArrayList object and calls the PopulateList() subroutine to populate the list. Even though the ArrayList object is passed to the subroutine by value, the subroutine has access to its items:

```
Private Sub Button1_Click(ByVal sender As System.Object, _
                ByVal e As System.EventArgs) Handles Button1.Click
    Dim aList As New ArrayList()
    PopulateList(aList)
    Console.WriteLine(aList(0).ToString)
    Console.WriteLine(aList(1).ToString)
    Console.WriteLine(aList(2).ToString)
End Sub
Sub PopulateList(ByVal list As ArrayList)
    list.Add("1")
    list.Add("2")
    list.Add("3")
End Sub
```

The same is true for arrays and all other collections. Even if you specify the ByVal keyword, they're passed by reference. A more elegant method of modifying the members of a structure from within a procedure is to implement the procedure as a function returning a structure, as explained in the section "Functions Returning Structures," later in this chapter.

Event-Handler Arguments

In this section, we're going to look at the implementation of event handlers as subroutines. Event handlers never return a result, so they're implemented as subroutines. In specific, we're going to examine the two arguments that are common to all event handlers, which pass information about the object and the action that invoked the event.

You may have noticed that the subroutines that handle events accept two arguments: *sender* and *e*. Here's the declaration of the Click event handler for a button:

```
Private Sub Button1_Click(ByVal sender As System.Object, _
                ByVal e As System.EventArgs) Handles Button1.Click
    End Sub
```

The *sender* argument conveys information about the object that initiated the event; we use this argument in our code to find out the type of the object that raised the event. The following two statements in a button's Click event handler will print the values shown in bold on the Output window:

```
Console.WriteLine(sender.ToString)
    System.Windows.Forms.Button, Text: Button1
Console.WriteLine(sender.GetType)
    System.Windows.Forms.Button
```

The second argument contains all the information you really need to process the event. The *e* argument is an object that exposes some properties, which vary depending on the type of the event and the control that raised the event. A TextBox control, for example, raises several events when a key is pressed, in addition to the events of the mouse. The information you need to process the different types of events is passed to your application through the second argument of the event handler.

Let's examine the members of this argument for two totally different event types. The *e* argument passed to the Click event handler has no special properties. All the information you really need is that a button was clicked and nothing more. The location of the pointer, for example, doesn't make any difference in your code, neither do you care about the status of the various control keys. Regardless of whether the Alt or the Shift key was down or not when the left mouse button was clicked, your application will be notified about the Click event. If you want to capture the state of the control keys and react differently depending on their status, you must program the handler of the MouseDown or MouseUp events. These events are raised when the mouse is pressed or released and are independent of the Click event.

THE MOUSE EVENTS

Every time you click the mouse, a series of events is triggered. When you perform a single click, your application receives a MouseDown event, then a Click event, and then a MouseUp event. You get mouse events even as you scroll the mouse over a control: the MouseEnter when the mouse enters the control, a series of MouseMove events as you move the mouse over the control, a MouseHover event if you hover the mouse over the control, and a MouseLeave event as soon as the pointer gets outside the bounds of the control. Different mouse events report different information to the application through the arguments of the appropriate event handler, and this information is passed to your application in the form of properties of the *e* argument. The *e* argument of most mouse events provides the following properties.

Button

This property returns the button that was pressed, and its value is one of the members of the MouseButtons enumeration: `Left`, `Middle`, `None`, `Right`, `XButton1`, and `XButton2`. The last two members of the enumeration are for five-button mice and correspond to the two side buttons. The Button property is present in events that involve the button of the mouse. The *e* argument of the Click and DoubleClick events, however, doesn't provide a Button property; these two events can only be triggered with the left button.

Clicks

This property returns the number of times the mouse button was pressed and released. Its value is 1 for a single click and 2 for a double-click. You can't click a control three times—as soon as you click it for the second time, a double-click event will be raised.

Delta

This property is used with wheel mice; it reads the number of detents (that is, notches or stops) that the mouse wheel was rotated. You can use this property to figure out how much a TextBox control was scrolled (or any other control that can be scrolled with a scrollbar).

X, Y

These two properties return the coordinates of the pointer at the moment the mouse button was pressed (in the MouseDown event) or released (in the MouseUp event). The coordinates are expressed in pixels in the client's area. If you click a Button control at the very first pixel (its top-left corner), the X and Y properties will be 0.

The same properties are exposed by both the MouseDown and MouseUp events. Notice that these two events are fired regardless of which button was pressed—unlike the Click and DoubleClick events, which can't be triggered with a button other than the left one.

The X and Y properties may be different for the MouseDown and MouseUp events. For example, you can press a button and hold it down while you move the pointer around. When you release the button, its coordinates will be different than the coordinates reported by the Mouse-Down event. If you move the mouse outside the control in which you pressed the button, the coordinates may exceed the dimensions of the control, or even be negative. They are the distances of the pointer, at the moment you released the button, from the top-left corner of the control.

Insert the following code in a Button's MouseDown and MouseUp event handlers:

```
Private Sub Button1_MouseDown(ByVal sender As Object, _
              ByVal e As System.Windows.Forms.MouseEventArgs) _
              Handles Button1.MouseDown
    Console.WriteLine("Button pressed at " & e.X & ", " & e.Y)
End Sub
Private Sub Button1_MouseUp(ByVal sender As Object, _
              ByVal e As System.Windows.Forms.MouseEventArgs) _
              Handles Button1.MouseUp
    Console.WriteLine("Button released at " & e.X & ", " & e.Y)
End Sub
```

If you press and release the mouse at a single point, both handlers will report the same point. If you move the pointer before releasing the button, you will see four values like the following:

```
Button pressed at 63, 16
Button released at -107, -68
```

As you can guess, the mouse button was pressed while the pointer was over the Button control, and it was released after the pointer was moved to the left and above the Button control.

THE KEY EVENTS

The TextBox control recognizes the usual mouse events, but the most important events in programming the TextBox (or other controls that accept text) are the key events, which are raised when a key is pressed, while the control has the focus. The KeyPress event is fired every time a key is pressed. This event reports the key that was pressed. You can have finer control over the user's interaction with the keyboard with the KeyDown and KeyUp events, which are fired when a key is pressed and released respectively. The KeyDown event handler's definition is:

```
Private Sub TextBox1_KeyDown(ByVal sender As Object, _
            ByVal e As System.Windows.Forms.KeyEventArgs) _
            Handles TextBox1.KeyDown
```

The second argument of the KeyDown and KeyUp event handlers provides information about the status of the keyboard and the key that was pressed through the following properties.

Alt, Control, Shift

These three properties return a True/False value indicating whether one or more of the control keys were down when the key was pressed.

KeyCode

The KeyCode property returns the code of the key that was pressed, and its value can be one of the members of the Keys enumeration. This enumeration contains a member for all keys, including the mouse keys, and its members are displayed in a drop-down list when you need them. Notice that each key has its own code, which usually corresponds to two different characters. The "a" and "A" characters, for example, have the same code, the KeysA member. The code of the key "0" on the numeric keypad is the member Key0, and the function key F1 has the code KeyF1.

KeyData

This property returns a value that identifies the key pressed, similar to the KeyCode property, but it also distinguishes the character or symbol on the key. The KeyCode for the 4 key is 52, regardless of whether it was pressed with the Shift key or not. The same KeyCode value applies to the $ symbol, because they're both on the same key. The KeyData values for the same two characters are two long values that include the status of the control keys. The value of the KeyData property is a member of the Keys enumeration.

KeyValue

This property returns the keyboard value for the key that was pressed. It's usually the same as the KeyData value, but certain keys don't report a value (the control keys, for example, don't report a KeyValue).

Passing an Unknown Number of Arguments

Generally, all the arguments that a procedure expects are listed in the procedure's definition, and the program that calls the procedure must supply values for all arguments. On occasions, however, you may not know how many arguments will be passed to the procedure. Procedures that calculate averages or, in general, process multiple values can accept a few to several arguments whose count is not known at design time. In the past, programmers had to pass arrays with the data to similar procedures. Visual Basic supports the ParamArray keyword, which allows you to pass a variable number of arguments to a procedure.

Let's look at an example. Suppose you want to populate a ListBox control with elements. To add an item to the ListBox control, you call the Add method of its Items collection as follows:

```
ListBox1.Items.Add("new item")
```

This statement adds the string "new item" to the ListBox1 control.

If you frequently add multiple items to a ListBox control from within your code, you can write a subroutine that performs this task. The following subroutine adds a variable number of arguments to the ListBox1 control:

```
Sub AddNamesToList(ParamArray ByVal NamesArray() As Object)
    Dim x As Object
    For Each x In NamesArray
        ListBox1.Items.Add(x)
    Next x
End Sub
```

This subroutine's argument is an array prefixed with the keyword ParamArray. This array holds all the parameters passed to the subroutine. To add items to the list, call the AddNamesToList() subroutine as follows:

```
AddNamesToList("Robert", "Manny", "Renee", "Charles", "Madonna")
```

If you want to know the number of arguments actually passed to the procedure, use the Length property of the parameter array. The number of arguments passed to the AddNamesToList() subroutine is given by the expression:

```
NamesArray.Length
```

The following loop goes through all the elements of the *NamesArray* and adds them to the list:

```
Dim i As Integer
For i = 0 to NamesArray.GetUpperBound(0)
    ListBox1.Items.Add(NamesArray(i))
Next i
```

If you want to use the array's Length property, write a loop like the following:

```
Dim i As Integer
For i = 0 to NamesArray.Length - 1
    ListBox1.Items.Add(NamesArray(i))
Next i
```

A procedure that accepts multiple arguments relies on the order of the arguments. To omit some of the arguments, you must use the corresponding comma. Let's say you want to call such a procedure and specify the first, third, and fourth arguments. The procedure must be called as:

```
ProcName(arg1, , arg3, arg4)
```

The arguments to similar procedures are usually of equal stature, and their order doesn't make any difference. A function that calculates the mean or other basic statistics of a set of numbers, or a subroutine that populates a ListBox or ComboBox control, are prime candidates for implementing using this technique. If the procedure accepts a variable number of arguments that aren't equal in stature, then you should consider the technique described in the following section.

Named Arguments

You've learned how to write procedures with optional arguments and how to pass a variable number of arguments to the procedure. The main limitation of the argument-passing mechanism, though, is the *order* of the arguments. If the first argument is a string and the second is a date, you can't change their order. By default, Visual Basic matches the values passed to a procedure to the declared arguments by their order. That's why the arguments you've seen so far are called *positional arguments*.

This limitation is lifted by Visual Basic's capability to specify *named arguments*. With named arguments, you can supply arguments in any order, because they are recognized by name and not by their order in the list of the procedure's arguments. Suppose you've written a function that expects three arguments: a name, an address, and an e-mail address:

```
Function Contact(Name As String, Address As String, EMail As String)
```

When calling this function, you must supply three strings that correspond to the arguments *Name*, *Address*, and *EMail*, in that order. However, there's a safer way to call this function: supply the arguments in any order by their names. Instead of calling the Contact function as follows:

```
Contact("Peter Evans", "2020 Palm Ave., Santa Barbara, CA 90000", _
        "PeterEvans@example.com")
```

you can call it this way:

```
Contact(Address:="2020 Palm Ave., Santa Barbara, CA 90000", _
        EMail:="PeterEvans@example.com", Name:="Peter Evans")
```

The := operator assigns values to the named arguments. Because the arguments are passed by name, you can supply them in any order.

To test this technique, enter the following function declaration in a form's code:

```
Function Contact(ByVal Name As String, ByVal Address As String, _
                 ByVal EMail As String) As String
    Console.WriteLine(Name)
    Console.WriteLine(Address)
    Console.WriteLine(EMail)
    Return ("OK")
End Function
```

Then, call the Contact() function from within a button's Click event with the following statement:

```
Console.WriteLine(Contact(Address:="2020 Palm Ave., Santa Barbara, CA 90000", _
                  Name:="Peter Evans", EMail:="PeterEvans@example.com"))
```

You'll see the following in the Immediate window:

```
Peter Evans
2020 Palm Ave., Santa Barbara, CA 90000
PeterEvans@example.com
OK
```

The function knows which value corresponds to which argument and can process them the same way that it processes positional arguments. Notice that the function's definition is the same whether you call it with positional or named arguments. The difference is in how you call the function and how you declare it.

Named arguments make code safer and easier to read, but because they require a lot of typing, most programmers don't use them. Besides, programmers are so used to positional arguments that the notion of naming arguments is like having to declare variables when variants will do. Named arguments are good for situations in which you have optional arguments that require many consecutive commas, which may complicate the code. The methods of the various objects exposed by the Office applications (discussed in Chapter 10) require a large number of arguments, and they're frequently called with named arguments.

More Types of Function Return Values

Functions are not limited to returning simple data types like integers or strings. They may return custom data types and even arrays. The ability of functions to return all types of data makes them very flexible and can simplify coding, so we'll explore it in detail in the following sections. Using complex data types, such as structures and arrays, allows you to write functions that return multiple values.

FUNCTIONS RETURNING STRUCTURES

Suppose you need a function that returns a customer's savings and checking balances. So far, you've learned that you can return two or more values from a function by supplying arguments with the ByRef keyword. A more elegant method is to create a custom data type (a structure) and write a function that returns a variable of this type. The structure for storing balances could be declared as follows:

```
Structure CustBalance
    Dim BalSavings As Decimal
    Dim BalChecking As Decimal
End Structure
```

Then, you can define a function that returns a CustBalance data type as:

```
Function GetCustBalance(ByVal custID As Integer) As CustBalance
    { statements }
End Function
```

The GetCustBalance() function must be defined in the same module as the declaration of the custom data type it returns. If not, you'll get an error message.

When you call this function, you must assign its result to a variable of the same type. First declare a variable of the CustBalance type and then use it as shown here:

```
Private Balance As CustBalance
Dim custID As Integer
```

```
custID = 13011
Balance = GetCustBalance(custID)
Console.WriteLine(Balance.BalSavings)
Console.WriteLine(Balance.BalChecking)
```

Here, *custID* is a customer's ID (a number or string, depending on the application). Of course, the function's body must assign the proper values to the CustBalance variable's fields.

Here's the simplest example of a function that returns a custom data type. This example outlines the steps you must repeat every time you want to create functions that return custom data types:

1. Create a new project and insert the declarations of a custom data type in the declarations section of the form:

```
Structure CustBalance
    Dim BalSavings As Decimal
    Dim BalChecking As Decimal
End Structure
```

2. Then implement the function that returns a value of the custom type. You must declare a variable of the type returned by the function and assign the proper values to its fields. The following function assigns random values to the fields *BalChecking* and *BalSavings*. Then, assign the variable to the function's name, as shown next:

```
Function GetCustBalance(ID As Long) As CustBalance
    Dim tBalance As CustBalance
    tBalance.BalChecking = CDec(1000 + 4000 * rnd())
    tBalance.BalSavings = CDec(1000 + 15000 * rnd())
    GetCustBalance = tBalance
End Function
```

3. Then place a button on the form from which you want to call the function. Declare a variable of the same type and assign to it the function's return value. The example that follows prints the savings and checking balances on the Output window:

```
Private Sub Button1_Click(ByVal sender As System.Object, _
                ByVal e As System.EventArgs) Handles Button1.Click
    Dim balance As CustBalance
    balance = GetCustBalance(1)
    Console.WriteLine(balance.BalChecking)
    Console.WriteLine(balance.BalSavings)
End Sub
```

For this example, I created a project with a single form. The form contains a single Command button whose Click event handler is shown here. Create this project from scratch, perhaps using your own custom data type, to explore its structure and experiment with functions that return custom data types.

In the following section, I'll describe a more complicated (and practical) example of a custom data type function.

VB.NET AT WORK: THE TYPES PROJECT

The Types project, which you'll find in this chapter's folder on the CD, demonstrates a function that returns a custom data type. The Types project consists of a form that displays record fields and is shown in Figure 4.2. Every time you click the View Next button, the fields of the next record are displayed. When all records are exhausted, the program wraps back to the first record.

FIGURE 4.2

The Types project demonstrates functions that return custom data types.

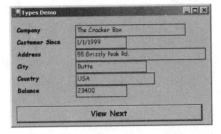

The project consists of a single form. The following custom data type appears in the form's code, outside any procedure:

```
Structure Customer
    Dim Company As String
    Dim Manager As String
    Dim Address As String
    Dim City As String
    Dim Country As String
    Dim CustomerSince As Date
    Dim Balance As Decimal
End Structure
Private Customers(8) As Customer
Private cust As Customer
Private currentIndex as Integer
```

The array *Customers* holds the data for nine customers, and the *cust* variable is used as a temporary variable for storing the current customer's data. The *currentIndex* variable is the index of the current element of the array.

The Click event handler of the View Next button calls the GetCustomer() function with an index value (which is the order of the current customer), and displays its fields in the Label controls on the form. Then it increases the value of the *currentIndex* variable, so that it points to the next customer.

The GetCustomer() function returns a variable of Customer type (the variable *aCustomer*). The code behind the View Next button follows:

```
Private Sub Button1_Click(ByVal sender As System.Object, _
                ByVal e As System.EventArgs) Handles Button1.Click
    If currentIndex = CountCustomers() Then currentIndex = 0
    Dim aCustomer As Customer
    aCustomer = GetCustomer(currentIndex)
    ShowCustomer(currentIndex)
    currentIndex = currentIndex + 1
End Sub
```

The CountCustomers() function returns the number of records stored in the *Customers* array. The event handler starts by comparing the value of the current index to the number of elements in the Customers array. If they're equal, the *currentIndex* variable is reset to zero. The definitions of the CountCustomers() and GetCustomer() functions are shown next:

```
Function CountCustomers() As Integer
    Return(Customers.Length)
End Function
Function GetCustomer(ByVal idx As Integer) As Customer
    Return(Customers(idx))
End Function
```

Finally, the ShowCustomer() subroutine displays the fields of the current record on the Label controls on the form:

```
Sub ShowCustomer(ByVal idx As Integer)
    Dim aCustomer As Customer
    aCustomer = GetCustomer(idx)
    lblCompany.Text = aCustomer.Company
    lblSince.Text = aCustomer.CustomerSince
    lblAddress.Text = aCustomer.Address
    lblCity.Text = aCustomer.City
    lblCountry.Text = aCustomer.Country
    lblBalance.Text = aCustomer.Balance
End Sub
```

The array *Customers* is populated when the program starts with a call to the InitData() subroutine (also in the project's module). The program assigns data to *Customers*, one element at a time, with statements like the following:

```
Dim cust As Customer
cust.Company = "Bottom-Dollar Markets"
cust.Manager = "Elizabeth Lincoln"
cust.Address = "23 Tsawassen Blvd."
cust.City = "Tsawassen"
cust.Country = "Canada"
cust.CustomerSince = #10/20/1996#
cust.Balance = 33500
Customers(1) = cust
```

The code assigns values to the fields of the *cust* variable and then assigns the entire variable to an element of the *Customers* array. The data could originate in a file or even a database. This wouldn't affect the operation of the application, which expects the GetCustomer() function to return a record of Customer type. If you decide to store the records in a file or a collection like the ones discussed in Chapter 11, the form's code need not change; only the implementation of the GetCustomer() function will change. You should also change the CountCustomers() function, so that it detects when it has reached the last record.

The Types project uses a single button that allows users to view the next record. You can place another button that displays the previous record. This button's code will be identical to the code of the existing button, with the exception that it will decrease the *currentIndex* variable.

FUNCTIONS RETURNING ARRAYS

In addition to returning custom data types, VB.NET functions can also return arrays. This is an interesting possibility that allows you to write functions that return not only multiple values, but also an unknown number of values. Earlier in the chapter you saw how to return multiple values from a function as arguments, passed to the function by reference. You can also consider a custom structure as a collection of values. In this section, we'll revise the Stats() function that was described earlier in this chapter, so that it returns the statistics in an array. The new Stats() function will return not only the average and the standard deviation, but the minimum and maximum values in the data set as well. One way to declare a function that calculates all the statistics is the following:

```
Function Stats(ByRef DataArray() As Double) As Double()
```

This function accepts an array with the data values and returns an array of doubles. This notation is more compact and helps you write easier-to-read code.

To implement a function that returns an array, you must do the following:

1. Specify a type for the function's return value, and add a pair of parentheses after the type's name. Don't specify the dimensions of the array to be returned here; the array will be declared formally in the function.

2. In the function's code, declare an array of the same type and specify its dimensions. If the function should return four values, use a declaration like this one:

```
Dim Results(3) As Double
```

The *Results* array will be used to store the results and must be of the same type as the function—its name can be anything.

3. To return the *Results* array, simply use it as argument to the Return statement:

```
Return(Results)
```

4. In the calling procedure, you must declare an array of the same type without dimensions:

```
Dim Stats() As Double
```

5. Finally, you must call the function and assign its return value to this array:

```
Stats() = Stats(DataSet())
```

Here, *DataSet* is an array with the values whose basic statistics will be calculated by the Stats() function. Your code can then retrieve each element of the array with an index value as usual.

VB.NET AT WORK: THE STATISTICS PROJECT

The next project demonstrates how to design and call functions that return arrays. It's the Statistics project, which you can find in this chapter's folder on the CD. When you run it, the Statistics application creates a data set of random values and then calls the ArrayStats() function to calculate the data set's basic statistics. The results are returned in an array, and the main program displays them in Label controls, as shown in Figure 4.3. Every time the Calculate Statistics button is clicked, a new data set is generated and its statistics are displayed.

FIGURE 4.3

The Statistics project calculates the basic statistics of a data set and returns them in an array.

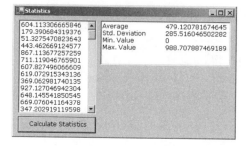

Let's start with the ArrayStats() function's code, which is shown in Listing 4.2.

LISTING 4.2: THE ARRAYSTATS() FUNCTION

```
Function ArrayStats(ByVal DataArray() As Double) As Double()
    Dim Result(3) As Double
    Dim Sum, SumSquares, DataMin, DataMax As Double
    Dim DCount, i As Integer
    Sum = 0
    SumSquares = 0
    DCount = 0
    DataMin = System.Double.MaxValue
    DataMax = System.Double.MinValue
    For i = 0 To DataArray.GetUpperBound(0)
        Sum = Sum + DataArray(i)
        SumSquares = SumSquares + DataArray(i) ^ 2
        If DataArray(i) > DataMax Then DataMax = DataArray(i)
        If DataArray(i) < DataMin Then DataMin = DataArray(i)
        DCount = DCount + 1
    Next
    Dim Avg, StdDev As Double
    Avg = Sum / DCount
    StdDev = Math.Sqrt(SumSquares / DCount - Avg ^ 2)
    Result(0) = Avg
    Result(1) = StdDev
    Result(2) = DataMin
    Result(3) = DataMax
    ArrayStats = Result
End Function
```

The function's return type is Double(), meaning the function will return an array of doubles; that's what the empty parentheses signify. This array is declared in the function's body with the statement:

```
Dim Result(3) As Double
```

The function performs its calculations and then assigns the values of the basic statistics to the elements of the array *Result*. The first element holds the average, the second element holds the standard deviation, and the other two elements hold the minimum and maximum data values. The *Result* array is finally returned to the calling procedure by the statement that assigns the array to the function name, just as you'd assign a variable to the name of the function that returns a single result.

The code behind the Calculate Statistics button, which calls the ArrayStats() function, is shown in Listing 4.3.

LISTING 4.3: CALCULATING STATISTICS WITH THE ARRAYSTATS() FUNCTION

```
Protected Sub Button2_Click(ByVal sender As Object, _
                ByVal e As System.EventArgs)
    Dim SData(99) As Double
    Dim Stats() As Double
    Dim i As Integer
    Dim rnd As New System.Random()
    ListBox1.Items.Clear()
    For i = 0 To 99
        SData(i) = rnd.NextDouble() * 1000
        ListBox1.Items.Add(SData(i))
    Next
    Stats = ArrayStats(SData)
    TextBox1.Text = "Average" & vbTab & vbTab & Stats(0)
    TextBox1.Text = TextBox1.Text & cvCrLf & "Std. Deviation" & vbTab & Stats(1)
    TextBox1.Text = TextBox1.Text & vbCrLf & "Min. Value" & vbTab & Stats(2)
    TextBox1.Text = TextBox1.Text & vbCrLf & "Max. Value" & vbTab & Stats(3)
End Sub
```

The code generates 100 random values and displays them on a ListBox control. Then, it calls the ArrayStats() function, passing the data values to it through the *SData* array. The function's return values are stored in the *Stats* array, which is declared as double but without dimensions. Then, the code displays the basic statistics on a TextBox control, one item per line.

Overloading Functions

There are situations where the same function must operate on different data types, or a different number of arguments. In the past, you had to write different functions, with different names and different arguments, to accommodate similar requirements. VB.NET introduces the concept of *function overloading*, which means that you can have multiple implementations of the same function, each with a different set of arguments and, possibly, a different return value. Yet, all overloaded functions share the same name. Let me introduce this concept by examining one of the many overloaded functions that come with the .NET Framework.

To generate a random number in the range from 0 to 1 (exclusive), use the NextDouble method of the System.Random class. To use the methods of the Random class, you must first create an instance of the class and then call the methods:

```
Dim rnd As New System.Random
Console.WriteLine("Three random numbers")
Console.Write(rnd.NextDouble() & " - " & rnd.NextDouble() & " - " & _
              rnd.NextDouble())
```

The random numbers that will be printed on the Output window will be double precision values in the range 0 to 1:

```
0.656691639058614 - 0.967485965680092 - 0.993525570721145
```

More often than not, we need integer random values. The Next method of the System.Random class returns an integer value from –2,147,483,648 to 2,147,483,647 (this is the range of values that can be represented by the Integer data type). We also want to generate random numbers in a limited range of integer values. To emulate the throw of a dice, we want a random value in the range from 1 to 6, while for a roulette game we want an integer random value in the range from 0 to 36. You can specify an upper limit for the random number with an optional integer argument. The following statement will return a random integer in the range from 0 to 99:

```
randomInt = rnd.Next(100)
```

Finally, you can specify both the lower and upper limits of the random number's range. The following statement will return a random integer in the range from 1,000 to 1,999:

```
randomInt = rnd.Next(1000, 2000)
```

The same method behaves differently based on the arguments we supply. The behavior of the method depends either on the type of the arguments, the number of the arguments, or both of them. As you will see, there's no single function that alters its behavior based on its arguments. There are as many different implementations of the same function as there are argument combinations. All the functions share the same name, so that they appear to the user as a single, multifaceted function. These functions are overloaded, and you'll see in the following section how they're implemented.

If you haven't turned off the IntelliSense feature of the editor, then as soon as you type the opening parenthesis after a function or method name, you see a yellow box with the syntax of the function or method. You'll know that a function is overloaded when this box contains a number and two arrows. Each number corresponds to a different overloaded form, and you can move to the next or previous overloaded form by clicking the two little arrows or by pressing the arrow keys.

Let's return to the Min() function we implemented earlier in this chapter. The initial implementation of the Min() function is shown next:

```
Function Min(ByVal a As Double, ByVal b As Double) As Double
    Min = IIf(a < b, a, b)
End Function
```

By accepting double values as arguments, this function can handle all numeric types. VB.NET performs automatically widening conversions (it can convert integers and decimals to doubles), so this trick makes our function work with all numeric data types. However, what about strings? If you attempt to call the Min() function with two strings as arguments, you'll get an exception. The Min() function just can't handle strings.

To write a Min() function that can handle both numeric and string values, you must, in essence, write two Min() functions. All Min() functions must be prefixed with the Overloads keyword. The following statements show two different implementations of the same function:

```
Overloads Function Min(ByVal a As Double, ByVal b As Double) As Double
    Min = IIf(a < b, a, b)
End Function
Overloads Function Min(ByVal a As String, ByVal b As String) As String
    Min = IIf(a < b, a, b)
End Function
```

As you may have guessed, we need a third overloaded form of the same function to compare dates. If you call the Min() function with two dates are arguments, as in the following statement, the Min() function will compare them as strings.

```
Console.WriteLine(Min(#1/1/2001#, #3/4/2000#))
```

This statement will print the date 1/1/2001, which is not the smaller (earlier) date. If you swap the years and call the function as

```
Console.WriteLine(Min(#1/1/2000#, #3/4/2001#))
```

you'll get the earlier date, but just because it happens that their alphanumeric order is now the same as their chronological order.

The overloaded form of the function that accepts dates as arguments is shown next:

```
Overloads Function Min(ByVal a As Date, ByVal b As Date) As Date
    Min = IIf(a < b, a, b)
End Function
```

If you now call the Min() function with the dates #1/1/2001# and #3/4/2000#, the function will return the second date, which is chronologically smaller than the first.

OK, the example of the Min() function is rather trivial. You can also write a Min() function that compares two objects and handle all other data types. Let's look into a more complicated overloaded function, which makes use of some topics discussed later in this book. The CountFiles() function counts the number of files that meet certain criteria. The criteria could be the size of the files, their type, or the date they were created. You can come up with any combination of these criteria, but here are the most useful combinations. (These are the functions I would use, but you can create even more combinations, or introduce new criteria of your own.) The names of the arguments are self-descriptive, so I need not explain what each form of the CountFiles() function does.

```
CountFiles(ByVal minSize As Integer, ByVal maxSize As Integer) As Integer
CountFiles(ByVal fromDate As Date, ByVal toDate As Date) As Integer
CountFiles(ByVal type As String) As Integer
CountFiles(ByVal minSize As Integer, ByVal maxSize As Integer, _
          ByVal type As String) As Integer
CountFiles(ByVal fromDate As Date, ByVal toDate As Date, _
          ByVal type As String) As Integer
```

Listing 4.4 shows the implementation of these overloaded forms of the CountFiles() function. Since we haven't discussed files yet, most of the code in the function's body will be new to you—but it's not hard to follow. For the benefit of readers who are totally unfamiliar with file operations, I've included a statement that prints on the Output window the type of files counted by each function. The Console.WriteLine statement prints the values of the arguments passed to the function, along with a description of the type of search it's going to perform. The overloaded form that accepts two integer values as arguments prints something like:

```
You've requested the files between 1000 and 100000 bytes
```

while the overloaded form that accepts a string as argument prints the following:

```
You've requested the .EXE files
```

LISTING 4.4: THE OVERLOADED IMPLEMENTATIONS OF THE COUNTFILES() FUNCTION

```
Overloads Function CountFiles(ByVal minSize As Integer, _
                             ByVal maxSize As Integer) As Integer
    Console.WriteLine("You've requested the files between " & minSize & _
                    " and " & maxSize & " bytes")
    Dim files() As String
    files = System.IO.Directory.GetFiles("c:\windows")
    Dim i, fileCount As Integer
    For i = 0 To files.GetUpperBound(0)
       Dim FI As New System.IO.FileInfo(files(i))
       If FI.Length >= minSize And FI.Length <= maxSize Then
          fileCount = fileCount + 1
       End If
    Next
    Return(fileCount)
End Function
Overloads Function CountFiles(ByVal fromDate As Date, _
                             ByVal toDate As Date) As Integer
    Console.WriteLine("You've requested the count of files created from " & _
                    fromDate & " to " & toDate)
    Dim files() As String
    files = System.IO.Directory.GetFiles("c:\windows")
    Dim i, fileCount As Integer
    For i = 0 To files.GetUpperBound(0)
       Dim FI As New System.IO.FileInfo(files(i))
       If FI.CreationTime.Date >= fromDate And _
             FI.CreationTime.Date <= toDate Then
          fileCount = fileCount + 1
       End If
    Next
    Return(fileCount)
End Function
```

```
Overloads Function CountFiles(ByVal type As String) As Integer
    Console.WriteLine("You've requested the " & type & " files")
    Dim files() As String
    files = System.IO.Directory.GetFiles("c:\windows")
    Dim i, fileCount As Integer
    For i = 0 To files.GetUpperBound(0)
        Dim FI As New System.IO.FileInfo(files(i))
        If FI.Extension = type Then
            fileCount = fileCount + 1
        End If
    Next
    Return(fileCount)
End Function
Overloads Function CountFiles(ByVal minSize As Integer, _
                    ByVal maxSize As Integer, ByVal type As String) As Integer
    Console.WriteLine("You've requested the " & type & " files between " & _
                    minSize & " and " & maxSize & " bytes")
    Dim files() As String
    files = System.IO.Directory.GetFiles("c:\windows")
    Dim i, fileCount As Integer
    For i = 0 To files.GetUpperBound(0)
        Dim FI As New System.IO.FileInfo(files(i))
        If FI.Length >= minSize And _
            FI.Length <= maxSize And _
            FI.Extension = type Then
            fileCount = fileCount + 1
        End If
    Next
    Return(fileCount)
End Function
Overloads Function CountFiles(ByVal fromDate As Date, ByVal toDate As Date, _
                            ByVal type As String) As Integer
    Console.WriteLine("You've requested the " & type & _
                    " files created from " & fromDate & " to " & toDate)
    Dim files() As String
    files = System.IO.Directory.GetFiles("c:\windows")
    Dim i, fileCount As Integer
    For i = 0 To files.GetUpperBound(0)
        Dim FI As New System.IO.FileInfo(files(i))
        If FI.CreationTime.Date >= fromDate And _
            FI.CreationTime.Date <= toDate And FI.Extension = type Then
            fileCount = fileCount + 1
        End If
    Next
    Return(fileCount)
End Function
```

If you're unfamiliar with the Directory and File objects, focus on the statement that prints to the Output window and ignore the statements that actually count the files that meet the specified criteria. After reading Chapter 13, you can revisit this example and understand the counting statements. The `Console.WriteLine` statements report all the values passed as arguments, and they differentiate between the various overloaded forms of the function.

Start a new project and enter the definitions of the overloaded forms of the function on the form's level. Listing 4.4 is lengthy, but all the overloaded functions have the same structure and differ only in how they select the files to count. Then place a TextBox and a button on the form, as shown in Figure 4.4, and enter the statements from Listing 4.5 in the button's Click event handler. The project shown in Figure 4.4 is called OverloadedFunctions, and you'll find it in this chapter's folder on the CD.

FIGURE 4.4

The Overloaded-Functions project

LISTING 4.5: TESTING THE OVERLOADED FORMS OF THE COUNTFILES() FUNCTION

```
Private Sub Button1_Click(ByVal sender As System.Object, _
            ByVal e As System.EventArgs) Handles Button1.Click
    TextBox1.AppendText(CountFiles(1000, 100000) & _
                " files with size between 1KB and 100KB" & vbCrLf)
    TextBox1.AppendText(CountFiles(#1/1/2001#, #12/31/2001#) & _
                " files created in 2001" & vbCrLf)
    TextBox1.AppendText(CountFiles(".BMP") & " BMP files" & vbCrLf)
    TextBox1.AppendText(CountFiles(1000, 100000, ".EXE") & _
                " EXE files between 1 and 100 KB" & vbCrLf)
    TextBox1.AppendText(CountFiles(#1/1/2000#, #12/31/2001#, ".EXE") & _
                " EXE files created in 2000 and 2001")
End Sub
```

The button calls the various overloaded forms of the CountFiles() function one after the other and prints the results on the TextBox control.

Function overloading is new to VB.NET, but it's used heavily throughout the language. There are relatively few functions (or methods, for that matter) that aren't overloaded. Every time you enter the name of a function followed by an opening parenthesis, a list of its arguments appears in the drop-down list with the arguments of the function. If the function is overloaded, you'll see a number in front of the list of arguments, as shown in Figure 4.5. This number is the order of the overloaded form of the function, and it's followed by the arguments of the specific form of the function. The figure shows all the forms of the CountFiles() function.

FIGURE 4.5

The overloaded forms of the Count-Files() function

1 of 5 ▾ CountFiles (**minSize As Integer**, maxSize As Integer) As Integer
2 of 5 ▾ CountFiles (**fromDate As Date**, toDate As Date) As Integer
3 of 5 ▾ CountFiles (**type As String**) As Integer
4 of 5 ▾ CountFiles (**minSize As Integer**, maxSize As Integer, type As String) As Integer
5 of 5 ▾ CountFiles (**fromDate As Date**, toDate As Date, type As String) As Integer

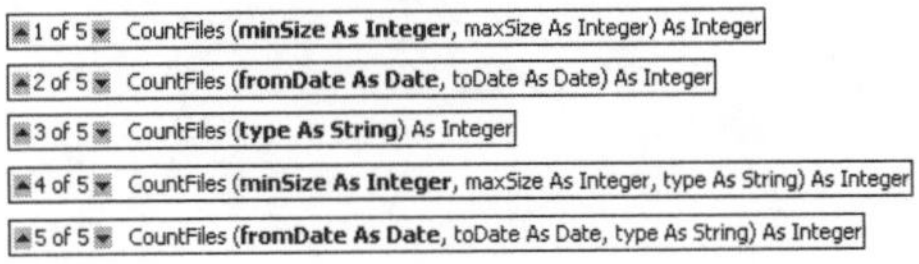

You will have to overload many of the functions you'll be writing once you start developing real applications, because you'll want your functions to work on a variety of data types. This is not the only reason to overload functions. You may also need to write functions that behave differently based on the number and types of their arguments.

NOTE   *Notice that you can't overload a function by changing its return type. That's why the Min() function returns a double value, which is the most accurate value. If you don't need more than a couple of decimal digits (or no fractional part at all), you can round the return value in your code accordingly. However, you can't have two Min() functions that accept the exact same arguments and return different data types. Overloaded forms of a function are differentiated by the number and/or the type of their arguments, but not by the return value.*

Summary

This chapter concludes the presentation of the core of the language. In the last two chapters, you've learned how to declare and use variables, and how to break your applications into smaller, manageable units of code. These units of code are the subroutines and functions. Subroutines perform actions and don't return any values. Functions, on the other hand, perform calculations and return values. Most of the language's built-in functionality is in the form of functions. The methods of the various controls look and feel like functions, because they're implemented as functions. Functions are indeed a major aspect of the language.

Subroutines aren't as common. Many programmers actually prefer to write only functions and use the return value to indicate the success or failure of the procedure, even if the procedure need not return any value. Event handlers are implemented as subroutines, because they don't return any values. Event handlers aren't called from within your code; they are simply activated by the Common Language Runtime.

Subroutines and functions communicate with the rest of the application through arguments. There are many ways to pass arguments to a procedure, and you've seen them all. You have also seen how to write overloaded functions, which are new to VB.NET; and as you will see in the rest of this book, they're quite common.

In the following chapters, we'll explore the Windows controls in depth, and you will write your first "real" Windows applications.

Chapter 5

Working with Forms

IN VISUAL BASIC, THE *form* is the container for all the controls that make up the user interface. When a Visual Basic application is executing, each window it displays on the desktop is a form. In previous chapters, we concentrated on placing the elements of the user interface on forms, setting their properties, and adding code behind selected events. Now, we'll look at forms themselves and at a few related topics, such as menus (forms are the only objects that can have menus attached), how to design forms that can be automatically resized, and how to access the controls of one form from within another form's code. The form is the top-level object in a Visual Basic application, and every application starts with the form.

NOTE *The terms* form *and* window *describe the same entity. A window is what the user sees on the desktop when the application is running. A form is the same entity at design time. The proper term is a Windows form, as opposed to a Web form, but I will refer to them as forms.*

Forms have built-in functionality that is always available without any programming effort on your part. You can move a form around, resize it, and even cover it with other forms. You do so with the mouse, or with the keyboard through the Control menu. As you will see, forms are not passive containers; they're "intelligent" objects that are aware of the controls placed on them and can actually manipulate the controls at runtime. For example, you can instruct the form to resize certain controls when the form itself is resized. Forms have many trivial properties that won't be discussed here. Instead, let's jump directly to the properties that are unique to forms and then look at how to manipulate forms from within an application's code.

The forms that constitute the visible interface of your application are called *Windows forms;* this term includes both the regular forms and dialog boxes, which are simple forms you use for very specific actions, such as to prompt the user for a specific piece of data or to display critical information. A *dialog box* is a form with a small number of controls, no menus, and usually an OK and a Cancel button to close it. For more information on dialog boxes, see the section "Forms vs. Dialog Boxes" later in this chapter. Everything you'll read about forms in the following sections applies to dialog boxes as well, even if some form features (such as menus) are never used with dialog boxes.

VB6 ➠ VB.NET

The Form Designer is one of the most improved areas of VB.NET. For the first time, you can design forms that can be easily resized—anyone who has programmed in earlier versions of VB knows what a hassle the resizing of forms could be. The Anchor and Dock properties allow you to anchor controls on the edges of the form and dock them on the form. When the form is resized, the controls on it can be either resized or moved to new locations, so that they remain visible.

If the controls can't fit the form, scroll bars can appear automatically, so that users can scroll the form in its window and bring another section into view, if the form's AutoScroll property is True. Scrolling forms are also new to VB.NET.

A new special control was added, whose sole purpose is to act as a pane separator on forms: the Splitter control. This control is a thin horizontal or vertical stripe that allows you to resize two adjacent controls. If two TextBox controls on the same form are separated by a Splitter control, users can shrink one TextBox to make more room for the other. Again, no code required.

Of course, many things have changed too. You can no longer show a form by calling its Show method. You must first create an instance of the form (a variable of the Form type) that you want to show and then call the Show method of this variable. You no longer have arrays of controls. This isn't much of a problem, though, because with VB.NET you can create instances of new controls from within your code and position them on the form.

The Appearance of Forms

Applications are made up of one or more forms (usually more than one), and the forms are what users see. You should craft your forms carefully, make them functional, and keep them simple and intuitive. You already know how to place controls on the form, but there's more to designing forms than populating them with controls. The main characteristic of a form is the title bar on which the form's caption is displayed (see Figure 5.1).

FIGURE 5.1

The elements of the form

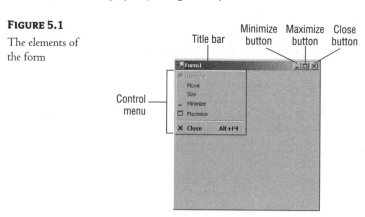

Clicking the icon on the left end of the title bar opens the Control menu, which contains the commands shown in Table 5.1. On the right end of the title bar are three buttons: Minimize, Maximize, and Close. Clicking these buttons performs the associated function. When a form is maximized, the Maximize button is replaced by the Restore button. When clicked, this button resets the form to the size and position before it was maximized. The Restore button is then replaced by the Maximize button.

TABLE 5.1: COMMANDS OF THE CONTROL MENU

COMMAND	EFFECT
Restore	Restores a maximized form to the size it was before it was maximized; available only if the form has been maximized
Move	Lets the user move the form around with the mouse
Size	Lets the user resize the form with the mouse
Minimize	Minimizes the form
Maximize	Maximizes the form
Close	Closes the current form

Properties of the Form Control

You're familiar with the appearance of the forms, even if you haven't programmed in the Windows environment in the past; you have seen nearly all types of windows in the applications you're using every day. The floating toolbars used by many graphics applications, for example, are actually forms with a narrow title bar. The dialog boxes that display critical information or prompt you to select the file to be opened are also forms. You can duplicate the look of any window or dialog box through the following properties of the Form object.

ACCEPTBUTTON, CANCELBUTTON

These two properties let you specify the default Accept and Cancel buttons. The Accept button is the one that's automatically activated when you press Enter, no matter which control has the focus at the time, and is usually the button with the OK caption. Likewise, the Cancel button is the one that's automatically activated when you hit the Esc key and is usually the button with the Cancel caption. To specify the Accept and Cancel buttons on a form, locate the AcceptButton and CancelButton properties of the form and select the corresponding controls from a drop-down list, which contains the names of all the buttons on the form. You can also set them to the name of the corresponding button from within your code.

AUTOSCALE

This property is a True/False value that determines whether the controls you place on the form are automatically scaled to the height of the current font. When you place a TextBox control on the form, for example, and the AutoScale property is True, the control will be tall enough to display a single line of text in the current font. The default value is True, which is why you can't make the controls smaller than a given size. This is a property of the form, but it affects the controls on the form. If you change the Font property of the form after you have placed a few controls on it, the existing controls won't be affected. The controls are adjusted to the current font of the form the moment they're placed on it.

AUTOSCROLL

This is one of the most needed of the Form object's new properties. The AutoScroll property is a True/False value that indicates whether scroll bars will be automatically attached to the form (as seen in Figure 5.2) if it's resized to a point that not all its controls are visible. This property is new to VB.NET and will help you design large forms without having to worry about the resolution of the monitor on which they'll be displayed.

FIGURE 5.2

If the controls don't fit in the form's visible area, scroll bars can be attached automatically.

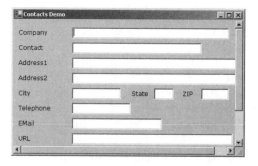

The AutoScroll property is used in conjunction with three other properties, described next: Auto-ScrollMargin, AutoScrollMinSize, and AutoScrollPosition.

AUTOSCROLLMARGIN

This is a margin, expressed in pixels, that's added around all the controls on the form. If the form is smaller than the rectangle that encloses all the controls adjusted by the margin, the appropriate scroll bar(s) will be displayed automatically.

If you expand the AutoScrollMargin property in the Properties window, you will see that it's an object (a Size object, to be specific). It exposes two members, the Width and Height properties, and you must set both values. The default value is (0,0). To set this property from within your code, use statements like these:

```
Me.AutoScrollMargin.Width = 40
Me.AutoScrollMargin.Height = 40
```

AUTOSCROLLMINSIZE

This property lets you specify the minimum size of the form, before the scroll bars are attached. If your form contains graphics you want to be visible at all times, set the Width and Height members of the AutoScrollMinSize property accordingly. Notice that this isn't the form's minimum size; users can make the form even smaller. To specify a minimum size for the form, use the Minimum-Size property, described later in this section.

Let's say the AutoScrollMargin properties of the form are 180 by 150. If the form is resized to less than 180 pixels horizontally or 150 pixels vertically, the appropriate scroll bars will appear automatically, as long as the AutoScroll property is True. If you want to enable the AutoScroll feature when the form's width is reduced to anything less than 250 pixels, set the AutoScrollMinSize property to (250, 0). Obviously, if the AutoScrollMinSize value is smaller than the dimensions of the form that will automatically invoke the AutoScroll feature, AutoScrollMinSize has no effect. In this example, setting `AutoScrollMinSize.Width` to anything less than 180 or `AutoScrollMinSize.Height` to anything less than 150 will have no effect on the appearance of the form and its scroll bars.

AUTOSCROLLPOSITION

This property lets you read (or set) the location of the auto-scroll position. The AutoScrollPosition is the number of pixels by which the two scroll bars were displaced from their initial locations. You can read this property to find out by how much the scroll bars were moved, or to move the scroll bars from within your code.

Use this property in very specialized applications, because the form's scroll bars are adjusted automatically to bring the control that has the focus into view. As long as the users of the application press the Tab key to move the focus to the next control, the focused control will be visible.

BORDERSTYLE

The BorderStyle property determines the style of the form's border and the appearance of the form; it takes one of the values shown in Table 5.2. You can make the form's title bar disappear altogether by setting the form's BorderStyle property to FixedToolWindow, the ControlBox property to False, and the Text property to an empty string. However, a form like this can't be moved around with the mouse and will probably frustrate users.

TABLE 5.2: THE FORMBORDERSTYLE ENUMERATION

VALUE	EFFECT
None	Borderless window that can't be resized; this setting should be avoided.
Sizable	(default) Resizable window that's used for displaying regular forms.
Fixed3D	Window with a visible border, "raised" relative to the main area. Can't be resized.
FixedDialog	A fixed window, used to create dialog boxes.

Continued on next page

TABLE 5.2: THE FORMBORDERSTYLE ENUMERATION *(continued)*

VALUE	EFFECT
FixedSingle	A fixed window with a single line border.
FixedToolWindow	A fixed window with a Close button only. It looks like the toolbar displayed by the drawing and imaging applications.
SizableToolWindow	Same as the FixedToolWindow but resizable. In addition, its caption font is smaller than the usual.

CONTROLBOX

This property is also True by default. Set it to False to hide the icon and disable the Control menu. Although the Control menu is rarely used, Windows applications don't disable it. When the ControlBox property is False, the three buttons on the title bar are also disabled. If you set the Text property to an empty string, the title bar disappears altogether.

KEYPREVIEW

This property enables the form to capture all keystrokes before they're passed to the control that has the focus. Normally, when you press a key, the KeyPress event of the control with the focus is triggered (as well as the other keystroke-related events), and you can handle the keystroke from within the control's appropriate handler. In most cases, we let the control handle the keystroke and don't write any form code for that.

If you want to use "universal" keystrokes in your application, you must set the KeyPreview property to True. Doing so enables the form to intercept all keystrokes, so that you can process them from within the form's keystroke events. The same keystrokes are then passed to the control with the focus, unless you "kill" the keystroke by setting its Handled property to True when you process it on the form's level. For more information on processing keystrokes at the Form level and using special keystrokes throughout your application, see the Contacts project later in this chapter.

MINIMIZEBOX, MAXIMIZEBOX

These two properties are True by default. Set them to False to hide the corresponding buttons on the title bar.

MINIMUMSIZE, MAXIMUMSIZE

These two properties read or set the minimum and maximum size of a form. When users resize the form at runtime, the form won't become any smaller than the dimensions specified with the MinimumSize property and no larger than the dimensions specified by MaximumSize. The MinimumSize property is a Size object, and you can set it with a statement like the following:

```
Me.MinimumSize = New Size(400, 300)
```

Or, you can set the width and height separately:

```
Me.MinimumSize.Width = 400
Me.MinimumSize.Height = 300
```

The `MinimumSize.Height` property includes the height of the Form's title bar; you should take that into consideration. If the minimum usable size of the Form is 400 by 300, use the following statement to set the MinimumSize property:

```
me.MinimumSize = New Size(400, 300 + SystemInformation.CaptionHeight)
```

TIP *The height of the caption is not a property of the Form object, even though you will find it useful in determining the useful area of the form (the total height minus the caption bar). Keep in mind that the height of the caption bar is given by the CaptionHeight property of the SystemInformation object.*

SIZEGRIPSTYLE

This property gets or sets the style of sizing handle to display in the bottom-right corner of the form; it can have one of the values shown in Table 5.3. By default, forms are resizable, even if no special mark appears at the bottom-right corner of the form. This little mark indicating that a form can be resized is new to VB.NET and adds a nice touch to the look of the form.

TABLE 5.3: THE SIZEGRIPSTYLE ENUMERATION

VALUE	EFFECT
Auto	(default) The SizeGrip is displayed as needed.
Show	The SizeGrip is displayed at all times.
Hide	The SizeGrip is not displayed, but the form can still be resized with the mouse (Windows 95/98 style).

STARTPOSITION

This property determines the initial position of the form when it's first displayed; it can have one of the values shown in Table 5.4.

TABLE 5.4: THE FORMSTARTPOSITION ENUMERATION

VALUE	EFFECT
CenterParent	The form is centered in the area of its parent form.
CenterScreen	The form is centered on the monitor.
Manual	The location and size of the form will determine its starting position. See the discussion of the Top, Left, Width, and Height properties of the form, later in this section.

Continued on next page

TABLE 5.4: THE FORMSTARTPOSITION ENUMERATION *(continued)*

VALUE	EFFECT
WindowsDefaultBounds	The form is positioned at the default location and size determined by Windows.
WindowsDefaultLocation	The form is positioned at the Windows default location and has the dimensions you've set at design time.

TOP, LEFT

These two properties set or return the coordinates of the form's top-left corner in pixels. You'll rarely use these properties in your code, since the location of the window on the desktop is determined by the user at runtime.

TOPMOST

This property is a True/False value that lets you specify whether the form will remain on top of all other forms in your application. Its default property is False, and you should change it only in rare occasions. Some dialog boxes, like the Find and Replace dialog box of any text processing application, are always visible, even when they don't have the focus. To make a form remain visible while it's open, set its TopMost property to True.

WIDTH, HEIGHT

These two properties set or return the form's width and height in pixels. They are usually set from within the form's Resize event handler, to keep the size of the form at a minimum size. The form's width and height are usually controlled by the user at runtime.

Placing Controls on Forms

As you already know, the second step in designing your application's interface is the design of the forms (the first step being the analysis and careful planning of the basic operations you want to provide through your interface). Designing a form means placing Windows controls on it, setting their properties, and then writing code to handle the events of interest. Visual Studio.NET is a rapid application development (RAD) environment. This doesn't mean that you're expected to develop applications rapidly. It has come to mean that you can rapidly prototype an application and show something to the customer. And this is made possible through the visual tools that come with VS.NET, especially the new Form Designer.

To place controls on your form, you select them in the Toolbox and then draw, on the form, the rectangle in which the control will be enclosed. Or, you can double-click the control's icon to place an instance of the control on the form. All controls have a default size, and you can resize the control on the form with the mouse. Next, you set the control's properties in the Properties window.

Each control's dimensions can also be set in the Properties window, through the Width and Height properties. These two properties are expressed in pixels. You can also call the Width and Height properties from within your code to read the dimensions of a control. Likewise, the Top and Left properties return (or set) the coordinates of the top-left corner of the control. In the section

"Building Dynamic Forms at Runtime," later in this chapter, you'll see how to create new controls at runtime and place them on a form from within your code. You'll use these properties to specify the location of the new controls on the form in your code.

Setting the TabOrder

Another important issue in form design is the tab order of the controls on the form. As you know, pressing the Tab key at runtime takes you to the next control on the form. The order of the controls isn't determined by the form; you specify the order when you design the application, with the help of the TabOrder property. Each control has its own TabOrder setting, which is an integer value. When the Tab key is pressed, the focus is moved to the control whose tab order immediately follows the tab order of the current control. The TabOrder of the various controls on the form need not be consecutive.

To specify the tab order of the various controls, you can set their TabOrder property in the Properties window, or you can select the Tab Order command from the View menu. The tab order of each control will be displayed on the corresponding control, as shown in Figure 5.3 (the form shown in the figure is the Contacts application, which is discussed shortly). Notice that some of the buttons at the bottom of the form are not aligned as they should be. The OK and Cancel buttons should be on top of the Add and Delete buttons, hiding them. I had to displace them to set the tab order of all controls on the form and then align some of the buttons again.

FIGURE 5.3

Setting the TabOrder of the controls on the main form of the Contacts project

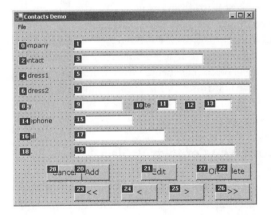

To set the tab order of the controls, click each control in the order in which you want them to receive the focus. Notice that you can't change the tab order of a few controls only. You must click all of them in the desired order, starting with the first control in the tab order. The tab order need not be the same as the physical order of the controls on the form, but controls that are next to each other in the tab order should be placed next to each other on the form as well.

NOTE *The default tab order is the same as the order in which you place the controls on the form. Unless you keep the tab order in mind while you design the form, you'll end up with a form that moves the focus from one control to the next in a totally unpredictable manner. Once all the controls are on the form, you should always check their tab order to make sure it won't confuse users.*

As you place controls on the form, don't forget to lock them, so that you won't move them around by mistake as you work with other controls. You can lock the controls in their places either by setting their Locked property to True, or by locking all the controls on the form with the Format ➤ Lock Controls command.

VB6 ➠ VB.NET

Many of the controls in earlier versions of Visual Basic exposed a Locked property too, but this property had a totally different function. The old Locked property prevented users from editing the controls at runtime (entering text on a TextBox control, for example). The new Locked property is effective at design time only; it simply locks the control on the form, so that it can't be moved by mistake.

Designing functional forms is a crucial step in the process of developing Windows applications. Most data-entry operators don't work with the mouse, and you must make sure all the actions can be performed with the keyboard. This doesn't apply to graphics applications, of course, but most applications developed with VB are business applications. If you're developing a data-entry form, for example, you must take into consideration the needs of the users in designing these forms. Make a prototype and ask the people who will use the application to test-drive it. Listen to their objections carefully, collect all the information, and then use it to refine your application's user interface. Don't defend your design—just learn from the users. They will uncover all the flaws of the application, and they'll help you design the most functional interface.

The process of designing forms is considered to be the simplest step by most beginners, but a bad user interface might force you to redesign the entire application later on—not to mention that an inefficient interface will discourage people from using your application. Take your time to think about the interface, the controls on your forms, and how users will navigate. I'm not going to discuss the topic of designing user interfaces in this book. Besides, this is one of the skills you'll acquire with time.

VB.NET at Work: The Contacts Project

I would like to conclude this section with an example of a simple data-entry form that demonstrates many of the topics discussed here, as well as a few techniques for designing easy-to-use forms. Figure 5.4 shows a data-entry form for contact information, and I'm sure you will add your own fields to make this application more useful. You can navigate through the contacts using the buttons with the arrows, as well as add new contacts or delete existing ones by clicking the appropriate buttons. When you're entering a new contact, the buttons shown in Figure 5.4 are replaced by the usual OK and Cancel buttons. The action of adding a new contact must end by clicking one of these two buttons. After committing a new contact, or canceling the action, the usual navigation buttons will appear again.

Once the controls are on the form, the first step is to set their tab order. You must specify a TabOrder even for controls that never receive focus, such as the labels. In addition to the tab order of the controls, we'll also use shortcut keys to give the user quick access to the most common fields. The shortcut keys are displayed as underlined characters on the corresponding labels, as you can see in Figure 5.4.

FIGURE 5.4

A simple data-entry
screen

To set the TabOrder of the controls, use the View ➤ Tab Order command. Click all the controls in the order you want them to receive the focus, starting with the first label. The proper order of the controls is shown back in Figure 5.3. You can change the order of the buttons, if you want, but the labels and text boxes must have consecutive settings. Don't forget to include the buttons in the tab order. Then open the View menu again and select the Tab Order command to return to the regular view of the Form Designer.

If you run the application now, you'll see that the focus moves from one TextBox to the next and the labels are skipped. Since the labels don't accept any data, they receive the focus momentarily and then the focus is passed to the next control in the tab order. After the last TextBox control, the focus is moved to the buttons, and then back to the first TextBox control. To add a shortcut key for the most common fields, determine which of the fields will have their own shortcut key and which keys will be used for that purpose. Being the Internet buffs that we all are, let's assign shortcut keys to the Company, EMail, and URL fields. Locate each label's Text property in the Properties window and insert the & symbol in front of the character you want to act as a shortcut for each Label. The Text properties of the three controls should be &Company, &EMail, and &URL.

Shortcut keys are activated at runtime by pressing the shortcut character while holding down the Alt key. The shortcut key will move the focus to the corresponding Label control, but because labels can't receive the focus, it's passed immediately to the next control in the tab order, which is the adjacent TextBox control. For this technique to work, you must make sure that all controls are properly arranged in the tab order.

TIP   *By the way, if you want to display the & symbol on a Label control, prefix it with another & symbol. To display the string "Tom & Jerry" on a Label control, assign the string "Tom && Jerry" to its Text property.*

If you run the application now, you'll be able to quickly move the focus to the Company, EMail, and URL boxes by pressing the shortcut key while holding down the Alt key. To access the other fields (the TextBoxes without shortcuts), the user can press Tab to move forward in the tab order or Shift+Tab to move backward. Try to move the focus with the mouse and enter data with the keyboard, and you'll soon understand what kind of interface a data-entry operator would rather work with.

The contacts are stored in an ArrayList object, which is similar to an array but a little more convenient. We'll discuss ArrayList in Chapter 11; for now, you can ignore the parts of the application that manipulate the contacts and focus on the design issues.

Now enter a new contact by clicking the Add button, or edit an existing contact by clicking the Edit button. Both actions must end with the OK or Cancel button. In other words, we won't allow users to switch to another contact while adding or editing a contact. The code behind the various buttons is straightforward. The Add button hides all the navigational buttons at the bottom of the form and clears the TextBoxes. The OK button saves the new contact to an ArrayList structure and redisplays the navigational buttons. The Cancel button ignores the data entered by the user and likewise displays the navigational buttons. In either case, when the user switches back to the view mode, the TextBoxes are also locked, by setting their ReadOnly properties to True.

Don't worry about the statements that manipulate the ArrayList with the contacts or the statements that save the contacts to a disk file and load them back to the application from a disk file. We'll come back to this project in Chapter 11, where we'll discuss ArrayLists. Just focus on the statements that control the appearance of the form.

For now, you can use the commands of the File menu to load or save a set of contacts. These commands are quite simple: they load the same file, CONTACTS.BIN in the application's folder. After reading about the Open File and Save File dialog controls, you can modify the code so that it prompts the user about the file to read from or write to. The CONTACTS.BIN file you will find on the CD contains a few contacts I created from the Northwind sample database.

The application keeps track of the current contact through the *currentContact* variable. As you move with the navigation keys, the value of this variable is increased or decreased accordingly. When you edit a contact, the new values are stored in the Contact object that corresponds to the location indicated by the *currentContact* variable. When you add a new contact, a new Contact object is added to the current collection, and its order becomes the new value of the *currentContact* variable. Most of the project's code performs trivial tasks—hiding and showing the buttons at the bottom of the form, displaying the fields of the current contact on the TextBox control, clearing the same controls to prepare them to accept a new contact, and so on. We'll come back to this project in Chapter 11, where I'll show you how to manipulate ArrayLists. There you'll find more information about storing data in an ArrayList, as well as how to save an ArrayList to a disk file and how to load the data from the file back to the ArrayList.

HANDLING KEYSTROKES

The last topic demonstrated in this example is how to capture certain keystrokes, regardless of the control that has the focus. We'll use the F10 keystroke to display the total number of contacts entered so far. Set the form's KeyPreview property to True and then enter the following code in the form's KeyDown event:

```
If e.Keycode = keys.F10 Then
    MsgBox("There are " & Contacts.Count.ToString & " contacts in the database")
    e.Handled = True
End If
```

The form captures all the keystrokes and processes them. After it's done with them, it may allow the keystrokes to be passed to the control that has the focus. The processing is quite trivial. It compares the key pressed to the F10 key and, if F10 was pressed, it displays the number of contacts entered so far in a message box. Then, it stops the keystroke from propagating back to control with the focus by setting its Handled property to True. Listing 5.1 is the complete event handler; if you omit that statement in the listing, the F10 keystroke will be passed to the control with the focus— the control that would receive the notification about the keystroke by default, if the form's KeyPreview property was left to its default value. Of course, the key F10 isn't processed by the TextBox control, so it's not necessary to "kill" it before it reaches the control.

LISTING 5.1: HANDLING KEYSTROKES IN THE FORM'S KEYDOWN EVENT HANDLER

```
Public Sub Form1_KeyDown(ByVal sender As Object, _
            ByVal e As System.WinForms.KeyEventArgs) Handles Form1.KeyUp
    If e.Keycode = Keys.F10 Then
        MsgBox("There are " & Contacts.Count.ToString & _
            " contacts in the database")
        e.Handled = True
    End If
    If e.KeyCode = Keys.Subtract And e.Modifiers = Keys.Alt Then
        bttnPrevious_Click(sender, e)
    End If
    If e.KeyCode = Keys.Add And e.Modifiers = Keys.Alt Then
        bttnNext_Click(sender, e)
    End If
End Sub
```

The KeyDown event handler contains a little more code to capture the Alt+Plus and Alt+Minus key combinations as shortcuts for the buttons that move to the next and previous contact respectively. If the user has clicked the Plus button while holding down the Alt button, the code calls the event handler of the Next button. Likewise, pressing Alt and the Minus key activates the event handler of the Previous button.

The KeyCode property of the *e* argument returns the code of the key that was pressed. All key codes are members of the Keys enumeration, so you need not memorize them. The name of the button with the plus symbol is `Keys.Add`. The Modifiers property of the same argument returns the modifier key(s) that were held down while the key was pressed. Also, all possible values of the Modifiers property are members of the Keys enumeration and will appear in a list as soon as you type the equal sign. The name of the Alt modifier is `Keys.Alt`.

If you run the Contacts application, you'll see that it's not trivial. To add or modify a record, you must click the appropriate button, and while in edit mode, the navigational buttons disappear. The reason is that data-entry operators want to know the state of the application at each moment. With this design, you can't move to another record while editing the current one, as discussed previously.

Another interesting part of the project is the handler of the KeyPress event. This event takes place when a normal key (letter, digit, or punctuation symbol) is pressed. If the OK button is invisible at the time, it means that the user can't edit the current record and the program "chokes" the keystroke, preventing it from reaching the control that has the focus. The form's KeyPress event is handled by the subroutine shown in Listing 5.2.

LISTING 5.2: HANDLING KEYSTROKES IN THE FORM'S KEYPRESS EVENT HANDLER

```
Private Sub Form1_KeyPress(ByVal sender As Object, _
            ByVal e As System.Windows.Forms.KeyPressEventArgs) _
            Handles MyBase.KeyPress
    If bttnOK.Visible = False Then
        e.Handled = True
    End If
End Sub
```

The Contacts project contains quite a bit of code, which will be discussed in more detail in Chapter 11. It's included in this chapter to demonstrate some useful techniques for designing intuitive interfaces, and I've only discussed the sections of the application that relate to the behavior of the form and the controls on it as a group.

Anchoring and Docking

One of the most tedious tasks in designing user interfaces with Visual Basic before VB.NET was the proper arrangement of the controls on the form, especially on forms that users were allowed to resize at runtime. You design a nice form for a given size, and when it's resized at runtime, the controls are all clustered in the top-left corner. A TextBox control that covered the entire width of the form at design time suddenly "cringes" on the left when the user drags out the window. If the user makes the form smaller than the default size, part of the TextBox is invisible, because it's outside the form. You can attach scroll bars to the form, but that doesn't really help—who wants to type text and have to scroll the form horizontally? It makes sense to scroll vertically, because you get to see many lines at once, but if the TextBox control is wider than the form, you can't see an entire line.

Programmers had to be creative and resize and/or rearrange the controls on a form from within the form's Resize event. This event takes place every time the user resizes the form at runtime, and, quite often, we had to insert code in this event to resize controls so that they would continue to take up the entire form's width. You may still have to insert a few lines of code in the Resize event's handler, but a lot of the work of keeping controls aligned is no longer needed. The Anchor and Dock properties of the various controls allow you specify how they will be arranged with respect to the edges of the form when the user resizes it.

The Anchor property lets you attach one or more edges of the control to corresponding edges of the form. The anchored edges of the control maintain the same distance from the corresponding edges of the form. Place a TextBox control on a new form and then open the control's Anchor property in the Properties window. You will see a little square within a larger square, like the one in Figure 5.5, and four pegs that connect the small control to the sides of the larger box. The large box is the form, and the small one is the control. The four pegs are the anchors, which can be either white or gray. The gray anchors denote a fixed distance between the control and the form. By default, the control is placed at a fixed distance from the top-left corner of the form. When the form is resized, the control retains its size and its distance from the top-left corner of the form.

FIGURE 5.5

The settings of the Anchor property

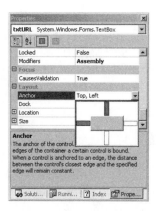

Let's say we want our control to fill the width of the form, be aligned to the top of the form, and leave some space for a few buttons at the bottom. Make the TextBox control as wide as the control (allowing, perhaps, a margin of a few pixels on either side). Then place a couple of buttons at the bottom of the form and make the TextBox control tall enough that it stops above the buttons, as shown in Figure 5.6. This is the form of the Anchor project on the CD.

FIGURE 5.6

This form is filled by three controls, regardless of the form's size at runtime.

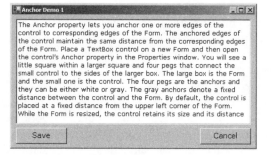

Now open the TextBox control's Anchor property and make the all four anchors gray by clicking them. This action tells the Form Designer to resize the control accordingly at runtime, so that the distances between the sides of the control and the corresponding sides of the form are the same as you've set at design time.

Resize the form at design time, without running the project. The TextBox control is resized according to the form, but the buttons remain fixed. Let's do the same for the two buttons. The two buttons must fit in the area between the TextBox control and the bottom of the form, so we must anchor them to the bottom of the form. Select both controls on the form with the mouse and then open their Anchor property. Make the anchor at the bottom gray and the other three anchors white; this will anchor the two buttons to the bottom of the form. If you resize the form now, the TextBox control will fill it, leaving just enough room for the two buttons at the bottom of the form.

We need to do something more about the buttons. They're aligned vertically, but their horizontal location doesn't change. Select the button to the left, open its Anchor property, and click the left anchor. This will anchor the button to the left side of the form—which is the default behavior anyway.

Now select the button to the right, open its Anchor property, and click the right anchor. This will anchor the second button to the right side of the control. Resize the form again and see how all controls are resized and rearranged on the form at all times. This is much better than the default behavior of the controls on the form. Figure 5.7 shows the same form in two very different sizes, with the TextBox taking up most of the space on the form and leaving room for the buttons, which in turn are repositioned horizontally as the form is resized.

FIGURE 5.7

The form of Figure 5.6 in two different sizes

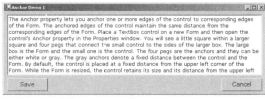

Yet, there's a small problem: if you make the form very narrow, there will be no room for both buttons across the form's width. The simplest way to fix this problem is to impose a minimum size for the form. To do so, you must first decide the form's minimum width and height and then set the MinimumSize property to these values.

In addition to the Anchor property, most controls provide the Dock property, which determines how a control will dock on the form. The default value of this property is None. Create a new form, place a TextBox control on it, and then open the control's Dock property. The various rectangular shapes are the settings of the property. If you click the middle rectangle, the control will be docked over the entire form: it will expand and shrink both horizontally and vertically to cover the entire form. This setting is appropriate for simple forms that contain a single control, usually a TextBox, and sometimes a menu. Try it out.

Let's create a more complicated form with two controls (it's the Docking project on the CD). The form shown in Figure 5.8 contains a TreeView control on the left and a ListView control on the right. The two controls display generic data, but the form has the same structure as a Windows Explorer window, with the directory structure in tree form on the left pane and the files of the selected folder on the right pane.

Place a TreeView control on the left side of the form and a ListView control on the right side of the form. Then dock the TreeView to the left and the ListView to the right. If you run the application now, then as you resize the form, the two controls remain docked to the two sides of the form, but their sizes don't change. If you make the form wider, there will be a gap between the two controls. If you make the form narrower, one of the controls will overlap the other.

End the application, return to the Form Designer, select the ListView control, and anchor the control on all four sides. This time, the ListView will change size to take up all the space to the right of the TreeView.

FIGURE 5.8

Filling a form with
two controls

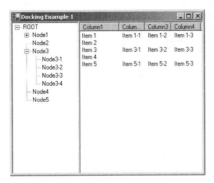

NOTE *When you anchor a control to the left side of the form, the distance between the control's left side and the form's left edge remains the same. This is the default behavior of the controls. If you dock the right side of the control to the right side of the form, then as you resize the width of the form, the control is moved so that its distance from the right side of the form remains fixed—you can even push the control out of the left edge of the form. If you anchor two opposite sides of the control (top and bottom, or left and right), then the control is resized, so that the docking distances of both sides remain the same. Finally, if you dock all four sides, the control is resized along with the form. Place a multiline TextBox control on a form and try out all possible settings of the Dock property.*

The form behaves better, but it's not what you really expect from a Windows application. The problem with the form of Figure 5.8 is that users can't change the relative widths of the controls. In other words, you can't make one of the controls narrower to make room for the other, which is a fairly common concept in the Windows interface. The narrow bar that allows users to control the relative sizes of two controls is a *splitter*. When the cursor hovers over a splitter, it changes to a double arrow to indicate that the bar can be moved. By moving the splitter, you can enlarge one of the two controls while shrinking the other.

The Form Designer provides a special control for placing a splitter between pairs of controls, and this is the Splitter control. We'll design a new form identical to that of Figure 5.8, only this time we'll place a Splitter control between them, so that users can change the relative size of the two controls. First, place a TextBox control on the form and set its Multiline property to True. You don't need to do anything about its size, because we'll dock it to the left side of the form. With the TextBox control selected, locate its Dock property and set it to Left. The TextBox control will fill the left side of the form, from top to bottom.

Then place an instance of the Splitter control on the form, by double-clicking its icon on the Toolbox. The Splitter will be placed next to the TextBox control. The Form Designer will attempt to dock the Splitter to the left side of the form. Since there's a control docked on this side of the form already, the Splitter will be docked left against the TextBox.

Now place another TextBox control on the form, to the right of the Splitter control. Set the TextBox's Multiline property to True and its Dock property to Fill. We want the second TextBox to fill all the area to the right of the Splitter. Now run the project and check out the functionality of the Splitter. Paste some text on the two controls and then change their relative size by sliding the Splitter between them, as shown in Figure 5.9. You will find this project, called Splitter1, in this chapter's folder on the CD.

FIGURE 5.9

The Splitter control lets you change the relative size of the controls on either side.

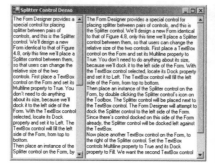
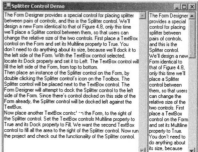

Let's design a more elaborate form with two Splitter controls, like the one shown in Figure 5.10 (it's the form of the Splitter2 project on the CD). This form is at the heart of the interface of Outlook, and it consists of a TreeView control on the left (where the folders are displayed), a ListView control (where the selected folder's items are displayed), and a TextBox control (where the selected item's details are displayed). Since we haven't discussed the ListView and TreeView controls yet, I'm using three TextBox controls. The process of designing the form is identical, regardless of the controls you put on it.

Before explaining the process in detail, let me explain how the form shown in Figure 5.10 is different from the one in Figure 5.9. The vertical Splitter allows you to change the size of the TextBox on the left; the remaining space on the form must be taken by the other two controls. A Splitter control, however, must be placed between two controls (no more, no less). By placing a Panel control on the right side of the form, we use the vertical Splitter to separate the TextBox control to the left and the Panel control to the right. The other two TextBox controls and the horizontal Splitter are arranged on the Panel as you would arrange them on a form. Let's build this form.

First, place a multiline TextBox control on the form and dock it to the right. Then place a Splitter control, which will be docked to the left by default. Since there's a control docked to the left of the form already, the Splitter control will be docked to the right side of that control. Then place a Panel control to the left of the Splitter control and set its Dock property to Fill. So far, you've done exactly what you did in the last example. If you run the application now, you'll be able to resize the two controls on the form.

Now we're going to place two TextBox controls on the Panel control, separated by a horizontal Splitter control. Place the first multiline TextBox control and dock it to the top of the Panel. Then place a Splitter control on the Panel. The Form Designer will attempt to dock it to the left of the control, so there's no point in trying to resize the Splitter control with the mouse. Just change its Dock property from Left to Top. Finally, place the third TextBox on the Panel, and set its Multiline property to True and its Dock property to Fill. The last TextBox will fill the available area of the Panel below the Splitter. Run the application, paste some text on all three TextBox controls, and then use the two Splitter controls to resize the TextBoxes any way you like. Any VB6 programmer will tell you that this is a very elaborate interface—they just can't guess how many lines of code you wrote.

So far, you've seen what the Form Designer and the Form object can do for your application. Let's switch our focus to programming forms.

FIGURE 5.10

An elaborate form with two Splitter controls.

The Form's Events

The Form object triggers several events, the most important of them being Activate, Deactivate, Closing, Resize, and Paint.

THE ACTIVATE AND DEACTIVATE EVENTS

When more than one form is displayed, the user can switch from one to the other with the mouse or by pressing Alt+Tab. Each time a form is activated, the Activate event takes place. Likewise, when a form is activated, the previously active form receives the Deactivate event.

THE CLOSING EVENT

This event is fired when the user closes the form by clicking its Close button. If the application must terminate because Windows is shutting down, the same event will be fired as well. Users don't always quit applications in an orderly manner, and a professional application should behave gracefully under all circumstances. The same code you execute in the application's Exit command must also be executed from within the Closing event as well. For example, you may display a warning if the user has unsaved data, or you may have to update a database, and so on. Place the code that performs these tasks in a subroutine and call it from within your menu's Exit command, as well as from within the Closing event's handler.

You can cancel the closing of a form by setting the **e.Cancel** property to True. The event handler in Listing 5.3 displays a message box telling the user that the data hasn't been saved and gives them a chance to cancel the action and return to the application.

LISTING 5.3: CANCELLING THE CLOSING OF A FORM

```
Public Sub Form1_Closing(ByVal sender As Object, _
            ByVal e As System.ComponentModel.CancelEventArgs) _
            Handles Form1.Closing
    Dim reply As MsgBoxResult
    reply = MsgBox("Current document has been edited. Click OK to terminate " & _
                "the application, or Cancel to return to your document.", _
                MsgBoxStyle.OKCancel)
    If reply = MsgBoxResult.Cancel Then
        e.Cancel = True
    End If
End Sub
```

THE RESIZE EVENT

The Resize event is fired every time the user resizes the form with the mouse. With previous versions of VB, programmers had to insert quite a bit of code in the Resize event's handler to resize the controls and possibly rearrange them on the form. With the Anchor and Dock properties, much of this overhead can be passed to the form itself.

Many VB applications used the Resize event to impose a minimum size for the form. To make sure that the user can't make the form smaller than, say 300 by 200 pixels, you would insert these lines into the Resize event's handler:

```
Private Form1_Resize(ByVal sender As Object, ByVal e As System.EventArgs) _
            Handles Form1.Resize
    If Me.Width < minWidth Then Me.Width = minWidth
    If Me.Height < minHeight Then Me.Height = minHeight
End Sub
```

There's a better approach to imposing a minimum form size, the MinimumSize property, discussed earlier in this chapter. If you want the two sides of the form to maintain a fixed ratio, you will have to resize one of the dimensions from within the Resize event handler. Let's say the form's width must have a ratio of 3:4 to its height. Assuming that you're using the form's height as a guide, insert the following statement in the Resize event handler to make the width equal to three fourths of the height:

```
Private Form1_Resize(ByVal sender As Object, ByVal e As System.EventArgs)
    Me.Width = (0.75 * Me.Height)
End Sub
```

You may also wish to program the Resize event to redraw the form. Normally, this action takes place from within the Paint event, which is fired every time the form must be redrawn. The Paint event, however, isn't fired when the form is reduced in size.

THE PAINT EVENT

This event takes place every time the form must be refreshed. When you switch to another form that partially or totally overlaps the current form and then switch back to the first form, the Paint event will be fired to notify your application that it must redraw the form. In this event's handler, we insert the code that draws on the form. The form will refresh its controls automatically, but any custom drawing on the form won't be refreshed automatically. We'll discuss this event in more detail in Chapter 14.

In this section, I'll show you a brief example of using the Paint event. Let's say you want to fill the background of your form with a gradient that starts with red at the top-left corner of the form and ends with yellow at the bottom-right corner, like the one in Figure 5.11. This is the form of the Gradient project, which you will find in this chapter's folder on the CD. Each time the user resizes the form, the gradient must be redrawn, because its exact coloring depends on the form's size and aspect ratio. The PaintForm() subroutine, which redraws the gradient on the form, must be called from within the Paint and Resize events.

FIGURE 5.11

Filling a form's background with a gradient

Before presenting the PaintForm() subroutine, I should briefly discuss the Graphics object. The surface on which you will draw the gradient is a Graphics object, which you can retrieve with the `Me.CreateGraphics` method. The FillRectangle method, which you'll use in this example, is one of the methods of the Graphics object, and it fills a rectangle with a gradient.

To draw on a surface, you must create a brush object (the instrument you'll draw with). One of the built-in brushes is the LinearGradientBrush, which creates a linear gradient. The following statement declares a variable to represents a brush that draws a linear gradient:

```
Dim grbrush As System.Drawing.Drawing2D.LinearGradientBrush
```

To initialize the *grbrush* variable, you must specify the properties of the gradient: its span and its starting and ending colors. One form of the Brush object's constructor is the following:

```
New Brush(origin, dimensions, starting_color, ending_color)
```

The last two arguments are the gradient's starting and ending colors, and they're obvious. The first argument is a point (a pair of x and y coordinates), while the dimensions of the gradient determine its direction and size. If the height of the gradient is zero, the gradient will be horizontal, and if the width is the same as its height, the gradient is diagonal. If the gradient's dimensions are smaller than the area you want to fill, the gradient will be repeated. To draw a red-to-yellow gradient that fills the form diagonally, the gradient's origin must be the form's top-left corner—the point $(0, 0)$—and the gradient's dimensions must be the same as the form's dimensions. The following statement creates the brush for the desired gradient:

```
grbrush = New System.Drawing.Drawing2D.LinearGradientBrush(New Point(0, 0), _
                    New Point(Me.Width, Me.Height), Color.Red, Color.Yellow)
```

Finally, the FillRectangle method will draw a filled rectangle with the specified brush. The FillRectangle method accepts as arguments the brush it will use to draw the gradient, the origin of the rectangle, and its dimensions:

```
Me.CreateGraphics.FillRectangle(grbrush, New Rectangle(0, 0, _
                                          Me.Width, Me.Height))
```

To fill a form with a gradient, enter a RepaintForm() subroutine in the form's code window, then call this subroutine from within the Form's Resize and Paint event handlers, as shown in Listing 5.4.

LISTING 5.4: REPAINTING A GRADIENT ON A FORM

```
Sub RepaintForm()
   Dim grbrush As System.Drawing.Drawing2D.LinearGradientBrush
   grbrush = New System.Drawing.Drawing2D.LinearGradientBrush(New Point(0, 0), _
            New Point(Me.width, Me.height), Color.Red, Color.Yellow)
   Me.CreateGraphics.FillRectangle(grbrush, New Rectangle(0, 0, _
            Me.Width, Me.Height))
End Sub
Public Sub Form1_Paint(ByVal sender As Object, _
              ByVal e As System.WinForms.PaintEventArgs) Handles Form1.Paint
   RepaintForm()
End Sub
Public Sub Form1_Resize(ByVal sender As Object, _
              ByVal e As System.EventArgs) Handles Form1.Resize
   RepaintForm()
End Sub
```

As mentioned earlier, the Paint event is fired every time the form must be redrawn, but not when the form is resized to smaller dimensions. Because the visible area of the form doesn't include any new regions, the Paint event isn't fired—Windows thinks there's nothing to redraw, so why fire a Paint event? The example with the gradient, however, is a special case. When the form is reduced in size, the gradient's colors must also change. They must go from red to yellow in a shorter span, which means that even though the end colors of the gradient will be the same, the actual gradient will look different. Therefore, the statements that draw the form's gradient must be executed from within the Resize event as well.

To experiment with the Paint and Resize events, comment out the call to the subroutine Repaint-Form() in one of the two event handlers at a time. Then resize the form, overlap it totally and partially by another form, and bring it to the foreground again. You will notice that unless both event handlers are executed, the form's background gradient isn't properly drawn at all times.

You can request that the Paint event is fired when the form is resized by calling the form's Set-Style method with the following arguments:

```
Me.SetStyle(ControlStyles.ResizeRedraw, True)
```

If you insert this statement in the form's Load event handler, then you need not program the Resize event. The Paint event will be fired every time the form is resized by the user. You'll read a lot about painting and drawing with VB.NET in Chapter 14. In the mean time, you can place background images on your forms by setting the BackgroundImage property.

Loading and Showing Forms

One of the operations you'll have to perform with multi-form applications is to load and manipulate forms from within other forms' code. For example, you may wish to display a second form to prompt the user for data specific to an application. You must explicitly load the second form, read the information entered by the user, and then close the form. Or, you may wish to maintain two forms open at once and let the user switch between them. The entire process isn't trivial, and it's certainly more complicated than it used to be with VB6. You have seen the basics of handling multiple forms in an application in Chapter 2; in this chapter, we'll explore this topic in depth.

To access a form from within another form, you must first create a variable that references the second form. Let's say your application has two forms, named Form1 and Form2, and that Form1 is the project's startup form. To show Form2 when an action takes place on Form1, first declare a variable that references Form2:

```
Dim frm As New Form2
```

This declaration must appear in Form1 and must be placed outside any procedure. (If you place it in a procedure's code, then every time the procedure is executed, a new reference to Form2 will be created. This means that the user can display the same form multiple times. All procedures in Form1 must see the same instance of the Form2, so that no matter how many procedures show Form2, or how many times they do it, they'll always bring up the same single instance of Form2.)

Then, to invoke Form2 from within Form1, execute the following statement:

```
frm.Show
```

This statement will bring up Form2 and usually appears in a button's or menu item's Click event handler. At this point, the two forms don't communicate with one another. However, they're both on the desktop and you can switch between them. There's no mechanism to move information from Form2 back to Form1, and neither form can access the other's controls or variables. To exchange information between two forms, use the techniques described in the section "Controlling One Form from within Another," later in this section.

The Show method opens Form2 in a modeless manner. The two forms are equal in stature on the desktop, and the user can switch between them. You can also display the second form in a modal manner, which means that users won't be able to return to the form from which they invoked it. While a modal form is open, it remains on top of the desktop and you can't move the focus to the any other form of the same application (but you can switch to another application). To open a modal form, use the statement

```
frm.ShowDialog
```

The modal form is, in effect, a dialog box, like the Open File dialog box. You must first select a file on this form and click the Open button, or click the Cancel button, to close the dialog box and return to the form from which the dialog box was invoked. Which brings us to the topic of distinguishing forms and dialog boxes.

A dialog box is simply a modal form. When we display forms as dialog boxes, we change the border of the forms to the setting FixedDialog and invoke them with the ShowDialog method. Modeless forms are more difficult to program, because the user may switch among them at any time. Not only that, but the two forms that are open at once must interact with one another. When the user acts on one of the forms, this may necessitate some changes in the other, and you'll see shortly how this is done. If the two active forms don't need to interact, display one of them as a dialog box.

When you're done with the second form, you can either close it by calling its Close method or hide it by calling its Hide method. The Close method closes the form, and its resources are no longer available to the application. The Hide method sets the Form's Visible property to False; you can still access a hidden form's controls from within your code, but the user can't interact with it. Forms that are displayed often, such as the Find and Replace dialog box of a text processing application, should be hidden, not closed. To the user, it makes no difference whether you hide or close a form. If you hide a form, however, the next time you bring it up with the Show or ShowDialog methods, its controls are in the state they were the last time. This may not be what you want, however. If not, you must reset the controls from within your code before calling the Show or ShowDialog method.

The Startup Form

A typical application has more than a single form. When an application starts, the main form is loaded. You can control which form is initially loaded by setting the startup object in the Project Properties window, shown in Figure 5.12. To open this, right-click the project's name in the Solution Explorer and select Properties. In the project's Property Pages, select the Startup Object from the drop-down list. You can also see other parameters in the same window, which are discussed elsewhere in this book.

By default, Visual Basic suggests the name of the first form it created, which is Form1. If you change the name of the form, Visual Basic will continue using the same form as startup form, with its new name.

FIGURE 5.12

In the Properties window, you can specify the form that's displayed when the application starts.

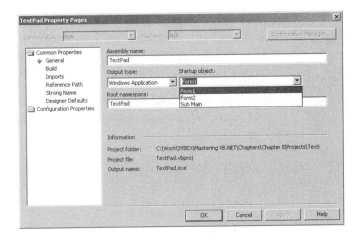

You can also start an application with a subroutine without loading a form. This subroutine must be called Main() and must be placed in a Module. Right-click the project's name in the Solution Explorer window and select the Add Item command. When the dialog box appears, select a Module. Name it StartUp (or anything you like; you can keep the default name Module1) and then insert the Main() subroutine in the module. The Main() subroutine usually contains initialization code and ends with a statement that displays one of the project's forms; to display the AuxiliaryForm object from within the Main() subroutine, use the following statements (I'm showing the entire module's code):

```
Module StartUpModule
    Sub Main()
        System.Windows.Forms.Application.Run(New AuxiliaryForm())
    End Sub
End Module
```

Then, you must open the Project Properties dialog box and specify that the project's startup object is the subroutine Main(). When you run the application, the form you specified in the Run method will be loaded.

Controlling One Form from within Another

Loading and displaying a form from within another form's code is fairly trivial. In some situations, this is all the interaction you need between forms. Each form is designed to operate independently of the others, but they can communicate via public variables (see the next section, "Private vs. Public Variables"). In most situations, however, you need to control one form from within another's code. Controlling the form means accessing its controls and setting or reading values from within another form's code.

Look at the two forms in Figure 5.13, for instance. These are forms of the TextPad application, which we are going to develop in Chapter 6. TextPad is a text editor that consists of the main form and an auxiliary form for the Find & Replace operation. All other operations on the text are performed with the commands of the menu you see on the main form. When the user wants to search for and/or replace a string, the program displays another form on which they specify the text to find, the type of search, and so on. When the user clicks one of the Find & Replace form's buttons, the corresponding code must access the text on the main form of the application and search for a word or replace a string with another. The Find & Replace dialog box not only interacts with the TextBox control on the main form, it also remains visible at all times while it's open, even if it doesn't have the focus, because its TopMost property was set to True. You'll see how this works in Chapter 6. In this chapter, we'll develop a simple example to demonstrate how you can access another form's controls.

FIGURE 5.13

The Find & Replace form acts on the contents of a control on another form.

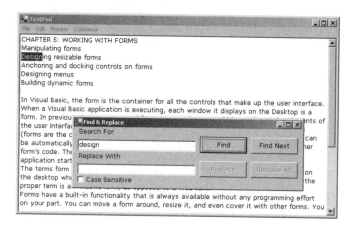

SHARING VARIABLES BETWEEN FORMS

The simplest method for two forms to communicate with each other is via *public variables*. These variables are declared in the form's declarations section, outside any procedure, with the keywords `Public Shared`. If the following declarations appear in Form1, the variable *NumPoints* and the array *DataValues* can be accessed by any procedure in Form1, as well as from within the code of any form belonging to the same project.

```
Public Shared NumPoints As Integer
Public Shared DataValues(100) As Double
```

To access a public variable declared in Form1 from within another form's code, you must prefix the variable's name by the name of the form, as in:

```
FRM.NumPoints = 99
FRM.DataValues(0) = 0.3395022
```

where *FRM* is a variable that references the form in which the public variables were declared. You can use the same notation to access the controls on the form represented by the *FRM* variable. If the form contains the TextBox1 control, you can use the following statement to read its text:

```
FRM.TextBox1.Text
```

Another technique for exposing the controls of a form to the code of the other forms of the application is to create `Public Shared` variables that represent the controls to be shared. The following declaration makes the *TBox* variable of Form1 available to all other forms in the application:

```
Public Shared TBox As TextBox
```

To make this variable represent a TextBox control, assign to it the name of the control:

```
TBox = TextBox1
```

This statement appears usually in the form's Load() subroutine, but it can appear anywhere in your code. It just has to be executed before you show another form. To access the TextBox1 control on Form1 from within another form's code, use the following expression:

```
Form1.TBox
```

This expression represents a TextBox control, and you can call any of the TextBox control's properties and methods:

```
Form1.TBox.Length                 ' returns the length of the text
Form1.TBox.Append("some text")    ' appends text
```

Keep in mind that the controls you want to access from within another form's code must be declared with as `Public Shared`, not just `Public`.

Forms vs. Dialog Boxes

Dialog boxes are special types of forms with rather limited functionality, which we use to prompt the user for data. The Open and Save dialog boxes are two of the most familiar dialog boxes in Windows. They're so common, they're actually known as *common dialog boxes*. Technically, a dialog box is a good old Form with its BorderStyle property set to FixedDialog. Like forms, dialog boxes may contain a few simple controls, such as Labels, TextBoxes, and Buttons. You can't overload a dialog box with controls and functionality, because you'll end up with a regular form.

Figure 5.14 shows a few dialog boxes you have certainly seen while working with Windows applications. The Protect Document dialog box of Word is a modal dialog box: You must close it before switching to your document. The Accept or Reject Changes dialog box is modeless, like the Find and Replace dialog box. It allows you to switch to your document, yet it remains visible while open even if it doesn't have the focus.

Notice that some dialog boxes, such as Open, Color, and even the humble MessageBox, come with the .NET Framework, and you can incorporate them in your applications without having to design them.

FIGURE 5.14

Typical dialog boxes used by Word

Another difference between forms and dialog boxes is that forms usually interact with each other. If you need to keep two windows open and allow the user to switch from one to the other, you need to implement them as regular forms. If one of them is modal, then you should implement it as a dialog box. A characteristic of dialog boxes is that they provide an OK and a Cancel button. The OK button tells the application that you're done using the dialog box and the application can process the information on it. The Cancel button tells the application that it should ignore the information on the dialog box and cancel the current operation. As you will see, dialog boxes allow you to quickly find out which button was clicked to close them, so that your application can take a different action in each case.

In short, the difference between forms and dialog boxes is artificial. If it were really important to distinguish between the two, they'd be implemented as two different objects—but they're the same object. So, without any further introduction, let's look at how to create and use dialog boxes.

To create a dialog box, start with a Windows Form, set its BorderStyle property to FixedDialog and set the ControlBox, MinimizeBox, and MaximizeBox properties to False. Then add the necessary controls on the form and code the appropriate events, as you would do with a regular Windows form. Figure 5.15 shows a simple dialog box that prompts the user for an ID and a password. The dialog box contains two TextBox controls, next to the appropriate labels, and the usual OK and Cancel buttons. The Cancel button signifies that the user wants to cancel the operation, which was initiated in the form that displayed the dialog box. The forms of Figure 5.15 are the Password project on the CD.

FIGURE 5.15

A simple dialog box that prompts users for a username and password

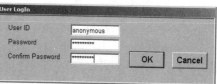

Start a new project, rename the form to MainForm, and place a button on the form. This is the application's main form, and we'll invoke the dialog box from within the button's Click event handler. Then add a new form to the project, name it PasswordForm, and place on it the controls shown in Figure 5.15.

We have the dialog box, but how do we initiate it from within another form's code? The process of displaying a dialog box is no different than displaying another form. To do so, enter the following code in the event handler from which you want to initiate the dialog box (this is the Click event handler of the main form's button):

```
Private Sub Button1_Click(ByVal sender As System.Object, _
            ByVal e As System.EventArgs) Handles Button1.Click
    Dim DLG as new PasswordForm()
    DLG.ShowDialog
End Sub
```

Here, *PasswordForm* is the name of the dialog box. The ShowDialog method displays a dialog box as modal; to display a modeless dialog box, use the Show method instead. An important distinction between modal and modeless dialog boxes has to do with the calling application. When you display a modal dialog box, the statement following the one that called the ShowDialog method is not executed. The statements from this point to the end of the event handler will be executed when the user *closes* the dialog box. Statements following the Show method, however, are executed immediately as soon as the dialog box is displayed.

You already know how to read the values entered on the controls of the dialog box. You also need to know which button was clicked to close the dialog box. To convey this information from the dialog box back to the calling application, the Form object provides the DialogResult property. This property can be set to one of the values shown in Table 5.5 to indicate what button was clicked. The `Dialog-Result.OK` value indicates that the user has clicked the OK button on the form. There's no need to place an OK button on the form; just set the form's DialogResult property to `DialogResult.OK`.

TABLE 5.5: THE DIALOGRESULT ENUMERATION

VALUE	DESCRIPTION
Abort	The dialog box was closed with the Abort button.
Cancel	The dialog box was closed with the Cancel button.
Ignore	The dialog box was closed with the Ignore button.
No	The dialog box was closed with the No button.
None	The dialog box hasn't been closed yet. Use this option to find out whether a modeless dialog box is still open.
OK	The dialog box was closed with the OK button.
Retry	The dialog box was closed with the Retry button.
Yes	The dialog box was closed with the Yes button.

The dialog box need not contain any of the buttons mentioned here. It's your responsibility to set the value of the DialogResult property from within your code to one of the settings shown in the table. This value can be retrieved by the calling application. Notice also that the action of assigning a value to the DialogResult property also closes the dialog box—you don't have to call the Close method explicitly.

Let's say your dialog box contains a button named Done, which signifies that the user is done entering values on the dialog box. The Click event handler for this button contains a single line:

```
Me.DialogResult = DialogResult.OK
```

This statement sets the DialogResult property, which will be read by the code of the form that invoked the dialog box, and also closes the dialog box. The event handler of the button that displays this dialog box should contain these lines:

```
Dim DLG as Form = new PasswordForm
If DLG.ShowDialog = DialogResult.OK Then
```

```
    { process the user selection }
End If
```

Figure 5.16 demonstrates how this is done in the Password project.

FIGURE 5.16

The code window
of the Password
project's main form

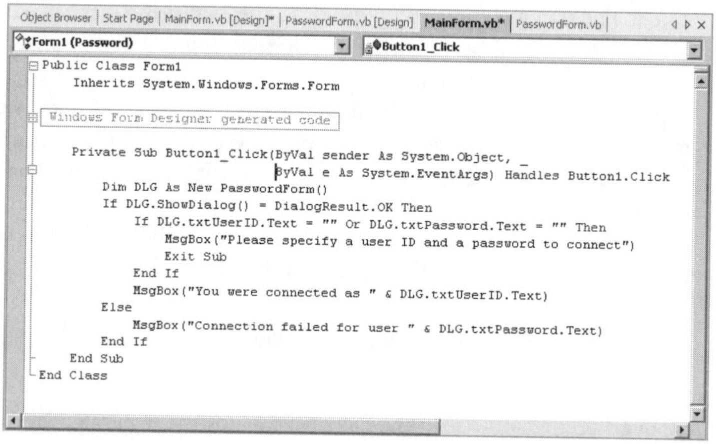

The dialog box may actually contain two buttons, one of them called Activate or Register Now and the other called Cancel or Remind Me Later. In addition, the dialog box may contain any number of buttons. You decide which buttons will close the form and enter the statement that sets the DialogResult property in their Click event handlers. The value of the DialogResult property is usually set from within two buttons—one that accepts the data and one that rejects them. Depending on your application, you may allow the user to close the dialog box by clicking more than two buttons. Some of them must set the DialogResult property to `DialogResult.OK`, others to `DialogResult.Abort`.

NOTE   *Of course, you can read the values of the controls on the dialog box anyway—it's your application and you can do whatever you wish with it. If the user has closed the dialog box with the Cancel button, however, the information is incorrect, and any results your application generates based on these values will also be incorrect.*

The DialogResult property applies to buttons as well. You can close the dialog box and pass the appropriate information to the calling application by setting the DialogResult property of a button to one of the members of the DialogResult enumeration in the Properties window. If you also set one of the buttons on the form to be the Accept button and another to be the Cancel button, you don't have to enter a single line of code in the modal form. The user can enter values on the various controls and then close the dialog box by pressing the Enter or Cancel key. The dialog box will close and will return the `DialogResult.OK` or `DialogResult.Cancel` value.

The dialog box doesn't contain a single line of code. Just make sure the Form's AcceptButton property is bttnOK, the CancelButton property is bttnCancel, and the DialogResult properties of the two buttons are OK and Cancel, respectively. The AcceptButton sets the form's DialogResult property to `DialogResult.OK` automatically, and the CancelButton sets the same property to `DialogResult.Cancel`. Any other button must set the DialogResult property explicitly. Listing 5.5 shows the code behind the Log In button on the main form.

LISTING 5.5: PROMPTING THE USER FOR AN ID AND A PASSWORD

```
Private Sub Button1_Click(ByVal sender As System.Object, _
               ByVal e As System.EventArgs) Handles Button1.Click
    Dim DLG As New PasswordForm()
    If DLG.ShowDialog() = DialogResult.OK Then
        If DLG.txtUserID.Text = "" Or DLG.txtPassword.Text = "" Then
            MsgBox("Please specify a user ID and a password to connect")
            Exit Sub
        End If
        MsgBox("You were connected as " & DLG.txtUserID.Text)
    Else
        MsgBox("Connection failed for user " & DLG.txtPassword.Text)
    End If
End Sub
```

The code of the main form reads the values of the controls on the dialog box through the *DLG* variable. If the dialog box contains many controls, it's better to communicate the data back to the calling application through properties. All you have to do is create a Property procedure for each control and then read the values entered by the user as properties. The topic of Property procedures is discussed in detail in Chapter 8, but it's nothing really complicated. To keep the complexity to a minimum, you can also implement the properties with `Public Shared` variables. Let's say that the dialog box prompts the user to select a state on a ComboBox control. To create a State property, use the following declaration:

```
Public Shared State As String
```

This variable will be exposed by the dialog box as a property, and the application that invoked the dialog box can read the value of the State property with a statement like `DLG.State`.

The value of the *State* variable must be set each time the user selects a state on the ComboBox control, from within the control's SelectedIndexChanged event handler:

```
State = cmbStates.Text
```

where *cmbStates* is the name of the ComboBox control. The user may change their mind and repeat the action of selecting a state. The most recently selected state's name will be stored in the variable *State*, because the SelectedIndexChanged event takes place every time the user makes another selection.

You can invoke the dialog box and then read the value of the *State* variable from within your code with the following statements:

```
Dim Dlg as StatesDialogBox = new StatesDialogBox
Dlg.ShowDialog
If Dlg.DialogResult = DialogResult.OK Then
    Console.WriteLine(Dlg.State)
End If
```

This is a good place to demonstrate how to design multiple interacting forms and dialog boxes with an example.

VB.NET at Work: The MultipleForms Project

It's time to write an application that puts together the most important topics discussed in this section. There's quite a bit to learn about projects with multiple forms, and this is the topic of the following sections. Most of the aspects discussed here are demonstrated in the MultipleForms project, which you will find on the CD. I suggest you follow the steps outlined in the text to build the project on your own.

The MultipleForms project consists of a main form, an auxiliary form, and a dialog box. All three components of the application's interface are shown in Figure 5.17. The buttons on the main form display both the auxiliary form and the dialog box.

FIGURE 5.17

The MultipleForms project's interface

Let's review the various operations we want to perform—they're typical for many situations, not specific to this application. At first, we must be able to invoke both the auxiliary form and the dialog box from within the main form; the Show Auxiliary Form and Show Age Form buttons do this. The main form contains a variable declaration, *strProperty*. This variable is, in effect, a property of the main form and is declared with the following statement:

```
Public Shared strProperty As String = "Mastering VB.NET"
```

The main form's code declares a variable that represents the auxiliary form and then calls its Show method to display the auxiliary form. The declaration must appear in the form's declarations section:

```
Dim FRM As New AuxiliaryForm()
```

The Show Auxiliary Form button contains a single statement, which invokes the auxiliary form by calling the Show method of the *FRM* variable.

The auxiliary-form button named Read Shared Variable In Main Form reads the *strProperty* variable of the main form with the following statement:

```
Private Sub bttnReadShared_Click(ByVal sender As System.Object, _
            ByVal e As System.EventArgs) Handles bttnReadShared.Click
```

```
    MsgBox(MainForm.strProperty, MsgBoxStyle.OKOnly, "Public Variable Value")
End Sub
```

Using the same notation, you can set this variable from within the auxiliary form. The following event handler prompts the user for a new value and assigns it to the shared variable of the main form. You can confirm that the value has changed by reading it again.

```
Private Sub bttnSetShared_Click(ByVal sender As System.Object, _
              ByVal e As System.EventArgs) Handles bttnSetShared.Click
    Dim str As String
    str = InputBox("Enter a new value for strProperty")
    MainForm.strProperty = str
End Sub
```

The two forms communicate with each other through public variables. Let's make this communication a little more elaborate by adding an event. Every time the auxiliary form sets the value of the *strProperty* variable, it will raise an event to notify the main form. The main form, in turn, will use this event to display the new value of the string on the TextBox control as soon as the code in the auxiliary form changes the value of the variable and before it's closed.

To raise an event, you must declare the event's name in the form's declaration section. Insert the following statement in the auxiliary form's declarations section:

```
Event strPropertyChanged()
```

Now add a statement that fires the event. To raise an event, we call the RaiseEvent statement passing the name of the event as argument. This statement must appear in the Click event handler of the Set Shared Variable In Main Form button, right after setting the value of the shared variable. Listing 5.6 shows the revised event handler.

LISTING 5.6: RAISING AN EVENT

```
Private Sub bttnSetShared_Click(ByVal sender As System.Object, _
              ByVal e As System.EventArgs) Handles bttnSetShared.Click
    Dim str As String
    str = InputBox("Enter a new value for strProperty")
    MainForm.strProperty = str
    RaiseEvent strPropertyChanged
End Sub
```

The event will be raised, but it will go unnoticed if we don't handle it from within the main form's code. To handle the event, you must change the declaration of the *FRM* variable from

```
Dim FRM As New AuxiliaryForm()
```

to

```
Dim WithEvents FRM As New AuxiliaryForm()
```

The WithEvents keyword tells VB that the variable is capable of raising events. If you expand the drop-down list with the objects in the code editor, you will see the name of the *FRM* variable, along with the other controls you can program. Select *FRM* in the list and then expand the list of events for the selected item. In this list, you will see the strPropertyChanged event. Select it, and the definition of an event handler will appear. Enter these statements in this event's handler:

```
Private Sub FRM_strPropertyChanged() Handles FRM.strPropertyChanged
    TextBox1.Text = strProperty
    Beep()
End Sub
```

It's a very simple handler, but it's adequate for demonstrating how to raise and handle custom events. If you run the application now, you'll see that the value of the TextBox control changes as soon as you change the value in the auxiliary form.

Of course, you can update the TextBox control on the main form directly from within the auxiliary form's code. Use the expression MainForm.TextBox1 to access the control and then manipulate it as usual. Events are used when we want to perform some actions on a form when an action takes place in one of the other forms of the application.

Let's see now how the main form interacts with the dialog box. What goes on between a form and a dialog box is not exactly "interaction"—it's a more timid type of behavior. The form displays the dialog box and then waits until the user closes the dialog box. Then, it looks at the value of the DialogResult property to find out whether it should even examine the values passed back by the dialog box. If the user has closed the dialog box with the Cancel (or an equivalent) button, the application ignores the dialog box settings. If the user closed the dialog box with the OK button, the application reads the values and proceeds accordingly.

Before showing the dialog box, the code of the Show Dialog Box button sets the values of certain controls on it. In the course of the application, it usually makes sense to suggest a few values on the dialog box, so that the user can accept the default values. The main form selects a date on the controls that display the date, and then displays the dialog box with the statements given in Listing 5.7.

LISTING 5.7: DISPLAYING A DIALOG BOX AND READING ITS VALUES

```
Protected Sub Button3_Click(ByVal sender As Object, _
                ByVal e As System.EventArgs)
' Preselects the date 4/11/1980
    DLG.cmbMonth.Text = "4"
    DLG.cmbDay.Text = "11"
    DLG.CmbYear.Text = "1980"
    DLG.ShowDialog()
    If DLG.DialogResult = DialogResult.OK Then
        MsgBox(DLG.cmbMonth.Text & " " & DLG.cmbDay.Text & ", " & _
            DLG.cmbYear.Text)
    Else
        MsgBox("OK, we'll protect your vital personal data")
    End If
End Sub
```

The *DLG* variable is declared on the Form level with the following statement:

```
Dim DLG As New AgeDialog()
```

The dialog box is modal: you can't switch to the main form while the dialog box is displayed. To close the dialog box, you can click one of the OK or Cancel buttons. Each button sets the Dialog-Result property to indicate the action that closed the dialog box. The code behind the two buttons is shown in Listing 5.8.

LISTING 5.8: SETTING THE DIALOG BOX'S DIALOGRESULT PROPERTY

```
Protected Sub bttnOK_Click(ByVal sender As Object, ByVal e As System.EventArgs)
    Me.DialogResult = DialogResult.OK
End Sub
Protected Sub bttnCancel_Click(ByVal sender As Object, _
                               ByVal e As System.EventArgs)
    Me.DialogResult = DialogResult.Cancel
End Sub
```

Since the dialog box is modal, the code in the Show Dialog Box button is suspended at the line that shows the dialog box. As soon as the dialog box is closed, the code in the main form resumes with the statement following the one that called the ShowDialog method of the dialog box. This is the If statement in Listing 5.7 that examines the value of the DialogResult property and acts accordingly.

Designing Menus

Menus are one of the most common and characteristic elements of the Windows user interface. Even in the old days of character-based displays, menus were used to display methodically organized choices and guide the user through an application. Despite the visually rich interfaces of Windows applications and the many alternatives, menus are still the most popular means of organizing a large number of options. Many applications duplicate some or all of their menus in the form of toolbar icons, but the menu is a standard fixture of a form. You can turn the toolbars on and off, but not the menus.

The Menu Editor

Menus can be attached only to forms, and they're implemented through the MainMenu control. The items that make up the menu are MenuItem objects. As you will see, the MainMenu control and MenuItem objects give you absolute control over the structure and appearance of the menus of your application.

The IDE provides a visual tool for designing menus, and then you can program their Click event handlers. In principle, that's all there is to a menu: you design it, then you program each command's actions. Depending on the needs of your application, you may wish to enable and disable certain commands, add context menus to some of the controls on your form, and so on. Because each item (command) in a menu is represented by a MenuItem object, you can control the application's menus from within your code by manipulating the properties of the MenuItem objects. Let's start by designing a simple menu, and I'll show you how to manipulate the menu objects from within your code we go along.

Double-click the MainMenu icon on the Toolbox. The MainMenu control will be added to the form, and a single menu command will appear on your form. Its caption will be Type Here. If you don't see the first menu item on the Form right away, select the MainMenu control in the Components tray below the form. Do as the caption says; click it and enter the first command's caption, **File**, as seen in Figure 5.18. As soon as you start typing, two more captions appear: one on the same level (the second command of the form's main menu, representing the second pull-down menu) and another one below File (representing the first command on the File menu). Select the item under File and enter the string **New**.

FIGURE 5.18

As soon as you start entering the caption of a menu or menu item, more items appear to the left and below the current item.

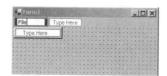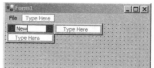

Enter the remaining items of the File menu—**Open**, **Save**, and **Exit**—and then click somewhere on the form. All the temporary items (the ones with the Type Here caption) will disappear, and the menu will be finalized on the form. At any point, you can add more items by right-clicking one of the existing menu items and selecting Insert New.

To add the Edit menu, select the MainMenu icon to activate the visual menu editor and then click the File item. In the new item that appears next to that, enter the string **Edit**. Press Enter and you'll switch to the first item of the Edit menu. Fill the Edit menu with the commands shown in Figure 5.19. Table 5.6 shows the captions (property Text) and names (property Name) for each menu and each command.

FIGURE 5.19

Type these standard commands on the Edit menu.

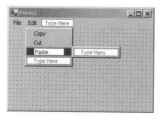

The left-most items in Table 5.6 are the names of the first-level menus (File and Edit); the captions that are indented in the table are the commands on these two menus. Each menu item has a name, which allows you to access the properties of the menu item from within your code. The same name is also used in naming the Click event handler of the item. The default names of the menu items you add visually to the application's menu are MenuItem1, MenuItem2, and so on. To change the default names to something more meaningful, you can change the Name property in the Properties window. To view the properties of a menu item, select it with the left mouse button, then right-click it and select Properties from the context menu.

TABLE 5.6: THE CAPTIONS AND NAMES OF THE FILE AND EDIT MENUS

CAPTION	NAME
File	FileMenu
New	FileNew
Open	FileOpen
Save	FileSave
Exit	FileExit
Edit	EditMenu
Copy	EditCopy
Cut	EditCut
Paste	EditPaste

Alternatively, you can select Edit Names from the context menu. This action lets you edit the names of the menu items right on the menu structure, as if you were changing the captions. The captions appear next to the names of the items, but you can only edit the names. Figure 5.20 shows a menu structure in name-editing mode. When you're done renaming the items, right-click somewhere on the menu and select the Edit Names command again. The check mark next to the Edit Names option will clear, and you'll be switched back to editing the captions.

FIGURE 5.20

Editing the names of the items in your menu

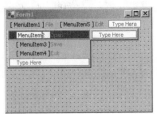

To create a separator bar in a menu, right-click the item you want to display *below* the separator and select Insert Separator. Separator bars divide menu items into logical groups, and even though they have the structure of regular menu commands, they don't react to the mouse click. You can also create a separator bar by setting the item's caption to a dash (-).

As you will notice, the menus expand by default to the bottom and to the right. To insert a menu command to the left of an existing command, or to insert a menu item above an existing menu item, right-click the item *following* the one you want to insert and select Insert New.

The MenuItem Object's Properties

The MenuItem object represents a menu command, at any level. If a command leads to a submenu, it's still represented by a MenuItem object, which has its own collection of MenuItem objects. Each individual command is represented by a MenuItem object. The MenuItem object provides the following properties, which you can set in the Properties window at design time or manipulate from within your code:

Checked   Some menu commands act as toggles, and they are usually checked to indicate that they are on or unchecked to indicate that they are off. To initially display a check mark next to a menu command, right-click the menu item, select Properties, and check the Checked box in its Properties window. You can also access this property from within your code to change the checked status of a menu command at runtime. For example, to toggle the status of a menu command called FntBold, use the statement:

```
FntBold.Checked = Not FntBold.Checked
```

DefaultItem   This property is a True/False value that indicates whether the MenuItem is the default item in a submenu. The default item is displayed in bold and is automatically activated when the user double-clicks a menu that contains it.

Enabled   Some menu commands aren't always available. The Paste command, for example, has no meaning if the Clipboard is empty (or if it contains data that can't be pasted in the current application). To indicate that a command can't be used at the time, you set its Enabled property to False. The command then appears grayed in the menu, and although it can be highlighted, it can't be activated. The following statements enable and disable the Undo command depending on whether the TextBox1 control can undo the most recent operation.

```
If TextBox1.CanUndo Then
    cmdUndo.Enabled = True
Else
    cmdUndo.Enabled = False
End If
```

cmdUndo is the name of the Undo command in the application's Edit menu. The CanUndo property of the TextBox control returns a True/False value indicating whether the last action can be undone or not.

IsParent   If the menu command, represented by a MenuItem object, leads to a submenu, then that MenuItems object's IsParent property is True. Otherwise, it's False. The IsParent property is read-only.

Mnemonic   This read-only property returns the character that was assigned as an access key to the specific menu item. If no access key is associated with a MenuItem, the character 0 will be returned.

Visible   To remove a command temporarily from the menu, set the command's Visible property to False. The Visible property isn't used frequently in menu design. In general, you should prefer to disable a command to indicate that it can't be used at the time (some other action is required to enable it). Making a command invisible frustrates users, who may try to locate the command in another menu.

MDIList   This property is used with Multiple Document Interface (MDI) applications to maintain a list of all open windows. The MDIList property is explained in Chapter 19.

PROGRAMMING MENU COMMANDS

Menu commands are similar to controls. They have certain properties that you can manipulate from within your code, and they trigger a Click event when they're clicked with the mouse or selected with the Enter key. If you double-click a menu command at design time, Visual Basic opens the code for the Click event in the code window. The name of the event handler for the Click event is composed of the command's name followed by an underscore character and the event's name, as with all other controls.

To program a menu item, insert the appropriate code in the MenuItem's Click event handler. A related event is the Select event, which is fired when the cursor is placed over a menu item, even if it's not clicked. The Exit command's code would be something like:

```
Sub menuExit(ByVal sender As Object, ByVal e As System.EventArgs) _
            Handles menuExit.Click
    End
End Sub
```

If you need to execute any clean-up code before the application ends, place it in the CleanUp() subroutine and call this subroutine from within the Exit item's Click event handler:

```
Sub menuExit(ByVal sender As Object, ByVal e As System.EventArgs) _
            Handles menuExit.Click
    CleanUp()
    End
End Sub
```

The same subroutine must also be called from within the Closing event handler of the application's main form, as some users might terminate the application by clicking the form's Close button.

An application's Open menu command contains the code that prompts the user to select a file and then open it. You will see many examples of programming menu commands in the following chapters. All you really need to know is that each menu item is a MenuItem object, and it fires the Click event every time it's selected with the mouse or the keyboard. In most cases, you can treat the Click event handler of a MenuItem object just like the Click event handler of a Button.

You can also program multiple menu items with a single event handler. Let's say you have a Zoom menu that allows the user to select one of several zoom factors. Instead of inserting the same statements in each menu item's Click event handler, you can program all the items of the Zoom menu with a single event handler. Select all the items that share the same event handler (click them with the mouse while holding down the Shift button). Then click the Event button on the Properties window and select the event that you want to be common for all selected items.

The handler of the Click event of a menu item has the following declaration:

```
Private Sub Zoom200_Click(ByVal sender As System.Object, _
            ByVal e As System.EventArgs) Handles Zoom200.Click
End Sub
```

This subroutine handles the menu item 200%, which magnifies an image by 200%. Let's say the same menu contains the options 100%, 75%, 50%, and 25%, and that the names of these commands are Zoom100, Zoom75, and so on. The common handler for their Click event will have the following declaration:

```
Private Sub Zoom200_Click(ByVal sender As System.Object, _
            ByVal e As System.EventArgs) Handles Zoom200.Click, _
            Zoom100.Click, Zoom75.Click, Zoom50.Click, Zoom25.Click
End Sub
```

The common event handler wouldn't do you any good, unless you could figure out which item was clicked from within the handler's code. This information is in the event's *sender* argument. Convert this argument to the MenuItem type, then look up all the properties of the MenuItem object that received the event. The following statement will print the name of the menu item that was clicked (if it appears in a common event handler):

```
Console.WriteLine(CType(sender, MenuItem).Text)
```

When you program multiple menu items with a single event handler, set up a `Select Case` statement based on the caption of the selected menu item, like the following:

```
Select Case sender.Text
    Case "Zoom In"
        { statements to process Zoom In command }
    Case "Zoom Out"
        { statements to process Zoom Out command }
    Case "Fit"
        { statements to process Fit command }
End Select
```

It's also common to manipulate the MenuItem's properties from within its Click event handler. These properties are the same properties you set at design time, through the Menu Editor window. Menu commands don't have methods you can call. Most menu object properties are toggles. To change the Checked property of the FontBold command, for instance, use the following statement:

```
FontBold.Checked = Not FontBold.Checked
```

If the command is checked, the check mark will be removed. If the command is unchecked, the check mark will be inserted in front of its name. You can also change the command's caption at runtime, although this practice isn't common. The Text property is manipulated only when you create dynamic menus, as you will see in the section "Adding and Removing Commands at Runtime." You can change the caption of simple commands such as Show Tools and Hide Tools. These two captions are mutually exclusive, and it makes sense to implement them with a single command. The code behind this MenuItem examines the caption of the command, performs the necessary operations, and then changes the caption to reflect the new state of the application:

```
If ShowMenu.Text = "Show Tools" Then
    { code to show the toolbar }
    ShowMenu.Text = "Hide Tools"
Else
    { code to hide the toolbar }
    ShowMenu.Text = "Show Tools"
End If
```

USING ACCESS AND SHORTCUT KEYS

Menus are a convenient way of displaying a large number of choices to the user. They allow you to organize commands in groups, according to their function, and are available at all times. Opening menus and selecting commands with the mouse, however, can be an inconvenience. When using a word processor, for example, you don't want to have to take your hands off the keyboard and reach for the mouse. To simplify menu access, Visual Basic supports access keys and shortcut keys.

Access Keys

Access keys allow the user to open a menu by pressing the Alt key and a letter key. To open the Edit menu in all Windows applications, for example, you can press Alt+E. E is the Edit menu's *access key*.

Once the menu is open, the user can select a command with the arrow keys or by pressing another key, which is the command's access key. Once a menu is open, the Alt key isn't needed. For example, with the Edit menu open, you can press P to invoke the Paste command or C to copy the selected text.

Access keys are designated by the designer of the application, and they are marked with an underline character. The underline under the character E in the Edit menu denotes that E is the menu's access key and that the keystroke Alt+E opens the Edit command. To assign an access key, insert the ampersand symbol (&) in front of the character you want to use as access key in the MenuItem's Text property.

NOTE *If you don't designate access keys, Visual Basic will use the first character in each top-level menu as its access key. The user won't see the underline character under the first character, but will be able to open the menu by pressing the first character of its caption while holding down the Alt key. If two or more menu captions begin with the same letter, the first (left-most and top-most) menu will open.*

Because the & symbol has a special meaning in menu design, you can't use it as is. To actually display the & symbol in a caption, prefix it with another & symbol. For example, the caption &Drag produces a command with the caption <u>D</u>rag (the first character is underlined because it's the access key). The caption Drag && Drop will create another command whose caption will be Drag & Drop. Finally, the string &Drag && Drop will create another command with the caption <u>D</u>rag & Drop.

Shortcut Keys

Shortcut keys are similar to access keys, but instead of opening a menu, they run a command when pressed. Assign shortcut keys to frequently used menu commands, so that users can reach them with a single keystroke. Shortcut keys are combinations of the Ctrl key and a function or character key. For example, the usual *access* key for the Close command (once the File menu is opened with Alt+F) is C; but the usual *shortcut* key for the Close command is Ctrl+W.

To assign a shortcut key to a menu command, drop down the Shortcut list in the MenuItem's Properties window and select a keystroke. You don't have to insert any special characters in the command's caption, nor do you have to enter the keystroke next to the caption. It will be displayed next to the command automatically. To view the possible keystrokes you can use as shortcuts, select a MenuItem in the Form Designer and expand the drop-down list of the Shortcut property in the Properties window.

TIP *When assigning access and shortcut keys, take into consideration well-established Windows standards. Users expect Alt+F to open the File menu, so don't use Alt+F for the Format menu. Likewise, pressing Ctrl+C universally performs the Copy command; don't use Ctrl+C as a shortcut for the Cut command.*

Manipulating Menus at Runtime

Dynamic menus change at runtime to display more or fewer commands, depending on the current status of the program. This section explores two techniques for implementing dynamic menus:

◆ Creating short and long versions of the same menu

◆ Adding and removing menu commands at runtime

Once the menu is in place and you have named all the items—you can use the default names, but this makes the code harder to read—you can program them by setting their properties from within your code. Each item in the menu is represented by a MenuItem object, which you program as usual.

CREATING SHORT AND LONG MENUS

A common technique in menu design is to create long and short versions of a menu. If a menu contains many commands, and most of the time only a few of them are needed, you can create one menu with all the commands and another with the most common ones. The first menu is the long one, and the second is the short one. The last command in the long menu should be Short Menu, and when selected, it should display the short version. The last command in the short menu should be Long Menu, and it should display the long version. Figure 5.21 shows a long and a short version of the same menu (from the LongMenu project, which you will find on the CD). The short version omits infrequently used commands and is easier to handle.

FIGURE 5.21

The two versions of the Font menu of the LongMenu application

To implement the LongMenu command, start a new project and create a menu that has the structure shown in Table 5.7. Listing 5.9 is the code that shows/hides the long menu in the MenuSize command's Click event.

TABLE 5.7: LONGMENU COMMAND STRUCTURE

COMMAND NAME	CAPTION
FontMenu	Font
mFontBold	Bold
mFontItalic	Italic

Continued on next page

TABLE 5.7: LONGMENU COMMAND STRUCTURE *(continued)*

COMMAND NAME	CAPTION
mFontRegular	Regular
mFontUnderline	Underline
mFontStrike	Strike
mFontSmallCaps	SmallCaps
mFontAllCaps	AllCaps
Separator	- (hyphen)
MenuSize	Short Menu

LISTING 5.9: THE MENUSIZE MENU ITEM'S CLICK EVENT

```
Protected Sub menuSize_Click(ByVal sender As Object, _
                ByVal e As System.EventArgs)
    If MenuSize.text = "Short Menu" Then
        MenuSize.text = "Long Menu"
    Else
        MenuSize.text = "Short Menu"
    End If
    mFontUnderline.Visible = Not mFontUnderline.Visible
    mFontStrike.Visible = Not mFontStrike.Visible
    mFontSmallCaps.Visible = Not mFontSmallCaps.Visible
    mFontAllCaps.Visible = Not mFontAllCaps.Visible
End Sub
```

The subroutine in Listing 5.9 doesn't do much. It simply toggles the Visible property of certain menu commands and changes the command's caption to Short Menu or Long Menu, depending on the menu's current status. Notice that because the Visible property is a True/False value, we don't care about its current status; we simply toggle the current status with the Not operator.

ADDING AND REMOVING COMMANDS AT RUNTIME

We'll conclude our discussion of menu design with a technique for building dynamic menus, which grow and shrink at runtime. Many applications maintain a list of the most recently opened files in their File menu. When you first start the application, this list is empty, and as you open and close files, it starts to grow.

The RunTimeMenu project demonstrates how to add items to and remove items from a menu at runtime. The main menu of the application's form contains the Run Time Menu submenu, which is initially empty.

The two buttons on the form add commands to and remove commands from the Run Time Menu. Each new command is appended at the end of the menu, and the commands are removed from the bottom of the menu first (the most recently added commands). To change this order, and display the most recent command at the beginning of the menu, use a large initial index value (like 99) and increase it with every new command you add to the menu. Listing 5.10 shows the code behind the two buttons that add and remove menu items.

LISTING 5.10: ADDING AND REMOVING MENUITEMS AT RUNTIME

```
Protected Sub bttnRemoveOption_Click(ByVal sender As Object, _
                ByVal e As System.EventArgs)
    If RunTimeMenu.MenuItems.Count > 0 Then
        RunTimeMenu.MenuItems.Remove(RunTimeMenu.MenuItems.count - 1)
    End If
End Sub
Protected Sub bttnAddOption_Click(ByVal sender As Object, _
                ByVal e As System.EventArgs)
    RunTimeMenu.MenuItems.Add("Run Time Option " & _
                RunTimeMenu.MenuItems.Count.toString, _
                New EventHandler(AddressOf Me.OptionClick))
End Sub
```

The Remove button's code uses the Remove method to remove the last item in the menu by its index, after making sure the menu contains at least one item. The Add button adds a new item, sets its caption to "Run Time Option *n*", where *n* is the item's order in the menu. In addition, it assigns an event handler to the new item's Click event. This event handler is the same for all the items added at runtime; it's the OptionClick() subroutine.

Adding menu items with the simpler forms of the Add method is trivial. The new menu items, however, would be quite useless unless there was a way to program them as well. The code uses the following form of the Add method, which accepts two arguments: the caption of the item and an event handler:

```
Menu.MenuItems.Add(caption, event_handler)
```

The event handler is the address of a subroutine, which will be invoked when the corresponding menu item is clicked, and it's specified as a New EventHandler object. The AddressOf operator passes the address of the OptionClick() subroutine to the new menu item, so that it knows which subroutine to execute when it's clicked.

As you can understand, all the runtime options invoke the same event handler—it would be quite cumbersome to come up with a separate event handlers for different items. In the single event handler, you can examine the name of the MenuItem object that invoked the event handler and act accordingly. The OptionClick() subroutine used in this example (Listing 5.11) displays the name of the menu item that invoked it. It doesn't do anything, but it shows you how to figure out the item of the Run Time Menu that was clicked:

LISTING 5.11: PROGRAMMING DYNAMIC MENU ITEMS

```
Private Sub OptionClick(ByVal sender As Object, ByVal e As EventArgs)
    Dim itemClicked As New MenuItem()
    itemClicked = CType(sender, MenuItem)
    Console.WriteLine("You have selected the item " & itemClicked.Text)
End Sub
```

CREATING CONTEXT MENUS

Nearly every Windows application provides a *context menu* that the user can invoke by right-clicking a form or a control. (It's sometimes called a *shortcut menu* or *pop-up menu*.) This is a regular menu, but it's not anchored on the form. It can be displayed anywhere on the form or on specific controls. Different controls can have different context menus, depending on the operations you can perform on them at the time.

To create a context menu, place a ContextMenu control on your form. The new context menu will appear on the form just like a regular menu, but it won't be displayed there at runtime. You can create as many context menus as you need by placing multiple instances of the ContextMenu control on your form and adding the appropriate commands to each one. To associate a context menu with a control on your form, set the *control's* ContextMenu property to the name of the corresponding context menu.

Designing a context menu is identical to designing a MainMenu. The only difference is that the first command in the menu is actually the context menu's name, and it's not displayed along with the menu. Figure 5.22 shows a context menu at design time and how the same menu is displayed at runtime. Context Menu is the menu's name, not a menu item.

FIGURE 5.22

A context menu, (left) at design time and (right) at runtime

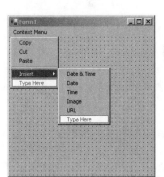
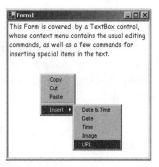

You can create as many context menus as you wish on a form. Each control has a ContextMenu property, which you can set to any of the existing ContextMenu controls. Select the control for which you want to specify a context menu and, in the Properties window, locate the ContextMenu property. Expand the drop-down list and select the name of the desired context menu.

To edit one of the context menus on a form, select the appropriate ContextMenu control at the bottom of the Designer. The corresponding context menu will appear on the form's menu bar, as if it were a regular form menu. This is temporary, however, and the only menu that will appears on the form's menu bar at runtime is the one that corresponds to the MainMenu control (and there can be only one of those on each form).

You can also merge two menus to create a new one that combines their items. This technique is used with MDI forms, where we want to add the commands of the child form to the parent form. For more information on the Merge method, see Chapter 19.

Iterating a Menu's Items

The last menu-related topic in this chapter demonstrates how to iterate through all the items of a menu structure, including their submenus at any depth. The main menu of an application can be accessed by the expression `Me.Menu`. This is a reference to the top-level commands of the menu, which appear in the form's menu bar. Each command, in turn, is represented by a MenuItem object. All the MenuItems under a menu command form a MenuItems collection, which you can scan and retrieve the individual commands.

The first command in a menu is accessed with the expression `Me.Menu.MenuItems(0)`; this is the File command in a typical application. The expression `Me.Menu.MenuItems(1)` is the second command on the same level as the File command (typically, the Edit menu).

To access the items *under* the first menu, use the MenuItems collection of the top command. The first command in the File menu can be accessed by the expression

```
Me.Menu.MenuItems(0).MenuItems(0)
```

The same items can be accessed by name as well, and this is how you should manipulate the menu items from within your code. In unusual situations, or if you're using dynamic menus to which you add and subtract commands at runtime, you'll have to access the menu items through the Menu-Items collection.

VB.NET AT WORK: THE MAPMENU PROJECT

The MapMenu project demonstrates how to access the items of a menu from within your application's code. The project's main form, shown in Figure 5.23, contains a menu, a TextBox control, and a Button that prints the menu's structure on the TextBox. You can edit the menu before running the program, and the code behind the Button will print the structure of the menu items without any modifications.

FIGURE 5.23

The MapMenu application

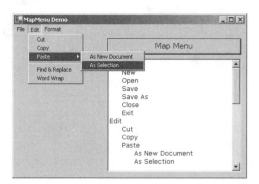

The code behind the Map Menu button (Listing 5.12) iterates through the items of a Main-Menu object and prints all the commands in the Output window. It scans all the items of the menu's MenuItems collection and prints their captions. After printing each command's caption, it calls the PrintSubMenu() subroutine, passing the current MenuItem as argument. The PrintSubMenu() sub-routine iterates through the items of the collection passed as argument and prints their captions.

LISTING 5.12: PRINTING THE TOP-LEVEL COMMANDS OF A MENU

```
Protected Sub MapMenu_Click(ByVal sender As Object, ByVal e As System.EventArgs)
    Dim itm As MenuItem
    For Each itm In Me.Menu.MenuItems
        Console.WriteLine(itm.Text)
        PrintSubMenu(itm)
    Next
End Sub
```

The PrintSubMenu() subroutine, shown in Listing 5.13, goes through the MenuItems collection of the MenuItem object passed to it as argument and prints the captions of the submenu it repre-sents. At each iteration, it examines the value of the property itm.MenuItems.Count. This is the num-ber of commands under the current menu items. If it's a positive value, the current item leads to a submenu. To print the submenu's items, it calls itself, passing the *itm* object as argument. This simple technique scans all the submenus, at any depth. The PrintSubMenu() subroutine is a recur-sive routine, because it calls itself.

LISTING 5.13: PRINTING SUBMENU ITEMS

```
Sub PrintSubMenu(ByVal MItem As MenuItem)
    Dim itm As New MenuItem()
    For Each itm In MItem.MenuItems
        Console.WriteLine(itm.Text)
        If itm.MenuItems.Count > 0 Then PrintSubMenu(itm)
    Next
End Sub
```

TIP   *There's a tutorial on coding recursive routines in Chapter 18 of this book, and you will find more examples of recur-sive routines in the course of the book. If you're totally unfamiliar with recursive routines, you can come back and exam-ine the code more carefully after reading this chapter.*

Open the MapMenu application, edit the menu on its form, run the project, and click the Map Menu Structure button. The few lines of the PrintSubMenu() subroutine will iterate through all the items in the form's menu and submenus, at any depth.

Building Dynamic Forms at Runtime

There are situations when you won't know in advance how many instances of a given control may be required on a form. This isn't very common, but if you're writing a data-entry application and you want to work with many tables of a database, you'll have to be especially creative. Since every table consists of different fields, it will be difficult to build a single form to accommodate all the possible tables a user may throw at your application.

Another good reason for adding or removing controls at runtime is to enable certain features of your application, depending on the current state or the user's privileges. For these situations, it is possible to design *dynamic forms*, which are populated at runtime. The simplest approach is to create more controls than you'll ever need and set their Visible property to False at design time. At runtime, you can display the controls by switching their Visible property to True. As you know already, quick-and-dirty methods are not the most efficient ones. You must still rearrange the controls on the form to make it look nice at all times. The proper method to create dynamic forms at runtime is to add and remove controls with the techniques discussed in this section.

Just as you can create new instances of forms, you can also create new instances of any control and place them on a form. The Form object exposes the Controls collection, which contains all the controls on the form. This collection is created automatically as you place controls on the form at design time, and you can access the members of this collection from within your code. It is also possible to add new members to the collection, or remove existing members, with the Add and Remove statements accordingly.

VB6 ➠ VB.NET

VB.NET doesn't support arrays of controls, which used to be the simplest method of adding new controls on a form at runtime. With VB.NET, you must create a new instance of a control, set its properties, and then place it on the form by adding it to the form's Controls collection.

The Form.Controls Collection

To understand how to create controls at runtime and place them on a form, you must first learn about the Controls collection. All the controls on a form are members of the Controls property, which is a collection. The Controls collection exposes members for accessing and manipulating the controls at runtime, and these members are:

Add method   Adds a new element to the Controls collection. In effect, it adds a new control on the current form. The Add method accepts a control as argument and adds it to the collection. Its syntax is:

```
Controls.Add(controlObj)
```

where *controlObj* is an instance of a control. To place a new Button control on the form, declare a variable of the Button type, set its properties, and then add it to the Controls collection:

```
Dim bttn As New System.WinForms.Button
```

```
bttn.Text = "New Button"
bttn.Left = 100
bttn.Top = 60
bttn.Width = 80
Me.Controls.Add(bttn)
```

Remove method   Removes an element from the Controls collection. It accepts as argument either the index of the control to be removed, or a reference to the control to be removed (a variable of the Control type that represents one of the controls on the form). The syntax of these two forms is:

```
Me.Controls.Remove(index)
Me.Controls.Remove(controlObj)
```

Count property   Returns the number of elements in the Controls collection. The number of controls on the current form is given by the expression `Me.Controls.Count`. Notice that if there are container controls, the controls in the containers are not included in the count. For example, if your form contains a Panel control, the controls on the panel won't be included in the value returned by the Count property.

All method   Returns all the controls on a form (or in a container control) as an array of the `System.WinForms.Control` type. You can iterate through the elements of this array with the usual methods exposed by the Array class.

Clear method   Removes all the elements of the Controls array.

The Controls collection is also a property of any control that can host other controls. Most of the controls that come with VB.NET can host other controls. The Panel control, for example, is a container for other controls. As you recall from our discussion of the Anchor and Dock properties, it's customary to place controls on a panel and handle them collectively, as a section of the form. They are moved along with the panel at design time, and they're rearranged as a group at runtime. The panel belongs to the form's Controls collection. The element that corresponds to the Panel control provides its own Controls collection, which lets you access the controls on the panel.

If a panel is the third element of the Controls collection, you can access it with the expression `Me.Controls(2)`. To access the controls *on* this panel, use the following Controls collection:

```
Me.Controls(2).Controls
```

VB.NET AT WORK: THE SHOWCONTROLS PROJECT

The ShowControls project (Figure 5.24) demonstrates the basic methods of the Controls array. Open the project and add any number of controls on its main form. You can place a panel to act as a container for other controls as well. Just don't remove the button at the top of the form (the Scan Controls On This Form button), which contains the code to list all the controls.

The code behind the Scan Controls On This Form button enumerates the elements of the form's Controls collection. The code doesn't take into consideration containers within containers. This would require a *recursive* routine, which would scan for controls at any depth. You will read a lot about recursive routines in this book and you will find a tutorial on the topic in Chapter 18. After you're familiar with recursion (if you aren't already), you can revisit this project and adjust its code accordingly. The code that iterates through the form's Controls collection and prints the names of the controls in the Output window is shown in Listing 5.14.

FIGURE 5.24

Accessing the controls on a form at runtime

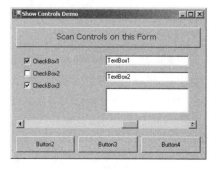

LISTING 5.14: ITERATING THE CONTROLS COLLECTION

```
Private Sub Button1_Click(ByVal sender As System.Object, _
            ByVal e As System.EventArgs) Handles Button1.Click
  Dim i As Integer
  For i = 0 To Me.Controls.Count - 1
    Console.WriteLine(Me.Controls(i).ToString)
    If Me.Controls(i).GetType Is GetType(system.Windows.Forms.Panel) Then
      Dim j As Integer
      For j = 0 To Me.Controls(i).Controls.Count - 1
        Console.WriteLine(Me.Controls(i).Controls(j).ToString)
      Next
    End If
  Next
End Sub
```

The form shown in Figure 5.24 produced the following output:

```
System.Windows.Forms.HScrollBar, Minimum: 0, Maximum: 100, Value: 60
System.Windows.Forms.CheckedListBox
System.Windows.Forms.TextBox, Text: TextBox2
System.Windows.Forms.CheckBox, CheckState: 1
System.Windows.Forms.CheckBox, CheckState: 0
System.Windows.Forms.CheckBox, CheckState: 1
System.Windows.Forms.TextBox, Text: TextBox1
System.Windows.Forms.Button, Text: Button4
System.Windows.Forms.Button, Text: Button3
System.Windows.Forms.Button, Text: Button2
```

Each member of the Controls collection exposes the GetType method, which returns the control's type, so that you can know what control is stored in each collection element. To compare the control's type returned by the GetType method, use the GetType() function passing as argument a control type. The following statement examines whether the control in the first element of the Controls collection is a TextBox:

```
If Me.Controls(0).GetType Is GetType(system.WinForms.TextBox) Then
    MsgBox("It's a TextBox control")
End If
```

Notice the use of the Is operator in the preceding statement. The equals operator will cause an exception, because objects can be compared only with the Is operator. Do not use string comparisons to find out the control's type. A statement like the following won't work:

```
If Me.Controls(i).GetType = "TextBox" Then ...    ' WRONG
```

The elements of the Controls collection are of the Control type, and they expose the properties of the control they represent. Their Top and Left properties read (or set) the position of the corresponding control on the form. The following expressions move the first control on the form to the specified location:

```
Me.Controls(0).Top = 10
Me.Controls(0).Left = 40
```

To access other properties of the control represented by an element of the Controls collection, you must first cast it to the appropriate type. If the first control of the collection is a TextBox control, use the CType() function to cast it to a TextBox variable, and then request its Text property:

```
If Me.Controls(i).GetType Is GetType(system.WinForms.TextBox) Then
    Console.WriteLine(CType(Me.Controls(0), TextBox).Text)
End If
```

The If statement is necessary, unless you can be sure that the first control is a TextBox control. If you omit the If statement and attempt to convert it to a TextBox, a runtime exception will be thrown if the object Me.Controls(0) isn't a TextBox control.

VB.NET at Work: The DynamicForm Project

To demonstrate how to handle controls at runtime from within your code, I've included the Dynamic-Form project (Figure 5.25), a simple data-entry window for a small number of data points. The user can specify at runtime the number of data points they wish to enter, and the number of TextBoxes on the control changes.

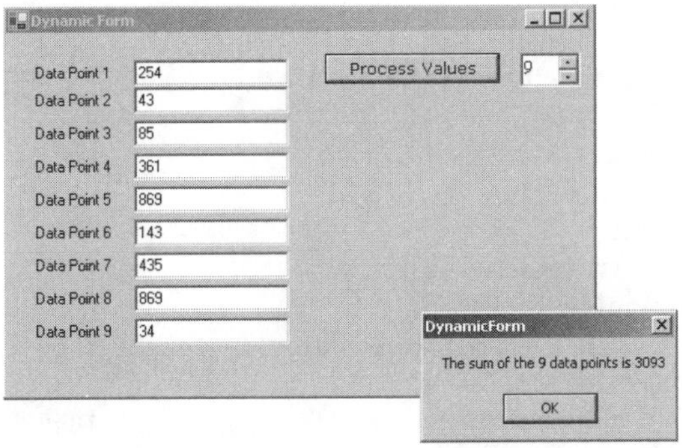

FIGURE 5.25

The DynamicForm project

The control you see at the top of the form is the NumericUpDown control. All you really need to know about this control is that it fires the ValueChanged event every time the user clicks one of the two arrows or types another value in its edit area. This event handler's code adds or removes controls on the form, so that the number of TextBoxes (as well as the number of the corresponding labels) matches the value on the control. Listing 5.15 shows the handler for the ValueChanged event of the NumericUpDown1 control. The ValueChanged event is fired when the user clicks one of the two arrows on the control or types a new value in the control's edit area.

LISTING 5.15: ADDING AND REMOVING CONTROLS AT RUNTIME

```
Private Sub NumericUpDown1_ValueChanged(ByVal sender As System.Object, _
            ByVal e As System.EventArgs) Handles NumericUpDown1.ValueChanged
   Dim TB As New TextBox()
   Dim LBL As New Label()
   Dim i, TBoxes As Integer
' Count all TextBox controls on the form
   For i = 0 To Me.Controls.Count - 1
      If Me.Controls(i).GetType Is GetType(System.Windows.Forms.TextBox) Then
         TBoxes = TBoxes + 1
      End If
   Next
' Add new controls if number of controls on the form is less
' than the number specified with the NumericUpDown control
   If TBoxes < NumericUpDown1.Value Then
      TB.Left = 100
      TB.Width = 120
      TB.Text = ""
      For i = TBoxes To NumericUpDown1.Value - 1
         TB = New TextBox()
         LBL = New Label()
         If NumericUpDown1.Value = 1 Then
            TB.Top = 20
         Else
            TB.Top = Me.Controls(Me.Controls.Count - 2).Top + 25
         End If
         Me.Controls.Add(TB)
         LBL.Left = 20
         LBL.Width = 80
         LBL.Text = "Data Point " & i
         LBL.Top = TB.Top + 3
         TB.Left = 100
         TB.Width = 120
         TB.Text = ""
         Me.Controls.Add(LBL)
         AddHandler TB.Enter, _
               New System.EventHandler(AddressOf TBox_Enter)
         AddHandler TB.Leave, _
               New System.EventHandler(AddressOf TBox_Leave)
```

```
        Next
    Else
        For i = Me.Controls.Count - 1 To _
                Me.Controls.Count - 2 * (TBoxes - NumericUpDown1.Value) Step -2
            Me.Controls.Remove(Controls(i))
            Me.Controls.Remove(Controls(i - 1))
        Next
    End If
End Sub
```

First, the code counts the number of TextBoxes on the form, then it figures out whether it should add or remove elements from the Controls collection. To remove controls, the code iterates through the last *n* controls on the form and removes them. The number of controls to be removed, *n*, is:

```
2 * (TBoxes - NumericUpDown1.Value)
```

where *TBoxes* is the total number of controls on the form minus the value specified in the NumericUpDown control.

If the value entered in the NumericUpDown control is less than the number of TextBox controls on the form, the code removes the excess controls from within a loop. At each step, it removes two controls, one of them being a TextBox and the other being a Label control with the matching caption (that's why the loop variable is decreased by two). The code also assumes that the first two controls on the form are the Button and the NumericUpDown controls. If the value entered by the user exceeds the number of TextBox controls on the form, the code adds the necessary pairs of TextBox and Label controls to the form.

To add controls, the code initializes a TextBox (*TB*) and a Label (*LBL*) variable. Then, its sets their locations and the label's caption. The left coordinate of all labels is 20, their width is 80, and their Text property (the label's caption) is the order of the data item. The vertical coordinate is 20 pixels for the first control, and all other controls are three pixels below the control on the previous row. Once a new control has been set up, it's added to the Controls collection with one of the following statements:

```
Me.Controls.Add(TB)      ' adds a TextBox control
Me.Controls.Add(LBL)     ' adds a Label control
```

The code contains a few long lines, but it isn't really complicated. It's based on the assumption that, except for the first few controls on the form, all others are pairs of Label and TextBox controls used for data entry.

To use the values entered by the user on the dynamic form, we must iterate the Controls collection, extract the values in the TextBox controls and use them. Listing 5.16 shows how the Process Values button scans the TextBox controls on the form performs some very basic calculations with them (counting the number of data points and summing their values).

LISTING 5.16: READING THE CONTROLS ON THE FORM

```
Private Sub Button1_Click(ByVal sender As System.Object, _
            ByVal e As System.EventArgs) Handles Button1.Click
    Dim ctrl As Object
```

```
Dim Sum As Double = 0, points As Integer = 0
Dim iCtrl As Integer
For iCtrl = 0 To Me.Controls.Count - 1
   ctrl = Me.Controls(iCtrl)
   If ctrl.GetType Is GetType(system.Windows.Forms.TextBox) Then
       If IsNumeric(CType(ctrl, TextBox).Text) Then
           Sum = Sum + CType(ctrl, TextBox).Text
           points = points + 1
       End If
   End If
Next
MsgBox("The sum of the " & points.ToString & " data points is " & _
       Sum.ToString)
End Sub
```

You can add more statements to calculate the mean and other vital statistics, or process the values in any other way. You can even dump all the values into an array and then use the array notation to manipulate them.

You can also write a For Each...Next loop to iterate through the TextBox controls on the form, as shown in Listing 5.17. The Process Values button at the bottom of the form demonstrates this alternate method of iterating through the elements of the Me.Controls collection. Because this loop goes through all the elements, we must examine the type of each control in the loop and process only the TextBox controls.

LISTING 15.17: READING THE CONTROLS WITH A FOR EACH...NEXT LOOP

```
Private Sub bttnProcess2_Click(ByVal sender As System.Object, _
               ByVal e As System.EventArgs) Handles bttnProcess2.Click
   Dim TB As Control
   Dim Sum As Double = 0, points As Integer = 0
   For Each TB In Me.Controls
      If TB.GetType Is GetType(Windows.Forms.TextBox) Then
          If IsNumeric(CType(TB, TextBox).Text) Then
              Sum = Sum + CType(TB, TextBox).Text
              points = points + 1
          End If
      End If
   Next
   MsgBox("The sum of the " & points.ToString & " data points is " & _
          Sum.ToString)
End Sub
```

Creating Event Handlers at Runtime

You've seen how to add controls on your forms at runtime and how to access the properties of these controls from within your code. In many situations, this is all you need: a way to access the properties of the controls (the text on a TextBox control, or the status of a CheckBox or RadioButton control). What good is a Button control, however, if it can't react to the Click event? The only problem with the controls you add to the Controls collection at runtime is that they don't react to events. It's possible, though, to create event handlers at runtime, and this is what you'll learn in this section. Obviously, this isn't a technique you'll be using every day; you can come back and read this section when the need arises.

To create an event handler at runtime, create a subroutine that accepts two arguments—the usual *sender* and *e* arguments—and enter the code you want to execute when a specific control receives a specific event. Let's say you want to add one or more buttons at runtime on your form and these buttons should react to the Click event. Create the ButtonClick() subroutine and enter the appropriate code in it. The name of the subroutine could be anything; you don't have to make up a name that includes the control's or the event's name.

Once the subroutine is in place, you must connect it to an event of a specific control. The Button-Click() subroutine, for example, must be connected to the Click event of a Button control. The statement that connects a control's event to a specific event handler, is the AddHandler statement, whose syntax is:

```
AddHandler control.event, New System.EventHandler(AddressOf subName)
```

For example, to connect the ProcessNow() subroutine to the Click event of the Calculate button, use the following statement:

```
AddHandler Calculate.Click, New System.EventHandler(AddressOf ProcessNow)
```

Let's add a little more complexity to the DynamicForm application. We will program the Enter and Leave events of the TextBox controls added at runtime through the `Me.Controls.Add` method. When a TextBox control receives the focus, we'll change its background color to a light yellow, and when it loses the focus we'll restore the background to white, so that the user knows which box has the focus at any time. We'll use the same handlers for all TextBox controls, and the code of the two handlers are shown in Listing 5.18.

LISTING 5.18: EVENT HANDLERS ADDED AT RUNTIME

```
Private Sub TBox_Enter(ByVal sender As Object, ByVal e As System.EventArgs)
   CType(sender, TextBox).BackColor = color.LightCoral
End Sub
Private Sub TBox_Leave(ByVal sender As Object, ByVal e As System.EventArgs)
   CType(sender, TextBox).BackColor = color.White
End Sub
```

The event handlers use the *sender* argument to find out which TextBox control received or lost the focus, and they set the appropriate control's background color (property BackColor). We write one handler per event and associate it with any number of controls added dynamically. Technically, the

TBox_Enter() and TBox_Leave() subroutines are not event handlers—at least, not before we associate them with an actual control and a specific event. This is done in the same segment of code that sets the properties of the controls we create dynamically at runtime. After adding the control to the Me.Controls collection, call the following statements to connect the new control's Enter and Leave events to the appropriate handlers:

```
AddHandler TB.Enter, New System.EventHandler(AddressOf TBox_Enter)
AddHandler TB.Leave, New System.EventHandler(AddressOf TBox_Leave)
```

Run the DynamicForm application and see how the TextBox controls handle the focus-related events. With a few statements and a couple of subroutines, we were able to create event handlers at runtime, from within our code.

Summary

In this chapter, you learned the most useful and practical techniques for designing forms. The Windows Form Designer that comes with VS.NET is leaps ahead of the equivalent designer of VB6, and it allows you to design truly elaborate interfaces with very little code (in some cases, no code at all). At the very least, you must make sure that the controls on the form will fit nicely when the form is resized at runtime by setting the Anchor and Dock properties accordingly.

Building applications with multiple forms is a bit more involved than it used to be, but not really complicated. In the following chapter, we're going to discuss in detail the basic components of the user interface, which are the controls—the basic building blocks of the application. If you think forms come with a lot of built-in functionality, wait until you find out the functionality built into the controls.

Chapter 6

Basic Windows Controls

IN THE PREVIOUS CHAPTERS, we explored the environment of Visual Basic and the principles of event-driven programming, which is the core of VB's programming model. In the process, we briefly explored a few basic controls through the examples. The .NET Framework provides many more controls, and all of them have a multitude of properties. Most of the properties have obvious names, and you can set them either from the Properties window or from within your code.

This chapter explores several of the basic Windows controls in depth. These are the controls you'll be using most often in your applications because they are the basic building blocks of the Windows user interface.

Rather than look at controls' background and foreground color, font, and other trivial properties, we'll look at the properties unique to each control and how these properties are used in building a user interface.

NOTE   *This chapter doesn't present every property and every method of the basic Windows controls. That would take another book, and its value would be questionable. Most properties are quite simple to use and easy to understand (and then there are some you'll never use). This chapter focuses on the unique properties, methods, and events of each control you need to know, in order to use them in your user interface.*

The TextBox Control

The TextBox control is the primary mechanism for displaying and entering text and is one of the most common elements of the Windows user interface. The TextBox control is a small text editor that provides all the basic text-editing facilities: inserting and selecting text, scrolling if the text doesn't fit in the control's area, and even exchanging text with other applications through the Clipboard.

VB6 ➠ VB.NET

The VB.NET TextBox control is very similar to the one in VB6, with a major improvement. The old TextBox control couldn't handle large chunks of text. It could handle up to 32K characters, and this was a serious limitation. The new TextBox control can hold more than 2 billion characters, which is more than you care to read in a single session.

The WordWrap property allows you to specify whether the control will wrap text lines as they approach the width of the control. In the old version of the control, the ScrollBars property determined whether the control wraps the text. Without a horizontal ScrollBar, the text was wrapped automatically. Now, you can enter long lines of text even if no horizontal scroll bar is present.

Another feature of the new TextBox control is that it allows you to access individual lines of text through the Lines property. The Lines property is a string array, and each element of the array holds a text line. Lines(0) is the first line, Lines(1) is the second line, and so on. The number of text lines on the control is given by the expression Lines.Length.

Finally, the properties that let you select or manipulate text—the SelStart, SelLength, and SelText properties—have changed names. They're now called SelectionStart, SelectionLength, and SelectedText. The Alignment property, which specifies the alignment of the text on the control, is now called TextAlignment. The AppendText method lets you add text to the control, and it's much faster than the equivalent statement

```
TextBox1.Text = TextBox1.Text & newLine
```

The text box is an extremely versatile data-entry tool that can be used for entering a single line of text, such as a number or a password, or for entering simple text files. Figure 6.1 shows a few typical examples created with the TextBox control. All the boxes in Figure 6.1 contain text—some a single line, some several lines. The scroll bars you see in some text boxes are part of the control. You can specify which scroll bars (vertical and/or horizontal) will appear on the control, and the appropriate scroll bars are attached to the control automatically whenever the control's contents exceed the visible area of the control.

With the exception of graphics applications, the TextBox control is the bread and butter of any Windows application. By examining its properties and designing a text editor based on the TextBox control, you'll see that most of the application's functionality is already built into the control.

FIGURE 6.1

Typical uses of the TextBox control

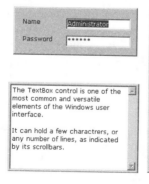

Basic Properties

Let's start with the properties that determine the appearance and, to some degree, the functionality of the TextBox control; these can be set through the Properties window. Then, we'll look at the properties that allow you to manipulate the control's contents. Let me mention quickly the TextAlign property, which sets (or returns) the alignment of the text on the control and can be Left, Right, or Center. The TextBox control doesn't allow you to format text, but you can set the font in which the text will be displayed with the Font property, as well as the control's background color with the BackColor property. If you want to display a background image, use the BackImage property and assign to it the path of the file with the desired image.

MULTILINE

This property determines whether the TextBox control will hold a single line or multiple lines of text. By default, the control holds a single line of text. To change this behavior, set the MultiLine property to True.

SCROLLBARS

This property controls the attachment of scroll bars to the TextBox control if the text exceeds the control's dimensions. Single-line text boxes can't have a scroll bar attached, even if the text exceeds the width of the control. Multiline text boxes can have a horizontal or a vertical scroll bar, or both. Scroll bars can appear in multiline text boxes even if they aren't needed or the text doesn't exceed the dimensions of the control.

If you attach a horizontal scroll bar to the TextBox control, the text won't wrap automatically as the user types. To start a new line, the user must press Enter. This arrangement is useful in implementing editors for programs in which lines must break explicitly. If the horizontal scroll bar is missing, the control inserts soft line breaks when the text reaches the end of a line, and the text is wrapped automatically. You can change the default behavior by setting the WordWrap property.

WORDWRAP

This property determines whether the text is wrapped automatically when it reaches the right edge of the control. The default value of this property is True. If the control has a horizontal scroll bar, however, you can enter very long lines of text. The contents of the control will scroll to the left, so that the insertion point is always visible as you type. You can turn off the horizontal scroll bar and still enter long lines of text; just use the left/right arrows to bring any part of the text into view.

This feature may seem dubious at first, but you'll find it useful when you resize the control. By the way, it's very easy to resize the control so that it always fills the form, with the Dock property (see section "Anchoring and Docking" in Chapter 5). If the text is a program listing, like the one shown in Figure 6.2, or a list of numbered items, you don't want the text to wrap at any point. You'd rather force users to open up the form so that the entire width of the text is visible across the control. You can experiment with the WordWrap and ScrollBars properties in the TextPad application, which is described later in this chapter.

FIGURE 6.2

Turn off the Word-Wrap property to display program listings or other lines that shouldn't break arbitrarily.

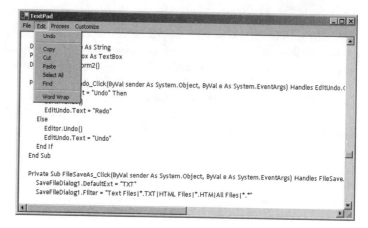

Notice that the WordWrap property has no effect on the actual line breaks. The lines are wrapped automatically, and there are no hard breaks (returns) at the end of each line. Open the TextPad project, enter a long paragraph, and resize the window. The text will be automatically adjusted to the new width of the control. Then select it and copy it by pressing Ctrl+C. Switch to Word, or another word processor, and paste it. You will see that the text is copied as a single paragraph, without additional hard breaks. The lines will break according to the size of the container and will be re-broken when the control is resized.

As you can understand, when WordWrap is set to True, there's no reason to attach a horizontal scroll bar to the control. Even if you set the ScrollBars property to Horizontal, this setting will be ignored.

AcceptsReturn, AcceptsTab

These two properties specify how the TextBox control reacts to the Return (Enter) and Tab keys. The Enter key activates the default button on the form, if there is one. The default button is usually an OK button that can be activated with the Enter key, even if it doesn't have the focus. In a multiline TextBox control, however, we want to be able to use the Enter key to change lines. The default value of this property is True, so that pressing Enter creates a new line on the control. If you set it to False, users can still create new lines in the TextBox control, but they'll have to press Ctrl+Enter. If the form contains no default button, then the Enter key creates a new line regardless of the AcceptsReturn setting.

Most forms that contain text boxes have also a default button, so users can work with the keyboard. Otherwise, they'd be forced to take their hands off the keyboard, use the mouse to click a button, and then return to the keyboard—or press the Tab button repeatedly to move the focus to one of the buttons.

TIP   This is a very important issue in designing practical user interfaces. You shouldn't force your users to switch between the keyboard and the mouse all the time. Follow the Windows standards (the Enter key for the default button, the Tab key to move from one control to the next, and shortcuts) to make sure that your application can be used without the mouse. Data-entry operators would rather work without the mouse at all.

The AcceptsTab property determines how the control reacts to the Tab key. Normally, the Tab key takes you to the next control in the tab order. In a TextBox control, however, you may wish for the Tab key to insert a Tab character in the text of the control instead; to do this, set this property to True. The default value of the AcceptsTab property is False, so that users can move to the next control with the Tab key. If you change the default value, users can still move to the next control in the tab order by pressing Ctrl+Tab. Notice that the AcceptsTab property has no effect on other controls. Users may have to press Ctrl+Tab to move to the next control while a TextBox control has the focus, but they can use the Tab key to move from any other control to the next one.

MaxLength

This property determines the number of characters the TextBox control will accept. Its default value is 32,767, which was the maximum number of characters the VB6 version of the control could hold. Set this property to zero, so that the text can have any length, up to the control's capacity limit— 2 GB, or 2,147,483,647 characters to be exact. To restrict the number of characters the user can type, set the value of this property accordingly.

NOTE *The MaxLength property of the TextBox control is often set to a specific value in data-entry applications. This prevents users from entering more characters than can be stored in a database field.*

A TextBox control with its MaxLength property set to 0, its MultiLine property set to True, and its ScrollBars property set to Vertical is, on its own, a functional text editor. Place a TextBox control with these settings on a form, run the application, and check out the following:

- Enter text and manipulate it with the usual editing keys, such as Delete, Insert, Home, and End.

- Select multiple characters with the mouse or the arrow keys while holding down the Shift key.

- Move segments of text around with Copy (Ctrl+C), Cut (Ctrl+X), and Paste (Ctrl+V) operations.

- Exchange data with other applications through the Clipboard.

You can do all this without a single line of code! Shortly you'll see what you can do with the TextBox control if you add some code to your application, but first, let's look at a few more properties of TextBox control.

Text-Manipulation Properties

Most of the properties for manipulating text in a TextBox control are available at runtime only. This section presents a breakdown of each property.

Text

The most important property of the TextBox control is the Text property, which holds the control's text. This property is also available at design time so that you can assign some initial text to the control. Notice that there are two methods of setting the Text property at design time. For single-line TextBox controls, set the Text property to a short string, as usual. For multiline TextBox controls, open the Lines property and enter the text on the String Collection Editor window, which will appear. When you're done, click OK to close the window. Each line you enter on the String Collection Editor window is a paragraph. Depending on the width of the control, this paragraph may be broken into multiple lines.

At runtime, use the Text property to extract the text entered by the user or to replace the existing text by assigning a new value to the property. The Text property is a string and can be used as argument with the usual string-manipulation functions of Visual Basic. It also supports all the members of the String class. The following expression returns the number of characters in the *TextBox1* control:

```
Dim strLen As Integer
strLen = TextBox1.Text.Length
```

VB6 programmers are accustomed to calling the Len() function, which does the same:

```
strLen = Len(TextBox1.Text)
```

To clear the control, you can set its Text property to a blank string:

```
TextBox1.Text = ""
```

or call the control's Clear method:

```
TextBox1.Clear
```

The IndexOf method of the String class will locate a string within the control's text. The following statement returns the location of the first occurrence of the string "Visual" in the text:

```
Dim location As Integer
location = TextBox1.Text.IndexOf("Visual")
You can also use the InStr() function of VB:
location = Instr(TextBox1.Text, "Visual")
```

The InStr() function allows you to specify whether the search will be case-sensitive or not, while the IndexOf method doesn't. For more information on locating strings in a TextBox control, see the later section "VB.NET at Work: The TextPad Project," where we'll build a text editor with search and replace capabilities.

To store the control's contents in a file, use a statement such as

```
StrWriter.Write(TextBox1.Text)
```

Similarly, you can read the contents of a text file into a TextBox control with a statement such as

```
TextBox1.Text = StrReader.ReadToEnd
```

where *StrReader* and *StrWriter* are two properly declared StreamReader and StreamWriter object variables. You will find out how to read from and write to files in Chapter 13, but you will also find the code for saving the text to a disk file (and reading text from a disk file as well) in the TextPad sample project, later in this chapter.

To locate all instances of a string in the text, use a loop like the one in Listing 6.1. This loop locates successive instances of the string "basic" and then continues searching from the character following the previous instance of the word in the text. To locate the last instance of a string in the text, use the LastIndexOf method. You can write a loop similar to the one of Listing 6.1 that scans the text backwards.

LISTING 6.1: LOCATING A STRING IN A TEXTBOX

```
Dim startIndex = -1
startIndex = TextBox1.Text.IndexOf("basic", startIndex + 1)
While startIndex > 0
    Console.WriteLine("String found at " & startIndex)
    startIndex = TextBox1.Text.IndexOf("basic", startIndex + 1)
End While
```

To test Listing 6.1, place a multiline TextBox and a Button control on a form, then enter the statements of the listing in the button's Click event handler. Run the application and enter some text on the TextBox control. Make sure the text contains the word "basic" or change the code to locate another word, and click the button. Notice that the IndexOf method performs a case-sensitive search.

Use the Replace method to replace a string with another within the line, the Split method to split the line into smaller components (like words), and any other method exposed by the String class. The following statement appends a string to the existing text on the control:

```
TextBox1.Text = TextBox1.Text & newString
```

This statement has appeared in just about any application that manipulated text with the TextBox control. It was an inefficient method to append text to the control, especially if the control contained a lot of text already. The problem with this statement isn't obvious when you're dealing with small text chunks. As the amount of text on the control increases, however, this statement takes longer to execute.

Now, you can use the AppendText method to append strings to the control, which is far more efficient that manipulating the Text property directly. To append a string to a TextBox control, use the following statement:

```
TextBox1.AppendText(newString)
```

The AppendText method appends the specified text to the control "as is," without any line breaks between successive calls. If you want to append individual paragraphs to the control's text, you must insert the line breaks explicitly, with a statement like the following:

```
TextBox1.AppendText(newString) & vbCrLf
```

vbCrLf is a VB constant that corresponds to the carriage return/new line characters.

READONLY, LOCKED

If you want to display text on a TextBox control but prevent users from editing it (an agreement or a contract they must read, software installation instructions, and so on), you can set the ReadOnly property to True. When ReadOnly is set to True, you can put text on the control from within your code, and users can view it, yet they can't edit it.

To prevent the editing of the TextBox control with VB6, you had to set the Locked property to True. Oddly, the Locked property is also supported, but now it has a very different function. The Locked property of VB.NET locks the control at design time (so that you won't move it or change its properties by mistake as you design the form).

LINES

In addition to the Text property, you can access the text on the control with the Lines property. Unlike the Text property, however, the Lines property is read-only: you can't set the control's text by assigning strings to the Lines array. Lines is a string array where each element holds a line of text. The first line of the text is stored in the element Lines(0), the second line of text is stored in the element Lines(1), and so on. You can iterate through the text lines with a loop like the following:

```
Dim iLine As Integer
For iLine = 0 To TextBox1.Lines.GetUpperBound(0)- 1
    { process string TextBox1.Lines(iLine) }
Next
```

You must replace the line in brackets with the appropriate code, of course. Because the Lines property is an array, it supports the GetUpperBound method, which returns the index of the last element in the array. Each element of the Lines array is a string, and you can call any of the String class's methods to manipulate it. You can search for a string within the current line with the IndexOf and LastIndexOf methods, retrieve the line's length with the Length property, and so on— just keep in mind that you can't alter the text on the control by editing the Lines array. The String class is discussed in detail in Chapter 12. Alternatively, you can store the current line to a string variable and manipulate it with the usual string-manipulation functions of VB:

```
Dim myString As String
myString = TextBox1.Lines(iLine)
```

PASSWORDCHAR

Available at design time, this property turns the characters typed into any character you specify. If you don't want to display the actual characters typed by the user (when entering a password, for instance), use this property to define the character to appear in place of each character the user types.

The default value of this property is an empty string, which tells the control to display the characters as entered. If you set this value to an asterisk (*), for example, the user sees an asterisk in the place of every character typed. This property doesn't affect the control's Text property, which contains the actual characters. If a text box's PasswordChar property is set to any character, the user can't even copy or cut the text. Any text that's pasted on the control will appear as a sequence of whatever character has been specified with PasswordChar.

Text-Selection Properties

The TextBox control provides three properties for manipulating the text selected by the user: Selected-Text, SelectionStart, and SelectionLength. For example, the user can select a range of text with a click-and-drag operation, and the selected text will appear in reverse color. You can access the selected text from within your code with the SelectedText property, and its location in the control's text with the SelectionStart and SelectionLength properties.

SELECTEDTEXT

This property returns the selected text, enabling you to manipulate the current selection from within your code. For example, you can replace the selection by assigning a new value to the

SelectedText property. To convert the selected text to uppercase, use the ToUpper method of the String class:

```
TextBox1.SelectedText = TextBox1.SelectedText.ToUpper
```

or use the UCase() function of VB6:

```
TextBox1.SelectedText = UCase(TextBox1.SelectedText)
```

To delete the current selection, assign an empty string to the SelectedText property:

```
TextBox1.SelectedText = ""
```

SELECTIONSTART, SELECTIONLENGTH

The SelectionStart property returns or sets the position of the first character of the selected text in the control's text, somewhat like placing the cursor at a specific location in the text and selecting text by dragging the mouse. The SelectionLength property returns or sets the length of the selected text. The most common use of these two properties is to extract the user's selection or to select a piece of text from within the application. You'll use these two properties to implement search and replace operations for a simple text editor.

Suppose the user is seeking the word "Visual" in the control's text. The IndexOf method will locate the string, but it won't select it. The found string may even be outside the visible area of the control. You can add a few more lines of code to select the word in the text and highlight it so that the user will spot it instantly:

```
Dim seekString As String
Dim textStart As Integer
seekString = "Visual"
textStart = TextBox1.Text.IndexOf(seekString)
If textStart > 0 Then
    TextBox1.SelectionStart = selStart - 1
    TextBox1.SelectionLength = seekString.Length
End If
TextBox1.ScrollToCaret()
```

These lines locate the string "Visual" (or any user-supplied string stored in the *seekString* variable) in the text and select it by setting the SelectionStart and SelectionLength properties of the TextBox control. The index of the first character on the control is zero, so we must subtract one from the location returned by the IndexOf method. Moreover, if the string is outside the visible area of the control, the user must scroll the text to bring the selection into view. The TextBox control provides the ScrollToCaret method, which brings the section of the text with the cursor into view.

The few lines of code shown above form the core of a text editor's Search command. Replacing the current selection with another string is as simple as assigning a new value to the SelectedText property, and this technique provides you with an easy implementation of a find-and-replace operation. Designing a Find and Replace dialog box will take more effort than implementing the find-and-replace logic!

TIP *The SelectionStart and SelectionLength properties always have a value even if no text has been selected. In this case, SelectionLength is 1, and SelectionStart is the current location of the pointer in the text. If you want to insert some text at the pointer's location, simply assign it to the SelectedText property.*

HIDESELECTION

The selected text on the TextBox will not remain highlighted when the user moves to another control or form. To change this default behavior, use the HideSelection property. You will use this property to keep text highlighted in a TextBox control while another form or a dialog box has the focus, such as a Find and Replace dialog box. Its default value is True, which means that the text doesn't remain highlighted when the text box loses the focus. If you set the HideSelection property to False, the selected text will remain highlighted even when the TextBox control loses the focus. The default value of this property in VB6 was False, something you must take into consideration when you convert old applications into VB.NET.

Text-Selection Methods

In addition to properties, the TextBox control exposes two methods for selecting text. You can select some text with the Select method, whose syntax is shown next:

```
TextBox1.Select(start, length)
```

The Select method is new to VB.NET and is equivalent to setting the SelectionStart and SelectionLength properties. To select the characters 100 through 105 on the control, call the Select method, passing the values 99 and 6 as arguments:

```
TextBox1.Select(99, 6)
```

If the range of characters you select contains hard line breaks, you must take them into consideration as well. Each hard line break counts for two characters (carriage return and line feed). If the TextBox control contains the string "ABCDEFGHI," then the following statement will select the range "DEFG":

```
TextBox1.Select(3, 4)
```

If you insert a line break every third character and the text becomes:

```
ABC
DEF
GHI
```

then the same statement will select the characters "DE" only. In reality, it has also selected the two characters that separate the first two lines, but special characters aren't displayed and can't be highlighted. The length of the selection, however, will be 4.

As far as the appearance of the selected text goes, it doesn't make any difference whether it was selected by the user or by the application; it appears in reverse color, as is common with all text editors.

The following two statements select the text on a TextBox control with the SelectionStart and SelectionLength properties:

```
TextBox1.SelectionStart = selStart - 1
TextBox1.SelectionLength = word.Length
```

These two lines can be replaced with a single call to the Select method:

```
TextBox1.Select(selStart - 1, word.Length)
```

where *word* is a string variable holding the selection.

A variation of the Select method is the SelectAll method, which selects all the text on the control.

Undoing Edits

An interesting feature of the TextBox control is that it can automatically undo the most recent edit operation. To undo an operation from within your code, you must first examine the value of the CanUndo property. If it's True, it means that the control can undo the operation; then you can call the Undo method to undo the most recent edit.

An edit operation is the insertion or deletion of characters. Entering text without deleting any is considered a single operation and will be undone in a single step. A user may have spent an hour entering text (without making any corrections), and you can make all the text disappear with a single call to the Undo method. Fortunately, the deletion of the text has become the most recent operation, which can be undone with another call to the Undo method. In effect, the Undo method is a toggle. When you call it for the first time, it undoes the last edit operation. If you call it again, it redoes the operation it previously undid. The deletion of text can be undone only if no other editing operation has taken place in the meantime.

Let's say you have typed 1,000 characters on a TextBox control. If you call the Undo method, it will clear the control. If you call it again, it will restore the deleted text. Then you enter another 1,000 characters, and delete the last 3 characters. Now the operation that will be undone by the Undo method is the deletion of the last 3 characters. Then if you call the Undo method again, it will re-remove the 3 characters.

In the TextPad application we'll build in the following section, we'll implement an Undo/Redo command. It will be the first command in the Edit menu and will be a toggle. If its caption is Undo, we'll call the Undo method and then change its name to Redo. Likewise, if its caption is Redo, we'll call the Undo method (which this time is going to undo the last undo and restore the text to the state it was before the call to the Undo method) and then change the command's name to Undo. Of course, the caption of the command will be Redo only between undoing an edit operation and the editing of the text. As soon as the user enters or deletes a single character on the TextBox control, the caption of the command must become Undo again.

The Undo method would be much more useful if we could set the beginning of an undo action. For example, we could mark the Enter keypress (the beginning of a new line) as the beginning of an undoable operation—or the saving of the text to a file, the paste operation, and so on. In its current implementation, the Undo method undoes everything up to the most recent deletion. If no text has been deleted, then all the text will be removed from the control. However, you will see an interesting method of using the Undo method to undo selected operations.

You can disable the redo operation by calling the ClearUndo method. This method clears the undo buffer of the control, and you should call it from within an Undo command's event handler, to prevent an operation from being redone. In most cases you should give users the option to redo an operation, especially since the Undo method may delete an enormous amount of text from the control.

VB.NET at Work: The TextPad Project

The TextPad application, shown in Figure 6.3, demonstrates most of the TextBox control's properties and methods described so far. TextPad is a basic text editor that you can incorporate in your programs and customize for special applications. The TextPad's form is covered by a TextBox control. Every time the user changes the size of the form, the application adjusts the size of the TextBox control accordingly. This feature doesn't require any programming—just set the Dock property of the TextBox control to Fill.

FIGURE 6.3

TextPad demonstrates the most useful properties and methods of the TextBox control.

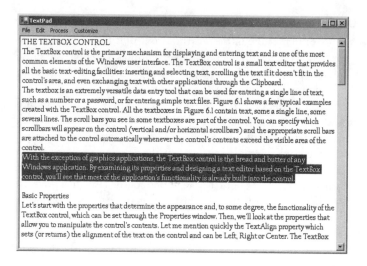

The name of the application's main form is TXTPADForm and the name of the Find and Replace dialog box is FindForm. You can design the two forms as shown in the figures of this chapter, or open the TextPad project on the CD and examine its code as well.

The menu bar of the form contains all the commands you'd expect to find in text-editing applications; they're listed in Table 6.1.

TABLE 6.1: THE MENU OF THE TEXTPAD FORM

MENU	COMMAND	DESCRIPTION
File	New	Clears the text
	Open	Loads a new text file from disk
	Save	Saves the text to its file on disk
	Save As	Saves the text with a new filename on disk
	Exit	Terminates the application
Edit	Undo/Redo	Undoes/redoes the last edit operation
	Copy	Copies selected text to the Clipboard
	Cut	Cuts selected text
	Paste	Pastes the Clipboard's contents to the text
	Select All	Selects all the text in the control
	Find	Displays a dialog box with Find and Replace options
	Word Wrap	Toggle menu item that turns text wrapping on and off

Continued on next page

TABLE 6.1: THE MENU OF THE TEXTPAD FORM *(continued)*

MENU	COMMAND	DESCRIPTION
Process	Upper Case	Converts selected text to uppercase
	Lower Case	Converts selected text to lowercase
	Number Lines	Numbers the text lines
Customize	Font	Sets the text's font, size, and attributes
	Page Color	Sets the control's background color
	Text Color	Sets the color of the text

Design this menu bar using the techniques explained in Chapter 5. The File menu commands are implemented with the Open File and Save File dialog boxes, the Font command with the Font dialog box, and the Color command with the Color dialog box. These dialog boxes are discussed in the following chapters, and as you'll see, you don't have to design them yourself. All you have to do is place a control on the form and set a few properties; the CLR takes it from there. The application will display the standard Open File/Save File/Font/Color dialog boxes on which the user can select or specify a filename or select a font or color.

THE EDIT MENU

The options on the Edit menu move the selected text to and from the Clipboard. For the TextPad application, all you need to know about the Clipboard are the SetDataObject method, which places the current selection (text, image, or any other information that can be exchanged between Windows applications) on the Clipboard, and the GetDataObject method, which retrieves information from the Clipboard (see Figure 6.4).

The Copy command, for example, is implemented with a single line of code (*Editor* is the name of the TextBox control). The Cut command does the same, and it also clears the selected text. The code for these and for the Paste command, which assigns the contents of the Clipboard to the current selection, is presented in Listing 6.2.

LISTING 6.2: THE CUT, COPY, AND PASTE COMMANDS

```
Protected Sub EditCopy_Click(ByVal Sender As Object, _
                ByVal e As System.EventArgs)
    Clipboard.SetDataObject(Editor.SelectedText)
End Sub
Protected Sub EditCut_Click(ByVal Sender As Object, _
                ByVal e As System.EventArgs)
    Clipboard.SetDataObject(Editor.SelectedText)
    Editor.SelectedText = ""
End Sub
```

```
Protected Sub EditPaste_Click(ByVal Sender As Object, _
                ByVal e As System.EventArgs)
    If Clipboard.GetDataObject.GetDataPresent(DataFormats.Text) Then
        Editor.SelectedText = Clipboard.GetDataObject.GetData(DataFormats.Text)
    End If
End Sub
```

FIGURE 6.4

The Copy, Cut, and Paste operations can be used to exchange text with any other application.

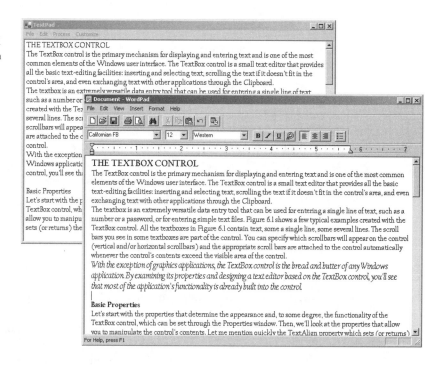

If no text is currently selected, the Clipboard's text is pasted at the pointer's current location. The SelectedText property allows you to paste text at the current location of the pointer, even if no text is currently selected. If the Clipboard contains a bitmap (placed there by another application), or any other type of data that the TextBox control can't handle, the paste operation will fail; that's why we handle the Paste operation with an If statement. If the Clipboard contains text, the program goes ahead and pastes the text on the control; if not, it does nothing. You could provide some hint to the user by including an Else clause that informs them that the data on the clipboard can't be used with a text-editing application.

The GetDataPresent property returns a True or False value, depending on whether the data on the Clipboard is of the same type as specified by the argument (text in our case). If you want to experiment with the Clipboard and the various formats it recognizes, check out the members of DataFormats, an enumeration that exposes a member for each different format it recognizes.

If you repeatedly paste chunks of text on the control, they're considered a single operation and will be undone with a single call to the Undo method.

THE PROCESS AND CUSTOMIZE MENUS

The commands of the Process and Customize menus are straightforward. The Customize menu commands open the Font or Color dialog box and change the control's Font, ForeColor, and Back-Color properties. The Upper Case and Lower Case commands of the Process menu are also trivial: they select all the text, convert it to uppercase or lowercase respectively, and assign the converted text to the control's Text property. Listing 6.3 is the code behind these two commands.

LISTING 6.3: THE UPPER CASE AND LOWER CASE COMMANDS

```
Private Sub ProcessUpper_Click(ByVal sender As System.Object, _
            ByVal e As System.EventArgs) Handles ProcessUpper.Click
    Editor.SelectedText = Editor.SelectedText.ToUpper
End Sub
Private Sub ProcessLower_Click(ByVal sender As System.Object, _
            ByVal e As System.EventArgs) Handles ProcessLower.Click
    Editor.SelectedText = Editor.SelectedText.ToLower
End Sub
```

The Number Lines command demonstrates how to process the individual lines of text on the control. This command inserts a number in front of each text line. However, it doesn't remove the line numbers, and there's no mechanism to prevent the user from editing the line numbers or inserting/deleting lines after they have been numbered. Use this feature to create a numbered listing, or to number the lines of a file just before saving it or sharing with another user. Listing 6.4 shows the Number Lines command's code and demonstrates how to iterate through the Lines array.

LISTING 6.4: THE NUMBER LINES COMMAND

```
Private Sub ProcessNumber_Click(ByVal sender As System.Object, _
            ByVal e As System.EventArgs) Handles ProcessNumber.Click
    Dim iLine As Integer
    Dim newText As New System.Text.StringBuilder()
    For iLine = 0 To Editor.Lines.Length - 1
        newText.Append((iLine + 1).ToString & vbTab & _
                    Editor.Lines(iLine) & vbCrLf)
    Next
    Editor.Text = newText.ToString
End Sub
```

This event handler uses a StringBuilder variable. The StringBuilder class is equivalent to the String class: it exposes similar methods and properties, but it's much faster in manipulating strings than the String class. The StringBuilder class is discussed in detail in Chapter 12.

Undoing Selected Operations

The numbering of the text lines is an operation you'd expect to be able to undo, but this isn't the case. If you paste a listing on the text box control and then number the lines with the Process ➢ Number Lines command, the numbered lines will appear as expected. If you attempt to undo the operation with the Edit ➢ Undo method, nothing will happen. The numbered lines weren't typed (or pasted) on the control, and they don't constitute an operation that can be undone.

One way to mark the numbering of the lines as an undoable operation is to copy the control's text to the Clipboard, clear the control and then paste the text onto the text box. The paste operation can be undone and the Undo command will restore the text to its status before the insertion of the line numbers. In effect, it will remove the numbers in front of each line.

The trick is to replace the line that assigns the text stored in the *newText* variable to the Text property of the text box with the following statements:

```
Editor.SelectAll()
Clipboard.SetDataObject(newText.ToString())
Editor.Paste()
```

The Click event handler of the Process ➢ Number Lines command of the TextPad project on the CD includes these statements. You can copy a few lines of VB code from the IDE and paste them onto the text box. Then number them with the Process ➢ Number Lines command and, finally, remove the numbers by undoing the operation. If you redo the last operation, the line numbers will be inserted in front of each code line. If you type something between the two operations, however, you will no longer be able to remove the line numbers with the Undo command.

Implementing an intelligent Undo/Redo feature requires quite a bit of code, and it's not among the features of simple text-editing applications. If you need this type of functionality, you're better off buying an off-the-shelf component. Not that it can't be implemented with VB.NET, but the time you'll spend on this project will be far more expensive.

Search and Replace Operations

The last option in the Edit menu—and the most interesting—displays a Find & Replace dialog box (shown in Figure 6.5). This dialog box works like the similarly named dialog box of Microsoft Word and many other Windows applications.

Figure 6.5

TextPad's Find & Replace dialog box

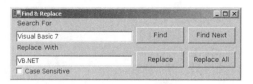

Before we look at the implementation of the Find & Replace dialog box, let me recap the techniques for manipulating a control from within another form's code, because this is what the Find & Replace dialog box does. Normally, the controls on a form are private and can't be accessed from code outside the form. To make a control available to other forms, you can either declare it as Public by setting the Modifiers property to Public, or create a Public variable on the form that represents the control to be shared. In our case, the control to be shared is the *Editor* TextBox control on the main form of the application, and we'll make it available to the code of the Find & Replace form through the *txtBox* variable. First, you must declare the *txtBox* variable in the main form with the following statement:

```
Public Shared txtBox As TextBox
```

This statement must appear outside any procedure. Then, in the main form's Load event, set the *txtBox* variable to the *Editor* TextBox control with the following statement:

```
txtBox = Editor
```

That's all it takes. If TXTPADForm is the main form's name, you can now access the properties of the *Editor* control on the main form with an expression like

```
TXTPADForm.txtBox.Text
```

It would have been simpler to make the *Editor* control public, and that is how you should make your controls available to other forms. I've chosen a technique that's slightly more complicated for demonstration purposes. This technique allows you to make public not the control itself, but some of its properties (like the Text property). If you wanted to expose only the Text property to other forms, then you'd have to declare a string variable as Public and set it to the control's Text property:

```
Public editText As String
editText = Editor.Text
```

The buttons in the Find & Replace dialog box are relatively self-explanatory:

Find   Locates the first instance of the specified string in the text. In other words, Find starts searching from the beginning of the text, not from the current location of the pointer. If a match is found, the Find Next, Replace, and Replace All buttons are enabled.

Find Next   Locates the next instance of the string in the text. Initially, this button is disabled; it's enabled only after a successful Find operation.

Replace   Replaces the current instance of the found string with the replacement string and then locates the next instance of the same string. Like the Find Next button, it's disabled until a successful Find operation.

Replace All   Replaces all instances of the string specified in the Search For box with the string in the Replace With box.

Whether the search is case-sensitive depends on the status of the Case Sensitive CheckBox control. The Find and Find Next commands check the status of this check box and set the *srchMode* variable accordingly. This variable is then used with the InStr() function to specify the type of search. We're using the InStr() function instead of the IndexOf method because the latter doesn't perform case-insensitive searches, while the InStr() does—so, there's good reason for using the good old VB functions after all.

If the string is found in the control's text, the program highlights it by selecting it. In addition, the program calls the TextBox control's ScrollToCaret method to bring the selection into view. If you omit to call the ScrollToCaret method and the selection is not in the currently visible text, users won't see it. The Find Next button takes into consideration the location of the pointer and searches for a match *after* the current location. If the user moves the pointer somewhere else and then clicks the Find Again button, the program will locate the first instance of the string after the current location of the pointer, and not after the last match. If you want to locate the next match regardless of where the pointer is, you should store the location of the match to a variable and use it with the InStr() function for subsequent searches.

TextPad handles search operations like all typical Windows applications. Let's start with the implementation of the Find button, shown in Listing 6.5.

LISTING 6.5: THE FIND BUTTON

```
Private Sub bttnFind_Click(ByVal sender As System.Object, _
             ByVal e As System.EventArgs) Handles bttnFind.Click
  Dim selStart As Integer
  Dim srchMode As CompareMethod
  If chkCase.Checked = True Then
     srchMode = CompareMethod.Binary
  Else
     srchMode = CompareMethod.Text
  End If
  selStart = InStr(TXTPADForm.txtBox.Text, searchWord.Text, srchMode)
  If selStart = 0 Then
     MsgBox("Can't find word")
     Exit Sub
  End If
  TXTPADForm.txtBox.Select(selStart - 1, searchWord.Text.Length)
  bttnFindNext.Enabled = True
  bttnReplace.Enabled = True
  bttnReplaceAll.Enabled = True
  TXTPADForm.txtBox.ScrollToCaret()
End Sub
```

The Find button examines the value of the *chkCase* CheckBox control, which specifies whether the search will be case-sensitive and sets the value of the *srchMode* variable accordingly. The *srchMode* variable is passed to the InStr() function and tells it how to search for the desired string. The variable's value can be one of the two constants, `Binary` (for case-sensitive, or exact, matches) and `Text` (for case-insensitive matches). If the InStr() function locates the string, the program selects it by calling the control's Select method with the appropriate arguments. If not, it displays a message. Notice that after a successful Find operation, the Find Next, Replace, and Replace All buttons on the form are enabled.

TIP *You may have noticed that the first selected character is at the location of the match minus 1 (`selStart` - 1). This is odd indeed, and the explanation is that for the InStr() function, the index of the first character is 1. The Select method, however, however, uses the index zero for the first character in the string. The same is true for all the methods of the String class, so you should be very careful not to mix the usual string functions of Visual Basic and the methods of the new String class.*

The code of the Find Again button is the same, but it starts searching at the character following the current selection. This way, the InStr() function locates the next instance of the same string. Here's the statement that locates the next instance of the search argument:

```
selStart = InStr(TXTPADForm.txtBox.SelStart + 2, TXTPADForm.txtBox.Text, _
                 SearchWord.Text, srchMode)
```

The Replace button replaces the current selection with the replacement string and then locates the next instance of the find string. The Replace All button does the same thing as the Replace button, but it continues to replace the found string until no more instances can be located in the text. Listing 6.6 presents the code behind the Replace and Replace All buttons.

LISTING 6.6: THE REPLACE AND REPLACE ALL OPERATIONS

```
Private Sub bttnReplace_Click(ByVal sender As System.Object, _
               ByVal e As System.EventArgs) Handles bttnReplace.Click
    If TXTPADForm.txtBox.SelectedText <> "" Then
       TXTPADForm.txtBox.SelectedText = replaceWord.Text
    End If
    bttnFindNext_Click(sender, e)
End Sub
Private Sub bttnReplaceAll_Click(ByVal sender As System.Object, _
               ByVal e As System.EventArgs) Handles bttnReplaceAll.Click
    Dim curPos, curSel As Integer
    curPos = TXTPADForm.txtBox.SelectionStart
    curSel = TXTPADForm.txtBox.SelectionLength
    Form1.txtBox.Text = Replace(TXTPADForm.txtBox.Text, Trim(searchWord.Text), _
                          Trim(replaceWord.Text))
    TXTPADForm.txtBox.SelectionStart = curPos
    TXTPADForm.txtBox.SelectionLength = curSel
End Sub
```

You might also want to limit the search operation to the selected text only. To do so, pass the location of the first selected character to the InStr() function as before. In addition, you must make sure that the located string falls within the selected range, which is from

```
TXTPADForm.Editor.SelectionStart
```

to

```
TXTPADForm.Editor.SelectionStart + TXTPADForm.Editor.SelectionLength
```

You must create two variables, the *curPos* and *curSel* variables, and store the values of the Selection-Start and SelectionLength properties when the Find command is clicked, and then ignore any matches outside this range.

THE UNDO/REDO COMMANDS

The Undo command (Listing 6.7) is implemented with a call to the Undo method. However, because the Undo method works like a toggle, we must also toggle its caption from Undo to Redo and vice versa, each time the command is activated.

LISTING 6.7: THE UNDO/REDO COMMAND OF THE EDIT MENU

```
Private Sub EditUndo_Click(ByVal sender As System.Object, _
              ByVal e As System.EventArgs) Handles EditUndo.Click
   If EditUndo.Text = "Undo" Then
      Editor.Undo()
      EditUndo.Text = "Redo"
   Else
      Editor.Undo()
      EditUndo.Text = "Undo"
   End If
End Sub
```

As I mentioned earlier, if you edit the text after an undo operation, you can no longer redo the last undo operation. This means that as soon as the contents of the TextBox control change, the caption of the first command in the Edit menu must become Undo, even it's Redo at the time. The Redo command is available only after undoing an operation and before editing the text. So, how do we know that the text has been edited? The TextBox control fires the TextChanged event every time its contents change. We'll use this event to restore the caption of the Undo/Redo command to Undo. Insert the following statements in the TextChanged event of the TextBox control:

```
Private Sub Editor_TextChanged(ByVal sender As System.Object, _
              ByVal e As System.EventArgs) Handles Editor.TextChanged
   EditUndo.Text = "Undo"
End Sub
```

Capturing Keystrokes

The TextBox control has no unique methods or events, but it's quite common in programming to use this control to capture and process the user's keystrokes. The KeyPress event occurs every time a key is pressed, and it reports the character that was pressed. You can use this event to capture certain keys and modify the program's behavior depending on the character typed.

Suppose you want to use the TextPad application (discussed in the preceding sections) to prepare messages for transmission over a telex line. As you may know, a telex can't transmit lowercase characters or special symbols. The editor must convert the text to uppercase and replace the special symbols with their equivalent strings: DLR for $, AT for @, O/O for %, BPT for #, and AND for &. You can modify the default behavior of the TextBox control from within the KeyPress event so that it converts these characters as the user types.

The TELEXPad application is identical to the TextPad application, but customized for preparing telex messages. (Not that the telex is growing in popularity, but there are situations in which some custom preprocessing of the data is required.) By capturing keystrokes, you can process the data as they are entered, in real time. For example, you could make sure that numeric values fall within a given range or that hexadecimal digits don't contain invalid characters, and so on. The only difference is the modified application's KeyPress event. The KeyPress event handler of the TELEX-Pad application is shown in Listing 6.8.

LISTING 6.8: TELEXPAD APPLICATION'S KEYPRESS EVENT HANDLER

```
Public Sub Editor_KeyPress(ByVal sender As Object, _
             ByVal e As System.WinForms.KeyPressEventArgs) _
             Handles Editor.KeyPress
    Dim ch As Char
    Dim CrLf As String
    If System.Char.IsControl(e.KeyChar) Then Exit Sub
    CrLf = vbCrLf
    ch = e.KeyChar.ToChar
    ch = ch.ToUpper(ch)
    Select Case ch
       Case "@".ToChar
          Editor.SelectedText = "AT"
       Case "#".ToChar
          Editor.SelectedText = "BPT"
       Case "$".ToChar
          Editor.SelectedText = "DLR"
       Case "%".ToChar
          Editor.SelectedText = "0/0"
       Case "&".ToChar
          Editor.SelectedText = "AND"
       Case Else
          Editor.SelectedText = ch
    End Select
    e.Handled = True
End Sub
```

The very first executable statement in the event handler examines the key that was pressed and exits if it was a special editing key (Del, Backspace, Ctrl+V, and so on). The KeyChar property of the *e* argument of the KeyPress event reports the key that was pressed. To convert it a character, we call its ToChar method, and in the following line, we convert the character to uppercase by calling the ToUpper method. Normally, you would combine the two statements:

```
ch = e.KeyChar.ToChar
ch = ch.ToUpper(ch)
```

into one:

```
ch = System.String.ToUpper(e.KeyChar.ToChar)
```

but I've used a rather verbose syntax to make code more readable.

Then the code uses a Case statement to handle individual keystrokes. If the user pressed the $ key, for example, the code displays the characters "DLR". If no special character was pressed, the code displays the character pressed "as is" from within the Case Else clause of the Select statement.

VB6 ➠ VB.NET

Before you exit the event handler, you must "kill" the original key pressed, so that it won't appear on the control. You do by setting the Handled property to True, which tells VB that it shouldn't process the keystroke any further. In VB6, you could kill a keystroke by setting the *KeyAscii* argument of the KeyPress event (or the *KeyCode* argument of the KeyUp event) to zero. The e.KeyChar argument in VB.NET is read-only, and you can't set it from within your code.

CAPTURING FUNCTION KEYS

Another common feature in text-editing applications is the assignment of special operations to the function keys. The Notepad application, for example, uses the F5 function key to insert the current date at the cursor's location. You can do the same with the TextPad application, but you can't use the KeyPress event—the *KeyChar* argument doesn't report function keys. The events that can capture the function keys are the KeyDown event, which is generated when a key is pressed, and the KeyUp event, which is generated when a key is released. Also, unlike the KeyPress event, KeyDown and KeyUp don't report the character pressed, but instead report the key's code (a special number that distinguishes each key on the keyboard, also known as the *scancode*), through the e.KeyCode property.

The keycode is unique for each key, not each character. Lower- and uppercase characters have different ASCII values but the same keycode because they are on the same key. The number 4 and the $ symbol have the same keycode because the same key on the keyboard generates both characters. When the key's code is reported, the KeyDown and KeyUp events also report the state of the Shift, Ctrl, and Alt keys.

To program the KeyDown and KeyUp events, you must know the keycode of the key you want to capture. The keycode for the function key F1 is 112 (or the constant Keys.F12), the keycode for F2 is 113 (or the constant Keys.F13), and so on. To capture a special key, such as the F1 function key, and assign a special string to it, program the key's KeyUp event. The event handler in Listing 6.9 uses the F5 and F6 function keys to insert the current date and time in the document. It also uses the F7 and F8 keys to insert two predefined strings in the document.

LISTING 6.9: KEYUP EVENT EXAMPLES

```
Public Sub Editor_KeyUp(ByVal sender As Object, _
            ByVal e As System.WinForms.KeyEventArgs) Handles Editor.KeyUp
    Select Case e.KeyCode
        Case Keys.F5 : editor.SelectedText = Now().ToLongDateString
        Case Keys.F6 : editor.SelectedText = Now().ToLongTimeString
        Case Keys.F7 : editor.SelectedText = "MicroWeb Designs, Inc."
        Case Keys.F8 : editor.SelectedText = "Another user-supplied string"
    End Select
End Sub
```

With a little additional effort, you can provide users with a dialog box that lets them assign their own strings to function keys. You'll probably have to take into consideration the status of the Shift, Control, and Alt properties of the event's *e* argument, which report the status of the Shift, Ctrl, and Alt keys respectively. Windows already uses many of the function keys, and you shouldn't reassign them. For example, the F1 key is the standard Windows context-sensitive Help key, and users will be confused if they press F1 and see the date appear in their documents. The keystroke Alt+F4 closes the window, so you shouldn't reassign it either.

To find out whether *two* of the modifier keys are down when a key is pressed, use the AND operator with the appropriate properties of the *e* argument. The following If structure detects the Ctrl and Alt keys:

```
If e.Control AND e.Alt Then
    { Alt and Control keys were down }
End If
```

The ListBox, CheckedListBox, and ComboBox Controls

The ListBox, CheckedListBox, and ComboBox controls present lists of choices, from which the user can select one or more. The first two are illustrated in Figure 6.6. The ListBox control occupies a user-specified amount of space on the form and is populated with a list of items. If the list of items is longer than can fit on the control, a vertical scroll bar appears automatically.

FIGURE 6.6

The ListBox and
CheckedListBox
controls

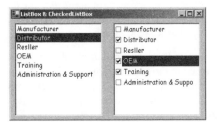

The items must be inserted in the ListBox control through the code or via the Properties window. To add items at design time, locate the Items property in the control's Properties window and click the button with the ellipsis. A new window will pop up, the String Collection Editor window, where you can add the items you want to display on the list. Each item must appear on a separate text line, and blank text lines will result in blank lines on the list. These items will appear on the list when the form is loaded, but you can add more items (or remove existing ones) from within your code at any time. They will appear in the same order as entered on the String Collection Editor window unless the control has its Sorted property set to True, in which case the items will be automatically sorted, regardless of the order in which you've specified them.

The ComboBox control also contains multiple items but typically occupies less space on the screen. The ComboBox control is an expandable ListBox control: the user can expand it to make a selection and collapse it after the selection is made. The real advantage to the ComboBox control, however, is that the user can enter new information in the ComboBox, rather than being forced to select from the items listed.

This section first examines the ListBox control's properties and methods. Later, you'll see how the same properties and methods can be used with the ComboBox control.

There's also a variation of the ListBox control, the CheckedListBox control, which is identical to the ListBox control, but a check box appears in front of each item. The user can select any number of items by checking the boxes in front of them.

VB6 ➡ VB.NET

The ListBox control has been greatly enhanced in .NET Framework. The most prominent change is that it no longer supports the List property. To access individual items on the control, you must use the Items property, which is a Collection. The first item on the control is Items(0), the second is Items(1), and so on. The Items collection has the usual properties of a collection: the Count property, which is the number of items on the control, and the Add, Remove, Insert, and Clear methods to add items to or remove items from the control. The ListCount property has also disappeared. The number of items on the control is given by the expression Items.Count, and the AddItem and RemoveItem methods of the old version of the control are no longer supported.

The handling of multiple selected items has also been enhanced. If the control allows a single selection, the SelectedIndex and SelectedItem properties return the index and the value of the selected item. If the control allows multiple selections, you can use the SelectedIndices and SelectedItems collections to access the indices and values of the selected items.

The most important enhancement to the new ListBox control is the search feature. You can use the FindString and FindStringExact methods to locate an item in the list. The FindString method locates the closest match to the search argument, while the FindStringExact method finds an exact match, if there is one. Notice that these methods work just as well with sorted and unsorted lists.

Finally, two new methods were introduced to speed up the display while new items are added to the control. If you have many items to add to the control at once, call the BeginUpdate method at the beginning, then call the Add or Insert method of the Items collection as many times as needed, and finally call the EndUpdate method. The control won't be updated each time you add a new item, but the items will be added to the control after EndUpdate is executed. This technique avoids the constant flickering of the control while new items are added.

Basic Properties

The ListBox and ComboBox controls provide a few common properties that determine the basic functionality of the control and are usually set at design time; we'll start with these fundamental properties.

INTEGRALHEIGHT

This property is a Boolean value (True/False) that indicates whether the control's height will be adjusted to avoid the partial display of the last item. When set to True, the control's actual height may be slightly different than the size you've specified, so that only an integer number of rows are displayed. If you want the ListBox control be the same height as another control, use the ListBox as the reference for the other controls. Sometimes you'll have to set this property to False to align a ListBox control with other controls on the form.

ITEMS

The Items property is a collection that holds the items on the control. At design time, you can populate this list through the String Collection Editor window. At runtime you can access and manipulate the items through the methods and properties of the Items collection, which are described in the following section. To load a number of items to a ListBox control at design time, locate the Items property in the Properties window, and click the button with the ellipsis next to it. This will bring up the String Collection Editor, where you can enter any number of items. Enter each item's text on a separate line, and click the OK button when you're done to close the window.

MULTICOLUMN

A ListBox control can display its items in multiple columns, if you set its MultiColumn property to True. The problem with multicolumn ListBoxes is that you can't specify the column in which each item will appear. Set this property to True for ListBox controls with a relatively small number of items, and do so only when you want to save space on the form. A horizontal scroll bar will be attached to a multicolumn ListBox, so that users can bring any column into view.

SELECTIONMODE

This property determines how the user can select the list's items and must be set at design time (at runtime, you can only read this property's value). The SelectionMode property's values determine whether the user can select multiple items and which method will be used for multiple selections. The possible values of this property—members of the SelectionMode enumeration—are shown in Table 6.2.

TABLE 6.2: THE SELECTIONMODE ENUMERATION

VALUE	DESCRIPTION
None	No selection at all is allowed.
One	(Default) Only a single item can be selected.
MultiSimple	Simple multiple selection: A mouse click (or pressing the spacebar) selects or deselects an item in the list. You must click all the items you want to select.
MultiExtended	Extended multiple selection: Press Shift and click the mouse (or press one of the arrow keys) to expand the selection. This will highlight all the items between the previously selected item and the current selection. Press Ctrl and click the mouse to select or deselect single items in the list.

SORTED

Items can be inserted by the application into a ListBox or ComboBox control, but inserting them in the proper place and maintaining some sort of organization can be quite a task for the programmer. If you want the items to be always sorted, set the control's Sorted property to True. This property can be set at design time as well as runtime.

The ListBox control is basically a text control and won't sort numeric data properly. To use the ListBox control to sort numbers, you must first format them with leading zeros. For example, the number 10 will appear in front of the number 5, because the string "10" is smaller than the string "5". If the numbers are formatted as "010" and "005", they will be sorted correctly.

The items in a sorted ListBox control are in ascending and case-sensitive order. Moreover, there is no mechanism for changing this default setting. The following items would be sorted as shown:

"AA"

"Aa"

"aA"

"aa"

"BA"

"ba"

Uppercase characters appear before the equivalent lowercase characters, but both upper- and lowercase characters appear together. All words beginning with *B* appear after the words beginning with *A* and before the words beginning with *C*. Within the group of words beginning with *B*, those beginning with a capital *B* appear before those beginning with a lowercase *b*.

NOTE *Populating long sorted lists is an expensive operation, because VB must figure out where to insert each item. It takes 13 seconds to populate an unsorted list with 100,000 items. The same operation takes forever (several minutes) if the Sorted property is set to True. If you want to add a large number of items to a ListBox control, set its Sorted property to False, populate it and then set the Sorted property to True to sort the items on the control. For 100,000 items, this trick will bring down the total time from minutes to seconds.*

TEXT

The Text property returns the selected text on the control. Notice that the items need not be strings. By default, each item is an object. For each object, however, the control displays a string, which is the same string returned by the object's ToString method. To retrieve the selected string on the control, use the Text property. To access the actual object, use the SelectedItem property, which is described later in this chapter.

The Items Collection

To manipulate a ListBox control from within your application, you should be able to:

◆ Add items to the list

◆ Remove items from the list

◆ Access individual items in the list

The items in the list are represented by the Items collection. You use the members of the Items collection to access the control's items and to add or remove items. The Items property exposes the standard members of a Collection, and they're described in the following sections.

Each member of the Items collection is an object. In most cases, we use ListBox controls to store strings, but it's possible to store objects. When you add an object to a ListBox control, a string will be displayed on the corresponding line of the control. This is the string returned by the object's ToString method. This is the property of the object that will be displayed by default. You can display any other property of the object by setting the control's ValueMember property to the name of the property.

If you add a Color and a Rectangle object to the Items collection with the following statements:

```
ListBox1.Items.Add(Color.Yellow)
ListBox1.Items.Add(New Rectangle(0, 0, 100, 100))
```

then the following strings will appear on the first two lines of the control:

```
Color [Yellow]
{X=0, Y=0, Width=100, Height=100}
```

However, you can access the members of the two objects, because the ListBox stores objects, not their descriptions. The following two statements will print the green color component of the Color object and the width of the Rectangle object (the output produced by each statement is shown in bold):

```
Console.WriteLine(ListBox1.Items.Item(0).G)
255
Console.WriteLine(ListBox1.Items.Item(1).Width)
100
```

The expressions in the last two statements are *late-bound*. This means that the compiler doesn't know whether the first object in the Items collection is a Color object and therefore can't verify the member Green. If you attempt to call the Green property of the second item in the collection, you'll get an exception at runtime to the effect that the code has attempted to access a missing member. The missing member is the G (green component) property of the Rectangle object.

The proper way to read the objects stored in a ListBox control is to examine the type of the object first, and attempt to retrieve a property (or call a method) of the object only if it's of the appropriate type. Here's how you would read the green component of a Color object:

```
If ListBox1.Items.Item(0).GetType Is GetType(Color) Then
    Console.WriteLine(ListBox1.Items.Item(0).G)
End If
```

ADD

To add items to the list, use the `Items.Add` or `Items.Insert` method. The syntax of the Add method is

```
ListBox1.Items.Add(item)
```

The *item* parameter is the object to be added to the list. You can add any object to the ListBox control, but items are usually strings. The Add method appends new items to the end of the list, unless the Sorted property has been set to True.

The following loop adds the elements of the array *words* to a ListBox control, one at a time:

```
Dim words(100) As String
{ statements to populate array }
```

```
Dim i As Integer
For i = 0 To 99
    ListBox1.Items.Add(words(i))
Next
```

Similarly, you can iterate through all the items on the control with a loop like the following:

```
Dim i As Integer
For i = 0 To ListBox1.Items.Count - 1
    { statements to process item ListBox1.Items(i) }
Next
```

You can also use the For Each…Next statement to iterate through the Items collection, as shown here:

```
Dim itm As Object
For Each itm In ListBox1.Items
    { process the current item, represented by the itm variable }
Next
```

When you populate a ListBox control with a large number of items, call the BeginUpdate before starting the loop and the EndUpdate method when you're done. These two methods will turn off the visual update of the control while you're populating it. When the EndUpdate method is called, the control will be redrawn with all the items.

CLEAR

The Clear method removes all the items from the control. Its syntax is quite simple:

```
List1.Items.Clear
```

COUNT

This is the number of items in the list. If you want to access all the items with a For…Next loop, the loop's counter must go from 0 to ListBox1.Items.Count - 1, as shown in the example of the Add method.

COPYTO

The CopyTo method of the Items collection retrieves all the items from a ListBox control and stores them to the array passed to the method as argument. The syntax of the CopyTo method is

```
ListBox1.CopyTo(destination, index)
```

where *destination* is the name of the array that will accept the items and *index* is the index of an element in the array where the first item will be stored. The array that will hold the items of the control must be declared explicitly and must be large enough to hold all the items.

INSERT

To insert an item at a specific location, use the Insert method, whose syntax is:

```
ListBox1.Items.Insert(index, item)
```

where *item* is the object to be added and *index* is the location of the new item. The first item's order in the list is zero. Note that you need not insert items at specific location when the list is sorted. If you do, the items will be inserted at the specified locations, but the list will no longer be sorted.

The following statement inserts a new item at the top of the list:

```
ListBox1.Items.Insert(0, "new item")
```

REMOVE

To remove an item from the list, you must first find its position (index) in the list, and call the Remove method passing the position as argument:

```
ListBox1.Items.Remove(index)
```

The *index* parameter is the order of the item to be removed, and this time it's not optional. The following statement removes the item at the top of the list:

```
ListBox1.Remove(0)
```

You can also specify the item to be removed by reference. To remove a specific item from the list, use the following syntax:

```
ListBox1.Items.Remove(item)
```

If the control contains strings, pass the string to be removed. If the same string appears multiple times on the control, only the first instance will be removed. If the control contains object, pass a variable that references the item you want to remove.

CONTAINS

The Contains method of the Items collection—not to be confused with the control's Contains method—accepts an object as argument and returns a True/False value indicating whether the collection contains this object or not. Use the Contains method to avoid the insertion of identical objects to the ListBox control. The following statements add a string to the Items collection, only if the string isn't already part of the collection:

```
Dim itm As String = "Remote Computing"
If Not ListBox1.Items.Contains(itm) Then
    ListBox1.Items.Add(itm)
End If
```

SELECTING ITEMS

The ListBox control allows the user to select either one or multiple items, depending on the setting of the SelectionMode property. In a single-selection ListBox control, you can retrieve the selected item with the SelectedItem property and its index with the SelectedIndex property. SelectedItem returns the selected item, which could be an object. The text that was clicked by the user to select the item is reported by the Text property.

If the control allows the selection of multiple items, they're reported with the SelectedItems property. This property is a collection of Item objects and exposes the same members as the Items collection. The `SelectedItems.Count` property reports the number of selected items.

To iterate through all the selected items in a multiselection ListBox control, use a loop like the following:

```
Dim itm As Object
For Each itm In ListBox1.SelectedItems
    Console.WriteLine(itm)
Next
```

The *itm* variable was declared as Object because the items in the ListBox control are objects. They happen to be strings in most cases, but they can be anything. If they're all of the same type, you can convert them to the specific type and then call their methods. If all the items are of the Color type, you can use a loop like the following to print the red component of each color:

```
Dim itm As Object
For Each itm In ListBox1.SelectedItems
    Console.WriteLine(Ctype(itm, Color).Red)
Next
```

A common situation in programming the ListBox control is to remove items from one control and add them to another. This is what the ListDemo project of the following section demonstrates, along with the techniques for adding and removing items to single-selection and a multiselection ListBox controls.

NOTE *Even though the ListBox control can store all types of objects, it's used most frequently for storing strings. Storing objects to a ListBox control requires some extra work, because the ToString method of most objects doesn't return the type of string we want to display on the control. You will find an example on using the ListBox control with objects in Chapter 8, where you'll learn how to build custom objects.*

VB.NET at Work: The ListDemo Project

The ListDemo application (shown in Figure 6.7) demonstrates the basic operations of the ListBox control. The two ListBox controls on the form operate slightly differently. The first has the default configuration: only one item can be selected at a time, and new items are appended after the existing item. The second ListBox control has its Sorted property set to True and its MultiSelect property set to MultiExtended. This means that the elements of this control are always sorted, and the user can select multiple cells with the mouse.

The code for the ListDemo application contains much of the logic you'll need in your ListBox manipulation routines. It shows you how to:

◆ Add and remove items

◆ Transfer items between lists

◆ Handle multiple selected items

◆ Maintain sorted lists

FIGURE 6.7

ListDemo demonstrates most of the operations you'll perform with ListBoxes.

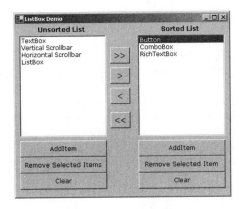

THE ADD ITEM BUTTONS

The Add Item buttons use the InputBox() function to prompt the user for input, and then they add the user-supplied string to the ListBox control. The code is identical for both buttons (Listing 6.10).

LISTING 6.10: THE ADD ITEM BUTTONS

```
Private Sub bttnAdd1_Click(ByVal sender As System.Object, _
            ByVal e As System.EventArgs) Handles bttnAdd1.Click
    Dim ListItem As String
    ListItem = InputBox("Enter new item's name")
    If ListItem.Trim <> "" Then
        sourceList.Items.Add(ListItem)
    End If
End Sub
```

Notice that the subroutine examines the data entered by the user to avoid adding blank strings to the list. The code for the Clear buttons is also straightforward; it simply calls the Clear method of the Items collection to remove all entries from the corresponding list.

THE REMOVE SELECTED ITEM(S) BUTTONS

The code for the Remove Selected Item button is different from that for the Remove Selected Items button (both are presented in Listing 6.11). The code for the Remove Selected Items button must scan all the items of the left list and remove the selected one(s). The reason is that the ListBox on the right can have only one selected item, and the other one allows the selection of multiple items. To delete an item, you must have at least one item selected. The code makes sure that the Selected-Index property is not negative. If no item is selected, the SelectedIndex property is −1 and attempting to remove an item by specifying an invalid index will generate an error.

LISTING 6.11: THE REMOVE BUTTONS

```
Private Sub bttnRemoveSelDest_Click(ByVal sender As System.Object, _
              ByVal e As System.EventArgs) Handles bttnRemoveSelDest.Click
    destinationList.Items.Remove(destinationList.SelectedItem)
End Sub
Private Sub bttnRemoveSelSrc_Click(ByVal sender As System.Object, _
              ByVal e As System.EventArgs) Handles bttnRemoveSelSrc.Click
    Dim i As Integer
    For i = 0 To sourceList.SelectedIndices.Count - 1
       sourceList.Items.RemoveAt(sourceList.SelectedIndices(0))
    Next
End Sub
```

Even though it's possible to remove an item by name, this is not a safe approach. If two items have the same name, then the Remove method will remove the first one. Unless you've provided the code to make sure that no identical items can be added to the list, remove them by their index, which is unique.

Notice that the code removes always the first item in the SelectedIndices collection. If you attempt to remove the item SelectedIndices(i), you will remove the first selected item, but after that you will not remove all the selected items. After removing an item from the selection, the remaining items are no longer at the same locations. The second selected item will take the place of the first selected item, which was just deleted, and so on. By removing the first item in the SelectedIndices collection, we make sure that all selected items, and only they, will be eventually removed.

The code of the Remove Selected Items button uses the Count property of the SelectedIndices collection to repeat the operation as many times as the number of selected items.

THE ARROW BUTTONS

The two Buttons with the single arrows, between the ListBox controls shown in Figure 6.7, transfer selected items from one list to another. The first arrow button can transfer a single element only, after it ensures that the list contains a selected item. Its code is presented in Listing 6.12. First, it adds the item to the second list, and then it removes the item from the original list. Notice that the code removes an item by passing it as argument to the Remove method, because it doesn't make any difference which one of two identical objects will be removed.

LISTING 6.12: THE RIGHT ARROW BUTTON

```
Private Sub bttnMoveDest_Click(ByVal sender As System.Object, _
              ByVal e As System.EventArgs) Handles bttnMoveDest.Click
    Dim i As Integer
    While sourceList.SelectedIndices.Count > 0
       destinationList.Items.Add(sourceList.SelectedItems(i))
       sourceList.Items.Remove(sourceList.SelectedItems(i))
    End While
End Sub
```

The second arrow button transfers items in the opposite direction; the code is almost identical to the one presented here, and I need not repeat it. The fact that one list is sorted and the other isn't doesn't affect our code. The destination control (the one on the left) doesn't allow the selection of multiple items, so you could use the SelectedIndex and SelectedItem properties. Since the single element is also part of the SelectedItems collection, you need not use a different approach. The statements that move a single item from the right to the left ListBox are shown next:

```
sourceList.Items.Add(destinationList.SelectedItem)
destinationList.Items.RemoveAt(destinationList.SelectedIndex)
```

Before we leave the topic of the ListBox control, let's examine one more powerful technique: using the ListBox control to maintain a list of keys (the data items used in recalling the information) to an array or random access file with records of related information. We'll use the ListBox control to store information like names, or book titles, which allows users to select the desired item. The item in the control will be linked to related information, like addresses and phone numbers for people, author and price information for books, and so on. In other words, we'll use the ListBox control as a lookup mechanism for several pieces of information.

Searching

The single most important enhancement to the ListBox control is that it can now locate any item in the list with the FindString and FindStringExact methods. Both methods accept a string as argument (the item to be located) and a second, optional argument, the index at which the search will begin. The FindString method locates a string that partially matches the one you're searching for; FindStringExact finds an exact match. If you're searching for "Man" and the control contains a name like "Mansfield," FindString will match the item, but FindStringExact will not.

NOTE   *Both the FindString and FindStringExact methods perform case-insensitive searches. If you're searching for "visual" and the list contains the item "Visual", both methods will locate it.*

The syntax of both methods is the same:

```
itemIndex = ListBox1.FindString(searchStr As String)
```

where *searchStr* is the string you're searching for. An alternative form of both methods allows you to specify the order of the item at which the search will begin:

```
itemIndex = ListBox1.FindString(searchStr As String, startIndex As Integer)
```

The *startIndex* argument allows you specify the beginning of the search, but you can't specify where the search will end.

The FindString and FindStringExact methods work even if the ListBox control is not sorted. You need not set the Sorted property to True before you call one of the searching methods on the control. Sorting the list will probably help the search operation a little, but it takes the control less than 100 milliseconds to find an item in a list of 100,000 items, so time spent to sort the list isn't worth it.

VB.NET AT WORK: THE LISTBOXFIND APPLICATION

The application you'll build in this section (seen in Figure 6.8) populates a list with a large number of items and then locates any string you specify. Click the button Populate List to populate the

ListBox control with 10,000 random strings. This process will take a few seconds and will populate the control with different random strings every time. Then, each time you click the Find Item button, you'll be prompted to enter a string. The code will locate the closest match in the list and select (highlight) this item.

FIGURE 6.8

The ListBoxFind application

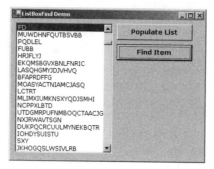

The code (Listing 6.13) attempts to locate an exact match with the FindStringExact method. If it succeeds, it reports the index of the matching element. If not, it attempts to locate a near match, with the FindString method. If it succeeds, it reports the index of the near match (which is the first item on the control that partially matches the search argument) and terminates. If it fails to find an exact match, it reports that the string wasn't found in the list.

LISTING 6.13: SEARCHING THE LIST

```
Private Sub bttnFind_Click(ByVal sender As System.Object, _
            ByVal e As System.EventArgs) Handles bttnFind.Click
    Dim srchWord As String
    Dim wordIndex As Integer
    srchWord = InputBox("Enter word to search for")
    wordIndex = ListBox1.FindStringExact(srchWord)
    If wordIndex >= 0 Then
        MsgBox("Index = " & wordIndex.ToString & "   =" & _
            (ListBox1.Items(wordIndex)).ToString, , "EXACT MATCH")
        ListBox1.TopIndex = wordIndex
        ListBox1.SelectedIndex = wordIndex
    Else
        wordIndex = ListBox1.FindString(srchWord)
        If wordIndex >= 0 Then
            MsgBox("Index = " & wordIndex.ToString & "   =" & _
                (ListBox1.Items(wordIndex)).ToString, , "NEAR MATCH")
            ListBox1.TopIndex = wordIndex
            ListBox1.SelectedIndex = wordIndex
        Else
            MsgBox("Item " & srchWord & " is not in the list")
        End If
    End If
End Sub
```

If you search for "SAC", for example, and the control begins with a string like "SAC" or "sac" or "sAc", the program will return the index of the item in the list and will report an exact match. If no exact match can be found, the program will return something like "SACDEF", if such a string exists on the control, as a near match. If none of the strings on the control starts with the characters *SAC*, the search will fail.

Populating the List

The Populate List button creates 10,000 random items with the help of the Random class. First, it generates a random value in the range 1 through 20, which is the length of the string (not all strings have the same length). Then the code (shown in Listing 6.14) generates as many random characters as the length of the string and builds the string. This random number is in the range from 65 to 91; these are the ANSI values of the uppercase characters.

LISTING 6.14: POPULATING A LIST WITH RANDOM STRINGS

```
Protected Sub PopulateButton_Click(ByVal sender As Object, _
                ByVal e As System.EventArgs)
    Dim wordLen As Integer
    Dim NWords As Integer = 9999
    Dim rnd As System.Random
    rnd = New System.Random()
    Dim rndChar As Char
    Dim thisWord As String
    Dim i, j As Integer
    For i = 0 To NWords
        wordLen = CInt(rnd.NextDouble * 20 + 1)
        thisWord = ""
        For j = 0 To wordLen
            rndchar = Chr(65 + CInt(rnd.Next, 25))
            thisWord = thisWord & rndChar
        Next
        ListBox1.Items.Add(thisWord)
    Next
End Sub
```

The ComboBox Control

The ComboBox control is similar to the ListBox control in the sense that it contains multiple items of which the user may select one, but it typically occupies less space on-screen. The ComboBox is practically an expandable ListBox control, which can grow when the user wants to make a selection and retract after the selection is made. Normally, the ComboBox control displays one line with the selected item. The real difference, however, between ComboBox and ListBox controls is that the ComboBox allows the user to specify items that don't exist in the list. Moreover, the Text property of the ComboBox is read-only at runtime, and you can locate an item by assigning a value to the control's Text property.

Three types of ComboBox controls are available in Visual Basic.NET. The value of the control's Style property, whose values are shown in Table 6.3, determines which box is used.

TABLE 6.3: STYLES OF THE COMBOBOX CONTROL

VALUE	EFFECT
DropDown	(Default) The control is made up of a drop-down list and a text box. The user can select an item from the list or type a new one in the text box.
DropDownList	This style is a drop-down list, from which the user can select one of its items but can't enter a new one.
Simple	The control includes a text box and a list that doesn't drop down. The user can select from the list or type in the text box.

The ComboBoxStyles project in this chapter's folder on the CD (see Figure 6.9) demonstrates the three styles of the ComboBox control. It's a common element of the Windows interface, and its properties and methods are identical to those of the ListBox control. Load the ComboBoxStyles project in the Visual Basic IDE and experiment with the three styles of the ComboBox control.

FIGURE 6.9

The ComboBox-Styles project demonstrates the various styles of the ComboBox control.

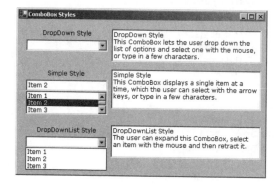

The DropDown and Simple ComboBox controls allow the user to select an item from the list or enter a new one in the edit box of the control.

The DropDownList ComboBox is similar to a ListBox control in the sense that it restricts the user to selecting an item, but not entering a new one. However, it takes much less space on the form than a ListBox. When the user wants to make a selection, the DropDownList expands to display more items. After the user has made a selection, the list contracts to a single line again.

Most of the properties and methods of the ListBox control also apply to the ComboBox control. The Items collection gives you access to the control's items, and the SelectedIndices and SelectedItems collections give you access to the items in the current selection. If the control allows only a single item to be selected, then use the properties SelectedIndex and SelectedItem. You can also use the FindString and FindStringExact methods to locate any items in the control.

There's one aspect worth mentioning, regarding the operation of the control. Although the edit box at the top allows you to enter a new string, the new string doesn't become a new item. It remains there until you select another item or you clear the edit box.

The most common use of the ComboBox control as a lookup table. The ComboBox control takes up very little space on the form, but it can be expanded at will. You can save even more space, when the ComboBox is contracted, by setting it to a width that's too small for the longest item. Use the DropDownWidth property, which is the width of the segment of the control that's dropped down. By default, this property is equal to the Width property. Figure 6.10 shows a ComboBox control with a couple of unusually long items. The control is wide enough to display the default selection. When the user clicks the arrow to expand the control, the drop-down section of the control is wider than the default width, so that the long items can be read. The control on the left is shown in its normal state, with a width of 130 pixels. The drop-down segment of the control is 240 pixels wide. You will have to experiment a little to find the ideal value of the DropDownWidth property.

FIGURE 6.10

The ComboBox control's Width and DropDownWidth properties

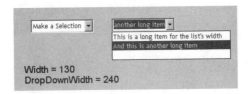

Although the ComboBox control allows users to enter text in the control's edit box, it doesn't provide a simple mechanism for adding new items at runtime. Let's say you provide a ComboBox with city names. Users can type the first few characters and very quickly locate the desired item. But what if you want to allow users to add new city names? You can provide this feature with two simple techniques. The simpler one is to place a button with an ellipsis (three periods) right next to the control. When users want to add a new item to the control, they can click the button and be prompted for the new item.

A more elegant approach is to examine the control's Text property as soon as it loses focus. If the string entered by the user doesn't match an item on the control, then you must add a new item to the control's Items collection and select the new item from within your code. The FlexComboBox project on the CD demonstrates how to use both techniques in your code. The main form of the project, which is shown in Figure 6.11, is a simple data-entry screen. It's not the best data-entry form, but it's meant for demonstration purposes.

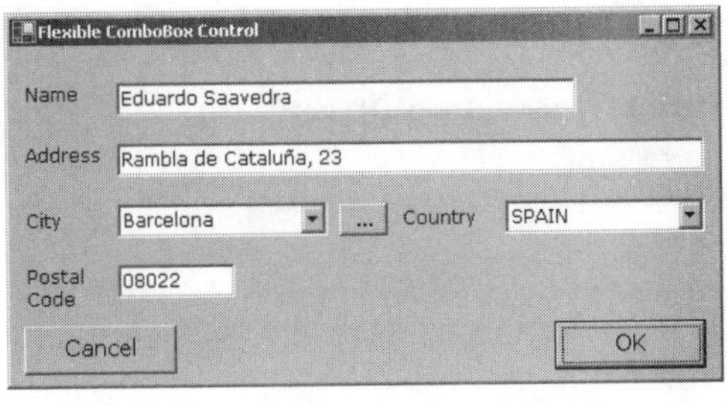

FIGURE 6.11

The FlexComboBox project demonstrates two techniques for adding new items to a ComboBox at runtime.

The ComboBox that displays countries isn't updateable; it's populated at design time and can't accept new items, so you must populate it with all the country names. The ComboBox that displays cities is updateable. You can either enter a city name and press the Tab key to move to another control, or click the button next to the control to be prompted for a new city name. The application will let you enter any city/country combination. You should provide code to limit the cities within the selected country, but this is a non-trivial task. You also need to store the new city names entered on the first ComboBox control to a file (or a database table), so that users will find them there the next time they execute the application. I'm not going to make the application really elaborate; I'll only add the code to demonstrate how to add new items to a ComboBox control at runtime.

The button with the ellipsis next to the City ComboBox control prompts the user for the new item with the InputBox() function. Then it searches the Items collection of the control with the `Items.IndexOf` method, and if the new item isn't found, it's added to the control. Then the code selects the new item in the list. To do so, it sets the control's SelectedIndex property to the value returned by the `Items.Add` method, or the value returned by the `Items.IndexOf` method, depending on whether the item was located, or added to the list. Listing 6.15 shows the code behind the button with the ellipsis.

LISTING 6.15: ADDING A NEW ITEM TO THE COMBOBOX CONTROL AT RUNTIME

```
Private Sub Button1_Click(ByVal sender As System.Object, _
            ByVal e As System.EventArgs) Handles Button1.Click
    Dim itm As String
    itm = InputBox("Enter new item", "New Item")
    If itm <> "" Then AddElement(itm)
End Sub
```

The AddElement() subroutine, which accepts a string as argument and adds it to the control, is shown in Listing 6.16. As you will see, the same subroutine will be used by the second method for adding items to the control at runtime.

LISTING 6.16: THE ADDELEMENT() SUBROUTINE

```
Sub AddElement(ByVal newItem As String)
    Dim idx As Integer
    If Not ComboBox1.Items.Contains(newItem) Then
        idx = ComboBox1.Items.Add(newItem)
    Else
        idx = ComboBox1.Items.IndexOf(newItem)
    End If
    ComboBox1.SelectedIndex = idx
End Sub
```

You can also add new items at runtime by adding the same code in the control's LostFocus event handler:

```
Private Sub ComboBox1_LostFocus(ByVal sender As Object, _
            ByVal e As System.EventArgs) Handles ComboBox1.LostFocus
    Dim newItem As String = ComboBox1.Text
    AddElement(newItem)
End Sub
```

The ScrollBar and TrackBar Controls

The ScrollBar and TrackBar controls let the user specify a magnitude by scrolling a selector between its minimum and maximum values. In some situations, the user doesn't know in advance the exact value of the quantity to specify (in which case, a text box would suffice), so your application must provide a more flexible mechanism for specifying a value, along with some type of visual feedback.

VB6 ➠ VB.NET

The ScrollBar control is the same as in VB6 with no substantial improvements. You will notice that there is only one ScrollBar control on the Toolbox, instead of the horizontal and vertical ones of VB6. In VB.NET, you can set the orientation of the control through the Orientation property. The main event of the ScrollBar control, Change, has a new name: it's now called ValueChanged.

The TrackBar control is the old Slider control; other than its name, nothing else has changed.

The vertical scroll bar that lets a user move up and down a long document is a typical example of the use of a ScrollBar control. In the past, users had to supply line numbers to locate the section of the document they wanted to view. With a highly visual operating system, however, this is no longer even an option.

The scroll bar and visual feedback are the prime mechanisms for repositioning the view in a long document or in a large picture that won't fit entirely in its window. When scrolling through a document or image to locate the area of interest, the user doesn't know or care about line numbers or pixel coordinates. Rather, the user uses the scroll bar to navigate through the document, and the visible part of the document provides the required feedback.

The TrackBar control is similar to the ScrollBar control, but it doesn't cover a continuous range of values. The TrackBar control has a fixed number of tick marks, which the developer can label (e.g., Off, Slow, and Speedy, as shown in Figure 6.12). The user can place the slider's indicator to the desired value. While the ScrollBar control relies on some visual feedback outside the control to help the user position the indicator to the desired value, the TrackBar control forces the user to select from a range of valid values.

In short, the ScrollBar control should be used when the exact value isn't as important as the value's effect on another object or data element. The TrackBar control should be used when the user can type a numeric value and the value your application expects is a number in a specific range; for example, integers between 0 and 100, or a value between 0 and 5 inches in steps of 0.1 inches (0.0, 0.1, 0.2 ... 5.0).

The TrackBar control is preferred to the TextBox control in similar situations because there's no need for data validation on your part. The user can only specify valid numeric values with the mouse.

FIGURE 6.12

The TrackBar control lets the user select one of several discrete values.

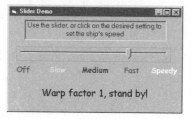

The ScrollBar Control

The ScrollBar control is a long stripe with an indicator that lets the user select a value between the two ends of the control, and it can be positioned either vertically or horizontally. Use the Orientation property to make the control vertical or horizontal. The left (or bottom) end of the control corresponds to its minimum value; the other end is the control's maximum value. The current value of the control is determined by the position of the indicator, which can be scrolled between the minimum and maximum values. The basic properties of the ScrollBar control, therefore, are properly named Minimum, Maximum, and Value (see Figure 6.13).

FIGURE 6.13

The basic properties of the ScrollBar control

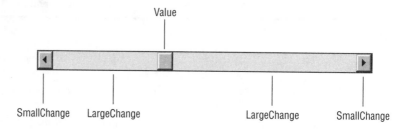

Minimum   The control's minimum value. The default value is 0, but because this is an Integer value you can set it to negatives values as well.

Maximum   The control's maximum value. The default value is 100, but you can set it to any value you can represent with the Integer data type.

Value   The control's current value, specified by the indicator's position.

The Minimum and Maximum properties are positive Integer values. To cover a range of negative numbers or non-integers, you must supply the code to map the actual values to Integer values. For example, to cover a range from 2.5 to 8.5, set the Minimum property to 25, set the Maximum property to 85, and divide the control's value by 10. If the range you need is from –2.5 to 8.5, do the same but set the Minimum property to 0, set the Maximum property to 110, and subtract 25 from the Value property every time you read it.

VB.NET AT WORK: THE COLORS PROJECT

Figure 6.14 shows another example that demonstrates how the ScrollBar control works. The Colors application lets the user specify a color by manipulating the value of its basic colors (red, green, and blue) through scroll bars. Each basic color is controlled by a scroll bar and has a minimum value of 0 and a maximum value of 255.

FIGURE 6.14

The Colors application demonstrates the use of the ScrollBar control.

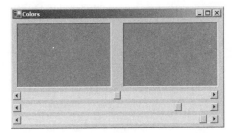

NOTE *If you aren't familiar with color definition in the Windows environment, see the section "Specifying Colors" in Chapter 14.*

As the scroll bar is moved, the corresponding color is displayed, and the user can easily specify a color without knowing the exact values of its primary components. All the user needs to know is whether the desired color contains, for example, too much red or too little green. With the help of the scroll bars and the immediate feedback from the application, the user can easily pinpoint the exact value. Notice that this "exact value" is of no practical interest; only the final color counts.

Scroll bars and slider bars have minimum and maximum values that can be set with the Minimum and Maximum properties. The indicator's position in the control determines its value, which is set or read with the Value property. In the Colors application, the initial value of the control is set to 128 (the middle of the range). Before looking at the code for the Colors application, let's examine the control's events.

THE SCROLLBAR CONTROL'S EVENTS

The user can change the ScrollBar control's value in three ways:

By clicking the two arrows at its ends. The value of the control changes by the amount specified with the SmallChange property.

By clicking the area between the indicator and the arrows. The value of the control changes by the amount specified with the LargeChange property.

By dragging the indicator with the mouse.

You can monitor the changes on the ScrollBar's value from within your code with two events: ValueChanged and Scroll. Both events are fired every time the indicator's position is changed. If you change the control's value from within your code, then only the ValueChanged event will be fired.

The Scroll event can be fired in response to many different actions, such as the scrolling of the indicator with the mouse or a click on one of the two buttons at the ends of the scrollbars. If you want to know the action that caused this event, you can examine the Type property of the second argument of the event handler. The settings of the e.Type property are shown in Table 6.4.

TABLE 6.4: THE ACTIONS THAT CAN CAUSE THE SCROLL EVENT

MEMBER	DESCRIPTION
EndScroll	The user has stopped scrolling the control.
First	The control was scrolled to the Minimum position.
LargeDecrement	The control was scrolled by a large decrement (user clicked the bar between the button and the left arrow).
LargeIncrement	The control was scrolled by a large increment (user clicked the bar between the button and the right arrow).
Last	The control was scrolled to the Maximum position.
SmallDecrement	The control was scrolled by a small decrement (user clicked the left arrow).
SmallIncrement	The control was scrolled by a small increment (user clicked the right arrow).
ThumbPosition	The button was moved.
ThumbTrack	The button is being moved.

EVENTS IN THE COLORS APPLICATION

The Colors application demonstrates how to program the two events. The two PictureBox controls display the color designed with the three scroll bars. The left PictureBox is colored from within the Scroll event, while the other one is colored from within the ValueChanged event.

As the user moves the indicator with the mouse, different colors are shown in the second Picture-Box, which is colored from within the ValueChanged event. This event is every time a scrollbar changes value. The other PictureBox doesn't follow the changes as they occur. In the Scroll event handler of the three scroll bars, the code examines the value of the e.Type property and reacts to it only if the event was fired because the scrolling of the indicator has ended. For all other actions, the event handler doesn't update the color of the left PictureBox.

If the user attempts to change the Color value by clicking the two arrows of the scroll bars or by clicking in the area to the left or to the right of the indicator, both PictureBox controls are updated. While the user slides the indicator, or keeps pressing one of the end arrows, only the PictureBox to the right is updated.

The conclusion from this experiment is that you can program either event to provide continuous feedback to the user. If this feedback requires too many calculations, which would slow down the reaction of the corresponding event handler, you can postpone the reaction until the user has stopped scrolling the indicator. You can detect this condition by examining the value of the e.Type property. When it's ScrollEventType.EndScroll, you can execute the appropriate statements. Listing 6.17 shows the code behind the Scroll and ValoueChanged events of the Srollbar that controls the red component of the color. The code of the corresponding events of the other two controls is identical.

LISTING 6.17: PROGRAMMING THE SCROLLBAR CONTROL'S SCROLL EVENT

```
Private Sub redBar_Scroll(ByVal sender As System.Object, _
            ByVal e As System.Windows.Forms.ScrollEventArgs) Handles redBar.Scroll
    If e.Type = ScrollEventType.EndScroll Then ColorBox1()
End Sub
Private Sub redBar_ValueChanged(ByVal sender As Object, _
            ByVal e As System.EventArgs) Handles redBar.ValueChanged
    ColorBox2()
End Sub
```

The ColorBox1() and ColorBox2() subroutines update the color of the two PictureBox controls and their listings are shown in Listing 6.18. The code creates a new color value based on the values of the three scroll bars and uses it to set the BackColor property of the appropriate control.

LISTING 6.18: UPDATING THE COLOR OF THE TWO TEXTBOX CONTROLS

```
Sub ColorBox1()
    Dim clr As Color
    clr = Color.FromARGB(redBar.Value, greenBar.Value, blueBar.Value)
    PictureBox1.BackColor = clr
End Sub
Sub ColorBox2()
    Dim clr As Color
    clr = Color.FromARGB(redBar.Value, greenBar.Value, blueBar.Value)
    PictureBox2.BackColor = clr
End Sub
```

The TrackBar Control

The TrackBar control is similar to the ScrollBar control, but it lacks the granularity of ScrollBar. Suppose you want the user of an application to supply a value in a specific range, such as the speed of a moving object. Moreover, you don't want to allow extreme precision; you need only a few settings, such as slow, fast, and very fast. A TrackBar control with just a few stops, such as the one shown in Figure 6.12, will suffice. The user can set the control's value by sliding the indicator or by clicking on either side of the indicator.

NOTE *Granularity is how specific you want to be in measuring. In measuring distances between towns, a granularity of a mile is often adequate. In measuring (or specifying) the dimensions of a building, the granularity could be on the order of a foot or an inch. The TrackBar control lets you set the type of granularity that's necessary for your application.*

Similar to the ScrollBar control, SmallChange and LargeChange properties are available. Small-Change is the smallest increment by which the Slider value can change. The user can only change the slider by the SmallChange value by sliding the indicator (unlike the ScrollBar control, there are no arrows at the two ends of the Slider control). To change the Slider's value by LargeChange, the user can click on either side of the indicator.

VB.NET AT WORK: THE INCHES PROJECT

Figure 6.15 demonstrates a typical use of the TrackBar control. The form in the figure is an element of a program's user interface that lets the user specify a distance between 0 and 10 inches in increments of 0.2 inches. As the user slides the indicator, the current value displays on a Label control above the TrackBar. If you open the Inches application, you'll notice that there are more stops than there are tick marks on the control. This is made possible with the TickFrequency property, which determines the frequency of the visible tick marks.

FIGURE 6.15

This TrackBar control lets users specify a distance.

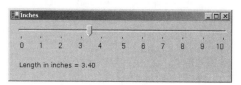

You may specify that the control has 50 stops (divisions) but that only 10 of them will be visible. The user can, however, position the indicator on any of the 40 invisible tick marks. You can think of the visible marks as the major tick marks and the invisible ones as the minor tick marks. If the TickFrequency property is 5, only every fifth mark will be visible. The slider's indicator, however, will stop at all tick marks.

TIP When using the TrackBar control on your interfaces, you should set the TickFrequency property to a value that helps the user select the desired setting. Too many tick marks are confusing and difficult to read. Without tick marks, the control isn't of much help. You might also consider placing a few labels to indicate the value of selected tick marks, as I have done in this example.

The properties of the TrackBar control in the Inches application are as follows:

```
Minimum = 0
Maximum = 50
SmallChange = 1
LargeChange = 5
TickFrequency = 5
```

The TrackBar needs to cover a range of 10 inches in increments of 0.2 inches. If you set the Small-Change property to 1, you have to set LargeChange to 10 (there's a total of 10 intervals of 0.2 inches in 10 inches). Moreover, the TickFrequency is set to 5, so there will be a total of 10 divisions in every inch. The numbers below the tick marks were placed there with properly aligned Label controls.

The label at the bottom needs to be updated as the TrackBar's value changes. This is signaled to the application with the Change event, which occurs every time the value of the control changes, either through scrolling or from within your code. The ValueChanged event handler of the TrackBar control is shown next:

```
Private Sub TrackBar1_ValueChanged(ByVal sender As System.Object, _
            ByVal e As System.EventArgs) Handles TrackBar1.ValueChanged
    lblInches.Text = "Length in inches = " & Format(TrackBar1.Value / 5, "#.00")
End Sub
```

The Label controls below the tick marks can also be used to set the value of the control. Every time you click one of the labels, the following statement sets the TrackBar control's value. Notice that all the Label controls' Click events are handled by a common handler:

```
Private Sub Label_Click(ByVal sender As System.Object, _
            ByVal e As System.EventArgs) Handles Label1.Click, Label2.Click, _
            Label3.Click, Label4.Click, Label5.Click, Label6.Click, _
            Label7.Click, Label8.Click, Label9.Click
    TrackBar1.Value = sender.text * 5
End Sub
```

VB.NET AT WORK: THE TEXTMARGIN PROJECT

To see the TrackBar control in use, let's review a segment of another application, the RTFPad application, which will be covered in Chapter 7. The Form shown in Figure 6.16 contains a RichTextBox control and two sliders. The RichTextBox control will be explained in Chapter 7. All you need to know about the control to follow the code is that the RichTextBox control is similar to a TextBox control, but provides many more editing and formatting options. Two of the control's properties we'll use in this example are the SelectionIndent and SelectionHangingIndent properties, and their functions are as follows:

FIGURE 6.16

The two TrackBar controls let the user format the paragraphs in a RichTextBox control.

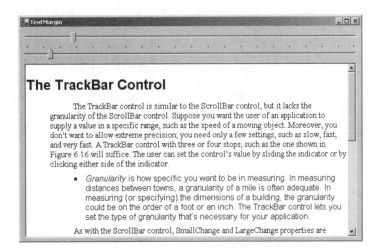

SelectionIndent   Specifies the amount by which the currently selected paragraphs are indented from the left side of the control.

SelectionHangingIndent   Specifies the amount of the hanging indentation (that is, the indentation of all paragraph lines after the first line).

The two TrackBar controls above the RichTextBox control let the user manipulate these two indentations. Because each paragraph in a RichTextBox control is a separate entity, it can be formatted differently. The upper slider controls the paragraph's indentation, and the lower slider controls the paragraph's hanging indentation.

You can open the TextMargin application in this chapter's folder on the CD and check it out. Enter a few paragraphs of text and experiment with it to see how the sliders control the appearance of the paragraphs.

To create the form shown in Figure 6.16, the left edge of the RichTextBox control must be perfectly aligned with the TrackBar control's indicators at their leftmost position. When both sliders are at the far left, the SelectionIndent and SelectionHangingIndent properties are zero. As the indicators are scrolled, these two properties change value, and the text is reformatted instantly. All the action takes place in the Slider controls' Scroll event.

Listing 6.18 presents the code of the Scroll event handlers for the two TrackBars: *TrackBar1*, on top, determines the paragraph's indentation, and *TrackBar2*, on the bottom, controls the hanging or "first-line" indentation of the current paragraph.

LISTING 6.18: SCROLL EVENT HANDLERS OF THE TRACKBARS

```
Private Sub TrackBar1_Scroll(ByVal sender As System.Object, _
             ByVal e As System.EventArgs) Handles TrackBar1.Scroll
   RichTextBox1.SelectionIndent = _
      CInt(RichTextBox1.Width * (TrackBar1.Value / TrackBar1.Maximum))
   TrackBar2_Scroll(sender, e)
End Sub
Private Sub TrackBar2_Scroll(ByVal sender As System.Object, _
             ByVal e As System.EventArgs) Handles TrackBar2.Scroll
   RichTextBox1.SelectionHangingIndent = CInt(RichTextBox1.Width * _
      (TrackBar2.Value / TrackBar2.Maximum)) - RichTextBox1.SelectionIndent
End Sub
```

The paragraph's hanging indentation is not the distance of the text from the left edge of the control, but the distance from the leftmost character of the first line. That's why every time the paragraph's indentation changes, the program calls the Scroll event of the second TrackBar control to adjust the hanging indentation, even though the second control hasn't been moved. The hanging indentation is expressed as a percentage, and we get the ratio of the difference between the two controls and their maximum value.

Every time you move the pointer in another paragraph in the text, the two TrackBar controls must be set to reflect the margins of the current paragraph. The selection of a new paragraph is reported to the application through the SelectionChanged event of the RichTextBox control. In the event handler shown in Listing 6.19 are two lines that set the Value property of the two TrackBar controls to the appropriate values.

LISTING 6.19: SELECTIONCHANGED EVENT HANDLER OF THE RICHTEXTBOX

```
Private Sub RichTextBox1_SelectionChanged(ByVal sender As Object, _
            ByVal e As System.EventArgs) _
            Handles RichTextBox1.SelectionChanged
    TrackBar1.Value = (RichTextBox1.SelectionIndent / RichTextBox1.Width) * 100
    TrackBar2.Value = TrackBar1.Value + _
            (RichTextBox1.SelectionHangingIndent / RichTextBox1.Width) * 100
End Sub
```

Summary

In this chapter, you learned about the basic Windows controls, which are the main components in creating Windows forms. The TextBox and ListBox controls are two of the most common elements of the interface of just about any Windows application and include a whole lot of functionality. The other controls are also quite common but considerably easier to program.

In the following chapters, you will read about more Windows controls—specifically, in Chapter 7, the controls for displaying common dialog boxes (like the Font and Color dialog boxes) and the RichTextBox control. These are not trivial controls, and they deserve a detailed discussion.

There are several more Windows controls I am not going to discuss in this book. The Date-TimePicker and MonthCalendar control are calendars that allow users to specify a date on a calendar, rather than typing it. The ToolBar and StatusBar controls are used to add tool bars (a narrow section with buttons at the top of the form) and status bars (a section with messages at the bottom of the form), and they are fairly easy to program. The functionality provided by these controls is too specific (and limited) compared to the functionality of the controls discussed in this and the following chapter.

Chapter 7

More Windows Controls

IN THIS CHAPTER, WE'LL continue our discussion of the basic Windows controls with the controls that implement the common dialog boxes and the RichTextBox control.

The Toolbox contains a few more controls, like ToolBar and DateTimePicker, that I won't discuss in this book. You won't often need them in your applications, and once you have learned to build user interfaces with the basic Windows controls, you'll have no problem using the less common ones. The controls I'm not discussing in this book are less elaborate and have a relatively small number of properties and methods.

The .NET Framework provides a set of controls for displaying common dialogs such as Open or Color. Each of these controls encapsulates a large amount of functionality that would take a lot of code to duplicate (in any language). The common dialog controls are an essential part of a Windows application, because they enable you to design user interfaces with the look and feel of a Windows application.

Besides the common dialog boxes, we'll also explore the RichTextBox control, which is an advanced version of the TextBox. RichTextBox provides all the functionality you'll need to build a word processor—WordPad is actually built around the RichTextBox control. It's the only control that can display formatted text, so if your application requires this feature, RichTextBox is your only option. It allows you to format text by mixing any number of fonts and attributes. You can also embed other objects in the document displayed on a RichTextBox, such as images. Sure, the RichTextBox control is nothing like a modern word processor, but it's a great tool for editing formatted text at runtime.

The Common Dialog Controls

A rather tedious, but quite common, task in nearly every application is to prompt the user for filenames, font names and sizes, or colors to be used by the application. Designing your own dialog boxes for these purposes would be a hassle, not to mention that your applications wouldn't have the same look and feel of all Windows applications. In fact, all Windows applications use some standard dialog boxes for common operations. Figure 7.1 shows a couple of examples. These dialog boxes are built into the Framework system, and any application can use them.

FIGURE 7.1

The Open and Font
common dialog
boxes

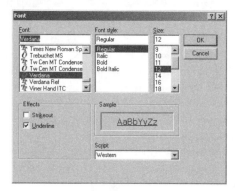

If you ever want to display an Open or Font dialog box, don't design it—it already exists. To use it, just place the appropriate common dialog control on your form and activate it from within your code by calling the ShowDialog method.

VB6 ⇒ VB.NET

In previous versions of VB, there was a single control on the Toolbox for all common dialog controls. VB.NET has a separate control for each common dialog, and there are four such controls on the Toolbox (excluding the ones that apply to printing). The new common dialog controls are the FontDialog, ColorDialog, Open-FileDialog, and SaveFileDialog. The new controls expose a large number of properties that are specific to each dialog box and are a little easier to program than the previous single control. The dialog controls for printing are discussed in detail in Chapter 15.

The common dialog controls are invisible at runtime, and they're not placed on your forms. You simply add them to the project by double-clicking their icons on the Toolbox. When a common dialog control is added to a project, a new icon appears in the components tray of the form, just below the Form Designer. The following common dialog controls are available on the Toolbox.

OpenFileDialog   Lets users select a file to open. It also allows the selection of multiple files, for applications that must process many files at once (change the format of the selected files, for example).

SaveFileDialog   Lets users select or specify a filename in which the current document will be saved.

ColorDialog   Lets users select a color from a list of predefined colors, or specify custom colors.

FontDialog   Lets users select a typeface and style to be applied to the current text selection. The Font common dialog has an Apply button, which you can intercept from within your code and use to apply the currently selected font to the text without closing the common dialog.

PrintDialog   Lets users select and set up a printer (the page's orientation, the document pages to be printed, and so on).

There are two more common dialog controls, the PrintPreviewDialog and the PageSetupDialog controls. These controls will be discussed in detail in Chapter 15, in the context of VB's printing capabilities. The PrintDialog control is discussed here because it doesn't require any printing code. This dialog box simply sets the basic properties of the printout. These properties must be taken into consideration by the printing code of the application, as you will see in Chapter 15.

Using the Common Dialog Controls

To display a common dialog from within your application, you must first add an instance of the appropriate control to your project. Then, you must set basic properties of the control through the Properties window. Most applications set the control's properties from within the code, because common dialogs interact closely with the application. When you call the Color common dialog, for example, you should preselect a color from within your application and make it the default selection on the control. If you open the Color dialog box to prompt the user for the color of the text on a control, the default selection should be the current setting of the control's ForeColor property. Likewise, the Save dialog box must suggest a filename when it first pops up, and you must specify the appropriate filename (or, at least, the file's extension) from within your application's code.

To display a common dialog box from within your code, you simply call the control's ShowDialog method, which is common for all controls. As soon as you call the ShowDialog method, the corresponding dialog box appears on-screen and the execution of the program is suspended until the box is closed. Using the Open and Save dialog boxes, the user can traverse the entire structure of their drives and locate the desired filename. When the user clicks the Open or Save button, the dialog box closes and the program's execution resumes. The code should read the name of the file selected by the user (FileName property) and use it to open the file or to store the current document there.

Here is the sequence of statements used to invoke the Open common dialog and retrieve the selected filename:

```
If OpenFileDialog1.ShowDialog = DialogResult.OK Then
    fileName = OpenFileDialog1.FileName
End If
```

The common dialogs are nothing more than dialog boxes, and they return a value indicating how they were closed. You should read this value from within your code and ignore the settings of the dialog box if it was canceled.

The variable *fileName* is the full pathname of the file selected by the user. You can also set the FileName property to a filename, which will be displayed when the Open dialog box is first opened. This allows the user to click the Open button to open the preselected file or choose another file.

```
OpenFileDialog1.FileName = "C:\Documents\Doc1.doc"
If OpenFileDialog1.ShowDialog = DialogResult.OK Then
    fileName = OpenFileDialog1.FileName
End If
```

Similarly, you can invoke the Color dialog box and read the value of the selected color with the following statements:

```
If ColorDialog1.ShowDialog = DialogResult.OK Then
    selColor = ColorDialog1.Color
End If
```

The ShowDialog method is common to all controls. The Title property is also common to all controls. This property returns or sets the string displayed in the title bar of the dialog box. The default title is the name of the dialog box (e.g., "Color," Font," and so on), but you can adjust it from within your code.

The Color Dialog Box

The Color dialog box, shown in Figure 7.2, is one of the simplest dialog boxes. It has a single property, Color, which returns the color selected by the user or sets the initially selected color when the user opens the dialog box. Before opening the Color common dialog with the ShowDialog method, you can set various properties, which are described next.

FIGURE 7.2

The Color dialog box

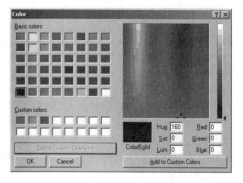

The following statements set the selected color of the Color common dialog control, display the control, and then use the color selected on the control to fill the form. First, place a ColorDialog control on the form, and then insert the following statements in a button's Click event handler:

```
Private Sub Button1_Click(ByVal sender As System.Object, _
                ByVal e As System.EventArgs) Handles Button1.Click
    ColorDialog1.Color = Me.BackColor
```

```
      ColorDialog1.AllowFullOpen = True
      If ColorDialog1.ShowDialog = DialogResult.OK Then
         Me.BackColor = ColorDialog1.Color
      End If
   End Sub
```

AllowFullOpen

Set this property to True if you want users to be able to open up the dialog box and define their own custom colors. The AllowFullOpen property doesn't open the custom section of the common dialog. It simply enables the Define Custom Colors button on the dialog box. Otherwise, this button is disabled. If you want to fully open the Color dialog box (like the one shown in Figure 7.2) when it first pops up, set the AllowFullOpen property to True. The Define Custom Colors button on the dialog box of Figure 7.2 is disabled because the dialog box is already fully opened.

AnyColor

This property is a Boolean value that determines whether the dialog box displays all available colors in the set of basic colors.

Color

This property is a Color value, and you can set it to any valid color. If you set this property before opening the Color dialog box, the selected color will appear on the control as the preselected color. On return, it's the color selected by the user on the dialog box.

```
   ColorDialog1.Color =  Color.Azure
   If ColorDialog1.ShowDialog = DialogResult.OK Then
      Me.BackColor = ColorDialog1.Color
   End If
```

CustomColors

This property indicates the set of custom colors that will be shown in the common dialog. The Color dialog box has a section called Custom Colors, where you can display 16 additional custom colors. The CustomColors property is an array of integers that represent colors. To display three custom colors in the lower section of the Color dialog box, use a statement like the following:

```
   Dim colors() As Integer = {222663, 35453, 7888}
   ColorDialog1.CustomColors = colors
```

You'd expect that the CustomColors property would be an array of Color values, but it's not. You can't create the array *CustomColors* with a statement like:

```
   Dim colors() As Color = {Color.Azure, Color.Navy, Color.Teal}
```

Since it's awkward to work with numeric values, you should convert color values to integer values with a statement like the following:

```
   Color.Navy.ToARGB
```

This statement returns an integer value that represents the color Navy. This value, however, is negative. The reason for that is that the first byte in the color value represents the transparency of the color. To get the value of the color, you must take the absolute value of the integer value returned by the previous expression. To create an array of integers that represent color values, use a statement like the following:

```
Dim colors() As Integer = {Math.Abs(Color.Gray.ToARGB), _
                           Math.Abs(Color.Navy.ToARGB), _
                           Math.Abs(Color.Teal.ToARGB)}
```

Now you can assign the *colors* array to the CustomColors property of the control, and they will appear in the Custom Colors section of the Color dialog box. The three colors of the same code are the custom colors shown in Figure 7.2.

SolidColorOnly

Indicates whether the dialog box will restrict users to selecting solid colors only. This setting should be used with systems that can display only 256 colors.

The Font Dialog Box

The Font dialog box, shown in Figure 7.3, lets the user review and select a font and its size and style. Optionally, the user can also select the font's color and even apply the current dialog-box settings to the selected text on a control of the form without closing the dialog box, by clicking the Apply button on the Font dialog box.

FIGURE 7.3

The Font common dialog box

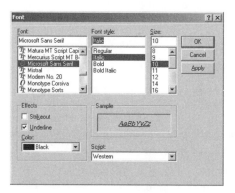

After the user selects a font, its size and style, and possibly some special effects (the text color or the underline attribute), and clicks the OK button, the dialog returns the attributes of the selected font through its properties. In addition to the OK button, there's an Apply button, which reports the current setting to your application. You can intercept the Click event of the Apply button and adjust the appearance of the text on your form while the common dialog is still visible.

The main property of this control is the Font property, which sets the initially selected font on the control and retrieves the font selected by the user. The following statements display the Font dialog box after selecting the current font of the TextBox1 control. When the user closes the dialog box, they retrieve the selected font and assign it to the TextBox control:

```
Private Sub Button2_Click(ByVal sender As System.Object, _
               ByVal e As System.EventArgs) Handles Button2.Click
    FontDialog1.Font = TextBox1.Font
    If FontDialog1.ShowDialog = DialogResult.OK Then
        TextBox1.Font = FontDialog1.Font
    End If
End Sub
```

ALLOWSCRIPTCHANGE

This property is a Boolean value that indicates whether the Script combo box will be displayed on the Font common dialog. This combo box allows the user to change the current character set and select a non-western language (like Greek, Hebrew, Cyrillic, and so on). The text on which the new font is applied will change to a different language only if the corresponding language has been installed on the system.

ALLOWSIMULATIONS

This property is a Boolean value that indicates whether the dialog box allows the display and selection of simulated fonts.

ALLOWVECTORFONTS

This property is a Boolean value that indicates whether the dialog box allows the display and selection of vector fonts.

ALLOWVERTICALFONTS

This property is a Boolean value that indicates whether the dialog box allows the display and selection of both vertical and horizontal fonts. Its default value is False, which displays only horizontal fonts.

COLOR

This property sets or returns the selected font color. The user will see the option to select a color for the selected font only if you set the ShowColor property to True.

FIXEDPITCHONLY

This property is a Boolean value that indicates whether the dialog box allows only the selection of fixed-pitch fonts. Its default value is False, which means that all fonts (fixed- and variable-pitch fonts) are displayed on the common dialog.

FONT

This property is a Font object. You can set it to the preselected font before displaying the dialog box and assign it to a Font property upon return. The following statements show how to preselect the font of the *TextBox1* control on the Font dialog box and how to change the same control's font to the one selected by the user on the dialog box:

```
FontDialog1.Font = TextBox1.Font
If FontDialog1.ShowDialog = DialogResult.OK Then
    TextBox1.Font = FontDialog1.Font
End If
```

You can create a new Font object and assign it to the control's Font property. The following statements do that:

```
Dim newFont As Font
newFont = New Font("Verdana", 12, FontStyle.Underline)
FontDialog1.Font = newFont
FontDialog1.ShowDialog()
```

The Font object's constructor is heavily overloaded. The form shown here is among the simpler overloaded forms of the constructor. To apply multiple attributes, combine their names with the Or operator.

The Color property is not part of the Font property. If you allow users to change the font's color, you must handle this property separately from within your code. To continue the previous example, the following statement sets the color of the new font:

```
TextBox1.ForeColor = FontDialog1.Color
```

FONTMUSTEXIST

This property is a Boolean value that indicates whether the dialog box forces the selection of an existing font. If the user enters a font name that doesn't correspond to a name in the list of available fonts, a warning is displayed. Its default value is True.

MAXSIZE, MINSIZE

These two properties are integers that determine the minimum and maximum point size the user can select. Use these two properties to prevent the selection of extremely large or extremely small font sizes.

SCRIPTSONLY

This property indicates whether the dialog box allows selection of fonts for Symbol character sets, in addition to the American National Standards Institute (ANSI) character set. Its default value is True.

SHOWAPPLY

This property is a Boolean value that indicates whether the dialog box provides an Apply button. Its default value is False, so the Apply button isn't normally displayed. If you set this property to True, you must also program the control's Apply button—the changes aren't applied automatically to any of the controls on the current form.

The following statements display the Font dialog box with the Apply button:

```
Private Sub Button2_Click(ByVal sender As System.Object, _
                ByVal e As System.EventArgs) Handles Button2.Click
    FontDialog1.Font = TextBox1.Font
    FontDialog1.ShowApply = True
    If FontDialog1.ShowDialog = DialogResult.OK Then
        TextBox1.Font = FontDialog1.Font
    End If
End Sub
```

If you display the Apply button, you must also capture its Click event and process it from within your code. The FontDialog control raises the Apply event every time the user clicks the Apply button. In this event's handler, you must read the currently selected font and assign it to the TextBox control on the form:

```
Private Sub FontDialog1_Apply(ByVal sender As Object, _
                ByVal e As System.EventArgs) Handles FontDialog1.Apply
    TextBox1.Font = FontDialog1.Font
End Sub
```

SHOWCOLOR

This property is a Boolean value that indicates whether the dialog box allows the user to select a color for the font.

SHOWEFFECTS

This property is a Boolean value that indicates whether the dialog box contains controls to allow the user to specify special text effects, such as strikethrough and underline. The effects are returned to the application as attributes of the selected Font object, and you don't have to anything special in your application.

The Open and Save As Dialog Boxes

Open and Save As are the two most widely used common dialog boxes, and they're implemented by the OpenFileDialog and SaveFileDialog controls. Nearly every application prompts the user for a filename, and VB provides two controls for this purpose. The two dialog boxes are nearly identical and most of their properties are common, so we'll start with the properties that are common to both controls.

When one of the two controls is displayed, it rarely displays all the files in any given folder. Usually the files displayed are limited to the ones that the application recognizes so that users can easily spot the file they want. The Filter property determines which files appear in the Open or Save dialog box (Figure 7.4).

It's also standard for the Windows interface not to display the extensions of files (although Windows distinguishes files using their extensions). The Save As Type combo box contains the various file types recognized by the application. The various file types can be described in plain English with long descriptive names and without their extensions.

FIGURE 7.4

The Save As
dialog box

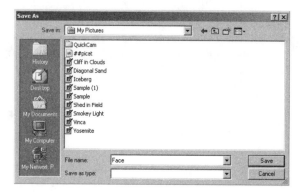

The extension of the default file type for the application is described by the DefaultExtension property, and the list of the file types displayed in the Save As Type box is described by the Filter property. Both the DefaultExtension and the Filter properties are available in the control's Properties window at design time. At runtime, you must set them manually from within your code.

To prompt the user for the file to be opened, use the following statements. This dialog box displays the files with the extension .BIN only.

```
Private Sub bttnSave_Click(ByVal sender As System.Object, _
            ByVal e As System.EventArgs) Handles bttnSave.Click
    OpenFileDialog1.DefaultExt = ".BIN"
    OpenFileDialog1.AddExtension = True
    OpenFileDialog1.Filter = "Binary Files|*.bin"
    If OpenFileDialog1.ShowDialog() = DialogResult.OK Then
        Console.WriteLine(OpenFileDialog1.FileName)
    End If
End Sub
```

The following sections describe the properties of the OpenFileDialog and SaveFileDialog controls.

ADDEXTENSION

This property is a Boolean value that determines whether the dialog box automatically adds an extension to a filename, if the user omits it. The extension added automatically is the one specified by the DefaultExtension property, which must be set before you call the ShowDialog method.

CHECKFILEEXISTS

This property is a Boolean value that indicates whether the dialog box displays a warning if the user enters the name of a file that does not exist.

CHECKPATHEXISTS

This property is a Boolean value that indicates whether the dialog box displays a warning if the user specifies a path that does not exist, as part of the user-supplied filename.

DEFAULTEXTENSION

This property sets the default extension of the dialog box. Use this property to specify a default filename extension, such as TXT or DOC, so that when a file with no extension is saved, the extension specified by this property is automatically appended to the filename, as long as the AddExtension property is also set to True. The default extension property starts with the period, and it's a string like ".BIN".

DEREFERENCELINKS

This property indicates whether the dialog box returns the location of the file referenced by the shortcut or the location of the shortcut itself. If you attempt to select a shortcut on your desktop with the DereferenceLinks property set to False, the dialog box will return to your application a value like C:\WINDOWS\SYSTEM32\lnkstub.exe, which is the name of the shortcut, and not the name of the file represented by the shortcut. If you set the DereferenceLinks property to True, the dialog box will return the actual filename represented by the shortcut, which you can use in your code.

FILENAME

This property is the path of the file selected by the user on the control. If you set this property to a filename before opening the dialog box, this value will be the proposed filename. The user can click OK to select this file, or select another one on the control. Read this property from within your code only if the control was closed with OK button. If the user closed it with the Cancel button, you should ignore the setting of this value. The two controls provide another related property, the File-Names property, which returns an array of filenames. To find out how to allow the user to select multiple files, see the discussion of the MultipleFiles and FileNames properties under "VB.NET at Work: Multiple File Selection" at the end of this section.

FILTER

This property is used to specify the type(s) of files displayed on the dialog box. To display text files only, set the Filter property to "Text files|*.txt". The pipe symbol separates the description of the files (what the user sees) from the actual extension (how the operating system distinguishes the various file types).

If you want to display multiple extensions, such as BMP, GIF, and JPG, use a semicolon to separate extensions with the Filter property. The string "Images|*.BMP;*.GIF;*.JPG" displays all the files of these three types when the user selects Images in the Save As Type box.

Don't include spaces before or after the pipe symbol because these spaces will be displayed with the description and Filter values. In the Open common dialog of an image-processing application, you'll probably provide options for each image file type, as well as an option for all images:

```
OpenFileDialog1.Filter = "Bitmaps|*.BMP|GIF Images|*.GIF|JPEG" & _
                         "Images|*.JPG|All Images|*.BMP;*.GIF;*.JPG"
```

The Open dialog box has four options, which determine what appears in the Save As Type box (see Figure 7.5).

FIGURE 7.5

Displaying multiple
file types in the
Open dialog box

FILTERINDEX

When you specify more than one filter for the Open dialog box, the filter specified first in the Filter property becomes the default. If you want to use a Filter value other than the first one, use the FilterIndex property to determine which filter will be displayed as the default when the common dialog is opened. The index of the first filter is 1, and there's no reason to ever set this property to 1. If you want to use the Filter property value of the example in the preceding section and set the FilterIndex property to 2, the Open dialog box will display GIF files by default.

INITIALDIRECTORY

This property sets the initial directory (folder) in which files are displayed the first time the Open and Save dialog boxes are opened. Use this property to display the files of the application's folder or to specify a folder in which the application will store its files by default. If you don't specify an initial folder, it will default to the last folder where the dialog box opened or saved a file. It's also customary to set the initial folder to the application's path, with the following statement:

```
OpenFileDialog1.InitialDirectory = Application.ExecutablePath
```

The expression `Application.ExecutablePath` returns the path in which the application's executable file resides. You can also create a default data folder for the application during installation and use this folder's name as the initial directory.

RESTOREDIRECTORY

Every time the Open and Save dialog boxes are displayed, the current folder is the one selected by the user the last time the control was displayed. The RestoreDirectory property is a Boolean value that indicates whether the dialog box restores the current directory before closing. Its default value is False, which means that the initial directory is not restored automatically. The InitialDirectory property overrides the RestoreDirectory property.

VALIDATENAMES

This property is a Boolean value that indicates whether the dialog box accepts only valid Win32 filenames. Its default value is True, and you shouldn't change it.

TIP *The following four properties—FileNames, MultiSelect, ReadOnlyChecked, and ShowReadOnly—are properties of the OpenFileDialog control only.*

FILENAMES

If the Open dialog box allows the selection of multiple files (see the later section "VB.NET at Work: Multiple File Selection"), the FileNames property contains the pathnames of all selected files. FileNames is a collection, and you can iterate through the filenames with an enumerator. See the MultipleFiles application for an example of iterating through the collection of the selected files. This property is unique to the OpenFileDialog control.

MULTISELECT

This property is a Boolean value that indicates whether the user can select multiple files on the dialog box. Its default value is False, and users can select a single file. When the MultiSelect property is True, the user can select multiple files, but they must all come from the same folder. You can't allow the selection of multiple files from different folders. This property is unique to the OpenFileDialog control.

READONLYCHECKED

This property is a Boolean value that indicates whether the Read-Only check box is initially selected when the dialog box first pops up (the user can clear this box to open a file in read/write mode). You can set this property to True only if the ShowReadOnly property is also set to True. This property is unique to the OpenFileDialog control.

SHOWREADONLY

This property is a Boolean value that indicates whether the Read-Only check box is available. If this check box appears on the form, the user can check it so that the file will be opened as read-only. Files opened as read-only shouldn't be saved onto the same file—you can prompt the user for a new filename, but you shouldn't save them with the same filename. This property is unique to the Open-FileDialog control.

VB.NET AT WORK: THE OPENFILE AND SAVEFILE METHODS

The OpenFileDialog control exposes the OpenFile method, which allows you to quickly open the selected file. Normally, after retrieving the name of the file selected by the user, you must open this file for reading (in the case of the Open dialog box) or writing (in the case of the Save dialog box). The topic of reading from, or writing to, files is discussed in detail in Chapter 13. In this section, I'll show you how to quickly read the selected file through the OpenFileDialog control's OpenFile method.

When the OpenFile method is applied to the Open dialog box, the file is opened with read-only permission. The same method can be applied to the Save dialog box, in which case the file is opened with read-write permission. The OpenFile method is demonstrated by the OpenMethod project, whose main form is shown in Figure 7.6.

FIGURE 7.6

The main form of the OpenMethod project

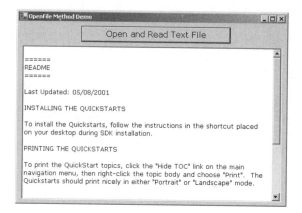

The following code segment demonstrates how to open a text file with the OpenFile method, read its contents, and display it on a TextBox control. The code displays the Open dialog box and then calls the control's OpenFile method to open the file and read it. Listing 7.1 is code behind the Open And Read Text File button on the form.

LISTING 7.1: THE OPENFILE METHOD OF THE OPENFILEDIALOG CONTROL

```
Private Sub readTextFile_Click(ByVal sender As System.Object, _
            ByVal e As System.EventArgs) Handles readTextFile.Click
   OpenFileDialog1.ShowDialog()
   Dim str As System.IO.Stream
   str = OpenFileDialog1.OpenFile
   Dim txt As New System.Text.StringBuilder()
   Dim buffer(1000) As Byte
   Dim numBytesToRead As Integer = CInt(str.Length)
   Dim numBytesRead As Integer = 0
   Dim n As Integer
   While (numBytesToRead > 0)
      n = str.Read(buffer, 0, 1000)
      Console.WriteLine(n.ToString & "read")
      If n = 0 Then
         Exit While
      End If
      Dim i As Integer
      For i = 0 To n
         txt.Append(Chr(buffer(i)))
      Next
      numBytesRead += n
      numBytesToRead -= n
   End While
   str.Close()
   TextBox1.Text = txt.ToString
End Sub
```

The code reads the file 1,000 characters at a time and appends the characters to a StringBuilder variable (this type of variable is especially efficient for manipulating strings, and you'll learn more about it in Chapter 12). The Read method of the Stream object reads 1,000 characters and stores them to the *buffer* array. Then the characters of the array are appended to a StringBuilder variable, the *txt* variable, which is finally displayed on the TextBox control.

VB.NET at Work: Multiple File Selection

The Open dialog box allows the selection of multiple files. This option isn't very common, but it can come in handy in situations when you want to process files en masse. You can let the user select many files and then process them one at a time. Or you may wish to prompt the user to select multiple files to be moved or copied.

To allow the user to select multiple files on the Open dialog box, set the MultiSelect property to True. The user can then select multiple files with the mouse by holding down the Shift or Ctrl key. The names of the selected files are reported by the property FileNames, which is an array of strings. The FileNames array contains the pathnames of all selected files, and you can iterate through them as you would iterate through the elements of any array.

In this chapter's folder on the CD, you'll find the MultipleFiles project, which demonstrates the use of the FileNames property. The application's form is shown in Figure 7.7. The button at the top of the form opens a File dialog box, where you can select multiple files. After closing the dialog box by clicking the Open button, the application displays the pathnames of the selected files in the List-Box control.

FIGURE 7.7

The MultipleFiles project lets the user select multiple files on an Open dialog box.

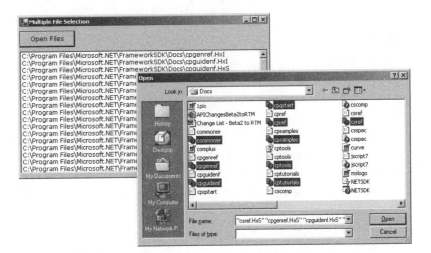

The code behind the Open Files button is shown in Listing 7.2. In this example, I've used the array's enumerator to iterate through the elements of the FileNames array. You can use any of the methods discussed in Chapter 3 to iterate through the array.

LISTING 7.2: PROCESSING MULTIPLE SELECTED FILES

```
Private Sub bttnFile_Click(ByVal sender As System.Object, _
                ByVal e As System.EventArgs) Handles bttnFile.Click
    OpenFileDialog1.Multiselect = True
    OpenFileDialog1.ShowDialog()
    Dim filesEnum As IEnumerator
    ListBox1.Items.Clear()
    filesEnum = OpenFileDialog1.FileNames.GetEnumerator()
    While filesEnum.MoveNext
        ListBox1.Items.Add(filesEnum.Current)
    End While
End Sub
```

The Print Dialog Box

The Print dialog box (Figure 7.8) enables users to select a printer, set certain properties of the printout (e.g., number of copies and pages to be printed), and set up a specific printer.

FIGURE 7.8

The Print common dialog box

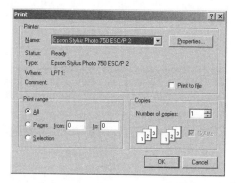

After the user selects a printer and clicks OK, the Print dialog box returns the attributes of the desired printout to the calling program through the following properties:

AllowPrintToFile This property is a Boolean value that controls whether the user will be given the option to print to a file. If set to False, the Print To File option on the dialog will be disabled.

AllowSelection This property is a Boolean value that determines whether the user is allowed to print the current selection of the document. If you don't want to provide the code for printing a segment of the document, set this property to False.

AllowSomePages This property is a Boolean value that determines whether the Pages option on the dialog will be enabled.

These properties determine which of the options on the dialog box will be available to the user. To retrieve the properties of the printout specified by the user on the dialog box, you must use the PrinterSettings object. This object exposes many properties, such as FromPage and ToPage (which determine the starting and ending page of the printout), Copies (which determines the number of copies of the printout), and PrinterName (the name of the selected printer). The PrinterSettings property is discussed in detail in Chapter 15.

The following statements create a new PrinterSettings object, pass it to the Print dialog box, and then display the dialog box. Upon return, they print a few of the settings specified by the user on the Print dialog box. Place an instance of the PrintDialog control to the form and enter the following statements in a button's Click event handler to test them:

```
PrintDialog1.AllowSomePages = True
PrintDialog1.AllowSelection = True
PrintDialog1.PrinterSettings = _
    New System.Drawing.Printing.PrinterSettings()
PrintDialog1.ShowDialog()
Console.WriteLine("FROM PAGE:    " & PrintDialog1.PrinterSettings.FromPage)
Console.WriteLine("TO PAGE:     " & PrintDialog1.PrinterSettings.ToPage)
Console.WriteLine("# OF COPIES: " & PrintDialog1.PrinterSettings.Copies)
Console.WriteLine("PRINTER NAME:" & PrintDialog1.PrinterSettings.PrinterName)
Console.WriteLine("PRINT RANGE: " & PrintDialog1.PrinterSettings.PrintRange)
Console.WriteLine("LANDSCAPE:   " & PrintDialog1.PrinterSettings.LandscapeAngle)
```

The output produced by the previous statements on my system looked like this:

```
FROM PAGE:    3
TO PAGE:      4
# OF COPIES: 1
PRINTER NAME:Epson Stylus Photo 750 ESC/P 2
PRINT RANGE: 2
LANDSCAPE:    270
```

To set the orientation of the printout, you must click the Properties button on the Print dialog box. This action will display the property pages dialog box of the specified printer, where you can set properties like the page's orientation, the quality of the printout, and other printer-dependent properties. The value 270 returned by the LandscapeAngle indicates the angle of rotation for the printout. The default orientation is Portrait, and the document must be rotated by 270 degrees clockwise for the Landscape orientation.

The PrinterSettings object, as well as the related PageSettings object, are explored in detail in Chapter 15, where you'll learn how to print documents with the .NET Framework and Visual Basic.

The RichTextBox Control

The RichTextBox control is the core of a full-blown word processor. It provides all the functionality of a TextBox control; in addition, it gives you the capability to mix different fonts, sizes, and attributes; and it gives you precise control over the margins of the text (see Figure 7.9). You can even place images in your text on a RichTextBox control (although you won't have the kind of control over the embedded images that you have with Microsoft Word).

FIGURE 7.9

A word processor based on the functionality of the RichTextBox control

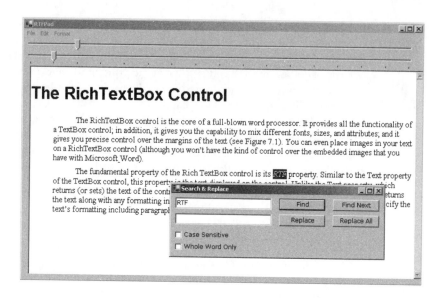

The fundamental property of the RichTextBox control is its *RTF* property. Similar to the Text property of the TextBox control, this property is the text displayed on the control. Unlike the Text property, which returns (or sets) the text of the control but doesn't contain formatting information, the RTF property returns the text *along with* any formatting information. Therefore, you can use the RichTextBox control to specify the text's formatting, including paragraph indentation, font, and font size or style.

RTF stands for *Rich Text Format*, which is a standard for storing formatting information along with the text. The beauty of the RichTextBox control for programmers is that they don't need to supply the formatting codes. The control provides simple properties that turn the selected text into bold, change the alignment of the current paragraph, and so on. The RTF code is generated internally by the control and used to save and load formatted files. It's possible to create elaborately formatted documents without knowing the RTF language.

NOTE *The WordPad application that comes with Windows is based on the RichTextBox control. You can easily duplicate every bit of WordPad's functionality with the RichTextBox control, as you will see later on in the section "VB.NET at Work: The RTFPad Project."*

The RTF Language

A basic knowledge of the RTF format, its commands, and how it works, will certainly help you understand how the RichTextBox control works. RTF is a language that uses simple commands to specify the formatting of a document. These commands, or *tags*, are ASCII strings, such as \par (the tag that marks the beginning of a new paragraph) and \b (the tag that turns on the bold style). And this is where the value of the RTF format lies. RTF documents don't contain special characters and can be easily exchanged among different operating systems and computers, as long as there is an RTF-capable application to read the document. Let's look at the RTF document in action.

Open the WordPad application (choose Start ➢ Programs ➢ Accessories ➢ WordPad) and enter a few lines of text (see Figure 7.10). Select a few words or sentences and format them in different ways with any of WordPad's formatting commands. Then save the document in RTF format: Choose File ➢ Save As, select Rich Text Format, and then save the file as `Document.rtf`. If you open this file with a text editor such as Notepad, you'll see the actual RTF code that produced the document. You can find the RTF file for the document shown in Figure 7.10 in this chapter's folder on the CD; a small section of the RTF document is presented in Listing 7.3.

FIGURE 7.10

The formatting applied to the text using WordPad's commands is stored along with the text in RTF format.

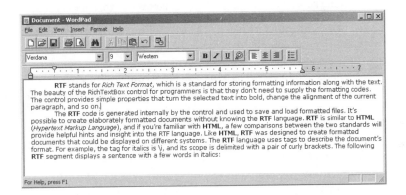

LISTING 7.3: EXCERPT FROM THE RTF CODE FOR THE DOCUMENT OF FIGURE 7.9

```
{\rtf1\ansi\ansicpg1252\deff0\deflang1033
{\fonttbl{\f0\fnil\fcharset0 Verdana;}{\f1\fswiss\fcharset0 Arial;}}
\viewkind4\uc1\pard\nowidctlpar\fi720\b\f0\fs18 RTF \b0 stands for \i Rich Text
Format\i0 , which is a standard for storing formatting information along with the
text. The beauty of the RichTextBox control for programmers is that they don\rquote
t need to supply the formatting codes. The control provides simple properties that
turn the selected text into bold, change the alignment of the current paragraph,
and so on.\par
```

As you can see, all formatting tags are prefixed with the backslash (\\) symbol. To display the \\ symbol itself, insert an additional slash. Paragraphs are marked with the \\par tag, and the entire document is enclosed in a pair of curly brackets. The \\li and \\ri tags followed by a numeric value specify the amount of the left and right indentation. If you assign this string to the RTF property of a RichTextBox control, the result will be the document shown in Figure 7.10, formatted exactly as it appears in WordPad.

RTF is similar to HTML (Hypertext Markup Language), and if you're familiar with HTML, a few comparisons between the two standards will provide helpful hints and insight into the RTF language. Like HTML, RTF was designed to create formatted documents that could be displayed on different systems. The RTF language uses tags to describe the document's format. For example, the tag for italics is \i, and its scope is delimited with a pair of curly brackets. The following RTF segment displays a sentence with a few words in italics:

```
{{\b RTF} (which stands for Rich Text Format) is a {\i document formatting
language} that uses simple commands to specify the formatting of the document.}
```

The following is the equivalent HTML code:

```
<b>RTF</b> (which stands for Rich Text Format) is a <i>document formatting
language</i> that uses simple commands to specify the formatting of the document.
```

The <b> and <i> tags of HTML are equivalent to the \b and \i tags of RTF. RTF, however, is much more complicated than HTML. It's not nearly as easy to understand an RTF document as it is to understand an HTML document because RTF was meant to be used internally by applications. As you can see in Listing 7.3, RTF contains information about the font being used, its size, and so on. Just as you need a browser to view HTML documents, you need an RTF-capable application to view RTF documents. WordPad, for instance, supports RTF and can both save a document in RTF format and read RTF files.

You're not expected to supply your own RTF code to produce a document. You simply select the segment of the document you want to format and apply the corresponding formatting command from within your word processor. Fortunately, the RichTextBox control isn't any different. It doesn't require you or the users of your application to understand RTF code. The RichTextBox control does all the work for you while hiding the low-level details.

VB.NET AT WORK: THE RTFDEMO PROJECT

The RTFDemo project, shown in Figure 7.11, demonstrates the principles of programming the RichTextBox control. The RichTextBox control is the large box covering the upper section of the form where you can type text as you would with a regular TextBox control.

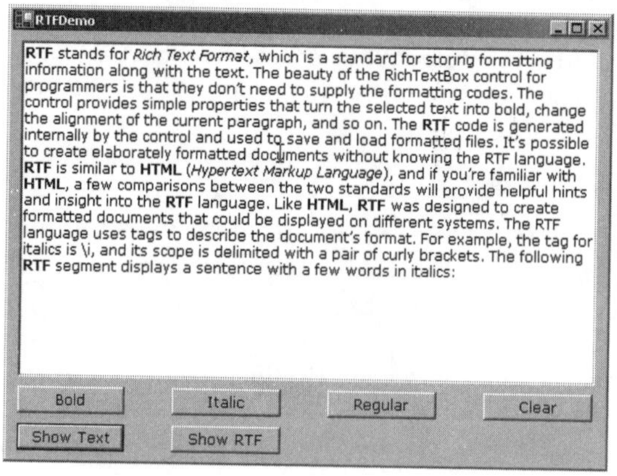

FIGURE 7.11

The RTFDemo project demonstrates how the Rich-TextBox control handles RTF code.

Use the first three buttons to set styles for the selected text. The Bold and Italic buttons are self-explanatory; the Regular button restores the regular style of the text. All three buttons create a new font based on the current font of the RichTextBox control and turn on the appropriate attribute. Here's the code behind the Bold button:

```
Private Sub bttnBold_Click(ByVal sender As System.Object, _
                ByVal e As System.EventArgs) Handles bttnBold.Click
    Dim fnt As New Font(RichTextBox1.Font, FontStyle.Bold)
    RichTextBox1.SelectionFont = fnt
End Sub
```

The code for the Italic button is quite similar, it simply sets a different attribute:

```
Private Sub bttnItalic_Click(ByVal sender As System.Object, _
                ByVal e As System.EventArgs) Handles bttnItalic.Click
    Dim fnt As New Font(RichTextBox1.Font, FontStyle.Italic)
    RichTextBox1.SelectionFont = fnt
End Sub
```

Both buttons create a new Font object based on the current font of the control. The second argument of the Font's constructor is a constant with the font's attributes. The code shown here turns on the Bold and Italic attributes of the font. The second statement in the two handlers assigns the new font to the selected text (property SelectionFont). Notice that these two buttons don't *toggle* the bold and the italic attribute; if the selected text is already bold, nothing will change.

The Clear button clears the contents of the control by calling its Clear method:

```
RichTextBox1.Clear()
```

The two buttons on the second row demonstrate the nature of the RichTextBox control. Select a few words on the control, turn on their bold and/or italic attribute, and then click the Show Text button. You'll see a message box that contains the control's text. No matter how the text is formatted, the control's Text property will be the same. This is the text you would copy from the control and paste into a text-editing application that doesn't support formatting commands (for example, Notepad). The code behind the Show Text button is:

```
MsgBox(RichTextBox1.Text)
```

To replace the text on the control, you can either type some new text, or select some formatted text in another application, like WordPad, and paste it on the control.

THE RTF CODE

If you click the Show RTF button, you'll see the actual RTF code that produced the formatted document in Figure 7.11. The message box with the RTF code is shown in Figure 7.12. This is all the information the RichTextBox control requires to render the document. As complicated as it may look, it isn't difficult to produce. In programming the RichTextBox control, you'll rarely have to worry about inserting actual RTF tags in the code. The control is responsible for generating the RTF code and for rendering the document. You simply manipulate a few properties (the recurring theme in Visual Basic programming), and the control does the rest.

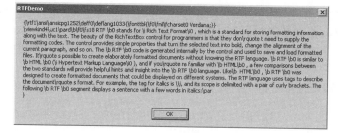

On rather rare occasions, you may have to supply RTF tags. You don't have to know much about RTF tags, though. Simply format a few words with the desired attributes using the RTFDemo application (or experiment with the Immediate window), copy the tags that produce the desired result, and use them in your application. If you are curious about RTF, experiment with the RTFDemo application.

One of the most interesting applications on the book's CD-ROM is the RTFPad application, a word-processing application that's discussed in detail later in this chapter. This application duplicates much of the functionality of Windows WordPad, but it's included in this book to show you how the RichTextBox control is used. The RTFPad application can become your starting point for writing custom word-processing applications (a programmer's text editor with color-coded keywords, for example).

The RichTextBox's Properties

The names of the RichTextBox control's properties for manipulating selected text mostly start with Selected or Selection. The most commonly used properties related to the selected text are shown in Table 7.1. Some of these are discussed in further detail in following sections.

TABLE 7.1: RICHTEXTBOX PROPERTIES FOR MANIPULATING SELECTED TEXT

PROPERTY	WHAT IT MANIPULATES
SelectedText	The selected text
SelectedRTF	The RTF code of the selected text
SelectionStart	The position of the selected text's first character
SelectionLength	The length of the selected text
SelectionFont	The font of the selected text
SelectionColor	The color of the selected text
SelectionIndent, SelectionRightIndent, SelectionHangingIndent	The indentation of the selected text
RightMargin	The distance of the text's right margin from the left edge of the control, which is in effect the length of each text line
SelectionBullet	Whether the selected text is bulleted
BulletIndent	The amount of bullet indent for the selected text

SELECTEDTEXT

The SelectedText property represents the selected text. To assign the selected text to a variable, use the following statement:

```
SText=RichTextbox1.SelectedText
```

RichTextbox1 is the name of the control. You can also modify the selected text by assigning a new value to the SelectedText property. The following statement converts the selected text to uppercase:

```
RichTextbox1.SelectedText=UCase(RichTextbox1.SelectedText)
```

If you assign a string to the SelectedText property, the selected text in the control is replaced with the string. The following statement replaces the current selection on the RichTextbox1 control with the string "Revised string":

```
RichTextbox1.SelectedText="Revised string"
```

If no text is selected, the statement *inserts* the string at the location of the pointer. It is possible, therefore, to insert text automatically by assigning a string to the SelectedText property.

NOTE *The SelectedText property is similar to the Text property. The difference is that SelectedText applies to the current selection or cursor position instead of the entire text of the control. The same is true for the RTF and SelectedRTF properties.*

SELECTIONSTART, SELECTIONLENGTH

To simplify the manipulation and formatting of the text on the control, two additional properties, SelectionStart and SelectionLength, report the position of the first selected character in the text and the length of the selection, respectively. You can also set the values of these properties to select a piece of text from within your code. One obvious use of these properties is to select (and highlight) the entire text (or a segment of the text):

```
RichTextBox1.SelectionStart = 0
RichTextBox1.SelectionLength = Len(RichTextBox1.Text)
```

A better method of selecting the entire text on the control is to call the SelectAll method, which is discussed later in this section.

SELECTIONALIGNMENT

Use this property to read or change the alignment of one or more paragraphs. This property value is one of the members of the HorizontalAlignment enumeration: Left, Right, and Center.

NOTE *The user doesn't have to actually select the entire paragraph to align it. Placing the pointer anywhere in the paragraph or selecting a few characters in the paragraph will do, because there is no way to align only a part of a paragraph.*

SELECTIONINDENT, SELECTIONRIGHTINDENT, SELECTIONHANGINGINDENT

These properties allow you to change the margins of individual paragraphs. The SelectionIndent property sets (or returns) the amount of the text's indentation from the left edge of the control. The

SelectionRightIndent property sets (or returns) the amount of the text's indentation from the right edge of the control. The SelectionHangingIndent property is the distance between the left edge of the first line and the left edge of the following lines.

The SelectionHangingIndent property includes the current setting of the SelectionIndent property. If all the lines of a paragraph are aligned to the left, the SelectionIndent property can have any value (this is the distance of all lines from the left edge of the control), but the SelectionHangingIndent property must be zero. If the first line of the paragraph is shorter than the following lines, the SelectionHangingIndent has a negative value. Figure 7.13 shows two differently formatted paragraphs. The settings of the SelectionIndent and SelectionHangingIndent properties are determined by the two sliders at the top of the form.

FIGURE 7.13

Various combinations of the SelectionIndent and SelectionHanging-Indent properties produce all possible paragraph formatting.

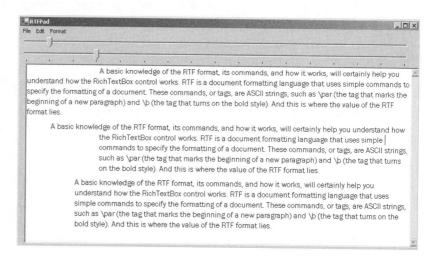

SELECTIONBULLET, BULLETINDENT

You use these properties to create a list of bulleted items. If you set the SelectionBullet property to True, the selected paragraphs are formatted with a bullet style, similar to the <ul> tag in HTML. To create a list of bulleted items, assign the value True to the SelectionBullet property. To change a list of bulleted items back to normal text, make the same property False.

The paragraphs formatted with the SelectionBullet property set to True are also indented from the left by a small amount. To set the amount of the indentation, use the BulletIndent property, whose syntax is

```
RichTextBox1.BulletIndent = value
```

You can also read the BulletIndent property from within your code to find out the bulleted items' indentation. Or you can use this property, along with the SelectionBullet property, to simulate nested bulleted items. If the current selection's SelectionBullet property is True and the user wants to apply the bullet format, you can increase the indentation of the current selection.

Methods

The first two methods of the RichTextBox control you will learn about are SaveFile and LoadFile:

SaveFile saves the contents of the control to a disk file.

LoadFile loads the control from a disk file.

SAVEFILE

The syntax of the SaveFile method is

```
RichTextBox1.SaveFile(path, filetype)
```

where *path* is the path of the file in which the current document will be saved. By default, the SaveFile method saves the document in RTF format and uses the RTF extension. You can specify a different format with the second, optional, argument, which can take on the value of one of the members of the RichTextBoxStreamType enumeration, which are described in Table 7.2.

TABLE 7.2: THE RICHTEXTBOXSTREAMTYPE ENUMERATION

FORMAT	EFFECT
PlainText	Stores the text on the control without any formatting
RichNoOLEObjs	Stores the text without any formatting and ignores any embedded OLE objects
RichText	Stores the formatted text
TextTextOLEObjs	Stores the text along with the embedded OLE objects
UnicodePlainText	Stores the text in Unicode format

LOADFILE

Similarly, the LoadFile method loads a text or RTF file to the control. Its syntax is identical to the syntax of the SaveFile method:

```
RichTextBox1.LoadFile(path, filetype)
```

The *filetype* argument is optional and can have one of the values of the RichTextBoxStreamType enumeration. Saving and loading files to and from disk files are as simple as presenting a Save or Open common dialog control to the user and then calling one of the SaveFile or LoadFile methods with the filename returned by the common dialog box.

NOTE *You can't assign formatted text to the control at design time. The Text property is available at design time, but the text is rendered in the same format. The RTF property isn't available at design time. To display initially some formatted text on the control, you must either load it from a file with the LoadFile method, or assign the equivalent RTF code to the RTF property at runtime, usually from within the form's Load event.*

SELECT, SELECTALL

The Select method selects a section of the text on the control, similar to setting the SelectionStart and SelectionLength properties. The Select method accepts two arguments, which are the location of the first character to be selected and the length of the selection:

```
RichTextBox1.Select(start, length)
```

The SelectAll method accepts no arguments and selects all the text on the control.

Advanced Editing Features

The RichTextBox control provides all the text-editing features you'd expect to find in a text-editing application. You can use the arrow keys to move through the text and press Ctrl+C to copy text or Ctrl+V to paste it. To facilitate the design of advanced text-editing features, the RichTextBox control provides the AutoSelectWord property, which controls how the control selects text. If it's True, the control selects a word at a time.

In addition to formatted text, the RichTextBox control can handle OLE objects. You can insert images in the text by pasting them with the Paste method. The Paste method doesn't require any arguments; it simply inserts the contents of the Clipboard at the current location in the document.

The RichTextBox control encapsulates undo and redo operations at multiple levels. Each operation has a name (Typing, Deletion, and so on), and you can retrieve the name of the next operation to be undone or redone and display it on the menu. Instead of a simple Undo or Redo caption, you can change the captions of the Edit menu to something like Undo Delete or Redo Typing.

To program undo and redo operation from within your code, you must use the following properties and methods.

CANUNDO, CANREDO

These two properties are Boolean values you can read to find out whether an operation can be undone or redone. If they're False, you must disable the corresponding menu command from within your code. The following statements disable the Undo command if there's no action to be undone at the time, where *EditUndo* is the name of the Undo command on the Edit menu:

```
If RichTextBox1.CanUndo Then
    EditUndo.Enabled = True
Else
    EditUndo.Enabled = False
End If
```

These statements appear in the menu item's Select event handler (not in the Click event handler), because they must be executed before the menu is displayed. The Select event is triggered when a menu is opened. As a reminder, the Click event isn't fired when you click an item. For more information on programming the events of a menu, see Chapter 5.

UNDOACTIONNAME, REDOACTIONNAME

These two properties return the name of the action that can be undone or redone. The most common value of both properties is the string "typing," which indicates that the Undo command will delete a number of characters. Another common value is the "delete" string, while some operations are named "unknown." If you change the indentation of a paragraph on the control, this action's name is "unknown." It's likely that more action names will be recognized in future versions of the control.

The following statement sets the caption of the Undo command to a string that indicates the action to be undone:

```
EditUndo.Text = "Undo " & Editor.UndoActionName
```

UNDO, REDO

These two methods undo or redo an action. The Undo method cancels the effects of the last action of the user on the control. The Redo method redoes the last action that was undone. Obviously, unless one or more actions have been undone already, the Redo method won't have any effect.

You will see how the Undo and Redo methods, as well as the related properties, are used in an application in the section "The RTFPad Project," later in this chapter.

Cutting and Pasting

To cut, or copy, and paste text on the RichTextBox control, you can use the same techniques as with the regular TextBox control. For example, you can replace the current selection by assigning a string to the SelectedText property. The RichTextBox, however, provides useful methods for performing these operations. The methods Copy, Cut, and Paste perform the corresponding operations. The Cut and Copy methods are straightforward and require no arguments. The Paste method accepts a single argument, which is the format of the data to be pasted. Since the data will come from the Clipboard, you can extract the format of the data in the Clipboard at the time and then call the CanPaste method to find out whether the control can handle this type of data. If so, you can then paste them on the control with the Paste method.

This technique requires quite a bit of code, because the Clipboard object doesn't return the format of the data it holds. You must call the following method of the Clipboard object to find out whether the data is of a specific type and then call the control's CanPaste method to find out whether it can handle the data:

```
If Clipboard.GetDataObject.GetDataPresent(DataFormats.Text) Then
    RichTextBox.Paste(DataFormats.Text)
End If
```

This is a very simple case, because we know that the RichTextBox control can accept text. For a robust application, you must call the GetDataPresent method for each type of data your application should be able to handle (you may not want to allow users to paste all types of data that the control can handle).

In the RTFPad project later in this chapter, we'll use a structured exception handler to allow users to paste anything on the control. If the control can't handle it, the data won't be pasted on the control. As you already know, the RichTextBox control can display images along with text. Each image takes up the entire width of the control. You can center it on the page with the usual alignment properties, but you can't enter text to either side of the image. If you need a control with the functionality of Word, then you can either automate Word from within your VB application (see Chapter 10 for more information on programming Word's objects) or purchase a third-party control with advanced processing features.

Searching in a RichTextBox Control

The Find method locates a string in the control's text and is similar to the InStr() function. You can use InStr() with the control's Text property to locate a string in the text, but the Find method is optimized for the RichTextBox control and supports a couple of options that the InStr() function doesn't. The simplest form of the Find method is the following:

```
RichTextBox1.Find(string)
```

The *string* argument is the string you want to locate in the RichTextBox control. The method returns an integer value that is the location of the first instance of the string in the text. If the specified string can't be found in the text, the value −1 is returned.

Another, equally simple syntax of the Find method allows you to specify how the control will search for the string:

```
RichTextBox1.Find(string, searchMode)
```

The *searchMode* argument is a member of the RichTextBoxFinds enumeration, which are shown in Table 7.3.

TABLE 7.3: THE RICHTEXTBOXFINDS ENUMERATION

VALUE	EFFECT
MatchCase	Performs a case-sensitive search.
NoHighlight	The text found will not be highlighted.
None	Locates instances of the specified string even if they're not whole words.
Reverse	The search starts at the end of the document.
WholeWord	Locate only instances of the specified string that are whole words.

Two more forms of the Find method allow you specify the range of the text in which the search will take place:

```
RichTextBox1.Find(string, start, searchMode)
RichTextBox1.Find(string, start, end, searchMode)
```

The arguments *start* and *end* are the starting and ending locations of the search (use them to search for a string within a specified range only). If you omit the *end* argument, the search will start at the location specified by the *start* argument and will extend to the end of the text.

You can combine multiples of the values of the *searchMode* argument with the OR operator. The default search is case-insensitive, covers the entire document, and highlights the matching text on the control. The RTFPad application's Find command demonstrates how to use the Find method and its arguments to build a Search & Replace dialog box that performs all the types of text-searching operations you might need in a text-editing application.

Formatting URLs

A new feature built into the RichTextBox control is the automatic formatting of URLs embedded in the text. To enable this feature, set the DetectURLs property to True. Then, as soon as the control determines that you're entering a URL (usually after you enter the three *W*s and the following period), it will format the text as a hyperlink. When the pointer rests over a hyperlink, its shape turns into a hand, just as it would in Internet Explorer. Run the RTFDemo project, enter a URL like www.sybex.com, and see how the RichTextBox control handles it.

In addition to formatting the URL, the RichTextBox control triggers the LinkClicked event when a hyperlink is clicked. To display the corresponding page from within your code, enter the following statement in the LinkClicked event handler:

```
Private Sub RichTextBox1_LinkClicked(ByVal sender As Object, _
            ByVal e As System.Windows.Forms.LinkClickedEventArgs) _
            Handles RichTextBox1.LinkClicked
   System.Diagnostics.Process.Start(e.LinkText)
End Sub
```

The `System.Diagnostics.Process` class provides the Start method, which starts an application. You can specify either the name of the executable or the path of a file. The Start method will look up the associated application and start it. As you can see, handling embedded URLs with the RichTextBox control is almost trivial.

Whatever application or file you specify in the Start method (Internet Explorer, for example) will run independently of your application, and the user may navigate to any other site, or close the browser and return to your application.

VB.NET at Work: The RTFPad Project

Creating a functional, even fancy, word processor based on the RichTextBox control is quite simple. The challenge is to provide a convenient interface that lets the user select text, apply attributes and styles to it, and then set the control's properties accordingly. This chapter's application does just that. It's called RTFPad, and you can find it in this chapter's folder on the CD.

The RTFPad application (see Figure 7.9) is based on the TextPad application developed in Chapter 6. It contains the same text-editing commands and some additional text-formatting commands that can only be implemented with the RichTextBox control; for example, it allows you to mix font styles in the text. This section examines the code and discusses a few topics unique to this application's implementation with the RichTextBox control.

The two TrackBar controls above the RichTextBox control manipulate the indentation of the text. We've already explored this arrangement in the discussion of the TrackBar control in Chapter 6, but let's review the operation of the two controls again. Each TrackBar control has a width of 816 pixels, which is equivalent to 8.5 inches on a monitor with a resolution of 96 dpi (dots per inch). The height of the TrackBar controls is 42 pixels and, unfortunately, they can't be made smaller. The Minimum and Maximum properties of the control are of no significance, because all we really care about is the relative value of the control. Each time the user slides the top TrackBar control, the code sets the SelectionIndent property to the proper percentage of the control's width. Because the Selection-HangingIndent includes the value of the SelectionIndent property, it also adjusts the setting of the SelectionHangingIndent property. Listing 7.4 is the code that's executed when the upper TrackBar control is scrolled.

LISTING 7.4: SETTING THE SELECTIONINDENT PROPERTY

```
Private Sub TrackBar1_Scroll(ByVal sender As System.Object, _
            ByVal e As System.EventArgs) Handles TrackBar1.Scroll
  Editor.SelectionIndent = Editor.Width * (TrackBar1.Value / TrackBar1.Maximum)
  Editor.SelectionHangingIndent = Editor.Width * _
            (TrackBar2.Value / TrackBar2.Maximum) - Editor.SelectionIndent
End Sub
```

The second TrackBar control controls the hanging indentation of the selected text (the indentation of all text lines after the first one). Its Scroll event handler is presented in Listing 7.5.

LISTING 7.5: SETTING THE SELECTIONHANGINGINDENT PROPERTY

```
Private Sub TrackBar2_Scroll(ByVal sender As System.Object, _
            ByVal e As System.EventArgs) Handles TrackBar2.Scroll
  Editor.SelectionHangingIndent = Editor.Width * _
            (TrackBar2.Value / TrackBar2.Maximum) - Editor.SelectionIndent
End Sub
```

Enter some text in the control, select one or more paragraphs, and check out the operation of the two sliders.

The Scroll events of the two TrackBar controls adjust the text's indentation. The opposite action must take place when the user rests the pointer on another paragraph: the sliders' positions must be adjusted to reflect the new indentation of the text. The selection of a new paragraph is signaled to the application by the SelChange event. The statements of Listing 7.6, which are executed from within the SelChange event, adjust the two slider controls to reflect the indentation of the text.

LISTING 7.6: SETTING THE SLIDER CONTROLS

```
Private Sub Editor_SelectionChanged(ByVal sender As Object, _
            ByVal e As System.EventArgs) Handles Editor.SelectionChanged
  If Editor.SelectionIndent = Nothing Then
     TrackBar1.Value = TrackBar1.Minimum
     TrackBar2.Value = TrackBar2.Minimum
  Else
     TrackBar1.Value = Editor.SelectionIndent * TrackBar1.Maximum / _
                    Editor.Width
     TrackBar2.Value = (Editor.SelectionHangingIndent / Editor.Width) * _
                    TrackBar2.Maximum + TrackBar1.Value
  End If
End Sub
```

If the user selects multiple paragraphs with different indentations, the SelectionIndent property returns Nothing. The code examines the value of the SelectionIndent property and, if it's Nothing, it moves both controls to the left edge. This way, the user can slide the controls and set the indentations for multiple paragraphs. Or you can set the sliders according to the indentation of the first or last paragraph in the selection. Some applications make the handles gray to indicate that the selected text doesn't have uniform indentation, but unfortunately you can't gray the sliders and keep them enabled. Of course, you can always design a custom control. The TrackBar controls are too tall for this type of interface and can't be made very narrow (as a result, the interface of the RTFPad application isn't very elegant).

THE FILE MENU

The RTFPad application's File menu contains the usual Open, Save, and Save As commands, which are implemented with the LoadFile and SaveFile methods. Listing 7.7 shows the implementation of the Open command in the File menu.

LISTING 7.7: THE OPEN COMMAND

```
Private Sub FileOpen_Click(ByVal sender As System.Object, _
            ByVal e As System.EventArgs) Handles FileOpen.Click
    If DiscardChanges() Then
        OpenFileDialog1.Filter = "RTF Files|*.RTF|DOC Files|" & _
                            "*.DOC|Text Files|*.TXT|All Files|*.*"
        If OpenFileDialog1.ShowDialog() = DialogResult.OK Then
            fName = OpenFileDialog1.FileName
            Editor.LoadFile(fName)
            Editor.Modified = False
        End If
    End If
End Sub
```

The *fName* variable is declared on the Form level and holds the name of the currently open file. It's set every time a new file is successfully opened and used by the Save command to automatically save the open file, without prompting the user for a filename.

DiscardChanges() is a function that returns a Boolean value, depending on whether the control's contents can be discarded or not. The function starts by examining the Editor control's Modified property. If True, it prompts the user as to whether he wants to discard the edits. Depending on the value of the Modified property and the user's response, the function returns a Boolean value. If the DiscardChanges() function returns True, the program goes on and opens a new document. If the function returns False, the handler exits. Listing 7.8 shows the Discard-Changes() function.

LISTING 7.8: THE DISCARDCHANGES() FUNCTION

```
Function DiscardChanges() As Boolean
    If Editor.Modified Then
        Dim reply As MsgBoxResult
        reply = MsgBox("Text hasn't been saved. Discard changes?", _
                        MsgBoxStyle.YesNo)
        If reply = MsgBoxResult.No Then
            Return False
        Else
            Return True
        End If
    Else
        Return True
    End If
End Function
```

The Modified property becomes True after typing the first character and isn't reset back to False. The RichTextBox control doesn't handle this property very intelligently and doesn't reset it to False even after saving the control's contents to a file. The application's code sets the Editor.Modified property to False after creating a new document, as well as after saving the current document.

The Save As command (Listing 7.9) prompts the user for a filename and then stores the Editor control's contents to the specified file. It also sets the *fName* variable to the file's path, so that the Save command can use it. The *fName* variable is declared at the beginning of the code, outside any procedure.

LISTING 7.9: THE SAVE AS COMMAND

```
Private Sub FileSaveAs_Click(ByVal sender As System.Object, _
                ByVal e As System.EventArgs) Handles FileSaveAs.Click
    SaveFileDialog1.Filter = "RTF Files|*.RTF|DOC Files|" & _
                            "*.DOC|Text Files|*.TXT|All Files|*.*"
    SaveFileDialog1.DefaultExt = "RTF"
    If SaveFileDialog1.ShowDialog() = DialogResult.OK Then
        fName = SaveFileDialog1.FileName
        Editor.SaveFile(fName)
        Editor.Modified = False
    End If
End Sub
```

The Save command's code is similar, only it doesn't prompt the user for a filename. It calls the SaveFile method passing the *fName* variable as argument. If the *fName* variable has no value (in other words, if a user attempts to save a new document with the Save command), then the code activates the event handler of the Save As command automatically. It also resets the control's Modified property to False. The code behind the Save command is shown in Listing 7.10.

LISTING 7.10: THE SAVE COMMAND

```
Private Sub FileSave_Click(ByVal sender As System.Object, _
                ByVal e As System.EventArgs) Handles FileSave.Click
    If fName <> "" Then
        Editor.SaveFile(fName)
        Editor.Modified = False
    Else
        FileSaveAs_Click(sender, e)
    End If
End Sub
```

THE EDIT MENU

The Edit menu contains the usual commands for exchanging data through the Clipboard (Copy, Cut, Paste), Undo/Redo commands, and a Find command to invoke the Find and Replace dialog box. All the commands are almost trivial, thanks to the functionality built into the control. The basic Cut, Copy, and Paste commands call the RichTextBox control's Copy, Cut, and Paste methods to exchange information with other applications through the Clipboard. If you aren't familiar with the Clipboard's methods, all you need to know to follow this example are the SetText method, which copies a string to the Clipboard, and the GetText method, which copies the Clipboard's contents to a string variable. The Copy, Cut, and Paste commands are shown in Listing 7.11.

LISTING 7.11: THE COPY, CUT, AND PASTE COMMANDS

```
Private Sub EditCopy_Click(ByVal sender As System.Object, _
                ByVal e As System.EventArgs) Handles EditCopy.Click
    Editor.Copy()
End Sub
Private Sub EditCut_Click(ByVal sender As System.Object, _
                ByVal e As System.EventArgs) Handles EditCut.Click
    Editor.Cut()
End Sub
Private Sub EditPaste_Click(ByVal sender As System.Object, _
                ByVal e As System.EventArgs) Handles EditPaste.Click
    Try
        Editor.Paste()
    Catch exc As Exception
        MsgBox("Can't paste current clipboard's contents")
    End Try
End Sub
```

As you recall from the discussion of the Paste command, we can't use the CanPaste method, because it's not trivial; you have to handle each data type differently. By using the exception handler, we allow the user to paste all types of data the RichTextBox control can accept, and we display a message when an error occurs.

The Undo and Redo commands of the Edit menu are coded as follows. First, we must display the name of the action to be undone or redone in the Edit menu. When the Edit menu is selected, the Select event is fired. This event takes place before the Click event, so I've inserted a few lines of code that read the name of the most recent action that can be undone or redone and print it next to the Undo or Redo command. If there's no such action, the program will disable the corresponding command. Listing 7.12 is the code that's executed when the Edit menu is dropped.

LISTING 7.12: SETTING THE CAPTIONS OF THE UNDO AND REDO COMMANDS

```
Private Sub EditMenu_Select(ByVal sender As Object, _
            ByVal e As System.EventArgs) Handles EditMenu.Select
   If Editor.UndoActionName <> "" Then
      EditUndo.Text = "Undo " & Editor.UndoActionName
      EditUndo.Enabled = True
   Else
      EditUndo.Text = "Undo"
      EditUndo.Enabled = False
   End If
   If Editor.RedoActionName <> "" Then
      EditRedo.Text = "Redo " & Editor.RedoActionName
      EditRedo.Enabled = True
   Else
      EditRedo.Text = "Redo"
      EditRedo.Enabled = False
   End If
End Sub
```

When the user selects one of the Undo and Redo commands, we simply call the appropriate method from within the menu item's Click event handler (Listing 7.13).

LISTING 7.13: UNDOING AND REDOING ACTIONS

```
Private Sub EditUndo_Click(ByVal sender As System.Object, _
            ByVal e As System.EventArgs) Handles EditUndo.Click
   If Editor.CanUndo Then Editor.Undo()
End Sub
Private Sub EditRedo_Click(ByVal sender As System.Object, _
            ByVal e As System.EventArgs) Handles EditRedo.Click
   If Editor.CanRedo Then Editor.Redo()
End Sub
```

Calling the CanUndo and CanRedo method is unnecessary, because if there's no corresponding action the two menu items will be disabled, but an additional check is no harm. Should there be an "unknown" action that the control can't undo, these If statements will prevent the control from attempting to perform the undo action.

THE FORMAT MENU

The commands of the Format menu control the alignment of the text and the font attributes of the current selection. The Font command displays the Font dialog box and then assigns the font selected by the user to the current selection. Listing 7.14 shows the code behind the Font command.

LISTING 7.14: THE FONT COMMAND

```
Private Sub FormatFont_Click(ByVal sender As System.Object, _
               ByVal e As System.EventArgs) Handles FormatFont.Click
    If Not Editor.SelectionFont Is Nothing Then
        FontDialog1.Font = Editor.SelectionFont
    Else
        FontDialog1.Font = Nothing
    End If
    If FontDialog1.ShowDialog() = DialogResult.OK Then
        Editor.SelectionFont = FontDialog1.Font
    End If
End Sub
```

Notice that the code preselects a font on the dialog box, which is the font of the current selection. If the current selection isn't formatted with a single font, then no font is preselected. You can modify the code so that it displays the font of the first character in the selection.

To enable the Apply button of the Font dialog box, set the control's ShowApply property to True and insert the following statement in its Apply event handler. Select the FontDialog1 control in the Objects drop-down list of the code editor, and then select the Apply event in the Events drop-down list. When the declaration of the event handler appears, insert the statement that applies the font selected on the Font dialog box to the current selection:

```
Private Sub FontDialog1_Apply(ByVal sender As Object, _
               ByVal e As System.EventArgs) Handles FontDialog1.Apply
    Editor.SelectionFont = FontDialog1.Font
End Sub
```

The options of the Align menu set the RichTextBox control's SelectionAlignment property to different members of the HorizontalAlignment enumeration. The Align ➤ Left command, for example, is implemented with the following statement:

```
Editor.SelectionAlignment = HorizontalAlignment.Left
```

THE SEARCH & REPLACE DIALOG BOX

The Find command in the Edit menu opens the dialog box shown in Figure 7.14, which the user can use to perform various search and replace operations (whole-word or case-sensitive match, or both). The code behind the Command buttons on this form is quite similar to the code for the Search & Replace dialog box of the TextPad application, with one basic difference: it uses the control's Find method. The Find method of the RichTextBox control performs all types of searches, and some of its options are not available with the InStr() function.

FIGURE 7.14

The Search &
Replace dialog box
of the RTFPad
application

To invoke the Search & Replace dialog box (Listing 7.15), the Find command calls the Show method of a variable that represents the dialog box.

LISTING 7.15: DISPLAYING THE SEARCH & REPLACE DIALOG BOX

```
Private Sub EditFind_Click(ByVal sender As System.Object, _
               ByVal e As System.EventArgs) Handles EditFind.Click
    If fndForm Is Nothing Then
       fndForm = New FindForm()
    End If
    fndForm.Show()
End Sub
```

fndForm is declared on the Form level with the following statement:

```
Dim fndForm As FindForm
```

The dialog box should have access to the Editor control on the main form. To allow the dialog box to manipulate the RichTextBox control on the main form, the program declared a public shared variable with the following statement:

```
Public Shared RTFBox As RichTextBox
```

This variable is initialized to the Editor RichTextBox control in the form's Load event handler, shown in Listing 7.16.

LISTING 7.16: THE MAIN FORM'S LOAD EVENT HANDLER

```
Private Sub EditorForm_Load(ByVal sender As Object, _
               ByVal e As System.EventArgs) Handles MyBase.Load
    RTFBox = Editor
End Sub
```

The Find method of the RichTextBox control allows you to perform case-sensitive or -insensitive searches, as well as search for whole words only. These options are specified through an argument of the RichTextBoxFinds type. The SetSearchMode() function (Listing 7.17) examines the settings of the two check boxes at the bottom of the form and sets this option.

LISTING 7.17: SETTING THE SEARCH OPTIONS

```
Function SetSearchMode() As RichTextBoxFinds
    Dim mode As RichTextBoxFinds
    If chkCase.Checked = True Then
        mode = RichTextBoxFinds.MatchCase
    Else
        mode = RichTextBoxFinds.None
    End If
    If chkWord.Checked = True Then
        mode = mode Or RichTextBoxFinds.WholeWord
    Else
        mode = mode Or RichTextBoxFinds.None
    End If
    SetSearchMode = mode
End Function
```

The Find and Find Next methods call this function to retrieve the constant that determines the type of the search specified by the user on the form. This value is then passed to the Find method. Listing 7.18 shows the code behind the Find and Find Next buttons.

LISTING 7.18: THE FIND AND FIND NEXT COMMANDS

```
Private Sub bttnFind_Click(ByVal sender As System.Object, _
                ByVal e As System.EventArgs) Handles bttnFind.Click
    Dim wordAt As Integer
    Dim srchMode As RichTextBoxFinds
    srchMode = SetSearchMode()
    wordAt = EditorForm.RTFBox.Find(txtSearchWord.Text, 0, srchMode)
    If wordAt = -1 Then
        MsgBox("Can't find word")
        Exit Sub
    End If
    EditorForm.RTFBox.Select(wordAt, txtSearchWord.Text.Length)
    bttnFindNext.Enabled = True
    bttnReplace.Enabled = True
    bttnReplaceAll.Enabled = True
    EditorForm.RTFBox.ScrollToCaret()
End Sub
Private Sub bttnFindNext_Click(ByVal sender As System.Object, _
                ByVal e As System.EventArgs) Handles bttnFindNext.Click
    Dim selStart As Integer
    Dim srchMode As CompareMethod
    srchMode = SetSearchMode()
    selStart = InStr(EditorForm.RTFBox.SelectionStart + 2, _
                EditorForm.RTFBox.Text, txtSearchWord.Text, srchMode)
```

```
        If selStart = 0 Then
            MsgBox("No more matches")
            Exit Sub
        End If
        EditorForm.RTFBox.Select(selStart - 1, txtSearchWord.Text.Length)
        EditorForm.RTFBox.ScrollToCaret()
    End Sub
```

Notice that both event handlers call the ScrollToCaret method to force the selected text to become visible—should the Find method locate the desired string outside the visible segment of the text.

Summary

This chapter concludes the presentation of the Windows controls you'll be using in building typical applications. There are a few more controls on the Toolbox that will be discussed in later chapters, and these are the rather advanced controls, like the TreeView and ListView controls. In addition, there are some rather trivial controls, which aren't used as commonly as the basic controls. The trivial controls will not be discussed in this book. Instead, we're going to move to some really exciting topics, like how to build custom classes and custom Windows controls.

Classes are at the core of VB.NET and extremely powerful. For the first time, VB classes support inheritance, which means you can extend existing classes, or existing Windows controls. You'll learn how to build your own classes and inherit existing ones in the following chapter. Then, you'll learn about building custom controls. Like classes, controls can also be inherited, and you'll see how easy it is to extend the functionality of existing controls by adding new members.

Part II

Rolling Your Own Objects

Chapter 8

Building Custom Classes

CLASSES ARE AT THE very heart of Visual Studio. Just about everything you do with VB.NET is a class, and you already know how to use classes. The .NET Framework itself is an enormous compendium of classes, and you can import any of them into your applications. You simply declare a variable of the specific class type, initialize it, and then use it in your code. As you have noticed, even a Form is a Class, and it includes the controls on the form and the code behind them. All the applications you've written so far are enclosed in a set of Class...End Class statements.

When you create a variable of any type, you're creating an instance of a class. The variable lets you access the functionality of the class through its properties and methods. Even the base data types are implemented as classes (the System.Integer class, System.Double, and so on). An integer value, like 3, is actually an instance of the System.Integer class, and you can call the properties and methods of this class using its instance. Expressions like 3.MinimumValue and #1/1/2000#.Today are odd, but valid.

In this chapter, you'll learn how to build your own classes, which you can use in your projects or pass to other developers. Classes are used routinely in team development. If you're working in a corporate environment, where different programmers code different parts of an application, you can't afford to repeat work that someone else has done already. You should be able to get their code and use it in your application as is. That's easier said than done, because you can guess what will happen as soon as a small group of programmers start sharing code. They'll end up with dozens of different versions for each function, and every time they upgrade a function they will most likely break the applications that were working with the old version. Or, each time they revise a function, they must update all the projects using the old version of the function and test them. It just doesn't work.

The major driving force behind object-oriented programming is *code reuse*. Classes allow you to write code that can be reused in multiple projects. You already know that classes don't expose their source code. In other words, you can't see the code in a class, and therefore you can't affect any other projects that use the class. You also know that classes implement complicated operations and make these operations available to programmers through properties and methods. The Array class exposes a Sort method, which sorts its elements. This is not a simple operation, but fortunately you don't have to know anything about sorting. Someone else has done it for you and made this functionality available to your applications. This is called *encapsulation*. Some functionality has been built into the class (or *encapsulated* into the class), and you can access it from within your applications with a simple method call.

The 3,500 (or so) classes that come with the .NET Framework give you access to all the objects used by the operating system. All you have to do is use them in your application. You don't have to see the code, and you don't have to know anything about sorting to sort your arrays, just as you don't need to know anything about encryption to encrypt a string with the System.Security.Cryptography class. In effect, you're reusing code that Microsoft has already written. As you will see, it is also possible to *extend* these classes by adding custom members, and even *override* existing members. When you extend a class, you create a new class based on an existing one. Projects using the original class will keep seeing the original class, and they will work fine. New projects that see the derived class will also work.

In this chapter, you'll learn how to create your own classes and share them with other programmers. This is one of the most improved areas of VB.NET, which is the first truly object-oriented version of Visual Basic. Most of the new functionality comes from the new techniques for implementing classes. Once you understand how classes are implemented and how to exploit features like inheritance, you'll understand the topics discussed in earlier chapters a lot better. If you still have questions regarding the object-oriented features of the language, like the methods and properties exposed by the various data types, there's a good chance that you'll find the answers here. This chapter is not as much about techniques as it is about a good understanding of how classes work and why features like inheritance are really needed in a modern language—and, of course, why you shouldn't go overboard with inheritance.

What Is a Class?

A *class* is a program that doesn't run on its own; it must be used by another application. The way we invoke a class is by creating a variable of the same type as the class. Then, we exploit the functionality exposed by the class by calling the members of the class through this variable. The methods and properties of the class, as well as its events, constitute the class's *interface*. It's not a visible interface, like the ones you've learned to design so far, and the class doesn't interact directly with the user. To interact with the class, the application uses the class's interface, just as users will be interacting with your application through its visual interface.

Until now, you have learned how to use classes. Now's the time to understand what goes on behind the scenes when you interact with a class and its members. Behind each object, there's a class. When you declare an array, you're invoking the System.Array class, which contains all the code for manipulating arrays. Even when you declare a simple integer variable, you're invoking a class, the System.Integer class. This class contains the code that implements the various properties (such as MinValue and MaxValue) and methods (such as ToString) of the Integer data type. The first time you use an object in your code, you're instantiating the class that implements this object. The class is loaded into memory, initializes its variables, and is ready to execute. An instance of the class is ready for you to use.

Classes are very similar to Windows controls, only they don't have a visible interface. Controls are instantiated when you place them on a form; classes are instantiated when you use a variable of the same type—and not when you declare the variable with the Dim statement. To use a control, you must make it part of the project by adding its icon to the Toolbox, if it's not already there. To use a class in your code, you must import the file that implements the class (this is a DLL file). To manipulate a control from within your code, you call its properties and methods. You do the same with classes. Finally, you program the various events raised by the controls to interact with the users of your applications. Most classes don't expose any events, since the user can't interact with them, but some classes do raise events, which you can program just as you program the events of a Windows control. Using classes is not new to you, and many of the concepts presented in this chapter are not new to you either.

In Chapter 3, I mentioned briefly that a class combines code and data. You have probably noticed this already in the last couple of chapters. The System.Integer class, for example, stores an integer value and knows how to process it. Variables in VB.NET are not just areas in memory you can access by name; they're instances of the corresponding classes. The array is a better example. The role of the array is to store sets of data. In addition to holding the data, the Array class also knows how to process them—how to retrieve an element, how to extract a segment of the array, even how to sort its elements. All these operations require a substantial amount of code. The data stored in the array and the code that implements the properties and the methods of the array are hidden from you, the developer. You can instruct the array to perform certain tasks. When you call the Sort method, you're telling the array to execute some code that will sort the elements of the array. The developer doesn't know how the data are stored in the array, or how the Sort method works. In the following section, you'll see how data and code coexist in a class and how you can manipulate the data through the properties and methods exposed by the class. Let's start by building a custom class and then using it in our code.

Building the Minimal Class

Our first example is the Minimal class; we'll start with the minimum functionality and keep adding features to it. The name of the class can be anything—just make sure it's suggestive of the class's functionality.

A Class may reside in the same file as a Form, but it's customary to implement custom classes in a separate module, a Class module. You can also create a Class project, which contains just a class. However, a class doesn't run on its own, and you can't test it without a form. You can create a Windows application, add the class to it, and then test it by adding the appropriate code to the form. After debugging the class, you can remove the test form and use the class with any project. Since the class is pretty useless outside the context of an application, in this chapter I will use Windows applications and add a class to them.

Start a new project and name it SimpleClass (or open the project by that name on the CD). Then create a new class by adding a Class item to your project. Right-click the project's name in the Solution Explorer window and, from the context menu, select Add ➤ Add Class. In the dialog box that pops up, select the Class icon and enter a name for the class. Set the class's name to Minimal, as shown in Figure 8.1.

The code that implements the class will reside in the `Minimal.vb` file, and we'll use the existing form to test our class. After you have tested and finalized the class's code, you no longer need the form and you can remove it from the project.

FIGURE 8.1

Adding a Class item
to a project

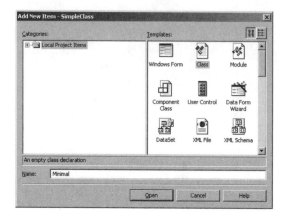

When you open the class by double-clicking its icon in the Project Explorer window, you will see the following lines in the code window:

```
Public Class Minimal

End Class
```

You can also create a class in the same file as the application's form. To do so, enter the Class keyword followed by the name of the class, after the existing End Class. The editor will insert the matching End Class for you. At this point, you already have a class, even though it doesn't do anything. Switch back to the Form Designer, add a button to the test form, and insert the following code in its Click event handler:

```
Dim obj1 As Minimal()
```

Press Enter and, on the following line, type the name of the variable, **obj1**, followed by a period. You will see a list of the methods your class exposes already:

```
Equals
GetHashCode
GetType
ReferenceEqual
ToString
```

These methods are provided by the Common Language Runtime (CLR). You don't have to supply any code for these methods. They don't expose any real functionality; they simply reflect how VB handles all classes. To see the kind of functionality these methods expose, enter the following lines in the Button's Click event handler and then run the application:

```
Dim obj1 As New Minimal()
Console.WriteLine(obj1.ToString)
Console.WriteLine(obj1.GetType)
Console.WriteLine(obj1.GetHashCode)
Dim obj2 As New Minimal()
Console.WriteLine(obj1.Equals(obj2))
Console.WriteLine(Minimal.ReferenceEquals(obj1, obj2))
```

The following lines will be printed on the Output window:

```
SimpleClass.Minimal
SimpleClass.Minimal
18
False
False
```

As you can see, the name of the object is the same as its type. This is all the information about your new class that's available to the CLR. Shortly you'll see how you can implement your own ToString method and return another value. The hash value of the *obj1* variable happens to be 18, but this is of no consequence.

The next line tells you that two variables of the same type are not equal. But why aren't they equal? We haven't differentiated them at all, yet they're different because they point to two different objects and the compiler doesn't know how to compare them. All it can do is figure out whether they point to the same object. To understand how objects are compared, add the following statement after the line that declares *obj2*:

```
obj2 = obj1
```

If you run the application again, the last statement will print True on the Output window. The Equals method checks for reference equality; that is, it returns True if both variables point to the same object (same instance of the class). If you change *obj1*, then *obj2* will point to the new object. OK, we can't change the object because it exposes no members that we can set to differentiate it from another object of the same type. We'll get to that shortly.

Most classes expose a custom Equals method, which knows how to compare two objects of the same class. The custom Equals method usually compares the properties of the two instances of the class and returns True if all properties are the same. You'll learn how to customize the default members of any class later in this chapter.

Notice the name of the class: `SimpleClass.Minimal`. Within the current project, you can access it as Minimal. Other projects can either import the Minimal class and access it as Minimal, or specify the complete name of the class.

Adding Code to the Minimal Class

Let's add some functionality to our class. We'll begin by adding a few properties and methods to perform simple text-manipulation tasks. The two properties are called *property1* (a String) and *property2* (a Double). To expose these two members as properties, you can simply declare them as public variables. This isn't the best method of implementing properties, but it really doesn't take more than declaring something as Public to make it available to code outside the class. The following line exposes the two properties of the class:

```
Public property1 As String, property2 As Double
```

The two methods are the ReverseString and NegateNumber methods. The first method reverses the order of the characters in *property1* and returns the new string. The NegateNumber method returns the negative of *property2*. These are the simplest type of methods that don't accept any arguments; they simply operate on the values of the properties. In just the way that properties are exposed as Public variables, methods are exposed as Public procedures (functions or subroutines).

Enter the function declarations of Listing 8.1 between the `Class Minimal` and `End Class` statements in the class's code window (I'm showing the entire listing of the class here).

LISTING 8.1: ADDING A FEW MEMBERS TO THE MINIMAL CLASS

```
Public Class Minimal
    Public property1 As String, property2 As Double
    Public Function ReverseString() As String
        Return (StrReverse(property1))
    End Function
    Public Function NegateNumber() As Double
        Return (-property2)
    End Function
End Class
```

Let's test what we've done so far. Switch back to your form and enter the lines shown in Listing 8.2 in a new button's Click event handler. Notice that as soon as you enter the name of the *obj* variable and the period after it, a complete list of the class's members, including the custom members, appears in a list box. The *obj* variable is of the Minimal type and exposes the public members of the class. You can set and read its properties and call its methods. In Figure 8.2, you see a few more members than the ones added so far; we'll extend our Minimal class in the following section. Your code doesn't see the class's code, just as it doesn't see any of the built-in classes' code. You trust that the class knows what it's doing and does it right.

LISTING 8.2: TESTING THE MINIMAL CLASS

```
Dim obj As New Minimal()
obj.property1 = "ABCDEFGHIJKLMNOPQRSTUVWXYZ"
obj.property2 = 999999
Console.WriteLine(obj.ReverseString)
Console.WriteLine(obj.NegateNumber)
```

FIGURE 8.2

The members of the class are displayed automatically by the IDE, as needed.

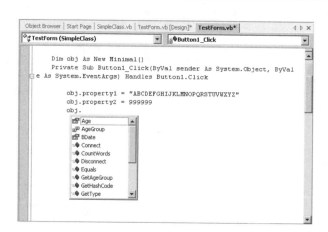

Every time you create a new variable of the Minimal type, you're creating a new instance of the Minimal class. The class's code is loaded into memory only the first time you create a variable of this type, but every time you declare another variable of the same type, a new set of variables is created. This is called an *instance of the class*. The code is loaded once, but it can act on different sets of variables. In effect, different instances of the class are nothing more than different sets of local variables.

THE NEW KEYWORD

The New keyword tells VB to create a new instance of the Minimal class. If you omit the New keyword, you're telling the compiler that you plan to store an instance of the Minimal class in the *obj* variable, but the class won't be instantiated. You must still initialize the *obj* variable with the New keyword on a separate line:

```
obj = New Minimal()
```

If you omit the New keyword, a "Null Reference" exception will be thrown when the code attempts to use the variable. This means that the variable is Null—it hasn't been initialized yet.

Property Procedures

The *property1* and *property2* properties will accept any value, as long as the type is correct and the value of the numeric property is within the acceptable range. But what if the generic properties were meaningful entities, like ages or zip codes? We should be able to invoke some code to validate the values assigned to the property. To do so, you must implement the properties with the so-called *Property procedures.*

Properties are implemented with a special type of procedure that contains a Get and Set section. The Set section of the procedure is invoked when the application attempts to set the property's value, and the Get section is invoked when the application requests the property's value. Usually, the value passed to the property is validated in the Set section and, if valid, stored to a local variable. The same local variable's value is returned to the application when it requests the property's value, from the property's Get section. Listing 8.3 shows what the implementation of an Age property would look like.

LISTING 8.3: IMPLEMENTING PROPERTIES WITH PROPERTY PROCEDURES

```
Private tAge As Integer
Property Age() As Integer
   Get
      Age = tAge
   End Get
   Set (ByVal Value As Integer)
      If Value < 0 Or Value >= 125 Then
         MsgBox("Age must be positive and less than 125")
      Else
         tAge = Value
      End If
   End Set
End Property
```

tAge is the local variable where the age is stored. When a line like the following is executed in the application that uses your class, the Set section of the Property procedure is invoked:

```
obj.Age = 39
```

Since the value is valid, it's stored in the *tAge* local variable. Likewise, when a line like the following one is executed,

```
Console.WriteLine(obj.Age)
```

the Get section of the Property procedure is invoked, and the value 39 is returned to the application.

The Value keyword in the Set section represents the actual value that the calling code is attempting to assign to the property. You don't declare this variable, and its name is always Value. The *tAge* variable is declared as private, because we don't want any code outside the class to access it; this variable is used by the class to store the value of the Age property and can't be manipulated directly. The Age property is, of course, public, so that other applications can set it.

Enter the Property procedure for the Age property in the Minimal class and then switch to the form to test it. Open the Button's Click event handler and add the following lines to the existing ones:

```
obj.Age = 39
Console.WriteLine("after setting the age to 39, age is " & obj.Age.ToString)
obj.Age = 199
Console.WriteLine("after setting the age to 199, age is " & obj.Age.ToString)
```

The value 39 will appear in the Output window. This means that the class accepted the value 39. When the third statement is executed, a message box will appear with the error's description:

```
Age must be positive and less than 125
```

then the value 39 will appear again in the Output window again. The attempt to set the age to 199 failed, so the property retains its previous value.

RAISING EXCEPTIONS

Our error-trapping code works fine, but what good is it? Any developer using our class won't be able to handle this error. You don't want to display messages from within your class, because messages are intended for the final user. As a developer, you'd rather receive an exception and handle it from within your code. So, let's change the implementation of the Age property a little. The Property procedure for the Age property (Listing 8.4) throws an argument exception if you attempt to assign an invalid value to it.

LISTING 8.4: THROWING AN EXCEPTION FROM WITHIN A PROPERTY PROCEDURE

```
Private tAge As Integer
Property Age() As Integer
   Get
      Age = tAge
   End Get
   Set (ByVal Value As Integer)
      If Value < 0 Or Value >= 125 Then
         Dim AgeException As New ArgumentException()
```

```
        Throw AgeException
    Else
        tAge = Value
    End If
End Set
End Property
```

You can test this property in your application; switch to the test form, and enter the statements of Listing 8.5 in a new button's Click event handler (this is the code behind the Handle Exceptions button on the test form).

LISTING 8.5: CATCHING THE AGE PROPERTY'S EXCEPTION

```
Dim obj As New Minimal()
Dim userAge as Integer
UserAge = InputBox("Please enter your age")
Try
    obj.Age = userAge
Catch exc as ArgumentException
    MsgBox("Can't accept your value, " & userAge.ToString & VbCrLf & _
            "Will continue with default value of 30")
    obj.Age = 30
End Try
```

This is a much better technique for handling errors in your class. The exceptions can be intercepted by the calling application, and developers using your class can write a robust application by handling the exceptions in their code. When you develop custom classes, keep in mind that you can't handle most errors from within your class, because you don't know how other developers will use your class. Make your code as robust as you can, but don't hesitate to throw exceptions for all conditions you can't handle from within your code (Figure 8.3). Our example continues with a default age of 30. But as a class developer, you can't make this decision—another developer might prompt the user for another value, and a sloppy developer might let his application crash (but this isn't your problem).

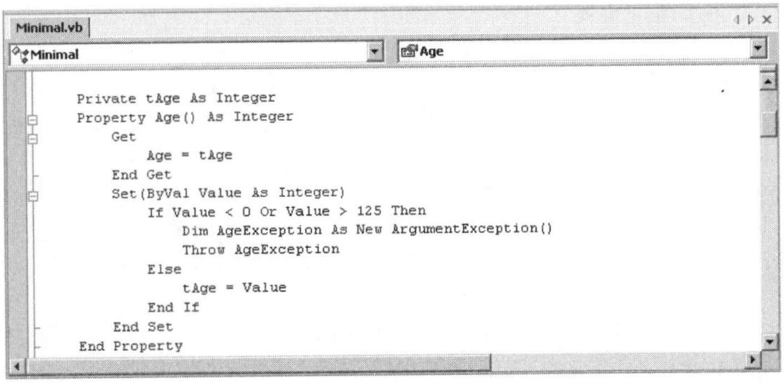

FIGURE 8.3

Raising an exception in the class's code

IMPLEMENTING READ-ONLY PROPERTIES

Let's make our class a little more complicated. Age is not usually requested on official documents. Instead, you must furnish your date of birth, from which your current age can be calculated at any time. We'll add a BDate property in our class and make Age a read-only property.

To make a property read-only, you simply declare it as ReadOnly and supply the code for the Get procedure only. Revise the Age property's code in the Minimal class as seen in Listing 8.6. Then enter the Property procedure from Listing 8.7 for the BDate property.

LISTING 8.6: MAKING A READ-ONLY PROPERTY

```
Private tAge As Integer
ReadOnly Property Age() As Integer
    Get
        Age = tAge
    End Get
End Property
```

LISTING 8.7: THE BDATE PROPERTY

```
Private tBDate As Date
Property BDate() As Date
    Get
        BDate = tBDate
    End Get
    Set
        If Not IsDate(Value) Then
            MsgBox("Invalid date")
            Exit Property
        End If
        If Value > Now() Or DateDiff(DateInterval.Year, Now(), Value) >= 125 Then
            MsgBox("Age must be positive and less than 125")
        Else
            tBDate = Value
        End If
    End Set
End Property
```

The code calls the DateDiff() function, which returns the difference between two dates in a specified interval—in our case, years. The expression `DateInterval.Year` is the name of constant, which tells the DateDiff() function to calculate the difference between the two dates in years. You don't have to memorize the constant names—you simply select them from a list as you type.

So, the code checks the number of years between the date of birth and the current date. If it's negative (which means that the person hasn't been born yet) or more than 125 years (just in case), it rejects the value. Otherwise it sets the value of the *tBDate* local variable.

Now we must do something about the Age property's value. The implementation of the Age property shown in Listing 8.6 allows you to read the value of the property, but not set it. However, you must update the *tAge* variable. Instead of maintaining a local variable for the age, we can calculate it every time the user requests the value of the Age property. Revise the Age property's code to match Listing 8.8, so that it calculates the difference between the date of birth and the current date and returns the person's age.

LISTING 8.8: A CALCULATED PROPERTY

```
ReadOnly Property Age() As Integer
    Get
        Age = CInt(DateDiff(DateInterval.Year, Now(), tBDate))
    End Get
End Property
```

Notice also that you no longer need the *tAge* local variable, because the age is calculated on-the-fly when requested. As you can see, you don't always have to store property values to local variables. A property that returns the number of files in a directory, for example, also doesn't store its value in a local variable. It retrieves the requested information on-the-fly and furnishes it to the calling application. By the way, the calculations may still return a negative value, if the user has changed the system's date, but this is rather far-fetched.

You can implement write-only properties with the WriteOnly keyword. This type of property is implemented with a Set section only. But WriteOnly properties are of questionable value, and you'll probably never use them.

Our Minimal class is no longer so minimal. It exposes some functionality, and you can easily add more. Add properties for name, profession, and income, and methods to calculate insurance rates and anything you can think of. Add a few members to the class, and check them out.

Before ending this section, let's experiment a little with object variables. We'll create two variables of the Minimal class and set some properties. Then, we'll call the Equals method to compare them. Enter the lines of Listing 8.9 in a new button's Click handler (this is the code behind the button named Test Equals Method on the test form).

LISTING 8.9: EXPERIMENTING WITH CLASS INSTANCES

```
Dim obj1 As New Minimal()
Obj1.property1 = "ABCDEFGHIJKLMNOPQRSTUVWXYZ"
Dim obj2 As New Minimal()
obj2 = obj1
If obj1.Equals(obj2) Then Console.WriteLine("They're equal")
obj2.property1 = "abcdefghijklmnopqrstuvwxyz"
If obj1.Equals(obj2) Then Console.WriteLine("They're equal")
```

The statements of Listing 8.9 will produce the following output:

```
They're equal
They're equal
```

The two variables are initially equal. No surprise. After modifying one of the *obj2* variable's properties, however, they're still equal, because *obj2* points to *obj1*. Every time we change *obj2*, *obj1* also changes. That's because we've made *obj1* point to *obj2*. They both point to the same object (or instance of the class), and you can access this object through either class.

Comment out the line that sets *obj2* equal to *obj1*. Now, they're not equal, even if you set all their fields to the same values. They don't reference the same object, and it's possible to set their properties differently.

In the following section, we'll add an Equals method that checks for *value equality* (as opposed to reference equality) by comparing the values of the properties of the two instances.

Customizing Default Members

As you recall, when you created the Minimal class for the first time, before adding any code, the class already exposed a few members—the default members, such as the ToString method (which returns the name of the class) and the Equals method (which compares two objects for reference equality). You can provide your custom implementation for these members; this is what we're going to do in this section. You already know how to do this. Your custom ToString method must be implemented as a public function, and it must override the default implementation. The implementation of a custom ToString method is shown next:

```
Public Overrides Function ToString() As String
    Return "The infamous Minimal class"
End Function
```

It's that simple. The Overrides keyword tells the compiler that this implementation overwrites the default implementation of the class. Ours is a very simple method, but you can return any string you can build in the function. For example, you can incorporate the value of the BDate property in the string:

```
Return("MINIMAL: " & tBDate.ToString)
```

tBDate is a local variable in the class's module, and you can use its value in any way you see fit in your code. The value of the local variable *tBDate* is the current value of the BDate property of the current instance of the class.

When called through different variables, the ToString method will report different values. Let's say you've created and initialized two instances of the Minimal class with the following statements:

```
Dim obj1 As New Minimal()
Obj1.Bdate = #1/1/1963#
Dim obj2 As New Minimal()
Obj2.Bdate = #12/31/1950#
Console.WriteLine(obj1.ToString)
Console.WriteLine(obj2.ToString)
```

The last two statements will print the following lines on the Output window:

```
MINIMAL: 1963-01-01 00:00:00
MINIMAL: 1950-12-31 00:00:00
```

The Equals method exposed by most of the built-in objects, however, can compare values, not references. Two Rectangle objects, for example, are equal if their dimensions and origins are the same. The following two rectangles are equal:

```
Dim R1 As New Rectangle(0, 0, 30, 60)
Dim R2 As New Rectangle
R2.X = 0
R2.Y = 0
R2.Width = 30
R2.Height = 60
If R1.Equals(R2) Then
    MsgBox("The Two rectangles are equal")
End If
```

If you execute these statements, a message box will pop up. The two variables point to different objects (i.e., different instances of the same class), but the two objects are equal. The Rectangle class provides its own Equals method, which knows how to compare two Rectangle objects. If your class doesn't provide a custom Equals method, all the compiler can do is compare the objects referenced by the two variables. In the case of our Minimal class, the Equals method returns True if the two variables point to the same object (which is the same instance of the class). If the two variables point to two different objects, the default Equals method will return False, even if the two objects are equal.

You're probably wondering what makes two objects equal. Is it all of their properties, or perhaps some of them? Two objects are equal if the Equals method says so. You should compare the objects in a way that makes sense, but you're in no way limited as to how you do this. You may even compare internal variables that are not exposed as properties to decide about the equality. In the Minimal class, for example, you may decide to compare the birth dates and return True if they're equal. Listing 8.10 is the implementation of a possible custom Equals method for the Minimal class.

LISTING 8.10: A CUSTOM EQUALS METHOD

```
Public Overloads Function Equals(ByVal obj As Object) As Boolean
    Dim O As Minimal = CType(obj, Minimal)
    If O.BDate = tBDate Then
        Equals = True
    Else
        Equals = False
    End If
End Function
```

Notice that the Equals method is prefixed with the Overloads keyword, not the Overrides keyword. To test the new Equals method, place a new button on the form and insert the statements of Listing 8.11 in its Click event handler.

LISTING 8.11: TESTING THE CUSTOM EQUALS METHOD

```
Dim O1 As New Minimal()
Dim O2 As New Minimal()
O1.BDate = #3/1/1960#
O2.BDate = #3/1/1960#
O1.property1 = "object1"
O2.property1 = "OBJECT2"
If O1.Equals(O2) Then
    MsgBox("They're equal")
End If
```

If you run the application, you'll see the message confirming that the two objects are equal, despite the fact that their *property1* properties were set to different values. The BDate property is the same, and this is the only setting the Equals method examines.

So, it's up to you to decide which properties fully and uniquely identify an object and to use these properties in determining when two objects are equal. It's customary to compare the values of all the properties of the two objects in the Equals function and return True if they're all the same. You can modify the code of the custom Equals function to take into consideration the other properties.

KNOW WHAT YOU'RE COMPARING

The Equals method shown in Listing 8.10 assumes that the object you're trying to compare to the current instance of the class is of the same type. Since you can't rely on developers to catch all their mistakes, you should know what you're comparing before you actually do the comparison. A more robust implementation of the Equals method is shown in Listing 8.12.

LISTING 8.12: A MORE ROBUST EQUALS METHOD

```
Public Overloads Function Equals(ByVal obj As Object) As Boolean
    Dim O As New Minimal()
    Try
        O = CType(obj, Minimal)
    Catch typeExc As InvalidCastException
        Throw typeExc
        Exit Function
    End Try
    If O.BDate = tBDate Then
        Equals = True
    Else
        Equals = False
    End If
End Function
```

NOTE *Note that the custom Equals method throws the same exception it receives from the CType() function. This is a little different from creating and throwing a new custom exception, as we did in the Age property's code.*

Custom Enumerations

Let's add a little more complexity to our class. Since we're storing dates of birth to our class, we can classify persons according to their age. Instead of using literals to describe the various age groups, we'll use an enumeration, with the following group names:

```
Public Enum AgeGroup
    Baby
    Child
    Teenager
    Adult
    Senior
    Overaged
End Enum
```

These statements must appear outside any procedure in the class, and we usually place them at the beginning of the file, right after the declaration of the Class. The enumeration is a list of integer values, each one mapped to a name. In our example, the name *Baby* corresponds to 0, the name *Child* corresponds to 1, and so on. You don't really care about the actual values of the names, because the very reason for using enumerations is to replace numeric constants with more meaningful names. You'll see shortly how enumerations are used both in the class and the calling application.

Now add to the class the GetAgeGroup method (Listing 8.13), which returns the name of the group to which the person represented by an instance of the Minimal class belongs. The name of the group is a member of the AgeGroup enumeration.

LISTING 8.13: USING AN ENUMERATION

```
Public Function GetAgeGroup() As AgeGroup
    Dim group As AgeGroup
    Select Case tAge
        Case Is < 5 : Return (group.Baby)
        Case Is < 12 : Return (group.Child)
        Case Is < 21 : Return (group.Teenager)
        Case Is < 65 : Return (group.Adult)
        Case Is < 100 : Return (group.Senior)
        Case Else : Return (group.Overaged)
    End Select
End Function
```

First, we declare a variable of the AgeGroup type. As you can see, the members of the AgeGroup enumeration become properties of the *group* variable. The advantage of using enumerations is that you can manipulate meaningful names instead of numeric constants. This makes your code less prone to errors and far easier to understand.

TIP   *The members of an enumeration are not variables. They're constants, and you can only access them through a variable of the AgeGroup enumeration.*

Because the AgeGroup enumeration was declared as Public, it's exposed to any application that uses the Minimal class. Let's see how we can use the same enumeration in our application. Switch to the form's code window, add a new button, and enter the statements from Listing 8.14 in its event handler.

LISTING 8.14: USING THE ENUMERATION EXPOSED BY THE CLASS

```
Protected Sub Button3_Click(ByVal sender As Object, _
                ByVal e As System.EventArgs)
    Dim obj As Minimal
    obj = New Minimal()
    obj.BDate = #2/9/1932#
    Console.WriteLine(obj.Age)
    Dim discount As Single
    If obj.GetAgeGroup = Minimal.AgeGroup.Baby Or _
        obj.GetAgeGroup = Minimal.AgeGroup.Child Then discount = 0.4
    If obj.GetAgeGroup = Minimal.AgeGroup.Senior Then discount = 0.5
    If obj.GetAgeGroup = Minimal.AgeGroup.Teenager Then discount = 0.25
    Console.WriteLine(discount)
End Sub
```

This routine calculates discounts based on the person's age. Notice that we don't use numeric constants in our code, just descriptive names. Moreover, the possible values of the enumeration are displayed in a drop-down list by the IntelliSense feature of the IDE as needed (Figure 8.4), and you don't have to memorize them, or look them up, as you would with constants.

FIGURE 8.4

The members of an enumeration are displayed automatically in the IDE as you type.

Using the SimpleClass in Other Projects

The project you've built in this section is a Windows application that contains a Class module. The class is contained within the project, and it's used by the project's main form. What if you wanted to use this class in another project?

First, you must change the type of the project. A Windows project can't be used as a component in another project. Right-click the SimpleClass project and select Properties. On the project's Properties dialog box, locate the Output drop-down list and change the project's type from Windows Application to Class Library, as shown in Figure 8.5. Then close the dialog box. When you return to the project, right-click the TestForm and select Exclude From Project. A class doesn't have a visible interface, and there's no reason to include the test form in your project.

FIGURE 8.5

Setting a project's properties through the Property Pages dialog box

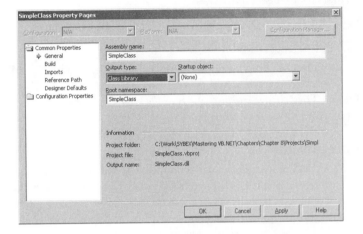

Now open the Build menu and select Configuration Manager. The current configuration is Debug. Change it to Release, as shown in Figure 8.6. The Debug configuration should be used in testing and debugging the project. When you're ready to distribute the application (be it a Windows application, a class library, or a control library), you must change the current configuration to Release. When you compile a project in Debug configuration, the compiler inserts additional information in the executable to ease the debugging process.

FIGURE 8.6

Changing the configuration of a project

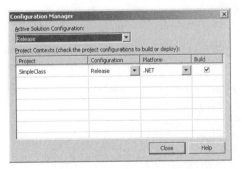

From the main menu, select Build ➤ Build SimpleClass. This command will compile the SimpleClass project (which is a class) and will create a DLL file. This is the file that contains the class's code and is the file you must use in any project that needs the functionality of the SimpleClass class. The DLL file will be created in the \Obj\Release folder under the project's folder.

Let's use the `SimpleClass.dll` file in another project. Start a new Windows application, open the Project menu, and add a reference to the SimpleClass. Select Project ➤ Add Reference and, in the dialog box that appears, switch to the Projects tab. Click the Browse button and locate the `Simple-Class.dll` file. Select the name of the file and click OK to close the dialog box.

The SimpleClass component will be added to the project. You can now declare a variable of the SimpleClass type and call its properties and methods:

```
Dim obj As New SimpleClass
obj.Age = 45
obj.property2 = 5544
MsgBox(obj.Negate())
```

If you want to keep testing the SimpleClass project, add the TestForm to the project (right-click the project's name, select Add ➤ Add Existing Item, and select the TestForm in the project's folder). Then change the project's type back to Windows application, and finally change its configuration from Release to Debug.

Firing Events

Methods and properties are easy to implement, and you have seen how to implement them. Classes can also fire events. It's possible to raise events from within your classes, although not quite as common. Controls have many events, because they expose a visible interface and the user interacts through this interface (clicks, drags and drops, and so on). But classes can also raise events. Class events can come from three different sources:

The class itself   A class may raise an event to indicate the progress of a lengthy process, or that an internal variable or property has changed value. The PercentDone event is a typical example. A process that takes a while to complete reports its progress to the calling application with this event, which is fired periodically. These are called *progress events,* and they're the most common type of class events.

Time events   These events are based on a timer. They're not very common, but you can implement alarms, job schedulers, and similar applications. You can set an alarm for a specific time or an alarm that will go off after a specified interval.

External events   External events, like the completion of an asynchronous operation, can also fire events. A class may initiate a file download and notify the application when the file arrives.

Notice that the class can't intercept events initiated by the user under any circumstances, because it doesn't have a visible user interface.

TIME EVENTS

Let's look at an example of a simple event, one that's raised at a specific time. We'll implement an event in our Minimal class that fires at five o'clock in the afternoon—that is, if an application is using the class at the time. Classes can't be instantiated at specific times. Even if they could, the events would go unnoticed. Classes must be instantiated by an application. In addition, the application must be executing when the event is fired, so that it can process it. If the application doesn't provide a handler for the event, the event will go unnoticed—just like the DragEnter and Enter events of most controls, which are not handled in a typical Windows application.

The first problem we face is that the class's code isn't running constantly to check the time periodically. It executes when a member of the class is called and then returns control to your application. To make your class check the time periodically, you must embed a Timer control in your class. But the class doesn't have a visible interface, so you can't place a Timer control on it. The solution is to instantiate a Timer control from within the class's code and program its Elapsed event so that it fires every so often. In our example, we'll implement an event that's fired every day at five o'clock. This is a reminder for the end of a shift, so it need not be extremely precise. We'll set the Timer control to fire a Tick event every 10 seconds. If this were a real-time application, you'd have to fire Tick events more often. The following line creates an instance of the Timer control:

```
Dim WithEvents tmr As System.Timers.Timer
```

This declaration must appear outside any procedure. The WithEvents keyword is crucial here. Controls and classes that raise events must be declared with the WithEvents keyword, or else the application won't see the events. Controls will fire them, but the class won't be watching out for events. While methods and properties are an integral part of the class and you don't have to request that these members be exposed, the events are not exposed by default. Moreover, the statements that declare object variables with the WithEvents keyword must appear outside any procedure.

The Timer control is disabled by default, and we must enable it. A good place to insert the Timer's initialization code is the class's New() procedure, which is called when the class is instantiated:

```
Public Sub New()
    tmr = New WinForms.Timer()
    tmr.Interval = 10000
    tmr.Enabled = True
End Sub
```

Our timer is ready to go and will fire an event every 10,000 milliseconds, or 10 seconds. The shorter the interval, the more time spent in processing the Timer's Elapsed event.

The Timer's Elapsed event will be fired every 10 seconds, and you must now program this event. What do we want to do in this event? Check the time and, if it's five o'clock, raise the TeaTime event. Before a class can raise an event, you must declare it with a statement like the following:

```
Public Event TeaTime()
```

This declaration must also appear outside any procedure in your class's code. Now you can program the Elapsed event handler (Listing 8.15) and raise the event when appropriate. Because we can't be sure that the Timer will fire its event at five o'clock precisely, we check the time and, if it's after 1700 hours and no later than 120 seconds after that time, we fire the event.

LISTING 8.15: THE TIMER'S TICK EVENT HANDLER

```
Private Sub tmr_Elapsed(ByVal sender As Object, _
              ByVal e As System.Timers.ElapsedEventArgs) Handles tmr.Elapsed
    'Console.WriteLine(DateDiff(DateInterval.Second, Now(), _
          DateAdd(DateInterval.Hour, 17, System.DateTime.Today)))
```

```
      If DateDiff(DateInterval.Second, Now(), DateAdd( _
                DateInterval.Hour, 17, System.DateTime.Today)) < 120 Then
         tmr.Enabled = False
         RaiseEvent TeaTime(Me)
      End If
   End Sub
```

Notice that once the event is raised, we disable the timer, or else the same event would fire again and again (Figure 8.7). The long statement I've commented out displays the number of seconds from the moment it's executed to five o'clock. Use this value to adjust the second statement, and make the class fire the event at any time.

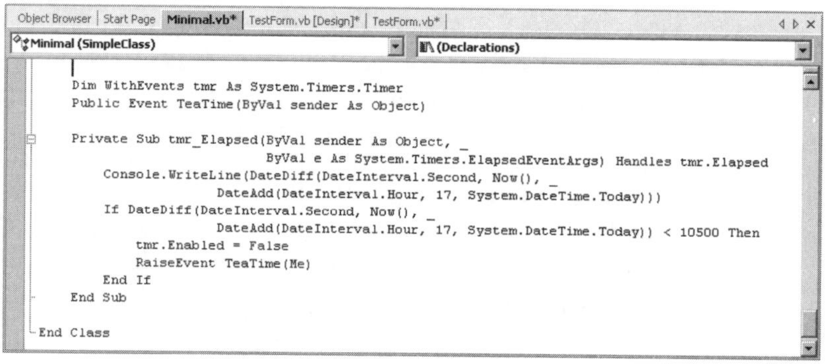

FIGURE 8.7

Declaring and raising an event in the class's code

The code uses the DateDiff() function, which calculates the difference between the current time and 1700 hours in seconds. If this difference is less than two minutes, the class raises the TeaTime event. The syntax of the DateDiff() function is complicated, but here's an explanation of its arguments. The first argument is a constant value that tells the DateDiff() function what time unit to use in reporting the difference. In our example, we want to express the difference in seconds. The following two arguments are the two date (or time) values to be subtracted. The first of the two arguments is the current date and time: the second is a date/time value that represents the current date at five o'clock. This value is constructed with the following expression:

```
DateAdd(DateInterval.Hour, 17, System.DateTime.Today)
```

This statement returns the current date with a time value of 17:00.00 (something like 2001-08-13 17:00:00). This value is then compared to the current date and time.

PROGRAMMING THE CLASS'S EVENT

How do we intercept the event in our main application? As you may have guessed, we'll instantiate the class with the WithEvents keyword. Declare a second variable of the Minimal type in the test form with the WithEvents keyword:

```
Dim WithEvents TimerObj As Minimal
```

After this declaration, the *TimerObj* variable will appear in the list of objects of the editor window, and its TeaTime event will appear in the list of events, as you see in Figure 8.8. You can now program the event in your application and use it any way you see fit.

FIGURE 8.8

Programming a class's event

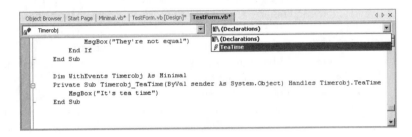

The events raised by a class may pass additional arguments to the program that handles the event. The *sender* argument is passed by default and contains information about the object that raised the event—so that you can write an event handler for multiple events. Place a new button on the form, name it Initialize Timer, and enter the following code in its Click event handler (this is the code behind the button of that name on the test form):

```
Private Sub bttnInitTimer_Click(ByVal sender As System.Object, _
            ByVal e As System.EventArgs) Handles bttnInitTimer.Click
    TimerObj = New Minimal()
End Sub
```

This subroutine creates a new instance of the *TimerObj* variable. This variable was declared outside the procedure, but it wasn't instantiated. Before this statement is executed, no events will take place. I've inserted the statement that prints the time difference (seconds left until five o'clock) in the Timer's Tick event so that you can see what's going on.

Let's see how the application uses the class. Start the application and wait for 10 seconds. You might expect to see something in the Output window, but nothing will appear. The `Console.Write-Line` statement in the Timer control's Tick event handler isn't executed, because the *TimerObj* variable hasn't been instantiated yet.

Click one of the buttons on the form other than the Initialize Timer button. Every 10 seconds, a new double value will appear in the Output window. This is the number of seconds left until (or passed since) five o'clock. The event, however, isn't raised. An instance (or more) of the Minimal class has been created, so the class's code is executing, and it prints the number of seconds left until the next TeaTime event in the Output window. However, the *TimerObj* variable (the one declared with the WithEvents keyword) has not been instantiated yet, so even if the class fires the event, your application won't handle it. Since none of the variables of the Minimal type was declared with the WithEvents keyword, the application isn't receiving notifications about the event—should it happen. The class's code, however, is running, and it prints a value every 10 seconds.

Now click the Initialize Timer button, wait for a few seconds, and the message will pop up—provided you're testing the application around five o'clock. Only the *TimerObj* variable was declared with the WithEvents keyword, and this is the only one that can intercept the event.

Before I end this example, I should show you how to test the application without having to wait forever. I ran the application at 1:57 P.M., and the value printed by the first statement in the Tick events was 10,900 or so (the numbe r of seconds to five o'clock). Then I stopped the application, changed the value 120 in the code to a value a little smaller than the one in the Output window (10,850), and restarted the application. A few moments later, the event was fired (it took more than 10 seconds, so I was sure the code was working properly). If you're running the application after five o'clock, the values will be negative, so adjust the comparison accordingly.

You have the basics for writing classes to fire alarms at specified intervals, a specific time, or even a time interval after a certain operation. You can also use this class (with some modifications) to monitor the system and raise an event if certain things happen. You could check a folder periodically to see if a file was added or deleted. There's no reason to write code for this, because the Framework exposes the FileSystemWatcher class, which does exactly that (the FileSystemWatcher class is discussed in Chapter 13). But you may wish to monitor a printer, know when a new user logs in, or keep track of any other operation or action you can detect from within your code.

PASSING PARAMETERS THROUGH EVENT ARGUMENTS

Events usually pass some information to the routine that processes them. The TeaTime event is a trivial example that doesn't include any information, but in most cases there will be some information you'll want to pass to the application. The arguments of an event are declared just like the arguments of a procedure. The following statement declares an event that's fired when the class completes the download of a file. The event passes three parameter values to the application that intercepts it:

```
Public Event CompletedDownload(ByVal fileURL As String, _
               ByVal fileName As String, ByVal fileLength As Long)
```

The parameters passed to the application through this event are the URL from which the file was downloaded, the path of a file where the downloaded information was stored, and the length of the file. To raise this event from within a class's code, call the RaiseEvent statement as before, passing three values of the appropriate type, as shown next:

```
RaiseEvent CompletedDownload("http://www.server.com/file.txt", _
               "d:\temp\A90100.txt", 144329)
```

In the following section, you'll find actual examples of events that pass arguments to the application that uses the class. You will also see how you can cancel an asynchronous operation from within your application by setting one of the arguments of the event.

PROGRESS EVENTS

Progress events can be fired in two ways. If you know the duration of the operation, you can fire progress events when every five or ten percent of the operation completes. If the operation takes place from within a loop, you can fire the progress event after a certain number of iterations. A more complicated case is when you don't know in advance how long the operation may take. This may happen when you download a file of unknown size. In this case, you can fire progress events every so many seconds and report the number of bytes downloaded, or some other indication that might help the application display some form of progress. Reporting the progress as a percentage of the total work

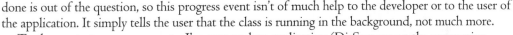

done is out of the question, so this progress event isn't of much help to the developer or to the user of the application. It simply tells the user that the class is running in the background, not much more.

To demonstrate progress events, I've prepared an application (DirScanner on the companion CD) that goes through an entire drive and adds up the sizes of all files. This is a lengthy operation even on the fastest Pentium system, so it will give you a chance to monitor the progress events. Since the class has no way of knowing the total number of folders (or files) on the disk ahead of time, it can only report the number of folders scanned so far.

The following code scans recursively all folders on the hard drive. The process of scanning a folder, including its subfolders, is quite simple—if you're familiar with recursion, that is. The code is discussed in detail in Chapter 18, but don't worry about understanding how it works right now. Just focus on the ScanProgress event, which is fired each time a new folder has been scanned. The application that receives the event can update a display with the total number of folders scanned so far, which is a good indication of the progress of the operation. It's not an indicator of the time left to complete the operation, but sometimes this is all you can do. When you search for a specific file with the Find utility, for example, all you get is a list of folders scanned so far at the bottom of the window.

The DirScanner class (shown in Listing 8.16) calls the ScanFolder() function, which accepts as argument the name of the folder to be scanned and returns the total size of all the files in this folder. ScanFolder() scans the files in the folder passed as argument. Then it goes through the subfolders under the same folder and does the same. To do so, it calls itself by passing each subfolder's name as argument. By the time it's done, the *totalSize* local variable holds the sum of the sizes of all files under the initial folder.

LISTING 8.16: THE DIRSCANNER CLASS

```
Imports System.IO
Imports System.IO.Directory
Public Class DirScanner
    Public Event ScanProgress(ByVal foldersScanned As Integer)
    Private totalSize As Long
    Private nFolders As Integer
    Public Function ScanFolder(ByVal folder As String) As Long
        Dim file, dir As String
        Dim FI As FileInfo
        For Each file In Directory.GetFiles(folder)
            FI = New FileInfo(file)
            totalSize = totalSize + FI.Length
        Next
        For Each dir In Directory.GetDirectories(folder)
            nFolders = nFolders + 1
            RaiseEvent ScanProgress(nFolders)
            ScanFolder(dir)
        Next
        Return totalSize
    End Function
End Class
```

The ScanProgress event is declared at the Class level (outside the ScanFolder() procedure), and it passes an Integer value to the calling application; this is the number of folders scanned so far. The ScanFolder() function maintains two private variables, where it stores the number of folders scanned so far (the *nFolders* variable) and the total size of the files. The *nFolders* value is reported to the application through the event's argument. The code of the ScanFolder() function is straightforward, except for the line that raises the event. The event is raised every time the function runs into a new folder and before it starts scanning it.

To test the DirScanner class and its event, add a button on the test form and enter the code of Listing 8.17 in its Click event handler.

LISTING 8.17: TESTING THE DIRSCANNER CLASS

```
Dim WithEvents objDirScanner As DirScanner
Protected Sub Button1_Click(ByVal sender As Object, _
                ByVal e As System.EventArgs)
    Dim folder As String
    objDirScanner = New DirScanner()
    folder = "C:\Program Files"
    MsgBox("Your files occupy " & _
            objDirScanner.ScanFolder(folder).Tostring & " bytes on the drive")
End Sub
```

The application calls the ScanFolder() method and, while the method is executing, it receives progress events. The last statement in this subroutine will be executed after the ScanFolder() method completes its execution and returns control to the Click event handler. In the meantime, the events raised by the class are processed by the objDirScanner_ScanProgress handler, which is shown in the following code. To program this event handler, select the name of the *objDirScanner* variable in the object list and the ScanProgress event in the event list of the editor's window. The code shown here uses the information passed through these events to update the caption on the application's form.

```
Public Sub objDirScanner_ScanProgress(ByVal foldersScanned As System.Integer) _
                Handles objDirScanner.ScanProgress
    Me.Text = "Scanned " & foldersScanned.ToString & " folders so far"
End Sub
```

Another method of reporting the progress of a lengthy operation is to raise an event every so often during the operation. The following pseudocode segment outlines the class's code that raises an event every *eventDuration* seconds:

```
If Now.TimeOfDay < (newInterval + eventDuration) Then
    newInterval = Now.TimeOfDay
    RaiseEvent Progress(foldersScanned)
End If
```

When an application initiates an operation that may take a while to complete, it usually provides a Cancel button, which the user can click to interrupt the process. But how do we notify the class that it must abort the current operation? This is done through the progress event, with the help of an additional argument. Many event handlers include a *Cancel* argument, which the application can set to True to indicate its intention to interrupt the execution of the current operation in the class. Let's revise our progress event in the DirScanner class to include a *Cancel* argument.

TIP *Notice that the* Cancel *argument doesn't pass information from the class to the application; it passes information the other way. We want the class to be able to read the value of the* Cancel *argument set by the application, so we must pass this argument by reference, not by value. If you pass the* Cancel *argument by value, its value won't change. Even if the application sets it to True, it's actually setting the value of the copy of the* Cancel *variable, and your class will never see this value.*

Instead of revising the code of the existing ScanProgress event, we'll add another event, the ScanTimerProgress event. Add the event declaration and the ScanTimerFolder() function from Listing 8.18 to your class.

LISTING 8.18: THE SCANTIMERFOLDER METHOD

```
Public Function ScanTimerFolder(ByVal folder As String) As Long
    Dim file, dir As String
    Dim FI As FileInfo
    Dim interval As Double = 3000
    If start = 0 Then start = Now.TimeOfDay.TotalMilliseconds
    Dim cancel As Boolean
    For Each file In Directory.GetFiles(folder)
        FI = New FileInfo(file)
        totalSize = totalSize + FI.Length
    Next
    For Each dir In Directory.GetDirectories(folder)
        If Now.TimeOfDay.TotalMilliseconds > (start + interval) Then
            RaiseEvent ScanTimerProgress(nFolders, cancel)
            If cancel Then Exit Function
            start = Now.TimeOfDay.TotalMilliseconds
        End If
        nFolders = nFolders + 1
        ScanTimerFolder(dir)
    Next
    Return totalSize
End Function
```

The code is the same, except for the If statement that examines the value of the *cancel* argument. If *cancel* is True, then the program aborts its execution. To test the new progress event, add a second button on the form and enter the code of Listing 8.19 in its Click event handler.

LISTING 8.19: INITIATING THE SCANNING OF A FOLDER

```
Protected Sub Button2_Click(ByVal sender As Object, ByVal e As System.EventArgs)
    Dim folder As Directory
    objDirScanner = New DirScanner()
    folder = New Directory("D:\")
    MsgBox("Your files occupy " & _
        objDirScanner.ScanTimerFolder(folder).Tostring & " bytes on the drive")
End Sub
```

The new event will be caught by the same object, the *objDirScanner* object, in addition to the Scan-Progress event. Delete (or comment out) the statements in the objDirScanner_ScanProgress event handler and enter Listing 8.20's lines in the new event's handler.

LISTING 8.20: THE SCANTIMERPROGRESS EVENT

```
Public Sub objDirScanner_ScanProgress(ByVal foldersScanned As System.Integer, _
            ByRef Cancel As Boolean) Handles objDirScanner.ScanProgress
    Me.Text = "Scanned " & foldersScanned.ToString & " folders so far"
    If foldersScanned > 3000 Then Cancel = True
End Sub
```

To test the *Cancel* argument, the program sets it to True to terminate the execution of the Scan-Folder() method if it has already scanned more than 3,000 files. Normally, you should provide a Cancel button on your form, which the user can click to terminate the execution of the method. Check out the DirScanner project and experiment with other techniques for handling the *Cancel* argument. If your `Program Files` folder contains fewer than 3,000 files, use a smaller value in the code to terminate the process of scanning a folder prematurely. Notice that if the scanning operation is interrupted prematurely, the corresponding method will not return the number of folders scanned or the total number of bytes they occupy on disk.

ASYNCHRONOUS OPERATIONS

An *asynchronous operation* is an operation you initiate from within your code and then continue with other tasks, without waiting for the operation's completion. When you start the download a file in Internet Explorer, for example, you can continue surfing while the file is being downloaded in the background. The more operations you can perform in the background, the more responsive your application appears to be.

When the operation completes, the class must notify the application that it's done, and this takes place through an event. These events are similar to the progress events discussed in the previous section, and we won't discuss them in this chapter.

Shared Properties

When you instantiate a class, its code is loaded into memory, its local variables are initialized, and then the New subroutine is executed. This happens the first time you instantiate a variable of the class's type. If the class has already been instantiated (that is, if you have already created a variable of the same type), the code isn't loaded again. Instead, a new copy of each local variable is created. The same code acts on different data, and it appears as if you have multiple instances of the class loaded and running at the same time. Each instance of the class has its own properties; the values of these properties are local to each instance of the class. If you declare two variables of the Minimal type in your application, thus:

```
Dim obj1, obj2 As Minimal
```

then you can set their *Age* property to different values:

```
obj1.property1 = 10
obj2.property2 = 90
```

The two expressions are independent of one another, as if there were two instances of the class in memory at the same time.

There are situations, however, where you want all instances of a class to see the same property value. Let's say you want to keep track of the users currently accessing your class. You can declare a method that must be called in order to enable the class, and this method signals that another user has requested your class. This could be a method that establishes a connection to a database or opens a file. We'll call it the Connect method. Every time an application calls the Connect method, you can increase an internal variable by one. Likewise, every time an application calls the Disconnect method, the same internal variable is decreased by one. This internal variable can't be private, because it will be initialized to zero with each new instance of the class. You need a variable that is common to all instances of the class. Such a variable is called *shared* and is declared with the Shared keyword.

Let's add a shared variable to our Minimal class. We'll call it *LoggedUsers*, and it will be read-only. Its value is reported with the Users property, and only the Connect and Disconnect methods can change its value. Listing 8.21 is the code you must add to the Minimal class to implement a shared property.

LISTING 8.21: IMPLEMENTING A SHARED PROPERTY

```
Shared LoggedUsers As Integer
ReadOnly Property Users() As Integer
   Get
      Users = LoggedUsers
   End Get
End Property
Public Function Connect() As Integer
   LoggedUsers = LoggedUsers + 1
   { your own code here }
End Function
Public Function Disconnect() As Integer
   If LoggedUsers > 1 Then
      LoggedUsers = LoggedUsers - 1
   End If
   { your own code here }
End Function
```

To test the shared variable, add a new button to the form and enter Listing 8.22 in its Click event handler. (The lines in bold are the values reported by the class; they're not part of the listing.)

LISTING 8.22: TESTING THE LOGGEDUSERS SHARED PROPERTY

```
Protected Sub Button5_Click(ByVal sender As Object, _
                ByVal e As System.EventArgs)
    Dim obj1 As New Minimal()
    obj1.Connect()
    Console.WriteLine(obj1.Users)
1
    obj1.Connect()
    Console.WriteLine(obj1.Users)
2
    Dim obj2 As New Minimal()
    obj2.Connect()
    Console.WriteLine(obj1.Users)
3
    Console.WriteLine(obj2.Users)
3
    Obj2.Disconnect()
    Console.WriteLine(obj2.Users)
2
End Sub
```

If you run the application, you'll see the values displayed under each Console.WriteLine statement in the Output window. The values in bold are not part of the listing; I've inserted them in the listing to help you match each item of the output to the statement that produces it. As you can see, both *obj1* and *obj2* variables access the same value of the Users property. Shared variables are commonly used in classes that run on a server and service multiple applications. In effect, they're the class's Global variables, which can be shared among all the instances of a class. You can use shared variables to keep track of the total number of rows accessed by all users of the class in a database, connection time, and other similar quantities.

A "Real" Class

In this section, I'll discuss a more practical class that exposes three methods for manipulating strings. I have used these methods in many projects, and I'm sure many readers will have good use for them—at least one of them. The first two methods are the ExtractPathName and ExtractFile-Name methods, which extract the file and path name from a full filename. If the full name of a file is "c:\Documents\Recipes\Chinese\Won Ton.txt", the ExtractPathName method will return the substring "c:\Documents\Recipes\Chinese\" and the ExtractFileName method will return the substring "Won Ton.txt".

NOTE *You can use the Split method of the String class to extract all the parts of a delimited string. Extracting the path name and filename of a complete filename is so common in programming that it's a good idea to implement the corresponding functions as methods in a custom class. You can also use the Path object, which exposes a similar functionality. The Path object is discussed in Chapter 13.*

The third method is called Num2String; it converts a numeric value (an amount) to the equivalent string. For example, it can convert the amount $12,544 to the string "Twelve Thousand, Five Hundred And Forty Four." No other class in the Framework provides this functionality, and any program that prints checks can use this class.

Parsing a Filename String

Let's start with the two methods that parse a complete filename. These methods are implemented as public functions, and they're quite simple. Start a new project, rename the form to TestForm, and add a Class to the project. Name the class and the project StringTools. Then enter the code of Listing 8.23 in the Class module.

> **LISTING 8.23: THE EXTRACTFILENAME AND EXTRACTPATHNAME METHODS**
>
> ```
> Public Function ExtractFileName(ByVal PathFileName As String) As String
>     Dim delimiterPosition As Integer
>     delimiterPosition = PathFileName.LastIndexOf("\")
>     If delimiterPosition > 0 Then
>         Return PathFileName.Substring(delimiterPosition + 1)
>     Else
>         Return PathFileName
>     End If
> End Function
> Public Function ExtractPathName(ByVal PathFileName As String) As String
>     Dim delimiterPosition As Integer
>     delimiterPosition = PathFileName.LastIndexOf("\")
>     If delimiterPosition > 0 Then
>         Return PathFileName.Substring(0, delimiterPosition)
>     Else
>         Return ""
>     End If
> End Function
> ```

These are two simple functions that parse the string passed as argument. If the string contains no delimiter, it's assumed that the entire argument is just a filename.

The Num2String method is far more complicated, but if you can implement it as a regular function, it doesn't take any more effort to turn it into a method. The listing of Num2String is shown in Listing 8.24. First, it formats the billions in the value (if the value is that large), then the millions, thousands, units, and finally the decimal part, which may contain no more than two digits.

LISTING 8.24: CONVERTING NUMBERS TO STRINGS

```
Public Function Num2String(ByVal number As Decimal) As String
    Dim biln As Decimal, miln As Decimal, thou As Decimal, hund As Decimal
    Dim ten As Integer, units As Integer
    Dim strNumber As String
    If number > 999999999999.99 Then
        Num2String = "***"
        Exit Function
    End If
    biln = CInt(number / 1000000000)
    If biln > 0 Then strNumber = FormatNum(biln) & " Billion" & Pad()
    miln = Int((number - biln * 1000000000) / 1000000)
    If miln > 0 Then _
        strNumber = strNumber & FormatNum(miln) & " Million" & Pad()
    thou = Int((number - biln * 1000000000 - miln * 1000000) / 1000)
    If thou > 0 Then _
        strNumber = strNumber & FormatNum(thou) & " Thousand" & Pad()
    hund = Int(number - biln * 1000000000 - miln * 1000000 - thou * 1000)
    If hund > 0 Then strNumber = strNumber & FormatNum(hund)
    If Right(strNumber, 1) = "," Then _
        strNumber = Left(strNumber, Len(strNumber) - 1)
    If Left(strNumber, 1) = "," Then _
        strNumber = Right(strNumber, Len(strNumber) - 1)
    If number <> Int(number) Then
        strNumber = strNumber & FormatDecimal(CInt((number - Int(number)) * 100))
    Else
        strNumber = strNumber & " dollars"
    End If
    Num2String = Delimit(SetCase(strNumber))
End Function
```

Each group of three digits (million, thousand, and so on) is formatted by the FormatNum()
function. Then, the appropriate string is appended ("Million", "Thousand", and so on). The
FormatNum() function, which converts a numeric value less than 1,000 to the equivalent string, is
shown in Listing 8.25.

LISTING 8.25: THE FORMATNUM() FUNCTION

```
Private Function FormatNum(ByVal num As Decimal) As String
    Dim digit100 As Decimal, digit10 As Decimal, digit1 As Decimal
    Dim strNum As String
    digit100 = Int(num / 100)
    If digit100 > 0 Then strNum = Format100(digit100)
    digit10 = Int((num - digit100 * 100))
    If digit10 > 0 Then
        If strNum <> "" Then
```

```
        strNum = strNum & " And " & Format10(digit10)
    Else
        strNum = Format10(digit10)
    End If
  End If
  FormatNum = strNum
End Function
```

The FormatNum() function formats a three-digit number as a string. To do so, it calls the Format100() to format the hundreds, and the Format10() function formats the tens. The Format10() function, as you may have guessed, calls the Format1() function to format the units. I will not show the code for these functions; you can find it on the CD in the StringTools project. You'd probably use similar functions to implement the Num2String method as a function. Instead, I will focus on a few peripheral issues, like the enumerations used by the class as property values.

To make the Num2String method more flexible, the class exposes the UseCase, UseDelimiter, and UsePadding properties. The UseCase property determines the case of the characters in the string returned by the method. The UseDelimiter method specifies the special characters that may appear before and after the string. Finally, the UsePadding property specifies the character that will appear between groups of digits. The values each of these properties may take on are shown here:

UsePadding	UseDelimiter	UseCase
clsToolsCommas	clsToolsNone	clsToolsCaps
clsToolsSpaces	clsTools1Asterisk	clsToolsLower
clsToolsDashes	clsTools3Asterisks	clsToolsUpper

The actual numeric values are of no interest. The values under each property name are implemented as enumerations, and you need not memorize their names. As you enter the name of property followed by the equal sign, the appropriate list of values will pop up and you can select the desired member.

Listing 8.26 presents the clsToolsCase enumeration and the implementation of the UseCase property:

LISTING 8.26: THE clsToolsCase ENUMERATION AND THE UseCase PROPERTY

```
Enum clsToolsCase
   clsToolsCaps
   clsToolsLower
   clsToolsUpper
End Enum
Private varUseCase As clsToolsCase
Public Property UseCase() As clsToolsCase
   Get
      Return (varUseCase)
   End Get
```

```
        Set
            varUseCase = Value
        End Set
    End Property
```

Once the declaration of the enumeration and the Property procedure are in place, the coding of the rest of the class is simplified a great deal. The Num2String() function, for example, calls the Pad() method after each three-digit group. The separator is specified by the UseDelimiter property, whose type is clsToolsPadding. The Pad() function uses the members of the clsToolsPadding enumeration to make the code easier to read. As soon as you enter the Case keyword, the list of values that may be used in the Select Case statement will appear automatically and you can select the desired member. Here's the code of the Pad() function:

```
Private Function Pad() As String
    Select Case mvarUsePadding
        Case clsToolsPadding.clsToolsSpaces : Pad = " "
        Case clsToolsPadding.clsToolsDashes : Pad = "-"
        Case clsToolsPadding.clsToolsCommas : Pad = ", "
    End Select
End Function
```

To test the StringTools class, create a test form like the one shown in Figure 8.9. Then enter the code from Listing 8.27 in the Click event handler of the two buttons.

FIGURE 8.9

The test form of the StringTools class

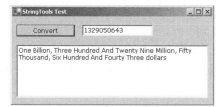

LISTING 8.27: TESTING THE STRINGTOOLS CLASS

```
Protected Sub Button1_Click(ByVal sender As Object, _
                ByVal e As System.EventArgs)
    Dim objStrTools As New StringTools()
    objStrTools.UseCase = StringTools.clsToolsCase.clsToolsCaps
    objStrTools.UseDelimiter = StringTools.clsToolsDelimit.clsToolsNone
    objStrTools.UsePadding = StringTools.clsToolsPadding.clsToolsCommas
    TextBox2.Text = objStrTools.Num2String(CDec(TextBox1.text))
End Sub
Protected Sub Button2_Click(ByVal sender As Object, _
                ByVal e As System.EventArgs)
    Dim objStrTools As New StringTools()
```

```
        openFileDialog1.ShowDialog()
        Console.writeline(objStrTools.ExtractPathName(OpenFileDialog1.FileName))
        Console.WriteLine(objStrTools.ExtractFileName(OpenFileDialog1.FileName))
    End Sub
```

Reusing the StringTools Class

Let's see now how the StringTools class can be used in another project, without making the VB file with the class part of every project that requires this functionality. First, you must create the class's executable file. Unlike Windows applications, classes are compiled into DLL files. Your project most likely contains a test form in addition to the class, so you must exclude the test form from the project. Right-click the name of the test form and select Exclude From Project. This action will exclude the file from the project. You project now contains the StringTools class only.

Classes can't be executed on their own, so you must also change the type of the project. Right-click the name of the project and select Properties. In the Project Property Pages dialog box, change the project's output type from Windows Application to Class Library. Then close the project's property pages, open the Project menu, and select Build. This action will create the StringTools.dll file in the project's Bin folder. This is the file you must reference in any project that requires the functionality of the StringTools class.

Start a new project, and choose Project ➢ Add Reference. On the dialog box that will appear, switch to the Projects tab and click the Browse button. Locate the Bin folder under the project's folder, where you will find the StringTools.dll file. Select it and close all the dialog boxes. When you're back to the project, you will see that the StringTools class has been added to the project. You can't edit the class's code, which means you can't break it. You can even extend the functionality of the StringTools class by adding more members to it, without touching its code. The topic of building new classes based on existing ones is discussed in the later section "Inheritance."

VB.NET at Work: The ClassContacts Project

In Chapter 4, I discussed briefly the Contacts application. This application uses a structure to store the contacts and provides four navigational buttons to allow users to move to the first, last, previous, and next contact. Now that you have learned how to use the ListBox control and how to use custom classes in your code, we're going to revise the Contacts application. First, we'll implement the contacts as a class. The fields of each contact (company name, contact name, and so on) will be implemented as properties. The advantage of implementing the contacts as classes, as opposed to structures, is that you can validate the values of the fields from within your class, and not rely on the application developer to validate the data before storing them to an instance of a structure.

Another advantage is that other developers can extend your class and add new properties, or methods, without having access to your code. You will see how to extend classes later in this chapter, in the section on inheritance.

We'll also improve the user interface of the application. Instead of the rather simplistic navigational buttons, we'll place all the company names in a sorted ListBox control. The user can easily locate the desired company and select it in the list to view the fields of the selected contact. The editing buttons at the bottom of the form work as usual. Figure 8.10 shows the revised Contacts application, which is the ClassContacts application you will find in this chapter's CD folder.

FIGURE 8.10

The interface of the ClassContacts application is based on the ListBox control.

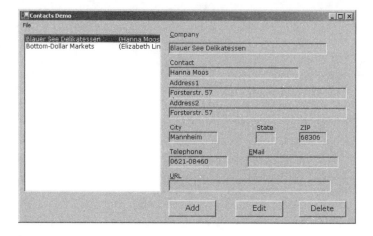

Make a copy of the Contacts folder from Chapter 4 and rename it to ClassContacts. Then open the application in the new folder and likewise rename the project from Contacts to ClassContacts. The next step is to delete the declaration of the Contact structure and add a class to the project. Name the new class Contact and enter in it the code from Listing 8.28.

LISTING 8.28: THE CONTACT CLASS

```
<Serializable()> Public Class Contact
    Private _companyName As String
    Private _contactName As String
    Private _address1 As String
    Private _address2 As String
    Private _city As String
    Private _state As String
    Private _zip As String
    Private _tel As String
    Private _email As String
    Private _URL As String
    Property CompanyName() As String
        Get
            CompanyName = _companyName
        End Get
        Set(ByVal Value As String)
            If Value Is Nothing Or Value = "" Then
                Throw New Exception("Company Name field can't be empty")
                Exit Property
            End If
            _companyName = Value
        End Set
    End Property
    Property ContactName() As String
```

```
      Get
          ContactName = _contactName
      End Get
      Set(ByVal Value As String)
          _contactName = Value
      End Set
End Property
Property Address1() As String
      Get
          Address1 = _address1
      End Get
      Set(ByVal Value As String)
          _address1 = Value
      End Set
End Property
Property Address2() As String
      Get
          Address2 = _address1
      End Get
      Set(ByVal Value As String)
          _address2 = Value
      End Set
End Property
Property City() As String
      Get
          City = _city
      End Get
      Set(ByVal Value As String)
          _city = Value
      End Set
End Property
Property State() As String
      Get
          State = _state
      End Get
      Set(ByVal Value As String)
          _state = Value
      End Set
End Property
Property ZIP() As String
      Get
          ZIP = _zip
      End Get
      Set(ByVal Value As String)
          _zip = Value
      End Set
End Property
Property tel() As String
```

```
        Get
            tel = _tel
        End Get
        Set(ByVal Value As String)
            _tel = Value
        End Set
    End Property
    Property EMail() As String
        Get
            EMail = _email
        End Get
        Set(ByVal Value As String)
            _email = Value
        End Set
    End Property
    Property URL() As String
        Get
            URL = _URL
        End Get
        Set(ByVal Value As String)
            _URL = Value
        End Set
    End Property
    Overrides Function ToString() As String
        If _contactName = "" Then
            Return _companyName
        Else
            Return _companyName & vbTab & "(" & _contactName & ")"
        End If
    End Function
End Class
```

The first thing you'll notice is that the class's definition is prefixed by the <Serializable()> keyword. The topic of serialization is discussed in Chapter 11, but for now all you need to know is that the .NET Framework can convert objects to a text or binary format and store them in files. Surprisingly, this process is quite simple. <Serializable()> is an attribute of the class. As you will see later in this book, there are more attributes you can use with your classes, or even with your methods. The most prominent method attribute is the <WebMethod> attribute, which turns a regular function into a Web method.

The various fields of the contact structure are now properties of the Contact class. The implementation of the properties is trivial, except for the CompanyName property, which contains some validation code. The Contact class requires that the CompanyName property has a value; if it doesn't, the class throws an exception. Finally, the class provides its own ToString method, which returns the name of the company followed by the contact name in parentheses. We're going to store all the contacts in the ListBox control. The ListBox control will display the value returned by the object's ToString method, so we must provide our own ToString method that describes each contact. The company name should be adequate, but if there are two companies by the same name, you can use another field to differentiate them. I've used the contact name, but you can use any of the other properties (the URL would be a good choice).

Each contact is stored in a variable of the Contact type and added to the ListBox control. Now, we must change the code of the main form a little. First, remove the navigational buttons; we no longer need them. Their function will be replaced by a few lines of code in the ListBox control's SelectedIndexChanged event. Every time the user selects another item on the list, the statements shown in Listing 8.29 display the contact's properties on the various TextBox controls on the form.

LISTING 8.29: DISPLAYING THE FIELDS OF THE SELECTED CONTACT OBJECT

```
Private Sub ListBox1_SelectedIndexChanged(ByVal sender As System.Object, _
            ByVal e As System.EventArgs) Handles ListBox1.SelectedIndexChanged
    currentContact = ListBox1.SelectedIndex
    ShowContact()
End Sub
```

The ShowContact() subroutine reads the object stored at the location specified by the *current-Contact* variable and displays its properties on the various TextBox controls on the form.

When a new contact is added, the code creates a new Contact object and adds it to the ListBox control. When a contact is edited, a new Contact object replaces the currently selected object on the control. The code is very similar to the code of the Contacts application. I should mention that the ListBox control is locked while a contact is being added or edited, because it doesn't make sense to select another contact at that time. Besides, we want to be able to replace the contact being edited when the user is done.

To delete a contact (Listing 8.30), we simply remove the currently selected object on the control. In addition, we must select the next object, or the first object if the deleted object was the last one in the list.

LISTING 8.30: DELETING AN OBJECT ON THE LISTBOX

```
Private Sub bttnDelete_Click(ByVal sender As System.Object, _
            ByVal e As System.EventArgs) Handles bttnDelete.Click
    If currentContact > -1 Then
        ListBox1.Items.RemoveAt(currentContact)
        If currentContact = ListBox1.Items.Count Then _
                currentContact = ListBox1.Items.Count - 1
        If currentContact = -1 Then
            ClearFields()
            MsgBox("There are no more contacts")
        Else
            ShowContact()
        End If
```

```
        Else
            MsgBox("No current contacts to delete")
        End If
    End Sub
```

When you add a new contact, the following code is executed in the Add button's Click event handler:

```
Private Sub bttnAdd_Click(ByVal sender As Object, _
                ByVal e As System.EventArgs) Handles bttnAdd.Click
    adding = True
    ClearFields()
    HideButtons()
    ListBox1.Enabled = False
End Sub
```

These statements simply prepare the application to accept a new record. The controls are cleared in anticipation of the new record's fields, and the *adding* variable is set to True. The OK button is clicked to end either the addition of a new record or an edit operation. The code behind the OK button is shown in Listing 8.31.

LISTING 8.31: COMMITTING A NEW OR EDITED RECORD

```
Private Sub bttnOK_Click(ByVal sender As System.Object, _
                ByVal e As System.EventArgs) Handles bttnOK.Click
    Dim contact As New Contact()
    SaveContact()
    ListBox1.Enabled = True
    ShowButtons()
End Sub
```

As you can see, the same subroutine handles both the insertion of a new record and the editing of an existing one. All the work is done by the SaveContact() subroutine, which is shown in Listing 8.32.

LISTING 8.32: THE SAVECONTACT() SUBROUTINE

```
Sub SaveContact()
    Dim contact As New Contact()
    contact.CompanyName = txtCompany.Text
    contact.ContactName = txtContact.Text
    contact.Address1 = txtAddress1.Text
    contact.Address2 = txtAddress2.Text
    contact.City = txtCity.Text
    contact.State = txtState.Text
    contact.ZIP = txtZIP.Text
    contact.tel = txtTel.Text
```

```
        contact.EMail = txtEMail.Text
        contact.URL = txtURL.Text
        If adding Then
            ListBox1.Items.Add(contact)
        Else
            ListBox1.Items(currentContact) = contact
            ListBox1.Items.RemoveAt(currentContact)
            ListBox1.Items.Add(contact)
        End If
    End Sub
```

The SaveContact() subroutine uses the *adding* variable to distinguish between an add and an edit operation, and either adds the new record to the ListBox control or replaces the current record in the ListBox with the values on the various controls.

The last step is the serialization and deserialization of the items on the ListBox control. Serialization is the process of storing the object to a disk file, and deserialization is the opposite process. To serialize objects, we first store them into an ArrayList object. The ArrayList object is a dynamic array that stores objects; it can be serialized as a whole. Likewise, the disk file is deserialized as an ArrayList; then each element of the ArrayList is moved to the Items collection of the ListBox control. The ArrayList object is discussed in detail in Chapter 11, along with the techniques for serializing and deserializing its elements.

The ClassContacts application demonstrates how to use classes to implement custom objects; it's also a demonstration of how the ListBox control should be used. In Chapter 6, when we explored the ListBox control, you saw examples of storing strings to this control. To make the most of the ListBox control, use it to save objects in its Items collection. In addition to storing data, the ListBox control is also a fine navigational tool, as long as it's sorted and the objects you store to the control provide a custom ToString method that returns a string identifying the object.

Encapsulation and Abstraction

As you have seen, developing a new custom class with VB is a straightforward process. In effect, it's very similar to writing regular VB code. So, why build classes in the first place? One of the advantages of using classes is that their functionality is cast in iron; other developers can use it, but they can't break it. You can think of classes as black boxes, and this is what programmers call *encapsulation*. The String data type encapsulates a lot of functionality and exposes it through its properties and methods (the Length property, or the Split method, for example). The functionality is added to the class and is available to all applications that make use of the String class.

If you have a set of utility functions and you use them in several of your projects, you're already familiar with the following scenario. You modify one function for the needs of a specific application, then you modify another function to suit another application, and as you go along you break applications that used to work with the old versions of the functions. If you place all your custom string-manipulation functions in a class, you'll encapsulate their functionality.

Encapsulation doesn't mean that the class must be used "as is." As you will see in the following section, it is possible (and desirable) to modify a member. In short, you can create new classes based on existing ones and add new members, or revise existing members. The old applications will work with the old class, while newer applications will work with the newer version of the class. All this can be done without any housekeeping requirements on your part.

Classes are extremely useful in team programming. In large database projects, a team of programmers develops classes that access the database and perform low-level operations. Other developers use these classes to get an abstracted view of the database. For example, programmers who develop front-end applications need not be concerned with the exact structure of the database. They can access methods like AddBook to add a new book to the database, or GetAuthorBooks to get the books of an author. The first method accepts fields like the book's title and ISBN and creates a new record in the database. The GetAuthorBooks method accepts the ID of an author and returns the books written by this author. The developers working on the front-end applications don't access the database directly. The appropriate classes give them an abstracted view of the database, and they call simple methods to perform fairly complicated tasks. Another advantage of using classes in database applications is that if you change the structure of the database, or even move the data to another database, you need only change the code in the class and the front-end applications will keep working. The capacity to isolate programmers from unnecessary details is called *abstraction*.

These are two of the advantages of using classes. In the following section you will learn about inheritance, a feature that will enable you to write truly reusable code. Inheritance is one of the foundations of object-oriented programming, and this is the first version of Visual Basic that supports true inheritance (or *implementation inheritance*, as it's called).

Inheritance

The promise of classes, and of object programming at large, is code reuse. The functionality you place into a class is there for your projects, and any other developer can access it as well. To appreciate the power of classes, you must understand what happens when you need to add functionality to your class. There are two ways to extend a class: add new members and revise existing members. Both approaches are quite simple if you've written the class. But what if others want to extend your class? Handing out the code is out of the question. Every developer will "improve" your class, and each developer will end up with his own version of it. The class will be no longer reusable. If you unleash the source code of a class to the members of a programming team, it won't be long before you have dozens of "improved" versions of your class. They may be improved versions, alright, but an application using one of them won't be able to use any of the others.

Changing your own classes is not simple either. The class is used by multiple applications, so you can't make changes that will break the existing code. To revise a class without breaking the existing code, you must make sure that the existing members don't change their interface—that is, you shouldn't change the types of the properties, or the number and type of the arguments you pass to the methods. The applications using your class don't see its code. All they care about is that the members they call will keep working. You can rewrite the code of a method, if you come up with a better way to accomplish the task—or other technological advances necessitate the update of the code. If the method doesn't change name, accepts the same arguments, and returns the same value, the calling application will never know that a different code is executing. Since methods are implemented as functions, it's possible to overload a method, so that it can be called with different arguments.

So, how can we update a class that's being used by dozens of applications out there? By overriding existing members or supplying the code for new members. Best of all, you don't need access to the class's code to extend it. You can add or replace members without seeing the existing code. To understand how useful this can be, let's start with an example of extending an existing class that's part of the Framework. Surely, you didn't think Microsoft would make the code of Windows itself available to all developers. This would break not only existing applications, but the operating system itself. Most of the 3,500 classes that come with the Framework, however, can be extended.

Classes are extended by creating new classes that inherit the functionality of the existing class. And this is the single most important new feature of VB.NET: *inheritance*. Inheritance is simply the ability to create a new class based on an existing one. The existing class is the parent class, or *base class*. The new class is said to *inherit* the base class and is called a *subclass*, or *derived class*. The derived class inherits all the functionality of the base class and can add new members and replace existing ones. The replacement of existing members with other ones is called *overriding*. When you replace a member of the base class, you're overriding it. Or, you can overload a method by providing multiple forms of the method that accept different arguments.

Inheriting Existing Classes

To demonstrate the power of inheritance, you're going to extend an existing class, the ArrayList class. This class comes with the Framework, and it's a dynamic array. (See Chapter 11 for a detailed description of the ArrayList class.) The ArrayList class maintains a list of objects, similar to an array, but it's dynamic. The class we'll develop in this section will inherit all the functionality of ArrayList, plus it will expose a custom method we'll implement here: the EliminateDuplicates method. The project described in this section is the CustomArrayList project on the CD.

Let's call the new class *myArrayList*. The first line in the new class must be the Inherits statement, followed by the name of the class we want to inherit, ArrayList. Start a new project, name it CustomArrayList, and add a new Class to it. Name the new class myArrayList:

```
Class myArrayList
Inherits ArrayList

End Class
```

If you don't add a single line of code to this class, the myArrayList class will expose exactly the same functionality as the ArrayList class. If you add a public function to the class, it will become a method of the new class, in addition to the methods of ArrayList. Add the code of the EliminateDuplicates() subroutine (Listing 8.33) to the myArrayList class; this subroutine will become a method of the new class.

LISTING 8.33: THE ELIMINATEDUPLICATES METHOD FOR THE ARRAYLIST CLASS

```
Sub EliminateDuplicates()
    Dim i As Integer = 0
    Dim delEntries As ArrayList
    While i <= MyBase.Count - 2
        Dim j As Integer = i + 1
```

```
            While j <= MyBase.count - 1
                If MyBase.Item(i).ToString = MyBase.item(j).ToString Then
                    MyBase.RemoveAt(j)
                End If
                j = j + 1
            End While
            i = i + 1
        End While
    End Sub
```

The code compares each item with all following items and removes any duplicates. The duplicate items are the ones whose ToString property returns the same value. You may wish to perform very specific comparisons, but the ToString method will do for our demo. To test the derived class, place a button on the test form, and insert the code presented by Listing 8.34 in its Click event handler.

LISTING 8.34: TESTING THE ELIMINATEDUPLICATES METHOD

```
Private Sub Button2_Click(ByVal sender As System.Object, _
                ByVal e As System.EventArgs) Handles Button2.Click
    Dim mlist As New myArrayList()
    mlist.Add(" 10")
    mlist.Add("A")
    mlist.Add("20")
    mlist.Add("087")
    mlist.Add("c")
    mlist.Add("A")
    mlist.Add("b")
    mlist.Add("a")
    mlist.Add("A")
    mlist.Add("87")
    mlist.Add(10)
    mlist.Add(100)
    mlist.Add(110)
    mlist.Add("1001")
    Console.WriteLine(mlist.GetString())
    mlist.EliminateDuplicates()
    Console.WriteLine(mlist.GetString())
End Sub
```

The following table shows the contents of the ArrayList before and after the elimination of the duplicates. Notice that the second list contains the item "10" twice. One of the items is a string, and the other one is a numeric value, and therefore they're not duplicates.

Original List	After Elimination of Duplicates
10	10
A	A
20	20
087	087
C	c
A	b
B	a
A	87
A	10
87	100
10	
100	

GetString (Listing 8.35) is not a method of the ArrayList. It's a method of the extended ArrayList class, which returns the values of all the items in the list (it uses each item's ToString method to retrieve the string representation of the items).

LISTING 8.35: THE GETSTRING METHOD

```
Function GetString() As String
    Dim i As Integer
    Dim strValue As String
    strValue = MyBase.Item(0).ToString
    For i = 1 To MyBase.Count - 1
        strValue = strValue & vbCrLf & MyBase.Item(i).ToString
    Next
    GetString = strValue
End Function
```

Another problem with the ArrayList class is that it can't sort its elements if they're not of the same type. You can always provide a custom comparer for custom types, but it's impossible to write a comparer that can handle all objects. Sometimes, however, we need to know the smallest or largest numeric element, or the alphabetically first or last element. These methods apply to numeric or string elements only; if some of the collection's elements are objects, we can ignore them. Let's implement two more custom methods (Listing 8.36) for myArrayList. The Min method returns the alphabetically smallest value; the NumMin method returns the numerically smallest value.

LISTING 8.36: THE MIN AND NUMMIN METHODS OF THE ARRAYLIST CLASS

```
Function Min() As String
    Dim i As Integer
    Dim minValue As String
        minValue = MyBase.Item(0).ToString
        For i = 1 To MyBase.Count - 1
            If MyBase.Item(i).ToString < minValue Then _
                minValue = MyBase.Item(i).ToString
        Next
        Min = minValue
End Function
Function NumMin() As Double
    Dim i As Integer
    Dim minValue As Double
        minValue = 1E+230
        For i = 1 To MyBase.Count - 1
            If IsNumeric(MyBase.item(i)) And _
                val(MyBase.Item(i).tostring) < minValue Then _
                    minValue = val(MyBase.Item(i).tostring)
        Next
        NumMin = minValue
End Function
```

You can populate the myArrayList with strings and integers and call the Min and NumMin methods to retrieve the smaller string or numeric value in the list.

What have we done in this section, really? We took an existing class, a very powerful one, and extended it. We did that by writing simple VB statements that could have appeared in any application. We just had to insert the Inherits keyword followed by the name of an existing class on which we want to base our class, and provide the implementation of the new methods. A few more keywords to learn and you can practically customize any class that comes with the Framework. Existing applications won't break (the ArrayList class is actually used by some system services, which will keep working fine); they see the original class, not myArrayList. Some of your new applications will see the enhanced ArrayList. Another developer might extend the functionality of your derived class. The old applications will work because ArrayList is still around; your applications will also work because myArrayList hasn't been modified; and someone else's applications will work with another class derived from yours.

Implementation inheritance is a powerful feature and can be used in many situations, besides enhancing an existing class. You can design base classes that address a large category of objects and then subclass them for specific objects. The typical example is the Person class, from which classes like Contact, Customer, Employee, and so on can be derived. Inheritance is used with large-scale projects to ensure consistent behavior across the application. In the following section, you're going to see an interesting application of inheritance. We're going to build classes that describe related objects (shapes), all of which will be based on a single class that encapsulates the basic characteristics of all derived classes.

Polymorphism

This is another powerful aspect of inheritance. *Polymorphism* is the ability of a base type to adjust itself to accommodate many different derived types. Let's make it simpler by using some analogies in the English language. Take the word *run*, for example. This verb can be used to describe athletes, cars, or refrigerators; they all "run." In different sentences, the same word takes different meanings. When you use it with a person, it means going a distance at a fast pace. When you use it with a refrigerator, it means that it's working. When you use it with a car, it may take on both meanings. So, in a sense the word *run* is polymorphic (and so are many other English words): Its exact meaning is differentiated according to the context.

To apply the same analogy to computers, think of a class that describes a basic object, like a Shape. This class would be very complicated if it had to describe and handle all shapes. It would be incomplete too, because the moment you released it to the world, you'd think of a new shape that can't be described by your class. To design a class that describes all shapes, you build a very simple class to describe shapes at large, and then you build a separate class for each individual shape: a Triangle class, a Square class, a Circle class, and so on. As you can guess, all these classes inherit the Shape class. Let's also assume that all the classes that describe individual shapes expose an Area method, which calculates the area of the shape they describe. The name of the Area method is the same for all classes, but it calculates a different formula.

The developer, however, doesn't have to learn a different syntax of the Area method for each shape. They can declare a Square object and calculate its area with the following statements:

```
Dim shape1 As New Square, area As Double
area = shape1.Area
```

If *shape2* represents a circle, the same method will calculate the circle's area:

```
Dim shape2 As New Circle, area As Double
area = shape2.Area
```

You can go through a list of objects derived from the Shape class and calculate their areas by calling the Area method. No need to know what shape each object represents—you just call its Area method. Let's say you've created an ArrayList with various shapes. You can go through the collection and calculate the total area with a loop like the following:

```
Dim shapeEnum As IEnumerator
Dim totalArea As Double
shapeEnum = aList.GetEnumerator
While shapeEnum.MoveNext
    totalArea = totalArea + CType(shapeEnum.Current, Shape).area
End While
```

The CType() function converts the current element of the collection to a Shape object; it's necessary only if the Strict option is on, which prohibits VB from late-binding the expression (Strict is off by default). As a reminder, when the Strict option is off, trivial mistakes will manifest themselves as runtime exceptions. If you mistype the name of the Area method as Arae, the compiler won't catch this error at design time. If the Strict option is on, however, the error will be caught as you type.

The Area method is polymorphic. Its exact meaning (or formula, in the case of shapes) is adjusted to the context in which it's used. OK, this is a simple concept. It's only natural that we're able to call the Area method to calculate the area of any shape, isn't it? Believe me, it took us many years to get there. VB.NET is the first version of VB that supports true polymorphism. We're going to look at the implementation of the classes that describe shapes in a moment, but first I would like to discuss some alternatives and show you the drawbacks, so that you won't think that building classes to calculate the areas of various shapes is wasted time.

The first alternative would be to build a separate function to calculate the area of each shape (SquareArea, CircleArea, and so on). It will work, but why bother with so many function names, not to mention the overhead in your code? You must first figure out the type of shape described by a specific variable, like *shape1*, and then call the appropriate method. The code will not be as easy to read, and the longer the application gets, the more If and Case statements you'll be coding.

The second, even less efficient method is a really long Area() function that would be able to calculate the area of all shapes. This function should be a very long Case statement, like the following one:

```
Public Function Area(ByVal shapeType As String) As Double
    Select Case shapeType
        Case "Square": { calculate the area of a square }
        Case "Circle": { calculate the area of a circle }
        { . . . more Case statements }
    End Select
End Function
```

The real problem with this approach is that every time you want to add a new segment to calculate the area of a new shape to the function, you'd have to edit it. If another developer wanted to add a shape, they'd be out of luck.

In the following section, we'll build the Shape class, which we'll extend with individual classes for various shapes. You'll be able to add your own classes to implement additional shapes, and any code written using the older versions of the Shape class will keep working.

The Shape Class

Let's start with the Shape class, which will be the base class for all other shapes. This is a really simple class that's pretty useless on its own. Its real use is that it exposes some members that can be inherited. The base class exposes two methods, Area and Perimeter. Even the two methods don't do much—actually, they do absolutely nothing. All they really do is provide a naming convention. All classes that will inherit the Shape class will have an Area and a Perimeter method. They must provide the implementation of these methods, so that all object variables that represent shapes will expose an Area method and a Perimeter method.

Start a new project as usual, add a Shape class, and enter the code of Listing 8.37 in it.

LISTING 8.37: THE SHAPE CLASS

```
Class Shape
    Overridable Function Area() As Double
    End Function
    Overridable Function Perimeter() As Double
    End Function
End Class
```

If there are properties common to all shapes, you place the appropriate Property procedures in the Shape class. If you want to assign a color to your shapes, place a Color property in this class. The Overridable keyword means that a class that inherits from the Shape class can override the default implementation of the corresponding methods or properties. As you will see shortly, it is possible for the base class to provide a few members that can't be overridden in the derived class.

Then you can implement the classes for the individual shapes. Add another Class to the project, name it Shapes, and enter Listing 8.38's code in it.

LISTING 8.38: THE SQUARE, TRIANGLE, AND CIRCLE CLASSES

```
Public Class Square
   Inherits Shape
   Private sSide As Double
   Public Property Side() As Double
      Get
         Side = sSide
      End Get
      Set
         sSide = Value
      End Set
   End Property
   Public Overrides Function Area() As Double
      Area = sSide * sSide
   End Function
   Public Overrides Function Perimeter() As Double
      Return (4 * sSide)
   End Function
End Class
Public Class Triangle
   Inherits Shape
   Private side1, side2, side3 As Double
   Property SideA() As Double
      Get
         SideA = side1
      End Get
      Set
         side1 = Value
      End Set
   End Property
   Property SideB() As Double
      Get
         SideB = side2
      End Get
      Set
         side2 = Value
      End Set
```

```
        End Property
        Public Property SideC() As Double
          Get
              SideC = side3
          End Get
          Set
              side3 = Value
          End Set
        End Property
        Public Overrides Function Area() As Double
          Dim perim As Double
          perim = Perimeter()
          Return (Math.Sqrt(perim * (perim - side1) * (perim - side2) * _
                          (perim - side3)))
        End Function
        Public Overrides Function Perimeter() As Double
            Return (side1 + side2 + side3)
        End Function
    End Class
    Public Class Circle
        Inherits Shape
        Private cRadius As Double
        Public Property Radius() As Double
          Get
              Radius = cRadius
          End Get
          Set
              cRadius = Value
          End Set
        End Property
        Public Overrides Function Area() As Double
            Return (Math.Pi * cRadius ^ 2)
        End Function
        Public Overrides Function Perimeter() As Double
            Return (2 * Math.Pi * cRadius)
        End Function
    End Class
```

The Shapes.vb file contains three classes: Square, Triangle, and Circle. All three expose their basic geometric characteristics as properties. The Triangle class, for example, exposes the properties SideA, SideB, and SideC, which allow you to set the three sides of the triangle. In addition, all three classes expose the Area and Perimeter methods. These methods are implemented differently for each class, but they do the same thing: they return the area and the perimeter of the corresponding shape. The Area method of the Triangle class is a bit involved, but it's just a formula.

TESTING THE SHAPE CLASS

To test the Shapes class, all you have to do is create three variables—one of each type of shape—and call their methods. Or, you can store all three variables into an array and iterate through them. If the collection contains Shape variables only, the current item is always a shape, and as such it exposes the Area and Perimeter methods. The code in Listing 8.39 does exactly that. First, it declares three variables of the Triangle, Circle, and Square types. Then it sets their properties and calls their Area method to print their areas.

LISTING 8.39: TESTING THE SHAPE CLASS

```
Protected Sub Button1_Click(ByVal sender As System.Object, _
                ByVal e As System.EventArgs)
    Dim shape1 As New Triangle()
    Dim shape2 As New Circle()
    Dim shape3 As New Square()
' Set up a triangle
    shape1.SideA = 3
    shape1.SideB = 3.2
    shape1.SideC = 0.94
    Console.WriteLine("The triangle's area is " & shape1.Area.ToString)
' Set up a circle
    shape2.Radius = 4
    Console.WriteLine("The circle's area is " & shape2.Area.ToString)
' Set up a square
    shape3.Side = 10.01
    Console.WriteLine("The square's area is " & shape3.Area.ToString)
    Dim shapes() As Shape
    shapes(0) = shape1
    shapes(1) = shape2
    shapes(2) = shape3
    Dim shapeEnum As IEnumerator
    Dim totalArea As Double
    shapeEnum = shapes.GetEnumerator
    While shapeEnum.MoveNext
        totalArea = totalArea + CType(shapeEnum.Current, shape).Area
    End While
    Console.WriteLine("The total area of your shapes is " & totalArea.ToString)
End Sub
```

In the last section, the test code stores all three variables into an array and iterates through its elements. At each iteration, it casts the current item to the Shape type and calls its Area method. The expression that calculates areas is CType(shapeEnum.Current, shape).Area, and the same expression calculates the area of any shape.

The Shape base class is quite trivial—it doesn't expose any functionality of its own. Depending on how you will use the individual shapes in your application, you can add properties and methods to the base class. In a drawing application, all shapes have an outline and a fill color. These properties can be implemented in the Shape class, because they apply to all derived classes. Any methods with common implementation for all classes should also be implemented as methods of the parent class.

The same techniques can be applied to more elaborate classes. For example, you can create a class that represents persons and then derive any number of classes from the Person class. The derived classes could be the Employee class, the Salesperson class, the Consultant class, and so on. The Person class stores the information that is common to all persons, and each of the derived classes inherits these properties and methods. The Pay method can't be common to all persons, and it must be implemented in each individual class. Some persons are paid a salary, others are paid commissions, and so on. The individual methods of each class must implement the Pay method according to the type of person they represent. Inheritance pays off in very large projects, while it may introduce substantial complications in small projects, especially if used without careful design.

Object Constructors and Destructors

As you already know, objects are created and then disposed of when no longer needed. To construct an object, you must first declare it and then set it to a new instance of the class it represents. To construct a triangle, for example, you can use either of these two statements:

```
Dim shape1 As Triangle = New Triangle()
Dim shape1 As New Triangle()
```

It is also possible to specify the properties of an object in the same line that creates the object, with the New keyword. This is the object's *constructor* (it initializes the object by setting some or all of its properties).

```
Dim rect1 As Rectangle = New Rectangle(10, 10, 50, 90)
```

The shapes in the Shapes class can't be initialized in the same line that declares them, because they don't provide a constructor. We must implement a so-called *parameterized* constructor, which allows you to pass arguments to an object as you declare it. These arguments are usually the basic properties of the object. Parameterized constructors don't pass arguments for all the properties of the object; they expect only enough parameter values to make the object usable.

Constructors are implemented with the New subroutine, which is called every time a new instance of the class is initialized. This is where you code initialization tasks such as opening files and establishing connections to databases. We used the New subroutine to instantiate a new Timer object in an earlier example. This time, we'll create a New subroutine for each shape, and we'll declare arguments for the New subroutine.

VB6 ➠ VB.NET

The Class_Initialize method of VB6 has been replaced by the New subroutine, and the Class_Terminate method of VB6 has been replaced by the Destruct subroutine in VB.NET.

Let's start with the Triangle class. When we initialize a Triangle, we want to be able to specify the sides of the triangle. Here's the constructor for the Triangle class:

```
Sub New(ByVal sideA As Double, ByVal sideB As Double, ByVal sideC As Double)
    MyBase.New()
    side1 = sideA
    side2 = sideB
    side3 = sideC
End Sub
```

The code is quite trivial, with the exception of the statement that calls the `MyBase.New` subroutine. MyBase is a keyword that lets you access the members of the base class (a topic that's discussed in detail later in this chapter). The reason you must call the New method of the base class is that the base class may have its own constructor, which can't be called directly. You must always insert this statement in your constructors to make sure that any initialization tasks that must be performed by the base class will not be skipped.

Likewise, when we create a Circle object, we want to be able to specify its radius. The following is the parameterized constructor of the Circle class:

```
Sub New(ByVal radius As Double)
    MyBase.New()
    cRadius = radius
End Sub
```

When you enter a statement like

```
Dim shape1 As New Triangle(
```

in the editor, you will see a list of the parameters you can set, as shown in Figure 8.11.

FIGURE 8.11

The members of the various Shape constructors displayed by IntelliSense

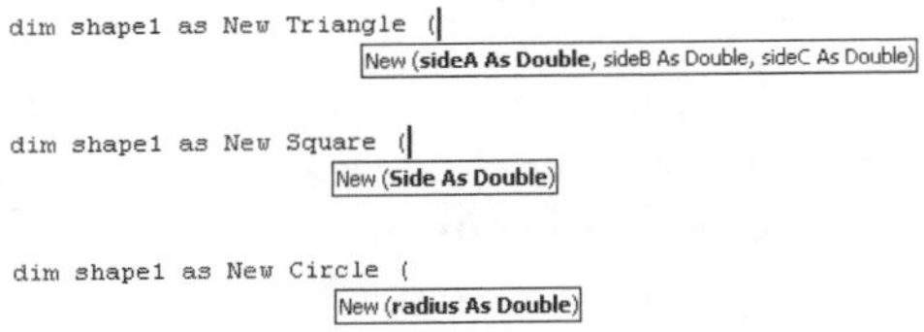

```
dim shape1 as New Triangle (
                           New (sideA As Double, sideB As Double, sideC As Double)

dim shape1 as New Square (
                         New (Side As Double)

dim shape1 as New Circle (
                         New (radius As Double)
```

If you no longer need an object, you can set it to Nothing. The Common Language Runtime (CLR) won't release the object as soon as you set it to Nothing. The new garbage collector (GC) checks periodically for objects that are no longer needed and releases them. However, you don't know when this will happen. If there are tasks you want to perform prior to releasing an object, place them in the Destruct subroutine. The GC will call this subroutine (if it exists) prior to releasing the object.

The New() subroutine is usually overloaded. We always provide a constructor that accepts no arguments, so that developers can create an instance of the class without having to specify any of the arguments. The following New() constructor allows you to create an instance of the Triangle shape without passing any parameters:

```
Sub New()
    MyBase.New()
End Sub
```

You may have noticed the lack of the Overloads keyword. Constructors can have multiple forms and don't require the use of Overloads—just supply as many implementations of the New() subroutine as you need. The following statements show how to create three overloaded forms of the New constructor of the Circle shape. The first constructor accepts no arguments, the second constructor accepts the radius of the circle, and the last constructor accepts a Rectangle object that encloses the circle:

```
Sub New()
    MyBase.New()
End Sub
Sub New(ByVal radius As Double)
    MyBase.New()
    cRadius = radius
End Sub
Sub New(ByVal rect As Rectangle)
    MyBase.New()
    cRadius = rect.Width
End Sub
```

Instance and Shared Methods

As you may have noticed in previous chapters (and it will become even more clear in the following chapters), some classes allow you to call some of their members without first creating an instance of the class. The String class, for example, exposes the IsLeapYear method, which accepts as argument a numeric value and returns a True/False value indicating whether the year is leap or not. You can call this method through the DateTime (or Date) class, as shown in the following statement:

```
If DateTime.IsLeapYear(1999) Then
    { process a leap year }
End If
```

Other members, like the Day property, can't be called through the name of the class. You must first create an instance of the DateTime class, assign a value to it, and then call the Day method of the specific instance of the class. The Day property returns the number of the day, and it has meaning only when applied to a specific date. To call the Day property, declare a variable of the Date type, initialize it, and then call its Day property:

```
Dim d1 As Date = Now()
Console.WriteLine(d1.Day)
```

If you attempt to call the property Date.Day, the statement will not be compiled and the error message will be "Day is not a member of Date." The methods that don't require that you create an instance of the class before you call them are called *shared* methods. Methods that can be applied to an instance of the class are called *instance* methods. By default, all methods are instance methods. To create a shared method, you must prefix the corresponding function declaration with the Shared keyword, just like a shared property.

Why do we need a shared method, and when should we create shared methods? If a method doesn't apply to a specific instance of a class, make it shared. Let's consider the DateTime class, which implements the Date data type. The DaysInMonth methods returns the number of days in the month that was passed to the method as argument. You don't really need to create an instance of a Date object to retrieve the current date, so the DaysInMonth method is a shared method. The AddDays method, on the other hand, is an instance method. We have a date to which we want to add a number days and construct a new date. In this case, it makes sense to apply the method to an instance of the class—the instance that represents the date to which we add the number of days.

 The SharedMembers project on the CD is a simple class that demonstrates the differences between a shared and an instance method. Both methods do the same thing: they reverse the characters in a string. The IReverseString method is an instance method: it reverses the current instance of the class, which is a string. The SReverseString method is a shared method: it reverses its argument. Listing 8.40 shows the code that implements the SharedMembersClass component.

LISTING 8.40: A CLASS WITH A SHARED AND AN INSTANCE METHOD

```
Public Class SharedMembersClass
    Private strProperty As String
    Sub New(ByVal str As String)
        strProperty = str
    End Sub
    Public Function IReverseString() As String
        Return (StrReverse(strProperty))
    End Function
    Public Shared Function SReverseString(ByVal str As String) As String
        Return (StrReverse(str))
    End Function
End Class
```

The instance method acts on the current instance of the class. This means that the class must be initialized to a string, and this is why the New constructor requires a string argument. To test the class add a form to the project, make it the Startup object and add two buttons on it. The code behind the two buttons is shown next:

```
Private Sub Button1_Click(ByVal sender As System.Object, _
            ByVal e As System.EventArgs) Handles Button1.Click
    Dim testString As String = "ABCDEFGHIJKLMNOPQRSTUVWXYZ"
    Dim obj As New SharedMembersClass(testString)
    Console.WriteLine(obj.IReverseString)
End Sub
Private Sub Button2_Click(ByVal sender As System.Object, _
            ByVal e As System.EventArgs) Handles Button2.Click
    Dim testString As String = "ABCDEFGHIJKLMNOPQRSTUVWXYZ"
    Console.WriteLine(SharedMembersClass.SReverseString(testString))
End Sub
```

The code behind the first button creates a new instance of the SharedMembersClass and calls its IReverseString method. The second button calls the SReverseString method through the class's name and passes the string to be reversed as argument to the method.

Who Can Inherit What?

The Shape base class and the Shapes derived class work fine, but there's a potential problem. A new derived class that implements a new shape may not override the Area or the Perimeter method. To make sure that all derived classes implement this method, we can specify the MustInherit modifier to the class declaration and the MustOverride modifier to the member declaration.

The Shapes project on the CD uses the MustInherit keyword in the definition of the Shape class. This keyword tells the CLR that the Shape class can't be used as is; it must be inherited by another class. A class that can't be used as is known as *abstract base* class, or *virtual* class. The definition of the Area and Perimeter methods are prefixed with the MustOverride keyword, which tells CLR that derived classes (the ones that will inherit the members of the base class) must provide their own implementation of the two methods:

```
Public MustInherit Class Shape
    Public MustOverride Function Area() As Double
    Public MustOverride Function Perimeter() As Double
End Class
```

Notice that there's no `End Function` statement, just the declaration of the function that must be inherited by all derived classes. If the derived classes may override one or more methods optionally, these methods must be implemented as actual functions. Methods that *must* be overridden need not be implemented as functions—they're just placeholders for a name.

There are other modifiers you can use with your classes, like the NotInheritable modifier, which prevents your class from being used as base class by other developers. You may wish to enhance the Array class by adding a few new members. If you insert the statement `Inherits Array` in a class, the compiler will complain to the effect that the `System.Array` class can't be inherited. This is an example of a noninheritable class.

In this section, we're going to look at the class-related modifiers and when to use them. The various modifiers are keywords, like the Public and Private keywords you can use in variable declarations. These keywords can be grouped according to the entity they apply to, and I've used this grouping to organize them in the following sections.

Parent Class Keywords

These keywords apply to classes that may be inherited, and they appear in front of the Class keyword. By default, all classes can be inherited, but their members can't be overridden. You can change this default behavior with the following modifiers:

NotInheritable Prevents the class from being inherited. No other classes can be derived from this class. The base data types, for example, are not inheritable. In other words, you can't create a new class based on the Integer data type. The Array class is also not inheritable.

MustInherit This class must be inherited. You can't create an object of this class in your code and, therefore, you can't access its methods. The Shape class is nothing more than a blueprint for the methods it exposes and can't be used on its own; that's why it was declared with the MustInherit keyword. A derived class can access the members of the base class through the keyword MyBase.

Derived Class Keyword

The Inherits keyword applies to classes that inherit from other classes and must be the first statement in the derived class:

Inherits   Any derived class must inherit an existing class. The Inherits statement tells the compiler which class it derives from, and it must be the first executable statement in the derived class's code. A class that doesn't include the Inherits keyword is by definition a base class.

Parent Class Member Keywords

These keywords apply to the members of classes that may be inherited, and they appear in front of the member's name. They determine how derived classes must handle the members (i.e., whether they may or must override their properties and methods):

Overridable   Every member with this modifier may be overwritten. If a member is declared as Public only, it can't be overridden. You should allow developers to override as many of the members of your class as possible, as long as you don't think there's a chance that they may break the code by overriding a member. Members declared with the Overridable keyword don't necessarily need to be overridden, so they must provide some functionality.

NotOverridable   Every member declared with this modifier can't be overridden in the inheriting class.

MustOverride   Every member declared with this modifier must be overridden. You may skip the overriding of a member declared with the MustOverride modifier in the derived class, as long as the derived class is declared with the MustInherit modifier. This means that the derived class must be inherited by some other class, which then receives the obligation to override the original member declared as MustOverride. It seems complicated, but it's really common sense. If you can't provide the implementation of a member that must be overridden, the class must be inherited by another class, which will provide the implementation.

The two methods of the Shape class must be overridden, and we've done so in all the derived classes that implement various shapes. Let's also assume that you wanted to create different types of triangles with different classes (an orthogonal triangle, an isosceles triangle, and a generic triangle). Let's also assume that these classes would inherit the Triangle class. You can skip the definition of the Area method in the Triangle class, but you'd have to include it in the derived classes that implement the various types of triangles. Moreover, the Triangle class would have to be marked as MustInherit.

Public   This modifier tells the CLR that the specific member can be accessed from any application that uses the class.

Private   This modifier tells the CLR that the specific member can be accessed only in the module it was declared. All the local variables must be declared as Private, and no other class (including derived classes), or application, will see them.

Protected   Protected members have scope between public and private, and they can be accessed in the derived class, but they're not exposed to applications using either the parent class or the derived classes. In the derived class, they have a private scope. Use the Protected keyword to mark the members that are of interest to developers who will use your class as base class, but not to developers who will use it in their applications.

Protected Friend This modifier tells the CLR that the member is available to the class that inherits the class, as well as to any other component of the same project.

Derived Class Member Keyword

The Overrides keyword applies to members of derived classes and indicates whether a member of the derived class overrides a base class member:

Overrides Use this keyword to specify the member of the parent class you're overriding. If a member has the same name in the derived class as in the parent class, this member must be overridden. You can't use the Overrides keyword with members that were declared with the NotOverridable or Protected keywords in the base class.

A few examples are in order. The sample application of this section is the InheritanceKeywords project on the CD. Create a simple class by entering the statements of Listing 8.41 in a Class module, and name the module ParentClass.

LISTING 8.41: THE INHERITANCEKEYWORDS CLASS

```
Public MustInherit Class ParentClass
    Public Overridable Function Method1() As String
        Return ("I'm the original Method1")
    End Function
    Protected Function Method2() As String
        Return ("I'm the original Method2")
    End Function
    Public Function Method3() As String
        Return ("I'm the original Method3")
    End Function
    Public MustOverride Function Method4() As String
' No code in a member that must be overridden !
' Notice the lack of the matching End Function here
    Public Function Method5() As String
        Return ("I'm the original Method5")
    End Function
    Private prop1, prop2 As String
    Property Property1() As String
        Get
            Property1 = "Original Property1"
        End Get
        Set
            prop1 = Value
        End Set
    End Property
    Property Property2() As String
```

```
        Get
            Property2 = "Original Property2"
        End Get
        Set
            prop2 = Value
        End Set
    End Property
End Class
```

This class has five methods and two properties. Notice that Method4 is declared with the Must-Override keyword, which means it must be overridden in a derived class. Notice also the structure of Method4. It has no code, and the `End Function` statement is missing. Method4 is declared with the MustOverride keyword, so you can't instantiate an object of the ParentClass type. A class that contains even a single member marked as MustOverride must also be declared as MustInherit.

Place a button on the class's test form, and in its code window attempt to declare a variable of the ParentClass type. VB will issue a warning that you can't create a new instance of a class declared with the MustInherit keyword. Because of the MustInherit keyword, you must create a derived class. Enter the lines from Listing 8.42 in the ParentClass module, after the end of the existing class.

LISTING 8.42: THE DERIVED CLASS

```
Public Class DerivedClass
    Inherits ParentClass
    Overrides Function Method4() As String
        Return ("I'm the derived Method4")
    End Function
    Public Function newMethod() As String
        Console.WriteLine("<This is the derived Class's newMethod " & _
                          "calling Method2 of the parent Class> ")
        Console.WriteLine("    " & MyBase.Method2())
    End Function
End Class
```

The Inherits keyword determines the parent class. This class overrides the Method4 member and adds a new method to the derived class, the newMethod. If you switch to the test form's code window, you can now declare a variable of the DerivedClass type:

```
Dim obj As DerivedClass
```

This class exposes all the members of ParentClass except for the Method2 method, which is declared with the Protected modifier. Notice that the newMethod() function calls this method through the MyBase keyword and makes its functionality available to the application. Normally, we don't expose Protected methods and properties through the derived class.

Let's remove the MustInherit keyword from the declaration of the ParentClass class. Since it's no longer mandatory that the ParentClass be inherited, the MustInherit keyword is no longer a valid modifier for the class's members. So, Method4 must be either removed or implemented. Let's delete the declaration of the Method4 member. Since Method4 is no longer a member of the ParentClass, you must also remove the entry in the DerivedClass that overrides it.

MyBase and MyClass

The MyBase and MyClass keywords let you access the members of the base class and the derived class explicitly. To see why they're useful, edit the ParentClass as shown here:

```
Public Class ParentClass
    Public Overridable Function Method1() As String
        Return (Method4())
    End Function
    Public Overridable Function Method4() As String
        Return ("I'm the original Method4")
    End Function
```

Then override Method4 in the derived class, as shown here:

```
Public Class DerivedClass
    Inherits ParentClass
    Overrides Function Method4() As String
    Return("Derived Method4")
End Function
```

Switch to the test form, add a button, declare a variable of the derived class, and call its Method4:

```
Dim objDerived As New DerivedClass()
Console.WriteLine(objDerived.Method4)
```

What will you see if you execute these statements? Obviously, the string "Derived Method4." So far, all looks reasonable, and the class behaves intuitively. But what if we add the following method in the derived class?

```
Public Function newMethod() As String
    Return (Method1())
End Function
```

This method calls Method1 in the ParentClass class, because Method1 is not overridden in the derived class. Method1 in the base class calls Method4. But which Method4 gets invoked? Surprised? It's the derived Method4! To fix this behavior (assuming you want to call the Method4 of the base class) change the implementation of Method1 to the following:

```
Public Overridable Function Method1() As String
    Return (MyClass.Method4())
End Function
```

If you run the application again, the statement:

```
Console.WriteLine(objDerived.newMethod)
```

will print the string:

```
I'm the original Method4
```

Is it reasonable for a method of the base class to call the overridden method? It is, because the overridden class is newer than the base class and the compiler tries to use the newest members. If you had other classes inheriting from the DerivedClass class, their members would take precedence.

Use the MyClass keyword to make sure you're calling a member in the same class, and not an overriding member in an inheriting class. Likewise, you can use the keyword MyBase to call the implementation of a member in the base class, rather than the equivalent member in a derived class.

VB.NET at Work: The Matrix Class

The Matrix project on the CD demonstrates many of the topics discussed in this chapter, plus a few rather advanced techniques, like complicated constructors. The Matrix class exposes the functionality you need to process two-dimensional matrices and can be your starting point for a class that implements advanced matrix operations, as opposed to the simple ones implemented in this example. I realize most readers aren't interested in math; you can skip this section if that's you. I will quickly describe the class, its methods, and how to use it, and you can explore the code on your own.

The Matrix class maintains a two-dimensional table of Doubles and the table's dimensions. The table's dimensions are exposed as properties—Rows and Cols—and they're stored in the _rows_ and _cols_ local variables. New tables are instantiated through the New constructor. If New is called without arguments, it creates a matrix with a single element. You can also pass the desired dimensions in the New constructor. The implementations of the two overloaded forms of the constructor are shown in Listing 8.43.

LISTING 8.43: THE OVERLOADED NEW() CONSTRUCTOR OF A MATRIX

```
Sub New(ByVal R As Integer, ByVal C As Integer)
    MyBase.new()
    _rows = R
    _cols = C
    ReDim _table(_rows, _cols)
End Sub
Sub New()
    MyBase.new()
    _rows = 1
    _cols = 1
    ReDim _table(_rows, _cols)
End Sub
```

If you don't know the dimensions of a table when you declare it, you can set them later with the Rows and Cols properties, which are implemented as seen in Listing 8.44. Actually, you will see shortly when you may have to declare a matrix without specific dimensions.

LISTING 8.44: THE ROWS AND COLS PROPERTIES OF A MATRIX

```
Public Property Rows() As Integer
    Get
        Rows = _rows
    End Get
```

```
      Set(ByVal Value As Integer)
         _rows = Value
      End Set
   End Property
   Public Property Cols() As Integer
      Get
         Cols = _cols
      End Get
      Set(ByVal Value As Integer)
         _cols = Value
      End Set
   End Property
```

To populate a matrix, call the Cell method (Listing 8.45) to assign a value to a specified cell. The Cell method accepts two arguments, which are the row and column number of the cell that will be set to the specified value.

LISTING 8.45: THE CELL METHOD OF A MATRIX

```
   Public Property Cell(ByVal row As Integer, ByVal col As Integer) As Double
      Get
         Cell = _table(row, col)
      End Get
      Set(ByVal Value As Double)
         _table(row, col) = Value
      End Set
   End Property
```

The following statements create a new matrix and populate it with random integer values in the range 0 to 300:

```
   Dim a As Matrix = New Matrix(3, 4)
   Dim i, j As Integer
   Dim rnd As System.Random = New System.Random()
   For i = 0 To a.Rows - 1
      For j = 0 To a.Cols - 1
         a.Cell(i, j) = rnd.Next(300)
      Next
   Next
```

The most useful methods of the Matrix class are those that perform matrix operations. I've implemented only a few matrix operations, but you can easily extend the class by adding new methods. These methods are the Add, Subtract, and Multiply methods, which perform the simpler matrix operations. All three methods accept either one or two Matrix objects as arguments, and they return the result of the operation. If you pass a single argument, the second matrix is the current instance of the class. If you pass two arguments, the methods add, subtract, or multiply the two matrices.

The result of a matrix operation is another matrix, unless the two matrices are incompatible for the operation. For example, you can't add two matrices of different dimensions. You can modify the code so that it makes the smaller matrix equal to the larger one by appending zeros for the missing elements. However, you can't multiply two matrices, unless the number of columns in the first matrix is equal to the number of rows in the second matrix. If the arguments passed to the Add method (or any other method of the Matrix class) are incompatible, the method returns an empty matrix. You must examine the size of the matrix returned by the method and act accordingly. Alternatively, you can throw an exception from within the method's code (the statement `Throw New System.ArgumentException()` is all you need).

Listing 8.46 shows the implementation of the Add method. The first overloaded form of the method acts on the two matrices passed as arguments; this code is rather trivial. The second overloaded form adds the matrix passed as argument to the matrix represented by the current instance of the class. To access the elements of the current matrix, the code uses the object MyClass. The first form of the Add method is a shared method, while the second one is an instance method (it requires an instance of the class).

LISTING 8.46: THE OVERLOADED MATRIX ADD METHOD

```
Public Overloads Function Add(ByVal A As Matrix, ByVal B As Matrix) As Matrix
    Dim Row, Col As Integer
    If Not (A.Rows = B.Rows And A.Cols = B.Cols) Then
        Add = New Matrix()
        Exit Function
    End If
    Dim newMatrix As New Matrix(A.Rows, A.Cols)
    For Row = 0 To A.Rows - 1
        For Col = 0 To A.Cols - 1
            newMatrix.Cell(Row, Col) = A.Cell(Row, Col) + B.Cell(Row, Col)
        Next
    Next
    Add = newMatrix
End Function
Public Overloads Function Add(ByVal A As Matrix) As Matrix
    Dim Row, Col As Integer
    If Not (A.Rows = MyClass.Rows And A.Cols = MyClass.Cols) Then
        Add = New Matrix()
        Exit Function
    End If
    Dim newMatrix As New Matrix(MyClass.Rows, MyClass.Cols)
    For Row = 0 To MyClass.Rows - 1
        For Col = 0 To MyClass.Cols - 1
            newMatrix.Cell(Row, Col) = A.Cell(Row, Col) + MyClass.Cell(Row, Col)
        Next
    Next
    Add = newMatrix
End Function
```

You can open the Matrix project on the CD, examine the code, and add more features to the Matrix class, starting with a method that inverts matrices (a complicated algorithm that I have not implemented in the sample project). You will notice that I've implemented the class in the form's file. After adding all the functionality you need to the class, you can copy the class's code into another project and create a class to use with any of your projects.

Summary

In this chapter, you learned the mechanics of building custom classes, and you were exposed to the main concepts of object-oriented programming. Inheritance and polymorphism are the two most powerful features introduced into the Visual Basic programming language, which bring it to the same level as the other two languages of Visual Studio.

The reason for using classes is code reuse. Classes are robust and not susceptible to changes. If another developer needs to extend your class, adding more members or overwriting existing members, they can do so by inheriting the functionality of your class. The existing applications will work with the old class, while newer applications can use the new one. You can also edit your class's code without breaking any existing code. Just make sure you don't change the interface of a class.

Now that you understand what classes are, how they work, and what they can do for you, we're going to explore some useful classes that come with the .NET Framework. Of the numerous Framework classes, I've selected a few that most developers will be using on a daily basis and will discuss them at length in the following chapters. There are many more classes than I even list in this book. Once you familiarize yourself with the most basic ones, you will find it easier to discover the functionality of the other classes, or locate in the documentation the one that exposes the functionality you need.

Chapter 9

Building Custom Windows Controls

Since version 5 of the language, VB has made it very simple to build custom controls, and it's gotten even better with VB.NET. In addition to a host of controls that come with VB.NET and the capability to use ActiveX controls with .NET, you can also easily create your own custom .NET controls.

The design of custom Windows controls has been one of the best implemented features of the language. Creating custom controls with VB.NET is even simpler, mostly because of the functionality added to the UserControl object.

Now, who should be developing custom Windows controls and why? If you come up with an interesting utility that can be used from within several applications, why not package it as a custom control and reuse it in your projects? You can also pass it to other developers and make sure that your application has a consistent look. For example, you might develop a custom control for designing reports or displaying lists of customers. Every form that uses this functionality should be implemented around this control. Users will learn to use the application faster, and the custom control will help you maintain a consistent look throughout the application.

In this chapter, you will learn how to design custom Windows controls for .NET. We'll start by designing a new control that inherits an existing control and adds some extra functionality. Just as in the previous chapter we created a custom ArrayList that incorporated all the functionality of the original ArrayList and added some methods to it, we'll do the same with the TextBox control. Then you'll see how to build custom controls that combine multiple .NET controls. These controls are called *compound controls*, and they're like regular forms with built-in functionality. The ComboBox control, for example, is a compound control made up of a TextBox (its edit area), a ListBox, and a Button that expands the list. Compound controls ride on the functionality of their constituent controls, and you can add specific functionality through custom properties and methods. Finally, you'll learn how to build user-drawn controls. A *user-drawn control* is an empty surface, and you're responsible for drawing the control's interface (and updating it in response to external events).

We'll also discuss a few interesting, out of the ordinary, topics, like how to take control of the drawing process of the MenuItem object and create menus with graphics. You'll also learn how easy it is to build nonrectangular controls.

On Designing Windows Controls

Before I get to the details of how to build custom controls, I want to show you how they relate to other types of projects. I'm going to discuss briefly the similarities and differences among Windows controls, classes, and standard projects. This information will help you get the big picture and put together the pieces of the following sections.

A standard application consists of a main form and several (optional) auxiliary forms. The auxiliary forms support the main form, as they usually accept user data that are processed by the code in the main form. You can think of a custom control as a form and think of its Properties window as the auxiliary form. An application interacts with the user through its interface. The developer decides how the forms interact with the user, and the user has to follow these rules. Something similar happens with custom controls. The custom control provides a well-defined interface, which consists of properties and methods. This is the only way to manipulate the control. Just as users of your applications don't have access to the source code and can't modify the application, developers can't see the control's source code and must access a Windows control through the interface exposed by the control. When you develop a custom control, in turn, you can use any of the controls on the Toolbox. Once an instance of the control is on the form, you can manipulate it through its properties and methods and you never get to see its code.

In Chapter 8, you learned how to implement interfaces consisting of properties and methods and how to raise events from within a class. This is how you build the interface of a custom Windows control. You implement properties as Property procedures, and you implement methods as Public procedures. Whereas a class may provide a few properties and any number of methods, a control must provide a large number of properties. A developer who places your custom control on a form expects to see the properties that are common to all the controls that are visible at runtime (properties to set the control's dimensions, its color, the text font, the Index and Tag properties, and so on). Fortunately, many of the standard properties are exposed automatically. The developer also expects to be able to program all the common events, such as the mouse and keyboard events, as well as some events that are unique to the custom control.

The design of a Windows control is similar to the design of a form. You place controls on a Form-like object, called UserControl, which is the control's surface. It provides nearly all the methods of a standard form, and you can adjust its appearance with the drawing methods. In other words, you can use familiar programming techniques to draw a custom control, or you can use existing controls to build a custom control.

The forms of an application are the windows you see on the Desktop when the application is executed. When you design the application, you can rearrange the controls on a form and program how they react to user actions. Windows controls are also windows, only they can't exist on their own and can't be placed on the Desktop. They must be placed on forms.

The major difference between applications and custom controls is that custom controls can exist in two runtime modes. When the developer places a control on a form, the control is actually running. When you set a control's property through the Properties window, something happens to the control; its appearance changes, or the control rejects the changes. This means that the code of the custom control is executing, even though the project on which the control is used is in design mode. When the developer starts the application, the custom control is already running. However, the control must be able to distinguish when the project is in design or execution mode and behave accordingly. Here's the first property of the UserControl object you will be using quite frequently in your code: the DesignMode property. When the control is positioned on a form and used in the

Designer, the DesignMode property is True. When the developer executes the project that contains the control, the DesignMode property is False.

Consider a simple TextBox control at design time. Its Text property is TextBox1. If you set its MultiLine property to True, and the ScrollBar property to Vertical, a vertical scroll bar will be attached to the control automatically. Obviously, some statements are executed while the project is in design mode. Then you start the application, enter some text in the TextBox control, and end it. When the project is back in design mode, the control's Text property is reset to TextBox1. The control has stored its settings before the project switched from design-time to runtime mode and restored them when the project returned to design mode again.

These dual runtime modes of a Windows control are something you'll have to get used to. When you design custom controls, you must also switch between the roles of Windows control developer (the programmer who designs the control) and application developer (the programmer who uses the control).

In summary, a custom control is an application with a visible user interface as well as an invisible programming interface. The visible interface is what the developer sees when he places an instance of the control on the form, which is also what the user sees on the form when the project is placed in runtime mode. The developer can manipulate the control through the properties exposed by the control (at design time) and through its methods (at runtime). The properties and methods constitute the control's invisible interface (or the *developer interface*, as opposed to the *user interface*). You, the control developer, will develop the visible user interface on a UserControl object, which is almost identical to the Form object. It's like designing a standard application. As far as the control's invisible interface goes, it's like designing a class. Of course, the code of the control may also affect its appearance.

Enhancing Existing Controls

The simplest type of custom Windows control you can build is one that enhances the functionality of an existing control. The .NET Windows controls are quite functional, and you'll be hard-pressed to come up with ideas to make them better. However, it's very likely that you may have to add some functionality that's specific to an application. The TextBox control, for example, is a text editor on its own, and you have seen how easy it is to build a text editor using the properties and methods exposed by this control. Many programmers add code to their projects to customize the appearance and the functionality of this control. Let's say you're building data-entry forms composed of many TextBox controls. To help the user identify the current control on the form, it would be nice to change its color while it has the focus. If the current control is colored differently than all others, users will quickly locate the control that has the focus.

Another feature you can add to the TextBox control is to format its contents as soon as it loses focus. Let's consider a TextBox control that must accept dollar amounts. After the user enters a numeric value, the control could automatically format the numeric value as a dollar amount, and perhaps change the text's color to red for negative amounts. You can also format the number as the user enters it, but I wouldn't advise you to do that. Some programmers like to format numeric values as the users enter digits, but this usually confuses, rather than helps, users. Let the users enter data on a control, and then format the control after they move the focus to another control. As you will see, it's not only possible, it's actually quite easy to build a control that incorporates all the functionality of a TextBox and some additional features that you provide through the appropriate code. You already know how to add features like the ones described here to a TextBox from within the application's code. But what if you want to enhance multiple TextBox controls on the same form, or reuse your code in multiple applications?

The best approach is to create a new Windows control with all the desired functionality and then reuse it in multiple projects. To use the proper terminology, you can create a new custom Windows control that inherits from the TextBox control. The derived (or subclassed) control includes all the functionality of the control being inherited, plus any new features you care to add to it. This is exactly what we're going to do in the following section.

Building the FocusedTextBox Control

Let's call our new custom control FocusedTextBox. Start a new VB project and, on the New Project dialog box, select the template Windows Control Library. Name the project FocusedTextBox. The Solution Explorer for this project contains a single item, the UserControl1 item (in addition to the standard project components such as References and AssemblyInfo). UserControl1 (Figure 9.1) is the control's surface—in a way, it's the control's form. This is where you'll design the visible interface of the new control.

FIGURE 9.1

A custom control in design mode

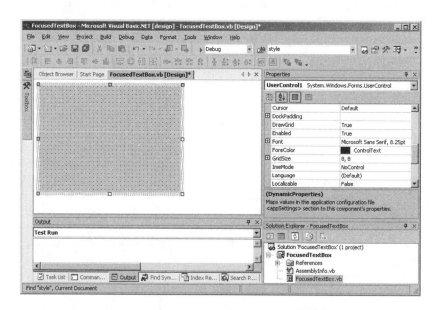

Start by renaming the UserControl1 object to FocusedTextBox. Renaming the object isn't enough; you must also rename the class that implements the control. Open the object's code window (click the View Code button at the top of the Solution Explorer while the UserControl1 object is selected) and change the line

```
Public Class UserControl1
```

to

```
Public Class FocusedTextBox
```

Then save the project by selecting the File ➢ Save All command. The UserControl object of a control that inherits from an existing control is empty. You need not place a TextBox control on it. Let's inherit all the functionality of the TextBox control into our new control. Locate the following line in the control's code window:

```
Inherits System.Windows.Forms.UserControl
```

and change it to

```
Inherits TextBox
```

This statement tells the compiler that we want our new control to inherit all the functionality of the TextBox. All custom controls inherit the `System.Windows.Forms.UserControl` object, and so does the TextBox control. In other words, you're not going to discard any functionality by deleting the original Inherits statement. As soon as you specify that your custom control inherits the TextBox control, the UserControl object will disappear from the Designer. The Designer knows exactly what the new control must look like (it will look and behave exactly like a TextBox control), and you're not allowed to change it. Let's test our control and verify that it exposes all the TextBox functionality.

To test the control, you must add it to a form. A control can't be executed in its own window. Add a new project to the solution (a Windows Application project) with the File ➢ Add Project ➢ New Project command. When the Add New Project dialog box appears, select the Windows Application template, specify the original project's path in the Location box, and set the project's name to TestProject. A new folder will be created under the `FocusedTextBox` folder—the `TestProject` folder—and the new project will be stored there. You could have added the test project to the custom control project's folder, but it's good to separate the custom control project's files from the test project's files.

To test the control you just "designed," you need to place an instance of the custom control on the *Form1* form of the test project. First, you must build the control and then add a reference to this control to the test project. Select the FocusedTextBox item in the Solution Explorer, and from the Build menu, select the Build FocusedTextBox command. This command will create a DLL file with the control's executable code. This file will be created in the `Bin` folder under the project's folder, and you will see later in this chapter how to reference the new custom control in other projects.

Then switch to the test project and select the Project ➢ Add Reference command. In the next dialog box, switch to the Projects tab, shown in Figure 9.2. Here you see the name of the other project in the solution (the custom control's project). Select the name of the FocusedTextBox project on the main pane, click Select, and then click the OK button to close the dialog box.

Your new control is now referenced in the test project. Open the test project's form in the Designer and expand the Toolbox. The last item on the Toolbox is the icon of your new control. It has already been integrated into the design environment, and you will see shortly how you can use it in any other Windows application. Place an instance of the FocusedTextBox control on the form and check it out. It looks, feels, and behaves just like a regular TextBox. In fact, it is a TextBox control by a different name. It exposes all the members of the regular TextBox control: you can move it around, resize it, change its Multiline and WordWrap properties, set its Text, and so on.

NOTE *If the new control and the test project are part of the same project, you don't have to add a reference to the control—it will appear in the Toolbox anyway, and you'll be able to use it with the test project as soon as you build it. You'll have to add a reference to the control, however, to use it with any other project.*

FIGURE 9.2

Referencing the custom control in the test project

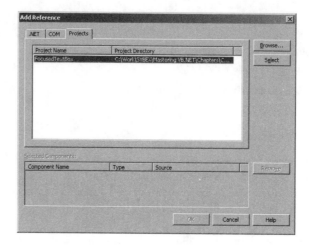

As you can see, it's quite trivial to create a new custom control by inheriting a .NET Windows control. Of course, what good is a control that's identical to an existing one? Let's add some extra functionality to our custom TextBox control. Switch to the control project and view the Focused-TextBox object's code. In the code editor's pane, expand the Objects list and select the item Base Class Events. This list contains the events of the TextBox control, since this is the base control for our custom control.

Then expand the Events drop-down list and select the Enter event. The following event handler declaration will appear:

```
Private Sub FocusedTextBox_Enter(ByVal sender As Object, _
            ByVal e As System.EventArgs) Handles MyBase.Enter

End Sub
```

This event takes place every time our custom control gets the focus. To change the color of the current control, insert the following statement in the event handler:

```
Me.BackColor = Color.Cyan
```

(or use any other color you like; just make sure it mixes well with the ForegroundColor property). We must also program the Leave event, so that the control's background color is reset to white when it loses the focus. Enter the following statement in the Leave event's handler:

```
Private Sub FocusedTextBox_Leave(ByVal sender As Object, _
            ByVal e As System.EventArgs) Handles MyBase.Leave
    Me.BackColor = Color.White
End Sub
```

Having a hard time picking the color that signifies that the control has the focus? Why not expose this value as a property, so that you (or other developers using your control) can set it individually in each project? Let's add two properties, the EnterFocusColor and the LeaveFocusColor (their role is rather obvious). Since our control is meant for data-entry operations, we can add one more neat feature. Some fields on a form are usually mandatory and some others are optional. Let's add some visual indication when a mandatory field is left blank. First, we need to specify whether a field is mandatory or not with the Mandatory property. If a field is mandatory, then its background color will switch to the color indicated by yet another property, the MandatoryColor property. Here's a quick overview of the control's custom properties:

EnterFocusColor   When the control receives the focus, its background color is set to this value. If you don't want the currently active control to change color, set its EnterFocusColor to white.

LeaveFocusColor   When the control loses the focus, its background color is set to this value. If the control has its Mandatory property set to True and it's blank, the MandatoryColor takes precedence.

Mandatory   This property indicates whether the control corresponds to a required field, if Mandatory is True (Required), or an optional field, if Mandatory is False (Optional).

MandatoryColor   This is the background color of the control if its Mandatory property is required. The MandatoryColor overwrites the LeaveFocusColor setting. In other words, if the user skips a mandatory field, the corresponding control is painted with the MandatoryColor and not with the LeaveFocusColor. Notice that required fields behave like optional fields after they have been assigned a value.

If you have read the previous chapter, you should be able to implement these properties easily. Listing 9.1 is the code that implements the four custom properties. The values of the properties are stored in the private variables declared at the beginning of the listing. Then the control's properties are implemented as Property procedures.

LISTING 9.1: THE PROPERTY PROCEDURES OF THE FOCUSEDTEXTBOX

```
Dim _mandatory As Boolean
Dim _enterFocusColor, _leaveFocusColor As Color
Dim _mandatoryColor As Color
Property Mandatory() As Boolean
   Get
      Mandatory = _mandatory
   End Get
   Set(ByVal Value As Boolean)
      _mandatory = Value
   End Set
End Property
Property EnterFocusColor() As Color
   Get
      EnterFocusColor = _enterFocusColor
   End Get
   Set(ByVal Value As Color)
      _enterFocusColor = EnterFocusColor
   End Set
End Property
Property LeaveFocusColor() As Color
```

```
    Get
        LeaveFocusColor = _leaveFocusColor
    End Get
    Set(ByVal Value As Color)
        _leaveFocusColor = LeaveFocusColor
    End Set
End Property
Property MandatoryColor() As Color
    Get
        MandatoryColor = _mandatoryColor
    End Get
    Set(ByVal Value As Color)
        _mandatoryColor = MandatoryColor
    End Set
End Property
```

The last step is to use these properties in the control's Enter and Leave events. When the control receives the focus, it changes its background color to EnterFocusColor to indicate that it's the current control on the form. When it loses the focus, its background is restored back to the Leave-FocusColor, unless it's a required field and the user has left it blank. In this case, its background color is set to MandatoryColor. Listing 9.2 shows the code in the two focus-related events of the UserControl object.

LISTING 9.2: THE ENTER AND LEAVE EVENTS

```
Private Sub FocusedTextBox_Enter(ByVal sender As Object, _
                ByVal e As System.EventArgs) Handles MyBase.Enter
    Me.BackColor = EnterFocusColor
End Sub
Private Sub FocusedTextBox_Leave(ByVal sender As Object, _
                ByVal e As System.EventArgs) Handles MyBase.Leave
    If Trim(Me.Text).Length = 0 And _mandatory Then
        Me.BackColor = _mandatoryColor
    Else
        Me.BackColor = _leaveFocusColor
    End If
End Sub
```

Build the control again with the Build ➤ Build FocusedTextBox command, and switch to the test form. Place several instances of the custom control on the form, align them, and then select each one and set its properties in the Properties window. All four custom properties are clustered in the Misc section of the window (Figure 9.3); you'll see shortly how you can change this default behavior. Set the custom properties of a few controls on the form and then press F5 to run the application. See how the FocusedTextBox controls behave as you move the focus from one to the other and how they handle the mandatory fields.

FIGURE 9.3

The custom properties of the FocusedTextBox control in the Properties window

Notice also that the color properties are set through the usual Color tab, just as you would set the color properties of the existing controls. The Mandatory property can change value with a double-click. Or you can expand the list of possible settings (True/False) and select one of them with the mouse.

Pretty impressive, isn't it? I'm also sure that many readers will incorporate this custom control in their projects—perhaps you may already be considering new features. Even if you have no use for an enhanced TextBox control, you'll agree that building it was quite simple. Next time you need to enhance one of the .NET Windows controls, you know how to do it. Just build a new control that inherits from an existing control, add some custom members, and use it. Of course, you can't change the base control's interface. This means that you can't draw the control's surface—it will be drawn by the code of the TextBox control. But then again, all rules have exceptions. Some of the controls allow you to hook your own code into them and control the process of drawing the base control's area. You'll see how to customize the appearance of menu items and the ListBox control toward the end of this chapter.

CLASSIFYING THE CONTROL'S PROPERTIES

Let's get back to our FocusedTextBox control—there are some loose ends to take care of. First, we must specify the category in the Properties window under which each custom property appears. By default, all the properties you add to a custom control are displayed in the Misc section of the Properties window. To specify that a control be displayed in a different section, use the Category attribute of the Property procedure. As you will see, properties have other attributes too, which you can set in your code as you design the control.

Properties can have attributes, which appear in front of the property name and are enclosed in a pair of angle brackets. The following attribute declaration in front of the property's name determines the category of the Properties window in which the specific property will appear:

```
<Category("Appearance")>
```

If none of the existing categories suits a specific property, you can create a new category in the Properties window by specifying its name in the Category attribute. If you have a few properties that should appear in a section called "Conditional," insert the following attribute in front of the declarations of the corresponding properties:

```
<Category("Conditional")>
```

When this control is selected, the "Conditional" section will appear in the Properties window and all the properties with this attribute under it.

All attributes are members of the `System.ComponentModel` class, and you must import this class. The following statement must be the first statement in the control's code window:

```
Imports System.ComponentModel
```

Another attribute is the Description attribute, which determines the property's description that appears at the bottom of the Properties window for the selected property. To specify multiple attributes, separate them with commas, as shown here:

```
<Description("Indicates whether the control can be left blank"), _
 Category("Appearance")> _
 Property Mandatory() As Boolean
{ the property procedure's code }
```

The most important attribute is the DefaultValue attribute, which determines the property's default (initial) value. The EnterFocusColor and LeaveFocusColor properties must have default values, so that when you place them on the form you won't have to change these two settings for all the controls. The DefaultValue attribute must be followed by the default value in parentheses:

```
<Description("Indicates whether the control can be left blank"), _
 Category("Appearance"), DefaultValue(False)> _
 Property Mandatory() As Boolean
{ the property procedure's code }
```

Some attributes apply to the Class that implements the custom controls. The DefaultProperty and DefaultEvent attributes determine the control's default property and event. To specify that Mandatory is the default attribute of the FocusedTextBox control, replace its declaration with the following:

```
<DefaultProperty("Mandatory")> Public Class FocusedTextBox
```

Events are discussed later in the chapter, but you already know how to raise an event from within a class. Raising an event from within a control's code is quite similar—although the control may raise events in response to external actions.

Open the FocusedTextBox project on the companion CD and examine its code. You can experiment with various formatting options for fields that are numeric. The following statement in the control's Leave event will format the control's contents as a dollar amount:

```
If IsNumeric(Me.Text) Then
   Me.Text = FormatCurrency(Me.Text, 2, False, True, True)
   If Val(Me.Text) < 0 Then
      Me.Text = "(" & Me.Text & ")"
   End If
End If
```

Let's move on to something more interesting. This time we'll build a control that combines the functionality of several controls, which is a much more common scenario than basing a new custom control to an existing control. You will literally design its visible interface by dropping controls on it, just like designing the visible interface of a Windows form.

Building Compound Controls

A compound control provides a visible interface that combines multiple Windows controls. As a result, this type of control doesn't inherit the functionality of any specific control. You must expose its properties by providing your own code. This isn't as bad as it sounds, because a compound control inherits the UserControl object, which exposes quite a few members of its own. You will add your own members, and in many cases you can map a property or method of the compound control to a property or method of one of its constituent controls. If your control contains a TextBox control, for example, you can map the custom control's WordWrap property to the equivalent property of the TextBox. The following property procedure demonstrates how to do it:

```
Property WordWrap() As Boolean
    Get
        WordWrap = TextBox1.WordWrap
    End Get
    Set(ByVal Value As Boolean)
        TextBox1.WordWrap = Value
    End Set
End Property
```

As you can see, you don't have to maintain a private variable for storing the value of the custom control's WordWrap property. When this property is set, the Property procedure assigns the property's value to the `TextBox1.WordWrap` property. Likewise, when this property's value is requested, the procedure reads it from the constituent control and returns it.

The same logic applies to events. Let's say your compound control contains a TextBox and a ComboBox control, and you want to raise the TextChanged event when the user edits the TextBox control and the (custom) SelectionChanged event when the user selects another item in the Combo-Box control. First, you must declare the two events:

```
Event TextChanged
Event SelectionChanged
```

Then, you must raise the two events from within the appropriate event handlers: the TextChanged event from the `TextBox.TextChanged` event hander and the SelectionChanged from the `ComboBox.SelectedIndexChanged` event handler:

```
Private Sub TextBox1_TextChanged(ByVal sender As System.Object, _
          ByVal e As System.EventArgs) Handles FocusedTextBox1.TextChanged
    RaiseEvent TextChanged()
End Sub
Private Sub ComboBox1_SelectedIndexChanged(ByVal sender As System.Object, _
          ByVal e As System.EventArgs) Handles ComboBox1.SelectedIndexChanged
    RaiseEvent SelectionChanged()
End Sub
```

VB.NET at Work: The ColorEdit Control

The control we'll build in this section is very similar to the Color dialog box. The ColorEdit control allows you to specify a color by adjusting its red, green, and blue components with three scroll bars, or to select a color by name. The control's surface at runtime on a form is shown in Figure 9.4.

FIGURE 9.4

The ColorEdit control on a form

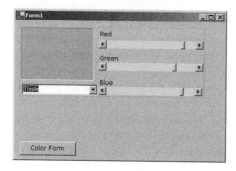

Now open the UserControl object and design its interface, as shown in Figure 9.4. The three ScrollBar controls are named RedBar, GreenBar, and BlueBar respectively. The MinimumValue property for all three controls is 0; the MaximumValue for all three is 255. This is the valid range of values for a color component. The control at the top-left corner is a Label control with its background color set to Black. (We could have used a PictureBox control in its place.) The role of this control is to display the selected color.

The ComboBox control at the bottom of the control is the NamedColors control, which is populated with color names when the control is loaded. Color is the name of an object that allows you to manipulate colors, and it exposes 140 properties, which are color names (Beige, Azure, and so on). Don't bother entering all the color names in the ComboBox control; just open the ColorEdit project on the CD and you will find the AddNamedColors() subroutine, which does exactly that. The first few lines of this function are shown next:

```
Private Sub AddNamedColors()
    With ComboBox1.Items
        .Add("AliceBlue")
        .Add("AntiqueWhite")
        .Add("Aqua")
```

The user can specify a color by sliding the three ScrollBar controls or by selecting an item in the ComboBox control. In either case, the Label control's Background color will be set to the selected color. If the color was specified with the ComboBox control, the three ScrollBars will be adjusted to reflect the color's basic components (red, green, and blue components).

Not all possible colors you can specify with the three ScrollBars have a name (there are approximately 16 million colors). That's why the ComboBox control contains the "Unknown" item, which is selected when the user specifies a color by settings its basic components.

Finally, the ColorEdit control exposes two properties, the SelectedColor and NamedColor properties. The NamedColor property retrieves the selected color's name. If the color wasn't isn't selected on the ComboBox control, the value "Unknown" will be returned. The SelectedColor property returns, or sets, the current color. The SelectedColor property's type is Color, and it can be assigned any expression that represents a color value. The following statement will assign the form's BackgroundColor property to the SelectedColor property of the control:

```
ctrlColorEditor.SelectedColor = Me.BackgroundColor
```

You can also specify a color value with the FromARGB method of the Color object:

```
ctrlColorEditor.SelectedColor = Color.FromARGB(red, green, blue)
```

The implementation of the SelectedColor property is shown in Listing 9.3, and it's straightforward. The Get section of the procedure assigns the Label's background color to the SelectedColor property. The Set section of the procedure extracts the three color components from the value of the property and assigns them to the three ScrollBar controls. Then it calls the ShowColor subroutine to update the display (you'll see shortly what this subroutine does).

LISTING 9.3: THE SELECTEDCOLOR PROPERTY PROCEDURE

```
Property SelectedColor() As Color
    Get
        SelectedColor = Label1.BackColor
    End Get
    Set(ByVal Value As Color)
        HScrollBar1.Value = Value.R
        HScrollBar2.Value = Value.G
        HScrollBar3.Value = Value.B
        ShowColor()
    End Set
End Property
```

The NamedColor property (Listing 9.4) is read-only and is marked with the ReadOnly keyword in front of the procedure's name. This property retrieves the value of the ComboBox control and returns it.

LISTING 9.4: THE NAMEDCOLOR PROPERTY PROCEDURE

```
ReadOnly Property NamedColor() As String
    Get
        NamedColor = ComboBox1.SelectedItem
    End Get
End Property
```

When the user selects a color name in the ComboBox control, the code retrieves the corresponding color value with the Color.FromName method. This method accepts a color name as argument (a string) and returns a color value, which is assigned to the *namedColor* variable. Then the code extracts the three basic color components with the R, G, and B properties (these properties return the red, green, and blue color components). Listing 9.5 shows the code behind the ComboBox control's SelectedIndexChanged event, which is fired every time a new color name is selected on the control.

LISTING 9.5: SPECIFYING A COLOR BY NAME

```
Private Sub ComboBox1_SelectedIndexChanged(ByVal sender As System.Object, _
              ByVal e As System.EventArgs) Handles ComboBox1.SelectedIndexChanged
    Dim namedColor As Color
    Dim colorName As String
    colorName = ComboBox1.SelectedItem
    If colorName <> "Unknown" Then
        namedColor = Color.FromName(colorName)
        HScrollBar1.Value = namedColor.R
        HScrollBar2.Value = namedColor.G
        HScrollBar3.Value = namedColor.B
        ShowColor()
    End If
End Sub
```

The ShowColor property simply sets the Label's background color to the color specified by the three ScrollBar controls. Even when you select a color value by name, the control's code sets the three ScrollBars to the appropriate values. This way, we don't have to write additional code to update the display. The ShowColor subroutine is quite trivial:

```
Sub ShowColor()
    Label1.BackColor = Color.FromARGB(255, HScrollBar1.Value, _
                            HScrollBar2.Value, HScrollBar3.Value)
End Sub
```

The single statement in this subroutine picks up the values of the three basic colors from the ScrollBar controls and creates a new color value with the FromARGB method of the Color object. The first argument is the transparency of the color (the "A" or alpha channel), and we set it to 255 for a completely opaque color. You can edit the project's code to take into consideration the transparency channel as well. If you do, you must replace the Label control with a PictureBox control and display an image on it. Then draw a rectangle with the specified color on top of it. If the color isn't completely opaque, you'll be able to see the underlying image and visually adjust the transparency channel.

TESTING THE COLOREDIT CONTROL

To test the new control, you must place it on a form. Build the ColorEdit control, add a new project to the current solution as before, reference the new control in the test project, and then add an instance of the control to the form. You don't have to enter any code in the test form. Just run it and see how you specify a color either with the scroll bars or by name. You can also read the value of the selected color through the SelectedColor property. The code behind the Color Form button on the test form does exactly that:

```
Private Sub Button1_Click(ByVal sender As System.Object, _
              ByVal e As System.EventArgs) Handles Button1.Click
    Me.BackColor = ColorEdit1.SelectedColor
End Sub
```

Building User-Drawn Controls

This is the most complicated, but also the most flexible, type of control. A user-drawn control consists of a UserControl object with no constituent controls. You are responsible for updating the control's visible area with the appropriate code, which must appear in the control's OnPaint method. This method is called right before the OnPaint event is fired, and if you override it, you can take control of the repaint process.

To demonstrate the design of user-drawn controls, we'll develop the Label3D control, which is an enhanced Label control and is shown in Figure 9.5. It provides all the members of the Label control plus a few highly desirable new features, such as the ability to align the text in all possible ways on the control, as well as in three-dimensional type. The new custom control is called Label3D, and its project on the CD is the FlexLabel project. It contains the Label3D project (which is a Windows Control Library project) and the usual test project (which is a Windows Application project).

FIGURE 9.5

The Label3D control is an enhanced Label control.

At this point, you're probably thinking about the code that aligns the text and renders it as carved or raised. A good idea is to start with a Windows project, which displays a string on a form and aligns it in all possible ways. A control is an application packaged in a way that allows it to be displayed on a form instead of on the Desktop. As far as the functionality is concerned, in most cases it can be implemented on a regular form.

Designing a Windows form with the same functionality is fairly straightforward. You haven't seen the drawing methods yet, but this control doesn't involve any advanced drawing techniques. All we need is a method to render strings on the control. To achieve the 3D effect, you must display the same string twice, first in white and then in black on top of the white. The two strings must be displaced slightly, and the direction of the displacement determines the effect (whether the text will appear as raised or carved). The amount of displacement determines the depth of the effect. Use a displacement of one pixel for a light effect and a displacement of two pixels for a heavy one.

VB.NET at Work: The Label3D Control

The first step in designing a user-drawn custom control is to design the control's interface: what it will look like when placed on a form (its visible interface) and how developers can access this functionality through its members (the programmatic interface). Sure, you've heard the same advice over and over, and many of you still start coding an application without spending much time designing it. In the real world, especially if you are not a member of programming team, people design as they code (or the other way around).

The situation is quite different with Windows controls. Your custom control must provide properties, which will be displayed automatically in the Properties window. The developer should be able to adjust every aspect of the control's appearance by manipulating the settings of these properties. In addition, developers expect to see the standard properties shared by most controls (such as the background color, the text's font, and so on). You must carefully design the methods so that they expose all the functionality of the control that should be accessed from within the application's code, and the methods shouldn't overlap. Finally, you must provide the events necessary for the control to react to external events. Don't start coding a custom control unless you have formulated a very clear idea of what the control will do and how it will be used by developers at design time.

THE LABEL3D CONTROL'S SPECIFICATIONS

The Label3D control displays a caption like the standard Label control, so it must provide the Caption and Font properties, which let the developer determine the text and its appearance. The UserControl object exposes these two properties, so we need not implement them in our code. In addition, the Label3D can align its caption both vertically and horizontally. This functionality will be exposed by the Alignment property, whose settings are shown in Table 9.1.

TABLE 9.1: THE SETTINGS OF THE ALIGNMENT PROPERTY (THE ALIGN ENUMERATION)

VALUE
TopLeft
TopMiddle
TopRight
CenterLeft
CenterMiddle
CenterRight
BottomLeft
BottomMiddle
BottomRight

The (self-explanatory) values in Table 9.1 are the names that will appear in the drop-down list of the Alignment property in the Properties window. As you have noticed, properties with a limited number of settings display a drop-down list there. This list contains descriptive names (instead of numeric values), and the developer can select only a valid setting. The Alignment property's settings will be the members of a custom enumeration.

Similarly, the text effect is manipulated through the Effect property, whose settings are shown in Table 9.2. There are basically two types of effects, raised and carved text, and two variations on each effect (normal and heavy).

TABLE 9.2: THE SETTINGS OF THE EFFECT PROPERTY (THE EFFECT3D ENUMERATION)

VALUE
None
Carved
CarvedHeavy
Raised
RaisedHeavy

Like the Alignment property, the Effect property has a small number of valid settings, which will be identified in the Properties window with descriptive names. These names are the members of another custom enumeration.

In addition to the custom properties, the Label3D control should also expose the standard properties of a Label control, such as Tag, BackColor, and so on. Developers expect to see standard properties in the Properties window, and you should implement them. The Label3D control doesn't have any custom methods, but it should provide the standard methods of the Label control, such as the Move method. Similarly, although the control doesn't raise any special events, it must support the standard events of the Label control, such as the mouse and keyboard events.

Most of the custom control's functionality exists already, and there should be a simple technique to borrow this functionality from other controls, rather than implementing it from scratch. This is indeed the case: The UserControl object, from which all user-drawn controls inherit, exposes a large number of members.

DESIGNING THE CUSTOM CONTROL

Start a new project of the Windows Control Library type, name it FlexLabel, and then rename the UserControl1 object to Label3D. Open the UserControl object's code window and change the name of the class from UserControl1 to Label3D. The first two lines in the code window should be:

```
Public Class Label3D
Inherits System.Windows.Forms.UserControl
```

All user-drawn controls inherit from the UserControl object, and you will soon see the members exposed by the UserControl object itself.

NOTE *Every time you place a Windows control on a form, it's named according to the UserControl object's name and a sequence digit. The first instance of the custom control you place on a form will be named Label3D1, the next one will be named Label3D2, and so on. Obviously, it's important to choose a meaningful name for your UserControl object.*

As you will soon see, the UserControl is the "form" on which the custom control will be designed. It looks, feels, and behaves like a regular VB form, but it's called a UserControl. UserControl objects have additional unique properties that don't apply to a regular form, but in order to start designing new controls, think of them as regular forms.

You've set the scene for a new user-drawn Windows control. Start by declaring the two enumerations shown in Tables 9.1 and 9.2. Listing 9.6 shows the Enum statements for the two enumerations.

LISTING 9.6: THE ALIGN AND EFFECT3D ENUMERATIONS

```
Public Enum Align
    TopLeft
    TopMiddle
    TopRight
    CenterLeft
    CenterMiddle
    CenterRight
    BottomLeft
    BottomMiddle
    BottomRight
End Enum
Public Enum Effect3D
    None
    Raised
    RaisedHeavy
    Carved
    CarvedHeavy
End Enum
```

The next step is to implement the Alignment and Effect properties. Each property's type is an enumeration, and Listing 9.7 shows the implementation of the two properties.

LISTING 9.7: THE ALIGNMENT AND EFFECT PROPERTIES

```
Private Shared mAlignment As Align
Private Shared mEffect As Effect3D
Public Property Alignment() As Align
    Get
        Alignment = mAlignment
    End Get
    Set(ByVal Value As Align)
        mAlignment = Value
        Invalidate()
    End Set
End Property
Public Property Effect() As Effect3D
    Get
        Effect = mEffect
    End Get
    Set(ByVal Value As Effect3D)
        mEffect = Value
        Invalidate()
    End Set
End Property
```

The current settings of the two properties are stored in the private variables *mAlignment* and *mEffect*. When either property is set, the Property procedure's code calls the Invalidate method of the UserControl object to redraw the string on the control's surface. The call to the Invalidate method is required for the control to operate properly in design mode. You can provide a method to redraw the control at runtime (although developers shouldn't have to call a method to refresh the control every time they set a property), but this isn't possible at design time. When a property is changed in the Properties window, the control should be able to update itself and reflect the new property setting. The Invalidate method causes the control to be redrawn, to reflect the new setting of the property. Shortly, you'll see an even better way to automatically redraw the control every time a property is changed.

Finally, you must add one more property, the Caption property, which is the string to be rendered on the control. Declare a private variable to store the control's caption (the *mCaption* variable) and enter the code from Listing 9.7 to implement the Caption property.

LISTING 9.7: THE CAPTION PROPERTY PROCEDURE

```
Private mCaption As String
Property Caption() As String
    Get
        Caption = mCaption
    End Get
    Set(ByVal Value As String)
        mCaption = Value
        Invalidate()
    End Set
End Property
```

The core of the control's code is in the OnPaint method, which is called automatically before the control repaints itself (that is, prior to the Paint event). The same event's code is also executed when the Invalidate method is called, and this is why we call this method every time one of the control's properties changes value. The OnPaint method enables you to take control of the repaint process and supply your own code for repainting the control's surface. The single characteristic of all user-drawn controls is that they override the default OnPaint method. This is where you must insert the code to draw the control's surface—i.e., draw the specified string taking into consideration the Alignment and Effect properties. The OnPaint method's code is shown in Listing 9.8.

LISTING 9.8: OVERRIDING THE USERCONTROL'S ONPAINT METHOD

```
Protected Overrides Sub OnPaint(ByVal e As PaintEventArgs)
    Dim lblFont As Font = Me.Font
    Dim lblBrush As New SolidBrush(Color.Red)
    Dim X, Y As Integer
    Dim textSize As SizeF
    textSize = e.Graphics.MeasureString(mCaption, lblFont)
    Select Case Me.mAlignment
        Case Align.BottomLeft
```

```
                X = 2
                Y = Me.Height - textSize.Height
            Case Align.BottomMiddle
                X = CInt((Me.Width - textSize.Width) / 2)
                Y = Me.Height - textSize.Height
            Case Align.BottomRight
                X = Me.Width - textSize.Width - 2
                Y = Me.Height - textSize.Height
            Case Align.CenterLeft
                X = 2
                Y = (Me.Height - textSize.Height) / 2
            Case Align.CenterMiddle
                X = (Me.Width - textSize.Width) / 2
                Y = (Me.Height - textSize.Height) / 2
            Case Align.CenterRight
                X = Me.Width - textSize.Width - 2
                Y = (Me.Height - textSize.Height) / 2
            Case Align.TopLeft
                X = 2
                Y = 2
            Case Align.TopMiddle
                X = (Me.Width - textSize.Width) / 2
                Y = 2
            Case Align.TopRight
                X = Me.Width - textSize.Width - 2
                Y = 2
        End Select
        Dim dispX, dispY As Integer
        Select Case mEffect
            Case Effect3D.None : dispX = 0 : dispY = 0
            Case Effect3D.Raised : dispX = 1 : dispY = 1
            Case Effect3D.RaisedHeavy : dispX = 2 : dispY = 2
            Case Effect3D.Carved : dispX = -1 : dispY = -1
            Case Effect3D.CarvedHeavy : dispX = -2 : dispY = -2
        End Select
        e.Graphics.Clear(Me.BackColor)
        lblBrush.Color = Color.White
        e.Graphics.DrawString(mCaption, lblFont, lblBrush, X, Y)
        lblBrush.Color = Me.ForeColor
        If Me.DesignMode Then
            e.Graphics.DrawString("DesignTime", New Font("Verdana", 24, _
            FontStyle.Bold), New SolidBrush(Color.FromARGB(200, 230, 200, 255)), 0, 0)
        Else
            e.Graphics.DrawString("RunTime", New Font("Verdana", 24, FontStyle.Bold), _
            New SolidBrush(Color.FromARGB(200, 230, 200, 255)), 0, 0)
        End If
        e.Graphics.DrawString(mCaption, lblFont, lblBrush, X + dispX,  Y + dispY)
    End Sub
```

This subroutine calls for a few explanations. The OnPaint event passes a PaintEventArgs argument (the ubiquitous *e* argument). This argument exposes the Graphics property, which represents the control's surface. The Graphics object exposes all the methods you can call to create graphics on the control's surface. The Graphics object is discussed in detail in Chapter 14, but for the purposes of this chapter all you need to know is that the MeasureString method returns the dimensions of a string when rendered in a specific font, and the DrawString method draws the string in the specified font. The first Select Case statement calculates the coordinates of the string's origin on the control's surface. These coordinates are calculated for each different alignment. Then another Select Case statement sets the displacement between the two strings, so that when superimposed they produce a three-dimensional look. Finally, the code draws the value of the Caption property on the Graphics object. It draws the string in white color first, then in black. The second string is drawn *dispX* pixels to the left and *dispY* pixels below the first one to give the 3D effect.

Notice the two statements that print the strings "DesignTime" and "RunTime" in a light color on the control's background, depending on the current status of the control. They indicate whether the control is currently in design (if UserMode is True) or run time (if UserMode is False).

TESTING YOUR NEW CONTROL

To test your new control, you must first add it to the Toolbox, so that you can place it on a form. You can add a form to the current project and test the control, but you shouldn't add more components to the control project. It's best to add a new project to the current solution.

Add the TestProject to the current solution, rename its Form to TestForm, and open it in design mode. Place a Label3D control on the test form and the other controls shown in Figure 9.5. If the Label3D icon doesn't appear in the Toolbox, you must build the control's project.

Now double-click the Label3D control on the form to see its events. Your new control has its own events, and you can program them just as you would program the events of any other control. Enter the following code in the control's Click event:

```
Private Sub Label3D1_Click(ByVal sender As Object, _
            ByVal e As System.EventArgs) Handles Label3D1.Click
    MsgBox("My properties are " & vbCrLf & _
        "Caption = " & Label3D1.Caption & vbCrLf & _
        "Alignment = " & Label3D1.Alignment & vbCrLf & _
        "Effect = " & Label3D1.Effect)
End Sub
```

To run the control, press F5 and then click the control. You will see the control's properties displayed in a message box.

The other controls on the test form (see Figure 9.5) allow you to set the appearance of the custom control at runtime. The two ComboBox controls are populated with the members of the appropriate enumeration when the form is loaded. In their SelectedIndexChanged event handler, you must set the corresponding property to the selected value, as shown in the following listing:

```
Private Sub AlignmentBox_SelectedIndexChanged(ByVal sender As System.Object, _
                            ByVal e As System.EventArgs) _
                        Handles AlignmentBox.SelectedIndexChanged
    Label3D1.Alignment = AlignmentBox.SelectedItem
End Sub
Private Sub EffectsBox_SelectedIndexChanged(ByVal sender As System.Object, _
```

```
                                            ByVal e As System.EventArgs) _
                                            Handles EffectsBox.SelectedIndexChanged
                Label3D1.Effect = EffectsBox.SelectedItem
            End Sub
```

The TextBox control at the bottom of the form stores the Caption property. Every time you change this string, the control is updated, because the Set procedure of the Caption property calls the Invalidate method.

INITIALIZING A CUSTOM CONTROL

To initialize the control's properties, insert the appropriate code in the New() subroutine. This subroutine is in the section marked with the following line:

```
#Region " Windows Form Designer generated code "
```

and it contains code generated by the designer. Expand this section by clicking the plus sign in front of its name and locate the New() subroutine. Listing 9.9 shows the New() subroutine of the custom control.

LISTING 9.9: THE NEW() SUBROUTINE OF THE LABEL3D CONTROL

```
Public Sub New()
    MyBase.New()
'This call is required by the Windows Form Designer.
    InitializeComponent()
'Add any initialization after the InitializeComponent() call
    mCaption = "Label3D"
    mAlignment = Align.CenterMiddle
    mEffect = Effect3D.Raised
    SetStyle(ControlStyles.ResizeRedraw, "True")
End Sub
```

I've only added the four last statements in this listing; the first couple of statements and the comments were inserted by the Designer. After assigning initial values to the private variables that store the control's properties, there's a call to the SetStyle method, which accepts several arguments. The ResizeRedraw argument determines whether the control will be redrawn when it's resized. Normally, the Paint event isn't fired when the control is made smaller, and when the control is enlarged, only the new area of the control is repainted. The call to the SetStyle method forces the control to be repainted every time the user resizes it on the form.

You need not initialize all the properties of the control, just the ones that should have a value the first time the control is placed on a form. When you place a TextBox control on the form, for example, its Text property is set to the control's name and its Font property is set to Microsoft Sans Serif. The Label3D control's default caption is "Label3D". Many of the control's properties are handled by the UserControl object itself, and Font is one of them. To set the initial font, locate the Font property of the UserControl and set it accordingly. The BackgroundColor and BackgroundImage properties are also handled by the UserControl object. You can specify a default background image if you want, but this property will be exposed in the Properties window, and the developer can set it at design time.

THE CHANGED EVENTS

The UserControl object exposes many of the events you need to program the control, like the key and mouse events. In addition, you can raise custom events. The .NET Windows controls raise an event every time a property value is changed. If you examine the list of events exposed by the Label3D control, you'll see the FontChanged and SizeChanged events. These events are provided by the UserControl object. As a control developer, you should expose similar events for your custom properties. This isn't very difficult to do, but you must follow a few steps.

Declare an event handler for each of the Changed events:

```
Private mOnAlignmentChanged As EventHandler
Private mOnEffectChanged As EventHandler
Private mOnCaptionChanged As EventHandler
```

Then declare the actual events and their handlers:

```
Public Event AlignmentChanged(ByVal sender As Object, ByVal ev As EventArgs)
Public Event EffectChanged(ByVal sender As Object, ByVal ev As EventArgs)
Public Event CaptionChanged(ByVal sender As Object, ByVal ev As EventArgs)
```

And finally invoke the event handlers from within the appropriate On*EventName* method:

```
Protected Overridable Sub OnAlignmentChanged(ByVal E As EventArgs)
    Invalidate()
    If Not (mOnAlignmentChanged Is Nothing) Then mOnAlignmentChanged.Invoke(Me, E)
End Sub
Protected Overridable Sub OnEffectChanged(ByVal E As EventArgs)
    Invalidate()
    If Not (mOnEffectChanged Is Nothing) Then mOnEffectChanged.Invoke(Me, E)
End Sub
Protected Overridable Sub OnCaptionChanged(ByVal E As EventArgs)
    Invalidate()
    If Not (mOnCaptionChanged Is Nothing) Then mOnCaptionChanged.Invoke(Me, E)
End Sub
```

As you can see, the On*property*Changed events call the Invalidate method to redraw the control when a property's value is changed. As a result, you can now remove the call to the Invalidate method from the Property Set procedures. If you switch to the test form, you will see that the custom control exposes the AlignmentChanged, EffectChanged, and CaptionChanged events. The OnCaptionChanged method is executed automatically every time the Caption property changes value, and it fires the CaptionChanged event. Normally, this event isn't programmed.

Raising Events

The UserControl object raises the usual events you'd expect to see in the editor's window. When you select the custom control in the Objects drop-down list of the editor and expand the list of events for this control, you'll see all the events fired by UserControl. They're the usual events, which you already know how to program. However, what good are the Key events if the custom control doesn't handle keystrokes? Most events will go unnoticed in most applications.

The situation is very different with compound controls. A compound control usually allows the user to interact with one or more of its constituent controls. Let's return to the ColorEdit custom control. The Click event is fired when the user clicks any area of the control outside the compound controls. When one of the scroll bars is clicked, no event is raised. Instead, the control adjusts the selected color. You can raise an event from within your control, if you want to. For example, you can raise an event to notify the application that the red scroll bar control has changed value, or that another color was selected in the ComboBox control with the named colors. Of course, these events are of questionable value, because the motivation for building a custom control is to hide as many of the low-level details as possible.

To demonstrate how to raise custom events, let's say you want to raise an event when the user clicks the Label control where the selected color is displayed. Let's call this event ColorClick. To raise a custom event, you must declare it in your control and call the RaiseEvent method to raise it. Note that the same event may be raised from many different places in the control's code.

To declare the ColorClick event, enter the following statement in the control's code. This line can appear anywhere, but placing it after the private variables that store the property values is customary.

```
Public Event ColorClick(ByVal sender As Object, ByVal e As EventArgs)
```

To raise the ColorClick event when the user clicks the Label control, insert the following statement in the Label control's Click event handler:

```
Private Sub Label1_Click(ByVal sender As System.Object, _
            ByVal e As System.EventArgs) Handles Label1.Click
    RaiseEvent ColorClick(Me, e)
End Sub
```

Raising a custom event from within a control is as simple as raising an event from within a class. The RaiseEvent statement in the Label's Click event handler maps the Click event of the Label control to the ColorClick event of the custom control. If you switch to the test form and examine the list of events of the Label3D control on the form, you'll see that the new event was added.

The ColorClick event doesn't convey much information. You could use it to display a context menu with a few common color names and let the user select one. In a real application, you could convey a lot of information to the developer using your control through custom events. As you can see, the arguments passed to the application by the ColorClick event are the same as the arguments passed to the Label control's Click event.

When raising custom events, it's likely that you'll want to pass additional information to the developer. Let's say you want to pass the Label control's color to the application through the second argument of the ColorClick event. The EventArgs type doesn't provide a Color property, so we must build a new type that inherits all the members of the EventArgs type and adds a property, the Color property. You can probably guess that we'll create a custom class that inherits from the EventArgs class and adds the Color member. Enter the statements of Listing 9.10 at the end of the file (after the existing End Class statement).

LISTING 9.10: DECLARING A CUSTOM EVENT TYPE

```
Public Class ColorEvent
    Inherits EventArgs
    Public Shared color As Color
End Class
```

Then, declare the following event in the control's code:

```
Public Event ColorClick(ByVal sender As Object, ByVal e As ColorEvent)
```

And finally raise the ColorClick event from within the Label's Click event handler (Listing 9.11).

LISTING 9.11: RAISING A CUSTOM EVENT

```
Private Sub Label1_Click(ByVal sender As System.Object, _
            ByVal e As System.EventArgs) Handles Label1.Click
    Dim ev As ColorEvent
    ev.color = Label1.BackColor
    RaiseEvent ColorClick(Me, ev)
End Sub
```

Using the Custom Control in Other Projects

By adding a test project to the Label3D custom control project, we were able to design and test the control in the same environment. A great help indeed, but the custom control can't be used in other projects. If you start another instance of Visual Studio and attempt to add your custom control to the toolbox, you won't see the Label3D entry in the Toolbox.

To add your custom component in another project, open the Customize Toolbox dialog box, then click the .NET Framework Components tab. Be sure to carry out the steps described here while the .NET Framework Components tab is visible. If the COM Components tab is visible instead, you can perform the same steps but you'll end up with an error message (because the custom component is not a COM component).

Click the Browse button on the dialog box and locate the FlexLabel.dll file. It's in the Bin folder under the FlexLabel project's folder. The Label3D control will be added to the list of .NET Framework components, as shown in Figure 9.6. Check the box in front of the control's name, then click the OK button to close the dialog box and add Label3D to the Toolbox. Now you can use this control in your new project.

FIGURE 9.6

Adding the Label3D control to another project's Toolbox

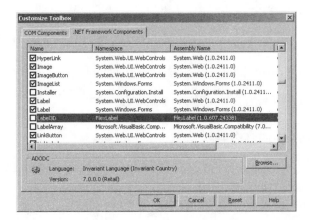

VB.NET at Work: The Alarm Control

This example demonstrates a custom control that contains all three types of members—properties, methods, and events—and raises events based on a timer, rather than some user action. It's a simple alarm that can be set to go off at a certain time, and when it times out, it triggers a TimeOut event. Moreover, while the timer is ticking, the control updates a display, showing the time elapsed since the timer started (the property CountDown must be False) or the time left before the alarm goes off (the property CountDown must be True). Figure 9.7 shows the test form for the Alarm control. The first instance of the Alarm control counts down the time left before the alarm goes off, and the second counts the time since it was started.

FIGURE 9.7

The test form for the Alarm custom control

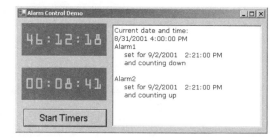

THE ALARM CONTROL'S INTERFACE

The Alarm control has two custom properties, AlarmTime and CountDown. AlarmTime is the time when the alarm goes off, expressed in AM/PM format. CountDown is a True/False property that determines what's displayed on the control. If CountDown is True, the alarm displays the time remaining. If you set the alarm to go off at 8:00 P.M. and you start the timer at 7:46 P.M., the control displays 0:14.00, then 0:13.59, and so on until the alarm goes off 14 minutes later. If CountDown is False, the control starts counting at 00:00.00 and counts until the AlarmTime is reached. The Alarm control takes into consideration the date as well and can be set to go off in more than 24 hours. However, it was designed to count a relatively small number of hours. If you set it to go off in a week, the number of hours left until the TimeOut event won't be displayed nicely on the control (you have to make the control wider so that it can fit more digits), but the code will work for any setting of the AlarmTime property.

The Alarm control has two methods for starting and stopping the alarm: StartTimer starts the timer, and StopTimer stops it.

Finally, the Alarm control fires the TimeOut event, which notifies the application that the alarm has gone off (which happens when the time reaches AlarmTime). The application can use this event to trigger another action or simply to notify the user.

TESTING THE ALARM CONTROL

The Alarm control's test form is shown earlier, in Figure 9.7. It contains two instances of the control, and you set their CountDown property at design time. The AlarmTime property of both controls is set to the same value, which is 15 minutes ahead of the current time. Listing 9.12 shows the code behind the Start Timers button of the test form.

```
Private Sub Button1_Click(ByVal sender As System.Object, _
                          ByVal e As System.EventArgs) Handles Button1.Click
    CtrlAlarm1.CountDown = True
    CtrlAlarm2.CountDown = False
    CtrlAlarm1.AlarmTime = Now.AddSeconds(10)
    CtrlAlarm2.AlarmTime = Now.AddSeconds(20)
    CtrlAlarm1.StartTimer()
    CtrlAlarm2.StartTimer()
    TextBox1.Text = "Current date and time: " & vbCrLf & Now & vbCrLf
    TextBox1.Text = TextBox1.Text + "Alarm1" & vbCrLf
    TextBox1.Text = TextBox1.Text & "     set for " & _
                    CtrlAlarm1.AlarmTime.ToShortDateString
    TextBox1.Text = TextBox1.Text & "     " & _
                    CtrlAlarm1.AlarmTime.ToLongTimeString & vbCrLf
    TextBox1.Text = TextBox1.Text & "     and counting down" & vbCrLf
    TextBox1.Text = TextBox1.Text & vbCrLf & "Alarm2" & vbCrLf
    TextBox1.Text = TextBox1.Text & "     set for " & _
                    CtrlAlarm2.AlarmTime.ToShortDateString
    TextBox1.Text = TextBox1.Text & "     " & _
                    CtrlAlarm2.AlarmTime.ToLongTimeString & vbCrLf
    TextBox1.Text = TextBox1.Text & "     and counting up" & vbCrLf
End Sub
```

The last group of statements that manipulate the TextBox control display the time each control was started and the alarm time of the two controls. Then, you can watch the alarms count the time until they go off. To start the two alarms, the code calls the control's StartTimer method. The information printed on the TextBox will help you verify that the controls work properly, especially if you edit the code.

Both controls will fire the TimeOut event when the alarm time is reached, and I've inserted two very simple handlers for these events (there's a similar event handler for the second control):

```
Private Sub CtrlAlarm1_TimeOut() Handles CtrlAlarm1.TimeOut
    Beep()
    MsgBox("Alarm1 is off!")
End Sub
```

DESIGNING THE ALARM'S USER INTERFACE

Your first step is to design the control's interface. Unlike the Timer control of Visual Basic, the Alarm control has a visible interface and uses two constituent controls: a Timer control (which is used to update the display every second as well as figure out whether the alarm must go off or not) and a Label control, where it displays the time.

To design the control's interface, follow these steps:

1. Place a Label control on the UserControl form, and set its Font property to a font and size that looks nice for our purposes. We will not expose the Label's Font as a property of the

control, so that developers using this control can't change it. If you want developers to be able to change the control's font, you must insert additional code to adjust the dimensions of the Label so that all the digits will be visible.

2. Set the Label's Dock property to Fill, so that it takes up all the space provided for the control.

3. Add a Timer control to the UserControl object—it will appear in the components tray at the bottom of the Designer's window.

The control's visible interface is quite trivial, thanks to the constituent controls. Let's look at the members of the Alarm control (Figure 9.8).

FIGURE 9.8

The Alarm control at design time

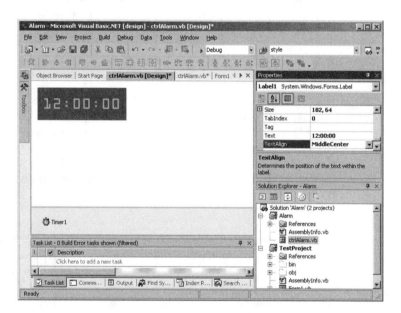

IMPLEMENTING THE CONTROL'S MEMBERS

Now we are ready to implement the control's properties, methods, and event. Let's start with the properties. First, declare the private variables that will hold the property values:

```
Private startTime As Date
Private Running As Boolean
Private m_CountDown As Boolean
Private m_AlarmTime As Date
```

As you have guessed, *m_CountDown* and *m_AlarmTime* are the two private variables that will hold the values of the CountDown and AlarmTime properties. The *Running* variable is True while the alarm is running and is declared outside any procedure so that all procedures can access its value. The *start-Time* variable is set to the time the alarm starts counting and is used when the control is not counting down (you'll see how it's used shortly).

The procedures for implementing the control's properties are quite simple; they're detailed in Listing 9.13.

LISTING 9.13: THE ALARM CONTROL'S PROPERTIES

```
Public Property CountDown() As Boolean
   Get
      CountDown = m_CountDown
   End Get
   Set(ByVal vNewValue As Boolean)
      m_CountDown = vNewValue
   End Set
End Property
Public Property AlarmTime() As Date
   Get
      AlarmTime = m_AlarmTime
   End Get
   Set(ByVal vNewValue As Date)
      If IsDate(vNewValue) Then m_AlarmTime = vNewValue
   End Set
End Property
```

The AlarmTime property may include a date part. If you specify a date only, the program assumes that the time is 00:00:00 (midnight). In the Properties window, VB will display a date value for the AlarmTime property. Type the desired time after the date in the format "hh:mm:ss". Notice that because AlarmTime is of the Date type, a DateTimePicker control will be automatically displayed on the Properties window to help you set the property's value visually.

Now we can add the code for the two methods. The StartTimer method (Listing 9.14) sets the Timer control's Enabled property to True, so that it will start firing Tick events.

LISTING 9.14: THE STARTTIMER METHOD

```
Public Sub StartTimer()
   If Not Running Then
      Timer1.Enabled = True
      Running = True
      startTime = Now
   End If
End Sub
```

This method doesn't do anything if the alarm is already running. The StopTimer method is shown in Listing 9.15.

LISTING 9.15: THE STOPTIMER METHOD

```
Public Sub StopTimer()
    If Running Then
        Timer1.Enabled = False
        Running = False
    End If
End Sub
```

As with the StartTimer method, the alarm stops only if it's running. If that's the case, the code disables the Timer control and sets the *Running* variable to False.

Next declare the TimeOut event with the following statement, which must appear outside any procedure.

```
Public Event TimeOut()
```

The TimeOut event doesn't pass any information to the caller; it simply notifies the application that the current instance of the Alarm control has timed off. To raise the event, you must insert the appropriate code in the Timer's Tick event handler. In the same event handler, which is invoked every second, we must also update the display. If the control is counting down, we create a TimeSpan object with the difference between the current time and the AlarmTime property. If the control is counting up, we create another TimeSpan object with the difference between the time the control was started and the current time (the time elapsed since the alarm was started). Listing 9.16 is the code of the Timer control's Tick event hander.

LISTING 9.16: THE TIMER'S TICK EVENT HANDLER

```
Private Sub Timer1_Tick(ByVal sender As System.Object, _
            ByVal e As System.EventArgs) Handles Timer1.Tick
    Dim TimeDiff As TimeSpan
    TimeDiff = m_AlarmTime.Subtract(Now)
    If TimeDiff.Seconds < 0 Then
        StopNow = True
        Timer1.Enabled = False
        Label1.Text = "*****"
        RaiseEvent TimeOut
        Exit Sub
    End If
    If Not m_CountDown Then
        ' the following statement calculates the difference
        ' between current time and alarm time and adds 1 second
        TimeDiff = Now.TimeOfDay.Subtract(startTime.TimeOfDay). _
                Add(New TimeSpan(0, 0, 1))
    End If
    Label1.Text = Format(TimeDiff.TotalHours, "00") & ":" & _
            Format(TimeDiff.Minutes, "00") & ":" & _
            Format(TimeDiff.Seconds, "00")
End Sub
```

The code also compares the current date/time to the setting of the *m_AlarmTime* property, and if the difference is negative, it means that the alarm must go off. If so, it raises the TimeOut event.

Designing Irregularly Shaped Controls

With VB.NET it's quite easy to create irregularly shaped controls. It's possible to create irregularly shaped forms too, but, unlike irregularly shaped controls, an irregularly shaped form is still quite uncommon. By the way, you can also create semitransparent forms with VB.NET—if you can come up with a good reason to do so.

To change the default shape of a custom control, you must use the Region object. This is another graphics-related object that specifies a closed area. You can even use Bezier curves to make highly unusual and smooth shapes for your controls. In this section, we'll do something less ambitious: We'll create controls with the shape of an ellipse, as shown in Figure 9.9.

FIGURE 9.9

Two instances of
an ellipse-shaped
control

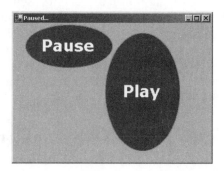

You can turn any control to any shape you like by creating the appropriate Region object and then applying it to the Region property of the control. This must take place from within the control's Load event. Listing 9.17 shows the statements that change the shape of the control.

LISTING 9.17: CREATING A NON-RECTANGULAR CONTROL

```
Private Sub RoundButton_Load(ByVal sender As System.Object, _
            ByVal e As System.EventArgs) Handles MyBase.Load
    Dim G As Graphics
    G = Me.CreateGraphics
    Dim roundPath As New GraphicsPath()
    Dim R As New Rectangle(0, 0, Me.Width, Me.Height)
    roundPath.AddEllipse(R)
    Me.Region = New Region(roundPath)
    Me.CreateGraphics.DrawEllipse(New Pen(Color.DarkGray, 3), R)
End Sub
```

First, we retrieve the Graphics object of the UserControl object and store it in the *G* variable. Then we create a GraphicsPath, the *roundPath* object, and add an ellipse to it. The ellipse is based on the rectangle that encloses the ellipse. The *R* object is used temporarily to specify the ellipse. The new path is then used to create a Region object, which is assigned to the Region property of the UserControl object. This gives our control the shape of an ellipse. The last statement draws an ellipse with the dark gray pen around the perimeter of the control. This step is optional, but it's equivalent to adding a border to the control.

To demonstrate the design of an irregularly shaped control, we'll build the RoundButton control, which was shown in Figure 9.9 earlier. You can find this control along with its test form in the NonRectangular project on the CD. The most important section of the control's code is the Load event handler, which was shown in Listing 9.17.

Irregularly shaped controls are used in fancy interfaces, and they usually react to movement of the mouse. The control of Figure 9.9 changes its background color and caption when the mouse is over the control. Listing 9.18 shows the code behind the control's MouseEnter and MouseLeave events. When the mouse enters the control's area (this is detected by the control automatically—you won't have to write a single line of code for it), the *currentState* variable is set to Active, the control's background color to green, and its caption to "Play." Similar actions take place in the control's Mouse-Leave event handler: the control's background color changes to red and its caption to "Pause". In addition, each time the control switches state (from Pause to Play or vice versa), one of the Now-Playing and NowPausing events is fired.

LISTING 9.18: THE ROUNDBUTTON CONTROL'S MOUSEENTER AND MOUSELEAVE EVENTS

```
Private Sub RoundButton_MouseEnter(ByVal sender As Object, _
             ByVal e As System.EventArgs) Handles MyBase.MouseEnter
   If currentState = State.Active Then
      Me.BackColor = Color.Green
      currentCaption = "Play"
      RaiseEvent NowPlaying()
   End If
End Sub
Private Sub RoundButton_MouseLeave(ByVal sender As Object, _
             ByVal e As System.EventArgs) Handles MyBase.MouseLeave
   If currentState = State.Active Then
      Me.BackColor = Color.Red
      currentCaption = "Pause"
      RaiseEvent NowPausing()
   End If
End Sub
```

These two events set up the appropriate variables, and the drawing of the control takes place in the OnPaint method, which is shown in Listing 9.19.

LISTING 9.19: THE ROUNDBUTTON CONTROL'S ONPAINT METHOD

```
Protected Overrides Sub OnPaint(ByVal pe As PaintEventArgs)
    Dim roundPath As New GraphicsPath()
    Dim R As New Rectangle(0, 0, Me.Width, Me.Height)
    roundPath.AddEllipse(R)
    Me.Region = New Region(roundPath)
    pe.Graphics.DrawEllipse(New Pen(Color.DarkGray, 3), R)
    Dim fnt As Font
    If currentState = State.Active Then
        If Me.BackColor.Equals(Color.Silver) Then Me.BackColor = Color.Green
        fnt = New Font("Verdana", 24, FontStyle.Bold)
    Else
        fnt = New Font("Verdana", 14, FontStyle.Regular)
    End If
    Dim X As Integer = (Me.Width - pe.Graphics.MeasureString( _
                        currentCaption, fnt).Width) / 2
    Dim Y As Integer = (Me.Height - pe.Graphics.MeasureString( _
                        currentCaption, fnt).Height) / 2
    pe.Graphics.DrawString(currentCaption, fnt, Brushes.White, X, Y)
End Sub
```

The OnPaint method uses graphics methods to center the string on the control. They're the same methods we used in the example of the user-drawn control, earlier in this chapter. The drawing methods are discussed in detail in Chapter 14.

The code makes use of the *currentState* variable, which can take on two values: Active and Inactive. These two values are members of the State enumeration, which is shown next:

```
Public Enum State
    Active
    Inactive
End Enum
```

The control can be in two states. In the Active state, it behaves as described. In the Inactive state, the control turns gray and doesn't respond to the movement of the mouse. In addition, its caption becomes "Resume" and the user can switch between states by clicking the control. The control's click event handler is shown next:

```
Private Sub RoundButton_Click(ByVal sender As Object, _
                ByVal e As System.EventArgs) Handles MyBase.Click
    If currentState = State.Active Then
        currentState = State.Inactive
        Me.BackColor = Color.Silver
        currentCaption = "Resume"
    Else
        currentState = State.Active
        currentCaption = "Play"
```

```
    End If
    Me.Invalidate()
End Sub
```

The code changes the control's state and, when the control is switched to the Inactive state, it fills it with a gray shade. To restore the control to its Active state, the user must click the control again.

The test form of the project shows how the RoundButton control behaves on a form. You can use the techniques described in this section to make a series of round controls to emulate the look of VCR controls. When the mouse hovers over the control, you can display the icon of the button (Play, Pause, Resume, and so on). When the mouse moves outside the area of the control, you can display the same icon with washed-out colors. Or you can place a nice colored dot on the control, which will be green when the button is pressed and red when it's released.

The control raises two events to notify the application that its state has changed. The two event names must be declared outside any procedure with the following statements:

```
Public Event NowPlaying()
Public Event NowPausing()
```

The two events are raised from within the MouseEnter and MouseLeave event handlers with the following statements:

```
RaiseEvent NowPlaying()
RaiseEvent NowPaused()
```

To test these events, switch to the test form and enter the following statements in the two event handlers of the RoundButton control. They're two simple statements that display the control's current status on the form's title bar. They simply demonstrate how to capture the changes in the control's status and use it in the host application to control other activities:

```
Private Sub RoundButton1_NowPlaying() Handles RoundButton1.NowPlaying
    Me.Text = "Playing..."
End Sub
Private Sub RoundButton1_NowPausing() Handles RoundButton1.NowPausing
    Me.Text = "Paused..."
End Sub
```

In Chapter 14, you'll learn more about shapes and paths, and you may wish to experiment with other oddly shaped controls. How about a progress indicator control that looks like a thermometer?

Building Owner-Drawn Controls

In this section, I'll show a couple of examples that demonstrate how to customize existing controls. You're not going to build new custom controls in this section; actually, you'll hook custom code into certain events of a control to direct the rendering of the control. Some of the .NET Windows controls can be customized far more than it is possible through their properties. These are the list-like controls (menus, ListBox controls), and they allow you to supply your own code for drawing each item. Using this technique, you can create a menu with a separate font for each menu item, a ListBox control with alternating background colors, and so on. You can even put bitmaps on the background of each item, draw the text in any colors, and create items of varying heights. This is a very interesting technique, because without it, as you recall from our discussion of the ListBox control, all items have the same height and you must make each control wide enough to fit the longest item (if this is known at design time).

To create an owner-drawn control, you must program two events: the MeasureItem and DrawItem events. As you may have noticed, you can only interfere with the drawing process of controls that display items in rectangles (like the MenuItem and ListBox controls). The MeasureItem event is where you decide about the dimensions of the rectangle where the drawing will take place.

These two events don't take place unless you set the DrawMode property of the control. Since only controls that expose the DrawMode property can be owner-drawn, you have a quick way of figuring out whether a control's appearance can be customized with the techniques discussed in this section. This property can be set to Normal (the control is draws its own surface), OwnerDrawnFixed (you can draw the control, but the height of the drawing area remains fixed), or OwnerDrawnVariable (you can draw the control and use a different height for each item). The settings of the DrawMode shown here apply to the ListBox control. The MenuItem control provides the OwnerDraw mode, whose settings are True (you're responsible for rendering the item's rectangle) or False. Let's start by building an owner-drawn menu.

Designing Owner-Drawn Menus

When a menu item's OwnerDraw property is set to True, the following events are fired every time the item is about to be drawn: first the MeasureItem event, then the DrawItem event. In the first event, you can find out the properties of the item and set up the size of the rectangle in which the menu item will be rendered. In the second event, you must insert the code to draw the item.

The second argument of both events, the ubiquitous *e* argument, exposes the Graphics object, which represents the area on which the item will be drawn. In the MeasureItem event's handler, you can't draw anything. You can calculate the dimensions of the rectangle that delimits the drawing you want to create and set the *e* argument's ItemWidth and ItemHeight properties respectively.

In the DrawItem event's handler, you can call any of the Graphic object's drawing commands to render anything on the item's rectangle. You can draw text in any font, style, or size, draw simple shapes, or even place a small bitmap in the item's rectangle. To demonstrate the design of owner-drawn menus, I've included the OwnerDrawnMenu project on the CD, which creates a simple menu with font names. Each name is rendered in the corresponding font, so that you can see what the text will look like when rendered in this font. The form of the OwnerDrawnMenu project is shown in Figure 9.10.

FIGURE 9.10

A simple owner-drawn menu

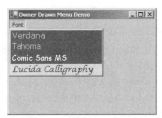

First, you must design the menu as usual and set the OwnerDrawn property of each menu item to True. Give meaningful names to all items, so that you can simplify your code.

Then insert the code of the Listing 9.20 in the MeasureItem and DrawItem event handlers of each owner-drawn menu item.

LISTING 9.20: PROGRAMMING THE MEASUREITEM AND DRAWITEM EVENTS

```
Private Sub FontVerdana_MeasureItem(ByVal sender As Object, _
            ByVal e As System.Windows.Forms.MeasureItemEventArgs) _
            Handles FontVerdana.MeasureItem
    Dim fnt As New Font("Verdana", 12, FontStyle.Regular)
    Dim itemSize As SizeF
    itemSize = e.Graphics.MeasureString("Verdana", fnt)
    e.ItemHeight = itemSize.Height
    e.ItemWidth = itemSize.Width
End Sub
Private Sub FontVerdana_DrawItem(ByVal sender As Object, _
            ByVal e As System.Windows.Forms.DrawItemEventArgs) _
            Handles FontVerdana.DrawItem
    Dim fnt As New Font("Verdana", 12, FontStyle.Regular)
    Dim R As New RectangleF(e.Bounds.X, e.Bounds.Y, _
                           e.Bounds.Width, e.Bounds.Height)
    Dim brush As SolidBrush
    e.Graphics.FillRectangle(Brushes.PaleTurquoise, R)
    e.Graphics.DrawString("Verdana", fnt, Brushes.White, R)
End Sub
```

I'm only showing the code for the first menu item; the others are identical. In the MeasureItem event handler, the code calls the MeasureString method to find out the dimensions of the item's caption when rendered in its font and then sets the dimensions of the item's rectangle in the menu. The code in the DrawItem event handler draws the caption in the item's rectangle. It uses a white solid brush and sets the item's background color to red. The string is rendered in white color. The last item (the handwriting font) is rendered in blue color on a yellow background.

The code is quite trivial really, and all the drawing methods will be discussed in detail in Chapter 14. You can return to this project after reading about the drawing methods and create more elaborate owner-drawn menus.

Designing Owner-Drawn ListBox Controls

In this section, we'll look at a similar technique for designing owner-drawn ListBox controls. You may have to create owner-drawn ListBoxes if you want to use different colors or fonts for different items, or to populate the list with items of widely different lengths. The example you'll build in this section, shown in Figure 9.11, uses an alternating background color, and each item has a different height, depending on the string it holds. Lengthy strings are broken into multiple lines at word boundaries. Since you're responsible for breaking the string into lines, you can use any other technique—for example, you can place an ellipsis to indicate that the string is too long to fit on the control, or use a smaller font, and so on.

FIGURE 9.11

An unusual, but quite functional ListBox control

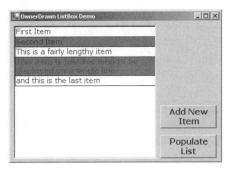

The fancy ListBox of Figure 9.11 was created with the OwnerDrawnList project, which you will find on the CD. Or you can follow the steps outlined in this section to build it from scratch.

To custom-draw the items on a ListBox control (or a ComboBox, for that matter), you use the MeasureItem event to calculate the item's dimensions and the DrawItem event to actually draw the item. Each item is a rectangle that exposes a Graphics object, and you can call any of the Graphics object's drawing methods to draw on the item's area. The drawing techniques we'll use in this example are similar to the ones we used in the previous section, but once you learn more about the drawing methods in Chapter 14, you'll be able to create even more elaborate designs than the ones shown here.

The items to be added to the list are stored in an ArrayList, which is populated in the form's Load event handler. Each time you add a new item to the ListBox control, it's first added to the ArrayList, then to the control. The reason for doing this is because at the time the MeasureItem event is fired, the item isn't part of the list yet and there's no simple method to access the new item—short of using a global variable. It's a minor inconvenience, and if you experiment with the OwnerDrawnList project, you may be able to find a work-around.

Each time an item is about to be drawn, the MeasureString and DrawString events are fired, in this order. In the MeasureString event handler, we set the dimensions of the item with the statements shown in Listing 9.21.

LISTING 9.21: SETTING UP AN ITEM'S RECTANGLE IN AN OWNER-DRAWN LISTBOX CONTROL

```
Private Sub ListBox1_MeasureItem(ByVal sender As Object, _
            ByVal e As System.Windows.Forms.MeasureItemEventArgs) _
            Handles ListBox1.MeasureItem
    Dim itmSize As SizeF
    Dim S As New SizeF(ListBox1.Width, 200)
    itmSize = e.Graphics.MeasureString(items(e.Index).ToString, fnt, S)
    e.ItemHeight = itmSize.Height
    e.ItemWidth = itmSize.Width
End Sub
```

This time we're using a different form of the MeasureString method. This form accepts as arguments a string, the font in which the string will be rendered, and a SizeF object. The SizeF object contains two members, the Width and Height members. These two members are used to pass to the method information about the area in which we want to print the string. In our example, we're going to print the string in a rectangle that's as wide as the ListBox control and as tall as needed to fit the entire string. I'm using a height of 200 pixels (enough the fit the longest string users may throw at the control). Upon return, the MeasureString method sets the members of the SizeF object to the width and height actually required to print the string. What we get back is the height of a rectangle in which the string will fit.

The two members of the SizeF object are then used to set the dimensions of the current item (properties e.ItemWidth and e.ItemHeight). We've set the dimensions of the item, and we're ready to draw it. The custom rendering of the current item takes place in the ItemDraw event handler, which is shown in Listing 9.22.

LISTING 9.22: DRAWING AN ITEM IN AN OWNER-DRAWN LISTBOX CONTROL

```vb
Private Sub ListBox1_DrawItem(ByVal sender As Object, _
            ByVal e As System.Windows.Forms.DrawItemEventArgs) _
            Handles ListBox1.DrawItem
    If e.Index = -1 Then Exit Sub
    Dim txtBrush As SolidBrush
    Dim bgBrush As SolidBrush
    Dim txtfnt As Font
    If e.Index / 2 = CInt(e.Index / 2) Then
    ' color even numbered items
        txtBrush = New SolidBrush(Color.Blue)
        bgBrush = New SolidBrush(Color.LightYellow)
    Else
    ' color odd numbered items
        txtBrush = New SolidBrush(Color.Blue)
        bgBrush = New SolidBrush(Color.Cyan)
    End If
    If e.State And DrawItemState.Selected Then
    ' use red color and bold for the selected item
        txtBrush = New SolidBrush(Color.Red)
        txtfnt = New Font(fnt.Name, fnt.Size, FontStyle.Bold)
    Else
        txtfnt = fnt
    End If
    e.Graphics.FillRectangle(bgBrush, e.Bounds)
    e.Graphics.DrawRectangle(Pens.Black, e.Bounds)
    Dim R As New RectangleF(e.Bounds.X, e.Bounds.Y, _
                            e.Bounds.Width, e.Bounds.Height)
    e.Graphics.DrawString(items(e.Index).ToString, txtfnt, txtBrush, R)
    e.DrawFocusRectangle()
End Sub
```

To test the enhanced ListBox control, place two buttons on the form, as shown in Figure 9.11. The Add New Item button prompts the user for a new item (a string) and adds it to the items ArrayList. Then it calls the Add method of the `ListBox.Items` collection to add the new item to the ListBox control. The reason you must add the new item to the ArrayList collection is that you can't directly add items to the control. As you recall, the MeasureItem event adds one element of the ArrayList to the control at a time. Since both the MeasureItem and DrawItem methods pick up the item to be added from the ArrayList collection, you need not specify any argument to the `List-Box1.Items.Add` method. Listing 9.23 provides the code that adds a new item to the list.

LISTING 9.23: ADDING AN ITEM TO THE LIST AT RUNTIME

```
Private Sub Button2_Click(ByVal sender As System.Object, _
                ByVal e As System.EventArgs) Handles Button2.Click
    Dim newItem As String
    newItem = InputBox("Enter item to add to the list")
    items.Add(newItem)
    ListBox1.Items.Add("")
End Sub
```

The last feature in the test application is the reporting of the selected item when the user double-clicks an item. I've included this code to demonstrate that, other than some custom drawing, the owner-drawn ListBox control carries with it all the functionality of the original ListBox control. It fires the same events, reports the same properties, and can be manipulated with the same methods.

When the user double-clicks the ListBox control, the code shown in Listing 9.24 is executed. This code retrieves SelectedIndex and SelectedItem properties and reports them to the application.

LISTING 9.24: RETRIEVING THE SELECTED ITEM FROM THE OWNER-DRAWN LISTBOX CONTROL

```
Private Sub ListBox1_DoubleClick(ByVal sender As Object, _
                ByVal e As System.EventArgs) Handles ListBox1.DoubleClick
    MsgBox("Item at location " & ListBox1.SelectedIndex & _
           " is " & vbCrLf & ListBox1.SelectedItem)
End Sub
```

Using ActiveX Controls

Before ending this chapter, I would like to show you how to use ActiveX control with .NET. If you're new to VB, ActiveX controls were the old Windows controls used with previous versions of VB. There are tons of ActiveX controls out there, and many of you are already using them in your projects. You can continue using them with your .NET projects as well. At this point, there's a relatively small number of .NET controls, so for a while we will have to use the same controls we used in our VB6 projects.

One of my favorite ActiveX controls is the WebBrowser control. I happen to have this control because I've installed VB6. If you're a VB6 programmer, you will have access to this control. If not, hopefully Microsoft will make these controls available with the release version of Visual Studio, or allow developers to download them. The WebBrowser control is nothing less than Internet Explorer in a control. This control can render any HTML document and Web page you can view with Internet Explorer, but it will do so in the context of a form. You can create forms that allow users to navigate the Web (or at least connect to your company's Web site) from within your application. Figure 9.12 shows a Windows form with an instance of the WebBrowser control on it. The document displayed on the control is Visual Studio's home page. You can navigate to any URL by typing an address in the TextBox control at the top of the form and clicking the Navigate button.

FIGURE 9.12

Navigating the Web with the Web-Browser control

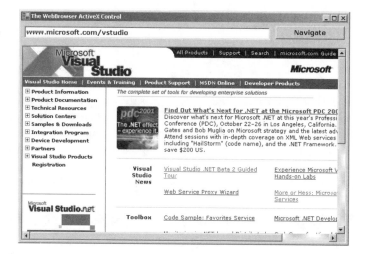

By default, .NET doesn't know how to handle ActiveX controls. To use an ActiveX control in a .NET application, you must create a "wrapper" around the ActiveX control. The wrapper is a layer of code that allows .NET to communicate with the ActiveX control. .NET thinks it's talking to a .NET control, and the ActiveX control thinks its talking to a COM component. In effect, the wrapper is a translator that allows the two parties to communicate with one another, even though they don't understand each other's language. This is called a *runtime callable wrapper (RCW)*, and it's created for you by the CLR as soon as you add an ActiveX control to your Toolbox.

To add an ActiveX control, such as the WebBrowser control, to your Toolbox, open the Customize Toolbox dialog box (right-click the Toolbox and select Customize). In the COM Components tab, locate the ActiveX control you want to add, as shown in Figure 9.13.

Now design a form like the one shown in Figure 9.12 and enter the code from Listing 9.25 in the button's Click event handler:

LISTING 9.25: NAVIGATING TO A URL WITH THE WEBBROWSER CONTROL

```
Private Sub Button1_Click(ByVal sender As System.Object, _
            ByVal e As System.EventArgs) Handles Button1.Click
    AxWebBrowser1.Navigate2(TextBox1.Text)
End Sub
```

FIGURE 9.13

Adding an ActiveX
control to the
Toolbox

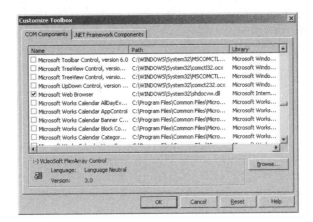

That's all it takes! You can also use this control to display local files to the users, such as help documents. Or allow them to connect to your site from within your application. I have found this control extremely useful in a large number of projects.

In Chapter 14, you'll see how to use another ActiveX control, the Script control. The Script control allows you to execute short programs written in VBScript (a subset of Visual Basic). As you will see, it's an extremely useful control that allows you to add scripting capabilities to your applications.

It is also possible to build your .NET controls so that they can be used in a COM environment, like Visual Studio 6. The process isn't complicated, but you must first understand how ActiveX controls are registered in the system Registry. I won't get into the details here, because this topic is of interest mostly to programmers who write .NET controls and want to expand their market by making their .NET controls compatible with earlier versions of Visual Studio. Please look up the documentation for specific information and step-by-step instructions on making your .NET control usable in the COM world.

Summary

One of the primary reasons for the phenomenal success of Visual Basic was that it could host custom controls. If you've been programming with VB for several years, you'll remember the VBX controls. If you started using VB the last few years, you'll remember the OCX controls. Now, it's the .NET controls. The controls keep getting better and so do the tools for creating custom controls.

The idea behind custom controls is that you can build a component with a visible and a programmatic interface and make it part of any development environment in the Windows world. Building custom controls isn't just a task for the few companies that sell them. Even modest applications may call for custom controls. When you build a control, you're actually encapsulating a lot of functionality in a black box, similar to a class. Unlike classes, however, controls have a visible interface too. Now that you know how to build your own classes and controls, you're ready to distribute your code not only to end users, but developers as well. Even if you won't make money by selling your components, there will always be a need for custom components in any programming environment. If you think that your code will be used repeatedly, either in multiple projects or by multiple programmers, consider packaging it as a custom class or control. The difference between the two is that controls expose the same functionality as classes but add a visible interface.

Chapter 10

Automating Microsoft Office Applications

ANOTHER WAY TO EXTEND Visual Basic is to program the various objects exposed by the Office applications, or any other application that exposes an object model. Word, Excel, and Outlook expose rich object models that can be programmed, either from within the Office applications themselves, or in external applications, written in any .NET language. You can program any Office application with VBA or use VB.NET to program against the object model of each application. In this chapter, I'll present the basic objects of the Office applications (Office 2000 and Office XP), because they are extremely popular and expose a whole lot of functionality.

I will limit the discussion to the three basic Office applications, Word, Excel, and Outlook, but once you understand how to manipulate their objects it shouldn't be hard to look into the object models of PowerPoint, Project, and VISIO. Practically speaking, the most useful object model for VB programmers is that of Outlook, which allows you to read incoming messages or to create and send new ones from within applications written in VB.NET. Excel and Word also expose quite a bit of functionality, and you will see how you can tap into this functionality from within your VB applications.

An *object model* is a collection of classes that represents the objects, or entities, each application can handle, the properties that determine the characteristics of these entities, and the methods that act on them. The object model exposes all the functionality of its application, and you can program the exposed objects with any language. Word, for example, manipulates documents, which are made up of text, graphics, and tables (among other things). Word's object model exposes the Document object, which represents a Word document. The Document object has a Range property, which represents a segment of the document (or all of it). The Range object, in turn, provides three collections—Paragraphs, Words, and Characters—which contain the corresponding entities of the document. All three collections provide the Font property, which lets you format the corresponding item by setting the font attributes. You can also apply a style to a paragraph or a word with the Style property.

As you will see, it is possible (and fairly straightforward) to start Word, create a new document, print it, and then close the application without ever displaying Word's window. You can use this functionality to generate elaborate printouts from within your VB applications. You can also access the spell-checking features of Word with a text document generated with VB.NET. Or you can create spreadsheets from within a VB application, complete with formulas. Then you can retrieve the results and use them in your VB application. All this can happen with Excel running in the background, and the users never see it. You can literally borrow the functionality of the Office applications and use it in your VB projects.

Of course, the object models of the Office applications aren't part of Visual Studio. They will be available to program against only if you have installed a version of Office on your system. The object models of the various versions of Office are very similar, and you should be able to adjust the code to accommodate syntactical changes. The samples of this chapter were developed with Office 2000 and they may require some minor changes to work with Office XP.

This chapter doesn't attempt to present the object models of the corresponding applications in their entirety. It's only an introduction to the topic of automating the Office applications by programming their objects. VBA programmers are already familiar with the object models discussed in this chapter, and they'll leverage their skills by bringing their knowledge of Office to Visual Basic. VB programmers, on the other hand, will learn how to program the object model of an external application and extend VB. They will also have to learn the object model of the application they're programming against, and the information in this chapter is more than adequate to get you started.

Programming Word

Word is a top-notch word processor, and you can tap into the power of Word through the object model it exposes. You can create documents, format them, and store them as DOC files. You can print these files, or e-mail them as attachments to a list of addresses. You can also reuse Word's spell-checking capabilities to correct documents at runtime. You will see later in this section how to spell-check a text document with a few lines of code using the objects exposed by Word.

Microsoft Word provides numerous objects, which you can use to program any action that can be carried out with menu commands. For example, you can open a document, count words and characters, replace certain words in it, and save it back on disk without user intervention. You can actually do all this without displaying Word's window on the Desktop.

The top-level Word object is the Application object, which represents the current instance of the application. You can use the Application object to access some general properties of Word's window, including its Visible property (to make the application visible or not). Normally, this property should be False, but you can turn it on during debugging to see what each statement in your code does to the current document.

To use the object model of Microsoft Word in your VB project, you must add a reference to the Microsoft Word application to the project. Open the Project menu, select Add References and, on the Add Reference dialog box, select the COM tab. Then locate the Microsoft Word 9.0 Object Library item by double-clicking its name and click OK to close the dialog box. (This version number applies to Office 2000. By the time you're reading this book, you may be using a newer version of Office. Select the Word component with the highest version number in the list.)

To program against Word's objects, you must first create a variable that represents the application, with a statement like the following:

```
Dim WordApp As New Word.Application
```

The New keyword tells VB to create a new instance of Word. This will start Word, but no visible interface will be displayed on the monitor. The *WordApp* variable must be declared on the Form level, so that all procedures can access it.

Under the Application object is the Documents collection, which contains a Document object for each open document. Using an object variable of the Document type, you can open an existing document or create a new document. The following statement opens an existing document with a specific name (assuming the specified document exists on the drive):

```
doc1 = WordApp.Documents.Open("My Word Samples.doc")
```

To create a new document, call the Add method of the Documents collection and then save the new document with the SaveAs method:

```
Dim newDoc As New Word.Document
newDoc = WordApp.Documents.Add
newDoc.SaveAs("My new Document")
```

The first statement declares a new document, and the second one adds a new document to the current instance of Word. After the execution of these statements, you can insert text, format it, and do anything you can do with the active document through Word's interface.

If you don't specify a path name, the document is saved in the default Save folder of Word. The SaveAs method accepts many more arguments, which are discussed in the section "Printing and Saving Documents," later in this chapter.

If the document has been saved already, you can call the Save method, which requires no arguments. Lastly, you must close the document and quit the application. The following statement closes the active document:

```
Documents.Close(saveChanges, originalFormat, routeDocument)
```

All three arguments are optional. The *saveChanges* argument is a member of the WDSaveOptions enumeration and can have one of the following values: wdDoNotSaveChanges, wdPromptToSaveChanges, or wdSaveChanges. The *originalFormat* argument determines the format that will be used to save the document; its value is a member of the WDOriginalFormat enumeration: wdOriginalDocumentFormat, wdPromptUser, or wdWordDocument. The last argument is a True/False value indicating whether the document should be routed to the next recipient. If the document doesn't have a routing slip attached, this argument is ignored.

If you have multiple open documents at once, you can select the active document with the Active-Document property. This property returns a Document object, and you can call it as shown here:

```
doc1 = WordApp.ActiveDocument
```

If the variable *doc1* represents an open document, you can make it the active document by calling the Activate method:

```
doc1.Activate
```

You can also create a new document by adding it to the Documents collection:

```
Dim doc As New Word.Document
doc = WordApp.Documents.Add
```

After you're done processing the document, you can save it by calling the SaveAs method, with the following statement:

```
Documents.SaveAs(fileName)
```

where *fileName* is a user-supplied filename (you can display the SaveFile common dialog to prompt the user for the file's name).

If the document has been modified since it was last saved, you must set the argument *saveChanges* to wdDoNotSaveChanges or wdSaveChanges. If you omit to close a changed document, the application won't terminate and, when you shut down your computer, you'll be prompted as to whether you want to save the file.

NOTE *If your application crashes, the next time you start Word you may see a bunch of recovered documents. These documents are leftovers of (rather unsuccessful) testing and debugging attempts.*

To terminate the application, call its Quit method, and then set the *WordApp* variable to Nothing. If you omit these steps and simply terminate your VB project, the instance of Word running in the background won't shut down. Every time you instantiate a variable to represent Microsoft Word, a new instance of the application will start and will remain alive in memory until you shut down the computer. Make sure you program the Closing event of your application, so that you won't leave any instances of Word floating around. The Closing event handler should contain the following lines:

```
Private Sub Form1_Closing(ByVal sender As Object, _
              ByVal e As System.ComponentModel.CancelEventArgs) _
              Handles MyBase.Closing
    WordApp.Documents.Close(Word.WdSaveOptions.wdDoNotSaveChanges)
    WordApp.Quit()
    WordApp = Nothing
End Sub
```

The Close method of the Documents collection closes all open documents without saving them. Then the Quit statement terminates Word. This code segment assumes that the documents have been saved already. If not, it will simply close them without prompting, which means you may lose the edits.

NOTE *While you're testing an application that uses any of the Office object models, you may have to end the application before it has had a chance to terminate the Office application. To find out if there are any instances of Word running in the background, invoke the Task Manager window by pressing Ctrl+Alt+Delete. On the Task Manager window, select the Processes tab and look for instances of the Office application you're programming against. The names of the three Office applications are WINWORD, EXCEL, and OUTLOOK, and if they appear in the list of processes while your application isn't running, you must terminate them manually. If you see too many instances of an Office application in the processes list, it means that your application doesn't terminate the Office application properly.*

TIP *If you stop the VB project by clicking the Stop button (or by selecting Debug ➤ Stop Debugging), the Closing event won't be triggered. While testing a project that contacts an Office application, try to terminate it with the End statement, or by clicking the Form's Close button. If you must terminate the application prematurely because of an error, open the Task Manager and shut down manually the running instances of the Office application.*

Objects That Represent Text

The most important object that each document exposes is the Range object, which represents a contiguous section of text. This section can be words, part of a word, characters, or even the entire document. Using the Range object's methods, you can insert new text, format existing text (or delete it), and so on. You can also use the Selection object to access part of the document. Both the Range and Selection objects will be discussed later in this chapter in detail.

To address specific units of text, use the following collections:

The **Paragraphs** collection, which is made up of Paragraph objects that represent text paragraphs

The **Words** collection, which is made up of Word objects that represent words

The **Characters** collection, which is made up of Character objects that represent individual characters

The Documents Collection and the Document Object

The first object under the Word Application object hierarchy is the Document object, which is any document that can be opened with Word or any document that can be displayed in Word's window. All open documents belong to a Documents collection that is made up of Document objects. Like all other collections, it supports the Count property (the number of open documents); the Add method, which adds a new document; and the Remove method, which closes an existing one. To access an open document, you can use the Item method of the Documents collection, specifying the document's index as follows:

```
Application.Documents.Item(1)
```

Or you can specify the document's name:

```
Application.Documents.Item("Chapter01.doc")
```

To open an existing document, use the Documents collection's Open method, whose syntax is:

```
Documents.Open(fileName)
```

The *fileName* argument is the document file's path name. To create a new document, use the Documents collection's Add method, which accepts two optional arguments:

```
Documents.Add(template, newTemplate)
```

The argument *template* specifies the name of a template file to be used as the basis for the new document. The *newTemplate* argument is a Boolean value. If it's set to True, Word creates a new template file.

Most of the operations you'll perform apply to the active document (the document in the active Word window), which is represented by the ActiveDocument object, a property of the Application object. To access the selected text in the active document, use the following expression:

```
Application.ActiveDocument.Selection
```

You can also make any document active by calling the Activate method of the Document object. To make the document MyNotes.doc active, use the following statement:

```
Documents("MyNotes.doc").Activate
```

You can also pass the index of a document as argument to the Documents collection to specify one of the open documents. After the execution of this statement, the `MyNotes.doc` document becomes the active one, and your code can refer to it through the object `Application.ActiveDocument`.

To access the first word in the active document use the following expression, which returns a Word object:

```
WordApp.ActiveDocument.Words(1)
```

The Word document exposes several properties, one of them being the Text property, which returns a string (the first word in the document):

```
WordApp.ActiveDocument.Words(1).Text
```

You can go through all the words in the active document with a loop like the following:

```
Dim word As Word.Range
For Each word In WordApp.ActiveDocument.Words
    Console.WriteLine(word.Text)
Next
```

Notice that there's no object that represents a word; a word is simply a Range object—the Words collection contains a Range object for each word in the document.

The following loop goes through the paragraphs of the active document, converts them to Range objects, and then prints the paragraph's text through the `Range.Text` property:

```
Dim para As Word.Paragraph
For Each para In WordApp.ActiveDocument.Paragraphs
    Console.WriteLine(para.Range.Text
Next
```

PRINTING AND SAVING DOCUMENTS

To print a document, call its Printout method, which has the following syntax:

```
Printout background, append, range, outputfilename, from, to, item, copies, _
        pages, pageType, PrintToFile, Collate, filename, ActivePrinterMacGX, _
        ManualDuplexPrint, PrintZoomColumn, PrintZoomRow, _
        PrintZoomPaperWidth, PrintZoomPaperHeight
```

All the arguments are optional; they correspond to the properties you can set on Word's Print dialog box. The *background* argument is a True/False value that specifies whether the printout will take place in the background, and this argument is usually set to True when we're automating applications.

When calling methods with a large number of arguments (most of which are omitted anyway), you should use named arguments to specify only a few arguments. For example, to print the first three pages of the active document, use the following syntax:

```
AppWord.ActiveDocument.Printout from:=1, to:=3
```

To save a document, use the SaveAs method of the Document object, which has the following syntax:

```
SaveAs FileName, FileFormat, LockComments, Password, AddToRecentFiles, _
        WritePassword, ReadOnlyRecommended, EmbedTrueTypeFonts, _
        SaveNativePictureFormat, SaveFormsData, SaveAsOCELetter
```

As with the Print method, the arguments of the SaveAs method correspond to the settings of the application's Save As dialog box. If the file has been saved already, use the Save method, which accepts no arguments at all. It saves the document to its file on disk using the options you specified in the SaveAs method when the document was saved for the first time. To save the active document under a different filename, use the following statement:

```
AppWord.ActiveDocument.SaveAs "c:\Documents\Report2002.doc"
```

Notice that there's no argument for overwriting an existing file. If you attempt to overwrite an existing file, a dialog box will pop up prompting you for whether you want to overwrite the file or cancel the operation. If you don't want your user to see any of Word's dialog boxes, you must make sure the file doesn't exist from within your code (or delete the file).

A related property of the Document object is the Saved property, which returns a True/False value indicating whether a document has been changed since the last time it was saved. Use the Saved property in your code to find out whether you must call the Save method before you quit the application.

The code segment in Listing 10.1 creates a new document, prints it, and then quits without saving it. The *WordApp* variable is declared outside the procedure, because it will most likely be used by other procedures in the same application. Notice that you can call the Add method of the Documents collection without a filename. The new document is called Document1, but it's not saved on disk.

LISTING 10.1: CREATING AND PRINTING A DOC FILE

```
Dim WordApp As New Word.Application()
Private Sub Button1_Click(ByVal sender As System.Object, _
                ByVal e As System.EventArgs) Handles Button1.Click
    Dim thisDoc As New Word.Document()
    thisDoc = WordApp.Documents.Add
    With thisDoc
        .Range.InsertAfter("Printing with Word")
        .Paragraphs.Item(1).Range.Font.Bold = True
        .Paragraphs.Item(1).Range.Font.Size = 14
        .Range.InsertParagraphAfter()
        .Paragraphs.Item(2).Range.Font.Bold = False
        .Paragraphs.Item(2).Range.Font.Size = 12
        .Range.InsertAfter("This is the first line of the test printout")
        .Range.InsertParagraphAfter()
        .Range.InsertAfter("and this is the second line of the test printout")
        Try
            .PrintOut(True, True)
        Catch exc As Exception
            MsgBox(exc.Message)
        End Try
        .Close(Word.WdSaveOptions.wdDoNotSaveChanges)
    End With
    WordApp.Quit()
End Sub
```

The sample code calls the PrintOut method of the Document object to print the current document. The two parameters passed to the method correspond to the *background* and *append* arguments. If something goes wrong during printing, the structured error handler will catch the exception and report it on a message box. The body of the procedure generates a sample document (you will see in the following section how the Range object can be used to create a new document).

MANIPULATING TEXT

As mentioned already, the two basic objects for accessing text in a Word document are the Range and Selection objects. The Selection object represents a contiguous segment of text, similar to making a selection with the mouse. The Range object is a also a collection of characters, words, or paragraphs, similar to the Selection. The difference between the two objects is that there's only one Selection object in a document, but you can define many Range objects. You can manipulate individual Range objects without affecting the current selection.

To extract some text from a document, you can use the Document object's Range method, which accepts as arguments the positions of the starting and ending characters in the text. The syntax of the Range method is:

```
Document1.Range(start, end)
```

where *Document1* is a variable of the Word.Document type and represents a Word document. The *start* and *end* arguments are two numeric values. The first character's position in the document is 0. The following statement extracts the first 100 characters of the document represented by the *Document* object variable:

```
Range1 = Document1.Range(0, 99)
```

These characters are assigned to the *Range1* object variable. The *Range1* variable must be declared as Range type:

```
Dim Range1 As Word.Range
```

In the preceding expressions, the *Document1* variable must first be set to refer to an existing object with statements like

```
Dim Document1 As Word.Document = WordApp.Documents.Item(1)
```

You can also replace the variable *Document1* with the built-in object ActiveDocument, which represents the active document. The selected text in the active document can be accessed by the following expression:

```
WordApp.ActiveDocument.Selection
```

Words, sentences, and paragraphs are more meaningful units of text than characters. The Word, Sentence, and Paragraph objects are better suited for text manipulation, and you commonly use these objects to access documents. These objects, however, don't support all the properties of the Range object. All units of text can be converted to a Range object with the Range property. For example, the following statement returns the third paragraph in the specified document as a Range object:

```
Document1.Paragraphs(3).Range
```

You can then apply the Range object's properties and methods to manipulate the third paragraph.

The Paragraph object doesn't have a Font property or a Select method. To change the appearance of the third paragraph in the document, you must first convert the paragraph to a Range object with a statement like this:

```
Set Range1 = Document1.Paragraphs(3).Range
Range1.Font.Bold = True
```

Document1 is a properly declared Document variable, and *Range1* is a properly declared Range variable. You can also combine both statements into one and avoid the creation of the *Range1* object variable as follows:

```
Document1.Paragraphs(3).Range.Font.Bold = True
```

The following statement selects (highlights) the same paragraph:

```
Document1.Paragraphs(3).Range.Select
```

(You won't see the selection, of course, but if you make Word's window visible at this point, you'll see that the Select method actually highlights a section of the document.) Once a paragraph (or any other piece of text) is selected, you can apply all types of processing to it (e.g., edit it, move it, format it).

The two methods of the Range object that you'll use most often are InsertAfter, which inserts a string of text after the specified Range, and InsertBefore, which inserts a string of text ahead of the specified Range. The following statements insert a title at the beginning of the document and a closing paragraph at the end:

```
AppWord.ActiveDocument.Select
AppWord.ActiveDocument.Range.InsertBefore "This is the document's title"
AppWord.ActiveDocument.Range.InsertAfter "This is the closing paragraph"
```

The Select method of the ActiveDocument object selects the entire text. The selected text is then converted to a Range object, so that the Range object's methods can be applied to it.

To create a new paragraph, use InsertParagraphBefore and InsertParagraphAfter. Both methods will insert a new paragraph, before or after the specified range.

THE CURRENT SELECTION

The Selection object represents the current selection in the active document. This property returns the range of text selected by the user, but you can also select a range of text from within your application. The Selection object is very similar to the Range object, and both objects expose the same functionality. Although you can maintain many Range objects in your application, there's only one selection. When the current selection is changed, the previous selection is lost.

NOTE *Selection is a property of the Application object and represents the selected text in the current document (the active document). If no text is selected, the Selection object represents an empty range of text. Its location is the same as the location of the insertion point.*

ACCESSING PARAGRAPHS, WORDS, AND CHARACTERS

While all collections in Word are 1-based, the Characters collection is 0-based. To access the first document in the Documents collection, we use an index value of 1. To access the first sentence in the document, we also use an index of 1, and the same is true for the first word. The first character, however, has an index of 0.

Let's say you have added a document to the Documents collection, represented by the *doc* variable:

```
Dim doc As New Word.Document()
doc = W.Documents.Add
```

W represents a running instance of Word, and it's declared on the Form level. Add two lines of text to the document with the following statements:

```
doc.Range.InsertAfter("The quick brown fox ")
doc.Range.InsertParagraphAfter()
doc.Range.InsertAfter("jumped over the lazy dog")
```

Let's experiment with extracting paragraphs, words, and characters from the current document. To read the first five characters of the document, enter the following statement:

```
Console.WriteLine(doc.Range(0, 5).Text)
```

This statement will print the string "The q" on the Output window (without the quotes, of course). To read the first paragraph, we must request the first member of the Paragraphs collection and get its Range property. Then we'll apply the Text property to read the text:

```
Console.WriteLine(doc.Range.Paragraphs.Item(1).Range.Text)
```

This statement will print the string "The quick brown fox " on the Output window. Finally, you can read the second word with the following statement:

```
Console.WriteLine(doc.Range.Paragraphs.Item(1).Range.Words.Item(2).Text)
```

The second word is "quick," which indicates that the Words collection is 1-based, like the Paragraphs collection.

Note that the Paragraph object must be converted to a Range object before you can access its Words collection.

To specify a Selection, use the Start and End properties, which are the locations of the starting and ending character of the selection in the document. If you set both properties to the same value, you're in effect positioning the insertion pointer to the specified location. The following statements select three characters, starting with the eleventh character in the document, and print them on the Output window:

```
WordApp.Selection.Start = 10
WordApp.Selection.End = 12
Console.WriteLine(WordApp.Selection.Text())
```

The Start and End properties are expressed in characters, and as such they're 0-based. The Selection.Type property returns information about the current selection, and its value can be one of the members of the WDSelectionType enumeration: `wdNoSelection`, `wdSelectionBlock`, `wdColumn`, `wdFrame`, `wdInLineShape`, `wdIP`, `wdNormal`, `wdRow`, and `wdShape`. IP stands for insertion point and represents the location of the insertion pointer at the time—this value means that there is no text currently selected.

The contents of the current selection are expressed in characters, words, sentences, and paragraphs. There are four properties, named Characters, Words, Sentences, and Paragraphs, and they're all collections. Use their Count property to find out the number of the corresponding items in the selection, or the Item property followed by an index value in parentheses to retrieve a specific member from the collection. The following expressions return the number of words and characters in the selected text:

```
WordApp.Selection.Words.Count
WordApp.Selection.Characters.Count
```

To access the third word in the current selection, use the following expression:

```
WordApp.Selection.Words.Item(3)
```

The various collections exposed by the Office applications are 1-based, except for the Characters collection, which is 0-based.

You can use the Selection object to enter new text into a document, as well as for formatting the text. While the Range object is a property of the Document object, the Selection object is a property of the `Word.Application` object and applies to the active document. To replace the current selection with new text, use the TypeText method, which accepts as argument the new text. If the selection contains any text, the old text will be replace with the new text. The selection can also be empty, in which case the new text will be inserted at the location of the insertion pointer.

The following statement inserts some text at the location of the insertion pointer, or replaces the selected text:

```
WordApp.Selection.TypeText("some text")
```

A good reason for using the Selection object to insert text is that you can specify the format before entering the text. To change the current character format, use the Font property of the Selection object, as shown in the following few statements:

```
With WordApp.Selection
    .Font.Size = .Font.Size + 1
    .Font.Bold = True
    .TypeText("this text stands out")
    .Font.Size = .Font.Size - 1
    .Font.Bold = False
    .TypeText("back to the previous text font")
End With
```

When you use the Selection object to insert text into a document, you can set the character format as you go along. If you want to apply styles, however, it's easier to use the Range object. Styles are usually applied to entire paragraphs, not isolated words or sentences. This is a good point at which to demonstrate the concepts discussed so far with an example.

VB.NET at Work: The WordDemo Project

With the objects and methods described so far, you have enough information to create a new document, place some text into it, format it, and then save it to a disk file. The first step is to start an instance of Word and connect to it. The WordDemo project (Figure 10.1) demonstrates how to:

- ◆ Create a new document.
- ◆ Insert some text and format it.
- ◆ Save the new document to a user-specified DOC file.

FIGURE 10.1

The WordDemo project's main form

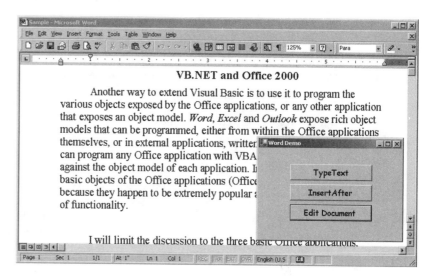

These actions take place from within the Visual Basic application while Word is running in the background. The user doesn't see Word's window, not even as an icon on the taskbar. The new document is saved in a file with a name you specify through the Save File dialog box. You can open this file later with Word and edit it.

The buttons InsertAfter and TypeText create a new document and apply some formatting, using the Range and Selection objects respectively. The code behind the TypeText button uses the Type-Text method of the Selection object to create a new document. Let's start with the code of the TypeText button, detailed in Listing 10.2.

LISTING 10.2: COMPOSING A DOCUMENT WITH THE TYPETEXT METHOD

```
Private Sub Button2_Click(ByVal sender As Object, _
                ByVal e As System.EventArgs) Handles Button2.Click
    Dim doc As New Word.Document()
    doc = WordApp.Documents.Add()
    Dim str As String
    str = "Text Formatting:"
    With WordApp.Selection
```

```
        .Font.Size = WordApp.Selection.Font.Size + 2
        .Font.Bold = True
        .TypeText(str)
        .Font.Size = WordApp.Selection.Font.Size - 2
        .Font.Bold = False
        .TypeParagraph()
        .Font.Color = Word.WdColor.wdColorDarkRed
        .Font.Italic = False
        .TypeText("This sentence will appear in red. ")
        .TypeParagraph()
        .Font.Color = Word.WdColor.wdColorBlack
        .Font.Italic = True
        .Font.Size = WordApp.Selection.Font.Size + 2
        .TypeText("Text color was reset to black, " & _
                    "but the font size was increased by two points")
    End With
    Dim fName As String
    SaveFileDialog1.Filter = "Documents|*.doc"
    SaveFileDialog1.ShowDialog()
    fName = SaveFileDialog1.FileName
    If fName <> "" Then
        Try
            doc.SaveAs(fName)
        Catch exc As Exception
            MsgBox("Failed to save document" & vbCrLf & exc.Message)
        End Try
    End If
    MsgBox("The document contains " & doc.Paragraphs.Count & " paragraphs " & _
                        vbCrLf & doc.Words.Count & " words and " & _
                            doc.Characters.Count & " characters")
    doc.Close(Word.wdSaveOptions.wdDoNotSaveChanges)
End Sub
```

This event handler makes use of the *WordApp* variable, which must be declared in the Form level with the following statement:

```
Dim WordApp As New Word.Application()
```

You must also add a reference to the Microsoft Word 9.0 Object library to your project.

The code changes the Font object to format the following text, and then it inserts the text with the TypeText method. The text entered is formatted according to the Font in effect. Every time you change the font attributes, they take effect for the following text. After entering the text, the code saves the document to a file. The name of the file is specified by the user on the FileSave dialog box.

You can also compose the same document using the Range object. The code behind the InsertAfter button uses the Range object to manipulate the text (insert new paragraphs and manipulate them). The following statements create a new document with a header, followed by three paragraphs, using the InsertAfter and InsertParagraphAfter methods. Listing 10.3 is the code behind the InsertAfter button.

LISTING 10.3: COMPOSING A DOCUMENT WITH THE RANGE METHOD

```
Private Sub Button1_Click(ByVal sender As System.Object, _
                ByVal e As System.EventArgs) Handles Button1.Click
    Dim doc As New Word.Document()
    doc = WordApp.Documents.Add()
    With doc.Range
        .InsertAfter("A New Architecture for Building Distributed Applications")
        .InsertParagraphAfter()
        .InsertAfter("ADO.NET is the latest data access technology from " & _
            "Microsoft, geared towards distributed applications. Unlike " & _
            "its predecessor, ADO.NET uses disconnected recordsets.")
        .InsertParagraphAfter()
        .InsertAfter("The disconnected recordsets are called Datasets, and " & _
            "they may contain multiple tables. If the tables are related, " & _
            "the Dataset knows how to handle the relations and provides " & _
            "methods that allow you to move from any row of a table to the " & _
            "related rows of the other tables.")
        .InsertParagraphAfter()
        .InsertParagraphAfter()
        .InsertAfter("ADO.NET uses XML to move rows between the database " & _
            "and the middle tier, as well as between the middle tier " & _
            "and the client. XML passes through firewalls, and it's an " & _
            "ideal candidate for moving binary information between " & _
            "layers and/or different operating systems.")
    End With
    Dim selRange As Word.Range
    selRange = doc.Paragraphs.Item(1).Range
    selRange.Font.Size = 14
    selRange.Font.Bold = True
    selRange.ParagraphFormat.Alignment = _
        Word.WdParagraphAlignment.wdAlignParagraphCenter
    selRange = doc.Paragraphs.Item(2).Range.Sentences.Item(2)
    selRange.Italic = True
    selRange = doc.Paragraphs.Item(3).Range.Words.Item(6)
    selRange.Font.Bold = True
    selRange = doc.Paragraphs.Item(5).Range.Words.Item(5)
    selRange.Font.Bold = True
    Dim fName As String
    SaveFileDialog1.Filter = "Documents|*.doc"
    SaveFileDialog1.ShowDialog()
    fName = SaveFileDialog1.FileName
    If fName <> "" Then
        Try
            doc.SaveAs(fName)
        Catch exc As Exception
            MsgBox("Failed to save document" & vbCrLf & exc.Message)
        End Try
    End If
```

```
MsgBox("The document contains " & doc.Paragraphs.Count & " paragraphs " & _
                        vbCrLf & doc.Words.Count & " words and " & _
                                doc.Characters.Count & " characters")
doc.Close(Word.WdSaveOptions.wdDoNotSaveChanges)
End Sub
```

Once the text has been added to the document, the code formats the header (the first paragraph in the document) and selected words in the document. The individual words are accessed through the Words collection of the corresponding paragraph. The following expression returns the second paragraph of the document:

```
doc.Paragraphs.Item(2)
```

If you apply the Range method to this expression, you'll get a Range object with the text of the second paragraph:

```
doc.Paragraphs.Item(2).Range
```

Finally, you can access individual words in this paragraph with the following expression:

```
doc.Paragraphs.Item(2).Range.Words.Item(5)
```

The Edit Document button shows you how to manipulate the text in a Word document from within your VB application. The initial document (SAMPLE.DOC) contains multiple spaces between words that shouldn't be there. To reduce multiple spaces to single space characters (a common task in editing), you can use the Find and Replace dialog box. The WordDemo application does the same by calling the Find.Execute method.

The Find method accepts a large number of arguments, and we usually specify only the arguments we're interested in by name. If you want to simply specify the word to search for, you can specify only the FindText argument as follows:

```
thisDoc.Content.Find.Execute FindText:= "VB7"
```

where *thisDoc* is an object variable that represents a document.

The arguments of the Find.Execute method are the following (the order they're listed here is the same order in which they appear in the method):

```
Find.Execute(FindText, MatchCase, MatchWholeWord, MatchWildChars, _
            MatchSoundsLike, MatchAllWordForms, MatchForward, Wrap, _
            Format, ReplaceWith, Replace, MatchKashida, MatchDiacritics, _
            MatchAlefHamza, MatchControl)
```

The names of the arguments are self-explanatory, except for the last few, which are True/False values and determine how Word should search for the specified text in non-English languages.

TIP   To find out the members of each Word enumeration, you can open the Object browser and expand Interop. Word ➢ Word (or the name of another application that's referenced in your project). Move down to the entries beginning with WD. These are Word's enumerations. Select an enumeration by clicking its name, and you will see the members of the enumeration in the right pane. The WDReplace enumeration, for instance, contains the following members: wdReplaceAll, wdReplaceNone, *and* wdReplaceOne.

If you want to replace one or more instances of a word (or sentence) in the text, set the *ReplaceWith* argument to the replacement text and the *Replace* argument to one of the values wdReplaceAll or wdReplaceOne, depending on whether you want to replace a single or all instances of the text. The code segment in Listing 10.4 replaces all instances of "VB7" to "VB.NET" and removes the multiple spaces from the document.

LISTING 10.4: MASSAGING A WORD DOCUMENT

```
Private Sub Button3_Click(ByVal sender As System.Object, _
              ByVal e As System.EventArgs) Handles Button3.Click
    Dim thisDoc As Word.Document
    Dim thisRange As Word.Range
    WordApp.Documents.Open("c:\sample.doc")
    WordApp.Visible = False
    thisDoc = WordApp.ActiveDocument
    thisDoc.Content.Find.Execute(FindText:="VB7", ReplaceWith:="VB.NET", _
                                Replace:=Word.WdReplace.wdReplaceAll)
    While thisDoc.Content.Find.Execute(FindText:="  ", _
                                Wrap:=Word.WdFindWrap.wdFindContinue)
        thisDoc.Content.Find.Execute(FindText:="  ", ReplaceWith:=" ", _
                                Replace:=Word.WdReplace.wdReplaceAll, _
                                Wrap:=Word.WdFindWrap.wdFindContinue)
    End While
    WordApp.Documents.Item(1).Save()
    MsgBox("Replaced all instances of 'VB7' with 'VB.NET' and saved the document")
    WordApp.Documents.Item(1).Close()
End Sub
```

For the WordDemo application, we must specify the string to search for and the replacement string. The program searches for two consecutive spaces, and if found, replaces them with a single space. Notice that the replacement of all instances of "VB7" with "VB.NET" is carried out by a single call to the Find.Execute method. The wdReplaceAll option tells Word to replace all instances of the string throughout the document. Replacing the multiple spaces, however, is not as simple, because you may have more than two spaces in a row. The code sets up a While loop, which repeats while the Find.Execute method reports that instances of two or more consecutive spaces exist. In the loop's body, we call the Find.Execute method, this time specifying a replacement string.

NOTE   To test this application, create a short document with several instances of the string "VB7" and insert multiple spaces between its words. Save the document as **sample.doc** *in the root folder of the C: drive and then run the application. You will find a simple file named* **sample.doc** *in the application's folder on the CD.*

Spell-Checking Documents

One of the most useful features of Word (and of every Office application) is its ability to spell-check a document. This functionality is also exposed by Word's objects, and you can borrow it for use within your Visual Basic applications. This is not only possible, it's actually quite simple. To call upon Word's spell-checking routines, you need to know about two objects: the ProofreadingErrors and SpellingSuggestions collections.

The ProofreadingErrors collection is a property of the Range object and it contains the misspelled words in the Range. To ask Word to spell-check a range of text and populate the ProofreadingErrors collection, call the Range object's SpellingErrors method. This method returns a result that must be stored in an object variable of type ProofreadingErrors:

```
Dim SpellCollection As ProofreadingErrors
Set SpellCollection = DRange.SpellingErrors
```

DRange is Range object (a paragraph or an entire document). The second line populates the *Spell-Collection* variable with the misspelled words. You can then set up a For Each…Next loop to read the words from the collection.

Besides locating spelling errors, Word can also suggest a list of alternate spellings or words that sound like the misspelled one. To retrieve the list of alternate words, you call the GetSpelling-Suggestions method of the Application object, passing the misspelled word as an argument. Notice that this is a method of the Application object, not of the Range object you're spell-checking. The results returned by the GetSpellingSuggestions method must be stored in another collection, this one of the SpellingSuggestions type:

```
Dim CorrectionsCollection As SpellingSuggestions
Set CorrectionsCollection = AppWord.GetSpellingSuggestions("antroid")
```

The second line retrieves the suggested alternatives for the word *antroid*. To scan the list of suggested words, you set up a loop that retrieves all the elements of the CorrectionsCollection collection. The example in the next section demonstrates the use of both methods from within a Visual Basic application.

VB.NET AT WORK: THE WORDSPELLCHECKER PROJECT

WordSpellChecker is an application that uses Word's methods to spell-check a text file. You'll find the WordSpellChecker application in this chapter's folder on the CD; its main form, shown in Figure 10.2, consists of a multiline TextBox control on which the user can enter some text and spell-check it by clicking the SpellCheck Document button.

FIGURE 10.2

The WordSpell-Checker application's main form

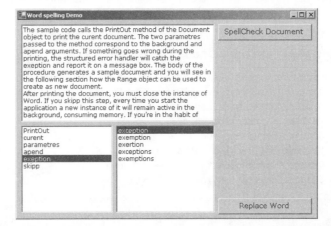

The application will contact Word and request the list of misspelled words. The list of misspelled words is displayed on a ListBox control on the same Form, as shown in Figure 10.2. The ListBox control on the left shows all the misspelled words returned by Word. Word can not only locate misspelled words but suggest alternatives as well. To view the alternate spellings for a specific word, select the word in the left list by double-clicking it.

To replace all instances of the selected misspelled word with the selected alternative, click the Replace button. You can design your own interface to allow the user to select which and how many instances of the misspelled word in the original document will be replaced.

The program uses three public variables, which are declared as follows:

```
Public WordApp As Application
Public CorrectionsCollection As SpellingSuggestions
Public SpellCollection As ProofreadingErrors
```

The *SpellCollection* variable is a collection that contains all the misspelled words, and the *CorrectionsCollection* variable is another collection that contains the suggested spellings for a specific word. The *CorrectionsCollection* variable's contents are changed every time the user selects another misspelled word in Word's Spelling Suggestions window.

When the SpellCheck Document button is clicked, the program creates a new document and copies the TextBox control's contents to the new document using the InsertAfter method of the Range object, as follows:

```
WordApp.Documents.Add
Dim Drange As Word.Range
Drange = WordApp.ActiveDocument.Range
DRange.InsertAfter(Text1.Text)
```

Now comes the interesting part. The Visual Basic code calls the Range object's SpellingErrors method, which returns a collection of ProofreadingErrors objects. The result of the SpellingErrors method is assigned to the object variable *SpellCollection*:

```
Dim SpellCollection As Word.ProofreadingErrors
Set SpellCollection = DRange.SpellingErrors
```

The lines in Listing 10.5—the SpellCheck Document button's Click event handler—spell-check the document and add the words contained in the *SpellCollection* collection (the misspelled words) to the ListBox1 control.

LISTING 10.5: THE CHECK DOCUMENT BUTTON

```
Private Sub Button1_Click(ByVal sender As System.Object, _
            ByVal e As System.EventArgs) Handles Button1.Click
    Dim DRange As Word.Range
    Me.Text = "Starting Word ..."
    WordApp.Documents.Add()
    Me.Text = "Checking words..."
    DRange = WordApp.ActiveDocument.Range
    DRange.InsertAfter(TextBox1.Text)
```

```
      Dim SpellCollection As Word.ProofreadingErrors
      SpellCollection = DRange.SpellingErrors
      If SpellCollection.Count > 0 Then
         ListBox1.Items.Clear()
         ListBox2.Items.Clear()
         Dim iword As Integer
         Dim newWord As String
         For iword = 1 To SpellCollection.Count
            newWord = SpellCollection.Item(iword).Text
            If ListBox1.FindStringExact(newWord) < 0 Then
               ListBox1.Items.Add(newWord)
            End If
         Next
      End If
      Me.Text = "Word spelling Demo"
   End Sub
```

The document is checked in a single statement, which calls the SpellingErrors method of a Range object that contains the entire text. Then the program goes through every word in the *SpellCollection* collection and adds them to the ListBox1 control. Notice that the ListBox control with the misspelled words doesn't contain duplicate entries. The code uses the control's FindStringExact method to find out whether a word belongs to the list or not.

Every time an entry in this ListBox is clicked, the code calls the WordApp object's GetSpelling-Suggestions method, passing the selected word as an argument. The GetSpellingSuggestions method returns another collection with the suggested words, which are placed in the second ListBox control on the Form with the statements shown in Listing 10.6. If this collection is empty (Word can't suggest any alternatives), the string "No suggestions!" is displayed on the control.

LISTING 10.6: RETRIEVING CORRECTION SUGGESTIONS

```
   Private Sub ListBox1_SelectedIndexChanged(ByVal sender As System.Object, _
               ByVal e As System.EventArgs) Handles ListBox1.SelectedIndexChanged
      Dim CorrectionsCollection As Word.SpellingSuggestions
      CorrectionsCollection = WordApp.GetSpellingSuggestions(ListBox1.Text)
      ListBox2.Items.Clear()
      If CorrectionsCollection.Count > 0 Then
         Dim iWord As Integer
         For iWord = 1 To CorrectionsCollection.Count
            ListBox2.Items.Add(CorrectionsCollection.Item(iWord).Name)
         Next
      Else
         ListBox2.Items.Add("No suggestions!")
      End If
   End Sub
```

You can also replace misspelled words in the document with one of the suggested alternatives by clicking the Replace Word button. When you do, the application calls the Replace function to replace all instances of the selected word with the selected alternative. After that, it removes the misspelled word from the list. The code behind the Replace Word button is shown in Listing 10.7.

LISTING 10.7: REPLACING MISSPELLED WORDS

```
Private Sub Button2_Click(ByVal sender As System.Object, _
              ByVal e As System.EventArgs) Handles Button2.Click
    If ListBox1.SelectedIndex >= 0 And ListBox2.SelectedIndex >= 0 Then
        TextBox1.Text = Replace(TextBox1.Text, _
                              ListBox1.SelectedItem, ListBox2.SelectedItem)
        ListBox1.Items.Remove(ListBox1.SelectedIndex)
        ListBox2.Items.Clear()
    End If
End Sub
```

The WordSpellChecker application can become the starting point for many custom Visual Basic applications that require spell-checking but don't need powerful editing features. In some cases, you might want to customize spelling, although it's not a very common situation. In a mail-aware application, for example, you can spell-check the text and exclude URLs and e-mail addresses. You would first scan the words returned by the SpellingErrors method to check which ones contained special characters and omit them.

As you can see, tapping into the power of the Office applications isn't really complicated. Once you familiarize yourself with the objects of these applications, you can access the Office applications by manipulating a few properties and calling the methods of these objects.

If you have a list of words to spell-check, you can call the CheckSpelling method of the Word.Application object to check the spelling of each word. The loop shown in Listing 10.8 goes through each word in a list and checks its spelling. If the word is misspelled, it's added to a second ListBox control. This application uses the Word.Application object and doesn't create a document with the text to be spell-checked.

LISTING 10.8: SPELL-CHECKING A LIST OF WORDS

```
Dim WordApp As New Word.application()
Private Sub Button1_Click(ByVal sender As System.Object, _
              ByVal e As System.EventArgs) Handles Button1.Click
    Dim SpellCollection As Word.ProofreadingErrors
    Dim wrd As Integer
    ListBox2.Items.Clear()
    Dim words As Integer = ListBox1.Items.Count
    For wrd = 0 To words - 1
        Me.Text = "Spelling ... " & CInt(wrd / words * 100) & " % done"
        If Not WordApp.CheckSpelling(ListBox1.Items(wrd)) Then
```

```
        ListBox2.Items.Add(ListBox1.Items(wrd))
      End If
      Application.DoEvents()
   Next
End Sub
```

Programming Excel

Excel is probably the most popular application among users and developers. Actually, there are countless programmers who earn their living by doing everything with Excel—they even write limited database applications using Excel as a data store. I'm not suggesting you start using Excel as a universal tool, but it's very likely that, at some point, you'll be called to import data from an Excel spreadsheet into your applications. In most situations, the tabular format of Excel isn't what you really need, and you'll have to write code to import the data into your applications.

Another good reason for using Excel's object model is to format and print tabular data. An application that generates reports on a regular basis (every day, for example) can create XLS files that can be used for neat printouts, as well as for archiving purposes.

To use Excel's object model in your code, you must add a reference to the Microsoft Excel 9.0 Object Library item to your project. Open the Project menu, select Add Reference, and double-click the name of the Excel library. Then click OK to add an instance of Excel's object model to your application. To contact Excel from within your VB application, declare a variable of the `Excel.Application` type. The following declaration must appear outside the procedures that use it:

```
Dim EXL As New Excel.Application
```

EXL represents a new instance of Excel, which runs in the background.

To access Excel's functionality, you can use a hierarchy of objects, which are described next. The objects that Excel exposes have different names from those of Word, but they form an equally sensible and structured hierarchy for accessing data stored in a tabular arrangement. Just as Word's basic unit of information is the text segment (not characters or words), Excel's basic unit of information is also called Range. A Range object can contain a single cell or an entire worksheet (and everything in between).

Two important methods of Excel's Application object are the Calculate method, which recalculates all open worksheets, and the Evaluate method, which evaluates math expressions and returns the result. The following statement returns a numeric value that is the result of the math expression passed to the Evaluate method as argument:

```
Dim result As Double
result = EXL.Evaluate("cos(3/1.091)*log(3.499)")
```

You can also use variables in your expressions as long as you store their values in specific cells and use the addresses of these cells in the expression. You will see shortly how to assign formulas to specific cells. Doing so allows you to calculate complicated expressions that involve other cells as well.

The Worksheets Collection and the Worksheet Object

Each workbook in Excel contains one or more worksheets. The Worksheets collection, which is similar to Word's Documents collection, contains a Worksheet object for each worksheet in the current workbook. To add a new worksheet, use the Add method, whose syntax is as follows:

```
Application.Worksheets.Add(before, after, count, type)
```

The *before* and *after* arguments let you specify the order of the new worksheet in the workbook. You can specify one of the two arguments; if you omit both, the new worksheet is inserted before the active worksheet (and also becomes active). The *type* argument specifies the new worksheet's type and can have one of the values in Table 10.1.

TABLE 10.1: THE XLSHEETTYPE ENUMERATION

VALUE	DESCRIPTION
xlWorksheet	The default value
xlExcel4MacroSheet	A worksheet with Excel 4 macros
xlExcel4IntlMacroSheet	A worksheet with Excel 4 international macros
xlChart	A worksheet with Excel charts
xlDialogSheet	A worksheet with Excel dialogs

To create a new worksheet, declare a variable of the Worksheet type and then add it to the Worksheets collection. Sheets belongs to Workbooks, so you must use a statement like the following one to create a new Workbook and then add a Worksheet to it:

```
Dim WSheet As New Excel.Worksheet()
WSheet = EXL.Workbooks.Add.Worksheets.Add
```

You can also open an existing workbook with the Open method of the Workbooks collection:

```
EXL.Workbooks.Open("c:\Sample.xls")
```

Then you can access the worksheets from within your code and populate them. By default, each new workbooks contains three worksheets, named "Sheet1," "Sheet2," and "Sheet3." To place a value in the first cell of the second worksheet, use the following statement:

```
WSheet = EXL.Workbooks.Item(1).Worksheets("Sheet2")
WSheet.Cells(1, 1) = "TOP LEFT CELL"
```

You can also add worksheets to the current Workbook with the Add method of the Worksheets collection. The following statements add a new worksheet and place a value to the top-left cell:

```
WSheet = EXL.ActiveWorkbook.Worksheets.Add()
WSheet.Cells(1, 1) = "First Cell"
```

To access an individual worksheet, use the Worksheet collection's Item method, passing the index or the worksheet's name as an argument. If the second worksheet is named `SalesData.xls`, the two following expressions are equivalent:

```
Application.Worksheets.Item(2)
Application.Worksheets.Item("SalesData")
```

The Range Object

Excel is an application for manipulating units of information stored in cells, but the basic object for accessing the contents of a worksheet is the Range object, which is a property of the Worksheet object. There are several ways to identify a Range, but here's the basic syntax of the Range method:

```
Worksheet.Range(cell1:cell2)
```

Here, *cell1* and *cell2* are the addresses of the two cells that delimit a rectangular area on the worksheet—the top-left and bottom-right corners of the selection. In this section, we are going to use the standard Excel notation, which is a number for the row and a letter for the column—for example, C3 or A103. To select the 10×10 top-left section of the active Worksheet, use the expression:

```
Worksheet.Range("A1:J10")
```

To retrieve a single cell as a Range object, use the Cells method, whose syntax is:

```
Worksheet.Cells(row, col)
```

The Range property is an object, and among the properties it exposes is the Range property. The `Range.Range` property is a relative reference to another cell. In the following code segment, the first line returns the cell D8. The second line returns a cell that is three columns to the right and five rows down from the previous cell—that is, G13:

```
range1 = Worksheet.Range(4, 8)
range2 = range1.Range(3, 5)
```

The second line can also be written as:

```
range2 = range1.Range("C5")
```

Finally, the Rows and Columns methods return an entire row or column by number. The following expressions return the third row and the fourth column as Row and Column objects, respectively:

```
Worksheet.Rows(3)
Worksheet.Columns("D")
```

The Row object contains a single row, and you can access this row's cells with the Cells property, which accepts as argument a single coordinate—the cell's order in the row. The same is true for columns. The following statement retrieves the third cell in the second row:

```
Console.WriteLine(WSheet.Rows(2).Cells(3).Text)
```

The Range object is not a collection, but you can access individual cells in a Range object through its Cells method. The Cells method accepts as arguments the row and column coordinates of a cell and returns its value. The indices are 1-based. The `Cells(i, j).Text` property returns the cell's contents as a string, and the `Cells(i, j).Value` property returns the cell's contents as a string (if it's text) or as a numeric value (if it's numeric).

Another way to work with cells is to make a selection and access the properties and methods of the Selection object. To create a Selection object (which represents the cells that are highlighted with the mouse when Excel's window is visible), use the Range object's Select method:

```
Range("A2:D2").Select
```

This statement creates a new Selection object. You can also assign names to the ranges and access them later in your code by their names. The following statement selects the same range as the preceding one and names it:

```
myRange = Range("A2:D2").Select
```

Because a worksheet has only one selection, you don't have to specify any arguments. To change the appearance of the selection, for instance, use the Font property:

```
Selection.Font.Bold = True
Selection.Font.Size = 13
```

Notice that the selection is always rectangular; you can't select nonadjoining cells on a worksheet. However, you can specify an area consisting of multiple ranges. The following statements combine two different ranges with the Union method and assign them to a new Range object:

```
Set Titles = Worksheet.Range ("A1:A10")
Set Totals = Worksheet.Range ("A100:A110")
Set CommonRange = Union(Titles, Totals)
CommonRange.Font.Bold = True
```

The Union method returns a Range object, which you can use to manipulate all the cells in the *Titles* and *Totals* ranges together. For example, you can apply common formatting to all the cells in the *CommonRange* object, as shown above.

THE MEMBERS OF THE RANGE OBJECT

The Range object provides a large number of properties and methods, which can't be discussed in the context of this chapter. One basic property is the Cells property, which is a collection of the cells that make up the current range. The first cell in the Range is `Range.Cells(1, 1)`, and the last is

```
Range.Cells(Range.Cells.Rows, Range.Cells.Columns)
```

All of Excel's collections are 1-based, rather than 0-based.

You can also access an entire row or column in the selection with the EntireRow and EntireColumn properties. These properties are also objects, and they expose a Cells property, similar to the Row and Column objects. To access an individual cell in either collection, use a single index. The Horizontal-Alignment and VerticalAlignment properties let you specify how the cells' contents will be aligned in available space. Look up the corresponding enumerations in the Object Browser to find out the possible settings for these properties.

The Clear method resets all the cells of the Range object, and the Copy method creates a copy of the Range object. If you want to fill a Range with identical values, use the methods FillDown, FillLeft, FillRight, and FillUp.

You can also sort the cells in a Range object by calling its Sort method, which rearranges the rows in the Range object according to the sorting criteria. Its syntax is:

```
Sort(key1, order1, key2, type, order2, key3, order3, header, orderCustom, _
    matchCase, orientation, sortMethod)
```

The arguments of the Sort method allow you to specify the same settings you would normally specify through Excel's Sort dialog box, shown in Figure 10.3. To bring up this dialog box in Excel, select a range of cells, and choose the Data ➢ Sort command.

FIGURE 10.3

The Sort method's arguments specify the same settings as this dialog box.

key1, key2, and *key3* are the columns according to which the range will be sorted. If you specify more than one column, the range will be sorted according to the *key1* column. Rows with identical values in this column will then be sorted according to the *key2* column. The *order1, order2,* and *order3* arguments determine the sort order of the three key columns. Their values are members of the XLSortOrder enumeration and can be set to xlAscending (the default) or xlDescending.

The *type* argument specifies which cells will be sorted and is used only when sorting PivotTables. Its value can be one of the following members of the XLSortType enumeration: xlSortLabels or xlSortValues. The *header* determines whether the first row should be treated as a header row or not; header rows are not sorted. This argument is one of the following members of the XLYesNoGuess enumeration: xlGuess, xlNo, or xlYes. The *orientation* argument, finally, lets you determine whether you want to sort rows (xlSortRows, which is the default value) or columns (xlSortColumns).

To sort the first 20 columns and 2 rows of the first worksheet, use the following statements:

```
Worksheets.("Sheet1").Range("A1:C20").Sort _
    Key1:=Worksheets("Sheet1").Range("A1"), _
    Key2:=Worksheets("Sheet1").Range("B1")
```

In the section "The ExcelDemo Project," later in this chapter, you'll find a demonstration of the Sort method.

THE USEDRANGE OBJECT

Another useful member of the Excel object model is the UsedRange object, which represents a rectangular section of the active worksheet containing all the non-empty cells. The UsedRange object is a Range object and exposes all the members of the Range object. The Rows and Columns properties are collections that contain the UsedRange object's rows and columns, respectively. The number of columns and rows are given by the properties `UsedRange.Columns.Count` and `UsedRange.Rows.Count`, and the total number of used cells is given by `UsedRange.Cells.Count`. To access these cells, use the expression `UsedRange.Cells(row, col)`; you can't use the A1 notation with the Cells collection.

To iterate through all the non-empty cells on the current worksheet, use the following loop. This loop scans the cells of *myRange* row by row and prints the indices and value of each cell in the Output window:

```
Dim myRange As Excel.Range = Wsheet.UsedRange
Dim row, col As Integer
For row = 1 To myRange.Rows.count
   For col = 1 To myRange.Columns.count
      Console.WriteLine("[" & row & ", " & col & " : " & _
                        myRange.cells(row, col).value & "]")
   Next
Next
```

Of course, not all the cells in the UsedRange are non-empty; some of them may be empty. All cells outside the UsedRange, however, are empty.

In the following section, we are going to create a new spreadsheet from within a Visual Basic application, insert data and formulas, and then print the document.

VB.NET AT WORK: THE EXCELDEMO PROJECT

The ExcelDemo application's Create Spreadsheet button demonstrates how to access a worksheet, populate it with data, and then format the data (see Figure 10.4). The program starts by setting the *AppExcel* object variable, which references the Excel application.

FIGURE 10.4

Contacting Excel's object model from within a VB application

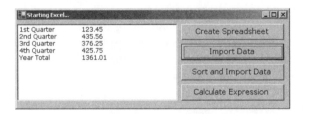

The new spreadsheet is populated and formatted with the statements shown in Listing 10.9. The code uses the Cells collection to access individual cells and assign their values. To format a group of cells, it creates a Range object that contains all the cells to be formatted alike, selects the range, and then manipulates the cells through the Selection object. Finally, it uses the UsedRange object to print the values of all non-empty cells in the Output window.

LISTING 10.9: PREPARING A NEW SPREADSHEET

```
Dim EXL As New Excel.Application()
Private Sub Button1_Click(ByVal sender As System.Object, _
            ByVal e As System.EventArgs) Handles Button1.Click
    If EXL Is Nothing Then
        MsgBox("Couldn't start Excel")
        Exit Sub
    End If
    Dim WSheet As New excel.Worksheet()
    WSheet = EXL.Workbooks.Add.Worksheets.Add
    With WSheet
        .Cells(2, 1).Value = "1st Quarter"
        .Cells(2, 2).Value = "2nd Quarter"
        .Cells(2, 3).Value = "3rd Quarter"
        .Cells(2, 4).Value = "4th Quarter"
        .Cells(2, 5).Value = "Year Total"
        .Cells(3, 1).Value = 123.45
        .Cells(3, 2).Value = 435.56
        .Cells(3, 3).Value = 376.25
        .Cells(3, 4).Value = 425.75
        .Range("A2:E2").Select()
        With EXL.Selection.Font
            .Name = "Verdana"
            .FontStyle = "Bold"
            .Size = 12
        End With
    End With
    WSheet.Range("A2:E2").Select()
    EXL.Selection.Columns.AutoFit()
    WSheet.Range("A2:E2").Select()
    With EXL.Selection
        .HorizontalAlignment = Excel.XlHAlign.xlHAlignCenter
    End With
' Format numbers
    WSheet.Range("A3:E3").Select()
    With EXL.Selection.Font
        .Name = "Verdana"
        .FontStyle = "Regular"
        .Size = 11
    End With
    WSheet.Cells(3, 5).Value = "=Sum(A3:D3)"
    Dim R As Excel.Range
    R = WSheet.UsedRange
    Dim row, col As Integer
    For col = 1 To R.Columns.count
        For row = 1 To R.Rows.count
```

```
                TextBox1.AppendText (R.cells(row, col).value & vbTab)
        Next
        TextBox1.AppendText(vbCrLf)
    Next
End Sub
```

While the worksheet is being populated and formatted, Excel is running in the background.
Users can't see Excel, although they will notice activity (the disk is spinning, and the pointer assumes
an hourglass shape for several seconds).

After the grid is populated, we can read the values from the spreadsheet and displays them in two
columns on the TextBox control of the ExcelDemo form. To read the data, you can use different
technique. The code in Listing 10.10 creates a selection on the spreadsheet and then brings it into
the Visual Basic application in a single move. The selected cells are read into the *CData* object
with the following statements:

```
AppExcel.Range("A2:E3").Select
Set CData = AppExcel.Selection
```

CData is a Range object that holds the selected cells. Then you can use straight VB code to iterate
through the elements of the *CData* object and create the two columns of text, shown in Figure 10.5.

LISTING 10.10: IMPORTING DATA FROM EXCEL

```
Private Sub Button2_Click(ByVal sender As System.Object, _
            ByVal e As System.EventArgs) Handles Button2.Click
    TextBox1.Clear()
    Dim WSheet As New Excel.Worksheet()
    WSheet = EXL.Workbooks.Open("C:\TEST.XLS").Worksheets.Item(1)
    EXL.Range("A2:E3").Select()
    Dim CData As Excel.Range
    CData = EXL.Selection
    Dim iCol, iRow As Integer
    For iCol = 1 To 5
        For iRow = 0 To 1
            TextBox1.AppendText(CData(iRow, iCol).value & vbTab
        Next
        TextBox1.AppendText(vbCrLf)
    Next
    EXL.Workbooks.Close()
End Sub
```

The ExcelDemo project also demonstrates how to use the Sort method (Listing 10.11), even
though the range is too small. We'll treat the 10 cells on the worksheet as a range and sort them
according to the values in the first column.

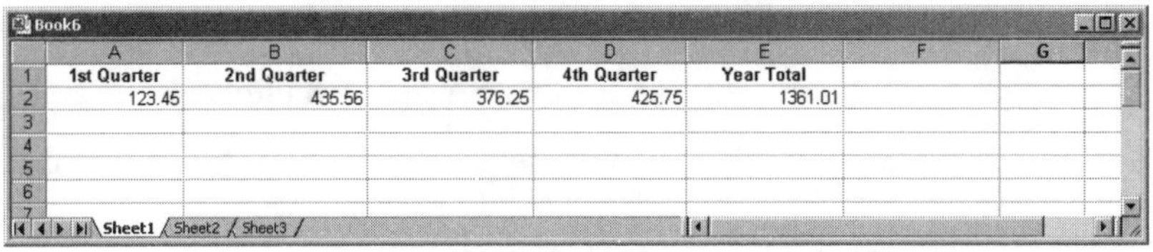

FIGURE 10.5

This spreadsheet was created by the Excel-Demo application, using Excel's objects.

LISTING 10.11: THE SORT AND IMPORT DATA BUTTON

```
Private Sub Button3_Click(ByVal sender As System.Object, _
                 ByVal e As System.EventArgs) Handles Button3.Click
    Dim WSheet As New Excel.Worksheet()
    WSheet = EXL.Workbooks.Open("C:\TEST.XLS").Worksheets.Item(1)
    EXL.Range("A2:E3").Select()
    Dim CData As Excel.Range
    CData = EXL.Selection
    CData.Sort(Key1:=CData.Range("A2"), order1:=Excel.XLSortOrder.xlAscending)
    TextBox1.Clear()
    Dim iCol, iRow As Integer
    For iCol = 1 To 5
        For iRow = 0 To 1
            TextBox1.AppendText(CData(iRow, iCol).value & vbTab)
        Next
        TextBox1.AppendText(vbCrLf)
    Next
    EXL.Workbooks.Close()
End Sub
```

If you change the *order1* argument's value to Excel.XLSortOrder.xlDescending, the rows won't be rearranged, because they happen to already be in descending order. You can add more rows to the worksheet and sort a larger range. You should also set the *header* argument to Excel.XLYesNoGuess.xlYes, so that the first row will be treated as header and won't be sorted along with the other rows.

To sort the same range by column, specify the *orientation* argument to the Sort method. To experiment with the various sort options, change the call to the Sort method in the previous listing to the following:

```
CData.Sort(Key1:=CData.Range("A2"), order1:=Excel.XlSortOrder.xlAscending, _
        orientation:=Excel.XlSortOrientation.xlSortRows)
```

If you print the values of the UsedRange without sorting, they will appear on the TextBox in the following order:

1st Quarter	2nd Quarter	3rd Quarter	4th Quarter	Year Total
123.45	435.56	376.25	425.75	1361.01

If you sort them by rows, which is the default sort order, the columns will be swapped as follows:

1st Quarter	3rd Quarter	4th Quarter	2nd Quarter	Year Total
123.45	376.25	425.75	435.56	1361.01

Using Excel as a Math Parser

Earlier in this chapter, you learned how to borrow the spell-checking capabilities of Word. Now, we'll do something similar with Excel. Excel is a great tool for doing math. At the same time, Visual Basic doesn't provide a function or method for calculating math expressions supplied by the user at runtime. If Excel is installed on the host computer, you can contact it from within your VB application and use it to evaluate complicated math expressions.

The simplest method to calculate a math expression is to call the Evaluate method of the Excel.Application object. Assuming you've initialized the *ExcelApp* object variable, you can calculate a math expression like

```
1/cos(0.335)*cos(12.45)
```

by calling the *ExcelApp* object's Evaluate method and passing the expression as a string argument:

```
y = ExcelApp.Evaluate("1/cos(0.335)*cos(12.45)")
```

The Calculate Expression button on the ExcelDemo project's form does exactly that with the statements shown in Listing 10.12.

LISTING 10.12: CALCULATING AN EXCEL EXPRESSION

```
Private Sub Button3_Click(ByVal sender As System.Object, _
              ByVal e As System.EventArgs) Handles Button3.Click
Dim mathStr As String
    mathStr = InputBox("Enter math expression to evaluate", , _
                      "cos(3.673/4)/exp(-3.333)")
    If mathStr <> "" Then
      Try
         MsgBox(EXL.Evaluate(mathStr).ToString)
      Catch exc As Exception
         MsgBox(exc.Message)
      End Try
    End If
End Sub
```

The code in Listing 10.12 prompts the user to enter any math expression at runtime. Calculating arbitrary math expressions supplied at runtime with straight Visual Basic code is quite difficult.

Another technique to calculate math expressions with Excel is to prefix the expression with the equal sign (=) and assign the entire expression to a cell. Excel will assign the result of the calculation to the cell, and if you read back the value of the same cell, it will be a number and not the actual expression you supplied.

```
Dim expression As String = "1/cos(0.335)*cos(12.45) "
wSheet.Cells(1, 1).Value = "=" & expression
wSheet.Calculate
result = wSheet.Cells(1, 1).Value
MsgBox("The value of the expression " & expression & vbCrLf & " is " & result)
```

NOTE   *Using Excel to evaluate simple expressions may seem like overkill, but if you consider that Visual Basic doesn't provide the tools for evaluating expressions at runtime, automating Excel is not such a bad idea. This is especially true if you want to evaluate complicated expressions and calculate the statistics of large data sets.*

Programming Outlook

Incorporating e-mail capabilities into your applications is a common feature in today's applications. To make your applications e-mail–aware, you can program Outlook's objects. In this section, you'll learn how to mail-enable your Visual Basic applications by manipulating the object model of Outlook. Outlook isn't a simple mail client. It maintains a list of contacts organized in folders; the contacts may contain a lot of information (from physical addresses to anniversary dates), even information about meetings. You will also learn how to write applications that automatically process, and even reply to, messages. Many corporations use Outlook to automate common tasks like appointment scheduling and routing e-mail. Because of the variety of tasks that can be performed from within Outlook's environment, you should learn the basics of programming its objects.

To contact Outlook and program the objects it exposes, you must first create a variable that represents the application itself, such as the *OLApp* variable:

```
Dim OLApp As New Outlook.Application
```

Unlike Word and Excel, Outlook doesn't expose a single object like a Document or Worksheet that gives you access to the information it can handle. Outlook contains several objects including mail messages, contacts, and tasks. The most likely candidate to use as the basic unit of information in Outlook is a folder. Depending on the operation you want to perform with Outlook, you must first select the appropriate folder in the Shortcuts bar. For example, to view the incoming e-mail messages, you must select the Inbox folder; to add a contact, you must first select the Contacts folder. You can't expect to find information about your contacts in the Inbox folder or the unread messages in the Calendar folder. Since every operation in Outlook is initiated with the selection of the proper folder, the various folders of the application are the top-level objects.

To access the folder objects, you must create a MAPI message store. A *MAPI message store* is a data source that provides all types of information that can be stored by Outlook. If you've used Outlook before, you know that it's essentially a front end for a database that can store many different types of information. To access this information, you must create a Namespace object variable with the following statements:

```
Dim OLApp As New Outlook.Application()
Dim OLNameSpace As Outlook.Namespace
OLNameSpace = OLApp.GetNamespace("MAPI")
```

The first statement that declares the *OLApp* variable should appear outside any procedure, so it can be used by all the procedures in your project. Through the *OLNameSpace* variable, you can access the various folders and other objects of Outlook. The method for accessing a folder is the GetDefault-Folder method, which accepts the name of the folder as argument and returns an object variable. The object variable returned by GetDefaultFolder method provides properties and methods that give your application access to the items stored in the folder.

The various folders maintained by Outlook can be accessed with the following constants (their names are self-explanatory, and they're all members of the OLDefaultFolders enumeration):

olFolderCalendar	olFolderInbox	olFolderOutbox
olFolderContacts	olFolderJournal	olFolderSentMail
olFolderDeletedItems	olFolderNotes	olFolderTask
olFolderDrafts		

To retrieve all the items in the Contacts folder, use the following statement:

```
Set allContacts = OLNameSpace.GetDefaultFolder(olFolderContacts).Items
```

The Items property returns a collection that contains all the items in the specified folder. The *allContacts* variable must be declared as:

```
Dim allContacts As Outlook.MAPIFolder
```

Each folder contains different types of information. The Contacts folder is made up of Contact-Item objects, the Inbox and Outbox folders contain MailItem objects, and the Calendar folder contains a collection of AppointmentItem objects. Each one of these objects provides numerous properties, which are the attributes of the item it represents. For example, a ContactItem object provides properties for setting just about any attribute of a contact (name, address, e-mail, and so on).

To see the properties of the ContactItem object, open the Object Browser, expand the Interop .Outlook item and locate the entry ContactItem as shown in Figure 10.6. The properties of the selected object will appear in the right pane, and the specific object provides a large number of properties. The properties you'll use most often in your applications are LastName, FirstName, Email1Address, Title, and the properties that begin with HomeAddress and BusinessAddress. These are the fields you can set in the Contact dialog box when you add or edit a contact with Outlook. If you need additional fields, you can create your own custom properties. (These are also accessed by name, but I'm not going to discuss them here. You should see Outlook's Help files for more information on adding custom properties.)

A property that's common to all items is the EntryID property, which is a string value that uniquely identifies each item. EntryID values are similar to IDs you assign to the various records in a database (they identify the record, but they have no other apparent meaning). Of course, you can't have the user select a contact or message based on its EntryID—it makes much more sense to present a list of names or companies to select from—but you can use them to bookmark items. You'll see how the EntryID property is used in the examples of the following sections. Basically, we use a meaningful field to display information (like an e-mail address or sender's name), and we keep track of the current contact or message by its EntryID property. The Namespace object exposes the GetFolderByID and GetItemByID methods; you will see shortly how these two methods are used along with EntryID.

FIGURE 10.6

The properties of
the ContactItem
object

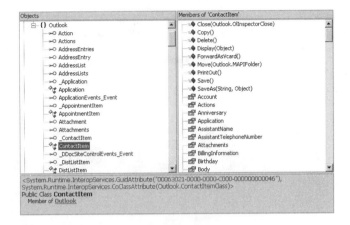

Retrieving Information

Outlook stores different types of information in different folders. Outlook's folders do not correspond to physical folders on the disk; they're just the basic organizational units of Outlook. Contact information is stored in the Contacts folder, incoming messages are stored in the Inbox folder, and so on. Most users, however, customize Outlook's folder structure by adding subfolders to the default folders. To organize your contacts, for instance, you can create the Business and Personal subfolders under the Contacts folder. Likewise, you can create Business, Personal, and Junk folders under the Inbox folder.

In the following sections, you'll learn how to extract contacts and messages from the corresponding folders. The process of extracting information stored in Outlook's folders is straightforward: we retrieve the contents of the appropriate folder, and then we extract the information we want by calling their properties. If the item is a message, you can retrieve its subject with the Subject property. If the item is a contact, you can retrieve the company of the contact with the CompanyName name property. The properties supported by each item are listed automatically in the code editor when needed, so I won't repeat them here.

The examples of the following sections deal with the Inbox and Contacts folders. Outlook supports other folders as well, which are not discussed in this chapter.

VB.NET AT WORK: THE CONTACTS PROJECT

The first example of programming Outlook's objects is the Contacts application, whose form is shown in Figure 10.7. The Contacts application assumes that all contact items are stored in the Contacts folder. If you've organized your contacts differently—perhaps in subfolders under the Contacts folder—copy a few contacts temporarily to the Contacts folder so that you can test the application. Later, in the section "Recursive Scanning of the Contacts Folder," you'll see how you can scan the entire Contacts folder recursively, including its subfolders.

The Contact project's main form contains two lists. The first list is populated with company names, which are read from the contact items. This list doesn't contain any duplicate entries, even though a typical Contacts folder contains multiple contacts from the same company. To view the

FIGURE 10.7

Demonstrating how
to retrieve contact
items from Out-
look's Contacts
folder

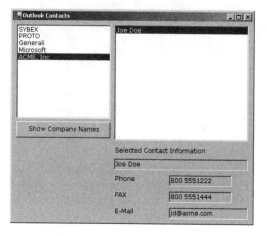

contacts in a company, double-click the company's name and the corresponding contacts will appear in the second ListBox control Then, each time you click a contact name, more information about the selected contact will be displayed in the lower half of the form.

First, you must declare a variable that represents the Outlook application, as well as a Namespace variable, with the following statements. All other objects can be accessed through these two variables.

```
Dim OutlookApp As New Outlook.Application()
Dim OLNameSpace As Outlook.Namespace
```

In addition, we need one more variable to store the contacts. This variable is also declared on the form, with the following statement:

```
Dim allContacts As Outlook.MAPIFolder
```

When the Show Company Names button is clicked, the program creates a collection with all the items in the Contacts folder, the *allContacts* collection, and then sorts it according to the company name. The list doesn't contains duplicate names (we use the Contains method of the Items collection to find out whether a company name exists in the list before adding it). The code of the Show Company Names button is detailed in Listing 10.13.

LISTING 10.13: POPULATING THE COMPANIES LIST

```
Private Sub Button1_Click(ByVal sender As System.Object, _
            ByVal e As System.EventArgs) Handles Button1.Click
    OLNameSpace = OutlookAPP.GetNamespace("MAPI")
    allContacts = OLNameSpace.GetDefaultFolder _
            (Outlook.OLDefaultFolders.olFolderContacts)
    allContacts.Items.Sort("CompanyName")
    Dim contact As Outlook.ContactItem
    Dim cnt As Integer
    ContactKeys.Clear()
    ListBox2.Items.Clear()
```

```
      For cnt = 1 To allContacts.Items.Count
          contact = allContacts.Items.Item(cnt)
          If contact.CompanyName <> "" Then
              If Not ListBox1.Items.Contains(contact.CompanyName) Then
                  ListBox1.Items.Add(contact.CompanyName)
              End If
          End If
      Next
  End Sub
```

The code that retrieves the contacts for the company selected on the left must be placed in the ListBox control's SelectedIndexChanged event. This event handler (Listing 10.14) applies the Restrict method to the *allContacts* collection, which selects only the items meeting the specified criteria. In our case, the criterion is that the contact's CompanyName field is the same as the selected item on the list. For more information on specifying selection criteria, see the section "Filtering Messages," later in this chapter.

LISTING 10.14: SELECTING CONTACTS FROM A COMPANY

```
  Private Sub ListBox1_SelectedIndexChanged(ByVal sender As System.Object, _
                  ByVal e As System.EventArgs) _
                  Handles ListofCompanies.SelectedIndexChanged
      Dim contacts As Outlook._Items
      contacts = allContacts.Items.Restrict("[CompanyName]='" & _
                                          ListofCompanies.Text & "'")
      Dim contact As Outlook.ContactItem
      Dim cnt As Integer
      ListofContacts.Items.Clear()
      ContactKeys.Clear()
      For cnt = 1 To contacts.Count
          contact = contacts.Item(cnt)
          If contact.Email1Address <> "" Then
              If (Not ListofContacts.Items.Contains(contact.Email1Address)) Then
                  ListofContacts.Items.Add(contact.Email1Address)
                  ContactKeys.Add(contact.EntryID)
              End If
          End If
      Next
  End Sub
```

This subroutine makes use of the Restrict method, which accepts a filter expression as argument. The filter is applied to the items of a specific folder and selects the items that meet the criteria. The items are then returned as a collection—in our example, a collection of ContactItem items. The items in the folder are not affected; if you apply another filter, you'll get back the items that create a new collection. It simply hides the items that don't meet the specified criteria.

To display additional information about a contact, the code shown in Listing 10.15 needs to be executed from within the second ListBox control's Click event. This code retrieves the selected contact by its ID and displays selected fields in the TextBoxes at the bottom of the form.

LISTING 10.15: DISPLAYING CONTACT INFORMATION

```
Private Sub ListBox2_SelectedIndexChanged(ByVal sender As Object, _
          ByVal e As System.EventArgs) Handles ListBox2.SelectedIndexChanged
   Dim contact As Outlook.ContactItem
   contact = OLNameSpace.GetItemFromID (ContactKeys(ListBox2.SelectedIndex))
   txtFullName.Text = contact.FullName
   txtTel.Text = contact.BusinessTelephoneNumber
   txtFAX.Text = contact.BusinessFaxNumber
End Sub
```

The Contacts project has a serious drawback: it assumes that all the contacts are in the Contacts folder. If they're organized in folders under the Contacts folder, then only the contacts in the top-level folder will be processed. Later in this chapter, you will see how to scan the Contacts folder, including its subfolders.

VB.NET AT WORK: THE MESSAGES PROJECT

The Messages project demonstrates some techniques for retrieving mail items. Messages are stored in the Inbox and Outbox folders, as well as any custom folders created under these by the user. The Messages example retrieves the messages from the Inbox folder only. If you don't have any messages in this folder, temporarily move some incoming messages from your custom folders to the Inbox folder to test the application. Later in the chapter, you'll see how to retrieve all the messages under Inbox, including its subfolders nested to any depth.

The Messages application (shown in Figure 10.8) lets you select messages based on their sender or the date they were sent. The user can specify the criteria with the controls on the top-right section of the form and then click the Show Selected Messages button to display the messages that meet the criteria in the Selected Messages ListBox. The program displays only each message's sender and subject on the ListBox control to the right. Then, when the user clicks a message on this list, more information is displayed in the controls in the lower half of the form (including the message's body). If the message contains attachments, the names of the attached files are displayed in a message box. Run the project and experiment with it.

There are two issues you should be aware of. First, the Messages application can see only the messages in the Inbox folder. If you've organized your messages into subfolders under the Inbox folder, you must temporarily move a few messages to the Inbox folder. The second issue is that the sender names are read from the Contacts folder. If the names in the Contacts folder don't match the names that appear in the messages, then you won't see the messages sent by the selected contact.

FIGURE 10.8

Demonstrating how to read Outlook's incoming messages from within VB applications

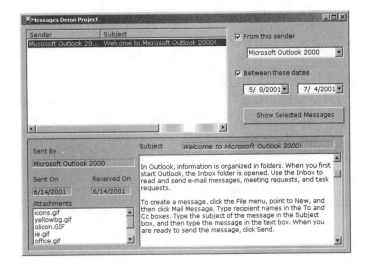

The Application's Code

In the form's Load event, we create two object variables: *OLApp* references the Outlook application and *OLObjects* references Outlook's folders. These variables are declared on the Form level with the following statements:

```
Dim OLApp As Application
Dim OLObjects As Outlook.NameSpace
```

Then the code sets up the *InBox* variable, where the messages in the Inbox folder will be stored. This variable is also declared outside any procedure, with the following statement:

```
Dim InBox As outlook.MAPIFolder
```

The code scans all the messages in the Inbox folder and adds the sender's name to the ComboBox control on the right. The Sorted property of the ComboBox control is set to True, and the code doesn't add duplicate entries (it uses the Contains method of the Items collection to find out whether the contact exists in the list or not). The bulk of the statements of Listing 10.16 are executed from within the form's Load event handler.

LISTING 10.16: INITIALIZING THE MESSAGES PROJECT

```
Dim OutlookApp As New outlook.Application()
Dim InBox As outlook.MAPIFolder
Dim OLObjects As Outlook.Namespace

Private Sub Form1_Load(ByVal sender As Object, ByVal e As System.EventArgs) _
            Handles MyBase.Load
   OLObjects = OutlookApp.GetNamespace("MAPI")
```

```
    InBox = OLObjects.GetDefaultFolder(Outlook.OLDefaultFolders.olFolderInbox)
    Dim mssg As Outlook.MailItem
    Dim imssg As Integer
    For imssg = 1 To InBox.Items.Count
        mssg = InBox.Items.Item(imssg)
        If Not mssg.SenderName Is Nothing Then
            If Not ComboBox1.Items.Contains(mssg.SenderName) Then
                ComboBox1.Items.Add(mssg.SenderName)
            End If
        End If
    Next
    ComboBox1.Sorted = True
    ComboBox1.SelectedIndex = 0
End Sub
```

FILTERING MESSAGES

The user can select a name and/or a date range to limit the selected messages. If the check boxes "From this sender" and "Between these dates" are cleared, then clicking the Show Selected Messages button will display all the messages in the Inbox folder on the ListView control on the left. We haven't discussed yet the ListView control, but you can think of it as ListBox control with multiple columns. Each item has a Text property, which is the string of the first column, and a SubItems property, which is a collection. If you check either or both check boxes, then the program will display only the messages that meet the specified criteria.

To filter the messages, use the Restrict method of the Items collection. This method accepts an expression that filters some messages and returns only the messages you're interested in. The syntax of the Restrict method is Restrict(filterstring), where *filterstring* is an expression that specifies the desired criteria. The Restrict method returns a collection of items: the items of the original collection that meet the criteria. The original collection doesn't change, and you can retrieve a different collection from it by applying another filter expression.

The *filterstring* argument is a string expression that combines field names, logical operators, and values. To retrieve the messages sent by "Site Builder Network", use the following string:

```
"[SenderName] = " 'Site Builder Network' "
```

To retrieve all messages sent in October 2000, use the following string:

```
"[SentOn] => " '10/01/00' " And [SentOn] <= " '10/31/00' "
```

(The single quotes are used to embed quotes within quotes. You can also use two consecutive double quotes in the string to indicate an embedded double quote.)

You can combine as many fields as needed with the usual comparison and logical operators. The field names for each item type can be found in the Object Browser. Select the desired item (e.g., MailItem, ContactItem) and look up its properties in the Members pane.

In the Messages project, you use the values of various controls on the form to build the filter string as follows. First, you validate the dates, then you build the filter string with the following statements:

```
If chkSender.Checked Then
    filter = "[SenderName]='" & ComboBox1.Text & "'"
End If
If chkDates.Checked Then
    If filter <> "" Then filter = filter & " And "
    filter = filter & "[SentOn] > '" & DateTimePicker1.Value.ToShortDateString & _
            "' And [SentOn] <= '" & DateTimePicker2.Value.ToShortDateString & "'"
End If
If filter <> "" Then
    selMessages = InBox.Items.Restrict(filter)
Else
    selMessages = InBox.Items
End If
```

Notice the placement of the single quotes in the expressions. If the selected string on the ComboBox1 control is "Sybex", then the statement:

```
"[SenderName] = '" & ContactName & "'"
```

will produce the following string:

```
[SenderName] = 'Sybex'
```

The *filter* variable is built slowly, according to the values entered by the user on the Form. If the user specifies a name, the SenderName property is set to the appropriate value. If the user specifies dates, the SentOn property is set accordingly.

The *filter* variable is then passed to the Restrict method of the InBox.Items collection. Then the program loops through the selected messages, which are the items of the *selMessages* collection. At each iteration, another message's sender and subject are displayed on a ListView control. I have used the ListView control to store the subjects of the messages and their sender, because I could also store the ID of the messages in a hidden column (a column with a width of 0 pixels). Here are the statements that display the filtered messages.

```
Dim mssg As Outlook.MailItem
Dim imssg As Integer
Dim itm As ListViewItem
For imssg = 1 To selMessages.Count
    mssg = selMessages.Item(imssg)
    itm = New ListViewItem()
    itm.Text = mssg.SenderName
    itm.SubItems.Add(mssg.Subject)
    itm.SubItems.Add(mssg.EntryID)
    ListView1.Items.Add(itm)
    itm = Nothing
Next
```

The rest of the code is straightforward. When an item on the ListView control is clicked, the program recalls the selected item and displays its basic entries in the corresponding Label controls at the bottom of the screen and its body in the TextBox control (whose ReadOnly property must be set to True to prevent editing of the message). Listing 10.17 is the ListView control's Selected-IndexChanged event handler.

LISTING 10.17: VIEWING A MESSAGE ITEM

```
Private Sub ListView1_SelectedIndexChanged(ByVal sender As System.Object, _
        ByVal e As System.EventArgs) Handles ListView1.SelectedIndexChanged
    Dim selID As String
    If ListView1.SelectedItems.Count() = 0 Then Exit Sub
    txtMessage.Text = ""
    selID = ListView1.SelectedItems(0).SubItems(2).Text
    Dim mssg As Outlook.MailItem
    mssg = OLObjects.GetItemFromID(selID)
    txtMessage.Text = mssg.Body
    lblSubject.Text = mssg.Subject
    lblSender.Text = mssg.SenderName
    lblSentOn.Text = mssg.SentOn.ToShortDateString
    lblRecvdOn.Text = mssg.ReceivedTime.ToShortDateString
    Dim i As Integer
    lstAttachments.Items.Clear()
    For i = 1 To mssg.Attachments.Count
        lstAttachments.Items.Add(mssg.Attachments.Item(i).FileName)
    Next
End Sub
```

Open the Messages project in the Visual Basic IDE to examine its code and see how it combines the items of the Contacts folder and uses them to retrieve mail items from the Inbox folder. You can modify the code to add more selection criteria or to work with different folders (for example, the Outbox folder or a subfolder under the Inbox folder).

WARNING   The Messages project uses the FullName property of the contacts to display the names of possible message senders. If the names you've used in the Contacts folder are not the same as the sender names in the incoming messages, then the program won't select all the messages as you'd expect. There are many methods for matching contacts and messages, but they require additional effort. For example, you can use each contact's e-mail address, which is the same in both the Contacts and Inbox folders. However, contacts may have multiple e-mail addresses, so you must make sure you search the mail items for all e-mail addresses (aliases) of the selected contact.

Recursive Scanning of the Contacts Folder

The Contacts project of the previous section assumes that all contacts are stored in the Contacts folder (likewise, the other projects assume that all messages reside in a single folder). This may be the case for users with a small number of contacts (or totally unorganized users), but it's not common. Most users organize their contacts in subfolders to better classify them and simplify searching. Scanning a Contacts folder with subfolders is not as simple. This operation calls for *recursive programming*. If you thought that the chapter on recursive programming was uncalled for in an introductory book, this is another attestation to its usefulness. The topic of recursive programming is discussed in detail in Chapter 18. In *this* chapter, I'll explain the code as we go along, but if you're totally unfamiliar with this programming technique, you should read the material on recursion first and you'll find it easier to understand the code of this section.

VB.NET AT WORK: THE ALLCONTACTS PROJECT

The application that demonstrates how to recursively scan the Contacts folder is called AllContacts and can be found in this chapter's folder on the CD. The TreeView control with the names of all subfolders under the Contacts folder is populated when the form is loaded (see Figure 10.9). Expand the various folders on the TreeView control, and click a folder's name to see its contact items in the ListBox control on the right.

FIGURE 10.9

Populating the Tree-View control with the names of the subfolders

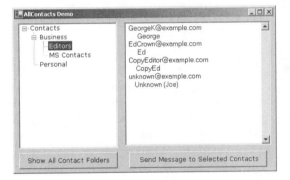

THE PROJECT'S CODE

Let's start with the trivial code. First, declare the following object variables, which are used by most procedures:

```
Dim OutlookApp As New Outlook.Application()
Dim OlObjects As Outlook.Namespace
Dim OlContacts As Outlook.MAPIFolder
```

Then, in the Show All Contact Folders button's Click event handler, enter the statements of Listing 10.18 to instantiate the *OlObjects* and *OlContacts* variables, needed to access the folders of Outlook. This code adds the root node to the TreeView control—the root node being the Contacts folder—and all the first-level subfolders under it. Each time a new subfolder is added to the TreeView control, the code calls the ScanSubFolders() subroutine, passing the current folder as argument. The ScanSubFolders() subroutine iterates through the subfolders of the folder passed as argument and adds them to the TreeView control, under the appropriate node.

LISTING 10.18: SCANNING THE SUBFOLDERS OF THE CONTACT FOLDER

```
Private Sub Button1_Click(ByVal sender As System.Object, _
              ByVal e As System.EventArgs) Handles bttnShowContacts.Click
    OlObjects = OutlookApp.GetNamespace("MAPI")
    OlContacts = _
        OlObjects.GetDefaultFolder(Outlook.OlDefaultFolders.olFolderContacts)
    Dim rootNode, newNode As TreeNode
    rootNode = TreeView1.Nodes.Add("Contacts")
    rootNode.Tag = OlContacts.EntryID
    Dim allFolders As Outlook.Folders
    Dim folder As Outlook.MAPIFolder
    allFolders = OlContacts.Folders
    folder = allFolders.GetFirst
    While Not folder Is Nothing
        newNode = rootNode.Nodes.Add(folder.Name)
        ScanSubFolders(folder, newNode)
        folder = allFolders.GetNext
    End While
End Sub
```

Later in our application, we want to be able to retrieve the contacts in any folder, when the user selects the folder. The folder's name is not enough, because it doesn't uniquely identify a folder. All folders have a unique ID, which you can retrieve with the EntryID property. To have this information handy later in code, we store the ID of each folder to the corresponding node's Tag property.

The ScanSubFolders() subroutine (Listing 10.19) iterates through all the subfolders of the folder passed as argument. If any of these subfolders have subfolders of their own, the program calls the ScanSubFolders() subroutine again to scan them. This process is repeated recursively, until the initial folder has been scanned to any depth necessary. At each iteration, the code adds a new folder to the TreeView control and sets the node's Tag property to the ID of the folder. This ID will be extracted later from the Tag property of the selected node and used to retrieve the corresponding folder.

LISTING 10.19: THE SCANSUBFOLDERS() SUBROUTINE

```
Private Sub ScanSubFolders(ByVal currentFolder As outlook.MAPIFolder, _
              ByVal currentNode As TreeNode)
    Dim subfolders As Outlook.Folders
    subfolders = currentFolder.Folders
    Dim parentNode As TreeNode = currentNode
    Dim newNode As TreeNode
    If subfolders.Count > 0 Then
        Dim strFolderKey As String
        Dim subFolder As Outlook.MAPIFolder
        subFolder = subfolders.GetFirst
        While Not subFolder Is Nothing
```

```
            newNode = parentNode.Nodes.Add(subFolder.Name)
            newNode.Tag = subFolder.EntryID
            ScanSubFolders(subFolder, newNode)
            subFolder = subfolders.GetNext
        End While
    End If
End Sub
```

VIEWING A FOLDER'S CONTACTS

After populating the TreeView control with the structure of the subfolders under the Contacts folder, you can select a folder in the TreeView control with the mouse to display its contacts on the ListBox control at the right side of the form. When an item in the TreeView control is clicked, the AfterSelect event is triggered; the code for this is presented in Listing 10.20. This event reports the node clicked, and you can use the event's argument to retrieve the node's tag, which is the ID of the selected folder. Once you know the ID of the selected folder, you can create a reference to this folder (variable *selFolder*) and use it to scan the contact items in the actual folder.

LISTING 10.20: LISTING THE ITEMS OF THE SELECTED FOLDER

```
Private Sub TreeView1_AfterSelect(ByVal sender As System.Object, _
            ByVal e As System.Windows.Forms.TreeViewEventArgs) _
            Handles TreeView1.AfterSelect
    If e.Node.Tag Is Nothing Then Exit Sub
    Dim folderid As String = e.Node.Tag
    Dim selFolder As Outlook.MAPIFolder
    selFolder = OlObjects.GetFolderFromID(folderid)
    Dim itm As Integer
    ListBox1.Items.Clear()
    For itm = 1 To selFolder.Items.Count
        ListBox1.Items.Add(selFolder.Items.Item(itm).Email1Address)
        ListBox1.Items.Add(vbTab & selFolder.Items.Item(itm).FullName)
    Next
End Sub
```

The code displays only the contact's name and e-mail address. You can modify the code to display any fields. For example, you can retrieve the contact's e-mail address and send a message to all the contacts in a specific folder, as we'll do in the last example of the chapter.

AUTOMATED MESSAGES

The Send Message to Selected Contacts button demonstrates how to send a message once the user has picked one or more recipients. The message's subject and body are hard-coded in this project, but you can easily modify the application so that it reads the message's body from a text file. You can also embed keywords into the text file and replace them with the recipient's name, title, address, and so on. The code (Listing 10.21) is short and straightforward, and it's meant to demonstrate the basic steps for automating the creation and dispatch of electronic messages, placing them in the Outbox folder. From there, the message will leave in the same way as the messages you create manually with Outlook.

LISTING 10.21: LISTING THE ITEMS OF THE SELECTED FOLDER

```
Private Sub bttnSend_Click(ByVal sender As System.Object, _
             ByVal e As System.EventArgs) Handles bttnSend.Click
    Dim msg As Outlook.MailItem
    msg = OutlookApp.CreateItem(Outlook.OlItemType.olMailItem)
    Dim iContact As Integer
    For iContact = 0 To ListBox1.SelectedIndices.Count - 1
        msg.Recipients.Add(ListBox1.Items(_
                         ListBox1.SelectedIndices.Item(iContact).ToString)
        msg.Subject = "Automated Message"
        msg.Body = "Enter the message's body here"
        msg.send()
    Next
End Sub
```

First, you must create a new MailItem object, variable *msg*, with the CreateItem method of Outlook. Then you set the fields of the MailItem object. There are many more properties you can set; they will all appear as soon as you enter the name of the variable that represents the MailItem object and the following period. Finally, call the MailItem object's Send method to place it in the Outbox folder, from which it will be sent the next time Outlook sends and receives messages.

Summary

If you add references to the various Office applications in your projects and then open the Object Browser, you'll realize that Word, Excel, and Outlook expose many objects, which in turn, provide numerous properties and methods. Automating Office applications is well within the reach of the average Visual Basic programmer, as long as you familiarize yourself with the objects exposed by these applications (or any other application that exposes an object model).

Part III

Basic Framework Classes

In this section:
- Chapter 11: Storing Data in Collections
- Chapter 12: Handling Strings, Characters, and Dates
- Chapter 13: Working with Folders and Files

Chapter 11

Storing Data in Collections

IN THIS CHAPTER, YOU'RE going to learn how to store sets of objects to structures similar to arrays. One of the most common operations in programming is the storage and manipulation of data. There are databases, of course, which can store any type of information and preserve its structure as well, but not all applications make use of databases. If your application needs to store a few shapes (like the ones you designed in the previous chapter), or a few names and contact information, you shouldn't have to set up a new database. A simple collection like the ones described in this chapter will suffice. Traditionally, arrays were used to store related data and objects. Since arrays can store custom data types (or structures), they seem to be the answer to many data-storage and -manipulation issues. Arrays, however, don't expose all the functionality you may need in your application. To address the issues of data storage outside databases, the .NET Framework provides certain classes known as *collections*.

All collections store sets of related data, and we've already examined a data structure that does the same, the array. Arrays used to be indexed sets of data, and this is how we've explored arrays so far. In this chapter, you're going to find out that VB.NET arrays expose useful members that make arrays extremely flexible. It took Microsoft years to get arrays right, but now you can have arrays that sort themselves, search for an element, and more. In the past, programmers spent endless hours writing code to perform the same operations on arrays, but VB.NET will free them from similar, counterproductive tasks.

There are more types of collections besides arrays, and they're all hosted in the System .Collections class, an assembly exposing many classes that implement collections, like the ArrayList and the HashTable collections. We aren't going to discuss them all in this book, only the most important ones, which are the ArrayList, HashTable, Dictionary, and SortedList. Their functionality overlaps a lot, which may make it difficult to decide which structure to use. The good news is that once you've learned to use one of them, you can easily apply your skills to the others.

Conventional arrays are not implemented by the System.Collections class. They're implemented by the System.Array class, which is not inheritable. This chapter starts with a discussion of the advanced features of the Array class. Once you know how to make the most of arrays, I'll discuss the limitations of arrays, and we'll explore other collections that overcome these limitations.

VB6 ⇢ VB.NET

All the topics discussed in this chapter are new to VB.NET. Arrays have been around since the first version of Visual Basic, but all the features discussed in this chapter, such as sorting and searching arrays, are new to VB.NET. ArrayLists are also new to VB.NET; they're dynamic arrays. Another class, the HashTable, is the evolution of a structure that was known as Dictionary in VB5 and VB6, whose elements are identified not by a number, but by a meaningful key. The basic functionality of the HashTable class is practically identical to that of the Dictionary, but the HashTable has more features, including the ability to sort its elements.

The last topic discussed in this chapter is the ability to specify functions for sorting custom objects in a collection. As you will see, it's quite simple. These functions don't actually sort the collection; they simply compare two elements. Once you provide this functionality, the Framework takes it from there and uses your custom functions to sort and search the collection. This type of close interaction with the inner workings of the language is a powerful feature, totally new to VB programmers.

Advanced Array Topics

In Chapter 3, we explored the basics of arrays—how to declare arrays, how to access elements by index, and a few more elementary topics. VB.NET supports arrays through the Array class, which exposes a whole lot of functionality that wasn't there before. The System.Array class is not inheritable, which means you can't create custom arrays; the classes under System.Collections are inheritable, and you can customize the other collections discussed in this chapter.

But before we explore the more advanced methods exposed by the Array class, let me remind you about the basic array members that are new to VB.NET arrays. The Length property returns the number of elements in the array. In the case of a multidimensional array, the Length property returns the total number of elements in all dimensions. To find out the number of dimensions in an array, call its Rank property. The index of the first element in an array is zero, and the index of the last element is retrieved by the method GetUpperBound. If the array is multidimensional, you must specify the dimension whose upper bound you wish to read. The expression array.GetUpperBound(0) returns the upper bound of the first dimension, and the expression array.GetUpperBound(array.Rank - 1) returns the number of elements in the last dimension of the array. For more information on these members, see the section "Arrays" in Chapter 3.

Sorting Arrays

The most prominent feature of the Array class is that VB.NET arrays can be sorted and searched. To sort an array, call its Sort method. This method is heavily overloaded and, as you will see, it is possible to sort an array based on the values of another array, or even supply your own custom sorting routines. If the array is sorted, you can call the BinarySearch method to locate an element. If not, you can call the IndexOf and LastIndexOf methods.

The simplest form of the Sort method accepts a single argument, which is the name of the array to be sorted:

```
System.Array.Sort(arrayName)
```

This method sorts the elements of the array according to the type of its elements. If the array is not strictly typed, the Sort method will fail. The Array class just doesn't know how to compare integers to strings or dates, so don't attempt to sort arrays whose elements are not of the same type. If you can't be sure that all elements are of the same type, use a Try…Catch statement.

NOTE *The Sort method is a reference method. It requires that you supply the name of the array to be sorted as an argument, even when you're applying the Sort method directly to an array. In other words, the expression* `arrayName.Sort()` *is invalid. You must still pass the name of the array as argument to the Sort method:* `arrayName.Sort(arrayName)`. *I'm using the notation* `System.Array.Sort(arrayName)` *because it's easier to understand. Besides, a statement like* `names.Sort(names)` *just isn't elegant.*

You can also sort a section of the array with the following form of the Sort method:

```
System.Array.Sort(arrayName, startIndex, endIndex)
```

where *startIndex* and *endIndex* are the indices that delimit the section of the array to be sorted. I don't see what good a half-sorted array can be, unless you're dealing with extremely large arrays. Even then, the Sort method is incredibly fast.

An interesting variation of the Sort method sorts the elements of an array according to the values of the elements in another array. Let's say you have one array of names and another with the matching Social Security numbers. It is possible to sort the array with the names according to their Social Security numbers. This form of the Sort method has the following syntax:

```
System.Array.Sort(array1, array2)
```

array1 is the array with the keys, and *array2* is the array with the actual elements to be sorted. This is a very handy form of the Sort method. Let's say you have a list of words stored in one array and their frequencies in another. Using the first form of the Sort method, you can sort the words alphabetically. With this form of the Sort method, you can sort them according to their frequencies (starting with the most common words and ending with the less common ones). The two arrays must be one-dimensional and have the same number of elements. If you want to sort a section of the array, just supply the *startIndex* and *endIndex* arguments to the Sort method, after the names of the two arrays.

The SortArrayByLength application, shown in Figure 11.1, demonstrates how to sort an array based on the length of its elements (short elements appear at the top of the array, while longer elements appear near the bottom of the array). First, it populates the array *MyStrings* with a few strings, then it assigns the lengths of these strings to the matching elements of the array *MyStringsLen*. The element `MyStrings(0)` is "Visual Basic", and the `MyStringsLen(0)` element's value is 12. Once the two arrays have been populated, the code sorts the elements of the *MyStrings* array according to the values of the *MyStringsLen* array.

FIGURE 11.1

The SortArray-
ByLength application

The statement that sorts the array is

```
System.Array.Sort(MyStringsLen, MyStrings)
```

The code, which also displays the arrays before and after sorting, is shown in Listing 11.1.

LISTING 11.1: SORTING AN ARRAY ACCORDING TO THE LENGTH OF ITS ELEMENTS

```
Protected Sub Button1_Click(ByVal sender As Object, ByVal e As System.EventArgs)
    Dim MyStrings(3) As String
    Dim MyStringsLen(3) As Integer
    MyStrings(0) = "Visual Basic"
    MyStrings(1) = "C++"
    MyStrings(2) = "C#"
    MyStrings(3) = "HTML"
    Dim i As Integer
    For i = 0 To UBound(MyStrings)
        MyStringsLen(i) = len(MyStrings(i))
    Next
    ListBox1.Items.Clear()
    ListBox1.Items.Add("Original Array")
    ListBox1.Items.Add("**************************")
    Dim str As Integer
    For str = 0 To UBound(MyStrings)
        ListBox1.Items.Add(MyStrings(str) & "    " & MyStringsLen(str).ToString)
    Next
    ListBox1.Items.Add("**************************")
    ListBox1.Items.Add("Array Sorted According to String Length ")
    ListBox1.Items.Add("**************************")
    System.Array.Sort(MyStringsLen, MyStrings)
    For str = 0 To UBound(MyStrings)
        ListBox1.Items.Add(MyStrings(str) & "    " & MyStringsLen(str).ToString)
    Next
    ListBox1.Items.Add("**************************")
```

```
'    Sort the array twice
ListBox1.Items.Add("Array Sorted Twice According to String Length ")
ListBox1.Items.Add("*************************")
System.Array.Sort(MyStringsLen, MyStrings)
For str = 0 To UBound(MyStrings)
    ListBox1.Items.Add(MyStrings(str) & "    " & MyStringsLen(str).ToString)
Next
ListBox1.Items.Add("*************************")
End Sub
```

The output produced by the SortArrayByLength application on the ListBox control is shown here:

```
Original Array
*************************
Visual Basic    12
C++    3
C#    2
HTML    4
*************************
Array Sorted According to String Length
*************************
C#    2
C++    3
HTML    4
Visual Basic    12
*************************
Array Sorted Twice According to String Length
*************************
C#    2
C++    3
HTML    4
Visual Basic    12
*************************
```

Notice that the Sort method sorts both the auxiliary array (the one with the lengths of the strings) and the main array. After the call to the Sort method, the first element in the *MyStrings* array is "C#", and the first element in the *MyStringsLen* array is 2. In other words, the Sort method doesn't simply sort the elements of one array based on the values of the other array. If it did, the elements of the two arrays would no longer match. Because of the way the Sort method operates, you can sort the array multiple times, as demonstrated in Listing 11.1.

The array with the keys that will determine the order of the elements can be anything. If the array to be sorted holds some rectangles, you can create an auxiliary array with the area of the rectangles, and sort the original array according to the area of its rectangles. Likewise, an array of colors can be sorted according to the hue, or the luminance, of each color component, and so on.

Another form of the Sort method uses a user-supplied function to sort arrays of custom objects. As you recall, arrays can store all types of objects. But the Framework doesn't know how to sort your custom objects. To sort an array of objects, you must provide your own function that implements the IComparer interface. This form of the Sort method is described in detail in the later section "The IEnumerator and IComparer Interfaces," where you will also learn how to write functions for sorting your custom objects.

Searching Arrays

Arrays can be searched in two ways: with the BinarySearch method, which works on sorted arrays and is extremely fast; and with the IndexOf (and LastIndexOf) methods, which work regardless of the order of the elements. All three methods search for an instance of an item and return its index. The IndexOf and LastIndexOf methods are similar to the methods by the same name of the String class. They return the index of the first (or last) instance of an object in the array, or the value −1 if the object isn't found in the array. Both methods are overloaded, and the simplest form of the IndexOf method is:

```
itemIndex = System.Array.IndexOf(array, object)
```

where *array* is the name of the array to be searched and *object* is the item you're searching for. The LastIndexOf method's syntax is identical, but the LastIndexOf method starts searching from the end of the array. If the item you're searching for is unique in the array, both methods will return the same index.

Another form of the IndexOf and LastIndexOf methods allows you to begin the search at a specific index:

```
itemIndex = System.Array.IndexOf(array, object, startIndex)
```

This form of the method starts searching in the segment of the array from *startIndex* to the end of the array. Finally, you can specify the range of indices where the search will take place with the following form of the method:

```
itemIndex = System.Array.IndexOf(array, object, startIndex, endIndex)
```

You can search large arrays more efficiently with the BinarySearch method, if the array is sorted. The simplest form of the BinarySearch method is

```
System.Array.BinarySearch(array, object)
```

where *array* is the name of the array and *object* the item you're searching for. To search a section of the array, supply the two indices that delimit the section of the array you wish to sort:

```
System.Array.BinarySearch(array, startIndex, selLength, object)
```

If the array contains custom objects, you must provide an IComparer object that compares two elements. This is the same object you supply to the Sort method for custom sorts.

The BinarySearch method returns an integer value, which is the index of the object you're searching for in the array. If the *object* argument is not found, the method returns a negative value, which is the negative of the index of the next larger item minus one. This transformation, the negative of a positive number minus one, is called the *one's complement*, and other languages provide an operator for it, the tilde (∼). The one's complement of 10 is −11, and the one's complement of −3 is 2.

Why all this complexity? Zero is a valid index, so only a negative value could indicate a failure in the search operation. A value of −1 would indicate that the operation failed, but the BinarySearch method does something better. If it can't locate the item, it returns the index of the item immediately after the desired item (the first item in the array that exceeds the item you're searching for). This is a near match, and the BinarySearch method returns a negative value to indicate near matches. Notice that there will always be a near match, unless you're searching for a value larger than the last value in the array. In this case, the BinarySearch method will return the one's complement of the array's upper bound. If your array was declared with 100 elements and the value you're searching for is an element that's larger than the last element, the BinarySearch method will return the one's complement of the value 100 (which is −101).

TIP   *Like the BinarySearch method, the IndexOf and LastIndexOf methods perform case-sensitive searches. However, because the BinarySearch method reports near matches, it appears as if it performs case-insensitive searches. If the array contains the element "Charles" and you search for "charles," the IndexOf method will not find the string, while the Binary-Search will find it but will report it as a near match.*

The `Option Compare` statement has no effect on the comparisons performed either by the Binary-Search or by the IndexOf/LastIndexOf methods. If you want to perform case-insensitive comparisons, you must provide your own custom comparer, as described in the section "Custom Sorting," later in this chapter.

The ArraySearch application, shown in Figure 11.2, demonstrates how to handle exact and near matches reported by the BinarySearch method. The Populate Array button populates an array with 1,000 random strings. The same strings are also displayed on a sorted ListBox control, so that you can view them. The elements have the same order in both the array and the ListBox, so we can use the index reported by the BinarySearch method to locate and select instantly the same item in the ListBox.

FIGURE 11.2

Searching an array and locating the same element in the ListBox control

The Populate Array button creates 1,000 random strings, each with a length of 3 to 15 characters. Both the length of each string and the characters in it are chosen randomly. You can find the code of the Populate Array button's Click handler on the CD. This isn't the most interesting part of the application anyway. When you run the application, message boxes will pop up displaying the time it took for each operation: how long it took to populate the array, how long it took to sort it, and how long it took to populate the ListBox. You may wish to experiment with large arrays (100,000 elements or more).

The Search Array button prompts the user for a string with an InputBox and then locates the string with the BinarySearch method in the array. The result is either an exact or a near match, and it's displayed on a message box. At the same time, the item reported by the BinarySearch method is also selected in the ListBox control.

To test the application, find a string in the list and then click the Search Array button. Enter the entire string (you can use lowercase or uppercase characters; it doesn't make a difference) and verify that the application reports an exact match and locates the item in the ListBox. Then enter a string that doesn't exist in the list (or the beginning of an existing string) and see how the Binary-Search handles near matches.

The code behind the Search Array button calls the BinarySearch method and stores the integer returned by the method to the *wordIndex* variable. Then it examines the value of this variable. If *wordIndex* is positive, there was an exact match and it's reported. If *wordIndex* is negative, the program calculates the one's complement of this value, which is the index of the near match. The element at this index is reported as a near match. Finally, regardless of the type of the match, the code selects the same item in the ListBox and makes it visible. Listing 11.2 is the code behind the Search Array button.

LISTING 11.2: LOCATING EXACT AND NEAR MATCHES WITH BINARYSEARCH

```
Private Sub bttnSearch_Click(ByVal sender As System.Object, _
             ByVal e As System.EventArgs) Handles bttnSearch.Click
   Dim srchWord As String
   Dim wordIndex As Integer
   srchWord = InputBox("Enter word to search for")
   wordIndex = System.Array.BinarySearch(words, srchWord)
   Console.WriteLine(wordIndex)
   If wordIndex >= 0 Then
      MsgBox("Words(" & wordIndex.ToString & ") = " & _
            words(wordIndex), , "EXACT MATCH")
      ListBox1.TopIndex = wordIndex
      ListBox1.SelectedIndex = wordIndex
   Else
      MsgBox("Words(" & (-wordIndex - 1).ToString & ") = " & _
            words(-wordIndex - 1), , "NEAR MATCH")
      ListBox1.TopIndex = -wordIndex - 1
      ListBox1.SelectedIndex = -wordIndex - 1
   End If
End Sub
```

Notice that all methods for sorting and searching arrays work with the base data types only. If the array contains custom data types, you must supply your own functions for comparing elements of this type, a process described in detail in the section "The IEnumerator and IComparer Interfaces," later in this chapter.

THE BINARY SEARCH ALGORITHM

The BinarySearch method uses a very powerful search algorithm, the *binary search algorithm*, but it requires that the array be sorted. You need not care about the technical details of the implementation of a method, but in the case of the binary search algorithm, a basic understanding of how it works will help you understand how it performs near matches. To locate an item in a sorted array, this method compares the search string to the array's middle element. If the search string is smaller, we know that the element is in the first half of the array and we can safely ignore the second half. The same process is repeated with the remaining half of the elements. The search string is compared to the middle element of the reduced array, and after the comparison, we can ignore one half of the reduced array. At each step, the binary search algorithm rejects one half of the items left until it reduces the list to a single item. This is the item we're searching for. If not, the item is not in the list. To search a list with 1,024 items, the binary search algorithm makes 10 comparisons. At the first step, it rejects 512 elements, then 256, then 128 and so on, until it reaches a single element. For an array of 1,024 × 1,024 (that's a little more than a million) items, the algorithm makes 20 comparisons to locate the desired item.

If you apply the BinarySearch method on an array that hasn't been sorted, the method will carry out all the steps and report that the item wasn't found, even though it may be in the array. The algorithm doesn't check the order of the elements; it just assumes that they're sorted. You may also have noticed that, regardless of the outcome, the same number of operations takes place. The binary search algorithm always halves the number of elements in which it attempts to locate the desired element in the array. That's why you should never apply to the BinarySearch method to an array that hasn't been sorted yet.

To see what happens when you apply the BinarySearch method to an array that hasn't been sorted, remove the statement that calls the Sort method in the ArraySearch sample application. The application will keep reporting near matches, even if the string you're searching is present in the array. The Binary-Search method, assuming that the array is sorted, keeps halving the array by successive comparisons. When it's left with a single item, which is not the one you're searching for, it returns the index of the following element and reports a near match. Of course, the near match isn't close to the element you're searching for by any stretch of the word—it's an element that happens to be there when the algorithm finishes. You should never apply the BinarySearch method to an array that hasn't been sorted.

Sorting an array is an expensive operation, and you can't afford to continuously sort lengthy arrays. If your array isn't sorted, you can still search for specific items with the IndexOf and LastIndexOf methods. These methods locate an item in an array and they're overloaded, similar to the Binary-Search method.

Other Array Operations

The Array class exposes additional methods, which are described briefly in this section.

The Reverse method reverses the order of the elements in an array. The syntax of the Reverse method is

```
System.Array.Reverse(array)
```

The Reverse method can't be applied to an array and reverse its elements. Instead, it returns a new array with the elements of the array passed as argument, only in reverse order. To reverse the order of the elements in the array *Names*, call the Reverse method passing the *Names* array as argument. The reversed array must be assigned to another array, *ReverseNames* in our example:

```
Dim Names(99) As String
{ statements to populate array Names }
Dim ReverseNames() As String
ReverseNames = System.Array.Reverse(Names)
```

After the execution of the last statement, the *ReverseNames* array contains the same elements as the *Names* array in reverse order. Notice that the *ReverseNames* array need not be dimensioned when it's declared; the Reverse method will dimension the array accordingly.

The Copy and CopyTo methods copy the elements of an array (or segment of an array) to another array. The Copy method copies a range of elements from one array to another, and its syntax is

```
System.Array.Copy(sourceArray, destinationArray, count)
```

sourceArray and *destinationArray* are the names of the two arrays, and *count* is the number of elements to be copied. The copying process starts with the first element of the source array and ends after the first *count* elements have been copied. If *count* is less than the length of the source array, or it exceeds the length of the second array, an exception will be thrown.

WARNING   *Both the Copy and CopyTo methods work with one-dimensional arrays only.*

Another form of the Copy method allows you to specify the range of elements in the source array to be copied and a range in the destination array where these elements will be copied. The syntax of this form of the method is

```
System.Array.Copy(sourceArray, sourceStart,_
              destinationArray, destinationStart, count)
```

This method copies *count* elements from the source array starting at location *sourceStart* and places them in the destination array starting at location *destinationStart*. All indices must be valid, and there should be *count* elements after the *sourceStart* index in the source array, as well as *count* elements after the *destinationStart* in the destination array. If not, a runtime error will be generated.

The CopyTo method is similar, but it doesn't require the name of the source array. It copies the elements of the array to which it's applied into the destination array:

```
System.Array.CopyTo(destinationArray, sourceStart)
```

Array Limitations

VB.NET arrays are more flexible than ever. The most demanding tasks programmers had to perform with arrays are now implemented as methods of the Array class. However, arrays aren't perfect for all types of data storage. One problem with arrays is that they're not dynamic structures. Resizing the array is a time-consuming operation. There is no simple method to insert additional elements or delete elements anywhere in the array. To remove the third item from an array, you must move up all the elements after the third one by one position. The element *array(3)* must become *array(2)*, *array(4)* must become *array(3)*, and so on. You can easily implement this technique with a loop, but what good is it going to be with a large array?

A similar approach must be followed to make space for a new element. To insert a new element at the beginning of the array, all elements must be moved by one position toward the end of the array.

These problems were addressed with the introduction of a new structure, the ArrayList, which is described in the following section. In short, the ArrayList is a dynamic array that expands and shrinks automatically during the course of the program as needed.

Another shortcoming of arrays is that you can only access their elements by means of an index, which in most situations is a meaningless number. Ideally, we should be able to access arrays with a meaningful key. If the array *Capitals* contains the state capitals, the capital of California could be the element *Capitals(0)* or *Capitals(33)*. It's up to the programmer to come up with a technique to match states to indices. A far more convenient structure would be an array that can be accessed by a string, which in our example would be the name of the state: *Capitals("California")*. The Framework provides two structures that resemble an array, but their elements can be accessed by a key: the HashTable and the Dictionary. The Dictionary is not new VB.NET—it has been around since VB4—but it's being replaced by the HashTable. In this chapter, I will discuss the HashTable class in detail.

Both ArrayLists and HashTables are quite similar in terms of the members they expose, so I will present the members of the ArrayList collection in detail. Many of these members apply to both collections.

The ArrayList Collection

The ArrayList collection allows you to maintain multiple elements, similar to an array. However, the ArrayList collection allows the insertion of elements anywhere in the collection, as well as the removal of any element. In other words, it's a dynamic structure that can also grow automatically as you add elements. Like an array, the ArrayList's elements can be sorted and searched. In effect, the ArrayList is a more "convenient" array, a dynamic array. You can also remove elements by value, not only by index. If you have an ArrayList populated with names, you remove the item "Charles" by passing the string itself as argument. Notice that "Charles" is not an index value; it's the element you want to remove.

Creating an ArrayList

To use an ArrayList in your code, you must first create an instance of the ArrayList class with the New keyword. When you declare an ArrayList, you need not specify any dimensions. Just use a statement like this one:

```
Dim aList As New ArrayList
```

The *aList* variable represents an ArrayList that can hold only 16 elements (the default size). You can set the initial capacity of the ArrayList by setting its Capacity property. The Capacity property is the number of elements the ArrayList can hold. It's like declaring an array for 100 elements, but using only 4 of them. There are 96 more elements to be used. The ArrayList's capacity can be increased, or reduced, at any time, just by setting the Capacity property. The following statement sets the capacity of the ArrayList to 1,000 elements:

```
aList.Capacity = 1000
```

The *aList* variable is now ready to hold a large number of items. Notice that you don't have to prepare the collection for accepting a specific number of items. Every time you exceed the collection's capacity, it's doubled automatically. However, it's not decreased automatically when you remove items.

The exact number of items currently in the ArrayList is given by the Count property, which is always less than (or, at most, equal to) the Capacity property. Both properties are expressed in terms of items, not bytes or any other unit that might involve additional calculations. If you decide that you're no longer going to add more items to the collection, you can call the TrimToSize method, which will set the collection's capacity to the number of items in the list. After calling the TrimTo-Size method, the Capacity property becomes equal to the Count property.

Adding and Removing Items

To add a new item to an ArrayList, use the Add method, whose syntax is

```
index = aList.Add(object)
```

where *aList* is a properly declared ArrayList and *object* is the item you want to add to the ArrayList collection (it could be a number, a string, or a custom object). The Add method appends the specified item to the collection and returns the index of the new item. If you're using an ArrayList named *Capitals* to store the names of the state capitals, you can add an item (a string) with the following statement:

```
Capitals.Add("Sacramento")
```

If the *Persons* ArrayList holds variables of a custom type, prepare a variable of that type and then add it to the collection. Let's say you've created a structure called Person with the following declaration:

```
Structure Person
    Dim LastName As String
    Dim FirstName As String
    Dim Phone As String
    Dim EMail As String
End Structure
```

To store a collection of Person items in an ArrayList, create a variable of the Person type, set its fields, and then add it to the ArrayList, as in Listing 11.3.

LISTING 11.3: ADDING A STRUCTURE TO AN ARRAYLIST

```
Dim Persons As New ArrayList
Dim p As New Person
p.LastName = "Last Name"
p.FirstName = "First Name"
p.Phone = "Phone"
p.EMail = "name@server.com"
Persons.Add(p)
p.LastName = "another name"
{ statements to set the other fields }
Persons.Add(p)
```

If you execute these statements, the ArrayList will hold two items, both of the Person type. Notice that you can add multiple instances of the same object to the ArrayList collection. To find out whether an item belongs to the collection already, use the Contains method, which accepts as argument an object and returns a True or False value, depending on whether the object belongs to the list:

```
If Persons.Contains(p) Then
    MsgBox("Duplicate element rejected")
Else
    Persons.Add(p)
End If
```

By default, items are appended to the ArrayList. To insert an item at a specific location, use the Insert method. The Insert method accepts as argument the location at which the new item will be inserted and, of course, an object to insert in the ArrayList, as shown next:

```
aList.Insert(index, object)
```

Unlike the Add method, the Insert method doesn't return a value—the location of the new item is already known.

You can also add multiple items with a single call to the AddRange method. This method appends a collection of items to the ArrayList. The items could come from an array, or another ArrayList. The following statement appends the elements of an array to the *aList* collection:

```
Dim colors() As Color = {Color.Red, Color.Blue, Color.Green}
aList.AddRange(colors)
```

The AddRange method in this example has appended three items of the same type to the ArrayList collection. The array could have been declared as Object too; it doesn't have to be strictly typed, because the ArrayList collection is not strictly typed.

To insert a range of items anywhere in the ArrayList, use the InsertRange method, whose syntax is

```
aList.InsertRange(index, objects)
```

where *index* is the index of the ArrayList where the new elements will be inserted and *objects* is a collection with the elements to be inserted.

Finally, you can overwrite a range in the ArrayList with a new range, with the SetRange method. To overwrite the items in locations 5 through 9 in an ArrayList, use a few statements like the following:

```
Dim words() As String = {"Just", "a", "few", "more", "words"}
aList.SetRange(5, words)
```

This code segment assumes that the *aList* collection contains at least 10 items, and it replaces five of them.

To remove an item, use the Remove method, whose syntax is:

```
aList.Remove(object)
```

The *object* argument is the value to be removed, and not an index value. The ArrayList allows you to remove items only by value. If the collection contains multiple instances of the same item, only the first instance of the object will be removed.

Notice that the Remove method compares values, not references. If the ArrayList contains a Rectangle object, you can search for this item by creating a new Rectangle variable and setting its properties to the properties of the Rectangle object you want to remove:

```
Dim R1 As New Rectangle(10, 10, 100, 100)
Dim R2 As Rectangle
aList.Add(R1)
aList.Add(R2)
R2 = New Rectangle(10, 10, 100, 100)
aList.Remove(R2)
```

If you execute these statements, they will add two identical rectangles to the *aList* ArrayList. The last statement will remove the first of the two rectangles.

If you attempt to remove an item that doesn't exist, an exception will be thrown. You can always make sure that the item exists before attempting to remove it, by calling the Contains method, which returns True if the item exists in the ArrayList, False otherwise:

```
If aList.Contains(object) Then aList.Remove(object)
```

You can also remove items by specifying their order in the list with the RemoveAt method. This method accepts as argument the location of the item to remove, which must be less than the number of items currently in the list. The syntax of the RemoveAt method is

```
aList.RemoveAt(index)
```

To remove more than one consecutive item, use the RemoveRange method, whose syntax is

```
aList.RemoveRange(startIndex, count)
```

The *startIndex* argument is the index of the first item to be removed, and *count* is the number of items to be removed.

The following statements are examples of the methods that remove items from an ArrayList collection. The first two statements remove an item by value. The first statement removes an object, and the second removes a string item. The third statement removes the third item, and the last one removes the third through fifth items.

```
aList.Remove(Color.Red)
aList.Remove("RichardM")
aList.RemoveAt(2)
aList.RemoveRange(2, 3)
```

If you execute all the statements in the order shown, the third statement may not remove the original collection's third item. It will remove the third item of the collection as it has been rearranged after the execution of the first two statements. The same is true for the last statement. It will remove the elements at locations 2, 3, and 4, as they are arranged at the moment the statement is executed.

COPYING ITEMS

Besides adding and removing items, you can also extract selected items from an ArrayList with the GetRange method. The GetRange method extracts a number of consecutive elements from the ArrayList and stores them to a new ArrayList:

```
newList = ArrayList.GetRange(index, count)
```

where *index* is the index of the first item to copy and *count* is the number of items to be copied. The GetRange method returns another ArrayList with the proper number of items.

The following statement copies three items from the *aList* ArrayList and inserts them at the beginning of the *bList* ArrayList. The three elements copied are the fourth through sixth elements in the original collection:

```
bList.InsertRange(0, aList.GetRange(3, 3))
```

The statements in Listing 11.4 populate the *aList* ArrayList with 10 strings. Then they copy elements 3 through 5 and add them to the start of the *bList* ArrayList. Then they copy elements 7 through 9 from the *aList* ArrayList and insert them in the *bList* ArrayList, right after the third element.

LISTING 11.4: THE GetRange AND InsertRange METHODS

```
Dim aList As New ArrayList()
Dim names(10) As String
names(0) = "Item 0" : names(1) = "Item 1"
names(2) = "Item 2" : names(3) = "Item 3"
names(4) = "Item 4" : names(5) = "Item 5"
names(6) = "Item 6" : names(7) = "Item 7"
names(8) = "Item 8" : names(9) = "Item 9"
aList.InsertRange(0, names)
ShowArrayList(aList)
Dim bList As New ArrayList()
bList.InsertRange(0, aList.GetRange(3, 3))
ShowArrayList(aList)
bList.InsertRange(2, aList.GetRange(7, 3))
ShowArrayList(bList)
```

The ShowArrayList() procedure (Listing 11.5) displays the contents of the ArrayList in the Output window (the GetEnumerator method is discussed in detail later in this chapter).

LISTING 11.5: THE ShowArrayList() SUBROUTINE

```
Sub ShowArrayList(ByVal List As Arraylist)
    Dim AListEnum As IEnumerator
    AListEnum = List.GetEnumerator
    While AListEnum.MoveNext
        Console.WriteLine(AListEnum.Current)
    End While
    Console.WriteLine()
End Sub
```

The output produced by Listing 11.5 is shown next in columns, so that you can compare the elements in the original ArrayList and the elements copied to the second ArrayList collection. The *bList* collection was populated with the items 3, 4, and 5 initially (the middle column in the following table). The second InsertRange statement inserted the items 7, 8, and 9 in front of the third element, which was pushed to the end of the list. The column bList (1) shows the contents of *bList* after the execution of the first InsertRange statement, and the column bList (2) shows the contents of *bList* after the execution of the second InsertRange statement.

aList	bList (1)	bList (2)
Item 0	Item 3	Item 3
Item 1	Item 4	Item 4
Item 2	Item 5	Item 7
Item 3		Item 8
Item 4		Item 9
Item 5		Item 5
Item 6		
Item 7		
Item 8		
Item 9		

The Repeat method fills an ArrayList with multiple instances of the same item, and its syntax is

```
newList = aList.Repeat(item, count)
```

This method returns a new ArrayList with *count* elements, all of them being identical to the *item* argument. To fill an ArrayList with the string "New Item", use the following statement:

```
newList = System.ArrayList.Repeat("New Item", 10)
```

Another method of the ArrayList class is the Reverse method, which reverses the order of the elements in an ArrayList collection, or a portion of it, and its syntax is

```
newList = aList.Reverse()
```

or

```
newList = aList.Reverse(startIndex, endIndex)
```

The first form of the method reverses the entire collection; the second form reverses a section of the collection. Both methods return another ArrayList with the same elements as the original, only in reverse order.

SORTING ARRAYLISTS

To sort the ArrayList, use the Sort method, which has three overloaded forms:

```
aList.Sort()
aList.Sort(comparer)
aList.Sort(startIndex, endIndex, comparer)
```

The ArrayList's Sort method doesn't require that you pass the name of the ArrayList to be sorted as argument. *aList* is a properly declared and initialized ArrayList object. The first form of the Sort method sorts the ArrayList alphabetically or numerically, depending on the data type of the objects stored in it. If the items are not all of the same type, an exception will be thrown. You'll see how you can handle this exception shortly.

If the items stored in the ArrayList are of a data type other than the base data types, you must supply your own mechanism to compare the objects. The other two forms of the Sort method use a custom function for comparing items. Notice that there is no overloaded form of the Sort method that sorts a section of the ArrayList.

NOTE *Despite their similarities, the Sort method of ArrayList collection is not as flexible as the Sort method of the Array class. For example, you can't sort an ArrayList collection based on the values in another collection.*

The Sort method will sort an ArrayList only if all the items are of the same type or if the items can be compared by the default comparer provided by a specific data type. The list may contain items of widely different types, in which case the Sort method will fail. To prevent a runtime exception, you must make sure that all items are of the same type. If you can't ensure that all the items are of the same type, catch the possible error and handle it from within your code, as demonstrated in Listing 11.6.

LISTING 11.6: FOOLPROOF SORTING

```
Dim Sorted As Boolean = True
Try
    aList.Sort()
Catch SortException As Exception
    MsgBox(SortException.Message)
    Sorted = False
End Try
If Sorted Then
    { process sorted ArrayList }
Else
    { process unsorted list }
End If
```

The *Sorted* Boolean variable is initially set to True, because the Sort method will most likely succeed. If not, an exception will be thrown, in which case the code resets the *Sorted* variable to False and uses it later to distinguish between sorted and unsorted collections. For example, if the collection was sorted properly, you can call the BinarySearch method. If not, you can only use the IndexOf and LastIndexOf methods to locate an item.

The Sort method can't even sort a collection of various numeric data types. If some of the objects are Doubles and some Integers or Decimals, the Sort method will fail. You must either make sure that all the items in the ArrayList are of the same type, or provide your own function for comparing the ArrayList's items.

SEARCHING ARRAYLISTS

Like arrays, the ArrayList class exposes the IndexOf and LastIndexOf methods to search in an unsorted list and the BinarySearch method for sorted lists. If you need to know the location of an item, use the IndexOf and LastIndexOf methods, which accept as argument the object to be located and return an index:

```
aList.IndexOf(object)
```

Here, *object* is the item you're searching.

The LastIndexOf method has the same syntax, but it starts scanning the array from its end and moves backward toward the beginning. The IndexOf and LastIndexOf methods are overloaded. The other two forms of the IndexOf method are:

```
aList.IndexOf(object, startIndex)
aList.IndexOf(object, startIndex, length)
```

The two additional arguments determine where the search starts and ends. The two methods return the index of the item, if it belongs to the collection. If not, they return the value −1. Both ArrayLists and Arrays are searched in a linear fashion, from beginning to end (or from end to beginning in the case of the LastIndexOf method).

TIP *The IndexOf and LastIndexOf methods perform case-sensitive searches, and they report exact matches only.*

If the ArrayList is sorted, use the BinarySearch method, which accepts as argument the object to be located and returns its index in the collection:

```
aList.BinarySearch(object)
```

where *object* is the item you're looking for. This form of the BinarySearch method can't be used with data types that don't provide their own comparer (i.e., base types like integers and strings). To use the BinarySearch method with an ArrayList of custom objects, you must provide your own comparer, which is the same as the one used with the Sort method to sort the collection.

There are two more forms of this method. To search for an item in an ArrayList with different data types, use the following form of the BinarySearch method:

```
aList.BinarySearch(object, comparer)
```

The first argument is the object you're searching for, and the second is the name of an IComparer object.

Another form of the BinarySearch method allows you to search for an item in a section of the collection; its syntax is

```
aList.BinarySearch(startIndex, length, object, comparer)
```

The first argument is the index at which the search will begin, and the second argument is the length of the subrange. *object* and *comparer* are the same as with the second form of the method. For more information on the BinarySearch method, see the description of the BinarySearch method of the Array class. The two methods are identical, and they apply to sorted lists only.

ITERATING AN ARRAYLIST

To iterate through the elements of an ArrayList collection, you can set up a For…Next loop like the following one:

```
For i = 0 To ArrayList.Count - 1
    { process item ArrayList(i) }
Next
```

This is a trivial operation, but the processing itself can get as complicated as the type of objects stored in the collection requires. The current item at each iteration is the ArrayList(i). If you don't know its exact type, assign it to an Object variable and then process it.

You could also use the For Each…Next loop with an Object variable, as shown next:

```
Dim itm As Object
For Each itm In ArrayList
    { process item itm }
Next
```

If all the items in the ArrayList are of the same type, you can use a variable of the same type to iterate through the collection, instead of a generic Object variable. If all the elements were Decimals, for example, you can declare the *itm* variable as Decimal.

An even better method is to create an enumerator for the collection and use it to iterate through its items. This technique applies to all collections and is discussed in the section "Enumerating Collections," later in this chapter.

The ArrayList class addresses most of the problems associated with the Array class, but one last problem remains—that of accessing the items in the collection through a meaningful key. This is the problem addressed by the HashTable collection.

The HashTable Collection

The ArrayList is a more convenient form of an array. It's dynamic, it allows you to insert items anywhere and remove items from the collection with a single method call, and it supports all the convenient features of an array, like sorting and searching.

Yet, both collections have a drawback: namely, you must access their elements by an index. Another collection, the HashTable collection, is similar to the ArrayList, but it allows you to access the items by a key. Each item has a value and a key. The value is the same value you store in an array, but the key is a meaningful entity for accessing the items in the collection.

The HashTable exposes most of the properties and methods of the ArrayList, with a few notable exceptions. The Count property returns the number of items in the collection as usual, but the HashTable collection doesn't expose a Capacity property. The HashTable collection uses fairly complicated logic to maintain the list of items, and it adjusts its capacity automatically. Fortunately, you need not know how the items are stored in the collection. In short, it creates automatically a unique key for each item. This key is derived from the item being added, and it's possible that two items will produce the same key—not very likely, but the possibility is not zero. The HashTable class uses a complicated algorithm to handle all possible cases, but you need not be concerned with these details. The Framework provides all these classes so that you won't have to write low-level code.

To use a HashTable in your code, you need not import any class. Just declare a HashTable variable with the following statement:

```
Dim hTable As New HashTable
```

To add an item to the HashTable, use the Add method, whose syntax is

```
hTable.Add(key, value)
```

value is the item you want to add (it can be any object), and *key* is a value you supply, which represents the item. This is the value you'll use later to retrieve the item. If you're setting up a structure for storing temperatures in various cities, use the city names as keys:

```
Dim Temperatures As New HashTable
Temperatures.Add("Houston", 81)
Temperatures.Add("Los Angeles", 78)
```

Notice that you can have duplicate values, but the keys must be unique. If you attempt to use an existing key, an argument exception will be raised. To find out whether a specific value or key is already in the collection, use the ContainsKey and ContainsValue methods. The syntax of the two methods is quite similar:

```
hTable.ContainsKey(object)
hTable.ContainsValue(object)
```

The HashTable collection exposes the Contains method too, which is identical to the ContainsKey method.

To find out whether a specific key is in use already, use the ContainsKey method, as shown in the following statements, which add a new item to the HashTable only if it's key doesn't exist already:

```
Dim value As New Rectangle(100, 100, 50, 50)
Dim key As String = "object1"
If Not hTable.ContainsKey(key) Then
    hTable.Add(key, value)
End If
```

The Values and Keys properties allow you to retrieve all the values and the keys in the HashTable. Both properties are collections and expose the usual members of a collection. To iterate through the values stored in the HashTable *hTable*, use the following loop:

```
Dim itm As Object
For Each itm In hTable.Values
    Console.WriteLine(itm)
Next
```

There is only one method to remove items from an ArrayList: the Remove method, which accepts as argument the key of the item to be removed:

```
hTable.Remove(key)
```

To extract items from a HashTable, use the CopyTo method. This method copies the items to a one-dimensional array, and its syntax is

```
newArray = HTable.CopyTo(arrayName)
```

You must set up the array that will accept the items beforehand, because this method can throw several different exceptions for various error conditions. The array that accepts the values must be one-dimensional, and there should be enough space in the array for the HashTable's values. Moreover, the array's type must be Object, because this is the type of the items you can store in a HashTable.

Listing 11.7 demonstrates how to scan the keys of a HashTable through the Keys property and then use these keys to access the items through the Item property (and passing the key as argument).

LISTING 11.7: ITERATING A HASHTABLE

```
Private Function ShowHashTableContents(ByVal table As Hashtable) As String
    Dim msg As String
    Dim element, key As Object
    msg = "The HashTable contains " & table.Count.tostring & " elements:" & vbCrLf
    For Each key In table.keys
        element = table.Item(key)
        msg = msg & vbCrLf
        msg = msg & "    Element Type = " & element.GetType.ToString & vbCrLf
        msg = msg & "    Element Key= " & Key.ToString
        msg = msg & "    Element Value= " & element.ToString & vbCrLf
    Next
    Return(msg)
End Sub
```

To print the contents of a HashTable variable on the Output window, call the ShowHashTableContents() function, passing the name of the HashTable as argument, and then print the string returned by the function:

```
Dim HT As New HashTable
{ statements to populate HashTable }
Console.WriteLine(ShowHashTableContents(HT))
```

VB.NET at Work: The WordFrequencies Project

In this section, you'll develop an application that counts word frequencies in a text. The WordFrequencies application scans text files and counts the occurrences of each word in the text. As you will see, the HashTable is the natural choice for storing this information, because you want to access a word's frequency by the word. To retrieve (or update) the frequency of the word *elaborate*, for example, you will use the expression:

```
Words("ELABORATE").Value
```

Arrays and ArrayLists are out of the question, because they can't be accessed by a key. You could also use the SortedList collection, which is described later in this chapter, but this collection maintains its items sorted at all times. If you need this functionality as well, you can modify the application accordingly. The items in a SortedList are also accessed by keys, so you won't have to introduce substantial changes in the code.

Let me start with a few remarks. First, all words we locate in the various text files will be converted to uppercase. Because the keys of the HashTable are case-sensitive, converting them to uppercase makes them unique. This way, we don't risk counting the same word in different cases as two or more different words.

The frequencies of the words can't be calculated instantly, because we need to know the total number of words in the text. Instead, each value in the HashTable is the number of occurrences of a specific word. To calculate the actual frequency of the same word, you must divide this value by the number of occurrences of all words, but this can happen only after we have scanned the entire text file and counted the occurrences of each word. Since this operation will introduce delays in the application, I've decided to keep track of number of occurrences only and calculate the word frequencies when requested.

When the code runs into another instance of the word *elaborate*, it simply increases the matching item of the HashTable by one:

```
Words("ELABORATE").Value = Words("ELABORATE").Value + 1
```

The application's interface is shown in Figure 11.3. To scan another text file and process its words, click the Read Text File button. You'll be prompted to select the name of the file to be processed with an Open dialog box. Then, you can click the Show Word Count button to count the number of occurrences of each word in the text. The last button on the form sorts the words according to their count.

FIGURE 11.3

The WordFrequencies project demonstrates how to use the HashTable collection.

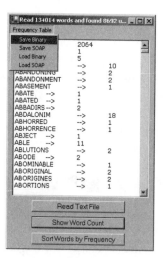

The application maintains a single HashTable collection, the Words collection, and it updates this collection rather than counting word occurrences from scratch. The Frequency Table menu contains the commands to save the collection's items to a disk file and read the same data from the file. Use one of the Save commands to save the HashTable to a disk file, and use the equivalent Load command to read the data from the disk file into the HashTable. The commands in this menu can store the data either to a text file (Save SOAP/Load SOAP commands) or to a binary file (Save Binary/Load Binary). Use these commands to store the data generated in a single session, load the data in a later session, and process more files. These commands will be discussed in detail at the end of the chapter, where we'll explore the Serialization class. For now, you can use the commands to continue processing text files in multiple sessions.

The WordFrequencies application uses techniques and classes we haven't discussed yet. The topic of reading from (or writing to) files is discussed in the following chapter. You don't really have to understand the code that opens a text file and reads its lines; just focus on the segments that manipulate the text file. To test the project, I used some very large files I downloaded from the Project Gutenberg Web site (`http://promo.net/pg/`). This site contains entire books in electronic format (plain text files), and you can borrow some files to test any program that manipulates text (in addition to reading them, of course).

The code reads the text into a string variable, the *str* variable. Then, it calls the Split method of the String class to split the text into individual words. The Split method uses the space, comma, period, quote, exclamation mark, colon, semicolon, and newline characters as delimiters. The individual words are stored in the *Words* array. The program goes through each word in the array and determines whether it's a valid word by calling the IsValidWord() function. This function returns False if one of the characters in the word is not a letter; strings like "B2B" or "U2" are not considered proper words. IsValidWord() is a custom function, and you can edit it as you wish.

Any valid word becomes a key to the *WordFrequencies* HashTable. The corresponding value is the number of occurrences of the specific word in the HashTable. If a key (a new word) is added to the table, its value is set to 1. If the key exists already, then its value is increased by 1, with the following If statement:

```
If Not WordFrequencies.ContainsKey(word) Then
    WordFrequencies.Add(word, 1)
Else
    WordFrequencies(word) = CType(WordFrequencies(word), Integer) + 1
End If
```

The code that reads the text file and splits it into individual words is shown in Listing 11.8. The code prompts the user to select a text file with the Open dialog box and then reads the entire text into a string variable, the *txtLine* variable, and the individual words are isolated with the Split method of the String class.

LISTING 11.8: SPLITTING A TEXT FILE INTO WORDS

```
Private Sub Button1_Click(ByVal sender As System.Object, _
            ByVal e As System.EventArgs) Handles Button1.Click
    OpenFileDialog1.DefaultExt = "TXT"
    OpenFileDialog1.Filter = "Text|*.TXT|All Files|*.*"
    OpenFileDialog1.ShowDialog()
    If OpenFileDialog1.FileName = "" Then Exit Sub
    Dim str As StreamReader
    Dim txtFile As File
    Dim txtLine As String
    Dim Words() As String
```

```
Dim Delimiters() As Char = {CType(" ", Char), CType(".", Char), _
                            CType(",", Char), CType("'", Char), _
                            Ctype("!", Char), Ctype(";", Char), _
                            Ctype(":", Char), Chr(10), Chr(13)}
str = File.OpenText(OpenFileDialog1.FileName)
txtLine = str.ReadLine()
txtLine = str.ReadToEnd
Words = txtLine.Split(Delimiters)
Dim iword As Integer, word As String
For iword = 0 To Words.GetUpperBound(0)
    word = Words(iword).ToUpper
    If IsValidWord(word) Then
        If Not WordFrequencies.ContainsKey(word) Then
            WordFrequencies.Add(word, 1)
        Else
            WordFrequencies(word) = CType(WordFrequencies(word), Integer) + 1
        End If
    End If
Next
End Sub
```

This event handler calculates the count of the unique words and displays them on a TextBox control. In a document with 130,000 words, it didn't take more than a couple of seconds to perform all the calculations. The process of displaying the list of unique words on a TextBox control was very fast too, thanks to the StringBuilder class. The code behind the Show Word Count button (Listing 11.9) displays the list of words along with the number of occurrences of each word in the text.

LISTING 11.9: DISPLAYING THE COUNT OF EACH WORD IN THE TEXT

```
Private Sub Button2_Click(ByVal sender As System.Object, _
            ByVal e As System.EventArgs) Handles Button2.Click
    Dim wEnum As IDictionaryEnumerator
    Dim occurrences As Integer
    Dim allWords As New System.Text.StringBuilder()
    wEnum = WordFrequencies.GetEnumerator
    While wEnum.MoveNext
        allWords.Append(wEnum.Key.ToString & vbTab & "->" & vbTab & _
                        wEnum.Value.ToString & vbCrLf)
    End While
    TextBox1.Text = allWords.ToString
End Sub
```

The last button on the form calculates the frequency of each word in the HashTable, sorts them according to their frequencies, and displays the list; its code is detailed in Listing 11.10.

```
Private Sub Button3_Click(ByVal sender As System.Object, _
                ByVal e As System.EventArgs) Handles Button3.Click
    Dim wEnum As IDictionaryEnumerator
    Dim Words(WordFrequencies.Count) As String
    Dim Frequencies(WordFrequencies.Count) As Double
    Dim allWords As New System.Text.StringBuilder()
    Dim i, totCount As Integer
    wEnum = WordFrequencies.GetEnumerator
    While wEnum.MoveNext
        Words(i) = CType(wEnum.Key, String)
        Frequencies(i) = CType(wEnum.Value, Integer)
        totCount = totCount + Frequencies(i)
        i = i + 1
    End While
    For i = 0 To Words.GetUpperBound(0)
        Frequencies(i) = Frequencies(i) / totCount
    Next
    Words.Sort(Frequencies, Words)
    TextBox1.Clear()
    For i = Words.GetUpperBound(0) To 0 Step -1
        allWords.Append(Words(i) & vbTab & "->" & vbTab & _
                    Format(100 * Frequencies(i), "#.000") & vbCrLf)
    Next
    TextBox1.Text = allWords.ToString
End Sub
```

HANDLING LARGE SETS OF DATA

Incidentally, my first attempt was to display the list of unique words on a ListBox control. The process was incredibly slow. The first 10,000 words were added in a few seconds, but as the number of items increased, the time it took to add them to the control increased exponentially (or so it seemed).

Adding thousands of items to a ListBox control is a very slow process. It's likely that you will run into situations where a seemingly simple task will turn out to be detrimental to your application's performance. You should try different approaches, but also consider a total overhaul of your user interface. Ask yourself, who needs to see a list with 10,000 words? You can use the application to do the calculations and then retrieve the count of selected words, or display the 100 most common ones, or even display 100 words at a time. I'm displaying the list of words because this is a demonstration, but a real application shouldn't display such a long list. The core of the application counts unique words in a text file, and it does it very efficiently.

Appending each word to a TextBox control was slow too, so I've used a string variable to store the text, then assign it to the control. This variable is the *allWords* variable, which was declared with the String-Builder type. As you will learn in the following chapter, the StringBuider class manipulates strings like the String class, but it's very fast.

The SortedList Class

The SortedList collection is a peculiar combination of the Array and HashTable classes. It maintains a list of items, which can be accessed either with an index or with a key. Moreover, the collection is always sorted according to the keys. The items of a SortedList are ordered according to the values of their keys, and there's no method for sorting the collection according to the values stored in it.

To create a new SortedList collection, use a statement like the following:

```
Dim sList As New SortedList
```

As you may have guessed, this collection can store keys that are of the base data types. If you want to use custom objects as keys, you must specify an argument of the IComparer type, which tells VB how to compare the custom items. This information is crucial; without it, the SortedList won't be able to maintain its items sorted. You can still store items in the SortedList, but they will appear in the order in which they were added.

This form of the SortedList constructor has the following syntax:

```
Dim sList As New SortedList(New comparer)
```

where *comparer* is the name of a custom IComparer interface (which is discussed in detail later in this chapter). There are also two more forms of the constructor, which allow you to specify the initial capacity of the SortedList collection, as well as a Dictionary object, whose data (keys and values) will be added to the SortedList.

Like the other two collections examined in this chapter, the SortedList collection supports the Capacity and Count properties. To add an item to a SortedList collection, use the Add method, whose syntax is

```
sList.Add(key, item)
```

where *key* is the key of the new item and *item* is the item to be added. Both arguments are objects. The Add method is the only way to add items to a SortedList collection. All items are inserted into the collection according to their keys, and each item's key must be unique. Attempting to add a duplicate key will throw an exception.

The SortedList class also exposes the ContainsKey and ContainsValue properties, which allow you to find out whether a key or item exists in the list already. To add a new item, use the following statement that makes sure the key isn't in use:

```
If Not sList.ContainsKey(myKey) Then
    sList.Add(myKey, myItem)
End If
```

(Just replace *myKey* and *myItem* with your key and item.) It's OK to store duplicate items in the same SortedList collection, but you can still detect the presence of an item in the list with a similar If statement.

To replace an existing item, use the SetByIndex method, which replaces the value at a specific index. The syntax of the method is

```
sList.SetByIndex(index, item)
```

where the first argument is the index at which the value will be inserted and *item* is the new item to be inserted in the collection. This object will replace the value that corresponds to the specified index.

The key, however, remains the same. There's no equivalent method for replacing a key; you must first remove the item, and then insert it again with its new key.

To remove items from the collection, use the Remove and RemoveAt methods. The Remove method accepts a key as argument and removes the item that corresponds to that key. The RemoveAt method accepts an index as argument and removes the item at the specified index. To remove all the items from a SortedList collection, call its Clear method. After clearing the collection, you should also call its TrimToSize method to restore its capacity to the default size (16).

Let's build a SortedList and print out its elements. The following listing declares the *sList* SortedList and then adds 10 items to the collection. The keys are integers, and the values are strings. The items are added in no specific order, but as soon as they're added they're inserted at the proper location in the collection, so that their keys are in ascending order.

Create a new project, place a button on its form, and enter Listing 11.11 in its Click event handler. The project you'll build in this section is called SortedList, and you can find it on the CD.

LISTING 11.11: POPULATING A SIMPLE SORTEDLIST

```
Public Sub Button1_Click(ByVal sender As System.Object, _
                ByVal e As System.EventArgs)
    Dim sList As New System.Collections.SortedList()
' Populate sortedlist
    sList.Add(16, "item 3")
    sList.Add(10, "item 9")
    sList.Add(15, "item 4")
    sList.Add(17, "item 2")
    sList.Add(11, "item 8")
    sList.Add(14, "item 5")
    sList.Add(18, "item 1")
    sList.Add(12, "item 7")
    sList.Add(19, "item 0")
    sList.Add(13, "item 6")
    Dim SLEnum As IDictionaryEnumerator
    SLEnum = sList.GetEnumerator()
' Print all key-value pairs
    While SLEnum.MoveNext
        Console.WriteLine("Key = " & SLEnum.Key.Tostring & ", Value= " & _
                        SLEnum.Value.ToString
    End While
End Sub
```

The first segment of the code populates the ArrayList, while the second segment of the code prints all the key–value pairs in the order in which the enumerator retrieves them. The enumerator is the built-in mechanism for scanning a collection's items (it will be discussed in detail later in this chapter).

If you execute these statements, they will produce the following output:

```
Key = 10, Value= item 9
Key = 11, Value= item 8
```

```
Key = 12, Value= item 7
Key = 13, Value= item 6
Key = 14, Value= item 5
Key = 15, Value= item 4
Key = 16, Value= item 3
Key = 17, Value= item 2
Key = 18, Value= item 1
Key = 19, Value= item 0
```

The items are sorted according to their keys, regardless of the order in which they were inserted into the collection.

Let's look now at a few methods for extracting keys and values. To find out the index of a value in the SortedList, use the IndexOfValue method, which accepts as argument an object. If the object exists in the collection, it returns its index. If not, it returns the value −1. If the same value appears more than once in the collection, the IndexOfValue property will return the first instance of the value. Moreover, there's no mechanism for retrieving the following instances. Notice that the Index-OfValue property performs a case-sensitive search. The following statement will return the index 2 (the item you're looking for is in the third place in the original SortedList):

```
Console.WriteLine(sList.IndexOfValue("item 7"))
```

You can also find out the index of a specific key, with the IndexOfKey method, whose syntax is similar. Instead of a value, it locates a key. The following statement will return the index 7 (the key you're looking for is in the eighth place in the SortedList):

```
Console.WriteLine(sList.IndexOfKey(17))
```

The GetKey and GetValue methods allow you to retrieve the index that corresponds to a specific key or value in the SortedList. Both methods accept an object as argument and return an index.

Finally, you can combine the two methods to retrieve the key that corresponds to a value, with a statement like the following one:

```
Console.WriteLine(sList.GetKey(sList.IndexOfValue("item 7")))
```

This statement will print the value 12, based on the contents of the *sList* collection in Listing 11.11.

NOTE *If either the key or the value you're searching for can't be found, the IndexOfKey and IndexOfValue methods will return −1.*

You can retrieve the keys in a SortedList collection and create another list, with the GetKeyList method. Likewise, the GetValueList method returns all the values in the SortedList. The following code extracts the keys from the *sList* SortedList and stores them in the *keys* list. Then, it scans the list with the help of the *key* variable and prints all the keys:

```
Dim keys As IList
keys = slist.GetKeyList()
Dim key As Integer
For Each key In Keys
    Console.WriteLine(key)
Next
```

You can also extract both the keys and the values from a SortedList and store them into an ArrayList, as shown here:

```
Dim AllKeys As New ArrayList()
AllKeys.InsertRange(0, sList.GetValueList)
```

Each item is stored at a specific location in the SortedList, and you can find out the location of each item with a loop like the following:

```
Dim idx As Integer
For idx = 0 To sList.Count - 1
    Console.WriteLine("ITEM: " & sList.GetByIndex(idx).ToString & _
                      " is at location " & idx.Tostring)
Next
```

The output produced by this code segment is:

```
ITEM: item 9 is at location 0
ITEM: item 8 is at location 1
ITEM: item 7 is at location 2
ITEM: item 6 is at location 3
ITEM: item 5 is at location 4
ITEM: item 4 is at location 5
ITEM: item 3 is at location 6
ITEM: item 2 is at location 7
ITEM: item 1 is at location 8
ITEM: item 0 is at location 9
```

You can also find out the location of each key, with a loop like the following one:

```
For idx = 0 To sList.Count - 1
    Console.WriteLine("The key at location " & idx.ToString & " is " & _
                      sList.GetKey(idx).ToString)
    Next
```

The output produced by the preceding code segment is:

```
The key at location 0 is 10
The key at location 1 is 11
The key at location 2 is 12
The key at location 3 is 13
The key at location 4 is 14
The key at location 5 is 15
The key at location 6 is 16
The key at location 7 is 17
The key at location 8 is 18
The key at location 9 is 19
```

Notice that the keys are rearranged as they're added to the list, and they're always physically sorted.

As you can understand, the keys must be of a base data type. If not, the SortedList can't compare the keys and therefore can't maintain the proper order. To use objects as keys, you must also supply a function custom comparer (a function that knows how to compare two objects). The topic of creating custom comparers in discussed in detail shortly in the section "The IEnumerator and IComparer Interfaces." In the last example of that section, you will build a custom comparer for sorting the SortedList based on a function of its keys, instead of the actual values of the keys.

Remember the WordFrequencies project we built earlier to demonstrate the use of the HashTable class? Change the declaration of the WordFrequencies variable from HashTable to SortedList, and the project will work as before. The only difference is that the words will appear on the TextBox control sorted alphabetically when you click the Show Word Count button.

OTHER COLLECTIONS

The `System.Collections` class exposes a few more collections, including the Queue and the Stack collections. The main characteristic of these two collections is how you add and remove items to them. When you add items to a Queue, the items are appended to the collection. When you remove items, they're removed from the top of the collection. You'd use this collection to emulate the customer line in a bank or a production line.

The Stack collection inserts new items at the top, and you can only remove the top item. The Stack collection is a FIFO (first in first out) structure, while the Queue class is a LIFO structure (last in first out). You'd use this collection to emulate the stack maintained by the CPU, one of the most crucial structures for the operating system and applications alike. Stacks and Queues are used heavily in computer science, but they aren't as common in business applications. I'm not going to discuss any more collections in this book, but you can look them up in the documentation. There are quite a few more interesting topics to cover in this chapter—and most important is how to save a collection to a disk file and read it back.

The IEnumerator and IComparer Interfaces

Judging by its title, you probably thought this is a section for C++ programmers adapted for VB programmers. IEnumerator and IComparer are two objects that unlock some of the most powerful features of collections. The proper term for IEnumerator and IComparer is *interface*, a term I will describe shortly. If you don't want to get too technical about interfaces, think of them as objects. The IEnumerator object retrieves a list of pointers for all the items in a collection, and you can use it to iterate through the items in a collection. Every collection has a built-in enumerator, and you can retrieve it by calling its GetEnumerator method. The IComparer object exposes the Compare and CompareTo methods, which tells the compiler how to compare two objects of the same type. Once the compiler knows how to compare the objects, it can sort a collection of objects with the same type.

The IComparer interface consists of a function that compares two items and returns a value indicating their order (which one is the smaller item, or whether they're equal). The Framework can't compare objects of all types. It only knows how to compare the base types—integers, strings, and so on. It doesn't know how to compare two rectangles, or two color objects. If you have a collection of colors, you may want to sort them according to their luminance, saturation, brightness, and so on. The compiler can't make any assumptions as to how you may wish to sort your collection, and, of course, it doesn't expose members to sort a collection in all possible ways. Instead, it gives you the option to specify a function that compares two colors (or two objects of any other type, for that matter) and uses this function to sort the collection. The same function is used by the BinarySearch method, to locate an item in a sorted collection. In effect, the IComparer interface is a function that knows how to compare two Color objects, for our example. If the collection contains items of a custom Structure, the IComparer interface is a function that knows how to compare two instances of the custom Structure.

So, what is an interface? An *interface* is another term in object-oriented programming and describes a very simple technique. When we write the code for a class, we may not know how to implement a few operations, but we do know that they'll have to be implemented later. We insert a placeholder for these operations (a function declaration) and expect that the application that uses the class will provide the actual implementation of these functions. All collections expose a Sort method, which sorts the items in the collection by comparing them to one another. To do so, the Sort method calls a function that compares two items and returns a value indicating their relative order. Any class that exposes a function that can compare its objects can be sorted. The Integer data type, which is implemented by the `System.Integer` class, exposes such a function, and so do all the base types. Custom objects must provide their own comparison function—or more than a single function, if you want to sort them in multiple ways. Since you can't edit the collection's Sort method's code, you must supply your comparison function through a mechanism that the class can understand. This is what the IComparer interface is all about. The code that compares two objects of the same type is actually trivial. You must follow the steps outlined here to make this function part of the class, so that the collection can see and use it.

Enumerating Collections

All collections expose the IEnumerator interface, which is a fancy term for a very simple operation. IEnumerator returns an object that allows you to iterate through the collection without having to know anything about its items, not even the count of the items. To retrieve the enumerator for a collection, call its GetEnumerator method, with a statement like the following:

```
Dim ALEnum As IEnumerator
ALEnum = AList.GetEnumerator
```

The IEnumerator object exposes two methods, the MoveNext and Reset methods. The MoveNext method moves to the next item in the collection and makes it the current item. When you initialize the IEnumerator object, it's positioned in front of the very first item, so you must call the MoveNext method to move to the first item. The Reset method does exactly the same: it repositions the IEnumerator in front of the first element.

The MoveNext method doesn't return an item, as you might expect. It returns a True/False value indicating whether it has successfully moved to the next item. Once you have reached the end of the collection, the MoveNext method will return False. Here's how you can enumerate through an ArrayList collection with an enumerator:

```
Dim aItems As IEnumerator
aItems = aList.GetEnumerator
While aItems.MoveNext
    { process item aItems.Current }
End While
```

At each iteration, the current item is given by the Current property of the enumerator, which represents the current object in the collection. Once you have reached the last item, the MoveNext method will return False and the loop will terminate. To rescan the items, you must reset the enumerator by calling its Reset method.

To process the current item, you can directly call its methods through the `aItems.Current` object. If the collection holds Rectangles, for example, you can access their sizes with these expressions:

```
CType(aItems.Current, Rectangle).Width
CType(aItems.Current, Rectangle).Height
```

The Strict option necessitates the explicit conversion of the Current item to a Rectangle object. In other words, you can't use an expression like `aItems.Current.Width` with the Strict option on.

The event handler in Listing 11.12 populates an ArrayList with Rectangle objects and then iterates through the collection and prints the area of each Rectangle.

LISTING 11.12: ITERATING AN ARRAYLIST WITH AN ENUMERATOR

```
Protected Sub Button2_Click(ByVal sender As Object, _
                ByVal e As System.EventArgs)
    Dim aList As New ArrayList()
    Dim R1 As New Rectangle(1, 1, 10, 10)
    aList.Add(R1)
    R1 = New Rectangle(2, 2, 20, 20)
    aList.Add(R1)
    aList.add(New Rectangle(3, 3, 2, 2))
    Dim REnum As IEnumerator
    REnum = aList.GetEnumerator
    Dim R As New Rectangle()
    While REnum.MoveNext
        R = CType(REnum.Current, Rectangle)
        Console.WriteLine(R.Width * R.Height)
    End While
End Sub
```

The third Rectangle variable is added to the collection directly, without using an intermediate variable, as I did with the first two objects. The Rectangle object is initialized in the same line that adds the object to the collection. Then the *REnum* variable is set up and used to iterate through the items of the collection. At each iteration, the code saves the current Rectangle to the *R* variable, and it uses this variable to access the properties of the Rectangle object (its width and height).

Of course, you can iterate a collection without the enumerator, but with a `For Each…Next` loop. To iterate through a HashTable, you can use either the Keys or the Values collections. The code of Listing 11.13 populates a HashTable with Rectangle objects. Then it scans the items and prints their keys, which are strings, and the area of each rectangle.

```
Protected Sub Button3_Click(ByVal sender As Object, _
                ByVal e As System.EventArgs)
    Dim hTable As New HashTable()
    Dim r1 As New Rectangle(1, 1, 10, 10)
    hTable.Add("R1", r1)
    r1 = New Rectangle(2, 2, 20, 20)
    hTable.Add("R2", r1)
    hTable.add("R3", New Rectangle(3, 3, 2, 2))
    Dim key As Object
    Dim R As Rectangle
    For Each key In hTable.keys
        R = CType(hTable(key), Rectangle)
        Console.WriteLine("The area of Rectangle {0} is {1}", Key.ToString, _
                    R.Width * R.Height)
    Next
End Sub
```

The code adds three Rectangle objects to the HashTable and then iterates through the collection using the Keys properties. Each item's key is a string ("R1", "R2", and "R3"). The Keys property is itself a collection and can be scanned with a For Each…Next loop. At each iteration, we access a different item through its key, with the expression hTable(key). The output produced by this code is shown here:

```
The area of Rectangle R1 is 100
The area of Rectangle R2 is 400
The area of Rectangle R3 is 4
```

(I have used a format string with the WriteLine method to avoid a very long statement by embedding the values into the string.)

Alternatively, you can iterate a HashTable with an enumerator, but be aware that the GetEnumerator method of the HashTable collection returns an object of the IDictionaryEnumerator type, not an IEnumerator object. The IDictionaryEnumerator is quite similar to the IEnumerator, but it exposes additional properties. They are the Key and Value properties, and they return the current item's key and value. The IDictionaryEnumerator object also exposes the Entry property, which returns both the key and the value. You can access the current item's key and value either as DEnum.Key and DEnum.Value, or as DEnum.Entry.Key and DEnum.Entry.Value. *DEnum* is a properly declared enumerator for the HashTable:

```
Dim DEnum As IDictionaryEnumerator
```

Assuming that you have populated the *hTable* collection with the same three Rectangle objects, you can use the statements in Listing 11.14 to iterate through the collection's items.

LISTING 11.14: ITERATING A HASHTABLE WITH AN ENUMERATOR

```
Dim hEnum As IDictionaryEnumerator
hEnum = hTable.GetEnumerator
While hEnum.MoveNext
    Console.WriteLine("The value of " & hEnum.Key & "{0} is " & hEnum.Value)
    Console.WriteLine(CType(hEnum.Value, Rectangle).Width * _
                      CType(hEnum.Value, Rectangle).Height)
End While
```

If you execute these statements after populating the HashTable collection with three Rectangles, they will produce the following output:

```
The value of R1 is {X=1,Y=1,Width=10,Height=10}
100
The value of R2 is {X=2,Y=2,Width=20,Height=20}
400
The value of R3 is {X=3,Y=3,Width=2,Height=2}
4
```

The Value property of the enumerator returns an object, which must be cast to the appropriate type, before you can call its members—unless the Strict option has been set to Off, of course.

VB.NET AT WORK: THE ENUMERATIONS PROJECT

The project Enumerations (Figure 11.4) on the CD shows how to iterate through an ArrayList and a HashTable with and without an enumerator. The code should be quite familiar to you by now, so I will not list it list here. You can open the project and examine its code and routines.

FIGURE 11.4

How to scan ArrayLists and HashTables with and without an enumerator

You can also enumerate arrays with an IEnumerator object. You must declare the enumerator variable as IEnumerator and then call the MoveNext method to iterate the array from within a loop. Listing 11.15 iterates through the elements of a string array with an enumerator.

LISTING 11.15: ENUMERATING AN ARRAY

```
Dim Names(4) As String
Names(0) = "Name 0" : Names(1) = "Name 1"
Names(2) = "Name 2" : Names(3) = "Name 3"
Dim arrayEnum As IEnumerator
arrayEnum = Names.GetEnumerator
While arrayEnum.MoveNext
    Console.WriteLine(arrayEnum.Current)
End While
```

Custom Sorting

The Sort method allows you to sort collections, as long as the items are of the same base data type. If the items are objects, however, the collection doesn't know how to sort them. If you want to sort objects, you must help the collection a little by telling it how to compare two objects. A sorting operation is nothing more than a series of comparisons. Sorting algorithms compare items and swap them if necessary. They don't even swap the items; they simply rearrange a list of pointers to the items. The first pointer points to the first item in the sorted collection, the second pointer points to the second item in the sorted collection, and so on. The items themselves remain in their original positions.

All the information needed by a sorting algorithm to operate on any type of item is a function that compares two objects. Let's say you have a list of persons, and each person is a Structure that contains names, addresses, e-addresses, and so on. The System.Collections class can't make any assumptions as to how you want your list sorted. This collection can be sorted by any field in the structure (names, e-addresses, postal codes, and so on). Even if the collection contains a built-in object, like a Rectangle or Color object, the collection doesn't know how to sort them.

The comparer is implemented as a separate class, outside all other classes, and is specific to a custom data type. Let's say you have created a custom structure for storing contact information. The Person object is declared as a structure with the following fields:

```
Structure Person
    Dim Name As String
    Dim BDate As Date
    Dim EMail As String
End Structure
```

To add an instance of the Person object to an ArrayList or HashTable, create a variable of Person type and initialize its fields as follows:

```
Dim p As New Person
Dim aList As ArrayList
p.Name = "Adams, George"
p.Bdate = #4/17/1957#
p.EMail = "gadams@example.com"
aList.Add(p)
```

To add another element, you can either create a new Person object (variable *p1*, for example) or set the *p* variable to Nothing and then initialize it again.

```
p = Nothing
p.Name = "New Name"
p.BDate = #1/1/1950#
' The EMail field is empty
aList.Add(p)
```

This collection can't be sorted with the simple form of the Sort method, because the compiler doesn't know how to compare two Person objects. You must provide your own function for comparing two variables of the Person type. Once this function has been written, the compiler will be able to compare items and therefore sort the collection. This custom function, however, can't be passed to the Sort and BinarySearch methods by name. You must create a new class that implements the IComparer interface and pass an IComparer object to the two methods. Here's the outline of a class that implements the IComparer interface (then we'll look at the implementation details of the function that actually compares two objects).

```
Class customComparer : Implements IComparer
    Public Function Compare(ByVal o1 As Object, ByVal o2 As Object) _
                            As Integer Implements IComparer.Compare
        { function's code }
    End Function
End Class
```

The name of the class can be anything. It should be a name that indicates the type of comparison it performs, or the type of objects it compares. The name of the custom function must be Compare, and it must implement the `IComparer.Compare` interface. What exactly do we mean by "implement an interface"? As you have seen, all classes expose some standard members. The method ToString, for example, is a standard method, and the Framework knows how to implement it. It simply returns the name of the class. There are situations, however, where we know that we're going to need a member, we know the name of the member, but we just can't implement it.

The collection classes, for example, expose a Sort method. In order to sort their items, they must be able to compare two elements and figure out which one is first. The comparison can be carried out for the base types, but not for objects. So, they provide a placeholder, where you must place a function that knows how to compare two instances of the object. This ability to write classes that provide placeholders for the actual implementation of a method is known as *interface*. If you write a function that compares two objects of the specific type and you pass it to the Sort method, this function will be called in the place of the Compare method. The Sort method calls the Compare method of the class that represents the objects you're comparing. If it finds one, it uses it. If not, the Sort method won't work. The IComparer interface is the class's way of incorporating your custom comparer function into its Sort method.

Let's get back to our example. To use the custom function, you must create an object of `customComparer` type (or whatever you have named the class) and then pass it to the Sort and BinarySearch methods as argument:

```
Dim CompareThem As New customComparer
aList.Sort(CompareThem)
```

You can combine the two statements in one by initializing the *customComparer* variable in the line that calls the Sort method:

```
aList.Sort(New customComparer())
```

You can also use the equivalent syntax of the BinarySearch method to locate a custom object that implements its own IComparer interface:

```
BinarySearch(object, New customComparer())
```

This is how you use a custom function to compare two objects. Everything is the same, except for the name of the class, which is different every time. The last step is to write the code that compares the two objects and returns an integer value, indicating the order of the elements. This value should be −1 if the first object is smaller than the second object, 0 if the two objects are equal, and 1 if the first object is larger than the second object. "Smaller" here means that the element appears before the larger one when sorted in ascending order. Listing 11.16 is the function that sorts Person objects according to the Age field.

LISTING 11.16: A CUSTOM COMPARER

```
Class PersonAgeComparer : Implements IComparer
    Public Function Compare(ByVal o1 As Object, ByVal o2 As Object) As Integer _
                        Implements IComparer.Compare
        Dim person1, person2 As Person
        Try
            person1 = CType(o1, Person)
            person2 = CType(o2, Person)
        Catch compareException As system.Exception
            Throw (compareException)
            Exit Function
        End Try
        If person1.BDate < person2.BDate Then
            Return -1
        Else
            If person1.BDate > person2.BDate Then
                Return 1
            Else
                Return 0
            End If
        End If
    End Function
End Class
```

The code could have been considerably simpler, but I'll explain momentarily why the Try statement is necessary. The comparison takes place in the If statement. If the first person's birth date is numerically smaller than the second person's, the function returns the value −1. If the first person's birth date is numerically smaller than the second person's, the function returns 1. Finally, if the two values are equal, the function returns 0.

The code is straightforward, so why the error-trapping code? Before we perform any of the necessary operations, we convert the two objects into Person objects. It's not unthinkable that the collection with the objects you want to sort contains objects of different types. If that's the case, the CType() function won't be able to convert the corresponding argument to the Person type, and the comparison will fail. The same exception that would be thrown in the function's code is raised again from within the error handler, and it's passed back to the calling code.

The Person objects can be sorted in many different ways. You may wish to sort them by ID, name, and so on. To accommodate multiple sorts, you must implement several classes, each one with a different Compare function. Listing 11.17 shows two classes that implement two different Compare functions for the Person class. The PersonNameComparer class compares the names, while the PersonAgeComparer class compares the ages.

LISTING 11.17: A CLASS WITH TWO CUSTOM COMPARERS

```
Class PersonNameComparer : Implements IComparer
    Public Function Compare(ByVal o1 As Object, ByVal o2 As Object) As Integer _
                    Implements IComparer.Compare
        Dim person1, person2 As Person
        Try
            person1 = CType(o1, Person)
            person2 = CType(o2, Person)
        Catch compareException As system.Exception
            Throw (compareException)
            Exit Function
        End Try
        If person1.Name < person2.Name Then
            Return -1
        Else
            If person1.Name > person2.Name Then
                Return 1
            Else
                Return 0
            End If
        End If
    End Function
End Class
Class PersonAgeComparer : Implements IComparer
    Public Function Compare(ByVal o1 As Object, ByVal o2 As Object) As Integer _
                    Implements IComparer.Compare
        Dim person1, person2 As Person
        Try
            person1 = CType(o1, Person)
            person2 = CType(o2, Person)
        Catch compareException As system.Exception
            Throw (compareException)
            Exit Function
        End Try
```

```
        If person1.BDate > person2.BDate Then
            Return -1
        Else
            If person1.BDate < person2.BDate Then
                Return 1
            Else
                Return 0
            End If
        End If
    End Function
End Class
```

To test the custom comparers, create a new application and enter the code of Listing 11.17 (the two classes) in a separate Class module. Don't forget to include the declaration of the Person Structure. Then place a button on the form and enter the code of Listing 11.18 in its Click event handler. This code adds three persons with different names and birth dates to an ArrayList.

LISTING 11.18: TESTING THE CUSTOM COMPARERS

```
Private Sub Button1_Click(ByVal sender As System.Object, _
                ByVal e As System.EventArgs) Handles Button1.Click
    Dim AList As New ArrayList()
    Dim p As Person
' Populate collection
    p.Name = "C Person"
    p.EMail = "PersonC@sybex.com"
    p.BDate = #1/1/1961#
    If Not AList.Contains(p) Then AList.Add(p)
    p.Name = "A Person"
    p.EMail = "PersonA@sybex.com"
    p.BDate = #3/3/1961#
    If Not AList.Contains(p) Then AList.Add(p)
    p.Name = "B Person"
    p.EMail = "PersonB@sybex.com"
    p.BDate = #2/2/1961#
    If Not AList.Contains(p) Then AList.Add(p)
' Print collection as is
    Dim PEnum As IEnumerator
    PEnum = AList.GetEnumerator
    ListBox1.Items.Add("Original Collection")
    While PEnum.MoveNext
        ListBox1.Items.Add(CType(PEnum.Current, Person).Name & vbTab & _
                        CType(PEnum.Current, Person).BDate)
    End While
' Sort by name, then print collection
    ListBox1.Items.Add(" ")
```

```
        ListBox1.Items.Add("Collection Sorted by Name")
        AList.Sort(New PersonNameComparer())
        PEnum = AList.GetEnumerator
        While PEnum.MoveNext
            ListBox1.Items.Add(CType(PEnum.Current, Person).Name & vbTab & _
                            CType(PEnum.Current, Person).BDate)
        End While
    ' Sort by age, then print collection
        ListBox1.Items.Add(" ")
        ListBox1.Items.Add("Collection Sorted by Age")
        AList.Sort(New PersonAgeComparer())
        PEnum = AList.GetEnumerator
        While PEnum.MoveNext
            ListBox1.Items.Add(CType(PEnum.Current, Person).Name & vbTab & _
                            CType(PEnum.Current, Person).BDate)
        End While
    End Sub
```

The four sections of the code are delimited by comments, which appear in bold in the listing. The first section populates the collection with three variables of the Person type. The second section prints the items in the order in which they were added to the collection:

```
C Person
1/1/1961
A Person
3/3/1961
B Person
2/2/1961
```

The third section of the code calls the Sort method passing the *PersonNameComparer* custom comparer as argument, and it again prints the contents of the ArrayList. The names are listed now in alphabetical order:

```
A Person
3/3/1961
B Person
2/2/1961
C Person
1/1/1961
```

In the last section, it calls the Sort method again, this time to sort the items by age, and prints them:

```
C Person
1/1/1961
B Person
2/2/1961
A Person
3/3/1961
```

As you can see, it's straightforward to write your own custom comparers and sort your custom object in any way that suits your application. Custom comparisons may include more complicated calculations, not just comparisons. For example, you can sort Rectangles by their area, color values by their hue or saturation, and customers by the frequency of their orders.

The example of this section is called CustomComparer; you can find it in this chapter's folder on the CD. The main form (Figure 11.5) contains a single button, which populates the collection and then prints the original collection, the collection sorted by name, and then the collection sorted by birth date.

FIGURE 11.5

The Custom-Compare project: how to sort collections of objects according to any property

Custom Sorting of a SortedList

The items of a SortedList are sorted according to their keys. Of course, the SortedList will not be able to maintain the order of the keys, unless the keys are of a base type, such as integers or strings. If you need to use objects as keys, you must simply provide a function to implement the IComparer interface, as you know well by now. In this section, we'll build a custom comparer for the same SortedList we built earlier in the SortedList example. The custom comparer will sort the keys in the collection according to the cosine of their values. If you're not interested in trigonometry and don't know what the cosine of a number is, don't worry. It's a function that transforms a number into another number. If the keys were points in the space, you could sort them according to their distance from the sun, or whatever. The idea is that you can transform the keys into another meaningful value and sort the collection according to the transformed value.

NOTE *Whether the SortedList is sorted according to its keys, or a transformation of the keys, these values must be unique. It's not enough that the original keys be unique. Their transformations must be also unique.*

Let's start with the custom comparer, which comparers the cosines of the two values. Add a new class to the SortedList project and name it CustomComparer. Then enter the code from Listing 11.19 in its code window.

LISTING 11.19: A CUSTOM COMPARER FOR THE SORTEDLIST

```
Class CustomComparer : Implements IComparer
    Public Function Compare(ByVal o1 As Object, ByVal o2 As Object) As Integer _
                    Implements IComparer.Compare
        Dim num1, num2 As Integer
        Try
            num1 = CType(o1, Integer)
            num2 = CType(o2, Integer)
        Catch compareException As system.Exception
            Throw (compareException)
            Exit Function
        End Try
        If Math.Cos(num1) < Math.Cos(num2) Then
            Return -1
        Else
            If Math.Cos(num1) > Math.Cos(num2) Then
                Return 1
            Else
                Return 0
            End If
        End If
    End Function
End Class
```

The Compare() function is very similar to the Compare() functions of the previous examples. Instead of comparing the arguments directly, it transforms them with the help of the Cos() function and then compares the transformed values. You can replace the Cos() function with a custom function that performs as many calculations as necessary.

To test the custom comparer, open the SortedList project, place another button on the form, and enter the following declaration in the new button's Click event handler:

```
Dim sList As New System.Collections.SortedList(New CustomComparer())
```

This statement tells the SortedList to sort its keys using the CustomComparer, not the default comparer for the integer data type. Then copy the statements that populate the SortedList and paste them after the previous declaration. Finally, enter a few more statements to iterate through the SortedList and print the key–value pairs. Here's the complete listing of the second button's event handler for your reference:

```
Dim sList As New System.Collections.SortedList(New CustomComparer)
' Populate SortedList
sList.Add(16, "item 3")
sList.Add(10, "item 9")
sList.Add(15, "item 4")
sList.Add(17, "item 2")
sList.Add(11, "item 8")
```

```
sList.Add(14, "item 5")
sList.Add(18, "item 1")
sList.Add(12, "item 7")
sList.Add(19, "item 0")
sList.Add(13, "item 6")
While SLEnum.MoveNext
    Console.WriteLine("Key = " & SLEnum.Key.Tostring & ", Value= " & _
                      SLEnum.Value.ToString & ",   Cos(key) = " & _
                      Math.Cos(CType(SLEnum.Key, Double)))
End While
```

If you execute these statements, they will generate the following output:

```
Key = 16, Value= item 3,   Cos(key) = -0.9576594803233847
Key = 10, Value= item 9,   Cos(key) = -0.8390715290764524
Key = 15, Value= item 4,   Cos(key) = -0.7596879128588213
Key = 17, Value= item 2,   Cos(key) = -2.7516333805159693E-01
Key = 11, Value= item 8,   Cos(key) = 4.4256979880507854E-03
Key = 14, Value= item 5,   Cos(key) = 0.1367372182078336
Key = 18, Value= item 1,   Cos(key) = 0.6603167082440802
Key = 12, Value= item 7,   Cos(key) = 0.8438539587324921
Key = 13, Value= item 6,   Cos(key) = 0.9074467814501962
Key = 19, Value= item 0,   Cos(key) = 0.9887046181866692
```

Once you have declared a custom comparer, you can use it with the BinarySearch method as well. The binary search algorithm uses consecutive comparisons to locate an item in a sorted collection. If the custom comparer is in place, it simply calls your Compare() function to perform the comparisons and locate the item in the collection. The form of the BinarySearch method that uses a custom comparer to locate an item is

```
BinarySearch(object, comparer())
```

where *object* is the item you're looking for and *comparer* is the name of the custom comparer. For every collection that uses a custom comparer for its Sort method, you must call this form of the Binary-Search method.

In Chapter 8 we created a class to represent shapes and added a method to calculate the area of each shape. You can create an ArrayList of Shape objects and write your own comparer to sort the elements of the ArrayList according to the area of each shape.

The Serialization Class

You have seen how the various collections of VB.NET store items, how to access their elements, and even how to sort and search the collections. The last piece of information you need before you can use collections in your applications to store large sets of data is how to store collections to disk files. In the last section of this chapter, you'll learn how to do this so you can reuse a collection at a later time. What good is it to create a long collection, if your application can't retrieve from a disk file in another session?

None of the collections exposes a Save or a similarly named method. Fortunately, there's a mechanism that can store arbitrary objects to disk: the Serialization class. This class exposes the Serialize method, which saves an object to disk. The Deserialize method does the opposite: it reads a file created by the Serialize method and re-creates the original object. The Serialization class is a complicated one, but in this book I will discuss its Serialize and Deserialize methods, which you can use to persist your collection (and custom data types) to disk. When it comes to saving objects to disk (or even exchange them with other applications), the proper term is *persist*, which basically means to make an entity like an object, or variable, available to the application between sessions.

Serializing Individual Objects

To serialize an object, you must call the Serialize method of the `System.Runtime.Serialization` `.Formatters.Binary` object. First, declare an object of this type with a statement like the following:

```
Dim BFormatter As New BinaryFormatter()
```

To avoid fully qualifying the BinaryFormatter class, import the class into your project with the following statement:

```
Imports System.Runtime.Serialization.Formatters.BinaryFormatter
```

The BinaryFormatter class persists objects in binary format. You can also persist objects in text format, using the SoapFormatter. The SoapFormatter persists the objects in XML format, which is quite verbose and the corresponding files are considerably lengthier. To use the SoapFormatter object, you must add a reference to the following .NET component through the Add Reference dialog box:

```
System.Runtime.Serialization.Formatters.Soap
```

Notice that this isn't a class you can import; you must add a reference to the class. After that, you can declare a SoapFormatter variable with the following statement:

```
Dim formatter As Soap.SoapFormatter
```

If you're wondering where the name of this class comes from, SOAP is an acronym for Simple Object Access Protocol. This is a protocol for accessing objects over HTTP—in other words, it's a protocol that allows the encoding of objects in text format. The SOAP protocol was designed to enable distributed computing over the Internet, and it's used with Web services. So, if SOAP can be used to access objects over the Internet, why not use it to persist objects in text format?

The methods of the BinaryFormatter and SoapFormatter are equivalent, so I will use the Binary-Formatter in the examples of this section. At the end of the section, I will show the code behind the menu of the WordFrequencies project, which persists the HashTable with the words and their frequencies to both binary and text format.

The syntax of the Serialize method is

```
BFormatter.Serialize(stream, object)
```

where *stream* is a variable that represents a stream and *object* is the object you want to serialize. Since we want to persist our objects to disk files, the *stream* argument represents a stream to a binary file.

The File object and its methods are discussed in detail in Chapter 13; here, I will only explain briefly the statements we'll use to store data to a disk file and read it back. The following statements create such a Stream object:

```
Dim saveFile As FileStream
saveFile = File.Create("C:\SHAPES.BIN")
```

The *saveFile* variable represents the stream to a specific file on the disk, and the Create method of the same variable creates a stream to this file.

After you have set up the Stream and BinaryFormatter objects, you can call the Serialize method to serialize any object. To serialize a Rectangle object, for example, use the following statements:

```
Dim R As New Rectangle(0, 0 , 100, 100)
BFormatter.Serialize(saveFile, R)
```

The event handler in Listing 11.20 persists two Rectangle objects to the Shapes.bin file in the root folder. The file's extension can be anything. Since the file is binary, I've used the BIN extension:

LISTING 11.20: SERIALIZING DISTINCT OBJECTS

```
Protected Sub Button1_Click(ByVal sender As Object, ByVal e As System.EventArgs)
    Dim R1 As New Rectangle()
    R1.X = 1
    R1.Y = 1
    R1.Size.Width = 10
    R1.Size.Height = 20
    Dim R2 As New Rectangle()
    R2.X = 10
    R2.Y = 10
    R2.Size.Width = 100
    R2.Size.Height = 200
    Dim saveFile As FileStream
    saveFile = File.Create("C:\SHAPES.BIN")
    Dim formatter As BinaryFormatter
    formatter = New BinaryFormatter()
    formatter.Serialize(saveFile, R1)
    formatter.Serialize(saveFile, R2)
    saveFile.Close()
End Sub
```

Notice that the Serialize method serializes a single object at a time. To save the two rectangles, the code calls the Serialize method once for each rectangle. To serialize multiple objects with a single statement, you must create a collection, append all the objects to the collection, and then serialize the collection itself, as explained in the following section.

Serializing a Collection

Serializing a collection is quite similar to serializing any single object. The second argument to the Serialize method is the object you want to serialize, and this object can be anything, including a collection. To demonstrate the serialization of an ArrayList, we'll modify the previous code a little, so that instead of persisting individual items, it will persist an entire collection. Declare the two Rectangle objects as before, but this time append them to an ArrayList collection. Then add a color value to the collection, as shown in Listing 11.21, which serializes an ArrayList collection to the file C:\ShapesColors.bin.

LISTING 11.21: SERIALIZING A COLLECTION

```
Private Sub Button2_Click(ByVal sender As System.Object, _
            ByVal e As System.EventArgs) Handles Button2.Click
    Dim R1 As New Rectangle()
    R1.X = 1
    R1.Y = 1
    R1.Width = 10
    R1.Height = 20
    Dim R2 As New Rectangle()
    R2.X = 10
    R2.Y = 10
    R2.Width = 100
    R2.Height = 200
    Dim shapes As New ArrayList()
    shapes.Add(R1)
    shapes.Add(R2)
    shapes.Add(Color.Chartreuse)
    shapes.Add(Color.DarkKhaki.GetBrightness)
    shapes.Add(Color.DarkKhaki.GetHue)
    shapes.Add(Color.DarkKhaki.GetSaturation)
    Dim saveFile As FileStream
    saveFile = File.OpenWrite("C:\ShapesColors.bin")
    saveFile.Seek(0, SeekOrigin.End)
    Dim formatter As BinaryFormatter = New BinaryFormatter()
    formatter.Serialize(saveFile, shapes)
    saveFile.Close()
    MsgBox("ArrayList serialized successfully")
End Sub
```

The last three Add methods add the components of another color to the collection. Instead of adding the color as is, we're adding three color components, from which we can reconstruct the color Color.DarkKhaki. Then we proceed to save the entire collection to a file using the same statements as before. The difference is that we don't call the Serialize method for each object. We call it once and pass the entire ArrayList as argument.

If you open the ShapesColors.bin file with a text editor (start Notepad and drop the file on its window), you will see that most of the file contains binary information—most of the characters are not printable. You will still be able to read the names of the properties saved to the file, as shown in Figure 11.6.

Deserializing Objects

To read a file with the description of an object that has been persisted with the Serialize method, you simply call the Formatter object's Deserialize method and assign the result to an appropriately declared variable. In the case of the last example, the value returned by the Deserialize method must be assigned to an ArrayList variable. The syntax of the Deserialize method is

```
object = Bformatter.Deserialize(str)
```

where *str* is a Stream object to the file with the data.

Because the Deserialize method returns an Object variable, you must cast it to the ArrayList type with the CType() function. To use the Deserialize method, declare a variable that can hold the value returned by the method. If the data to be deserialized is a Rectangle, declare a Rectangle variable. If it's a collection, declare a variable of the same collection type. Then call the Deserialize method and cast the value returned to the appropriate type. The following statements outline the process:

```
Dim object As <type>
{ code to set up a Stream variable (str) and BinaryFormatter }
object = CType(Bformatter.Serialize(str), <type>)
```

Listing 11.22 is the code that retrieves the items from the ShapesColors.bin file and stores them into an ArrayList. I've added a few statements to print all the items of the ArrayList.

LISTING 11.22: DE-SERIALIZING A COLLECTION

```
Private Sub Button1_Click(ByVal sender As System.Object, _
                ByVal e As System.EventArgs) Handles Button1.Click
    Dim readFile As FileStream
    readFile = File.OpenRead("C:\ShapesColors.bin")
    Dim BFormatter As BinaryFormatter
    BFormatter = New BinaryFormatter()
```

```
        Dim Shapes As New ArrayList()
        Dim R1 As Rectangle
        Shapes = CType(BFormatter.Deserialize(readFile), ArrayList)
        Dim i As Integer
        TextBox1.AppendText("The ArrayList contains " & Shapes.Count & _
                            " objects" & vbCrLf & vbCrLf)
        For i = 0 To Shapes.Count - 1
            TextBox1.AppendText(Shapes(i).ToString & vbCrLf)
        Next
    End Sub
```

You can find the code presented in this section in the Serialization project on the CD. The application consists of two buttons; the first persists the collection to disk, and the second reads the file, re-creates the collection, and displays the objects read from the file.

PERSISTING A HASHTABLE

We can now return to the WordFrequencies project and examine the code behind the menu of the project. The Frequency Table menu contains four commands, which save the HashTable to, and read it from, a text file and a binary file. The four commands of the menu are:

Command	Effect
Save Binary	Saves the HashTable to a binary file with default extension BIN
Load Binary	Loads the HashTable with data from a binary file
Save SOAP	Saves the HashTable to a text file with default extension TXT
Load Binary	Loads the HashTable with data from a text file

The code behind the Save Binary command is shown in Listing 11.23. The code is actually quite simple: it creates an instance of the BinaryFormatter class (variable *Formatter*) and uses its Serialize method to persists the entire HashTable with a single statement.

LISTING 11.23: PERSISTING THE HASHTABLE TO A BINARY FILE

```
Private Sub SaveBin(ByVal sender As System.Object, _
                ByVal e As System.EventArgs) Handles SaveBinary.Click
    Dim saveFile As FileStream
    SaveFileDialog1.DefaultExt = "BIN"
    If SaveFileDialog1.ShowDialog = DialogResult.OK Then
        saveFile = File.OpenWrite(SaveFileDialog1.FileName)
        saveFile.Seek(0, SeekOrigin.End)
        Dim Formatter As BinaryFormatter = New BinaryFormatter()
        Formatter.Serialize(saveFile, WordFrequencies)
        saveFile.Close()
    End If
End Sub
```

The equivalent Load Binary command is just as simple. It sets up a BinaryFormatter object and calls its Deserialize method to read the data.

The code of the Save SOAP command (Listing 11.24) sets up a SoapFormatter object and uses its Serialize method to persist the HashTable. The code that reads the data from the file and populates the HashTable is equally simple, and it's shown in Listing 11.25.

LISTING 11.24: PERSISTING THE HASHTABLE TO A TEXT FILE

```
Private Sub SaveText(ByVal sender As System.Object, _
                ByVal e As System.EventArgs) Handles SaveText.Click
   Dim saveFile As FileStream
   SaveFileDialog1.DefaultExt = "XML"
   If SaveFileDialog1.ShowDialog = DialogResult.OK Then
      saveFile = File.OpenWrite(SaveFileDialog1.FileName)
      saveFile.Seek(0, SeekOrigin.End)
      Dim Formatter As Soap.SoapFormatter = New Soap.SoapFormatter()
      Formatter.Serialize(saveFile, WordFrequencies)
      saveFile.Close()
   End If
End Sub
```

LISTING 11.25: LOADING A HASHTABLE FROM A TEXT FILE

```
Private Sub LoadText(ByVal sender As System.Object, _
                ByVal e As System.EventArgs) Handles LoadText.Click
   Dim readFile As FileStream
   OpenFileDialog1.DefaultExt = "XML"
   If OpenFileDialog1.ShowDialog = DialogResult.OK Then
      readFile = File.OpenRead(OpenFileDialog1.FileName)
      Dim Formatter As Soap.SoapFormatter
      Formatter = New Soap.SoapFormatter()
      WordFrequencies = CType(Formatter.Deserialize(readFile), SortedList)
   End If
End Sub
```

As you can see, the code is identical whether you use the BinaryFormatter or a SoapFormatter class. The code is quite simple, and the Serialize/Deserialize methods do all the work automagically.

You can open the binary file with a text editor, and you will see the words but not the numeric values. If you open the text file, you will see a structured XML file with the words and their counts. The words are in the first half of the file, and their counts in the second half. Here are the first few lines of this file (I've omitted the headers):

```
<item id="ref-5" xsi:type="SOAP-ENC:string">A</item>
<item id="ref-6" xsi:type="SOAP-ENC:string">ABADDIRS</item>
```

```
<item id="ref-7" xsi:type="SOAP-ENC:string">ABANDON</item>
<item id="ref-8" xsi:type="SOAP-ENC:string">ABANDONED</item>
<item id="ref-9" xsi:type="SOAP-ENC:string">ABANDONING</item>
```

The corresponding counts are:

```
<item xsi:type="xsd:int">2064</item>
<item xsi:type="xsd:int">1</item>
<item xsi:type="xsd:int">5</item>
<item xsi:type="xsd:int">10</item>
<item xsi:type="xsd:int">2</item>
```

Most of us shouldn't really care how the Serialize method stores the data to the XML file, or to the binary file, as long as the Deserialize method can read them back into and load them into an object so that we won't have to write code to parse this file.

Summary

The Collection classes we explored in this chapter are just a few among the 3,500 classes of the .NET Framework, but they're certainly among the most useful ones. Just about any application that needs to persist data between sessions can benefit from these classes. Even the humble array has been totally revamped; it can now sort and search its elements. The ArrayList is a dynamic array, while the HashTable is offers many of the advantages of an ArrayList plus the capability to access its elements by meaningful keys.

All the collections support custom sorting and searching. If the collection contains objects or custom structures, you can provide simple custom functions to enable the comparison and sorting of the collection's elements. Not only that, but you can provide multiple comparers and use each one to sort the collection in many different ways, as needed.

The last class we explored in this chapter was the Serialization class, which basically enables you to persist complicated objects with a single function call. You saw examples of using the members of the Serialization class with an ArrayList, but this is probably the most efficient way to use the Serialization class. An ArrayList may can be populated with objects of any type, so you can store your custom objects to an ArrayList and then persist the entire collection to a file with a few simple statements.

Chapter 12

Handling Strings, Characters, and Dates

THIS CHAPTER IS A formal discussion of the .NET Framework's string- and date-manipulation capabilities. You have seen many of the string functions in earlier chapters, as well as many of the properties and methods of the String class. Almost every application manipulates strings, so the String and StringBuilder classes are two that you'll use more than any other.

Previous versions of Visual Basic provided numerous functions for manipulating strings. These functions are supported by VB.NET, and not just for compatibility reasons; they're part of the core of Visual Basic. The string-manipulation functions are still a major part of VB, while the math functions were removed from the language and placed in a special class, the System.Math class. This is a good indication of the type of processing that takes place in a typical application. You'll write more code to manipulate strings than to do math.

Another group of functions deals with dates. The date-manipulation functions are still part of the core of the language and were not moved to a special class. Many of these functions are duplicated in the DateTime class, in the form of properties and methods. The Month() function, for example, returns the month of a date passed to the function as argument. The DateTime.Month property does the same: it returns the month of a date value. The following statements print the number of the current month:

```
Console.WriteLine(Month(Now()))
Console.WriteLine(Now().Month)
```

The first statement used the Month() function, while the second one uses the Date class's Month method. The function Now() returns the current date, which is a value of the Date type (which is the same as the DateTime type), and that's why we can apply the Month method to this value.

The string- and date-handling functions of Visual Basic are described in the reference "VB.NET Functions and Statements" (on the companion CD). These functions aren't new to VB.NET anyway, and it's important that you familiarize yourself with the built-in functions, even if you're going to use the new classes of the .NET Framework. There are miles of VB6 code out there, and it's more than likely that you will run into code ported from VB6 applications, or you'll be asked to port VB6 code into .NET.

In this chapter, we'll explore the members of the String and StringBuilder classes, which handle strings, and the members of the DateTime and TimeSpan classes, which handle dates and time. As I go along, I will mention the equivalent VB functions for the readers already familiar with VB6. If you're porting old VB applications to VB.NET, the string and date functions of VB6 still work with VB.NET, but you should gradually replace them with the newer classes. If you've written applications that manipulate strings extensively, you should take the time to replace the older string functions with the equivalent methods of the StringBuilder class.

Handling Strings and Characters

The new Framework provides two classes for manipulating text: the String and the StringBuilder classes. The String object represents fixed-length strings, which you can't edit. Once you assign a value to a String object, that's it. You can examine the string, locate words in it, parse it, but you can't edit it. The String class also exposes methods like the Replace and Remove methods, which replace a section of the string with another or remove a range of characters from the string. These methods, however, don't act on the string directly: they replace or remove parts of the original string and then return the result as a new string.

The StringBuilder class is similar to the String class: it stores strings, but it can manipulate them in place. The distinction between the two classes is that the String class is for static strings, while the StringBuilder class is for dynamic strings. Use the String class for strings that don't change frequently in the course of an application and the StringBuilder class for strings that grow and shrink frequently. The two classes expose similar methods, but the String class's methods return new strings; if you need to manipulate large strings extensively, using the String class may fill the memory quite fast.

Any code that manipulates strings must also be able to manipulate individual characters. In previous versions of Visual Basic, characters were indistinguishable from strings; they were one-character strings. VB.NET introduces the Char class, which not only stores characters but also exposes numerous methods for handling characters. Both the String and StringBuilder classes provide methods for storing strings into arrays of characters, as well as converting character arrays into strings. After extracting the individual characters from a string, you can process them with the members of the Char class. We'll start our discussion of text-handling features of VB.NET with an overview of the Char data type, and we'll continue with the other two major components, the String and StringBuilder classes.

VB6 ➡ VB.NET

The Char class is new to VB.NET, and it exposes numerous methods for handling characters. You will find this data type especially useful in validating user-supplied strings, as you no longer need to write code to figure out whether a character is a digit or letter, a special character, and so on. There are now methods you can call to find out the type of character stored in a Char variable.

The StringBuilder is also new to VB.NET. The old string functions of Visual Basic are now implemented as methods of the String and StringBuilder classes.

The Char Class

The Char data type stores characters as individual, double-byte (16-bit), Unicode values, and it exposes methods for classifying the character stored in a Char variable. You can use methods like IsDigit and IsPunctuation on a Char variable to determine its type, and other similar methods can simplify your string validation code.

To use a character variable in your application, you must declare it with a statement like the following one:

```
Dim ch As Char = "A"
```

You can also initialize it by setting the variable to a character:

```
Dim ch As Char = CChar("A")
```

The expression "A" represents a string, even though it contains a single character. Everything you enclose in double quotes is a string. To convert it to a character, you must cast it to the Char type. If the Strict option is off (which is the default value), you need not perform the conversion explicitly. If the Strict option is on, you must use the CChar() or CType() function to convert the string in the double quotes to a character value, as shown in the second example line. You can also pass a string to CChar() function. It will convert the *first* character of the string to a Char type and ignore the following characters. The CType() function can convert an object to a character.

PROPERTIES

The Char class provides two trivial properties, MaxValue and MinValue. They return the largest and smallest character values you can represent with the Char data type.

METHODS

The Char data type exposes methods for handling characters. As you will see, the String and StringBuilder classes expose the Chars property, which returns individual characters in the string, and you can apply any of the methods discussed here to a variable of the Char type.

All the methods discussed in the following sections have the same syntax. They accept either a single argument, which is the character they act upon, or a string and the index of a character in the string on which they act. The IsDigit() method, for example, has two forms, which are:

```
Char.IsDigit(char)
Char.IsDigit(string, 3)
```

The first statement acts on a character variable, while the second form acts on the third character of the specified string. Both methods return True if the specified character is a numeric digit, False otherwise.

With a few exceptions, the methods of the Char class are *shared*. This means that you can call them without having to create an instance of the class. As you saw, the IsDigit method accepts as argument a character and doesn't act on a Char variable. If the *ch* variable represents a character, you can find out whether the character is a digit with either of the following statements:

```
ch.IsDigit(ch)
Char.IsDigit(ch)
```

The first notation isn't very elegant, so I will use the second notation in the examples of this section. You can even use the following counter-intuitive method of calling IsDigit:

```
CType("a", Char).IsDigit("4")
```

The CType() function returns a character, and you can apply any of the System.Char class's methods to this character.

GetNumericValue

This method returns a numeric value if called with an argument that is a digit, and the value −1 otherwise. If you call the GetNumericDigit with the argument "5", it will return the numeric value 5. If you call it with the symbol "@", it will return the value −1.

GetUnicodeCategory

This method returns a numeric value that is a member of the UnicodeCategory enumeration and identifies the Unicode group to which the character belongs. The Unicode categories group characters into many categories such as math symbols, currency symbols, and quotation marks. Look up the UnicodeCategory enumeration in the documentation for more information.

IsControl

This method returns a True/False value indicating whether the specified character is a control character. The Backspace and Escape keys, for example, are control characters. The second form of the method examines the character at location *index* in a string and returns True if it's a control character.

IsDigit

This method determines whether the specified character is a digit. The code segment in Listing 12.1 uses the IsDigit method to find out whether the current character is a digit or a character. You can insert this code in a control's KeyPress event to process each keystroke.

LISTING 12.1: DIFFERENTIATING LETTER FROM DIGIT KEYSTROKES

```
Private Sub TextBox1_KeyPress(ByVal sender As Object, _
            ByVal e As KeyPressEventArgs) Handles TextBox1.KeyPress
    Dim c As Char
    c = e.KeyChar
    If Char.IsDigit(c) Then
        { process c as number }
    Else
        { process c as character or punctuation symbol }
    End If
End Sub
```

The `e.KeyChar` property returns the character that was pressed by the user and fired the KeyPress event. To reject nonnumeric keys as the user enters text on a TextBox control, use the event handler shown in Listing 12.2.

LISTING 12.2: REJECTING NONNUMERIC KEYSTROKES

```
Private Sub TextBox1_KeyPress(ByVal sender As Object, ByVal e As EventArgs)
    Dim c As Char
    c = e.KeyChar
    If Not (Char.IsDigit(c) Or Char.IsControl(c)) Then
      e.Handled = True
    End If
End Sub
```

This code ignores any keystrokes that don't represent numeric digits and are not control characters. Control characters are not rejected, because we want users to be able to edit the text on the control. The Backspace key is captured by the KeyPress event, and you shouldn't "kill" it. If the TextBox control is allowed to accept fractional values, you should allow the period character as well, by using the following If clause:

```
Dim c As Char
c = e.KeyChar
If Not (Char.IsDigit(c) Or c = "." Or Char.IsControl(c)) Then
    e.Handled = True
End If
```

IsLetter

This method returns a True/False value indicating whether the specified character is a letter. You can write an event handler similar to the one shown in Listing 12.2 using the IsLetter method to accept letters and reject numeric keys and special symbols.

IsLetterOrDigit

This method returns a True/False value indicating whether the specified character is a letter or a digit. The example of the Chars property of the String class shows how to scan an entire string to find out whether it's made up of letter and digits, or whether it contains symbols as well.

IsLower, IsUpper

This method returns a True/False value indicating whether the specified character is lowercase or uppercase, respectively.

IsNumber

This method returns a True/False value indicating whether the specified character is a number. The IsNumber method takes into consideration hexadecimal digits (the characters 0123456789ABCDEF) in the same way as the IsDigit method does for decimal numbers.

IsPunctuation

This method returns a True/False value indicating whether the specified character is a punctuation mark.

IsSeparator

This method returns a True/False value indicating whether the character is categorized as a separator (space, newline character, and so on). The following characters are considered separators (oddly, the semicolon is not a separator):

)	closing parenthesis
:	colon
,	comma
!	exclamation mark
(	opening parenthesis
.	period
#	pound sign

IsWhiteSpace

This method returns a True/False value indicating whether the specified character is white space. Any sequence of spaces, tabs, line feeds, and form feeds is considered white space. Use this method along with the IsPunctuation method to remove all characters in a string that are not words.

ToLower, ToUpper

These methods convert their argument to a lowercase or uppercase character and return it as another character.

ToString

This method converts a character to a string. It returns a single-character string, which you can use with other string-manipulation methods or functions.

The String Class

The String class implements the String data type, which is one of the richest data types in terms of the members it exposes. We have used strings extensively in earlier chapters, but this is a formal discussion of the String data type and all of the functionality it exposes.

To create a new instance of the String class, you simply declare a variable of the String type. You can also initialize it by assigning to the corresponding variable a text value:

```
Dim title As String = "Mastering VB.NET"
```

The String class exposes a Replace method, but this method returns a new string; it doesn't replace the specified characters in the original string:

```
Dim title As String = "Mastering VB.NET"
Dim newTitle As String
newTitle = title.Replace("VB", "Visual Basic")
```

The Replace method, and many other methods of the String class, don't operate directly on a string. Instead, they create a new string and return it as their result. In the last statement of the example, the Replace method doesn't act directly on the *title* variable. It creates a new String variable, which is assigned to another variable. You can also apply the result of a method to the same variable to which the method applies:

```
title = title.Replace("VB", "Visual Basic")
```

You can also manipulate strings with Visual Basic's string-manipulation functions. For example, you can replace the substring "VB" with "Visual Basic" with the following statement:

```
newTitle = Replace(title, "VB", "Visual Basic")
```

Like the methods of the String class, the string-manipulation functions don't act on the original string; they return a new string.

If you plan to manipulate strings in your code often, use the StringBuilder class instead, which is extremely fast compared to the String class and VB's string-manipulation functions.

Some of the members of the String class are shared members, while some others are instance members. The Copy method, for example, accepts as argument the string to be copied and doesn't require an instance of the class:

```
Dim s1, s2 As String
s1 = "This is a string"
s2 = String.Copy(s1)
```

The Length property, however, can only be applied to an instance of the String class. The following statement returns the length of the string stored in the variable *s1*:

```
Console.WriteLine(s1 & " is " & s1.Length.ToString & " characters long.")
```

PROPERTIES

The String class exposes only two properties, the Length and Chars properties, which return a string's length and its characters respectively. Both properties are read-only.

Length

The Length property returns the number of characters in the string, and it's read-only. To find out the number of characters in a string variable, use the following statement:

```
chars = myString.Length
```

You can apply the Length method to any expression that evaluates to a string. The following statement formats the current date in long date format (this format includes the day's and month's names) and then retrieves the string's length:

```
StrLen = Format(Now(), "dddd, MMMM dd, yyyy").Length
```

The Format() function formats numbers and dates and was discussed in Chapter 3.

Chars

The Chars property is an array of characters that holds all the characters in the string. Use this property to read individual characters from a string based on their location in the string. The index of the first character in the Chars array is zero.

TIP *The Chars array is read-only, and you can't edit a string by setting individual characters.*

The loop detailed in Listing 12.3 rejects strings (presumably passwords) that are less than six characters long and don't contain a special symbol:

LISTING 12.3: VALIDATING A PASSWORD

```
Private Function ValidatePassword(ByVal password As String) As Boolean
    If password.Length < 6 Then
        MsgBox("The password must be at least 6 characters long")
        Return False
    End If
    Dim i As Integer
    Dim valid As Boolean = False
    For i = 0 To password.Length - 1
        If Not Char.IsLetterOrDigit(password.Chars(i)) Then Return True
    Next
    MsgBox("The password must contain at least one " & _
            "character that is not a letter or a digit.")
    Return False
End Function
```

The code checks the length of the user-supplied string and makes sure it's at least six characters long. If not, it issues a warning and returns False. Then it starts a loop that scans all the characters in the string. Each character is accessed by its index in the string. If one of them is not a letter or digit—in which case the IsLetterOrDigit method will return False—the function terminates and returns True to indicate a valid password. If the loop is exhausted, then the *password* argument contains no special symbols and the function displays a message and returns False.

METHODS

All the functionality of the String class is available through methods, which are described in the following sections. Most of these methods are shared methods: you must supply the string on which they act as argument. In other words, they don't modify the current instance of the String class; instead, they return a new String value.

Compare

This method compares two strings and returns a negative value if the first string is less than the second, a positive value if the second string is less than the first, and zero if the two strings are equal. The Compare method is overloaded, and the first two arguments are always the two strings to be compared.

The simplest form of the method accepts two strings as arguments:

```
String.Compare(str1, str2)
```

The following form of the method accepts a third argument, which is a True/False value and determines whether the search will be case-sensitive (if True) or not:

```
String.Compare(str1, str2, case)
```

Another form of the Compare method allows you to compare segments of two strings; its syntax is

```
String.Compare(str1, index1, str2, index2, length)
```

index1 and *index2* are the starting locations of the segment to be compared in each string. The two segments must have the same length, which is specified by the last argument.

The following statements return the values shown in bold below each:

```
Console.WriteLine(String.Compare("the quick brown fox", "THE QUICK BROWN FOX"))
-1
Console.WriteLine(String.Compare("THE QUICK BROWN FOX", "the quick brown fox"))
1
Console.WriteLine(String.Compare("THE QUICK BROWN FOX", "THE QUICK BROWN FOX"))
0
```

If you want to specify a case-sensitive search, append yet another argument and set it to True. The forms of the Compare method that perform case-sensitive searches may accept yet another argument, which determines the culture info.

CompareOrdinal

The CompareOrdinal method compares two strings similar to the Compare method, but it doesn't take into consideration the current locale. This method returns zero if the two strings are the same, but a positive or negative value if they're different. These values are not 1 and –1; the value can be anything, since it represents the numeric difference between the Unicode values of the first two characters that are different in the two strings.

Concat

This method concatenates two or more strings (places them one after the other) and forms a new string. The simpler form of the Concat method has the following syntax, and it's equivalent to the & operator:

```
newString = String.Concat(string1, string2)
```

This statement is equivalent to the following:

```
newString = string1 & string2
```

A more useful from of the same method concatenates a large number of strings stored in an array:

```
newString = String.Concat(strings)
```

To use this form of the method, store all the strings you want to concatenate into a string array and then call the Concat method, as shown in this code segment:

```
Dim strings() As String = {"string1", "string2", "string3", "string4"}
Dim longString As String
longString = String.Concat(strings)
```

If you want to separate the individual strings with special delimiters, append them to each individual string before concatenating them. Or, you can use the Join method discussed later in this section. The Concat method simply appends each string to the end of the previous one.

Copy

The Copy method copies the value of one String variable to another. Notice that the value to be copied must be passed to the method as argument. The Copy method doesn't apply to the current instance of the String class. Most programmers will use the assignment operator and will never bother with the Copy method. The last two statements in the following sample code are equivalent:

```
Dim s1, s2 As String
s1 = "some text"
s2 = s1
s2 = String.Copy(s1)
```

The following syntax will also work, because the *s1* variable is an instance of the String class, but it's awkward—almost annoying:

```
s2 = s1.Copy(s1)
```

However, the Copy method doesn't return a copy of the string to which it's applied. The following statement is invalid:

```
s2 = s1.Copy        ' INVALID STATEMENT
```

EndsWith, StartsWith

These two methods return True if the string ends or starts with a user-supplied substring. The syntax of these methods is

```
found = str.EndsWith(string)
found = str.StartsWith(string)
```

These two methods are equivalent to using the Left and Right functions to extract a given number of characters from the left or right end of the string. The two statements following the declaration of the *name* variable are equivalent:

```
Dim name As String = "Visual Basic.NET"
```

```
If Left(name, 3) = "Vis" Then ...
If name.StartsWith("Vis") Then ...
```

Notice that the comparison performed by the StartsWith method is case-sensitive. If you don't care about the case, you can convert both the string and the substring to uppercase, as in the following example:

```
If name.ToUpper.StartsWith("VIS") Then ...
```

This If clause is True regardless of the casing of the *name* variable.

IndexOf, LastIndexOf

These two methods locate a substring in a larger string. The IndexOf method starts searching from the beginning of the string, and the LastIndexOf method starts searching from the end of the string. Both methods return an integer, which is the order of the substring's first character in the larger string (the order of the first character is zero).

VB6 ➡ VB.NET

The IndexOf and LastIndexOf methods are equivalent to the InStr() and InStrRev() functions of VB6.

In the following examples, *ch* is a Char variable, *chars* is an array of type Char, and *str* is a String variable.

To locate a single character in a string, use the following forms of the IndexOf method:

```
String.IndexOf(ch)
String.IndexOf(ch, startIndex)
String.IndexOf(ch, startIndex, count)
```

The *startIndex* argument is the location in the string, where the search will start, and the *count* argument is the number of characters that will be examined. The IndexOf method returns the location of the first instance in the string—these two methods are instance methods.

To locate a string, use the following forms of the IndexOf method:

```
String.IndexOf(str)
String.IndexOf(str, startIndex)
String.IndexOf(str, startIndex, count)
```

The last three forms of the IndexOf method search for an array of characters in the string:

```
String.IndexOf(chars())
String.IndexOf(chars(), startIndex)
String.IndexOf(chars(), startIndex, count)
```

The following statement will return the position of the string "Visual" in the text of the *TextBox1* control, or −1 if the string isn't contained in the text:

```
Dim pos As Integer
pos = TextBox1.Text.IndexOf("Visual")
```

Both methods perform a case-sensitive search, taking into consideration the current locale. To make case-insensitive searches, use uppercase for both the string and the substring. The following statement returns the location of the string "visual" (or "VISUAL", "Visual", and even "vISUAL") within the text of *TextBox1*:

```
Dim pos As Integer
pos = TextBox1.Text.ToUpper.IndexOf("VISUAL")
```

The expression `TextBox1.Text` is the text on the control, and its type is String. We apply the method ToUpper to convert the text to uppercase. The expression `TextBox1.Text.ToUpper` is the text on the TextBox1 control converted to uppercase, which is a string value. Finally, we apply the IndexOf method to this string to locate the first instance of the word "VISUAL."

IndexOfAny

This method accepts as argument an array of characters and returns the first occurrence of any of the array's characters in the string:

```
str.IndexOfAny(chars)
```

where *chars* is an array of characters. This method attempts to locate the first instance of any member of *chars* in the string. If the character is found, then its index is returned. If not, the process is repeated with the second character and so on, until an instance is found, or the array has been exhausted. If you want to locate the first delimiter in a string, call the IndexOfAny method with an array like the following:

```
Dim chars() As Char = {CChar(" "), CChar("."), CChar(","), CChar(";")}
Dim mystring As String = "This is a short sentence"
Console.WriteLine(mystring.IndexOfAny(chars))
```

When the last statement is executed, the value 4 will be printed on the Output window. This is the location of the first space in the string (keep in mind that the index of the first character in the string is zero).

To locate the first number in a string, pass the *nums* array to the IndexOfAny method, as shown in the following example:

```
Dim nums() As Char = {"1", "2", "3", "4", "5", "6", "7", "8", "9", "0"}
mystring = "This sentence contains 36 characters"
Console.WriteLine(mystring.IndexOfAny(nums))
```

The statements shown here will work if the Strict option is off. If this option is turned on, you must explicitly convert each number to a character with the CChar() or CType() function, as shown in the first example of this section.

Insert

The Insert method inserts one or more characters at a specified location in a string and returns the new string. The syntax of the Insert method is

```
newString = str.Insert(startIndex, subString)
```

startIndex is the position in the *str* variable, where the string specified by the second argument will be inserted. The following statement will insert a dash between the second and third characters of the string "CA93010"

```
Dim Zip As String = "CA93010"
Dim StateZip As String
StateZip = Zip.Insert(2, "-")
```

The *StateZip* string variable will become "CA-93010" after the execution of these statements.

Join

This method joins two or more strings and returns a single string with a separator between the original strings. Its syntax is

```
newString = String.Join(separator, strings)
```

where *separator* is the string that will be used as separator and *strings* is an array with the strings to be joined.

If you have an array of many strings and you want to join a few of them, you can specify the index of the first string in the array and the number of strings to be joined with the following form of the Join method:

```
newString = String.Join(separator, strings, startIndex, count)
```

The following statement will create a full path by joining folder names:

```
Dim path As String
Dim folders() As String = {"My Documents", "Business", "Expenses"}
path = String.Join("/", folders)
```

The value of the *path* variable after the execution of these statements will be:

```
My Documents/Business/Expenses
```

Split

Just as you can join strings, you can split a long string into smaller ones with the Split method, whose syntax is

```
strings() = String.Split(delimiters, string)
```

where *delimiters* is an array of characters and *string* is the string to be split. The string is split into sections that are separated by any one of the delimiters specified with the first argument. These strings are returned as an array of strings. The Split method, like the Join method, is a shared method (you can't split a string variable by applying the Split method to it).

NOTE *The* delimiters *array allows you to specify multiple delimiters, which makes it a great tool for isolating words in a text. You can specify all the characters that separate words in text (spaces, tabs, periods, exclamation marks, and so on) as delimiters and pass them along with the text to be parsed to the Split method.*

The statements in Listing 12.4 isolate the parts of a path, which are delimited by a backslash character.

LISTING 12.4: EXTRACTING A PATH'S COMPONENTS

```
Dim path As String = "c:\My Documents\Business\Expenses"
Dim delimiters() As Char = {CChar("\")}
Dim parts() As String
parts = path.Split(delimiters)
Dim iPart As IEnumerator
iPart = parts.GetEnumerator
While iPart.MoveNext
    Console.WriteLine(iPart.Current.tostring)
End While
```

If the path ends with a slash, then the Split method will return an extra empty string. You should either make sure that the string doesn't start or end with a delimiter, or ignore the elements of the *parts* array that hold empty strings.

Notice that the *parts* array is declared without a size. It's a one-dimensional array that will be dimensioned automatically by the Split method, according to the number of substrings separated by the specified delimiter(s). The second half of the code iterates through the parts of the path and displays them on the Output window.

If you execute the statements of Listing 12.4 (place them in a button's Click event handler and run the program), the following strings will be printed in the Output window:

```
c:
My Documents
Business
Expenses
```

Remove

The Remove method removes a given number of characters from a string, starting at a specific location, and returns the result as a new string. Its syntax is

```
newString = str.Remove(startIndex, count)
```

where *startIndex* is the index of the first character to be removed in the *str* string variable and *count* is the number of characters to be removed.

The Remove method is new to VB.NET. To remove a particular number of characters in previous versions of Visual Basic, you had to build a new string by concatenating the characters to the left and to the right of the part of the string to be removed.

Replace

This method replaces all instances of a specified character (or substring) in a string with a new one. It creates a new instance of the string, replaces the characters as specified by its arguments, and returns this string:

```
newString = str.Replace(oldChar, newChar)
```

where *oldChar* is the character in the *str* variable to be replaced and *newChar* is the character to replace the occurrences of *oldChar*. The string after the replacement is returned as the result of the method. The following statements replace all instances of the tab character with a single space. You can change the last statement to replace tabs with a specific number of spaces—usually 3, 4, or 5 spaces.

```
Dim txt, newTxt As String
Dim vbTab As String = vbCrLf
txt = "some text        with two tabs"
newTxt = txt.Replace(vbTab, " ")
```

Note that the Replace method can also replace substrings in a longer string. This form of the syntax is shown next:

```
newString = str.Replace(oldString, newString)
```

Use the following statements to replace all instances of "VB7" in a string with the substring "VB.NET":

```
Dim txt, newTxt As String
txt = "Welcome to VB7"
newTxt = txt.Replace("VB7", "VB.NET")
```

PadLeft, PadRight

These two methods align the string left or right in a specified field. They both return a fixed-length string with spaces to the right (for left-padded strings) or to the left (for right-padded strings). Both methods accept the length of the field as argument and return a new string:

```
Dim LPString, RPString As String
LPString = "[" & "Mastering VB".PadRight(20) & "]"
RPString = "[" & "Mastering VB".PadLeft(20) & "]"
```

After the execution of these statements, the values of the *LPString* and *RPString* variables are:

```
[Mastering VB        ]
[        Mastering VB]
```

There are 8 spaces to the right of the left-padded string and 8 spaces to the right of the left-padded string.

VB6 ➡ VB.NET

The PadLeft and PadRight methods replace the LSet() and RSet() functions of VB6.

Another form of these methods allows you to specify the character to be used in padding the strings. If you change the calls to the PadLeft and PadRight methods in the last example with the following:

```
LPString = "Mastering VB".PadRight(20, "@")
RPString = "Mastering VB".PadLeft(20, ".")
```

then the two strings will be:

```
Mastering VB@@@@@@@@
........Mastering VB
```

If the string is shorter than the specified field length, then the PadLeft and PadRight methods return the original string. The two padding methods don't trim the string to fit it in the specified field.

You can use the padding methods for visual alignment only if you're using a monospaced font, like Courier. These two methods can used to create text files with rows made up of fields with a fixed length.

The StringBuilder Class

The StringBuilder class stores dynamic strings and exposes methods to manipulate them much faster than the String class. To use the StringBuilder class in an application, you must import the `System.Text` class (unless you want to fully qualify each instance of the StringBuilder class in your code). Assuming you have imported the `System.Text` class in your code module, you can create a new instance of the class with the following statement:

```
Dim txt As New StringBuilder
```

There are many ways to initialize an instance of the StringBuilder class, but first I must explain the capacity of a StringBuilder object. Since the StringBuilder handles dynamic strings, it's good to declare in advance the size of the string you intend to store in the current instance of the class. The default capacity is 16 characters, and it's doubled automatically every time you exceed it. To set the initial capacity of the StringBuilder class, use the Capacity property. A related property is the MaxCapacity property, which is read-only and returns the maximum length of a string you can store in a StringBuilder variable. This value is approximately 2 billion characters; it's the length of the longest string you can store to an instance of the StringBuilder class.

To create a new instance of the StringBuilder class, you can call its constructor without any arguments, as I did in the preceding example. You can also initialize it by passing a string as argument:

```
Dim txt As New StringBuilder("some string")
```

If you can estimate the maximum length of the string you'll store in the variable, you can specify this value with the following form of the constructor, so that the variable need not be resized as you add to it:

```
Dim txt As New StringBuilder(initialCapacity)
```

The size you specify is not a hard limit; the variable may grow longer at runtime, and the StringBuilder will adjust its capacity.

If you want to specify a *maximum* capacity for your StringBuilder variable, use the following constructor:

```
Dim txt As New StringBuilder(initialCapacity, maxCapacity)
```

Finally, you can initialize a new instance of the StringBuilder class using both an initial and a maximum capacity, as well as its initial value, with the following form of the constructor:

```
Dim txt As New StringBuilder(string, initialCapacity, maxCapacity)
```

All the members of the StringBuilder class are instance members. In other words, you must create an instance of the StringBuilder class before calling any of its properties or methods.

PROPERTIES

You have already seen the two basic properties of the StringBuilder class, the Capacity and Max-Capacity properties. In addition, the StringBuilder class provides the Length and Chars properties, which are the same as the corresponding properties of the String class.

Length

This property returns the number of characters in the current instance of the StringBuilder and is an integer value smaller than (or, at most, equal to) the Capacity property.

Chars

This property gets or sets the character at a specified location in the string, and it's an array of characters. Note that the index of the first character is zero.

```
ch = SB.Chars(index)
```

where *ch* is a properly declared Char variable and *SB* is an instance of the StringBuilder class. To set a character's value in the string, use the following statement:

```
SB.Chars(index) = ch
```

NOTE *The Chars property of the StringBuilder class is read-write, as opposed to the same property of the String class, which is read-only. You can use the Chars array to change selected characters in a string.*

METHODS

Many of the methods of the StringBuilder class are equivalent to the methods of the String class, but they act directly on the string to which they're applied, and they don't return a new, separate string.

Append

The Append method appends a base type to the current instance of the StringBuilder class, and its syntax is

```
SB.Append(value)
```

where the *value* argument can be a single character, a string, a date, or any numeric value. When you append numeric values to a StringBuilder, they're converted to strings; the value appended is the string returned by the type's ToString method. You can also append an object to the String-Builder—the actual string that will be appended is the object's ToString property.

Another form of the Append method allows you to append an array of characters, and it has the following syntax:

```
SB.Append(chars, startIndex, count)
```

Or, you can append a segment of a string by specifying the starting location of the substring in the longer string and the number of characters to be copied:

```
SB.Append(string, startIndex, count)
```

AppendFormat

The AppendFormat method is similar to the Append method. Before appending the string, however, it formats it. The string to be appended contains format specifications and the appropriate values. The syntax of the AppendFormat method is

```
SB.AppendFormat(string, values)
```

The first argument is a string with embedded format specifications and *values* is an array with values (objects, in general), one for each format specification in the *string*. If you have a small number of values to format, up to four, you can supply them as separate arguments separated by commas:

```
SB.AppendFormat(string, value, value, value, value)
```

The following statement appends the string "Your balance as of Thursday, May 16, 2002 is $19,950.40" to a StringBuilder variable:

```
Dim statement As New StringBuilder
statement.AppendFormat("Your balance as of {0:D} is ${1: #,###.00}", _
                #5/16/2002#, 19950.40)
```

Each format specification is enclosed in a pair of curly brackets, and they're numbered sequentially (from zero). Then there's a colon followed by the actual specification. The D format specification tells the AppendFormat method to format the specified string in long date format. The second format specification, "#,###.00", uses the thousands separator and two decimal digits.

The following statements append the same string, but they pass the values through an array:

```
Dim statement As New StringBuilder
Dim values() As Object = {"5/16/2002", 19950.4}
statement.AppendFormat("Your balance as of {0:D} is ${1:#,###.00}", values)
```

In both cases, the *statement* variable will hold a string like this one:

```
Your balance as of Thursday, May 16, 2002 is $19,950.40
```

The format specifications in the original string usually contain formatting characters. For more information on date and time formatting options, see the section on the ToString method of the Date type, later in this chapter.

Insert

This method inserts a string into the current instance of the StringBuilder class, and its syntax is

```
SB.Insert(index, value)
```

The *index* argument is the location where the new string will be inserted in the current instance of the StringBuilder, and *value* is the string to be inserted. As with the Append method, the *value* argument can be any object. The Insert method will insert the string returned by the object's ToString method.

This means that you can use the Insert method to insert numeric values and dates directly into a StringBuilder variable.

A variation of the syntax shown here inserts multiple copies of the specified string into the StringBuilder:

```
SB.Insert(index, string, count)
```

Yet another form of the Insert method inserts an array of characters at the specified location in the current instance of the StringBuilder (*chars* is an array of characters):

```
SB.Insert(index, chars)
```

Remove

This method removes a number of characters from the current StringBuilder, starting at a specified location; its syntax is

```
SB.Remove(startIndex, count)
```

where *startIndex* is the position of the first character to be removed from the string and *length* is the number of characters to be removed.

Replace

This method replaces all instances of a string in the current StringBuilder with another string. The syntax of the Replace method is

```
SB.Replace(oldValue, newValue)
```

where the two arguments can be either strings or characters. Another form of the Replace method limits the replacements to a specified segment of the StringBuilder instance:

```
SB.Replace(oldValue, newValue, startIndex, count)
```

This method will replace all instances of *oldValue* with *newValue* in the section starting at location *startIndex* and extending *count* characters.

ToString

Use this method to convert the StringBuilder instance to a String and assign it to a String variable.

VB.NET at Work: The StringReversal Project

To get an idea of how efficiently the StringBuilder manipulates strings, here's an application that reverses a string (Figure 12.1). The program reverses two strings, one declared as String and another one declared as StringBuilder. Note that neither the String nor the StringBuilder class exposes a method for reversing the order of the characters in a string. However, you can use the StrReverse() function in this project to reverse a string with a single function call. In this example, we'll reverse the strings by swapping individual characters to time the two classes.

On my computer, it took a fifth of a second to reverse a 30,000 character-string with the String-Builder class and almost 14 seconds to do the same with the String class. Obviously, the StringBuilder class is optimized for manipulating strings dynamically. With previous versions of Visual Basic, many programmers had to write special functions in VC++ to manipulate large strings efficiently. Now, you can get awesome performance out of the StringBuilder class. If you have applications that manipulate strings extensively, port them to VB.NET and watch them run circles around the old applications written with VB's string-manipulation functions.

FIGURE 12.1

The StringReversal project's main form

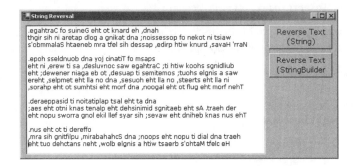

The StringReversal project reads the text on the TextBox control and appends it to the *STR* String-Builder variable. Then it goes through the first half of the string, one character at a time, and swaps it with the matching character in the second half of the array. The first character, `STR.Chars(0)` is swapped with the last character in the string, `STR.Chars(STR.Length-1)`. The second character, `STR.Chars(1)`, is swapped with the second-to-last character, `STR.Chars(STR.Length - 2)`, and so on. Without the temporary variable, we'd overwrite one of the characters to be swapped and wouldn't be able to copy it to its new location. Notice that we subtract one from the indices, because the indexing of the characters in a StringBuilder variable starts at zero, and the location of the last character is the length of the string minus 1. By the way, the same is true for String variables. The code stores the length of the StringBuilder to the *STRLen* variable to avoid calling the Length property at each iteration.

To reverse a String variable, we use the string-manipulation functions of VB. Unlike the methods of the StringBuilder class, the equivalent VB functions use the index 1 for the first character of the string. The Mid() function extracts a character from a string, and the Mid statement replaces one of the existing characters with another one. Listing 12.5 is the Click event handler of the Reverse Text (String) button. You can ignore the statements that time the operations for now—they're discussed in the following section.

LISTING 12.5: REVERSING A STRING VARIABLE

```
Private Sub Button1_Click(ByVal sender As System.Object, _
            ByVal e As System.EventArgs) Handles Button1.Click
    Dim TStart, TEnd As Date
    Dim TDiff As TimeSpan
    Dim STRLen As Integer
    STRLen = Len(TextBox1.Text)
    Dim revCrLf As String
    revCrLf = vbCrLf.Chars(1) & vbCrLf.Chars(0)
    TStart = Now()
    Dim txt As String
    txt = TextBox1.Text
```

```
   Dim aChar As String
   Dim iChar As Integer
   For iChar = 1 To CInt(STRLen / 2)
      aChar = Mid(txt, iChar, 1)
      Mid(txt, iChar, 1) = Mid(txt, STRLen - iChar - 1, 1)
      Mid(txt, STRLen - iChar - 1) = aChar
   Next
   TEnd = Now()
   TDiff = TEnd.Subtract(TStart)
   Console.WriteLine("Reversed string in " & TDiff.TotalSeconds.ToString)
   TextBox1.Text = txt.Replace(revCrLf, vbCrLf)
End Sub
```

Notice the line that replaces carriage returns and line feeds. On the TextBox control, each line is terminated with the sequence Chr(10) & Chr(13). When the order of these two characters is reversed, they will no longer change line on the TextBox control. This statement restores the line-feed/carriage-return combination back to its original state. Listing 12.6 reverses the same string using a StringBuilder variable (this is the code behind the Reverse Text (StringBuilder) button).

LISTING 12.6: REVERSING A STRINGBUILDER VARIABLE

```
Private Sub Button2_Click(ByVal sender As System.Object, _
               ByVal e As System.EventArgs) Handles Button2.Click
   Dim TStart, TEnd As Date
   Dim TDiff As TimeSpan
   Dim STR As New System.Text.StringBuilder()
   Dim STRLen As Integer
   STRLen = Len(TextBox1.Text)
   STR.Capacity = STRLen
   STR.Append(TextBox1.Text)
   Dim ichar As Integer
   Dim chr As Char
   TStart = Now()
   For ichar = 0 To CInt(STR.Length / 2 - 1)
      chr = STR.Chars(ichar)
      STR.Chars(ichar) = STR.Chars(STRLen - ichar - 1)
      STR.Chars(STRLen - ichar - 1) = chr
   Next
   Dim revCrLf As String
   revCrLf = vbCrLf.Chars(1) & vbCrLf.Chars(0)
   STR.Replace(revCrLf, vbCrLf)
   TEnd = Now()
   TDiff = TEnd.Subtract(TStart)
   Console.WriteLine("Reversed string in " & TDiff.TotalSeconds.ToString)
   TextBox1.Text = STR.ToString
End Sub
```

VB.NET at Work: The CountWords Project

As you have noticed, the StringBuilder doesn't provide as many methods as the String class. The StringBuilder class should be used to build long strings and manipulate them dynamically. If you want to locate words or other patterns in the text, align strings in fixed-length fields, and other similar operations, use the String class. You can also combine both classes in your application, so that you can speed both string-manipulation and -handling operations. To extract the text from a StringBuilder, use its ToString method. To assign a string to the StringBuilder variable, use its Append method:

```
Dim strB As New StringBuilder
Dim str1, str2 As String
str1 = "some text"
strB.Append(str1)
{ statements to process the strB variable }
str2 = strB.ToString
```

Any of the String class's methods, however, can be used with StringBuilder variables. The ToString method of the StringBuilder class returns a string, which can be processed with the methods of the String class. For instance, the StringBuilder class lacks the IndexOf and LastIndexOf methods. To locate an instance of a word in a StringBuilder variable, use the following statement:

```
pos = SB.ToString.IndexOf("visual")
```

where *SB* is a properly declared an initialized StringBuilder variable and *pos* is the index of the first instance of the word "visual" in the StringBuilder's text.

The CountWords application, shown in Figure 12.2, counts all instances of a user-supplied word in a StringBuilder variable. You can do the same with the Sting class, but if you want to further process the text, you'll have to use the StringBuilder class anyway. The program prompts the user for a string and attempts to locate it in the text with the following statement:

```
startIndex = SB.ToString.ToUpper.IndexOf(searchWord.ToUpper)
```

FIGURE 12.2

The CountWords project counts the instances of a user-supplied word in a text.

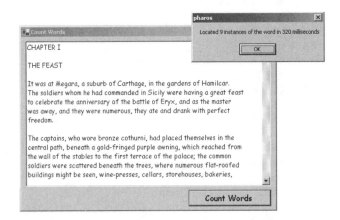

Then, it sets up a loop that locates one instance of the user-supplied word at a time. The following statement searches for the word in text, starting at the location startIndex + searchWord.Length + 1. This expression is the location of the first character following the most recently located instance of the word in the large string. At each iteration of the loop, the IndexOf method starts searching for the word in the text following the previous instance of the word. Here's the statement that locates the next instance of the word in the text:

```
startIndex = SB.ToString.ToUpper.IndexOf(searchWord.ToUpper, _
                              startIndex + searchWord.length + 1)
```

This statement appears in a loop that's repeated for as long as the *startIndex* variable is positive. When all instances of the word in the text have been located, the IndexOf method returns the value −1 and the loop terminates. The complete code of the Count Words button is shown in Listing 12.7.

LISTING 12.7: THE COUNTWORDS PROJECT'S CODE

```
Private Sub Button1_Click(ByVal sender As System.Object, _
            ByVal e As System.EventArgs) Handles Button1.Click
    Dim SB As New System.[Text].StringBuilder()
    Dim searchWord As String
    searchWord = InputBox("Please enter the word to search for", _
                    "StringBuilder Search Example", "BASIC")
    Dim startIndex As Integer
    SB.Append(Textbox1.Text)
    startIndex = SB.ToString.ToUpper.IndexOf(searchWord.ToUpper)
    Dim T1, T2 As Date
    Dim SP As New TimeSpan()
    T1 = Now()
    Dim count As Integer
    If startIndex = 0 Then
        MsgBox("The string you're searching for wasn't found")
    End If
    While startIndex > 0 And startIndex + searchWord.Length < SB.Length
        count = count + 1
        startIndex = SB.ToString.ToUpper.IndexOf(searchWord.ToUpper, _
                                    startIndex + searchWord.Length + 1)
    End While
    T2 = Now
    SP = T2.Subtract(T1)
    Dim msg As String
    msg = "Located " & count.ToString & " instances of the word in " & _
        SP.Milliseconds.ToString & " milliseconds"
    MsgBox(msg)
End Sub
```

When executed, this code will pop up a message box with a statement like the following:

```
Located 22 instances of the word in 270 milliseconds
```

The last few statements calculate the time it took the program to locate all the instances of the word with the methods of the TimeSpan object, which is discussed in the following section.

Handling Dates

Another common task in coding business applications is the manipulation of dates and time. To aid the coding of these tasks, the Framework provides the DateTime and TimeSpan classes. The Date-Time class handles date and time values, while the TimeSpan class handles time differences. Date is a data type, and there's no equivalent class in the Framework. All Date variables are implemented by the DateTime class. The two types of variables are identical, and the DateTime name is more appropriate, since these variables can store both dates and times. Since the Date data type has been around for a while, I will use this name for the class. But keep in mind that there's no Date class and you must use the `System.DateTime` class to call the shared members of a Date variable.

 VB.NET supports all the date and time functions of previous versions of Visual Basic, which are described in detail in a bonus reference on the CD.

The DateTime Class

The DateTime class is used for storing date and time values, and it's one of the Framework's base data types. Date and time values are stored internally as double numbers. The integer part of the value corresponds to the data and the fractional part corresponds to the time. To convert a Date variable to a double value, use the method ToOADateTime, which returns a value that is an OLE Automation–compatible date. The value 0 corresponds to the midnight of December 30, 1899.

To initialize a Date variable, supply a date value enclosed in a pair of pound symbols. If the value contains time information, separate it from the date part with a space:

```
Dim date1 As Date = #4/15/2001#
Dim date2 As Date = #4/15/2001 14:01:59#
```

You can declare the two variables as DateTime type. If you have a string that represents a date and you want to assign it to a Date variable for further processing, use the DateTime class's Parse and ParseExact methods. The Parse method parses a string and returns a date value, if the string can be interpreted as a date value. Let's say your code prompts the user for a date and then it uses in date calculations. The user-supplied date is read as a string, and you must convert it to a Date value:

```
Dim sDate1 As String
Dim dDate1 As Date
sDate1 = InputBox("Please enter a date after 1/1/2002")
Try
    dDate1 = System.DateTime.Parse(sDate1)
        { use dDate1 in your calculations }
    Catch exc As Exception
        MsgBox("You've entered an invalid date")
End Try
```

The Parse method will convert a string that represents a date to a DateTime value regardless of the format of the date. You can enter dates like "1/17/2001", "Jan. 17, 2003", or "January 17, 2003" (with or without the comma). Actually, even the string "17/1/2003" will be read as January 17, because there are only 12 months, and this is the only interpretation that will yield a valid date. VB assumes you've entered a European-style date and swaps the day and month values, if the month value is invalid.

PROPERTIES

The Date type exposes the following properties, which are straightforward.

Date

The Date property returns the date from a date/time value and sets the time to midnight. The statements:

```
Dim date1 As Date
date1 = Now()
Console.WriteLine(date1)
Console.WriteLine(date1.Date)
```

will print something like the following values in the Output window:

```
5/29/2001 2:30:17 PM
5/29/2001 12:00:00 AM
```

DayOfWeek, DayOfYear

These two properties return the day of the week (a number from 1 to 7) and the number of the day in the year (an integer from 1 to 365, or 366 for leap years).

Hour, Minute, Second, Millisecond

These properties return the corresponding time part of the Date value passed as arguments. If the current time is 1:35:22 P.M., the three properties of the DateTime class will return the following values when applied on the current date and time:

```
Console.WriteLine("The current time is " & Date.Now.TimeOfDay.ToString)
Console.WriteLine("The hour is " & Date.Now.Hour)
Console.WriteLine("The minute is " & Date.Now.Minute)
Console.WriteLine("The second is " & Date.Now.Second)
```

If you place these statement in a button's Click event handler and execute them, the following will be printed on the Output window:

```
The current time is 13:35:22.0527552
The hour is 13
The minute is 35
The second is 22
```

Day, Month, Year

These three properties return the day of the month, the month, and the year of the Date value passed as argument. The Day and Month properties are numeric values, but you can convert them to the appropriate string (the name of the day or month) with the WeekDayName() and MonthName() functions. Both functions accept as argument the number of the day (a value from 1 to 7) or month (from 1 to 13), and they return the name. Use the value 13 with a 13-month calendar (for non-U.S. or non-European calendars). They also accept a second optional argument that is a True/False value and indicates whether the function should return the abbreviated name (if True) or full name (if False). The WeekDayName() function accepts a third optional argument, which determines the first day of the week. Set this argument to one of the members of the FirstDayOfWeek enumeration. By default, the first day of the week is Sunday.

Ticks

This property returns the number of ticks from a date/time value. Each tick is 100 nanoseconds (or 0.0001 milliseconds). To convert ticks to milliseconds, multiply them by 10,000 (or use the TimeSpan object's TicksPerMillisecond property, discussed later in this chapter).

TimeOfDay

This property returns the time from a date/time value. The following statement will return a value like the one shown after the statement, in bold:

```
Console.WriteLine(Now().TimeOfDay)
14:35:44.4589088
```

METHODS

The DateTime class exposes several methods for manipulating dates. The most practical methods add and subtract time intervals to and from an instance of the DateTime class.

Compare

Compare is a shared method that compares two date/time values and returns an integer value indicating the relative order of the two values. The syntax of the Compare method is

```
order = System.DateTime.Compare(date1, date2)
```

where *date1* and *date2* are the two values to be compared. The method returns an integer, which is −1 if *date1* is less than *date2*, 0 if they're equal, and 1 if *date1* is greater than *date2*.

DaysInMonth

This shared method returns the number of days in a specific month. Because February contains a variable number of days depending on the year, the DaysInMonth method accepts as arguments both the month and the year:

```
monDays = System.DateTime.DaysInMonth(year, month)
```

To find out the number of days in February 2009, use the following expression:

```
FebDays = System.DateTime.DaysInMonth(2, 2009)
```

FromOADate

This shared method creates a date/time value from an OLE Automation Date.

```
newDate = System.DateTime.FromOADate(dtvalue)
```

The argument *dtvalue* must be a Double value in the range from –657,434 (first day of year 100) to 2,958,465 (last day of year 9999).

IsLeapYear

This shared method returns a True/False value that indicates whether the specified year is leap or not.

```
Dim leapYear As Boolean
leapYear = System.DateTime.IsLeapYear(year)
```

Add

This method adds a TimeSpan object to the current instance of the Date class. The TimeSpan object represents a time interval and there are many methods to create a TimeSpan object, which are all discussed in the section "The TimeSpan Class" later in this chapter. The following statements create a new TimeSpan object that represents 3 days, 6 hours, 2 minutes, and 50 seconds, and add this TimeSpan to the current date and time. Depending on when these statements are executed, the two date/time values will differ, but the difference between them will always be 3 days, 6 hours, 2 minutes, and 50 seconds:

```
Dim TS As New TimeSpan()
Dim thisMoment As Date = Now()
TS = New TimeSpan(3, 6, 2, 50)
Console.WriteLine(thisMoment)
Console.WriteLine(thisMoment.Add(TS))
```

The values printed in the Output window when I tested this code segment were:

```
2001-04-13 16:26:38
2001-04-16 22:29:28
```

Subtract

This method is the counterpart of the Add method; it subtracts a TimeSpan object from the current instance of the Date class and returns another Date value. The following statements create a new TimeSpan object that represents 3 days, 6 hours, 2 minutes, and 50 seconds, and subtracts this TimeSpan from the current date and time. Depending on when these statements are executed, the two date/time values will differ, but the difference between them will always be the same:

```
Dim TS As New TimeSpan()
Dim thisMoment As Date = Now()
TS = New TimeSpan(3, 6, 2, 50)
Console.WriteLine(thisMoment)
Console.WriteLine(thisMoment.Subtract(TS))
```

The values printed in the Output window when I tested this code segment were:

```
5/29/2001 2:52:03 PM
5/26/2001 8:49:13 AM
```

Adding Intervals to Dates

Various methods add specific intervals to a date/time value. Each method accepts the number of intervals to add (days, hours, milliseconds, and so on). These methods are simply listed: AddYears, AddMonths, AddDays, AddHours, AddMinutes, AddSeconds, AddMilliseconds, and AddTicks. A tick is 100 nanoseconds and is used for really fine timing operations.

To add 3 years and 12 hours to the current date, use the following statements:

```
Dim aDate As Date
aDate = Now()
aDate = aDate.AddYears(3)
aDate = aDate.AddHours(12)
```

If the argument is a negative value, the corresponding intervals are subtracted from the current instance of the class. The following statement subtracts 2 minutes from a Date variable:

```
aDate = aDate.AddMinutes(-2)
```

ToString

This method converts a date/time value to a string, using a specific format. The Date class recognizes numerous format patterns, which are listed in the following two tables. Table 12.1 lists the standard format patterns, and Table 12.2 lists the format characters that can format individual parts of the date/time value. You can combine the custom format characters to format dates and times in any way you wish.

The syntax of the ToString method is

```
aDate.ToString(formatSpec)
```

where *formatSpec* is a format specification. The "D" named date format, for example, formats a date value as a long date, and the following statement will return the string shown below the statement in bold:

```
Console.Writeline(#9/17/2005#.ToString("D"))
```
Saturday, September 17, 2005

Table 12.1 lists the named formats for the standard date and time patterns. The format characters are case-sensitive; for example, "g" and "G" represent slightly different patterns.

TABLE 12.1: THE DATE AND TIME NAMED FORMATS

NAMED FORMAT	OUTPUT	FORMAT NAME
d	MM/dd/yyyy	ShortDatePattern
D	dddd, MMMM dd, yyyy	LongDatePattern
f	dddd, MMMM dd, yyyy HH:mm	fulldatetimePattern (long date and short time)
F	dddd, MMMM dd, yyyy HH:mm:ss	FullDateTimePattern (long date and long time)
g	MM/dd/yyyy HH:mm	general (short date and short time)

Continued on next page

TABLE 12.1: THE DATE AND TIME NAMED FORMATS *(continued)*

NAMED FORMAT	OUTPUT	FORMAT NAME
G	MM/dd/yyyy HH:mm:ss	General (short date and long time)
m, M	MMMM dd	MonthDayPattern
r, R	ddd, dd MMM yyyy HH':'mm':'ss 'GMT'	RFC1123Pattern
s	yyyy-MM-dd HH:mm:ss	SortableDateTimePattern
t	HH:mm	ShortTimePattern
T	HH:mm:ss	LongTimePattern
u	yyyy-MM-dd HH:mm:ss	UniversalSortableDateTimePattern
U	dddd, MMMM dd, yyyy HH:mm:ss	UniversalSortableDateTimePattern
y, Y	MMMM, yyyy	YearMonthPattern

The following examples format the current date using all of the format patterns listed in Table 12.1. An example of the output produced by each statement is shown under each statement, in bold.

```
Console.WriteLine(now().ToString("d"))
5/29/2001
Console.WriteLine(now().ToString("D"))
Tuesday, May 29, 2001
Console.WriteLine(now().ToString("f"))
Tuesday, May 29, 2001 3:14 PM
Console.WriteLine(now().ToString("F"))
Tuesday, May 29, 2001 3:14:43 PM
Console.WriteLine(now().ToString("g"))
5/29/2001 3:14 PM
Console.WriteLine(now().ToString("G"))
5/29/2001 3:14:43 PM
Console.WriteLine(now().ToString("m"))
May 29
Console.WriteLine(now().ToString("r"))
Tue, 29 May 2001 15:14:43 GMT
Console.WriteLine(now().ToString("s"))
2001-05-29T15:14:43
Console.WriteLine(now().ToString("t"))
3:14 PM
Console.WriteLine(now().ToString("T"))
3:14:43 PM
Console.WriteLine(now().ToString("u"))
2001-05-29 15:14:43Z
Console.WriteLine(now().ToString("U"))
```

```
Tuesday, May 29, 2001 12:14:43 PM
Console.WriteLine(now().ToString("y"))
May, 2001
```

Table 12.2 lists the format characters that can be combined to build custom format date and time values. The patterns are case-sensitive; for example, "MM" is valid, but "mm" isn't. If the custom pattern contains spaces or characters enclosed in single quotation marks, these characters will appear in the formatted string.

TABLE 12.2: DATE FORMAT SPECIFIER

FORMAT CHARACTER	DESCRIPTION
d	The date of the month
dd	The day of the month with a leading zero for single-digit days
ddd	The abbreviated name of the day of the week (a member of the AbbreviatedDay-Names enumeration)
dddd	The full name of the day of the week (a member of the DayNamesFormat enumeration)
M	The number of the month
MM	The number of the month with a leading zero for single-digit months
MMM	The abbreviated name of the month (a member of the AbbreviatedMonthNames enumeration)
MMMM	The full name of the month
y	The year without the century (the year 2001 will be printed as 1)
yy	The year without the century (the year 2001 will be displayed as 01)
yyyy	The complete year
gg	The period or era (this pattern is ignored if the date to be formatted does not have an associated period, such as A.D. or B.C.)
h	The hour in 12-hour format
hh	The hour in 12-hour format with a leading zero for single-digit hours
H	The hour in 24-hour format
HH	The hour in 24-hour format with a leading zero for single-digit hours
m	The minute of the hour
mm	The minute of the hour with a leading zero for single-digit minutes
s	The second of the hour
ss	The second of the hour with a leading zero for single-digit seconds

Continued on next page

TABLE 12.2: DATE FORMAT SPECIFIER *(continued)*

FORMAT CHARACTER	DESCRIPTION
t	The first character in the AM/PM designator
tt	The AM/PM designator
z	The time-zone offset (applies to hours only)
zz	The time-zone offset with a leading zero for single-digit hours (applies to hour only)
zzz	The full time-zone offset (hour and minutes) with leading zeros for single-digit hours and minutes

The following examples format the current time using all of the format patterns listed in Table 12.2. An example of the output produced by each statement is shown under each statement, indented and in bold.

```
Console.WriteLine(now().ToString("m/d/yyyy"))
```
5/29/2001
```
Console.WriteLine(now().ToString("dd"))
```
29
```
Console.WriteLine(now().ToString("ddd"))
```
Tue
```
Console.WriteLine(now().ToString("dddd"))
```
Tuesday
```
Console.WriteLine(now().ToString("M/yyyy"))
```
May 2001
```
Console.WriteLine(now().ToString("MM"))
```
05
```
Console.WriteLine(now().ToString("MMM"))
```
May
```
Console.WriteLine(now().ToString("MMMM"))
```
May
```
Console.WriteLine(now().ToString("m/d/y"))
```
29/5/1
```
Console.WriteLine(now().ToString("m/d/yy"))
```
29/5/01
```
Console.WriteLine(now().ToString("yy"))
```
01
```
Console.WriteLine(now().ToString("yyyy"))
```
2001
```
Console.WriteLine(now().ToString("gg"))
```
A.D.
```
Console.WriteLine(now().ToString("hh"))
```
03
```
Console.WriteLine(now().ToString("HH"))
```

```
15
Console.WriteLine(now().ToString("h:m"))
3:26
Console.WriteLine(now().ToString("mm"))
26
Console.WriteLine(now().ToString("h:m:s"))
3:26:38
Console.WriteLine(now().ToString("hh:mm:ss"))
03:26:38
Console.WriteLine(now().ToString("h:m:s t"))
3:26:38 P
Console.WriteLine(now().ToString("tt"))
PM
Console.WriteLine(now().ToString("zz"))
+03
Console.WriteLine(now().ToString("zzz"))
+03:00
```

To display the day of the month and the month name only, for instance, use the following statement:

```
Console.WriteLine(now().ToString("MMMM d"))
May 29
```

You may have noticed some overlap between the named formats and the format characters. The character "d" signifies the short date pattern when used as a named format and the number of the day when used as format character. The compiler figures out how it's used based on the context. If the format argument is "d/mm", the program will display the day and month number, while the format argument "d, mmm" will display the number of the day followed by the month's name. If you use the character "d" on its own, however, it will be interpreted as the named format for the short date format.

Date Conversion Methods

The Date class supports methods for converting a date/time value to many of the other base types. The most common ones are ToInt16, ToSingle, ToString, ToUInt16, ToUInt32, and ToUInt64. When a date/time value is converted an integer value, the time value is obviously lost. The other conversion methods require some explanation:

ToFileTime   Converts the value of the current Date instance to the format of the local system file time. There's also an equivalent FromFileTime method, which converts a file time value to a Date value.

ToLocalTime   Converts a UTC time value to local time.

ToLongDateString, ToShortDateString   These two methods convert the date part of the current Date instance to a string with the long (or short) date format. The following statement will return a value like the one shown in bold, which is the long date format:

```
Console.WriteLine(Now().ToLongDateString)
Friday, July 16, 2001
```

The following statement will convert the current date to the short date format:

```
Console.WriteLine(Now().ToShortDateString)
7/16/2001
```

ToLongTimeString, ToShortTimeString   These two methods convert the time part of the current instance of the Date class to a string with the long (or short) time format. The following statement will return a value like the one shown in bold:

```
Console.WriteLine(Now().ToLongTimeString)
6:40:53 PM
```

The following statement will convert the current time to the short date format:

```
Console.WriteLine(Now().ToShortTimeString)
6:40 PM
```

ToOADate   Converts the DateTime instance into an OLE Automation–compatible date.

ToUniversalTime   Converts the current instance of the DateTime class into universal coordinated time (UCT). If you convert the local time of a system in New York to UCT when daylight savings is not in effect, the value returned by this method will be a date/time value that's five hours ahead. The date may be the same or the date of the following day. If the statement is executed after 7 P.M. local time, the date will be that of the following day.

DATES AS NUMERIC VALUES

The Date type encapsulates very complicated operations. Manipulating dates is one of the most cumbersome tasks in programming, if you consider that not all months have the same number of days. For years, programmers had to write code to manipulate dates, or buy libraries with date- and time-handling functions. To get an idea of how the Framework handles dates, let's experiment a little with them. Start by declaring two variables, a Date and a Double, and initialize the Date variable to the current date:

```
Dim Date1 As Date
Date1 = Now()
Dim dbl As Double
```

Insert a couple of statements to convert the date to a Double value and print it:

```
dbl = Date1.ToOADate
Console.WriteLine(dbl)
```

On the date I tested this code, April 10, 2001, the value was 36,991.63150635417. The integer part of this value is the date, and the fractional part is the time. If you add one day to the current date and then convert it to a Double again, you'll get a Double value:

```
dbl = Now().AddDays(1).ToOADate
Console.WriteLine(dbl)
```

This time, the value 36,992.63150635417 was printed. You can add two days to the current date by adding (48×60) minutes. The original integer part of the numeric value will be increased by two:

```
dbl = Now().AddMinutes(48 * 60).ToOADate
Console.WriteLine(dbl)
```

The value printed this time will be 36,993.631506585647.

Let's see how the date-manipulation methods deal with leap years. We'll add 10 years to the current date with the AddYears method, and we'll print the new value with a single statement:

```
Console.WriteLine(Now().AddYears(10).ToLongDateString)
```

The value that will appear in the Output window will be Sunday, April 10, 2011. This method simply changed the value of the year. If you add 3,650 days, you'll get a different value, because the 10-year span contains at least two leap years:

```
Console.WriteLine(Now().AddDays(3650).ToOADate)
```

The new value that will be printed on the Output window will be Friday, April 08, 2011, and the corresponding double value will be 40,643.631506585647.

The TimeSpan Class

The last class discussed in this chapter is the TimeSpan class, which represents a time interval and can be expressed in many different units, from ticks and milliseconds to days. The TimeSpan is usually the difference between two date/time values, but you can also create a TimeSpan for a specific interval and use it in your calculations.

To use the TimeSpan variable in your code, just declare it with a statement like the following:

```
Dim TS As New TimeSpan
```

To initialize the TimeSpan object, you can provide a string with the number of days, hours, minutes, seconds, and milliseconds. The following statement initializes a TimeSpan object with a duration of 9 days, 12 hours, 1 minute, and 59 seconds:

```
Dim TS As TimeSpan = New TimeSpan(9, 12, 1, 59)
```

As you have seen, the difference between two dates calculated by the Date.Subtract method returns a TimeSpan value. You can initialize an instance of the TimeSpan object by creating two date/time values and getting their difference, as in the following statements:

```
Dim TS As New TimeSpan
Dim date1 As Date = #4/11/1985#
Dim date2 As Date = Now()
TS = date2.Subtract(date1)
Console.WriteLine(TS)
```

Depending on the day on which you execute these statements, they will print something like the following on the Output window:

```
5992.15:58:14.4766848
```

The days are separated from the rest of the string with a period, while all other items are separated with colons.

PROPERTIES

The TimeSpan type exposes the properties described in the following sections. Most of these members are shared.

Field Properties

TimeSpan exposes the simple properties shown in Table 12.3, which are known as *fields* and are all shared.

TABLE 12.3: THE FIELDS OF THE TIMESPAN OBJECT

PROPERTY	RETURNS
Empty	An empty TimeSpan object
MaxValue	The largest interval you can represent with a TimeSpan object
MinValue	The smallest interval you can represent with a TimeSpan object
TicksPerDay	The number of ticks in a day
TicksPerHour	The number of ticks in an hour
TicksPerMillisecond	The number of ticks in a millisecond
TicksPerMinute	The number of ticks in one minute
TicksPerSecond	The number of ticks in one second
Zero	A TimeSpan object of zero duration

Interval Properties

In addition to the fields, the TimeSpan class exposes two more groups of properties that return the various intervals in a TimeSpan value; these are the shown in Tables 12.4 and 12.5. The members of the first group of properties return the number of specific intervals (days, hours, and so on) in a TimeSpan value. The second group of properties returns the entire TimeSpan's duration in one of the intervals recognized by the TimeSpan method.

TABLE 12.4: THE INTERVALS OF A TIMESPAN VALUE

PROPERTY	RETURNS
Days	The number of whole days in the current TimeSpan
Hours	The number of whole hours in the current TimeSpan
Milliseconds	The number of whole milliseconds in the current TimeSpan. The largest value of this property is 999.
Minutes	The number of whole minutes in the current TimeSpan. The largest value of this property is 59.

Continued on next page

TABLE 12.4: THE INTERVALS OF A TIMESPAN VALUE *(continued)*

PROPERTY	RETURNS
Seconds	The number of whole seconds in the current TimeSpan. The largest value of this property is 59.
Ticks	The number of whole ticks in the current TimeSpan

TABLE 12.5: THE TOTAL INTERVALS OF A TIMESPAN VALUE

PROPERTY	RETURNS
TotalDays	The total number of days in the current TimeSpan
TotalHours	The total number of hours in the current TimeSpan
TotalMilliseconds	The total number of whole milliseconds in the current TimeSpan
TotalMinutes	The number of whole minutes in the current TimeSpan
TotalSeconds	The number of whole seconds in the current TimeSpan

If a TimeSpan value represents 2 minutes and 10 seconds, the Seconds property will return the value 10. The TotalSeconds property, however, will return the value 70, which is the total duration of the TimeSpan in seconds.

WARNING *Be very careful when choosing the property to express the duration of a TimeSpan in a specific interval. Since both properties will return a value, you may not notice that you're using the wrong property for the task at hand.*

Duration

This property returns the duration of the current instance of the TimeSpan. The duration is expressed as the number of days, followed by the number of hours, minutes, seconds, and milliseconds. The following statements create a TimeSpan object of a few seconds (or minutes, if you don't mind waiting) and print its duration in the Output window. The first few statements initialize a new instance of the Date type, the *T1* variable, to the current date and time. Then a message box is displayed that prompts to click the OK button to continue. Wait for several seconds before closing the message box. The last group of statements subtract the *T1* variable from the current time and display the duration (this is how long you kept the message box open on your screen).

```
Dim T1, T2 As Date
T1 = Now
MsgBox("Click OK to continue")
T2 = Now
```

```
Dim TS As TimeSpan
TS = T2.Subtract(T1)
Console.WriteLine("Total duration = " & TS.Duration.ToString)
Console.WriteLine("Minutes = " & TS.Minutes.ToString)
Console.WriteLine("Seconds = " & TS.Seconds.ToString)
Console.WriteLine("Ticks = " & TS.Ticks.ToString)
Console.WriteLine("Milliseconds = " & TS.TotalMilliseconds.ToString)
Console.WriteLine("Total seconds = " & TS.TotalSeconds.ToString)
```

If you place these statements in a button's Click event handler and execute them, you'll see a series of values like the following in the Output window:

```
Total duration = 00:01:50.1183424
Minutes = 1
Seconds = 50
Ticks = 1101183424
Milliseconds = 110118.3424
Total seconds = 110.1183424
```

METHODS

There are various methods for creating and manipulating instances of the TimeSpan class; these are described in the following sections.

Interval Methods

The methods in Table 12.6 create a new TimeSpan object of a specific duration. Each duration is specified as a number of intervals, accurate to the nearest millisecond.

TABLE 12.6: INTERVAL METHODS OF THE TIMESPAN OBJECT

METHOD	CREATES A NEW TIMESPAN OF THIS LENGTH
FromDays	Number of days specified by the argument
FromHours	Number of hours specified by the argument
FromMinutes	Number of minutes specified by the argument
FromSeconds	Number of seconds specified by the argument
FromMilliseconds	Number of milliseconds specified by the argument
FromTicks	Number of ticks specified by the argument

All methods accept a single argument, which is a Double value that represents the number of the corresponding intervals (days, hours, and so on).

Parse(string)

This method creates a new TimeSpan object from a string with the TimeSpan format (days, followed by a period, followed by the hours, minutes, and seconds separated by colons). The following statements creates a new TimeSpan variable with a duration of 3 days, 12 hours, 20 minutes, 30 seconds, and 500 milliseconds:

```
Dim SP As New TimeSpan()
SP = TimeSpan.Parse("3.12:20:30.500")
Console.WriteLine(SP)
3.12:20:30.5000000
```

Add

This method adds a TimeSpan object to the current instance of the class; its syntax is

```
newTS = TS.Add(TS1)
```

where *TS*, *TS1*, and *newTS* are all TimeSpan variables. The following statements create two TimeSpan objects and then add them:

```
Dim TS1 As New TimeSpan("1:00:01")
Dim TS2 As New TimeSpan("2:01:09")
Dim TS As New TimeSpan
TS = TS1.Add(TS2)
```

The duration of the new TimeSpan variable is 3 hours, 1 minute, and 10 seconds. A more practical example is the following, which constructs a TimeSpan object using the Fromxxx methods described in Table 12.6. The following statements create a TimeSpan object with a duration of 3 hours, 2 minutes, 16 seconds, and 500 milliseconds:

```
Dim TS As New System.TimeSpan()
TS = System.TimeSpan.FromHours(3)
TS = TS.Add(System.TimeSpan.FromMinutes(2))
TS = TS.Add(System.TimeSpan.FromSeconds(16))
TS = TS.Add(System.TimeSpan.FromMilliseconds(500))
Console.WriteLine("The total Time Span is " & TS.ToString)
```

The total duration of the *TS* TimeSpan variable is 3 hours, 2 minutes, 16 seconds, and 500 milliseconds. If you print the *TS* variable, its value will be: 03:02:16.5000000.

Subtract

The Subtract method subtracts a TimeSpan object from the current instance of the TimeSpan class. The following statements create two TimeSpan objects with different durations. Then, the two time spans are subtracted and their difference is printed in three different ways:

```
Dim T1, T2 As TimeSpan
T1 = New TimeSpan(3, 9, 10, 12)
T2 = New TimeSpan(0, 1, 0, 59, 3)
Dim TS As TimeSpan = T2.Subtract(T1)
Console.WriteLine(TS.Duration())
```

```
Console.WriteLine(TS.Days)
Console.WriteLine(TS.TotalDays)
```

The last three statements printed the following values in the Output window:

```
3.08:09:12.9970000
-3
-3.33973376157407
```

The Duration of the span is 3 days, 8 hours, 9 minutes, 12 seconds, and 997 milliseconds. The Days method returns the number of days in the TimeSpan as a whole number. The TotalDays method returns the same difference as a number of days with a fractional part. If you multiply the fractional part (0.33973376157407) by 24, you'll get 8.153610277. If you multiply the fractional part of this number by 60, you'll get 9.2166166. Finally, you can multiply the new fractional part by 60 to get the number of seconds: 12.996999 (a rounding error was introduced in the calculations, but this was expected). You will get the same results by calling the TimeSpan object's Hour, Minute, and Second properties.

CompareTo

This method compares the current instance of the TimeSpan with another TimeSpan object; its syntax is

```
TS.CompareTo(TS1)
```

where *TS* is a properly initialized TimeSpan object. The CompareTo method returns 0 if they're equal, –1 if the current instance is longer, and 1 if the TimeSpan object passed as argument is longer.

Equals

This method returns a True/False value that indicates whether two TimeSpan objects represent the same interval. The syntax of the Equals method is

```
TS.Equals(TS1)
```

Negate

This method negates the current TimeSpan instance. A positive TimeSpan (which will yield a future date when added to the current date) becomes negative (which will yield a past date when added to the current date).

VB.NET at Work: Timing Operations

The TimeSpan class has a fine granularity, which makes it ideal for timing operations. To time an operation—a sequence of statements—you measure the time right before they start executing and right after they have executed. Then you take the difference, which is the time it took for the operation to complete. If the operation takes a very short time (a time comparable to the time it takes to measure the time), you must execute the statements repeatedly and divide the total duration by the number of iterations. In general, the time spent executing the statements that keep track of the time should be negligible compared to the time spent executing the actual statements.

The following code outlines the code for timing a group of statements:

```
Dim TStart, TEnd As Date
Dim Duration As TimeSpan
TStart = Now()
{ enter here the statements to be timed }
TEnd = Now()
Duration = TEnd.Subtract(TStart)
Console.Write("Statements took " & TS.TotalSeconds & " seconds to execute.")
```

In the StringReversal project, earlier in this chapter, we used these statements to time the operation of reversing a String (or StringBuilder) variable's characters. In this project, we timed the block of statements that reverse the string in-place. The statements we timed form a loop, which goes through the characters in the string. If you divide the duration of the operation by the number of characters processed, you will find out how long it takes to process each character.

The timing of operations is called *benchmarking*, and it's one of the most difficult aspects of computing, because of the many factors that may affect a specific operation. In many cases, these factors aren't obvious, and different companies will come up with different benchmarks for the same software. The technique discussed in this chapter is adequate for comparing two alternate ways of coding the same operation, but an actual benchmark is far more complicated.

Summary

In this chapter, you learned about some of the most interesting base data types. Strings, characters, and date/time values are some of the richest data types, as they encapsulate a lot of functionality. For the first time, you have at your disposal methods to simplify the processing of characters—like figuring out whether a character is white space, a letter, a digit, or even a separator. The TimeSpan class encapsulates all the functionality you need to manipulate time differences, and it gives you the tools for timing at a very fine level. The StringBuilder class, finally, provides the fastest string-manipulation methods VB has ever provided.

This chapter ends our discussion of the fundamental classes of the .NET Framework. This doesn't mean that the other classes are less important. There's no way to cover all of the Framework's classes in a single book, especially in a book that teaches programming with VB. I've chosen the classes you'll be using most often in your applications and presented them in detail, rather than attempting to mention just the basics of many classes.

Chapter 13

Working with Folders and Files

FILES HAVE ALWAYS BEEN an important aspect of programming. We use files to store data, and in many cases we have to manipulate files and folders from within applications. I need not give examples: just about any application that allows user input must store its data to a file (or multiple files) for later retrieval—databases excluded, of course.

Manipulating files and folders is quite common too. Organizing files into folders and processing files en masse are two typical examples. I recently ran into a few Web-related tasks, that are worth mentioning here. A program for placing watermarks on pictures was the first. A watermark is a graphic that's placed over an image to indicate its origin. The watermark is very transparent, so that it doesn't obscure the image, but it makes the image unusable on any site other than the original site. You will see in Chapter 14 how to place a semitransparent graphic on top of an image, and with the help of the information in this chapter, you'll be able to scan a folder with thousands of images and automate the process of watermarking the images.

Another example has to do with matching filenames to values stored in a database. Product images are usually named after the product's ID, and they're stored in separate files. There's a need for programs to match product IDs to images, find out whether there's an image for a specific product in the database, or simply move the image files around (store the images for different product categories into different folders and so on).

You may even need to initiate some action when a file in a specific folder is created, edited, or deleted. For example, you can process files as soon as they're uploaded to a server or copied to a specific folder. There are better ways to automate the workflow, but I'm not going to elaborate on this. The fact is that many programmers still use these methods. They work, and you may have to not only act on files, but also initiate other actions from within your applications based on changes in the file system. In the last section, you'll learn about the FileSystemWatcher, a component that can detect changes in the file system and notify your application about these changes through events.

Accessing Folders and Files

In this section, you'll learn how to access and manipulate files and folders with the help of the Directory and File classes. The Directory class provides methods for manipulating folders, and the File class provides methods for manipulating files. These two objects allow you to perform just about any operation you can perform on a folder and a file, respectively, short of storing data into or reading from files.

TIP Directory *is another name for* folder; *they mean the same thing, but* folder *is the more familiar term in Windows. When it comes to developers and administrators, Microsoft still uses the term* directory *(the Active Directory, the Directory object, and so on).*

Keep in mind that Directory and File objects don't represent folders or files. The two objects that represent these entities are the DirectoryInfo and FileInfo classes. If you're in doubt as to which class you should use in your code, consider that the members of the Directory and File classes are *shared*: you can call them without having to explicitly create an instance of the corresponding object first. The methods of the DirectoryInfo and FileInfo are *instance* methods: they apply to an instance of the corresponding object.

Both the Directory and the DirectoryInfo classes allow you to delete a folder, including its subfolders. The Delete method of the DirectoryInfo class will act on a directory you specified when you instantiated the DirectoryInfo class:

```
Dim DI As New DirectoryInfo("C:\Work Files\Assignments")
DI.Delete()
```

But you can't call Delete on a DirectoryInfo object that you haven't specifically declared. The `DirectoryInfo.Delete` method doesn't accept the name of a folder as argument. In short, you can't use the DirectoryInfo class without first creating an instance of it, which references a specific folder.

The Delete method of the Directory class can be called at any time, by passing as argument the path of the folder to be deleted:

```
Directory.Delete("C:\Work Files\Assignments")
```

The two classes expose similar members for performing basic file and folder operations, and it shouldn't come as a surprise that there's a substantial overlap between the classes' methods.

I will start this chapter with a detailed discussion of the Directory and File classes, which are richer, and then I'll go quickly through the members of the DirectoryInfo and FileInfo classes.

The Directory Class

The Directory class exposes all the members you need to manipulate folders, and you must import it into any project that may require its members with the following statement, which must appear at the beginning of the file, outside any class:

```
Imports System.IO
```

METHODS

The Directory object exposes methods for accessing folders and their contents, which are described in the following sections.

CreateDirectory

This method creates a new folder, whose path is specified by a string passed as argument to the method:

```
Directory.CreateDirectory(path)
```

path is the fully qualified path of the folder you want to create and can be either an absolute or a relative path. If it's a relative path, its absolute value is determined by the current drive and path.

The CreateDirectory method returns a DirectoryInfo object, which contains information about the newly created folder. The DirectoryInfo object is discussed later in this chapter along with the FileInfo object.

Notice that the CreateDirectory method can create multiple nested folders in a single call. The statement

```
Directory.CreateDirectory("C:\folder1\folder2\folder3")
```

will create the folder `folder1` (if it doesn't exist), then `folder2` (if it doesn't exist) under `folder1`, and finally `folder3` under `folder2` in the C: drive. If `folder1` exists already, but it doesn't contain a subfolder named `folder2`, then `folder2` will be automatically created. An exception will also be thrown if the total path is too long, or if your application doesn't have permission to create a folder in the specified path. However, no exception will be thrown if the specified path exists on the disk already. The method will simply not create any new folders. It will still return a DirectoryInfo object, which describes the existing folder.

Delete

This method deletes a folder and all the files in it. If the folder contains subfolders, the Delete method will optionally remove the entire directory tree under the node you're removing. The simplest form of the Delete method is

```
Directory.Delete(path)
```

where *path* is the path of the folder to be deleted. This method will delete the specified path only. If the specified folder contains subfolders, they will not be deleted and, therefore, the specified folder won't be deleted either.

To delete a folder recursively (that is, also delete any subfolders under it), use the second form of the Delete method, which accepts a second argument:

```
Directory.Delete(path, force)
```

The *force* argument is a True/False value that determines whether the Delete method will delete the subfolders under the specified folder or not. If True, the folder will be removed, along with its files and subfolders.

The statements in Listing 13.1 attempt to delete a single folder. If the folder contains subfolders, the Delete method will fail and an exception handler will be activated. The exception handler examines the type of exception, and if it was caused because the folder isn't empty, it can call the second form of the Delete method forcing it to delete the folder recursively. Create a new project, insert the statement `Imports System.IO` at the beginning of the file, and then place the statements of Listing 13.1 in a button's Click event handler to experiment with the code.

LISTING 13.1: DELETING A DIRECTORY

```
Private Sub Button1_Click(ByVal sender As System.Object, _
              ByVal e As System.EventArgs) Handles Button1.Click
    Directory.CreateDirectory("c:/folder1/folder2/folder3")
    Try
        Directory.Delete("c:\folder1", False)
    Catch exc As IOException
        If exc.ToString.IndexOf("The directory is not empty") >= 0 Then
            Dim reply As MsgBoxResult
            reply = MsgBox("Delete all files and subfolders?", _
                        MsgBoxStyle.YesNo, exc.Message)
            If reply = MsgBoxResult.Yes Then
                Directory.Delete("c:\folder1", True)
            Else
                MsgBox(exc.Message)
            End If
        End If
    End Try
End Sub
```

Exists

This method accepts a path as argument and returns a True/False value indicating whether the specified folder exists.

```
Directory.Exists(path)
```

The Delete method will throw an exception if you attempt to delete a folder that doesn't exist, so you can use the Exists method to make sure the folder exists, before attempting to delete it:

```
If Directory.Exists(path) Then Directory.Delete(path)
```

Of course, the Delete method may fail for other reasons as well, and you should provide an error handler—for example, the Delete method will fail if the folder contains read-only files.

GetCreationTime, SetCreationTime

These methods read or set the date a specific folder was created. The GetCreationTime method accepts a path as argument and returns a Date value:

```
Dim CreatedOn As Date
CreatedOn = Directory.GetCreationTime(path)
```

SetCreationTime accepts a path and a date value as argument and sets the specified folder's creation time to the value specified by the second argument:

```
Directory.SetCreationTime(path, datetime)
```

You shouldn't change the creation dates of files except on rare occasions. If you do, you will never be able to read the file's original creation date.

GetCurrentDirectory, SetCurrentDirectory

Use these methods to retrieve and set the path of the current directory. The current directory is a basic concept when working with the Directory class. We will use this technique in the CustomExplorer project, later in this chapter. The first time you call the GetCurrentDirectory method, it will return the folder in which the application is running. If you set the current folder with the SetCurrentDirectory method, the GetCurrentDirectory method will retrieve the name of the new current folder. The SetCurrentDirectory accepts a string argument, which is a path, and sets the current directory to the specified path.

The expression `Directory.GetCurrentDirectory` will return the application's current folder. For the default installation, it's something like

```
C:\Documents and Settings\TOOLKIT\My Documents\Visual Studio Projects\
DirectoryFileSamples\bin
```

(`DirectoryFileSamples` is the name of the project I used to test the short samples of this chapter.) You can change the current folder with a relative path like the following:

```
Directory.SetCurrentDirectory("..\..\..\My Pictures")
```

The two periods are a shortcut for the parent folder. From the `bin` folder just named, this statement moves up three levels to the `My Documents` folder and then to the `My Pictures` folder under `My Docu-ments` (assuming that there is a folder by that name). So this SetCurrentDirectory statement switches the current folder to

```
C:\Documents and Settings\TOOLKIT\My Documents\My Pictures
```

Notice that the value you pass to the SetCurrentDirectory method as argument must be the name of an existing folder. If not, a FileNotFound exception will be thrown. You can also switch to a folder on another drive, if you specify the full folder's path, including its drive letter. To handle possible errors, use the SetCurrentDirectory method with a structured error handler like the one in Listing 13.2.

LISTING 13.2: CHANGING THE CURRENT DIRECTORY

```
Try
    Directory.SetCurrentDirectory("..\..\..\Projects1")
    MsgBox("Switched current folder to " & Directory.GetCurrentDirectory)
Catch exc As FileNotFoundException
    MsgBox("Invalid folder specified, currrent directory is " & vbCrLf & _
            Directory.GetCurrentDirectory)
Catch exc As Exception
    MsgBox("Can't access specified folder")
End Try
```

The code of Listing 13.2 handles the FileNotFoundException separately with the first Catch clause. All other exceptions are handled by the second Catch clause.

GetDirectories

This method retrieves all the subfolders of a specific folder and returns their names as an array of strings:

```
Dirs = Directory.GetDirectories(path)
```

The *path* argument is the path of the folder whose subfolders you want to retrieve. The *Dirs* array that accepts the names of the subfolders must be declared with a statement like the following:

```
Dim Dirs() As String
```

Another form of the GetDirectories method allows you to specify search criteria for the folders you want to retrieve, and its syntax is

```
Dirs = Directory.GetDirectories(path, pattern)
```

This statement returns an array of strings with the names of the subfolders that match the search criteria. To retrieve all the subfolders of the `C:\Windows` folder with the string "System" in their names, use the statement

```
Dirs = Directory.GetDirectories("C:\Windows", "*SYSTEM*")
```

This statement will go through the subfolders of `C:\Windows` and return those that contain the string "SYSTEM" (including "System32" and "MySystem"). The only special characters you can use in the criteria specification are the question mark, which stands for any single character, and the asterisk, which stands for any string. Listing 13.3 retrieves the names of the folders that contain the string "System" under the `C:\WINNT` folder and prints them in the Output window.

LISTING 13.3: RETRIEVING SELECTED SUBFOLDERS OF A FOLDER

```
Dim Dirs() As String
Dirs = Directory.GetDirectories("C:\WINNT", "*SYSTEM*")
Dim dir As String
Console.WriteLine(Dirs.Length & " folders match the pattern '*SYSTEM*'")
For Each dir In Dirs
    Console.WriteLine(dir)
Next
```

GetDirectoryRoot

This method returns the root part of the path passed as argument, and its syntax is

```
root = Directory.GetDirectoryRoot(path)
```

The *path* argument is a string, and the return value is also a string like "C:\" or "D:\". Notice that the GetDirectoryRoot method doesn't require that the *path* argument exists. It will return the name of the root folder of the specified path.

GetFiles

This method returns the names of the files in the specified folder as an array of strings. The syntax of the GetFiles method is

```
files = Directory.GetFiles(path)
```

where *path* is the path of the folder whose files you want to retrieve and *files* is an array of strings, which must be declared as follows:

```
Dim files() As String
```

This array will be dimensioned as it gets populated by the GetFiles method, so you don't have to specify an upper bound when declaring the array.

Another form of the GetFiles method allows you to specify a pattern and retrieve only the names of the files that match the pattern. This form of the method accepts a second argument, which is a string similar to the *pattern* argument of the GetDirectories method:

```
files = Directory.GetFiles(path, pattern)
```

The statements in Listing 13.4 retrieve all the EXE files under the \WINNT folder and print their names in the Output window.

LISTING 13.4: RETRIEVING SELECTED FILES OF A FOLDER

```
Dim files() As String
files = Directory.GetFiles("C:\WINNT", "*.EXE")
MsgBox("Found " & files.Length & " EXE files")
Dim file As String
For Each file In files
    Console.WriteLine(file)
Next
```

GetFileSystemEntries

This method returns an array of all items (files and folders) in a path. The simplest form of the method is

```
items = Directory.GetFileSystemEntries(path)
```

where *items* is an array of FileSystemEntry, which you must declare as

```
Dim items() As String
```

As with the GetFiles method, you can specify a second argument, which filters the FileSystemEntry objects you want to retrieve:

```
Items = Directory.GetFileSystemEntries(path, matchFiles)
```

To iterate through the items of a folder, associate a Directory object with this folder and use a loop like the following one:

```
Dim itm As String
For Each itm In Directory.GetFileSystemEntries("C:\windows")
    Console.WriteLine(itm)
Next
```

Since the GetFileSystemEntries method returns an array of strings, how do we know that a specific member of the array is a file or a folder? To find out whether the current item is a file or a folder, you can use the Exists method of the Directory object. The File object, which is equivalent to the Directory object and is discussed in the following section, also exposes an Exists method. The loop shown in Listing 13.5 goes through the file system items in your `C:\Program Files` folder and displays their names, along with the indication "FOLDER" or "FILE," depending on the type of each item.

LISTING 13.5: RETRIEVING THE FILE SYSTEM ITEMS OF A FOLDER

```
Dim items() As String
Dim path As String = "c:\Program Files"
items = Directory.GetFileSystemEntries(path)
Dim itm As String
For Each itm In items
   If Directory.Exists(itm) Then
       Console.WriteLine("FOLDER " & itm)
   Else
       Console.WriteLine("FILE " & itm)
   End If
Next
```

If you execute these statements, you will see a list like the following in the Output window (only considerably longer):

```
FOLDER c:\Program Files\Microsoft.NET
FOLDER c:\Program Files\HTML Help Workshop
FOLDER c:\Program Files\Microsoft Web Controls 0.6
FILE c:\Program Files\folder.htt
FILE c:\Program Files\desktop.ini
```

NOTE   *The GetDirectories, GetFiles, and GetFileSystemEntries methods return the items under the specified folder. If this folder contains subfolders (as is usually the case), the GetDirectories method won't return any subfolders beyond the ones directly under the specified folder. To scan a folder recursively (scan all the subfolders under it to any depth), you must use a recursive routine. You will find examples of recursive folder scanning in Chapters 16 and 18.*

GetLastAccessTime, SetLastAccessTime

These two methods are equivalent to the GetCreationTime and SetCreationTime methods, only they return and set the most recent date and time the file was accessed. The most common reason to change the last access time for a file is so that the specific file will be excluded from a routine that deletes old files, or to include it in a list of backup files (with an automated procedure that backs up only the files that have been changed since their last backup).

GetLastWriteTime, SetLastWriteTime

These two methods are equivalent to the GetCreationTime and SetCreationTime methods, but they return and set the most recent date and time the file was written to.

GetLogicalDrives

This method returns an array of strings, which are the names of the logical drives on the computer. The statements in Listing 13.6 print the names of all logical drives.

LISTING 13.6: RETRIEVING THE NAMES OF ALL DRIVES ON THE COMPUTER

```
Dim drives() As String
drives = Directory.GetLogicalDrives
Dim iDrive As Integer
For iDrive = 0 To drives.GetUpperBound(0)
    Console.WriteLine(drives(iDrive))
Next
```

When executed, these statements will produce a list like the following:

```
A:\
C:\
D:\
E:\
```

GetParent

This method retrieves an object that represents the properties of a folder's parent folder. The syntax of the GetParent method is

```
parent = Directory.GetParent(path)
```

The return value is a DirectoryInfo object, and it must be declared with a statement like the following:

```
Dim parent As DirectoryInfo
```

The name of the parent folder, for example, is `parent.Name` and its full name is `parent.FullName`.

Move

This method moves an entire folder to another location in the file system; its syntax is

```
Directory.Move(source, destination)
```

where *source* is the name of the folder to be moved and *destination* is the name of the destination folder. The Move method doesn't work along different volumes, and the *destination* can't be the same as the *source* argument, obviously.

Notice the lack of a Copy method that would copy an entire folder to a different location. To copy a folder, you must manually create an identical folder structure and then copy the corresponding files to the proper subfolders.

The File Class

The File class exposes methods for manipulating files (copying, moving them around, opening and closing them), similar to the methods of the Directory class. The names of the methods are self-descriptive, and most of them accept as argument the path of the file on which they act. Use these methods to implement the common operations users normally perform through the Windows interface from within your application.

METHODS

Many of the methods listed in the following sections allow you to open existing or create new files. We'll use some of these methods later in the chapter to write data to, and read from, text and binary files.

AppendText

This method prepares an existing text file for appending text to it and returns a StreamWriter object. If the file doesn't exist, it creates a new one and opens it. The syntax of the AppendText method is

```
FStream = File.AppendText(path)
```

Copy

This method copies an existing file to a new location; its syntax is

```
File.Copy(source, destination)
```

where *source* is the path of the file to be copied and *destination* is the path where the file will be copied to. If the destination file exists, the Copy method will fail.

To overwrite the destination file, use the following form of the method, which allows you to specify whether the destination file can be overwritten.

```
File.Copy(source, destination, overwrite)
```

If the last argument is True, the destination file is overwritten (if it exists).

The Copy method works across volumes. The following statement copies the file `faces.jpg` from the folder `c:\My Documents\Screen\` to the folder `d:\Fun Images` and changes its name to `Bouncing Face.jpg`. Notice that both the source and destination paths must already exist. If not, an exception will be thrown.

```
File.Copy("c:\My Documents\Screen\faces.jpg", _
        "d:\Fun Images\Bouncing Face.jpg")
```

NOTE *The Copy method doesn't accept wildcard characters. In other words, you can't copy multiple files with a single call to the Copy method.*

Create

This method creates a new file and returns a Stream object to this file. You can use this object to write to or read from the file. The Stream object is discussed in detail later in this chapter, along with the methods for writing to or reading from the file. The simplest form of the Create method accepts a single argument, which is the path of the file you want to create:

```
FStream = File.Create(path)
```

You can also create a new file and specify the size of the buffer to be associated with this file, with the following form of the method:

```
FStream = File.Create(path, bufferSize)
```

where *bufferSize* is an Integer (Int32) value.

If the specified file exists already, it's replaced. The new file is opened for read-write operations, and it's opened exclusively by your application. Other applications can access it only after your application closes it. Once the file has been created, you can use the methods of the Stream object to write to it. These methods are discussed in the section "Accessing Files," later in this chapter.

There are several exceptions the Create method can raise, which are described in Table 13.1.

TABLE 13.1: EXCEPTIONS OF THE CREATE METHOD

EXCEPTION	DESCRIPTION
IOException	The folder you specified doesn't exist.
ArgumentNullException	The path you specified doesn't reference a file.
SecurityException	The user of your application doesn't have permission to create a new file in the specified folder.
ArgumentException	The path you specified is invalid.
AccessException	The file can't be opened in read-write mode. Most likely, you've attempted to open a read-only file, but the File.Create method opens a file in read-write mode.
DirectoryNotFoundException	The folder you specified doesn't exist.

Note that pathnames are limited to 248 characters, and filenames are limited to 259 characters.

CreateText

This method is similar to the Create method, but it creates a text file and returns a StreamWriter object for writing to the file. The StreamWriter object is similar to the Stream object, but used for text files only, whereas the StreamWriter object can be used with both text and binary files.

The syntax of the CreateText method is

```
File.CreateText(path)
```

and it returns an object that must be declared as follows:

```
Dim SW As StreamWriter
SW = File.CreateText(path)
```

You will learn more about reading from and writing to files later in this chapter.

Delete

This method removes the specified file from the file system. The syntax of the Delete method is

```
File.Delete(path)
```

where *path* is the path of the File object you want to delete. This method will raise an exception if the file is open at the time for reading or writing, or if the file doesn't exist.

Exists

This property is a True/False value that indicates whether a file exists or not. The following statements delete a file, after making sure that the file exists already:

```
If File.Exists(path) Then
    File.Delete(path)
Else
    MsgBox("The file " & path & " doesn't exist")
End If
```

The Delete method will not raise an exception if the file doesn't exist, so you don't have to make sure that a file exists before deleting it. You can use similar statements to confirm that a file exists before attempting to open it.

GetAttributes

This method accepts a file path as argument and returns the attributes of the specified file. The method returns a FileAttributes object, which contains all the attributes. A file may have more than a single attribute (for instance, it can be hidden and compressed). Table 13.2 lists all possible attributes a file can have.

TABLE 13.2: THE ATTRIBUTES OF A FILE

VALUE	DESCRIPTION
Archive	The file's archive status. Most of the files in your file system have the Archive attribute.
Compressed	The file is compressed.
Encrypted	The file is encrypted.
Hidden	The file is hidden, and it doesn't appear in an ordinary directory listing.
Normal	Normal files have no other attributes, so this setting excludes all other attributes.

Continued on next page

TABLE 13.2: THE ATTRIBUTES OF A FILE *(continued)*

VALUE	DESCRIPTION
NotContentIndexed	The file isn't indexed by the operating system's content indexing service.
Offline	The file is offline and its contents may not be available at all times.
ReadOnly	The file is read-only.
SparseFile	The file is sparse (a large files whose data are mostly zeros).
System	A system file is part of the operating system or is used exclusively by the operating system.
Temporary	The file is temporary. Temporary files are created by applications and they're deleted by the same applications that created them when they terminate.

To examine whether a file has an attribute set, you must AND the value returned by the GetAttributes methods with the desired attribute, which is a member of the FileAttributes enumeration. To find out whether a file is read-only, use the following If statement:

```
If File.GetAttributes(fpath) And FileAttributes.ReadOnly Then
    Console.WriteLine("The file " & fpath & " is read only")
Else
    Console.WriteLine("You can write to the file " & fpath)
End If
```

You can also retrieve a file's attributes through the FileInfo object, described later in this chapter.

GetCreationTime, SetCreationTime

The GetCreationTime method returns a date value, which is the date and time the file was created. This value is set by the operating system, but you can change it with the SetCreationTime method. The following statement returns a value like the one shown in bold underneath it:

```
Console.WriteLine(File.GetCreationTime("c:\config.sys"))
6/13/2001 1:27:48 PM
```

The SetCreationTime allows you to change the file's creation time; it accepts as argument the file's path and the new creation time:

```
File.SetCreationTime(path, datetime)
```

GetLastAccessTime, SetLastAccessTime

The GetLastAccessTime method returns a date value, which is the date and time the specified file was accessed for the last time. Use the SetLastAccessTime method to set this value. SetLastAccessTime accepts as arguments the file whose last access time you want to set and the desired date. Changing the last access of a file is sometimes called "touching" the file. If you have a utility that manipulates files according to when they were last used (for example, one that moves data files that haven't been accessed in the last three months to tape), you can "touch" a few files to exclude them from the operation.

GetLastWriteTime, SetLastWriteTime

The GetLastWriteTime method returns a date value, which is the date and time the specified file was written to for the last time. You can set this value with the SetLastWriteTime method.

Move

This method moves the specified file to a new location. You can also use the Move method to rename a file, by simply moving it to another name in the same folder. Moving a file is equivalent to copying it to another location and then deleting the original file. The Move method works across volumes.

```
File.Move(sourceFileName, destFileName)
```

The first argument is the path of the file to be moved, and the second argument is the path of the destination file. The following statement move the file `Boston Trip.xls` from the folder `C:\My Document\Business` to the folder `\\Accounts\Expenses\JamesK\`:

```
File.Move("C:\My Document\Business\Boston Trip.xls", _
          "\\Accounts\Expenses\JamesK\Boston Trip.xls")
```

Open

This method opens an existing file for read-write operations. The simplest form of the method is

```
FStream = File.Open(path)
```

which opens the file specified by the *path* argument and returns a Stream object to this file. The following form of the method allows you to specify the mode in which you want to open the file:

```
FStream = fileObj.Open(path, fileMode)
```

where the *fileMode* argument can have one of the values shown in Table 13.3.

TABLE 13.3: THE FILEMODE ENUMERATION

VALUE	EFFECT
Append	Opens the file in write mode, and all the data you write to the file are appended to its existing contents.
Create	Requests the creation of a new file. If a file by the same name exists, this will be overwritten.
CreateNew	Requests the creation of a new file. If a file by the same name exists, an exception will be thrown. This mode will create and open a file only if it doesn't already exist.
Open	Requests that an existing file be opened.
OpenOrCreate	Opens the file in read-write mode if the file exists, or creates a new file and opens it in read-write mode if the file doesn't exist.
Truncate	Opens an existing file and resets its size to zero bytes. As you can guess, this file must be opened in write mode.

Another form of the Open method allows you to specify the access mode, in addition to the file mode:

```
FStream = File.Open(path, fileMode, accessMode)
```

where the *accessMode* argument can have one of the values listed in Table 13.4.

TABLE 13.4: THE FILEACCESS ENUMERATION

VALUE	EFFECT
Read	The file is opened in read-only mode. You can read from the Stream object that is returned, but an exception will be thrown if you attempt to write to the file.
ReadWrite	The file opened in read-write mode. You can either write to the file or read from it.
Write	The file is opened in write mode. You can write to the file, but if you attempt to read from it, an exception will be thrown.

You can also specify a fourth argument to the Open method, which specifies how the file will be shared with other applications. This form of the method requires that the other two arguments (*file-Mode* and *accessMode*) be supplied as well:

```
FStream = File.Open(path, fileMode, accessMode, shareMode)
```

The *shareMode* argument determines how the file will be shared among multiple applications and can have one of the values from Table 13.5.

TABLE 13.5: THE FILESHARE ENUMERATION

VALUE	EFFECT
None	The file can't be shared for reading or writing. If another application attempts to open the file, it will fail until the current application closes the file.
Read	The file can be opened by other applications for reading, but not for writing.
ReadWrite	The file can be opened by other applications for reading or writing.
Write	The file can be opened by other applications for writing, but not for reading.

OpenRead

This method opens an existing file in read mode and returns a stream object associated with this file. You can use this stream to read from the file.

The syntax of the OpenRead method is:

```
FStream = fileObj.OpenRead(path)
```

where *fileObj* is a properly initialized File variable. The OpenRead method is equivalent to opening an existing file with read-only access with the Open method.

OpenText

This method opens an existing text file for reading and returns a StreamReader object associated with this file. Its syntax is

```
FStream = File.OpenText(path)
```

Why do we need an OpenText method in addition to the Open, OpenRead, and OpenWrite methods? The answer is that text can be stored in different formats. It can be plain text (UTF-8 encoding), ASCII text, or Unicode text. The StreamReader object associated with the text file will perform the necessary conversions, and you will always read the correct text from the file. The default encoding for the OpenText method is UTF-8.

OpenWrite

This method opens an existing file in write mode and returns a StreamWriter object associated with this file. You can use this stream to write to the file, as you will see later in this chapter.

The syntax of the OpenRead method is:

```
FStream = File.OpenWrite(path)
```

where *path* is the path of the file.

This ends our discussion of the Directory and File objects, which are the two major objects for manipulating files and folders. In the following section, I will present the DirectoryInfo and FileInfo classes briefly, and then we'll build an application that puts together much of the information presented so far.

The DirectoryInfo Class

The DirectoryInfo and FileInfo classes are similar to the Directory and File classes, but they must be instantiated before they are used. Their constructors specify the folder or file they will act upon, and you don't have to specify a folder or file when you call their methods.

To create a new instance of the DirectoryInfo class that references a specific folder, supply the folder's path in the class's constructor:

```
Dim DI As New DirectoryInfo(path)
```

METHODS

The members of the DirectoryInfo class are equivalent to the members of the Directory class, and you will recognize them as soon as you see them in the IntelliSense drop-down list. Here are a couple of methods that are unique to the DirectoryInfo class.

CreateSubdirectory

This method creates a subfolder under the folder specified by the current instance of the class, and its syntax is

```
CreateSubdirectory(path)
```

The CreateSubdirectory method returns a DirectoryInfo object that represents the new subfolder. The *path* argument need not be a single folder's name. If you specified multiple nested folders, the CreateSubdirectory method will create the appropriate hierarchy, similar to the CreateDirectory method of the Directory class.

GetFileSystemInfos

This method returns an array of FileSystemInfo objects, one for each item in the folder referenced by the current instance of the class. The items can be either folders or files. To retrieve information about all the entries in a folder, create an instance of the DirectoryInfo class and then call its Get-FileSystemInfos method:

```
Dim DI As New DirectoryInfo(path)
Dim itemsInfo() As FileSystemInfo
itemsInfo = DI.GetFileSystemInfos()
```

You can also specify an optional search pattern as argument when you call this method:

```
itemsInfo = DI.GetFileSystemInfos(pattern)
```

The FileSystemInfo objects expose a few properties, which are not new to you. The Name, Full-Name, and Extension return a file's or folder's name or full path or a file's extension. The Creation-Time, LastAccessTime, and LastWriteTime are also properties of the FileSystemInfo object, as well as the Attributes property.

You will notice that there are no properties that determine whether the current item is a folder or a file. To find out the type of an item, use the Directory member of the Attributes property:

```
If itemsInfo(i).Attributes And FileAttributes.Directory Then
    { current item is a folder }
Else
    { current item is a file }
End If
```

The code in Listing 13.7 retrieves all the items in the C:\Program Files folder and prints their name along with the FOLDER and FILE characterization.

LISTING 13.7: PROCESSING A FOLDER'S ITEMS WITH THE FILESYSTEMINFO OBJECT

```
Dim path As String = "C:\Program Files"
Dim DI As New DirectoryInfo(path)
Dim itemsInfo() As FileSystemInfo
itemsInfo = DI.GetFileSystemInfos()
Dim item As FileSystemInfo
For Each item In itemsInfo
```

```
        If item.Attributes And FileAttributes.Directory Then
            Console.Write("FOLDER ")
        Else
            Console.Write("FILE  ")
        End If
        Console.WriteLine(item.Name)
    Next
```

Notice the similarities and differences between the GetFileSystemInfos method of the Directory-Info class and the GetFileSystemEntries of the Directory object. GetFileSystemInfos returns an array of objects that contains information about the current item (file or folder). GetFileSystemEntries returns an array of strings (the names of the folders and files).

The FileInfo Class

The FileInfo class exposes many properties and methods, which are equivalent to the members of the File class, so I'm not going to repeat all of them here. The Copy/Delete/Move methods allow you to manipulate the file represented by the current instance of the FileInfo class, similar to the methods by the same name of the File class. Although there's substantial overlap between the members of the FileInfo and File classes, the difference is that with FileInfo you don't have to specify a path. Its members act on the file represented by the current instance of the FileInfo class.

PROPERTIES

The FileInfo object exposes a few rather trivial properties, which are mentioned briefly here.

Length

This property returns the size of the file represented by the FileInfo object in bytes. The File class doesn't provide an equivalent property or method.

CreationTime, LastAccessTime, LastWriteTime

These properties return a date value which is the date on which the file was created, accessed for the last time, or written to for the last time. They are equivalent to the methods of the File object by the same name and the "Get" prefix.

Name, FullName, Extension

These properties return the filename, full path, and extension of the file represented by the current instance of the FileInfo class. They have no equivalents in the File class, because the File class's methods require that you specify the path of the file, so its path and extension are known.

METHODS

The FileInfo object exposes methods for manipulating files, and most of them are equivalent to the methods of the File object.

CopyTo, MoveTo

These two methods copy and move the file represented by the current instance of the FileInfo class. Both methods accept a single argument, which is the destination of the operation (the path to which the file will be copied or moved). If the destination file exists already, you can overwrite it by specifying a second optional argument, which has a True/False value:

```
FileInfo.CopyTo(path, force)
```

Both methods return an instance of the FileInfo class, which represents the new file—if the operation completed successfully.

Directory

This method returns a DirectoryInfo value that contains information about the file's parent directory.

DirectoryName

This method returns a string with the file's parent directory's name. The following statements return the two (identical) strings shown in bold:

```
Dim FI As FileInfo
FI = New FileInfo("c:\folder1\folder2\folder3\test.txt")
Console.WriteLine(FI.Directory().FullName)
c:\folder1\folder2\folder3
Console.WriteLine(FI.DirectoryName())
c:\folder1\folder2\folder3
```

Of course, the Directory method returns an object, which you can use to retrieve other properties of the parent folder.

The Path Class

The Path class contains an interesting collection of methods, which you can think of as utilities. The Path class's methods perform simple tasks such as retrieving a file's name and extension, returning the full path description of a relative path, and so on. The Path class's members require that you specify the path on which they will act. In other words, there's no constructor for the Path class that would allow you instantiate a Path object to represent a specific path.

PROPERTIES

The Path class exposes the following properties. Notice that none of these members apply to a specific path; they're general properties that return settings of the operating system.

AltDirectorySeparatorChar

This property returns an alternate directory separator character. For Windows 2000, the AltDirectorySeparatorChar property returns the slash character (/).

DirectorySeparatorChar

This property returns the directory separator character. For Windows 2000, the DirectorySeparatorChar returns the backslash character (\).

InvalidPathChars

This property returns the list of invalid characters in a path as an array of characters. The following statements print the invalid path characters to the Output window; their output is shown in bold below the code:

```
Dim p As Path
Dim invalidPathChars() As Char
invalidPathChars = p.InvalidPathChars
Dim c As Char
For Each c In invalidPathChars
    Console.Write(c & vbtab)
Next
```

/   \   "   <   > |

You can use these characters to validate user input, or pathnames read from a file. If you have a choice, let the user select the files through the Open dialog box, so that their pathnames will always be valid.

PathSeparator

This property returns separator character that may appear between multiple paths. For Windows 2000, this character is the semicolon (;).

VolumeSeparatorChar

This property returns the volume separator character. For Windows 2000, this character is the colon (:).

METHODS

The most useful methods exposed by the Path class are like utilities for manipulating file and pathnames, and they described in the following sections. Notice that the methods of the Path class are shared: you must specify the path on which they will act.

ChangeExtension

This method changes the extension of a file, and its syntax is

```
newExtension = Path.ChangeExtension(path, extension)
```

The return value is the new extension of the file (a string value). The first argument is the file's path, and the second argument is the file's new extension. If you want to remove the file's extension, set the second argument to Nothing. The following statement changes the extension of the specified file from "BIN" to "DAT":

```
Dim path As String = "c:\My Documents\NewSales.bin"
Dim newExt As String = ".dat"
Path.ChangeExtension(path, newExt)
```

Combine

This method combines two path specifications into one, and its syntax is

```
newPath = Path.Combine(path1, path2)
```

Use this method to combine a folder path with a file path. The following expression will return the string shown in bold:

```
Path.Combine("c:\textFiles", "test.txt")
c:\textFiles\test.txt
```

Notice that the Combine method inserted the separator, as needed. It's a simple operation, but if you had to code it yourself, you'd have to examine each path and determine whether a separator must be inserted.

GetDirectoryName

This method returns the directory name of a path. The statement

```
Path.GetDirectoryName("C:\folder1\folder2\folder3\Test.txt")
```

will return the string

```
C:\folder1\folder2\folder3
```

GetFileName, GetFileNameWithoutExtension

These two methods return the filename in a path, with and without its extension, respectively.

GetFullPath

This method returns the full path of the specified path; you can use it to convert relative pathnames to fully qualified pathnames. The following statement returned the string shown in bold on my computer (it will be quite different on your computer, depending on the current directory):

```
Console.WriteLine(Path.GetFullPath("..\..\Test.txt"))
C:\Mastering VB.NET\Chapters\Chapter 13\Projects\Test.txt
```

The pathname passed to the method as argument need not exist. The GetFullPath method will return the fully qualified pathname of a nonexisting file, as long as the path doesn't contain invalid characters.

GetTempFile, GetTempPath

The GetTempFile method returns a unique filename, which you can use as temporary storage area from within your application. The name of temporary file can be anything, since no user will ever access it. In addition, the GetTempFile method creates a zero-length file on the disk, which you can open with the Open method. A typical temporary filename is the following:

```
C:\DOCUME~1\TOOLKI~1\LOCALS~1\Temp\tmp105.tmp
```

which was returned by the following statement on my system:

```
Console.WriteLine(File.GetTempFile)
```

The GetTempPath method returns the system's temporary folder. All temporary files should be created in this folder, so that the operating system can remove them when it's running out of space. Your applications should remove all the temporary files they create, but more often than not, programmers leave temporary files around.

HasExtension

This method returns a True/False value indicating whether a path includes a file extension.

VB.NET at Work: The CustomExplorer Project

The CustomExplorer application, which demonstrates the basic properties and methods of the Directory and File objects, duplicates the functionality of Windows Explorer. Its user interface, shown in Figure 13.1, leaves a lot to be desired, but we'll come back to this example in Chapter 16, where we'll discuss the TreeView and ListView controls and you'll see how you can build a more elaborate user interface, but the core of the application will remain pretty much the same. In this chapter, you'll see how the basic members of the Directory and File objects can be used to manipulate the file system.

FIGURE 13.1

The Custom-Explorer project

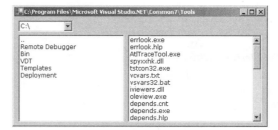

When you start the application, the names of all the logical drives will be displayed in the top-left ComboBox control, as shown in Figure 13.1. The other controls are initially empty. To view the folders of a drive, just select it in the ComboBox control. When the root folder's contents appear in the second ListBox control, you can click a folder's name to view its subfolders and its files. The selected folder's subfolders will replace the contents of the FoldersList ListBox under the ComboBox control, and the selected folder's files will replace the contents of the FilesList ListBox.

When you're not viewing the root folder, the parent folder's symbol (two periods) will appear at the top of the ListBox control with the folder names. You can click this item to move to the parent folder. The application allows you to use simple clicks to move up and down the hierarchy of your file system. You may wish to make the application a little more elaborate by programming the DoubleClick event too.

The three controls are named DrivesList, FoldersList, and FilesList. When the application is initialized (Listing 13.8), it calls the ShowAllDrives() subroutine, which populates the DrivesList control with the names of the logical drives. The ShowAllDrives() subroutine calls the GetLogicalDrives method of the Directory object and then goes through the array returned by this method and adds each logical drive's letter to the DrivesList control. The ShowAllDrives() subroutine is shown in Listing 13.9.

LISTING 13.8: CUSTOMEXPLORER'S FORM_LOAD EVENT HANDLER

```
Private Sub Form1_Load(ByVal sender As System.Object, _
            ByVal e As System.EventArgs) Handles MyBase.Load
    ShowAllDrives()
    DrivesList.SelectedIndex = 1
    Me.Text = Directory.GetCurrentDirectory
End Sub
```

LISTING 13.9: THE SHOWALLDRIVES() SUBROUTINE

```
Sub ShowAllDrives()
    Dim drives() As String
    drives = Directory.GetLogicalDrives()
    Dim aDrive As String
    DrivesList.Items.Clear()
    For Each aDrive In drives
        DrivesList.Items.Add(aDrive)
    Next
End Sub
```

When a drive is selected in the DrivesList control, the program calls the ShowFoldersInDrive subroutine (Listing 13.10) to display the folders in the selected drive's root folder on the FoldersList control. The ShowFoldersInDrive() subroutine accepts a drive as argument and displays the folders in this drive by iterating through the folders in the array returned by the `Directory.GetDirectories` method.

LISTING 13.10: DISPLAYING THE FOLDERS OF THE SELECTED DRIVE

```
Private Sub DrivesList_SelectedIndexChanged(ByVal sender As System.Object, _
        ByVal e As System.EventArgs) Handles DrivesList.SelectedIndexChanged
    ShowFoldersInDrive(DrivesList.Text)
End Sub
Sub ShowFoldersInDrive(ByVal drive As String)
    Dim folders() As String
    Try
        folders = Directory.GetDirectories(drive)
    Catch exception As Exception
        MsgBox(exception.Message)
        Exit Sub
    End Try
    Dim fldr As String
    FoldersList.Items.Clear()
    Dim DI As DirectoryInfo
```

```
      For Each fldr In folders
         DI = New DirectoryInfo(fldr)
         FoldersList.Items.Add(DI.Name)
      Next
      Directory.SetCurrentDirectory(drive)
      Me.Text = Directory.GetCurrentDirectory
   End Sub
```

When you select a new folder in the FoldersList control (all you have to do is click the folder's name), the program replaces the contents of the FoldersList control with the subfolders of the selected folder. It must also display the parent folder's name (..), so that you can move up in the directory tree. Listing 13.11 shows the code of the FoldersList control's SelectedIndexChanged event handler:

LISTING 13.11: DISPLAYING THE SUBFOLDERS OF THE SELECTED FOLDER

```
Private Sub FoldersList_SelectedIndexChanged(ByVal sender As System.Object, _
        ByVal e As System.EventArgs) Handles FoldersList.SelectedIndexChanged
   Dim DI As DirectoryInfo
   Select Case FoldersList.Text
      Case ""
         MsgBox("Please select a folder to expand")
         Exit Sub
      Case ".."
         Directory.SetCurrentDirectory("..")
      Case Else
         Directory.SetCurrentDirectory(Directory.GetCurrentDirectory & "\" & _
                                  FoldersList.Text)
         Me.Text = Directory.GetCurrentDirectory
   End Select
   Dim folders() As String
   Dim selectedFolder As String = FoldersList.Text
   folders = Directory.GetDirectories(Directory.GetCurrentDirectory)
   FoldersList.Items.Clear()
   If Directory.GetCurrentDirectory <> _
              Directory.GetDirectoryRoot(selectedFolder) Then _
      FoldersList.Items.Add("..")
   Dim fldr As String
   For Each fldr In folders
      DI = New DirectoryInfo(fldr)
      FoldersList.Items.Add(DI.Name)
   Next
   ShowFilesInFolder()
End Sub
```

This event handler always switches to the selected folder by calling the SetCurrentDirectory method of the Directory object. This simplifies the code considerably, because we can move to the parent folder when the user clicks the two periods with the statement `Directory.SetCurrentDirectory("..")`. In other words, we don't have to keep track of the current directory in our code—we're always in it. The routine that displays the files in the selected folders is also simplified—it goes through the files of the current directory.

If the selected item in the list is the parent folder symbol (..), the program switches to the parent directory. Otherwise, it switches to the selected folder under the current folder. The program then retrieves all the folders under the selected one and stores them in the *folders* array. A `For Each...Next` loop is used to iterate through the items of the array and display them on the FoldersList control, replacing its existing contents. Then, it calls the ShowFilesInFolder subroutine, which retrieves the files in the current folder and displays them in the FilesList control (see Listing 13.12).

LISTING 13.12: THE SHOWFILESINFOLDER() SUBROUTINE

```
Sub ShowFilesInFolder()
    Dim file As String
    Dim FI As FileInfo
    FilesList.Items.Clear()
    For Each file In Directory.GetFiles(Directory.GetCurrentDirectory)
        FI = New FileInfo(file)
        FilesList.Items.Add(FI.Name)
    Next
End Sub
```

The code uses the FileInfo class to retrieve the file's name. You can also use the FileInfo class's members to retrieve additional information about the file.

The program also prints information about any file in the Output window. Every time the user selects a file in the FilesList control by clicking its name, the program prints the file's name, followed by the file's attributes. It only prints the attributes that are set, and it does so by comparing the Attributes property to each of the members of the FileSystemAttributes enumeration. If the file's attribute is normal, then the string "NORMAL FILE" is printed under the file's name. If not, each attribute that is set is displayed with the ATTRIBUTES heading in the Output window. The action of the selection of a new file in the FilesList control is signaled by the SelectedIndexChanged event, whose event handler is shown in Listing 13.13.

LISTING 13.13: RETRIEVING A FILE'S PROPERTIES

```
Private Sub FilesList_SelectedIndexChanged(ByVal sender As System.Object, _
        ByVal e As System.EventArgs) Handles FilesList.SelectedIndexChanged
    Dim selectedFile As String = FilesList.Text
    Dim FI As New FileInfo(Directory.GetCurrentDirectory & "\" & _
                        selectedFile)
    Console.WriteLine(FI.Name)
```

```
Console.WriteLine("    LENGTH      " & FI.Length.ToString)
Console.WriteLine("    EXTENSION   " & FI.Extension)
Console.WriteLine("    CREATED     " & FI.CreationTime)
Console.WriteLine("    ACCESSED    " & FI.LastAccessTime.ToShortDateString)
If FI.Attributes = FileAttributes.Normal > 0 Then
    Console.Write(" NORMAL FILE ")
    Exit Sub
End If
Console.Write("    ATTRIBUTES ")
If FI.Attributes And FileAttributes.Archive Then Console.Write("Archive ")
If FI.Attributes And FileAttributes.Compressed Then _
                Console.Write("Compressed ")
If FI.Attributes And FileAttributes.Directory Then _
                Console.Write("Directory ")
If FI.Attributes And FileAttributes.Encrypted Then _
                Console.Write("Encrypted ")
If FI.Attributes And FileAttributes.Hidden Then Console.Write("Hidden ")
If FI.Attributes And FileAttributes.NotContentIndexed Then _
                Console.Write("Not Indexed ")
If FI.Attributes And FileAttributes.Offline Then Console.Write("OffLine ")
If FI.Attributes And FileAttributes.ReadOnly Then Console.Write("ReadOnly ")
If FI.Attributes And FileAttributes.System Then Console.Write("System ")
If FI.Attributes And FileAttributes.Temporary Then _
                Console.Write("Temp File ")
Console.WriteLine()
End Sub
```

When you select a file in the FileList control, a few lines like the following will be printed in the Output window:

```
desktop.ini
    LENGTH     271
    EXTENSION  .ini
    CREATED    6/9/2000 2:51:24 PM
    ACCESSED   03/17/2001
    ATTRIBUTES Hidden
```

Notice that all files are displayed in the FilesList control, because the `Directory.GetFiles` method returns by default all the files (see Listing 13.12). If you want to hide certain types of files, you must insert the appropriate code in the ShowFilesInFolder() subroutine.

Accessing Files

In the first half of the chapter, you learned how to manipulate files and folders. Now we're going to discuss how to access files (read from or write into them). There are two types of files, text files and binary files. Of course, you can classify files in any way you like, but when it comes to writing to and reading from files, it's convenient to treat them either as text or binary. A binary file is any file that doesn't contains plain text. Text files are usually read by line, or in their entirety into a String variable. Binary files must be read according to the type of the information stored in them. A bitmap file, for instance, must be read one byte at a time. Each pixel is usually represented by three or four bytes, and you must combine the values read to reconstruct the pixel's color. Or you can read a Color variable at a time. A binary file that contains doubles must be read one double at a time. Most binary files contain multiple data types, and you must know the organization of a file before you can read it. A Double value is stored in 8 bytes, and an Integer value is stored in 4 bytes. Unless you know how to read a binary file, you won't get the correct values out of it.

So the division of files into text and binary is dictated by our need to store data in them or get data out of them. In the following sections, you'll see that the .NET Framework provides different objects and different methods for manipulating text and binary files. It is possible to read text files as binary files, one byte at a time, but then you must reconstruct the original characters. It is also possible to store text into binary files and embed into it binary data types like integers, doubles, and dates.

Practically, you can distinguish text from binary files by the fact that text files can be read. Binary files contain mostly unprintable characters, and even the numeric digits in them don't make much sense. You can read any strings that may be part of the file, but an integer number isn't stored as text. Binary files can't be read with a text editor.

To access a file, you must first set up a Stream object. *Stream objects* are created by the various methods that open or create a file, as you have seen in the previous sections, and they return information about the file they're connected to. Once the Stream object is in place, you create a Reader or Writer object, which enables you to read information from or write information into the Stream. There are two types of Reader objects: the StreamReader for text files and the BinaryReader for binary files. Likewise, there are two Writer objects, the StreamWriter and the BinaryWriter. These objects expose a few properties and methods for writing to files and reading from them, and these members are discussed shortly.

Previous versions of Visual Basic supported statements for accessing the so-called random-access files. A random-access file contains records (structures) of fixed length, and you can quickly access any record in the file. Although you can still use random access with VB.NET, it's not recommended that you write applications based on random-access files. To support this type of application, you need a database. I'm not going to discuss random-access files in this chapter, because they're already obsolete. Remember that the Serializer object can save an array of custom structures to disk and load them back into the array. For small sets of data, use arrays of structures (or any of the Collections discussed in Chapter 11), and for larger data sets, deploy a database.

The FileStream Object

The StreamReader/StreamWriter and BinaryReader/BinaryWriter objects allow you to read from or write to text and binary files through a FileStream object. To prepare your application to write to a text file, you must set up a FileStream object, which is the channel between your application and the file. There are many ways to set up a FileStream object and associate it with a file, and they're described in the following sections. All the objects are contained in the System.IO namespace, so don't forget to import the System.IO namespace in your projects that perform file input/output. It's the same namespace that exposes the Directory, File, Path, and other classes discussed so far.

The FileStream object exposes a few members, that convey information about the file you're accessing through a FileStream variable. We'll cover these members here, and then we'll discuss the Reader and Writer objects that actually write data to or read it from files.

The FileStream object's constructor is overloaded; its most common forms require that you specify the path of the file and the mode in which the file will be opened (for reading, appending, writing, and so on). The simpler form of the constructor is

```
Dim FS As New FileStream(path, fileMode)
```

The *fileMode* argument is a member of the FileMode enumeration (see Table 13.3). It's the same argument used by the Open method of the File class. Also similar to Open method of the File class, another overloaded form of the constructor allows you to specify the file's access mode, and the syntax of this method is

```
Dim FS As New FileStream(path, fileMode, fileAccess)
```

The last argument is a member of the FileAccess enumeration (see Table 13.4). The last overloaded form of the constructor accepts a fourth argument, which determines the file's sharing mode:

```
Dim FS As New FileStream(path, fileMode, fileAccess, fileShare)
```

The *fileShare* argument's value is a member of the FileShare enumeration (see Table 13.5).

PROPERTIES

You can use the following properties of the FileStream object to retrieve information about the underlying file.

CanRead

This read-only property determines whether the current stream supports reading. If the file associated with a specific FileStream object can be read, this property returns True.

CanSeek

This read-only property determines whether the current stream supports seeking. A seek operation in the context of files doesn't locate a specific value in the file. It simply moves the current position to any location within the file.

CanWrite

This read-only value determines whether the current stream supports writing. If the file associated with a specific FileStream object can be written to, this property returns True.

Length

This read-only property returns the length of the file associated with the FileStream in bytes.

Position

This property gets or sets the current position within the stream. You can compare the Position property to the Length property to find out whether you have reach the end of an existing file. When these two properties are equal, there are no more data to read.

METHODS

The FileStream object exposes the following methods that support input/output operations. The methods for accessing a file's contents are discussed in the following section (you can't access the file's contents with a FileStream object).

Lock

This method allows you to lock the file you're accessing, or part of it. The syntax of the Lock method is

```
Lock(position, length)
```

where *position* is the starting position and *length* is the length of the range to be locked. To lock the entire file, use the statement

```
FileStream.Lock(1, FileStream.Length)
```

Seek

This method sets the current position in the file represented by the FileStream object:

```
FileStream.Seek(offset, origin)
```

The new position is *offset* bytes from the *origin*. In the place of the *origin* argument, use one of the SeekOrigin enumeration members, listed in Table 13.6.

TABLE 13.6: THE SEEKORIGIN ENUMERATION

VALUE	EFFECT
Begin	The offset is relative to the beginning of the file.
Current	The offset is relative to the current position in the file.
End	The offset is relative to the end of the file.

SetLength

This method sets the length of the file represented by the FileStream object. Use this method after you have written to an existing file, to truncate its length. The syntax of the SetLength method is

```
FileStream.SetLength(newLength)
```

If the specified value is less than the length of the file, the file is truncated. Otherwise, the file is expanded. The bytes after the length of the original file all the way to the end of the new file are undefined.

The StreamWriter Object

The StreamWriter object is the channel through which you send data to the text file. To create a new StreamWriter object, declare a variable of the StreamWriter type. The constructor of the StreamWriter object is overloaded, and its various forms are discussed next. The first form creates a new StreamWriter object for a file:

```
Dim SW As New StreamWriter(path)
```

This form of the constructor creates a new StreamWriter object for the file specified by the *path* argument. The new object has the default encoding and the default buffer size. The encoding scheme determines how characters are saved (the default encoding is UTF-8), and the buffer size determines the size of a buffer where data are stored before they're sent to the file. The following statement creates a new StreamWriter object and associates it with the specified file:

```
Dim SW As New StreamWriter("c:\TextFile.txt")
```

Another form of the same constructor creates a new StreamWriter object for the specified file using the default encoding and buffer size, but it allows you to overwrite existing files. If the *overwrite* argument is True, you can overwrite the contents of an existing file.

```
Dim SW As New StreamWriter(path, overwrite)
```

You can also specify the encoding for the StreamWriter with the following form of the constructor:

```
Dim SW As New StreamWriter(path, overwrite, encoding)
```

The last form of the constructor that accepts a file's path allows you to specify both the encoding and the buffer size:

```
Dim SW As New StreamWriter(path, overwrite, encoding, bufferSize)
```

The same forms of the constructor can be used with a FileStream object. The simplest form of this type of constructor is

```
Dim SW As New StreamWriter(stream)
```

This form creates a new StreamWriter object for the FileStream specified by the *stream* argument. To use this form of the constructor, you must first create a new FileStream object and then use it to instantiate a StreamWriter object:

```
Dim FS As FileStream
FS = New FileStream("C:\TextData.txt", FileMode.Create)
Dim SW As StreamWriter
SW = New StreamWriter(FS)
```

Finally, there are two more forms of the StreamWriter constructor that accept a FileStream object as the first argument. These forms are simply listed here:

```
New StreamWriter(stream, encoding)
New StreamWriter(stream, encoding, bufferSize)
```

Once you have created the StreamWriter object, you can call its members to manipulate the underlying file. These are described in the following sections.

PROPERTY: NEWLINE

The StreamWriter object provides a very handy property, the NewLine property, which allows you to change the string used to terminate each line in the file. This terminator is written to the text file by the WriteLine method, following the text. The default line-terminator string is a carriage return followed by a line feed ("\r\n").

NOTE *The TextReader object doesn't provide a similar property. It reads lines terminated by the carriage return (\r), line feed (\n) or carriage return/line feed (\r\n) characters only.*

METHODS

To send information to the underlying file, use the following methods of the StreamWriter object.

AutoFlush

This property is a True/False value that determines whether the methods that write to the file (the Write and WriteString methods) will also flush their buffer. If you set this property to False, then the buffer will be flushed when the operating system gets a chance, when the Flush method is called, or when you close the FileStream object. The False setting may help your application's performance, but only for very large files. When AutoFlush is True, then the buffer is flushed with every write operation.

Close

This method closes the StreamWriter object and releases the resources associated with it to the system. Always call the Close method after you're done using the StreamWriter object. If you have created the StreamWriter object on a FileStream object, you must also close the underlying stream.

Flush

This method clears writes any data in the buffer to the underlying file.

Write(data)

This method writes the data specified by the *data* argument to the stream on which it's applied. The Write method is overloaded and can accept any data type as argument. When you pass a numeric value as argument, the Write method stores it to the file as a string. This is the same string as you'd get with the number's ToString method. You can write any data type to the file, except for the Date type. To save dates to a text file, you must convert them to strings with one of the methods of the Date data type. You can even write objects to the file, and you will see shortly how the Write method handles objects.

There's one form of the Write method I would like to discuss here, and this is similar to the `Console.WriteLine` method, which accepts a string with embedded format arguments, followed by a list of values, one for each argument. The following statement writes a string with two embedded numeric values in it:

```
SW.Write("Your price is ${0} plus ${1} for shipping", 86.50, 12.99)
```

This statement will write the following string to the file:

```
Your price is $86.50 plus $12.99 for shipping
```

WriteLine(data)

This method is identical to the Write method, but it appends a line break after saving the data to the file (the same as the methods of the Console object by the same name).

You will find examples on using the StreamWriter object after we discuss the methods of the StreamReader object.

The StreamReader Object

The StreamReader object provides the necessary methods for reading from a text file. It exposes methods that match those of the StreamWriter object, methods that can read the information written to the file through the StreamWriter's Write and WriteLine methods.

The StreamReader object's constructor is overloaded. You can specify the FileStream object it will use to write data to the file, the encoding scheme, and the buffer size. The simplest form of the constructor is

```
Dim SR As New StreamReader(FS)
```

This declaration associates the *SR* variable with the file on which the *FS* FileStream object was created. This is the most common form of the StreamReader object's constructor. To prepare your application for reading the contents of the file C:\My Documents\Meeting.txt, use the following statements:

```
Dim FS As FileStream
Dim SR As StreamReader
FS = New FileStream("c:\My Documents\Meeting.txt", _
                    System.IO.FileMode.OpenOrCreate, System.IO.FileAccess.Write)
SR = New StreamReader(FS)
```

You can also create a new StreamReader object directly on a file, with the following form of the constructor:

```
Dim SR As New StreamReader(path)
```

To create a StreamReader object and associate it with the file of the previous example, use the statement

```
Dim SR As New StreamReader("c:\My Documents\Meeting.txt")
```

With both forms of the constructor, you can specify the character encoding with a second argument:

```
Dim SR As New StreamReader(FS, encoding)
Dim SR As New StreamReader(path, encoding)
```

You can also specify a third argument with the size of the buffer to be used with the file input/output operations:

```
Dim SR As New StreamReader(FS, encoding, bufferSize)
Dim SR As New StreamReader(path, encoding, bufferSize)
```

METHODS

Close

This method closes the current instance of StreamReader and releases any system resources associated with the StreamReader.

Peek

This method returns the next character without actually removing it from the input stream. The Peek method doesn't reposition the current position in the stream. If there are no more characters left in the stream, the value –1 is returned. The Peek method will also return –1 if the current stream doesn't allow peeking.

Read

This method reads a number of characters from the StreamReader object to which it's applied and returns the number of characters read. This value is usually the same as the number of characters you specified, unless there aren't as many characters in the file. If you have reached the end of the stream (which is the end of the file), the method returns the value –1. The syntax of the Read method is

```
charsRead = Read(chars, startIndex, count)
```

where *count* is the number of characters to be read. The characters are stored in the *chars* array of characters, starting at the index specified by the second argument. The return value is the number of characters actually read from the file.

A simpler form of the Read method reads the next character from the stream and returns it as an integer value:

```
Dim newChar As Integer
newChar = SR.Read()
```

where *SR* is a properly declared StreamReader object.

ReadBlock

This method reads a number of characters from a text file and stores them in a Character array. It accepts the same arguments as the Read method and returns the number of characters read:

```
charsRead = SR.Read(chars, startIndex, count)
```

ReadLine

This method reads the next line from the text file associated with the StreamReader object and returns a string. If you're at the end of the file, the method returns the Null value. The syntax of the ReadLine method is

```
Dim txtLine As String
txtLine = SR.ReadLine()
```

A text line is a sequence of characters followed by carriage return (\r), or line feed (\n), or carriage return and line feed (\r\n). Notice that the NewLine character you may have specified for the specific file with the StreamWriter object is ignored by the ReadLine method. The string returned by the method doesn't include the line terminator.

ReadToEnd

The last method for reading characters from a text file reads all the characters from the current position to the end of the file. We usually call this method once to read the entire file with a single statement and store its contents to a string variable. The syntax of the ReadToEnd method is

```
allText = SR.ReadToEnd()
```

Sending Data to a File

The statements in Listing 13.14 demonstrate how to send various data types to a file. You can place the statements of this listing to button's Click event handler and then open the file with Notepad to see its contents. Everything is in text format, including the numeric values. Don't forget to import the System.IO namespace to your project.

LISTING 13.14: WRITING DATA TO A TEXT FILE

```
Dim SW As StreamWriter
Dim FS As FileStream
FS = New FileStream("C:\TextData.txt", FileMode.Create)
SW = New StreamWriter(FS)
SW.WriteLine(9.009)
SW.WriteLine(1 / 3)
SW.Write("The current date is ")
SW.Write(Now())
SW.WriteLine()
SW.WriteLine(True)
SW.WriteLine(New Rectangle(1, 1, 100, 200))
SW.WriteLine(Color.YellowGreen)
SW.Close()
FS.Close()
```

Here's the output produced by Listing 13.14:

```
9.009
0.333333333333333
The current date is 2001-03-16T12:14:02
True
{X=1,Y=1,Width=100,Height=200}
Color [YellowGreen]
```

Notice how the WriteLine method without an argument inserts a new line character in the file. The statement SW.Write(now()) prints the current date but doesn't switch to another line. The

WriteLine method without any arguments starts a new line. The following statements demonstrate a more complicated use of the Write method with formatting arguments:

```
Dim BDate As Date = #2/8/1960 1:04:00 PM#
SW.WriteLine("Your age in years is {0}, in months is {1}, " & _
             "in days is {2}, and in hours is {3}.", _
             DateDiff(DateInterval.year, BDate, Now), _
             DateDiff(DateInterval.month, BDate, Now), _
             DateDiff(DateInterval.day, BDate, Now), _
             DateDiff(DateInterval.hour, BDate, Now))
```

The *SW* StreamWriter must be declared with the statements at the beginning of Listing 13.14. The day I tested these statements, the following string was written to the file:

```
Your age in years is 41, in months is 493, in days is 15012.027722980833, and in
hours is 360288.66535154.
```

Of course, the data to be stored to a text file need not be hard-coded in your application. The code of Listing 13.15 stores the contents of a TextBox control to a text file.

LISTING 13.15: STORING THE CONTENTS OF A TEXTBOX CONTROL TO A TEXT FILE

```
Dim SW As StreamWriter
Dim FS As FileStream
FS = New FileStream("C:\TextData.txt", FileMode.Create)
SW = New StreamWriter(FS)
SW.Write(TextBox1.Text)
```

To save the contents of a ListBox control to a text file, iterate through its Items collection and store each item to the file. The items of the control will be stored in the file as strings. Neither the StreamWriter nor the BinaryWriter provides a method for storing objects to or reading objects from a file. If you want to store objects, see the discussion of serializing collections in Chapter 11.

The following statements populate a ListBox control with various items:

```
ListBox1.Items.Add("First Item")
ListBox1.Items.Add(New Rectangle(0, 0, 3, 3))
ListBox1.Items.Add(New Point(3.2, 4.01))
ListBox1.Items.Add("Last Item")
```

The code that saves each item to a separate line in the C:\Items.txt file is shown in Listing 13.16.

LISTING 13.16: SAVING AN ITEMS COLLECTION TO A TEXT FILE

```
Dim SW As StreamWriter
Dim FS As FileStream
FS = New FileStream("C:\Items.txt", FileMode.Create)
SW = New StreamWriter(FS)
Dim itm As Object
For Each itm In ListBox1.Items
```

```
        SW.WriteLine(itm.ToString)
Next
SW.Close()
FS.Close()
```

Notice that the Write method stores the item's text, even though the item added to the control is an object. If you open the `Items.txt` file, you will read the following:

```
First Item
{X=0,Y=0,Width=3,Height=3}
{X=3,Y=4}
Last Item
```

Listing 13.17 clears the ListBox control and populates it again by reading the items from the file. (For more information on reading from a text file, see the discussion of the StreamReader object, in the following section.) Since the ListBox control's items are stored as text, you can use the StreamWriter and StreamReader objects to write them to and read them from the file.

LISTING 13.17: READING AN ITEMS COLLECTION FROM A TEXT FILE

```
Dim SR As StreamReader
Dim FS As FileStream
FS = New FileStream("C:\Items.txt", FileMode.Open)
SR = New StreamReader(FS)
Dim itm As Object
itm = SR.ReadLine()
While Not itm = Nothing
    ListBox1.Items.Add(itm)
    itm = SR.ReadLine()
End While
SR.Close()
FS.Close()
```

In the following sections, we'll explore the BinaryWriter and BinaryReader objects, which are the equivalents of the StreamWriter and StreamReader objects for binary files. Because of the variety of the binary data types, these two objects provide many more methods than their text counterparts.

The BinaryWriter Object

To prepare your application to write to a binary file, you must set up a BinaryWriter object, with the statements shown here:

```
Dim BW As New BinaryWriter(FS)
```

where *FS* is a properly initialized FileStream object. You can also create a new BinaryWriter object directly on a file, with the following form of the constructor:

```
Dim BW As New StreamReader(path)
```

To specify the encoding of the text in the binary file, use the following form of the method:

```
Dim BW As New BinaryWriter(FS, encoding)
Dim BW As New BinaryWriter(path, encoding)
```

You can also specify a third argument with the size of the buffer to be used with the file input/output operations:

```
Dim BW As New BinaryWriter(FS, encoding, bufferSize)
Dim BW As New BinaryWriter(path, encoding, bufferSize)
```

METHODS

The BinaryWriter object exposes the following methods for manipulating binary files.

Close

This method closes the current BinaryWriter and releases any system resources associated with it.

Flush

This method clears all buffers for the current writer and writes all buffered data to the underlying file.

Seek

This method sets the position within the current stream.

Write

This method writes a value to the current stream. This method is heavily overloaded, but it accepts a single argument, which is the value to be written to the file. The data type of its argument determines how it will be written. The Write method can save all the base types to the file except for the Date and Object types.

WriteString

Where all other data types can be written to a binary file with the Write method, strings must be written with the WriteString method. This method writes a length-prefixed string to the file and advances the current position by the appropriate number of bytes. The string is encoded by the current encoding scheme, and the default value is UTF8Encoding.

You will find examples of using the Write and WriteString methods of the BinaryWriter object at the end of the following section, which describes the methods of the BinaryReader object.

The BinaryReader Object

The BinaryReader object reads data from a binary file. As you have seen, binary files may also hold text, and the BinaryReader object provides the ReadString method to read strings written to the file by the `BinaryWriter.WriteString` method.

To use the methods of the BinaryReader object in your code, you must first create an instance of the object. The BinaryReader object is associated with a FileStream object, and the simplest form of its constructor is

```
Dim BR As New BinaryReader(streamObj)
```

where *streamObj* is the FileStream object. You can also specify the character encoding scheme to be used with the BinaryReader object, using the following form of the constructor:

```
Dim BR As New BinaryReader(streamObj, encoding)
```

If you omit the *encoding* argument, the default UTF8Encoding will be used.

METHODS

The BinaryReader object exposes the following methods for accessing the contents of a binary file.

Close

This method is the same as the Close method of the StreamReader object. It closes the current reader and releases the underlying stream.

PeekChar

This method returns the next available character from the stream without repositioning the current pointer. The character read is returned as an integer, or −1 if there are no more characters to be read from the stream. The name of the method doesn't quite comply with the BinaryReader object, but here's why. Peeking at the next byte makes sense only if the next byte is a character. Reading the first byte of a Double value, for example, wouldn't help you much. A character is usually stored in a single byte (ASCII text), but it can also be stored in two bytes (Unicode text). The PeekChar method knows how many bytes it must read from the text (they're determined by the current encoding), and it always returns a character, regardless of its size in bytes. The PeekChar method's return value is an integer, not a character.

The Read Methods

The BinaryReader object exposes methods for reading the same base data types you can write to a file through the BinaryWriter object. Each method returns a value of the corresponding type (the ReadBoolean method returns a Boolean value, and so on) and only a single value of this type. To read multiple values of the same type, you must call the same method repeatedly. The various methods for reading the base data types from the file are briefly described in Table 13.7.

TABLE 13.7: THE READ METHODS OF THE BINARYREADER OBJECT

VALUE	EFFECT
ReadBoolean	Reads and returns a True/False value.
ReadByte	Reads and returns a single byte.
ReadBytes(byteArray, count)	Reads and returns *count* bytes from the file and stores them into the Byte array passed as the first argument.
ReadChar	Reads and returns a character. Depending on how text was stored in the file, the ReadChar method may read one or two bytes (in the case of Unicode text), but it always returns a character.

Continued on next page

TABLE 13.7: THE READ METHODS OF THE BINARYREADER OBJECT *(continued)*

VALUE	EFFECT
ReadChars(charArray, count)	Reads and returns *count* characters from the file and stores them in the character array specified as the first argument.
ReadDecimal	Reads and returns a Decimal value from the file.
ReadDouble	Reads and returns a Double value from the file.
ReadInt16	Reads and returns a short Integer (a 2-byte) value.
ReadInt32	Reads and returns an Integer (a 4-byte) value.
ReadInt64	Reads and returns a Long Integer (8-byte) value.
ReadSByte	Reads and returns a signed byte.
ReadSingle	Reads a Single (4-byte) value from the file.
ReadString	Reads and returns a string from the file. The string must be stored in the file prefixed by its length. This is how the WriteString method stored strings to a text file, so there's nothing you have to do anything special from within your code. If the string isn't prefixed by its length, the ReadString method will read a string with the wrong number of characters. The method will interpret the first byte as the string's length.
ReadUInt16	Reads and returns an unsigned short Integer (2-byte) value.
ReadUInt32	Reads and returns an unsigned Integer (4-byte) value
ReadUInt64	Reads and returns an unsigned long Integer (8-byte) value

To use these methods, you're supposed to know the structure of the data stored in the file. A file with a price list, for example, contains the same items for each product. The first two fields are the product's ID and description, followed by the product's price, and other pieces of information, which are repeated for each product. Once you know the types of values stored in the file, you can call the appropriate methods to read the correct values. If you misread even a single value, none of the following values will be read correctly.

VB.NET at Work: The RecordSave Project

Let's look at the code for saving structured information to a binary file. In this section, you're going to build the RecordSave application, which demonstrates how to store a price list to a disk file and read it later from the same file. The main form of the application is shown in Figure 13.2. The Save Records button creates a few records and then saves them to disk. The Read Records button reads the records from the file and displays them on the ListBox control.

Each record of the price list contains the following fields:

◆ The product's ID (a String)

◆ The product's description (a String)

- The product's price (a Single value)

- The product's availability (a Boolean value)

- The minimum reorder quantity (an Integer value)

FIGURE 13.2

The RecordSave project demonstrates how to store records in a binary file.

The program saves each field as a separate entity, using the Write method of a BinaryStream object. Only the string is written to the file with the WriteString method, because we want to be able to read the string back with the ReadString method.

Since the price list contains many products, you will most likely store it in an array of custom Structures. The Product structure shown next is a simple, yet quite adequate, structure for our price list:

```
Structure Product
    Dim ProdID As String
    Dim prodDescription As String
    Dim listPrice As Single
    Dim available As Boolean
    Dim minStock As Integer
End Structure
```

The code that writes the Structure to a binary file is shown in the Listing 13.18.

LISTING 13.18: SAVING A RECORD TO A BINARY FILE

```
Private Sub Button1_Click(ByVal sender As System.Object, _
            ByVal e As System.EventArgs) Handles Button1.Click
    Dim BW As BinaryWriter
    Dim FS As FileStream
    FS = New FileStream("Records.bin", System.IO.FileMode.OpenOrCreate, _
                    System.IO.FileAccess.Write)
    BW = New BinaryWriter(FS)
    BW.BaseStream.Seek(0, SeekOrigin.Begin)
    Dim p As New Product()
' Save first record
    p.ProdID = "100-A39"
    p.prodDescription = "Cellular Phone with built-in TV"
```

```
      p.listPrice = 497.99
      p.available = True
      p.minStock = 40
      SaveRecord(BW, p)
' Save second record
      p = New Product()
      p.ProdID = "100-U300"
      p.prodDescription = "Wireless Handheld"
      p.listPrice = 315.5
      p.available = False
      p.minStock = 12
      SaveRecord(BW, p)
' Save third record
      p = New Product()
      p.ProdID = "ZZZ"
      p.prodDescription = "Last Gadget"
      p.listPrice = .99
      p.available = True
      p.minStock = 1000
      SaveRecord(BW, p)

      BW.Close()
      FS.Close()
End Sub
```

The code of the SaveRecord() subroutine is shown in Listing 13.19. It accepts as arguments the BinaryWriter object that represents the binary file to which the data will be written and a Product structure to be saved to the file.

LISTING 13.19: THE SAVERECORD() SUBROUTINE

```
Sub SaveRecord(ByVal writer As BinaryWriter, ByVal record As Product)
    writer.Write(record.ProdID)
    writer.Write(record.prodDescription)
    writer.Write(record.listPrice)
    writer.Write(record.available)
    writer.Write(record.minStock)
End Sub
```

To read the records stored in the file, set up a BinaryReader associated with the Records.bin file and call the appropriate Read method for each field of the record. Since we don't know in advance how many records are in the file, we set up a loop that keeps reading one record at a time, while the current position (property Position of the FileStream object) is less than the length of the file (property Length of the FileStream object). Listing 13.20 is the code behind the Read Records button.

LISTING 13.20: READING RECORDS FROM A BINARY FILE

```
Private Sub Button2_Click(ByVal sender As System.Object, _
            ByVal e As System.EventArgs) Handles Button2.Click
    Dim BR As BinaryReader
    Dim FS As FileStream
    FS = New System.IO.FileStream("Binarydata2.bin", FileMode.Open, _
                            FileAccess.Read)
    BR = New System.IO.BinaryReader(FS)
    BR.BaseStream.Seek(0, SeekOrigin.Begin)
    Dim p As New Product()
    TextBox1.Clear()
    Dim c As Integer
    c = BR.PeekChar
    While FS.Position < FS.Length
        Console.WriteLine(c)
        p = Nothing
        ' Read fields and populate structure
        p.ProdID = BR.ReadString
        p.prodDescription = BR.ReadString
        p.listPrice = BR.ReadSingle
        p.available = BR.ReadBoolean
        p.minStock = BR.ReadInt32
        ' Display structure
        ShowRecord(p)
        c = BR.PeekChar
    End While
    BR.Close()
    FS.Close()
End Sub
```

Notice that the product's price is read with the ReadSingle method, because it was saved as a Single variable. The ShowRecord() subroutine appends the fields of the current structure to the TextBox control at the bottom of the form.

Using a custom Structure to store the fields simplifies the structure of the application at large, but it doesn't help the file I/O operation much. It's quicker to use the Serializer object to store an entire collection to the file at once, rather than each member of the collection individually. The Serializer object was discussed in Chapter 11, and it addresses many of the file I/O needs of your applications. There will be situations, however, when you must store widely different pieces of information to a text or binary file, and the information presented in this chapter should be adequate for these situations.

The FileSystemWatcher Component

The FileSystemWatcher is a special component that has no visible interface and allows your application to watch for changes in the file system. You can use the FileSystemWatcher component to monitor changes in the local computer's file system, a network drive, and even a remote computer's file system (as long as the remote machine is running Windows NT or Windows 2000). The component exposes a few properties that let you specify what type of changes you want to monitor and the folders/files that will be monitored. Once activated, it fires an event every time one of the specified items has been changed.

The items you can monitor are folders and files. You can specify the folders you want to monitor as well as the file types to be monitored. You can also specify the types of actions you want to monitor; each action fires its own event. The actions you can monitor are the creation, deletion, and renaming of a file or folder and the modification of a file. The corresponding events are appropriately named: Changed, Created, Deleted, and Renamed. There's also a special event, the Error event, that is fired when too many changes occur and the FileSystemWatcher component can't keep track of them all (the internal buffer overflows and this condition is signaled with the Error event).

Properties

To use a FileSystemWatcher component in your project, open the Components tab of the Toolbox and double-click the FileSystemWatcher component's icon. An instance of the component will be placed in your project, and you can set the following properties in the Properties window.

NotifyFilter

This property determines the types of changes you want to monitor; its value can have one of the values shown in the Table 13.8, the members of the IO.NotifyFilters enumeration.

TABLE 13.8: THE NOTIFYFILTERS ENUMERATION

VALUE	DESCRIPTION
Attributes	The attributes of the file or folder
CreationTime	The date of file's or folder's creation
DirectoryName	The directory name
FileName	The filename
LastAccess	The date of file's or folder's last access
LastWrite	The date of file's or folder's last edit
Security	The security settings of the file or folder
Size	The size of the file or folder

You can combine multiple types of changes with the Or operator, but only in your code. The following statement prepares the *FileSystemWatcher1* component to monitor for changes in the date and time of a file's last write and last access:

```
FileSystemWatcher1.NotifyFilter = IO.NotifyFilters.LastWrite Or _
                        IO.NotifyFilters.LastAccess
```

PATH

Set this property to the path you want to monitor. The component will watch for changes in all the files in the specified path. If you want to include the path's subfolders, set the IncludeSubdirectories property to True. The default value of this property is False.

FILTER

This property filters the files you want to monitor through a string with wildcards. A Filter value of `*.txt` tells the component to monitor for changes in text files only. The default value of the Filter property is `*.*`, which includes all the files with an extension. To monitor all files, including the ones without extension, set the Filter property to an empty string. Notice that you can't specify multiple extensions with the Filter property.

ENABLERAISINGEVENTS

To start monitoring for changes in the file system, set the EnableRaisingEvents property to True. While the EnableRaisingEvents property is True, the FileSystemWatcher component fires an event for the changes you have specified through its properties.

Events

To notify your application about the changes, the FileSystemWatcher component raises the following events, which you can handle from within your code: Changed, Created, Deleted, and Renamed. To code the handlers of these events, select the name of the FileSystemWatcher component in the Object drop-down list of the editor's window and the name of the event you want to code in the Events drop-down list.

Like all events, they include two arguments: the *sender* and the *e* argument. The second argument of these events carries information about the type of the change through the ChangeType member. The `e.ChangeType` member can be a member of the `IO.WatcherChangeTypes` enumeration: `All`, `Changed`, `Created`, `Deleted`, and `Renamed`. The `e.FullPath` and `e.Name` properties are the path and filename of the file that was changed, created, or deleted. In the case of a folder, use the FullPath property to retrieve the name of the changed folder. Finally, the Renamed event's argument exposes the Old-FullPath and OldName members, which let you retrieve the old path and name of the renamed file.

You can write a common event handler for the Changed, Created, and Deleted events, because they share the same arguments. The Rename event must have its own handler, because the *e* argument is of a different type.

All the changes detected by the FileSystemWatcher component are stored in an internal buffer, which may overflow if too many changes take place in a short period of time. To avoid overflowing the buffer, you should limit the number of files you monitor by setting the Filter and Path properties appropriately. You should always limit the type of changes (you'll rarely have to monitor for all types of changes in a folder). If the buffer overflows, the Error event will be raised. In this event's handler you can increase the size of the buffer, by setting the InternalBufferSize property. You can double the buffer's size from within the Error event handler to prevent the loss of additional events with the following statement:

```
FileSystemWatcher1.InternalBufferSize = 2 * FileSystemWatcher1.InternalBufferSize
```

VB.NET at Work: The FileSystemWatcher Project

The FileSystemWatcher project, shown in Figure 13.3, demonstrates how to set up a FileSystem-Watcher component and how to process the events raised by the component. The FileSystemWatcher component is initialized when the button is clicked. This button's Click event handler prepares the FileSystemWatcher component to monitor changes in text files on the root of the C: drive. The Path property was set through the Properties window, but you may have to change it. I've chosen the root folder because it's easy to locate and it has very few files on most systems. You can create, edit, rename, and then delete a few text files in the root folder to test the application.

FIGURE 13.3

The FileSystem-Watcher project

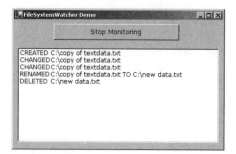

After setting the properties at design time, the code sets the component's EnableRaisingEvents property to True to start watching for changes. These changes will be signaled though the component's events, which are programmed to print in the Output window the type of change detected and the name of the corresponding file. The type of change is reported to the event handler through the ChangeType member of the *e* argument. When a file is renamed, the program prints both the old and the new name.

The Start Monitoring button is a toggle. When clicked for the first time, its caption changes to Stop Monitoring and if you click it again, it will stop monitoring the file system. The properties of the FileSystemWatcher component are set in the form's Load event, which is shown in Listing 13.21.

LISTING 13.21: PROGRAMMING THE FILESYSTEMWATCHER COMPONENT

```vb
Private Sub Form1_Load(ByVal sender As Object, ByVal e As System.EventArgs) _
            Handles MyBase.Load
    FileSystemWatcher1.Path = "c:\"
    FileSystemWatcher1.IncludeSubdirectories = False
    FileSystemWatcher1.Filter = "*.txt"
    FileSystemWatcher1.NotifyFilter = IO.NotifyFilters.CreationTime Or _
            IO.NotifyFilters.LastWrite Or IO.NotifyFilters.LastAccess Or _
            IO.NotifyFilters.FileName
    FileSystemWatcher1.EnableRaisingEvents = False
End Sub
```

The code behind the button's Click event handler (Listing 13.22) toggles the EnableRaisingEvents property and the button's caption. When this property is set to True, the FileSystemWatcher component starts monitoring the changes in the file system.

LISTING 13.22: THE CODE OF THE START MONITORING BUTTON

```
Private Sub Button1_Click(ByVal sender As System.Object, _
            ByVal e As System.EventArgs) Handles Button1.Click
    If Button1.Text = "Start Monitoring" Then
        FileSystemWatcher1.EnableRaisingEvents = True
        Button1.Text = "Stop Monitoring"
    Else
        FileSystemWatcher1.EnableRaisingEvents = False
        Button1.Text = "Start Monitoring"
    End If
End Sub
```

Now you must program the handlers of the FileSystemWatcher component. You need not program all the events, only the ones you want to monitor. Since the Changed, Created, and Deleted event handlers have the same arguments, you can write a common handler for all three and a separate one for the Renamed event. Listing 13.23 details the event handlers of the sample applications.

LISTING 13.23: THE EVENT HANDLERS OF THE FILESYSTEMWATCHER COMPONENT

```
Private Sub WatcherHandler(ByVal sender As Object, _
            ByVal e As System.IO.FileSystemEventArgs) _
            Handles FileSystemWatcher1.Changed, FileSystemWatcher1.Created, _
            FileSystemWatcher1.Deleted
    ListBox1.Items.Add(e.ChangeType & vbTab & e.FullPath)
End Sub
Private Sub FileSystemWatcher1_Renamed(ByVal sender As Object, _
            ByVal e As System.IO.RenamedEventArgs) _
            Handles FileSystemWatcher1.Renamed
    ListBox1.Items.Add(e.ChangeType & vbTab & e.OldFullPath & " TO " & e.FullPath)
End Sub
```

If you want to handle the Error event, you must stop monitoring the file system momentarily, double the value of the InternalBufferSize property, and then enable the monitoring again, as in Listing 13.24.

LISTING 13.24: PROGRAMMING THE FILESYSTEMWATCHER'S ERROR EVENT

```
Private Sub FileSystemWatcher1_Error(ByVal sender As Object, _
                ByVal e As System.IO.ErrorEventArgs) _
                Handles FileSystemWatcher1.Error
    Dim status As Boolean
    status = FileSystemWatcher1.EnableRaisingEvents
    FileSystemWatcher1.EnableRaisingEvents = False
    FileSystemWatcher1.InternalBufferSize = _
                2 * FileSystemWatcher1.InternalBufferSize
    FileSystemWatcher1.EnableRaisingEvents = status
End Sub
```

Summary

The System.IO class exposes all the objects you need to interact with the file system and access files. As you have seen, writing to and reading from files is fairly straightforward with the reader and writer objects discussed in this chapter. However, there's another option for saving complicated objects to files; namely the Serializer class, which was discussed in Chapter 11.

The topic of storing data is not exhausted with the techniques discussed in this chapter. For large amounts of data, especially structured data, you should consider setting up a database, a topic discussed in the fifth part of this book. A database is more than an elaborate mechanism for storing data; it also allows you to retrieve data instantly based on keys, field values, even combinations of field values.

Part IV

Intermediate Programming

Chapter 14

Drawing and Painting with Visual Basic

ONE OF THE MOST interesting and fun parts of a programming language is its graphics elements. In general, graphics fall into two major categories: vector and bitmap. *Vector graphics* are images generated by graphics methods such as the DrawLine and DrawEllipse methods. The drawing you create is based on mathematical descriptions of the various shapes. *Bitmap graphics* are images that can be displayed on various controls and processed on a pixel-by-pixel basis. The difference between vector and bitmap graphics is that vector graphics aren't tied to a specific monitor resolution; that is, they can be displayed at various resolutions.

Vector graphics can be redrawn at any resolution. Bitmap graphics, on the other hand, have a fixed resolution. An image 600 pixels wide and 400 pixels tall has that specific resolution. If you attempt to use it to fill a monitor that's 1280 pixels wide and 1024 pixels tall, you'll have to repeat some pixels. Image-processing software can interpolate between pixels, but when you blow up a bitmap, you see its block-like structure.

Despite their inherent limitations, bitmap graphics are quite useful and much more common than vector graphics. For example, you can't create the image of a landscape with graphics commands. On the other hand, it doesn't make sense to display the bitmap of a circle when a simple Circle command can produce the same image faster and more cleanly. Both types of graphics have their place, and you can mix them to produce the desired result.

Text belongs to the vector graphics category, because the characters in various fonts are described mathematically and can be rendered at various sizes with no loss of quality. Figure 14.1 shows a string printed at 96 points (at the top) and the same string printed at 48 points and enlarged 200%. The upper string is as smooth as it can be, while the lower one has too many artifacts around its edges. I could have made the upper string even smoother by turning on the anti-aliasing feature, but then the comparison wouldn't be fair. The .NET Framework provides rich tools for rendering text, and we'll examine them along with the other vector drawing methods. If the differences between the two strings aren't obvious on the printed page, you can open the file VectorBitmap.tif in this chapter's folder on the CD, which is the electronic version of the same image.

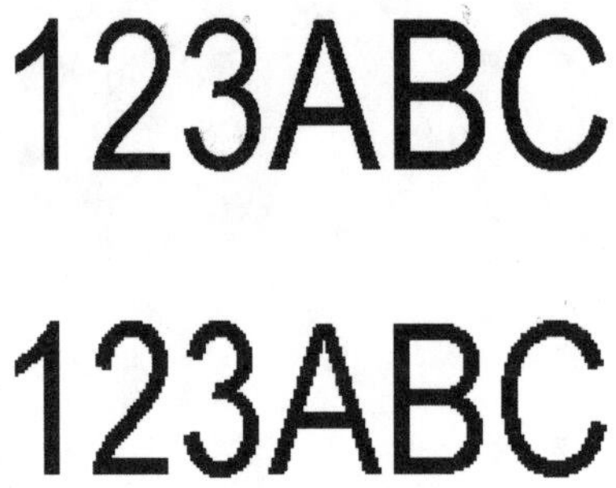

FIGURE 14.1

Enlarging strings versus printing them at a larger font

123ABC

123ABC

With VB.NET you can draw on just about any control. However, it's quite unusual to draw on a TextBox control and highly unlikely that you will ever draw on a ListBox control. The two objects we usually draw on are the Form object and the PictureBox control. You can place graphics on controls at design time and runtime. To load a graphic (bitmap or icon) on a control at design time, you assign its filename to the Image, or BackgroundImage, property of the control in the Properties window. Or, you can change the setting of the same two properties at runtime.

If the graphic is assigned to a control at design time, it's stored along with the application. Vector drawings aren't loaded; they are generated on-the-fly. Where bitmap graphics are copies of their subjects (pictures of buildings, persons, landscapes, and so on), vector graphics are the descriptions of the objects we want to display (a circle centered at a given point having a certain radius, or a rectangle of certain width and height filled with a specific gradient) and are rendered at runtime.

Displaying Images

To load an image to a PictureBox control, locate the Image property in the Properties window and click the button with the ellipsis next to it. An Open dialog box will appear, where you can select the image to be displayed. The image is stored in a hidden file that has the same name as the form plus the extension .resx. As a result, you don't have to distribute the image with your application.

After the image is loaded, you must make sure it will fill the available space, unless you let the user select the graphic at runtime. The PictureBox control exposes the SizeMode property, which determines how the image will be sized and aligned on the control. Its default setting is Normal, and in this mode the control displays the image at its normal magnification. If the image is larger than the control, part of the image will be invisible. If the image is smaller than the control, part of the control will be empty. If the image is smaller than the control, you can set the SizeMode property to CenterImage to center the image on the control.

The SizeMode property can also be set to StretchImage and AutoSize. The StretchImage setting resizes the image so that it fills the control. If the control's aspect ratio isn't the same as the aspect ratio of the image, the image will be distorted in the process. If you want to use the StretchImage setting, you must also resize one of the dimensions of the control, so that the image will be properly resized. You'll see how to do this in the following sample. The last setting, AutoSize, resizes the control to the image. This is not the most convenient setting, because the control may cover other controls on the form. Figure 14.2 shows a PictureBox control with a small image in all four settings.

FIGURE 14.2

The settings of the SizeMode property

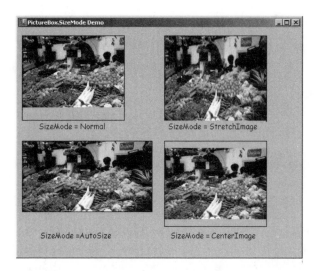

The most flexible setting of the SizeMode property is StretchImage. Before letting the Form Designer stretch the image, however, you must make sure that the control has the same aspect ratio as the image it displays. If the image is twice as wide as it is tall, the same should be true for the PictureBox control that hosts the image. If that's the case, the image can be resized safely. If not, the image will be distorted in the process.

Loading an image to a PictureBox control doesn't require any code or special handling. For more information on resizing images while maintaining their aspect ratio, see the discussion of the Image-Load project, later in this chapter. The image itself is an object, and you can also manipulate it from within your code. The following section describes the Image object, its properties, and a few of the methods you can use to manipulate an image.

The Image Object

The Image property of the PictureBox control is an Image object, which contains the current bitmap and exposes properties and methods for manipulating this image. There are several ways to create an Image object. You can declare a variable of the Image type and then assign the Image property of the PictureBox control of the Form object to the variable:

```
Dim img As Image
img = PictureBox1.Image
```

The *img* Image variable holds the bitmap of the PictureBox1 control. As you will see shortly, you can call the Save method of the Image class to save the image to a disk file.

You can also create a new Image object from an image file, using the Image object's FromFile method:

```
Dim img As Image
img = Image.FromFile("Butterfly.jpg")
```

Once the *img* variable has been set up, you can assign it to the Image property of a PictureBox control:

```
PictureBox1.Image = img
```

PROPERTIES

The Image object exposes more members, some of which are discussed in the following sections. Let's start with the properties, which are simpler.

HorizontalResolution, VerticalResolution

These are read-only properties that return the horizontal and vertical resolution of the image, respectively, in pixels-per-inch.

Width, Height

These are read-only properties that return the width and height of the image, respectively, in pixels. If you divide the dimensions of the image (properties Width and Height) by the corresponding resolutions (properties HorizontalResolution and VerticalResolution), you'll get the actual size of the image—the dimensions of the image when printed, for instance.

PixelFormat

This is another read-only property that returns the pixel format for this Image object. The PixelFormat property determines the quality of the image; there are many pixel formats, which are members of the PixelFormat enumeration. For now, I will assume that you're using a color display with a depth of 24 bits per pixel. Images with 24-bit color are of the `Format24bppRgb` type. Rgb stands for "red green blue" (the three basic colors) and 24bpp stands for 24 bits per pixel. Each of the basic colors in this format is represented by one byte (8 bits).

METHODS

In addition to the basic properties, the Image object exposes methods for manipulating images. These are discussed next.

RotateFlip

This method rotates and/or flips an image, and its syntax is:

```
Image.RotateFlip(type)
```

where the *type* argument determines how the image will be rotated. This argument can have one of the values of the RotateFlipType enumeration, shown in Table 14.1.

To flip vertically the image displayed on a PictureBox control, use the following statement:

```
PictureBox1.Image.RotateFlip(RotateFlipType.RotateNoneFlipY)
PictureBox1.Refresh()
```

The Refresh method redraws the control, and you must call it to display the new (flipped) image on the control.

TABLE 14.1: THE ROTATEFLIPTYPE ENUMERATION

MEMBER	DESCRIPTION
Rotate180FlipNone	Rotates image by 180 degrees
Rotate180FlipX	Rotates image by 180 degrees and then flips it horizontally
Rotate180FlipXY	Rotates image by 180 degrees and then flips it vertically and horizontally
Rotate180FlipY	Rotates image by 180 degrees and then flips it vertically
Rotate270FlipNone	Rotates image by 270 degrees (which is equivalent to rotating it by −90 degrees)
Rotate270FlipX	Rotates image by 270 degrees (which is equivalent to rotating it by −90 degrees) and then flips it horizontally
Rotate270FlipXY	Rotates image by 270 degrees (which is equivalent to rotating it by −90 degrees) and then flips it vertically and horizontally
Rotate270FlipY	Rotates image by 270 degrees (which is equivalent to rotating it by −90 degrees) and then flips it vertically
Rotate90FlipNone	Rotates image by 90 degrees
Rotate90FlipX	Rotates image by 90 degrees and then flips it horizontally
Rotate90FlipXY	Rotates image by 90 degrees and then flips it horizontally and vertically
Rotate90FlipY	Rotates image by 90 degrees and then flips it vertically
RotateNoneFlipNone	No rotation and no flipping
RotateNoneFlipX	Flips image horizontally
RotateNoneFlipXY	Flips image vertically and horizontally
RotateNoneFlipY	Flips image vertically

GetThumbnailImage

This method returns the thumbnail of the specified image. The *thumbnail* is a miniature version of the image, whose exact dimensions you can specify as arguments. Thumbnail images are used as visual enhancements in selecting an image. The thumbnail takes a small fraction of the space taken by the actual image, and we can display many thumbnails on a form to let the user select the desired one(s). The syntax of the GetThumbnailImage method is:

```
Image.GetThumbnailImage(width, height, Abort, Data)
```

The first two arguments are the dimensions of the thumbnail. The other two arguments are callbacks, which are used when the process is aborted. Since thumbnails don't take long to generate, we'll ignore these two arguments for the purposes of this book (we'll set them both to Nothing). The following statements create a thumbnail of the image selected by the user and display it on a

PictureBox control. To test these statements, place a PictureBox and a Button control on the form. Then place an instance of the Open dialog box on the form and insert the following statements in the Button's Click event handler:

```
Dim img As Image
img = Image.FromFile(OpenFileDialog1.FileName)
PictureBox1.Image = img.GetThumbnailImage(32, 32, Nothing, Nothing)
```

Using the techniques described in Chapter 13, you can scan a folder, retrieve all the image files, and create a thumbnail for each. As for displaying them, I would suggest you create as many Picture-Box controls as there are images in the folder and arrange them horizontally and vertically on a form. Chapter 5 describes how to create instances of Windows controls at runtime and position them on the form from within your code. Since this isn't a trivial project, I've included a sample project on the CD that demonstrates how to display thumbnails on a form. The project is called Thumbnails, and you will find it in this chapter's folder. I've copied the CustomExplorer project of Chapter 11, renamed the Form, and removed the FilesList control (where the names of the files in the selected folder were displayed). In its place, the program displays the PictureBox controls with the thumbnails. When the user clicks an image, the program loads the image on the PictureBox control of another form and displays it. Figure 14.3 shows the two forms of the Thumbnails application. You can see the thumbnails of the images on one of the forms and one image in preview mode on the other form.

FIGURE 14.3

The Thumbnails application displays the images in a folder as thumbnails.

Then I adjusted the code to accommodate the display of thumbnails instead of file names. The ShowFilesInFolder() subroutine of the original application displayed the names of the files in the current folder on a ListBox control. This subroutine was replaced by the ShowImagesInFolder() subroutine, which is shown in Listing 14.1.

LISTING 14.1: THE SHOWIMAGESINFOLDER SUBROUTINE

```
Sub ShowFilesInFolder()
    Dim file As String
    Dim FI As FileInfo
    Dim PBox As PictureBox, img As Image
    Dim Left As Integer = 280
    Dim Top As Integer = 40
    Dim ctrl As Integer
' remove all PictureBox controls on the form
    For ctrl = Me.Controls.Count - 1 To 2 Step -1
        Me.Controls.Remove(Me.Controls(ctrl))
    Next
    Me.Invalidate()
    For Each file In Directory.GetFiles(Directory.GetCurrentDirectory)
        FI = New FileInfo(file)
        If FI.Extension = ".GIF" Or FI.Extension = ".JPG" Or _
                FI.Extension = ".BMP" Then
            PBox = New PictureBox()
            img = Image.FromFile(FI.FullName)
            PBox.Image = img.GetThumbnailImage(64, 64, Nothing, Nothing)
            If Left > 580 Then
                Left = 280
                Top = Top + 74
            End If
            PBox.Left = Left
            PBox.Top = Top
            PBox.Width = 64
            PBox.Height = 64
            PBox.Visible = True
            PBox.Tag = FI.FullName
            Me.Controls.Add(PBox)
            AddHandler PBox.Click, New System.EventHandler(AddressOf OpenImage)
            Left = Left + 74
        End If
    Next
End Sub
```

The subroutine starts by removing any PictureBox control already on the form. This is necessary because when the user switches to another folder, we want to display this folder's images on a clean form. Then the code goes through each file in the selected folder and examines its extension. If it's JPG, GIF, or BMP (you can add more file extensions if you want), it creates a new PictureBox control, sets its size and location, loads the thumbnail of the image, and then adds it to the Controls collection of the form. Each image's path is stored in the PictureBox control's Tag property, and it's retrieved later to load the image on the second form, where it can be previewed.

Notice how the code adds a handler for the Click event of each PictureBox control. All the PictureBox controls share a common handler for their Click event, the OpenImage() subroutine. This subroutine reads the selected image's path from the Tag property of the control that fired the Click event and displays the corresponding image on the auxiliary form. The implementation of the OpenImage() subroutine is shown here:

```
Sub OpenImage(ByVal sender As Object, ByVal e As System.EventArgs)
    Dim imgForm As New previewForm()
    imgForm.PictureBox1.Image = Image.FromFile(sender.tag)
    imgForm.Show()
End Sub
```

previewForm is the name of the second form of the application, where the selected image is previewed. If you need more information about this project, please review the material of the last part of Chapter 5, which explains how to create instances of controls at runtime. This application is a rather advanced example of dynamic forms, rather than a demo of the GetThumbnailImage method, but it's an interesting application and some readers may have a good use for the techniques demonstrated here. You will notice that all the bitmaps have the same dimensions (64 by 64), which means that the thumbnails will be distorted (most images aren't square). You must choose the dimensions of the thumbnail for an image, so that the reduced image has the same aspect ratio as the original image. For example, if the original image's dimensions are 640×480, the thumbnail's dimensions should be 64×48 (or 32×24, or 128×96, and so on). In the later section on the ImageLoad project, you will learn how to resize an image and maintain its aspect ratio.

The user interface of the Thumbnails application isn't the most functional either. If you scroll the form to see all the thumbnails that aren't near the top of the form, the controls with the drives and folder names will be scrolled out of view. Use a different form to display the thumbnails, or add the appropriate menu commands, which can't be scrolled out of view.

Save

If your application processes the displayed image during the course of its execution and you want to save the image, you can use the Save method of the Image property. The simplest syntax of the Save method accepts a single argument, which is the path of the file where the image will be saved:

```
Image.Save(path)
```

To save the contents of the *PictureBox1* control to a file, you must use a statement like the following:

```
PictureBox1.Image.Save("c:\tmpImage.bmp")
```

The image will be saved in BMP format. Another form of the Save method allows you to specify the format in which the image will be saved:

```
PictureBox1.Image.Save("c:\tmpImage.bmp", format)
```

where the *format* argument's value can be one of the members of the ImageFormat enumeration. The fully qualified name of the enumeration is `System.Drawing.Imaging.ImageFormat`, so you should import the library `System.Drawing.Imaging` into any project that uses the enumerations mentioned in this chapter. This way you won't have to fully qualify the name of the enumeration.

The ImageFormat enumeration contains members for all common image formats (see Table 14.2). Once you've imported the `System.Drawing.Imaging` class to your project, then to save the image on the PictureBox1 control in GIF format, use the statement:

```
PictureBox1.Image.Save("c:\tmpImage.gif", ImageFormat.Gif)
```

TABLE 14.2: THE IMAGEFORMAT ENUMERATION

MEMBER	DESCRIPTION	EXTENSION
Bmp	Bitmap image	BMP
Emf	Enhanced Windows metafile	EMF
Exif	Exchangeable Image Format	EXIF
Gif	Graphics Interchange Format	GIF
Icon	Windows icon	ICO
Jpeg	Joint Photographic Experts Group format	JPEG
MemoryBmp	Saves the image to a memory bitmap	
Png	W3C Portable Network Graphics format	PNG
Tiff	Tagged Image File Format	TIF
Wmf	Windows metafile	WMF

VB.NET AT WORK: THE IMAGELOAD PROJECT

The ImageLoad application (shown in Figure 14.4) demonstrates how to use the SizeMode property to best fit an image on a PictureBox control. The PictureBox control maintains a constant size, and you won't have to do anything special about the other controls on the form. If the image fits on the control, the control's SizeMode property is set to CenterImage—the image is displayed centered on the control. If the image's dimensions exceed the dimensions of the PictureBox control, the code resizes the larger dimension of the control, according to the image's aspect ratio. The PictureBox control's size isn't drastically different from its initial dimensions, and it never grows to cover other controls.

FIGURE 14.4

The ImageLoad project

The application prompts the user to select an image file through the Open dialog box. Then it compares the image's dimensions to the dimensions of the control, and if the image is smaller than the control in both dimensions, it sets the control's SizeMode property to CenterImage. If not, it calculates the image's aspect ratio and resizes the larger dimension accordingly.

The Load command under the Image menu is implemented with the statements in Listing 14.2.

LISTING 14.2: THE IMAGE ➤ LOAD MENU COMMAND

```
Private Sub ImageLoad_Click(ByVal sender As System.Object, _
            ByVal e As System.EventArgs) Handles ImageLoad.Click
    OpenFileDialog1.Filter = "Images|*.GIF;*.JPG;*.TIF;*.BMP"
    If OpenFileDialog1.ShowDialog() = DialogResult.OK Then
        PictureBox1.Image = Image.FromFile(OpenFileDialog1.FileName)
        ResizeImage()
    End If
End Sub
```

The code displays the image on the control and immediately calls the ResizeImage subroutine to resize the image. This subroutine will display the image on a PictureBox control whose dimensions are 400 by 400 pixels. If one of the image's dimensions exceeds the corresponding dimension of the control, this dimension will be resized while maintaining the aspect ratio. Listing 14.3 shows the ResizeImage() subroutine used in the LoadImage application.

LISTING 14.3: THE RESIZEIMAGE() SUBROUTINE

```
Private Sub ResizeImage()
    PictureBox1.Width = 400
    PictureBox1.Height = 400
    If PictureBox1.Image.Width < PictureBox1.Width And _
            PictureBox1.Image.Height < PictureBox1.Height Then
        PictureBox1.SizeMode = PictureBoxSizeMode.CenterImage
    Else
        Dim ratio As Single
        If PictureBox1.Image.Width > PictureBox1.Image.Height Then
            ratio = PictureBox1.Image.Width / PictureBox1.Image.Height
            PictureBox1.Height = PictureBox1.Width / ratio
        Else
            ratio = PictureBox1.Image.Height / PictureBox1.Image.Width
            PictureBox1.Width = PictureBox1.Height / ratio
        End If
    End If
End Sub
```

The user can restore the image to its original size with the Zoom ➤ Normal command, whose code is almost trivial:

```
Private Sub ZoomNormal_Click(ByVal sender As System.Object, _
             ByVal e As System.EventArgs) Handles ZoomNormal.Click
   PictureBox1.Width = PictureBox1.Image.Width
   PictureBox1.Height = PictureBox1.Image.Height
End Sub
```

The Auto command of the Zoom menu fits the image on the control by calling the ResizeImage() subroutine. The last two commands in the menu, Zoom In and Zoom Out, enlarge or reduce the magnification of the image by 25%: their implementation is also trivial. The following statements zoom into the image by 25%:

```
PictureBox1.Width = PictureBox1.Width * 1.25
PictureBox1.Height = PictureBox1.Height * 1.25
```

As you can see, the various zooming commands don't directly manipulate the Image object. Instead, they control the dimensions of the image's container (the PictureBox control) and rely on the Auto-Size setting of the control's SizeMode property to resize the image. The code would have been even simpler if we didn't want to maintain the image's aspect ratio. We're going to use the same subroutine in the PrintBitmap project of the following chapter, where you will learn how to print bitmaps at any magnification.

NOTE *The PictureBox control's Image object doesn't change when you resize the control. Its dimensions are the dimensions of the image loaded initially, regardless of the current magnification.*

The Process menu of the application contains commands for rotating and flipping the image. These commands call the RotateFlip method with different arguments. The only implication worth mentioning here is that when we rotate an image right or left, we're actually swapping its width with its height. To avoid clipping images that are not square, you must swap the dimensions of the PictureBox control as well. Listing14.4 shows the code of the Rotate Right command:

LISTING 14.4: ROTATING AN IMAGE

```
Private Sub ProcessRotateRight_Click(ByVal sender As System.Object, _
             ByVal e As System.EventArgs) Handles ProcessRotateRight.Click
   PictureBox1.Image.RotateFlip(RotateFlipType.Rotate90FlipNone)
   PictureBox1.Invalidate()
   Dim tmp As Integer
   tmp = PictureBox1.Width
   PictureBox1.Width = PictureBox1.Height
   PictureBox1.Height = tmp
End Sub
```

Exchanging Images through the Clipboard

Whether you use bitmap images or create graphics from scratch with the Visual Basic drawing methods, sooner or later you'll want to exchange them with other Windows applications. To do so, you use the Clipboard and its GetDataObject and SetDataObject methods. The SetDataObject method accepts the data to be placed on the Clipboard as argument. To copy the bitmap displayed on the *PictureBox1* control to the Clipboard, use the following statement:

```
Clipboard.SetDataObject(PictureBox1.Image)
```

A second form of the SetDataObject method accepts an additional argument: a True/False value that specifies whether the contents of the Clipboard will remain on it after the application that placed them there has terminated.

The GetDataObject method is a bit more complicated. This method returns an IDataObject, which in turn exposes three methods:

GetData   Retrieves the clipboard's contents.

GetDataPresent   Returns True if the Clipboard contains data of a specific type.

GetFormats   Returns all the formats supported by the Clipboard.

The GetData method accepts a single argument, which is the format of the desired data. The Clipboard doesn't just return any data it may contain; instead, you must specify the type of data you expect to read into your application when you request it. To read the bitmap stored in the Clipboard and display it on the PictureBox1 control, you must use a statement like the following:

```
PictureBox1.Image = Clipboard.GetDataObject.GetData(DataFormats.Bitmap)
```

The DataFormats enumeration contains a member for each type of data it recognizes (it includes types like Text, HTML, WaveAudio, and many more. If you can't be sure whether the Clipboard contains data of a specific type, use the GetDataPresent method passing as argument the desired type. If the Clipboard's data are of this type, the GetDataPresent method will return True:

```
clipboard.GetDataObject.GetDataPresent(dataFormat)
```

where *dataFormat* is a member of the DataFormats enumeration. You can also specify a second argument, which is a True/False value that determines whether the Clipboard should attempt to automatically convert its data to the specified format.

VB.NET AT WORK: THE IMAGECLIPBOARD PROJECT

The ImageClipboard project, whose main form is shown in Figure 14.5, allows you to exchange images between your VB application and any other image-aware application running under Windows through the Clipboard.

The Load Image button prompts the user to select an image with the Open dialog box (you've seen this code in the ImageLoad application). The Clear Image button clears the PictureBox control by calling the Clear method of the Graphics object (this object is discussed in the following section). The other two buttons move a bitmap to and from the Clipboard, as explained already. Listing 14.5 shows the event handlers for all four buttons on the form.

FIGURE 14.5

The ImageClipboard application lets you exchange images with other applications.

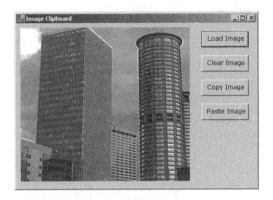

LISTING 14.5: THE IMAGECLIPBOARD APPLICATION

```
Private Sub bttnPaste_Click(ByVal sender As System.Object, _
            ByVal e As System.EventArgs) Handles bttnPaste.Click
    If Clipboard.GetDataObject.GetDataPresent(DataFormats.Bitmap) Then
        PictureBox1.Image = Clipboard.GetDataObject.GetData(DataFormats.Bitmap)
    Else
        MsgBox("The Clipboard doesn't contain a bitmap!")
    End If
End Sub
Private Sub bttnCopy_Click(ByVal sender As System.Object, _
            ByVal e As System.EventArgs) Handles bttnCopy.Click
    Clipboard.SetDataObject(PictureBox1.Image)
End Sub
Private Sub bttnLoad_Click(ByVal sender As System.Object, _
            ByVal e As System.EventArgs) Handles bttnLoad.Click
    OpenFileDialog1.Filter = "Images|*.bmp;*.tif;*.jpg;*.gif"
    If OpenFileDialog1.ShowDialog() = DialogResult.OK Then
        PictureBox1.Image = Image.FromFile(OpenFileDialog1.FileName)
    End If
End Sub
Private Sub bttnClear_Click(ByVal sender As System.Object, _
            ByVal e As System.EventArgs) Handles bttnClear.Click
    PictureBox1.CreateGraphics.Clear(Color.Black)
End Sub
```

This example concludes our discussion of the Image object. So far, you have learned how to add images to the application's user interface, properly resize bitmaps, and perform simple geometrical transformations like rotating and flipping. In the following section, you'll learn how to create your own graphics.

Drawing with GDI+

GDI stands for *Graphics Design Interface*, and it's a collection of classes that enables you to create graphics, text, and images. In short, GDI is the graphics engine of Windows. GDI has been around for many years, and its latest version is GDI+, which is the only way to create graphics in .NET. All the drawing statements of VB6 are gone, and although it's more difficult to create graphics with GDI+, the new graphics engine is faster, richer, and common for all .NET languages.

One of the basic characteristics of GDI+ is that it's stateless. This means that a graphics operation is totally independent of the previous one and can't affect the following one. To draw a line, you must specify a Pen object and the two endpoints of the line. You must do the same for the next line you'll draw. You can't assume that the second line will use the same pen, or that it will start at the point where the previous line ended. There isn't even a default font for text-drawing methods. Every time you draw some text, you must specify the font in which the text will be rendered, as well as the Brush object that will be used to draw the text.

The GDI+ classes reside in the following namespaces, and you must import one or more of them in your projects: `System.Drawing`, `System.Drawing2D`, `System.Drawing.Imaging`, and `System.Drawing.Text`. In this chapter we'll explore all three aspects of GDI+, namely vector drawing, imaging, and typography, starting with the basic drawing objects.

Before you start drawing, you must select the surface you want to draw on, the type of shapes you want to draw, and the instrument you'll use to draw with. The surface on which you can draw is a Graphics object. This object exposes numerous methods for drawing basic (and not so basic) shapes. To draw on a form, or a control, we request the proper Graphics object, which exposes all the drawing methods.

The next step is to decide what instrument you'll use to draw with. There are two major drawing instruments, the Pen object and the Brush object. You use pens to draw stroked shapes (lines, rectangles, curves) and brushes to draw filled shapes (any area enclosed by a shape). The main characteristics of the Pen object are its color and its width (the size of the trace left by the pen). The main characteristic of the Brush object is the color or pattern that will fill the shape. An interesting variation of the Brush object is the gradient brushes, which change color as you move from one point of the shape you want to fill to another. You can start filling a shape with red in the middle and specify that as you move toward the edges of the shape, the fill color fades to yellow.

After you have specified the drawing surface and the drawing instrument, you draw an actual shape by calling the appropriate method of the Graphics object. Here's a simple example of a few statements that draw a line on the form.

```
Dim redPen As Pen = New Pen(Color.Red, 2)
Dim point1 As Point = New Point(10,10)
Dim point2 As Point = New Point(120,180)
Me.CreateGraphics.DrawLine(redPen, point1, point2)
```

The first statement declares a new Pen object, which is initialized to draw in red with a width of 2 pixels. The following two statements declare and initialize two points, which are the line's starting and ending points. The coordinates are expressed in pixels, and the origin is at the form's top-left corner. The last statement draws a line by calling the DrawLine method. The expression `Me.CreateGraphics` retrieves the Graphics object of the form, which exposes all the drawing methods, including the DrawLine method. The Graphics object is the drawing surface, and all drawing methods produce some output on this surface. You can also create a new Graphics object and associate it with the form:

```
Dim G As Graphics
G = Me.CreateGraphics
G.DrawLine(redPen, point1, point2)
```

The DrawLine method accepts as argument the pen it will use to draw and the line's starting and ending points. I have used two Point objects to make the code easier to read. The DrawLine method, like all other drawing methods, is heavily overloaded. You can omit the declarations of the two points and pass their coordinates as arguments to the DrawLine method with the following statement:

```
Me.CreateGraphics.DrawLine(redPen, 10, 10, 120, 180)
```

You can also omit the declaration of a Pen object variable and initialize it in the same statement that draws the line:

```
Me.CreateGraphics.DrawLine(New Pen(Color.Red, 2), 10, 10, 120, 180)
```

All coordinates are expressed by default in pixels. It's possible to specify coordinates in different units and let GDI+ convert them to pixels before drawing. If you're drawing molecules, your units will be tiny fractions of a millimeter (microns), while if you're drawing the trajectories of planets, your units will be millions or billions of miles. For now, we'll use pixels, which are quite appropriate for simple objects. Once you've familiarized yourself with the drawing methods, you'll learn how to specify different coordinate systems.

The Basic Drawing Objects

This is a good point to introduce some of the objects we'll be using all the time in drawing. Instead of interrupting the discussion of the more interesting drawing methods that will follow, I'd rather discuss here all the auxiliary objects used in drawing. No matter what you draw, or what drawing instrument you're using, one or more of the objects discussed in this section will be required.

THE GRAPHICS OBJECT

The Graphics object is the drawing surface. Every control you can draw on exposes a Graphics property, which is an object. The Graphics object exposes all the methods for drawing on the surface of the control. It goes without saying that the PictureBox control exposes a Graphics property, but so does the TextBox control, as well as many controls you wouldn't expect. It's not recommended that you draw on a TextBox control, of course, unless you're coding a peculiar application. Bear in mind that anything you draw on the TextBox control will disappear as you start typing. You must first place the text on the control and then draw on its surface.

To retrieve the Graphics object of a control, call the control's CreateGraphics method. Because this method returns a Graphics object, it also exposes all the methods and properties you will use to create graphics on the control. If you enter the string `Me.CreateGraphics` and a period, you will see a list of the members of the Graphics object in a drop-down list. The DpiX and DpiY properties, for example, return the horizontal and vertical resolution of the form. On an average monitor, these two properties return a resolution of 96 dots per inch.

To use the Graphics object, you must first import the library Drawing2D into your project with the following statement (if not, you will have to fully qualify the references to the drawing methods):

```
Imports System.Drawing.Drawing2D
```

Then, declare a variable of the Graphics type and initialize it to the Graphics object returned by the control's CreateGraphics method:

```
Dim G As Graphics
G = PictureBox1.CreateGraphics
```

At this point you're ready to start drawing on the PictureBox1 control with the methods we'll discuss in the following sections. If you want to draw on the form, create a Graphics object with the form's CreateGraphics method:

```
Dim G As Graphics
G = Me.CreateGraphics
```

You can actually draw on any control that provides a CreateGraphics method.

NOTE *The Graphics object is initialized to the control's drawing surface the moment you create it. If the form is resized at runtime, the Graphics object won't change and part of the drawing surface may not be available for drawing. If you create a Graphics object to represent a form in the form's Load event handler, this object will represent the surface of the control the moment the Graphics object was created. If the form is resized at runtime, the drawing methods you apply to the Graphics object will take effect in part of the form. The most appropriate event for initializing the Graphics object and inserting the painting code is the form's Paint event. This event is fired when the form must be redrawn. Insert your drawing code there and create a Graphics object in the Paint event. Then draw on the Graphics object and release it when you're done.*

The Graphics object exposes the following basic properties, in addition to the drawing methods discussed in the following sections.

DpiX, DpiY The horizontal and vertical resolutions of the drawing surface. These properties are expressed in pixels per inch (or dots per inch, if the drawing surface is your printer). A distance of `Graphics.DpiX` pixels will be exactly one inch on the monitor. If you plan to work with a unit other than pixels, you should take advantage of the PageUnit property.

PageUnit The unit in which you want to express the coordinates on the Graphics object. Its value can be a member of the GraphicsUnit enumeration (Table 14.3).

TextRenderingHint This property specifies how the Graphics object will render text; its value is one of the members of the TextRenderingHint enumeration: `AntiAlias`, `AntiAliasGridFit`, `ClearTypeGridFit`, `SingleBitPerPixel`, `SingleBitPerPixelGridFit`, and `SystemDefault`.

SmoothingMode This property is similar to the TextRenderingHint, but it applies to all shapes, not just text. Its value is one of the members of the SmoothingMode enumeration: `AntiAlias`, `Default`, `HighQuality`, `HighSpeed`, `Invalid`, and `None`.

Figure 14.6 shows an ellipse drawn with the SmoothingMode property set to `AntiAlias` (the one on the left) and to `HighSpeed` (on the right). Parts of the two ellipses were blown up with an image-processing application, so that you can see the difference in the two modes. Anti-aliased shapes (or text, for that matter) are smoother because their edges contain shades between the drawing and background colors. These shades are introduced by GDI+ automatically when you render shapes to lessen the contrast between the two colors. As a result, anti-aliased drawings look smoother.

TABLE 14.3: THE GRAPHICSUNIT ENUMERATION

VALUE	DESCRIPTION
Display	The unit is 1/75 of an inch.
Document	The unit is 1/300 of an inch.
Inch	The unit is one inch.
Millimeter	The unit is one millimeter.
Pixel	The unit is one pixel (the default value).
Point	The unit is a printer's point (1/72 of an inch).
World	The developer specifies the unit to be used.

FIGURE 14.6

SmoothingMode set to (left) Anti-Alias and (right) HighSpeed

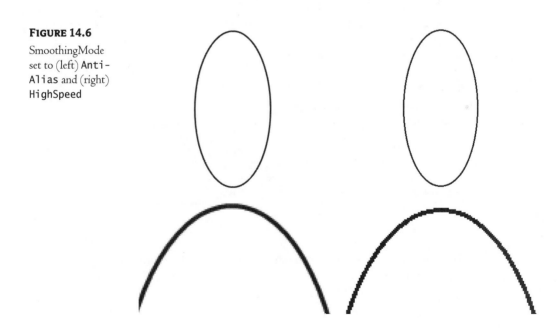

Figure 14.7 shows the effect of the TextRenderingHint property on text. The anti-aliased text looks much better on the monitor. The ClearType setting has no effect on CRT monitors. You can see the difference only when you render text on LCD monitors, such as the new flat panel monitors or notebook monitors.

Visual Basic.NET
Visual Basic.NET
Visual
Visual

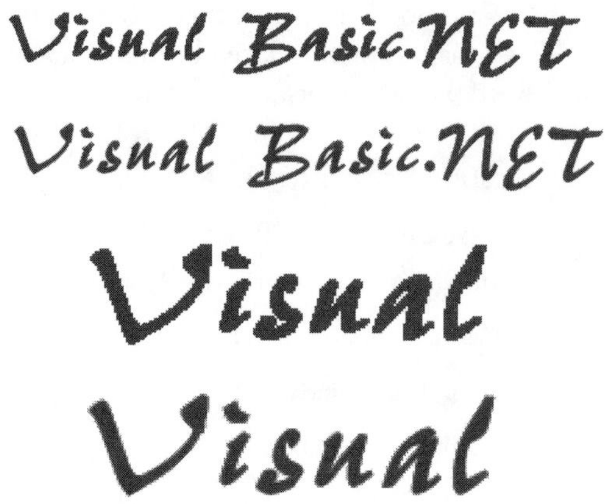

FIGURE 14.7
TextRenderingHint set to (top) `ClearType` and (bottom) `AntiAlias`

THE POINT OBJECT

The Point object represents a point on the drawing surface and is expressed as a pair of (x, y) coordinates. The x coordinate is its horizontal distance from the origin, and the y coordinate is its vertical distance from the origin. The origin is the point with coordinates (0, 0), and this is the top-left corner of the drawing surface. Figure 14.8 shows the coordinates of the two opposite corners of the Graphics object and a point in its interior.

(0, 0)
X-coordinates
Y-coordinates
Graphics Object
(320, 140)
(400, 200)

FIGURE 14.8
The origin of the default coordinate system is at the top-left corner of the drawing surface.

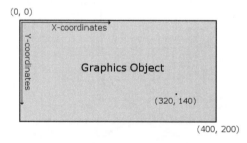

To create a new Point object, you must specify its x and y coordinates, represented as X and Y properties of the object. The constructor of the Point object is:

```
Dim P1 As Point
P1 = New Point(X, Y)
```

where X and Y are integer values, the point's horizontal and vertical distances from the origin. Alternatively, you can declare a Point object and then set its X and Y properties:

```
Dim P1 As Point
P1.X = 34
P1.Y = 50
```

As you will see later, coordinates can also be specified as Single numbers (if you choose to use a coordinate system other than pixels). In this case, use the PointF object, which is identical to the Point object with the exception that its coordinates are non-integers (F stands for *floating-point,* and floating-point numbers are represented by the Single or Double data type).

THE RECTANGLE OBJECT

Another object quite common in drawing is the Rectangle object. Its constructor accepts as arguments the coordinates of the rectangle's top-left corner and its width and height.

```
Dim box As Rectangle
box = New Rectangle(X, Y, width, height)
```

The following statement creates a rectangle whose top-left corner is 1 pixel to the right and 1 pixel down from the origin and whose dimensions are 100 and 20 pixels:

```
box = New Rectangle(1, 1, 100, 20)
```

The *box* variable represents a rectangle, but it doesn't generate any output on the monitor. If you want to draw the rectangle, you can pass it as argument to the DrawRectangle or FillRectangle method, depending on whether you want to draw the outline of the rectangle or a filled rectangle.

Another form of the Rectangle constructor uses the Size object to specify the dimensions of the rectangle:

```
box = New Rectangle(point, size)
```

To create the same Rectangle object as in the last example with this form of the constructor, use the following statement:

```
Dim P As Point
P.X = 1
P.Y = 1
Dim S As Size
S.Width = 100
S.Height = 20
box = New Rectangle(P, S)
```

Both sets of statements create a rectangle that extends from point $(1, 1)$ to the point $([1 + 100]$, $[1 + 20])$ or $(101, 21)$, in the same manner as the ones shown in Figure 14.9.

FIGURE 14.9

Specifying rectangles with the coordinates of their top left corner and their dimensions

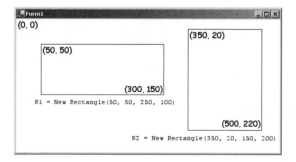

Alternatively, you can declare a Rectangle object and then set its properties, as shown here:

```
Dim box As new Rectangle
box.X = 1
box.Y = 1
box.Width = 100
box.Height = 20
```

THE COLOR OBJECT

The Color object represents a color, and there are many ways to specify a color. We'll discuss the Color object in more detail later in this chapter, in the discussion of bitmaps. In the meantime, you can specify colors by name. Declare a variable of the Color type, and initialize it to one of the named colors exposed by the Color object:

```
Dim myColor As Color
myColor = Color.Azure
```

The 128 named members of the Color object will appear in a drop-down list as soon as you enter the period following the keyword Color. You can also use the FromARGB method, which creates a new color from its basic color components (the Red, Green, and Blue components). For more information on specifying colors with this method, see the section "Specifying Colors" later in this chapter.

The Color object is used to set the color of the Pen object you draw with or the color in which a string will be rendered. You can also use the same object to assign values to any color-related property, such as the BackColor property of any control. To set the background color of a TextBox control, use the following statement:

```
TextBox1.BackColor = Color.Beige
```

THE FONT OBJECT

The Font object represents the font to be used when rendering strings with the DrawString method. To specify a font, you must create a new Font object, set its family name, size, and style, and then pass it as argument to the DrawString method. Alternatively, you can prompt the user for a font with the Font common dialog box and use the object returned by the dialog box's Font property as argument with the DrawString method.

To create a new Font object, use a few statements like the following:

```
Dim drawFont As New Font("Comic Sans MS", FontStyle.Bold)
```

The Font constructor has 13 forms in all. Two of the simpler forms of the constructor, which allow you specify the size and the style of the font, are shown next:

```
Dim drawFont As New Font(name, size)
Dim drawFont As New Font(name, size, style)
```

where *size* is an integer and *style* is a member of the FontStyle enumeration (Bold, Italic, Regular, Strikeout, and Underline). To specify multiple styles, combine them with the Or operator:

```
FontStyle.Bold Or FontStyle.Italic
```

You can also initialize a Font variable to an existing font. The following statement creates a Font object and initializes it to the current font of the form:

```
Dim textFont As New Font
textFont = Me.Font
```

The Font object provides the Size, Bold, and Italic properties. Unfortunately, these properties are read-only and return the attributes of the font in use. You can't turn on the bold attribute by setting the `Font.Bold` property to True. It would be very convenient to be able to quickly adjust the properties of an existing font and create a new one, but this isn't the case.

Of course, you can use the current settings of an existing font to create a new Font object. The following statements build a new Font object based on the settings of the form's current font. The new font belongs to the same family as the form's current font, is twice the size of this font, and has the same attributes as the form's font plus the bold attribute.

```
Dim textFont As Font
textFont = New Font(Me.Font.FontFamily, 2 * Me.Font.Size, _
                    Me.Font.Style Or FontStyle.Bold)
```

THE PEN OBJECT

The Pen object represents a virtual pen, which you use to draw on the Graphics object's surface. To construct a Pen object, you must specify a color and the pen's width in pixels. The following statements declare three Pen objects with the same color and different widths:

```
Dim thinPen, mediumPem, thickPen As Pen
thinPen = New Pen(Color.Black, 1)
mediumPen = New Pen(Color.Black, 3)
thickPen = New Pen(Color.Black, 5)
```

If you omit the second argument, a pen with a width of a single pixel will be created by default. Another form of the Pen object's constructor allows you to specify a brush, instead of a color:

```
Dim patternPen as Pen
patternPen = New Pen(brush, width)
```

where *brush* is a Brush object (which is discussed later in this chapter). As you will see, the drawing methods generate two types of drawings: stroked shapes and filled shapes. Stroked shapes (or outlines) are drawn with a pen, while filled shapes are drawn with a brush. To draw the outline of a shape with a pattern, you must create a Pen object based on an existing brush, and then use it with a drawing method.

The quickest method of creating a new Pen object is to use the built-in Pens collection, which creates a Pen with a width of one pixel and the color you specify. The following statement can appear anywhere a Pen object is required and will draw shapes in blue color:

```
Pens.Blue
```

NOTE   *There's an important distinction between Pens and Brushes you should bear in mind as you draw with VB.NET. You can't draw a shape with a Brush object, and you can't fill a closed shape with a Pen. It is possible, however, to draw a shape with a pattern, as long as you assign the pattern to the Pen object. Likewise, you can fill a shape with a solid color, as long as you set the color of the Brush object you're using to fill with.*

The Pen object exposes these properties:

LineJoin   Determines how two consecutive line segments will be joined. Its value is one of the members of the LineJoin enumeration: `Bevel`, `Miter`, `MiterClipped`, and `Round`.

StartCap, EndCap   Determine the caps at the beginning and end of a line segment respectively. Their value is one of the members of the LineCap enumeration: `Round`, `Square`, `Flat`, `Diamond`, and so on.

DashCap   Determines the cap to be used at the beginning and end of a dashed line. Its value is one of the members of the DashCap enumeration: `Flat`, `Round`, and `Triangle`.

DashStyle   Determines the style of the dashed lines drawn with the specific Pen. Its value is one of the members of the DashStyle enumeration (`Solid`, `Dash`, `DashDot`, `DashDotDot`, `Dot`, and `Custom`)

PenType   Determines the style of the Pen. Its value is one of the members of the PenType enumeration: `HatchFilled`, `LinearGradient`, `PathGradient`, `SolidColor`, and `TextureFill`.

THE PATH OBJECT

The Path object is a combination of the various drawing entities, like lines, rectangles, and curves. You can create as many of these drawing entities and build a new entity, which is called *Path*. Paths are usually closed and filled with a color, a gradient or a bitmap. You can create a path in several ways. The simplest method is to create a new Path object and then use one of these methods to append the appropriate item to the path:

AddArc	AddEllipse	AddPolygon
AddBezier	AddLine	AddRectangle
AddCurve	AddPie	AddString

These methods add to the path the same shapes you can draw on the Graphics object with the methods discussed in the later section "Drawing Shapes with the Graphics Object." There's even an AddPath method, which adds an existing path to the current one. The syntax of the various methods that add shapes to a path is identical to the corresponding methods that draw. We simply omit the first argument (the Pen object), because all the shapes will be rendered with the same pen. The following method draws an ellipse:

```
Me.CreateGraphics.DrawEllipse(pen, 10, 30, 40, 50)
```

To add the same ellipse to a Path object, use the following statement:

```
Dim myPath As New Path
myPath.AddEllipse(10, 30, 40, 50)
```

To *display* the path, call the DrawPath method passing a Pen and the Path object as arguments:

```
Me.CreateGraphics.DrawPath(myPen, myPath)
```

Why combine shapes into paths instead of drawing individual shapes? There are many reasons for maintaining multiple shapes as a single entity. Once the shape has been defined, you can draw multiple instances of it on the monitor, draw the same path with a different pen, or fill the path's constituent shapes with the same bitmap or gradient. Paths are also used to create the ultimate type of gradient, the PathGradient, as you will see in the section "Path Gradients," later in this chapter.

Later in this chapter, we'll build an application for plotting functions. To plot a function, we'll create a shape with all the points along the curve and draw it with a single call the DrawPath method.

THE BRUSH OBJECT

The Brush object is the instrument for filling shapes, and you can create brushes that fill with a solid color, a pattern, or a bitmap. In reality, there's no Brush object. The Brush class is actually an abstract class that is inherited by all the objects that implement a brush, but you can't declare a variable of the Brush type in your code. The brush objects are:

Brush Object Type	Fills Shapes With
SolidBrush	A solid color
HatchBrush	A hatched pattern
LinearGradientBrush	A linear gradient
PathGradientBrush	A gradient that has one starting color and many ending colors
TextureBrush	A bitmap

Solid Brushes

To fill a shape with a solid color, you must create a SolidBrush object with the following constructor:

```
Dim sBrush As SolidBrush
sBrush = New SolidBrush(brushColor)
```

where *brushColor* is a color value, specified with the help of the Color object. Every filled object you draw with the *sBrush* object will be filled with the color of the brush.

Hatched Brushes

To fill a shape with a hatch pattern, you must create a HatchBrush object with the following constructor:

```
Dim hBrush As HatchBrush
HBrush = New HatchBrush(hatchStyle, hatchColor, backColor)
```

The first argument is the style of the hatch, and it can have one of the values shown in Table 14.4. The other two arguments are the colors to be used in the hatch. The hatch is a pattern of lines drawn on a background, and the two color arguments are the color of the hatch lines and the color of the background on which the hatch is drawn.

TABLE 14.4: THE HATCHSTYLE ENUMERATION

VALUE	EFFECT
BackwardDiagonal	Diagonal lines from top-right to bottom-left
Cross	Vertical and horizontal crossing lines
DiagonalCross	Diagonally crossing lines
ForwardDiagonal	Diagonal lines from top-left to bottom-right
Horizontal	Horizontal lines
Vertical	Vertical lines

Gradient Brushes

A gradient brush fills a shape with a specified gradient. The `LinearGradientBrush` fills a shape with a linear gradient, and the `PathGradientBrush` fills a shape with a gradient that has one starting color and many ending colors. Gradient brushes are discussed in detail in the section "Gradients" later in this chapter.

Textured Brushes

In addition to solid and hatched shapes, you can fill a shape with a texture using a TextureBrush object. The texture is a bitmap that is tiled as needed to fill the shape. Textured brushes are used in creating rather fancy graphics, and we'll not explore them in this chapter.

Drawing Shapes

In this section, you will learn the drawing methods of the Graphics object. Before getting into the details of the drawing methods, however, let's write a simple application that draws a couple of simple shapes on a form. First, we must create a Graphics object with the following statement:

```
Dim G As Graphics
G = Me.CreateGraphics
```

Everything you draw on the surface represented by the *G* object will appear on the form. Then, we must create a Pen object to draw with. The following statement creates a Pen object that draws in blue:

```
Dim P As New Pen(Color.Blue)
```

You've created the two basic objects for drawing: the drawing surface and the drawing instrument. Now you can draw shapes by calling the Graphics object's methods. The following statement will print a rectangle with its top-left corner near the top-left corner of the form (at a point that's 10 pixels to the right and 10 pixels down from the form's corner) and is 200 pixels wide and 150 pixels tall. These are the values you must pass to the DrawRectangle method as arguments, along with the Pen object that will be used to render the rectangle:

```
G.DrawRectangle(P, 10, 10, 200, 150)
```

Let's add the two diagonals of the rectangle. The diagonals are two lines, one from the top-left to the bottom-right corner of the rectangle and another from top-right to bottom-left. Here are the two statements that draw the diagonals:

```
G.DrawLine(P, 10, 10, 210, 160)
G.DrawLine(P, 210, 10, 10, 160)
```

We've written all the statements to create a shape on the form, but where do we insert them? Let's try a Button. Start a new project, place a button on it, and then insert the statements of Listing 14.6 in the Button's Click event handler.

LISTING 14.6: DRAWING SIMPLE SHAPES

```
Private Sub Button1_Click(ByVal sender As System.Object, _
             ByVal e As System.EventArgs) Handles Button1.Click
    Dim G As Graphics
    G = Me.CreateGraphics
    Dim P As New Pen(Color.Blue)
    G.DrawRectangle(P, 10, 10, 200, 150)
    G.DrawLine(P, 10, 10, 210, 160)
    G.DrawLine(P, 210, 10, 10, 160)
End Sub
```

 Run the application and click the button. You will see the shape shown in Figure 14.10. This figure was created by the SimpleShapes application on the CD.

FIGURE 14.10

The output of Listing 14.6

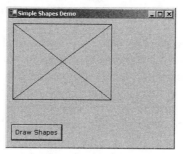

PERSISTENT DRAWING

If you switch to the Visual Studio IDE, or any other window, and then return to the form of the SimpleShapes application, you'll see that the drawing has disappeared! If you're a VB6 programmer, you've recognized that the form's AutoRedraw property isn't True. But there's no AutoRedraw property in VB.NET. Only the bitmap of the PictureBox is persistent. Everything you draw on the Graphics object is temporary. It doesn't become part of the Graphics object and is visible only while the control, or the form, need not be redrawn. As soon as the form is redrawn, the shapes disappear.

So, how do we make the output of the various drawing methods permanent on the form? Microsoft suggests placing all the graphics statements in the OnPaint method, which is activated automatically when the form is redrawn. OnPaint is a method of the form, which is invoked automatically by the operating system and, in turn, it invokes the Paint event. To draw something every time the form is redrawn, place the necessary statements in the OnPaint method.

The OnPaint method accepts a single argument, the *e* argument, which, among other properties, exposes the form's Graphics object. You can create a Graphics object in the OnPaint method and then draw on this object. Listing 14.7 is the OnPaint event handler that creates the shape shown in Figure 14.10 and refreshes the form every time it's totally or partially covered by another form. Delete the code in the button's Click event handler and insert the subroutine from the listing into the form's code window.

LISTING 14.7: PROGRAMMING THE ONPAINT EVENT

```
Protected Overrides Sub OnPaint(ByVal e As PaintEventArgs)
    Dim G As Graphics
    G = e.Graphics
    Dim P As New Pen(Color.Blue)
    G.DrawRectangle(P, 10, 10, 200, 150)
    G.DrawLine(P, 10, 10, 210, 160)
    G.DrawLine(P, 210, 10, 10, 160)
End Sub
```

If you run the application now, it works like a charm. The shapes appear to be permanent, even though they're redrawn every time you switch to the form. All the samples that come with Visual Studio place the graphics statements in the OnPaint method, so that they're executed every time the form is redrawn.

This technique is fine for a few graphics elements you want to place on the form to enhance its appearance. But many applications draw something on the form in response to user actions, like the click of a button or a menu commands. Using the OnPaint method in a similar application is out of the question. The drawing isn't the same, and you must figure out from within your code which shapes you have to redraw at any given time. Consider a drawing application. The current drawing evolves according to the commands you issue. The code in the OnPaint method can't execute a few drawing commands to regenerate the drawing. Keeping track of the drawing commands that were executed and the order in which they were executed is quite a task. The solution is to make the drawing permanent on the Graphics object, so it won't have to be redrawn every time the form is hidden or resized.

It is possible to make the graphics permanent by drawing not on the Graphics object, but directly on the control's (or the form's) bitmap. The Bitmap object contains the pixels that make up the image and is very similar to the Image object. As you will see, you can create a Bitmap object and assign it to an Image object. In the image-processing application we'll develop toward the end of this chapter, you'll learn how to extract the bitmap from a PictureBox control, process the pixels of a bitmap, and then assign the processed bitmap back to the control's Image property. In the meantime, you can use the code of Listing 14.7 to create a drawing surface that doesn't have to be constantly redrawn.

To create this "permanent" drawing surface, you must first create a Bitmap object that has the same dimensions as the PictureBox control you want to draw on:

```
Dim bmp As Bitmap
bmp = New Bitmap(PictureBox1.Width, PictureBox1.Height)
```

The *bmp* variable represents an empty bitmap. Then, we set the control's Image property to this bitmap with the following statement:

```
PictureBox1.Image = bmp
```

Immediately after that, you must set the bitmap to the control's background color with the Clear method:

```
G.Clear(PictureBox1.BackColor)
```

After the execution of this statement, anything we draw on the *bmp* bitmap is shown on the surface of the PictureBox control and is permanent. All we need is a Graphics object that represents the bitmap, so that we can draw on the control. The following statement creates a Graphics object based on the *bmp* variable:

```
Dim G As Graphics
G = Graphics.FromImage(bmp)
```

Now, we're in business. We can call the *G* object's drawing methods to draw and create permanent graphics on the PictureBox control. You can put all the statements presented so far in a function that returns a Graphics object (Listing 14.8) and use it in your applications.

LISTING 14.8: RETRIEVING A GRAPHICS OBJECT FROM A PICTUREBOX'S BITMAP

```
Function GetGraphicsObject(ByVal PBox As PictureBox) As Graphics
    Dim bmp As Bitmap
    bmp = New Bitmap(PBox.Width, PBox.Height)
    PBox.Image = bmp
    Dim G As Graphics
    G = Graphics.FromImage(bmp)
    Return G
End Function
```

To create permanent drawings on the surface of the PictureBox control, you must call the Get-GraphicsObject() function to obtain a Graphics object from the control's bitmap. The Form object doesn't expose an Image property, so you must use its BackgroundImage property. Listing 14.9 is the revised GetGraphicsObject() function for the Form object.

LISTING 14.9: RETRIEVING A GRAPHICS OBJECT FROM A FORM'S BITMAP

```
Function GetGraphicsObject() As Graphics
    Dim bmp As Bitmap
    bmp = New Bitmap(Me.Width, Me.Height)
    Dim G As Graphics
    Me.BackgroundImage = bmp
    G = Graphics.FromImage(bmp)
    Return G
End Function
```

Let's revise the SimpleShapes application so that it draws permanent shapes on the form. Create a new project and place two Button controls on it. Insert the GetGraphicsObject() function in the form's code window and then the statements shown in Listing 14.10 behind each button. The listing shows the entire code of the SimpleGraphics application, which is on the CD.

LISTING 14.10: THE SIMPLEGRAPHICS APPLICATION

```
Private Sub Button1_Click(ByVal sender As System.Object, _
              ByVal e As System.EventArgs) Handles Button1.Click
    Dim G As Graphics
    G = GetGraphicsObject()
    G.Clear(Color.Silver)
    Dim P As New Pen(Color.Blue)
    G.DrawRectangle(P, 10, 10, 200, 150)
    G.DrawLine(P, 10, 10, 210, 160)
    G.DrawLine(P, 210, 10, 10, 160)
    Me.Invalidate()
End Sub
Private Sub Button2_Click(ByVal sender As System.Object, _
              ByVal e As System.EventArgs) Handles Button2.Click
    Me.CreateGraphics.DrawEllipse(Pens.Red, 10, 10, 200, 150)
End Sub
Function GetGraphicsObject() As Graphics
    Dim bmp As Bitmap
    bmp = New Bitmap(Me.Width, Me.Height)
    Dim G As Graphics
    Me.BackgroundImage = bmp
    G = Graphics.FromImage(bmp)
    Return G
End Function
```

The first button (the Draw On Bitmap button of the SimpleGraphics application) draws on the Graphics object derived from the form's background bitmap. Anything drawn on this object is permanent. The second button (the Draw On Graphics button) uses the Graphics object returned by the form's CreateGraphics method to draw an ellipse in red color, inscribed in the rectangle. The ellipse isn't permanent. If you click both buttons, you will see the rectangle and its two diagonals, as well as the ellipse. Switch to another window and then bring the application to the foreground. The ellipse will not be there, because it wasn't drawn permanently on the form.

As you can guess, it's possible to combine the two methods and draw shapes that are permanent and shapes that are not. To erase the non-permanent shapes, call the control's Invalidate method, which redraws the control. Anything drawn on the Graphics object returned by the control's CreateGraphics method will disappear. The Invalidate method can be called without an argument to refresh (invalidate) the entire control. Or it can be called with a Rectangle object as argument, in which case it will invalidate the area of the control specified by the Rectangle object.

Now that you know how to draw on the Graphics object and you're familiar with the basic drawing objects, we can discuss the drawing methods in detail. In the following sections, I use the CreateGraphics method to retrieve the drawing surface of a PictureBox or form to keep the examples short. You can modify any of the projects to draw on the Graphics object derived from a bitmap. All you have to do is change the statements that create the G variable.

Drawing Methods

With basic objects out of the way, we can now focus on the drawing methods themselves. There are many drawing methods, one for each basic shape. You can create much more elaborate shapes by combining the methods described in the following sections.

All drawing methods have a few things in common. The first argument is always a Pen object, which will be used to render the shape on the Graphics object. The following arguments are the parameters of a shape: they determine the location and dimensions of the shape. The DrawLine method, for example, needs to know the endpoints of the line to draw, while the DrawRectangle method needs to know the origin and dimensions of the rectangle to draw. The parameters needed to render the shape are passed as arguments to each drawing method, following the Pen object.

The drawing methods can also be categorized in two major groups: the methods that draw stroked shapes (outlines) and the methods that draw filled shapes. The methods in the first group start with the "Draw" prefix (DrawRectangle, DrawEllipse, and so on). The methods of the second group start with the "Fill" prefix (FillRectangle, FillEllipse, and so on). Of course, some DrawXXX methods don't have an equivalent FillXXX method. For example, you can't fill a line or an open curve, so there are no FillLine or FillCurve methods.

Another difference between the drawing and filling methods is that the filling methods use a Brush object to fill the shape—you can't fill a shape with a pen. So, the first argument of the methods that draw filled shapes is a Brush object, not a Pen object. The remaining arguments are the same, because you must still specify the shape to be filled, just as you would specify the shape to be drawn. In the following sections, I will present in detail the shape-drawing methods but not the shape-filling methods. If you can use a drawing method, you can just as easily use its filling counterpart.

Table 14.5 shows the names of the drawing methods. The first column contains the methods for drawing stroked shapes and the second column contains the corresponding methods for drawing filled shapes (if there's a matching method).

TABLE 14.5: THE DRAWING METHODS

DRAWING METHOD	FILLING METHOD	DESCRIPTION
DrawArc		Draws an arc
DrawBezier		Draws very smooth curves with fixed endpoints, whose exact shape is determined by two control points
DrawBeziers		Draws multiple Bezier curves in a single call
DrawClosedCurve	FillClosedCurve	Draws a closed curve
DrawCurve		Draws curves that pass through certain points
DrawEllipse	FillEllipse	Draws an ellipse
DrawIcon		Renders an icon on the Graphics object
DrawImage		Renders an image on the Graphics object
DrawLine		Draws a line segment
DrawLines		Draws multiple line segments in a single call
DrawPath	FillPath	Draws a GraphicsPath object
DrawPie	FillPie	Draws a pie section
DrawPolygon	FillPolygon	Draws a polygon (a series of line segments between points)
DrawRectangle	FillRectangle	Draws a rectangle
DrawRectangles	FillRectangles	Draws multiple rectangles in a single call
DrawString		Draws a string in the specified font on the drawing surface
	FillRegion	Fills a Region object

Some of the drawing methods allow you to draw multiple shapes of the same type, and they're properly named DrawLines, DrawRectanlges, and DrawBeziers. We simply supply more shapes as arguments, and they're drawn one after the other with a single call to the corresponding method. The multiple shapes are stored in arrays of the same type, as the individual shapes. The DrawRectangle method, for example, accepts as argument the Rectangle object to be drawn. The DrawRectangles method accepts as argument an array of Rectangle objects and draws them in a single call.

DRAWLINE

The DrawLine method draws straight line-segments between two points with a pen supplied as argument. The simplest forms of the DrawLine method are the following:

```
Graphics.DrawLine(pen, X1, Y1, X2, Y2)
Graphics.DrawLine(pen, point1, point2)
```

where the coordinates are expressed in pixels (or the current coordinate system) and *point1* and *point2* are either Point or PointF objects, depending on the coordinate system in use.

DRAWRECTANGLE

The DrawRectangle method draws a stroked rectangle and has two forms:

```
Graphics.DrawRectangle(pen, rectangle)
Graphics.DrawRectangle(pen, X1, Y1, width, height)
```

The *rectangle* argument is a Rectangle object that specifies the shape to be drawn. In the second form of the method, the arguments *X1* and *Y1* are the coordinates of the rectangle's top-left corner and the other two arguments are the dimensions of the rectangle. All these arguments can be integers or singles, depending on the coordinate system in use. However, they must be all of the same type.

The following statements draw two rectangles, one inside the other. The outer rectangle is drawn with a red pen with the default width, while the inner rectangle is drawn with a 3-pixel-wide green pen.

```
Graphics.DrawRectangle(Pens.Red, 100, 100, 200, 100)
Graphics.DrawRectangle(New Pen(Color.Green, 3), 125, 125, 75, 50)
```

DRAWELLIPSE

An ellipse is an oval or circular shape, determined by the rectangle that encloses it. The two dimensions of this rectangle are the ellipse's major and minor diameters. Instead of giving you a mathematically correct definition of an ellipse, I've prepared a few ellipses with different ratios of their two diameters. These ellipses are shown in Figure 14.11. The figure was prepared with the GDIPlus application, which demonstrates a few more graphics operations; you will find it in this chapter's folder on the CD. The ellipse is oblong along the direction of the major diameter and squashed along the direction of the minor diameter. If the two diameters are exactly equal, the ellipse becomes a circle. Indeed, the circle is just a special case of the ellipse.

To draw an ellipse, call the DrawEllipse method, which has two basic forms:

```
Graphics.DrawEllipse(pen, rectangle)
Graphics.DrawEllipse(pen, X1, Y1, width, height)
```

FIGURE 14.11

Two ellipses with their enclosing rectangles

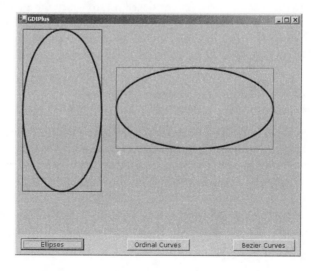

The arguments are the same as with the DrawRectangle method, because an ellipse is basically a circle deformed to fit in a rectangle. The two ellipses and their enclosing rectangles shown in Figure 14.11 were generated with the statements of Listing 14.11.

LISTING 14.11: DRAWING ELLIPSES AND THEIR ENCLOSING RECTANGLES

```
Private Sub Button1_Click(ByVal sender As System.Object, _
                ByVal e As System.EventArgs) Handles Button1.Click
    Dim G As Graphics
    G = PictureBox1.CreateGraphics
    G.SmoothingMode = Drawing.Drawing2D.SmoothingMode.AntiAlias
    G.FillRectangle(Brushes.Silver, ClientRectangle)
    Dim R1, R2 As Rectangle
    R1 = New Rectangle(10, 10, 160, 320)
    R2 = New Rectangle(200, 85, 320, 160)
    G.DrawEllipse(New Pen(Color.Black, 3), R1)
    G.DrawRectangle(Pens.Black, R1)
    G.DrawEllipse(New Pen(Color.Black, 3), R2)
    G.DrawRectangle(Pens.Red, R2)
End Sub
```

The ellipses were drawn with a pen that is three pixels wide. As you can see in the figure, the width of the ellipse is split to the inside and outside of the enclosing rectangle, which is drawn with a 1-pixel-wide pen.

DRAWPIE

A pie is a shape similar to a slice of a pie: an arc along with the two line segments that connect its endpoints to the center of the circle, or the ellipse, to which the arc belongs. The DrawPie method accepts as arguments the pen with which it will draw the shape, the circle to which the pie belongs, the arc's starting angle, and its sweep angle. The circle (or the ellipse) of the pie is defined with a rectangle. The starting and sweeping angles are measured clockwise. The DrawPie method has two forms, which are:

```
Graphics.DrawPie(pen, rectangle, start, sweep)
Graphics.DrawPie(pen, X, Y, width, height, start, sweep)
```

The two forms of the method differ in how the rectangle is defined (a Rectangle object versus its coordinates and dimensions). The *start* argument is the pie's starting angle, and *sweep* is the angle of the pie. The ending angle is *start+sweep*. Angles are measured in degrees (there are 360 degrees in a circle) and increase in a clockwise direction. The 0 angle corresponds to the horizontal axis, and the vertical axis forms a 90-degree angle with the horizontal axis.

The following statements create a pie chart by drawing individual pie slices. Each pie starts where the previous one ends, and the sweeping angles of all pies add up to 360 degrees, which corresponds to a full rotation (a full circle). Figure 14.12 shows the output produced by the Listing 14.12.

FIGURE 14.12

A simple pie chart generated with the PieChart method

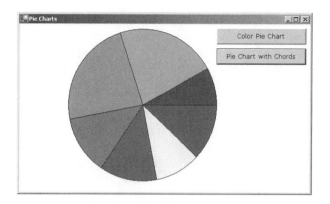

LISTING 14.12: DRAWING A SIMPLE PIE CHART WITH THE FILLPIE METHODS

```
Private Sub Button2_Click(ByVal sender As System.Object, _
              ByVal e As System.EventArgs) Handles Button2.Click
    Dim G As System.Drawing.Graphics
    G = Me.CreateGraphics
    Dim brush As System.drawing.SolidBrush
    Dim rect As Rectangle
    brush = New System.Drawing.SolidBrush(Color.Green)
    Dim Angles() As Single = {0, 43, 79, 124, 169, 252, 331, 360}
    Dim Colors() As Color = {Color.Red, Color.Cornsilk, Color.Firebrick, _
                         Color.OliveDrab, Color.LawnGreen, _
                         Color.SandyBrown, Color.MidnightBlue}
    G.Clear(Color.Ivory)
    rect = New Rectangle(100, 10, 300, 300)
    Dim angle As Integer
    For angle = 1 To Angles.GetUpperBound(0)
       brush.Color = Colors(angle - 1)
       G.FillPie(brush, rect, Angles(angle - 1), _
               Angles(angle) - Angles(angle - 1))
    Next
    G.DrawEllipse(Pens.Black, rect)
End Sub
```

The code sets up two arrays, one with angles and another with colors. The *Angles* array holds the starting angle of each pie. The sweep angle of each pie is the difference between its own starting angle and the starting angle of the following pie. The sweep angle of the first pie is `Angles(1)` – `Angles(0)`, which is 43 degrees. The loop goes through each pie and draws it with a color it picks from the *Colors* array, based on the angles stored in the *Angles* array.

The second button on the PieChart project's form draws the same pie chart, but it also connects each slice's endpoints to the center of the circle. The code behind this button is identical to the code shown in Listing 14.6 with the exception that after calling the FillPie method (which draws the filled pie shape), it calls the DrawPie method to draw the outline of the pie.

Notice that the FillPie method doesn't connect the pie's endpoints to the center of the ellipse. Use the DrawEllipse method to draw the complete outline of the pie.

DRAWPOLYGON

This method draws an arbitrary polygon. It accepts two arguments, which are the Pen that it will use to render the polygon and an array of points that define the polygon. The polygon has as many sides (or vertices) as there are points in the array, and it's always closed, even if the first and last points are not identical. In fact, you need not repeat the starting point at the end, because the polygon will be automatically closed. The syntax of the DrawPolygon method is:

```
Graphics.DrawPolygon(pen, points())
```

where *points* is an array of points, which can be declared with a statement like the following:

```
Dim points() As Point = {New Point(x1, y1), New Point(x2, y2), …}
```

DRAWCURVE

Curves are smooth lines drawn as *cardinal splines*. A real spline was a flexible object (made of soft wood) that designers used to flex on the drawing surface with spikes. The spline would go through all the fixed points, but the shape between the fixed points was a smooth curve. The entire spline yielded a smooth curve that passed through all the spikes that held it in place. If the spline weren't flexible enough, it would break. In modern computer graphics, there are mathematical formulas that describe the path of the spline through the fixed points and take into consideration the tension (the degree of flexibility) of the spline. A more flexible spline yields a curve that bends easily. Less flexible splines do not bend easily around their fixed points. Computer-generated splines do not break, but they can take unexpected shapes.

To draw a curve with the DrawCurve method, you specify the locations of the spikes (the points which the spline must go through) and the spline's tension. If the tension is 0, the spline is totally flexible, like a rubber band: all the segments between points are straight lines. The higher the tension, the smoother the curve will be. Figure 14:13 shows four curves passing through the same points, but each curve is drawn with a different tension value. The curves shown in the figure were drawn with the GDIPlus project (using the Ordinal Curves button).

The simplest form of the DrawCurve method has the following syntax:

```
Graphics.DrawCurve(pen, points, tension)
```

where *points* is an array of points. The first and last elements of the array are the curve's endpoints, and the curve will go through the remaining points.

An alternate form of the method lets you specify the curve's first fixed point in the array, as well as the number of segments that make up the curve:

```
Graphics.DrawCurve.(pen, points, offset, segments, tension)
```

The *offset* and *segments* arguments allow you to work with a portion of the *points* array, rather than with the entire array. The *points* array must contain at least four points—the two endpoints and two more control points along the curve. The *tension* argument is optional, and if you omit it, the curve will be drawn with a tension of 1.

FIGURE 14.13

These curves go through the same points, but they have different tensions.

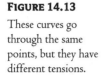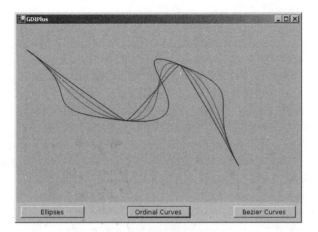

The curves shown in Figure 14.13 were produced by the code shown in Listing 14.13. Notice that a tension of 0.5 is practically the same as 0 (the spline bends around the fixed points like a rubber band). If you drew the same curve with a tension of 5, you'd get an odd curve indeed. The reason is, although a physical spline would break, the mathematical spline takes an unusual shape to accommodate the fixed points.

LISTING 14.13: CURVES WITH COMMON FIXED POINTS AND DIFFERENT TENSIONS

```
Private Sub Button2_Click(ByVal sender As System.Object, _
                ByVal e As System.EventArgs) Handles Button2.Click
    Dim G As Graphics
    G = PictureBox1.CreateGraphics
    G.SmoothingMode = Drawing.Drawing2D.SmoothingMode.HighQuality
    Dim points() As Point = {New Point(20, 50), New Point(220, 190), _
                        New Point(330, 80), New Point(450, 280)}
    G.DrawCurve(Pens.Blue, points, 0.1)
    G.DrawCurve(Pens.Red, points, 0.5)
    G.DrawCurve(Pens.Green, points, 1)
    G.DrawCurve(Pens.Black, points, 2)
End Sub
```

DRAWBEZIER

The DrawBezier method draws Bezier curves, which are smoother than cardinal splines. A Bezier curve is defined by two endpoints and two control points. The control points act as magnets. The curve is the trace of a point that starts at one of the endpoints and moves toward the second one. As it moves, the point is attracted by the two control points. Initially, the first control point's influence is predominant. Gradually, the curve comes into the second control point's field, and it ends at the second endpoint.

The DrawBezier method accepts a pen and four points as arguments:

```
Graphics.DrawBexier(pen, X1, Y1, X2, Y2, X3, Y3, X4, Y4)
Graphics.DrawBezier(pen, point1, point2, point3, point4)
```

Figure 14.14 shows four Bezier curves, which differ in the *y* coordinate of the third control point. All control points are marked with little squares: one each for the three points that are common to all curves and four in a vertical column for the point that differs in each curve. The code, shown in Listing 14.14, draws the little squares at the control points and then draws the four Bezier curves. The endpoints and one control point (P1, P2, and P4) remain the same, while the other control point (P3) is set to four different values. Notice how far the control point must go to have a significant effect on the curve's shape.

FIGURE 14.14

Bezier curves and their control points

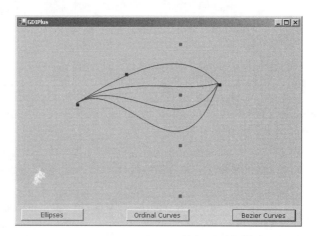

LISTING 14.14: DRAWING BEZIER CURVES AND THEIR CONTROL POINTS

```
Private Sub Button3_Click(ByVal sender As System.Object, _
            ByVal e As System.EventArgs) Handles Button3.Click
    Dim G As Graphics
    G = PictureBox1.CreateGraphics
    G.SmoothingMode = Drawing.Drawing2D.SmoothingMode.AntiAlias
    G.FillRectangle(Brushes.Silver, ClientRectangle)
    Dim P1 As New Point(120, 150)
    Dim P2 As New Point(220, 90)
    Dim P3 As New Point(330, 30)
    Dim P4 As New Point(410, 110)
    Dim sqrSize As New Size(6, 6)
    G.FillRectangle(Brushes.Black, New Rectangle(P1, sqrSize))
    G.FillRectangle(Brushes.Black, New Rectangle(P2, sqrSize))
    G.FillRectangle(Brushes.Red, New Rectangle(P3, sqrSize))
    G.FillRectangle(Brushes.Black, New Rectangle(P4, sqrSize))
    G.DrawBezier(Pens.Blue, P1, P2, P3, P4)
```

```
        P3 = New Point(330, 130)
        G.FillRectangle(Brushes.Red, New Rectangle(P3, sqrSize))
        G.DrawBezier(Pens.Blue, P1, P2, P3, P4)
        P3 = New Point(330, 230)
        G.FillRectangle(Brushes.Red, New Rectangle(P3, sqrSize))
        G.DrawBezier(Pens.Blue, P1, P2, P3, P4)
        P3 = New Point(330, 330)
        G.FillRectangle(Brushes.Red, New Rectangle(P3, sqrSize))
        G.DrawBezier(Pens.Blue, P1, P2, P3, P4)
    End Sub
```

The calls to the FillRectangle method draw the little boxes that represent the control points. To draw the curve, all you need is to specify the four control points and pass them along with a Pen object to the DrawBezier method.

DrawPath

This method accepts a Pen object and a Path object as arguments and renders the specified path on the screen:

```
Graphics.DrawPath(pen, path)
```

To construct the Path object, use the AddXXX methods (AddLine, AddRectangle, and so on), as discussed in the section "The Path Object," earlier in this chapter. You will find an example of how to use the Path object later in this chapter, when you'll learn how to plot functions.

DrawString

The DrawString method renders a string on the drawing surface. The string may be rendered on a single line or multiple lines (there are different forms of the DrawString method for each type of text rendering). As a reminder, the TextRenderingHint property of the Graphics object allows you to specify the quality of the rendered text.

The simplest form of the DrawString method is:

```
Graphics.DrawString(string, font, brush, X, Y)
```

The first argument is the string to be rendered in the font specified with the second argument. The text will be rendered with the Brush object specified with the *brush* argument. Here, *X* and *Y* are the coordinates of the string's top-left corner when it will be rendered.

While working with strings, you frequently need to know the actual dimensions of the string when rendered with the DrawString method in a specific font. The MeasureString method allows you to retrieve the metrics of a string before actually drawing it. This method returns a SizeF structure with the width and height of the string when rendered. Having this information allows you to align your strings on the drawing surface. You can also pass a Rectangle object as argument to the MeasureString method to find out how many lines it will take to render the string on the rectangle.

The simplest form of the MeasureString method is:

```
Dim textSize As SizeF
textSize = Me.Graphics.MeasureString(string, font)
```

where *string* is the string to be rendered and *font* is the font in which the string will be rendered. To center a string on the form, use the X coordinate returned by the following expression:

```
Dim textSize As SizeF
Dim X As Integer, Y As Integer = 0
textSize = Me.Graphics.MeasureString(string, font)
X = (Me.Width - textSize.Width) / 2
G.DrawString("Centered string", font, brush, X, Y)
```

We subtract the rendered string's length from the form's width, and we split the difference in half at the two sides of the string.

Figure 14.15 shows a string printed at the center of the form (by the Draw Centered String button of the TextEffects project), and the two lines pass through the same point. Listing 14.15 shows the statements that produced the string at the middle of this form. This listing is part of the TextEffects project, which you will find in this chapter's folder on the CD.

FIGURE 14.15

Centering a string on a form

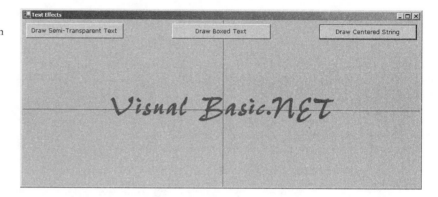

LISTING 14.15: PRINT A STRING CENTERED ON THE FORM

```
Private Sub Center(ByVal sender As System.Object, _
            ByVal e As System.EventArgs) Handles bttnCentered.Click
    Dim G As Graphics
    G = Me.CreateGraphics
    G.FillRectangle(New SolidBrush(Color.Silver), ClientRectangle)
    G.TextRenderingHint = Drawing.Text.TextRenderingHint.AntiAlias
    FontDialog1.Font = Me.Font
    FontDialog1.ShowDialog()
    Dim txtFont As Font
    txtFont = FontDialog1.Font
    G.DrawLine(New Pen(Color.Green), CInt(Me.Width / 2), CInt(0), _
            CInt(Me.Width / 2), CInt(Me.Height))
    G.DrawLine(New Pen(Color.Green), 0, CInt(Me.Height / 2), _
            CInt(Me.Width), CInt(Me.Height / 2))
    Dim txtLen, txtHeight As Integer
    Dim txtSize As SizeF
```

```
txtSize = G.MeasureString("Visual Basic.NET", txtFont)
Dim txtX, txtY As Integer
txtX = (Me.Width - txtSize.Width) / 2
txtY = (Me.Height - txtSize.Height) / 2
G.DrawString("Visual Basic.NET", txtFont, New SolidBrush(Color.Red), _
             txtX, txtY)
End Sub
```

As you can see, the coordinates passed to the DrawString method (variables *txtX* and *txtY*) are the coordinates of the top-left corner of the rectangle that encloses the first character of the string. After drawing the string, the code calls the MeasureString method to retrieve the rectangle that encloses the string (the *boxSize* variable) and prints this rectangle on the form.

Another form of the DrawString method accepts a rectangle as argument and draws the string in this rectangle, breaking the text into multiple lines if needed. The syntax of this form of the method is:

```
Graphics.DrawString(string, font, brush, rectanglef)
Graphics.DrawString(string, font, brush, rectanglef, stringFormat)
```

If you want to render text in a box, you will most likely use the equivalent form of the MeasureString method to retrieve the metrics of the text on the rectangle. This form of the MeasureString method returns the number of lines it will take to render the string on the rectangle, and it has the following syntax:

```
e.Graphics.MeasureString(string, Font, fitSize, StringFormat, lines, cols)
```

string is the text to be rendered, and *Font* is the font in which the string will be rendered. The *fitSize* argument is a SizeF object that represents the width and height of a rectangle, where the string must fit. The *lines* and *cols* variables are passed by reference, and they are set by the MeasureString method to the number of lines and number of characters that will fit in the specified rectangle. The exact location of the rectangle doesn't make any difference—only its dimensions matter, and that's why the third argument is a SizeF object and not a Rectangle object.

Figure 14.16 shows a string printed in two different rectangles. The sample code can be found in the TextEffects project on the CD, and Figure 14.16 was created with the Draw Boxed Text button. The code that produced the figure is shown in Listing 14.16.

FIGURE 14.16

Printing text in a rectangle

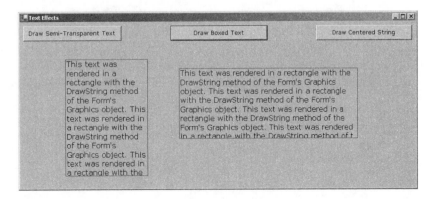

LISTING 14.16: PRINTING TEXT IN A RECTANGLE

```
Private Sub BoxedText(ByVal sender As System.Object, _
              ByVal e As System.EventArgs) Handles bttnBoxed.Click
   Dim G As Graphics
   G = Me.CreateGraphics
   G.FillRectangle(New SolidBrush(Color.Silver), ClientRectangle)
   Dim txt As String = "This text was rendered in a rectangle with the " & _
                   "DrawString method of the form's Graphics object."
' Make the string longer
   txt = txt & txt & txt & txt & txt
   G.DrawString(txt, New Font("verdana", 12, FontStyle.Regular), _
              Brushes.Black, New RectangleF(100, 80, 180, 250))
   G.DrawRectangle(Pens.Red, 100, 80, 180, 250)
   G.DrawString(txt, New Font("verdana", 12, FontStyle.Regular), _
              Brushes.Black, New RectangleF(350, 100, 400, 150))
   G.DrawRectangle(Pens.Red, 350, 100, 400, 150)
End Sub
```

Some of the overloaded forms of the DrawString method accept an argument of the StringFormat type. This argument determines characteristics of the text and exposes a few properties of its own, which include the following:

Alignment   Determines the alignment of the text. Its value is one of the members of the StringAlignment enumeration: Center (text is aligned in the center of the layout rectangle), Far (text is aligned far from the origin of the layout rectangle) and Near (text is aligned near the origin of the layout rectangle).

Trimming   Determines how text will be trimmed if it doesn't fit in the layout rectangle. Its value is one of the members of the StringTrimming enumeration: Character (text is trimmed to the nearest character), EllipsisCharacter (trimmed to the nearest character and an ellipsis is inserted at the end to indicate that some of the text is missing), EllipsisPath (text at the middle of the string is removed and replaced by an ellipsis), EllipsisWord (trimmed to the nearest word and an ellipsis is inserted at the end), None (no trimming), and Word (trimmed to the nearest word).

FormatFlags   Specifies layout information for the string. Its value can be one of the members of the StringFormatFlags enumeration. The two members of this enumeration you may need often are DirectionRightToLeft (prints to the left of the specified point) and DirectionVertical.

To use the *stringFormat* argument of the DrawString method, instantiate a variable of this type, set the desired properties, and then pass it as argument to the DrawString method, as shown here:

```
Dim G As Graphics = Me.CreateGraphics
Dim SF As New StringFormat()
SF.FormatFlags = StringFormatFlags.DirectionVertical
G.DrawString("Visual Basic", Me.Font, Brushes.Red, 80, 80, SF)
```

The call to the DrawString method will print the string from top to bottom. It will also rotate the characters. The `DirectionRightToLeft` will print the string to the left of the specified point, but it will not mirror the characters. In effect, it shifts the string to the left of the point specified with the DrawString method, by the length of the string, and then prints it.

You can find additional examples of the MeasureString method in Chapter 15, where we'll use this method to fit strings on the width of the page. The third button on the form of the TextEffect project draws text with a three-dimensional look by overlaying a semitransparent string over an opaque string. This technique is explained in the section "Alpha Blending," later in this chapter, where you'll learn how to use transparency. You may also wonder why none of the DrawString methods' forms accept as argument an angle of rotation for the text. You can draw text, or any shape, at any orientation as long as you set up the proper rotation transformation. This topic is discussed in the section "Coordinate Transformations," also later in this chapter.

DRAWIMAGE

The DrawImage method renders an image on the Graphics object, at a specified location. The DrawImage method is heavily overloaded and quite flexible. The following form of the method draws the image at its original magnification at the specified location. Both the image and the location of its top-left corner are passed to the method as arguments:

```
Graphics.DrawImage(img, point)
```

img is an Image object, and *point* is a Point object that specifies the location of the image's top-left corner on the drawing surface.

Another form of the method draws the specified image within the specified rectangle. If the rectangle doesn't match the original dimensions of the image, the image will be resized to fit in the rectangle. The rectangle should have the same aspect ratio as the Image object, so that the image won't be distorted in the process.

```
Graphics.DrawImage(img, rectangle)
```

Another form of the method allows you to change not only the magnification of the image, but its shape as well. This method accepts as argument not a rectangle, but an array of three points that specify a parallelogram. The image will be sheared to fit in the parallelogram.

```
Graphics.DrawImage(img, points())
```

where *points* is an array of points that define a parallelogram. The array holds three points, which are the top-left, top-right, and bottom-left corners of the parallelogram. The fourth point is determined uniquely by the other three, and you need not supply it.

The last important form of the method allows you to set the attributes of the image:

```
Graphics.DrawImage(image, points(), srcRect, units, attributes)
```

The first two arguments are the same as in the previous version of the method. The *srcRect* argument is a rectangle that specifies the portion of image to draw, and *units* is a constant of the GraphicsUnit enumeration. It determines how the units of the rectangle are measured (pixels, inches, and so on). The last argument is an ImageAttributes object that contains information about the attributes of the image you want to change (such attributes include the gamma value, and a transparent color value, or color key). The ImageAttributes object provides methods for setting image attributes, and they're discussed shortly.

The DrawImage method is quite flexible, and you can use it for many special effects, including wipes. A *wipe* is the gradual appearance of an image on a form or PictureBox control. You can use this method to draw stripes of the original image, or start with a small rectangle in the middle and enlarge it until the entire image is covered.

You can also correct the color of the image by specifying the *attributes* argument. To specify the *attributes* argument, create an ImageAttributes object, with a statement like the following:

```
Dim attr As New System.Drawing.Imaging.ImageAttributes
```

The ImageAttributes object provides the following methods.

SetWrapMode

Specifies the wrap mode that is used to decide how to tile a texture across a shape. This attribute is used with textured brushes, and I don't discuss it in this book.

SetGamma

This method sets the gamma value for the image's colors and accepts a Single value, which is the gamma value to be applied. A gamma value of 1 doesn't affect the colors of the image. A smaller value darkens the colors, while a larger value makes the image colors brighter. Notice that the gamma correction isn't the same as manipulating the brightness of the colors. The gamma correction takes into consideration the entire range of values in the image; it doesn't apply equally to all the colors. In effect, it takes into consideration both the brightness and the contrast and corrects them in tandem, with a fairly complicated algorithm. The syntax of the SetGamma method is:

```
ImageAttributes.SetGamma(gamma)
```

The following statements render the image stored in the *img* Image object on the *G* Graphics object, and they gamma-correct the image in the process by a factor of 1.25:

```
Dim attrs As New System.Drawing.Imaging.ImageAttributes()
attrs.SetGamma(1.25)
Dim dest As New Rectangle(0, 0, PictureBox1.Width, PictureBox1.Height)
G.DrawImage(img, dest, 0, 0, img.Width, img.Height, GraphicsUnit.Pixel, attrs)
```

SetOutputChannel

If you plan to create high-quality printouts of your images, you must separate them into four different channels. Each channel represents a different color, but these colors aren't red, green and blue. Typographers use four different basic colors, which are cyan, magenta, yellow, and black. The process of breaking an image into four channels is known as *color separation*, and you can separate your images with SetOutputChannel. Call this method four times, each time with a different channel. The syntax of the SetOutputChannel method is:

```
ImageAttributes.SetOutputChannel(colorChannel)
```

where the *colorChannel* argument can have one of the following values: `ColorChannelC` (cyan channel), `ColorChannelM` (magenta channel), `ColorChannelY` (yellow channel), `ColorChannelK` (black channel), and `ColorChannelLast` (the same channel as in the last time you called the method). The four channels produced by the SetOutputChannel method are monochrome (grayscale), and each one is printed with a different ink. All four channels, however, are printed on the same page, and the result is the original image's colors.

Gradients

In this section we'll look at the tools for creating gradients. The techniques for gradients can get quite complicated, but I will limit the discussion to the types of gradients you'll need for business or simple graphics applications.

LINEAR GRADIENTS

Let's start with linear gradients. Like all other gradients, they're part of the `System.Drawing` class and are implemented as brushes. To use a gradient, you must create the appropriate brush with the appropriate constructor. To draw a linear gradient, you must create a LinearGradientBrush with a statement like

```
Dim lgBrush As LinearGradientBrush
lgBrush = New LinearGradientBrush(rect, startColor, endColor, gradientMode)
```

To understand how to use the arguments, you must understand how the linear gradient works. This method creates a gradient that fills a rectangle, specified by the *rect* object passed as the first argument. This rectangle isn't filled with any gradient; it simply tells the method how long (or how tall) the gradient should be. The gradient starts with the *startColor* at the left side of the rectangle and ends with the *endColor* at the opposite side. The gradient changes color slowly as it moves from one end to the other. The last argument, *gradientMode*, specifies the direction of the gradient and can have one of the values shown in Table 14.6.

TABLE 14.6: THE GRADIENT'S MODE

VALUE	EFFECT
BackwardDiagonal	The gradient fills the rectangle diagonally, from the top-right corner (startColor) to the bottom-left corner (endColor).
ForwardDiagonal	The gradient fills the rectangle diagonally, from the top-left corner (startColor) to the bottom-right corner (endColor).
Horizontal	The gradient fills the rectangle from left (startColor) to right (endColor).
Vertical	The gradient fills the rectangle from top (startColor) to bottom (endColor).

Notice that in the descriptions of the various modes, I stated that the gradient fills the rectangle, not the shape. The gradient is calculated according to the dimensions of the rectangle specified with the first argument. If the actual shape is smaller than this rectangle, only a section of the gradient will be used to fill the shape. If the shape is larger than this rectangle, the gradient will repeat as many times as necessary to fill the shape.

Let's say you want to use the same gradient that extends 300 pixels horizontally to fill two rectangles, one that's 200 pixels wide and another one that's 600 pixels wide. We'll fill this shape with two similar LinearGradientBrushes that differ only in the size of the rectangle specified with the first argument. The first brush will use a rectangle 200 pixels wide, filled with two thirds of the gradient; the second will use a rectangle 600 pixels wide and be filled with a gradient that's repeated twice. The code in Listing 14.17 corresponds to the GDIPlusGradients projects on the CD.

LISTING 14.17: FILLING RECTANGLES WITH A LINEAR GRADIENT

```
Private Sub LinearGradient_Click(ByVal sender As System.Object, _
            ByVal e As System.EventArgs) Handles bttnLinearGradient.Click
    Dim G As Graphics
    G = Me.CreateGraphics
    Dim R As New RectangleF(20, 20, 300, 100)
    Dim startColor As Color = Color.BlueViolet
    Dim EndColor As Color = Color.LightYellow
    Dim LGBrush As New System.Drawing.Drawing2D.LinearGradientBrush _
                (R, startColor, EndColor, LinearGradientMode.Horizontal)
    G.FillRectangle(LGBrush, New Rectangle(20, 20, 200, 100))
    G.FillRectangle(LGBrush, New Rectangle(20, 150, 600, 100))
End Sub
```

For a horizontal gradient, only the width of the rectangle is used; the height is irrelevant. For a vertical gradient, only the height of the rectangle matters. When you draw a diagonal gradient, then both dimensions are taken into consideration.

You can also use a LinearGradientBrush to fill any shape, including closed polygons and closed curves. How does the brush handle irregular shapes? It doesn't, really. It fills, with the specified gradient, a rectangle that completely encloses the shape, and it shows only the pixels that fall within the shape. It's like building a larger gradient and looking at it through an irregularly shaped (nonrectangular) window.

You can create gradients at any direction by setting the *gradientMode* argument of the LinearGradientBrush object's constructor. The Diagonal Linear Gradient button on the GDIPlusGradients project does exactly that.

The button Gradient Text on the form of the GDIPlusGradients project on the CD renders some text with a linear gradient. As you recall from our discussion of the DrawString method, strings are rendered with a Brush object, not a Pen object. If you specify a LinearGradientBrush object, the text will be rendered with a linear gradient. The text shown in Figure 14.17 was produced by the Gradient Text button, whose code is shown in Listing 14.18.

FIGURE 14.17

Drawing a string
filled with a gradient

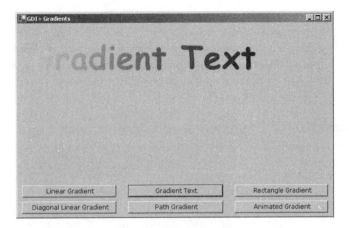

LISTING 14.18: RENDERING STRINGS WITH A LINEAR GRADIENT

```
Private Sub bttnGradientText_Click(ByVal sender As System.Object, _
            ByVal e As System.EventArgs) Handles bttnGradientText.Click
    Dim G As Graphics
    G = Me.CreateGraphics
    G.Clear (me.BackColor)
    G.TextRenderingHint = System.Drawing.Text.TextRenderingHint.AntiAlias
    Dim largeFont As New Font("Comic Sans MS", 48, _
                              FontStyle.Bold, GraphicsUnit.Point)
    Dim gradientStart As New PointF(0, 0)
    Dim txt As String = "Gradient Text"
    Dim txtSize As New SizeF()
    txtSize = G.MeasureString(txt, largeFont)
    Dim gradientEnd As New PointF()
    gradientEnd.X = txtSize.Width
    gradientEnd.Y = txtSize.Height
    Dim grBrush As New LinearGradientBrush(gradientStart, gradientEnd, _
                                       Color.Yellow, Color.Blue)
    G.DrawString(txt, largeFont, grBrush, 20, 20)
End Sub
```

The code of Listing 14.18 is a little longer than it could be (or than you might expect). Because linear gradients have a fixed size and don't expand or shrink to fill the shape, you must call the MeasureString method to calculate the width of the string and then create a linear gradient with the exact same width. This way, the characters will be filled exactly with the specified gradient.

PATH GRADIENTS

This is the ultimate gradient tool. Using a PathGradientBrush, you can create a gradient that starts at a single point and fades into multiple different colors in different directions. You can fill a rectangle starting from a point in the interior of the rectangle, which is colored, say, black. Each corner of the rectangle may have a different ending color. The PathGradientBrush will change color in the interior of the shape and will generate a gradient that's smooth in all directions. Figure 14.18 shows a rectangle filled with a path gradient, but the gray shades on the printed page won't show the full impact of the gradient. Open GDIPlusGradients project on the CD to see the same figure in color (button Path Gradient).

FIGURE 14.18

A path gradient starting at the middle of the rectangle

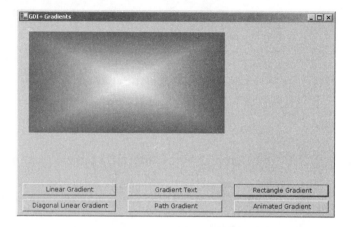

To fill a shape with a path gradient, you must first create a path object. The PathBrush will be created for the specific path and can be used to fill this path—but not any other shape. Actually, you can fill any other shape with the PathBrush created for a specific path, but the gradient won't fit the new shape. A path gradient must be applied only to the Path object for which it was created. To create a PathGradientBrush, use the following syntax:

```
Dim pgBrush As PathGradientBrush
pgBrush = New LinearGradientBrush(path)
```

where *path* is a properly initialized Path object.

The *pgBrush* object provides properties that determine the exact coloring of the gradient. First, you must specify color of the gradient at the center of the shape, using the CenterColor property. The SurroundColors property is an array, with as many elements as there are vertices (corners) in the Path object. Each element of the SurroundColors array must be set to a color value, and the resulting gradient will have the color of the equivalent element of the SurroundColors array.

The following declaration creates an array of three different colors and assigns them to the SurroundColors property of a PathGradientBrush:

```
Dim Colors() As Color = {Color.Yellow, Color.Green, Color.Blue}
pgBrush.SurroundColors = Colors
```

After setting the PathGradientBrush, you can fill the corresponding Path object by calling the FillPath method. The Path Gradient button on the form of GDIPlusGradient creates a rectangle filled with a gradient that's red in the middle of the rectangle and has a different color at each corner. Listing 14.19 shows the code behind the Path Gradient button.

```
Private Sub bttnPathGradient_Click(ByVal sender As System.Object, _
            ByVal e As System.EventArgs) Handles bttnPathGradient.Click
    Dim G As Graphics
    G = Me.CreateGraphics
    Dim path As New System.Drawing.Drawing2D.GraphicsPath()
    path.AddLine(New Point(10, 10), New Point(400, 10))
    path.AddLine(New Point(400, 10), New Point(400, 250))
    path.AddLine(New Point(400, 250), New Point(10, 250))
    Dim pathBrush As New System.Drawing.Drawing2D.PathGradientBrush(path)
    pathBrush.CenterColor = Color.Red
    Dim surroundColors() As Color = _
                        {Color.Yellow, Color.Green, Color.Blue, Color.Cyan}
    pathBrush.SurroundColors = surroundColors
    G.FillPath(pathBrush, path)
End Sub
```

The gradient's center point is, by default, the center of the shape. You can also specify the center of the gradient (the point that will be colored according to the CenterColor property). You can place the center point of the gradient anywhere by setting its CenterPoint property to a Point or PointF value.

The GDIPlusGradients application has a few more buttons that create interesting gradients, which you can examine on your own. The Rectangle Gradient button fills a rectangle with a gradient that has a single ending color all around. All the elements of the SurroundColors property are set to the same color. The Animated Gradient animates the same gradient by changing the coordinates of the PathGradientBrush object's CenterPoint property.

Clipping

Anyone who has used drawing or image-processing applications already knows that many of the tools of a similar application make use of *masks*. A mask is any shape that limits the area in which you can draw. If you want to place a star or heart on an image and print something in it, you create the shape in which you want to limit your drawing tools, then convert this shape into a mask. When you draw with the mask, you can start and end your strokes anywhere on the image. Your actions will have no effect outside the mask, however.

The mask of the various image-processing applications is a *clipping region*. A clipping region can be anything, as long as it's a closed shape. While the clipping region is activated, drawing takes place in the area of the clipping region. To specify a clipping area, you must call the SetClip method of the Graphics object. The SetClip method accepts the clipping area as argument, and the clipping area can be the Graphics object itself (no clipping), a Rectangle, a Path, or a Region.

NOTE *A Region is a structure made up of simple shapes. There many methods to create a Region object—you can combine and intersect shapes, or exclude shapes from a region—but we aren't going to discuss the Region object in this chapter, because it's not among the common objects we use to generate the type of graphics discussed in the context of this book.*

The SetClip method has the following forms:

```
Graphics.SetClip(Graphics)
Graphics.SetClip(Rectangle)
Graphics.SetClip(GraphicsPath)
Graphics.SetClip(Region)
```

All methods accept a second optional argument, which determines how the new clipping area will be combined with the existing one. The second argument is the *combineMode* argument, and its value can be one of the members of the CombineMode enumeration: Complement, Exclude, Intersect, Replace, Union, and XOR.

Once a clipping area has been set for the Graphics object, drawing is limited to that area. You can specify any coordinates, but only the part of the drawing that falls inside the clipping area is visible. The Clipping project demonstrates how to clip text and images within an elliptical area (see Figure 14.19). The button Boxed Text draws a string in a rectangle. The button Clipped Text draws the same text but first applies a clipping area. The clipping area is an ellipse. The Clipped Image button uses the same rectangle to clip an image. Since there's no form of the SetClip method that accepts an ellipse as argument, we must construct a Path object, add the ellipse to the path, and then create a clipping area based on the path.

FIGURE 14.19

Clipping text and images in an ellipse

The following statements create the clipping area for the text, which is an ellipse. The path is created by calling the AddEllipse method of the GraphicsPath object. This path is then passed as argument to the Graphics object's SetClip method:

```
Dim P As New System.Drawing.Drawing2D.GraphicsPath()
Dim clipRect As New RectangleF(30, 30, 250, 150)
P.AddEllipse(clipRect)
Dim G As Graphics
G = PictureBox1.CreateGraphics
G.SetClip(P)
```

The listing behind the Clipped Text and Clipped Image buttons is shown next. The first button prints some text in a rectangular area that is centered over the clipping area. The first button, Boxed Text, shows how the text is printed within the rectangle. The same rectangle and its text are then printed at a different location, right behind the clipping area. Both the rectangle and the ellipse are based on the same Rectangle object. Listing 14.20 shows the code behind the Boxed Text and the Clipped Text buttons.

LISTING 14.20: THE BOXED TEXT AND CLIPPED TEXT BUTTONS

```
Private Sub bttnBoxedText_Click(ByVal sender As System.Object, _
              ByVal e As System.EventArgs) Handles bttnBoxedText.Click
    Dim Rect As New RectangleF(30, 30, 250, 150)
    Dim G As Graphics
    G = PictureBox1.CreateGraphics
    Dim format As StringFormat = New StringFormat()
    format.Alignment = StringAlignment.Center
    G.DrawString(txt & txt, New Font("Verdana", 11, FontStyle.Regular), _
              Brushes.Coral, Rect, format)
End Sub
Private Sub bttnClippedText_Click(ByVal sender As System.Object, _
              ByVal e As System.EventArgs) Handles bttnClippedText.Click
    Dim P As New System.Drawing.Drawing2D.GraphicsPath()
    Dim clipRect As New RectangleF(30, 30, 250, 150)
    P.AddEllipse(clipRect)
    Dim G As Graphics
    G = PictureBox1.CreateGraphics
    G.DrawEllipse(Pens.Red, clipRect)
    G.SetClip(P)
    Dim format As StringFormat = New StringFormat()
    format.Alignment = StringAlignment.Center
    G.DrawString(txt & txt, New Font("Verdana", 11, FontStyle.Regular), _
              Brushes.Coral, clipRect, format)
End Sub
```

The difference between the two subroutines is that the second sets an ellipse as the clipping area and draws the same ellipse. Because the Graphics object has a clipping area, anything we draw on it is automatically clipped.

The Clipped Image button sets up a similar clipping area and then draws an image centered behind the clipping ellipse. As you saw in Figure 14.19, only the segment of the image that's inside the clipping area is visible. The code behind the Clipped Image button is shown in Listing 14.21.

LISTING 14.21: THE CLIPPED IMAGE BUTTON

```
Private Sub bttnClippedImage_Click(ByVal sender As System.Object, _
              ByVal e As System.EventArgs) Handles bttnClippedImage.Click
    Dim G As Graphics
    G = PictureBox1.CreateGraphics
    G.TranslateTransform(200, 200)
```

```
    Dim P As New System.Drawing.Drawing2D.GraphicsPath()
    Dim clipRect As New RectangleF(-150, -150, 320, 260)
    P.AddEllipse(clipRect)
    G.SetClip(P)
    Dim path As String
    path = Application.StartupPath.Remove(Application.StartupPath.Length - 4, 4)
    G.DrawImage(Image.FromFile(path & "\seattle.jpg"), -150, -150)
End Sub
```

Coordinate Transformations

So far, we've been specifying our coordinates in pixels. This is a convenient coordinate system for drawing simple shapes and experimenting with the various drawing methods, but in real applications you need a more familiar method of specifying coordinates. No physical object's dimensions are declared in pixels; we measure objects in inches, meters, or even miles. Other objects are measured in millionths of a centimeter. Since pixels are the natural units for displays, we must map the actual units to pixels. In this section, we'll look at techniques for mapping real-world coordinates to pixels.

The coordinate system is similar to a city map. Each square on the map has its own unique address: a combination of a column and a row number. The row number is the vertical coordinate, or y coordinate. The column number is the horizontal coordinate, or x coordinate. Any point on the form can be identified by its x and y coordinates, and we refer to it as the point at coordinates (x, y) or simply the point (x, y).

The point with the smallest coordinates is the *origin of the coordinate system.* The origin of a coordinate system is the point $(0, 0)$, and it's the top-left point of the Graphics object. The x coordinates increase to the right, and the y coordinates increase downward. Each coordinate is a number that may or may not correspond to a meaningful unit. For example, the letter and number coordinates on a city map don't correspond to meaningful units; they are arbitrary. The coordinates on a topological map, though, correspond to physical distances (e.g., kilometers or miles). The physical interpretation of the coordinates depends on the intended application.

If you want to draw a plan for your new house, you need to use a coordinate system in inches or centimeters so that there will be some relation between units and the objects you draw. If you're going to draw some nice geometrical shapes, any coordinate system will do. Finally, if you're going to display and process images, you'll want a coordinate system that uses pixels as units. Actually, pixels aren't the best units for any application, except for image-processing applications.

GDI+ lets you define your own coordinate system. All you have to do is set the PageUnit property to the appropriate constant. If you set PageUnit property to Inches, the dimensions of your shapes, as well as their locations on the Graphics object, must be specified in inches. In this case, two points that are one unit apart are one inch from each other. You can also specify decimal distances such as 0.1, which corresponds to $1/10$ of an inch. Changing the PageUnit property doesn't resize or otherwise affect the form or the printer's page. It simply changes the density of the grid you use to address the points on the control. The benefit of using the PageUnit property is that you don't have to map your coordinates to pixels on the monitor or to dots on the printed page. GDI+ knows how many pixels are in an inch on the monitor, and it will scale the coordinates accordingly. A statement that draws a rectangle one inch tall and three inches wide will produce the correct shape on any monitor or printer, regardless of its resolution.

If you want to know the density of the pixels on the current monitor, read the DpiX and DpiY properties of the Graphics object. These properties return the pixels per inch in *x* and *y* directions of the monitor. If the Graphics object is the printer's page, they will return the dots per inch for the specific printer. These properties are determined by the device's capabilities and are read-only.

The PageUnit property affects all the entities drawn on the control, even the width of the Pen. A Pen with a width of 1 will draw lines one inch wide. To specify pen widths in pixels, use the inverse of the property DpiX, which is one pixel. To specify a 2-pixel-wide pen, use a statement like this one:

```
Dim myPen = New Pen(Color.Black, 2 * (1 / Graphics.DpiX))
```

Using coordinates that correspond to physical units of length—such as inches, points, and millimeters—is straightforward. The most interesting, and flexible, coordinate system is one that suits your needs—in other words, a *custom coordinate system*. A custom coordinate system is dictated by the application and can be anything, from a fraction of a millimeter, to a mile, or a light year. Custom coordinate systems need not correspond to length units. When you plot the number of users hitting your site each hour, you need a coordinate system to represent the hour of the day along the *x* axis and the number of visitors (or the number of hits, or any other quantity you care to measure) along the *y* axis. This coordinate system goes from 1 to 24 along the horizontal axis and from 0 to a large value like 100, or 10,000, in the vertical axis. Another chart might involve month numbers and units sold. If you want to draw the trajectory of the earth around the sun, and the sun is a circle at the middle of the drawing surface, the coordinates along the two axes must go from a very large negative value to a very large positive value.

To summarize, your starting point is a coordinate system that represents the physical dimensions of the entity you want to plot on the form. This is the *world coordinate system*. The dimensions of the form are also known: they're the form's Width and Height properties. This is the *page coordinate system*. The world coordinates must be mapped onto page coordinates, and this mapping is known as a *transformation*.

Specifying Transformations

In computer graphics, there are three types of transformations: scaling, translation, and rotation. The scaling transformation changes the dimensions of a shape but not its form. If you scale an ellipse by 0.5, you'll get another ellipse that's half as wide and half as tall as the original one. The translation transformation moves a shape by a specified distance. If you translate a rectangle by 30 pixels along the *x* axis and 90 pixels along the *y* axis, the new origin will be 30 pixels the right and 90 pixels down from the original rectangle's top-left corner. The rotation transformation rotates a shape by a specified angle, expressed in degrees. 360 degrees correspond to a full rotation. and the shape appears the same. A rotation by 180 degrees is equivalent to flipping the shape vertically and horizontally.

Transformations are stored in a 5×5 matrix, but you need not set it up yourself. The Graphic object provides the ScaleTransform, TranslateTransform, and RotateTransform methods, and you can specify the transformation to be applied to the shape by calling one or more of these methods and passing the appropriate argument(s). The ScaleTransform accepts as arguments scaling factors for the horizontal and vertical directions:

```
Graphics.ScaleTransformation(Sx, Sy)
```

If an argument is smaller than one, the shape will be reduced in the corresponding direction; if it's larger than one, the shape will be enlarged in the corresponding direction. We usually scale both directions by the same factor to retain the shape's aspect ratio. If you scale a circle by different factors in the two dimensions, the result will be an ellipse, and not a smaller or larger circle.

The TranslateTransform method accepts two arguments, which are the displacements along the horizontal and vertical directions:

```
Graphics.TranslateTransform(Tx, Ty)
```

The Tx and Ty arguments are expressed in the coordinates of the current coordinate system. The shape is moved to the right by Tx units and down by Ty units. If one of the arguments is negative, the shape is moved in the opposite direction (to the left or up).

The RotateTransform method accepts a single argument, which is the angle of rotation, and it's expressed in degrees:

```
Graphics.RotateTransform(rotation)
```

If the *rotation* argument is 360, the shape is rotated a full circle—no change at all. The rotation takes place about the origin. As you will see, the final position and orientation of a shape is different if two identical rotation and translation transformations are applied in different order.

Every time you call one of these methods, the elements of the transformation matrix are set accordingly. All transformations are stored in this matrix, and they have a cumulative effect. If you specify two translation transformations, for example, the shape will be translated by the sum of the corresponding arguments in either direction. The following two transformations:

```
Graphics.TranslateTransform(10, 40)
Graphics.TranslateTransform(20, 20)
```

are equivalent to the following one:

```
Graphics.TranslateTransform(30, 60)
```

To start a new transformation after drawing some shapes on the Graphics object, call the Reset-Transform method, which clears the transformation matrix.

The effect of multiple transformations may be cumulative, but the order in which transformations are performed makes a big difference. The GDIPlusTransformations project allows you to experiment with the various transformations. The shape being transformed is a rectangle that contains a string and a small bitmap, as shown in Figure 14.20. Each button on the right performs a different transformation or combination of transformations. The code is quite short, and you can easily add additional transformations, or change their order, and see how the shape is transformed. Keep in mind that some transformations may bring the shape entirely outside the form. In this case, just apply a translation transformation in the opposite direction.

The code behind the buttons Translate, Rotate, and Scale is shown in Listing 14.22. The buttons set the appropriate transformations and then call the DrawShape() subroutine, passing the current Graphic object as argument:

FIGURE 14.20

The GDIPlusTrans-
formations project

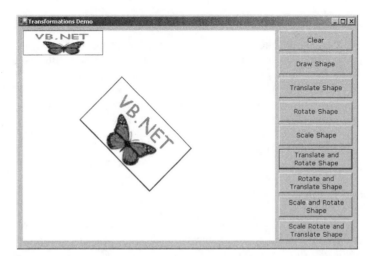

```
Private Sub bttnTranslate_Click(ByVal sender As System.Object, _
            ByVal e As System.EventArgs) Handles bttnTranslate.Click
    Dim G As Graphics = PictureBox1.CreateGraphics
    G.TranslateTransform(200, 90)
    DrawShape(G)
End Sub
Private Sub bttnRotate_Click(ByVal sender As System.Object, _
            ByVal e As System.EventArgs) Handles bttnRotate.Click
    Dim G As Graphics = PictureBox1.CreateGraphics
    G.RotateTransform(45)
    DrawShape(G)
End Sub
Private Sub bttnTranslateRotate_Click(ByVal sender As System.Object,_
            ByVal e As System.EventArgs) Handles bttnTranslateRotate.Click
    Dim G As Graphics = PictureBox1.CreateGraphics
    G.TranslateTransform(200, 90)
    G.RotateTransform(45)
    DrawShape(G)
End Sub
```

The DrawShape() subroutine, which draws the rectangle, the string, and the bitmap, is called by all the buttons after setting up the appropriate transformation(s). Listing 14.23 shows the Draw-Shape() subroutine.

LISTING 14.23: THE DRAWSHAPE() SUBROUTINE

```
Sub DrawShape(ByVal GraphicObject As Graphics)
    Dim Font As Font = New Font("Comic Sans MS", 36, FontStyle.Bold, _
                                GraphicsUnit.Pixel)
    Dim Pen As Pen = New Pen(Color.Red, 2)
    GraphicObject.DrawRectangle(Pen, New Rectangle(1, 1, 200, 120))
    GraphicObject.DrawRectangle(Pen, New Rectangle(1, 1, 200, 120))
    GraphicObject.DrawString("VB.NET", Font, Brushes.Violet, 25, 5)
    GraphicObject.DrawImage(Image.FromFile(Application.StartupPath & _
                            "\Butterfly.jpg"), New PointF(50, 50))
End Sub
```

The reason we pass the Graphics object as argument to the DrawShape() subroutine (as opposed to creating the appropriate Graphics object in the subroutine's code) is because the transformations we defined earlier apply to this object. By passing the *G* argument to the DrawShape() subroutine, we're actually passing all the transformations applied to the Graphics object. The shapes drawn on the Graphics objects by the code in the DrawShape() subroutine will undergo the specified transformation.

Run the GDIPlusTransformations project and examine its code. You can add more buttons with your own transformations to the form, or change the parameters of the various transformations. Notice how the order of the various transformations affects the placement, orientation, and size of the final image.

In the following section, we'll look at an interesting example of the DrawImage method combined with coordinate transformations. The example you'll build in the following section will render a cube with different images plastered on each side of the cube. Later in this chapter we'll use transformations to plot a function, in an interesting and practical application. Even if you're not interested in graphics or math, you should understand how to use the basic transformations, because in the following chapter we'll use them to create printouts.

VB.NET AT WORK: THE IMAGECUBE PROJECT

As you recall, the DrawImage method can render images on any parallelogram, not just a rectangle, with the necessary distortion. A way to look at these images is not as distorted, but as *perspective* images. Looking at a printout from an unusual angle is equivalent to rendering an image within a parallelogram. Imagine a cube with a different image glued on each side. To display such a cube on your monitor, you must calculate the coordinates of the cube's edges and then use these coordinates to define the parallelograms on which each image will be displayed. Figure 14.21 shows a cube with a different image on each side.

If you're good at math, you can rotate a cube around its vertical and horizontal axes and then map the rotated cube on the drawing surface. You can even apply a perspective transformation, which will make the image look more like the rendering of a three-dimensional cube. This is more involved than the topics discussed in this book; actually, it's a good topic for a book on 3D graphics, but not for a general programming book. Instead of doing all the calculations, I've come up with a set of coordinates for the parallelogram that represents each vertex (corner) of the cube. For a different orientation, you can draw a perspective view of a cube on paper and measure the coordinates of its vertices. Once you can define the parallelogram that corresponds to each visible side, you can draw an image with the DrawImage method on each parallelogram. The DrawImage method will shear the image as necessary to fill the specified area. The result is the representation of a cube covered with images on the flat surface of your monitor.

FIGURE 14.21

This cube was created with a call to the DrawImage method for each visible side.

The ImageCube project on the CD does exactly that. It sets up the coordinates of the vertices of a cube projected onto a two-dimensional drawing surface. Then, it calls the DrawImage method once for each side of the cube, passing as arguments the image to be rendered on the corresponding side of the cube and an array with the coordinates of the three out of the four corners of the side.

The code that produced Figure 14.21 starts by setting up the coordinates of each side. Notice that we only need the coordinates of three points to identify each parallelogram, and the arrays *face1*, *face2*, and *face3* correspond to the three visible faces of the cube. Each of these arrays contains three elements, all of the Point type, which are the coordinates of the three vertices of the corresponding side of the cube. Then the DrawImage method is called for each face, with the appropriate coordinates and a different image. The complete listing behind the Draw Cube button is shown in Listing 14.24. I'm using the random-number generator to randomly assign images to each of the cube's side, so that each time you click the Draw Cube button, a new cube is drawn. To keep the code simple, I'm not checking each random number to make sure a different image is mapped to each side of the cube, but you can add the necessary logic to avoid reusing the same image for more than one side.

LISTING 14.24: RENDERING THE IMAGECUBE

```
Private Sub bttnDrawCube_Click(ByVal sender As System.Object, _
            ByVal e As System.EventArgs) Handles bttnDrawCube.Click
    Dim G As Graphics
    G = GetGraphicsObject()
```

```
        G.Clear(Color.SandyBrown)
        G.TranslateTransform(250, 200)

        Dim images(2) As Image
        Dim path As String
        path = Application.StartupPath.Remove(Application.StartupPath.Length - 4, 4)
        images(0) = Image.FromFile(path & "\image1.jpg")
        images(1) = Image.FromFile(path & "\image2.jpg")
        images(2) = Image.FromFile(path & "\image3.jpg")

        Dim face1(2) As Point
        face1(0) = New Point(-150, -20)
        face1(1) = New Point(150, -20)
        face1(2) = New Point(-150, 230)

        Dim face2(2) As Point
        face2(0) = New Point(-30, -140)
        face2(1) = New Point(270, -140)
        face2(2) = New Point(-150, -20)

        Dim face3(2) As Point
        face3(0) = New Point(150, -20)
        face3(1) = New Point(270, -140)
        face3(2) = New Point(150, 230)
        Dim imgIndex As Integer
        Dim rnd As New System.Random()
        imgIndex = rnd.Next(0, 3)
        G.DrawImage(images(imgIndex), face1)
        imgIndex = rnd.Next(0, 3)
        G.DrawImage(images(imgIndex), face2)
        imgIndex = rnd.Next(0, 3)
        G.DrawImage(images(imgIndex), face3)
    End Sub
```

The GetGraphicsObject() function retrieves a Graphics object from the PictureBox control's bitmap, and its code was shown earlier in Listing 14.8. This is necessary if you want to draw persistently, instead of having to redraw the cube from within the OnPaint event. If you want to use the OnPaint method, you must also store the images (or the random numbers that correspond to the three images) in global variables; otherwise every time the OnPaint event handler is executed, a new cube will be displayed.

Notice that the cube is (approximately) centered at the origin of the form, so I've introduced a translation transformation to push the cube toward the middle of the form. You can add a rotation transformation too, but you may have to modify the translation transformation, should the image end up partially outside the form.

VB.NET at Work: Plotting Functions

Many programmers will use graphics to plot functions or user-supplied data sets. A *plot* is a visual representation of the values of a function over a range of an independent variable. Figure 14.22 shows the following function plotted against time in the range from –0.5 to 5:

```
10 + 35 * Sin(2 * X) * Sin(0.80 / X)
```

FIGURE 14.22

Plotting math functions with VB.NET

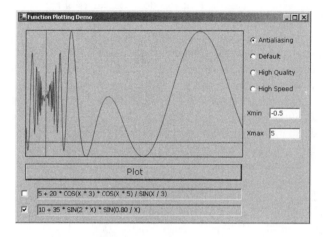

The plot of Figure 14.22 was created with the Plotting project, which is described in this section. The variable *x* represents time and goes from –0.5 to 5. The time is mapped to the horizontal axis, and the vertical axis is the magnitude of the function. For each pixel along the horizontal axis, we calculate the value of the function and turn on the pixel that corresponds to the calculated value.

Functions can be plotted in very small, or quite large, ranges. The same is true for their values. One function may extend from –2 to –1, while another function may extend from 0 to 10,000. Obviously, we can't use pixels as our units because most plots will not even fall in the range covered by the pixels of the bitmap. Somehow, we must map the function values to pixels and scale them, so that the function we're plotting fills the available area. This mapping takes place through two transformations: a scaling transformation and a translation transformation.

A scaling transformation changes the size of a shape or curve. If the curve extends vertically from –1 to 5 and the area on which you're plotting goes from 0 to 399 pixels, you must scale the plot up so that it fills the available area. If the curve extends from –1,000 to 500 vertically, you must also scale it to fill the available area, only this time you must reduce the size of the plot. In the first example, you must fit 6 units along the *x* axis to 400 units. The scaling factor is 400 / 6, or 67 approximately. If the function extends vertically from 1 to 3 and the control's drawing surface's height is 250 pixels, the scaling factor along the vertical axis is 250 / 2, or 125.

The scaling will make the area of the plot equal to the drawing area. But the plot may not fall in the range of pixels on the control. If you're plotting the function in the range from –10 to 0, the curve falls to the left of the drawing surface. The proper translation transformation must push all values to the right so that the smallest value (–10) corresponds to the leftmost pixel on the control and the largest value corresponds to the rightmost pixels on the control. Likewise, you must translate the plot vertically to bring it within the control's visible area.

GDI+ allows you to define global transformations, which apply to all drawing actions. The global transformations apply to all graphics objects, including the pen you're drawing with, so you can't use them to map the function values onto pixels. Another type of transformation applies to individual shapes, and this is what we want. We want to transform the curve, but not the pen we draw with.

To plot a function on a PictureBox, you can either color individual pixels, or draw line segments between consecutive points of the function. In this example, we'll use a path to represent the plot of a function. We'll calculate the function along the values of the independent variable, and we'll form a point defined by its two coordinates, x and y. x is the value of the independent variable and y is the function's value at this point. Once we have the path, we'll apply a transformation to the entire path and render it with a Pen object on the drawing surface.

One advantage of this approach is that you can store the Path object that represents the plot to a global variable and reuse it to redraw the plot, or even apply a new transformation and plot the function at a different scale or location. If you discard the path after rendering it, you must recalculate all the points of the function along the x axis. The sample project doesn't reuse the path, but you may have to do so in your applications.

The quantity represented on the horizontal axis is the independent variable. You can select any range to plot by setting a minimum and a maximum value for the x variable. The function must be evaluated along the horizontal axis, and it's determined by the current value of the independent variable. When you're plotting a function like sin(x)*cos(x), you must evaluate the function for each point in the range of values of the independent variable x. You may choose to plot the function in the range from −1 to 1, or in the range from −1,000 to 1,000.

Depending on the range of the independent variable, the function's range may also change. In the range −1 to 1, the function may extend from −0.5 to 2.5, but in a different range, it may extend over a much larger range of values. The range of values of the function determines the units along the y axis. The vertical size of the plot doesn't change; it's the height of the control on which you're drawing. However, you must map the physical values of the function you're plotting to pixel coordinates.

Let me explain how the code of the Plotting application sets up the appropriate transformation. The function's plot extends over a user-specified area in the horizontal direction (from −0.5 to 5 in our case) and over a different range in the vertical axis. The vertical range is calculated by the program—unless you want to specify the vertical range as well. First, we must scale the plot so that the range from −0.5 to 5 is mapped to the width of the PictureBox. The function is plotted over a range of 5.5 units horizontally, and they must be mapped to `Picture1.Width` pixels. The function must be scaled horizontally by the factor `Picture1.Width/5.5`. The vertical scaling factor is calculated in a similar manner. You must first iterate through all the function values you're going to plot and find out the smallest and largest values. Let's say the function extends vertically from −4 to 20. The vertical scaling factor is `Picture1.Height/24`.

The origin of the drawing area is at the top-left corner of the form or control. The origin of the plot, the point (0, 0), is at a different location, so we must translate the drawing. The physical coordinate −0.5 must be mapped to a pixel with a x coordinate 0. The translation transformation along the horizontal axis is the negative of the smallest x value. In our example, it is −(−0.5), or 0.5.

Let's see how the two transformations are combined. The first endpoint's x coordinate is −0.5. I will assume that the width of the PictureBox is 500 pixels. The first point must be translated horizontally by 0.5 and then scaled horizontally by 500 / 5.5:

```
(-0.5 + 0.5) * 500 / 5.5 = 0
```

So the first endpoint's *x* coordinate is 0. The last point's *x* coordinate is:

```
(5 + 0.5) * 500 / 5.5 = 500
```

The middle physical coordinate along the horizontal axis is 2.25, and it will be mapped to the following pixel coordinate:

```
(2.25 + 0.5) * 500 / 5.5 = 250
```

which is the middle point of the horizontal axis. The exact same calculation will be performed for the vertical axis. The translation and scaling transformations map the box that encloses the function to the corners of the PictureBox control.

NOTE   *As you may have noticed, the translation transformation is applied first, and then the scaling transformation. If you reverse the order of the transformations, the result won't be the same. If you first scale the coordinate 1 and then translate it, it will end up at the following* x *coordinate: 1 × 500 / 5.5 + 0.5 = 91.5, which isn't the coordinate of the middle point along the* x *axis.*

To specify the transformations we want to perform on each point, we set up a transformation matrix, the World transformation matrix:

```
World = New System.Drawing.Drawing2D.Matrix()
```

Then, we apply the two transformations:

```
World.Scale(((PictureBox1.Width - 4) / (Xmax - Xmin)), _
            -(PictureBox1.Height - 4) / (Ymax - Ymin))
World.Translate(-Xmin, -Ymax)
```

(We subtract 4 pixels from the control's dimensions to make up for the PictureBox control's border and leave a tiny margin between the extremes of the plot and the border.) At this point, the World transformation contains the definitions of the required transformations, and it will apply them to each point drawn on the Graphics object.

Now that you have seen how the function's points are mapped to pixels, let's look at the actual code. First, we calculate the range of *y* values in the specified range of *x* values. Since we can't address sub-pixels, it makes no sense to calculate the function value at more points than there are pixels along the *x* axis; so the value is calculated at as many points as there are pixels. This is done in a loop, and we keep track of the minimum and maximum values. The same calculations must be repeated for all the functions to be plotted and then we keep the minimum and maximum value over all functions. These values are stored in *YMin* and *YMax* variables, and they're used later in the code to set up the appropriate transformation. If the function returns a nonnumeric value (a value like NaN or Infinity), the program aborts.

Then, the program sets up the scaling and translation transformations as explained already. The transformations are stored in the World matrix, which is then used to apply them to a Path object.

In the last section, the code builds a path for the function to be plotted by adding line segments that connect the last point to the current one. The last step is to draw the path, when it's complete. Before drawing the path, we apply the World transformation to it, so that the world coordinates will be mapped correctly to pixel coordinates:

```
plot1.Transform(World)
G.DrawPath(plotPen, plot1)
```

where *plot1* is the name of the Path object that contains the points to be plotted. Listing 14.25 is the complete code of the Plot() subroutine, which is called from within the Plot button's Click event handler.

```
Private Sub plot()
    If Not (CheckBox1.Checked Or CheckBox2.Checked) Then Exit Sub
    Dim G As Graphics
    G = PictureBox1.CreateGraphics
    G.Clear(PictureBox1.BackColor)

    Dim t As Double
    Dim Xmin, Xmax As Single
    Dim Ymax, Ymin As Single
    Ymin = System.Single.MaxValue
    Ymax = -System.Single.MaxValue
    Xmin = txtXMin.Text
    Xmax = txtXMax.Text
    Dim val As Single
    Dim XPixels As Integer = PictureBox1.Width - 1

    For t = Xmin To Xmax Step (Xmax - Xmin) / (PictureBox1.Width - 2)
        If CheckBox1.Checked Then
            val = Function1Eval(t)
            If System.Double.IsInfinity(val) Or _
                        System.Double.IsNaN(val) Then
                MsgBox("Can't plot this function in " & _
                    "the specified range!")
                Exit Sub
            End If
            Ymax = Math.Max(val, Ymax)
            Ymin = Math.Min(val, Ymin)
        End If
        If CheckBox2.Checked Then
            val = Function2Eval(t)
            If System.Double.IsInfinity(val) Or _
                        System.Double.IsNaN(val) Then
                MsgBox("Can't plot this function in " & _
                    "the specified range!")
                Exit Sub
            End If
            Ymax = Math.Max(val, Ymax)
            Ymin = Math.Min(val, Ymin)
        End If
    Next
    World = New System.Drawing.Drawing2D.Matrix()
```

```
World.Scale(((PictureBox1.Width - 2) / (Xmax - Xmin)), - _
            (PictureBox1.Height - 2) / (Ymax - Ymin))
World.Translate(-Xmin, -Ymax)
' the following paths correspond to the two axes
Dim Xaxis As New System.Drawing.Drawing2D.GraphicsPath()
Dim Yaxis As New System.Drawing.Drawing2D.GraphicsPath()
Xaxis.AddLine(New PointF(Xmin, 0), New PointF(Xmax, 0))
Yaxis.AddLine(New PointF(0, Ymax), New PointF(0, Ymin))
Dim oldX, oldY As Single
Dim X, Y As Single
' Each segment in the path goes from (oldX, oldY) to (X, y)
' At each iteration (X, Y) becomes (oldX, oldY) for the next point
' the following two paths correspond to the functions to be plotted
Dim plot1 As New System.Drawing.Drawing2D.GraphicsPath()
Dim plot2 As New System.Drawing.Drawing2D.GraphicsPath()
Dim plotPen As Pen = New Pen(Color.BlueViolet, 1)
' Calculate the min and max points of the plot
If CheckBox1.Checked Then
    oldX = Xmin
    oldY = Function1Eval(Xmin)
    For t = Xmin To Xmax Step (Xmax - Xmin) / _
                            (PictureBox1.Width - 1)
        X = t
        Y = Function1Eval(t)
        plot1.AddLine(oldX, oldY, X, Y)
        oldX = X
        oldY = Y
    Next
End If
If CheckBox2.Checked Then
    oldX = Xmin
    oldY = Function2Eval(Xmin)
    For t = Xmin To Xmax Step (Xmax - Xmin) / _
                            (PictureBox1.Width - 1)
        X = t
        Y = Function2Eval(t)
        plot2.AddLine(oldX, oldY, X, Y)
        oldX = X
        oldY = Y
    Next
End If
' create the plot1 and plot2 paths
G.Clear(PictureBox1.BackColor)
If RadioButton1.Checked Then SmoothingMode = _
            Drawing.Drawing2D.SmoothingMode.AntiAlias
If RadioButton2.Checked Then SmoothingMode = _
            Drawing.Drawing2D.SmoothingMode.Default
If RadioButton3.Checked Then SmoothingMode = _
```

```
                        Drawing.Drawing2D.SmoothingMode.HighQuality
        If RadioButton4.Checked Then SmoothingMode = _
                        Drawing.Drawing2D.SmoothingMode.HighSpeed
        G.SmoothingMode = SmoothingMode
        ' and finally draw everything
        Xaxis.Transform(World)
        plotPen.Color = Color.Red
        G.DrawPath(plotPen, Xaxis)          ' The X axis
        Yaxis.Transform(World)
        plotPen.Color = Color.Red
        G.DrawPath(plotPen, Yaxis)          ' The Y axis
        If CheckBox1.Checked Then
            plotPen.Color = Color.DarkMagenta
            plot1.Transform(World)       ' The first function
            G.DrawPath(plotPen, plot1)
        End If
        If CheckBox2.Checked Then
            plotPen.Color = Color.DarkGreen
            plot2.Transform(World)
            G.DrawPath(plotPen, plot2)   ' The second function
        End If
    End Sub
```

Notice that the Plot() subroutine draws on the Graphics object returned by the CreateGraphics method of the PictureBox control. You can click the Plot button to redraw the function(s) at any time. You can draw the function on the control's bitmap and not have to worry about redrawing the function when the form is covered by another form. You should also call the Plot() subroutine from within the form's Resize event to redraw the function when the form is resized, because the Picture-Box control is anchored on all four sides of the form.

The functions Function1Eval() and Function2Eval() calculate the value of each function for any value of the independent variable, and their implementation is shown here:

```
Function Function1Eval(ByVal X As Double) As Double
    Function1Eval = 5 + 20 * Cos(X * 3) * Cos(X * 5) / Sin(X / 3)
End Function
Function Function2Eval(ByVal X As Double) As Double
    Function2Eval = 10 + 35 * Sin(2 * X) * Sin(0.80 / X)
End Function
```

The FunctionPlot application plots always the same two functions. You can specify a different range, but this doesn't make the application any more flexible. Allowing users to specify their own functions to plot isn't trivial, unless you use the Script ActiveX control. This control can evaluate any expression written in VBScript (a variation of VB), and you can bring this functionality in your application by adding an instance of the Script control to your form.

To add an instance of the Script control to your project, select Project ➤ Add Reference. When the Add Reference dialog box appears, click the COM tab and locate the item Microsoft Script

Control 1.0. If the control isn't there, you must download from `http://msdn.microsoft.com/scripting` and install it on your computer. Once installed, it will appear in the Add Reference dialog box and you can add it to your project.

Using the Script control to evaluate a function is quite simple. All you have to do to evaluate a function for a value of its independent variable is to execute a script like the following:

```
X = 0.04
Y = 5 + 20 * Cos(X * 3) * Cos(X * 5) / Log(Abs(Sin(X)) / 10)
```

You can execute these statements with the help of the Script control and retrieve the value of the function for the specified value of the X variable. Revise the Function1Eval() and Function2Eval() functions as shown in Listing 14.26.

LISTING 14.26: EVALUATING ARBITRARY MATH EXPRESSIONS AT RUNTIME

```
Function Function1Eval(ByVal X As Double) As Double
   Try
      AxScriptControl1.ExecuteStatement("X=" & X)
      Function1Eval = AxScriptControl1.Eval(txtFunction1.Text)
   Catch exc As Exception
      Throw New Exception("Can't evaluate function at X=" & X)
   End Try
End Function
Function Function2Eval(ByVal X As Double) As Double
   Try
      AxScriptControl1.ExecuteStatement("X=" & X)
      Function2Eval = AxScriptControl1.Eval(txtFunction2.Text)
   Catch exc As Exception
      Throw New Exception("Can't evaluate function at X=" & X)
   End Try
End Function
```

If an error occurs in the script (division by zero, an attempt to calculate the logarithm of a negative value, and so on), a custom exception is raised. This exception must be caught by the Plot() subroutine and abort the plotting of the function.

The revised function is called FunctionPlotting, and you will find it in this chapter's folder on the CD. The only difference is how the function is evaluated at each point along the *x* axis and how the program handles math errors. The Script control is an old one and can't handle values like NaN and Infinity.

Bitmaps

The type of graphics we explored so far are called *vector graphics*, because they can be scaled to any extent. Since they're based on mathematical equations, you can draw any details of the picture without losing any accuracy. Vector graphics, however, can't be used to describe the type of images you capture with your digital camera. These images belong to a different category of graphics, the *bitmap graphics*. A bitmap is a collection of colored pixels, arranged in rows and columns.

So, what's the difference between a Bitmap object and an Image object? The Image object is static. It provides properties that retrieve the attributes of the image stored in the object, but you can't edit the image's pixels. The Bitmap object, on the other hand, provides methods that allow you to read and set its pixels. In the last section of this chapter, you're going to build an image-processing application. But first, let's look at the information stored in a Bitmap or Image object. Both bitmaps and image are made up of color values (the color of each pixel), so it's time to look at how GDI+ stores and handles colors in detail.

Specifying Colors

You're already familiar with the Color common dialog box, which lets you specify colors by manipulating their basic components. If you attempt to specify a Color value through the common dialog box, you'll see three boxes—Red, Green, and Blue (RGB)—whose values change as you move the cross-shaped pointer over the color spectrum. These are the values of the three basic colors that computers use to specify colors. Any color that can be represented on a computer monitor is specified by means of the RGB colors. By mixing percentages of these basic colors, you can design almost any color.

The model of designing colors based on the intensities of their RGB components is called the *RGB model*, and it's a fundamental concept in computer graphics. If you aren't familiar with this model, this section is well worth reading. Every color you can imagine can be constructed by mixing the appropriate percentages of the three basic colors. Each color, therefore, is represented by a triplet in which red, green, and blue are three bytes that represent the basic color components. The smallest value, 0, indicates the absence of color. The largest value, 255, indicates full intensity, or saturation. The triplet (0, 0, 0) is black, because all colors are missing, and the triplet (255, 255, 255) is white. Other colors have various combinations: (255, 0, 0) is a pure red, (0, 255, 255) is a pure cyan (what you get when you mix green and blue), and (0, 128, 128) is a mid-cyan (a mix of mid-green and mid-blue tones). The possible combinations of the three basic color components are $256 \times 256 \times 256$, or 16,777,216 colors.

NOTE *Each color you can display on a computer monitor can be defined in terms of three basic components: red, green, and blue.*

Notice that we use the term *basic colors* and not *primary colors*, which are the three colors used in designing colors with paint. The concept is the same; you mix the primary colors until you get the desired result. The primary colors used in painting, however, are different. They are the colors red, yellow, and blue. Painters can get any shade imaginable by mixing the appropriate percentages of red, yellow, and blue paint. On a computer monitor, you can design any color by mixing the appropriate percentages of red, green, and blue.

NOTE *Just as painters don't work with three colors only, you're not limited to the three basic colors. The Color object exposes the names of 128 colors, and you can specify colors by name.*

The process of generating colors with three basic components is based on the RGB color cube, shown in Figure 14.23. The three dimensions of the color cube correspond to the three basic colors.

The cube's corners are assigned each of the three primary colors, their complements, and the colors black and white. Complementary colors are easily calculated by subtracting the Color values from 255. For example, the color (0, 0, 255) is a pure blue tone. Its complementary color is (255 – 0, 255 – 0, 255 – 255), or (255, 255, 0), which is a pure yellow tone. Blue and yellow are complementary colors, and they are mapped to opposite corners of the cube. The same is true for red and cyan, green and magenta, and black and white. If you add a color to its complement, you get white.

FIGURE 14.23

Color specification of the RGB color cube

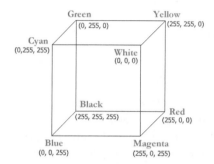

Notice that the components of the colors at the corners of the cube have either zero or full intensity. As you move from one corner to another along the same edge of the cube, only one of its components changes value. For example, as you move from the green to the yellow corner, the red component changes from 0 to 255. The other two components remain the same. As you move between these two corners, you get all the available tones from green to yellow (256 in all). Similarly, as you move from the yellow to the red corner, the only component that changes is the green, and you get all the available shades from yellow to red. As you can guess, this is how GDI+ calculates the gradients: it draw a (imaginary) line between the two points that represent the starting and ending colors of the gradient and picks the colors along this line.

Although you can specify a little more than 16 million colors, you can't have more than 256 shades of gray. The reason is that a gray tone, including the two extremes (black and white), is made up of equal values of all three primary colors. You can see this on the RGB cube. Gray shades lie on the cube's diagonal that goes from black to white. As you move along this path, all three basic components change value, but they are always equal. The value (128, 128, 128) is a mid-gray tone, but the values (127, 128, 128) and (129, 128, 128) aren't gray tones, although they are too close for the human eye to distinguish. That's why it's wasteful to store grayscale pictures using a 3-bytes-per-pixel format. A 256-color file format stores a grayscale just as accurately and more compactly. Once you know an image is grayscale, you needn't store all three bytes per pixel—one value is adequate (the other two components have the same value).

Defining Colors

For defining colors, the Color object provides the FromARGB method, which accepts three arguments:

```
Color.FromARGB(Red, Green, Blue)
```

The FromARGB method can produce any color imaginable. I mentioned earlier that the triplet (255, 255, 0) is a pure yellow tone. To specify this Color value with the FromARGB method, you can use a statement such as

```
newColor = Color.FromARGB(255, 255, 0)
```

The *newColor* variable is a Color value, and you can use it anywhere you could use a color value. To change the form's background color to yellow, you can assign the *newColor* variable to the BackColor property, like this:

```
Form1.BackColor = newColor
```

or you can combine both statements into one like this:

```
Form1.BackColor = Color.FromARGB(255, 255, 0)
```

There another form of the FromARGB method that accepts four arguments. The first argument in the method is the *transparency* of the color, and it can be a value from 0 (totally transparent) to 255 (totally opaque). The other three arguments are the usual red, green, and blue color components. For more information on transparent colors, see the following section, "Alpha Blending."

You can also retrieve the three basic components of a Color value with the R, G, and B methods. The following statements print in the Output window the values of the three components of one of the named colors:

```
Dim C As Color = Color.Beige
Console.WriteLine "Red Component = " & C.R.ToString
Console.WriteLine "Green Component = " & C.G.ToString
Console.WriteLine "Blue Component = " & C.B.ToString
```

In an image-processing application, such as the one we'll develop later in this chapter, we want to read pixel values, isolate their color components, and then process them separately.

ALPHA BLENDING

Besides the red, green, and blue components, a color value may also contain a transparency component. This value determines whether the color is opaque, or transparent. In the case of transparent colors, you can specify the degree of transparency. This component is the *alpha component*. The following statement creates a new color value, which is yellow and 25 percent transparent:

```
Dim trYellow As Color
trYellow = Color.FromARGB(192, Color.Yellow)
```

If you want to "wash out" the colors of an image on a form, draw a white rectangle with a transparency of 50 percent or more. The size of the rectangle must be the same as the size of the form, so you can use the ClientRectangle object to retrieve the area taken by the form. Then create a solid brush with a semitransparent color with the `Color.FromARGB` method. The following code segment does exactly that:

```
Dim brush As New SolidBrush(Color.FromARGB(128, Color.White))
Me.CreateGraphics.FillRectangle(brush, ClientRectangle)
```

If you execute these statements repeatedly, the form will eventually become white. Another use of transparent drawing is to place watermarks on images you're going to publish on the Web. A *watermark* is a string or logo that's drawn transparently on the image. It doesn't really disturb the viewers, but it makes the image unusable on another site. It's a crude but effective way to protect your images on the Web.

The following statements place a watermark with the string "MySite.Com" on an image. The font is fairly large and bold, and the code assumes that the text fits in the width of the image.

```
Private Sub Button1_Click(ByVal sender As System.Object, _
            ByVal e As System.EventArgs) Handles Button1.Click
    Dim WMFont As New Font("Comic Sans MS", 20, FontStyle.Bold)
    Dim WMBrush As New SolidBrush(Color.FromARGB(92, 230, 80, 120))
    PictureBox1.CreateGraphics.DrawString("MySite.com", WMFont, WMBrush, 100, 40)
End Sub
```

You can combine these statements with a simple program that scans all the images in a folder (you'll find this information in Chapter 13) to write an application that watermarks a large number of files en masse. Figure 14.24 shows the watermarked image produced by the previous code segment.

FIGURE 14.24

Watermarking an image with a semi-transparent string

Another interesting application of transparency is to superimpose a semitransparent drawing over an opaque one. Figure 14.25 shows some text with a 3D look. To achieve this effect, you render a string with a totally opaque brush. Then you superimpose the same string drawn with a partially transparent brush. The superimposed string is displaced by a few pixels in relation to the first one. The amount of displacement, its direction, and the colors you use determine the type of 3D effect (raised or depressed). The second brush can have any color, as long as the color combination produces a pleasant effect. The strings shown in Figure 14.25 were generated with the TextEffects project (button Draw Semi-Transparent Text). If you run the application and look at the rendered strings carefully, you'll see that they're made up of three colors. The two original colors appear around the edges. The inner area of each character is what the transparency of the second color allows us to see.

The code behind the Draw Semi-Transparent Text button is quite simple, really. It's a bit lengthy, but I will include its listing anyway. The code draws the first string with the solid blue brush:

```
brush = New SolidBrush(Color.FromARGB(255, 0, 0, 255))
```

Then another instance of the same string is drawn, this time with a different brush:

```
brush.Color = Color.FromARGB(192, 0, 255, 255)
```

FIGURE 14.25

Creating a 3D effect by superimposing transparency on an opaque and a semi-transparent string

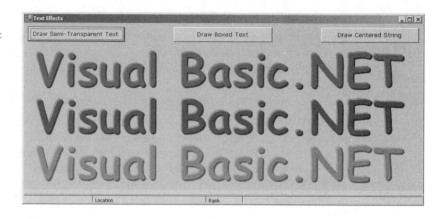

This is a semitransparent shade of cyan. The two superimposed strings are displaced a little with respect to one another. The statements in Listing 14.26 produced the two upper strings of Figure 14.25.

LISTING 14.27: SIMPLE TEXT EFFECTS WITH TRANSPARENT BRUSHES

```
brush = New SolidBrush(Color.FromARGB(255, 0, 0, 255))
drawFont = New Font("Comic Sans MS", 72, Drawing.FontStyle.Bold)
G.DrawString("Visual Basic.NET", drawFont, brush, 10, 30)
brush.Color = Color.FromARGB(192, 0, 255, 255)
G.DrawString("Visual Basic.NET", drawFont, brush, 7, 27)
brush.Color = Color.FromARGB(255, 0, 0, 255)
drawFont = New Font("Comic Sans MS", 72, Drawing.FontStyle.Bold)
G.DrawString("Visual Basic.NET", drawFont, brush, 10, 130)
brush.Color = Color.FromARGB(128, 0, 255, 255)
G.DrawString("Visual Basic.NET", drawFont, brush, 7, 127)
```

Processing Bitmaps

Images are arrays of color values. These values are stored in disk files, and when an image is displayed on a PictureBox or Form control, each of its color values is mapped to a pixel on the PictureBox or form. As you'll see, image processing is nothing more than simple arithmetic operations on the values of the image's pixels. The ImageProcessing application we'll build to demonstrate the various image-processing techniques is slow compared with professional applications, but it demonstrates the principles of image-processing techniques and can be used as a starting point for custom applications.

We'll build a simple image-processing application that can read all the image types VB can handle (BMP, GIF, TIFF, JPEG, and so on), process them, and then display the processed images. There are simpler ways to demonstrate Visual Basic pixel-handling methods, but image processing is an intriguing topic, and I hope many readers will experiment with its techniques in the ImageProcessing application.

An image is a two-dimensional array of pixels in which each pixel is represented by one or more bits. In a black-and-white image, each pixel is represented by a single bit. Image formats that use 256 colors store each pixel in a byte. The best quality images, however, use three bytes per pixel, one for each RGB color component. (For this example, we'll ignore the alpha channel.)

Let's look at a simple technique, the inversion of an image's colors. To invert an image, you must change all pixels to their complementary colors—black to white, green to magenta, and so on (the complementary colors are on opposite corners of the RGB cube, shown in Figure 14.23, earlier in this chapter).

To calculate complementary colors, you subtract each of the three color components from 255. For example, a pure green pixel whose value is (0, 255, 0) will be converted to (255 – 0, 255 – 255, 255 – 0) or (255, 0, 255), which is magenta. Similarly, a mid-yellow tone (0, 128, 128) will be converted to (255 – 0, 255 – 128, 255 – 128) or (255, 127, 127), which is a mid-brown tone. If you apply this color transformation to all the pixels of an image, the result will be the negative of the original image (what you'd see if you looked at the negative from which the picture was obtained).

Other image-processing techniques aren't as simple, but the important thing to understand is that, in general, image processing is as straightforward as a few arithmetic operations on the image's pixels. After we go through the ImageProcessing application, you'll probably come up with your own techniques and be able to implement them.

VB.NET at Work: The ImageProcessing Project

The application we'll develop in this section is called ImageProcessing; it's shown in Figure 14.26. It's not a professional tool, but it can be easily implemented in Visual Basic, and it will give you the opportunity to explore various image-processing techniques on your own. To process an image with the application, choose File ➤ Open to load it to the PictureBox control and then select the type of action from the Process menu. Using the ImageProcessing application, you can apply the following effects to an image:

Smooth Reduces the amount of detail in the image by smoothing areas with abrupt changes in color and/or intensity.

Sharpen Brings out the detail in the image by amplifying the differences between similarly colored pixels.

Emboss Adds a raised (embossed) look to the image.

Diffuse Gives the image a "painterly" look.

Next, let's look at how each algorithm works and how it's implemented in Visual Basic.

How the Application Works

Let's start with a general discussion of the application's operation before we get down to the actual code. Once the image is loaded on a PictureBox control, you can access the values of its pixels with the GetPixel method of the bitmap object that holds the image. The GetPixel method returns a Color value, and you can use the R, G, and B methods of the Color object to extract the basic color components. This is a time-consuming step, and for most algorithms, it must be performed more than once for each pixel.

FIGURE 14.26

The ImageProcess-
ing application
demonstrates several
image-processing
techniques that can
be implemented
with VB.

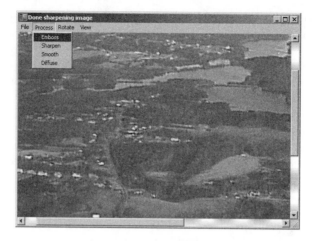

All image-processing algorithms read a few pixel values and process them to calculate the new value of a pixel. This value is then written into the new bitmap with the SetPixel method. The syntax of the SetPixel and GetPixel methods of the Bitmap object are as follows:

```
color = Bitmap.GetPixel(X, Y)
Bitmap.SetPixel(X, Y, color)
```

where *X* and *Y* are the coordinates of the pixel whose value you're reading, or setting. The GetPixel method returns the color of the specified pixel, while the SetPixel method sets the pixel's color to the specified value.

All image-processing algorithms share a common structure as well. We set up two nested loops, one that scans the rows of pixels and an inner loop that scans the pixels in each row. In the inner loop's body, we calculate the current pixel's new value, taking into consideration the values of the surrounding pixels. Because of this, we can't save the new pixel values to the original bitmap. When processing the next pixel, some of the surrounding pixels will have their original values, while some other will have the new values. As a result, we must create copy of the original bitmap and use this bitmap to retrieve the original values of the pixels. The processed values are displayed on the bitmap of the PictureBox control, so that you can watch the progress of the processing.

The following is the outline of all the algorithms we'll implement shortly:

```
bmap = New Bitmap(PictureBox1.Image)
PictureBox1.Image = bmap
Dim tempbmp As New Bitmap(PictureBox1.Image)
Dim i, j As Integer
With tempbmp
    For i = DX To .Height - DX - 1
        For j = DY To .Width - DY - 1
            { calculate new pixel value }
            bmap.SetPixel(j, i, new_pixel_value)
        Next
        If i Mod 10 = 0 Then
            PictureBox1.Invalidate()
```

```
        PictureBox1.Refresh()
      End If
    Next
End With
```

Here's how it works. First, we create a Bitmap object from the image on the PictureBox control. This is the *bmap* variable, which is then assigned back to the Image property of the control. Everything you draw on the *bmap* object will appear on the control's surface. We then create another identical Bitmap object, the *tempbmp* variable. This object holds the original values of all the pixels of the image.

The two nested loops go through every pixel in the image. In the inner loop's body, we calculate the new value of the current pixel and then write this value to the matching location of the *bmap* object. The new pixel will appear on the control when we refresh it, by calling the control's Invalidate method. This method isn't called every time we display a new pixel. It would introduce a significant delay, so we invalidate the control after processing 10 rows of pixels. This is a good balance between performance and a constant visual feedback.

APPLYING EFFECTS

In the following sections, you'll find a short description and the implementation of a few image-processing techniques (the ones you can apply to the image with the commands of the Process menu).

Smoothing Images

One of the simplest and most common operations in all image-processing programs is the smoothing (or blurring) operation. The smoothing operation is equivalent to low-pass filtering: just as you can cut off a stereo's high-frequency sounds with the help of an equalizer, you can cut off the high frequencies of an image. If you're wondering what the high frequencies of an image are, think of them as the areas with abrupt changes in the image's intensity. These are the areas that are mainly affected by the blurring filter.

The smoothed image contains less abrupt changes than the original and looks a lot like the original image seen through a semitransparent glass. Figure 14.27 shows a smoothed image, obtained with the ImageProcessing application.

FIGURE 14.27

Smoothing an image reduces its detail, but can make the image less "noisy" and "busy."

To smooth an image, you must reduce the large differences between adjacent pixels. Let's take a block of nine pixels, centered on the pixel we want to blur. This block contains the pixel to be blurred and its eight immediate neighbors. Let's assume that all the pixels in this block are green, except for the middle one, which is red. This pixel is drastically different from its neighbors, and for it to be blurred, it must be pulled toward the average value of the other pixels. Taking the average of a block of pixels is, therefore, a good choice for a blurring operation. If the current pixel's value is similar to the values of its neighbors, the average won't affect it significantly. If its value is different, the remaining pixels will pull the current pixel's value toward them. In other words, if the middle pixel was green, the average wouldn't affect it. Being the only red pixel in the block, though, it's going to come closer to the average value of the remaining pixels. It's going to assume a green tone.

Here's an example with numbers: if the value of the current pixel is 10 and the values of its eight immediate neighbors are 8, 11, 9, 10, 12, 10, 11, and 9, the average value of all pixels will be

$$(8 + 11 + 9 + 10 + 12 + 10 + 11 + 9 + 10) / 9 = 10$$

The pixel under consideration happens to be right on the average of its neighboring pixels. The results would be quite different if the value of the center pixel was drastically different. If the center pixel's value was 20, the new average would be 11. Because the neighboring pixels have values close to 10, they would pull the "outlier" toward them. This is how blurring works. By taking the average of a number of pixels, you force the pixels with values drastically different from their neighbors to get closer to them.

Another factor affecting the amount of blurring is the size of the block over which the average is calculated. We used a 3×3 block in our example, which yields an average blur. To blur the image even more, use a 5×5 block. Even larger blocks will blur the image to the point that useful information will be lost. The actual code of the Smooth operation scans all the pixels of the image (excluding the edge pixels that don't have neighbors all around them) and takes the average of their RGB components. It then combines the three values with the method `Color.FromARGB` to produce the new value of the pixel.

The code that implements the smoothing operation (shown in Listing 14.28) is lengthy, but it's not really complicated. The long statements combine the color components of all nine neighboring pixels. The current pixel has coordinates (i, j), and the neighboring pixels have indices from $i - 1$ to $i + 1$ and from $j - 1$ to $j + 1$. A more elegant approach would be to use two nested loops to iterate through the nine pixels, but this would make the code a little harder to follow.

LISTING 14.28: SMOOTHING AN IMAGE

```
Private Sub ProcessSmooth_Click(ByVal sender As System.Object, _
            ByVal e As System.EventArgs) Handles ProcessSmooth.Click
    bmap = New Bitmap(PictureBox1.Image)
    PictureBox1.Image = bmap
    Dim tempbmp As New Bitmap(PictureBox1.Image)
    Dim DX As Integer = 1
    Dim DY As Integer = 1
    Dim red, green, blue As Integer
    Dim i, j As Integer
```

```
With tempbmp
    For i = DX To .Height - DX - 1
        For j = DY To .Width - DY - 1
            red = CInt((CInt(.GetPixel(j - 1, i - 1).R) + _
                        CInt(.GetPixel(j - 1, i).R) + _
                        CInt(.GetPixel(j - 1, i + 1).R) + _
                        CInt(.GetPixel(j, i - 1).R) + _
                        CInt(.GetPixel(j, i).R) + _
                        CInt(.GetPixel(j, i + 1).R) + _
                        CInt(.GetPixel(j + 1, i - 1).R) + _
                        CInt(.GetPixel(j + 1, i).R) + _
                        CInt(.GetPixel(j + 1, i + 1).R)) / 9)
            green = CInt((CInt(.GetPixel(j - 1, i - 1).G) + _
                        CInt(.GetPixel(j - 1, i).G) + _
                        CInt(.GetPixel(j - 1, i + 1).G) + _
                        CInt(.GetPixel(j, i - 1).G) + _
                        CInt(.GetPixel(j, i).G) + _
                        CInt(.GetPixel(j, i + 1).G) + _
                        CInt(.GetPixel(j + 1, i - 1).G) + _
                        CInt(.GetPixel(j + 1, i).G) + _
                        CInt(.GetPixel(j + 1, i + 1).G)) / 9)
            blue = CInt((CInt(.GetPixel(j - 1, i - 1).B) + _
                        CInt(.GetPixel(j - 1, i).B) + _
                        CInt(.GetPixel(j - 1, i + 1).B) + _
                        CInt(.GetPixel(j, i - 1).B) + _
                        CInt(.GetPixel(j, i).B) + _
                        CInt(.GetPixel(j, i + 1).B) + _
                        CInt(.GetPixel(j + 1, i - 1).B) + _
                        CInt(.GetPixel(j + 1, i).B) + _
                        CInt(.GetPixel(j + 1, i + 1).B)) / 9)
            red = Math.Min(Math.Max(red, 0), 255)
            green = Math.Min(Math.Max(green, 0), 255)
            blue = Math.Min(Math.Max(blue, 0), 255)
            bmap.SetPixel(j, i, Color.FromARGB(red, green, blue))
        Next
        If i Mod 10 = 0 Then
            PictureBox1.Invalidate()
            PictureBox1.Refresh()
            Me.Text = Int( _
                100 * i / (PictureBox1.Image.Height - 2)).ToString & "%"
        End If
    Next
End With
PictureBox1.Refresh()
Me.Text = "Done smoothing image"
End Sub
```

Sharpening Images

Since the basic operation for smoothing an image is addition, the opposite operation will result in sharpening the image. The sharpening effect is more subtle than smoothing, but also more common and more useful. Nearly every image published, especially in monochrome ("one-color") publications, must be sharpened to some extent. For an example of a sharpened image, see Figure 14.28. Sharpening an image consists of highlighting the edges of the objects in it, which are the very same pixels blurred by the previous algorithm. Edges are areas of an image with sharp changes in intensity between adjacent pixels. The smoothing algorithm smoothed out these areas; now we want to emphasize them.

FIGURE 14.28

The sharpening operation brings out detail that isn't evident in the original image.

In a smooth area of an image, the difference between two adjacent pixels will be zero or a very small number. If the pixels are on an edge, the difference between two adjacent pixels will be a large value (perhaps negative). This is an area of the image with some degree of detail that can be sharpened. If the difference is zero, the two pixels are nearly identical, which means that there's nothing to sharpen there. This is called a "flat" area of the image. (Think of an image with a constant background. There's no detail to bring out on the background.)

The difference between adjacent pixels isolates the areas with detail and completely flattens out the smooth areas. The question now is how to bring out the detail without leveling the rest of the image. How about adding the difference to the original pixel? Where the image is flat, the difference is negligible, and the processed pixel practically will be the same as the original one. If the difference is significant, the processed pixel will be the original plus a value that's proportional to the magnitude of the detail. The sharpening algorithm can be expressed as follows:

```
new_value = original_value + 0.5 * difference
```

If you simply add the difference to the original pixel, the algorithm brings out too much detail. You usually add a fraction of the difference; a 50% factor is common. The code that implements the Sharpen command is shown in Listing 14.29.

LISTING 14.29: SHARPENING AN IMAGE

```
Private Sub ProcessSharpen_Click(ByVal sender As System.Object, _
                ByVal e As System.EventArgs) Handles ProcessSharpen.Click
    bmap = New Bitmap(PictureBox1.Image)
    PictureBox1.Image = bmap
    Dim tempbmp As New Bitmap(PictureBox1.Image)
    Dim DX As Integer = 1
    Dim DY As Integer = 1
    Dim red, green, blue As Integer
    Dim i, j As Integer
    With tempbmp
        For i = DX To .Height - DX - 1
            For j = DY To .Width - DY - 1
                red = CInt(.GetPixel(j, i).R) + 0.5 * _
                    CInt((.GetPixel(j, i).R) - _
                        CInt(bmap.GetPixel(j - DX, i - DY).R))
                green = CInt(.GetPixel(j, i).G) + 0.5 * _
                    CInt((.GetPixel(j, i).G) - _
                        CInt(bmap.GetPixel(j - DX, i - DY).G))
                blue = CInt(.GetPixel(j, i).B) + 0.5 * _
                    CInt((.GetPixel(j, i).B - _
                        CInt(bmap.GetPixel(j - DX, i - DY).B)))
                red = Math.Min(Math.Max(red, 0), 255)
                green = Math.Min(Math.Max(green, 0), 255)
                blue = Math.Min(Math.Max(blue, 0), 255)
                bmap.SetPixel(j, i, Color.FromARGB(red, green, blue))
            Next
            If i Mod 10 = 0 Then
                PictureBox1.Invalidate()
                PictureBox1.Refresh()
                Me.Text = Int( _
                    100 * i / (PictureBox1.Image.Height - 2)).ToString & "%"
            End If
        Next
    End With
    PictureBox1.Refresh()
    Me.Text = "Done sharpening image"
End Sub
```

The variables *DX* and *DY* express the distances between the two pixels being subtracted. You can subtract adjacent pixels on the same row, adjacent pixels in the same column, or diagonally adjacent pixels, which is what I did in this subroutine. Besides adding the difference to the original pixel value, this subroutine must check the result for validity. The result of the calculations may exceed the valid value range for a color component, which is 0 to 255. That's why you must clip the value if it falls outside the valid range.

Embossing Images

To sharpen an image, we add the difference between adjacent pixels to the pixel value. What do you think would happen to a processed image if you took the difference between adjacent pixels only? The flat areas of the image would be totally leveled, and only the edges would remain visible. The result would be an image like the image in Figure 14.29. This effect clearly sharpens the edges and flattens the smooth areas of the image. By doing so, it gives the image depth. The processed image looks as if it's raised and illuminated from the right side. This effect is known as *emboss* or *bas relief*.

FIGURE 14.29

The Emboss special effect

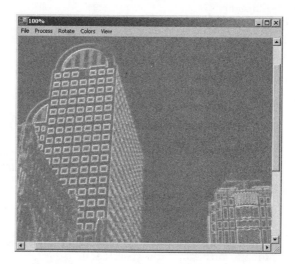

The actual algorithm is based on the difference between adjacent pixels. For most of the image, however, the difference between adjacent pixels is a small number, and the image will turn black. The Emboss algorithm adds a constant to the difference to bring some brightness to areas of the image that would otherwise be dark. The algorithm can be expressed as follows:

```
new_value = difference + 128
```

As usual, you can take the difference between adjacent pixels in the same row, adjacent pixels in the same column, or diagonally adjacent pixels. The code that implements the Emboss filter in the ImageProcessing application uses differences in the x and y directions (set the values of the variables *DispX* or *DispY* to 0 to take the difference in one direction only). The Emboss filter's code is shown in Listing 14.30.

LISTING 14.30: EMBOSSING AN IMAGE

```
Private Sub ProcessEmboss_Click(ByVal sender As System.Object, _
            ByVal e As System.EventArgs) Handles ProcessEmboss.Click
    bmap = New Bitmap(PictureBox1.Image)
    PictureBox1.Image = bmap
```

```
        Dim tempbmp As New Bitmap(PictureBox1.Image)
        Dim i, j As Integer
        Dim DispX As Integer = 1, DispY As Integer = 1
        Dim red, green, blue As Integer
        With tempbmp
            For i = 0 To .Height - 2
                For j = 0 To .Width - 2
                    Dim pixel1, pixel2 As System.Drawing.Color
                    pixel1 = .GetPixel(j, i)
                    pixel2 = .GetPixel(j + DispX, i + DispY)
                    red = Math.Min(Math.Abs(CInt(pixel1.R)-CInt(pixel2.R))+128, 255)
                    green = Math.Min(Math.Abs(CInt(pixel1.G)-CInt(pixel2.G))+128, 255)
                    blue = Math.Min(Math.Abs(CInt(pixel1.B)-CInt(pixel2.B))+128, 255)
                    bmap.SetPixel(j, i, Color.FromARGB(red, green, blue))
                Next
                If i Mod 10 = 0 Then
                    PictureBox1.Invalidate()
                    PictureBox1.Refresh()
                    Me.Text = Int( _
                        100 * i / (PictureBox1.Image.Height - 2)).ToString & "%"
                End If
            Next
        End With
        PictureBox1.Refresh()
        Me.Text = "Done embossing image"
    End Sub
```

The variables *DispX* and *DispY* determine the location of the pixel being subtracted from the one being processed. Notice that the pixel being subtracted is behind and above the current pixel. If you set the *DispX* and *DispY* variables to −1, the result is similar, but the processed image looks engraved rather than embossed.

Diffusing Images

The Diffuse special effect is different from the previous ones, in the sense that it's not based on the sums or the differences of pixel values. This effect uses the Rnd() function to introduce some randomness to the image and give it a "painterly" look, as demonstrated in Figure 14.30.

This time we won't manipulate the values of the pixels. Instead, the current pixel will assume the value of another one, selected randomly in its 5×5 neighborhood with the help of the Random class.

The Diffuse algorithm is the simplest one. It generates two random variables, *DX* and *DY*, in the range −3 to 3. These two variables are added to the coordinates of the current pixel to yield the coordinates of another pixel in the neighborhood. The original pixel is replaced by the value of the pixel that (*DX*, *DY*) pixels away. The code that implements the Diffuse operation is shown in Listing 14.31.

FIGURE 14.30

The Diffuse special effect gives the image a painterly look.

LISTING 14.31: DIFFUSING AN IMAGE

```
Private Sub ProcessDiffuse_Click(ByVal sender As System.Object, _
            ByVal e As System.EventArgs) Handles ProcessDiffuse.Click
    bmap = New Bitmap(PictureBox1.Image)
    PictureBox1.Image = bmap
    Dim tempbmp As New Bitmap(PictureBox1.Image)
    Dim i As Integer, j As Integer
    Dim DX As Integer
    Dim DY As Integer
    Dim red As Integer, green As Integer, blue As Integer
    With tempbmp
        For i = 3 To .Height - 3
            For j = 3 To .Width - 3
                DX = Rnd() * 4 - 2
                DY = Rnd() * 4 - 2
                red = .GetPixel(j + DX, i + DY).R
                green = .GetPixel(j + DX, i + DY).G
                blue = .GetPixel(j + DX, i + DY).B
                bmap.SetPixel(j, i, Color.FromARGB(red, green, blue))
            Next
            Me.Text = Int(100 * i / (.Height - 2)).ToString & "%"
            If i Mod 10 = 0 Then
                PictureBox1.Invalidate()
```

```
            PictureBox1.Refresh()
            Me.Text = Int( _
                100 * i / (PictureBox1.Image.Height - 2)).ToString & "%"
        End If
    Next
End With
PictureBox1.Refresh()
Me.Text = "Done diffusing image"
End Sub
```

Open the ImageProcessing application and experiment with the algorithms described in this chapter. Change the parameters of the various algorithms and see how they affect the processed image. You can easily implement new algorithms by inserting the appropriate code in the inner loop's body. The rest of the code remains the same. Some simple ideas include clipping one or more colors (force the red color component of each pixel to remain within a range of values), substituting one component for another (replace the red component of each pixel with the green or blue component of the same pixel), inverting the colors of the image (subtract all three color components of each pixel from 255), and so on. With a little imagination, you can create interesting effects for your images.

Summary

It's been a long chapter, but graphics have never been simple. This may explain why they're not among the most favorite programming topics, but they sure are fun. GDI+ brings VB graphics to a new level. GDI+ exposes a whole lot of functionality, and you have seen most of it in this chapter.

The basic object you'll be using in your code to generate graphics is the Graphics object, and you can retrieve the Graphics object of a form or control with the CreateGraphics method. Then you can call this object's drawing methods to generate graphics. If you're going to display a few graphics elements on your form, you can put the corresponding statements in a subroutine that overwrites the OnPaint method, so that the form is redrawn every time it's refreshed.

If you want to create graphics in response to user actions, keep in mind that anything you draw on the Graphics object returned by the CreateGraphics method is not permanent; it will be ignored when the form is refreshed. To generate permanent graphics on a form or PictureBox control, you must create a Graphics object based on the bitmap of the control. The bitmap is permanent, and it's refreshed properly when the form is resized or temporarily covered by another form. As far as the drawing methods go, they're the same no matter how you created the Graphics object.

Chapter 15

Printing with VB.NET

THE TOPIC OF PRINTING with Visual Basic hasn't received much publicity in previous versions of the language, mostly because it's a non-trivial topic and many developers used third-party tools to add print capabilities to their applications. VB.NET has simplified printing a little, but in some ways printing with VB.NET is more complicated than it used to be. The .NET Framework introduced mechanisms for generating printouts, but printing from within a VB application isn't trivial. As you already know, there's no control with built-in printing capabilities. It would be nice if certain controls, like the TextBox or the TreeView control, would print their contents, but this is not the case. The VB6 version of the RichTextBox control provided a printing method (the SelPrint method), which is no longer supported by the new version of the control that comes with VB.NET. If you want to print a few text paragraphs entered by the user on a TextBox control, you must provide your own code for that.

Printing with VB isn't really complicated, but it requires a lot of code—most of it calling graphics methods. You must carefully calculate the coordinates of each graphic element placed on the paper, take into consideration the settings of the printer and the current page, and start a new page when the current one is filled. It's like generating graphics for the monitor, so you need a basic understanding of the graphics methods, even if you're only going to develop business applications. If you need to generate elaborate printouts, I would suggest that you look into third-party controls with built-in printing capabilities. In this chapter, you will find all the information you need, but before you decide to generate your own reports, weigh the complexity of your code versus a specialized tool. On the other hand, if you can group your project's printouts into a few different types with common characteristics, you can then develop a class for each type of report and reuse these classes to produce all the printouts.

The first step in adding printing capabilities to an application is to decide what it is that you want to print and then design an application that allows users to specify what they want to print. The simplest printing job is to generate a printout from the contents of a TextBox control. Even this seemingly trivial task requires that you break the text lines, make sure that they're confined within the page's margins, detect when you have reached the end of the page, and start a new page as needed. You can't even take for granted things like printing page numbers at the bottom of the page or the document's title at the top of the page.

Printing simple reports (tabular data) is another common printing task. You can draw an outline of the printout on paper and then implement it with VB code. The data will most likely come from a database, so you don't really need to create an application with an elaborate interface. Printing graphics is straightforward—but not typical in business applications. All the graphics commands you use to generate a graphic on the screen can be applied to the printer as well. The most complicated case is the printing of formatted text.

The examples of this section will address many of your day-to-day needs, and I'm including examples that will serve as your starting point for some of the most typical printing needs, from printing tabular data to bitmaps.

VB6 ➡ VB.NET

VB6 included some mechanisms to simplify the generation of simple printouts. These mechanisms are no longer available. On the plus side, VB.NET provides a unified approach for generating all types of printouts. Generating a preview, for example, is no longer a separate process. Whether you print on a printer or in the preview pane, the process is identical.

The Printing Objects

We'll start our exploration of Visual Basic's printing capabilities with an overview of the printing process, which is the same no matter what you print. Printing with VB.NET is equivalent to drawing on a Form or PictureBox object. VB.NET introduced several controls for generating output for the printer, and here's a quick overview of these objects (you'll find more information on these objects and examples in the following sections). You don't need to use all these objects in your project. Only the PrintDocument object is required, and you will have to master the members of this control.

PrintDocument

This object represents your printer, and you must add a PrintDocument control to any project that generates printer output. In effect, everything you draw on the PrintDocument object is sent to the printer. The PrintDocument object represents the printing surface, and it exposes a Graphics object. You can program against the Graphics object using all the methods discussed in Chapter 14. If you can create drawings on a form, you can just as easily print them on your printer. To print text, for example, you must call the DrawString method. To print headers and footers, you supply the text to be printed, the coordinates on the page where the string will be printed, and the font in which the string will be rendered. You can also print frames around the text with the DrawLine or DrawRectangle method. In general, you can use all the methods of the Graphics object to prepare the printout.

To send something to the printer, you must first add an instance of the PrintDocument control to the project. This control is invisible at runtime, and its icon will appear on the Components tray at design time. When you're ready to print, call the PrintDocument object's Print method. This method isn't going to produce any output, but it will raise the PrintPage event. This is where you must insert the code that generates output for the printer. The PrintPage event passes the *e* argument, which exposes the Graphics property of the current Printer object, among other members.

This is same object we used in the previous chapter to generate all kinds of graphics. The printer has its own Graphics object, which represents the page you print on. All the methods that generate graphics can be applied to the printer's Graphics object to print graphics on the page. The following statement initiates the printing:

```
PrintDocument1.Print
```

This statement is usually placed in a button's or a menu item's Click event handler. To experiment with simple printouts, create a new project, place a button on the form, and add an instance of the PrintDocument object to the project. Enter the previous statement in the button's Click event handler.

After the execution of this statement, the PrintDocument1_PrintPage event handler takes over. This event is fired for each page, so you insert the code to print the first page in this event's handler. If you need to print additional pages, you set the **e.HasMorePages** property to True just before you exit the event handler. This will fire another PrintPage event. The same process will repeat until you've printed everything. When you've finished, you set the **e.HasMorePages** property to False, and no more PrintPage events will be fired. Figure 15.1 outlines the printing process.

FIGURE 15.1

All printing takes place in the Print-Page event handler of the PrintDocument object.

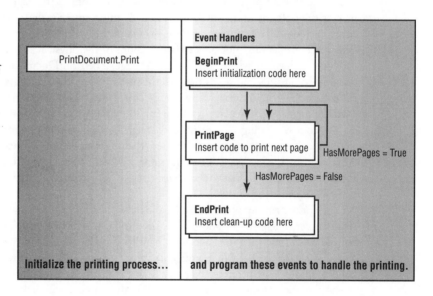

The code in Listing 15.1 shows the structure of a typical PrintPage event handler. The PrintPage event handler prints three pages with the same text and a different page number on each page.

LISTING 15.1: A SIMPLE PRINTPAGE EVENT HANDLER

```
Private Sub PrintDocument1_PrintPage(ByVal sender As Object, _
            ByVal e As System.Drawing.Printing.PrintPageEventArgs) _
            Handles PrintDocument1.PrintPage
    Static pageNum As Integer
```

```
        Dim prFont As New Font("Verdana", 24, GraphicsUnit.Point)
        e.Graphics.DrawString("PAGE " & pageNum + 1, prFont, _
                            Brushes.Black, 700, 1050)
        e.Graphics.DrawRectangle(Pens.Blue, 0, 0, 300, 100)
        e.Graphics.DrawString("Printing with VB.NET", prFont, _
                            Brushes.Black, 10, 10)
' Add more printing statements here
' Following is the logic that determines whether we're done printing
        pageNum = pageNum + 1
        If pageNum <= 3 Then
            e.HasMorePages = True
        Else
            e.HasMorePages = False
        End If
End Sub
```

Notice that the page number is printed at the bottom of the page, but the corresponding statement is the first one in the subroutine. I'm assuming you're using an letter-size page, so I've hard-coded the coordinates of the various elements in the code. Later in this chapter, you'll learn how to take into consideration not only the dimensions of the physical page but its orientation, too.

You can draw anywhere you like on the page. The PrintDocument object accumulates all the graphics commands and sends them to the printer when the PrintPage event handler terminates. So, the order in which you place the various elements on the page doesn't matter. You can also draw overlapping shapes, like placing text over a bitmap or drawing arrows over a chart.

The code of Listing 15.1 prints three pages, with the same text and different page numbers. While there are more pages to be printed, the program sets the `e.HasMorePages` property to True. After printing the last page, it sets the same argument to False to prevent further invocations of the PrintPage event. Note that the *pageNum* variable was declared as static, so that it will retain its value between calls.

The entire printout is generated by the same subroutine, one page at a time. Because pages are not totally independent of one another, we need to keep some information in variables that are not initialized every time the PrintPage event handler is executed. The page number, for example, must be stored in a variable that will maintain its value between successive invocations of the PrintPage event handler, and it must be increased every time a new page is printed. If you're printing a text file, you must keep track of the current text line, so that each page will pick up where the previous one ended and not from the beginning of the document. You use static variables or declare variables on the form's level, whatever suits you best. This is a recurring theme in programming the PrintPage event, and you'll see many more examples of this technique in the following sections.

PrintDialog

The PrintDialog control displays the standard Print dialog box, shown in Figure 15.2, which allows users to select a printer and set its properties. If you don't display this dialog box, the output will be sent automatically to the default printer and will use the default settings of the printer. The Print dialog box was discussed in Chapter 7, and you already know how to retrieve the selected printer, as well as the settings specified by the user, in the dialog box. In this chapter, you'll see how to use these settings in the code that generates output for the printer.

FIGURE 15.2

The Print dialog box

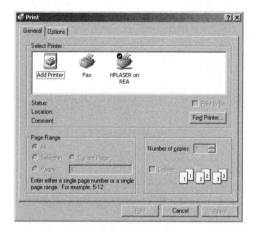

Among other settings, the Print dialog box allows you to specify the range of pages to be printed. Before allowing users to select a range of pages, be sure that you have a way to skip any number of pages. If the user specifies pages 10 through 19, your code must calculate the section of the document that would normally be printed on the first nine pages, skip it, and start printing after that. If the printout is a report with a fixed number of rows per page, skipping pages is trivial. If the printout contains formatted text, you must repeat all the calculations to generate the first nine pages and ignore them (skip the statements that actually print the graphics). Starting a printout at a page other than the first one can be a challenge.

When you select a printer from this dialog box, it automatically becomes the active printer and any printout generated after the selection of the printer will be sent to this printer; you don't have to insert any code to switch printers.

The actual printer to which you will send the output of your application is almost transparent to the printing code. The same commands will generate the same output on any printer. If you're using a color printer, you may insert additional code to generate colored output. If you're using a plotter, you'll also want to print all the components of the same color together, to minimize the time spent by the plotter in changing pens. For the most common printers—that is, ink-jet and PostScript printers—you don't have to modify a single statement. The same code will work with all printers.

It is also possible to set the printer from within your code with a statement like the following:

```
PrintDocument1.PrinterSettings.PrinterName = printer
```

where *printer* is the name of one of the installed printers. For more information on selecting a printer form within your code, see the section "Printer and Page Properties," later in this chapter. There are situations where you want to set a printer from within your code and not give users a chance to change it. An application that prints invoices and reports, for example, must use a different printer for each type of printout.

PageSetupDialog

This control displays the Page Setup dialog box, which allows users to set up the page (its orientation and margins). The dialog box, shown in Figure 15.3, returns the current page settings in a PageSettings object, which exposes the user-specified settings as properties. These settings don't take effect on their own; you simply examine their values and take them into consideration as you prepare the output for the printer from within your code. The PageSetup dialog box is shown in Figure 15.3. As you can see, there aren't many parameters to set on this dialog box, but you should display it and take into account the settings specified by the user.

FIGURE 15.3

The Page Setup
dialog box

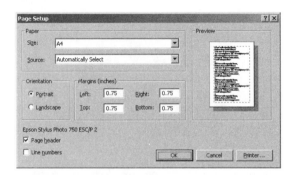

To display this dialog box in your application, you must drop the PageSetupDialog control on the Form and then call its ShowDialog method. The single property of this control you'll be using exclusively in your projects is the PageSettings property. PageSettings is an object that exposes a number of properties reflecting the current settings of the page (margins and orientation). These settings apply to an entire document. The PrintDocument object has an analogous property, the DefaultPageSettings property. After the user closes the PageSetup dialog box, we assign its PageSettings object to the DefaultPageSettings object of the PrintDocument object to make the user-specified settings available to our code. Here's how we usually display the dialog box from within our application and retrieve its PageSettings property:

```
PageSetupDialog1.PageSettings = PrintDocument1.DefaultPageSettings
If PageSetupDialog1.ShowDialog() = DialogResult.OK Then _
        PrintDocument1.DefaultPageSettings = PageSetupDialog1.PageSettings
```

Notice that first line that initializes the dialog box is mandatory. If you attempt to display the dialog box without initializing its PageSettings property, an exception will be thrown. You will find more information on the PageSettings object later in this chapter, and we'll use it in most of the examples of this chapter.

The statements that manipulate the printing objects can get fairly lengthy. It's common to use the With structure to make the statements shorter. The last example can also be coded as follows:

```
With PageSetupDialog1
   .PageSettings = PrintDocument1.DefaultPageSettings
   If .ShowDialog() = DialogResult.OK Then _
             PrintDocument1.DefaultPageSettings = .PageSettings
End With
```

PrintPreviewDialog

This is another dialog box that displays a preview of the printed document. It exposes a lot of functionality and allows users to examine the output and, when they're happy with it, send it to the printer. The Print Preview dialog, shown in Figure 15.4, is made up of a preview pane, where you can display one or more pages at the same time at various magnifications, and a toolbar. The buttons on the toolbar allow you to select the magnification, set the number of pages that will be displayed on the preview pane, move to any page of a multi-page printout, and send the preview document to the printer.

FIGURE 15.4

The Print Preview dialog box

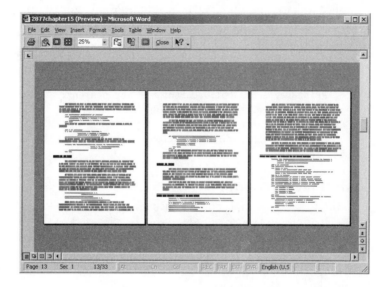

Once you've written the code to generate the printout, you can direct it to the PrintPreview control. You don't have to write any additional code; just place an instance of the control on the form and set its Document property to the PrintDocument control on the form. Then show the control instead of calling the Print method of the PrintDocument object:

```
PrintPreviewDialog1.Document = PrintDocument1
PrintPreviewDialog1.ShowDialog
```

After the execution of these two lines, the PrintDocument object takes over. It fires the PrintPage event as usual, but it sends its output to the preview dialog box and not to the printer. The dialog box contains a Print button, which the user can click to send the document being previewed to the printer. The exact same code that generated the preview document will print the document on the printer.

The PrintPreview control will save you a lot of paper and toner while you're testing your printing code because you don't have to actually print every page to see what it looks like. Since the same code generates both the preview and the actual printed document, and the Print Preview option adds a professional touch to your application, there's no reason why you shouldn't add this feature to your projects.

TIP *The PrintPreview control generates output that would normally appear to the default printer (or the printer selected in the Print dialog box). If this printer is a networked printer that your computer can't access at the time, the Print Preview dialog box will not be displayed. Instead, an exception will be thrown, which you must catch from within your code.*

The first example of this chapter, discussed a few pages earlier in Listing 15.1, prints three simple pages to the printer. To redirect the output of the program to the PrintPreview control, replace the statement that calls the `PrintDocument1.Print` method in the button's Click event handler with the following statements:

```
PrintPreviewDialog1.Document = PrintDocument1
PrintPreviewDialog1.ShowDialog
```

If you run the project, this time you'll be able to preview the document on your monitor. If you're satisfied with its appearance, you can click the Print button to send the document to the printer. As you can see, providing a Print Preview feature is really trivial. All the work is done by the PrintPreviewDialog control.

To avoid runtime errors, you can use the following exception handler:

```
Try
    PrintPreviewDialog1.Document = PrintDocument1
    PrintPreviewDialog1.ShowDialog
Catch exc As Exception
    MsgBox "The printing operation failed" & vbCrLf & exc.Message
End Try
```

PrintPreviewControl

The PrintPreviewControl control is the preview pane of the Print Preview dialog box. The control has no buttons, and you must provide your own interface to allow users to navigate through the document's pages or change the current magnification. There are no compelling reasons to use this control, but it's an alternative to the PrintPreviewDialog control. Once you've understood how the PrintPreviewDialog control works, you will find it easy to program to control and preview the documents on a form of your own.

At this point, you'd expect to see some more examples of printing. However, there are a few more objects we'll be using in our examples, and I must discuss them before I can show you some nontrivial examples. Please bear with me for a few more pages and you'll find several examples of common printing tasks shortly. In the next two sections, you'll learn how to retrieve the dimensions of the page in the printer and how to specify coordinates on the page. This will allow you to generate printouts that are not tied to a specific page size and/or orientation.

Printer and Page Properties

One of the most common tasks in generating printouts is to retrieve the settings of the current printer and page, and this is a good place to present the members of these two objects, as we'll use them extensively in the examples of the following sections. The properties of these two items are reported to your application through the PrinterSettings and the PageSettings objects. The PageSettings object is a property of the PrintPageEventArgs class, and you can access it through the *e* argument of the PrintPage event handler. The DefaultPageSettings property of the PrintDocument object is an object, which exposes the current page's settings.

The PrinterSettings object is a property of the PrintDocument object, as well as a property of the PageSetupDialog and PrintDialog controls. Finally, one of the properties exposed by the PageSettings object is the PrinterSettings object. These two objects provide all the information you may need about the selected printer and the current page through the properties listed in Tables 15.1 and 15.2.

TABLE 15.1: THE PROPERTIES OF THE PAGESETTINGS OBJECT

PROPERTY	DESCRIPTION
Bounds	Returns the bounds of the page (`Bounds.Width` and `Bounds.Height`). If the current orientation is landscape, the width is larger than the height.
Color	Returns, or sets, a True/False value indicating whether the current page should be printed in color. On a monochrome printer, this property is always False.
Landscape	A True/False value indicating whether the page is printed in landscape or portrait orientation.
Margins	The margins for the current page (`Margins.Left`, `Margins.Right`, `Margins.Bottom`, and `Margins.Top`).
PaperSize	The size of the current page (`PaperSize.Width` and `PaperSize.Height`).
PaperSource	The page's paper tray.
PrinterResolution	The printer's resolution for the current page.
PrinterSettings	This property returns, or sets, the printer settings associated with the page. For more information on the PrinterSettings object and the properties it exposes, see the following table.

TABLE 15.2: THE MEMBERS OF THE PRINTERSETTINGS OBJECT

MEMBER	DESCRIPTION
InstalledPrinters	This method retrieves the names of all printers installed on the computer. The same printer names also appear in the Print dialog box, where the user can select any one of them.
CanDuplex	A read-only property that returns a True/False value indicating whether the printer supports double-sided printing.
Collate	Another read-only property that returns a True/False value indicating whether the printout should be collated or not.
Copies	This property returns the requested number of copies of the printout.
DefaultPageSettings	This property is the PageSettings object that returns, or sets, the default page settings for the current printer.
Duplex	This property returns, or sets, the current setting for double-sided printing.

Continued on next page

TABLE 15.2: THE MEMBERS OF THE PRINTERSETTINGS OBJECT *(continued)*

MEMBER	DESCRIPTION
FromPage, ToPage	The printout's starting and ending pages, as specified in the Print dialog box by the user.
IsDefaultPrinter	Returns a True/False value indicating whether the selected printer (the one identified by the PrinterName property) is the default printer. Note that selecting a printer other than the default one in the Print dialog box doesn't change the default printer.
IsPlotter	Returns a True/False value indicating whether the printer is a plotter.
IsValid	Returns a True/False value indicating whether the PrinterName corresponds to a valid printer.
LandscapeAngle	Returns an angle, in degrees, by which the portrait orientation must be rotated to produce the landscape orientation.
MaximumCopies	Returns the maximum number of copies that the printer allows you to print at a time.
MaximumPage	Returns, or sets, the largest value the FromPage and ToPage properties can have.
MinimumPage	Returns, or sets, the smallest value the FromPage and ToPage properties can have.
PaperSizes	Returns all the paper sizes that are supported by this printer.
PaperSources	Returns all the paper source trays on the selected printer.
PrinterName	Returns, or sets, the name of the printer to use.
PrinterResolutions	Returns all the resolutions that are supported by this printer.
PrintRange	Returns, or sets, the numbers of the pages to be printed, as specified by the user. When you set this property, the value becomes the default setting when the Print dialog box is opened.
SupportsColor	Returns a True/False value indicating whether this printer supports color printing.
CreateMeasurementGraphics	Returns a Graphics object that contains printer information you can use in the `PrintDocument.Print` event handler.

To retrieve the names of the installed printers, use the InstalledPrinters collection of the PrinterSettings object. This collection contains the names of the printers as strings, and you can access them with the following loop:

```
Dim i As Integer
With PrintDocument1.PrinterSettings.InstalledPrinters
    For i = 0 To .Count - 1
        Console.WriteLine(.Item(i))
    Next
End With
```

These statements will produce output like the following when executed:

```
Fax
HPLaser
\\EXPERT\XEROX
```

The first two printers are local (Fax isn't even a printer; it's a driver for the fax and it's installed by Windows). The last printer's name is XEROX and it's a network printer, connected to the EXPERT workstation.

You can also change the current printer by setting the PrinterName property of the PrinterSettings property with either of the following statements:

```
PrintDocument1.PrinterSettings.PrinterName = "HPLaser"
PrintDocument1.PrinterSettings.PrinterName = _
        PrintDocument1.PrinterSettings.InstalledPrinters(1)
```

Another property that needs additional explanation is the PrinterResolution object. The PrinterResolution object provides the Kind property, which returns, or sets, the current resolution of the printer, and its value is one of the PrinterResolutionKind enumeration's members: `Custom`, `Draft`, `High`, `Low`, and `Medium`. To find out the exact horizontal and vertical resolutions, read the X and Y properties of the PrinterResolution object. When you set the `PrinterResolution.Kind` property to Custom, you must specify the X and Y properties.

Note that the PrinterResolution object is a property of the PageSettings object. The PrinterSettings object exposes a similarly named object, the PrinterResolutions property. This property is a collection that returns all resolution kinds, which are the members of the PrinterResolutionKind enumeration.

Page Geometry

Printing on a page is similar to generating graphics on your screen. Like the drawing surface on the monitor (the client area), the page on which you're printing has a fixed size and resolution. The most challenging aspect of printing is the calculation of the coordinates, where each graphic element will appear. In business applications, the most common elements are strings (rendered in various fonts, styles, and sizes), lines, and rectangles, which are used as borders for tabular data. Although you can print anywhere on the page (if you want, you can start filling the page from the bottom up), we usually print one element at a time, calculate the space it takes on the page, and then print the next element next or below it. Printing code makes heavy use of the MeasureString method, and nearly all of the examples in this chapter make use of this method.

The printable area is determined by the size of the paper you're using, and in most cases it's 8.5×11 inches (keep in mind that most printers can't print near the edge of the page). Printed pages have a margin on all four sides, and you can set a different margin on every side. The user determines the margins through the Page Setup dialog box, and your program is confined to drawing within the specified margins.

You can access the current page's margins through the Margins property of the `PrintDocument1.DefaultPageSettings` object. This object exposes the Left, Right, Top, and Bottom properties, which are the values of the four margins. The margins, as well as the page coordinates, are expressed in *hundredths of an inch*. The width of a standard letter-sized page, for example, is 8,500 units and its height is 11,000 units. Of course, you can use non-integer values for even greater granularity, but you won't see two straight lines printed at less than one hundredth of an inch apart. You can use other units, which are all members of the PageUnit enumeration, which was discussed in the previous chapter.

NOTE   *In the examples of this chapter, I'm using the default units, and since there are 100 units in an inch, all the variables that represent coordinates and sizes are declared as Integer. You can also declare them as Single, but a fraction of a hundredth of an inch isn't going to make any difference in your printout.*

Another property exposed by the DefaultSettings object is the PageSize property, which in turn exposes the Width and Height properties. The width and height of the page are given by the following expressions:

```
PrintDocument1.DefaultPageSettings.PaperSize.Width
PrintDocument1.DefaultPageSettings.PaperSize.Height
```

The top of the page is at coordinates (0, 0), which corresponds to the top-left corner of the page. We never actually print at this corner. The coordinates of the top-left corner of the printable area of the page are given by the following expressions:

```
PrintDocument1.DefaultPageSettings.Margins.Top
PrintDocument1.DefaultPageSettings.Margins.Left
```

VB.NET AT WORK: THE SIMPLEPRINTOUT PROJECT

Let's start with a very simple application that prints a string at the top-left corner of the page (the origin of the page) and a rectangle that delimits the page's printable area. To print something, start by dropping the PrintDocument object on your form. An instance of the control will appear in the Components tray, as this control is invisible at runtime. Then place a button on the form and in its Click event handler enter the following statement:

```
PrintDocument1.Print()
```

This tells the PrintDocument object that you're ready to print. The PrintDocument object will fire the BeginPrint event, where you can place any initialization code. Then, it will fire the PrintPage event, whose definition is

```
Private Sub PrintDocument1_PrintPage(ByVal sender As Object, _
            ByVal e As System.Drawing.Printing.PrintPageEventArgs) _
            Handles PrintDocument1.PrintPage

End Sub
```

This event doesn't signal an external action; it's the PrintDocument object's way of receiving your printing statements (it tells the application "I'm ready to print another page, so please tell me what to print"). As implied by its name, the PrintPage event is fired once for each page. You must place the VB code required to produce the desired output in this event's handler. So, how do we access the printer from within this event?

The *e* argument exposes several members, the most important of them being the Graphics property. The `e.Graphics` property is a Graphics object, which you can use to draw on the page. Anything you draw on this object is printed on paper. As you recall from the previous chapter, the `e.Graphics` object represents the drawing surface. When printing, the same object represents the paper in your printer's tray.

Let's start by printing a single word at the origin of the page, which is its top-left corner. To draw a string, call the Graphic object's DrawString method, as shown here:

```
Dim pFont As Font
pFont = New Font("Comic Sans MS", 20)
e.Graphics.DrawString("ORIGIN", pFont, Brushes.Black, 0, 0)
```

The last two arguments of the DrawString method are the coordinates of a point, where the string will be printed. As you notice, the string is printed below the origin so that it's visible. If you attempt to print a string at the bottom-right corner of the page, the entire string will fall just outside the page and no visible output will be produced.

No matter what your default printer is, it's highly unlikely that it's been set to no margins. As you can see, the page's margins aren't enforced by the PrintDocument object; you must respect them from within your code, as it is possible to print anywhere on the page. To take into consideration the page's margins, change the coordinates from (0, 0) to the left and top margins.

You can also use the other members of the Graphics object, as you did in the previous chapter to generate graphics. The following statement will render the text on the page using an anti-alias technique (anti-aliased text looks much smoother than text rendered with the default method):

```
e.Graphics.TextRenderingHint = Drawing.Text.TextRenderingHint.AntiAlias
```

Next, we'll print a rectangle around the area of page in which we're allowed to print—a rectangle delimited by the margins of the page. To draw this rectangle, we need to know the size of all four margins, and the size of the page, obviously. To read (or set) the page's margins, use the `PrintDocument1.DefaultPageSettings.Margin` object, which provides the Left, Right, Top, and Bottom properties. We're also going to need the dimensions of the page, which we can read through the Width and Height properties of the `PrintDocument1.DefaultPageSettings.PaperSize` object. The four margins are calculated and stored in four variables with the following statements:

```
Dim Lmargin, Rmargin, Tmargin, Bmargin As Integer
With PrintDocument1.DefaultPageSettings.Margins
    Lmargin = .Left
    Rmargin = .Right
    Tmargin = .Top
    Bmargin = .Bottom
End With
```

The rectangle we want to draw should start at the point (*Lmargin*, *Tmargin*) and extend *PrintWidth* units to the right and *PrintHeight* units down. These two variables are the width and height of the page minus the respective margins, and they're calculated with the following statements:

```
Dim PrintWidth, PrintHeight As Integer
With PrintDocument1.DefaultPageSettings.PaperSize
    PrintWidth = .Width - Lmargin - Rmargin
    PrintHeight = .Height - Tmargin - Bmargin
End With
```

Then insert the following statements in the PrintPage event handler to draw the rectangle:

```
Dim R As Rectangle
R = New Rectangle(Lmargin, Tmargin, PrintWidth, PrintHeight)
e.Graphics.DrawRectangle(Pens.Black, R)
```

You've seen all the statements that will generate the desired output and they're all familiar to you from the previous chapter. You will find these statements in the SimplePrintout project, which consists of a form with a button. In summary, here's how you'll build the SimplePrintout project from scratch. First, create the interface (a single button on the form will suffice). Then drop an instance of the PrintDocument control on the form. This control must exist on every form that sends data to the printer. The code behind the button initiates the printing with the following statement:

```
Private Sub Button1_Click(ByVal sender As System.Object, _
            ByVal e As System.EventArgs) Handles Button1.Click
    PrintDocument1.Print()
End Sub
```

The action takes place from within the PrintPage event handler, which is shown in Listing 15.2. The event handler contains all the statements presented in the previous paragraphs and a few comments.

LISTING 15.2: GENERATING A SIMPLE PRINTOUT

```
Private Sub PrintDocument1_PrintPage(ByVal sender As Object,_
            ByVal e As System.Drawing.Printing.PrintPageEventArgs) _
            Handles PrintDocument1.PrintPage
' Turn on antialias for text
    e.Graphics.TextRenderingHint = Drawing.Text.TextRenderingHint.AntiAlias
' Print a string at the origin
    Dim pFont As Font
    pFont = New Font("Comic Sans MS", 20)
    e.Graphics.DrawString("ORIGIN", pFont, Brushes.Black, 0, 0)
' Read margins into local variables
    Dim Lmargin, Rmargin, Tmargin, Bmargin As Integer
    With PrintDocument1.DefaultPageSettings.Margins
        Lmargin = .Left
        Rmargin = .Right
        Tmargin = .Top
        Bmargin = .Bottom
    End With
' Calculate the dimensions of the printable area
    Dim PrintWidth, PrintHeight As Integer
    With PrintDocument1.DefaultPageSettings.PaperSize
        PrintWidth = .Width - Lmargin - Rmargin
        PrintHeight = .Height - Tmargin - Bmargin
    End With
' Now print the rectangle
    Dim R As Rectangle
    R = New Rectangle(Lmargin, Tmargin, PrintWidth, PrintHeight)
    e.Graphics.DrawRectangle(Pens.Black, R)
End Sub
```

VB.NET AT WORK: THE PAGESETTINGS PROJECT

Let's put together the information presented so far by printing something more elaborate. This example prints a rectangle bounded by the margins of the page as before. In addition to the rectangle, it also prints four strings, one in each margin (as seen in Figure 15.5). These strings will have different orientations, as shown in the following figure. The project that generated the output is called PageSettings, and you will find it in this chapter's folder on the CD. The same project also demonstrates how to display the PageSetup dialog box from within your code and generate a printout according to the settings on this dialog box. It may not be the most practical example, but it demonstrates some basic printing techniques.

FIGURE 15.5

The output of the PageSettings project

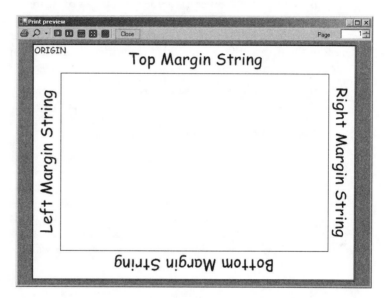

The statements of the previous example print a rectangle enclosing the printable area of the page. Printing the labels is a bit involved. As you can see, the four strings appear in all four orientations, and therefore some rotation transformation is involved. We'll discuss the code for printing the captions later. For now, let's demonstrate the PageSetupDialog control and how you take the settings on this dialog box from within your code.

Setting Up the Page

To display this dialog box from within your code, first place an instance of the PageSetupDialog control on your form—it will actually appear in the Components tray below the form, because it's invisible at runtime. Then set its PageSettings property to a PageSettings object that contains the default settings for the printer. We usually set this property to the DefaultPageSettings property of the PrintDocument object, although you can create a new PageSettings object and set its properties from within your code. Finally, display the dialog box by calling its ShowDialog method:

```
PageSetupDialog1.PageSettings = PrintDocument1.DefaultPageSettings
PageSetupDialog1.ShowDialog()
PrintDocument1.DefaultPageSettings = PageSetupDialog1.PageSettings
```

Upon return, we assign the PageSettings property of the control to the DefaultPageSettings property of the PrintDocument object. Now, we must take into consideration the settings specified on the dialog box from within the PrintPage event's code. The area on the page in which you must restrict your output is a rectangle, with its top-left corner at the left and top margin, and its dimensions are the width and height of the page less the corresponding margins. The only implication is when the user changes the orientation of the page. When you're printing in landscape mode, the size of the paper doesn't change. If you examine the Width and Height properties of the PaperSize object, you'll realize that the page is always taller than it is wide. This means that we must swap the width and height from within our code. The margins, however, remain the same.

To find out whether the user has changed the page's orientation, examine the Landscape property of the DefaultPageSettings object. If it's True, it means that the user wants to print in landscape mode and you must swap the page's width and height units. The following statements calculate the dimensions of the area of the page within the margins, where all the printing will take place, as well as the new width and height of the page:

```
If PrintDocument1.DefaultPageSettings.Landscape Then
    With PrintDocument1.DefaultPageSettings.PaperSize
        PrintWidth = .Height - Tmargin - Bmargin
        PrintHeight = .Width - Rmargin - Lmargin
        PageWidth = .Height
        PageHeight = .Width
    End With
End If
```

If you run the PageSettings project now, you will see that it prints the string "ORIGIN" at the top-left corner of the page, regardless of the page's orientation. These few statements in effect turn around the "image" of the printout, and the rest of the code will work in either orientation.

Printing the Labels

Now we can focus on the code that prints the captions in the space of the four margins, which is considerably more elaborate. The top margin's caption isn't rotated; it's printed at the default orientation. The caption in the right margin is rotated by 90 degrees, and the caption of the bottom margin is rotated by 180 degrees. The caption of the left margin is rotated by –90 degrees. These rotations take place around the origin, so the labels must also be moved to their places with a translation transformation.

Let's look at the code that prints the "Right Margin String" caption, shown in Listing 15.3. The following statements are responsible for printing the caption in the right margin. They make use of the variables that hold the margins and the page's dimensions, which were discussed already.

LISTING 15.3: PRINTING A CAPTION IN THE RIGHT MARGIN

```
strWidth = e.Graphics.MeasureString(RMarginCaption, pFont).Width
strHeight = e.Graphics.MeasureString(RMarginCaption, pFont).Height
X = PageWidth - (Rmargin - strHeight) / 2
Y = TMargin + (PrintHeight - strWidth) / 2
e.Graphics.ResetTransform()
```

```
e.Graphics.TranslateTransform(X, Y)
e.Graphics.RotateTransform(90)
e.Graphics.DrawString(RMarginCaption, pFont, Brushes.Black, 0, 0)
```

First we calculate the string's width and height. The string will be rotated by 90 degrees before being printed. The rotation alone would place the string just outside the left margin, so we must translate it to the right. The amount of the translation is the page's width minus half the difference between the string's height and the right margin. Translating the caption by the width of the page would bring it to the very right edge of the paper. To center it in the right margin, we must split the difference of the string's height from the right margin on either side of the string. We're using the string's height in calculating the X coordinate and the string's width in calculating the Y coordinate, because after the string is rotated by 90 degrees, the width and height will be swapped. X and Y are the amounts by which the string must be moved along the horizontal and vertical axis. This movement will be performed by a translation transformation. The rotation of the string will be performed by a rotation transformation (for more information on transformations, see Chapter 14). Because transformations are cumulative, the code resets any existing transformations and applies two new ones. Then, the DrawString method is called to print the string. The DrawString method draws the string at the point (0, 0), but the two transformations will place it at the proper place.

The code for placing the other three captions is quite analogous. It uses the proper translation and rotation transformations, and the only complication is the calculation of the coordinates of the translation transformation. The listing of the PrintPage event handler of the PageSettings project is fairly lengthy, but it's included in Listing 15.4 for your convenience.

LISTING 15.4: PRINTING THE RECTANGLE AND THE MARGIN CAPTIONS

```
Private Sub PrintDocument1_PrintPage(ByVal sender As Object, _
            ByVal e As System.Drawing.Printing.PrintPageEventArgs) _
            Handles PrintDocument1.PrintPage
    Dim R As Rectangle
    Dim strWidth, strHeight As Integer
    Dim pFont As Font
    pFont = New Font("Comic Sans MS", 20)
    e.Graphics.DrawString("ORIGIN", pFont, Brushes.Black, 0, 0)
    pFont = New Font("Comic Sans MS", 40)
    Dim X, Y As Integer
    Dim TMarginCaption As String = "Top Margin String"
    Dim LMarginCaption As String = "Left Margin String"
    Dim RMarginCaption As String = "Right Margin String"
    Dim BMarginCaption As String = "Bottom Margin String"
    Dim LMargin, RMargin, TMargin, BMargin As Integer
    With PrintDocument1.DefaultPageSettings.Margins
        LMargin = .Left
        RMargin = .Right
        TMargin = .Top
        BMargin = .Bottom
```

```
            End With
            Dim PrintWidth, PrintHeight, PageWidth, PageHeight As Integer
            With PrintDocument1.DefaultPageSettings.PaperSize
                PrintWidth = .Width - LMargin - RMargin
                PrintHeight = .Height - TMargin - BMargin
                PageWidth  = .Width
                PageHeight = .Height
            End With
            If PrintDocument1.DefaultPageSettings.Landscape Then
                With PrintDocument1.DefaultPageSettings.PaperSize
                    PrintWidth = .Height - TMargin - BMargin
                    PrintHeight = .Width - RMargin - LMargin
                    PageWidth = .Height
                    PageHeight = .Width
                End With
            End If
    ' Draw rectangle
            R = New Rectangle(LMargin, TMargin, PageWidth - LMargin - RMargin, _
                            PageHeight - BMargin - TMargin)
            e.Graphics.DrawRectangle(Pens.Black, R)
    ' Draw top margin's caption
            strWidth = e.Graphics.MeasureString(TMarginCaption, pFont).Width
            strHeight = e.Graphics.MeasureString(TMarginCaption, pFont).Height
            X = LMargin + (PrintWidth - strWidth) / 2
            Y = (TMargin - strHeight) / 2
            e.Graphics.TranslateTransform(X, Y)
            e.Graphics.DrawString(TMarginCaption, pFont, Brushes.Black, 0, 0)
    ' Draw right margin's caption
            strWidth = e.Graphics.MeasureString(RMarginCaption, pFont).Width
            strHeight = e.Graphics.MeasureString(RMarginCaption, pFont).Height
            X = PageWidth - (RMargin - strHeight) / 2
            Y = TMargin + (PrintHeight - strWidth) / 2
            e.Graphics.ResetTransform()
            e.Graphics.TranslateTransform(X, Y)
            e.Graphics.RotateTransform(90)
            e.Graphics.DrawString(RMarginCaption, pFont, Brushes.Black, 0, 0)
    ' Draw bottom margin's caption
            strWidth = e.Graphics.MeasureString(BMarginCaption, pFont).Width
            strHeight = e.Graphics.MeasureString(BMarginCaption, pFont).Height
            X = PageWidth - RMargin - (PrintWidth - strWidth) / 2
            Y = PageHeight - (BMargin - strHeight) / 2
            e.Graphics.ResetTransform()
            e.Graphics.TranslateTransform(X, Y)
            e.Graphics.RotateTransform(180)
            e.Graphics.DrawString(BMarginCaption, pFont, Brushes.Black, 0, 0)
    ' Draw left margin's caption
            strWidth = e.Graphics.MeasureString(LMarginCaption, pFont).Width
            strHeight = e.Graphics.MeasureString(LMarginCaption, pFont).Height
```

```
        X = (LMargin - strHeight) / 2
        Y = TMargin + (PrintHeight + strWidth) / 2
        e.Graphics.ResetTransform()
        e.Graphics.TranslateTransform(X, Y)
        e.Graphics.RotateTransform(-90)
        e.Graphics.DrawString(LMarginCaption, pFont, Brushes.Black, 0, 0)
    End Sub
```

As always, you must call the PrintDocument object's Print method for this event handler to be activated. You can use the Print method of the PrintDocument object, but the project you'll find on the CD uses the PrintPreviewDocument object to display a preview of the printout. Listing 15.5 shows the code behind the button on the form:

LISTING 15.5: THE PRINT BUTTON

```
Private Sub Button1_Click(ByVal sender As System.Object, _
                ByVal e As System.EventArgs) Handles Button1.Click
    Try
        PrintPreviewDialog1.Document = PrintDocument1
        PageSetupDialog1.PageSettings = PrintDocument1.DefaultPageSettings
        PageSetupDialog1.ShowDialog()
        PrintDocument1.DefaultPageSettings = PageSetupDialog1.PageSettings
        PrintPreviewDialog1.ShowDialog()
    Catch exc As Exception
        MsgBox("Printing Operation Failed" & vbCrLf & exc.Message)
    End Try
End Sub
```

The code uses an error handler to prevent the program from crashing with a runtime exception if there's a problem with the printer. The application should work if there's a default printer; it will fail to generate a preview only if the default printer is a network printer and you have no access to it at the time.

The first statement sets up the PrintPreview control by setting its Document property to the Print-Document object. The second statement assigns the default page settings to the PageSetupDialog control and the following statement displays the Page Setup dialog box. Once the user has specified the desired settings and closes the dialog box, the new settings are assigned to the PrintDocument object's DefaultPageSettings property. The last statement displays the Print Preview dialog box. This statement initiates the printing process, which sends its output to the preview pane, instead of the printer. That's all it takes to add a preview feature to your application. The PrintPreviewDialog control is discussed later in this chapter.

If you feel uncomfortable with the transformations, especially the rotation transformation, Figure 15.6 shows what happens to a string when it's rotated in all four directions around the origin. The origin—the point with coordinates (0, 0)—is where the two axes meet.

FIGURE 15.6

Rotating a string
around the origin

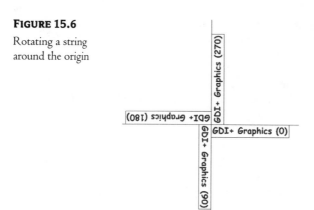

 The statements in Listing 15.6 rotate the string "GDI+ Graphics" around the origin by 90, 180, and 270 degrees. The numbers in parentheses indicate the angle of rotation for each string. Of course, I couldn't print to the left of the origin, or above the origin, so the rotated strings were translated by 50 percent of the page's width to the right and 50 percent of the page's height down to appear at the middle of the page. The two axes were also translated by the same amounts in the two directions. This illustration's purpose is to help you visualize how the string is rotated around the origin. Besides the string itself, the enclosing rectangle is also printed. This is the rectangle returned by the Measure-String method, subject to the same transformations as the string it encloses. Listing 15.6 shows the statements that generated the output shown in Figure 15.6. The project described here is the Rotated-Strings project, and you will find it in this chapter's folder on the CD.

LISTING 15.6: ROTATION AND TRANSLATION TRANSFORMATIONS

```
Private Sub PrintDocument1_PrintPage(ByVal sender As Object, _
            ByVal e As System.Drawing.Printing.PrintPageEventArgs) _
            Handles PrintDocument1.PrintPage
  Dim Tx, Ty As Integer
' Tx, Ty are the coordinates of the center point on the page
  Tx = e.PageSettings.PaperSize.Width / 2
  Ty = e.PageSettings.PaperSize.Height / 2
' Draw a crosshair line at the middle of the page
  e.Graphics.DrawLine(New Pen(Color.Red, 2), Tx, 0, Tx, Ty * 2)
  e.Graphics.DrawLine(New Pen(Color.Red, 2), 0, Ty, Tx * 2, Ty)
  Dim fnt As Font = New Font("Comic Sans MS", 24, FontStyle.Bold)
  Dim RectSize As SizeF
  Dim Rect As Rectangle
' Print string without rotation
  e.Graphics.TranslateTransform(Tx, Ty)
  e.Graphics.DrawString("GDI+ Graphics (0)", fnt, Brushes.Black, 0, 0)
  RectSize = e.Graphics.MeasureString("GDI+ Graphics (0)", fnt)
  Rect = New Rectangle(0, 0, RectSize.Width, RectSize.Height)
  e.Graphics.DrawRectangle(Pens.Green, Rect)
' Print string rotated 90 degrees
```

```
      e.Graphics.ResetTransform()
      e.Graphics.TranslateTransform(Tx, Ty)
      e.Graphics.RotateTransform(90)
      e.Graphics.DrawString("GDI+ Graphics (90)", fnt, Brushes.Black, 0, 0)
      RectSize = e.Graphics.MeasureString("GDI+ Graphics (90)", fnt)
      Rect = New Rectangle(0, 0, RectSize.Width, RectSize.Height)
      e.Graphics.DrawRectangle(Pens.Green, Rect)
   ' Print string rotated 270 degrees
      e.Graphics.ResetTransform()
      e.Graphics.TranslateTransform(Tx, Ty)
      e.Graphics.RotateTransform(270)
      e.Graphics.DrawString("GDI+ Graphics (270)", fnt, Brushes.Black, 0, 0)
      RectSize = e.Graphics.MeasureString("GDI+ Graphics (270)", fnt)
      Rect = New Rectangle(0, 0, RectSize.Width, RectSize.Height)
      e.Graphics.DrawRectangle(Pens.Green, Rect)
   ' Print string rotated 180 degrees
      e.Graphics.ResetTransform()
      e.Graphics.TranslateTransform(Tx, Ty)
      e.Graphics.RotateTransform(180)
      e.Graphics.DrawString("GDI+ Graphics (180)", fnt, Brushes.Black, 0, 0)
      RectSize = e.Graphics.MeasureString("GDI+ Graphics (180)", fnt)
      Rect = New Rectangle(0, 0, RectSize.Width, RectSize.Height)
      e.Graphics.DrawRectangle(Pens.Green, Rect)
   End Sub
```

As you know by now, to activate the PrintPage event handler, you must call the Print method of the PrintDocument object or display the Print Preview dialog box by calling its ShowDialog method. The following statements display the rotated strings on a Print Preview dialog box:

```
PrintPreviewDialog1.Document = PrintDocument1
PrintPreviewDialog1.UseAntiAlias = True
PrintPreviewDialog1.ShowDialog()
```

Printing Examples

Using the Framework's printing objects is straightforward, in principle. Depending on the type of the printout you want to generate, however, the code of the PrintPage event handler can get quite complicated. Since there are no techniques that you can apply to all situations, I've included a few typical examples to demonstrate how to use the same objects to perform very different tasks. The first example demonstrates how to print tabular reports. A tabular report has the form of a grid, with columns of different width and rows of different height.

The second example is the printing of text and, even though this is the least exciting type of printout, you should be able to send text to the printer. As you will see, it's not a trivial operation. The last example prints bitmaps, probably the simplest type of printout. The only challenge with printing bitmaps is that you may have to reduce the size of the bitmap to make it fit in the width, or the height, of the page.

Printing Tabular Data

This is the printing operation you'll be using most often in typical business applications that require custom printing. Figure 15.7 shows an example of a printout with tabular data. This printout was generated by the PrintTable project, which you can find in this chapter's folder on the CD, and its code is discussed in detail here.

The ISBN column contains a 10-character string, and it's quite simple to handle. All you have to do is make sure that the ISBN will fit in the corresponding column. If you allow the user to select the font at runtime and you can't set a fixed width for this column, you should print only as many characters as will fit in the reserved width. In this example, we aren't going to do anything special about the ISBN column.

FIGURE 15.7

Using the Print-Table application to print data in a tabular arrangement

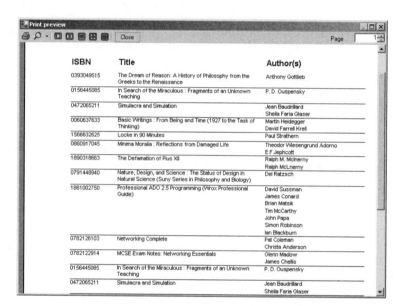

The Title column has a variable length, and you may have to break long titles into two or more printed lines—and this is the real challenge of this application. As you recall from the discussion of the DrawString method in Chapter 14, this method can print a string in a rectangle you pass as an argument. The width of this rectangle must be the same as the width of the Title column. The height of the rectangle should be enough for the entire text to fit in it. In our code, we'll use a rectangle with the appropriate width and adequate height to make sure that the entire title will be printed. Alternatively, you can trim the title if it's too long, but there's no point in trimming substantial information.

Of course, depending on its length, the title may take up one, two, or even more lines on the page. You must also keep track of the height of the title's cell and take it into consideration in printing the next row of the table.

The last intricacy of this application is the Authors column. Each book may have no authors or one or more authors, and we'll print each author on a separate line. As you realize, the total height of each row depends on the height of the Title or Author cell. We must keep track of the height of these two cells and move down accordingly before printing the following row. Where the height of the Authors cells is determined by the number of authors—we'll print each author on a single line and assume that the name does not exceed the width of the page—we must provide the code to break the title into multiple lines.

So, where does the data come from? It could come from a text file, an XML document, or a data-base. It doesn't really make a difference, as long as you can access one row at a time and extract its fields. For the purposes of this example, and since we haven't discussed databases yet, I'm using a ListView control to store the data. The ListView control is populated in the form's Load event handler. Each book is a different item in the ListView, and the various fields are subitems. The main item's Text property is the book's ISBN, and the remaining fields are stored as subitems. I will not show the code that populates the ListView control here, just the statements that populate the first two items. I've taken sample data from an online bookstore and, in some cases, edited their titles to make them long or added fictitious authors. For all intents and purposes, the data used in this sample application should be considered fictitious.

```
Dim BookItem As New ListViewItem()
BookItem.Text = "0393049515"
BookItem.SubItems.Add("The Dream of Reason: " & _
                "A History of Philosophy from the Greeks to the Renaissance")
BookItem.SubItems.Add("Anthony Gottlieb")
ListView1.Items.Add(BookItem)
BookItem = New ListViewItem()
BookItem.Text = "0156445085"
BookItem.SubItems.Add("In Search of the Miraculous: " & _
                "Fragments of an Unknown Teaching")
BookItem.SubItems.Add("P. D. Ouspensky")
ListView1.Items.Add(BookItem)
```

You can open the PrintTable project on the CD and examine the code of the button that populates the ListView control. Once the list has been populated, you can click the Preview & Print button to generate the preview and print the report. The main form of the PrintTable project, populated with the data shown in the sample printout, is shown in Figure 15.8.

FIGURE 15.8

The PrintTable project's main form

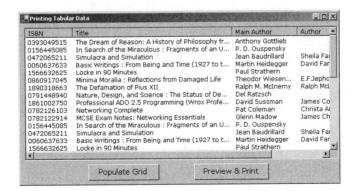

FORMATTING THE CELLS

The report is generated one row at a time. The vertical coordinate of the row is stored in the variable *Y*, which is incremented accordingly for each new row. This coordinate applies to all cells, and if a cell contains multiple lines, the *y* coordinate is adjusted accordingly for each line. The *x* coordinate of each column is the same for all rows. These coordinates are calculated at the beginning and they don't change from row to row.

Breaking a string into multiple lines isn't trivial. You should include as many words as you can on each line without exceeding the available width. Fortunately, the Graphics object's MeasureString method can break a string into the required number of lines to fit the string into a rectangle and report the number of lines. This form of the MeasureString method is

```
Graphics.MeasureString(string, font, size, format, cols, lines)
```

The first argument is the string to be printed, and it will be rendered in the font specified by the second argument. The *size* argument is the width and height of the rectangle in which the string must fit. In our case, the width of the *size* argument is the width of the cell in which the string must fit. The last two arguments are the number of characters that will fit across the rectangle and the number of lines the string must be broken into. Even though we don't know the height of the rectangle in advance, we can use an absurdly large value. The MeasureString method will tell us how many text lines it needs, and we'll use this value to calculate the height of the rectangle. To calculate the height of the cell in which the title will fit, the program uses the following statements:

```
Dim cols, lines As Integer
e.Graphics.MeasureString(strTitle, tableFont, New SizeF(W2, 100), _
                    New StringFormat(), lines, cols)
```

strTitle is a string variable that holds the title, and *tableFont* is the font in which the string will be rendered. *W2* is the width of the second column of the grid, where the title appears. This is a fixed value, calculated ahead of time. The initial height of the rectangle is 100 pixels, and we hope that even the longest title will fit in this rectangle. You can make the cell even taller, but this sample project will work as advertised with reasonably sized fields. It is possible for a given cell's text to be so long that it will take a page and a half to print. The PrintTable project can't handle similar extreme situations. You will have to provide additional code to handle the overflow of a cell to the following page.

The *lines* and *cols* variables are passed by reference, and they are set by the MeasureString method to the number of lines and number of characters that will fit in the specified rectangle. The exact location of the rectangle doesn't make any difference; only its dimensions matter, and that's why the third argument is a SizeF object and not a Rectangle object.

Once we have the number of lines it takes for the title to be printed in the specified width, we can advance the vertical coordinate by the following amount:

```
lines * tableFont.GetHeight(e.Graphics)
```

tableFont is the font we use to print the table. Its GetHeight method returns the height of the font when rendered on the Graphics object passed as argument. This will take care of breaking long titles into multiple lines, which is the most challenging aspect of the code. The last cell in each row contains a line for each author. The following loop goes through all the authors and prints them, each one on a separate line:

```
For subitm = 2 To ListView1.Items(itm).SubItems.Count - 1
    str = ListView1.Items(itm).SubItems(subitm).Text
    e.Graphics.DrawString(str, tableFont, Brushes.Black, X3, Yc)
    Yc = Yc + tableFont.Height + 2
Next
```

The *y* coordinate of the last author is stored in the variable *Yc*. To calculate the *y* coordinate of the next row of the table, we compare the *Y* and *Yc* variables and keep the larger value. This value, plus a small displacement, is used as the *y* coordinate for the following line. Listing 15.7 is the complete listing of the PrintPage event handler of the PrintTable project.

LISTING 15.7: THE PRINTPAGE EVENT HANDLER OF THE PRINTTABLE PROJECT

```
Private Sub PrintDocument1_PrintPage(ByVal sender As Object, _
            ByVal e As System.Drawing.Printing.PrintPageEventArgs) _
            Handles PrintDocument1.PrintPage
    Y = PrintDocument1.DefaultPageSettings.Margins.Top + 20
    e.Graphics.DrawString("ISBN", TitleFont, Brushes.Black, X1, Y)
    e.Graphics.DrawString("Title", TitleFont, Brushes.Black, X2, Y)
    e.Graphics.DrawString("Author(s)", TitleFont, Brushes.Black, X3, Y)
    Y = Y + 30
    While itm < ListView1.Items.Count
        Dim str As String
        str = ListView1.Items(itm).Text
        e.Graphics.DrawString(str, tableFont, Brushes.Black, X1, Y)
        str = ListView1.Items(itm).SubItems(1).Text
        Dim R As New RectangleF(X2, Y, W2, 80)
        e.Graphics.DrawString(str, tableFont, Brushes.Black, R)
        Dim lines, cols As Integer
        e.Graphics.MeasureString(str, tableFont, New SizeF(W2, 50), _
                            New StringFormat(), cols, lines)
        Dim subitm As Integer, Yc As Integer
        Yc = Y
        For subitm = 2 To ListView1.Items(itm).SubItems.Count - 1
            str = ListView1.Items(itm).SubItems(subitm).Text
            e.Graphics.DrawString(str, tableFont, Brushes.Black, X3, Yc)
            Yc = Yc + tableFont.Height + 2
        Next
        Y = Y + lines * tableFont.Height + 5
        Y = Math.Max(Y, Yc)
        With PrintDocument1.DefaultPageSettings
            e.Graphics.DrawLine(Pens.Black, .Margins.Left, Y, _
                            .PaperSize.Width - .Margins.Right, Y)
            If Y > 0.95 * (.PaperSize.Height - .Margins.Bottom) Then
                e.HasMorePages = True
```

```
            Exit Sub
        End If
    End With
    itm = itm + 1
  End While
  e.HasMorePages = False
End Sub
```

The code makes use of a few variables that are declared on the Form level with the following statements:

```
Dim tableFont, titleFont As Font
Dim X1, X2, X3 As Integer
Dim W1, W2, W3 As Integer
Dim Y As Integer
Dim itm As Integer
```

Before we can print, we must specify the widths of the columns. Since we know the information we're going to display in each column, we can make a good estimate of the column widths. The first column, where the ISBN is displayed, starts at the left margin of the page and extends 100 units to the right. The default unit is 1/100 of an inch, so the ISBN column's width is 1 inch. The title column should take up most of the page's width. In the PrintTable example, I've given 50 percent of the available page width to this column. The remaining space goes to the Author column. The variables *X1*, *X2*, and *X3* are the *x* coordinates of the left edge of each column, while the variables *W1*, *W2*, and *W3* are the widths of the columns. These variables are set in the Print button's Click event handler. Then, the subroutine displays the PrintPreview dialog box to display the document, as it will be printed on the page. Listing 15.8 shows the Print button's Click event handler.

LISTING 15.8: SETTING UP THE COLUMNS AND PRINTING THE TABLE

```
Private Sub Button2_Click(ByVal sender As System.Object, _
            ByVal e As System.EventArgs) Handles Button2.Click
  PageSetupDialog1.PageSettings = PrintDocument1.DefaultPageSettings
  If PageSetupDialog1.ShowDialog() Then
      PrintDocument1.DefaultPageSettings = PageSetupDialog1.PageSettings
  End If
  tableFont = New Font("Arial", 8)
  titleFont = New Font("Arial", 12, FontStyle.Bold)
  X1 = PrintDocument1.DefaultPageSettings.Margins.Left
  Dim pageWidth As Integer
  With PrintDocument1.DefaultPageSettings
      pageWidth = .PaperSize.Width - .Margins.Left - .Margins.Right
  End With
  X2 = X1 + 100
  X3 = X2 + pageWidth * 0.5
```

```
        W1 = X2 - X1
        W2 = X3 - X2
        W3 = pageWidth - X3
        PrintPreviewDialog1.Document = PrintDocument1
        PrintPreviewDialog1.ShowDialog()
        itm = 0
    End Sub
```

The global variables are set in the Print button's Click event handler, but they're all declared outside any procedure, because they must be accessible by the PrintPage event handler. After setting the variables, you can call the ShowDialog method of the PrintPreviewDialog control to preview the document.

The PrintPage event is fired whenever a new page must start. First, we print the header of the table with the following statements:

```
Y = PrintDocument1.DefaultPageSettings.Margins.Top + 20
e.Graphics.DrawString("ISBN", titleFont, Brushes.Black, X1, Y)
e.Graphics.DrawString("Title", titleFont, Brushes.Black, X2, Y)
e.Graphics.DrawString("Author(s)", titleFont, Brushes.Black, X3, Y)
Y = Y + 30
```

titleFont is a Font object that represents the font we use for the table header and is declared on the Form level. The rest of the program uses the *tableFont* object, which represents the font in which the table's text will be rendered. Here are the declarations of these two objects:

```
Dim tableFont As Font
tableFont = New Font("Arial", 8)
Dim titleFont As Font
titleFont = New Font("Arial", 12, FontStyle.Bold)
```

Then we set up two nested loops. The outer loop goes through all the items on the ListView control, and the inner loop goes through the subitems of the current item. The structure of the two loops is the following:

```
While itm < ListView1.Items.Count
    { print current item }
    For subitm = 2 To ListView1.Items(itm).SubItems.Count - 1
        { print all subitems }
    Next
End While
```

The PrintTable project is based on the assumption that the author names will fit in the specified width. If not, part of the author name will flow over the right margin. You can either break long author names (similar to breaking the title into multiple lines) or truncate author names. If you want to print a box around the report, you must definitely truncate the author names, so that they won't run over the right margin. Alternatively, you can print the report in landscape mode—you may have to adjust the widths of the Title and Author columns.

The PrintTable project is the starting point for tabular reports, and it demonstrates the core of an application that prints tables. You will have to add a title to each page, a header and a footer for each page (with page numbers and dates), and quite possibly a grid to enclose the cells. Experiment with the PrintTable project by adding more features to it. You can become as creative as you wish with this application. I should also bring to your attention the fact that the PrintTable application ends the page when the report's height exceeds the 95 percent of the page's printable area. This test takes place after printing each item. If the last title printed on a page has a dozen different authors, it will run over the bottom of the page.

USING STATIC VARIABLES

The PrintPage event handler produces all the pages, one after the other. These pages, however, are not independent of one another. When you print a long text file, for example, you must keep track of the pages printed so far or the current line. If you set up a variable that keeps track of the current line, you shouldn't reset this variable every time the PrintPage event handler is executed. One way to maintain the value of a variable between consecutive calls of the same procedure is to declare it with the Static keyword. Static variables maintain their values between calls, unlike the private variables.

In the PrintTable project, I've used the *itm* variable to keep track of the item being printed. Each time a page is filled, the PrintPage event handler is terminated and we start printing on a new page. By making the variable *itm* static, we're sure that it won't be reset every time the PrintPage event handler is entered. Instead, all items are printed sequentially on one or more pages.

Printing Plain Text

In this section we'll examine a less-exciting operation, the printing of a text file. It should be a trivial task after the program that prints the tabular reports, but it's not nearly as trivial as you may think. But why bother with a simple operation like printing plain text? The reason is that no control has built-in printing capabilities, and text files are still quite common. Printing formatted text is even more complicated, so we'll start with plain text files.

Plain text means that all characters are printed in the same font, size, and style, just like the text you enter on a TextBox control. Your task is to start a new page when the current page fills and break the lines at, or before, the left margin. Because the text is totally uniform, you know in advance the height of each line and you can easily calculate the number of lines per page ahead of time.

If you look up the printing examples that come with Visual Studio, they're all based on the assumption that each text line fits across the page. As we all know, this is rarely true. The sample code provided simply dumps each text line to the printer and is much faster than the code you'll find in this section, but it's of little practical use and here's why. Text files are made up of lines, which may exceed by far the width of the page. It's your responsibility to break the long lines into shorter ones and fit them on the page. As you know, each paragraph in a text file is a separate line and rarely fits on a single line on the printed page. The TextBox control, for example, breaks lines according to its width, and if you resize the control at runtime, the line breaks will be recalculated. Your code must do exactly that: calculate the proper page breaks, so that the lines will fit on the page.

NOTE *The PrintText project discussed in the following section takes approximately 10 seconds to prepare a page of text on an 850 MHz computer. Following the discussion of the PrintText project, you will find a much faster technique for printing text, but it's not as flexible as the methods described in the following section.*

VB.NET AT WORK: THE PRINTTEXT PROJECT

In this section, we're going to build the PrintText application. The main form of this application contains a TextBox control and a button that prints the text on the control. The program displays a preview of the text on a PrintPreview dialog box, and you can print the text by clicking the Print button on the dialog box. Figure 15.9 shows a section of a text previewed with the PrintText application.

FIGURE 15.9

Printing and previewing documents with the PrintText application

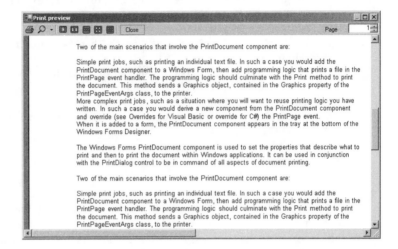

You can use the TextBox control to enter a few paragraphs or a few pages of text and then print them. Before we examine the code, let me describe shortly the process of breaking the text into lines that fit across the page. We'll start reading the text one word at a time (including white space, punctuation, and line feeds) and calculate the length of the word when printed on paper. If the length of the current line plus the length of the word don't exceed the width of the printable area, we'll append the word to the string and continue. At each step we'll call the MeasureString method to calculate the length of the string when printed. When this string exceeds the width of the printable area of the page, we'll print the string and create a new string with the word that wouldn't fit on the previous line, and then we'll start over again. The string will grow by one word at a time, until it's just right to be printed.

Let's start with the function that extracts the next word of the document on the TextBox control. This is the GetNextWord() function, which reads consecutive words from a text file and slowly builds a string by appending each word to the string. When the length of the string plus the length of the next word exceed the width of the page (excluding the margins, of course), we print the line and start a new line with the last word. The process continues until all the words in the document are exhausted. The GetNextWord() function, shown in Listing 15.9, keeps track of the current location in the document, so that it can read the next word every time it's called. To do so, it uses the *currPosition* variable, which is declared as Static. This variable is the index of the next word's first character in the text.

LISTING 15.9: THE GETNEXTWORD() FUNCTION

```
Function GetNextWord(Optional ByVal reset As Boolean = False) As String
    Static currPos As Integer
    Dim word As String
    If reset Then currPos = 0
    If currPos >= TextBox1.Text.Length Then Return ""
    While Not System.Char.IsLetterOrDigit(TextBox1.Text.Chars(currPos))
        word = word & TextBox1.Text.Chars(currPos)
        currPos = currPos + 1
        If currPos >= TextBox1.Text.Length Then Return word
    End While
    While Not (System.Char.IsWhiteSpace(TextBox1.Text.Chars(currPos)))
        word = word & TextBox1.Text.Chars(currPos)
        currPos = currPos + 1
        If currPos >= TextBox1.Text.Length Then Return word
    End While
    Return word
End Function
```

The GetNextWord() function accepts an optional argument, the *reset* argument. This argument forces the function to start reading words from the beginning of the text. Otherwise, you wouldn't be able to reuse it in the same session. After scanning the text once, it would return the empty string, indicating that there are no more words to be read. This function encapsulates all the complexity of isolating words and their surrounding spaces from the rest of the application, and you can use it in your applications in similar situations. However, you will have to modify it a little. This implementation of the GetNextWord() function doesn't ignore spaces and punctuation marks. In printing a document, all characters are significant, and you can't afford to ignore a single space. To extract individual words from a text document, you should treat punctuation marks as delimiters and ignore them, as well as trim all the spaces around the words.

We must also keep track of the height of the text, so that we can start a new page when needed. To start a new page we simply set the **e.HasMorePages** argument to True and exit the PrintPage event handler. The PrintDocument object will fire another PrintPage, in which we'll print a new page, and we'll continue until we run out of words.

To initiate the printout, the Print button contains the following statements:

```
Private Sub Button1_Click(ByVal sender As System.Object, _
              ByVal e As System.EventArgs) Handles Button1.Click
    PrintPreviewDialog1.Document = PrintDocument1
    PrintPreviewDialog1.ShowDialog()
    GetNextWord(True)
End Sub
```

Now we can focus on the code that creates the actual printout, which is shown in Listing 15.10. The code reads a word at time, adds its length to the length of the current line, and then compares it to the width of the printable area of the page. If the total length fits on the page, we proceed with the next word. If not, we print the line, advance vertically by a little more than the line's height, and start a new line with the last word that didn't make it on the line just printed. This technique assumes that the text doesn't contain words that can't fit on the width of the printable area of the page. You must add your own code to arbitrarily break such awfully long lines.

LISTING 15.10: THE PRINTTEXT PROJECT'S PRINTPAGE EVENT HANDLER

```
Private Sub PrintDocument1_PrintPage(ByVal sender As Object, _
                ByVal e As System.Drawing.Printing.PrintPageEventArgs) _
                Handles PrintDocument1.PrintPage
    Dim txtFont As New Font("Arial", 10)
    Dim txtH As Integer = _
        PrintDocument1.DefaultPageSettings.PaperSize.Height - _
        PrintDocument1.DefaultPageSettings.Margins.Top - _
        PrintDocument1.DefaultPageSettings.Margins.Bottom
    Dim LMargin As Integer = PrintDocument1.DefaultPageSettings.Margins.Left
    Dim TMargin As Integer = PrintDocument1.DefaultPageSettings.Margins.Top
    Dim txtW As Integer = _
        PrintDocument1.DefaultPageSettings.PaperSize.Width - _
        PrintDocument1.DefaultPageSettings.Margins.Left - _
        PrintDocument1.DefaultPageSettings.Margins.Right
    Dim linesPerPage As Integer = _
        e.MarginBounds.Height / txtFont.GetHeight(e.Graphics)
    Dim R As New RectangleF(LMargin, TMargin, txtW, txtH)
    Static line As String
    Dim word As String
    Dim cols, lines As Integer
    word = GetNextWord()
    While word <> "" And lines < linesPerPage
        line = line & word
        word = GetNextWord()
        e.Graphics.MeasureString(line & word, txtFont, New SizeF(txtW, txtH), _
                            New StringFormat(), cols, lines)
    End While
    If word = "" And Trim(line) <> "" Then
        e.Graphics.DrawString(line, txtFont, Brushes.Black, R, _
                            New StringFormat())
        e.HasMorePages = False
        Exit Sub
    End If
    e.Graphics.DrawString(line, txtFont, Brushes.Black, R, New StringFormat())
    e.HasMorePages = True
    line = word
End Sub
```

When the PrintPage event handler starts executing, it calculates the page's geometry (the margins and the dimensions of the printable area of the page), as well as the number of text lines that can fit on the page (variable *linesPerPage*). Then, it starts calling the GetNextWord() function from within a loop, which terminates when the printed text exceeds the height of the page (minus the margins, of course). Every time a new page is filled, it sets the `e.HasMorePages` property to True and then exits.

When the GetNextWord() function runs out of words, which means we've reached the end of the text, it returns an empty string and the PrintPage event handler sets the `e.HasMorePages` property to False and exits.

As you can see, the most complicated part of the application is the retrieval of the next word to be printed. By implementing the GetNextWord() function and inserting all the logic of isolating words—including their surrounding space and punctuation—into this function, we simplified the logic of the PrintPage event handler.

To experiment with the printing methods, you can insert the code to print the document's name and the current page number at the top of the page, or you can place a rectangle around the text. For an interesting effect, you can use a larger font, space vertically the text lines, and draw a light gray line under each text line. You can also insert the code presented earlier in this chapter to handle both landscape and portrait orientation.

You can also adjust the code to handle program listings. Program listings are plain text files, like the ones you can print with this application, but you must mark long code lines that are broken to fit on the page. You can insert a special symbol either at the end of a code line that continues on the following line on the page or in front of the continued line. This symbol is usually a bent arrow that resembles the Return key.

The PrintText project doesn't send its output directly to the printer; instead, it generates a preview that allows you to examine the printout on the screen until you get your code right. You will notice that the generation of the preview is a slow process. There are many things you can do to speed up the code. For example, you can read several words at a time. It's very unlikely that a line contains fewer than five or six words, so why waste time calculating the width of a very short line? You can also estimate the number of words that will fit on a page, read as many words, and then calculate how many lines they will take on the printed page with the MeasureString method. If they all fit on the page, you can add one word at a time (as we did earlier) until you fill the page. If the printed text exceeds the height of the page, you must subtract words until you fill the page, but no more. This is a fairly complicated logic that would overwhelm the discussion of the basic printing objects. Once you understand how the text is broken into lines and how to figure out when to change pages, you can make the algorithms as complicated as you wish.

VB.NET AT WORK: THE PRINTTEXT2 PROJECT

The PrintText project is fairly slow. It takes just over 10 seconds to prepare each page, which is quite slow compared to printing text with Notepad or even WordPad. Some readers may have already guessed how to speed up the printing of plain text. Why use the MeasureString method on individual words to find out whether they fit on the current line; why not pass the entire text as argument to this method, along with a rectangle that represents the printable area of the page? The method will return the number of characters that can be printed on the page, and then we can repeat the process with the rest of the text. Indeed, this is the way to print straight text.

The idea is to instantiate a Rectangle object that represents the printable area of the page. Then call the MeasureString method to find out how many characters will fit into the rectangle and print so many characters with the DrawString method. Just two method calls, and the first page is ready. Repeat the same process for the following pages, starting with the character following the last character printed on the previous page. This method is fast and works with all text files. However, it's not as flexible as the method that prepares the printout one word at a time—I'll discuss the drawbacks of this method at the end of the section.

The text to be printed is stored in the textToPrint variable, which is declared outside any procedure with the statement

```
Dim textToPrint As String
```

To make the application more flexible, I've added a Page Setup dialog box, where users can specify the margins and the orientation of the printout. The code starts by displaying the Page Setup dialog box by calling the ShowDialog method of the PageSetupDialog control. Then it initiates printing on an instance of the PrintPreviewDialog control, by calling its ShowDialog method. Listing 15.11 shows the code behind the Preview & Print button on the form, which initiates the printing.

LISTING 15.11: INITIATING THE PRINTING OF PLAIN TEXT

```
Private Sub Button1_Click(ByVal sender As System.Object, _
             ByVal e As System.EventArgs) Handles Button1.Click
    textToPrint = TextBox1.Text
    PageSetupDialog1.PageSettings = PrintDocument1.DefaultPageSettings
    If PageSetupDialog1.ShowDialog() = DialogResult.OK Then
        PrintDocument1.DefaultPageSettings = PageSetupDialog1.PageSettings
    End If
    Try
        PrintPreviewDialog1.Document = PrintDocument1
        PrintPreviewDialog1.ShowDialog()
    Catch exc As Exception
        MsgBox("Print operation failed " & vbCrLf & exc.Message)
    End Try
End Sub
```

The ShowDialog method of the PrintPreviewDialog control is equivalent to calling the Print method of the PrintDocument control. After that, a series of PrintPage events will follow. Listing 15.12 shows the code in the PrintPage event's handler.

LISTING 15.12: A SIMPLER METHOD OF PRINTING PLAIN TEXT

```
Private Sub PrintDocument1_PrintPage(ByVal sender As Object, _
             ByVal e As System.Drawing.Printing.PrintPageEventArgs) _
             Handles PrintDocument1.PrintPage
    Static currentChar As Integer
    Dim txtFont As New Font("Arial", 10)
    Dim txtH, txtW As Integer
    Dim LMargin, TMargin As Integer
    With PrintDocument1.DefaultPageSettings
        txtH = .PaperSize.Height - .Margins.Top - .Margins.Bottom
```

```
            txtW = .PaperSize.Width - .Margins.Left - .Margins.Right
            LMargin = PrintDocument1.DefaultPageSettings.Margins.Left
            TMargin = PrintDocument1.DefaultPageSettings.Margins.Top
        End With
        If PrintDocument1.DefaultPageSettings.Landscape Then
            Dim tmp As Integer
            tmp = txtH
            txtH = txtW
            txtW = tmp
        End If
        Dim linesperpage As Integer = txtH / txtFont.Height
        Dim R As New RectangleF(LMargin, TMargin, txtW, txtH)
        Dim lines, chars As Integer
        Dim fmt As New StringFormat(StringFormatFlags.LineLimit)
        e.Graphics.MeasureString(Mid(textToPrint, currentChar + 1), _
                            txtFont, New SizeF(txtW, txtH), fmt, chars, lines)
        e.Graphics.DrawString(Mid(textToPrint, currentChar + 1), _
                        txtFont, Brushes.Black, R, fmt)
        currentChar = currentChar + chars
        If currentChar < textToPrint.Length Then
            e.HasMorePages = True
        Else
            e.HasMorePages = False
            currentChar = 0
        End If
    End Sub
End Sub
```

The core of the printing code is concentrated in the following three statements:

```
e.Graphics.MeasureString(Mid(textToPrint, currentChar + 1), _
                    txtFont, New SizeF(txtW, txtH), fmt, chars, lines)
e.Graphics.DrawString(Mid(textToPrint, currentChar + 1), _
                txtFont, Brushes.Black, R, fmt)
currentChar = currentChar + chars
```

The first statement determines how many characters will fit in a rectangle with dimensions *txtW* and *txtH* when rendered on the page in the specified font. The *fmt* argument is crucial for the proper operation of the application, and I will explain it momentarily.

The second statement prints the segment of the text that will fit in this rectangle. Notice that the code is using the Mid() function to pass not the entire text, but a segment starting at the location following the location of the last character in the previous page. The location of the first character in the page is given by the *currentChar* variable, which is increased by the number of characters printed on the current page. The number of characters printed on the current page is retrieved by the MeasureString method and stored in the *chars* variable.

And the trick that makes this code work is how the *fmt* StringFormat object is declared. The height of the printable area of the page may not (and usually does not) accommodate an integer number of lines. The MeasureString method will attempt to fit as many text lines in the specified rectangle as possible, even if the last line fits only partially in the rectangle. To force the Measure-String and DrawString methods to work with an integer number of lines, create a FormatString object passing the constant `StringFormatFlags.LineLimit` as argument:

```
Dim fmt As New StringFormat(StringFormatFlags.LineLimit)
```

If you pass the *fmt* object as argument to both the MeasureString and DrawString methods, they will ignore partial lines and the rest of the printing code works as expected.

If the user changes the orientation of the page, the code switches the page's width and height. This is all it takes to print text in landscape orientation. The page's margins are also accounted for.

Before ending this section, I should explain why I haven't started with this version of the application (which is also simpler that the PrintText project of the previous section). The PrintText2 application prints one page at a time. You have no control over the individual lines or words. The granularity of the PrintText2 application is an entire page. If the text contains formatting information (simple tags to turn on and off the attributes like bold and italics), you won't be able to process them. Assume that the text contains HTML-like tags (like the <B> and <I> tags) to determine the appearance of the text, or custom tags to specify the formatting of section headers. When you treat a block of text as a single entity, you won't be able to process individual words.

The same is true for simpler types of processing. Let's say you want to format a program listing by inserting a continuation symbol at the end of every code line that has to be broken into two or more text lines. Since we rely on the DrawString method to break long code lines into multiple text lines for us, we can't insert the appropriate symbols, or indent the continued lines, as is customary in program listings. It's also common to number the lines of program listings. Even this simple operation can't be incorporated into the PrintText2 application's project. So a text-printing application that prepares the page one word at a time may be slow, but it's flexible, and you're more likely to write code based on the PrintText sample application. The technique demonstrated by the PrintText2 application is a convenient method of printing simple text files, similar to printing them with Notepad.

Printing Bitmaps

If you have a color printer, you probably want to print images, too. Printing bitmaps is quite simple. As you have probably guessed, you call the DrawImage method to send the bitmap to the printer. As a reminder, the simplest form of the DrawImage method of the Graphics object accepts two arguments, which are the bitmap to be drawn (an Image object) and a rectangle in which the image will be drawn:

```
Graphics.DrawImage(image, rectangle)
```

The method will stretch the bitmap specified by the *image* argument to fill the rectangle specified by the second argument. Because of this, it is imperative that you calculate carefully the dimensions of the rectangle, so that they will retain their original aspect ratio. If not, the image will be distorted in the process. Most applications will let the user specify a zoom factor, which is then applied to both dimensions. If the image fits on the page, you can make the rectangle equal to the dimensions of the image and not worry about distortions.

Since the reduced image will, most likely, be smaller than the dimensions of the paper on which it will be printed, you must also center the image on the paper. To do so, you can subtract the image's width from the paper's width and split the difference on the two sides of the image (you will do the same for the vertical margins).

If you specify a rectangle the same size as the image, the image will be printed in its actual size. A common image resolution is 72 dots per inch. If the bitmap is 1,024 pixels wide, it will take approximately 14 inches across the page—this means that part of the image won't be printed.

FIGURE 15.10

The PrintBitmap application resizes bitmaps to fit the width of the page and prints them.

Before you send a bitmap to the printer, you must first make sure the bitmap will fit on the page. If the bitmap is too large for a letter-size page, you must reduce its size. Fortunately, the Framework can handle this for you. All you have to do is specify the size of the rectangle on the paper, in which the image will be printed. The following statements, which must appear in the PrintDocument event, print the image centered on the page. If the image doesn't fit on the page, its top-left corner is printed at the origin, and only the rightmost and bottommost parts of the image will be missing. Notice also that the image isn't printed in actual size; instead, it's printed at the current magnification. Listing 15.13 provides the code of the PrintPage event handler.

LISTING 15.13: SCALING AND PRINTING A BITMAP

```
Private Sub PrintDocument1_PrintPage(ByVal sender As Object, _
            ByVal e As System.Drawing.Printing.PrintPageEventArgs) _
            Handles PrintDocument1.PrintPage
    Dim R As Rectangle
    Dim PictWidth, PictHeight, PictLeft, PictTop As Integer
    PictWidth = PictureBox1.Width
    PictHeight = PictureBox1.Height
    With PrintDocument1.DefaultPageSettings.PaperSize
        If PictWidth < .Width Then
            PictLeft = (.Width - PWidth) / 2
        Else
            PictLeft = 0
```

```
        End If
        If PictHeight < .Height Then
            PictTop = (.Height - PHeight) / 2
        Else
            PictTop = 0
        End If
    End With
    R = New Rectangle(PictLeft, PictTop, PictWidth, PictHeight)
    e.Graphics.DrawImage(PictureBox1.Image, R)
End Sub
```

The *PictWidth* and *PictHeight* variables hold the dimensions of the scaled image, while *PictLeft* and *PictTop* are the coordinates of the image's top-left corner on the page. To initiate the printing process, you must call the PrintDocument object's Print method, or you can display the PrintPreview dialog box, which is what the following code does:

```
Private Sub bttnPrint_Click(ByVal sender As System.Object, _
            ByVal e As System.EventArgs) Handles Button2.Click
    PrintPreviewDialog1.Document = PrintDocument1
    PrintPreviewDialog1.ShowDialog()
End Sub
```

The user can resize and rotate the image before printing it. These rotation commands can be found in the main form's Process menu, while the Zoom menu has four options: Auto, Normal, Zoom In, and Zoom Out (Figure 15.11). The last two commands zoom in and out by 25 percent at a time. These commands change the size of the PictureBox control that holds the image, and the PrintPage event handler uses the dimensions of this control to determine the dimensions of the printed image. The Normal command resets the image to its actual size, and the Auto command resizes the image proportionally so that its height is 400 pixels.

FIGURE 15.11

The PrintBitmap application's main form

Using the PrintPreviewControl

The PrintPreviewControl is the core of the PrintPreviewDialog control packaged as a Windows control. It consists of the preview pane, where the printed document can be previewed. Other than that, it has a vertical and horizontal scroll bar but no controls to zoom or to move from page to page. You can use this control to create a custom print-preview form for specialized applications, but you must design an interface that will allow users to navigate through the document being viewed. You should use the PrintPreviewDialog control instead, but if you want to use a different interface or restrict the preview pane on a form, you'll find all the information you need to program the PrintPreviewControl in this section.

Just like its cousin, the PrintPreviewDialog, the PrintPreviewControl requires the presence of a PrintDocument control. This control will provide the document to be viewed and will expose the PrintPage event, where all the action takes place. Once you've added a PrintPreviewControl and a PrintDocument control to the project, you can assign the instance of the PrintDocument control to the Document property of the PrintPreviewControl with a statement like the following, and you're ready to preview:

```
PrintPreviewControl1.Document = PrintDocument1
```

Unlike the PrintPreviewDialog control, the PrintPreviewControl is visible at runtime. Not only that, but you need quite a bit of space on your form for this control to work. Figure 15.12 shows a form with a TextBox control on the left and a PrintPreviewControl on the right. The interface for previewing the document is quite trivial, but it demonstrates the basic properties of the control. We'll get to the interface shortly.

First, size the control on the form. You should probably dock it on the edges of the form, so that users can control the preview pane's size. Then place the Preview button on the form and enter the following code in its Click event handler:

```
Private Sub Button1_Click(ByVal sender As System.Object, _
            ByVal e As System.EventArgs) Handles Button1.Click
    PrintPreviewControl1.Columns = 2
    PrintPreviewControl1.Document = PrintDocument1
End Sub
```

The Columns property determines how many pages appear next to each other on the control. There's also a Rows property, which determines how many rows of pages are on the control. To display four pages at a time on the control, set both properties to 2.

After setting the control's Document property, you can insert the code to generate the printout in the PrintDocument control's PrintPage event handler. The output will be sent to the Preview control, not to the printer, or even to the PrintPreview dialog box. In this example we'll print eight pages, so that you can experiment with the various settings of the control. We'll print the text on the TextBox control on eight pages (all pages will display the same text). Each page will be differentiated by the page number, which will appear in bold at the top of the page, as shown in Figure 15.12. Listing 15.14 shows the code in the PrintPage event handler.

LISTING 15.14: PRINTING A SIMPLE DOCUMENT TO THE PRINTPREVIEW CONTROL

```
Private Sub PrintDocument1_PrintPage(ByVal sender As Object, _
                ByVal e As System.Drawing.Printing.PrintPageEventArgs) _
                Handles PrintDocument1.PrintPage
    Static iPage As Integer
    e.Graphics.DrawString("PAGE # " & (iPage+ 1).ToString, _
                        New Font("Comic sans MS", 24), Brushes.Black, 10, 10)
    e.Graphics.DrawString(RichTextBox1.Text, RichTextBox1.Font, _
                        Brushes.Black, 50, 50)
    iPage = iPage + 1
    If iPage = 8 Then
        e.HasMorePages = False
    Else
        e.HasMorePages = True
    End If
End Sub
```

FIGURE 15.12

Previewing a simple document on the PrintPreview control

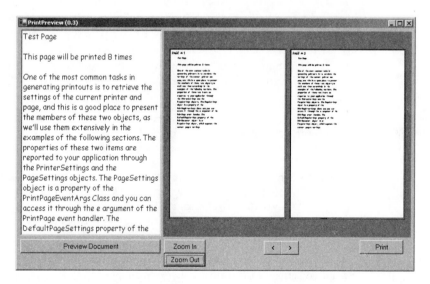

The static variable *iPage* is increased each time a new page is printed, and while it's less than 8, the HasMorePages property is set to True, to continue printing. If you run the project at this point, you will see the first two pages on the PrintPreviewControl, but you have no way to zoom or jump to the following pages. The default magnification is set automatically, so that you can view the width of a page. To change the default magnification, you must set the Zoom property to the appropriate value. A value of 1 displays the document in actual size. The magnification you see will be something close to 0.3.

The Zoom In and Zoom Out buttons control the magnification. The Zoom In button increases the magnification by increasing the Zoom property by 25 percent. If the zoom value is more than 3 (three times the actual size), the Zoom property is clipped to 3.

```
Private Sub Button2_Click(ByVal sender As Object, _
        ByVal e As System.EventArgs) Handles Button2.Click
    PrintPreviewControl1.Zoom = PrintPreviewControl1.Zoom * 1.25
    If PrintPreviewControl1.Zoom > 3 Then PrintPreviewControl1.Zoom = 3
End Sub
```

Similarly, the Zoom Out button decreases the Zoom factor by 25 percent each time, down to a smallest magnification of 0.3:

```
Private Sub Button3_Click(ByVal sender As Object, _
        ByVal e As System.EventArgs) Handles Button3.Click
    PrintPreviewControl1.Zoom = PrintPreviewControl1.Zoom / 1.25
    If PrintPreviewControl1.Zoom < 0.3 Then PrintPreviewControl1.Zoom = 0.3
End Sub
```

The other two buttons allow you to move forward and backward through the pages. The current page on the preview pane is set by the StartPage property, so the other two buttons control the StartPage property. If the control displays multiple pages, the Page property is the number of the first page on the control. Our control displays two pages, so the StartPage property is increased or decreased by 2 (which is the value of the Columns property). If you set up a PrintPreview control with pages in multiple rows and columns, use the product of the Columns property times the Rows property. Here's the code behind the two navigational buttons:

```
Private Sub bttnNext_Click(ByVal sender As System.Object, _
                ByVal e As System.EventArgs) Handles bttnNext.Click
    PrintPreviewControl1.StartPage = _
        PrintPreviewControl1.StartPage + PrintPreviewControl1.Columns
End Sub
Private Sub bttnPrevious_Click(ByVal sender As System.Object, _
                ByVal e As System.EventArgs) Handles bttnPrevious.Click
    PrintPreviewControl1.StartPage = _
        PrintPreviewControl1.StartPage - PrintPreviewControl1.Columns
End Sub
```

You may have noticed that the code doesn't check the current value of the StartPage property. Even if you attempt to set this property to an invalid value, no exception will be thrown. The reason for this behavior is that we never know the number of the last page, so the control itself takes care of possible erroneous settings of the StartPage property.

The PrintPreview control exposes the UseAntiAlias property, which is a True/False value that indicates whether the control will use anti-aliasing in rendering the text. Set this property to True for the best possible preview, since the resolution of the screen (100 pixels or so per inch) is much lower than the resolution of a typical printer (600 to 1,200 dots per inch).

Summary

Printing is a major aspect of any language, and it's not a trivial topic. In my experience, many developers purchase controls with built-in printing capabilities to simplify the task of printing from within their applications. If you're developing business applications, you should probably implement a few classes for printing the basic types of reports and reuse them throughout your application. You can even share them with coworkers, to make sure all reports have a consistent look.

The Framework provides a number of controls to simplify tasks such as setting up the printer and page properties and previewing your printouts before sending them to the printer. These tools can be used to generate very simple or very complicated printouts. The basic tools and the outline of the process don't change. Your code, however, may become considerably more complicated.

Chapter 16

The TreeView and ListView Controls

THE LAST TWO WINDOWS CONTROLS we're going to explore in this chapter are among the more advanced ones, and they are certainly more difficult to program than the previous ones. These two controls, however, are the basic makings of unique user interfaces, as you'll see in the examples. The TreeView and ListView controls implement two of the more advanced data structures (a topic that's not terribly popular even among computer science students). These controls were designed to hide much of the complexity of the data structures they implement, and they do this very well. However, they are more difficult to use than the other controls.

The ImageList control is a simple control for storing images, which is used frequently with these two controls. In itself, the ImageList control is very simple to use, and I will show briefly how to use this control in conjunction with the other two controls, which are the main subject of this chapter.

I will start with a general discussion of the two controls to help you understand what they do and when to use them. A basic understanding of the data structures they implement is also required to use them efficiently in your applications. Then, I'll discuss their members and demonstrate how to use the controls. If you find the examples too difficult to understand, you can always postpone the use of these controls in your applications. Some of the code I will present in this chapter can be used as is in many situations, so you should take a look at the examples and see if you can incorporate some of them in your applications. Unlike other controls, the TreeView and ListView controls can be considered advanced, which is why I haven't discussed them in the first part of the book. They're also excellent tools for designing elaborate Windows interfaces and I feel they deserve to be covered in detail.

Examining the Advanced Controls

In Chapter 5, you learned that the ListBox control is a simple control for storing objects. The items of a ListBox control can be sorted, but they have no particular structure. I'm sure most of you wish the ListBox control had more "features," such as the means to store additional information along with each item and display them at will. For instance, a list with city and state names should be structured so that each city appears under the corresponding state name. In a ListBox control, you can indent some of the entries, but the control itself can't impose or maintain any structure on its data. The answer to the shortcomings of the ListBox control can be found in the TreeView and ListView controls.

Figure 16.1 shows the TreeView and ListView controls used in tandem. What you see in Figure 16.1 is Windows Explorer, a utility for examining and navigating your hard disk's structure. The left pane, where the folders are displayed, is a *TreeView* control. The folder names are displayed in a manner that reflects their structure on the hard disk. You can expand and contract certain branches and view only the segment(s) of the tree structure you're interested in.

The right pane is a ListView control. The items on the ListView control can be displayed in four different ways (as large icons, as small icons, in a list, or in report form). These are the various views you can set through the View menu of Windows Explorer. Although most people prefer to look at the contents of the folders as icons, the most useful view is the Report view, which displays not only filenames but their attributes as well. In the Report view, the list can be sorted according to any of its columns, making it very easy for the user to locate any item based on various criteria (file type, size, creation date, and so on).

FIGURE 16.1

Windows Explorer is made up of a TreeView (left pane) and a ListView (right pane).

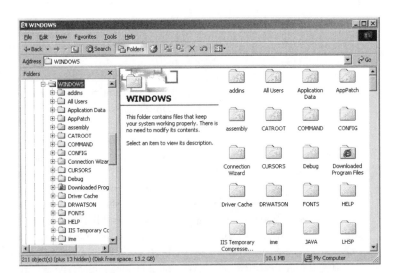

VB6 ⇒ VB.NET

If you've programmed the TreeView control that came with VB6, you're probably dependent on the Key property, which uniquely identified each node and allowed you to place new nodes under existing nodes by specifying the key of the parent node. The Key property is no longer supported. The Find method of the old version of the control, which located an item based on its key, is also gone. The new version of the control is strictly a tool for displaying data, and it provides all the functionality needed to interact with the user. You will miss some of the functionality of the old TreeView control that didn't make it to the new control. On the positive side, the new control gives more control over the appearance of the items—you can set their font, background color, and so on. It also comes with a tool that allows you to add nodes at design time.

The new version of the control is in many respects different from the old version, and you'll practically have to learn to program it like a new control.

How Tree Structures Work

The TreeView control implements a data structure known as a *tree*. A tree is the most appropriate structure for storing hierarchical information. The organizational chart of most companies is a tree structure. Every person reports to another person above them, all the way to the president or CEO. Figure 16.2 depicts a possible organization of continents, countries, and cities as a tree. (For brevity, I sometimes abstract a bit; "America" is treated as a single continent, and I've omitted Antarctica because is has no countries or cities.) Every city belongs to a country and every country to a continent. In the same way, every computer file belongs to a folder that may belong to an even bigger folder. You can't draw large tree structures on paper, but it's possible to create a similar structure in the computer's memory without size limitations.

FIGURE 16.2

The world viewed as a tree

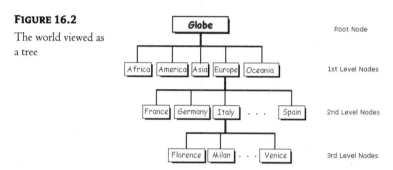

Each item in the tree of Figure 16.2 is called a *node*, and nodes can be nested to any level. Oddly, the top node is the *root* of the tree and the subordinate nodes are called *child nodes*. If you try to visualize this structure as a real tree, think of it as an upside-down tree with the branches emerging from the root.

To locate a city, you must start at the root node and select the continent to which the city belongs. Then, you must find the country (in the selected continent) to which the city belongs. Finally, you can find the city you're looking for. If it's not under the appropriate country node, then it doesn't exist. You also can traverse a tree in the opposite direction. There may an identically named city in another country, but this isn't the one you're looking for; it's just a synonym.

NOTE   *The TreeView control doesn't require that the items be unique. You can actually have identically named nodes in the same branch—as unlikely as this may be for a real application. The nodes are strings and they can be anything. There's no property that makes a node unique in the tree structure, or even in its own branch.*

You can start with a city and find its country. The country node is the city node's *parent node*. Notice that there is only one route from child nodes to their parent nodes, which means you can instantly locate the country or continent of a city. The same data shown in Figure 16.2 is shown in Figure 16.3 on a TreeView control. Only the nodes we're interested in are expanded. The plus sign indicates that the corresponding node contains child nodes. To view them, click the button with the plus sign to expand the node.

The tree structure is ideal for data with parent-child relations (relations that can be described as "belongs to" or "owns"). The continents-countries-cities data is a typical example. The folder structure on a hard disk is another typical example. Any given folder is the child of another folder or the root folder. If you need a method to traverse the folder structure of your hard disk quickly and conveniently, you must store the folders in a TreeView control. This is exactly what happens when you use Windows Explorer to navigate your hard disk. Of course, there are other ways to navigate your hard disk (you can do the same with an Open dialog box), but the TreeView control helps you visualize the structure of the entire disk. With the Open dialog box, you can view only one segment of the disk, namely, the current folder.

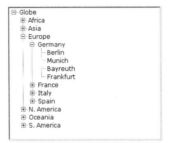

FIGURE 16.3

The tree of Figure 16.2 implemented with a TreeView control

Many programs are actually based on tree structures. Computerized board games use a tree structure to store all possible positions. Every time the computer has to make a move, it locates the board's status on the tree and selects the "best" next move. For instance, in tic-tac-toe, the tree structure that represents the moves in the game has nine nodes on the first level, which correspond to all the possible positions for the first token on the board (the X or O mark). Under each possible initial position, there are eight nodes, which correspond to all the possible positions of the second token on the board (one of the nine positions is already taken). On the second level, there are 9×8, or 72 nodes. On the third level, there are seven nodes under each node that correspond to all the possible positions of the third token, a total of 72×7, or 504 nodes, and so on. In each node, you can store a value that indicates whether the corresponding move is good or bad. When the computer has to make a move, it traverses the tree to locate the current status of the board, and then it makes a good move.

Of course, tic-tac-toe is a very simple game. In principle, you could design a chess-playing game using a tree. This tree, however, would grow so large so quickly that it couldn't be stored in any reasonable amount of memory. Moreover, scanning the nodes of this enormous tree would be a slow process. If you also consider that chess moves aren't just good or bad (there are better and not-so-good moves), and you must look ahead many moves to decide which move is the best for the current status of the board, you'll realize that this ad hoc approach is totally impractical. Practically speaking, such a program requires either infinite resources or infinite time. That's why the chess-playing algorithms use *heuristic approaches*, which store every recorded chess game in a database and consult this database to pick the best next move.

Maintaining a tree structure is a fundamental operation in software design; computer science students spend a good deal of their time implementing tree structures. Even the efficient implementation of a tree structure is a research subject. Fortunately, with Visual Basic you don't have to implement tree structures on your own. The TreeView control is a mechanism for storing hierarchically structured data on a control with a visible interface. The TreeView control hides (or *encapsulates*, in object-oriented terminology) the details of the implementation and allows you to set up tree structures with a few lines of code. In short, all the gain without the pain (almost).

You may find this too good to be true, but if you've ever had to implement tree structures, you'll appreciate the simplicity of the TreeView control.

Programming the TreeView control is not as simple as programming other controls, but keep in mind that the TreeView control implements a complicated data structure. It's far simpler to program the TreeView control than to implement tree structures from scratch. There's not much you can do about efficiency, and unless you're developing highly specialized applications that rely on tree structures, the TreeView control is your best bet.

The ListView control implements a simpler structure, known as a *list*. A list's items aren't structured in a hierarchy. They are all on the same level and can be traversed serially, one after the other. You can also think of the list as an array, but the list offers more features. A list item can have subitems and can be sorted in many ways. For example, you can set up a list of customer names (the list's items) and assign a number of subitems to each customer, like a contact, an address, a phone number, and so on. Or you can set up a list of files with their attributes as subitems. Figure 16.4 shows a Windows folder mapped on a ListView control. Each file is an item, and its attributes are the subitems. As you already know, you can sort this list by filename, size, file type, and so on. All you have to do is click the header of the corresponding column. You can also display the list of files in different views: as icons, as a list of filenames only, or as a report (the view shown in Figure 16.4).

FIGURE 16.4

A folder's files displayed in a Tree-View control (Report view)

The ListView control is a glorified ListBox control. If all you need is a control to store sorted objects, use a ListBox control. If you want more features, like storing multiple items per row, sorting them in different ways, or locating them based on any subitem's value, then you must consider the ListView control. It's simpler to program than the TreeView control but still more involved than the simple ListBox control.

To program the TreeView and ListView controls, you must understand the concept of collections. You can't simply add items to these controls with the Add method as you would do with the ListBox control. Each level of nodes in the TreeView control is a *collection*. Each item in this collection represents a node, which may have child nodes. Each node's child nodes form another collection. Each item in this collection is a *TreeNode object*, which in turn may have its own Nodes collection, which is another collection of TreeNode objects. We'll discuss these techniques in detail, but there's something else I would like to mention briefly and get out of the way as early as possible.

The TreeView and ListView controls are commonly used along with the ImageList control. The ImageList control is a very simple control for storing images so they can be retrieved quickly and used at runtime. You populate the ImageList control with images, usually at design time, and then you recall them by an index value at runtime. Before we get into the details of the TreeView and ListView controls, a quick overview of the ImageList control is in order. The reason I present it here is that the ImageList control is used almost exclusively with the TreeView and ListView controls.

The ImageList Control

The ImageList control is a really simple control that stores a number of images used by other controls at runtime. For example, a TreeView control may use a number of icons to identify its nodes. The simplest and quickest method of preparing the images to be used with the TreeView control is to create an ImageList with icons. The ImageList control maintains a series of bitmaps in memory that the TreeView control can access very quickly at runtime. Keep in mind that the ImageList control can't be used on its own and remains invisible at runtime.

The images stored in the ImageList control can be used for any purpose by your application, but in this book, we'll use them in conjunction with the TreeView and ListView controls, which use them to identify their nodes and list items, respectively. So, before we start the discussion of the TreeView and ListView controls, let's look at how to store images in an ImageList control and how to use this control in our code.

To use the ImageList control in a project, double-click its icon in the Toolbox to place an instance of the control to your project. To load images to an ImageList control, locate the Images property in the Properties window and click the button with the ellipses next to the property name. The Image Collection Editor window (Figure 16.5) will pop up, and you can load all the images you want by selecting the appropriate files. All the images should have the same dimensions—but this is not a requirement. Notice that the ImageList control doesn't resize the images; they must have the same size as when you load them.

FIGURE 16.5

The Image Collection Editor

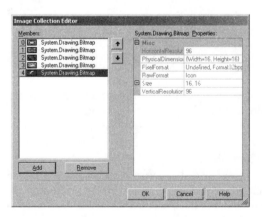

To add an image to the collection, click the Add button. You'll be prompted to select an image file through the Open File dialog box. Each image you select is added to the list. When you select an image in this list, the properties of the image are displayed in the same window—but you can't change the properties. One property of the ImageList control you can set in the Properties window is the TransparentColor property, which is a color that will be treated as transparent for all images (this is also known as the *key color*).

Each image stored in the ImageList control can be identified by an Index value, which is the order in which the image was added to the Images collection. You'll see later how to assign an image to an item of the TreeView or ListView control.

The other method of adding images to an ImageList control is to call the Add method of the Images collection, which contains all the images stored in the control. The Images collection provides the usual Add and Remove methods. To add an image at runtime, you must first create an Image object with the image (or icon) you want to add to the control and then call the Add method as follows:

```
ImageList1.Images.Add(image)
```

where *image* is an Image object with the desired image. You will usually call this method as follows:

```
ImageList1.Images.Add(Image.FromFile(path))
```

where *path* is the full path of the file with the image. *Images* is a collection of Image objects, not the files where the pictures are stored. This means that the image files need not reside on the computer on which the application will be executed. This is another good reason to store your images in an ImageList control, instead of copying them along with the executables.

The TreeView Control

Let's start our discussion with a few simple properties that you can set at design time. To experiment with the properties discussed in this section, open the TreeViewDemo project in this chapter's folder on the CD. The project's main form is shown in Figure 16.6. After setting some properties (they are discussed next), run the project and click the Populate button to populate the control. After that, you can click the other buttons to see the effect of the various property settings on the control. We'll discuss the other buttons on the form in the following sections.

CheckBoxes   If this option is enabled, a check box appears in front of each item. If the control displays check boxes, you can also select multiple items. If not, you're limited to a single selection.

FullRowSelect   This True/False value determines whether the entire row of the selected item will be highlighted and whether an item will be selected even if the user clicks outside the item's text.

HideSelection   This property determines whether the selected item will remain highlighted when the focus is moved to another control.

HotTracking   This True/False value determines whether items are highlighted as the pointer hovers over them. When this property is True, the TreeView control behaves like a Web document with the items acting as hyperlinks—they turn blue while the pointer hovers over them. However, you can't capture this action from within your code. There's no event to report that the pointer is hovering over an item.

FIGURE 16.6

The TreeViewDemo project demonstrates the basic properties and methods of the TreeView control.

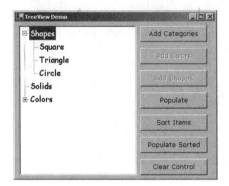

Indent   This property indicates the indentation level in pixels. The same indentation applies to all levels of the tree—each level is indented by the same amount of pixels with respect to its parent level.

ShowLines   The ShowLines property is a True/False value that determines whether the items on the control will be connected to their parent items with lines. The lines connect each node to its parent node, and it's customary to display them.

ShowPlusMinus   The ShowPlusMinus property is a True/False value that determines whether the plus/minus button is shown next to tree nodes that have children. The plus button is displayed when the node is collapsed, and it causes the node to expand when clicked. Likewise, the minus sign is displayed when the node is expanded and causes the node to collapse when clicked.

ShowRootLines   This is another True/False property that determines whether there will be lines between each node and root of the tree view. Experiment with the ShowLines and ShowRootLines properties to find out how they affect the appearance of the control.

Sorted   This property determines whether the items in the control will be automatically sorted or not. The control sorts each level of nodes separately. In our globe example, it will sort the continents, then the countries within each continent, and then the cities within each country. Once the control has been sorted, you can't undo the operation. The existing items will remain sorted with respect to one another. You can turn off the Sorted property and insert more items. The new items will not be sorted.

Text   This is the text of the currently selected node. Use this property to retrieve the user's selection.

TopNode   This is the first visible node in the TreeView control. It's the first node in the control if its contents haven't been scrolled, but it can be any node, at any level, if the control has been scrolled. The TreeNode property returns a TreeNode object, which you can use to manipulate the node from within your code.

VisibleCount   This property returns the number of items that are visible on the control.

Adding New Items at Design Time

Let's look now at the process of populating the TreeView control. Adding an initial collection of items to a TreeView control is trivial. Locate the Nodes property in the Property box, and you'll see that its value is Collection. This string simply indicates that the control's items form a collection. To add items, click the button with the ellipses, and the TreeView item editor window will appear, as shown in Figure 16.7. To add the root item, just click the Add Root button. The new item will be named Node0 by default. You can change its name by selecting the item in the list. When its name appears in the Label box, change the item's name to anything you like.

FIGURE 16.7

The TreeNode Editor window

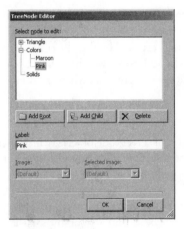

You can add items at the same level as the selected one by clicking the Add Root button, or you can add items under the selected node by clicking the Add Child button. The Add Child button adds a new node under the selected node. Follow these steps to enter the root node GLOBE, a child node for Europe, and two more nodes under Europe: Germany and Italy. I'm assuming that you're starting with a clean control. If your TreeView control contains any items, clear them all by selecting one item at a time in the list and clicking the Delete button.

Click the Add Root button first. A new node will be added automatically to the list of nodes, and it will be named Node0. Select it with the mouse, and its name will appear in the Label box. Here you can change its name to GLOBE.

Then click the Add Child button, which will add a new node under the GLOBAL root node. Select it with the mouse as before, and change its name to Europe. Then select the newly added node in the list and click the Add Child button again. Name the new node Germany. You've successfully added a small hierarchy of nodes. To add another node under Europe, select the Europe node in the list and click the Add Child button again. Name the new button Italy. Continue adding a few cities under each country. It's likely that you will add child nodes under the wrong parent. This will happen if you forget to select the proper parent node before clicking the Add Child button. Each new node you add in the Editor's window isn't selected automatically. You must switch to the list of nodes and select the proper parent node with the mouse.

Note that when a node is deleted, all the nodes under it are deleted, too. Moreover, this action can't be undone. So, be careful when deleting nodes.

Click the OK button to close the Editor's window and return to your form. The nodes you've added to the TreeView control are there, but they're collapsed. Only the root nodes are displayed with the plus sign in front of their names. Click the plus sign to expand the tree and see its child nodes. The TreeView control behaves the same at design time as it does at runtime—as far as navigating the tree goes, at least.

The nodes added to a TreeView control at design time will appear each time the form is initialized. You can add new nodes through your code, and you will see how this is done in the following section.

Adding New Items at Runtime

Adding items to the control at runtime is a bit more involved. You've read about the tree structure; now you'll learn how this structure is exposed by the object model of the TreeView control. All the items belong to the control's Nodes collection, which is made up of TreeNode objects. To access the Nodes collection, use the following expression, where *TreeView1* is the control's name and *Nodes* is a collection of TreeNode objects:

```
TreeView1.Nodes
```

This expression returns a collection of TreeNode objects, which is called TreeNodeCollection, and it exposes the proper members for accessing and manipulating the individual nodes. The control's Nodes property is the collection of all root nodes.

To access the first item, use the expression `TreeView.Nodes(0)` (this is the GLOBE node in our example). The Text property returns the item's value, which is a string. `TreeView1.Nodes(0).Text` is the value of the first item on the control. The second item on the same level is `TreeView1.Nodes(1).Text`, and so on. The Text property is the string you've added to the control at design time. If you use the TreeView control to store objects, then the object's ToString property will be displayed at each node.

The following statements will print the strings shown below them in bold (these strings are not part of the statements; they're the output the statements produce).

```
Console.WriteLine(TreeView1.Nodes(0).Text)
GLOBE
Console.WriteLine(TreeView1.Nodes(0).Nodes(0).Text)
Europe
Console.WriteLine(TreeView1.Nodes(0).Nodes(0).Nodes(1).Text)
Italy
```

Let's take a closer look at these expressions. `TreeView1.Nodes(0)` is the first root node, the GLOBE node. Under this node, there's a collection of nodes, the `TreeView1.Nodes(0).Nodes` collection. Each node in this collection is a continent name. The first node in this collection is Europe, and you can access it with the expression `TreeView1.Nodes(0).Nodes(0)`. Likewise, this node has its own Nodes collection, which are the countries under the specific continent.

NOTE Notice that a TreeView control contains many Nodes collections. The `TreeView.Nodes` collection represents all the root nodes. Each node in this collection has its own Nodes collection, which represents the child nodes under the root. Each one of these nodes may have its own Nodes collection, and so on, up to any level.

THE NODES.ADD METHOD

The Add method adds a new node to the Nodes collection. The Add method accepts as an argument a string or a TreeNode object. The simplest form of the Add method is

```
newNode = Nodes.Add(nodeCaption)
```

where *nodeCaption* is a string that will be displayed on the control (you can't add objects to the TreeView control). Another form of the Add method allows you to add a TreeNode object directly:

```
newNode = Nodes.Add(nodeObj)
```

To use this form of the method, you must first declare and initialize a TreeNode object:

```
Dim nodeObj As New TreeNode
nodeObj.Text = "Tree Node"
nodeObj.ForeColor = Color.BlueViolet
TreeView1.Nodes.Add(nodeObj)
```

The TreeNode object exposes a number of properties for setting its appearance. You can change its foreground and background colors, the image to be displayed in front of the node (ImageIndex property), the image to be displayed in front of the node when the node is selected (SelectedImageIndex property), and more, including the NodeFont property. You will see shortly how to assign images to the nodes of a TreeView control.

The last overloaded form of the Add method allows you to specify the index in the current Nodes collection, where the node will be added:

```
newNode = Nodes.Add(index, nodeObj)
```

The *nodeObj* Node object must be initialized as usual. The Add method inserts the new node into the current Nodes collection.

NOTE   *The Add method is a method of the Nodes collection, not of the TreeView control. You can't apply the Add method to the control.*

If you call the Add method on the `TreeView1.Nodes` collection, as we've done in the last few examples, you'll add a root item. If you call it on a child's Nodes collection, you'll add another item to the existing collection of child items. If your control contains a root item already, then this item is given by the expression

```
TreeView1.Nodes(0)
```

To add a child node to the root node, use a statement like the following:

```
TreeView1.Nodes(0).Nodes.Add("Asia")
```

The expression `TreeView1.Nodes(0)` is the first root node. Its Nodes property represents the nodes under the root node, and the Add method of the Nodes property adds a new node to this collection.

To add another element on the same level as the previous one, just use the same statement with a different argument. To add a country under Asia, use a statement like the following:

```
TreeView1.Nodes(0).Nodes(1).Nodes.Add("Japan")
```

This can get quite complicated, as you can understand. The proper way to add child items to a node is to create a TreeNode variable that represents the parent node, under which the child nodes will be added. The *ContinentNode* variable, for example, represents the node Europe:

```
Dim ContinentNode As TreeNode
ContinentNode = TreeView1.Nodes(0).Nodes(0)
```

The expression `TreeView1.Nodes(0)` is the first root node. The property `Nodes(0)` is the third child of the previous node (in our case, the Europe node). Then, you can add child nodes to the *ContinentNode* node:

```
ContinentNode.Nodes.Add("France")
ContinentNode.Nodes.Add("Germany")
```

To add yet another level of nodes, the city nodes, create a new variable that represents the country of the city. The Add method actually returns a TreeNode object, so you can add a country and a few cities with the following statements:

```
Dim CountryNode As TreeNode
CountryNode = ContinentNode.Nodes.Add("Germany")
CountryNode.Nodes.Add("Berlin")
CountryNode.Nodes.Add("Frankfurt")
```

Then, you can continue adding countries through the *ContinentNode* variable:

```
CountryNode = ContinentNode.Nodes.Add("Italy")
CountryNode.Nodes.Add("Rome")
```

VB6 ➠ VB.NET

A feature of the old TreeView control many of you will miss is the Keys property. Because there's no Keys property, the new Add method doesn't support relations. With the VB6 version of the control, you could add nodes in any order. All you had to do was to specify a relation between the new node and an existing node. This relation was usually a parent/child relation, which would make the new node a child node of the specified parent node. Without the Keys property, you can't uniquely identify the parent node in the tree.

THE COUNT PROPERTY

This property returns the number of nodes in the Nodes collection. Again, this is not the total number of nodes in the control, just the number of nodes in the current Nodes collection. The expression

```
TreeView1.Nodes.Count
```

returns the number of all nodes in the first level of the control. In the case of the Globe example, it returns the value 1. The expression

```
TreeView1.Nodes(0).Nodes.Count
```

returns the number of continents in the Globe example. Again, you can simplify this expression with an intermediate TreeNode object:

```
Dim Continents As TreeNode
Continents = TreeView1.Nodes(0)
Console.WriteLine("There are " & Continents.Nodes.Count.ToString & _
                  " continents on the control")
```

THE CLEAR METHOD

The Clear method removes all the child nodes from the current node. If you apply this method to the control's root node, it will clear the control. To remove all the countries under the Germany node, use a statement like the following:

```
TreeView1.Nodes(0).Nodes(2).Nodes(1).Nodes.Clear
```

This example assumes that the third node under Globe corresponds to Europe and the second node under Europe corresponds to Germany.

THE ITEM PROPERTY

The Item property retrieves a node specified by an index value. The expression

```
Nodes.Item(1)
```

is equivalent to the expression

```
Nodes(1)
```

THE REMOVE METHOD

The Remove method removes a node from the Nodes collection. Its syntax is

```
Nodes.Remove(index)
```

where *index* is the order of the node in the current Nodes collection. To remove the selected node, call the Remove method on the SelectedNode object without arguments:

```
TreeView1.SelectedNode.Remove
```

Or you can apply the Remove method to a TreeNode object that represents the node you want to remove:

```
Dim Node As TreeNode
Node = TreeView1.Nodes(0).Nodes(7)
Node.Remove
```

THE FIRSTNODE, NEXTNODE, PREVNODE, AND LASTNODE PROPERTIES

These four properties allow you to retrieve any node at the current segment of the tree. Let's say the current node is the Germany node. The FirstNode property will return the first city under Germany (the first node in the current segment of the tree) and the LastNode will return the last city under

Germany. PrevNode and NextNode allow you to iterate through the nodes of the current segment: they return the next and previous nodes on the current segment of the tree (the sibling nodes, as they're called). See the section "Enumerating the Nodes Collection," later in this chapter, for an example.

Assigning Images to Nodes

To display an image in front of a node's caption, you must first initialize an ImageList control and populate it with all the images you plan to use with the TreeView control. The Node object exposes two image-related properties: ImageIndex and SelectedImageIndex. Both properties are the indices of an image in an ImageList control, which contains the images to be used with the control. To connect the ImageList control to the TreeView object (as well as the ListView object, which is discussed later in the chapter), you must assign the name of the ImageList control to the ImageList property of the TreeView control. Then you can specify images by their index in the ImageList control.

The ImageIndex property is the index of the image you want to display in front of the node's caption. The SelectedImageIndex is the index of the image you want to display when the node is selected (expanded). Windows Explorer, for example, uses the icon of a closed folder for all collapsed nodes and the icon of an open folder for all expanded nodes. If you don't specify a value for the SelectedImageIndex property, then the image specified with the ImageIndex property will be displayed. If you haven't specified a value for this property either, then no image will be displayed for this node.

VB.NET AT WORK: THE TREEVIEWDEMO PROJECT

It's time to demonstrate the members discussed so far with an example. The project you'll build in this section is the TreeViewDemo project, and you can find it in this chapter's folder on the CD. The project's main form is shown in Figure 16.8.

FIGURE 16.8

The TreeViewDemo project

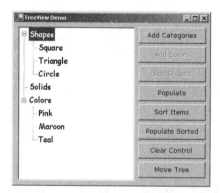

The Add Categories button adds the three top-level nodes to the TreeView control with the statements shown in Listing 16.1. These are the control's root nodes. The other two buttons add items under the root nodes.

LISTING 16.1: THE ADD CATEGORIES BUTTON

```
Protected Sub AddCategories_Click(ByVal sender As Object, _
                  ByVal e As System.EventArgs)
    TreeView1.Nodes.Add("Shapes")
    TreeView1.Nodes.Add("Solids")
    TreeView1.Nodes.Add("Colors")
End Sub
```

When these statements are executed, three root nodes will be added to the list. After clicking the Add Categories button, your TreeView control looks like the one shown at the left.

To add a few nodes under the node Colors, you must retrieve the Colors Nodes collection and add child nodes to this collection, as shown in Listing 16.2.

LISTING 16.2: THE ADD COLORS BUTTON

```
Protected Sub AddColors_Click(ByVal sender As Object, _
                  ByVal e As System.EventArgs)
    Dim cnode As TreeNode
    cnode = TreeView1.Nodes(2)
    cnode.Nodes.Add("Pink")
    cnode.Nodes.Add("Maroon")
    cnode.Nodes.Add("Teal")
End Sub
```

When these statements are executed, three nodes will be added under the Colors node, but the Colors node won't be expanded. Therefore, its child nodes won't be visible. To see its child nodes, you must double-click the Colors node to expand it (or click the plus sign in front of it, if there is one). The same TreeView control with its Colors node expanded is shown to the left. Alternatively, you can add a statement that calls the Expand method of the *cnode* object, after adding the color nodes to the control:

```
cnode.Expand()
```

Run the project, click the first button (Add Categories) and then the second button (Add Colors). If you click the Add Colors button first, you'll get a NullReferenceException, indicating that node can't be inserted unless its parent node exists already. You can add a few statements in the TreeViewDemo project's code to disable the buttons that generate similar runtime errors.

To add child nodes under the Shapes node, use the statements shown in Listing 16.3. This is the Shapes button's Click event handler.

LISTING 16.3: THE ADD SHAPES BUTTON

```
Protected Sub AddShapes_Click(ByVal sender As Object, _
                  ByVal e As System.EventArgs)
    Dim snode As TreeNode
```

```
        snode = treeview1.Nodes(0)
        snode.Nodes.Add("Square")
        snode.Nodes.Add("Triangle")
        snode.Nodes.Add("Circle")
    End Sub
```

```
⊟ Shapes
    Square
    Triangle
    Circle
  Solids
⊟ Colors
    Pink
    Maroon
    Teal
```

Add a third Command button on the form, name it Add Shapes, and insert these lines in its Click event handler. If you run the project and click the three buttons in the order in which they appear on the Form, the TreeView control will be populated with Colors and Shapes. If you double-click the items Colors and Shapes, the TreeView control's nodes will be expanded.

Notice that the code knows the order of the root node to which it's adding child nodes. Your application should know the node under which it must add new child nodes. You could scan the entire tree to locate an item, but then again the node names are not unique, not even within a Nodes collection.

This approach doesn't work with a sorted tree. If your TreeView control is sorted, you must create a hierarchy of nodes explicitly, with the following statements:

```
snode = TreeView1.Nodes.Add("Shapes")
snode.Add("Square")
snode.Add("Circle")
snode.Add("Triangle")
```

These statements will work regardless of the control's Sorted property setting. The three shapes will be added under the Shapes nodes, and their order will be determined automatically. Of course, you can always populate the control in any way you like and then turn on the Sorted property.

Let's revise the code we've written so far to display all the nodes under a header called Items. In other words, we'll add a new node that will act as the root node for existing nodes. It's not a common operation, but it's an interesting example of how to manipulate the nodes of a TreeView control.

First, we must add the root, a node that will contain all other nodes as children. Before we do so, however, we must copy into local variables all the first-level nodes. We'll use these variables to add the current root nodes under the new (and single) root node. There are three root nodes currently in our control, so we need three local variables. The three variables are of the TreeNode type, and they're set to the root nodes of the original tree. Then we must clear the entire tree, add the new root node (the Items node), and finally add all the copied nodes under the new root. The code behind the Move Tree button is shown in Listing 16.4.

LISTING 16.4: MOVING AN ENTIRE TREE

```
Protected Sub MoveTree_Click(ByVal sender As Object, _
                ByVal e As System.EventArgs) Handles bttnMoveTree.Click
    Dim colorNode, shapeNode, solidNode As TreeNode
    colorNode = TreeView1.Nodes(0)
    shapeNode = TreeView1.Nodes(1)
    solidNode = TreeView1.Nodes(2)
    TreeView1.Nodes.Clear()
    TreeView1.Nodes.Add("Items")
```

```
            TreeView1.Nodes(0).Nodes.Add(colorNode)
            TreeView1.Nodes(0).Nodes.Add(shapeNode)
            TreeView1.Nodes(0).Nodes.Add(solidNode)
        End Sub
```

You can revise this code so that it uses an array of Node objects to store all the root nodes instead of their count. For a routine that will work with any tree, you must assume that the number of nodes is unknown, so the ArrayList would be a better choice. The following loop stores all the root nodes of the TreeView1 control to the *TVList* ArrayList:

```
Dim node As TreeNode
For Each node in TreeView1.Nodes
    TVList.Add(node)
Next
```

Likewise, the following loop extracts the root nodes from the TVList object:

```
Dim node As TreeNode
Dim itm As Object
TreeView1.Nodes.Clear
For Each itm In TVList
    node = CType(itm, TreeNode)
    TreeView1.Nodes.Add(node)
Next
```

ENUMERATING THE NODES COLLECTION

Each group of child nodes forms a Nodes collection, which exposes several methods. As you have seen in the last example, a Node object may include an entire tree under it. When we move a node, it takes with it the entire Nodes collection under it. The FirstNode property returns the first node in the collection, the LastNode property returns the last node in the collection, and the NextNode and PrevNode properties return the next and previous nodes in the collection, respectively. You can scan all the nodes in the CurrentNode collection with a loop, which starts with the first node and then moves to the next node with the help of the FirstNode and NextNode properties. The following loop prints the names of all continents on the GlobeTree control:

```
Dim node As TreeNode
node = GlobeTree.Nodes(0).Nodes(0).FirstNode
While node <> Nothing
    Console.WriteLine(node.text)
    node = node.NextNode
End While
```

The last property demonstrated by the TreeViewDemo project is the Sorted property, which sorts the child nodes of the node to which it's applied. When you set the Sorted property of a node to True, every child node you attach to it will be inserted automatically in alphabetical order.

NOTE *If you reset the Sorted property to False and add another node, it will be appended to the end of the existing (and sorted) nodes. This is how new child nodes are added to a parent node when its Sorted property is False.*

VB.NET AT WORK: THE GLOBE PROJECT

The Globe project, which you can find in this chapter's folder on the CD, demonstrates many of the techniques we've discussed so far. It's not the simplest example of a TreeView control, and its code is lengthy, but it will help you understand how to manipulate nodes at runtime. As you know by now, TreeView is not a simple control, so before ending this section I would like to show you a fairly advanced example that you can use as a starting point for your own custom applications. You'll also see how to save the nodes of a TreeView control to a disk file and retrieve them later.

FIGURE 16.9

The Globe project

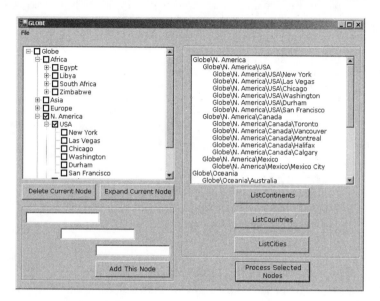

The Globe project consists of a single form, which is shown in Figure 16.9. The TreeView control at the left contains a tree structure with continents, countries, and cities, with a rather obvious structure. Each city belongs to a country, and each country belongs to a continent. The control is initially populated with the continents, which were added at design time. The countries and cities are added from within the form's Load event handler. The continents were added at design time, but as you will see, there's no particular reason not to add them to the control at runtime. It would have been actually simpler to add all the nodes at runtime, but I've decided to add a few nodes at design time just for demonstration purposes.

When a node is selected in the TreeView control, its text is displayed on the TextBox controls at the bottom of the form. When a continent name is selected, the continent's name appears in the first TextBox, and the other two TextBoxes are empty. When a country is selected, its name appears in the second TextBox, and its continent appears in the first TextBox. Finally, when a city is selected, it appears in the third TextBox, along with its country and continent in the other two TextBoxes.

You can also use the TextBox controls to add new nodes. To add a new continent, just supply the name of the continent in the first TextBox and leave the other two empty. To add a new country, supply its name in the second TextBox and the name of the continent it belongs to in the first one. Finally, to add a city, supply a continent, country, and city name in the three TextBoxes.

Run the Globe application and expand the continents and countries to see the tree structure of the data stored in the control. Add new nodes to the control, and enumerate these nodes by clicking the appropriate button on the right-hand side of the form. These buttons list the nodes at a given level (continents, countries, and cities). When you add new nodes, the code places them in their proper place in the list. If you specify a new city and a new country under an existing continent, then a new country node will be created under the specified continent, and a new city node will be inserted under the specified country.

Coding the Globe Project

Let's take a look at the code of the Globe project. We'll start by looking at the code that populates the TreeView control. The root node (GLOBE) and the continent names were added at design time through the TreeNode Editor. In many cases, it is convenient to add the first few nodes, or at least the root node, at design time.

After the continents are in place, the code adds the countries to each continent and the cities to each country. The code in the form's Load event goes through all the continents already on the control and examines their Text property. Depending on the continent represented by the current node, it adds the corresponding countries and some city nodes under each country node.

If the current node is Africa, the first country to be added is Egypt. The Egypt node is added to the *ContinentNode* object. The new node is returned as a TreeNode object and is stored in the *CountryNode* object. Then the code uses this object to add nodes that correspond to cities under the Egypt node. The form's Load event handler is quite lengthy, so I'm showing (Listing 16.5) only the code that adds the first country under each continent and the first city under each country.

LISTING 16.5: ADDING THE NODES OF AFRICA

```
For Each ContinentNode In GlobeNode.Nodes
    Select Case ContinentNode.Text
        Case "Europe"
            CountryNode = ContinentNode.Nodes.Add("Germany")
            CountryNode.Nodes.Add("Berlin")
        Case "Asia"
            CountryNode = ContinentNode.Nodes.Add("China")
            CountryNode.Nodes.Add("Beijing")
        Case "Africa"
            CountryNode = ContinentNode.Nodes.Add("Egypt")
            CountryNode.Nodes.Add("Cairo")
            CountryNode.Nodes.Add("Alexandria")
        Case "Oceania"
            CountryNode = ContinentNode.Nodes.Add("Australia")
            CountryNode.Nodes.Add("Sydney")
        Case "N. America"
            CountryNode = ContinentNode.Nodes.Add("USA")
            CountryNode.Nodes.Add("New York")
        Case "S. America"
            CountryNode = ContinentNode.Nodes.Add("Argentina")
    End Select
Next
```

The remaining countries and their cities are added with similar statements, which you can examine if you open the Globe project. Notice that the GlobeTree control could have been populated entirely at design time, but this wouldn't be much of a demonstration. Let's move on to a few more interesting aspects of programming the TreeView control.

Retrieving the Selected Node

The selected node is given by the property SelectedNode. Once you can retrieve the selected node, you can also retrieve its parent node and the entire path to the root node. The parent node of the current control is `TreeView1.SelectedNode.Parent`. If this node has a parent, you can retrieve it by calling the Parent property of the previous expression (`TreeView1.SelectedNode.Parent.Parent`). Or you can use the FullPath property to retrieve the selected node's full path. The FullPath property of the Rome node is

```
GLOBE\Europe\Italy\Rome
```

The slashes separate the segments of the node's path. You can specify any other character for this purpose by setting the control's PathSeparator property.

To remove the selected node from the tree, call the Remove method:

```
TreeView1.SelectedNode.Remove
```

If the selected node is a parent control for other nodes, the Remove method will take with it all the nodes under the selected one. You can also use the IsSelected property of the Node object to find out whether a specific node is selected or not. The IsSelected property returns a True/False value, depending on the status of the node. A similar property, the IsExpanded property, allows you to find out whether a specific node is expanded or not.

One of the operations you'll want to perform with the TreeView control is to capture the selection of a node. The TreeView control fires the AfterSelect event, which notifies your application of the selection of another node. If you need to know which node was previously selected, you must use the BeforeSelect event. The second argument of both events has two properties, the Node and Action properties, which let you find out the node that fired the event and the action that caused it. The `e.Node` property is a TreeViewNode object that represents the selected node. Use it in your code as you would use any other node of the control. The `e.Action` property is a member of the TreeViewAction enumeration (ByKeyboard, ByMouse, Collapse, Expand, Unknown). Use this property to find out the action that caused the event. The actions of expanding and collapsing a tree branch fire their own events, which are the BeforeExpand/AfterExpand and the BeforeCollapse/AfterCollapse events, respectively.

VB6 ⮞ VB.NET

The VB6 version of the TreeView control recognized the NodeClick event, which was fired every time the user selected another node in the control. The NodeClick event has been replaced by the AfterSelect event.

The Globe project retrieves the selected node and extracts the parts of the node's path. The individual components of the path are displayed in the three TextBox controls at the bottom of the form. Listing 16.6 shows the event handler for the TreeView control's AfterSelect event.

LISTING 16.6: PROCESSING THE SELECTED NODE

```
Private Sub GlobeTree_AfterSelect(ByVal sender As Object, _
               ByVal e As System.Windows.Forms.TreeViewEventArgs) _
               Handles GlobeTree.AfterSelect
    If GlobeTree.SelectedNode Is Nothing Then Exit Sub
    Dim components() As String
    txtContinent.Text = ""
    txtCountry.Text = ""
    txtCity.Text = ""
    components = Split(GlobeTree.SelectedNode.FullPath.ToString, _
                   GlobeTree.PathSeparator)
    Console.WriteLine(GlobeTree.SelectedNode.FullPath.ToString)
    If components.Length > 1 Then txtContinent.Text = components(1)
    If components.Length > 2 Then txtCountry.Text = components(2)
    If components.Length > 3 Then txtCity.Text = components(3)
End Sub
```

The Split() function of VB extracts the parts of a string that are delimited by a special character. For the case of the TreeView control, this special character is given by the property PathSeparator, and the default value of this property is the character "\". If any of the captions contain this character, you should change the default to a different character by setting the PathSeparator property to something else.

The code behind the Delete Current Node and Expand Current Node buttons is simple. To delete a node, call the selected node's Remove method:

```
GlobeTree.SelectedNode.Remove
```

The other button expands the current node by calling the Expand method of the selected node:

```
GlobeTree.SelectedNode.Expand
```

The TreeNode object exposes the ExpandAll method, too, which expands not only the specified node but all the Nodes collections under it (its child nodes).

Processing Multiple Selected Nodes

The GlobeTree TreeView control has its CheckBoxes property set to True so that users can select multiple nodes. I've added this feature to demonstrate how you can retrieve the selected nodes and process them.

As you will notice by experimenting with the TreeView control, you can check a node that has subordinate nodes, but these nodes will not be affected. They will remain unchecked (or checked, if you have already checked them). In most cases, however, when we check a parent node, we actually intend to check all the nodes under it. When you check a country, for example, you're in effect selecting not only the country but all the cities under it. The code of the Process Selected Nodes button assumes that when a parent node is checked, it must also check all the nodes under it.

Let's look at the code that iterates through the control's nodes and isolates the selected ones. It doesn't really process them, it simply prints them on the ListBox control. However, you can call a function to process the selected nodes in any way you like. The code behind the Process Selected Nodes button starts with the continents. It creates a TreeNodeCollection with all the continents and then goes through the collection with a For Each…Next loop. At each step, it creates a new TreeNode-Collection, which contains all the subordinate nodes (the countries under the selected continent) and goes through the new collection. This loop is also interrupted at each step to retrieve the cities in the current country and process them with another loop. The following pseudo-code listing outlines the code:

```
Set up the Continents Collection
For Each continent In Continents
   If continent is selected Then process it
   Set up the Countries Collection
   For Each country In Countries
      If country is selected Then process it
      Set up the Cities Collection
      For Each city In Cities
         If city is selected Then process it
      Next
   Next
Next
```

The code behind the Process Selected Nodes button implements the pseudo-code shown above and is shown in Listing 16.7.

LISTING 16.7: PROCESSING ALL SELECTED NODES

```
Protected Sub bttnProcessSelected_Click(ByVal sender As Object, _
               ByVal e As System.EventArgs)
   Dim continent, country, city As TreeNode
   Dim Continents, Countries, Cities As TreeNodeCollection
   ListBox1.Items.Clear()
   Continents = GlobeTree.Nodes(0).Nodes
   For Each continent In Continents
      If continent.Checked Then ListBox1.Items.Add(continent.FullPath)
      Countries = continent.Nodes
      For Each country In Countries
         If country.Checked Or country.Parent.Checked Then _
            ListBox1.Items.Add("     " & country.FullPath)
         Cities = country.Nodes
         For Each city In Cities
            If city.Checked Or city.Parent.Checked Or _
               city.Parent.Parent.Checked Then _
                  ListBox1.Items.Add("          " & city.FullPath)
         Next
      Next
   Next
End Sub
```

The code examines the Checked property of the current node, as well as the Checked property of its parent node. If either one is True, then the node is considered selected. You should try to add the appropriate code to select all subordinate nodes of a parent node when the parent node is selected (whether you deselect the subordinate nodes when the parent node is deselected is entirely up to you and the type of application you're developing). The Nodes collection exposes the GetEnumerator method, which should be very familiar to you by now. You can revise the last listing so that it uses an enumerator in the place of each For Each…Next loop.

Adding New Nodes

The Add Node button lets the user add new nodes to the tree at runtime. The number and type of the node(s) added depend on the contents of the TextBox controls:

- If only the first TextBox control contains text, then a new continent will be added.

- If the first two TextBox controls contain text, then:

  - If a continent exists, a new country node is added under the specified continent.

  - If a continent doesn't exist, a new continent node is added, and then a new country node is added under the continent's node.

- If all three TextBox controls contain text, the program adds a continent node (if needed), then a country node under the continent node (if needed), and finally, a city node under the country node.

Obviously, you can omit a city, or a city and country, but you can't omit a continent name. Likewise, you can't specify a city without a country or a country without a continent. The code will prompt you accordingly when it detects a condition that prevents it from adding the new node for any reason. If the node exists already, then the program selects the existing node and doesn't issue any warnings. The Add Node button's code is shown in Listing 16.8.

LISTING 16.8: ADDING NODES AT RUNTIME

```
Private Sub bttnAddNode_Click(ByVal sender As System.Object, _
            ByVal e As System.EventArgs) Handles bttnAddNode.Click
    Dim nd As TreeNode
    Dim Continents As TreeNode
    If txtContinent.Text.Trim <> "" Then
        Continents = GlobeTree.Nodes(0)
        Dim ContinentFound, CountryFound, CityFound As Boolean
        Dim ContinentNode, CountryNode, CityNode As TreeNode
        For Each nd In Continents.Nodes
            If nd.Text.ToUpper = txtContinent.Text.ToUpper Then
                ContinentFound = True
                Exit For
            End If
        Next
        If Not ContinentFound Then
```

```
            nd = Continents.Nodes.Add(txtContinent.Text)
        End If
        ContinentNode = nd
        If txtCountry.Text.Trim <> "" Then
            Dim Countries As TreeNode
            Countries = ContinentNode
            If Not Countries Is Nothing Then
                For Each nd In Countries.Nodes
                    If nd.Text.ToUpper = txtCountry.Text.ToUpper Then
                        CountryFound = True
                        Exit For
                    End If
                Next
            End If
            If Not CountryFound Then
                nd = ContinentNode.Nodes.Add(txtCountry.Text)
            End If
            CountryNode = nd
            If txtCity.Text.Trim <> "" Then
                Dim Cities As TreeNode
                Cities = CountryNode
                If Not Cities Is Nothing Then
                    For Each nd In Cities.Nodes
                        If nd.Text.ToUpper = txtCity.Text.ToUpper Then
                            CityFound = True
                            Exit For
                        End If
                    Next
                End If
                If Not CityFound Then
                    nd = CountryNode.Nodes.Add(txtCity.Text)
                End If
                CityNode = nd
            End If
        End If
    End If
End Sub
```

The listing is quite lengthy, but it's not hard to follow. First, it attempts to find a continent that matches the name in the first TextBox. If it succeeds, it need not add a new continent node. If not, then a new continent node must be added. To avoid simple data-entry errors, the code converts the continent names to uppercase before comparing them to the uppercase of each node's name. The same happens with the countries and the cities. As a result, each node's pathname is unique. You can't have the same city name under the same country more than once. It is possible, however, to add the same city name to two different countries. The example is not quite realistic, as there are common city names in every country.

Listing Continents/Countries/Cities

The three buttons List Continents, List Countries, and List Cities populate the ListBox control with the names of the continents, countries, and cities, respectively. The code is straightforward and is based on the techniques discussed in previous sections. To print the names of the continents, it iterates through the children of the GLOBE node. Listing 16.9 shows the complete code of the List Continents button.

LISTING 16.9: RETRIEVING THE CONTINENT NAMES

```
Private Sub bttnListContinents_Click(ByVal sender As System.Object, _
            ByVal e As System.EventArgs) Handles bttnListContinents.Click
    Dim Nd As TreeNode, continentNode As TreeNode
    Dim continent As Integer, continents As Integer
    ListBox1.Items.Clear()
    Nd = GlobeTree.Nodes(0)
    continents = Nd.Nodes.Count
    continentNode = Nd.Nodes(0)
    For continent = 1 To continents
        ListBox1.Items.Add(continentNode.Text)
        continentNode = continentNode.NextNode
    Next
End Sub
```

The code behind the List Countries names is equally straightforward, although longer. It must scan each continent, and within each continent, it must scan in a similar fashion the continent's child nodes. To do this, you must set up two nested loops, the outer one to scan the continents and the inner one to scan the countries. The complete code for the List Countries button is shown in Listing 16.10. Notice that in this example, I'm using For...Next loops to iterate through the current level's nodes, and I also use the NextNode method to retrieve the next node in the sequence.

LISTING 16.10: RETRIEVING THE COUNTRY NAMES

```
Private Sub bttnListCountries_Click(ByVal sender As System.Object, _
            ByVal e As System.EventArgs) Handles bttnListCountries.Click
    Dim Nd, CountryNode, ContinentNode As TreeNode
    Dim continent, continents, country, countries As Integer
    ListBox1.Items.Clear()
    Nd = GlobeTree.Nodes.Item(0)
    continents = Nd.Nodes.Count
    ContinentNode = Nd.Nodes(0)
    For continent = 1 To continents
        countries = ContinentNode.Nodes.Count
        CountryNode = ContinentNode.Nodes(0)
        For country = 1 To countries
            ListBox1.Items.Add(CountryNode.Text)
```

```
                CountryNode = CountryNode.NextNode
            Next
            ContinentNode = ContinentNode.NextNode
        Next
    End Sub
```

When the `ContinentNode.Next` method is called, it returns the next node in the Continents level. Then the `ContinentNode.Nodes(0)` method is called, and it returns the first node in the Countries level. As you can guess, the code of the List Cities button uses the same two nested lists as the previous listing and an added inner loop, which scans the cities of each country.

The code behind these Command buttons requires some knowledge of the information stored in the tree. It will work with trees that have two or three levels of nodes such as the Globe tree, but what if the tree's depth is allowed to grow to a dozen levels? A tree that represents the structure of a folder on your hard disk, for example, may easily contain a dozen nested folders. Obviously, to scan the nodes of this tree you can't put together unlimited nested loops. The next section describes a technique for scanning any tree, regardless of how many levels it contains. The code in the following section uses *recursion*, and if you're not familiar with recursive programming, then you should first read Chapter 18.

Scanning the TreeView Control

The items of a TreeView control can all be accessed through the Nodes collection. You have seen how to scan the entire tree of the TreeView control with a `For Each…Next` loop. This technique, however, requires that you know the structure of the tree, and you must write as many nested loops as there are nested levels of nodes. It works with simple trees, but it's quite inefficient when it comes to mapping a file system to a TreeView control.

VB.NET AT WORK: THE TREEVIEWSCAN PROJECT

To demonstrate the process of scanning a TreeView control, I have included the TreeViewScan project on the CD. The application's form is shown in Figure 16.10. The Form contains a TreeView control on the left, which is populated with the same data as the Globe's TreeView control, and a ListBox control on the right, where the tree's nodes are listed. Child nodes on the ListBox control are indented according to the level to which they belong.

FIGURE 16.10

The TreeViewScan application demonstrates how to scan the nodes of a TreeView control recursively.

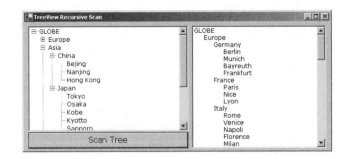

Scanning the child nodes in a tree calls for a *recursive procedure*, or a procedure that calls itself. Think of a tree structure that contains all the files and folders on your C: drive. If this structure contained no subfolders, you'd need to set up a loop to scan each folder, one after the other. Since most folders contain subfolders, the process must be interrupted at each folder to scan the subfolders of the current folder. The process of scanning a drive recursively was described in detail in Chapter 13.

Recursive Scanning

To start the scanning of the TreeView1 control, start at the top node of the control with the statement

```
Protected Sub bttnScanTree_Click(ByVal sender As Object, _
               ByVal e As System.EventArgs)
   ScanNode(GlobeTree.Nodes(0))
End Sub
```

This is the code behind the Scan Tree button, and it doesn't get any simpler. It calls the Scan-Node() subroutine to scan the child nodes of a specific node, which is passed to the subroutine as an argument. `GlobeTree.Nodes(0)` is the root node. By passing the root node to the ScanNode() subroutine, we're in effect asking it to scan the entire tree.

This example assumes that the TreeView control contains a single root node and that all other nodes are under the root node. If your control contains multiple root nodes, then you must set up a small loop and call the ScanNode() subroutine once for each root node:

```
For Each node In GlobeTree.Nodes
   ScanNode(node)
Next
```

Let's look now at the ScanNode() subroutine, shown in Listing 16.11.

LISTING 16.11: SCANNING A TREE RECURSIVELY

```
Sub ScanNode(ByVal node As TreeNode)
   Dim thisNode As TreeNode
   Static IndentLevel As Integer
   Application.DoEvents()
   ListBox1.Items.Add(Space(IndentLevel) & node.Text)
   If node.Nodes.Count > 0 Then
      IndentLevel += 5
      For Each thisNode In node.Nodes
         ScanNode(thisNode)
      Next
      IndentLevel -= 5
   End If
End Sub
```

This subroutine is deceptively simple. First, it adds the caption of the current node to the ListBox1 control. If this node (represented by the *Node* variable) contains child nodes, the code must scan them all. The `Node.Nodes.Count` method returns the number of nodes under the current node. If this value is positive, then we scan all the items of the **Node.Nodes** collection. To do this, the ScanNode() subroutine must call itself by passing a different argument. If you're familiar with recursive procedures, you'll find the code quite simple. If not, this coding probably will raise many questions. You can use the ScanNode() subroutine as is to scan any TreeView control. All you need is a reference to the root node (or the node you want to scan recursively), which you must pass to the ScanNode() subroutine as an argument. The subroutine will scan the entire subtree and display its nodes on a ListBox control. The nodes will be printed one after the other. To make the list easier to read, indent the names of the nodes by an amount that's proportional to the levels of nesting. Nodes of the first level aren't indented at all. Nodes on the first level can be indented by 5 spaces, nodes on the second level can be indented by 10 spaces, and so on. The variable *IndentLevel* keeps track of the level of nesting and is used to specify the indentation of the corresponding node. It's increased by 5 when we start scanning a new subordinate node and decreased by the same amount when we return to the next level up. The *IndentLevel* variable is declared as Static so that it maintains its value between calls.

Run the TreeViewScan project and expand all nodes. Then click the Scan Tree button to populate the list on the right with the names of the continents/countries/cities. Obviously, the ListBox control is not a substitute for the TreeView control. The data have no particular structure; even when they're indented, there are no tree lines connecting its nodes, and users can't expand and collapse the control's contents. So why bother to map the contents of the TreeView control to a ListBox control? The goal was to demonstrate how to scan a tree structure and extract all the nodes along with their structure. You can use the ScanNode() subroutine to store the nodes of a TreeView control to a disk file or transfer them to a database or another control. The ScanNode() subroutine is the core of the subroutine you need and can be adjusted to accommodate any of the operations just mentioned.

The ListView Control

The ListView control is similar to the ListBox control except that it can display its items in many forms, along with any number of subitems for each item. To use the ListView control in your project, place an instance of the control on a form and then sets its basic properties, which are described in the following sections.

The View and Arrange properties There are two properties that determine how the various items will be displayed on the control: the View property, which determines how the items will appear, and the Arrange property, which determines how the items will be aligned on the control's surface. The View property can have one of the values shown in Table 16.1.

TABLE 16.1: SETTINGS OF THE VIEW PROPERTY

SETTING	DESCRIPTION
LargeIcon	(Default) Each item is represented by an icon and a caption below the icon.
SmallIcon	Each item is represented by a small icon and a caption that appears to the right of the icon.
List	Each item is represented by a caption.
Report	Each item is displayed in a column with its subitems in adjacent columns.

The Arrange property determines how the items will be arranged on the control, and its possible settings are show in Table 16.2.

TABLE 16.2: SETTINGS OF THE ARRANGE PROPERTY

SETTING	DESCRIPTION
Default	When an item is moved on the control, it remains where it is dropped.
Left	Items are aligned to the left side of the control.
SnapToGrid	Items are aligned to an invisible grid on the control. When the user moves an item, the item moves to the closest grid point on the control.
Top	Items are aligned to the top of the control.

HeaderStyle This property determines the style of the headers in Report view. It has no meaning when the View property is set to something else, because only the Report view has columns. The possible settings for the HeaderStyle property are shown in Table 16.3.

TABLE 16.3: SETTINGS OF THE HEADERSTYLE PROPERTY

SETTING	DESCRIPTION
Clickable	Visible column header that responds to clicking
Nonclickable	Visible column header that does not respond to clicking
None	No visible column header

AllowColumnReorder This property is a True/False value that determines whether the user can reorder the columns at runtime. If this property is set to True, then the user can move a column to a new location by dragging its header with the mouse and dropping it in the place of another column. This property is also meaningful only in Report view.

Activation This property specifies the action that will activate an item on the control, and it can have one of the values shown in Table 16.4.

TABLE 16.4: SETTINGS OF THE ACTIVATION PROPERTY

SETTING	DESCRIPTION
OneClick	Items are activated with a single click. When the cursor is over an item, it changes shape and the color of the item's text changes.
Standard	Items are activated with a double-click. No change in the selected item's text color takes place.
TwoClick	Items are activated with a double-click and their text changes color as well.

FullRowSelect   This property is a True/False value indicating whether the user can select an entire row or just the item's text, and it's meaningful only in Report view.

GridLines   Another True/False property. If True, then grid lines between items and subitems are drawn. This property is meaningful only in Report view.

LabelEdit   The LabelEdit property lets you specify whether the user will be allowed to edit the text of the items. The default value of this property is False.

MultiSelect   A True/False value indicating whether the user can select multiple items on the control or not. To select multiple items, click them with the mouse while holding down the Shift or the Control key.

Scrollable   A True/False value that determines whether the scrollbars are visible or not. Even if the scrollbars are invisible, users will still be able to bring any item into view. All they have to do is select an item and then press the arrow keys as many times as needed to scroll a different section of the Items collection into view.

Sorting   This property determines how the items will be sorted, and as usual it's meaningful only in Report view. This Sorting property isn't a simple True/False value like the Sorted property of the TreeView control. Its setting can be `None`, `Ascending`, or `Descending`. A ListView control can be sorted in many ways (it has multiple columns), and each column may hold data of a different type. You must build a custom comparer and assign it to the ListViewItemSorter property of the ListView control. The process of sorting a ListView control is discussed in detail in the section "Sorting the ListView Control," later in this chapter.

The Columns Collection

To display items in Report view, you must first set up the appropriate columns. The first column corresponds to the item, and the following columns correspond to its subitems. If you don't set up at least one column, no items will be displayed in Report view. Conversely, the Columns collection is meaningful only when the ListView control is used in Report view.

The items of the Columns collection are of the ColumnHeader type. The simplest method to set up the appropriate columns is to do so at design time with a visual tool. Locate and select the Columns property in the Properties window, and click the button with the ellipses next to it. The ColumnHeader Collection Editor window will appear, as shown in Figure 16.11, where you can add and edit the appropriate columns.

Adding columns to a ListView control and setting their properties through the window of Figure 16.11 is quite trivial. Don't forget to size the columns according to the data you anticipate to store in them and set their headers.

It is also possible to manipulate the Columns collection from within your code, with the methods and properties discussed here.

Add method   Use the Add method of the Columns collection to add a new column to the control. The syntax of the Add method is

```
TreeView.Columns.Add(header, width, textAlign)
```

FIGURE 16.11

The ColumnHeader
Collection Editor
window

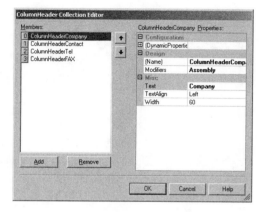

The *header* argument is the column's header (the string that appears on top of the items). The *width* argument is the column's width in pixels, and the last argument determines how the text will be aligned. The *textAlign* argument can be Center, Justify, Left, NotSet, or Right. The NotSet setting specifies that horizontal alignment is not set.

The Add method returns a ColumnHeader object, which you can use later in your code to manipulate the corresponding column. The ColumnHeader object exposes a Name property, which can't be set with the Add method.

```
Header1 = TreeView1.Add("Column 1", 60, ColAlignment.Left)
Header1.Name = "COL1"
```

After the execution of these statements, the first column can be accessed not only by index but by name as well.

Clear method   This method removes all columns.

Count property   This property returns the number of columns in the ListView control. You can add more subitems than there are columns in the control, but the excess subitems will not be displayed.

Remove method   This method removes a column by its index:

```
ListView1.Columns(3).Remove
```

The indices of the following columns are automatically decreased by one.

The ListItem Object

As with the TreeView control, the ListView control can be populated either at design time or at runtime. To add items at design time, click the button with the ellipsis next to the ListItems property in the Properties window. When the ListViewItem Collection Editor window pops up, you can enter the items, including their subitems, as shown in Figure 16.12.

FIGURE 16.12

The ListViewItem
Collection Editor

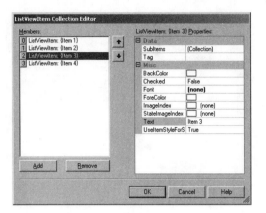

Click the Add button to add a new item. Each item has subitems, which you can specify as members of the SubItems collection. To add an item with three subitems, you can populate the SubItems collection with the appropriate elements. Click the button with the ellipsis in the SubItems property on the ListViewItem Collection Editor, and the ListViewSubItem Collection Editor will appear. This window is very similar to the ListViewItem Collection Editor window, and you can add each item's subitems. Assuming that you have added the item called Item 1 in the ListViewItem Collection Editor, you can add these subitems: Item 1-a, Item 1-b, and Item 1-c. The first subitem (the one with zero index) is actually the main item of the control.

Notice that you can set other properties, like the color and font for each item, the check box in front of the item that indicates whether the item is selected, and the image of the item. Use this window to experiment with the appearance of the control and the placement of the items, especially in Report view, since subitems are visible only in this view. Even then, you won't see anything unless you specify headers for the columns.

Unlike the TreeView control, the ListView control allows you to specify a different appearance for each item and each subitem. To set the appearance of the items, use the Font, BackColor, and ForeColor properties of the ListViewItem object.

Almost all ListViews are populated at runtime. Not only that, but you should be able to add and remove items during the course of the application. The items of the ListView control are of the ListViewItem type, and they expose a number of members that allow you to control the appearance of the items on the control. These members are listed next:

BackColor property   This property sets or returns the background color of the current item.

Checked property   This property controls the status of an item. If it's True, then the item has been selected. You can also select an item from within your code by setting its Checked property to True. The check boxes in front of each item won't be visible unless you set the control's CheckBoxes property to True.

Font property   This property sets the font of the current item. Subitems can be displayed in a different font if you specify one with the SetSubItemFont method (see the section "The SubItems Collection," later in this chapter).

Text property   This property is the caption of the current item.

SubItems collection   This property holds the subitems of the current ListViewItem. To retrieve a specific subitem, use a statement like the following:

```
sitem = ListView1.Items(idx1).SubItems(idx2)
```

where *idx1* is the index of the item and *idx2* the index of the desired subitem.

To add a new subitem to the SubItems collection, use the Add method, passing the text of the subitem as argument:

```
LItem.SubItems.Add("subitem's caption")
```

The argument of the Add method can also be a ListViewItem object. If you want to add a subitem at a specific location, use the Insert method. The Insert method of the SubItems collection accepts two arguments: the index of the subitem before which the new subitem will be inserted and a string or ListViewItem to be inserted:

```
LItem.SubItems.Insert(idx, subitem)
```

Like the ListViewItem objects, each subitem can have its own font, which is set with the Font property.

Remove method   This method removes an item by index. When you remove an item, it takes with it all of its subitems.

SetSubItemBackColor method   This method sets the background color of the current subitem.

SetSubItemForeColor method   This method sets the foreground color of the current subitem.

The items of the ListView control can be accessed through the ListItems property, which is a collection. As such, it exposes the standard members of a collection, which are described in the following section.

The Items Collection

All the items on the ListView control form a collection, the Items collection. This collection exposes the typical members of a collection that let you manipulate the control's items. These members are discussed next:

Add method   This method adds a new item to the Items collection. The syntax of the Add method is

```
ListView1.Items.Add(caption)
```

You can also specify the index of the image to be used along with the item and a collection of subitems to be appended to the new item, with the following form of the Add method:

```
ListView1.Items.Add(caption, imageIndex)
```

where *imageIndex* is the index of the desired image on the associated ImageList control.

Finally, you can create a ListViewItem object in your code and then add it to the ListView control with the following form of the Add method:

```
ListView1.Items.Add(listItemObj)
```

The following statements create a new item, set its individual subitems, and then add the newly created ListViewItem object to the control:

```
Dim LItem As New ListViewItem()
LItem.Text = "new item"
LItem.SetSubItem(0, "sub item 1a")
LItem.SetSubItem(1, "sub item 1b")
LItem.SetSubItem(2, "sub item 1c")
ListView1.ListItems.Add(LItem)
```

Count property   Returns the number of items in the collection.

Clear method   Removes all the items from the collection.

Item property   Retrieves an item specified by an index value.

Remove method   Removes an item from the Items collection.

The SubItems Collection

Each item in the ListView control may also have subitems. You can think of the item as the key of a record and the subitems as the other fields of the record. The subitems are displayed only in Report mode, but they are available to your code in any view. For example, you can display all items as icons, and when the user clicks on an icon, show the values of the selected item's subitems on other controls.

To access the subitems of a given item, use its SubItems collection. The following statements add an item and three subitems to the ListView1 control:

```
Dim LItem As ListViewItem
Set LItem = ListView1.Items.Add( , , "Alfreds Futterkiste")
LItem.SubItems(1) = "Maria Anders"
LItem.SubItems(2) = "030-0074321"
LItem.SubItems(3) = "030-0076545"
```

To access the SubItems collection, you must have a reference to the item to which the subitems belong. The Add method returns a reference to the newly added item, the *LItem* variable, which is then used to access the item's subitems, as shown in the last example.

Displaying the subitems on the control requires some overhead. Subitems are displayed only in Report view mode. However, setting the View property to Report is not enough. You must first create the columns of the Report view, as explained earlier. The ListView control displays only as many subitems as there are columns in the control. The first column, with the header Company, displays the items of the list. The following columns display the subitems. Moreover, you can't specify which subitem will be displayed under each header. The first subitem ("Maria Anders" in the above example) will be displayed under the second header, the second subitem ("030-0074321" in the same example) will be displayed under the third header, and so on. At runtime, the user can rearrange the columns by dragging them with the mouse. To disable the rearrangement of the columns at runtime, set the control's AllowColumnReorder property to False (its default value is True).

Unless you set up each column's width, all columns will have the same width. The width of individual columns is in pixels, and it's usually specified as a percentage of the total width of the control, especially if the control is docked to the form. The following code sets up a ListView control with four headers, all having the same width:

```
Dim LWidth As Integer
LWidth = ListView1.Width - 5
ListView1.ColumnHeaders.Add("Company", LWidth / 4)
ListView1.ColumnHeaders.Add("Contact", LWidth / 4)
ListView1.ColumnHeaders.Add("Phone", LWidth / 4)
ListView1.ColumnHeaders.Add("FAX", LWidth / 4)
ListView1.View = DetailsView
```

This subroutine sets up four headers of equal width. The first header corresponds to the item (not a subitem). The number of headers you set up must be equal to the number of subitems you want to display on the control plus one. The constant 5 is subtracted to compensate for the width of the column separators.

VB.NET AT WORK: THE LISTVIEWDEMO PROJECT

Let's put together the members of the ListView control to create a sample application that populates a ListView control and enumerates its items. The application is called ListViewDemo and you'll find it in this chapter's folder on the CD. The application's form, shown in Figure 16.13, contains a ListView control whose items can be displayed in all possible views, depending on the status of the OptionButton controls in the List Style section on the right side of the form.

FIGURE 16.13

The ListViewDemo project demonstrates the basic members of the ListView control.

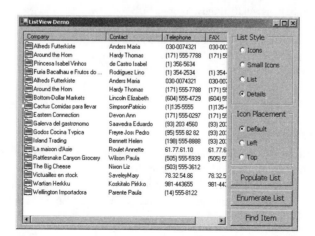

When the application starts, it sets up the headers (columns) of the ListView control. You can comment out the lines that insert the headers in the Form's Load event and then run the project to see what happens when the control is switched to Report view.

Let's start by looking at the form's initialization code. The control's headers and their widths were set at design time, through the ColumnHeader Collection Editor, as explained earlier.

To populate the ListView control, click the Populate List button, whose code is shown next. The code creates a new ListViewItem object for each item to be added. Then it calls the Add method of the SubItems collection to add the item's subitems (contact, phone, and fax numbers). After the ListViewItem has been set up, it's added to the control with the Add method of its Items collection.

Listing 16.12 shows the statements that insert the first two items in the list. The remaining items are added with similar statements, which need not be repeated here. The sample data I used in the ListViewDemo application came from the NorthWind sample database, which is installed along with Visual Basic.

LISTING 16.12: POPULATING A LISTVIEW CONTROL

```
Dim LItem As New ListViewItem()
LItem.Text = "Alfreds Futterkiste"
LItem.SubItems.Add("Anders Maria")
LItem.SubItems.Add("030-0074321")
LItem.SubItems.Add("030-0076545")
LItem.ImageIndex = 0
ListView1.Items.Add(LItem)

LItem = New ListViewItem()
LItem.Text = "Around the Horn"
LItem.SubItems.Add("Hardy Thomas")
LItem.SubItems.Add("(171) 555-7788")
LItem.SubItems.Add("(171) 555-6750")
LItem.ImageIndex = 0
ListView1.Items.Add(LItem)
```

ENUMERATING THE LIST

The Enumerate List button scans all the items in the list and displays them along with their subitems in the Output window. To scan the list, you must set up a loop that enumerates all the items in the Items collection. For each item in the list, set up a nested loop that scans all the subitems of the current item. The complete code for the Enumerate List button is shown in Listing 16.13.

LISTING 16.13: ENUMERATING ITEMS AND SUBITEMS

```
Private Sub bttnEnumerate_Click(ByVal sender As System.Object, _
                ByVal e As System.EventArgs) Handles bttnEnumerate.Click
    Dim i, j As Integer
    Dim LItem As ListViewItem
    For i = 0 To ListView1.Items.Count - 1
        LItem = ListView1.Items(i)
        Console.WriteLine(LItem.Text)
        For j = 0 To LItem.SubItems.Count - 1
            Console.WriteLine("   " & ListView1.Columns(j).Text & _
                              " " & Litem.SubItems(j).Text)
        Next
    Next
End Sub
```

The output of this code in the Output window is shown next. The subitems appear under the corresponding item, and they are indented by three spaces.

```
Alfreds Futterkiste
    Company  Alfreds Futterkiste
    Contact  Anders Maria
    Telephone  030-0074321
    FAX  030-0076545
Around the Horn
    Company  Around the Horn
    Contact  Hardy Thomas
    Telephone  (171) 555-7788
    FAX  (171) 555-6750
```

The code in Listing 16.13 uses a For…Next loop to iterate through the items of the control. You can also set up a For Each…Next loop, as shown here:

```
For Each ListViewItem In ListView1.Items
    { same statements }
Next
```

SORTING THE LISTVIEW CONTROL

The ListView control provides a Sorting method, which allows you to specify how the list's items will be sorted. Each item may contain any number of subitems, and you should be able to sort the list according to any column. The values stored in the subitems may represent different data types (numeric values, strings, dates, and so on). The control doesn't provide a default sorting mechanism for all data types. Instead, it uses a custom Comparer object, which you supply, to sort the items. The topic of building custom comparers has been discussed in detail in Chapter 11. As a reminder, the custom comparer is implemented as a function, which compares two items and returns an integer value (−1, 0, or 1), which indicates the order of the two items. Once this function is in place, the control uses it to sort its items.

The ListView control's ListViewItemSorter property accepts the name of a custom comparer, and the items on the control are sorted according to the custom comparer as soon as you set the Sorting property. As you may recall, you can provide several custom comparers and sort the items in many different ways. If you plan to display subitems along with your items in Report view, you should make the list sortable by any column. It's customary for a ListView control to sort its items according to the values in a specific column each time the header of this column is clicked. And this is exactly the type of functionality you'll add to the ListViewDemo project in this section.

The ListViewDemo control displays contact information. The items are company names, and the first subitem under each item is the name of a contact. We'll create two custom comparers to sort the list according to either company name or contact. The two methods are identical since they compare strings, but it's not any more complicated to compare dates, distances, and so on.

Let's start with the two custom comparers. Each comparer must be implemented in its own class, and you assign the name of the custom comparer to the ListViewItemProperty of the control. Listing 16.14 shows the ListCompanyComparer and the ListContactComparer.

LISTING 16.14: THE TWO CUSTOM COMPARERS FOR THE LISTVIEWDEMO PROJECT

```
Class ListCompanySorter
    Implements IComparer
    Public Function CompareTo(ByVal o1 As Object, ByVal o2 As Object) As Integer _
                    Implements System.Collections.IComparer.compare
        Dim item1, item2 As ListViewItem
        item1 = CType(o1, ListViewItem)
        item2 = CType(o2, ListViewItem)
        If item1.ToString.ToUpper > item2.ToString.ToUpper Then
            Return 1
        Else
            If item1.ToString.ToUpper < item2.ToString.ToUpper Then
                Return -1
            Else
                Return 0
            End If
        End If
    End Function
End Class
Class ListContactSorter
    Implements IComparer
    Public Function CompareTo(ByVal o1 As Object, ByVal o2 As Object) As Integer _
                    Implements System.collections.IComparer.compare
        Dim item1, item2 As ListVewItem
        item1 = CType(o1, ListViewItem)
        item2 = CType(o2, ListViewItem)
        If item1.SubItems(1).ToString.ToUpper > _
                    item2.SubItems(1).ToString.ToUpper Then
            Return 1
        Else
```

```
        If item1.SubItems(1).ToString.ToUpper < _
                    item2.SubItems(1).ToString.ToUpper Then
            Return -1
        Else
            Return 0
        End If
      End If
    End Function
End Class
```

The code is straightforward. If you need additional information, see the discussion of the IComparer interface in Chapter 11. The two functions are identical, except that the first one sorts according to the item and the second one sorts according to the first subitem.

To test the custom comparers, you simply assign their names to the ListViewItemSorter property of the ListView control. To take advantage of our custom comparers, we must write some code that intercepts the clicks on the control's headers and calls the appropriate comparer. The ListView control fires the ColumnClick event each time a column header is clicked. This event handler reports the index of the column that was clicked through the e.Column argument, and we can use this argument in our code to sort the items accordingly. Listing 16.15. shows the event handler for the ColumnClick event.

LISTING 16.15: THE LISTVIEW CONTROL'S COLUMNCLICK EVENT HANDLER

```
Public Sub ListView1_ColumnClick(ByVal sender As Object, _
            ByVal e As System.WinForms.ColumnClickEventArgs) _
            Handles ListView1.ColumnClick
  Select Case e.column
    Case 0
      ListView1.ListViewItemSorter = New ListCompanySorter()
      ListView1.Sorting = SortOrder.Ascending
    Case 1
      ListView1.LisViewtItemSorter = New ListContactSorter()
      ListView1.Sorting = SortOrder.Ascending
  End Select
End Sub
```

PROCESSING SELECTED ITEMS

The user can select multiple items on a ListView control by default. Even though you can display a check mark in front of each item, it's not customary. Items on a ListView control are selected with the mouse while holding down the Ctrl or Shift key.

The selected items form the SelectedListItemCollection, which is a property of the control. You can iterate through this collection with a For...Next loop or through the enumerator object exposed by the collection. In the following example, I use a For Each…Next loop. Listing 16.16 is the code behind the Selected Items button of the ListViewDemo project. It goes through the selected items and displays each item, along with its subitems, in the Output window. Notice that you can select multiple items in any view, even when the subitems are not visible. They're still there, however, and they can be retrieved through the SubItems collection.

LISTING 16.16: ITERATING THE SELECTED ITEMS ON A LISTVIEW CONTROL

```
Private Sub bttnIterate_Click(ByVal sender As System.Object, _
              ByVal e As System.EventArgs) Handles bttnIterate.Click
    Dim LItem As ListViewItem
    Dim LItems As ListView.SelectedListViewItemCollection
    LItems = ListView1.SelectedItems
    For Each LItem In LItems
        Console.Write(LItem.Text & vbTab)
        Console.Write(LItem.SubItems(0).ToString & vbTab)
        Console.Write(LItem.SubItems(1).ToString & vbTab)
        Console.WriteLine(LItem.SubItems(2).ToString & vbTab)
    Next
End Sub
```

VB.NET AT WORK: THE CUSTOMEXPLORER PROJECT

The last example in this chapter combines the TreeView and ListView controls. It's a fairly advanced example, but I've included it here for the most ambitious readers. It can also be used as the starting point for many custom applications, so give it a try. You can always come back to this project after you've mastered other aspects of the language.

The Explorer project, shown in Figure 16.14, is the core of a custom Explorer window, which displays a structured list of folders on the left pane and the list of files in the selected folder on the right pane. The left pane is populated when the application starts, but it takes a while. On my Pentium system, it takes nearly five seconds to populate the TreeView control with the structure of the C:\Windows folder. You can expand any folder on this pane and view its subfolders. To view the files in a folder, click its name, and the right pane will be populated with the names of the files, along with vital data, such as the file size, date of creation, and date of last modification. You already know how to manipulate folders and files, and you should be able to follow the code easily. If you have to, you can review the Directory and FileInfo objects and their properties in Chapter 13.

This section's project is not limited to displaying folders and files; you can populate the two controls with data from several sources. For example, you can display customers in the left pane (and organize them by city or state) and their related data on the right pane (e.g., invoices and payments). Or you can populate the left pane with product names and the right pane with the respective sales. In general, you can use it as an interface for many types of applications. You can even use it as a custom Explorer to add features that are specific to your applications.

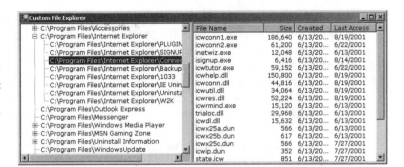

FIGURE 16.14

The Explorer project demonstrates how to combine a TreeView and a ListView control on the same form.

The left pane is populated from within the Form's Load event handler subroutine. The code makes use of the Directory and File objects, which were discussed earlier in the book. Following is the code that populates the TreeView control with the subfolders of the C:\Program Files folder.

```
Dim Nd As New TreeNode()
Nd = TreeView1.Nodes.Add("C:\Program Files")
ScanFolder("c:\Program Files", ND)
```

Nd represents the control's root node, and it's the name of the folder to be scanned. To populate the control with the files of another folder or drive, change the name of the path accordingly. The code is short and, as you have guessed, all the work is done by the ScanFolder() subroutine. The ScanFolder() subroutine is a short, recursive procedure that scans all the folders under C:\Program Files and is shown in Listing 16.17. The second argument is the root node, under which the entire tree of the specified folder will appear.

LISTING 16.17: THE SCANFOLDER() SUBROUTINE

```
Sub ScanFolder(ByVal folderSpec As String, ByRef currentNode As TreeNode)
    Dim thisFolder As String
    Dim allFolders() As String
    allFolders = Directory.GetDirectories(folderSpec)
    For Each thisFolder In allFolders
        Dim Nd As TreeNode
        Nd = New TreeNode(thisFolder)
        currentNode.Nodes.Add(Nd)
        folderSpec = thisFolder
        ScanFolder(folderSpec, Nd)
    Next
End Sub
```

The variable *thisFolder* represents the current folder (the one passed to the ScanFolder() subroutine as argument). Using this variable, the program creates the *allFolders* collection, which contains all the subfolders of the current folder. Then it scans every folder in this collection and adds its name to the TreeView control. The newly added node is the name of the folder. Within a given folder, all subfolder names are unique. After adding a folder to the TreeView control, the procedure must scan the subfolders of the current folder. It does so by calling itself and passing another folder's name as an argument. If you find the recursive implementation of the subroutine difficult to understand, go through the material of Chapter 18. You can use the ScanFolder() subroutine as is in your projects; just pass to it a reference to the folder you want to scan. The first argument to the ScanFolder() subroutine is the name of the folder to be scanned.

Notice that the ScanFolder subroutine doesn't simply scan a folder. It also adds a node to the TreeView control for each new folder it runs into. That's why it accepts two arguments, the name of the current folder and the node that represents this folder on the control. All folders are placed under their parent folder, and the structure of the tree represents the structure of your hard disk (or the section of the hard disk you're mapping on the TreeView control). All this is done with a small recursive subroutine, the ScanFolder() subroutine.

Viewing a Folder's Files

To view the files of a folder, click the folder's name in the TreeView control. As explained earlier, the action of the selection of a new node is detected with the AfterSelect event. The code in the TreeView1_AfterSelect event handler, shown in Listing 16.18, displays the selected folder's files on the ListView control.

LISTING 16.18: DISPLAYING A FOLDER'S FILES

```
Private Sub TreeView1_AfterSelect(ByVal sender As System.Object, _
           ByVal e As System.Windows.Forms.TreeViewEventArgs) _
           Handles TreeView1.AfterSelect
    Dim Nd As TreeNode
    Dim pathName As String
    Nd = TreeView1.SelectedNode
    pathName = Nd.Text
    ShowFiles(pathName)
End Sub
```

The ShowFiles() subroutine actually displays the file names, and some of their properties, in the specified folder on the ListView control. Its code is shown in Listing 16.19.

LISTING 16.19: THE SHOWFILES SUBROUTINE

```
Sub ShowFiles(ByVal selFolder As String)
    ListView1.Items.Clear()
    Dim files() As String
    Dim file As String
    files = Directory.GetFiles(selFolder)
    For Each file In files
        Dim LItem As New ListViewItem()
        LItem.Text = ExtractFileName(file)
        Dim FI As New FileInfo(file)
```

```
        LItem.SubItems.Add(FI.Length.ToString("#,###"))
        LItem.SubItems.Add(FormatDateTime(Directory.GetCreationTime(file), _
                        DateFormat.ShortDate))
        LItem.SubItems.Add(FormatDateTime(Directory.GetLastAccessTime(file), _
                        DateFormat.ShortDate))
        ListView1.Items.Add(LItem)
    Next
End Sub
```

The ShowFiles subroutine creates a ListItem for each file. The item's caption is the file's name. The first subitem is the file's length. The other two items are the file's creation and last access times. You can add more subitems if your application needs them. The ListView control in this example uses the Report view to display the items, so you don't have to worry about images. If we used the Large Icon or Small Icon view, we'd have to come up with icons for all types of files (or the most common ones).

As mentioned earlier, the ListView control isn't going to display any items unless you specify the proper columns through the Columns collection. The columns, along with their widths and captions, were set at design time through the ColumnHeader Collection Editor.

Saving a Tree's Nodes to Disk

You've learned how to populate the TreeView and ListView controls, how to manipulate them at runtime, and how to sort the ListView control in any way you wish, but what good are all these techniques unless you can save the tree's nodes or the ListItems to a disk file and reuse them in a later session?

In Chapter 11, you saw how to serialize complicated objects, like an ArrayList. It would be nice if the TreeNode object were serializable; you could serialize the root node and all the nodes under it with a single call to the Serialize method. Unfortunately, this is not the case. Well, how about subclassing the TreeNode object? Create a new class that inherits from the TreeNode class and is serializable. This is an option, but it's not simple. Besides, the subclassed TreeNode object will be specific to an application.

Since we already know how to serialize an ArrayList, we can extract the items of the TreeView control to an ArrayList and then serialize the ArrayList. The code of this section serializes the strings displayed on a TreeView control. You know how to scan the nodes of a TreeView control, and the code for serializing the control's nodes seems trivial. It's not quite so.

The ArrayList has a linear structure: each item is independent of any other. The TreeView control, however, has a hierarchical structure. Most of its nodes are children of other nodes, as well as parents of other nodes. Therefore, we must store not only the data (strings), but their structure as well. To store this information, we'll create a new structure with two fields: one for the node's value and another for the node's indentation:

```
<Serializable()> Structure sNode
    Dim node As String
    Dim level As Integer
End Structure
```

We want to be able to serialize this structure, so we must prefix it with the <Serializable> attribute. The *level* field is the node's indentation; the *level* field of all root nodes is zero. The nodes immediately under the root have a level of 1, and so on. To serialize the TreeView control, we'll iterate through its nodes and store each node to an *sNode* variable. Each time we switch to a child node, we'll increase the current value of the level by one. Each time we move up to a parent node, we'll decrease the same value accordingly. All the *sNode* structures will be added to an ArrayList, which will then be serialized.

Likewise, when we read the ArrayList from the disk file, we must reconstruct the original tree. Items with a level value of zero are root nodes. The first item with a level value of 1 is the first child node under the most recently added root node. As long as the *level* field doesn't change, the new nodes are added under the same parent. When this value increases, we must create a new child node under the current node. When this value decreases, we must move up to the current node's parent and create a new child under it. The only complication is that a *level* value may decrease by more than one. In this case, we must move up to the parent's parent, or even higher in the hierarchy. Figure 16.15 shows a typical TreeView control and how its nodes are stored in the ArrayList.

FIGURE 16.15

The structure of the nodes of a TreeView control

TreeView	List
⊟ Root	0 Root
⊟ Node 1	1 Node 1
├ Node 1.1	2 Node 1.1
├ Node 1.2	2 Node 1.2
⊟ Node 1.3	2 Node 1.3
⊟ Node 1.3.1	3 Node 1.3.1
├ Node 1.3.1.1	4 Node 1.3.1.1
└ Node 1.3.1.2	4 Node 1.3.1.2
⊟ Node2	1 Node2
├ Node 2.1	2 Node 2.1
└ Node 2.2	2 Node 2.2
⊟ Node3	1 Node3
├ Node 3.1	2 Node 3.1
├ Node 3.2	2 Node 3.2
└ Node 3.3	2 Node 3.3

The control on the left is a TreeView control, populated at design time. The control on the right is a ListBox control with the items of the ArrayList. The first column is the *level* field (the node's indentation), while the second column is the node's text.

Now we can look at the code for serializing the control. The code presented in this section is part of the Globe project—namely, it's the code behind the Save Nodes and Load Nodes commands of the File menu. The File ➤ Save Nodes command prompts the user with the File Save dialog box for the path of a file, where the nodes will be stored. Then it calls the SaveNodes() subroutine, passing the root node of the control and the path of the file where the items will be stored. Listing 16.20 shows this menu item's Click event handler.

LISTING 16.20: THE FILE ➤ SAVE NODES MENUITEM'S EVENT HANDLER

```
Private Sub FileSave_Click(ByVal sender As System.Object, _
            ByVal e As System.EventArgs) Handles FileSave.Click
    SaveFileDialog1.DefaultExt = "XML"
    If SaveFileDialog1.ShowDialog = DialogResult.OK Then
        CreateList(GlobeTree.Nodes(0), SaveFileDialog1.FileName)
    End If
End Sub
```

TheCreateList() subroutine goes through the nodes of the root node and stores them into the *GlobeNodes* ArrayList. This ArrayList is declared at the Form level with the following statement:

```
Dim GlobeNodes As New ArrayList()
```

CreateList() is a recursive subroutine that scans the immediate children of the node passed as argument. If a child node contains its own children, the subroutine calls itself to iterate through the children. This process may continue to any depth. The code of the subroutine is shown in Listing 16.21; its structure is similar to the ScanNode() subroutine of Listing 16.11.

LISTING 16.21: THE CREATELIST() SUBROUTINE

```
Sub CreateList(ByVal node As TreeNode, ByVal fName As String)
    Static level As Integer
    Dim thisNode As TreeNode
    Dim myNode As sNode
    Application.DoEvents()
    myNode.level = level
    myNode.node = node.Text
    GlobeNodes.Add(myNode)
    If node.Nodes.Count > 0 Then
        level = level + 1
        For Each thisNode In node.Nodes
            CreateList(thisNode, fName)
        Next
        level = level - 1
    End If
    SaveNodes(fName)
End Sub
```

After the ArrayList has been populated, the code calls the SaveNodes() subroutine, which persists the ArrayList to a disk file. The path of the file is the second argument of the CreateList() subroutine. SaveNodes(), shown in Listing 16.22, is a straightforward subroutine that serializes the *GlobeNodes* ArrayList to disk.

LISTING 16.22: THE SAVENODES() SUBROUTINE

```
Sub SaveNodes(ByVal fName As String)
    Dim formatter As SoapFormatter
    Dim saveFile As FileStream
    saveFile = File.Create(fName)
    formatter = New SoapFormatter()
    formatter.Serialize(saveFile, GlobeNodes)
    saveFile.Close()
End Sub
```

TIP *For more information on serializing ArrayLists, see Chapter 13.*

The File ➢ Load Nodes command prompts the user for a filename and then calls the LoadNodes() subroutine to read the ArrayList persisted in this file and load the control with its nodes. The Click event handler of the Load Nodes command is shown in Listing 16.23.

LISTING 16.23: THE FILE ➢ LOAD NODES MENUITEM'S EVENT HANDLER

```
Private Sub FileLoad_Click(ByVal sender As System.Object, _
            ByVal e As System.EventArgs) Handles FileLoad.Click
   OpenFileDialog1.DefaultExt = "XML"
   If OpenFileDialog1.ShowDialog = DialogResult.OK Then
      LoadNodes(GlobeTree, OpenFileDialog1.FileName)
   End If
End Sub
```

The LoadNodes() subroutine loads the items read from the file into the *GlobeNodes* ArrayList and then calls the ShowNodes() subroutine to load the nodes from the ArrayList onto the control. The LoadNodes() subroutine is shown in Listing 16.24.

LISTING 16.24: LOADING THE GLOBENODES ARRAYLIST

```
Sub LoadNodes(ByVal TV As TreeView, ByVal fName As String)
   TV.Nodes.Clear()
   Dim formatter As SoapFormatter
   Dim openFile As FileStream
   openFile = File.Open(fName, FileMode.Open)
   formatter = New SoapFormatter()
   GlobeNodes = CType(formatter.Deserialize(openFile), ArrayList)
   openFile.Close()
   ShowNodes(TV)
End Sub
```

The most interesting code is in the ShowNodes() subroutine, which goes through the items in the ArrayList and re-creates the original structure of the TreeView control. At each iteration, the subroutine examines the value of the item's *level* field. If it's the same as the current node's level, then the new node is added under the same node as the current node (we're on the same indentation level). If the current item's *level* field is larger than the current node's level, then the new node is added under the current node (it's a child of the current node). Finally, if the current item's *level* field is smaller than then current node's level, the code moves up to the parent of the current node. This step may be repeated several times, depending on the difference of the two levels. If the current node's level is 4 and the *level* field of the new node is 1, the code will move up three levels (it will actually be added under the most recent root node). Listing 16.25 is the code of the Show-Nodes() subroutine.

LISTING 16.25: THE SHOWNODES() SUBROUTINE

```
Sub ShowNodes(ByVal TV As TreeView)
    Dim o As Object
    Dim currNode As TreeNode
    Dim level As Integer = 0
    Dim fromLowerLevel As Integer
    Dim i As Integer
    For i = 0 To GlobeNodes.Count - 1
        o = GlobeNodes(i)
        If o.level = level Then
            If currNode Is Nothing Then
                currNode = TV.Nodes.Add(o.node.ToString)
            Else
                currNode = currNode.Parent.Nodes.Add(o.node.ToString)
            End If
        Else
            If o.level > level Then
                currNode = currNode.Nodes.Add(o.node.ToString)
                level = o.level
            Else
                While o.level <= level
                    currNode = currNode.Parent
                    level = level - 1
                End While
                currNode = currNode.Nodes.Add(o.node.ToString)
            End If
        End If
        TV.ExpandAll()
        Application.DoEvents()
    Next
End Sub
```

Why did I use a SoapFormatter and not a BinaryFormatter to persists the data? I just wanted to see the structure of the data in text format. You will probably change the code to save the data in binary format, because it's much more compact. Of course, XML and SOAP are quite fashionable these days. You can also claim that the data can be read on any other system and you follow industry standards. I suggest you use mostly the binary format for storing application data. If you want to exchange data with another system, create a DataSet in XML format—a topic discussed in Part IV of this book.

The technique shown here persists the strings displayed on the control, and it work with most applications. If you're using a TreeView control to store objects, you must adjust the code of this section to persist the objects, not just strings.

If you're wondering what the persisted nodes look like in the XML file, here's how the first few items of the Globe tree are persisted. The file format is verbose indeed, but the items of interest appear in bold (they're the *node* and *level* fields):

```
- <item xsi:type="a3:NodeSerializer+sNode" xmlns:a3="http://schemas.microsoft.com/
clr/nsassem/Globe/Globe%2C%20Version%3D1.0.638.15776%2C%20Culture%3Dneutral%2C%20Pu
blicKeyToken%3Dnull">
  <node id="ref-4">Globe</node>
  <level>0</level>
  </item>
- <item xsi:type="a3:NodeSerializer+sNode" xmlns:a3="http://schemas.microsoft.com/
clr/nsassem/Globe/Globe%2C%20Version%3D1.0.638.15776%2C%20Culture%3Dneutral%2C%20Pu
blicKeyToken%3Dnull">
  <node id="ref-5">Africa</node>
  <level>1</level>
  </item>
- <item xsi:type="a3:NodeSerializer+sNode" xmlns:a3="http://schemas.microsoft.com/
clr/nsassem/Globe/Globe%2C%20Version%3D1.0.638.15776%2C%20Culture%3Dneutral%2C%20Pu
blicKeyToken%3Dnull">
  <node id="ref-6">Egypt</node>
  <level>2</level>
  </item>
- <item xsi:type="a3:NodeSerializer+sNode" xmlns:a3="http://schemas.microsoft.com/
clr/nsassem/Globe/Globe%2C%20Version%3D1.0.638.15776%2C%20Culture%3Dneutral%2C%20Pu
blicKeyToken%3Dnull">
  <node id="ref-7">Alexandria</node>
  <level>3</level>
  </item>
```

Persisting the items of a ListView control is even simpler. You must create a new structure that reflects the structure of each row (the item and subitems of each row), and then create an ArrayList with items of this type. Persisting the ArrayList is straightforward and so is the loading of the control, since the ListView control doesn't have a hierarchical structure. Its items are organized in a linear fashion, just like the items of the ArrayList.

To reuse the subroutines that serialize and deserialize the nodes of a TreeView control, you can create a new class that exposes the CreateList() and LoadNodes() subroutines as methods. The other two subroutines that actually save the ArrayList to disk and load a disk file into the ArrayList are Private to the class and can be called only from within the code of the two methods.

The Globe project on the CD contains a class, the NodeSerializer class. This class contains the code and the declarations discussed in this section, and I will not repeat the code here. To use this class in your code, you must create an instance of the class and call the appropriate method.

To persist the TreeView control to a file, use the following statements:

```
Dim NS As New NodeSerializer()
NS.CreateList(GlobeTree.Nodes(0), SaveFileDialog1.FileName)
```

To load a TreeView control previously saved to a file, use the following statements:

```
Dim NS As New NodeSerializer()
NS.LoadNodes(GlobeTree, OpenFileDialog1.FileName)
```

I've included these statements in the Globe project on the CD, but they're commented out. To test the commands of the File menu of the Globe application, add a few items to the TreeView control (countries and cities) and save the tree to a disk file. Then select the root node, delete it with the Delete Current Node button, and load the file you just saved to disk.

One last remark about the code that loads a TreeView control from a disk file. Since the TreeView is persisted to an XML file, the user may attempt to open an XML file that contains irrelevant data. You must insert a structured exception handler to avoid runtime errors, or use a new extension for these files. After looking at the XML files generated by the Serialize method for a couple of TreeView controls, you should change the SoapFormatter to a BinaryFormatter.

Summary

The controls discussed in this chapter are among the more advanced ones. With the possible exception of the data-bound controls, which are discussed in the fourth part of the book, you have all the information you need to start building elaborate user interfaces.

The TreeView and ListView controls are highly visual. Not only do they display the necessary information, but they also make it easy for the user to see how the information is structured. They're not commonly used in the user interface design, even by intermediate programmers, but they can add a professional touch to your applications. As you have seen, they're not especially hard to program either. Once you understand the relation between a node and its Nodes collection and how to create items with subitems, you'll be able to use them just like any other control.

The recursive procedure for scanning a TreeView control may have thrown off some of you. If you have read Chapter 13, you have seen a similar procedure for scanning folders. As the object models become more and more complicated, recursive programming will become a necessity in everyday programming. If you're not comfortable with this topic, please read a detailed tutorial on recursive programming in Chapter 18 of this book. Recursion is a very powerful coding technique, and it will simplify enormously some of your coding tasks, as demonstrated in the examples of this chapter.

Chapter 17

Error Handling and Debugging

WRITING A PIECE OF software, even a relatively small one, can be an extremely complicated task. Developers usually put careful forethought and planning into the nature of the task and the means they will use to solve the task through the program that they intend to write.

The complex nature of software development invariably leads to errors in programming. This chapter sets out to explain the different types of errors that you might encounter when writing Visual Basic .NET code, some of the tools that you can use to locate these errors, and the coding structures used to prevent these errors when users run your program.

In addition to programming errors, your application should be able to gracefully handle all the abnormal conditions it may encounter, from user errors (when they enter a string where the program expects a date or numeric value) to malfunctioning devices, or simpler situations such as not being able to save data to a file because another application is using it. All these conditions may be beyond your program's control, but your application should be to handle them. At the very least, your program shouldn't crash; it's OK to abort an operation and display a warning, but an application shouldn't crash.

Types of Errors

The errors caused by a computer program (regardless of the language in which the program is written) can be categorized into three major groups: design-time, runtime, and logic.

The design-time error is the easiest to find and fix. A design-time error occurs when you write a piece of code that does not conform to the rules of the language in which you're writing. They are easy to find because Visual Studio .NET tells you not only where they are, but also what part of the line it doesn't understand.

Runtime errors are harder to locate, because VS doesn't give you any help in finding the error until it occurs in your program. These errors occur when your program attempts something illegal, like accessing data that doesn't exist or a resource to which it doesn't have the proper permissions. These types of errors can cause your program to crash, or hang, unless they are handled properly.

The third type of error, the logic error, is often the most insidious type to locate, because it may not manifest itself as a problem in the program at all. A program with a logic error simply means that the output or operation of your program is not exactly as you intended it. It could be as simple as an incorrect calculation or having a menu option enabled when you wanted it disabled, or something complex like a database that's duplicating order information.

This section will cover and demonstrate all three types of errors, and show you tools and techniques that you can use to hunt them down and squash them.

Design-Time Errors

Also called syntax errors, design-time errors occur when the Visual Basic .NET interpreter cannot recognize one or more lines of code that you have written. Some design-time errors are simply typographical errors, where you have mistyped a keyword. Others are the result of missing items: undeclared or untyped variables, classes not yet imported, incorrect parameter lists in a function or method call, or referencing members of a class that do not exist.

A program with as few as one design-time error cannot be compiled and run—you must locate and correct the error before continuing. Fortunately, design-time errors are the easiest to detect and correct, because VB.NET shows you the exact location of these errors and gives you good information about what part of the code it can't understand. What follows is a brief example showing several design-time errors in just a few lines of code.

The event code shown in Figure 17.1 was typed into the Click event of a button named *Button1*.

FIGURE 17.1

VB.NET identifies the locations of design-time errors.

```
Private Sub Button1_Click(ByVal sender As System.Object, _
ByVal e As System.EventArgs) _
Handles Button1.Click

    For i = 1 To 100
        lbNumbers.add("item " & i)
    Next

End Sub
```

Note the three blue squiggly lines under various parts of this brief code (under two instances of the letter *i* and under the term *lbNumbers*). Each one of those squiggly lines represents a design-time error. To determine what the errors are, locate the Task List window in the IDE and bring it forward. The Task List displays the errors seen in Figure 17.2 for the code from Figure 17.1.

FIGURE 17.2

Corresponding errors in the Task List

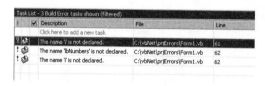

NOTE *You can determine which squiggly blue line corresponds to which design-time error in the Task List by double-clicking the error in the Task List. The corresponding error will become selected in the code window.*

Note that two of the errors are the same: they state "The name 'i' is not declared." In this case, these errors are telling you that you've referenced a variable named *i* but you have not declared it. To fix these two errors, you need to modify the code as shown in Figure 17.3.

FIGURE 17.3

Once declared, the variable doesn't produce an error.

```
Private Sub Button1_Click(ByVal sender As System.Object, _
ByVal e As System.EventArgs) _
Handles Button1.Click

    Dim i As Integer

    For i = 1 To 100
        lbNumbers.add("item " & i)
    Next

End Sub
```

The only error remaining now is "The name 'lbNumbers' is not declared." As the programmer of the application, you would probably have some type of idea what *lbNumbers* is. In this case, I was attempting to add 100 items to a ListBox, and *lbNumbers* is supposed to be the name of the ListBox on the form. This error tells me that I do not have a ListBox on the form named *lbNumbers*. I've either forgotten to put a ListBox on the form entirely, or I did add one but did not name it *lbNumbers*. To correct the problem, I can either make sure a ListBox is on my form with the correct name, or I can change this code so that the name matches whatever I've named the ListBox.

I added a ListBox named *lbNumbers* to my form. After doing so, however, I'm still left with a syntax error on the line, as seen in Figure 17.4.

FIGURE 17.4

The ListBox statement still produces a design-time error.

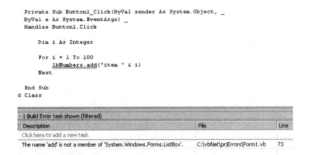

```
Private Sub Button1_Click(ByVal sender As System.Object, _
ByVal e As System.EventArgs) _
Handles Button1.Click

    Dim i As Integer

    For i = 1 To 100
        lbNumbers.add("item " & i)
    Next

End Sub
d Class
```

Description	File	Line
Click here to add a new task		
The name 'add' is not a member of 'System.Windows.Forms.ListBox'.	C:\vbNet\prj\Errors\Form1.vb	73

- 1 Build Error task shown (filtered)

Note that the text of the error is different. It reads "The name 'add' is not a member of 'System .Windows.Forms.ListBox'." This is telling you that it now recognizes that *lbNumbers* is a ListBox object, but there is no member (property, event, or method) named *add* on a ListBox. So what's the correct way to write a line of code that adds an item to a ListBox? Some brief research in the help should yield the correct line of code—the one shown in Figure 17.5.

FIGURE 17.5

This syntax is correct.

```
Private Sub Button1_Click(ByVal sender As System.Object, _
ByVal e As System.EventArgs) _
Handles Button1.Click

    Dim i As Integer

    For i = 1 To 100
        lbNumbers.Items.Add("item " & i)
    Next

End Sub
```

Notice that all blue squiggly lines are now gone, and the Task List should be empty of errors as well. This means our program is free of syntax errors and is ready to run.

Runtime Errors

Runtime errors are much more insidious to find and fix than design-time errors. Runtime errors are problems encountered by your program while it's running. Runtime errors can take on dozens of different shapes and forms. Here are some examples:

- Attempting to open a file that doesn't exist
- Trying to log in to a server with an incorrect username or password
- Trying to access a folder for which you have insufficient rights
- Requesting data from a database table that has been renamed
- Opening a file on a server that is down for maintenance
- Accessing an Internet URL that no longer exists
- Allocating a resource without the necessary available RAM
- Dividing a number by zero
- Users entering character data where a number is expected (and vice versa)

As you can see, runtime errors can occur due to an unexpected state of the computer or network upon which your program is running, or simply because the user has supplied the wrong information (an invalid password, a bad filename, and so on). Because of this, you can write a program that runs fine on your own machine, and all the machines in your test environment, but fails on a customer site due to the state of that customer's computing resources.

As you might imagine, runtime errors can be many degrees harder to diagnose and fix in comparison to design-time errors. After all, any error you make in design time is right there in front of you, on your own development PC. Not only that, but the Visual Studio compiler goes ahead and tells you right where a design-time error is and why it's an error. The runtime error, by comparison, may only manifest itself in strange computing conditions on a PC halfway across the world. We'll see in later sections how runtime errors can be detected and managed.

Logic Errors

Logic errors also occur at runtime, and because of this, they are often difficult to track down. A logic error occurs when a program does not do what the developer intended it to do. For example, you might provide the code to add a customer to a customer list, but when the end user runs the program and adds a new customer, the customer is not there. The error might lie in the code that adds the customer to the database; or perhaps the customer is indeed being added, but the grid that lists all the customers is not being refreshed after the add customer code, so it merely appears that the customer wasn't added.

A second example of a logic error: suppose you allow the end user to manually type the two-letter state code of every customer address that they enter into your program. One of the functions of your program might be to display a map of the U.S. that shades the states based on the number of customers within each state. How do you suppose your shaded map will display customers with invalid state codes? Most likely, these customers would not be displayed on the map at all. Later, the manager of the department calls you and says "The Total Customers Entered report for last month tells me that 7,245 customers were entered into our system. However, the Density Map report only shown 6,270 customers on it. Why don't these two reports match?"

In this example, we've made a design decision—the decision to allow the end user to type the two-digit state code—and that decision has lead to a major logic error, the fact that two reports from the same system give different results for the number of customers entered into the system for the same time period.

Here are some actual VB.NET code snippets that produce logic errors. Consider the following code snippet.

```
Private Sub Button1_Click(ByVal sender As System.Object, _
            ByVal e As System.EventArgs) Handles Button1.Click
    Dim i As Integer
    i = 1
    Do While i > 0
        i += 1
    Loop
End Sub
```

Here we have an integer variable set to 1 and incremented by one in a loop. Each time the loop iterates, the number gets bigger. The loop will continue to iterate as long as the variable is greater than 0. See any problem with this? The problem is that the value of the variable will *always* be greater than 0, so the loop will never terminate. This is called an infinite loop, and it's one of my personal favorite types of errors (favorite in the sense that I seem to always find a way to write new and exciting flavors of infinite loop). Of course, this loop isn't exactly infinite—after 2 billion iterations, an overflow will occur, but that's a good indication as to what happened.

Here's another simple example of a logic error:

```
Private Sub ColorTheLabel(ByVal lbl As Label)
    If CInt(lbl.Text) < 0 Then
        lbl.ForeColor = Color.Green
    Else
        lbl.ForeColor = Color.Red
    End If
End Sub
```

This routine was intended to color the text of a label red if the label text contained a negative number, and green if it contained a positive number (or 0). However, I got the logic backward— the label text is green for numbers less than 0, and red otherwise. This code won't produce any design-time errors or runtime crashes. It simply does the opposite of what I intended it to do.

Note finally that logic errors may or may not manifest themselves as program crashes. In the logic error examples above, the programs wouldn't have crashed or produce any type of error message— they simply did not perform as intended. Some logic errors might indeed produce a program crash, at which point the line between a logic error and a runtime error becomes blurry. The fact that a new customer doesn't appear in a grid might cause a crash if your program tries to highlight that new customer in the grid but the customer row isn't there. In this case, we've made a logic error (not adding the customer to the grid) that's caused a runtime error (program crashes when it tries to highlight a row in a grid that doesn't exist). In this case, fixing the logic error would automatically fix the runtime error.

Exceptions and Structured Exception Handling

A runtime error in VB.NET generates an *exception*. An exception is a response to the error condition that the program just generated. Figure 17.6 is an example of an exception message. This is the dialog that appears when you are running your program in the IDE. If the same error were to be encountered by a user running your program, the dialog would look slightly different, as seen in Figure 17.7.

FIGURE 17.6

Design-time error message

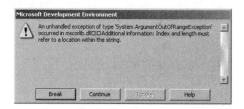

FIGURE 17.7

Runtime error message

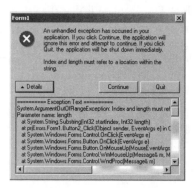

Note that this dialog gives the user the opportunity to continue the program. In some rare cases, this might be desirable, but in most cases you probably would not want your users attempting to continue after a program exception has occurred. Think about it—your program has just encountered some form of data that it cannot handle correctly, and now it's asking the user if it should attempt to ignore that bad data and continue. It is difficult to predict what type of further problems might result as the program continues on and attempts to handle the bad data. Most likely, further exceptions will be generated as the subsequent lines of code attempt to deal with the same unexpected data.

If we don't want our users handling an exception that the program generates, then we'll simply have to handle it ourselves. The Visual Basic .NET error-handling model allows us to do just that. An error handler is a section of VB.NET code that allows you to detect exceptions and perform the necessary steps to recover from them. What follows are some exception-handling code examples.

Studying an Exception

The exception dialogs shown in Figures 17.6 and 17.7 were generated by the VB.NET code shown in Listing 17.1.

LISTING 17.1: AN UNHANDLED EXCEPTION

```
Private Sub Button2_Click(ByVal sender As System.Object, _
              ByVal e As System.EventArgs) Handles Button2.Click
    Dim s As String
    s = "answer"
    Button2.Text = s.Substring(10, 1)
End Sub
```

This code is attempting to display the eleventh character in the string "answer". Seeing as the word "answer" contains only six characters, you can imagine how an exception might be generated. Let's examine at the exact phrasing of the exception to learn as much as possible about this particular error.

```
An unhandled exception of type 'System.ArgumentOutOfRangeException' occurred in
mscorlib.dll
Additional information: Index and length must refer to a location within the
string.
```

NOTE *This seems almost too trivial to mention, but always thoroughly read the exceptions that your program generates. Their purpose is to give you a brief description of the condition that caused the error, which of course is necessary to know before you can figure out how to handle it.*

The first thing to notice is the fact that this message refers to this runtime error as an *unhandled* exception. This means that the line of code that generated this error is not contained within an exception-handling block.

The second interesting piece of information is that this exception is of type System.Argument-OutOfRangeException, whatever that means. What's important to note is that the different types of errors can be classified in groups. This is important when we you realize that the .NET Framework exception-handling mechanism follows the same object-oriented design principles that the rest of the Framework follows. An exception creates an instance of an object, and that object is a descendent of class Exception.

The error message above is telling us that the exception object instance generated is of class (type) System.ArgumentOutOfRangeException, which is a descendent of class Exception.

The "additional information" block gives us some specific notes on the nature of the error. It tells us that the index and length parameters of the Substring method must both lie within the boundaries of the string. In our case, we attempted to retrieve the eleventh character of a six-character string, clearly outside the boundary.

Getting a Handle on this Exception

Listing 17.2 is the same defective code statement as Listing 17.1, but with a simple exception handler wrapped around it.

LISTING 17.2: HANDLING AN EXCEPTION, VERSION 1

```
Private Sub Button2_Click(ByVal sender As System.Object, _
             ByVal e As System.EventArgs) Handles Button2.Click
    Dim s As String
    s = "answer"
    Try
        Button2.Text = s.Substring(10, 1)
    Catch
        Button2.Text = "error"
    End Try
End Sub
```

This code attempts to do the same thing as the code above, but this time the faulty Substring statement is wrapped around a Try…Catch…End Try block. This block is a basic exception handler. If any of the code after the Try statement generates an exception, then program control automatically jumps to the code after the Catch statement. If no exceptions are generated in the code under the Try statement, then the Catch block is skipped. When this code is run, the System.ArgumentOut-OfRangeException is generated, but now the code does not terminate with a message box. Instead, the text property of *Button2* is set to the word "error", and the program continues along.

Listing 17.3 handles the same error in a slightly different way.

LISTING 17.3: HANDLING AN EXCEPTION, VERSION 2

```
Private Sub Button2_Click(ByVal sender As System.Object, _
             ByVal e As System.EventArgs) Handles Button2.Click
    Dim s As String
    s = "answer"
    Try
        Button2.Text = s.Substring(10, 1)
    Catch oEX As Exception
        Call MsgBox(oEX.Message)
    End Try
End Sub
```

In this example, the exception generates an instance of the Exception class and places that instance in a variable named *oEX*. Having the exception instance variable is useful because it can give you the text of the exception, which we display in a message box here. Of course, displaying the exception message in a message box is pretty much the same thing that your program does when an unhandled exception is generated, so it's doubtful that you would do this in your own program. However, you could log the exception text to the event log or a custom error file.

Note that the exception handlers above do not differentiate between types of errors. If *any* exception is generated within the Try block, then the Catch block is executed. You can also write exception handlers that handle different classes of errors, as seen in Listing 17.4.

LISTING 17.4: HANDLING AN EXCEPTION, VERSION 3

```
Private Sub Button3_Click(ByVal sender As System.Object, _
            ByVal e As System.EventArgs) Handles Button3.Click
    Try
        Button3.Text = lbStates.SelectedItem.ToString
    Catch oEX As System.NullReferenceException
        Call MsgBox("Please select an item first")
    Catch oEX As Exception
        Call MsgBox("Some other error: " & oEX.Message)
    End Try
End Sub
```

This code attempts to take the selected item in a ListBox named *lbStates* and display it as the caption of a button. If no item is selected in the ListBox, then a `System.NullReferenceException` will be generated, and we use that information to tell the user to select an item in the ListBox. If any other type of exception is generated, then this code displays the text of that error message.

Note that, in the list of exceptions in Listing 17.4, the more specific exception handler comes first and the more general exception handler comes last. This is how you'll want to code all of your multiple Catch exception handlers so that they are handled in the correct order. If you put your more general Catch handlers first, then they will execute first and override the more specific handlers.

Also note that the variable *oEX* is reused in each of the exception blocks. This is possible because the Catch statement actually serves as a declaration of that variable (note that I didn't have to Dim the *oEX* variable anywhere) and that the *oEX* variable has a local scope only within the Catch block.

Note that because the Exception instance is declared in each Catch block, it has scope only within that block. The code in Listing 17.5 is illegal for scoping reasons.

LISTING 17.5: HANDLING AN EXCEPTION, VERSION 4 (ILLEGAL)

```
Private Sub Button3_Click(ByVal sender As System.Object, _
            ByVal e As System.EventArgs) Handles Button3.Click
    Try
        Button3.Text = lbStates.SelectedItem.ToString
    Catch oEX As System.NullReferenceException
        Call MsgBox("please select an item first")
    Catch oEX As Exception
        Call MsgBox("some other error")
    End Try
    MsgBox(oEX.message)
End Sub
```

The final MsgBox is not valid because the *oEX* variable that it attempts to display is not in scope at this point of the procedure. The two *oEX* variables have scope only in their Catch blocks.

Finally (!)

You'll recall that when an exception is generated and handled by a Catch statement, the code execution is immediately transferred to the first relevant Catch exception handler block and then continues on out of the Try...Catch...End Try block. Sometimes, it might be necessary to perform some cleanup before moving out of the exception-handling block. Consider the procedure demonstrated in Listing 17.6.

LISTING 17.6: A POSSIBLE EXCEPTION

```
Protected Sub ReadFromATextFile(cFilename as string)
   Dim s As StreamReader
   Dim cLine As String
   Dim bDone As Boolean = False
   lbresults.Items.Clear()
   s = New Streamreader(cFilename)
   Try
      While Not bDone
         cLine = s.ReadLine()
         If cLine Is Nothing Then
            bDone = True
         Else
            Call lbresults.Items.Add(cLine)
         End If
      End While
      s.Close()
   Catch oEX as Exception
      Call MsgBox("some error occurred")
   End Try
End Sub
```

This method attempts to read the contents of a text file and put the results into a ListBox, line by line. Most of the reading code is wrapped within a generic exception handler. If an exception is encountered in the main loop, then the s.Close() line will in all likelihood not be executed. This means that our file stream will never be properly closed, possibly leading to a resource leak.

Fortunately, there is an additional type of block available in exception handlers that specifically allow us to avoid this type of problem. This new block is called the Finally block. The code within a Finally block always executes, whether an exception is generated or not. The code in Listing 17.7 is the same as the method in Listing 17.6 but now modified to wrap the s.Close() method inside a Finally block.

LISTING 17.7: HANDLING AN EXCEPTION WITH A FINALLY BLOCK

```
Protected Sub ReadFromATextFile(cFilename as string)
    Dim s As StreamReader
    Dim cLine As String
    Dim bDone As Boolean = False
    lbresults.Items.Clear()
    s = New Streamreader(cFilename)
    Try
        While Not bDone
            cLine = s.ReadLine()
            If cLine Is Nothing Then
                bDone = True
            Else
                Call lbresults.Items.Add(cLine)
            End If
        End While
    Catch oEX as Exception
        Call MsgBox("some error occurred")
    Finally
        s.Close()
    End Try
End Sub
```

Here, you see that any exception within the file-reading loop will be handled with a message box, and then the StreamReader object is closed inside the Finally block. This close statement runs whether the code within the Try...Catch block succeeds or fails. This allows you to guarantee that certain resources or handlers are properly disposed of when they are no longer needed.

Customizing Exception Handling

There are hundreds of exception classes built into the .NET Framework, and you may not want to handle all of them the same way. You can customize the way certain exceptions are handled by bringing up the Exceptions dialog (Figure 17.8) found in the Debug menu.

The exception shown in the Figure is one we saw in the earlier examples, System.NullReference-Exception. When this exception is first encountered, the system is currently set to do whatever the parent setting specifies. Tracing up the tree in this dialog, we eventually find that all .NET Framework exceptions are set to continue when they are first encountered, but to break into the debugger if they are not handled in a Try...Catch...Finally...End Try block. This is consistent with what we saw in the earliest exception examples—a dialog would be displayed when an exception was encountered, but that dialog would disappear once we wrote the proper exception-handling code.

FIGURE 17.8

The Debug ➢ Exceptions dialog

Throwing Your Own Exceptions

As you become more adept at writing VB.NET classes, you will probably encounter the need to throw your own exceptions. Imagine writing the code for an integer property that has a certain range. If a fellow developer is using your class and attempts to set the property to a value beyond this range, you would probably want to inform the developer that he has entered an invalid value. The best way to inform him of this problem is to send him an exception. That way, the developer using your class can choose to handle this error in his own way by writing an exception handler in his code. Listing 17.8 is an example of "throwing" an exception.

LISTING 17.8: THROWING AN EXCEPTION

```
Private FValue As Integer = 0
Property Value() As Integer
   Get
      Return FValue
   End Get
   Set(ByVal iValue As Integer)
      If iValue <= FMax Then
         FValue = iValue
      Else
         FValue = FMax
         Throw New OverflowException(_
            "Cannot set ProgressBar value to greater than maximum.")
      End If
      Invalidate()
   End Set
```

This code is taken from a ProgressBar control. It is the code that implements the Value property of the ProgressBar control. A check is done to make sure that the value that the property is set to is less than or equal to the value of the Max property, since you can't set the current value to be bigger than the maximum defined value. If the property is trying to be set to a value larger than the max, then an exception is generated via the Throw statement. This statement instantiates an exception of class OverflowException and produces a custom error that the fellow developer can see in his own exception handler.

Debugging

As you've seen, encountering errors is nearly a certainty when developing a piece of software. Syntax errors, of course, are the easiest to detect, because the IDE tells you right where they are and what the nature of the error is. It's the runtime errors that are harder to locate and correct, because of the many forms these errors can take. You've seen examples of errors that will cause your program to crash, as well as errors that spiral your program off into an infinite loop, and even errors that produce no outward signs at all—they simply cause the program to behave in some unintended way.

Fortunately, Visual Studio .NET provides you with a fine selection of tools to detect and remove the errors in your program. The act of hunting and eliminating errors is called *debugging*, because you're goal is to remove the bugs (or de-bug) the program.

Breakpoints

The breakpoint is the first and most important weapon in the war against bugs. When you set a *breakpoint* in your program, you're telling VS.NET to stop execution of the program when it reaches a certain line in the code. Once stopped, you can examine the state of the program, including the values of the variables, the procedure stack, and the contents of memory.

Before we can look at debugging essentials, we need some buggy code. Let's write a program to count all the vowels in a string. To set this program up, start a new WinForms project, then add a button named *cbCount* and a TextBox named *tbPhrase* to the form. Add the code from Listing 17.9 to the project.

LISTING 17.9: BUG-FILLED CODE

```
Private Sub cbCount_Click(ByVal sender As System.Object, _
                ByVal e As System.EventArgs) Handles cbCount.Click
    cbCount.Text = CountTheVowels(cbCount.Text)
End Sub
Private Function CountTheVowels(ByVal cSomeString As String) As Integer
    Dim x As Integer = 1
    Dim iTot As Integer = 0
    Dim iPos As Integer
    Do While x <= cSomeString.Length
        iPos = InStr("aeio", cSomeString.Substring(x, 1).ToLower)
        If iPos > 0 Then
            iTot += 1
```

```
        End If
    Loop
    Return iTot
End Function
```

The button click event passes the contents of the text box into the function CountTheVowels(), which is where all the dirty work will be performed. When the count is obtained, the caption of the button should be replaced with the vowel count. Once you get the code for the program typed in exactly as seen above, try running the program, entering some text into the text box, and clicking the button. Then wait. And wait. My guess is that the caption of the button will not change until you stop the application by pressing Ctrl+Break (or select Debug ➤ Stop Debugging). If you wait long enough, an overflow exception will occur. This means that the value of the variable *iTot* has exceeded the maximum value you can represent with an Integer.

Obviously, this little function shouldn't take very long to run, so something screwy must be going on, like an infinite loop. Let's set a breakpoint in the function and see if we can spot it.

To set a breakpoint, place the cursor on a line of code in the function where you want the program to stop, and press the F9 key. The line of code should become highlighted in red, as seen in Figure 17.9.

FIGURE 17.9

Setting a breakpoint

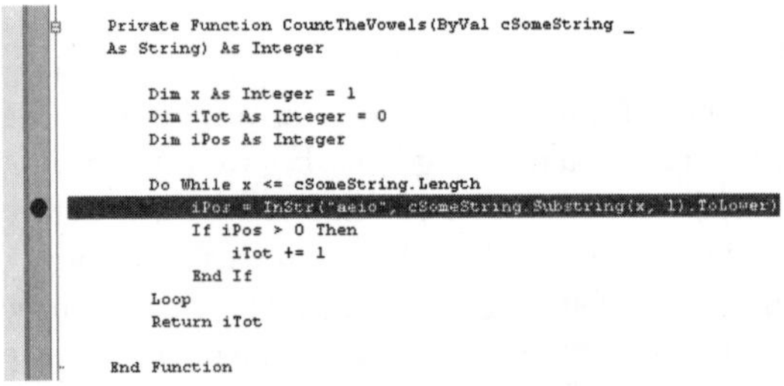

```
Private Function CountTheVowels(ByVal cSomeString _
As String) As Integer

    Dim x As Integer = 1
    Dim iTot As Integer = 0
    Dim iPos As Integer

    Do While x <= cSomeString.Length
        iPos = InStr("aeio", cSomeString.Substring(x, 1).ToLower)
        If iPos > 0 Then
            iTot += 1
        End If
    Loop
    Return iTot

End Function
```

Once a breakpoint is set, you can begin the program, type some text into the text box, and click the button. Like a good soldier, the debugger should come up on that same line of code, this time highlighted in yellow. This means that the program has stopped execution on that exact line of code.

Now we can start looking around. First, take the cursor and hover it over some of the areas of code. You should be able to see a tooltip displaying the value of the various variables you rest the mouse over, like the one in Figure 17.10.

FIGURE 17.10

Tooltips display the value of variables.

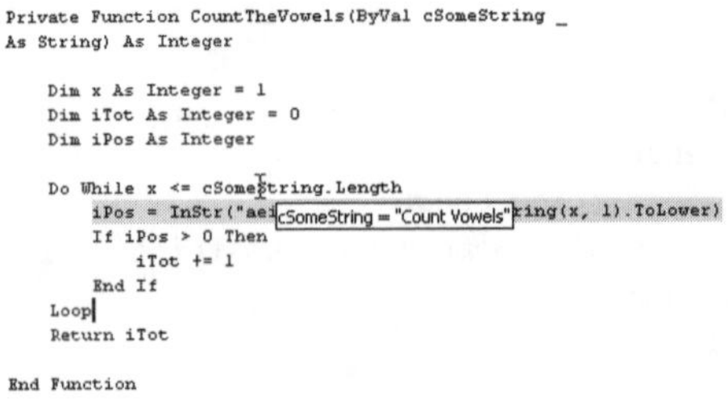

```
Private Function CountTheVowels(ByVal cSomeString _
As String) As Integer

    Dim x As Integer = 1
    Dim iTot As Integer = 0
    Dim iPos As Integer

    Do While x <= cSomeString.Length
        iPos = InStr("aei cSomeString = "Count Vowels" ring(x, 1).ToLower)
        If iPos > 0 Then
            iTot += 1
        End If
    Loop
    Return iTot

End Function
```

The figure displays the first of the errors I've made coding this program. The value of the variable *cSomeString* is "Count Vowels", but this is not the string I typed into my text box. Why is this string being passed into the function? A quick examination of the function call reveals this problem.

```
cbCount.Text = CountTheVowels(cbCount.Text)
```

Note that I inadvertently passed the Text property of the button *cbCount*, when my intention was to pass in the value of tbPhrase.Text. This is a perfect example of a logic error. The code works fine (well, anyway, it will work fine once we find the rest of these bugs), but it won't count the vowels in the string that we intended to count. The fix for this first bug is easy. First, stop the program from running by selecting Stop Debugging from the Debug menu (shortcut key is Shift+F5).

NOTE   *Spend some time memorizing the shortcut keys for all the debugging functions. You'll be make using these functions quite a bit, and use of the shortcut keys will save a ton of time.*

Once the program is stopped, change the CountTheVowels() function call as follows (note the change marked in bold font). Now we're passing in the string we intended.

```
cbCount.Text = CountTheVowels(tbPhrase.Text)
```

Stepping Through

As it often happens, we started looking for an infinite loop but found another, unrelated bug first. Now that we've squashed that bug, we can go back to running the program and looking for the original problem. Start up the program again, type some text into the text box, and click the button. Once again, the program should stop at the breakpoint.

Let's watch a few of the program lines run in sequence and see if that tells us anything. To make the program step through the current line of code, press the F10 key. Each time you press F10, one line of code will execute, and the yellow highlight will move to the next line of code that is about to be executed.

NOTE   *The F11 key also steps through the code, but it will step into any procedures that are called. The F10 key steps over the procedure calls, running them all at once and returning back to the original spot. This allows you to skip over the line-by-line tracing of procedures that you are not currently debugging.*

You can continue to trace through the loop line by line and examine variable values with the tooltips. Can you figure out the cause of the infinite loop? Perhaps it's time to bring in some more debugging tools.

The Local and Watch Windows

While still stopped in debug mode, select Debug ➢ Windows ➢ Locals from the menu. The Locals window (Figure 17.11) should be displayed in the lower section of the IDE. This window shows you the current value of all of the locally declared variables. Now we can see the value of the variables changing as we step through the program.

Try stepping through the loop a few more times. What you might notice is that the values of the variables aren't changing. To get even more information, highlight the entire phrase cSomeString .Substring(x, 1).ToLower, right-click, and select Add Watch from the context menu. This will bring up the Watch window, as seen in Figure 17.12.

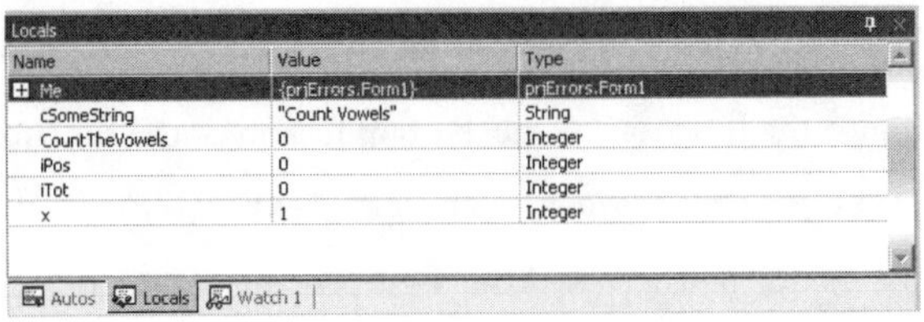

FIGURE 17.11

The Locals window

FIGURE 17.12

The Watch window

The Watch window is similar to the Locals window, but it allows you to look at the value of complex expressions like the one we just placed in it. Once again, try stepping through the loop a few times. You might expect that the Substring command would be incrementing the letter in the string as the loop iterates, but that isn't happening. The only logical reason for this is that the value of counter variable *x* isn't changing. Let's look at the loop again.

```
Do While x <= cSomeString.Length
    iPos = InStr("aeio", cSomeString.Substring(x, 1).ToLower)
    If iPos > 0 Then
        iTot += 1
    End If
Loop
```

I've made one of the classic looping blunders here. I set up a counter variable *x* to loop through the string character by character, but I never added any code to increment the string! That's as sure a recipe for an infinite loop as anything. Fixing that problem is an easy remedy (see the code high-lighted in bold).

```
Do While x <= cSomeString.Length
    iPos = InStr("aeio", cSomeString.Substring(x, 1).ToLower)
    If iPos > 0 Then
        iTot += 1
    End If
    x += 1
Loop
```

Okay, that bug is squashed, so it's time to remove the breakpoint and rerun the program to see if it works. This time, however, the program crashes and burns with the following error.

```
An unhandled exception of type 'System.ArgumentOutOfRangeException' occurred in
mscorlib.dll. Additional information: Index and length must refer to a location
within the string.
```

We've seen that error before—it means that we tried to look at a character beyond the length of the string. By checking the Locals window, you should be able to eventually track down this problem. The problem here is that the loop counter x starts at character 1 and ends at value cSomeString .Length. While that range is correct for VB version 6 and below, .NET strings are indexed *starting at 0*. Oops. We need to modify our procedure as shown by the two bold items here, the zero and the less-than sign:

```
Private Function CountTheVowels(ByVal cSomeString As String) As Integer
    Dim x As Integer = 0
    Dim iTot As Integer = 0
    Dim iPos As Integer
    Do While x < cSomeString.Length
        iPos = InStr("aeio", cSomeString.Substring(x, 1).ToLower)
        If iPos > 0 Then
            iTot += 1
        End If
        x += 1
    Loop
    Return iTot
End Function
```

This modified loop starts at 0 and ends at cSomeString.Length - 1, which is the correct way to iterate through a .NET string. Once again, you can try to remove all breakpoints and rerun the application. This time, it should actually produce a value, like the successful test in Figure 17.13.

FIGURE 17.13

We've debugged our program ... or have we?

Finally, we got an answer! But is it the correct answer? A manual count gives 11 vowels in the test string "The quick brown fox jumps over the lazy dog". Since this is a fairly long test string, you might want to try a smaller string, like the string "aeiou" shown in Figure 17.14.

Now that's definitely wrong—it's counted only four of the five vowels in the string. Looks like there's another logic error. Back to the debugging drawing board ... Actually, this error is pretty easy compared with some of the others we've already squashed. Look at the actual comparison of the character to the vowel list.

```
iPos = InStr("aeio", cSomeString.Substring(x, 1).ToLower)
```

Where's the *u*? It looks like I simply forgot to include the *u* in the vowel list. After adding the *u* back in, the final, working code looks like Listing 17.10.

FIGURE 17.14

It's clear that a mistake occurred.

LISTING 17.10: BUG-FREE CODE

```
Private Sub cbCount_Click(ByVal sender As System.Object, _
            ByVal e As System.EventArgs) Handles cbCount.Click
    cbCount.Text = CountTheVowels(tbPhrase.Text)
End Sub
Private Function CountTheVowels(ByVal cSomeString As String) As Integer
    Dim x As Integer = 0
    Dim iTot As Integer = 0
    Dim iPos As Integer
    Do While x < cSomeString.Length
        iPos = InStr("aeiou", cSomeString.Substring(x, 1).ToLower)
        If iPos > 0 Then
            iTot += 1
        End If
        x += 1
    Loop
    Return iTot
End Function
```

This is the type of error you can only catch with exhaustive tests—that is, only a user will likely catch this error. You can actually test the program with a string that doesn't contain the character "u," see that it works nicely, and distribute it. Very soon you will receive messages to the effect that your application doesn't work. Yet this application has been tested and seems to work fine. The tests, however, were not exhaustive.

You should also try to test your applications with extreme situations (a blank string, for example, or a very large one, an invalid numeric value, and so on). The final test, of course, is to pass the applications to users and ask for their comments. Unfortunately, we don't write software for each other. We write software for people knowledgeable enough to crash an application in minutes but not knowledgeable enough to keep it running.

NOTE *There are many more advanced debugging tools available in Visual Studio .NET. A great list of these tools can be found in the Debug menu, under the Window submenu. (Look at the menu when you have a program running). You can get memory dumps, disassembled versions of your program, traces of the procedure call stack, a list of running threads, and other views of your program.*

Summary

Testing and debugging is as critical a step in the complete development process as the design and coding steps. It's obvious that your code won't leave the shop with any syntax errors (since you can't compile if you have any), but tracking down runtime errors and logic errors are just as important. All facets and functions of the program need to be put through a rigorous test procedure to help shake out these problems.

One excellent method of testing software involves asking users who have no preconceived notions about its functionality to test it for you. For example, if you're writing software for the accounting department to use, ask members of the marketing department to test it for you. These users will have much less familiarity with the goals of the software, as well as the expected inputs and outputs. This gives them a larger chance of entering unexpected data, which can lead to unhandled exceptions in your code.

Another hidden benefit of using testers from another department is for some quick usability studies. Again, these users will be unfamiliar with the day-to-day operation of the accounting department, and the task flow of your software won't be intuitively obvious to them. This makes for a good test of how easy your software is to use.

Chapter 18

Recursive Programming

THIS CHAPTER IS SLIGHTLY different from the previous ones because it doesn't describe specific Visual Basic techniques or controls. Instead, it introduces a powerful technique for implementing efficient, compact programs. *Recursion* is a special topic in computer programming that's one of the least understood among beginners and even among some advanced programmers. It's surrounded by an aura of mystery, and most BASIC programmers ignore it. The truth is, recursive programming is no more complicated than any other programming approach, once you understand how it works and when to use it.

Some readers may think that the material in this chapter is of little use to the average programmer. Recursive procedures are extremely useful, however, and you have already seen recursive routines in the previous chapters. If you have read the previous chapters, you should have a good idea of the type of procedures that are implemented recursively. Recursion was a novel technique with earlier versions of Visual Basic, but with VB.NET it's commonplace. Toward the end of this chapter, you'll learn how to write applications that scan an entire folder and its subfolders. The FolderMap application is a customized Windows Explorer that you can incorporate in your applications even if you don't quite understand how it works. In the last section of this chapter, I will review some of the recursive procedures used in earlier chapters. As you will see, some of the most practical and interesting applications involve recursive coding.

Basic Concepts

Recursive programming is used for implementing algorithms, or mathematical definitions, that are described recursively, that is, in terms of themselves. A recursive definition is implemented by a procedure that calls itself; thus, it is called a *recursive procedure*.

Code that calls functions and subroutines to accomplish a task, such as the following segment, is quite normal:

```
Function MyPayments()
   { other statements }
   CarPayment = CalculateCarPayment(Interest, Duration)
   HomePayment = CalculateHomePayment(Interest, Duration)
   MonthlyPayments = CarPayment + HomePayment
   { more statements }
End Function
```

In the preceding code, the MyPayments() function calls two functions to calculate the monthly payments for a car and home loan. There's nothing puzzling about this piece of code because it's linear. Here's what it does:

1. The MyPayments() function suspends execution each time it calls a function (the CalculateCarPayment() and CalculateHomePayment() functions).

2. It waits for each function to complete its task and return a value.

3. It then resumes execution.

But what if a function calls itself? Examine the following code:

```
Function DoSomething(n As Integer) As Integer
   { other statements }
   value = value - 1
   If value = 0 Then Exit Function
   newValue = DoSomething(value)
   { more statements }
End Function
```

If you didn't know better, you'd think that this program would never end. Every time the DoSomething() function is called, it gets into a loop by calling itself again and again, and it never exits. In fact, this is a clear danger with recursion. It's not only possible but also quite easy for a recursive function to get into an endless loop. A recursive function must exit explicitly. In other words, you must tell a recursive function when to stop calling itself and exit. The condition that causes the DoSomething() function to end is met when *value* becomes zero. If the initial value of this variable is negative, the function will never end, because *value* will never become zero. This is a typical logical error you must catch from within your code.

Apart from this technicality, you can draw a few useful conclusions from this example. A function performs a well-defined task. When a function calls itself, it has to interrupt the current task to complete another, quite similar task. The DoSomething() function can't complete its task (whatever this is) unless it performs an identical calculation, which it does by calling itself.

Recursion in Real Life

Do you ever run into recursive processes in your daily tasks? Suppose you're viewing a World Wide Web page that describes a hot new topic. The page contains a term you don't understand, and the term is a hyperlink. When you click the hyperlink, another page that defines the term is displayed. This definition contains another term you don't understand. The new term is also a hyperlink, so you click it and a page containing its definition is displayed. Once you understand this definition, you click the Back button to go back to the previous page where you re-read the term, knowing its definition. You then go back to the original page.

The task at hand involves understanding a topic, a description, and a definition. Every time you run into an unfamiliar term, you interrupt the current task to accomplish another identical task, such as learning another term.

The process of looking up a definition in a dictionary is similar, and it epitomizes recursion. For example, if the definition of an ASP page is "ASP pages are Web pages that contain Web controls," you'd probably have to look up the definition of *Web controls*. Once you understand what Web controls are, you can go back and understand the other definitions. Let's say that Web controls are defined as "elements used to build ASP Web pages." This is a sticky situation, indeed. At this point, you'd either have to interrupt your search or look up its definition elsewhere. Going back and forth between these two definitions won't take you anywhere. This is the endless loop mentioned earlier.

Because endless loops can arise easily in recursive programming, you must be sure that your code contains conditions that will cause the recursive procedure to stop calling itself. In the example of the DoSomething() function, this condition is as follows:

```
If value = 0 Then Exit Function
```

The code reduces the value of the variable *value* by increments of 1 until it eventually reaches 0, at which point the sequence of recursive calls ends (provided the initial value of the variable is positive, because if you start with a negative value you'll never reach zero). Without such a condition, the recursive function would call itself indefinitely. Once the DoSomething() function ends, the suspended instances of the same function resume their execution and terminate.

When you interrupt a task to perform another similar task, you're performing some type of recursion. Each new task in the process involves a different definition, but the goal is to gather all the information you need to complete the initial task. Now, let's look at a few practical examples and see these concepts in action. The first example is a trivial one, but you'll be able to follow the thread of recursive calls and understand how recursion works. In the following sections, we'll build more difficult, and practical, recursive procedures.

A Simple Example

I'll demonstrate the principles of recursive programming with a simple example: the calculation of the factorial of a number. The factorial of a number, denoted with an exclamation mark, is described recursively as follows:

```
n! = n * (n-1)!
```

The factorial of n ($n!$, read as "n factorial") is the number n multiplied by the factorial of $(n-1)$, which in turn is $(n-1)$ multiplied by the factorial of $(n-2)$ and so on, until we reach $0!$, which is 1 by definition.

Here's the process of calculating the factorial of 4:

```
4! = 4 * 3!
   = 4 * 3 * 2!
   = 4 * 3 * 2 * 1!
   = 4 * 3 * 2 * 1 * 0!
   = 4 * 3 * 2 * 1 * 1
   = 24
```

For the mathematically inclined, the factorial of the number n is defined as follows:

```
n! = n * (n-1)!      if n is greater than zero
n! = 1               if n is zero
```

The factorial is described in terms of itself, and it's a prime candidate for recursive implementation. The Factorial application, shown in Figure 18.1, lets you specify the number whose factorial you want to calculate in the box on the left and displays the result in the box on the right. To start the calculations, click the Factorial button.

FIGURE 18.1

The Factorial
application

Here's the Factorial() function that implements the previous definition:

```
Function Factorial(n As Integer) As Double
    If n = 0 Then
        Factorial = 1
    Else
        Factorial = n * Factorial(n - 1)
    End If
End Function
```

The recursive definition of the factorial of an integer is implemented in a single line:

```
Factorial = n * Factorial(n-1)
```

As long as the argument of the function isn't zero, the function returns the product of its argument times the factorial of its argument minus 1. With each successive call of the Factorial() function, the initial number decreases by an increment of 1, and eventually n becomes 0 and the sequence of recursive calls ends. Each time the Factorial() function calls itself, the calling function is suspended temporarily. When the called function terminates, the most recently suspended function resumes execution. To calculate the factorial of 10, you'd call the Factorial() function with the argument *10*, as follows:

```
MsgBox("The factorial of 10 " & Factorial(10))
```

The execution of the Factorial(10) function is interrupted when it calls Factorial(9). This function is also interrupted when Factorial(9) calls Factorial(8), and so on. By the time Factorial(0) is called, 10 instances of the function have been suspended and made to wait for the function they called to finish. When that happens, they resume execution. The first instance to resume its execution is the Factorial(1), then the Factorial(2), and so on.

Let's see how this happens by adding a couple of lines to the Factorial() function. Open the Factorial application and add a few statements that print the function's status in the Output window, as shown in Listing 18.1.

LISTING 18.1: THE FACTORIAL() RECURSIVE FUNCTION

```
Function Factorial(n As Integer) As Double
    Console.WriteLine("Starting the calculation of " n & " factorial")
    If n = 0 Then
        Factorial = 1
    Else
        Console.WriteLine("Calling Factorial(" & n - 1 & ")")
        Factorial = Factorial(n - 1) * n
    End If
    Console.WriteLine("Done calculating " & n & " factorial")
End Function
```

WATCHING THE ALGORITHM

You can watch the execution of the algorithm by inserting a few statements that display the progress on the Output window (the WriteLine statements in Listing 18.1). The first WriteLine statement tells us that a new instance of the function has been activated and gives the number whose factorial it's about to calculate. The second WriteLine statement tells us that the active function is about to call another instance of itself and shows which argument it will supply to the function it's calling. The last WriteLine statement informs us that the factorial function is done. Here's what you'll see in the Output window if you call the Factorial() function with the argument 4:

```
Starting the calculation of 4 factorial
Calling Factorial(3)
Starting the calculation of 3 factorial
Calling Factorial(2)
Starting the calculation of 2 factorial
Calling Factorial(1)
Starting the calculation of 1 factorial
Calling Factorial(0)
Starting the calculation of 0 factorial
Done calculating 0 factorial
Done calculating 1 factorial
Done calculating 2 factorial
Done calculating 3 factorial
Done calculating 4 factorial
```

This list of messages is lengthy, but it's worth examining for the sequence of events. The first time the function is called, it attempts to calculate the factorial of 4. It can't complete its operation and calls Factorial(3) to calculate the factorial of 3, which is needed to calculate the factorial of 4. The first instance of the Factorial() function is suspended until Factorial(3) returns its result.

Similarly, Factorial(3) doesn't complete its calculations because it must call Factorial(2). So far, there are two suspended instances of the Factorial() function. In turn, Factorial(2) calls Factorial(1), and Factorial(1) calls Factorial(0). Now, there are four suspended instances of the Factorial() function, all waiting for an intermediate result before they can continue with their calculations. Figure 18.2 shows this process.

FIGURE 18.2

You can watch the progress of the calculation of a factorial in the Output window.

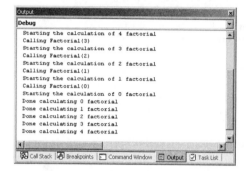

When Factorial(0) completes its execution, it prints the following message and returns a result:

```
Done calculating 0 factorial
```

This result is passed to the most recently interrupted function, which is Factorial(1). This function can now resume operation, complete the calculation of 1! (1 × 1), and then print another message indicating that it finished its calculations.

As each suspended function resumes operation, it passes a result to the function from which it was called, until the very first instance of the Factorial() function finishes the calculation of the factorial of 4. Figure 18.3 shows this process. (In the figure, factorial is abbreviated as *fact*.) The arrows pointing to the right show the direction of recursive calls, and the ones pointing to the left show the propagation of the result.

FIGURE 18.3

Recursive calculation of the factorial of 4

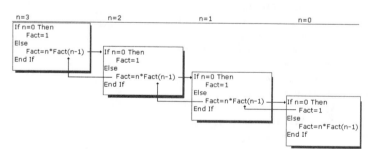

WHAT HAPPENS WHEN A FUNCTION CALLS ITSELF

If you're completely unfamiliar with recursive programming, you're probably uncomfortable with the idea of a function calling itself. Let's take a closer look at what happens when a function calls itself.

As far as the computer is concerned, it doesn't make any difference whether a function calls itself or another function. When a function calls another function, the calling function suspends execution and waits for the called function to complete its task. The calling function then resumes (usually by taking into account any result returned by the function it called). A recursive function simply calls itself instead of another one.

Let's look at what happens when the factorial in the previous function is implemented with the following line in which Factorial1() is identical to Factorial():

```
Factorial = n * Factorial1(n-1)
```

When the Factorial() function calls Factorial1(), its execution is suspended until Factorial1() returns its result. A new function is loaded into the memory and executed. If the Factorial() function is called with 3, the Factorial1() function calculates the factorial of 2.

Similarly, the code of the Factorial1() function is

```
Factorial1 = n * Factorial2(n-1)
```

This time, the function Factorial2() is called to calculate the factorial of 1. The function Factorial2() in turn calls Factorial3(), which calculates the factorial of 0. The Factorial3() function completes its calculations and returns the result 1. This is in turn multiplied by 1 to produce the factorial of 1. This result is returned to the function Factorial1(), which completes the calculation of the factorial of 2 (which is 2×1). The value is returned to the Factorial() function, which now completes the calculation of 3 (3×2, or 6). As you understand, we can't write dozens of identical functions; accounting for this is what recursive functions do for your applications.

RECURSIVE CALLS AND THE OPERATING SYSTEM

You can think of a recursive function calling itself as the operating system supplying another identical function with a different name; it's more or less what happens. Each time your program calls a function, the operating system does the following:

1. Saves the status of the active function

2. Loads the new function in memory

3. Starts executing the new function

If the function is recursive—in other words, if the new function is the same as the one currently being executed—nothing changes. The operating system saves the status of the active function somewhere and starts executing it as if it was another function. Of course, there's no reason to load the code in memory again because the function is already there. The new instance of the function consists of a new set of local variables. The same code will act on different variables and produce a different result.

When the newly called function finishes, the operating system reloads the function it interrupted in memory and continues its execution. I mentioned that the operating system stores the status of a function every time it must interrupt it to load another function in memory. The *status information* includes the values of its variables and the location where execution was interrupted. In effect, after the operating system loads the status of the interrupted function, the function continues execution as if it was never interrupted. We'll return to the topic of storing status information later on in the section "The Stack Mechanism."

Recursion by Mistake

Recursion isn't as complicated as you may think. Here's an example of a recursive situation you may have experienced without knowing it. Figure 18.4 shows a simple application that fills the background of a PictureBox with a solid color. Instead of setting the control's BackColor property, though, it draws vertical lines from one end of the control to the other. Every time the Color Box button is clicked, the PictureBox control is filled slowly with vertical lines. The color of the lines is chosen randomly. The application runs too fast for you to notice the progress of the painting, so I've inserted a statement to invalidate the control after drawing each line. I've also included a loop that redraws each line 20 times, to make sure the process is slow and so you can interrupt it (you'll understand shortly why this is necessary). If you're running this application on a computer that's much faster than mine, you must increase this value to slow down the application.

FIGURE 18.4

Click the Color Box button before the program has a chance to fill the control to watch a recursive behavior.

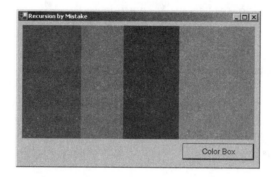

VB.NET AT WORK: THE RECURSE PROJECT

You'll find the Recurse application in this chapter's folder on the CD. Load it and run it. Click the Color Box button, and the program will start filling the PictureBox with a random color from left to right. Because of the way the control is filled, the progress of the drawing is slow, even on a fast Pentium. The code behind the Color Box Command button is shown in Listing 18.2.

LISTING 18.2: THE COLOR BOX BUTTON

```
Private Sub Button1_Click(ByVal sender As System.Object, _
                    ByVal e As System.EventArgs) Handles Button1.Click
    Static bmp As New Bitmap(PictureBox1.ClientSize.Width, _
                        PictureBox1.ClientSize.Height)
    Dim clr As Color
    Dim rnd As New System.Random()
    Dim G As Graphics
    PictureBox1.Image = bmp
    G = Graphics.FromImage(bmp)
    clr = Color.FromARGB(rnd.Next(0, 255), rnd.Next(0, 255), rnd.Next(0, 255))
```

```
    Dim X As Integer
    For X = 0 To PictureBox1.Width - 1
        G.DrawLine(New Pen(clr), X, 0, X, PictureBox1.Height)
        PictureBox1.Invalidate()
        Application.DoEvents()
    Next
End Sub
```

Suppose the program starts filling the picture box with red lines. Before the program has a chance to complete its operation, click the Color Box button again. The button's Click event handler is interrupted, and the program starts filling the control with a new color, perhaps fuchsia. Interrupt the process again. This time, yellow kicks in and starts filling the control from left to right. Let this operation complete.

As soon as the picture box is filled with yellow, the interrupted process will resume. The program completes the drawing of the fuchsia lines, but it doesn't start drawing from the left edge of the control. It picks up from where it was interrupted. When the fuchsia color reaches the right edge of the control, red kicks in! Can you see what's going on here? Each time you click the Color Box button, the Click event handler of the button is interrupted, and a new copy of the same subroutine starts executing. The interrupted (or suspended) instance of the subroutine doesn't die. It waits for a chance to complete, which it gets when the newer instance of the subroutine completes its task.

This recursion is made possible by the `Application.DoEvents()` statement placed in the loop's body. Without it, you wouldn't be able to interrupt the subroutine and invoke another instance of it. Normally, you wouldn't call the DoEvents() method to avoid the very behavior you witnessed in this example. Most of the procedures you've written so far don't use the DoEvents() statement; these procedures won't allow another procedure to start executing before they have finished.

AVOIDING RECURSION

If you comment out the `Application.DoEvents()` statement in the listing, you won't be able to interrupt the process of coloring the control. The application, however, will become less responsive. While the loop is executing, you won't be able to even move the window on the desktop. Can you make the application more responsive by including the call to the DoEvents method, yet avoid the side effect of the recursive behavior? You can set up a static variable, which will be set to True while the loop is executing. You examine this variable's value before entering the loop. If it's True, you must exit immediately. If it's False, set it to True and continue. When the loop terminates, reset it to False:

```
Static Executing As Boolean      ' variable initialized to False
If Executing Then Exit Sub
Executing = True
{ procedure's statements }
Executing = False
```

This is a simple technique to prevent the multiple executions of the same procedure. Obviously, this technique applies to regular procedures and shouldn't be used with recursive procedures.

I need to mention one important aspect of recursion here. The *clr* variable is local and maintains its value while the subroutine is interrupted. Visual Basic stores the values of the local variables of the interrupted procedures and recalls them when the procedure gets a chance to complete. This is possible because each new copy of the procedure that starts executing has its own set of local variables. Local variables are part of the procedure's status.

Scanning Folders Recursively

The examples of recursive functions we have looked at so far probably haven't entirely convinced you of the usefulness of recursion. The factorial of a number can be easily calculated with a For…Next loop, and the Recurse subroutine is a side effect (basically, a bug). So, what good is recursion?

The answer is the FileScan application, which can't be implemented non-recursively. I hope that the previous examples helped you understand the principles of recursive programming and that you're ready for some real recursion. We'll design an application similar to Windows Explorer, which scans an entire folder, including its subfolders. As the application scans the files and subfolders of a folder or an entire volume, it can locate files by name, size, and date. It can also move files around and, in general, perform all the operations of Windows Explorer plus any other custom operation you might require. Much of the functionality of this application is provided by Windows Explorer already, but as you'll see shortly, this application is highly customizable. It can serve as your starting point for many file operations that Windows Explorer doesn't provide. For example, your custom Explorer could expand all the subfolders each time you open a folder, display the full pathname of each folder, or even process files of a certain type (resize image files, encrypt documents, and so on). Later in the chapter, you'll see an application that generates a list of all the files in a folder, including its subfolders, organized by folder.

A file-scanning application is ideal for implementing with a recursive function because its operation is defined recursively. Suppose you want to scan all the entries of a folder and locate the files whose size exceeds 1 MB or count the files. If an entry is another folder, the same process must be repeated for that subfolder. If the subfolder contains one or more subfolder(s) of its own, the process must be repeated for each subfolder. This application calls for a recursive function, because every time it runs into a subfolder, it must interrupt the scanning of the current folder and start scanning the subfolder by calling itself. If you spend some time thinking about the implementation of this algorithm, you'll conclude that there's no simple way to do it without recursion. Actually, once you've established the recursive nature of a process, you'll know you must code it as a recursive procedure.

Describing a Recursive Procedure

When you're about to write a recursive procedure, it's helpful to start with a general written description of the procedure. For the FileScan application, we need a subroutine (since it's not going to return a result) that scans the contents of a folder: let's call it ScanFolder(). The ScanFolder() subroutine must scan all the entries of the initial folder and process the files in it. If the current entry is a file, it must act upon the file, depending on its name, size, or any of its attributes. If the current entry is a folder, it must scan the contents of this folder. In other words, it must interrupt the scanning of the current folder and start scanning the subfolder. And the most efficient way to scan a subfolder is to have it to call itself. Here's the ScanFolder() function in pseudocode:

```
Sub ScanFolder(current_folder)
    Process files in current_folder
    If current_folder contains subfolders
    For each subfolder
        ScanFolder(subfolder)
    Next
End If
```

Translating the Description to Code

Now, let's translate this description to actual code. Because we need access to each folder's files and subfolders, we need three controls to display the drives, the folders of the selected drive, and the files in the selected folder, as shown in Figure 18.5. This is the FileScan project, which you can find in this chapter's folder on the CD. The drives are displayed on a ComboBox control. When the user selects a drive on this ComboBox, the drive's folders are displayed on the ListBox control under it. When the user double-clicks a folder's name, the ListBox control is populated with the subfolders of the selected folder. Finally, when the user clicks the Scan Now button, the code scans the selected folder, including its subfolders. This application is similar to the CustomExplorer application you developed in Chapter 13. I will repeat the process for the benefit of readers who are not familiar with recursive coding, and in the following section we'll add a unique feature to the application. Where the FileScan application displays the files under the current folder only, we'll add a button to display all the files in the selected folder, as well as the files in all subfolders under the selected one.

FIGURE 18.5

The FileScan application is the core of a custom Explorer.

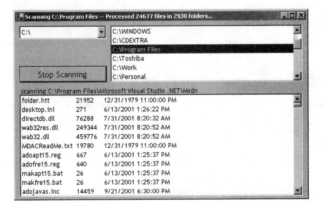

DISPLAYING DRIVES AND FOLDERS

The Drives ComboBox control is populated when the application starts from within the Form_Load event handler with the following statements, shown in Listing 18.3.

LISTING 18.3: POPULATING THE DRIVES COMBOBOX CONTROL

```
Private Sub Form1_Load(ByVal sender As System.Object, _
             ByVal e As System.EventArgs) Handles MyBase.Load
    Dim drives() As String
    drives = System.IO.Directory.GetLogicalDrives
    Dim iDrive As Integer
    DrivesList.Items.Clear()
    On Error Resume Next
    For iDrive = 0 To drives.GetUpperBound(0)
        DrivesList.Items.Add(drives(iDrive))
    Next
    DrivesList.SelectedIndex = 1
End Sub
```

Notice the error-trapping code, which consists of the On Error Resume Next statement. This is the simplest type of error trapping, but that's all we need. VB.NET will throw an exception if you attempt to access a drive that's not ready. This will happen if you have two floppy drives, A: and B:, and there's no disk in drive B: when you select the second item in the list (on most systems, the second item will be the hard drive C:). The On Error Resume Next statement tells VB to ignore the error and continue. It will add the names of drives A: and B: to the Drives ComboBox control even if it can't access the selected drive.

When a drive is selected in the Drives ComboBox, the root folders on this drive are displayed in the Folders ListBox control with the following statements, which are executed from within the SelectedIndexChanged event handler of the Drives ListBox control. First, the code retrieves the names of the folders in the root folder with the GetDirectories method and adds them to the FoldersList control. Then it retrieves the files of the root folder with the GetFiles method and displays their names on the FilesList control. Both FoldersList and FilesList are ListBox controls. The code shown in Listing 18.4 is executed when the user selects a drive in the ComboBox control.

LISTING 18.4: DISPLAYING A DRIVE'S ROOT FOLDERS

```
Private Sub DrivesList_SelectedIndexChanged(ByVal sender As System.Object, _
             ByVal e As System.EventArgs) Handles DrivesList.SelectedIndexChanged
    Dim directories() As String
    Try
        directories = System.IO.Directory.GetDirectories(DrivesList.Text)
    Catch drvException As Exception
        MsgBox(drvException.Message)
        Exit Sub
    End Try
    Dim dir As String
    FoldersList.Items.Clear()
    For Each dir In directories
        FoldersList.Items.Add(dir)
    Next
    FilesList.Items.Clear()
End Sub
```

The error handler catches any runtime exceptions, displays the appropriate message, and aborts the execution of the application. An exception will be thrown if the user attempts to display the contents of a drive that's not ready (a CD drive that's empty, for example).

Finally, we must add some code to the DoubleClick event handler of the FoldersList ListBox control. This action signals the user's intention to switch to one of the displayed folders and view its subfolders. Listing 18.5 shows the code behind the DoubleClick event handler.

LISTING 18.5: DISPLAYING THE SELECTED FOLDER'S SUBFOLDERS AND FILES

```
Private Sub FoldersList_DoubleClick(ByVal sender As System.Object, _
                ByVal e As System.EventArgs) Handles FoldersList.DoubleClick
    Dim selDir As String
    selDir = FoldersList.Text
    Dim dirs(), files() As String
    If selDir = ".." Then
        dirs = Directory.GetDirectories(parentDir)
        files = Directory.GetFiles(parentDir)
        Try
            parentDir = Directory.GetParent(parentDir).FullName
        Catch exc As Exception
            parentDir = Nothing
        End Try
    Else
        dirs = Directory.GetDirectories(selDir)
        files = Directory.GetFiles(selDir)
        Try
            parentDir = Directory.GetParent(selDir).FullName
        Catch exc As Exception
            parentDir = Nothing
        End Try
    End If
    Dim dir As String
    FoldersList.Items.Clear()
    If Not parentDir Is Nothing Then
        FoldersList.Items.Add("..")
    End If
    For Each dir In dirs
        FoldersList.Items.Add(dir)
    Next
End Sub
```

The code in this event handler displays the subfolders of the selected folder in the same ListBox control, replacing its current contents. The very first item added to the Folders ListBox control is the symbol for the parent directory, which moves you to the parent folder. The code examines the selected item and, if it's "..", it displays the subfolders of the parent folder. Otherwise, it displays the subfolders of the selected folder. The *parentDir* variable is declared on the Form level, and it's used for storing the parent folder every time the user switches to a subfolder. It's used to navigate back to the parent folder when the user clicks the parent folder symbol.

The error handler is actually part of the application's logic. The code always attempts to retrieve the parent folder. If an error occurs, which means that the current folder has no parent folder, the *parentDir* variable is set to Nothing.

When the button on the form is clicked, the program starts scanning the selected folder recursively—it scans the files of the selected folder and then the files of all folders under the selected one. As it proceeds, it displays the name of the selected folder and the number of files and subfolders scanned so far on the form's title bar. It also displays the path name of the folder being scanned on a Label control, above the FilesList control. Listing 18.6 is the code behind the Scan Selected Folder button, which initiates the recursive scanning.

LISTING 18.6: INITIATING THE RECURSIVE SCANNING OF A FOLDER

```
Private Sub Button1_Click(ByVal sender As System.Object, _
              ByVal e As System.EventArgs) Handles Button1.Click
    FilesList.Items.Clear()
    If Button1.Text = "Scan Selected Folder" Then
        Button1.Text = "Stop Scanning"
        interrupt = False
    Else
        Button1.Text = "Scan Selected Folder"
        interrupt = True
        Me.Text = "INTERRUPTED"
    End If
    Try
        If FoldersList.Text = "" Then
            Scanfolder(DrivesList.Text)
        Else
            Scanfolder(FoldersList.Text)
        End If
    Catch scanException As Exception
        MsgBox(scanException.Message)
    End Try
    Button1.Text = "Scan Selected Folder"
End Sub
```

First, this code clears the contents of the ListBox, where the files will be displayed. Then it changes the caption of the button to Stop Scanning, so that users will have a chance to interrupt the scan of an entire volume. This code demonstrates a technique for interrupting a recursive process. We set the *interrupt* variable to False when the scanning of the folder starts. If the user clicks the button while the scan is in progress, the *interrupt* variable is set to True. This variable is examined from within the recursive procedure, and you'll see shortly how the program uses it to interrupt the process.

The last If...End If clause initiates the scanning of the selected folder. If a folder name was selected in the FoldersList control, this is the folder that's scanned recursively. If not, it attempts to scan recursively the selected drive. The appropriate error handler will display a message, should the user attempt to scan a drive that's not ready or a folder that can't be scanned successfully.

The recursive part of the application is the ScanFolder() subroutine, which is shown in Listing 18.7.

LISTING 18.7: THE SCANFOLDER() SUBROUTINE

```
Sub ScanFolder(ByVal currDir As String)
    If interrupt Then Exit Sub
    Dim Dir As String
    Dim File As String
    Dim FI As FileInfo
    Label1.Text = "scanning " & currDir
    For Each File In Directory.GetFiles(currDir)
        FI = New FileInfo(File)
        FilesList.Items.Add(FI.Name & vbTab & FI.Length & vbTab & _
                            FI.CreationTime)
    Next
    countFiles += Directory.GetFiles(currDir).Length
    Me.Text = "Scanning " & FoldersList.Text & " - Processed " & countFiles & _
              " files in " & countFolders & " folders..."
    For Each Dir In Directory.GetDirectories(currDir)
        countFolders += 1
        Application.DoEvents()
        ScanFolder(Dir)
    Next
End Sub
```

The ScanFolder() subroutine examines the value of the *interrupt* variable. If it's True, it terminates. Because ScanFolder() is recursive, all pending instances of the subroutine must terminate. As soon as the current instance terminates, the most recently interrupted instance of the subroutine kicks in and completes its execution. Then the next instance kicks in, until all pending instances of the subroutine have terminated. Depending on the complexity of the calculations performed by the recursive procedure, it may take a few seconds until the process is terminated.

The code that fills the FilesFolder ListBox control is straightforward: First, the subroutine adds the names of the files in the folder passed as argument (this is the selected folder on the FoldersList control). In addition to the name, it displays the file's size and its creation date. After scanning all the files in the current folder, the program goes through each subfolder of the selected folder. Each one of these folders must also be scanned in the same manner, so the subroutine calls itself, passing the name of a different folder each time. This process is repeated for all the subfolders of the selected folder, at any depth.

The ScanFolder application is an interesting example of recursive programming, but why duplicate functionality that's already available for free? One reason is that the FileScan application is highly customizable. In the previous section, you learned how to count all the files of a given folder, including those in its subfolders. You can add many more useful features to the FileScan application that aren't available through Windows Explorer. For example, you can implement a version of the Find utility that locates files and/or folders based on criteria that aren't available through the Find utility. A limitation of the Find utility is that you can't specify exclusion criteria. For instance, you can't ask it to find all the files whose size exceeds 1 MB that aren't system files (e.g., EXE, DLL) or images (e.g., BMP, TIF, JPG). But with FileScan, you can modify the application to handle all types of file selection or rejection criteria by designing the proper user interface. In the following section, we'll modify the FileScan project a little, so that it maps a folder on a RichTextBox control.

VB.NET AT WORK: THE FOLDERMAP PROJECT

Here's another customization idea for the FileScan application: Have you ever had to prepare a hard copy of your hard disk's structure? (If you ever have to submit the contents and structure of an entire CD to a publisher, this utility will save you a good deal of work.) As far as I know, there is no simple way to do it. However, you can easily modify the FileScan application so that it prints the contents of a folder, including its subfolders, to a text box. Figure 18.6 shows the FolderMap application, which does exactly that. The structure of a user-specified folder is printed on a RichTextBox control so that folder names can be displayed in bold and stand out. The contents of the text box can be copied and pasted in any other document or used in a mail message. In this example, I'm using the RichTextBox control to format the folder and filenames differently. The FolderMap project is also an interesting demonstration of creating formatted text from within your application with the help of the RichTextBox control.

FIGURE 18.6

The FolderMap application generates a text file with the structure of any given folder.

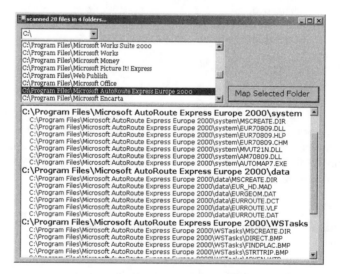

The code behind the Map Selected Folder button is identical to the code of the Scan Now button of the FileScan project, and it's shown in Listing 18.8. It calls the ScanFolder() subroutine once, passing the name of the folder to be mapped.

LISTING 18.8: THE MAP SELECTED FOLDER BUTTON

```
Private Sub bttnMapFolder_Click(ByVal sender As System.Object, _
                ByVal e As System.EventArgs) Handles bttnMapFolder.Click
    RichTextBox1.Clear()
    Me.Cursor = System.Windows.Forms.Cursors.WaitCursor
    countFiles = 0
    countFolders = 1
    Try
        ScanFolder(FoldersList.SelectedItem)
    Catch scanException As Exception
        MsgBox(scanException.Message)
    End Try
    Me.Cursor = System.Windows.Forms.Cursors.Default
End Sub
```

This code isn't new to you. Let's examine the code of the ScanFolder() subroutine, which is shown in Listing 18.9. It's based on the ScanFolder() subroutine of the previous example, with the exception of the lines that format and display the filenames on the RichTextBox control at the bottom of the form. The subroutine prints the name of the current folder in bold. Then, it goes through the files in the current folder first and prints them on the RichTextBox control. All filenames are indented by a few spaces to the right, and they're printed in regular font. The last For Each...Next loop in the subroutine goes through the subfolders of the current folder and calls the ScanFolder() subroutine for each one.

LISTING 18.9: THE REVISED SCANFOLDER() SUBROUTINE

```
Sub ScanFolder(ByVal currDir As String)
    Dim Dir As String
    Dim File As String
    RichTextBox1.SelectionFont = boldFont
    RichTextBox1.AppendText(currDir & vbCrLf)
    For Each File In System.IO.Directory.GetFiles(currDir)
        RichTextBox1.SelectionFont = textFont
        RichTextBox1.AppendText("   " & File & vbCrLf)
    Next
    countFiles += System.IO.Directory.GetFiles(currDir).Length
    Me.Text = "scanned " & countFiles & " files in " & countFolders & _
              " folders..."
    For Each Dir In System.IO.Directory.GetDirectories(currDir)
        countFolders += 1
        Application.DoEvents()
        ScanFolder(Dir)
    Next
End Sub
```

At the beginning of the program, the variables *boldFont* and *textFont* are declared as follows:

```
Dim boldFont As New Font("Verdana", 11, System.Drawing.FontStyle.Bold)
Dim textFont As New Font("Verdana", 9, System.Drawing.FontStyle.Regular)
```

The code switches the RichTextBox control to bold font for printing folder names and back to regular font for printing filenames. The actual folder and filenames are appended to the existing contents with the control's AppendText method.

While the application scans the selected folder, the pointer's icon is switched to an hourglass, indicating that the process will take a while. Depending on the total number of files under the folder you're mapping, the program may take a while to complete. Normally, you will create a printout of a folder with a few dozen, or even a few hundred, files. If you attempt to map the **Program Files** folder after the installation of Visual Studio, you will have to wait for a few minutes. Scanning the folders isn't a slow process, but as the number of text lines in the RichTextBox increases, it takes more and more time to add new lines to the control.

An alternative is to append the filenames to a disk file rather than a memory variable, then open the file and read its contents into the RichTextBox control. Or, if you don't care about displaying folder names in bold, you could abandon the RichTextBox control and use a TextBox or a ListBox control. You could also use a StringBuilder variable to store all the folder and filenames in a really long variable and then display this string on the TextBox control. I think the benefit of richly formatting the folder structure offsets the less-than-optimal execution speed, as long as the size of the folder you want to map is reasonable.

FURTHER CUSTOMIZATION

Another customization idea is to process selected files with a specific application. Suppose your **DownLoad** folder is full of ZIP files you have downloaded from various sources. Unzipping these files into the **DownLoad** folder would be a disaster. Ideally, you should create a separate folder for each ZIP file, copy a single ZIP file there, and then unzip it. You can do this manually or you can let a variation of the FileScan application do it for you. All you need is a small program that creates the folder, moves the ZIP file there, and then unzips it with PK_UNZIP (of course, any zipping/unzipping utility will work in a similar manner.) You could even write a DOS batch file to process the ZIP files with the following statements:

```
md c:\Shareware\%2
copy %1 c:\Shareware\%2\
del %1
pkunzip c:\Shareware\%1
```

TIP   *A batch file is a program that can be started with the Shell function. To start the PK_UNZIP application from within Visual Basic, use a statement like* Shell("pkunzip c:\zipfiles*.ZIP").

If this batch file is named MVFiles.bat, you can call it with two arguments:

```
MVFILES CuteUtility.zip CuteUtility
```

The first argument is the name of the ZIP file to be moved and unzipped, and the second argument is the name of the folder where the ZIP file will be moved and unzipped. You can modify the FileScan application so that every time it runs into a ZIP file, it calls the `MVFiles.bat` program with the appropriate arguments and lets it process the ZIP file.

The Stack Mechanism

Now that you have seen examples of recursive programming and have a better understanding of this powerful technique, let's look at the mechanism that makes recursion possible. I mentioned earlier that each time a procedure (function or subroutine) calls another, its status must be stored in memory so that it can later resume execution. The status of an interrupted procedure includes the location of the line where it was interrupted and the values of the local variables the moment it was interrupted. This information is enough for a procedure to resume operation and never be aware that it was interrupted.

Stack Defined

The area of memory in which the procedure's status is stored is called the *stack*. The stack is a protected area of the system's memory that's handled exclusively by the operating system. The stack memory is regular memory, but the operating system handles it differently from the way it handles the rest of memory. For one thing, programs can't grab any byte from the stack. The items in this memory are stacked on top of one another, and only the topmost item can be extracted.

Each time a program places a value on the stack, the new item is placed at the top of the stack. When a program reads a value from the stack, it can read only the item on top, which is the item that was placed on the stack last. This type of memory organization is called *last in, first out,* or *LIFO*. The item that is placed on the stack last is the first one to be read. This is exactly the mechanism used to pass arguments between procedures.

Recursive Programming and the Stack

If you aren't familiar with the role of the stack in the computer's operation, the following discussion will probably help you understand the mechanics of recursion a little better. The stack is one of the oldest models used in programming, and it's still as useful and as popular as ever. In fact, it's an important part of the operating system. Microprocessors provide special commands for manipulating the stack. Fortunately, you don't have to worry about the stack, since it's handled exclusively by the operating system and your favorite programming language. The description of the stack you'll find in this section is a bit simplified. The goal is to explain how recursive procedures work without getting too technical.

Suppose the recursive procedure is a subroutine and it accepts no arguments, similar to the Scan-Folder() subroutine. When the ScanFolder() subroutine calls itself, it must first store its status on the stack so that it can later resume. One component of the subroutine's status is the line that was executing when the program was interrupted. The ScanFolder() subroutine calls itself from within a loop. When it resumes, it should be able to continue with the remaining loops and not start all over again. The loop's counter, *i*, is part of the subroutine's status, and it must also be stored on the stack along with all the information that makes up the function's status.

The ScanFolder() subroutine's status is stored on top of the stack, and the same subroutine starts executing again with a fresh set of local variables (a new loop counter, for example). When this copy of the ScanFolder() subroutine calls itself again, its status is stored on the stack on top of the status of the previously interrupted subroutine. As more instances of the same subroutine are called, the status of each is stored on top of the previously interrupted subroutine's status. Eventually, the active Scan-Folder() subroutine terminates, and the most recently interrupted one takes over. Its status is on the top of the stack. The operating system removes the values of its local variables from the stack so that the subroutine can resume execution.

What's left on the top of the stack now is the status of the subroutine that must resume execution when the active subroutine terminates. When these values are removed from the stack, the status of another interrupted function surfaces on the stack. This simple mechanism allows procedures to interrupt each other and keep track of each other's status without any complicated operations. Each procedure finds its status on the stack, as if no other information was ever placed on top of it.

Passing Arguments through the Stack

The same mechanism is used to pass arguments from one procedure to another. Suppose your program calls the function `Payment(Amount, Interest)`, which expects to read two arguments (the loan amount and an interest rate) and return the monthly payment. As you know so well by now, you must supply the arguments in this order: first the amount, then the interest. The calling program leaves its status and the two arguments on the stack in the same order: first its status (the values of its local variables), then the value of the *Amount* argument, and finally, the value of the *Interest* argument. When the Payment() function takes over, it retrieves the two arguments from the top of the stack: first the value of the last argument, then the value of the first argument. After the removal of these two values from the stack, the status of the calling procedure is at the top of the stack. When the Payment() function finishes, it leaves its result on the top of the stack and relinquishes control to the calling procedure.

The calling procedure removes the value from the top of the stack (the result of the Payment() function) and uses it for its own purposes. It then removes the values of the local variables (its status) so that it can resume execution. As you can see, the LIFO structure is ideal for exchanging data between procedures.

Suppose the Payment() function calls another function. Again, the arguments of the new function are placed on the stack where the new function will find them. When the other function returns, it leaves its result on the top of the stack where the Payment() function will find it and remove it from the stack. It also finds its status information on the stack. No matter how many functions are called in such a nested manner, the information required is always at the top of the stack.

The only requirement when passing arguments through the stack is that they are placed there in the order they are needed. The procedure being called has no other means to decipher which value corresponds to which argument. That's why these arguments are also known as *positional arguments*.

VB functions support *named arguments* as well, and you can pass arguments to them in any order, as long as you provide both the name and the value of the argument. If the Payment() function has a default interest rate, you can call it as follows: `Payment(Amount:=29000)`. Even these procedures use the stack mechanism to pass the named arguments, but the mechanics are a bit more complicated. The basic idea is the same: The information is always placed on top of the stack, and when it's read, it's removed from the stack. In this way, each procedure is guaranteed to find the information it leaves on the stack the moment it needs it.

A REAL-LIFE EXAMPLE

Imagine that you are so disciplined and organized that you can place every document you use in your office on top of a document stack. Every time you're interrupted by a visitor or a phone call, you leave the document you were working with on top of this paper stack and remove another document from your filing cabinet to work on. When you've finished, you take the document in front of you and place it back in the filing cabinet (or if you're interrupted again, you place this document on the stack and retrieve another one from the filing cabinet).

What you now have in front of you is the document you were working on when you were interrupted. When you've finished with this document, you put it back where it belongs and another document surfaces on the stack—the document you interrupted working on to work with another document. After you work with this document, revise it, and put it away, you have another document before you from an even earlier interruption. If you can maintain this type of organization, you'll never need to waste time looking for documents (and your productivity will be at an all-time high!). Everything will be in its filing space, and most of the time, the document you need will be right in front of you. Thankfully, we're not as simplistic as our computers, nor do we need to be so rigid. But you'll probably agree that this type of memory organization makes perfect sense for keeping track of interrupted tasks on your computer.

Special Issues in Recursive Programming

Recursion is not a technique that most programmers regularly use. Only a few situations call for recursive programming, and unfortunately, these programs can't be implemented otherwise. As the various object models become more and more complicated, you'll have to implement an increasing number of recursive procedures. The following sections discuss the dangers of recursion and give you a few hints to help you recognize a procedure that calls for recursive programming.

It's Easy to Write a Never-Ending Program

If you forget to specify an exit condition with a few statements that stop the procedure from calling itself, you'll end up with a never-ending program, or an endless loop. If this happens, your computer will run out of memory for storing the intermediate results, and the program will end with the "Out of stack space" error message. The memory available for storing intermediate results between procedure calls is limited and it's easy to exhaust.

The stack isn't used only for recursive procedures. Each time a function is called, the status of the one that's interrupted, along with the arguments of the function being called, are stored on the stack. It's practically impossible to run out of stack space with regular procedures; to do so, you'd have to call an extremely large number of procedures, one from within the other. You can run out of stack space with recursive procedures, though, because you don't have to write several thousand routines—only one that calls itself and doesn't provide an exit mechanism.

I've tried to produce a stack overflow by calculating the factorial of a very large number. While this was easy with previous versions of VB, this time I've exhausted the accuracy of the Long data type before generating a stack overflow. I even changed the Factorial() function's type to Double to fill the stack, but guess what happened: the string "Infinity" appeared on the form! The ScanFolder() subroutine will never generate a stack overflow, because I can't imagine a file system with nested folders to a depth of several hundreds.

I had to write a dummy subroutine that calls itself to cause the stack to overflow. After more than 40,000 recursive calls, the stack was exhausted. To be on the safe side, you can catch the Stack-OverflowException in your code.

Knowing When to Use Recursive Programming

In addition to knowing how to implement recursive programming, you need to know *when* to use it. The recursive nature of many problems isn't obvious, so it may take a while to get the hang of it. (We humans aren't trained to think recursively, but once you've established the recursive nature of a problem, the recursive algorithm will follow quite naturally.) An algorithm that, in the middle of carrying out a task, has to start and complete an identical task is a prime candidate for recursive implementation. Consider a procedure for scanning the contents of a folder. First, it counts the files. If the folder has subfolders, the same process must be repeated for each subfolder.

If you find yourself nesting loops in many levels or if you're trying to set up conditions to exit these loops prematurely, your code would probably benefit from a recursive implementation. Recursion bears some resemblance to iteration, and in some situations, you can implement a recursive algorithm with a loop. The factorial algorithm, for instance, can be easily implemented with a For…Next loop. But there are situations in which iterations won't help.

TRY IT!

If you're interested in recursion and would like to experiment a little, here's a problem that can be solved both recursively and nonrecursively: Write a program that accepts a phone number and produces all possible seven-letter combinations that match the phone number (vanity numbers, as they are called). This is not a trivial task, no matter how you look at it. There are 3 to the power of 7, or 2,187, possible combinations, because each number can be mapped to one of three letters and phone numbers have seven digits (excluding the area code).

I've mentioned already that recursive routines are quite common when programming with classes of .NET Framework. You have already seen a few recursive routines in earlier chapters, and I would like to go through a couple of typical examples presented in earlier chapters. In Chapter 5, you saw a recursive procedure for scanning the items of a menu, and in Chapter 16, you saw a recursive procedure for scanning the nodes of a TreeView control. Now that you have a better understanding of how recursion works, you may wish to take a closer look at these applications. In the following sections, I will focus on the recursive nature of these routines and not on the object models used in each example.

PRINTING A MENU'S COMMANDS

In Chapter 5, you saw a subroutine that iterates through the items of a menu. If an item leads to a submenu, the submenu's items are also scanned, and this process is repeated to any depth. Of course, no menu item should be nested in more than two or three levels, but this procedure will work with any menu structure. The following code iterates through the items of a MainMenu object and prints all the commands in the Output window. MapMenu is the name of a button on a form with a menu, and it prints the names of the commands at the top level. It scans all the items of the menu's Menu-Items collection and prints their captions. After printing each command's caption, it calls the PrintSubMenu() subroutine, passing the current MenuItem as argument. The PrintSubMenu() subroutine iterates through the items of the collection passed as argument and prints their captions. The MapMenu command's code is shown here:

```
Private Sub Button1_Click(ByVal sender As System.Object, _
                ByVal e As System.EventArgs) Handles Button1.Click
    Dim itm As MenuItem
    For Each itm In Me.Menu.MenuItems
        TextBox1.AppendText(itm.Text & vbCrLf)
        PrintSubMenu(itm)
    Next
End Sub
```

The PrintSubMenu() subroutine, shown in the following code, goes through the MenuItems collection of the MenuItem object passed as argument and prints the captions of its items. If the current item leads to a submenu (in other words, if it has its own MenuItems collection), it calls the PrintSubMenu() subroutine recursively. The PrintSubMenu() subroutine is called with a different argument every time, and this argument is the current menu item—the item whose submenu we want to scan.

```
Sub PrintSubMenu(ByVal MItem As MenuItem)
    Static indentLevel As Integer
    indentLevel += 5
    Dim itm As New MenuItem()
    For Each itm In MItem.MenuItems
        TextBox1.AppendText(Space(indentLevel) & itm.Text & vbCrLf)
        If itm.MenuItems.Count > 0 Then PrintSubMenu(itm)
    Next
    indentLevel -= 5
End Sub
```

When the PrintSubMenu() subroutine starts executing, it increases the variable *indentLevel* by 5. This variable is the number of spaces printed in front of each item's caption. We increase the indentation level by five spaces every time we run into a new submenu, and we decrease it every time we move to the previous menu level. When the PrintSubMenu() subroutine finishes processing a submenu, the indentation is decreased by five spaces, so that items on the same level have the same indentation.

PRINTING THE NODES OF A TREEVIEW CONTROL

Scanning the nodes of a TreeView control is another typical example of a recursive procedure, because each node may have a collection of nodes under it, and this can go on to any depth. For the purposes of our example, we'll assume that the TreeView control has a single root node. This isn't an unreasonable assumption, because most tree structures have a single root and you should try to implement trees with a single root node to simplify your code. If you have a tree with multiple root nodes, you must write a loop that iterates through the root nodes, and for each node you must call the ScanNode() recursive procedure.

To start the scanning of the TreeView1 control, start at the top node of the control with the statement

```
ScanNode(GlobeTree.Nodes(0))
```

This statement must appear in a button's Click event handler. It calls the ScanNode() subroutine to scan the child nodes of a specific node, which is passed to the subroutine as argument. `GlobeTree.Nodes(0)` is the root node. By passing the root node to the ScanNode() subroutine, we're in effect asking it to scan the entire tree. The name of the TreeView control is GlobeTree, the same one we used in the examples of Chapter 16.

Let's look now at the ScanNode() subroutine:

```
Sub ScanNode(ByVal node As TreeNode)
    Dim thisNode As TreeNode
    Static indentLevel As Integer
    Application.DoEvents()
    ListBox1.Items.Add(Space(indentLevel) & node.Text)
    If node.Nodes.Count > 0 Then
        indentLevel += 5
        For Each thisNode In node.Nodes
            ScanNode(thisNode)
        Next
        indentLevel -= 5
    End If
End Sub
```

The ScanNode() subroutine adds the caption of the current node to the ListBox1 control. Then it examines the values of the `Node.Nodes.Count` property, which returns the number of nodes under the current node. If this value is positive, the subroutine proceeds by scanning all the items of the `Node.Nodes` collection. It does that by calling itself and passing the current node as argument.

The ScanNode() subroutine can scan any TreeView control. All you need is a reference to the root node (or the node you want to scan recursively), which you must pass to the ScanNode() subroutine as argument. The subroutine will scan the entire subtree and display its nodes on a ListBox control.

The variable *indentLevel* keeps track of the level of nesting and is used to specify the indentation of the current node. It's increased by 5 when we start scanning a new subordinate node and decreased by the same amount when we return to the next level up—similar to the PrintSubMenu() subroutine. The *indentLevel* variable is declared as static, because it must maintain its value between calls. If you want to display the nodes on a different control, such as a RichTextBox control, or save them to a text file, modify the statement that adds items to the ListBox1 control.

Summary

In this chapter, you learned about a powerful coding technique, recursion. Recursive procedures aren't among the most popular topics in programming, but as you saw, they help you write code that's impossible without recursion. First, you have to establish the recursive nature of the process. Once you do, you can write a procedure that performs the basic calculations and then calls itself with a different argument each time.

You must also make sure that the recursive procedure will eventually come to an end. You must examine some condition and explicitly insert an `Exit Sub` or `Exit Function` statement. If not, the procedure will keep calling itself until it causes a stack overflow.

Recursion is a very practical coding technique. I've used recursive techniques throughout the book, not because I wanted to show you a more elaborate, or a more elegant, way of doing things. None of the recursive procedures presented in this book can be implemented nonrecursively (except the introductory example of this chapter, of course).

To the computer, a recursive procedure is no different than any other procedure. Your program doesn't know, and doesn't care, whether a procedure calls itself or another one. It just loads and executes another copy of the specified procedure. If it's the same one it's currently executing, it uses the copy of the code in memory and creates a new set of local variables. In other words, it creates a new instance of the newly called procedure in memory and executes it.

Chapter 19

The Multiple Document Interface

THE *MULTIPLE DOCUMENT INTERFACE (MDI)* was designed as an alternative interface for applications that manipulate documents of the same type. It simplifies the exchange of information among documents, all under the same roof. With an MDI application, you can maintain multiple open windows but not multiple copies of the application. Data exchange is easier when you can view and compare many documents simultaneously.

You almost certainly use Windows applications that can open multiple documents at the same time and allow the user to switch among them with a mouse-click. Microsoft Word is a typical example, although most people use it in single-document mode. Each document is displayed in its own window, and all document windows have the same behavior. The main form, or MDI form, is not duplicated, but it acts as a container for all other windows, and it's called the *parent window*. The windows in which the individual documents are displayed are called *child windows* (or *document windows*). When you reposition the parent window on the Desktop, its child windows follow. Child windows, however, exist independently of the parent window. You can open and close child windows as you wish, and child windows can even have different functions. For example, you can open a few text windows and a few graphics windows next to one another, although this is rare.

Figure 19.1 shows Excel 2000 in MDI mode. The application's main window contains five documents, three of them in custom-size windows and two of them minimized. The menus and the toolbars of the parent window apply to all the child windows. In reality, the menu bar of the MDI form contains the menu of the active child form. Depending on the state of the active child window, the MDI form's menu may also change.

Paint Shop Pro is a very popular application (see Figure 19.2) that uses an MDI interface. Many mail applications display each message in a separate window and allow the user to open multiple messages. Most of the popular text editors (Notepad excluded) are MDI applications, too.

FIGURE 19.1

Using Excel in
MDI mode

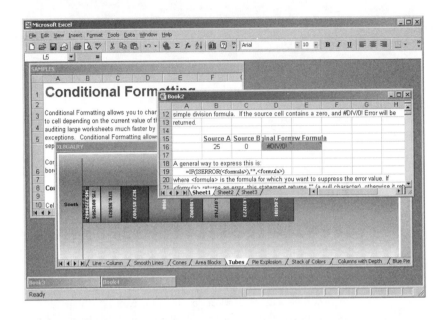

FIGURE 19.2

Paint Shop Pro, one
of the most popular
graphics applica-
tions, uses the MDI
user interface.

MDI applications aren't very common; not too many applications lend themselves to MDI implementation. Most of them are easier to implement with multiple forms, but some applications should
be implemented with an MDI interface. These are the applications that can open multiple documents

of the same type and use a common menu structure that applies to all open documents. In the following sections, we are going to discuss the basic behavior of MDI applications, their differences from regular *Single Document Interface (SDI)* applications, and how to build MDI applications.

MDI Applications: The Basics

MDI applications must have at least two forms, the parent form and one or more child forms. There may be many child forms contained within the parent form, but there can be only one parent form. The parent form is the MDI form, or MDI *container*, because it contains all child forms.

The parent form may not contain any controls. While the parent form is open in design mode, the icons on the Toolbox aren't disabled, but you can't place any controls on the form. The parent form can, and usually does, have its own menu. While one or more child forms are displayed, the menu of the child forms takes over and it's displayed on the MDI form's menu bar. This is not a requirement, of course, and you can manipulate the parent form's menu with the techniques we discussed in Chapter 4. In this chapter, you'll learn about a feature that is specific to the menus of MDI applications, namely how to merge two different menus—the menu of the MDI form and the menu of the child forms.

In the following section, we're going to build a simple MDI application. In the process, we'll discuss the steps that are unique to an MDI application.

Building an MDI Application

Building an MDI application is a fairly straightforward process, but quite a few steps are unique to MDI applications. In this section, we're going to build a typical MDI application that demonstrates all the built-in features of the MDI. In a later section, we're going to add more functionality to this application. As you will see, once you get the interface right and you have the skeleton of a working MDI application, adding specific functionality to it is as simple as adding functionality to an SDI application. In effect, all the code belongs to the child form, and the MDI form is simply a container with a few lines of supporting code.

The application we'll build in this section is the skeleton of an MDI text-editing application, and it's shown in Figure 19.3. All child forms of the application are the same, and they determine the functionality of the application. The commands of the menu are placeholders, with no code behind them—we'll add the code later. For now, we're going to focus on the mechanics of designing MDIs.

Before building the application, let's go over the basic characteristics of an MDI application. When you start an MDI application, you see the container form. Most applications automatically display a new document of the type they can handle. Excel, for instance, opens a new XLS file when you start it. Closing this document disables most of the commands in Excel's menus. Without an active document, these commands are meaningless. They're activated automatically again as soon as a new document is opened on a child form. The child forms usually have more menu commands, which are merged with the initial menu of the MDI form's menu commands.

The child forms don't display their own menus. When you design a child form, you add a menu as usual, but this menu will appear on the menu bar of the MDI form—it will either replace the initial menu of the MDI form or it will be merged with it. You may have also noticed that the menu of an MDI application changes according to the state of the document on the active child form. If you select some text in the active document, the Cut and Copy commands will be enabled. If you switch to another child form whose document contains no selection, these two commands will be disabled. In effect, each child form has its own menu, and each time you switch to another child form, its menu becomes the application's menu. You can design an MDI application that uses child forms with totally different menus, but this is quite unusual—at the very least, it will confuse the users.

FIGURE 19.3

MDIPad is an MDI text-editing application.

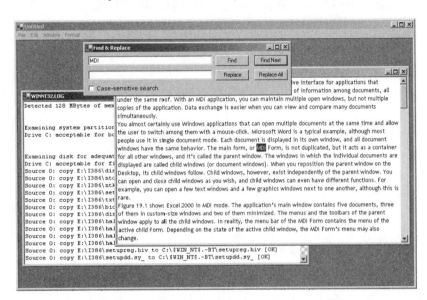

Let's now build the application. Start a new project and name it MDIProject. Select the project's form in the Solution window, and rename it from **Form1.vb** to **MDIForm.vb**. This form will become the window that will host the child forms at runtime. To specify this function of the form, select the MDIForm component in Solution Explorer, and in the Properties window locate the IsMdiContainer property. This property determines whether the form will act as an MDI parent form (in other words, whether it will be a container for child forms). The default value is False, and you must change it to True. While you're setting the form's properties, change the MDI form's caption to "MDIForm".

We've taken care of the parent form. We must now create a child form. Because all child forms are usually the same, we'll create a single form that will serve as a template for all child windows. It is possible for an MDI application to host child forms that are not identical, but this is rather unusual. In this chapter, we'll explore MDI applications with child forms that are identical.

Right-click the project's name in the Solution Explorer window, and from the context menu select Add ➤ Add Item. In the dialog box that appears, select Windows Form. Change its name to ChildForm, and click Open to add it to the project. Child forms are regular forms, and you need not set any properties to make them appear in their container. If you run the project now, you will see the parent form and nothing more.

To display a child window at runtime, you must insert a few lines of code. Since the user is in charge of creating and closing child forms, we must add a menu, usually a File menu, that contains a

New command. Before we can open a child form, we'll build a simple menu with a command that allows you to create a new instance of the child form and display it on the parent form.

With the MDI form in the Design window, drop a MainMenu control onto the project. Then create a menu with the structure shown in Table 19.1.

TABLE 19.1: THE CAPTIONS AND NAMES OF THE FILE AND WINDOW MENUS

CAPTION	NAME
File	FileMenu
New	FileNew
Exit	FileExit
Window	WindowMenu
Tile Horizontally	WindowTileH
Tile Vertically	WindowTileV
Cascade	WindowCascade
Arrange Icons	WindowArrange

The first column contains the top-level items, which are the usual File and Window menus. The Window menu is a characteristic of all MDI applications, and we'll come back to this topic shortly. The File menu contains the two commands you really need when no child form is displayed. The New command instantiates a child form, and the Exit command terminates the application.

Enter the lines in Listing 19.1 in the New menu item's Click event handler.

LISTING 19.1: INSTANTIATING A NEW CHILD FORM

```
Private Sub FileNew_Click(ByVal sender As System.Object, _
            ByVal e As System.EventArgs) Handles FileNew.Click
    Static nWindow As Integer
    Dim child As New ChildForm()
    child.MdiParent = Me
    child.Text = "Child window # " & nWindow.ToString
    child.Show()
    nWindow = nWindow + 1
End Sub
```

Creating and displaying an instance of the child form isn't new to you; this is the same code we used in Chapter 4 to display a form or dialog box from within another form. We create a variable that represents the form and then we call its Show method. In our example, we also set the caption of the form. The *nWindow* variable is static so that it's increased every time a child control is added.

This variable is used to display a different caption for each child form. Note that the *nWindow* variable's value isn't decreased when a child form is closed. Therefore, there will be gaps in the numbering of the child forms as you close and open new documents, but they will all have a different caption. In a real application, each child form's caption will be the title of the document displayed.

The line that's new to you is the following:

```
Child.MdiParent = Me
```

which makes the form a child of the MDI form. The child form will appear in its parent's window, and its menu will be automatically merged with the parent form's menu. So far, we haven't designed a menu for the child form, but we'll do so shortly. You'll see how the two menus are merged—you can actually specify how the two menus will be merged.

If you run the project now, you'll be able to open new child forms—each one with a unique caption—resize them in the MDI form's window, move them around, and close them when you no longer need them. The Window menu's items aren't doing anything because we haven't programmed them yet. You have built a working skeleton of an MDI application, and you're ready to add some real functionality to your project.

The child form may contain any number of controls since this is the form the user will be interacting with. You can place a multiline TextBox control on the form to experiment with the child forms of the application. Place a button or two on the child form as well, so that you can enter a few lines of code behind them as you go through the example.

NOTE   *All MDI child forms are sizable, have borders, and have the usual Control-menu, Close, and Minimize/Maximize buttons, regardless of the settings of the equivalent properties.*

THE WINDOW MENU

All MDI applications in the Windows environment have a menu called *Window* that contains two groups of commands. The first group of commands positions the child windows on the MDI form, and the second group consists of the captions of the open child windows (see Figure 19.4). With the commands on this menu, you can change the arrangement of the open windows (or the icons of the minimized windows) and activate any child window.

FIGURE 19.4

A Window menu of
an MDI application

Stop the project and right-click the Window menu item on the MDI form. On the context menu, select Properties. In the Properties window, locate the MDIList property. This property causes the menu to keep track of all open child forms and display their names at the bottom of the Window submenu. This is a characteristic function of the Window menu, and it's implemented by setting a single property.

The other four options of the Window menu, which automatically rearrange the child forms within the parent form's window, are implemented with a call to the LayoutMdi method of the child form. Windows offers three ways of arranging the windows on an MDI form. You can cascade them, tile them vertically, or tile them horizontally. Of course, the user can resize and move the windows around, but the automatic placement comes in handy when the MDI form becomes messy and the user can no longer easily locate the desired window. The placement of the child windows on the form is controlled with the LayoutMdi method, which accepts as argument one of the members of the MdiLayout enumeration: `TileHorizontal`, `TileVertical`, `Cascade`, or `ArrangeIcons`. If you're not familiar with the Window menu, check out the application, or open several documents with your favorite MDI application (Excel being one of them) and then rearrange them on the MDI form in all possible ways. By tiling the child forms vertically or horizontally, you can easily compare documents.

Enter the statements shown in Listing 19.2 into each of the four commands of the Window menu.

LISTING 19.2: THE WINDOW MENU'S COMMANDS

```
Private Sub WindowTileH_Click(ByVal sender As System.Object, _
            ByVal e As System.EventArgs) Handles WindowTileH.Click
   Me.LayoutMdi(MdiLayout.TileHorizontal)
End Sub
Private Sub WindowTileV_Click(ByVal sender As Object, _
            ByVal e As System.EventArgs) Handles WindowTileV.Click
   Me.LayoutMdi(MdiLayout.TileVertical)
End Sub
Private Sub WindowCascade_Click(ByVal sender As System.Object, _
            ByVal e As System.EventArgs) Handles WindowCascade.Click
   Me.LayoutMdi(MdiLayout.Cascade)
End Sub
Private Sub WindowArrange_Click(ByVal sender As System.Object, _
            ByVal e As System.EventArgs) Handles WindowArrange.Click
   Me.LayoutMdi(MdiLayout.ArrangeIcons)
End Sub
```

The LayoutMdi method of the parent form automatically rearranges the child forms; all you have to do is supply the proper argument. Run the project again, open a few child forms, and see their names in the Window menu. You can switch to any child form by selecting its name in this menu. The active form's name is checked automatically in the Window menu. Check out the commands that arrange the child forms as well. The Arrange Icons command applies to forms that are minimized and has no effect on the other forms.

MERGING MDI AND CHILD MENUS

We now have a working MDI application, but it doesn't do anything useful yet. We must add a few controls and a menu to the child form in order to build a real application. The parent form has no controls, just a few menu commands to create and close new child forms. In this section, we're going to add a menu to the child form and merge it with the MDI form's menu.

Open the child form in the Design window and drop a MainMenu control on it. Then design the menu shown in Table 19.2 (the dashes indicate separators).

TABLE 19.2: THE CAPTIONS AND NAMES OF THE FILE, EDIT, AND FORMAT MENUS

CAPTION	NAME
File	FileMenu
-	
Open	FileOpen
Save	FileSave
Save As	FileSaveAs
Close	FileClose
-	
Preview	FilePreview
Print	FilePrint
Edit	EditMenu
Copy	EditCopy
Cut	EditCut
Paste	EditPaste
-	
Find	EditFind
Word Wrap	EditWordWrap
Format	FormatMenu
Font	FormatFont
Text Color	TextColor
Page Color	PageColor

This is the menu of the MDIPad application, which we'll build in the next few sections. MDIPad is a text editor similar to the TextPad of Chapter 6, but it can maintain many open documents at once with an MDI interface.

As you can see, some of the commands are missing, and they are the ones we've already added to the MDI form's menu. The MDI form has a File menu with the New and Exit commands. These two commands are missing from the child form's menu. We're going to merge the two menus and specify that the New command will be the first command in the File menu, while the Exit command will be the last command in the same menu. This also explains why the child form's File menu starts and ends with a separator. The top separator will be placed under the New command, while the last separator will end up just above the Exit command. The separators aren't placed automatically when the menus are merged; you must insert them in the child form's menu. You can also insert them in the MDI form's menu, but they will appear even when they don't separate sections of the menu, as they're supposed to do.

The MDI form's menu is really minimal because the MDI form is simply a container for the child forms. You can't do anything without first opening a new document. The child form's menu contains all the commands users need to interact with the document and edit it. The child form contains all the code of the application, and its menu structure indicates the capabilities of the application.

NOTE   *Some applications display the full menu even when no child form is open. These menus usually lead to disabled commands, as there's no document for the commands to act upon. It's possible to design an MDI form with the complete menu of the application, but this will complicate your code.*

If you run the application at this point and open a new child form with the New command, you will see that the child form's menu options are added to its parent's menu. There are two File menus, the first one with two commands (New and Exit) and the second one with the commands of the child form's File menu. The two menus were merged, but not exactly as we would like them. We must set a few properties to specify how the menus are merged. By default, Form Designer displays the commands of the MDI form followed by the commands of the child form.

Notice that the menus are actually added, not merged. The first commands are those of the MDI form, followed by the commands of the child form. Moreover, menus are combined according to their order in their respective forms, not their names—that's why you see two File menus. To properly merge two menus, you must set their MergeType and MergeOrder properties.

The MergeType property determines how the items of two menus are merged. Its value can be one of the members of the MenuMerge enumeration. The MenuMerge enumeration's members are listed in Table 19.3.

TABLE 19.3: THE MENUMERGE ENUMERATION

MEMBER	DESCRIPTION
Add	The menu item of the child form is added to the menu items of the parent MDI form. This is the default setting of the MenuMerge property.
MergeItems	All items of a submenu on the child form are merged with the items of the submenu of the parent MDI form. This setting applies to menu items that lead to submenus. The items are merged according to their positions in the respective menus, not by their captions.
Remove	The menu item is ignored when the two menus are merged
Replace	The menu item replaces another item at the same position in the merged menu.

The Replace option allows you to design the complete menu on the child form and have it replace the MDI form's menu as soon as the first child form is opened. This, however, means that you must duplicate the menus of the MDI form on the child form.

When menu items are merged, the parent form's menu items appear first, followed by the child form's menu items. To change the order in which two items are merged, set their MergeOrder property. This property is an integer value that determines whether an item appears in front of or after another item. The menu items being merged need not have consecutive MergeOrder values. Those with a smaller value appear in front of others with larger MergeOrder values. The MergeOrder property of the main menu's items determines the order of the top-level menu. The MergeOrder property of the items in a specific menu determines the order of the commands in this menu.

The Window item, for example, is always the last menu in an MDI application, with the exception of the Help menu. To make sure it is the last item in the merged menu structure, set its MergeOrder property to 99. If your application has a Help menu, set the Help item's MergeOrder property to 100. You need not do anything about the items of the Window menu; they follow their parent item.

Let's go through the settings of the menus of the MDI form and its child form of the application you're building. The Window menu is unique to the MDI form. To make sure it is the last menu on the form, set its MergeType property to Add and its MergeOrder property to 99. The File menu of the MDI form must be merged with the File menu of the child form, so you must set the MergeType property of both items to MergeItems. The MergeOrder property doesn't make any difference.

Then you must set the MergeOrder property of each item in the File menu of both forms. Switch to the MDI form, select the New item under the File menu, and set its MergeOrder property to 0. We want this item to be the first one in the File menu, even when the two menus are merged. The Exit item must be the last one, so set its MergeOrder property to 9. The items of the File menu on the child form should be merged with the commands of the File menu of the MDI form. Set their MergeType property to MergeItems. The MergeOrder property of the File menu's items need not change. We've already specified that the New command must appear at the top of the menu and the Exit command must appear at the bottom of the menu. The remaining commands will appear between them, and they'll have the same order as they do in the child form's File menu.

Then select the Edit and Format menus on the child form. These menus must appear after the File menu, in this order, so set their MergeType property to Add. Again, you don't have to do anything about their order. The two menus that are unique to the child form (Edit and Format) are placed on the merged menu in the order in which they appear in the menu of their own form. Figure 19.5 shows the parent and child menus, as well as the merged menu. The child menu is shown in design mode, because this menu can't be displayed on its own.

At this point you can run the application and check out how an MDI application handles the menus. Notice how the parent form's menu changes when you open new child forms and how it shrinks back to the items of the parent form after you close the last child form.

Built-In Capabilities of MDI Applications

You've just created an MDI application. It doesn't do much, but if you run the project now, you'll see two forms, one inside the other, as shown in Figure 19.6. To properly start the application, make sure that the MDI form is the application's startup form. To do this, open the project's Properties window and set the MDI form (whatever you have named it) as the startup object. If the startup object is the child window, it won't be displayed by default; you must load it from within the application code. Notice that the child form is contained entirely within the parent form and exists only in that context. If you close or minimize the parent form, the child form also will be closed or minimized.

FIGURE 19.5

The parent menu (top left), the child menu (top right) and the merged parent/child menu (bottom)

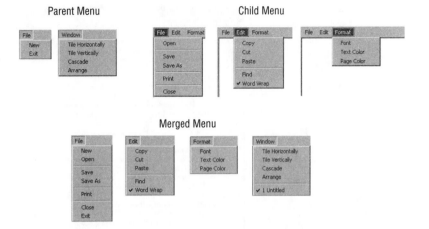

FIGURE 19.6

The framework of an MDI application with a single child form

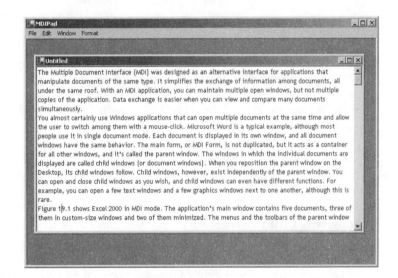

Use the mouse to move the child form around and change its size. If you click the child form's Maximize button, the two forms are combined into one, as shown in Figure 19.7.

You can also move the child form outside the parent form, in which case the appropriate scroll bars will be attached to the parent form. In addition, both the child window and the MDI form have a Control menu (which you can open by clicking the icon in the top-left corner) and their own Minimize, Restore, and Close buttons (in the top-right corner).

NOTE *Later in this chapter, you'll see that the way you name parent and child windows is important to maintaining the Windows graphical user interface (GUI) guidelines. The most important rule for parent and child windows is that the parent form's caption should be the name of the application and the captions of the child forms should be the names of the documents in each of them.*

FIGURE 19.7

The MDI application from Figure 19.6 after the child window has been maximized

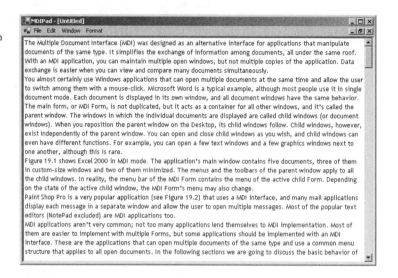

Clicking the child form's Minimize button reduces the child form to an icon, but always within the parent form. You'll never see a child form's icon on the Desktop's status bar, even if its ShowIn-Taskbar property is set to True. To restore the minimized form to its original size, double-click the icon. A child window is usually minimized instead of being closed to make room for other documents. In short, the child form behaves like a regular form on the Desktop, only its "desktop" is the parent window.

I have just demonstrated the basic operations of an MDI application with just a few lines of codes. These capabilities are built into the language and are available to your applications through the settings of certain properties. We're almost ready to build a functional MDI application. But first, let's see how we can access the controls on the child forms.

Accessing Child Forms

There are two different methods to access the child forms. The first method, and the most common one, is to use the Me keyword. This keyword refers to the form in which the code resides, and since the bulk of the code is on the child form, you can use the Me keyword to access the controls on the child form. The MDI child forms of a text editor, for example, contain a TextBox control where the user can enter and edit text. The following expression returns the text on the active child form:

```
Me.TextBox1.Text
```

To select all the text on the active child window, call the TextBox control's SelectAll method with the following statements:

```
Me.TextBox1.SelectAll
```

To access the child form from within the MDI parent form's code, you can use the ActiveMdiChild property, which represents the active child form. The following statement returns the caption of the active child form:

```
Me.ActiveMdiChild.Text
```

To access the contents of a TextBox control on the child form from within the MDI form's code, use the following statement:

```
Me.ActiveMdiChild.TextBox1.Text
```

In the last two examples, the Me keyword refers to the MDI parent form, not to the child forms, because the code resides in the MDI form.

If the various child forms weren't identical, you'd have to insert additional code to make sure that the active form contains the control you want to access. If some of the child forms contain a TextBox control while others don't, you can't use the last statement without some error-trapping code. MDI applications that deploy more than a single type of child form are more complicated to code and rather uncommon.

You can also access all child windows through the MdiChildren property of the parent form. This property returns an array whose elements represent the child forms open on the MDI form at any one time. To find out the number of open child forms, read the Length property of this array:

```
Console.WriteLine("There are " & Me.MdiChildren.Length & " child Forms open")
```

This statement works only if it appears in the MDI parent form's code. To access a child form from within another child form's code, you must first access the parent form (`Me.ParentForm`) and then the parent form's MdiChildren property. The following statements return the values shown in bold if executed from within a child form's code:

```
Console.WriteLine(Me.ParentForm.MdiChildren.GetLength(0))
3
Console.WriteLine(Me.ParentForm.ActiveMdiChild)
MDIProject.ChildForm, Text: Child window # 1
```

TRACKING THE ACTIVE CHILD FORM

The child form you design is the prototype. An *instance* of a form is a copy that inherits all the properties of the original but exists in your application independently of the original. On an MDI form, all child forms are usually instances of one basic form. All forms all have the same behavior, but the operation of each one doesn't affect the others. When a child form is loaded, for example, it will have the same background color as its prototype, but you can change this from within your code by setting the form's BackColor property. No other child form will be affected by that change.

Each child form is totally independent of any other child form, and you can access it from within your code through the Me keyword. This keyword identifies the current form, as long as you program it from within its own form. When you program a command of the child form's menu, for example, you can access the active child form with the Me keyword.

Sometimes, we want to access an MDI child form from within another form that's neither a parent nor a child form. In a text-editing application, like the one you're going to develop in the following section, we want to be able to access the active child form from within the Search & Replace dialog box. The simplest method is to maintain a variable that keeps track of the active MDI child form, and access the child form through this variable. You will see this technique in action in the following section.

VB.NET AT WORK: THE MDIPAD PROJECT

In Chapter 5, you built the TextPad application, which is a simple text editor based on the TextBox control. Now you're going to convert it to an MDI application. An MDI application lets you open and edit multiple documents simultaneously. You can also copy information from one window and paste it into another, and you can arrange multiple documents on-screen so that you can view any other document while editing the active one. All this is possible without invoking multiple instances of the application. Figure 19.8 shows the TextPad application, and Figure 19.9 shows the MDIPad application.

FIGURE 19.8

The TextPad application

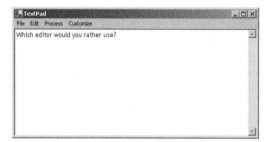

FIGURE 19.9

The MDIPad application

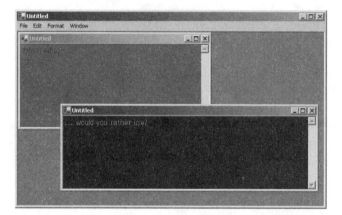

Start a new project, name it MDIPad, and change the name of its form to MDIForm. Then set its form's IsMdiContainer property to True. Add another form and name it DocumentForm. This is the MDI child form.

Design two menus, one for the MDI form and another one for the MDI child form. The two menus of the application are identical to the menus of the MDIProject sample, discussed earlier (see Tables 19.1 and 19.2). Then add a TextBox control on the child form. Set its name to Editor and its Dock property to Fill, so that it takes up all the available space on the child form. Add a ListBox control to the child form, too, and set its Visible property to False. We'll use this control to store the file's name so that we can quickly retrieve it from within the Save command's event handler. We're ready to implement the commands of the two menus, starting with the MDI form's menu. If you're in doubt as to the settings of the MergeType and MergeOrder properties of the menu items, open the MDIPad on the CD and examine their settings.

PROGRAMMING THE NEW COMMAND

The New command of the MDI form's File menu opens a new child form. Its implementation is shown in Listing 19.3.

LISTING 19.3: THE NEW COMMAND

```
Private Sub FileNew_Click(ByVal sender As System.Object, _
              ByVal e As System.EventArgs) Handles FileNew.Click
   Dim child1 As New DocumentForm()
   child1.MdiParent = Me
   child1.Show()
   child1.Text = "Untitled"
End Sub
```

The New command doesn't clear the contents of the active child window, as was the case with the TextPad application. Instead, it opens a new, blank child window. Every time you click the New command, a new child form is displayed and its initial caption is set to "Untitled".

PROGRAMMING THE OPEN COMMAND

The Open command's code is longer but not drastically different from the Open command of the TextPad application. It prompts the user to select a text file through the Open dialog box and then displays the text in the active child window. Listing 19.4 shows the code of the Open command.

LISTING 19.4: THE OPEN COMMAND

```
Private Sub FileOpen_Click(ByVal sender As System.Object, _
              ByVal e As System.EventArgs) Handles FileOpen.Click
   OpenFileDialog1.DefaultExt = "*.txt"
   OpenFileDialog1.ShowDialog()
   If OpenFileDialog1.ShowDialog() = DialogResult.OK Then
      Dim fname As String = OpenFileDialog1.FileName
      Me.Text = fname.Substring(fname.LastIndexOf("\") + 1)
      Dim StrReader As System.IO.StreamReader
      StrReader = New System.IO.StreamReader(fname)
      Editor.Text = StrReader.ReadToEnd
      Editor.SelectionStart = 0
      Editor.SelectionLength = 0
      ListBox1.Items.Add(fname)
      ListBox1.Items.Add(Now())
   End If
End Sub
```

The Open command displays the Open dialog box and retrieves the name of a text file selected by the user. The caption of the active child form is the name of the file. Because the OpenFileDialog control returns the full pathname, we extract the last section of the pathname, which is the filename. Then the file is read and displayed on the Editor TextBox control.

Most of the information you need about each child form can be retrieved through the Me keyword. You will also have to maintain some information that can't be retrieved directly from the child form. The filename of each open document, for example, isn't stored on the child form—unless you want to display the file's pathname on the form's title bar. You may also want to maintain additional information about each document (like the date and time it was opened, the current magnification for an image, and so on). This information is stored in the invisible ListBox control. You can add all kinds of information to the ListBox control and access it at any time from within your code. The only requirement is that you must decide the order of the item in which each piece of information is stored. The Open command's event handler stores the path of the file in the first item of the ListBox control and the time the file was opened in the second item of the control. The pathname will be used later by the Save command.

PROGRAMMING THE SAVE COMMANDS

New documents are saved with the Save As command. The code of the Save As command, shown in Listing 19.5, is the counterpart of the Open command.

LISTING 19.5: THE SAVE AS COMMAND

```
Private Sub FileSaveAs_Click(ByVal sender As System.Object, _
            ByVal e As System.EventArgs) Handles FileSaveAs.Click
    SaveFileDialog1.DefaultExt = "*.txt"
    If SaveFileDialog1.ShowDialog() = DialogResult.OK Then
        Dim saveFileName As String
        Dim StrWriter As System.IO.StreamWriter
        StrWriter = New System.IO.StreamWriter(saveFileName)
        StrWriter.Write(Editor.Text)
        Me.Editor.Modified = False
        ListBox1.Items.Add(saveFileName)
    End If
End Sub
```

The Save As command prompts the user for a filename. This filename is then stored in the first item of the hidden ListBox control, to be used later in saving the document. The Save command's code retrieves the file's path from the hidden control and saves the document, as shown in Listing 19.6. If the user attempts to save a new document, the first item of the list will be empty, and the program invokes the SaveAs command automatically.

```
Private Sub FileSave_Click(ByVal sender As System.Object, _
                ByVal e As System.EventArgs) Handles FileSave.Click
   Dim saveFileName As String
   saveFileName = ListBox1.Items.Item(0)
   If saveFileName = "" Then
      FileSaveAs_Click(sender, e)
   Else
      Dim StrWriter As System.IO.StreamWriter
      StrWriter = New System.IO.StreamWriter(saveFileName)
      StrWriter.Write(Editor.Text)
      Me.Editor.Modified = False
   End If
End Sub
```

The Save and Save As commands also set the Modified property of the TextBox control on the active child form to False. The reason for this is that the TextBox isn't aware of the save operation and doesn't reset the Modified property. We want the Modified property to be up to date, because we'll examine it when the user attempts to close the application and prompt him accordingly. See the section "Closing an MDI Application" for more information.

Finally, the Close command closes the active child form (and the current document, of course). Its code is shown in Listing 19.7.

```
Private Sub FileClose_Click(ByVal sender As System.Object, _
                ByVal e As System.EventArgs) Handles FileClose.Click
   Me.Close()
End Sub
```

The application doesn't examine the status of the document and prompt the user if they're about to close a document that has been edited. As you will see, this action takes place in the child form's Closing event, which is discussed later in this chapter.

PROGRAMMING THE FORMAT MENU

Let's add some code behind the Text Color and Page Color commands of the Format menu. These are really trivial operations compared to the Open and Save commands. To implement the two color commands, you must add an instance of the ColorDialog control on the child form and then insert the statements shown in Listing 19.8 in the Click event handlers of the Text Color and Page Color commands.

LISTING 19.8: SETTING THE TEXT AND PAGE COLORS

```
Private Sub TextColor_Click(ByVal sender As System.Object, _
            ByVal e As System.EventArgs) Handles TextColor.Click
    ColorDialog1.Color = Me.Editor.ForeColor
    ColorDialog1.ShowDialog()
    Me.Editor.ForeColor = ColorDialog1.Color
End Sub
Private Sub PageColor_Click(ByVal sender As System.Object, _
            ByVal e As System.EventArgs) Handles PageColor.Click
    ColorDialog1.Color = Me.Editor.BackColor
    ColorDialog1.ShowDialog()
    Me.Editor.BackColor = ColorDialog1.Color
End Sub
```

This is the same code you'd use to set the background and foreground colors of a TextBox control on a regular SDI application. You use the Me keyword to access the active child form. If you run the application now, you can open any number of child forms and change their colors. Each child form behaves independently of all others, and it maintains its settings.

The code that sets the font for the active child form is also quite trivial. We display the Font dialog box and then assign the font selected by the user to the Font property of the Editor control, as shown in Listing 19.9.

LISTING 19.9: SETTING THE EDITOR'S FONT

```
Private Sub EditFont_Click(ByVal sender As System.Object, _
            ByVal e As System.EventArgs)
    FontDialog1.Font = Me.Editor.Font
    If FontDialog1.ShowDialog() = DialogResult.OK Then
        Me.Editor.Font = FontDialog1.Font
    End If
End Sub
```

For some operations, we need to know when the user switches to another child form. This action is signaled by the MdiChildActivate event, which is an event of the MDI parent form, and you can use it to update internal variables in your code. In this event's handler, we display the title of the currently active child form on the MDI form's title bar. Listing 19.10 displays the title of the currently active child form on the MDI form's caption. In addition, it sets the *activeChildForm* variable to the currently active child window. This variable points always to the current child window and is used by the Find command, which acts on the document of the active child window.

LISTING 19.10: KEEPING TRACK OF THE ACTIVE CHILD FORM

```
Private Sub MDIForm_MdiChildActivate(ByVal sender As Object, _
            ByVal e As System.EventArgs) Handles MyBase.MdiChildActivate
```

```
    If Me.ActiveMdiChild Is Nothing Then
        Me.Text = "MDIPad - no document"
    Else
        Me.Text = Me.ActiveMdiChild.Text
        activeChildForm = Me.ActiveMdiChild
    End If
End Sub
```

The *activeChildForm* variable is declared as `Public Shared` on the MDI form with the following statement:

```
Public Shared activeChildForm As DocumentForm
```

Every time another child form is activated, this variable is updated to reflect the currently active child form. You'll see shortly how this variable is used in the discussion of the Find command.

PROGRAMMING THE EDIT MENU

The Edit menu's commands handle the selected text on the Editor TextBox control. They're straightforward: The Copy command copies the selected text to the Clipboard. The Cut command does the same, and then it deletes the current selection. The Paste command extracts the text from the Clipboard and uses it to replace the current selection on the TextBox control. All commands use the expression `Me.Editor` to access the TextBox control on the active child form, and their code is shown in Listing 19.10.

LISTING 19.10: PROGRAMMING THE TEXT EDITING COMMANDS

```
Private Sub EditCopy_Click(ByVal sender As System.Object, _
              ByVal e As System.EventArgs) Handles EditCopy.Click
    If Me.Editor.SelectedText.Length > 0 Then
        Me.Editor.Copy()
    End If
End Sub
Private Sub EditPaste_Click(ByVal sender As System.Object, _
              ByVal e As System.EventArgs) Handles EditPaste.Click
    If Clipboard.GetDataObject.GetData(DataFormats.Text) Then
        Me.Editor.Paste()
    Else
        MsgBox("no text to paste")
    End If
End Sub
Private Sub EditCut_Click(ByVal sender As Object, _
              ByVal e As System.EventArgs) Handles EditCut.Click
    If Me.Editor.SelectedText.Length > 0 Then
        Clipboard.SetDataObject(Me.Editor.SelectedText)
        Me.Editor.Cut()
    End If
End Sub
```

THE FIND COMMAND

This is the most interesting part of the application. The Find command must display a Find & Replace dialog box, shown in Figure 19.10. This dialog box must remain on top of the application's main form, even when it doesn't have the focus. Design a form like the one shown in Figure 19.10, and set its TopMost property to True.

FIGURE 19.10

The Find & Replace dialog box of the MDIPad application

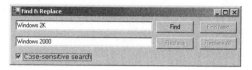

To invoke the Find & Replace dialog box from within a child form's code, you must create an instance of the dialog box and then call its Show method. Insert the following declaration in the child form's code window, outside any procedure's definition:

```
Dim extForm As Form = New FindForm()
```

Then add the code in Listing 19.11 to the Find command's Click event handler. This code displays the FindForm dialog box by calling the *extForm* object's Show method.

LISTING 19.11: DISPLAYING THE FIND & REPLACE DIALOG BOX

```
Private Sub EditFind_Click(ByVal sender As System.Object, _
              ByVal e As System.EventArgs) Handles EditFind.Click
    extForm.Show()
End Sub
```

Once the dialog box is displayed, users can search for a word or replace one or more instances of a word with another one. The search can be case-sensitive or not, depending on the status of the Case-Sensitive Search check box. The code of the Find button is shown in Listing 19.12.

LISTING 19.12: THE FIND BUTTON

```
Private Sub bttnFind_Click(ByVal sender As System.Object, _
              ByVal e As System.EventArgs) Handles bttnFind.Click
    Dim selStart As Integer
    Dim srchMode As CompareMethod
    srchMode = SetSearchMode()
    selStart = InStr(MDIForm.activeChildForm.Editor.Text, _
               srchWord.Text, srchMode)
    If selStart = 0 Then
        MsgBox("Can't find word")
        Exit Sub
    End If
    MDIForm.activeChildForm.Editor.Select(selStart - 1, srchWord.Text.Length)
    MDIForm.activeChildForm.Editor.ScrollToCaret()
```

```
        bttnFindNext.Enabled = True
        bttnReplace.Enabled = True
        bttnReplaceAll.Enabled = True
    End Sub
```

To access the document of the active child form, the code uses the *activeChildForm* variable of the MDI parent form. This variable references the active child form, and we can use it to access the TextBox control with the document. The code uses the InStr() function because it provides an argument that allows us to perform case-sensitive and case-insensitive searches. The search mode is specified by the *srchMode* argument, which is calculated by the SetSearchMode() function based on the status of the check box on the dialog box. The SetSearchMode() function examines the value of the check box and returns a member of the CompareMethod enumeration:

```
Function SetSearchMode() As CompareMethod
    If chkCase.Checked = True Then
        Return CompareMethod.Binary
    Else
        Return CompareMethod.Text
    End If
End Function
```

The code behind the Find Next button, shown in Listing 19.13, is quite similar. It uses the InStr() function as well, except that it specifies the index of the character in the text where the search will begin. This index is the location of the character following the current selection.

LISTING 19.13: THE FIND NEXT BUTTON

```
    Private Sub bttnFindNext_Click(ByVal sender As System.Object, _
                        ByVal e As System.EventArgs) Handles bttnFindNext.Click
        Dim selStart, srchStart As Integer
        Dim srchMode As CompareMethod
        srchMode = SetSearchMode()
        srchStart = MDIForm.activeChildForm.Editor.SelectionStart + _
                MDIForm.activeChildForm.Editor.SelectionLength
        selStart = InStr(srchStart + 1, MDIForm.activeChildForm.Editor.Text, _
                    srchWord.Text, srchMode)
        If selStart = 0 Then
            MsgBox("There are no more instances of the specified word")
            bttnFindNext.Enabled = False
            Exit Sub
        End If
        MDIForm.activeChildForm.Editor.Select(selStart - 1, srchWord.Text.Length)
        MDIForm.activeChildForm.Editor.ScrollToCaret()
        bttnFindNext.Enabled = True
        bttnReplace.Enabled = True
        bttnReplaceAll.Enabled = True
    End Sub
```

Finally, the Replace and Replace All commands are straightforward. They call the Replace()
function to replace the word in the Search box with the word in the Replace box. Their code is
shown in Listing 19.14.

LISTING 19.14: THE REPLACE AND REPLACE ALL BUTTONS

```
Private Sub bttnReplace_Click(ByVal sender As System.Object, _
               ByVal e As System.EventArgs) Handles bttnReplace.Click
    MDIForm.activeChildForm.Editor.SelectedText = replaceWord.Text
    bttnFindNext_Click(sender, e)
End Sub
Private Sub bttnReplaceAll_Click(ByVal sender As System.Object, _
               ByVal e As System.EventArgs) Handles bttnReplaceAll.Click
    Dim srchMode As CompareMethod
    Dim srchStart As Integer
    srchMode = SetSearchMode()
    Dim pointerLocation As Integer = _
               MDIForm.activeChildForm.Editor.SelectionStart
    MDIForm.activeChildForm.Editor.Text = _
               Replace(MDIForm.activeChildForm.Editor.Text, _
                       srchWord.Text, replaceWord.Text, , , srchMode)
    MDIForm.activeChildForm.Editor.SelectionStart = pointerLocation
End Sub
```

Ending an MDI Application

In most cases, ending an application with the End statement isn't necessarily the most user-friendly
approach. Before you end an application, you must always offer your users a chance to save their
work. Ideally, you should maintain a *True/False* variable whose value is set every time the user edits
the open document (the Change event of many controls is a good place to set this variable to True)
and reset every time the user saves the document (with the Save or Save As command).

Handling unsaved data in normal applications is fairly simple, as there's only one document to
deal with. But in an MDI application, you have to cope with several possible scenarios:

◆ The user closes a child window by clicking its Close button. You should detect this condition
and provide the same code you'd use with an SDI application.

◆ The user closes a single document by selecting the Close command of the File menu. This situation is easy to handle—it's just like a normal application.

◆ The user closes the MDI form. If the MDI form is closed, all the open documents will close with
it! If losing the edits in a single document is bad, imagine losing the edits in multiple documents.

Therefore, terminating an MDI application with the End statement is unacceptable. First, you need
a mechanism to detect whether a document needs to be saved or not. In a text-processing application,
you can examine the Modified property of the TextBox control. For other types of applications, you

may have to maintain a list of *True/False* variables, one for each document. When the document is modified, set the corresponding variable to True. When the document is saved, reset it to False to indicate that the document can be closed without being saved first. When the user attempts to close the document, you can examine this variable and act accordingly—prompt the user about saving the document or create a backup copy of the document.

TIP *The Modified property of the TextBox is not automatically reset to False when the document is saved. To use the Modified property, you must explicitly set it to False when the document is saved.*

When the user closes a document through the Close command, it's easy to handle the document. Insert the proper code in the Close command's event handler to detect whether the document being closed contains unsaved data and prompt the user accordingly. When the user clicks the child form's Close button, the child form's Closing event is fired, this time by the child form. Finally, when the MDI form is closed, each of the child forms receives the Closing event. In addition, the MDI form's Closing event is also fired. Normally, there's no reason to program this event. As long as you handle the Closing event of the child form, no data will be lost.

In the Closing event, you can cancel the operation of closing a document, or the MDI form itself, by settings the **e.Cancel** property to True.

To close the active child form, execute the following statements (they must appear in the Close command's Click event handler):

```
Private Sub FileExit_Click(ByVal sender As System.Object, _
                ByVal e As System.EventArgs) Handles FileExit.Click
    Me.Close()
End Sub
```

The Close method invokes the Closing event of the child form. In this event, you can add code to detect whether the document has been saved or not and close the document or prompt the user accordingly. The Closing event handler shown in Listing 19.15 examines the Modified property of the TextBox control on the active child form. If it's False, it doesn't do anything (it allows the child form to be closed). If it's True, it prompts the user with a message box. If the user agrees to discard the changes, the event handler terminates and the child form is closed. If the user clicks the No button, the event handler sets the **e.Cancel** property to True, which cancel the form's Closing event.

LISTING 19.15: THE CHILD FORM'S CLOSING EVENT HANDLER

```
Private Sub Form1_Closing(ByVal sender As Object, _
                ByVal e As System.ComponentModel.CancelEventArgs) _
                Handles MyBase.Closing
    If Me.Editor.Modified Then
        Dim reply As MsgBoxResult
        reply = MsgBox("Document " & Me.Text & " was modified but not saved. " & _
                    "Discard the edits?", MsgBoxStyle.YesNo)
        If reply = MsgBoxResult.No Then
            e.Cancel = True
        End If
    End If
End Sub
```

Even if the user closes the MDI form, the Closing event for each child form will be fired, and the same handler will take care of the closing of all documents.

A Scrollable PictureBox

One of the shortcomings of earlier versions of Visual Basic was that you couldn't attach scroll bars to large forms. This is no longer a problem because the new Windows Form Designer automatically attaches scroll bars when the form is resized below a minimum size. Many developers were wishing the PictureBox had its own scroll bars to handle large images, but this is not the case. The Picture-Box control can't be scrolled. In this section, we're going to build a scrollable PictureBox control using the techniques discussed so far.

The scrollable PictureBox isn't a new control; it's not even a PictureBox with its own scroll bars. It's a child form filled with a PictureBox control. The size of the PictureBox is determined by the user at runtime, but if it gets smaller than the size of the image, the scroll bars will be attached automatically. This is a feature of the Form object, and child forms support it, because they inherit the Windows.Forms.Form class. Figure 19.11 shows a child form with an image and the appropriate scroll bars attached to it. From a user's point of view, it looks just like a PictureBox with scroll bars.

FIGURE 19.11

Using an MDI form to simulate a scrolling PictureBox control

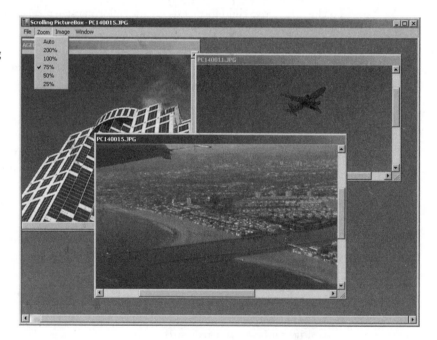

 The form shown in Figure 19.11 belongs to the ScrollingPictureBox project, which you'll find in this chapter's folder on the CD. This project is an MDI application that uses child forms to display images. To implement the scrolling form, follow these steps:

1. Start a new project.

2. Rename the form to MDIImage and set its IsMdiContainer property to True.

3. Add a child form to the project with the Project ➤ Add Windows Form command. Set the child form's Name property to ImageForm and its caption (property Text) to "Untitled."

4. Add an instance of the MainMenu control to the parent form and create the menu structure shown in Table 19.4.

5. Switch to the child form, add an instance of the MainMenu control to this form as well, and create the menu structure shown in Table 19.5.

TABLE 19.4: THE CAPTIONS AND NAMES OF THE PARENT FORM'S MENU

CAPTION	NAME
File	FileMenu
New Image	FileNew
Exit	FileExit
Window	WindowMenu
Title Horizontally	WindowTileH
Tile Vertically	WindowTileV
Cascade	WindowCascade
Arrange Icons	WindowArrange

TABLE 19.5: THE CAPTIONS AND NAMES OF THE CHILD FORM'S MENU

CAPTION	NAME
File	FileMenu
Load	FileLoad
Close	FileClose
-	
Zoom	ZoomMenu
Auto	ZoomAuto
200%	Zoom200
100%	Zoom100
75%	Zoom75
50%	Zoom50
25%	Zoom25

Continued on next page

TABLE 19.5: THE CAPTIONS AND NAMES OF THE CHILD FORM'S MENU *(continued)*

CAPTION	NAME
Image	ImageMenu
Rotate Left	ImageRotateLeft
Rotate Right	ImageRotateRight
Flip Horizontal	ImageFlipH
Flip Vertical	ImageFlipV

6. Enter the following code behind the New command of the parent form's menu. This command creates a new child form and displays it on the MDI form, but doesn't load an image.

```
Private Sub FileNew_Click(ByVal sender As System.Object, _
            ByVal e As System.EventArgs) Handles FileNew.Click
    Dim childForm As New Form3()
    childForm.MDIParent = Me
    childForm.show()
End Sub
```

This code opens another child form. Initially, the child form is empty, and it has the initial size of the child form you specified at design time. Your next step is to add the code behind the Load command, which loads an image to the active child form.

7. Add an instance of the OpenFileDialog control on the main form, and enter the statements shown in Listing 19.16 to the handler of the Click event of the Load command.

LISTING 19.16: LOADING A NEW IMAGE

```
Private Sub FileLoad_Click(ByVal sender As System.Object, _
            ByVal e As System.EventArgs) Handles FileLoad.Click
    Dim imgFile As String
    OpenFileDialog1.Filter = "Images|*.jpg;*.tif"
    OpenFileDialog1.ShowDialog()
    imgFile = OpenFileDialog1.FileName
    PictureBox1.Image = Image.FromFile(imgFile)
    PictureBox1.Width = PictureBox1.Image.Width
    PictureBox1.Height = PictureBox1.Image.Height
    Me.ZoomMenu.Enabled = True
    Me.ProcessMenu.Enabled = True
    Me.PrintMenu.Enabled = True
End Sub
```

The code resizes the PictureBox control to fit the size of the image it contains in actual size. The child form that hosts the PictureBox isn't resized, but the proper scroll bars are attached automatically. The user can then change the current magnification with one of the commands of the Zoom menu. Even without the Zoom or the Image menu, you have a functional application that displays multiple images in scrolling PictureBoxes. Each image is displayed in its own window, and all windows are hosted in MDI form.

The project's code on the CD contains a few more statements that I've omitted from Listing 19.16. Each child form contains an invisible ListBox control, where we store information about the image displayed on the form, such as the name and dimensions of the image. Not that you can't read the dimensions directly from the Image object, but I wanted to demonstrate how to maintain information about each open document. In an SDI application, you'd probably use global variables to store this information. The situation is different with MDI applications, because you must maintain the same information for multiple documents, and an invisible control on the child form is the simplest method. The last command of the Image menu, the Image Properties command, displays the properties stored in the ListBox control in a message box.

To make the application more useful, let's add the code behind the other menu commands. The Zoom menu contains various zooming factors supported by the application. It's really trivial to add more factors or prompt the user to supply a value for the image's magnification level. Every time an option in the Zoom menu is clicked, we must make sure that the selected option is checked (and all other options cleared) and resize the active child form to the specified zooming factor.

All the items of the Zoom menu are serviced by the same procedure, the ZoomImage() subroutine, which is shown in Listing 19.17.

LISTING 19.17: THE ZOOMIMAGE SUBROUTINE

```
Sub ZoomImage(ByVal sender As System.Object, ByVal e As System.EventArgs) _
            Handles Zoom100.Click, Zoom200.Click, Zoom75.Click, _
                    Zoom50.Click, Zoom25.Click
    UncheckZoomMenu()
    Me.PictureBox1.Width = PictureBox1.Image.Width * _
                        Val(CType(sender, MenuItem).Text) / 100
    Me.PictureBox1.Height = PictureBox1.Image.Height * _
                        Val(CType(sender, MenuItem).Text) / 100
    ImageInfo.Items.Item(3) = Val(sender.text) / 100
    CType(sender, MenuItem).Checked = True
End Sub
```

Notice that the ZoomImage() subroutine handles multiple menu items. To find out which command was selected, the code picks up the caption of the item that was clicked with the Sender.Text expression, retrieves its numeric value (50 for 50 percent, 25 for 25 percent, and so on), and uses the value to resize the image on the child form. For more information on writing event handlers for multiple menu items see Chapter 5.

The Auto option is the most interesting part of the application. This command resizes the Picture-Box on the current child form so that the image will fit exactly on it. One of the dimensions of the control remains the same, while the other one is resized according to the image's aspect ratio. The dimension that remains unchanged is the dimension that corresponds to the smaller of the image's width and height. If the image is taller than it is wide, the width of the image is resized. Otherwise, the code resizes the height of the control. In effect, the image is fit into the child window as best as possible, without introducing any distortion. Before you select the Auto command of the Zoom menu, resize the child form to a comfortable size for the available area. After the execution of the Zoom ➤ Auto command, the image will fill either the horizontal or the vertical dimension of the form. You can then change the other dimension with the mouse to view the entire image. Listing 19.18 contains the code behind the Zoom ➤ Auto command:

LISTING 19.18: THE ZOOM ➤ AUTO COMMAND

```
Private Sub ZoomAuto_Click(ByVal sender As System.Object, _
            ByVal e As System.EventArgs) Handles ZoomAuto.Click
   If PictureBox1.Image.Width > PictureBox1.Image.Height Then
      PictureBox1.Height = Me.Height
      PictureBox1.Width = PictureBox1.Height * _
         (PictureBox1.Image.Width / PictureBox1.Image.Height)
   Else
      PictureBox1.Height = PictureBox1.Width * _
         (PictureBox1.Image.Height / PictureBox1.Image.Width)
   End If
End Sub
```

For more information on printing bitmaps, as well as how to resize images and maintain their aspect ratio, see Chapter 15.

The Process menu contains a few simple commands for rotating and flipping the image. All event handlers use the RotateFlip method of the Image object, passing as argument one of the members of the RotateFlipType enumeration. After the image has been rotated, we must also swap the width and height of the corresponding PictureBox control. Listing 19.19 demonstrates the implementations of the Rotate Right and Flip Vertical commands.

LISTING 19.19: THE ROTATE RIGHT AND FLIP VERTICAL COMMANDS

```
Private Sub RotateRight_Click(ByVal sender As System.Object, _
            ByVal e As System.EventArgs) Handles RotateRight.Click
   PictureBox1.Image.RotateFlip(RotateFlipType.Rotate90FlipNone)
   PictureBox1.Invalidate()
End Sub
Private Sub FlipVertical_Click(ByVal sender As Object, _
            ByVal e As System.EventArgs) Handles FlipVertical.Click
   PictureBox1.Image.RotateFlip(RotateFlipType.Rotate180FlipX)
   PictureBox1.Invalidate()
End Sub
```

Summary

In this, the last chapter of Part IV, you learned about the Multiple Document Interface (MDI), which allows you to write applications that open multiple documents. An MDI application consists of a MDI form, which hosts a number of MDI child forms. Each MDI child form contains a document. The documents are usually of the same type, but if your application can handle multiple document types, the MDI form should be able to host all the document types.

The MDI child form is equivalent to the main form of a SDI application, like the ones we explored in previous chapters. This form contains the code that provides most of the functionality of the application. The MDI form is the container for the child forms and contains a simple menu. Everything else, including the main menu of the application, resides in the child forms.

This chapter concludes the code of the Visual Basic language. In the next part of the book, we'll look into database programming, and in the last part of the book we'll explore Web applications.

Summary

Part V

Database Programming with VB.NET

In this section:

Chapter 20

Databases: Architecture and Basic Concepts

IN THE FIFTH PART of the book, we'll explore databases. In this chapter, you'll learn the basics of databases: how they store data, how to update a database, and how to retrieve the information you need from a database. In the following chapters, you'll also learn how to develop applications that access databases. The topic of database programming could easily justify another book of this size, and there will be many fine books on database programming in the bookstores. The database-related topics discussed in this book were chosen to help you get started with database programming. I've selected topics that will help you master basic concepts of databases and ADO.NET, rather than attempt to touch on a large number of topics.

ADO.NET is the data-access mechanism of Visual Studio .NET. In short, it's a class that provides all the members you need to access and manipulate a database. It's the most complicated class, because it exposes a large number of members and performs very complicated operations. We'll have a lot to say about ADO.NET in the following chapters. In the meantime, we'll start with something less exciting, but equally important.

In this chapter, we'll look at the basic concepts of the relational model and the Structured Query Language. This chapter isn't about VB, and you can skip it if you're familiar with databases and SQL. Because I can't assume that all readers are comfortable with these topics, I'm including a chapter that will help readers understand the foundations of database programming. You may have watched demonstrations of Visual Studio where someone establishes a connection to a database, drops a few objects on the form, sets some properties, and builds an application for browsing, or even editing, a table almost automagically. However, you can't expect to go far on the visual tools alone. You must understand how data are structured in databases, how they're retrieved, and how you update a database.

Step-by-step instructions are fine for building menus or other simple programming tasks, but not nearly adequate for learning database programming. Databases are based on certain principles, and the more you learn about their structure and the mechanisms for manipulating them, the easier it will be for you to follow the material in the next few chapters, as well as continue beyond the material of the book on your own. In the following chapters, you'll see how to write code that manipulates databases using the objects discussed in this chapter, so the information presented in this chapter isn't just of theoretical interest. Everything you will learn in this chapter is as practical as it gets.

Another important motivation for this chapter is the fact that databases, the most important aspect of computer science today, are among the most complicated objects in programming, yet they're based on common-sense principles. Once you've understood these principles, you'll find that database programming isn't as complicated as you may have thought.

What Is a Database?

A *database* is an object for storing complex, structured information. The same is true for a file, or even for the file system on your hard disk. What makes a database unique is the fact that databases are designed to make data easily retrievable. The purpose of a database is not so much the storage of information as its quick retrieval. In other words, you must structure your database so that it can be queried quickly and efficiently.

Databases are maintained by special programs, such as Access and SQL Server. These programs are called *database management systems (DBMS)*, and they're among the most complicated applications. A fundamental characteristic of a DBMS is that it isolates much of the complexity of the database from the developer. Regardless of how each DBMS stores data on disk, you see your data organized in tables with relationships between tables. To access the data stored in the database and to update the database, you use a special language, Structured Query Language (SQL). Unlike other areas of programming, SQL is a truly universal language and all major DBMSs support this language.

NOTE *The recommended DBMS for Visual Studio .NET is SQL Server 2000. You can use Access, or even non-Microsoft databases like Oracle. Although this chapter was written with SQL Server 2000, most of the examples will work with Access 2000 as well.*

Data are stored in *tables,* and each table contains entities of the same type. In a database that stores information about books, there will be a table with titles, another table with authors, and a table with publishers. The table with the titles contains information like the title of the book, number of pages, and the book's description. Author names are stored in a different table, because each author may appear in multiple titles. If author information were stored along with each title, we'd be repeating author names. This means that every time we wanted to change an author's name, we'd have to modify multiple entries in the titles table. Even retrieving a list of unique author names would be a challenge, because you'd have to scan the entire database, retrieve all the authors, and then get rid of the duplicates entries. The same is true for publishers. Publishers are stored in a separate table, and each title contains a pointer to the appropriate row in the publishers table. If publisher information was stored along with each title, then deleting all the books of a specific publisher would also remove the information about the specific publisher from the database.

The reason for breaking the information we want to store in a database into separate tables is to avoid duplication of information. This is a key point in database design. Duplication of information will sooner or later lead to inconsistencies in the database. The process of breaking the data into related tables that eliminate all possible forms of information duplication is called *normalization,* and there rules for normalizing databases. The topic of database normalization is not discussed in this book. However, all it really takes to design a functional database is common sense. Once you learn how to extract data from your database's tables with SQL statements, you'll develop a better understanding of how databases should be structured.

Breaking the information into separate tables is a very convenient approach, but we must figure out a way to reconstruct the information. For each title, we must retrieve the title's author(s) and publisher and put them together to display all the information about the book. To be able to reconstruct the original information, we establish links between the various tables. These links are called *relationships,* and they're at the heart of a modern DBMS.

Relational Databases

The databases we're interested in are *relational,* because they are based on relationships among the data they contain. The data is stored in tables, and tables contain related data, or *entities,* such as persons, products, orders, and so on. The idea is to keep the tables small and manageable; thus, separate entities are kept in their own tables. If you start mixing customers and invoices, products and their suppliers, or books, publishers, and authors in the same table, you'll end up repeating information—a highly undesirable situation. If there's one rule to live by as a database designer and programmer, this is it: *Do not duplicate information.*

Of course, entities are not independent of each other. For example, orders are placed by specific customers, so the rows of the Customers table must be linked to the rows of the Orders table that store the orders of the customers. Figure 20.1 shows a segment of a table with customers (top left) and the rows of a table with orders that correspond to one of the customers (bottom right). The lines that connect the rows of the two tables represent *relationships.*

FIGURE 20.1

Linking customers and orders with relationships

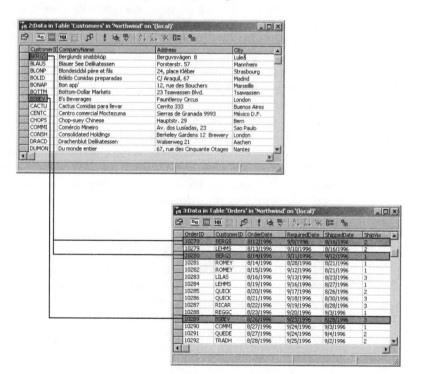

As you can see in Figure 20.1, relationships are implemented by inserting columns with matching values in the two related tables; the CustomerID column is repeated in both tables. The rows with a common value in their CustomerID field are related. In other words, the lines that connect the two tables simply indicate that there are two fields, one on each side of the relationship, with a common value. The customer with the ID value BERGS has placed the orders 10278 and 10280. The customer BSBEV has placed the order 10289. To find all the orders placed by a customer, we can scan the Orders table and retrieve the rows in which the CustomerID field has the same value as the ID of the specific customer in the Customers table. Likewise, you can locate customer information for each order by looking up the row of the Customers table that has the same ID as the one in the CustomerID field of the Orders table.

These two fields used in a relationship are called *key fields*. The CustomerID field of the Customers table is the *primary key*, because it identifies a single customer. The CustomerID field of the Orders table is the *foreign key* of the relationship. A CustomerID value appears in a single row of the Customers table; it's the table's primary key. However, it may appear in multiple rows of the Orders table, because in this table the CustomerID field is the foreign key. In fact, it will appear in as many rows of the Orders table as there are orders for the specific customer.

The operation of matching rows in two tables based on their primary and foreign keys is called a *join*. Joins are very basic operations in manipulating tables, and they are discussed in detail in the section "Structured Query Language," later in this chapter.

Exploring the Northwind Database

In this section, we'll explore the structure of a sample database that comes with both SQL Server 2000 and Access 2000. The Northwind database stores products, customers, and sales data, and many of you are already familiar with the structure of the database. We'll discuss the basic objects that make up a database shortly, but it's easier to explain these objects through examples. Besides, you need a good understanding of the structure of this database, so that you can follow the examples of the following sections and chapters. Unless you understand how data is stored in the tables of the database and how the tables relate to one another, you won't be able to retrieve information from the database or insert new data into it.

The Northwind database is made up of tables, each storing a collection of unique entities (customers, products, and so on). A table that stores products has a column for the product's name, another column for the product's price, and so on. Each product is stored in a different row. As products are added or removed from the table, the number of rows changes, but the number of columns remains the same; they determine the information we store about each product.

PRODUCTS TABLE

The Products table stores information about the products sold by the Northwind Corporation. This information includes the product's name, packaging information, price, and other relevant fields. Each product (or row) in the table is identified by a unique numeric ID. Since the rows of the Products table are referenced by invoices (the Order Details table, which is discussed later), the product IDs appear in the Order Details table as well.

SUPPLIERS TABLE

Each product has a supplier too. Because the same supplier may offer more than one product, the supplier information is stored in a different table, and a common field, the SupplierID field, is used to link each product to its supplier as shown in Figure 20.2. For example, the products Chai, Chang, and Aniseed Syrup are purchased from the same supplier, Exotic Liquids. Their SupplierID fields all point to the same row in the Suppliers table.

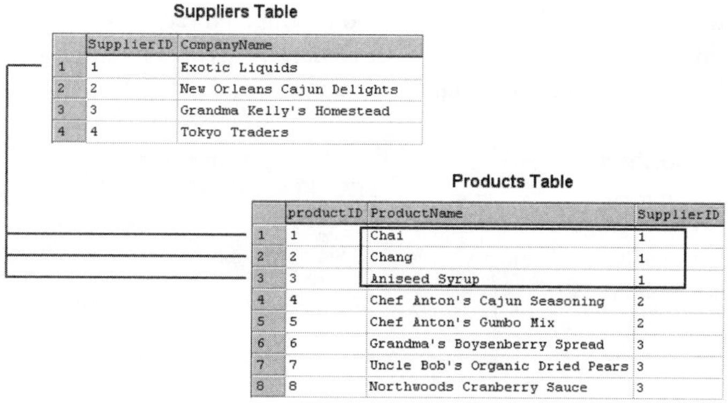

FIGURE 20.2

Linking products to their suppliers and their categories

Suppliers Table

	SupplierID	CompanyName
1	1	Exotic Liquids
2	2	New Orleans Cajun Delights
3	3	Grandma Kelly's Homestead
4	4	Tokyo Traders

Products Table

	productID	ProductName	SupplierID
1	1	Chai	1
2	2	Chang	1
3	3	Aniseed Syrup	1
4	4	Chef Anton's Cajun Seasoning	2
5	5	Chef Anton's Gumbo Mix	2
6	6	Grandma's Boysenberry Spread	3
7	7	Uncle Bob's Organic Dried Pears	3
8	8	Northwoods Cranberry Sauce	3

CATEGORIES TABLE

In addition to having a supplier, each product belongs to a category. Categories are not stored along with product names, but in a separate table, the Categories table. Again, each category is identified by a numeric value (field CategoryID) and has a name (field CategoryName). In addition, the Categories table has two more columns: Description, which contains text, and Picture, which stores a bitmap. The CategoryID field in the Categories table is the primary key, and the field by the same name in the Products table is the corresponding foreign key.

CUSTOMERS TABLE

The Customers table stores information about the company's customers. Each customer is stored in a separate row of this table, and customers are referenced by the Orders table. Unlike the product IDs, the customer IDs are five-character strings.

ORDERS TABLE

The Orders table stores information about the orders placed by Northwind's customers. The OrderID field, which is an integer value, identifies each order. Orders are numbered sequentially, so this field is also the order's number. Each time you append a new row to the Orders table, the value of the new OrderID field is generated automatically by the database.

The Orders table is linked to the Customers table through the CustomerID field. By matching rows with identical values in their CustomerID fields in the two tables, we can recombine customers with their orders. Figure 20.1 shows how customers are linked to their orders.

ORDER DETAILS TABLE

You probably have noticed that the Northwind database's Orders table doesn't store any details about the items ordered. This information is stored in the Order Details table (see Figure 20.3). Each order is made up of one or more items, and each item has a price, a quantity, and a discount. In addition to these fields, the Order Details table contains an OrderID column, which holds the ID of the order to which the detail line belongs.

FIGURE 20.3

The Customers, Orders, and Order Details tables, and their relations

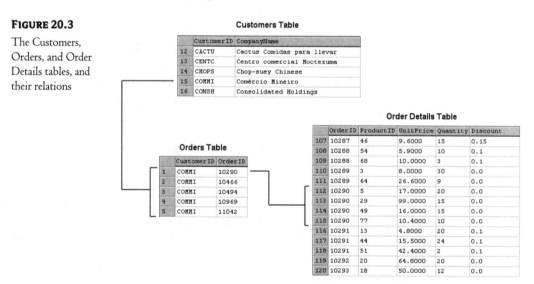

The reason details aren't stored along with the order's header is that the Orders and Order Details tables store different entities. The order's header, which contains information about the customer who placed the order, the date of the order, and so on, is quite different from the information you must store for each item ordered.

EMPLOYEES TABLE

This table holds employee information. Each employee is identified by a numeric ID, which appears in the each order. When a sale is made, the ID of the employee who made the sale is recorded in the Orders table.

SHIPPERS TABLE

Each order is shipped with one of the three shippers stored in the Shippers table. The appropriate shipper's ID is stored in the Orders table.

Exploring the Pubs Database

Before looking at SQL and more practical techniques for manipulating tables, let's look at the structure of another sample database that comes with SQL Server, the Pubs database. Pubs is a database for storing book, author, and publisher information, not unlike the database you may have to build for an online bookstore (since online bookstores are so common).

The Pubs database is made up of really small tables, but it was carefully designed to demonstrate many of the features of SQL, so it's a prime candidate for sample code. Just about any book about SQL Server uses the Pubs database. In the examples of the following sections, I will use the Northwind database, because it's a commercial database and the type of information stored in the Northwind database is closer to the needs of the average VB programmer than the Pubs database. Some of the fine points of SQL, however, can't be demonstrated with the data of the Northwind database, and this is where I'll show examples that make use of the ubiquitous Pubs database.

TITLES TABLE

The Titles table contains the information about individual books (the book's title, ID, price, and so on). Each title is identified by an ID, which is not a numeric value. The IDs of the books look like this: BU2075.

AUTHORS TABLE

The Authors table contains information about authors. Each author is identified by an ID, which is stored in the au_id field. This field is a string, with a value like 172-32-1176—that is, resembling U.S. Social Security numbers.

TITLEAUTHOR TABLE

The Titles and Authors tables are not directly related. The reason is the two tables can't be joined with a one-to-many relation. The relation between the two tables is many-to-many. Some authors have written many books, and some books are written by multiple authors. If you stop and think about the relationship between the two tables, you'll realize that it can't be implemented with a primary and a foreign key.

To establish a many-to-many relationship, you must create a table between the other two. This table must have a one-to-many relationship with either table. Figure 20.4 shows how the Titles and Authors tables of the Pubs database are related to one another. The table between them holds pairs of title IDs and author IDs. If a book was written by two authors, the TitleAuthor table contains two entries with the same title ID and different author IDs. The book with title_id of TC7777 was written by three authors. The IDs of the authors appear in the TitleAuthor table along with the ID of the book. The IDs of these three authors are 267-41-2394, 472-27-2349, and 672-71-3249. Likewise, if an author has written more than one book, the author's ID will appear many times in the TitleAuthor table, each time paired with a different title ID.

There will be situations where you won't be able to establish the desired relationship directly between two tables, and the reason is that the relationship is many-to-many. When you discover a conflict between two tables, you must create a third one between them.

FIGURE 20.4

The TitleAuthor table links titles to authors

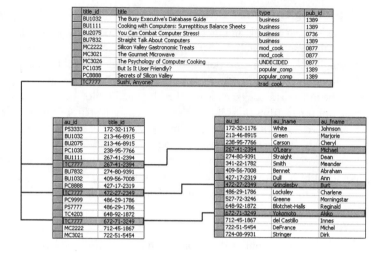

PUBLISHERS TABLE

This table contains information about publishers. Each title has a pub_id field, which points to the matching row of the Publishers table. Unlike the other major tables of the Pubs database, the Publishers table uses a numeric value to identify each publisher.

OTHER TABLES

The Pubs database contains a few more tables. The Sales table contains sale information, while the RoySched table contains royalty information about each author. The author's payment is determined by the sales of the corresponding titles and the author's royalty schedule (how the royalties escalate with sales). We are not going to use these tables in our examples, so I won't discuss them here.

Understanding Relations

In a database, each table has a field with a unique value for every row. This field is the table's *primary key*. The primary key does not have to be a meaningful entity, because in most cases there's no single field that's unique for each row. The primary key need not resemble the entity it identifies either. The only requirement is that primary keys are unique in the entire table. In most designs, we use an integer as the primary key. To make sure they're unique, we even let the DBMS generate a new integer for each row added to the table. Each table can have one primary key only, and this field can't be Null. The DBMS can automatically generate an integer value for a primary key field every time a new row is added. SQL Server uses the term *Identity* for this data type, and you can have only one Identity field in each table.

The related rows in a table repeat the primary key of the row they are related to, in another table. The copies of the primary keys in all other tables are called *foreign keys*. Foreign keys need not be unique (in fact, they aren't), and any field can serve as a foreign key. What makes a field a foreign key is that it matches the primary key of another table. The CategoryID field is the primary key of the Categories table, because it identifies each category. The CategoryID field in the Products table is the foreign key, because the same value may appear in many rows (many products may belong to the same category).

REFERENTIAL INTEGRITY

Maintaining the links between tables is not trivial task. When you add an invoice line, for instance, you must make sure that the product ID corresponds to a row in the Products table. An important aspect of a database is its *integrity*. To be specific, you must ensure that the relations are always valid, and this type of integrity is called *referential integrity*. There are other types of integrity (for example, setting a product's value to a negative value will compromise the integrity of the database), but this is not nearly as important as the referential integrity. The wrong price can be easily fixed. But issuing an invoice to a customer that does not exist isn't easy (if at all possible) to fix. Modern databases come with many tools to help ensure their integrity. These tools are constraints you enter when you design the database, and the DBMS makes sure the constraints are not violated as the various programs manipulate the database.

When you relate the Products and Categories tables, for example, you must also make sure that:

♦ Every product added to the foreign table points to a valid entry in the primary table. If you are not sure which category the product belongs to, you can leave the CategoryID field of the Products table empty. Or, you can create a generic category, the UNKNOWN or UNDE-CIDED category, and use this category if no information is available.

♦ No rows in the Categories table are removed if there are rows in the Products table pointing to the specific category. This would make the corresponding rows of the Products table point to an invalid category.

These two restrictions would be quite a burden on the programmer if the DBMS didn't protect the database against actions that could impair its integrity. The integrity of your database depends on the validity of the relations. Fortunately, all DBMSs can enforce rules to maintain their integrity. You'll learn how to enforce rules that guarantee the integrity of your database later in this chapter. In fact, when you create the relationship, you can check a couple of boxes that tell SQL Server to enforce the relationship (that is, not to accept any changes in the data that violate the relationship).

THE VISUAL DATABASE TOOLS

To simplify the development of database applications, Visual Studio.NET comes with some visual tools, the most important of which are discussed in the following sections.

The Server Explorer   This is the first and most prominent tool. The Server Explorer is the Toolbox for database applications, in the sense that it contains all the basic tools for connecting to databases and manipulating their objects.

The Query Builder   This is a tool for creating SQL queries (statements that retrieve the data we want from a database, or update the data in the database). SQL is a language in its own right, and we'll discuss it later in this chapter. The Query Builder lets you specify the operations you want to perform on the tables of a database with point-and-click operations. In the background, the Query Builder builds the appropriate SQL statement and executes it against the database.

The Database Designer and Tables Designer   These tools allow you to work with an entire database or its tables. When you work with the database, you can add new tables, establish relationships between the tables, and so on. When you work with individual tables, you can manipulate the structure of the tables, edit their data, and add constraints. You can use these tools to manipulate a very complicated object—the database—and its components with point-and-click operations.

The Server Explorer

Your starting point for developing database applications with VB.NET is the Server Explorer. This toolbox is your gateway to the databases on your system or network, and you can use it to locate and retrieve the tables you're interested in. Place the pointer over the Server Explorer tab to expand the corresponding toolbox, which looks something like the one shown in Figure 20.5. The two main objects in the Server Explorer are Data Connections and the Servers object. Under the Data Connections branch, you will see the connections to databases you're programming against. Under the Servers branch, you will see the database servers you can access from your computer and various objects they expose.

FIGURE 20.5

The Server Explorer contains the database objects you can access on your computer.

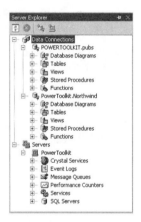

NOTE   *Note that the Server Explorer's tools are available even if no project is open at the time. These tools allow you to work with the objects of a database, and the actions you'll perform (like the design of a table) are not specific to a project.*

Right-click the Data Connections icon and, from the context menu, select the Add Connection command. You may also see one or more connections to your databases, if you have already created some. Every new connection you add remains under the Data Connections branch until you decide to remove it, and you can use it in any number of projects.

To add a new connection, select the Add Connection command and the Data Link Properties dialog box will pop up, as shown in Figure 20.6. In the Data Link Properties dialog box, specify a new connection to one of the databases on your system. First, you must select the database provider (basically, the driver you'll use to access the database). For the examples of this part of the book, I will use SQL Server databases.

FIGURE 20.6

The Provider and Connection tabs of the Data Link Properties window

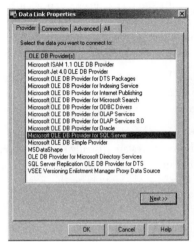
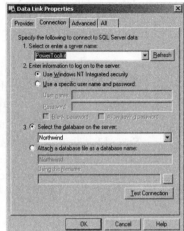

Then switch to the Connection tab. Here you must enter the User Name and Password in the appropriate boxes. If you (or the administrator) have set up SQL Server to use the Windows NT integrated security, just check the radio button named Use Windows NT Integrated Security. Then drop down the top list box to select one of the SQL Servers your computer can access. You will see the local SQL Server, as well as any other SQL Server on the network. Select the local SQL Server, then select the Northwind database in the second drop-down list on the dialog box. If SQL Server is running on the same computer as Visual Studio, you won't see the names of the servers, but the local one is selected by default.

If you have Access 2000 installed on your system, use the Microsoft Jet 4.0 OLE DB Provider. On the Connection tab, click the Test Connection button to make sure you can connect to the database. If not, make sure SQL Server is running and that the user name and password you specified are correct.

Click OK to close the Data Link Properties dialog box, and the name of the new connection will appear under the Data Connections branch of the tree in the Server Explorer window. The default name of the connection is made up of the name of the computer followed by the name of the database—for my server, `PowerToolkit.Northwind`—but you can change it. Right-click a connection and, from the context menu, select Rename.

Switch back to Server Explorer tab and expand the new connection. You will see the following entries under it:

Database Diagrams This is where you can examine the various diagrams of the database. A database diagram is a visual representation of a set of related tables, with the relations between the tables. Relations are indicated with line segments between two related tables, and you can quickly learn a lot about the structure of a database by looking at a database diagram.

Tables This is where you can select a table and edit it, or add a new table to the database. You can edit the table itself (change its design by adding/removing rows or change the data types of one or more columns). Finally, you can view the table's rows and edit them, add new rows, or delete existing rows.

Views   This is where you specify the various views you want to use in your applications. Sometimes, the tables are not the most convenient, or even the most expedient, method of looking at your data. If the database contains a table with employees and this table includes wages or other sensitive data, you can create a view that's identical to the table but excludes selected columns.

Views are created with SQL SELECT statements, which are discussed in detail later in this chapter. A SELECT statement basically allows you to specify the information you want to retrieve from the database. This information can be stored in a View object, which is just like another table to your application.

Stored Procedures   Stored procedures are (usually small) programs that are stored in the database and perform very specific, and often repeated, tasks. By coding many of the operations you want to perform against the database as stored procedures, you won't have to access the database directly. Moreover, you can call the same stored procedure from several places in your VB code, and you can be sure that the same action is performed every time. Once created, the stored procedure becomes part of the database, and programmers (as well as users) can call it by name, passing the appropriate arguments if necessary. A typical example is a stored procedure for removing orders. The stored procedure must remove the order details first, then remove the order (and possibly update the customer's balance, the stock, and so on). In general, orders shouldn't be removed from a database—they should be cancelled with another transaction—but with the fake orders people place to online stores, many developers allow the removal of orders.

Functions   The functions of SQL Server are just like the VB functions. They perform specific tasks on the database (retrieve or update data) taking into consideration the arguments passed to the functions when they were called. ADO.NET is built around SQL statements and stored procedures, so we're not going to discuss SQL Server functions in this book.

Working with Tables

Expand the Tables tree to see the list of tables in the Northwind database. If you right-click one of them, you will see the following (among other trivial options).

RETRIEVE DATA FROM TABLE

This command brings the entire table onto a grid. You can edit any row and even delete rows or add new ones. Figure 20.7 shows the data of the Customers table of the Northwind database in edit mode.

To experiment with tables, open the Categories table by double-clicking its name. Select a row by clicking the gray button in front of the row and then click the Delete button. First, you'll be warned that you're about to remove a row and that the action can't be undone. If you click Yes, the row should be removed. If you attempt to remove a row from the Categories table, however, you'll get the following warning:

```
DELETE statement conflicted with COLUMN REFERENCE constraint
'FK_Products_Categories'. The conflict occurred in database 'Northwind', table
'Products', column 'CategoryID'.
The statement has been terminated
```

FIGURE 20.7
Editing the Customers table in Visual Basic's IDE

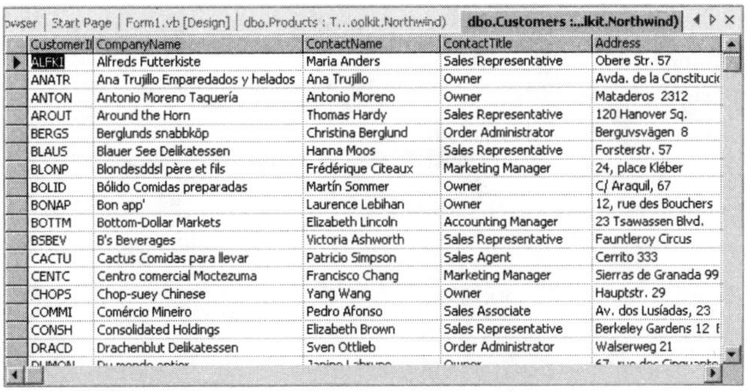

CustomerII	CompanyName	ContactName	ContactTitle	Address
ALFKI	Alfreds Futterkiste	Maria Anders	Sales Representative	Obere Str. 57
ANATR	Ana Trujillo Emparedados y helados	Ana Trujillo	Owner	Avda. de la Constitucio
ANTON	Antonio Moreno Taquería	Antonio Moreno	Owner	Mataderos 2312
AROUT	Around the Horn	Thomas Hardy	Sales Representative	120 Hanover Sq.
BERGS	Berglunds snabbköp	Christina Berglund	Order Administrator	Berguvsvägen 8
BLAUS	Blauer See Delikatessen	Hanna Moos	Sales Representative	Forsterstr. 57
BLONP	Blondesddsl père et fils	Frédérique Citeaux	Marketing Manager	24, place Kléber
BOLID	Bólido Comidas preparadas	Martín Sommer	Owner	C/ Araquil, 67
BONAP	Bon app'	Laurence Lebihan	Owner	12, rue des Bouchers
BOTTM	Bottom-Dollar Markets	Elizabeth Lincoln	Accounting Manager	23 Tsawassen Blvd.
BSBEV	B's Beverages	Victoria Ashworth	Sales Representative	Fauntleroy Circus
CACTU	Cactus Comidas para llevar	Patricio Simpson	Sales Agent	Cerrito 333
CENTC	Centro comercial Moctezuma	Francisco Chang	Marketing Manager	Sierras de Granada 99
CHOPS	Chop-suey Chinese	Yang Wang	Owner	Hauptstr. 29
COMMI	Comércio Mineiro	Pedro Afonso	Sales Associate	Av. dos Lusíadas, 23
CONSH	Consolidated Holdings	Elizabeth Brown	Sales Representative	Berkeley Gardens 12
DRACD	Drachenblut Delikatessen	Sven Ottlieb	Order Administrator	Walserweg 21

This simply means that there's a constraint in the database that will be violated if you remove this line. The constraint is between the Products and Categories tables. Each product belongs to a category, and if you remove this category, some of the products will be left without a category. Notice that this restriction is added to the database when it was designed—it's not SQL Server's idea to protect you from such mistakes. The designers of the Northwind database added the appropriate constraints, so that users won't violate the integrity of the database accidentally. As you will see, it's easy to add new constraints to a table and to protect the integrity of the database from mistakes of programmers and users alike.

If you attempt to delete a row from the Products table, you'll get a similar error, but this time the conflict is between the Products and Order Details tables. Each row in the Order Details table contains a product's ID, and if you were allowed to remove a product from the Products table, some invoices would reference nonexistent products.

However, you can delete rows from the Order Details table. Just write down the fields of the row you're deleting, so that you can add it later. You don't have to add the deleted row, but be aware that some of the queries in the following sections and chapters may not return the exact same rows as shown in this book. To delete a row, select it by clicking the gray button in the first column of the grid and then tap the Delete key.

To add a row, press Ctrl+End to go to the last line, place the cursor in the first cell of the row marked with an asterisk (this is the new row), and start typing. To move to the next cell, press Tab. To commit the new row to the database, move the pointer to another row. As long as you're editing a row, the icon with the pen appears in the first column of the grid. While this icon is displayed, the original row in the table hasn't changed yet. After you're done entering values, move the pointer to another row and the icon of the pen will disappear, indicating that the row has been successfully added. If the data are not consistent with the structure of the database, the changes will be aborted by the database. If you attempt to enter a new product with a CategoryID that doesn't exist in the Categories table, the new row will not be accepted. Likewise, if you attempt to create a new order for a nonexistent customer, the new row will also be rejected.

DESIGN TABLE

Close the table, return to the Server Explorer, right-click one of the tables, and this time select Design Table. The table's structure will appear on a grid, as shown in Figure 20.8. The first column contains the table's column names (the fields of each row).

FIGURE 20.8

The Customers table in design view

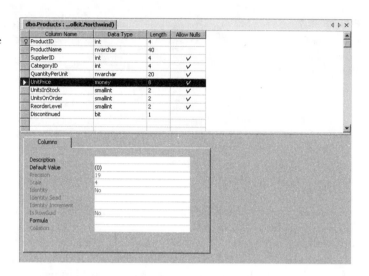

Each column has a name, a data type, and a length. To set the data type of a column, click the Date Type cell of a field. This cell is a ComboBox displaying all available data types. Drop down the list of data types and select the desired one. The most common data types are the char and varchar types, which store strings, and the numeric types, including the money data type. There's also a special field for storing dates and times. Basically, you can use all the data types available in VB and a few more data types that are unique to SQL Server. The difference between the char and varchar data types is that the char type stores strings of fixed length (the length is specified by the value in parentheses following the data type's name) and the varchar type stored strings of variable length. The value in parentheses is the maximum allowed length of the string for variable-length strings.

You can also set the Allow Nulls field to indicate whether a field may have no value. The Null value is a very special value in database programming. It's not the numeric zero and it's not an empty string. Null means that the field has no value. Thus, it can't be used in comparisons and you can't read its value. In the Customers table, for instance, neither the CustomerID nor the CompanyName fields may be Null. Any other field may be Null. When we enter a new customer, we may not know the address or the phone number. But we have to assign an ID to the customer that will make the new row unique in the entire table, and we must also specify the company's name.

The Northwind database uses five-letter keys to identify each customer. This is rather unusual, because we don't want to burden the user with the task of coming up with unique keys for each customer. This task can be left to the database, which is capable of providing a unique numeric value to each new row added to the table. Of course, the autogenerated fields are integers, but they're just as good (if not better). They uniquely identify a row in the table, and they're used to relate the rows of one table to the rows of another. Normally, user never look up customers by their ID.

In the lower section of the window, you see additional information about the selected field. Each field has a Description, a Default Value, and a Collation setting (the last setting applies to character fields only). The Description field holds information that will help programmers figure out the role of each field and is supplied by the database designer. The Default Value is a value that will be placed in this field automatically when a new row is added to the table. If most of the customers are in the U.S., you can set the Country's default value the string "US" (without the quotes) so that users will supply another value only for customers from another country. The Collation setting determines how the rows will be sorted, as well as how the database will search for values in the specific column. Normally, you set a collation sequence when you set up the database. You can specify a different sort order for a specific field by setting its Collation property. If you click the button with the ellipses next to the Collation setting, you'll see a large number of settings. The string "CS" and "CI" stand for *case-sensitive* and *case-insensitive*, respectively. Searches are usually case-insensitive, so that the argument "Mc Donald" will locate "MC Donald" and "Mc DONALD." The strings "AS" and "AI" stand for *accent-sensitive* and *accent-insensitive*; they're used with languages that recognize accent marks.

Numeric fields can be integers (data type int), big integers (data type bigint) and floating-point numbers (data type real), among others. As you can see, SQL Server's data types are not named after VB's data types, but they're mapped to the corresponding data types of Visual Basic. The bigint data type is the same as a long integer in VB.

Integer data types have an Identity property: in each table you can have one identity field, which is an integer value. This value is incremented by the DBMS every time a new row is added, and it's guaranteed to be unique. We use these fields as primary indices. The primary index is unique for each row and is used in establishing relations between tables. The actual value of no interest to users; they don't even have to see this field. All you really want is that the primary key in one row has the same value as the foreign key(s) in the related table(s).

NEW TABLE

This command adds a new table to the database. If you select it, you will see a grid like the one shown back in Figure 20.8, only all rows will be empty. You can start adding fields by specifying a name, a data type, and its Allow Nulls property. For the purposes of this book, I will assume that the database has already been designed for you. Designing databases is no trivial tasks, and programmers shouldn't be adding tables to simplify their code. We first organize our data into tables, create the tables, set up relations between them, and only then can we code against the database. It's not uncommon to add a table to an existing database at a later stage, but this reveals some flaw in the initial database design.

Notice that once you add a table to the database, you can't remove it through the Server Explorer. You must open the same database with the Enterprise Manager and delete it from there.

Relationships, Indices, and Constraints

To manipulate relationships, indices, and constraints, open one of the tables in design mode. Then right-click somewhere on the table and select Property Pages. There are four tabs on the property pages dialog box, one for each of the major objects of the database. The first tab, Tables, displays the name of the table you selected in the Server Explorer. Notice that you can't select a different table on this dialog box.

RELATIONSHIPS TAB

The second tab, Relationships, is where you can specify relationships between tables (Figure 20.9). Select the Property Pages of the Categories table and you will see that there is already a relationship between the Categories table and the Products table. The relationship is called FK_Products_Categories, and it relates the primary and foreign keys of the two tables (field CategoryID). The names of the two related tables appear in two read-only boxes. When you create a new relationship, you'll be able to select a table from a drop-down list. Under each table's name, you see a list of fields. Here you select the matching fields in the two tables. Most relationships are based on a single field, which is common to both tables. However, you can relate two tables on multiple fields (you may have to use relationships based on multiple fields in an accounting application). The check boxes at the bottom of the page specify how the DBMS will handle the relationship and are discussed shortly.

FIGURE 20.9

The Relationships tab on the table's property pages

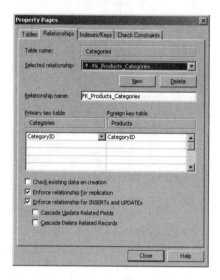

To create a new relationship with another table, click the New button. A new relationship will be added with a default name, which you can change. Like all other objects, relationships have unique names too.

Expand the Primary Key Table box and select the name of the table with the primary key in the relationship. Then expand the Foreign Key Table box and select the name of the other table. The relationship's name will change to reflect the selected tables. The default relationship names starts with the string "FK" (which stands for *foreign key*), followed by an underscore character and the name of the foreign table, followed by another underscore and the name of the primary table. You can change the relationship's name to anything you like.

If the relationship is based on a compound key, select all the fields that make up the primary and foreign keys, in the same order. At the bottom of the Properties window, you see a few options that you can set or clear:

Check existing data on creation If the existing data violate the relationship, the new relationship won't be established. You will have to fix the data and then attempt to establish the relationship again.

Enforce relationship for replication The relationship is enforced when the database is replicated.

Enforce relationship for INSERTs and UPDATEs   The relationship is enforced when you add new data or update existing data. If you attempt to add data that violate the relationship, the new data (or the update) will be rejected. SQL Server won't let you enter data that violate the relationship between two tables, and this option should be checked (except for rare occasions).

Cascade update related fields   When you change the primary key in one table, some rows of a related table will be left with an invalid foreign key. If you change the ID of a publisher, for example, all the titles that pointed to this publisher will become invalid after you change the publisher's ID. If this option is checked, SQL Server will change the foreign key of the related tables as well.

Cascade delete related records   When you delete the primary key in one table, some rows of a related table will be left with an invalid foreign key. If you delete a publisher, for example, all the titles that pointed to this publisher will become invalid after the deletion of the publisher. If this option is checked, SQL Server will delete all the rows of the related table(s) with the same foreign key.

You can also establish a relationship between two tables on the database diagram with point-and-click operations. Figure 20.2 shows a database diagram that relates the Products table to the Suppliers table. With the database diagram, you can easily visualize how the tables are organized in the database. Relationships are depicted as lines connecting two tables, and you can easily figure out which is the primary table (the line that connects the two tables has the symbol of a key to the end of the primary table) and which is the foreign table (the same line has the infinity symbol at the foreign table).

The Northwind database doesn't include any database diagrams, so you must create one. To add a diagram to a database, right-click the Diagrams item and, from the context menu, select New Diagram. You can do the same in the Enterprise Manager, if you prefer.

As soon as you select the New Diagram command, you'll be prompted to select the names of the tables to be added to the diagram through the Add Table dialog box. Select the first table you want to add to the diagram and click the Add button. Repeat the same process for all the tables you want to include in the diagram, and then click the Close button. A very simple diagram could include the Products, Categories, and Suppliers tables. The first two tables are related through the CategoryID field, and the latter two through the SupplierID field. Select the three tables and click the Add button to add them to the diagram. On the next screen, click the Close button to close the dialog.

This will create a new diagram and place the links between the tables. All you have to do is rearrange the tables a little on the diagram pane, so that you can easily visualize them, along with their relationships. Since the relationships between the tables exist already, it will also draw the lines between the tables. Each table on the diagram is represented by a box that contains all the fields in the corresponding table. Primary key fields are marked with the symbol of a key. Figure 20.10 shows how a database diagram depicts the relationship between the Products & Categories tables and the relationship between the Products & Suppliers tables. Close the Database Diagram window and you'll be prompted to enter a name for the diagram (name it Products).

FIGURE 20.10

A database diagram created with SQL Server's Enterprise Manager

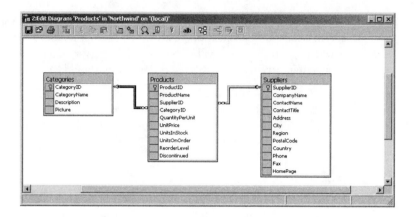

The most common relationships are *one-to-many* relationships, just like the ones shown in Figure 20.10. They're called one-to-many because each primary key may appear in multiple rows of the foreign table. Each category ID appears in multiple rows of the Products table. Likewise, each supplier's ID may also appear in multiple rows of the Products table—but a primary key is unique in its table.

To view or edit the details of a relationship, right-click the line that represents the relationship and you will see the following commands:

Delete relationship from database   This command removes the relationship between the two tables.

Property Pages   This command will bring up the property pages of the primary table, where you can specify additional relationships or constraints.

Earlier in this chapter, you saw that you couldn't remove a row from the Categories table, because this action conflicted with the FK_Products_Categories constraint. If you open the first diagram you created in this section and examine the properties of the relation between the Product and Categories tables, you'll see that its name is FK_Products_Categories and that the relation is enforced. If you want to be able to delete Categories, you must delete all the products that are connected to the specific category first. SQL Server can take care of deleting the related rows for you, if you check Cascade Delete Related Records. This is a rather dangerous practice, and you shouldn't check it without good reason. For the case of the Products table, you shouldn't enable cascade deletions. The products are also linked to the Order Details table, which means that the corresponding detail lines would also disappear from the database. Allowing cascade deletion in a database like Northwind will result in loss of valuable information irrevocably.

There are other situations where cascade deletion is not such a critical issue. You can enable cascade deletions in the Pubs database, for instance, so that each time you delete a title, the corresponding rows in the TitleAuthor table will also be removed. When you delete a book, you obviously don't need any information about this book in the TitleAuthor table. If you insert the same book into the database again, you may use a different ID and the old links to the Authors table will not work—you'll have to link the new title to its author(s) again anyway.

INDEXES/KEYS TAB

You've created a few tables and have actually entered some data into them. Now the most important thing you can do with a database is extract data from it (or else, why store the information in the first place?). We rarely browse the rows of a single table. Instead, we're interested in summary information that will help us make business decisions. We need answers to questions like "What's the most popular product in California?" or "What month has the largest sales for a specific product?" To retrieve this type of information, you must combine multiple tables. To answer the first question, you must locate all the customers in California, retrieve their orders, sum the quantities of the items they have purchased, and then select the product with the largest sum of quantities. As you can guess, a DBMS must be able to scan the tables and locate the desired rows quickly.

Computers use a special technique, called *indexing*, to locate information very quickly. This technique requires that the data be maintained in some order. The indexed rows need not be in a specific physical order, as long as we can retrieve them in a specific order. If you want to retrieve the name of the category of a specific product, the rows of the Categories table must be ordered according to the CategoryID field. This is the value that links each row in the Products table to the corresponding row in the Categories table. The DBMS will retrieve the CategoryID field of a specific product, and then it will instantly locate the matching row in the Categories table, because the rows of this table are indexed according to their CategoryID field.

Fortunately, you don't have to maintain the rows of the tables in any order yourself. The DBMS does it for you. You simply specify that a table be maintained in a specific order according to a column's value, and the DBMS will take over. The DBMS can maintain multiple indexes for the same table. You may wish to search the products by name and supplier. It's customary to search for a customer by name, city, postal code, country, and so on. To speed up the searches, you can maintain an index for each field you want to search on.

Indexes are manipulated by the DBMS; all you have to do is define them. Every time a new row is added or an existing row is deleted or edited, the table's indexes are automatically updated. You can use the index at any time to locate rows very quickly. Practically, indexes allow you to select a row based on an indexed field instantly. When searching for specific rows, the DBMS will take into consideration automatically any index that can speed the search.

Figure 20.11 shows the properties of the PK_Categories index of the Categories table. This index is based on the column CategoryID of the table, and it maintains the rows of the Categories table in ascending order according to their ID. The prefix PK stands for *primary key*. To specify that an index is also the table's primary key, you must check the option Create Unique. You can create as many indices as necessary for each table, but only one of them can be the primary key. The Create Unique box in Figure 20.11 is disabled, because the primary key is involved in one or more relationships—therefore, you can't change the table's primary key because you'll break some of the existing relationships with other tables. To create a new index, click the New button, specify the column on which the new index will be based, and then enter a name for the new index (or accept the default one). You can create an index that uses multiple fields, but there are no multifield indices in the sample databases.

FIGURE 20.11

The Indexes/Keys tab of the property pages

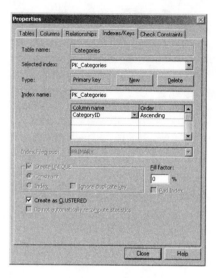

CHECK CONSTRAINTS TAB

A *constraint* is another important object of a database. The entity represented by a field may be subject to physical constraints. The Discount field, for example, should be a positive value no greater than 1 (or 100, depending on how you want to store it). Prices are also positive values. Other fields are subject to more complicated constraints. The DBMS can make sure that the values assigned to those fields do not violate the constraints. Otherwise, you'd have to make sure that all the applications that access the same fields conform to the physical constraints.

FIGURE 20.12

The Check Constraints tab of the property pages

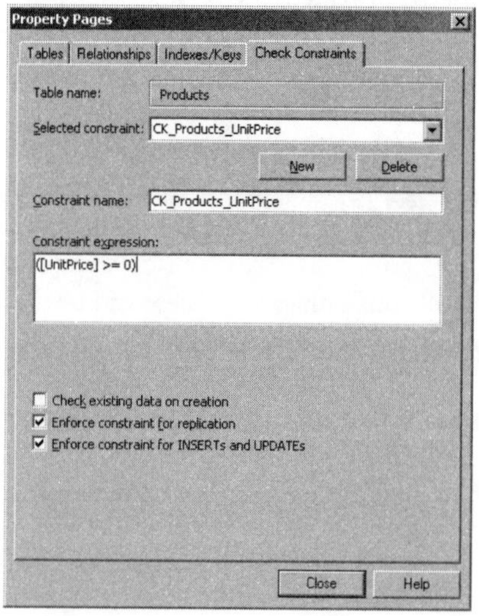

To make a constraint part of the database, open the table that contains the field on which you want to impose a constraint, in design view. Then right-click somewhere on the table and select Property Pages. On the dialog box that appears, select the Check Constraints tab, as shown in Figure 20.12. This figure shows one of the constraints of the Products table. To view another constraint, expand the Selected Constraint drop-down list and select the name of another constraint. The names of the constraints start with the CK prefix, followed by an underscore, the name of the table, then another underscore and finally the name of the field on which the constraint applies. The CK_Products_UnitPrice constraint is the expression that appears in the Constraint Expression box: the UnitPrice field must be positive. Constraints have a syntax similar to the syntax of SQL restrictions (I'll get into SQL in the following section) and are quite trivial.

So far, you should have a good idea about how databases are organized, what the relationships are for, and why they're so critical for the integrity of the data stored in the tables. Now we're going to look at ways to retrieve data from a database. To specify the rows and columns you want to retrieve from one or more tables, you must use SQL statements, which is the topic of the following section.

NOTE *There are visual tools for specifying the information you want to retrieve from a database, and these are the tools of choice for many developers. The visual tools are nothing more than a user-friendly interface for specifying SQL statements. In the background, they generate the appropriate SQL statement, and you will get the most out of these tools if you understand the basics of SQL. I will start with an overview of SQL; after that I'll show you how to use the Query Builder utility to specify a few advanced queries.*

Structured Query Language

SQL (Structured Query Language) is a universal language for manipulating tables, and every database management system (DBMS) supports it, so you should invest the time and effort to learn it. You can generate SQL statements with point-and-click operations (the Query Builder is a visual tool for generating SQL statements), but this is no substitute for understanding SQL and writing your own statements.

SQL is a *nonprocedural* language. This means that SQL doesn't provide traditional programming structures like IF statements or loops. Instead, it's a language for specifying the operation you want to perform at an unusually high level. The details of the implementation are left to the DBMS. This is good news for nonprogrammers, but many programmers new to SQL wish it had the structure of a more traditional language. You will get used to SQL and soon be able to combine the best of both worlds: the programming model of VB and the simplicity of SQL.

TIP *SQL is not case-sensitive, but it's customary to use uppercase for the SQL statements and keywords. In the examples of this book, I use uppercase for SQL statements.*

To retrieve all the company names from the Customers table of the Northwind database, you issue a statement like this one:

```
SELECT CompanyName
FROM Customers
```

If the Customers table happens to have multiple rows that refer to the same company, you can request that the query return unique names by using the DISTINCT keyword:

```
SELECT DISTINCT CompanyName
FROM Customers
```

To select customers from a specific country, you issue the following statement:

```
SELECT CompanyName
FROM Customers
WHERE Country = 'Germany'
```

The DBMS will retrieve and return the rows you requested. As you can see, this is not how you'd retrieve rows with Visual Basic. With a procedural language, like VB, you'd have to specify the statements to scan the entire table, examine the value of the Country column, and either select or reject the row. Then you would display the selected rows. With SQL you don't have to specify how the selection operation will take place. You simply specify *what* you want the database to do for you—not *how* to do it.

SQL statements are categorized into two major categories, which are actually considered separate languages: the statements for manipulating the data, which form the Data Manipulation Language (DML); and the statements for defining database objects, such as tables or their indexes, which form the Data Definition Language (DDL). The DDL is not of interest to every database developer, and we will not discuss it in this book. The DML is covered in depth, because you'll use these statements to retrieve data, insert new data to the database, and edit or delete existing data.

The statements of the DML part of the SQL language are also known as *queries*, and there are two types of queries: selection queries and action queries. *Selection queries* retrieve information from the database. The queries return a set of rows with identical structure. The columns may come from different tables, but all the rows returned by the query have the same number of columns. *Action queries* modify the database's objects, or create new objects and add them to the database (new tables, relationships and so on).

Executing SQL Statements

If you are not familiar with SQL, I suggest that you follow the examples in this chapter and modify them to perform similar operations. To follow these examples, you have two options, the Query Analyzer and the Query Builder. The Query Analyzer executes SQL statements you design. The Query Builder lets you build the statements with visual tools. After a quick overview of the SQL statements, I will describe the Query Builder and show you how to use its interface to build fairly elaborate queries.

USING THE QUERY ANALYZER

One of the applications installed with SQL Server is the Query Analyzer. To start it, select Start ➢ Programs ➢ SQL Server ➢ Query Analyzer. Initially, its window will be empty. First, select the desired database's name in the Database drop-down list and then enter the SQL statement you want to execute in the upper pane. The SQL statement will be executed against the selected database when you press Ctrl+E, or click the Run button (the button with the green arrow on the toolbar).

Alternatively, you can prefix the SQL statement with the USE statement, which specifies the database against which the statement will be executed. To retrieve all the Northwind customers located in Germany, enter this statement:

```
USE Northwind
SELECT CompanyName FROM Customers
WHERE Country = 'Germany'
```

The USE statement isn't part of the query; it simply tells the Query Analyzer the database against which it must execute the query. I'm including the USE statement with all the queries so that you know the database used for each example. Then select the Execute command from the Query menu, or press Ctrl+E to execute the statement. The results will appear in the lower pane, as shown in Figure 20.13. For a selection query, like the previous one, you will see the rows selected and their count at the bottom of the Results pane. An action query that updates a table (adds a new row, edits, or deletes an existing row) doesn't return any rows; it simply displays the number of rows affected.

FIGURE 20.13

Executing queries with the Query Analyzer

To execute another query, enter another statement in the upper pane or edit the previous statement, and press Ctrl+E again. You can also save SQL statements into files, so that you won't have to type them again. To do so, open the File menu, select Save As or Save command, and enter the name of the file where the contents of the Query pane will be stored. The statement will be stored in a text file with the extension .sql. The lengthier examples of this chapter can be found in this chapter's folder on the companion CD. Instead of typing the statements of the examples, you can load the corresponding SQL file from the CD and execute it.

Selection Queries

We'll start our discussion of SQL with the SELECT statement. Once you learn how to express the criteria for selecting the desired rows with the SELECT statement, you'll be able to apply this information to other data-manipulation statements.

The simplest form of the SELECT statement is

```
SELECT fields
FROM tables
```

where *fields* and *tables* are comma-separated lists of the fields you want to retrieve from the database and the tables they belong to. To select the contact information from all the companies in the Customers table, use this statement:

```
USE Northwind
SELECT CompanyName, ContactName, ContactTitle
FROM Customers
```

To retrieve all the fields, use the asterisk (*) or the ALL keyword. The statement

```
SELECT * FROM Customers
```

will select all the fields from the Customers table.

WHERE CLAUSE

The unconditional form of the SELECT statement we used in last few examples is quite trivial. You rarely retrieve data from all rows in a table. Usually you specify criteria, such as "All companies in Germany," "All customers who have placed three or more orders in the last six months," or even more complicated expressions. To restrict the rows returned by the query, use the WHERE clause of the SELECT statement. The most common form of the SELECT statement is the following:

```
SELECT fields
FROM tables
WHERE condition
```

The *fields* and *tables* arguments are the same as before. The syntax of the WHERE clause can get quite complicated, so we'll start with the simpler forms of the selection criteria.

The *condition* argument can be a relational expression, like the ones you use in VB. To select all the customers from Germany, use the following condition:

```
WHERE Country = 'Germany'
```

To select customers from multiple countries, use the OR operator to combine multiple conditions:

```
WHERE Country = 'Germany' OR
      Country = 'Austria'
```

You can also combine multiple conditions with the AND operator.

It is also possible to retrieve data from two or more tables with a single statement (this is the most common type of query, actually). When you combine multiple tables in a query, you can use the WHERE clause to specify how the rows of the two tables will be combined. Let's say you want a list of all product names, along with their categories. The information you need is not contained in a single table. You must extract the product name from the Products table and the category name from the Categories table and specify that the ProductID field in the two tables must match. The statement

```
USE Northwind
SELECT ProductName, CategoryName
FROM Products, Categories
WHERE Products.CategoryID = Categories.CategoryID
```

will retrieve the names of all products, along with their category names. Here's how this statement is executed. For each row in the Products table, the SQL engine locates the matching row in the Categories table and then appends the ProductName and CategoryName fields to the result.

If a product has no category, then it will not be included in the result. If you want all the products, even the ones that don't belong to a category, you must use the JOIN clause, which is described later in this chapter. Using the WHERE clause to combine rows from multiple tables may lead to unexpected results, because it can only combine rows with matching fields. If the foreign key in the Products table is Null, this product won't be selected. This is a fine point in combining multiple tables, and many programmers abuse the WHERE clause. As a result, they retrieve fewer rows from the database, and they don't even know it. See the section "SQL Joins" later in this chapter for more information.

NOTE *When fields in two different tables have the same names, you must prefix them with the table's name to remove the ambiguity. Also, some field names may contain spaces. These field names must appear in square brackets. The Publishers table of the Pubs sample database contains a field named Publisher Name. To use this field in a query, enclose it in brackets:* Publishers.[Publisher Name]. *The table prefix is optional (no other table contains a column by that name), but the brackets are mandatory.*

You can also combine multiple restrictions with logical operators. To retrieve all the titles published by a specific publisher, use a statement like the following:

```
USE PUBS
SELECT titles.title
FROM titles, publishers
WHERE titles.pub_id = publishers.pub_id AND publishers.pub_name = 'New Moon Books'
```

This statement combines two tables and selects the titles of a publisher specified by name. To match titles and publisher, it requests that

1. The publisher's name in the Publishers table is *New Moon Books*, and

2. The *pub_id* field in the Titles table matches the *pub_id* field in the Publishers table.

Notice that we did not specify the publisher's name (field *pub_name*) in the SELECT list; all the desired books have the same publisher, so we need not include the publisher's names in the result set.

KNOWING WHERE YOU'RE GOING

If you specify multiple tables without the WHERE clause, the SQL statement, will return an enormous cursor. If you issue the following statement,

```
SELECT ProductName, CategoryName FROM Categories, Products
```

you will not get a line for each product name followed by its category. You will get a cursor with 616 rows, which are all possible combinations of product names and category names. In this example, the Categories table has eight rows and the Products table has 77 rows, so their cross-product contains 616 rows.

AS KEYWORD

By default, each column of a query is labeled after the actual field name in the output. If a table contains two fields named CustLName and CustFName, you can display them with different labels using the AS keyword. The SELECT statement

```
SELECT CustLName, CustFName
```

will produce two columns labeled CustLName and CustFName. The query's output will look much better if you change the labels of these two columns with a statement like the following one:

```
SELECT CustLName AS [Last Name],
       CustFName AS [First Name]
```

It is also possible to concatenate two fields in the SELECT list with the concatenation operator. Concatenated fields are not labeled automatically, so you must supply your own header for the combined field. The following statement creates a single column for the customer's name and labels it *Customer Name*:

```
SELECT CustFName + ', ' + CustLName AS [Customer Name]
```

TOP KEYWORD

Some queries may retrieve a large number of rows, while you're interested in the top few rows only. The TOP N keyword allows you to select the first *N* rows and ignore the remaining ones. Let's say you want to see the list of the 10 most wanted products. Without the TOP keyword, you'd have to calculate how many items from each product have been sold, sort them according to items sold, and examine the first 10 rows returned by the query.

The TOP keyword is used only when the rows are ordered according to some meaningful criteria. Limiting a query's output to the alphabetically top *N* rows isn't very practical. When the rows are sorted according to items sold, revenue generated, and so on, it makes sense to limit the query's output to *N* rows. You'll see many examples of the TOP keyword later in this chapter, after you learn how to order a query's rows.

DISTINCT KEYWORD

The DISTINCT keyword eliminates any duplicates from the cursor retrieved by the SELECT statement. Let's say you want a list of all countries with at least one customer. If you retrieve all country names from the Customers table, you'll end up with many duplicates. To eliminate them, use the DISTINCT keyword, as shown in the following statement:

```
USE NORTHWIND
SELECT DISTINCT Country
FROM Customers
```

LIKE OPERATOR

The LIKE operator uses pattern-matching characters, like the ones you use to select multiple files in DOS. The LIKE operator recognizes several pattern-matching characters (or *wildcard* characters) to match one or more characters, numeric digits, ranges of letters, and so on; these are listed in Table 20.1.

TABLE 20.1: SQL WILDCARD CHARACTERS

WILDCARD CHARACTER	DESCRIPTION
%	Matches any number of characters. The pattern program% will find program, programming, programmer, and so on. The pattern %program% will locate strings that contain the words *program, programming, nonprogrammer,* and so on.
_	(Underscore character) Matches any single alphabetic character. The pattern b_y will find *boy* and *bay,* but not *boysenberry.*
[ ]	Matches any single character within the brackets. The pattern Santa [YI]nez will find both *Santa Ynez* and *Santa Inez.*
[^]	Matches any character not in the brackets. The pattern %q[^u]% will find words that contain the character *q* not followed by *u* (they are misspelled words).
[-]	Matches any one of a range of characters. The characters must be consecutive in the alphabet and specified in ascending order (A to Z, not Z to A). The pattern [a-c]% will find all words that begin with *a, b,* or *c* (in lowercase or uppercase).
#	Matches any single numeric character. The pattern D1## will find *D100* and *D139,* but not *D1000* or *D10.*

You can use the LIKE operator to retrieve all titles about Windows from the Pubs database, with a statement like the following one:

```
USE PUBS
SELECT titles.title
FROM titles
WHERE titles.title LIKE '%WINDOWS%'
```

The percent signs mean that any character(s) may appear in front of or after the word *Windows* in the title.

To include a wildcard character itself in your search argument, enclose it in square brackets. The pattern %50[%]% will match any field that contains the string "50%".

NULL VALUES

A very common operation in manipulating and maintaining databases is to locate Null values in fields. The expressions IS NULL and IS NOT NULL find field values that are (or are not) Null. A zero-length string is not the same as a Null field. To locate the rows which have a Null value in their CompanyName column, use the following WHERE clause:

```
WHERE CompanyName IS NULL
```

A Null price in the Products table means that the product's price was not available at the time of the data entry. You can easily locate the products without prices and edit them. The following statement will locate products without prices:

```
USE NORTHWIND
SELECT * FROM Products WHERE UnitPrice IS NULL
```

Certain fields can't be Null in a table. The primary key, for example, can't be Null. It also doesn't make sense to enter a new customer without a name, or a book without a title. When you design the database, you can request that certain columns can't be Null; the DBMS will ensure that no row with a Null value in these columns will be added to the table.

ORDER KEYWORD

The rows of a query are not in any particular order. To request that the rows be returned in a specific order, use the ORDER BY clause, whose syntax is

```
ORDER BY col1, col2, . . .
```

You can specify any number of columns in the ORDER list. The output of the query is ordered according to the values of the first column (col1). If two rows have identical values in this column, then they are sorted according to the second column, and so on. The statement

```
USE NORTHWIND
SELECT CompanyName, ContactName
FROM Customers
ORDER BY Country, City
```

will display the customers ordered by country and by city within each country.

Calculated Fields

In addition to column names, you can specify calculated columns in the SELECT statement. The Order Details table contains a row for each invoice line. Invoice #10248, for instance, contains four lines (four items sold), and each detail line appears in a separate row in the Order Details table. Each row holds the number of items sold, the item's price, and the corresponding discount. To display the line's subtotal, you must multiply the quantity by the price minus the discount, as shown in the following statement:

```
USE NORTHWIND
SELECT Orders.OrderID, ProductID,
       [Order Details].UnitPrice * [Order Details].Quantity *
          (1 - [Order Details].Discount) AS SubTotal
FROM   Orders, [Order Details]
WHERE  Orders.OrderID = [Order Details].OrderID
```

This statement will calculate the subtotal for each line in the invoices issued to all Northwind customers and display them along with the order number, as shown in Figure 20.14. The order numbers are repeated as many times as there are products in the order (or lines in the invoice). In the following section, "Totaling and Counting," you will find out how to calculate totals, too.

FIGURE 20.14

Calculating the subtotals for each item sold

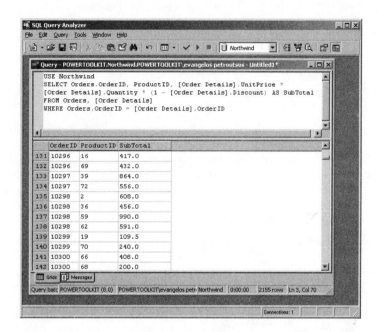

NOTE   *Long lines in a SQL statement can be broken anywhere, and there's no need to insert a line-continuation charac-ter, as you do with VB statements.*

TIP   *You can shorten the preceding SQL statement by omitting the table name qualifier for the ProductID, Quantity, and UnitPrice fields, since their names do not appear in any other table. You can't omit the table qualifier from the OrderID field's name, because it appears in both tables involved in the query.*

TOTALING AND COUNTING

SQL supports some aggregate functions, which act on selected fields of all the rows returned by the query. The aggregate functions, listed in Table 20.2, perform basic calculations like summing, counting, and averaging numeric values. Aggregate functions accept field names (or calculated fields) as arguments, and they return a single value, which is the sum (or average) of all values.

TABLE 20.2: SQL'S AGGREGATE FUNCTIONS

FUNCTION	RETURNS
COUNT()	The number (count) of values in a specified column
SUM()	The sum of values in a specified column
AVG()	The average of the values in a specified column
MIN()	The smallest value in a specified column
MAX()	The largest value in a specified column

These functions operate on a single column (which could be a calculated column) and return a single value. The rows involved in the calculations are specified with the proper WHERE clause. The SUM() and AVG() functions can process only numeric values. The other three functions can process both numeric and text values.

These functions are used to summarize data from one or more tables. Let's say we want to know how many of the Northwind database customers are located in Germany. The following SQL statement will return the desired value:

```
USE NORTHWIND
SELECT COUNT(CustomerID)
FROM Customers
WHERE Country = 'Germany'
```

This is a simple demonstration of the COUNT() function. If you want to count unique values, you must use the DISTINCT keyword along with the name of the field to count. If you want to find out in how many countries there are Northwind customers, use the following SQL statement:

```
USE NORTHWIND
SELECT COUNT(DISTINCT Country)
FROM Customers
```

If you omit the DISTINCT keyword, the statement will return the number of rows that have a Country field. The aggregate functions ignores the Null values, unless you specify the * argument. The following statement will return the count of all rows in the Customers table, even if some of them have a Null in the Country column:

```
USE NORTHWIND
SELECT COUNT(*)
FROM Customers
```

The SUM() function is used to total the values of a specific field in the specified rows. To find out how many units of the product with ID = 11 (Queso Cabrales) have been sold, use the following statement:

```
USE NORTHWIND
SELECT SUM(Quantity)
```

```
FROM [Order Details]
WHERE ProductID = 11
```

The SQL statement that returns the total revenue generated by a single product is a bit more complicated. To calculate it, you must add the products of quantities times prices, taking into consideration each invoice's discount:

```
USE NORTHWIND
SELECT SUM(Quantity * UnitPrice * (1 - Discount))
FROM [Order Details]
WHERE ProductID = 11
```

You will find out that Queso Cabrales generated a total revenue of $12,901.77. If you want to know how many items of this product were sold, add one more aggregate function to the query to sum the quantities of each row that refers to the specific product ID:

```
USE NORTHWIND
SELECT SUM(Quantity),
       SUM(Quantity * UnitPrice * (1 - Discount))
FROM   [Order Details]
WHERE  ProductID = 11
```

SQL Joins

Joins specify how you connect multiple tables in a query, and there are four types of joins:

- Left outer, or left join

- Right outer, or right join

- Full outer, or full join

- Inner join

A *join* operation combines all the rows of one table with the rows of another table. Joins are usually followed by a condition, which determines which records in either side of the join will appear in the result. The WHERE clause of the SELECT statement is very similar to a join, but there some fine points that will be explained momentarily.

NOTE   *The left, right, and full joins are sometimes called "outer" joins to differentiate them from an inner join. "Left join" and "left outer join" mean the same thing.*

LEFT JOINS

This join displays all the records in the left table and only those records of the table on the right that match certain user-supplied criteria. This join has the following syntax:

```
FROM (primary table) LEFT JOIN (secondary table) ON (primary table).(field)
(comparison) (secondary table).(field)
```

The left outer join retrieves all rows in the primary table and the matching rows from a secondary table. The following statement will retrieve all the titles from the Pubs database along with their publisher. If some titles have no publisher, they will be included to the result:

```
USE PUBS
SELECT  title, pub_name
FROM    titles LEFT JOIN publishers
            ON titles.pub_id = publishers.pub_id
```

RIGHT JOINS

This join is similar to the left outer join, except that all rows in the table on the right are displayed and only the matching rows from the left table are displayed. This join has the following syntax:

```
FROM (secondary table) RIGHT JOIN (primary table) ON (secondary table).(field)
(comparison) (primary table).(field)
```

The following statement retrieves all the publishers from the Pubs database along with their titles. Notice that this statement is almost exactly the same as the example of the left outer join entry; I only changed LEFT to RIGHT:

```
USE PUBS
SELECT  title, pub_name
FROM    titles RIGHT JOIN publishers
            ON titles.pub_id = publishers.pub_id
```

FULL JOINS

The full join returns all the rows of the two tables, regardless of whether there are matching rows or not. In effect, it's a combination of left and right joins. To retrieve all the titles and all publishers, and match publishers to their titles, use the following join:

```
USE PUBS
SELECT  title, pub_name
FROM    titles FULL JOIN publishers
            ON titles.pub_id = publishers.pub_id
```

INNER JOINS

This join returns the matching rows of both tables, similar to the WHERE clause, and has the following syntax:

```
FROM (primary table) INNER JOIN (secondary table) ON (primary table).(field)
(comparison) (secondary table).(field)
```

The following SQL statement combines records from the Titles and Publishers tables of the PUBS database if their PubID fields match. It returns all the titles and their publishers. Titles without publishers will not be included in the result:

```
USE PUBS
SELECT titles.title, publishers.pub_name FROM titles, publishers
WHERE titles.pub_id = publishers.pub_id
```

You can retrieve the same rows using an inner join, as follows:

```
USE PUBS
SELECT titles.title, publishers.pub_name
FROM titles INNER JOIN publishers ON titles.pub_id = publishers.pub_id
```

For more examples with joins, see the section "Specifying Left, Right, and Inner Joins," later in this chapter.

GROUPING ROWS

Sometimes you need to group the results of a query, so that you can calculate subtotals. Let's say you need not only the total revenues generated by a single product, but a list of all products and the revenues they generated. The example of the previous section "Totaling and Counting" calculates the total revenue generated by a single product. If you omit the WHERE clause, it will calculate the total revenue generated by all products. It is possible to use the SUM() function to break the calculations at each new product ID as demonstrated in the following statement. To do so, you must group the product IDs together with the GROUP BY clause.

```
USE NORTHWIND
SELECT    ProductID,
          SUM(Quantity * UnitPrice *(1 - Discount)) AS [Total Revenues]
FROM      [Order Details]
GROUP BY ProductID
ORDER BY ProductID
```

The above statement will produce an output like this one:

ProductID	Total Revenues
1	12788.10
2	16355.96
3	3044.0
4	8567.89
5	5347.20
6	7137.0
7	22044.29

As you can see, the SUM() function works in tandem with the GROUP BY clause (when there is one) to produce subtotals. The GROUP BY clause groups all the rows with the same values in the specified column and forces the aggregate functions to act on each group separately. SQL Server will sort the rows according to the column specified in the GROUP BY clause and start calculating the aggregate functions. Every time it runs into a new group, it prints the result and resets the aggregate function(s).

If you use the GROUP BY clause in a SQL statement, you must be aware of the following rule:

All the fields included in the SELECT list must be either part of an aggregate function or part of the GROUP BY clause.

Let's say you want to change the previous statement to display the names of the products, rather than their IDs. The following statement will display product names, instead of product IDs. Notice that the ProductName field doesn't appear as an argument to an aggregate function, so it must be part of the GROUP BY clause.

```
USE NORTHWIND
SELECT    ProductName,
          SUM(Quantity * [Order Details].UnitPrice * (1 - Discount))
             AS [Total Revenues]
FROM      [Order Details], Products
WHERE     Products.ProductID = [Order Details].ProductID
GROUP BY ProductName
ORDER BY ProductName
```

These are the first few lines of the output produced by this statement:

ProductName	Total Revenues
Alice Mutton	32698.38
Aniseed Syrup	3044.0
Boston Crab Meat	17910.63
Camembert Pierrot	46927.48
Carnarvon Tigers	29171.87

If you omit the GROUP BY clause, the query will return the total revenue generated by all the products in the database.

You can also combine multiple aggregate functions in the SELECT field. The following statement will calculate the units of products sold, along with the revenue they generated and the number of invoices that contain the specific product:

```
USE NORTHWIND
SELECT    ProductID AS PRODUCT,
          COUNT(ProductID) AS [INVOICES],
          SUM(Quantity) AS [UNITS SOLD],
          SUM(Quantity * UnitPrice *(1 - Discount)) AS Revenue
FROM      [Order Details]
GROUP BY ProductID
ORDER BY ProductID
```

The following SELECT statement returns all product IDs along with the number of invoices that contain them, and the minimum, maximum, and average quantity ordered:

```
USE NORTHWIND
SELECT    ProductID AS PRODUCT,
          COUNT(ProductID) AS [Invoices],
          MIN(Quantity) AS [Min],
          MAX(Quantity) AS [Max],
          AVG(Quantity) AS [Average]
FROM      [Order Details]
GROUP BY ProductID
ORDER BY ProductID
```

Limiting Groups with HAVING

The HAVING clause limits the groups that will appear in the cursor. In a way, it is similar to the WHERE clause, but the HAVING clause allows you to use aggregate functions. The following statement will return the IDs of the products whose sales exceed 1,000 units:

```
USE NORTHWIND
SELECT ProductID, SUM(Quantity)
FROM [Order Details]
GROUP BY ProductID
HAVING SUM(Quantity) > 1000
```

If you want to include regular restrictions, you can use the WHERE clause as well. To see product names instead of IDs, add a slightly longer statement that includes the Products table and maps them to the ProductIDs in the Order Details table with a WHERE clause:

```
USE NORTHWIND
SELECT     Products.ProductName,
           [Order Details].ProductID,
           SUM(Quantity) AS [Items Sold]
FROM       Products, [Order Details]
WHERE      [Order Details].ProductID = Products.ProductID
GROUP BY   [Order Details].ProductID, Products.ProductName
HAVING     SUM(Quantity) > 1000
ORDER BY   Products.ProductName
```

IN and NOT IN Keywords

The IN and NOT IN keywords are used in a WHERE clause to specify a list of values that a column must match (or not match). They are more of a shorthand notation for multiple OR operators. The following is statement that retrieves the names of the customers in all German-speaking countries:

```
USE NORTHWIND
SELECT CompanyName
FROM Customers
WHERE Country IN ('Germany', 'Austria', 'Switzerland')
```

The BETWEEN Keyword

The BETWEEN keyword lets you specify a range of values and limit the selection to the rows that have a specific column in this range. The BETWEEN keyword is a shorthand notation for an expression like

```
column >= minValue AND column <= maxValue
```

To retrieve the orders placed in 1997, use the following statement:

```
USE NORTHWIND
SELECT OrderID, OrderDate, CompanyName
FROM   Orders, Customers
WHERE  Orders.CustomerID = Customers.CustomerID AND
       (OrderDate BETWEEN '1/1/1997' AND '1/1/1998')
```

Action Queries

In addition to the selection queries we examined so far, you can also execute queries that alter the data in the database's tables. These queries are called *action queries*, and they're quite simple compared to the selection queries. There are three types of actions you can perform against a database: insertions of new rows, deletions of existing rows, and updates (edits) of existing rows. For each type of action there's a SQL statement, appropriately named INSERT, DELETE, and UPDATE. Their syntax is very simple, and the only complication is how you specify the affected rows (for deletions and updates). As you can guess, the rows to be affected are specified with a WHERE clause, followed by the criteria we have discussed in selection queries.

The first difference between action and selection queries is that action queries don't return any rows. They return the number of rows affected, but you disable this feature by calling the statement:

```
SET NOCOUNT ON
```

This statement can be used when working with a SQL Server database. Let's look at the syntax of the three action SQL statements, starting with the simplest, the DELETE statement.

DELETING ROWS

The DELETE statement deletes one or more rows from a table, and its syntax is:

```
DELETE table_name WHERE criteria
```

The WHERE clause specifies the criteria that the rows must meet in order to be deleted. The criteria expression is no different than the criteria you specify in the WHERE clause of selection query. To delete the orders placed before 1998, use a statement like

```
USE NORTHWIND
DELETE Orders
WHERE  OrderDate < '1/1/1998'
```

Of course, the specified rows will be deleted only if the Orders table allows cascade deletions, or if the rows to be deleted are not linked to related rows.

INSERTING NEW ROWS

The syntax of the INSERT statement is:

```
INSERT table_name (column_names) VALUES (values)
```

column_names and *values* are comma-separated lists of columns and their respective values. Values are mapped to their columns by the order in which they appear in the two lists.

Notice that you don't have to specify values for all columns in the table, but the *values* list must contain as many items as there are column names in the first list. To add a new row to the Customers table use a statement like the following:

```
INSERT Customers (CustomerID, CompanyName) VALUES ('FRYOG', 'Fruit & Yogurt')
```

This statement will insert a new row, provided that the FRYOG key isn't already in use. Only two of the new row's columns are set, and they're the columns that can't accept Null values.

If you want to specify values for all the columns of the new row, you can omit the list of columns. The following statement retrieves a number of rows from the Products table and inserts them into the SelectedProducts table, which has the exact same structure:

```
INSERT INTO SelectedProducts VALUES (values)
```

If the values come from a table, you can replace the VALUES keyword with a SELECT statement:

```
INSERT INTO SelectedProducts
    SELECT * FROM Products WHERE CategoryID = 4
```

There are more variations of the INSERT statement, but in this book we'll use the simplest form, where you specify both the column names and their values. The wizard we'll explore the in the following chapter generates statements like the following to insert a new row:

```
INSERT INTO dbo.Customers(CustomerID, CompanyName, ContactName, ContactTitle,
                    Address, City, Region, PostalCode, Country, Phone, Fax)
    VALUES (@CustomerID, @CompanyName, @ContactName, @ContactTitle, @Address,
            @City, @Region, @PostalCode, @Country, @Phone, @Fax)
```

The variables $@CustomerID$, $@CompanyName$, and so on are the values of the fields of the newly created row—these values were specified by the user through the appropriate interface.

EDITING EXISTING ROWS

The UPDATE statement edits a row's fields, and its syntax is

```
UPDATE table_name SET field1 = value1, field2 = value2, …
WHERE criteria
```

The *criteria* expression is no different than the criteria you specify in the WHERE clause of selection query. To change the country from "UK" to "United Kingdom" in the Customers table, use the following statement:

```
UPDATE Customers SET Country='United Kingdom'
WHERE  Country = 'UK'
```

This statement will locate all the rows in the Customers table that meet the specified criteria (their Country field is "UK") and change this field's value to "United Kingdom."

In Chapter 21, you'll see UPDATE statements like the one in Listing 20.1, which are executed to update the underlying table in the database. These statements are created automatically by the appropriate wizard and become part of the application. The SQL statement in Listing 20.1 was generated automatically to update the Customers table. The variables $@CustomerID$, $@CompanyName$, and so on are the new values of the fields. The variables $@Original\_CustomerID$ and $@Original\_CompanyName$ are the values read from the database. The SET clause of the statement is quite simple: it sets the values of the fields to the new values. The WHERE statement is a little complicated, because this UPDATE statement won't change the table if the values of the fields are not the same as the ones read from the database.

LISTING 20.1: A SQL UPDATE STATEMENT

```
UPDATE dbo.Customers
SET    CustomerID = @CustomerID, CompanyName = @CompanyName,
       ContactName = @ContactName, ContactTitle = @ContactTitle,
       Address = @Address, City = @City, Region = @Region,
       PostalCode = @PostalCode, Country = @Country, Phone = @Phone, Fax = @Fax
WHERE (CustomerID = @Original_CustomerID) AND
       (Address = @Original_Address OR @Original_Address1 IS NULL AND
            Address IS NULL) AND
       (City = @Original_City OR @Original_City1 IS NULL AND City IS NULL) AND
       (CompanyName = @Original_CompanyName) AND
       (ContactName = @Original_ContactName OR @Original_ContactName1 IS NULL
            AND ContactName IS NULL) AND
       (ContactTitle = @Original_ContactTitle OR @Original_ContactTitle1 IS NULL
            AND ContactTitle IS NULL) AND
       (Country = @Original_Country OR @Original_Country1 IS NULL
            AND Country IS NULL) AND
       (Fax = @Original_Fax OR @Original_Fax1 IS NULL AND Fax IS NULL) AND
       (Phone = @Original_Phone OR @Original_Phone1 IS NULL AND Phone IS NULL) AND
       (PostalCode = @Original_PostalCode OR @Original_PostalCode1 IS NULL
            AND PostalCode IS NULL) AND
       (Region = @Original_Region OR @Original_Region1 IS NULL AND Region IS NULL)
```

The variables with the original values are set when the row is read from the table. Then you can edit the row's fields through the appropriate interface. This may take a few seconds, or minutes (or an hour, if you decide to take a lunch break before updating the table). There's always a chance that another user might edit the same row before you commit your changes to the database. If a single field's value is different from the value we read, it means that the row has been modified since we read it and the UPDATE operation will fail.

In a banking application, a customer's balance might be $2,000. When a check is cashed, we must subtract the amount of the check from the current balance. But if another teller has already subtracted an amount from the same account, there may not be enough funds to cover both checks. You will learn more about updating tables with SQL statements (as well as stored procedures) in the following chapter.

I should bring to your attention that some of the complexity of the statements is due to the fact that Null values can't be compared. If two values are Null, they're not equal. The very essence of the Null value is to indicate that a field doesn't have a value, and therefore can't be compared. To find out whether two fields are both Null, you must use an expression like the following:

```
@value1 IS NULL AND field1 IS NULL
```

The Query Builder

The Query Builder is a visual tool for building SQL statements. It's a highly useful tool that generates SQL statements for you—you just specify the data you want to retrieve with point-and-click operations, instead of typing complicated expressions. A basic understanding of SQL is obviously required, and this is why I've described the basic keywords of SQL in the last section, but it is possible to build SQL queries with the Query Builder without knowing anything about SQL. I would suggest you use this tool to quickly build SQL statements, but don't expect that it will do your work for you. It's a great tool for beginners, but you can't get far by ignoring SQL. The Query Builder is also a great tool for learning SQL, as you specify the query with point-and-click operations but the Query Builder builds the appropriate SQL statements. You can also edit the SQL statement manually and execute it.

There are many ways to start the Query Builder. In the following chapter, you'll see how the Query Builder is activated every time you need to specify a query. You can open the Views items in the Server Explorer, right-click the name of a view, and select Design View from the context menu. Views are based on SQL statements, and you will see the Query Builder with the statement that implements the view you selected.

You can also create new queries by creating a new view. A view is the result of a query: it's a virtual table that consists of columns from one or more tables selected with a SQL SELECT statement. The Query Builder's window is shown in Figure 20.15.

FIGURE 20.15

Using the Query Builder to build a SQL statement with point-and-click operations

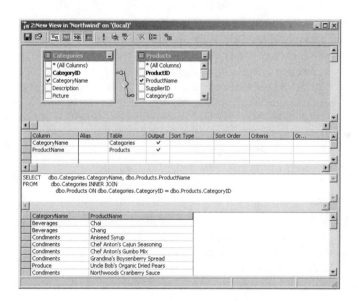

The query shown in Figure 20.15 retrieved the names of all the products in the Product table, along with the name of the category they belong to (the category name is stored in the Categories table). To create a new query with the Query Builder, open the Northwind database's section in the Server Explorer, right-click the Views item, and select New View. You will see the window of Figure 20.15, but it will be empty.

The Query Builder Interface

The Query Builder contains four panes: Diagram, Grid, SQL, and Results.

DIAGRAM PANE

This is where you select the tables you want to use in your queries—the tables in which the required data reside. To select a table, right-click anywhere on the Diagram pane and you will see the Add Table dialog box. Select as many tables as you need and then close the Add Table dialog box.

The selected tables will appear on the Diagram pane as small boxes, along with their fields, as shown in Figure 20.15. The tables involved in the query are related to one another (although this is not a requirement, it's rather unlikely that you'll retrieve data from unrelated tables). The relations are indicated as lines between the tables. These lines connect the primary and foreign keys of the relation. The line between the Products and Categories tables in Figure 20.15 indicates that the two tables are related through the CategoryID field. The CategoryID field in the Categories table is the primary key, and the same field in the Products table is the foreign key. The symbol of a key at one end of the line shows the primary key of the relationship, and the other end of the arrow is either a key (indicating a one-to-one relationship) or the infinity symbol (indicating a one-to-many relationship).

The little shape in the middle of the line indicates the type of join that must performed on the two tables, and it can take several shapes. To change the type of the relation, you can right-click the shape and select one of the options in the context menu. The diamond-shaped icon indicates an inner join, which requires that only rows with matching primary and foreign keys will be retrieved. By default, the Query Builder treats all joins as inner joins, but you can change the type of the join; you'll see how this is done in the section "Specifying Left, Right, and Inner Joins," later in this chapter.

The first step in building a query is the selection of the fields that will be included in the result. Select the fields you want to include in your query by checking the box in front of their names, in the corresponding tables. As you select and deselect fields, their names appear in the Grid pane. Notice that all fields are prefixed by the name of the table they came from, so that there will be no ambiguities.

Right-click the Diagram pane and select Add Table. In the dialog box that pops up, select the Products and Categories tables, click Add, then click Close to close the dialog box.

GRID PANE

The Grid pane contains the selected fields. Some fields may not be part of the output—you may use them only for selection purposes—but their names will appear on this pane. To exclude them from the output, clear the box in the Output column.

The Alias column contains a name for the field. By default, the column's name is the alias. This is the heading of each column in the output, and you can change the default name to any string that suits you.

SQL PANE

As you build the statement with point-and-click operations, the Query Builder generates the SQL statement that must be executed against the database to retrieve the specified data. The statement that retrieves product names along with their categories is shown next:

```
SELECT  dbo.Products.ProductName, dbo.Categories.CategoryName
FROM    dbo.Categories INNER JOIN dbo.Products
        ON dbo.Categories.CategoryID = dbo.Products.CategoryID
```

If you paste this statement in the SQL pane and then execute it, you'll see a list of product names along with their categories. To execute the query, right-click somewhere on the Query Builder window and select Run Query. The Query Builder will first fill out the remaining panes (if you've chosen to enter the SQL statement), and then it will execute the query. It will display the tables involved in the query on the Tables pane, it will insert the appropriate rows in the Grid pane, and then it will execute the query and display the results on the Results pane.

RESULTS PANE

To execute a query, right-click somewhere on the SQL pane and select Run from the context menu. The Query Builder will execute the statement it generated and will display the results in the Results pane at the bottom of the window. The heading of each column is the column's name, unless you've specified an alias for the column.

In the following section, we're going to build a few fairly complicated queries with the visual tools of Query Builder, and in the process I will discuss additional features of the Query Builder.

SQL at Work: Calculating Sums

In this section we'll build a query that retrieves all the products, along with the quantities sold. The names of the products will come from the Products table, while the quantities must be retrieved from the Order Details table. Because the same product appears in multiple rows of the tables (each product appears in multiple invoices with different quantities), we must sum the quantities of all rows that refer to the same product.

Create a new view in the Server Explorer to start the Query Builder, right-click the upper pane, and select Add Table. On the Add Table dialog box, select the tables Products and Order Details, then close the dialog box. The two tables will appear on the Diagram pane with a line connecting them. This is their relation.

Now check the fields you want to include in the query: Select the field ProductName in the Products table and the field Quantity in the Order Details table. Expand the options in the Sort Type box in the ProductName row and select Ascending. The Query Builder will generate the following SQL statement:

```
SELECT   dbo.Products.ProductName, dbo.[Order Details].Quantity
FROM     dbo.Products INNER JOIN dbo.[Order Details]
         ON dbo.Products.ProductID = dbo.[Order Details].ProductID
ORDER BY dbo.Products.ProductName
```

Execute this statement, and the first few lines in the Results pane will be

```
Alice Mutton    30
Alice Mutton    15
Alice Mutton    15
Alice Mutton    40
```

The Query Builder knows how the two tables are related and retrieved the matching rows from the two tables. It has also inserted a line that links the two tables in the Tables pane. This line indicates the relationship between the two tables. However, it didn't sum the quantities for each product.

Now you'll specify that we want the sum the quantities. Right-click the Quantity field in the Grid pane and select the Group By option from the context menu. A new column will be inserted after the Sort Order column. This column is set automatically to Group By for all the fields.

Now select the Group By cell of the Quantity row, expand the drop-down list, and select the Sum option. You have just specified that the field Quantity must be summed. The Group By option tells the Query Builder to group together all the rows that refer to the same product. This ensures that the sum will include all the products, because the rows of the Order Details table that refer to the same product are grouped together).

Notice that the Alias cell of the Quantity row has become Expr1 (it's no longer a column, but an aggregate). Set the alias to Total Items. Something has changed in the Diagram pane too (see Figure 20.16). The summation symbol has appeared next to the Quantity field (even though this field isn't selected to appear in the output of the query), and the grouping symbol has appeared next to the ProductName field.

FIGURE 20.16

A query with totals

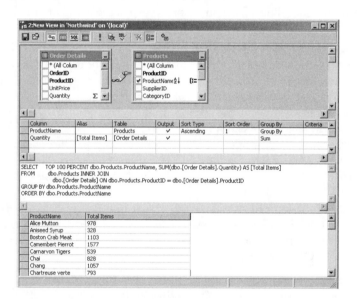

Run the query now and see the results in the lower pane. Each product name appears only once, and the number next to it is the total number of items sold.

If you close the Query Builder window now, you'll be prompted as to whether you want to save the new view and to specify a name for it. The definition will be saved to the Northwind database, along with the other objects of the database.

SQL at Work: Counting Rows

Let's say you want to find out the number of orders in which each product appears. Go back to the Server Explorer and open the previous view (or the Query Analyzer). Add the Orders table, which will be automatically related to the Order Details table with the OrderID field. Click the OrderID field in the Orders table. A new line will be added to the Grid pane, and its Group By column will be set automatically to Group By. Set it to Count Distinct and its alias to "# Of Orders." We're going to sum the orders in which each product appears. The Count Distinct aggregate function is similar to the Count function, but it will not include the same order twice (if the same product appears in two rows of the same order). Run the query. This time you'll get one line per product. The Alice Mutton item has been ordered 37 times, and the total items sold are 978.

```
Alice Mutton         978    37
Aniseed Syrup        328    12
Boston Crab Meat     1103   41
Camembert Pierrot    1577   51
```

The SELECT statement generated by the SQL Builder is the following. Notice that the Orders table isn't involved in the query. All the information we need resides in the Order Details table. The Products table is included so that we can display product names instead of product IDs.

```
SELECT    TOP 100 PERCENT dbo.Products.ProductName,
          SUM(dbo.[Order Details].Quantity) AS [Total Items],
          SUM(dbo.[Order Details].OrderID) AS [# Of Orders]
FROM      dbo.Products
          INNER JOIN dbo.[Order Details] ON
            dbo.Products.ProductID = dbo.[Order Details].ProductID
GROUP BY  dbo.Products.ProductName
ORDER BY  dbo.Products.ProductName
```

The phrase TOP 100 PERCENT tells SQL Server to return all qualifying rows and is optional. The Query Builder inserted it so that you can change the value and limit the number of selected rows. Change the default aliases of the two calculated columns and execute the query again by clicking the button with the exclamation mark.

Limiting the Selection

So far, we've extracted data from all rows. Practically, we never work with all the rows in the database—we select a subset based on chronological, geographical, or other criteria. In this section we'll modify the previous query so that it retrieves the totals over a time period. As you can guess, we'll use the WHERE clause to limit the selected rows.

Our selection will be chronological. We'll sum the items sold in a year (or any other interval you wish). This will introduce a little additional complexity to our query, because the information on which the selection will be based doesn't appear in the Order Details table. The date of each order is stored in the Orders table, so we must add this table to our query.

Select the OrderDate field to the Grid pane. We want to specify two criteria for the date: it must be after the starting date and before the ending date. So, add the Orders.OrderDate field twice. To add a second instance of the same field, expand the first empty cell in the left column and, from the drop-down list, select its name. Then move to the Group By column of the row of the OrderDate field. Change its value to WHERE and, in the Criteria column, enter the following:

```
>= '1/1/1998'
```

In the second instance of the same field, expand the Group By column, set it to WHERE, and then enter the following string in the Criteria column:

```
<= '1/1/1999'
```

The Query Builder has generated the following SQL statement:

```
SELECT    TOP 100 PERCENT dbo.Products.ProductName,
            SUM(dbo.[Order Details].Quantity) AS [Total Items],
            SUM(dbo.[Order Details].OrderID) AS [# Of Orders]
FROM      dbo.Products
            INNER JOIN dbo.[Order Details] ON
              dbo.Products.ProductID = dbo.[Order Details].ProductID
            INNER JOIN dbo.Orders ON
              dbo.[Order Details].OrderID = dbo.Orders.OrderID
WHERE     (dbo.Orders.OrderDate >=
            CONVERT(DATETIME, '1998-01-01 00:00:00', 102))
          AND (dbo.Orders.OrderDate <=
            CONVERT(DATETIME, '1999-01-01 00:00:00', 102))
GROUP BY dbo.Products.ProductName
ORDER BY dbo.Products.ProductName
```

As you can see, the Query Builder inserted the appropriate statements to convert your values to dates. You can make this statement a little more compact by using the BETWEEN operator. Remove the cells corresponding to the OrderDate field from the first column. Then add the OrderDate field again, set its Group By column to WHERE, and in the Criteria columns, enter the expression BETWEEN '1/1/1998' AND '1/1/1999'. When no time is specified, it's assumed that it's the first second of the specified date. The date 1/1/1998 includes the first day of the year. The date 12/31/1998 doesn't include the last day of the year, because it will be converted to 1998-12-31 00:00:00. If you specify the first and last day of the year, the totals will be calculated over a period of 364 days, not 365 days (assuming the year is not leap). So, you must either specify the following date, or add a time part to the date to take into consideration the 24 hours of the final day: 12/31/1998 23:59:59.

Execute the query and you will see the following lines at the top of the Results pane:

```
Alice Mutton      217    11
Aniseed Syrup     108    4
```

Go back to the Grid pane and change the dates to calculate the same results for the year 1997. The two criteria should be:

```
>= '1/1/1997'
<= '1/1/1998'
```

Execute the new query and you will see the same product names, only with different totals. Here's the revised query's code:

```
SELECT    TOP 100 PERCENT dbo.Products.ProductName,
            SUM(dbo.[Order Details].Quantity) AS [Total Items],
            SUM(dbo.[Order Details].OrderID) AS [# Of Orders]
FROM      dbo.Products
            INNER JOIN dbo.[Order Details] ON
```

```
                 dbo.Products.ProductID = dbo.[Order Details].ProductID
              INNER JOIN dbo.Orders ON
                 dbo.[Order Details].OrderID = dbo.Orders.OrderID
  WHERE      (dbo.Orders.OrderDate BETWEEN
                 CONVERT(DATETIME, '1997-01-01 00:00:00', 102)
                 AND CONVERT(DATETIME, '1998-1-1 00:00:00', 102))
  GROUP BY dbo.Products.ProductName
  ORDER BY dbo.Products.ProductName
```

Parameterized Queries

How about running the same query with different dates? Let's modify our query once again, and make the two dates parameters of the queries. Each time you'll be executing the new query, you'll be prompted to specify the starting and ending dates.

Replace the two dates in the Criteria column of the Grid pane with a question mark. The revised expression should now read:

```
Between ? And ?
```

If you run the query, you'll get an error message telling you that parameters aren't supported for this type of query. We're designing a view; that's why you can't use parameters. Click OK to get rid of the message, and you'll be prompted to enter the values of the two parameters (Figure 20.17). A question mark in a query corresponds to a parameter, and you must supply the values for the parameters in the order in which they appear in the query. Enter the two dates in Define Query Parameters window and you'll see its output in the Results pane.

FIGURE 20.17

Specifying the parameters for a query

In the following section, we'll convert this statement to a stored procedure, and you'll see how you can pass values for the query's parameters. Because the behavior of the query depends on the values of its parameters, this is a *parameterized query*.

Calculated Columns

Let's add yet another step of complexity to our query. We'll modify our query so that it calculates the total revenues generated by each product. Move down in the Field column of the Grid pane, and in the first free cell, enter the following expression:

```
Quantity * UnitPrice * (1 - Discount)
```

The wizard will replace the field names with fully qualified names:

```
(dbo.[Order Details].Quantity * dbo.Products.UnitPrice) * (1 - dbo.[Order
Details].Discount)
```

This expression calculates the subtotal for each line in the Order Details table. We multiply the price with the quantity, taking into consideration the discount. Shortly, we're going to sum the subtotals for each product.

Because this is a calculated column, its Alias becomes Expr1. Change this value to Revenue. In the Group By column, select Sum. Make sure the Output column is checked and then run the query. Same results as before, only this time with an extra column, which is the revenue generated by the corresponding product:

```
Alice Mutton      978    37    38142
Aniseed Syrup     328    12    3280
Boston Crab Meat  1103   41    20295.2
```

The SQL statement generated by the SQL Builder is:

```
SELECT    dbo.Products.ProductName,
          SUM(dbo.[Order Details].Quantity) AS [Total Items],
          COUNT(DISTINCT dbo.Orders.OrderID) AS [Times Ordered],
          SUM(dbo.[Order Details].Quantity * dbo.Products.UnitPrice) AS Revenue
FROM      dbo.Products
          INNER JOIN dbo.[Order Details] ON
             dbo.Products.ProductID = dbo.[Order Details].ProductID
          INNER JOIN dbo.Orders ON
             dbo.[Order Details].OrderID = dbo.Orders.OrderID
WHERE     (dbo.Orders.OrderDate > @FromDate) AND
          (dbo.Orders.OrderDate < @ToDate)
GROUP BY  dbo.Products.ProductName
ORDER BY  dbo.Products.ProductName
```

This is a fairly complicated statement, and we won't get into any more complicated statements in this book. As you can see, you can create quite elaborate SQL statements to retrieve information from the database with point-and-click operations. But even if you don't want to enter your own SQL statements, some understanding of this language is required. All the keywords have been explained previously, and you can test your knowledge of SQL by examining the code generated by the Query Builder.

Specifying Left, Right, and Inner Joins

This time we'll build another query to demonstrate the differences between the various types of joins and, most importantly, the types of (subtle) errors introduced by the wrong type of join. We'll build a query that retrieves all the titles from the Pubs database, along with their authors.

Open the Query Builder window, or remove all the tables from the Diagram pane if it's already open. This time, select the Pubs database and drop the following tables on the Diagram pane: Titles,

TitleAuthor, and Authors. Then check the fields title, au_lname, and au_fname to include in your query. Set the Title Sort Order to 1 and run the query. The first few lines in the Results pane will be:

But Is It User Friendly?	Carson	Cheryl
Computer Phobic AND Non-Phobic Individuals: Behavior Variations	MacFeather	Stearns
Computer Phobic AND Non-Phobic Individuals: Behavior Variations	Karsen	Livia
Cooking with Computers: Surreptitious Balance Sheets	O'Leary	Michael
Cooking with Computers: Surreptitious Balance Sheets	MacFeather	Stearns

If a book has multiple authors, the book's title will appear in the results as many times as there are authors. This is how SQL works, and you can't change this behavior. Be aware that many queries will return rows with identical information (the same title with each of its authors), and you must provide the code to display all the authors along with the corresponding title, rather than repeating the same title over and over. Later in the book, you'll learn how to bring in selected titles and the authors that are related to the selected titles (not all authors). For now, let's focus on SQL statements.

Let's start by formatting the output a little. First, change the au_lname column to au_lname + ', ' + au_fname. This will concatenate first and last names to form the author's name. This is a calculated column, and its Alias will be set to Expr1; change it to Author. Then run the query.

The Query Builder has generated the following SQL statement:

```
SELECT  dbo.titles.title,
        dbo.authors.au_lname + ', ' + dbo.authors.au_fname AS Author
FROM    dbo.authors
        INNER JOIN dbo.titleauthor ON
            dbo.authors.au_id = dbo.titleauthor.au_id
        INNER JOIN dbo.titles ON
            dbo.titleauthor.title_id = dbo.titles.title_id
        ORDER BY dbo.titles.title
```

If you execute the query now, the following lines will appear at the top of the Results pane:

But Is It User Friendly?	Carson, Cheryl
Computer Phobic AND Non-Phobic Individuals: Behavior Variations	MacFeather, Stearns
Computer Phobic AND Non-Phobic Individuals: Behavior Variations	Karsen, Livia
Cooking with Computers: Surreptitious Balance Sheets	O'Leary, Michael
Cooking with Computers: Surreptitious Balance Sheets	MacFeather, Stearns

This is an inner join, which returned 25 rows. They are all the books with one or more authors. To include the books without an author, we must create a right join (the table to the right being the Titles table). The right join will include all the titles whether they have an author or not.

Right-click the line that relates the table Titles to the table TitleAuthor, and from the menu choose Select All Rows From Titles. This action changes the inner join between the tables to a right join. Run the new query and it will generate 26 rows in the Results pane. The last title has no author, and the corresponding line is:

The Psychology of Computer Cooking   <NULL>

The SQL statement generated by the Query Builder is:

```
SELECT  dbo.titles.title,
        dbo.authors.au_lname + ', ' + dbo.authors.au_fname AS Author
FROM    dbo.titleauthor
        INNER JOIN dbo.authors ON
           dbo.titleauthor.au_id = dbo.authors.au_id
        RIGHT OUTER JOIN dbo.titles ON
           dbo.titleauthor.title_id = dbo.titles.title_id
        ORDER BY dbo.titles.title
```

To do the opposite, select all authors whether they appear in a title or not, reset the relation between Titles and TitleAuthor (clear the check mark in front of Select All Rows From Title), and check the item Select All Rows From Authors. If you run the query, you'll see that the following line is included in the Results pane:

<NULL>   Stringer, Dirk

The last type of join will return all titles and all authors. Right-click the line that connects the Titles and TitleAuthor tables and check both options, as shown in Figure 20.18.

FIGURE 20.18

A query that retrieves all the titles and all the authors

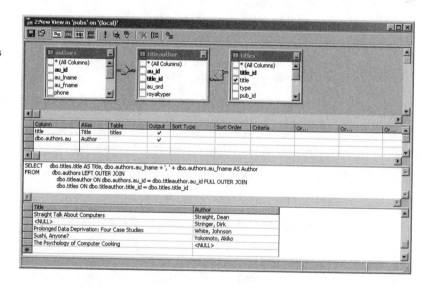

This time the Query Builder will generate the following SQL statement:

```
SELECT  dbo.titles.title AS Title,
        dbo.authors.au_lname + ', ' + dbo.authors.au_fname AS Author
FROM    dbo.authors LEFT OUTER JOIN dbo.titleauthor
            ON dbo.authors.au_id = dbo.titleauthor.au_id
            FULL OUTER JOIN dbo.titles
            ON dbo.titleauthor.title_id = dbo.titles.title_id
```

When executed, this statement will return authors without books as well as titles without author:

<NULL>   Greene, Morningstar

The Psychology of Computer Cooking   <NULL>

Notice that the outer join is between the Titles and TitleAuthor tables, as well as between the TitleAuthor and Authors tables. Once each title is linked to the proper row(s) in the TitleAuthor table, the corresponding names will be easily retrieved from the Authors table with an inner join. Each row in the TitleAuthor table points to a single row of Authors table. You can use the Diagram pane of the SQL Query Builder to experiment with the various types of joins. Right-click the line that connects two tables (it represents a join) and change the type of the join—check or clear the two options on the context menu.

Stored Procedures

This is another of the objects you must familiarize yourself with. *Stored procedures* are short programs that are executed on the server and perform very specific tasks. Any action you perform against the database frequently should be coded as a stored procedure, so that you can call it from within any application or from different parts of the same application. A stored procedure that retrieves customers by name is a typical example, and you'll call this stored procedure from many different placed in your application.

You should use stored procedures for all the operations you want to perform against the database. Stored procedures isolate programmers from the database and minimize the risk of impairing the database's integrity. When all programmers access the same stored procedure to add a new invoice to the database, they don't have to know the structure of the tables involved or in what order to update these tables. They simply call the stored procedure passing the invoice's fields as arguments. Another benefit of using stored procedures to update the database is that you don't risk implementing the same operation in two different ways. This is especially true for a team of developers, because some developers may have not understood the business rules thoroughly. If the business rules change, you can modify the stored procedures accordingly, without touching the other parts of the application.

Another advantage of using stored procedures is that they're compiled by SQL Server and they're executed faster. There's no penalty in using stored procedures versus SQL statements, and any SQL statement can be easily turned into a stored procedure, as you will see in this section. Stored procedures contain traditional programming statements that allow you to validate arguments, use default argument values, and so on. The language you use to write stored procedure is called T-SQL, and it's a superset of SQL.

ADO.NET makes heavy use of stored procedures by design. You can also use SQL statements to query or update the database, but once you've gotten the SQL statement right, you can very easily turn it into a stored procedure so that all other programmers in your team can use it. Stored procedures are stored in the database, and you can prevent developers from modifying them (the database administrator will give each team the proper rights to create, edit, or delete database objects).

So, what's the difference between stored procedures and SQL statements? As you recall, SQL is a peculiar language: it allows you to specify what you want to do, but not how to do it. Unlike VB, it's a nonprocedural language. It lacks the control flow statements you expect to find in any programming languages, it doesn't use variables, and you can't break a complicated query into smaller procedures. SQL Server extends SQL by adding traditional programming structures. The new language is called T-SQL (Transact-SQL). I won't discuss T-SQL in depth in this book, but you'll get a good idea of the capabilities of T-SQL through the examples of the following sections; plus, the basic components of the T-SQL language are overviewed in the bonus chapter "Transact-SQL" on the companion CD. Knowing VB, you'll have no problem learning the basics of T-SQL.

Let's explore stored procedures by looking at an existing one. Open the Server Explorer toolbox, connect to the Northwind database and them expand the Stored Procedures node of the Northwind database. Locate the SalesByCategory stored procedure and double-click its name. The SalesByCategory stored procedure contains the statements from Listing 20.2, which will appear on the editor's window:

LISTING 20.2: THE SALESBYCATEGORY STORED PROCEDURE

```
ALTER PROCEDURE dbo.SalesByCategory
    @CategoryName nvarchar(15),
    @OrdYear nvarchar(4) = '1998'
AS
IF @OrdYear != '1996' AND @OrdYear != '1997' AND @OrdYear != '1998'
BEGIN
    SELECT @OrdYear = '1998'
END
SELECT ProductName,
        TotalPurchase = ROUND(SUM(CONVERT(decimal(14,2),
        OD.Quantity * (1-OD.Discount) * OD.UnitPrice)), 0)
FROM [Order Details] OD, Orders O, Products P, Categories C
WHERE OD.OrderID = O.OrderID
        AND OD.ProductID = P.ProductID
        AND P.CategoryID = C.CategoryID
        AND C.CategoryName = @CategoryName
        AND SUBSTRING(CONVERT(nvarchar(22), O.OrderDate, 111), 1, 4) = @OrdYear
GROUP BY ProductName
ORDER BY ProductName
```

This type of code is probably new to you. You'll learn it quite well as you go along, because it's really required in coding database applications. You can rely on the various wizards to create stored procedures for you, but you should be able to understand how they work.

The first statement alters the procedure SalesByCategory, which is already stored in the database. If it's a new procedure, you can use the CREATE statement instead of ALTER, to attach a new stored procedure to the database. The following lines until the AS keyword are the parameters of the stored procedure. All variables in T-SQL start with the @ symbol. *@CategoryName* is a 15-character string, and *@OrdYear* is a string that also has a default value. If you omit the second argument when calling the SalesByCategory procedure, then the year 1998 will be used automatically.

The AS keyword marks the beginning of the stored procedure. The first IF statement makes sure that the year is a valid one (from 1996 to 1998). If not, it will use the year 1998. The BEGIN and END keywords mark the beginning and end of the IF block (the same block that's delimited by the If and End If statements in VB code).

Following the IF statement is a long SELECT statement that uses the arguments passed to the stored procedure as parameters. This is a straight SQL statement that implements a parameterized query. Because the stored procedure is called like a function, it will not prompt the user for the values of the parameters; these values are passed as arguments when the stored procedure is called.

Notice that each table is assigned an alias, so that we won't have to type the name of table over and over. The alias for the Orders table is O, the alias for the Order Details table is OD, and they're defined in the same line that specifies the tables from which the data will come:

```
FROM [Order Details] OD, Orders O, Products P, Categories C
```

After that, we use the shorter aliases in the place of the tables' names.

The second half of the stored procedure's code appears in a box on the editor's window. Right-click anywhere in this box and select Design SQL Block. This block is a SQL statement that retrieves the total sales for the specified year and groups them by category. You can edit it either as a SQL segment or through the visual interface of the Query Builder. You already know how to handle SQL statements, so everything you learned about building SQL statements applies to stored procedures as well. The only difference is that you can embed traditional control structures, like IF statements, AND loops, and WHILE loops, and mix them with SQL.

The stored procedure we examined returns a cursor (a set of rows). It is also possible to write stored procedures that return one or more values, through their parameters list. A stored procedure that returns the total items of specific product sold in a period need not return a cursor; all we need is an integer value. You'll see later how to return a few parameters from a stored procedure.

For now, let's test the stored procedure. Right-click anywhere in the SQL Builder panes and select Run Stored Procedure. A dialog box pops up and prompts you to enter the values for the two parameters the query expects: the name of the category and the year. Enter **Beverages** and **1997** as shown in Figure 20.19 and then click OK. The stored procedure will return the qualifying rows, which will be displayed in the Output window.

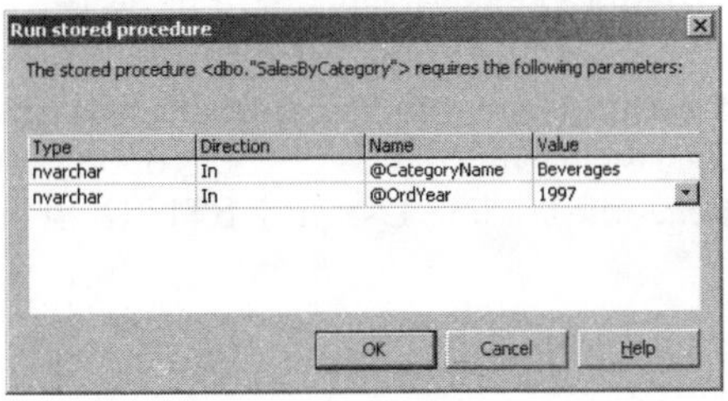

FIGURE 20.19

Supplying the values of a stored procedure's parameters

The SalesByCategory stored procedure returned the following lines when executed with the parameters shown in Figure 20.19. These lines appear in the Output window.

```
ProductName                              TotalPurchase
--------------------------------------   ----------------------
Chai                                     4887
Chang                                    7039
Chartreuse verte                         4476
Côte de Blaye                            49198
Guaraná Fantástica                       1630
Ipoh Coffee                              11070
Lakkalikööri                             7379
Laughing Lumberjack Lager                910
Outback Lager                            5468
Rhönbräu Klosterbier                     4486
Sasquatch Ale                            2107
Steeleye Stout                           5275
No more results.
(12 row(s) returned)
@RETURN_VALUE = 0
Finished running dbo."SalesByCategory".
```

This is quite a statement, but stored procedures are not difficult to design with the SQL Builder. Let's build a new stored procedure to calculate the number of orders placed by each customer and the total revenue they generated.

Let's create a new stored procedure. Right-click the Stored Procedures item in the Server Explorer and select New Stored Procedure. You will see a new pane on the Designer surface with the following text, which is the outline of a stored procedure:

```
CREATE PROCEDURE dbo.StoredProcedure1
/*
    (
        @parameter1 datatype = default value,
        @parameter2 datatype OUTPUT
    )
*/
AS
    /* SET NOCOUNT ON */
    RETURN
```

The symbols /* and */ delimit a section with comments in T-SQL. In the first commented section, you see how the stored procedure's variables must be declared. You must replace this section with the declarations of your stored procedure's arguments.

Then comes the AS keyword, where you must enter the SQL statements you want to execute in your stored procedure. The last statement, RETURN, is optional, because the stored procedure will terminate as soon as it reaches the last line. Use the RETURN statement to exit the stored procedure prematurely.

Select all the text on the editor and replace it with the following stored procedure declaration:

```
CREATE PROCEDURE dbo.OrdersPerCustomer
    @CustomerID nchar(5)='ALFKI'
AS
```

The first line declares the name of the procedure. The next few lines declare the name and type of the parameters expected by the procedure. If the parameter has a default value, this is also specified on the same line as the parameter's declaration. The OrdersPerCustomer stored procedure accepts a single argument, which is the customer's ID (a five-character string, as you recall from the overview of the Northwind database earlier in this chapter).

Following the AS keyword is the SQL code that retrieves data from the database. Right-click anywhere in the editor's window, and from the context menu, select Insert SQL. This will open the SQL Builder, where you can build a SQL statement with point-and-click operations.

Let's build a SQL statement that will retrieve the orders for a specific customer. On the SQL Builder window, clear the SQL pane, then right-click the Diagram pane and select Add Table from the context menu. In the dialog box, select Customers, then click Add. Do the same for the Orders table, and then close the Add Table dialog box. You have two tables in the upper pane, and the SQL Builder inserted a line between them. This is a relation. It indicates that the CustomerID field in the Orders is the same as one of the CustomerID fields in the Customers table.

Next we must specify what we want to see in our query. Click CompanyName in the first table and OrderID in the second table (and clear all other fields). Column (field) names will appear in the grid under the Column heading, and the corresponding tables they came from will appear under the Table heading. The check mark in the output column denotes that they will be included in the output. If you run the query now (choosing Run from the context menu), you'll see the all the orders for all customers. We don't want all the orders per customer, just the count of the orders placed by a single customer.

Go to the OrderID row and GroupBy column in the Grid pane. When you select the cell, a button will appear with a down arrow. Click the button and a list of options will appear. Select the Count option. The Alias cell in the same row has become Expr1. This is the header of the Count column; all other columns in the query are named after the table column. Change Expr1 to Total Orders.

At this point, the statement is:

```
SELECT    dbo.Customers.CompanyName,
          COUNT(dbo.Orders.OrderID) AS [Total Orders]
FROM      dbo.Customers INNER JOIN dbo.Orders ON
              dbo.Customers.CustomerID = dbo.Orders.CustomerID
```

Now go to the CompanyName row, and in the GroupBy cell, select Group By. We want to count all the orders per customer, so we must first group the customers and then sum their orders. This is one of the fine points in SQL. If you make a mistake and forget to group the query appropriately, the following message will appear when you attempt to execute it:

```
Column Customers.CompanyName is invalid in the select list because it is not
contained in an aggregate function and there is no GROUP BY clause.
```

The final SQL statement is:

```
SELECT    dbo.Customers.CompanyName,
          COUNT(dbo.Orders.OrderID) AS [Total Orders]
FROM      dbo.Customers INNER JOIN dbo.Orders ON
              dbo.Customers.CustomerID = dbo.Orders.CustomerID
GROUP BY dbo.Customers.CompanyName
```

If you execute it now, you'll get a list of customers and the number of orders per customer.

```
Alfreds Futterkiste                     6
Ana Trujillo Emparedados y helados      4
Antonio Moreno Taquería                 7
Around the Horn                        13
Berglunds snabbköp                     18
Blauer See Delikatessen                 7
```

This is not the stored procedure you're executing. You're still working with SQL Builder. When you close the SQL Builder window later, the SQL statement will be placed in the SQL box in the stored procedure's definition.

The last step is to limit the number of customers. Add the CustomerID to the list of columns by checking the box in front of its name in the Customers table. When it's added to grid, clear the check mark in the Output cell. We'll use this field to limit our selection, but we don't want it to appear along with the other fields in the output list. Then go to the Criteria cell of the same row and enter =?. The equal sign means that we want to select the customer with a specific value of the CustomerID field, which will be supplied as argument to the stored procedure. The specific value is the question mark, which means a user-supplied value. If you entered the string "='ALFKI'", the query would always return the number of orders placed by the customer Alfreds Futterkiste. It makes more sense to write parameterized queries, which can select different rows every time you execute them depending on the parameter value.

Run the query. You'll be prompted to enter the ID of a customer. Enter **ALFKI**, and you'll see the total number of orders for the specified customer in the Results pane. Now close the SQL Builder window and the SQL statement will appear in the SQL block of the stored procedure. The complete stored procedure is now:

```
CREATE PROCEDURE dbo.OrdersPerCustomer
        @CustomerID nchar(5)= 'ALFKI'
AS
SELECT    dbo.Customers.CompanyName,
          COUNT(dbo.Orders.OrderID) AS [Total Orders],
          dbo.Customers.CustomerID
FROM      dbo.Customers INNER JOIN dbo.Orders ON
              dbo.Customers.CustomerID = dbo.Orders.CustomerID
GROUP BY dbo.Customers.CompanyName,
          dbo.Customers.CustomerID
HAVING   (dbo.Customers.CustomerID = @CustomerID)
```

Notice that the question mark in the SQL statement was replaced by the first argument of the stored procedure. If there were another parameter (another question mark in the stored procedure), it would be replaced by the second argument of the stored procedure, and so on. You may have to edit the names of the arguments—you will have to do so if the order of the SQL statement's parameters doesn't match the order in which the arguments are passed to the stored procedure. Close the stored procedure's window by clicking the Close button (the little X mark) in its top-right corner. Then select the name of the new stored procedure in the Stored Procedures branch of the tree in the Server Explorer and select Run Stored Procedure. You'll be prompted to enter a customer ID. If you enter **ALFKI**, you'll see the following in the Output window:

```
Running dbo."OrdersPerCustomer"
( @CustomerID = ALFKI ).CompanyName    Total Orders    CustomerID
-------------------------------------------------------------
Alfreds Futterkiste                        6            ALFKI
No more results.
(1 row(s) returned)
@RETURN_VALUE = 0
Finished running dbo."OrdersPerCustomer".
```

If the Output window is not visible, open it with View ➤ Output Window to see the output of the stored procedure.

The stored procedure we've built, which is basically a SQL statement that retrieves information from the database packaged as a procedure (so that you can call it by name), is a fairly complicated one. Stored procedures are made up of SQL statements and some T-SQL code. The different types of code are clearly marked on the stored procedure's design window, and you can use the Query Builder to build and test the SQL part of the stored procedure. The rest is simple T-SQL code that sets up variables and uses traditional programming structures to perform housekeeping tasks.

As you will see in the following chapter, stored procedures can be called like functions. In addition, they can return results to the calling procedure through their arguments. The stored procedure that returns the number of invoices placed by a customer in a specified period need not return a cursor. It can return a single value. Like VB functions, stored procedures return a single value, which is the return value.

We could have assigned the number of orders to the stored procedure's return value. Most practical stored procedures return multiple rows, and this is why I've shown you how to return a row, rather than a single value.

Can you edit the stored procedure so that it returns the total revenue generated by the selected customer in addition to the number of orders? You can use the Query Builder to design the query visually, or enter the following query's definition in the SQL pane and then watch the query update the other panes:

```
SELECT    Customers.CompanyName, COUNT(Orders.OrderID) AS [Total Orders],
          Customers.CustomerID,
          SUM([Order Details].Quantity * Products.UnitPrice) AS Total
FROM      Customers INNER JOIN Orders ON
              Customers.CustomerID = Orders.CustomerID INNER JOIN [Order Details]
              ON Orders.OrderID = [Order Details].OrderID INNER JOIN Products
              ON [Order Details].ProductID = Products.ProductID
GROUP BY  Customers.CompanyName, Customers.CustomerID
HAVING    (Customers.CustomerID = @CustomerID)
```

We'll use this stored procedure in the following chapter in a short application that demonstrates how to execute a stored procedure from within your VB code and how to get the results back.

Summary

It's been a long chapter but certainly interesting. You've learned how data are stored in databases, how to break the information into smaller pieces and store it into tables, and how relationships between tables allow you to quickly locate the information you're interested in.

All actions against databases are performed with SQL statements and stored procedure. SQL is a universal language for accessing data in databases. SQL is not a traditional language, in that it describes the actions you want to perform to the database but not how these actions will be carried out. ADO.NET is based on SQL (SQL statements and stored procedures), and all the information in this chapter will be used in the following chapters to build database applications.

So far, you've learned how to extract data from a database. In the following chapter, you'll learn how to move this information from the server (the computer running SQL Server) to the client (the machine on which your application is running), how to store the information and process it on the client, and how to update the database.

Chapter 21

Building Database Applications with ADO.NET

IN THIS CHAPTER, WE'RE going to explore the basics of database applications. The database applications you build with VB.NET are client-server applications. The data resides in a database, which is installed on one of the computers on the network. To test the examples of this section, you will most likely use a copy of SQL Server installed on the same machine you use for development. In an actual production environment, your application will be installed on many clients, and all of the clients will be accessing the same database, installed on the server. The server knows how to access the data very efficiently, and that's all it does. Presenting the data to the user and/or processing the data is your application's responsibility. The server is the machine on which SQL Server is running. The machines on which the application is running are the clients.

The client-server model is a very efficient one because it allows you to share the computational load among multiple computers and each computer does what it can do best. The client computer gets data, presents them to the user, optionally processes them, and sends them back to the server. The server can focus on moving data out of and into the database. The type of client described here is called *rich client*, because it can use advanced controls to present the data to the user. It's a workstation running Windows applications, which can process the data in many ways. For example, it can convert the data read from the database into elaborate graphical representations. There's absolutely no reason to pass the task of processing the data to the server.

The client-server architecture a two-tier architecture. The programs running on the client make up the *presentation tier*; the database server is the *data tier*. Of course, you've all read that ADO.NET is a great tool for three-tier, or multitier, applications. So, what's the third tier? Let's consider for a moment an application that runs on the Web—an online store, for example. The client is the browser. This is the program that runs on each client and interacts with the user. Unlike a Windows application, the browser can't deploy an elaborate user interface (you can't place any of the Windows controls on a Web page); you're limited to the HTML controls. This type of client is called *thin client*, because it has limited processing capabilities. The browser must receive HTML pages and render them on the monitor. The HTML page may contain scripts too, but even so you can't duplicate the functionality of a Windows form on a Web page. In other words, you can't pull data from the database, download them to the client, and process them there. If you want to convert the numeric data retrieved from the database into charts, you must create the pages with the graphs and download them to the client, where they can be rendered by the browser.

The processing of the data takes place on the Web server. The clients on the Web don't see the database server directly. Instead, they contact a program running on the Web server, which in turns contacts the database to retrieve the requested data, format them in a way the browser can understand them, and then send the HTML page to the client. The programs running on the Web server that service the requests made by the clients form the third tier, and a Web application is the most familiar example of the three-tier architecture. The three-tier architecture is the evolution of the client-server model.

You can also introduce additional tiers to your applications. Let's say your application records orders made over the Web. When the user places an order, the application running on the Web server may have to contact the server of a shipping company to get a quote on the shipping cost and add it to the total cost of the order. The programs on the shipper's server form yet another tier of the application.

What makes VB.NET a great tool for multitier applications is that it uses XML to pass data between layers. XML is a text-based protocol that can describe any type of data, even images. By using the XML format, data are moved easily and reliably between layers, even between different operating systems and databases. Since you're probably wondering about XML, what it can do for your applications and, especially, how well you must understand XML, let me simplify the picture a little. You can write database applications without ever seeing a line of XML code. ADO.NET uses XML to format the data and move them between the database and the client application (or any of the other tiers of the application). As you work with the objects of ADO.NET, you access data in their native format. XML is totally transparent to you.

The Architecture of ADO.NET

You already know how to retrieve data from a database with SQL statements and stored procedures. Now you'll learn where the data are stored on the client computer and how to process them. We'll get to the first few examples of database applications shortly, but first I would like to overview the architecture of ADO.NET. Once you have a good idea of the big picture and the motivation behind the design of ADO.NET, you'll be able to better understand the objects of ADO.NET and how to use them.

ADO.NET is considered to be the evolution of ADO, but it doesn't even resemble ADO. ADO was designed on the assumption that the client could maintain a connection to the database. When the Web wasn't an issue, you could set up a connection to the database and request data over this connection, or update the database through the same connection. The client application was connected to the database at all times, and it could access any table at any time. In fact, this is how most database applications that run on local area networks are written today.

As programmers were looking for ways to access their databases over the Web, they realized that they couldn't write applications that maintained their own connection to the database. They still used ADO, but they were using ADO in a disconnected mode: they wrote code to read data from the database, move them to the client, and close the connection to the database. The processing of the data took place on the client. To update the database, programmers had to establish a new connection, send the modified data back to the server to update the tables of the database, and then close the connection again. Microsoft kept adding features to ADO to enhance the support of disconnected sets of data.

Clearly, there was a need for a different programming paradigm, one that would completely decouple the server from the client. This new paradigm was implemented with ADO.NET, which uses a disconnected architecture. The client application requests the data, which are downloaded to the client computer and stored locally. The client is your application that uses a database over the company's network, or a Web application that connects to a Web server through any connection, from dial-up to T1. Even if you have a fast connection, ADO.NET doesn't allow you to maintain a connection to the database and access it directly. Instead, you're required to retrieve the data you need to the client and work with them there.

You know how to request the data you're interested in. All you need is a structure that will hold the data. This structure is an object called a *DataSet*. The DataSet is a cache for your data, and it looks just like the database. You can edit the data in the DataSet, add new data, even combine the data you retrieved from your database with data from another database. It is possible (but certainly not recommended) to download all the tables to the client and work with a complete copy of the database. Everything you do the DataSet is local to the client and doesn't affect the tables in the database. When you're ready to update the underlying tables in the database, you establish a new connection, send the modified data, and close the connection again.

The DataSet is at the core of ADO.NET, because everything takes place in the DataSet. With ADO, there was a similar object, the Recordset object, where you could store a table or the result of a query and process it locally. The DataSet is far more than a Recordset: it's a miniature database, made up of tables and relations between them. Let's say you want to work with the invoices issued last month. The data you need are some rows of the Customers table (the customers that placed one or more orders in this period), some rows of the Orders table (the orders placed in the same period), and some rows of the Order Details table (the details that correspond to the selected orders). Chances are you don't need all the columns of these tables either. So you can specify, with SQL statements or stored procedures, the data you need and bring them into a DataSet on the client. The data will end up in three different tables in the DataSet, and you can establish relations between tables. In essence, you're working with a subset of the database. You can review the data, edit them, do anything you would do if you were working directly against the database. The DataSet can impose the same constraints and enforce referential integrity between its tables. After you're done processing the data, the DataSet knows how to move the changes back to the database—after all, they have the same structure.

While the data is in the DataSet, other users can add new rows to the tables of the database, even edit some of the rows you have copied into the DataSet. Unfortunately, there's no way for you to know in advance that one of the customer rows in a local DataSet is no longer the same as the original row in the database. You will only find out when you attempt to update the database. As a result, this architecture is not ideal for applications like flight reservations. If you need this type of immediate access to the database, you should request data as you need them and update the database immediately. These types of applications are quite uncommon. ADO.NET is a great architecture for typical applications most of us are faced with on a daily basis, and it's especially well suited for the Web. However, the current version of ADO.NET doesn't address all the issues. It's very likely that the next version of ADO.NET will also support connected DataSets. If not, there will be applications that ADO.NET can't handle.

To get the data into a DataSet, you must first establish a connection to the database. The Connection object allows you to specify the database you want to work with, and it's one of the simpler objects of ADO.NET. Between the database and the DataSet there's another object, the DataAdapter object. While the client application works with the data in the DataSet most of the time, every now and then it must exchange information with the database (query the database, or update it). The communication between the database and the DataSet takes place through the DataAdapter. This object knows how to update the database, as well as how to move data from the database and store them into the DataSet. As you will see, the DataAdapter object contains four commands for retrieving rows from the database, updating and deleting existing rows, and inserting new rows. These commands are SQL statements, and this is all the information the DataAdapter object needs to move data between the DataSet and the underlying data source.

The first advantage of the DataSet object is that it doesn't care where its data came from, as long as there's a DataAdapter object that can move data to and from the DataSet. As a result, you can create DataSets in code, or from an XML file. You can even save (or persist) a DataSet object to a disk file and write a database application without the database.

How About XML?

ADO.NET and XML go hand in hand, so where does XML come into the picture? XML is a method of representing structured data, and ADO.NET uses XML to pass data between the server and the client. Fortunately, you don't have to write any XML code yourself, neither do you have to parse XML documents to retrieve the information. ADO.NET uses XML for its own purposes, and you can take advantage of it and write XML code, if you want. It is possible, for example, to create a new DataSet with XML statements and store your data there. This DataSet is totally independent of a database and resides in the client computer's memory. When you're done using it, you can store it to a file and retrieve it from there later. In effect, this is a mechanism to create your own data store (it's not a database, of course, but you can have related tables), without the overhead of setting up a SQL Server database.

Later in this chapter, you will see this technique in action. XML is an interesting technology, but it's not required for learning the basics of programming with ADO.NET. After mastering simpler topics such as data binding and programming DataSets, you can explore XML on your own.

Creating a DataSet

We'll start our exploration of database programming by creating a DataSet. In this chapter, you'll see how to create a DataSet with visual tools and how to display its data on a grid. In the following chapter, you'll learn how to create DataSets programmatically, but the visual tools are much simpler, and in most cases there's no reason to write code to connect to a database and populate a DataSet.

To create a new database application, start a new project as usual. When the project's form appears, open the Server Explorer and expand one of the databases. Select the Northwind database and expand its icon to see the objects of the database. In the Tables section, select the Customers table, drag it with the mouse, and drop it on the form. VB will add two new objects in the Components tray: *SqlConnection1* and *SqlDataAdapter1*.

The first object, *SqlConnection1*, is the application's connection to the database. This object contains all the information needed to connect to the database. If you look at its properties, you will see that its ConnectionString property is:

```
data source=PowerToolkit;initial catalog=Northwind;integrated security=SSPI;
persist security info=False;workstation id=POWERTOOLKIT;packet size=4096
```

SqlDataAdapter1 is the channel between your application and the database. The DataSet doesn't know anything about the database—it's not its job to know about the database. The application can request the data through the DataAdapter object, process them and then rely on the DataAdapter to update the database.

If you look up the properties of the *SqlDataAdapter1* object (Figure 21.1), you'll see that it has a SelectCommand property, which is a Command object that retrieves the data from the table. The SelectCommand object has a property called CommandText, which is a SELECT SQL statement:

```
SELECT CustomerID, CompanyName, ContactName, ContactTitle, Address, City, Region,
PostalCode, Country, Phone, Fax FROM dbo.Customers
```

FIGURE 21.1

The properties of the SqlDataAdapter object

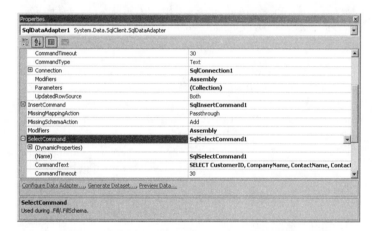

This statement was generated automatically when you dropped the Customers table on the form. VB picked up the information from the table's structure in the database and create a SELECT statement to retrieve all the columns of all rows.

If you select the SelectCommand item in the Properties window and then click the button with the ellipsis that appears next to the item's setting, the Query Builder window will pop up and you can edit the SELECT statement (to exclude a few columns, or specify selection criteria to limit the number of rows returned by the query). You can also edit the SELECT statement by selecting the *SqlDataAdapter1* object on the designer and clicking the Configure Data Adapter command at the bottom of the Properties window.

The *SqlDataAdapter1* also has an InsertCommand property, which is shown next:

```
INSERT INTO dbo.Customers(CustomerID, CompanyName, ContactName, ContactTitle,
       Address, City, Region, PostalCode, Country, Phone, Fax)
```

```
VALUES (@CustomerID, @CompanyName, @ContactName, @ContactTitle, @Address,
        @City, @Region, @PostalCode, @Country, @Phone, @Fax);
SELECT CustomerID, CompanyName, ContactName, ContactTitle, Address, City,
        Region, PostalCode, Country, Phone, Fax FROM dbo.Customers
WHERE (CustomerID = @Select_CustomerID)
```

Any string that starts with the @ symbol is a variable. The DataAdapter sets the values of all these variables to the values of the new row to be inserted and then executes the InsertCommand against the database. The INSERT statement will add a new row to the Customers table. The SELECT statement following the INSERT statement selects the newly added row from the table and returns it to the application. There are two more commands in the SqlDataAdapter object, UpdateCommand and DeleteCommand. These two commands update a row in the Customers table and delete a row, respectively. We'll return to the DataAdapter object and look at its properties, as well as how to set it up manually, later in this chapter. For now, keep in mind that the action of adding a table to a form creates and configures a DataAdapter object.

NOTE *If you're working with an Access database, you'll follow the same steps, but the objects will have different names. The Connection object's default name will be OleDbConnection, and the DataAdapter object's default name will be OleDbDataAdapter. The SQL statements that move data in and out of an Access database may use a slightly different syntax, but they're equally simple statements.*

So far, you've created and configured a DataAdapter object that knows how to access the database and retrieve the desired data. The next step is to tell the DataAdapter where to leave the data it retrieves from the database, and where the changes reside, so that it can update the database. This is the DataSet object. Select the DataAdapter object on the designer and locate the Generate Dataset link at the bottom of the Properties window. Alternatively, you can open the Data menu and select the Generate Dataset command. (The Data menu isn't available unless the form is visible.) You will see the Generate Dataset dialog box, which is shown in Figure 21.2. This dialog box proposes to create a new DataSet object, named *DataSet1*, that will contain the table Customers. As you will see in the following example, a DataSet may contain multiple tables—that's why you're given the option to select the table(s) you want to add to the DataSet. Click OK to create the new DataSet object. In the following examples we'll use more descriptive names, but for this introductory example I'm going to use the default names.

Two new items will be added to the project: the `DataSet1.xsd` item in the Solution Explorer and the *DataSet11* object on the design surface. *DataSet1* is a class that describes the structure of the data you'll retrieve from the database. *DataSet11* is an instance of this class—this is where the data will be stored.

Let's see what we have done so far. Open the Data menu and select Preview Data. Alternatively, you can right-click the DataAdapter's icon in the Components tray and select Preview Data. This command will open the Data Adapter Preview window, which is shown in Figure 21.3. When the Data Adapter Preview dialog box comes up, it will be initially empty. Click the Fill Dataset button to execute the query, populate the DataSet, and preview the Customers table. You can see that the query retrieved the desired data from the database. If the DataSet contains multiple tables, you'll have to select the name of the table you want to preview in the Data Tables list, and its rows will appear in the preview pane.

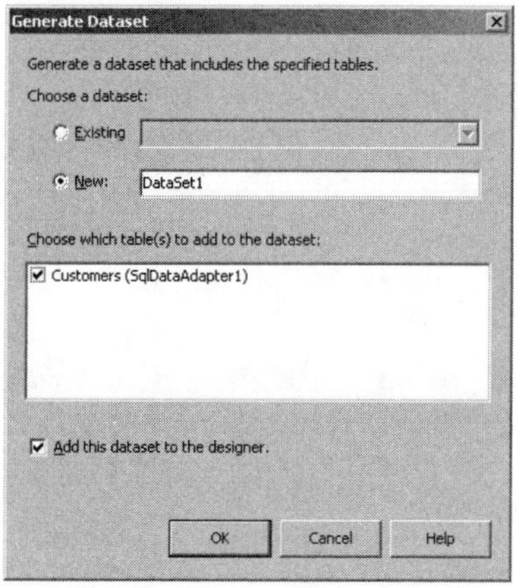

FIGURE 21.2

To generate a
DataSet, specify its
name and the tables
you want to add to it.

FIGURE 21.3

Previewing the Customers table

The last step is to display the information to the user, and this is what we'll do next. There are many ways to present the information on a front-end application, but we'll start with a tool designed specifically for this purpose.

The DataGrid Control

One of the most common tasks in programming database applications is to present data to the users. We have created the DataSet that will hold our data, so we can now design an interface to present the data residing in the DataSet to the user. At design time, the DataSet is empty, of course. The DataSet object contains information about the structure of the table(s) it will hold at runtime, but no actual data.

The primary control for displaying DataSets is the DataGrid control, which is similar to the grid you use to edit the rows of a table with SQL Server's Enterprise Manager or even Access. The application you'll develop in this section is called Customers (it's available in this chapter's folder on the companion CD), and its main form is shown in Figure 21.4. The DataGrid control can display not only single tables, but it also allows you to navigate through the rows of related tables. For example, you can display categories, select a category, and view the products under the selected category. Let's start by displaying a single table on the DataGrid control.

FIGURE 21.4

Displaying the Customers table on a DataGrid control

ID	Company	Contact	Title
ALFKI	Alfreds Futterkiste	Maria Anders	Sales Representative
ANATR	Ana Trujillo Emparedados y helados	Ana Trujillo	Owner
ANTON	Antonio Moreno Taquería	Antonio Moreno	Owner
AROUT	Around the Horn	Thomas Hardy	Sales Representative
BERGS	Berglunds snabbköp	Christina Berglund	Order Administrator
BLAUS	Blauer See Delikatessen	Hanna Moos	Sales Representative
BLONP	Blondesddsl père et fils	Frédérique Citeaux	Marketing Manager
BOLID	Bólido Comidas preparadas	Martín Sommer	Owner
BONAP	Bon app'	Laurence Lebihan	Owner
BOTTM	Bottom-Dollar Markets	Elizabeth Lincoln	Accounting Manager
BSBEV	B's Beverages	Victoria Ashworth	Sales Representative

Load Data   Update Table

NOTE   *By the way, the DataGrid control isn't appropriate for all types of interfaces, and you shouldn't give users free access to all the rows of a DataTable. However, it's the best tool for visualizing the structure of a DataSet, and you will find it convenient at the beginning. As you learn more about the objects of ADO.NET and how to program them, you'll start using the more traditional controls to build your interfaces. The DataGrid control, however, remains a powerful tool, especially for displaying DataSets.*

Switch the project's form and place a DataGrid control on it. To specify where the data will come from, you must set the control's DataSource property to a DataSet. Locate the DataSource property in the Properties window and expand the list of possible settings for the property. You will see two settings: DataSet11 and DataSet11.Customers. If you set the DataSource property to a DataSet object, then you will have to specify which of the tables in the DataSet you want to display on the grid. Since our DataSet contains a single table, set the DataSource property to DataSet11.Customers. Alternatively, you can set the DataSource property to DataSet11 and the DataMember property Customers.

The names of all the fields will appear at the header of the DataGrid control. The data is still at the server; the control must be populated when the user requests it. That's why you see only the field names and no data. By default, all columns have the same length. Clearly, you must customize the appearance of the DataGrid control. But first, let's see what our data looks like on the control.

If you run the application now, you won't see any data on the control. The DataSet must be populated explicitly by calling the Fill method of the associated DataAdapter. Place a button on the form, name it Load Data, and insert the following code in its Click event handler:

```
Private Sub Button1_Click(ByVal sender As System.Object, _
                ByVal e As System.EventArgs) Handles Button1.Click
    DataSet11.Clear()
    SqlDataAdapter1.Fill(DataSet11, "Customers")
End Sub
```

The first statement clears the current contents of the *DataSet11* object. The Fill method of the DataAdapter accepts as arguments the names of a DataSet and of a table in the DataSet and populates the specified table. You can omit the second argument if the DataSet contains a single table.

Run the application, click the Load Data button, and the grid will be populated with the rows of the Customers table. You can edit the fields on the grid, but the changes are local to the DataSet and they're not automatically submitted to the database. To update the underlying tables, you must explicitly call the Update method of the DataAdapter object. The Update method accepts two arguments, just like the Fill method. You specify the names of the DataSet and of the table to be updated. Enter the following statement behind the Update Table button:

```
Private Sub Button2_Click(ByVal sender As System.Object, _
            ByVal e As System.EventArgs) Handles Button2.Click
    SqlDataAdapter1.Update(DataSet11, "Customers")
End Sub
```

Updating the rows in the underlying tables is not a trivial task, and it takes much more code than a single call to the Update method. For this example, we'll assume that you're updating simple tables and no other users are accessing the same tables at the same time. A more practical, robust approach requires quite a bit of code, and we'll discuss it in the following chapter. The Update method updates one row at a time, and it stops as soon as it encounters an error. If the first edited row can't be written to the underlying table, the DataAdapter object will not attempt to update the remaining edited rows. To continue the update process even if one or more rows fail, set the DataAdapter object's ContinueUpdateOnError to True.

CUSTOMIZING THE DATAGRID CONTROL

The default appearance of the DataGrid control is rather blunt, and you'll always have to customize it. The simplest customization tool for the DataGrid control is the AutoFormat command. Right-click the DataGrid control and, from the context menu, select AutoFormat. On the dialog box that appears, you will see a list of available styles, such as Professional, Simple, and Classic. You can select each style on the dialog box to preview it and apply any style to the control by selecting it with the mouse and clicking OK to close the dialog box.

You can also customize each individual element of the control. Select the DataGrid control on the form and locate its TableStyles property in the Properties window. Click the button with the ellipsis and you will see the DataGridTableStyle Collection Editor, shown in Figure 21.5. The DataGrid control can display one or more tables, and each table can have its own style. Since our DataSet contains a single table, we must add a single DataGridTableStyle object to the collection. Click Add and the *DataGridTableStyle1* object will be added to the collection. You can change its name too, but let's leave the default for the first example.

Here you can set properties like the HeaderFont, the background color of the rows, as well as an alternate background color (the AlternatingBackColor value will be used for even-numbered rows). The DataGridTableStyle object won't be automatically associated to any of the tables; you must set the name of the table explicitly with the MappingName property. Locate this property in the Properties section of the dialog box, expand the list of possible values (which are the names of the tables in the DataSet), and select the Customers table.

FIGURE 21.5

Specifying the
appearance of each
table in the Data-
Grid control

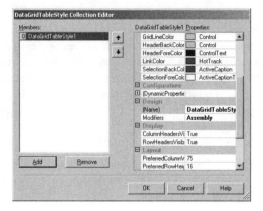

Right above the MappingName property, you'll see the GridColumnStyles property, which is
also a collection. Click the button with the ellipsis, and you will see the GridColumnStyles Collection Editor, shown in Figure 21.6. This collection, which is initially empty, contains one member for
each column, and each member determines the appearance of a different column in the parent table.

FIGURE 21.6

Specifying the
appearance of each
column on the
DataGrid control

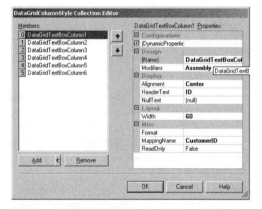

In the dialog box of Figure 21.6, you can set the widths, captions, and alignments of the individual columns. Don't forget to set the MappingName property of each DataGridColumnStyle item to
the appropriate field of the table. Any DataGridColumnStyle item that's not mapped to a column
will be ignored. The NullText property is a string that will appear in every field that's Null.

DISPLAYING RELATED TABLES

In this section, we'll build a project that involves two related tables, the Products and Categories
tables. Most of the applications you'll write will handle related rows from multiple tables, as isolated
tables are quite rare. We'll display the data on a DataGrid control again, but in a hierarchical way.
The DataGrid allows you to display the rows of the parent table (in our case, the Categories table)
and navigate to each parent row's child rows. If a parent row has child rows, a plus sign is displayed
in front of its name. You can click this symbol to view the related rows. At any point you can return

to the parent table, select another row, and view its child rows. The project you'll build in this section is called RelatedTables, and you can find it on the CD. The project's form is shown in Figure 21.7.

FIGURE 21.7

Displaying a table with related rows on the DataGrid control

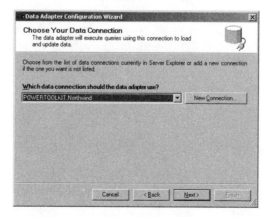

The first step is to create a DataSet with two related tables. Start a new project, open the Server Explorer, and drop the Categories and Products tables of the Northwind database onto the form. VB will add automatically a Connection object to the form, as well as two DataAdapters. Since both DataAdapters see the same database, a single Connection object will suffice. Now you must configure the two DataAdapters. First, rename them to *DACategories* and *DAProducts*—no reason to work with names that differ in the last digit. To configure a DataAdapter object, select it with the mouse and click the Configure Data Adapter link at the bottom of the Properties window (or select the same command from the DataAdapter's context menu). The default DataAdapter object is configured with a SQL statement that retrieves all columns and all rows of a table. In most cases you'll have to edit this statement to retrieve a subset of a table.

To configure a DataAdapter, you can use the Data Adapter Configuration Wizard. In the following section, I will describe all the options offered by the wizard, and then we'll use it to configure the *DACategories* DataAdapter.

THE DATA ADAPTER CONFIGURATION WIZARD

The Configure Data Adapter command will start the Data Adapter Configuration Wizard, and the first screen of the wizard is a welcome screen. Click Next to view the next one, which prompts you to select a Connection object. Accept the default connection, which was established when you dropped the tables on the form.

Click Next to see the next screen of the wizard, which is the Choose A Query Type screen. Here you can specify the method that will be used to retrieve the data from the database. You can use SQL statements, use existing stored procedures, or create new stored procedures. When you'll be working with large application or in a team environment, you will have to design the stored procedures first, and then you'll start building database applications. The wizard can generate both the SQL statements and stored procedures needed to access the database. I suggest you familiarize yourself with SQL statements first and use stored procedures later. Let's see how each option works.

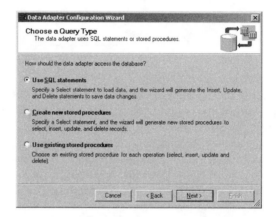

Select the SQL statements option and click Next. The Wizard will display the Generate The SQL Statements screen, where it will display a SELECT statement that retrieves all rows and all columns of the database. You can either edit the default SELECT statement or type a new statement. You can also click the Query Builder button to start Query Builder. Use this tool to visually specify the data you want to retrieve from one or more tables, as explained in Chapter 20. When you close the Query Builder, you'll be returned to the Generate the SQL Statements screen and the new SELECT statement will appear on the this screen.

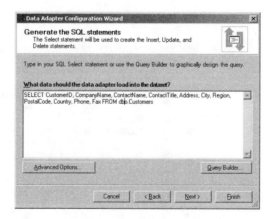

By default, the wizard will create all the SQL statements for retrieving and editing the table (the INSERT, DELETE, and UPDATE statements). If you don't plan to update the table from within the application—you only want to present data to the user—click the Advanced Options buttons. A dialog box will pop up where you can disable the generation of the UPDATE/INSERT/DELETE statements. On the same dialog box, you can set two more options to control how the statements will be generated.

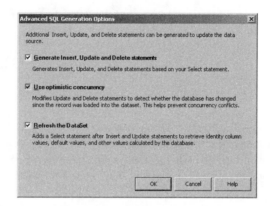

The option Use Optimistic Concurrency applies to the UPDATE and DELETE statements. If you leave this option checked, the resulting statements will not modify any rows in the underlying table(s) in the database if these rows have been edited since your application read them. "Optimistic concurrency" means that we don't anticipate multiple users editing the same row at the same time. If this happens rarely, then you can check the Optimistic Concurrency option. In the few cases that this happens, your application won't be able to update the rows that have already been edited.

If you clear this option, the wizard will generate SELECT statements that update the underlying tables even if they have changed since they were read into the local DataSet. In this situation, the last user to commit his changes to the database wins.

The last option, Refresh The DataSet, generates SQL statements that update the database and then retrieve the rows they changed with a SQL statement. Check this option so that the application can immediately retrieve the new rows and display them on your form.

Click OK to close the Advanced Options dialog box and return to the wizard. Click the Next button to view the last screen that summarizes the results. Click Finish on this screen and the wizard will generate the SQL statements according to the options you specified on the wizard.

If you choose Create New Stored Procedures in the Choose A Query Type screen of the wizard, the next screen will display the SQL statement that retrieves all the data from the specified table. You can click the Query Builder to specify the query with visual tools. After specifying the SQL SELECT statement on which the stored procedures will be based, click Next to see the Create The Stored Procedures screen.

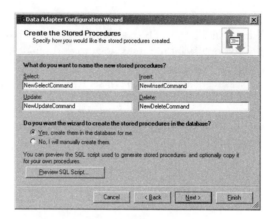

On this screen, you can specify the names of the stored procedures for each action your application will perform against the database (select rows, insert new rows, editing existing rows, and delete rows). You can also specify whether the wizard should generate the stored procedures and add them to the database, or whether you want to write the stored procedures to the database yourself. You can click the Preview SQL Script button to see the stored procedures that the wizard will generate. You should let the wizard generate the stored procedures and edit them from within Server Explorer if you have to. Click Next to see the last screen of the wizard that summarizes the results.

If you choose Use Existing Stored Procedures in the Choose A Query Type screen of the wizard, the next screen will prompt you to select the four stored procedures for the actions you want to perform against the database. If a procedure requires parameters, you must specify the columns that contain the parameter values as well.

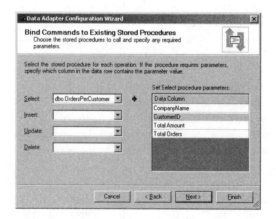

CONFIGURING THE DACATEGORIES DATAADAPTER

Let's return to the RelatedTables project and configure the DACategories DataAdapter. The Categories table contains an Image field, which we won't display on our form. Accept the default settings on the Data Adapter Configuration Wizard, and change the SQL statement by removing the name of the Picture field. Here is the edited SQL statement you will see on the Generate the SQL Statements screen of the wizard:

```
SELECT CategoryID, CategoryName, Description
FROM dbo.Categories
```

Then configure the DAProducts DataAdapter by accepting all the defaults. Use the SQL statement generated by the wizard, which retrieves all the fields of the Products table (unless you want to omit a few columns). Once the two DataAdapters have been configured, you can generate the DataSet. Click the link Generate Dataset (or select the command Generate Dataset from the Data menu) and you will see the Generate Dataset dialog box (shown earlier in Figure 21.2). The wizard suggests that you create a DataSet with a single table. Check both table names and then change the default name of the DataSet to *CategoriesProducts*. You have just created a single DataSet with two tables.

When the `CategoriesProducts.xsd` file appears on the Solution Explorer, double-click it. The XSD file contains the schema of the two tables in the DataSet, but not the relationship between them. Even though the relationship between the two tables exists in the database, the wizard didn't relate the tables in the DataSet to one another. You must do so by establishing a relationship manually. With the two tables on the designer's surface, open the Toolbox. The Toolbox is a new one and contains the tools for editing XML schemas. Drag the Relation icon from the Toolbox and drop it on the Products table. The Edit Relation window, shown in Figure 21.8, will pop up. Here, you can specify the characteristics of the relationship between the two tables. Specifying a relationship between two tables in the DataSet is no different than specifying a relationship in the database. The Parent Element is the primary table, and the Child Element is the foreign table. After you have specified the primary and foreign tables, you must set the key fields of each table. Notice that the primary key can't be changed: it's always the parent table's primary key. Finally, you can specify the rules for updating, deleting, and inserting rows. For now, leave the Default option in these boxes.

FIGURE 21.8

Establishing a relation between two tables in a DataSet

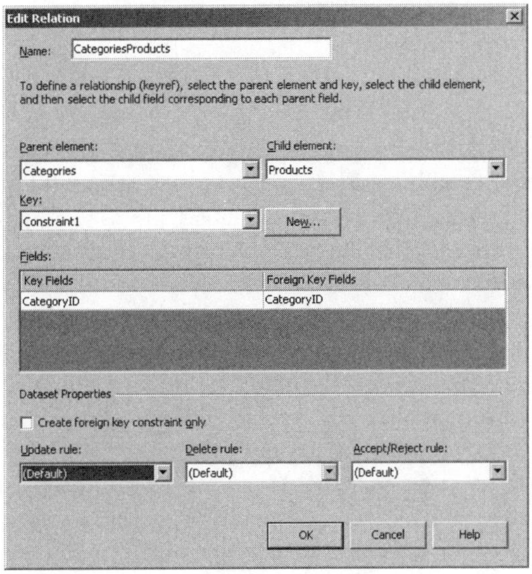

Click the OK button to return to the XML Designer. The relationship you created is depicted with a line between the two tables as shown in Figure 21.9. You can click the diamond-shaped icon at the middle of this line and select Edit Relation to see a dialog box where you can modify the relation.

FIGURE 21.9

How a relation is depicted on the XML Designer

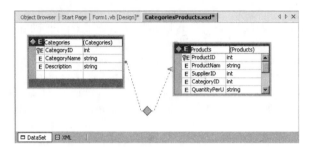

If you click the XML tab at the bottom of the Designer, you will see the XML description of the relationship:

```
<xsd:unique name="Constraint1" msdata:PrimaryKey="true">
    <xsd:selector xpath=".//Categories" />
    <xsd:field xpath="CategoryID" />
</xsd:unique>
<xsd:unique name="Products_Constraint1" msdata:ConstraintName="Constraint1"
msdata:PrimaryKey="true">
    <xsd:selector xpath=".//Products" />
    <xsd:field xpath="ProductID" />
</xsd:unique>
<xsd:keyref name="CategoriesProducts" refer="Constraint1">
    <xsd:selector xpath=".//Products" />
    <xsd:field xpath="CategoryID" />
</xsd:keyref>
```

I can't get into the details of XML here, but it's easy to see the definitions of the primary and foreign keys. *keyref* is XML's term for a relation. The CategoriesProducts relation is between Constraint1 (the Categories table's primary key) and the CategoryID field of the Products table.

We now have a DataSet with two related tables, just as they appear in the database. The DataSet will be populated with a copy of the two tables the moment it's created. You can work with the copies of the tables and update the underlying tables in the database whenever you see fit (if you edit the DataSet). The catch here is that the DataSet must be populated at once. Should you be working with a table of half a million book titles, you'd download an enormous amount of information to the client. If the user wants to view the first few titles in a couple of categories only, you're wasting system resources. In your applications, you should limit the number of rows downloaded to the client, and you'll see how to do this later in this chapter. Never download more data to the client than you're going to use. Dumping thousands of rows on a DataGrid control isn't going to be of much help to the user either.

To load the data to the grid, enter the statements shown in Listing 21.1 in the form's Load event.

LISTING 21.1: POPULATING A DATASET WITH TWO TABLES

```
Private Sub Form1_Load(ByVal sender As System.Object, _
                ByVal e As System.EventArgs) Handles MyBase.Load
    DACategories.Fill(CategoriesProducts1, "Categories")
    DAProducts.Fill(CategoriesProducts1, "Products")
End Sub
```

Run the application now. When the form comes up, it will be empty, displaying a plus symbol where the first row should appear. Click it and you will see the names of the two tables: Categories and Products. Select the parent table, Categories, and the grid will be populated with the rows of the Categories table. In front of each row, you'll see the plus symbol, which indicates that all the rows in the Categories table are parent rows and you can expand them to see their child rows from the Products table.

If you click one of the plus signs, you'll see the names of all relations that use the Categories table as the parent table. In our example, there's only one such relation, the CategoriesProducts relation. Click this link and the grid will be populated with the selected category's child rows, as shown in Figure 21.10. At the top of the grid, you see the name of the parent table and the selected row. This is the parent row of all the rows currently on the grid (it's the category to which all the products belong). At the top-left corner of the grid are two icons: The back arrow icons takes you back to the parent row. The other icon is a toggle that hides/displays the details of the parent row.

FIGURE 21.10

Viewing child rows on the DataGrid control

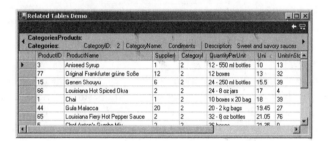

The headers of each column are clickable. When a header is clicked, the rows on the grid are sorted alphabetically according to the selected column. If you sort a column, a little arrow appears next to its header, indicating the order in which the rows are sorted (ascending or descending). To disable the sorting of the columns, set the DataGrid control's AllowSorting property to False (its default value is True).

As you can see, the DataGrid control can handle related tables without any code. It picks up all the information about relations from the schema (the XSD file created for you by the wizard) and uses it to build an elaborate interface. The DataGrid is fine for building an interface to browse one or more tables, but when it comes to updating the underling tables, you must provide additional code. You're going to learn how to write robust code for updating the underlying tables in the following chapter. In the following section, we'll look at another simple technique for displaying data on a form, using the familiar Windows controls.

Data Binding

What you've done so far was to bind the DataGrid control to the rows of a DataSet. This process is called *data binding,* and it's not an exclusive feature of the DataGrid control. In fact, all controls can be bound to a DataSet and display a specific field of the current row from the DataSet. You can create a form with TextBox controls on it and bind each control's Text property to a different DataSet field. As you move through the rows of the DataSet, the values on the controls will change to reflect the values of the corresponding fields in the current row. If you edit the TextBox controls, the new values will overwrite the ones in the DataSet. No changes, however, will be immediately sent to the data source, because the DataSet resides on the client computer and is disconnected from its source. To update the underlying table(s), you must call the DataAdapter object's Update method.

Figure 21.11 shows a simple interface built with data-bound TextBox controls. Each control is bound to a different field in the Customers table, and the control values change as you navigate through the rows of the table with the help of the buttons at the bottom of the form. Again, the Customers table resides in a DataSet object on the client. The form shown in the figure is the main form of the ViewEditCustomers project, which you will find on the CD.

FIGURE 21.11

Viewing and editing the Customers table through data-bound TextBox controls

Before looking at the application of Figure 21.11, let me overview the process of data binding. To begin with, there are two types of data binding: simple and complex. This distinction is necessary because some controls, such as the DataGrid and ListBox, can display multiple fields and/or rows, while other controls, including the TextBox control, can only display a single field from the current row.

The complex data-bound controls have a DataSource and a DataMember property. DataSource determines where the data will come from and is usually set to the name of DataSet object. If the DataSet contains multiple tables, then you must also specify which of the tables you want to display on the control. You do so by setting the control's DataMember property to the name of the appropriate table. As you saw in the preceding section, the DataGrid control can display multiple related tables. If that's what you want, then don't set the DataMember property. A DataSet may contain (and usually does) multiple unrelated tables, in which case you must set the DataMember property to one of the tables in the DataSet.

Simple data-bound controls don't have a DataSource property. Instead, they have a group of properties under the heading DataBinding. Under the DataBinding section in the control's Properties window, you will see the names of the properties you can bind to a DataSet object. The TextBox properties that can be bound are Text and Tag. We usually set the Text property to a general field and the Tag property to the table's primary key, so that we can read it at any time and identify the current row in the table. The most common scenario is to bind the Text property to the customer's name (or other information useful to the user) and the Tag property to the customer's ID. With this arrangement, we can instantly locate related rows in other tables (the customer's orders, for example) because we have the ID of the current customer.

The CheckBox control has more properties you can bind to data. The Checked property can be bound to a True/False field, and the value of the field sets or clears the check mark on the control. You can also bind the control's CheckAlign property to a data field, but this a bit far-fetched. As you will see in the example of the following section, you can bind one or more controls on the form to the fields of a DataSet with point-and-click operations.

As can see, it's actually easier to bind a so-called complex control, because you don't have to specify which property binds to which field. You simply display all the fields. There are two controls, the ListBox and ComboBox controls, that are a little more complicated, and you will see shortly how to bind these two controls and use them as lookup devices. First, we'll build a simple application for viewing and editing the rows of a single table.

VB.NET at Work: The ViewEditCustomers Project

Start a new project and design its form like the one shown in Figure 21.11. Place the controls on the form, then create a DataSet with the rows of the Customers table as follows. Open the Server Explorer, open the Northwind branch, and drop the Customers table on the form. Rename the *Sql-DataAdapter1* object that will be automatically created to DACustomers. This is the DataAdapter object that will retrieve the rows of the table and update the underlying tables. Then configure the DataAdapter—just accept the default SQL statement that retrieves all the rows of the table. Create the DataSet object and name it *DSCustomers*. The *DSCustomers1* object will be placed at the controls tray below the form's design surface.

At this point, you can bind the controls on the form to the *DSCustomers1* DataSet. Select the top TextBox control (make sure its ReadOnly property is set to True, because we'll use it to display the customer's ID, which the user isn't allowed to edit). Open the DataBinding section in the control's Properties window, locate the Text item, and expand its list of possible settings (Figure 21.12). You will see the *DSCustomers1* DataSet object. Click the plus symbol in front of its name and you will see the name of the Customers table (here you will see the names of all tables in the DataSet, but this specific DataSet contains a single table). Expand the table and you will see the names of the fields in the table. Select the CustomerID field; this will bind the first TextBox control on the form to the CustomerID field of the Customers table. At any given time, it will display the value of the CustomerID field on the current row.

FIGURE 21.12

Binding the Text property of a TextBox control to a field of a table in a DataSet

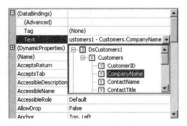

Bind the remaining TextBoxes to the appropriate fields of the Customers table by repeating the process just described.

Next, you must insert the appropriate code behind the Load Table button, which will move the rows of the Customers table from the database to the local DataSet by calling the DataAdapter's Fill method:

```
Private Sub Button1_Click(ByVal sender As System.Object,_
            ByVal e As System.EventArgs) Handles Button1.Click
    DSCustomers1.Clear()
    DACustomers.Fill(DsCustomers1, "Customers")
End Sub
```

THE BINDINGCONTEXT OBJECT

The interesting code is behind the navigational buttons, which allow you to move from row to row. To change the current location in a DataTable, use the BindingContext object. This object is a property of the form and keeps track of the current position in each DataTable of each DataSet. (Technically, there's a CurrencyManager object for each DataTable, and the BindingContext object keeps track of all the CurrencyManager objects. Since you'll never have to program directly against the CurrencyManager object, the BindingContext is the object you must become familiar with).

To specify the appropriate BindingContext object, pass to it as arguments the name of the DataSet and the name of a table in the DataSet. The most important property of the BindingContext object is the Position property, which is the current position in the table. The current position in the Customers DataTable of the *DSCustomers1* DataSet object is:

```
Me.BindingContext(DsCustomers1, "Customers").Position
```

To move to any row, set this property to any value between 0 (the first row) and the following expression, which is the index of the last row:

```
Me.BindingContext(DsCustomers1, "Customers").Count - 1
```

To move to the next or previous row, increase or decrease the Position property by one. Of course, you must take into consideration the current position, so that you won't attempt to move beyond the first or last row in the table. Listing 21.2 shows the minimum code for the previous button.

LISTING 21.2: MOVING TO THE PREVIOUS ROW

```
Private Sub bttnPrevious_Click(ByVal sender As System.Object, _
            ByVal e As System.EventArgs) Handles bttnPrevious.Click
    If Me.BindingContext(DsCustomers1, "Customers").Position > 0 Then
        Me.BindingContext(DsCustomers1, "Customers").Position = _
          (Me.BindingContext(DsCustomers1, "Customers").Position - 1)
        PositionChanged()
    End If
End Sub
```

The PositionChanged() subroutine displays the current row's number at the bottom of the screen, and its code is shown in Listing 21.3.

```
Sub PositionChanged()
    lblPosition.Text = (((Me.BindingContext(DsCustomers1, _
        "Customers").Position + 1).ToString + " / ") + _
        Me.BindingContext(DsCustomers1, "Customers").Count.ToString)
End Sub
```

If you run the project now, you can iterate through the Customers table's rows with the navigational buttons and edit any field on any row. The Update Table button submits the changes to the database by calling the DataAdapter's Update method:

```
Private Sub Button2_Click(ByVal sender As System.Object, _
            ByVal e As System.EventArgs) Handles Button2.Click
    DACustomers.Update(DsCustomers1)
End Sub
```

However, it's easy to crash the program. If you set the CompanyName field to an empty string, a runtime error will occur when you attempt to move to another row. The DataTable can't accept a row with a blank CompanyName field, because it would violate one of the restrictions.

To handle this error, we must add some error-trapping code to the handlers of the navigational buttons. We'll discuss the topic of updating the DataSet and the underlying tables in detail in the following chapter. Here we'll use a very simple error handler: If a runtime exception occurs, we'll cancel the edit process by calling the BindingContext object's CancelCurrentEdit method. We'll display a message box with a description of the error and then call CancelCurrentEdit, which will restore the original values of the fields on the data-bound controls. The revised event handler of the Previous button is shown in the Listing 21.4.

```
Private Sub bttnPrevious_Click(ByVal sender As System.Object, _
            ByVal e As System.EventArgs) Handles bttnPrevious.Click
    Try
        If Me.BindingContext(DsCustomers1, "Customers").Position > 0 Then
            Me.BindingContext(DsCustomers1, "Customers").Position = _
                (Me.BindingContext(DsCustomers1, "Customers").Position - 1)
            PositionChanged()
        End If
    Catch dataException As Exception
        MsgBox(dataException.Message)
        Me.BindingContext(DsCustomers1, "Customers").CancelCurrentEdit()
    End Try
End Sub
```

Run the ViewEditCustomers application, browse all the customers in the DataSet, and edit a few. You can commit the changes to the database at any time by clicking the Update Table button. Or you can discard the edits and reload the data into the DataSet by clicking the Load Table button.

In Chapter 22, you'll learn how to validate the data and how to commit the changes to the database in a more robust manner. A sure way to crash this application is to load the data, remove one of the customers from the underlying table (use the Enterprise Manager to delete a row of the Customers table in the Northwind database), and then attempt to update the database. The operation will fail, because the Update method will attempt to update a row that no longer exists in the database.

There are two more problems with this application. First, we're downloading the entire Customers table to the client. Northwind is a small database, but an actual table with customer information might be quite large. It's recommended that you move only as many rows as you need from the database (customers from a specific country, or customers that placed an order in the last few weeks). You can even move a single row. If the user wants to change a customer's phone number, your application should give the user a chance to specify the desired row and then retrieve only that row. You should always keep in mind the fact that the DataSet resides on the client, and you shouldn't move too much information too frequently from the database to the client.

The other problem of this application is the user interface. If the number of customers were in the thousands, moving to the next or previous row would clearly be out of the question. We're going to look at a more functional interface in the following section, where we'll also discuss the process of data-binding the ListBox and ComboBox controls.

Binding Complex Controls

The process of binding the ListBox and ComboBox controls is different than binding simple controls, or even the DataGrid control. These two controls are commonly used as lookup and navigational devices. They can display one field and keep track of another field. For example, you can display the customers' names and keep track of the customer ID. In effect, the user sees names, but your program sees IDs. The application we'll use in the following section does exactly that: it displays the company names in a ComboBox control and lets the user select a customer by clicking a name. The selected customer's fields will appear in the data-bound controls, and the user can either edit a row, or move to a different row by clicking another item on the ListBox control. The new interface is far more functional that the previous one, and you will use it in many situations, especially if you want to present many rows to the user.

An even more common use of the complex data-bound controls is as lookup devices. Each row in the Products table has a CategoryID field and a SupplierID field, which link each product to a category and a supplier. The actual names of the categories and suppliers are stored in separate tables, related to the Products table through a pair of primary/foreign keys. You'll see how you can create a form with data-bound controls for the Products table and use two ComboBox controls populated with the names of the categories and suppliers. As you move through the products, the proper items will be selected in the two ComboBox controls.

VB.NET AT WORK: THE LOOKUPCUSTOMERS PROJECT

The LookupCustomers project is very similar to the ViewEditCustomers project—the only difference is in the navigational model. Copy the ViewEditCustomers project's folder to a new location and rename it to LookupCustomers. Then open the new project and rename it to LookupCustomers. (Or use the project provided on the companion CD.) The main form of the new project is shown in Figure 21.13.

FIGURE 21.13

Using a data-bound ComboBox control as navigational tool

Delete all the navigational controls at the bottom of the form, and place a ComboBox control to the left side of the form (you will have to move the other controls to make room for the ComboBox control). The ComboBox control must be populated with the names of all customers. Set the control's DataSource property to DSCustomers1.Customers and its DisplayMember property to CompanyName. The ComboBox control will get its data from the Customers table and will display the CompanyName field of each row.

Bind the TextBox controls on the form to the appropriate fields in the Customers table. The last step is to populate the DataSet by calling the Fill method of the associated DataAdapter. Enter the following statements in the Load button's Click event handler:

```
Private Sub LoadData(ByVal sender As System.Object, _
              ByVal e As System.EventArgs) Handles bttnLoad.Click
    DSCustomers1.Clear()
    DACustomers.Fill(DSCustomers1, "Customers")
End Sub
```

If you run the application now, you'll be able to populate the DataSet, but nothing will happen as you click its items. You must add a few lines of code to set the current row in the DataSet every time the user selects another customer in the ComboBox control. Since the order of the items on the ComboBox control is the same as the order of rows in the DataSet, you can set the Position property to the index of the selected item. This is done with a single statement:

```
Me.BindingContext(DsCustomers1, "Customers").Position = ComboBox1.SelectedIndex
```

If you allow users to edit the current row, however, and that row contains errors, you may not be able to move to another row. One such error would be to clear the current row's CompanyName field. This field can't be empty (this column's AllowNull property is False), and any attempt to set it to Null will cause an exception when you attempt to leave the current row. You must insert an exception handler to reject the changes if the current row contains errors. Listing 21.5 shows the event handler of the ComboBox control's SelectedIndexChanged event handler.

LISTING 21.5: MOVING TO A ROW IN THE DATASET

```
Private Sub ComboBox1_SelectedIndexChanged(ByVal sender As System.Object, _
          ByVal e As System.EventArgs) Handles ComboBox1.SelectedIndexChanged
    Try
        Me.BindingContext(DsCustomers1, "Customers").EndCurrentEdit()
        Me.BindingContext(DsCustomers1, "Customers").Position = _
            ComboBox1.SelectedIndex
    Catch updateException As Exception
        MsgBox(updateException.Message)
        Me.BindingContext(DsCustomers1, "Customers").CancelCurrentEdit()
        Me.BindingContext(DsCustomers1, "Customers").Position = _
            ComboBox1.SelectedIndex
    End Try
End Sub
```

The code in the Catch clause of the exception handler displays the error message that prevented the DataSet from moving to another row. Then it cancels the current edit action (the fields are restored to their initial values) and, finally, moves to the new row. This isn't the most elegant method of handling update errors, but we'll discuss more robust techniques in the following chapter.

VB.NET AT WORK: THE PRODUCTS PROJECT

In this section, you'll learn how to use a data-bound ComboBox as a lookup mechanism in your applications. The main form of the application, shown in Figure 21.14 and available in this chapter's folder on the CD, allows you to navigate through the rows of the Products table with the help of a ListBox control, a technique you're already familiar with. Most of the fields of each row are displayed on TextBox controls. If you bind the CategoryID and SupplierID fields to two TextBox controls, you will see two numbers, which are the foreign keys to the other two tables. By using data-bound ComboBox controls, users see the actual names of the related fields.

FIGURE 21.14

Browsing and editing the Products table

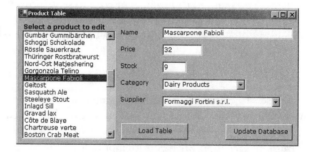

Start a new project and design a form like the one shown in Figure 21.14. Then you must create a DataSet with three tables that store product-related information: the Products, Categories, and Suppliers tables. Drop the three tables on the form, configure each DataAdapter, and create the Products

DataSet. You can select a few fields from each table, as you aren't going to display many fields. The SELECT statements for the three DataAdapters are as follows:

DAProducts:
```
SELECT ProductID, ProductName, SupplierID, CategoryID,
       QuantityPerUnit, UnitPrice, UnitsInStock
FROM   dbo.Products
```
DACategories:
```
SELECT CategoryID, CategoryName FROM dbo.Categories
```
DASuppliers:
```
SELECT SupplierID, CompanyName FROM dbo.SuppliersASuppliers
```

Then create the *DSProducts* DataSet and place all three tables in it. Since we want the current row of the Categories and Suppliers tables to change each time another row of the Products table is selected, we must establish the appropriate relationships between the tables. Double-click the DSProducts.xsd file in the Solution Explorer window to open the DataSet in design view. Then establish a relationship between the Products and Categories table based on the CategoryID field and another relationship between the Products and Suppliers tables based on the SupplierID field. Preview the DataSet to see that all tables and relations are in place. If you view one of the Categories or Suppliers tables, you will see that each row leads to a set of related rows.

Now you must bind all the controls on the form. Bind the Text property of each of the TextBox controls to the appropriate field of the Products table of the DataSet. The top TextBox is bound to the expression

```
DsProducts1 - Products.ProductName
```

and it will display the ProductName field of the Products table. Do the same for the controls that display the Price and Stock fields.

Select the ListBox control and bind it as follows:

Property	Value
DataSource	DSProducts1.Products
DataMember	ProductName

These two properties will cause the ListBox control to be populated with the ProductName field of the Products DataTable. Then set the control's ValueMember property to the ProductID field. This property connects the selected item on the control to one of the rows of the Products table in the *DSProducts1* DataSet.

The last step is to bind the two ComboBox controls to the related tables. Select the first Combo-Box control on the form and bind it to the DataSets as follows:

Property	Value
DataSource	DSProducts1.Categories
DataMember	CategoryName
ValueMember	CategoryID
SelectedValue	DSProducts1 – Products.CategoryID

The ComboBox control will be populated with the names of the categories and will be connected to the Products table through the CategoryID field. In effect, the current selection on the control will be the name of the category of the row whose CategoryID field matches the CategoryID field of the Products DataTable.

Binding the second ComboBox control to the Suppliers table is quite similar, so I will only list the data-binding properties and their settings:

Property	Value
DataSource	DSProducts1.Suppliers
DataMember	CompanyName
ValueMember	SupplierID
SelectedValue	DSProducts1 – Products.SupplierID

You should be very familiar with the code that populates the DataSet and updates the database by now. The code behind the two buttons on the form is shown in Listings 21.6 and 21.7.

LISTING 21.6: POPULATING THE DSCUSTOMERS DATASET

```
Private Sub Button1_Click(ByVal sender As System.Object,_
            ByVal e As System.EventArgs) Handles Button1.Click
   DACategories.Fill(DsProducts1, "Categories")
   DASuppliers.Fill(DsProducts1, "Suppliers")
   DAProducts.Fill(DsProducts1)
End Sub
```

LISTING 21.7: UPDATING THE DATABASE

```
Private Sub Button2_Click(ByVal sender As System.Object,_
            ByVal e As System.EventArgs) Handles Button2.Click
   DAProducts.Update(DsProducts1)
End Sub
```

The code for updating the underlying table is quite primitive. You will learn how to properly update the underlying table in the following chapter.

The last step is to add some code to the ListBox control to turn it into a navigational tool. We want to move to the row of the product selected on the control. We can take advantage of the fact that the items on the ListBox appear in the same order as in the DataSet: we'll use the control's SelectedIndex property to move to the appropriate row in the Products DataTable. Listing 21.8 shows how to move to the correct row of Products when the user selects another item on the ListBox.

```
Private Sub ListBox1_SelectedIndexChanged(ByVal sender As System.Object, _
        ByVal e As System.EventArgs) Handles ListBox1.SelectedIndexChanged
    Me.BindingContext(DsProducts1, "Products").Position = ListBox1.SelectedValue
End Sub
```

Run the application now and check out how the current product's category and supplier are displayed on the two ComboBox controls. You can also change a product's category or supplier by selecting another item on the appropriate control. This application will crash if you enter an invalid field value (a negative price, for example). However, it's easy to validate the data on the controls and make sure that they don't violate any constraints, before you submit them to the database. Because the current product's category and supplier must be selected from a list, users can't violate the integrity of the database by mistake.

Programming the DataAdapter Object

Before we exhaust the topic of the data binding, I'd like to bring to your attention the fact that all the applications we've developed so far move all the data they may need from the database server to the client. This is the essence of disconnected DataSets: you bring the data to the client and work with them locally. But shouldn't there be a limit on the amount of data we move around? Indeed, you can't download a table with 30,000 customers just because a user wants to view (or edit) a phone number. Likewise, you can't move information about half a million titles to the client just because the user wants to view a couple of them.

Disconnected DataSets are not your license to make copies of the database (or even a substantial section of it) to every client. You must design your application so that it stores to the client only the rows absolutely necessary for the task at hand, and no more. This is easier said than done, and we usually pass this responsibility to the user. We design an interface that allows users to specify the rows they need and then retrieve only the ones that meet the criteria (like products in a price range or customers from a country). You will also bring the related rows in other tables.

The Command Objects

Each DataAdapter has four command objects, which provide the information needed to interact with the database: DeleteCommand, InsertCommand, UpdateCommand, and SelectCommand. If an application isn't going to alter the database, then you need only specify SelectCommand, which retrieves data with a SELECT statement.

Each of these objects has a CommandText property, which is the name of the stored procedure or SQL statement that acts against the database; a Connection object, which determines the database the command object acts upon; and a collection of Parameter objects (the Parameters collection), which are the parameters expected by the SQL statement or stored procedure. These four Command objects are adequate to interact with the tables in the database.

In the examples so far, we let the wizard generate the appropriate SQL statements for us. In this section we'll create a Connection object and a DataAdapter from scratch. This will help you understand a little better the basic objects of ADO.NET. In Chapter 22, we'll go past data binding and you'll learn how to program the same objects.

Start a new project and name it CustomerOrders. As you would guess, this application will display customers, orders, and order details. However, this time we'll use a more elaborate interface, and we'll write code that doesn't move too much information over the network. In other words, we will not create a DataSet with all the customers, all their orders, and all the detail lines in each order. We'll ask the user to specify the name of the customer by entering the first few characters of the company name. Then, with the appropriate SELECT statement, we move only the matching names to the client and display them on a ListBox control, as shown in Figure 21.15. When the user selects a name in this ListBox control, the selected customer's orders are displayed on a DataGrid control that shows the order's ID, the date it was placed, and its total. When an order is selected with the mouse, the order's details are moved from the database to the client and displayed on the second DataGrid control.

FIGURE 21.15

The CustomerOrders application's main form

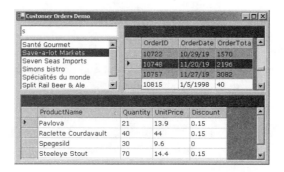

To build this project, we'll use the tools of the Data tab of the Toolbox. Instead of dropping tables from the Server Explorer onto the form and letting VB configure them, we'll place the appropriate objects and configure them manually.

Start by placing an OleDbConnection object on the form and set its ConnectionString property to the following string:

```
Provider=SQLOLEDB.1;Integrated Security=SSPI;
Initial Catalog=Northwind;Data Source=PowerToolkit
```

You must change the name of the Data Source to match your installation. The OleDbConnection is functionally equivalent to the SqlConnection object, but it uses the OLEDB drivers to access the database. The SqlConnection object is optimized for accessing SQL Server databases, but I've used the OleDbConnection object to demonstrate that the two are totally equivalent.

Then drop an OleDbDataAdapter object on the form. The Data Adapter Configuration Wizard will start, and you must specify the following SQL statement to select a few customers:

```
SELECT CompanyName, ContactName, Country, CustomerID
FROM Customers
WHERE (CompanyName LIKE ?)
```

This is a parameterized query, and you must specify the value of the parameter before calling it (the parameter is indicated by the question mark).

On the screen of the wizard where you specify the SQL SELECT statement, click Advanced Options, and on the Advanced SQL Generation Options form, clear the option Generate Insert, Update, and Delete Statements. Our application will only display data, and we won't use any other of these commands.

Then create a second DataAdapter object for the Orders table. This DataAdapter's SQL statement should be:

```
SELECT    Orders.OrderID, Orders.OrderDate,
          SUM(([Order Details].UnitPrice * [Order Details].Quantity) *
              (1 - [Order Details].Discount)) AS OrderTotal
FROM      Orders INNER JOIN [Order Details]
                ON Orders.OrderID = [Order Details].OrderID
WHERE     (Orders.CustomerID = ?)
GROUP BY Orders.OrderID, Orders.OrderDate
```

This is a fairly straightforward statement that selects a few fields of the orders of a customer along with each order's total. The query's parameter is the customer's ID, a value we'll extract from the ListBox control when the user selects a name in the list.

Place yet another DataAdapter on the form, the OrderDetails Adapter, and set its SELECT statement to the following:

```
SELECT Products.ProductName, [Order Details].Quantity,
       [Order Details].UnitPrice,
       [Order Details].Discount
FROM    [Order Details] INNER JOIN Products
                        ON [Order Details].ProductID = Products.ProductID
WHERE ([Order Details].OrderID = ?)
```

This statement selects the details of an order specified by its ID. Notice that instead of the ProductID field (which identifies the product in the Order Details table), we retrieve the name of the product from the Products table.

Once the three DataAdapters are in place, create three DataSet objects, one for each DataAdapter object on the form. Select the Customers DataAdapter and then use Data ➤ Generate Dataset. Set the new DataSet's name to *DSCustomers* and add only the Customers table to the DataSet. Do the same for the other two DataAdapters and name their DataSets *DSOrders* and *DSDetails*. Figure 21.16 shows the form's design surface. Notice the three DataAdapter and the three matching DataSet objects.

Select the Customers DataAdapter object on the form and, in the Properties window, locate and expand its SelectCommand object. You will see the SELECT statement you created next to the CommandText property. The setting of the CommandType property is Text. In the following section, you will see how to set the CommandText property to the name of a stored procedure. When the command is a stored procedure, the CommandType property should be set to Stored Procedure.

Another of the properties under the SelectCommand section of the Properties window is the Parameters property, which is a collection. This property contains information about the parameters of the SQL statement or stored procedure. Click the button with the ellipsis and you will see the OleDbParameter Collection Editor (Figure 21.17 shows the Properties window and the Collection

Editor.) In this window you can specify the parameter's name and data type. You will use the parameter's name to assign a value to it later, and its type must match the type of the parameter in the query or stored procedure. The parameter of the statement that selects one or more customers is a string, while the parameter of the statement that retrieves the details of an order is an integer. You can also set the parameter's value in this window, but parameter values are almost always set from within the code. The reason for using parameterized queries and stored procedures is that we want to be able to set the parameters at runtime.

FIGURE 21.16

The CustomerOrder project's main form in design mode

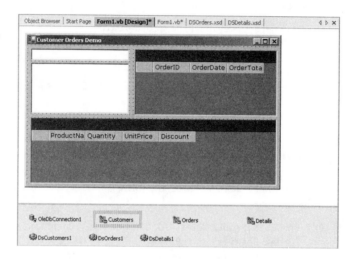

FIGURE 21.17

Setting the properties of Command's parameters

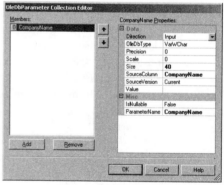

It's time now to add some code to the application. The statement that retrieves customers must be entered in the TextBox control's KeyUp event handler. Every time the user presses the Enter key, the statements of Listing 21.9 must be executed.

LISTING 21.9: SELECTING CUSTOMER'S BY NAME

```
Private Sub TextBox1_KeyUp(ByVal sender As Object, _
          ByVal e As System.Windows.Forms.KeyEventArgs) Handles TextBox1.KeyUp
   If e.KeyCode = Keys.Enter Then
      ListBox1.Visible = True
      Customers.SelectCommand.Parameters("CompanyName").Value = _
         TextBox1.Text & "%"
      DsCustomers1.Clear()
      Customers.Fill(DsCustomers1)
      ListBox1.Focus()
   End If
End Sub
```

SelectCommand is a property of the DataAdapter object, so we can access it with the expression `Customers.SelectCommand`. It's also an object that exposes its own members, one of them being the Parameters collection. To set the value of a parameter, you call the command's Parameters collection, passing the name of the parameter as argument. Then set this member's Value property to the desired value. Each member of the Parameters collection exposes more properties, such as DbType (use it to set the parameter's type), IsNullable, and the Precision and Scale properties of numeric parameters.

Notice the percent sign following the value entered by the user on the TextBox control. If the user enters **Antonio** on the TextBox control, the parameter value passed to the query is Antonio%. This parameter will return all the customers whose name begins with "Antonio" followed by any other string.

Then the code clears the *DSCustomers1* DataSet and populates it again with the rows returned by the query of the SelectCommand (this happens when the Fill method is called). The ListBox control is bound to the *DSCustomers* DataSet's Customers table, so it's automatically populated. The data-binding properties of the ListBox control are as follows:

Property	Value
DataSource	DsCustomers1.Customers
DisplayMember	CompanyName

There are no other data-binding properties to be set. The order of the rows in the ListBox control is the same as their order in the DataSet's table, so the SelectedIndex property determines the order of the selected rows in the Customers table of the *DSCustomers* DataSet.

When the user selects one of the customers in the ListBox control, the statements of Listing 21.10 are executed. They retrieve the CustomerID of the selected customer and pass it as parameter to the SelectCommand of the Orders DataSet. Finally, the code calls the Fill method to populate *DSOrders1* DataSet.

LISTING 21.10: RETRIEVING THE SELECTED CUSTOMER'S ORDERS

```
Private Sub ListBox1_SelectedIndexChanged(ByVal sender As System.Object, _
            ByVal e As System.EventArgs) Handles ListBox1.SelectedIndexChanged
    Dim row As Integer = ListBox1.SelectedIndex
    Dim CustID As String = DsCustomers1.Customers(row).CustomerID
    Orders.SelectCommand.Parameters("CustomerID").Value =  CustID
    DsOrders1.Clear()
    Orders.Fill(DsOrders1)
End Sub
```

We must also detect the selection of a row in the DataGrid control with the Orders, retrieve the detail lines of the selected order and display them on the second DataGrid control. When a row (or cell) is selected on the DataGrid control, the CurrentCellChanged event is fired. Listing 21.11 shows the code that displays the selected order's details on the second DataGrid control.

LISTING 21.11: RETRIEVING THE SELECTED ORDER'S DETAILS

```
Private Sub DataGrid1_CurrentCellChanged(ByVal sender As Object, _
            ByVal e As System.EventArgs) Handles DataGrid1.CurrentCellChanged
    Dim row As Integer = DataGrid1.CurrentRowIndex
    Dim OrdID As Integer = DataGrid1.Item(row, 0)
    Details.SelectCommand.Parameters("OrderID").Value = OrdID
    DsDetails1.Clear()
    Details.Fill(DsDetails1)
End Sub
```

This is all the code required by the application, and it's not complicated either. We determine the parameter required by the query we want to call and then pass it to the query through the Parameters collection of the SelectCommand object. Of course, you must set the data-binding properties of the two DataGrid controls, so that they will update their contents when the underlying DataSets change. To bind the two DataGrid controls, set their DataSource property to the name of the corresponding DataSet.

The Command and DataReader Objects

Sometimes, we want to retrieve data from the database and read them sequentially. If you don't plan to edit the data and submit any changes back to the client, you can use the DataReader object to read the rows sequentially. The DataReader is an object that lets you iterate through the rows retrieved by a query. It's faster than storing all the rows to a DataSet, but you can't move back and forth in the rows. Moreover, the connection to the database is open while you iterate through the rows, so the processing should be as quick as possible. For example, you can't prompt the user between rows; this would tie the connection for too long. It goes without saying that you can't use the DataReader object to update the underlying table. The DataReader object returns a forward-only, read-only result.

As with the other major ADO.NET objects, there are two flavors of the DataReader object: the SqlDataReader and the OleDbDataReader objects. Use the SqlDataReader object for SQL Server databases and the OleDbDataReader for OLEDB-compliant databases. To create a DataReader object, you must execute a query against a database through a Command object. You've already set up Command objects, even though you didn't do so explicitly. This time we'll create a Command object and set its Connection and CommandText properties from within our code. Once the Command object has been set up, you can execute it by calling one of the following methods:

ExecuteReader   Executes the command and returns a DataReader object, which you can use to read the results, one row at a time.

ExecuteXMLReader   Executes the command and returns a XMLDataReader object, which you can use to read the results, one row at a time.

ExecuteScalar   Executes the command, returns the first column of the first row in the result, and ignores all other rows.

ExecuteNonQuery   Executes a SQL command against the database and returns the number of rows affected. Use this method to execute a command that updates the database.

The first two methods return a DataReader object, the ExecuteNonQuery method returns an integer (the number of rows affected), and the ExecuteScalar method returns an object (the first column of the first row in the result set). The DataReader is an abstract class and can't be used in an application. Instead, use the SqlDataReader or the OleDbDataReader object, depending on the database you're connected to.

VB.NET at Work: The DataReader Project

This section's project demonstrates the simplest possible use of a SqlDataReader object. We'll read the category names from the Categories table and place them on a ListBox control. To test this code, place an instance of the SqlConnection and SqlCommand controls on a new form. These two controls must be selected from the Data tab of the Toolbox. They're not configured, because they're not associated with any objects in the database. Let's configure them.

Select the *SqlConnection1* object on the designer and open its Properties window. Locate the ConnectionString property and, from the drop-down list, select the Northwind database. Then select the *SqlCommand1* object on the designer, open its Properties window, and locate the Connection property. Expand the list of available connections and set it to SqlConnection1 (your project contains a single Connection object). Then locate the CommandText property and click the button with the ellipsis. This action will start the Query Builder, where you can create a query with the rows you want to retrieve. Add the Categories table to the query and select the fields CategoryID and Category-Name. Then click OK to close the Query Builder.

So far, you've established a connection to the Northwind database and created a command to retrieve the names of all categories. All you have do now is to execute the command and process its results.

In our code we'll use the ExecuteReader method to retrieve textual information. Place a Button and a ListBox control on the form, and enter the statements from Listing 21.12 in the button's Click event handler.

LISTING 21.12: ITERATING THE ROWS OF A SQLDATAREADER OBJECT

```
Private Sub Button1_Click(ByVal sender As System.Object,_
              ByVal e As System.EventArgs) Handles Button1.Click
    SqlConnection1.Open()
    Dim SQLReader As System.Data.SqlClient.SqlDataReader
    SQLReader = SqlCommand1.ExecuteReader()
    While SQLReader.Read
        ListBox1.Items.Add(SQLReader.Item("CategoryID") & vbTab & _
                          SQLReader.Item("CategoryName"))
    End While
    SqlConnection1.Close()
End Sub
```

First, the code opens the connection. Normally, the connection is opened by the DataAdapter object when the application requests data, but this time we don't have a DataAdapter object. Then it calls the Command object's ExecuteReader method and assigns the result to a SqlDataReader object. The data isn't stored in this object. Instead, we'll use this object to iterate through the rows returned by the query. This must take place from within a loop, which must go quickly through the data and then close the connection.

The Read method of the SqlDataReader object returns true while there is more data to be read. Each time you call the Read method, the DataReader moves to the next row, and you can read the current row's fields through the Item property. The Item property accepts as argument the name or index of a column and returns its value. At each iteration of the loop, we read the two fields of the current row and add them to the ListBox control.

VB.NET at Work: The StoredProcedure Project

The example of this section shows a slightly different method of retrieving just the information you need to present to the user and no more. This time we'll use one of the stored procedures we developed in Chapter 20. The OrdersPerCustomer stored procedure retrieves the number of orders placed by a customer and the grand total of these orders. This stored procedure doesn't place any computational burden on the database server, because it applies to a single customer. What if the user wanted to see the totals for several, or even many, customers? Would you write another procedure that calculates the same totals for all customers? In a real database with thousands of customers and many orders per customer, the computational burden is no longer insignificant.

To avoid having the computer perform unnecessary operations and return results that the user may not even see, we'll force users to select the customer whose totals they want. Figure 21.18 shows the interface of the application. The user is expected to select a customer from the list on the left, and then the selected customer's totals will appear on the form. The totals are calculated as requested, which may lead to many requests to the database server. However, each request is serviced in no time at all, and it's certainly more efficient than calculating the totals for all customers and moving the information to the client; the user may only look at a few totals and just ignore the rest.

FIGURE 21.18

Retrieving information from the database with stored procedures

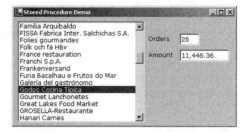

Start a new project and place on its form the controls you see in Figure 21.18. The ListBox control must be populated with the names of all the companies in the Customers table. Drop the Customers table from the Server Explorer onto the form and a new DataAdapter object will be added to the project. Rename the DataAdapter to *DACustomers* and configure it so that it retrieves only the CustomerID and CompanyName fields from the database. Here's the DataAdapter's SELECT statement:

```
SELECT CustomerID, CompanyName FROM dbo.Customers
```

Then generate the Customers DataSet and use it to populate the ListBox control. Set the control's DataSource property to `Customers1.Customers`, its DisplayMember property to CompanyName, and ValueMember to CustomerID. Then call the DataAdapter's Fill method from within the form's Load event handler:

```
Private Sub Form1_Load(ByVal sender As System.Object, _
            ByVal e As System.EventArgs) Handles MyBase.Load
   DACustomers.Fill(Customers1)
End Sub
```

If you run the application now, the ListBox will be populated with the customers' names. In the control's SelectedIndexChanged event handler, we must execute the OrdersPerCustomer procedure to retrieve the two totals for the selected customer. To execute the stored procedure, add a SqlCommand object to the form.

If you haven't followed the examples in the previous chapter, you must add OrdersPerCustomer to the Northwind database (the application expects that the stored procedure is part of the database and will call it by name). To add a new stored procedure to a database, start Enterprise Manager, locate the Stored Procedures section under the Northwind database, and from its context menu select New Stored Procedure. Then add the definition shown in Listing 21.13 to the new stored procedure and save it as OrdersPerCustomer.

LISTING 21.13: THE OrdersPerCustomer STORED PROCEDURE

```
ALTER PROCEDURE dbo.OrdersPerCustomer
        @CustomerID nchar(5)='ALFKI'
AS
```

```
SELECT    dbo.Customers.CompanyName,
          COUNT(dbo.Orders.OrderID) AS [Total Orders],
          dbo.Customers.CustomerID,
          CAST(SUM((dbo.[Order Details].UnitPrice *
             dbo.[Order Details].Quantity) *
             (1 - dbo.[Order Details].Discount)) AS money) AS [Total Amount]
FROM      dbo.Customers
          INNER JOIN dbo.Orders
             ON dbo.Customers.CustomerID = dbo.Orders.CustomerID
          INNER JOIN dbo.[Order Details]
             ON dbo.Orders.OrderID = dbo.[Order Details].OrderID
GROUP BY  dbo.Customers.CompanyName, dbo.Customers.CustomerID
HAVING    (dbo.Customers.CustomerID = @CustomerID)
```

Select the SqlCommand object from the Data tab of the Toolbox and drop it on the form. To execute the stored procedure, set the SqlCommand object's CommandText property to the name of the stored procedure, set its CommandType to `CommandType.StoredProcedure`, and then create a new parameter and set it to the ID of the selected customer.

To set up a parameter, you must first create a Parameter object and add it to the Parameters collection of the *SqlCommand1* object. The Parameter must be added to the collection only once. Then, you must set the properties of the Parameter object. The two most important properties of the Parameter object are the Direction and Value properties. The Direction property determines whether the parameter passes a value to the stored procedure, receives a value from the stored procedure, or both. Its value can be one of the members of the ParameterDirection enumeration: `Input`, `Output`, `InputOutput`, and `ReturnValue`. The parameter's Value is the ID of the selected customer, which is given by the SelectedValue property of the ListBox control. The SelectedValue property returns the value of the field specified with the ValueMember property.

The last step is to execute the command and accept the results into a SqlReader object. Listing 21.14 shows the code that's executed when the user selects a different customer in the ListBox control.

> **LISTING 21.14: EXECUTING A STORED PROCEDURE WITH THE SQLCOMMAND OBJECT**

```
Private Sub ListBox1_SelectedIndexChanged(ByVal sender As System.Object, _
        ByVal e As System.EventArgs) Handles ListBox1.SelectedIndexChanged
    SqlConnection1.Open()
    SqlCommand1.CommandType = CommandType.StoredProcedure
    SqlCommand1.CommandText = "OrdersPerCustomer"
    If SqlCommand1.Parameters.Count = 0 Then
        SqlCommand1.Parameters.Add(New _
            System.Data.SqlClient.SqlParameter("@CustomerID", SqlDbType.NChar))
        SqlCommand1.Parameters(0).Direction = ParameterDirection.Input
    End If
    SqlCommand1.Parameters(0).Value = ListBox1.SelectedValue.ToString
    Dim SQLReader As System.Data.sqlclient.SqlDataReader
    SQLReader = SqlCommand1.ExecuteReader
```

```
    While SQLReader.Read
        txtOrders.Text = SQLReader.Item("Total Orders").ToString
        txtAmount.Text = SQLReader.Item("Total Amount").ToString
    End While
    SqlConnection1.Close()
End Sub
```

Summary

In this chapter, you've learned about the basic objects of ADO.NET through examples. You know how to connect to a database, set up DataAdapter objects for each table you want to query, and populate a DataSet object with one or more tables. The tables in a DataSet are usually related, but the relations between tables are not copied from the database automatically. You must establish relations between them by editing the XSD file with the schema of the DataSet

Once the data is in the DataSet, you can process it in any way you like. In this chapter, you learned how to bind controls to the fields of the tables in the DataSet, so that users can navigate through the rows of the tables and even edit them. The DataGrid control is a very flexible tool for presenting multiple related tables, and you know how to use it in your applications. You also know how to use the ListBox and ComboBox controls as lookup devices by binding them to a field in a table.

In the following chapter, you'll learn how to access the contents of a DataSet programmatically, as well as how to update the database. You will also learn how to create DataSet objects in your code and how to save them to disk files. This technique allows you to create custom data stores or exchange data with other systems.

Chapter 22

Programming the ADO.NET Objects

IN THE PRECEDING CHAPTER, you learned how to build applications that access databases with point and click operations. Binding fields to controls isn't your only option; it isn't event the best option. As you recall, the Update method can't handle update errors. The DataGrid control isn't quite appropriate for editing rows either. It's a great tool for displaying data, but it's not the most appropriate control for editing rows. A major limitation of the DataGrid control is that it can't display lookup fields. It can handle related rows, but at any given time it can only display the rows of a single table—you can't use the DataGrid control to display master/detail forms. To keep a customer's data, the customer's orders, and an order's details all visible on the form, we had to use multiple DataGrid controls on our form.

Database applications aren't trivial, and the process of building database applications can't be oversimplified. Throwing a few controls on the form and setting their data-binding properties works for very simple applications, but for everything else you must provide quite a bit of code. You must validate your data and minimize the amount of data moved back and forth between the client and the server. The DataSet object's Update method passes all the rows it contains to the database and uses the SQL statements generated by the configuration wizard to update the underlying tables. In most cases, very few of the rows have been edited, and you should be able to transmit only the rows that were added, deleted, or modified.

Another important consideration is how the DataSet is populated. Do we move all the data we may need in the course of the application? This is what the DataSet object does best. It maintains a copy of selected tables in the client computer's memory, so that the application won't have to hit the server for every row the user may need to view. The more data you move into the DataSet, the longer the user can work with the disconnected data. There are applications, however, where this isn't desirable. An invoicing application can't keep the price list in memory for too long, because prices may change in the database. It should also be able to update the current stock.

To build reliable, robust database applications, you must learn to program the objects exposed by ADO.NET. You have seen how to use the Command and DataReader objects in the previous chapter. In this chapter, you'll learn how to access the data stored in the DataSet from within your code and how to execute commands directly against the database. We'll also explore the DataForm wizard, a tool for building simple data-browsing and -editing applications.

The Structure of a DataSet

The main object of any ADO.NET application is the DataSet object, which is s a miniature database that lives on the client. The main purpose of the Connection and DataAdapter objects is to populate the DataSet object, as well as move information from the DataSet to the database and update the underlying table(s). The basic concept behind ADO.NET is to move the required data to the client, process them there, and then, optionally, update the database with the changes made by the client application to the local data. The data on the client is a copy of the data on the server the moment the DataSet was generated, and the DataSet is totally disconnected from the underlying tables in the database.

The structure of the DataSet object is quite simple. VB6 programmers will have to get used to living with client-side data, but those of you new to VB.NET will find the DataSet a convenient method of working with subsets of tables. It's made up of tables, which may or may not correspond to tables of the database. You can bring in an entire table, like the Categories table. Or you can select a few columns and/or a few rows from a table in the database and store them to a table in the DataSet. Finally, you can create a table by combining rows from multiple tables. For example, you can execute a query that retrieves all product names from the Products table along with the name of the category they belong to from the Categories tables and stores the returned rows to a new table in the DataSet. It is also possible to add and drop tables from a DataSet at any time during the course of the application.

Finally, you can create new tables from within your code. To do so, we create a DataTable object to represent the new table and then a series of DataRow objects to represent the table's rows. Each row must have a data type, an optional default value, a length, and so on. You can create the same table structures from within your code as you would do with the visual tools of Enterprise Manager. After specifying the structure of the tables, you can add relations between them. Everything you can do visually with the XSD Designer, you can also do from within your code. The process of establishing relations between tables using the Designer was described in the last chapter. The product documentation discusses extensively how to create DataSets programmatically. You will find this information useful in situations where the data comes from someone else's database. As you will see later in this chapter, it is possible to create a DataSet programmatically, populate it, and then store its contents to a XML file. This chapter shows you how to use DataSets to manipulate databases, which is what most of us will be doing anyway.

If the tables were totally independent of one another, the DataSet would be nothing more than a collection of arrays. Yet it's not. In addition to the tables, the DataSet maintains relations between tables, as you have seen. If you need to see the product names along with the names of the categories they belong to, you can bring both tables into the DataSet and establish a relationship between them.

DataSets are not aware of the data sources. The exchange of information between DataSets and data sources (which, in most cases, are databases) takes place through the Data Adapter object, described in Chapter 21. Each table in a DataSet has an associated Data Adapter object, whose function is to retrieve data from the underlying table and populate the DataSet, as well as update the underlying table in the database with data from the DataSet.

The DataSet's structure and its data are described with XML keywords. You don't have to learn much about XML, but if you open the XSD file, you'll see the XML code that describes the structure of the DataSet. The data aren't available at design time, but once you populate the tables of the

DataSet, the data will also be described in XML. The Data Adapter formats the data as XML documents and passes them to the DataSet. It also receives data in XML format from the DataSet and updates the underlying tables in the database.

Navigating the Tables of a DataSet

In this section, we're going to take a closer look at the structure of the DataSet and how it organizes data in tables. You'll learn how to enumerate the tables in the DataSet and how to iterate through their rows and access the values of individual columns. The information in this section will enable you to write applications for displaying data. Later in the chapter, we'll take a closer look at techniques for updating the tables in the data source.

The DataSet object exposes members for accessing its contents. The tables in a DataSet are exposed through the Tables collection, which is made up of DataTable objects. If the tables are related, the relations are exposed by the Relations collection, which is made up of DataRelation objects. The following two loops print the names of the tables and relations in a DataSet:

```
Dim tbl As System.Data.DataTable
For Each tbl In AllOrders1.Tables
    Console.WriteLine(tbl.TableName)
Next
Dim rel As System.Data.DataRelation
For Each rel In AllOrders1.Relations
    Console.WriteLine(rel.RelationName)
Next
```

The DataTable object's most important property is the Rows property, which is a collection of DataRow objects. The DataRow object, in turn, exposes the Item property, which is the value of a specific column (field) in a row. If the *DSCustomers* DataSet contains the Customers table, the following statement returns the CustomerID field of the third row in the Customers table:

```
DSCustomers.Tables("Customers").Rows(2).Item("CustomerID")
```

There's a simpler expression for retrieving the same value, which is the following:

```
DSCustomers.Customers(2).CustomerID
```

Obviously, the second expression is easier to write and makes your code easier to read and maintain. However, this notation applies only to a *typed* DataSet—one with a schema available at design time. The DataSet is based on existing tables, so that their structures are known at design time and the compiler can create typed DataSets. If you create a DataSet at runtime from within your code, then the compiler has no way of knowing the structure of the DataSet and therefore can't create a typed DataSet. This chapter deals with typed datasets only.

If you're wondering how the compiler knows about the structure of the DataSet and how it can expose the names of the tables as members of the DataSet object, or the names of the columns as members of the DataTable object, the answer is quite simple. It creates a class for every DataSet and for every table you add to the DataSet. This is done on the fly, and all the information is hidden from you. To view the class that implements the DataSet, click the Show All Files button on the Solution Explorer. Under the XDS file with the DataSet's schema, there's another file with the same name and extension VB. If you open this for a DataSet that contains the Customers table, you will see that it contains the definition of the class DSCustomers, which in turn contains the classes CustomersDataTable and CustomersRow. All these classes expose their own members, which you can access through the *DSCustomers1* object. *DSCustomers1* is an instance of the DSCustomers class.

Using the DataTable, DataRelation, and DataRow objects, you can navigate through all the tables of a DataSet, going from each row of any given table to the related rows in any other table. Let's say you have created a DataSet with the Customers, Orders, and Order Details tables. Obviously, data binding is not the only way to build a user interface for browsing or editing a DataSet. You can write code to display the current row's fields to a TextBox control and store the edited values back to the same row. You can also write code to navigate through the rows of a table or through the tables of a DataSet. Let's look at an example of navigating through the tables of a DataSet and reading their fields with code.

VB.NET AT WORK: THE DATASETS PROJECT

The Datasets project, whose main form is shown in Figure 22.1, can display the names of all tables in a DataSet, the names of all relations in the DataSet, and finally all the data in the DataSet. The Show Tables button displays the names of all the tables in the DataSet to the top-left ListBox control. The Show Relations button displays the names of all relations in the second ListBox control. The Show All Data button adds the customers, their orders, and each order's details to a TreeView control. As you can see, the structure of the tree reflects the structure of the data in the DataSet.

FIGURE 22.1

The Datasets project demonstrates how to navigate through a DataSet and its tables.

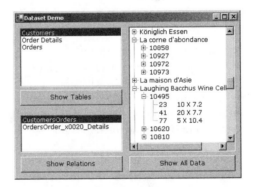

The root nodes are customers (the parent table of the DataSet). Under each root node, you can find the customer's orders (the IDs of the orders), and under each order you can find the order's details. The nodes with the details contain the product ID, quantity, and price. You can modify the SELECT statement of the Order Details table so that it displays product names instead of product IDs, or include each order's total. Or you can map the DataSet's structure to a ListView control, which gives you more control over the appearance of the data. Listing 22.1 shows the code behind the Show Tables button, which iterates through the Tables collection of the *AllOrders1* DataSet object. The DataSet was created by dropping the Customers, Orders, and Order Details tables of the Northwind database on the design surface, as described in the previous chapter. All three tables are stored in the same DataSet, and the relations between tables were established on the XSD file, as described in the previous chapter.

LISTING 22.1: NAVIGATING THROUGH THE TABLES OF A DATASET

```
Private Sub Tables(ByVal sender As System.Object, _
               ByVal e As System.EventArgs) Handles bttnTables.Click
    ListBox1.Items.Clear()
    Dim tbl As System.Data.DataTable
    For Each tbl In AllOrders1.Tables
        ListBox1.Items.Add(tbl.TableName)
    Next
End Sub
```

The Show Relations button is quite similar; it iterates through the Relations collection of the DataSet and prints the names of the relations on the second ListBox control. Listing 22.2 shows the code behind this button.

LISTING 22.2: NAVIGATING THROUGH THE RELATIONS OF A DATASET

```
Private Sub Relations(ByVal sender As System.Object, _
               ByVal e As System.EventArgs) Handles bttnRelations.Click
    ListBox2.Items.Clear()
    Dim rel As System.Data.DataRelation
    For Each rel In AllOrders1.Relations
        ListBox2.Items.Add(rel.RelationName)
    Next
End Sub
```

When you select a relation by clicking its name, the program displays the properties of the selected relation in a message box. If you click the CustomerOrders relation, the following will appear on a message box:

```
PARENT Customers
CHILD Orders
ON CustomerID = CustomerID
```

The last button on the form displays the entire hierarchy of the DataSet on a TreeView control with the statements shown in Listing 22.3.

LISTING 22.3: NAVIGATING THROUGH THE ROWS OF RELATED TABLES

```
Private Sub Data(ByVal sender As System.Object, _
               ByVal e As System.EventArgs) Handles bttnData.Click
    DAcustomers.Fill(AllOrders1, "Customers")
    DAOrders.Fill(AllOrders1, "Orders")
    DAOrderDetails.Fill(AllOrders1, "Order Details")
    Dim CORelation As String
```

```
        CORelation = AllOrders1.Customers.ChildRelations(0).RelationName()
        Dim ODRelation As String
        ODRelation = AllOrders1.Orders.ChildRelations(0).RelationName
        Dim row As AllOrders.CustomersRow
        For Each row In AllOrders1.Customers
            Dim Cnode As TreeNode
            Cnode = TreeView1.Nodes.Add(row.CompanyName)
            Dim OrderRows() As AllOrders.OrdersRow
            OrderRows = row.GetChildRows(CORelation)
            Dim Orow As AllOrders.OrdersRow
            For Each Orow In OrderRows
                Dim Onode As TreeNode
                Onode = Cnode.Nodes.Add(Orow.OrderID)
                Dim DetailRows() As AllOrders.Order_DetailsRow
                Dim Drow As AllOrders.Order_DetailsRow
                DetailRows = Orow.GetChildRows(ODRelation)
                For Each Drow In DetailRows
                    Onode.Nodes.Add(Drow.ProductID & "        " & Drow.Quantity & " X " & _
                                    Drow.UnitPrice)
                Next
            Next
        Next
    End Sub
```

The code starts by populating all three tables of the DataSet. Then it retrieves the name of the first child relation of the Customer table (the *CORelation* string, which is the name of the relation between the Customers and Orders tables) and the first child relation of the Orders table (the *ODRelation* string, which is the relation between the Orders and Order Details tables). We'll use the names of these relations to navigate from each row to its child rows.

Then the code starts scanning the rows of the Customers table with a For Each loop. In the loop's body, it adds a new root node to the TreeView control with the customer's name. Then it retrieves the child rows of the current row. The child rows are stored in an array of OrdersRow objects with the following statement:

```
Dim OrderRows() As AllOrders.OrdersRow
OrderRows = row.GetChildRows(CORelation)
```

The GetChildRows method of the DataRow object accepts as argument the name of a relation, and it retrieves the child rows related to the current row with the specified relation. The rows are stored in properly declared array or OrdersRow items.

Then the code goes through the child rows and, for each row, adds a child node under the current customer's node in the TreeView control. As you can guess, it retrieves the current order's child rows, which are the order's details. The innermost loop adds these rows under the current order's node. All three nested loops have the same structure, and you should examine the code to understand how it navigates through all the rows of all tables following the relations between tables.

As you can see, there's no compelling reason to bind your controls to the fields of a DataSet. You can access any field of any row of any table of the DataSet from within your code and display its value on a control. You can even apply any formatting necessary to the field's value before displaying it. If the user changes the value of the field, you can validate it before it's even stored to the DataSet.

The examples so far have dealt mostly with the presentation of data. Now we're going to look into the process of updating the DataSet, as well how to update the underlying tables in the database.

Updating DataSets

In the previous chapter, you learned how to update the tables in the database through the DataAdapter object. This technique, however, isn't very robust, and here's why. You may start with a DataSet of 30 changed rows. Some of these rows may contain errors, and the DataSet won't update the rows in error. You'll have to select all rows in error, figure out what went wrong, and try again. Fixing the errors means that you must present all the information to the user and give them a chance to edit the rows again, then try to update the database again.

Some rows may contain errors that can't be fixed by the user. Let's say the user has edited a row, but in the meantime another user has removed this row from the underlying table in the database. Obviously, the DataAdapter won't be able to update this row, because it no longer exists in the database. This is a typical error that may stop the DataAdapter from updating the remaining rows.

Another messy situation arises when a table contains an identity column, one that is assigned a value automatically by the database. The ProductID column in the Product database is such a column. Let's say you've created a DataSet that contains the products of the Northwind corporation. It is possible to add new rows to the Products table, and the DataSet will automatically assign a new value to the ProductID field. This field is certainly unique in your DataSet, but another user may have already added a row with the same ID to the database. Handling this type of error isn't trivial.

There's a simple work-around for new databases, but this can't be applied to existing databases. You can use GUIDs (globally unique identifiers) instead of Identity columns. A GUID is a system-generated number that's globally unique. It's generated in such a manner that's extremely unlikely that there will ever be a conflict with two GUIDs. In the unlikely case that there's a conflict (the system generates a GUID that already exists in the table), the operation will fail. But this is a remote possibility, and we can live with it. The problem with Identity columns is that they're used extensively in existing databases, and we can't redesign our databases.

Another problem arises with constraints other than the referential constraints. The UnitPrice column in the Products table has a constraint that prevents it from accepting a negative value (a very reasonable constraint). Should you attempt to store a negative value in this column, the database will reject the changes. This constraint, however, isn't stored in the DataSet. In other words, you can edit a row of the Products table in your DataSet, set UnitPrice to a negative value, and the changes will be stored in the Products table of the DataSet. When you attempt to update the database, however, the row will be rejected. To handle this type of error, you must supply all the necessary validation code. But then again, how can we be sure that we have caught every possible error?

The answer to all these questions is to update the database as frequently as possible through stored procedures. If a row fails to update, we must notify the user immediately, giving the user a chance to review the error and make the necessary corrections. But this approach violates the whole idea of using disconnected DataSets. Indeed, DataSets are a great tool for a disconnected world, but not all of our applications are disconnected. An application that runs in a small business environment isn't going to benefit much from the disconnected nature of ADO.NET. It's very likely that ADO.NET will be augmented in the near future to support connected DataSets as well. Until then, you must do most of the work manually, and you'll see in this chapter how to update the underlying tables.

The DataForm Wizard

One of the tools that come with Visual Studio is the DataForm wizard, which creates data-entry forms for you. Let's look at this tool in action, then we'll discuss its limitations. You will also find interesting coding examples in the output generated by the wizard. The example of this section is the EditProducts project, whose main form is shown in Figure 22.2. This form allows you to edit the rows of the Products table of the Northwind database, enter new rows, and delete existing rows. The interface and the code behind the controls were generated by the DataForm wizard. What you see in Figure 22.2 is the form of the EditProducts project as it was generated by the wizard. The main form of the EditProducts project on the CD is quite different, because we'll edit this form extensively in this section to make its interface more user-friendly.

FIGURE 22.2

Editing the Products table on a form generated by the DataForm wizard

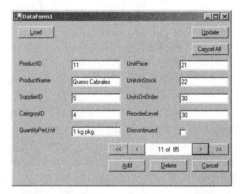

Start a new project, name it EditProducts, and delete the Form1 component. Then right-click the project's name and select Add ➢ Add New Item. In the dialog box that appears, select DataForm Wizard. A wizard starts that will take you through the steps of setting up a new DataForm. The first screen displays a welcome message; click Next to skip it. On the next screen, you're prompted to specify the DataSet on which the DataForm will be based. Since the project doesn't contain a DataSet, specify the name of a new DataSet, which the wizard will create for you. Enter the name **DSProducts** and click Next to view the next screen of the wizard.

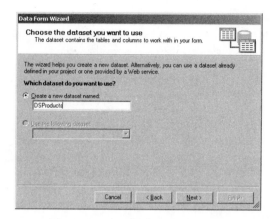

You're prompted to select a connection to a database or specify a new one. Select your connection to the Northwind database and click Next to see the Choose Tables Or Views screen. Here you will see a list of all tables and views in the database, and you can select one or more items on which the DataForm will be based. If you select multiple tables, make sure they're related. Select the Products table and then click the button with the right arrow to add the Products table to the list of selected items. Each product has a related row in the Categories table and another related row in the Suppliers table. Add these two tables to the list of selected items and then click the Next button to see the next screen.

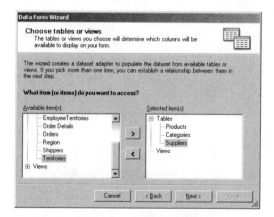

On the next screen of the wizard, you're asked to establish relationships between tables. Establish two relationships here, one between categories and products and another one between suppliers and products. In the Name box, enter the name of the first relationship, **CategoriesProducts**. The Parent table of the relationship is the Categories table, and the Child table is Products. The Keys are the matching columns in each table, and they are the CategoryID columns of the two tables. Then click the button with the right arrow to add the relationship to the list of Relations.

Establish another relationship between the Suppliers and Products tables in a similar manner and add it to the list of Relations. You have established the relations between the DataSet's tables, and you can click Next to view the next screen of the wizard.

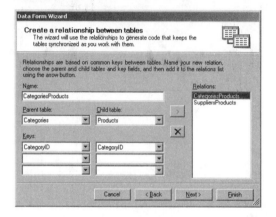

On the next screen of the wizard, you're prompted to choose the tables and columns that will be stored in the DataForm. We will not display related rows (as we did with the DataGrid control in Chapter 21). We want to design a form that displays all the columns of the Products table, and you'll see shortly how the other two tables will be used (you can guess that we'll use them to look up the name of the category and supplier of each product, rather than displaying all categories and all suppliers).

By default, the wizard selects all the fields of the Products table. If you wanted to create a master/detail form, you'd have to specify the Detail table as well. For now click Next to see the next screen of the wizard.

On the last screen, you must select the display style. You can display all rows on a DataGrid control or create a new form with separate controls for each row. Check the radio button Single Record In Individual Controls, and the check boxes at the bottom of the window will be enabled. These check boxes allow you to specify whether the DataForm will contain an Add button (to add new rows to the Products table), a Delete button (to delete the current row), a Cancel button (to cancel any changes in the DataSet and reload all rows from the underlying table) and the Navigation controls (to move from row to row). Leave all the check boxes checked, as they are by default.

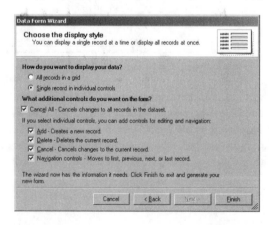

Now click Finish to generate the DataForm. The wizard will add a new form to your project, populate it with the necessary TextBox controls to display the field of the current row in the Products table, and also generate the necessary code. As you can see, all the TextBox controls have the same width and you must adjust them according to the length of the fields they display.

The navigational buttons at the bottom of the form allow you to move to the first/last and previous/next rows in the table. You will see the navigational controls (as shown in Figure 22.2) only if you build the project following the guidelines presented here. The EditProducts project on the CD is an improved version of the form generated by the wizard, and you will see shortly how you can enhance the default user interface.

You can notice immediately that the navigational method of the DataForm wizard is totally inadequate. We can't expect users to keep clicking the Next button until they hit the desired row. To make the navigational model a little more user-friendly, we'll add a list with the product names, so that the user can quickly locate the desired product. Figure 22.3 shows the new interface we're going to build based on the form generated by the wizard.

FIGURE 22.3

A more functional form for editing the products

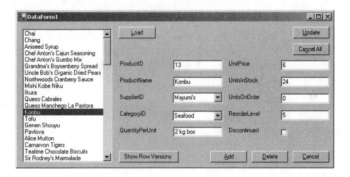

First, make the form wider. Then grab all the controls on the form with the mouse and move them to the right to make room for a ListBox control on the left side of the form. Place a ListBox control on the form, as shown in Figure 22.3, and set its properties as follows:

Property	Value
DataSource	objDSProducts.Products
DisplayMember	ProductName
ValueMember	ProductID

This ListBox will be populated with the names of all products in the Products list. The ValueMember property stores the IDs of the products, so that we can retrieve the selected product's details by the ProductID field when the user selects a product on the list. Then enter the line of Listing 22.4 in the ListBox control's SelectedIndexChanged event handler. This event is fired every time the user clicks another item on the control, and in its handler we'll add code to move to the selected product's row in the Products table in our DataSet. The various TextBox controls on the Form are bound to the corresponding columns of the Products table. As a result, when we move to another row of the Products, the text boxes are updated.

LISTING 22.4: MOVING TO THE SELECTED PRODUCT

```
Private Sub ListBox1_SelectedIndexChanged(ByVal sender As System.Object, _
            ByVal e As System.EventArgs) Handles ListBox1.SelectedIndexChanged
    Me.BindingContext(objDSProducts, "Products").Position = ListBox1.SelectedIndex
End Sub
```

We no longer need the so-called navigation buttons at the bottom of the form, so delete them. Delete the Label control that displays the current row's number as well—we can easily visualize our approximate position in the table by looking at the ListBox control.

If you run the project now, you'll be able to quickly locate a product in the ListBox control and click it to view its fields. Before you run the project, however, you must specify that the DataForm1 form is its Startup object. The form behaves as expected most of time, but there are a few quirks to this design. The product's supplier and category are displayed as numeric values. Sure, this is how we want to store the information to our database, but when we design forms for the end user, we want to be able to show them a supplier name and a category name. We've been through this in the previous chapter, so you already know how to replace these two TextBox controls with ComboBox controls that display the equivalent strings. Delete the TextBox control that corresponds to the SupplierID field. Then place a ComboBox control in its place and set the following properties of the control:

Property	Value
DataSource	objDSProducts.Suppliers
DataMember	CompanyName
ValueMember	SupplierID
SelectedValue	objDSProducts - Products.SupplierID

Delete the TextBox control that displays the CategoryID and replace it with a ComboBox control with the following settings:

Property	Value
DataSource	objDSProducts.Categories
DataMember	CategoryName
ValueMember	CategoryID
SelectedValue	objDSProducts - Products.CategoryID

Run the project now, load the DataSet, and edit a few rows. You have a functional interface, and you can edit the rows of a table in the DataSet. My advice is to disallow the editing of the current row in browsing mode by turning on the ReadOnly property of the TextBox controls. Place an Edit button on the form, which will make the controls editable by resetting their ReadOnly property. While the user can edit the current row, disable all navigational controls on the form and force users to end the edit operation by clicking the OK or Cancel button.

The new interface is much more functional than the original one, produced by the wizard, but it's not very robust. Let's say you wish to take a look at the suppliers, or categories, by expanding the appropriate ComboBox control. It sure isn't your intention to change the current row. Click a category name by mistake and you've edited the current row. When you move to the next row, the changes will be committed to the DataSet, and when you click the Update button the changes will be sent to the database. Sure, my suggested approach takes a few more keystrokes, or mouse clicks, but real-world applications must be robust.

Let's continue our exploration of the application the wizard has generated for us. Try adding a few products. Don't bother specifying the new product's ID; it will be assigned one by the database. The Add button will add a new row to the Products table in the local DataSet. The new rows will be submitted to the database along with the edits and deletions (if any) when you click the Update button.

When adding a new product, make sure you click the CheckBox control (field Discontinued) once to check it, and once again to clear it. The default state of this control isn't cleared, even though you don't see a check mark. If you don't touch the CheckBox, the application will crash with an error message to the effect that the Discontinued field can't be Null. The same will happen if you don't supply a value to the ProductName field, because this field can't be Null. As you can see, some of the table's basic constraints are embedded into the DataSet's DataTable object, and they're enforced. This is a good thing, but should they crash the application?

The program crashes when it attempts to move to another row in the table and the current row has errors. We can trap this error with a structured error handler and prevent the program from crashing. Open the SelectedIndexChanged event handler of the ListBox control and insert the code shown in Listing 22.5.

LISTING 22.5: HANDLING DATA-ENTRY ERRORS

```
Private Sub ListBox1_SelectedIndexChanged(ByVal sender As System.Object, _
            ByVal e As System.EventArgs) Handles ListBox1.SelectedIndexChanged
    Try
        Me.BindingContext(objDSProducts, "Products").Position = _
        ListBox1.SelectedIndex
    Catch dataException As Exception
        MsgBox(dataException.Message)
        Me.BindingContext(objDSProducts, "Products").CancelCurrentEdit()
        Me.BindingContext(objDSProducts, "Products").Position = _
        ListBox1.SelectedIndex
    End Try
End Sub
```

NOTE *OK, the problem is the statement we inserted to improve the navigational capabilities of the DataForm, so it's not really the wizard's fault. But our custom code and the simplistic navigational tools inserted on the form by the wizard do the same thing—they change the Position property of the BindingContext object—so the original code would have failed in the same manner.*

If an error occurs, the exception handler will display the description of the error in a message box, then it will clear the edits and move to the product selected in the ListBox control. The user can select the previous row and edit it again, knowing what type of error prevented the update of the DataSet.

If you click the Delete button, the current row will be removed from the DataSet (it will also be removed from the ListBox control, just as new rows are added automatically to this control). But products are referenced in the Order Details table, so how can we delete them? Remember, the DataSet resides in the local computer and is disconnected from the database. Since the DataSet contains a single table, there are no relations to be enforced and the DataSet happily removes the row when you request it. What will happen when you attempt to update the database, however, is a different story. SQL Server will emphatically refuse to remove a row that's being referenced by another table, and the update operation will fail. Delete a row, then click the Update button. You'll get an error message to the effect that the row can't be removed because this would violate the PK_Order_Details_Products constraint.

Handling Identity Fields

I should point out the following behavior of the application. If you add a row, its ProductID field will be assigned a value automatically. The ProductID column is an Identity column, and you can't set it; it must be assigned a value by the DBMS. The DataSet knows that the ProductID column is an Identity column and, every time you add a row, it assigns the next available value to it. If the last row's ProductID field is 90, it will assign the value 91 to the first row you add, the value 92 to the second row, and so on. But what will happen if another user has already added a few rows to the table? Run the application again, add a couple of rows, and then switch to the Enterprise Manager. Do not update the database yet.

In the Enterprise Manager, add a couple of rows to the Products table. Then switch to the application and click the Update button. The new rows will be added to the underlying table. Write down the IDs of the new rows. Then load the DataSet again by clicking the Load button, locate the newly added rows, and examine their IDs. This time they're different! They have the values assigned to them by the database.

This is a reasonable behavior too, as we don't really care about the IDs of the rows. Or do we? In an application like EditProducts, no one would really care to see the actual ID of a product. There are situations, however, where you may want to use the ID of a row as a foreign key in another table. Let's say you want to issue an invoice. First, you must add a row to the Orders table. The new order will get an ID from the database. This ID, however, must appear in all the rows of the Order Details table that refer to the specific invoice. And obviously, we must make sure that the proper ID is inserted in the Order Details table (it must be the final ID of the order assigned by the database, not a temporary ID generated by the DataSet).

RETRIEVING PROPER IDS

There are situations where we do need to know the proper ID assigned to an identity field by the database. The best way to handle these situations is to create a stored procedure that accepts the fields of a new row, writes it to the database, and returns the ID assigned by the database. Although this can be done through the DataSet object, why bother with a mechanism that's optimized for disconnected scenarios? We want to connect to the database, commit the new row, and get back its ID as soon as possible. You see, the DataSet was designed for a disconnected world, but not all data-access requirements fall into this category. It's highly unlikely that ADO.NET will remain for long a disconnected data-access mechanism—Microsoft will have to add features to make ADO.NET work in connected scenarios like the one described here.

Instead of using the DataSet to update the database, we can use the Command object. I discussed the Command object in Chapter 21, but I will repeat the process here by demonstrating how to add a new row to the Orders table. First, you must create a stored procedure that inserts a new row to the table. The only required field for the Orders table is the ID of the customer that placed the order. The order's date (OrderDate field) can be assigned the current date and time by the database. The remaining fields (the ID of the employee who made the sale, the shipping address, and so on) are optional. To keep the complexity of the sample code to the bare minimum, I will ignore these fields.

The stored procedure in Listing 22.6 accepts as argument the ID of a customer and creates a new row in the Orders table. After the execution of the INSERT statement, the stored procedure retrieves the value of the identity field of the new row (it's given by the expression @@IDEN-TITY) and returns it to the calling application.

LISTING 22.6: THE NEWORDER STORED PROCEDURE

```
CREATE PROCEDURE NewOrder
@custID nchar(5)
AS
INSERT INTO Orders (CustomerID, OrderDate) VALUES(@custID, GetDate())
RETURN (@@IDENTITY)
GO
```

The value returned by the stored procedure is known as its *return value*, and you'll see shortly how you can retrieve it from within your application.

Once the stored procedure is in place, you can create a new Command object to call the stored procedure. First we establish a Connection object to the database, then we open the connection and assign the Connection object to the Connection property of the Command object.

The Command object's CommandText property is set to the name of the stored procedure, and its CommandType property is set to the constant `CommandType.StoredProcedure`. At this point, we can execute the stored procedure, but we must first add some parameters to it. We create a new Parameter object for each parameter expected by the stored procedure, set its name, type, and value, and then add it to the Command object's Parameters collection. Finally, we call the Command object's ExecuteScalar method, which returns the stored procedure's return value. Listing 22.7 shows how to add a new row to the Orders table and then retrieve the new row's OrderID field. If the new row can't be added to the table, the stored procedure will raise an error (it will also return the value zero). The ID of the new row is then stored in the *orderID* variable for further processing.

LISTING 22.7: RETRIEVING A NEW ROW'S IDENTITY COLUMN

```
Dim myConnection As New SqlConnection()
myConnection.ConnectionString = "data source=PowerToolkit; " & _
      "initial catalog=Northwind;integrated security=SSPI"
   myConnection.Open()
   Dim myCommand As New SqlCommand()
   myCommand.Connection = myConnection
Try
   myCommand.CommandText = "NewOrder"
   myCommand.CommandType = CommandType.StoredProcedure
   Dim p As New SqlParameter()
   p.ParameterName = "@CustID"
   p.Direction = ParameterDirection.Input
   p.SqlDbType = SqlDbType.Char
   p.Value = "BLAUS"
   myCommand.Parameters.Add(p)
   p = New SqlParameter()
   p.ParameterName = "RETURN"
   p.Direction = ParameterDirection.ReturnValue
   p.SqlDbType = SqlDbType.Int
   myCommand.Parameters.Add(p)
   myCommand.ExecuteScalar()
   Dim orderID As Integer = CType(myCommand.Parameters("RETURN").Value, Integer)
Catch exc As Exception
   MsgBox(exc.Message)
End Try
```

And what might that further processing be? In most situations, it's the use of the ID in adding new rows in related tables. To complete the insertion of an order to the database, we must also add a few rows to the Order Details table. These rows must refer to the order to which they belong, so their OrderID field must be set to the ID of the order we just inserted.

I will show you how to add the detail lines; it's quite analogous to adding a row to the Orders table. However, there's a complication. What if one of the detail lines can't be added to its table? We should be able to cancel the entire order, not just a detail line. Performing multiple actions against a database is a transaction, and we must first discuss the topic of transactions. After you understand how transactions are handled, you'll see the code for entering a new order to the Northwind database.

Transactions

The closing remark of the last section brings us to a very important topic in database programming, the topic of transactions. A *transaction* is a series of actions that must either succeed, or fail, as a whole. Should one of the actions fail, then the entire transaction fails and all the changes made to the database so far must be undone ("rolled back" in proper database terminology). If all actions succeed, then they can be finalized ("committed" in proper database terminology) and become part of the database. A transaction takes place while you transfer money from one account to another. The two actions are the withdrawal of an amount from one account and the deposit of the same amount to another account. If the bank charges you for the transaction, then a third action is involved in the transaction. If one of them fails, you want the accounts to be restored in their initial states, as if the transaction were never attempted. You don't want the money to come out of your account and not appear in the other account, and you don't want to be charged for an unsuccessful transaction. Even if you don't care about an amount appearing magically in someone else's account, the bank cares.

To implement a transaction, you mark the beginning of it. If the transaction fails, the database must be restored to the state it was in just prior to when the transaction was initiated. Then you insert the code for all the actions involved in the transaction, and at the end you commit the transaction. Once the transaction is committed, other users can see its effects. Until then, however, other users can't see the effects of any of the steps. In other words, there are no partial transactions. If an error prevents the completion of the transaction, then you must roll it back—bring the tables to the state they were in just before the start of the transaction. The following pseudo-code is the skeleton of a transaction:

```
Begin Transaction
Try
    { statements to complete transaction }
    Commit Transaction
Catch Exception
    Rollback Transaction
End Try
```

Let's say we want to place a new order. First, we must add a row to the Orders table. Then we must add some rows to the Order Details table—one row per item ordered. The rows in the Order Details table must reference the matching row in the Orders table—that is, they must use the ID of the order as foreign key.

To add rows to the Order Details table, we'll do something similar. We'll write a stored procedure that adds a new row to the Order Details table, the NewOrderLine stored procedure (Listing 22.8). The code we'll discuss in this section can be found in the Transaction project on the CD. This procedure accepts as arguments the ID of the order to which the detail line belongs, the product ID, and the quantity ordered. To complete the row, it picks the price of the product from the Products table. I've ignored the discount in this example, but it can be added with an additional parameter.

LISTING 22.8: THE NEWORDERLINE STORED PROCEDURE

```
CREATE PROCEDURE NewOrderLine
@OrderID integer, @ProductID integer, @quantity integer
AS
DECLARE @ProductPrice money
SET @ProductPrice=(SELECT UnitPrice FROM Products WHERE ProductID=@ProductID)
INSERT INTO [Order Details] (OrderID, ProductID, Quantity, UnitPrice)
VALUES (@OrderID, @ProductID, @Quantity, @ProductPrice)
GO
```

This stored procedure must be called once for each detail line. Let's continue with the *myCommand* object of the previous example. First, we must set the Command object's CommandText and CommandType properties:

```
myCommand.CommandText = "NewOrderLine"
myCommand.CommandType = CommandType.StoredProcedure
```

Then we clear the Command object's Parameters collection and add a new set of parameters, designed for the NewOrderLine stored procedure.

```
myCommand.Parameters.Clear()
p = New SqlParameter()
p.ParameterName = "@OrderID"
p.Direction = ParameterDirection.Input
p.SqlDbType = SqlDbType.Int
p.Value = orderID
myCommand.Parameters.Add(p)

p = New SqlParameter()
p.ParameterName = "@ProductID"
p.Direction = ParameterDirection.Input
p.SqlDbType = SqlDbType.Int
p.Value = 15
myCommand.Parameters.Add(p)

p = New SqlParameter()
p.ParameterName = "@Quantity"
p.Direction = ParameterDirection.Input
p.SqlDbType = SqlDbType.Int
p.Value = 1
myCommand.Parameters.Add(p)
myCommand.ExecuteNonQuery()
```

Each parameter has a name (property ParameterName), type (property SqlDbType), direction (property Direction), and value (property Value). Once these properties are set, we add the parameter object to the Command object's Parameters collection. After all the necessary parameters are set, we call the ExecuteNonQuery method of the Command object, which executes the stored procedure and returns the number of rows affected. The same process must be repeated for all the detail lines— only you need not re-create the Parameter object, you can simply set its properties and add it to the parameters collection. All other properties remain the same.

So, we have the code that adds a new row to the Orders table (Listing 22.6), the code that retrieves the new order's ID (Listing 22.7), and the code that adds rows to the Order Details table (Listing 22.8). Let's put all the actions together in a transaction. To create a transaction with ADO.NET, you must create a Transaction object. A Transaction object is created on the Connection object, by calling its BeginTransaction method. This statement marks the beginning of the transaction. Then, we set the Command object's Transaction property to the Transaction object. This is how ADO knows which actions to undo when the transaction is rolled back:

```
Dim myTrans As SqlTransaction
myTrans = myConnection.BeginTransaction()
myCommand.Transaction = myTrans
```

Then comes an exception handler to catch any error that may occur during the processing of the transaction. All the statements presented earlier must appear in the Try clause of the exception handler. If the Catch clause is entered, we roll back the transaction by calling the Transaction object's RollBack method. If the transaction succeeds, we call the same object's Commit method to commit the transaction. Listing 22.9 shows the code that creates a new order and adds three detail lines to it. The detail lines refer to the products with IDs of 15, 25, and 35, and the quantities are 1, 3, and 5 items of each product, respectively. You have seen most of the code already, but I'm repeating it for your convenience here.

LISTING 22.9: PERFORMING A TRANSACTION WITH THE COMMAND OBJECT

```
Dim myConnection As New SqlConnection()
myConnection.ConnectionString = "dataSource=PowerToolkit;initial" & _
    "catalog=Northwind;integrated security=SSPI"
myConnection.Open()
Dim myCommand As New SqlCommand()
myCommand.Connection = myConnection
Dim myTrans As SqlTransaction
myTrans = myConnection.BeginTransaction()
myCommand.Transaction = myTrans
Try
    myCommand.CommandText = "NewOrder"
    myCommand.CommandType = CommandType.StoredProcedure
    Dim p As New SqlParameter()
    p.ParameterName = "@CustID"
    p.Direction = ParameterDirection.Input
    p.SqlDbType = SqlDbType.Char
    p.Value = "BLAUS"
    myCommand.Parameters.Add(p)
    p = New SqlParameter()
    p.ParameterName = "RETURN"
    p.Direction = ParameterDirection.ReturnValue
    p.SqlDbType = SqlDbType.Int
    myCommand.Parameters.Add(p)
    myCommand.ExecuteScalar()
    Dim orderID As Integer = CType(myCommand.Parameters("RETURN").Value, Integer)
' Set up parameters collection and add first item
    myCommand.CommandText = "NewOrderLine"
    myCommand.CommandType = CommandType.StoredProcedure
    myCommand.Parameters.Clear()
```

```
    p = New SqlParameter()
    p.ParameterName = "@OrderID"
    p.Direction = ParameterDirection.Input
    p.SqlDbType = SqlDbType.Int
    p.Value = orderID
    myCommand.Parameters.Add(p)
    p = New SqlParameter()
    p.ParameterName = "@ProductID"
    p.Direction = ParameterDirection.Input
    p.SqlDbType = SqlDbType.Int
    p.Value = 15
    myCommand.Parameters.Add(p)
    p = New SqlParameter()
    p.ParameterName = "@Quantity"
    p.Direction = ParameterDirection.Input
    p.SqlDbType = SqlDbType.Int
    p.Value = 1
    myCommand.Parameters.Add(p)
    myCommand.ExecuteNonQuery()
' Add second item
    p = myCommand.Parameters("@ProductID")
    p.Value = 25
    p = myCommand.Parameters("@Quantity")
    p.Value = 2
    myCommand.ExecuteNonQuery()
' Add third item
    p = myCommand.Parameters("@ProductID")
    p.Value = 35
    p = myCommand.Parameters("@Quantity")
    p.Value = 3
    myCommand.ExecuteNonQuery()
    myTrans.Commit()
    Console.WriteLine("Order written to database.")
Catch exc As Exception
    myTrans.Rollback()
    Console.WriteLine(exc.Message)
        MsgBox("Could not add order to database.")
Finally
    myConnection.Close()
End Try
```

The last statement in the Finally section of the error handler is very important. In ADO.NET you should never keep connections open longer than absolutely necessary. The code shown in Listing 22.9 will add a new order to the Northwind database by updating two tables in a transaction (you will find this code in the Transaction project on the CD).

Performing Update Operations

Now it's time to look at a few really advanced database operations. Getting data out of a database, storing them to a DataSet, and even processing them on the client computer is fairly straightforward. Updating the underlying tables is also straightforward, as long as all rows and all fields have been validated. In this section, we'll take a look at what can go wrong in moving the data from the DataSet back into the database.

As you have seen, there are two major approaches when working with ADO.NET: use the DataSet's update method, or use the Command object to execute SQL statements and stored procedures directly against the database. Neither approach is necessarily better than the other; sometimes you'll find DataSets more convenient to work with, sometimes not. DataSets were designed for disconnected scenarios. You can populate a DataSet with several tables, establish relations between them, and send it to Germany where someone might use it for their own purposes. Or you can take it with you to a Greek island, edit it, and bring it back two weeks later. The question is what will happen when you attempt to update the database with your DataSet's data. If the tables are edited frequently by other users as well, then all kinds of conflicts will arise when you call the Update method. If the tables aren't modified frequently, then there's a good chance that most of the rows in your DataSet will successfully update the underlying tables.

You can safely use DataSets to send data to other users. You can also safely receive DataSets from other users, probably from different databases. You'll be able to write applications to look at them, even edit them. You can also use them to update your database. The data in a DataSet sent by someone else most likely contains new data, and you can insert the appropriate rows in your database. If the same data exist in your database, you'll probably use the new DataSet to update your database. A publisher might send you a complete list of books for your online store. It's safe to assume that the publisher's data contain fewer mistakes than yours and you can use the new data to update your database.

The most complicated scenario is when you want to write applications to maintain a database. Invoicing and similar applications are easy to write, because an invoice can't be edited. Invoices are entered once, they can be viewed many times, used in calculations, but no one can change an invoice. We usually cancel an invoice in its entirety. If you want to write a front-end application for maintaining a database where things change every day, the disconnected approach of ADO.NET may not be your best bet. Here's why. The DataSet can hold a small (or not so small) segment of your database. To make the best of the disconnected nature of the DataSet, you must keep it on the client for as long as possible. The longer you keep the disconnected DataSet on the client computer, the more you increase the chances of other users to modify the same data in the database. The problem of two or more users attempting to update the same data is as old as computers (almost) and is known as *concurrency*. There are two ways to deal with concurrency, optimistic concurrency and pessimistic concurrency. ADO.NET is based on optimistic concurrency.

Optimistic concurrency means that no other users will attempt to access the same data while you're editing them. As you recall, the stored procedures generated by the DataAdapter wizard for updating the database won't update a row if even one of its fields has changed since we last read it. If even a single field has changed value in the underlying table, then the row we have in the DataSet has been edited by someone else. Can we overwrite someone else's edits?

Let's think about it for a moment. If you're editing the Customers table, you're most likely changing addresses, phone numbers, and so on. If someone else happens to edit the same row at the same time, they're probably doing the same. Would it make any difference if you committed your edits before, or after, another user? There are many situations where the "last-write wins." The user that updates the database last overwrites changes made by others. When you create the SQL statements or stored procedures for updating the database, you're given the option to use optimistic concurrency or not. If you decide that the "last-write wins" scenario works for your application, don't use optimistic concurrency.

In an airline reservation system, the "last-write wins" scenario is out of the question, obviously. We don't want agents to assign the same seat over and over again. The same is true for an application that updates bank accounts and so on. That's why the wizard that generates the SQL statements for updating the database uses optimistic concurrency and doesn't update a row if it has been changed since it was read into the DataSet.

A DataRow's Versions

How does the DataSet know that a row has been edited since it was last read? This is an interesting aspect of ADO.NET. Each row in a DataTable has several versions. The values read from the database are the Original values (this is how the DataSet knows whether a row has been modified since it read it from its table). The value of a field in the DataSet is the Current value. While the user is editing a field, the new value is the Proposed value. The Proposed value will become the Current value when the changes are written to the DataSet. Finally, the Default value is the field's default value.

To specify which version of a field's value you want to read, specify the second parameter of the DataRow.Item property. The following statement retrieves the Original value of the first column of the first row in the Products table of the *DSProducts1* DataSet:

```
DSProducts1.Products.Rows(0).Item("ProductName", DataRowVersion.Original)
```

To experiment with the various versions of a row, open the EditProducts project and add a Show Versions button on its form. Then enter the statements of Listing 22.10 in the button's Click event handler.

LISTING 22.10: READING THE VERSIONS OF A DATAROW

```
Private Sub Button1_Click(ByVal sender As System.Object, _
                ByVal e As System.EventArgs) Handles Button1.Click
    Dim i As Integer
    Dim row As DataRow
    For i = 0 To 2
        row = objDSProducts.Products.Rows(i)
        If row.HasVersion(DataRowVersion.Current) Then
            Console.WriteLine("CURRENT  " & row.Item("ProductName", _
                            DataRowVersion.Current))
        End If
        If row.HasVersion(DataRowVersion.Default) Then
            Console.WriteLine("DEFAULT  " & row.Item("ProductName", _
                            DataRowVersion.Default))
        End If
```

```
        If row.HasVersion(DataRowVersion.Original) Then
            Console.WriteLine("ORIGINAL " & row.Item("ProductName", _
                            DataRowVersion.Original))
        End If
        If row.HasVersion(DataRowVersion.Proposed) Then
            Console.WriteLine("PROPOSED " & row.Item("ProductName", _
                            DataRowVersion.Proposed))
        End If
    Next
End Sub
```

The event handler of Listing 22.10 displays all the versions of the first two rows in the *objDS-Products* DataSet (a DataSet that holds the Products table). It displays only the ProductName field's values in all versions, so this is the field you must edit if you want to experiment with the versions of the DataRow object.

As you can see, a row may not have all possible versions, so we use the HasVersion method to find out whether a specific version exists before we attempt to retrieve it. This code prints all available versions of the first three rows of the Products table. Run the application and edit one or more of the first three rows. Then click the Show Versions button to see the versions of the first three rows at the time.

The second product's name is "Chang." Change it to "Chang1" and, without moving the focus to another field, click the Show Versions button. This is what you will see in the Output window:

```
CURRENT   Chang
DEFAULT   Chang1
ORIGINAL  Chang
PROPOSED  Chang1
```

The Current version is the value of the ProductName field in the DataSet, and it's "Chang." The Proposed value is "Chang1." Return to the form and click another product, then back to Chang. The action of switching to another row caused the changes to be written to the DataSet. If you click the Show Versions button again, you will see the following:

```
CURRENT   Chang1
DEFAULT   Chang1
ORIGINAL  Chang
```

For one, there's no Proposed value. Once the changes are saved, there's no longer a Proposed value. The current value became "Chang1," but the Original value did not change. You must commit the changes to the database and reload the DataSet to change a row's Original value.

As you can guess, the various versions of the values are used in validating the data and in determining whether a row has changed since it was last read from the database. The SQL statements generated by the wizard that generates the DataAdapter object for each table use the various versions of the rows to implement optimistic concurrency. The following UPDATE statement commits the changes made to a row to the underlying table, but only if the row's fields have the same values read into the DataSet:

```
UPDATE dbo.Products SET ProductName = ?, SupplierID = ?, CategoryID = ?,
                       QuantityPerUnit = ?, UnitPrice = ?, UnitsInStock = ?,
                       UnitsOnOrder = ?, ReorderLevel = ?, Discontinued = ?
WHERE (ProductID = ?) AND
      (CategoryID = ? OR ? IS NULL AND CategoryID IS NULL) AND
      (Discontinued = ?) AND
      (ProductName = ?) AND
      (QuantityPerUnit = ? OR ? IS NULL AND QuantityPerUnit IS NULL) AND
      (ReorderLevel = ? OR ? IS NULL AND ReorderLevel IS NULL) AND
      (SupplierID = ? OR ? IS NULL AND SupplierID IS NULL) AND
      (UnitPrice = ? OR ? IS NULL AND UnitPrice IS NULL) AND
      (UnitsInStock = ? OR ? IS NULL AND UnitsInStock IS NULL) AND
      (UnitsOnOrder = ? OR ? IS NULL AND UnitsOnOrder IS NULL)
```

The question marks correspond to parameters, and they're substituted with actual values prior to executing this statement. If you turn off optimistic concurrency, the wizard will generate the following simple statement:

```
UPDATE dbo.Products SET ProductName = ?, SupplierID = ?, CategoryID = ?,
                       QuantityPerUnit = ?, UnitPrice = ?, UnitsInStock = ?,
                       UnitsOnOrder = ?, ReorderLevel = ?, Discontinued = ?
WHERE (ProductID = ?)
```

A DataRow's States

In addition to versions, rows have states, too; a row can be in one of the following states:

Added   The row has been added to the DataTable, but it hasn't been accepted yet (rows are accepted after they're written to the database as well).

Deleted   The row has been deleted. However, it remains in the DataSet marked as Deleted, so that the Update method can delete the matching row of the underlying table.

Detached   The row has been created but it has not been added to a DataTable yet. A row is in this state while you set its fields and before you actually add it to a table.

Modified   The row has been modified, but it hasn't been accepted yet.

Unchanged   The row hasn't been changed yet.

The state of a row is used in updating the underlying tables. When you call the DataAdapter's Update method, all rows are moved to the database, where they're committed with the appropriate SQL statement or stored procedure. To conserve bandwidth, you can send only the modified, added, and deleted rows to the database. This is the technique used by the DataForm wizard, and it's worth taking a look at the code it produces. All the action of updating the database takes place in the UpdateDataSource() function, which returns the number of rows that were updated successfully. Listing 22.11 shows the code of the UpdateDataSource() function.

LISTING 22.11: THE UPDATEDATASOURCE() FUNCTION OF THE DATAFORM WIZARD

```
Public Function UpdateDataSource(ByVal dataSet As EditProducts.DSProducts) _
                As System.Int32
  Me.OleDbConnection1.Open()
  Dim UpdatedRows As System.Data.DataSet
  Dim InsertedRows As System.Data.DataSet
  Dim DeletedRows As System.Data.DataSet
  Dim AffectedRows As Integer = 0
  UpdatedRows = DataSet.GetChanges(System.Data.DataRowState.Modified)
  InsertedRows = DataSet.GetChanges(System.Data.DataRowState.Added)
  DeletedRows = DataSet.GetChanges(System.Data.DataRowState.Deleted)
  Try
    If (Not (UpdatedRows) Is Nothing) Then
      AffectedRows = OleDbDataAdapter1.Update(UpdatedRows)
      AffectedRows = (AffectedRows + OleDbDataAdapter2.Update(UpdatedRows))
      AffectedRows = (AffectedRows + OleDbDataAdapter3.Update(UpdatedRows))
    End If
    If (Not (InsertedRows) Is Nothing) Then
      AffectedRows = (AffectedRows + OleDbDataAdapter1.Update(InsertedRows))
      AffectedRows = (AffectedRows + OleDbDataAdapter2.Update(InsertedRows))
      AffectedRows = (AffectedRows + OleDbDataAdapter3.Update(InsertedRows))
    End If
    If (Not (DeletedRows) Is Nothing) Then
      AffectedRows = (AffectedRows + OleDbDataAdapter1.Update(DeletedRows))
      AffectedRows = (AffectedRows + OleDbDataAdapter2.Update(DeletedRows))
      AffectedRows = (AffectedRows + OleDbDataAdapter3.Update(DeletedRows))
    End If
  Catch updateException As System.Exception
    Throw updateException
  Finally
    Me.OleDbConnection1.Close()
  End Try
End Function
```

This function generates three new DataSets and populates them with the added, deleted, and modified rows of the original DataSets. In a large DataSet, the three partial DataSets will be considerably smaller than the original DataSet. Then, it calls the Update method of the corresponding DataAdapter object, passing the appropriate DataSet.

The order of the DataSets passed to the Update method is important. First it passes the rows that were edited, then the new rows, and finally the deleted rows.

If you examine the code generated by the wizard, you'll see that it doesn't reload the DataSet. Instead, it merges the rows that successfully updated the underlying tables with the existing rows in the DataSet (it basically consolidates the changes) and then calls the DataSet object's AcceptChanges method. AcceptChanges sets the Original value of all fields to the Current value. In effect, the new DataSet is the same as the one you would get by reloading it from the database. If your DataSet isn't excessively large, you can reload it from the database and save yourself some serious debugging. You can also copy the code generated by the wizard and reuse it.

Updating Tables Manually

To update the underlying table(s) from within a DataSet, you must call the DataAdapter object's Update method. The Update method sends all the changes to the database, and through the appropriate stored procedures, the tables are updated. The DataAdapter object exposes the Continue-UpdateOnError property, which determines how the DataAdapter will react when an error is encountered. If the ContinueUpdateOnError property is False, which (mysteriously) is the default value, the DataAdapter will terminate the update process. If the first 10 edited rows in the DataSet contain no errors, they will be committed to the database. If the 11th row contains an error, the DataAdapter won't even attempt to update the remaining rows.

The ContinueUpdateOnError property should be set to True, so that the DataAdapter will update all the rows that don't contain errors. My guess is that all developers will make a habit of setting this property to True. After calling the Update method with the ContinueUpdateOnError property set to True, you must examine each row's Errors property to find out whether there was an error. Even better, you can insert the appropriate code in the DataAdapter object's RowUpdated event, which is fired after each attempt to update a row.

In this event, you can examine the `e.Status` property for the current operation. If the operation failed, then the `e.Status` property will be `UpdateStatus.ErrorsOccurred`. You can then retrieve the error message describing why the operation failed and present it along with the row (or the row's key field) to the user, or take some other course of action. There are no simple rules as to how to handle update errors; it all depends on the application. A safe approach is to accept the changes in rows of the DataSet that successfully updated the underlying table(s) and reset the ones that failed to update the database to their original values. At the same time, you can create a list of all the rows that failed to update along with the corresponding error message. Let's see how to use this technique to build a robust data-entry screen.

The DataEntry project's main form, shown in Figure 22.4, displays the names of all products in a ListBox control. To view the fields of a product on the form, click the product's name in the list. The technique of using a ListBox control as a navigational tool has been described earlier in this chapter. There are actually better techniques for selecting a specific row, but the focus in this example is how to edit a table of the DataSet and commit the changes to the database.

FIGURE 22.4

The DataEntry project demonstrates robust table-editing techniques.

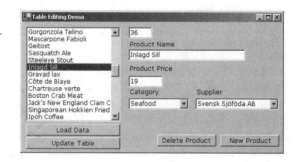

To edit a row, you just change the values of its fields on the form. To change the product's category and supplier, simply select another item in the corresponding ComboBox control. To delete the selected product, click the Delete Product button. To add a new product to the table, click the New Product button. When this button is clicked, the add and delete buttons are replaced by OK and Cancel buttons. Moreover, the ListBox control is disabled, so that you can't select another row until you finish editing the new row. To commit the new row to the DataSet, click OK. This action hides the OK and Cancel buttons and restored the other two buttons on the form.

Notice that the new row is added to the DataSet, which resides on the client—no information is sent to the database server. After editing, deleting, and adding rows to the DataSet, you can commit the changes to the Products table of the DataSet by clicking the Update Table button. In this button's event handler, the Update method of the matching DataAdapter object is called. Instead of passing the entire DataSet to the server, we call the Update method three times, passing one set of rows at a time: the edited, the added, and finally the deleted rows. Listing 22.12 is the handler of the Click event of the Update Table button.

LISTING 22.12: CALLING THE DATAADAPTER'S UPDATE METHOD

```
Private Sub UpdateTable(ByVal sender As System.Object, _
            ByVal e As System.EventArgs) Handles bttnUpdate.Click
    If Not DsProducts1.GetChanges(DataRowState.Modified) Is Nothing Then _
        SqlDataAdapter1.Update(DsProducts1.GetChanges(DataRowState.Modified))
    If Not DsProducts1.GetChanges(DataRowState.Added) Is Nothing Then _
        SqlDataAdapter1.Update(DsProducts1.GetChanges(DataRowState.Added))
    If Not DsProducts1.GetChanges(DataRowState.Deleted) Is Nothing Then _
        SqlDataAdapter1.Update(DsProducts1.GetChanges(DataRowState.Deleted))
End Sub
```

The code calls the Update method with a different group of rows, only if the group isn't empty. If there are rows to be updated, the Update method is called with a DataSet object that contains the edited (modified) rows. The GetChanges method retrieves the rows whose state is the same as the second argument.

The DataAdapter attempts to update one row at a time. After each attempt (whether it was successful or not), it fires the RowUpdated event, which is handled by the code shown in Listing 22.13.

LISTING 22.13: HANDLING THE DATAADAPTER'S ROWUPDATED EVENT

```
Private Sub SqlDataAdapter1_RowUpdated(ByVal sender As Object, _
            ByVal e As System.Data.SqlClient.SqlRowUpdatedEventArgs) _
            Handles SqlDataAdapter1.RowUpdated
    Select Case e.Row.RowState
        Case DataRowState.Added
            Console.Write("Adding Product ID = " & _
                        e.Row.Item("ProductID", ataRowVersion.Proposed))
        Case DataRowState.Deleted
```

```
                Console.Write("Deleting Product ID = " & _
                            e.Row.Item("ProductID", DataRowVersion.Original))
          Case DataRowState.Modified
             Console.Write("Updating Product ID = " & _
                            e.Row.Item("ProductID", DataRowVersion.Original))
       End Select
       If e.Status = UpdateStatus.ErrorsOccurred Then
          Console.WriteLine("Failed to update row ")
          Console.WriteLine(e.Errors.Message)
          e.Row.RejectChanges()
       Else
          Console.WriteLine("  Updated successfully")
          e.Row.AcceptChanges()
       End If
    End Sub
```

The event reports the row being updated through the Row property of its *e* argument. The expression **e.Row.RowState** returns the state of the row. We use the row's state to display the type of action (add/edit/delete) that caused the current row to be updated. We also display the key field's value of the current row, so that the user knows which rows failed to update the database. Notice that new rows don't have an original version, so we display the proposed version.

Then the code examines the **e.Status** property, which will be set to **UpdateStatus.ErrorsOccurred** if the operation failed, and display the message returned by the database. The output produced by the RowUpdated event handler looks like this:

```
Updating Product ID = 1   Updated successfully
Updating Product ID = 9   Updated successfully
Updating Product ID = 44   Updated successfully
Updating Product ID = 91   Updated successfully
Deleting Product ID = 78   Updated successfully
```

The product with ID of 91 was added to the table, but the RowUpdated event handler reports it as being updated.

For each row that successfully updates the underlying table, we call the AcceptChanges method. This method copies the original field values into the current values. For all intents and purposes, this row looks as if it was just read from the database and hasn't been edited yet.

This techniques works only if the SqlDataAdapter1 object's ContinueUpdateOnError property is set to True. If not, the update process will be interrupted the first time an error occurs. The project uses three DataAdapter objects, one for each of the tables Products, Categories, and Suppliers. Of the three DataAdapter objects, only the one that corresponds to the Products table contains statements to update the database. The other two DataAdapters contain only a SELECT statement to retrieve their data from the database.

To add a new row to the Products table, you must click the New Product button. This button's event handler prepares the various controls to accept the field values of the new row and displays the

OK and Cancel buttons. Most important, it suspends the data binding. The TextBox controls on the form may assume invalid values for a while, so we must disable the data binding while the fields of the new row are being set. Data binding will resume later, when the user clicks the OK button and the new row is actually added to the DataSet. Here's the code behind the New Product button:

```
Private Sub bttnNew_Click(ByVal sender As System.Object, _
            ByVal e As System.EventArgs) Handles bttnNew.Click
    Me.BindingContext(DsProducts1, "Products").SuspendBinding()
    ListBox1.Enabled = False
    bttnOK.Visible = True
    bttnCancel.Visible = True
    bttnDelete.Visible = False
    bttnNew.Visible = False
End Sub
```

Finally, when the OK button is clicked, the new row is committed to the database with the statements of Listing 22.14.

LISTING 22.14: ADDING A NEW ROW

```
Private Sub bttnOK_Click(ByVal sender As System.Object, _
            ByVal e As System.EventArgs) Handles bttnOK.Click
    Dim newRow As DSProducts.ProductsRow
    newRow = DsProducts1.Products.NewProductsRow
    newRow.Item("ProductName") = TextBox2.Text
    newRow.Item("UnitPrice") = TextBox3.Text
    If cmbCategory.SelectedValue > 0 Then _
            newRow.Item("CategoryID") = cmbCategory.SelectedValue
    If cmbSupplier.SelectedValue > 0 Then _
            newRow.Item("SupplierID") = cmbSupplier.SelectedValue
    newRow.Item("Discontinued") = 0
    DsProducts1.Products.AddProductsRow(newRow)
    Me.BindingContext(DsProducts1, "Products").ResumeBinding()
    ListBox1.Enabled = True
    bttnOK.Visible = False
    bttnCancel.Visible = False
    bttnDelete.Visible = True
    bttnNew.Visible = True
End Sub
```

To add a new row, we must first create a variable that represents this row. Since we're working with a typed DataSet, we can declare a variable of the NewProductsRow type. Then we set the fields of the new row and finally add the newly created row to the table with the AddProductsRow method. After adding the row to the table, we enable the data binding again with the ResumeBinding method.

To delete a row, we call the DataRow's Delete method. The code behind the Delete Product button executes the following statement:

```
DsProducts1.Products(Me.BindingContext(DsProducts1, _
                     "Products").Position).Delete()
```

The expression

```
Me.BindingContext(DsProducts1, "Products").Position
```

returns the index of the selected row in the DataTable—an integer value. `DSProducts1.Products` is a DataTable object that represents the Products table in the DataSet. By calling this object with a numeric value as argument, we isolate a DataRow object, which represents the selected row in the Products table. Finally, we call the Delete method on this row to delete it. The row isn't actually removed from the DataSet. It will be removed only when we call the DataSet's AcceptChanges method—and this method must be called only after the underlying row has been successfully removed from the underlying table.

Open the DataEntry project on the CD and experiment with its code. See how the ComboBox controls were bound to the DataSet so that they always display the selected product's category and supplier. You can add more features to the application, starting with a better navigational model. The rows on the ListBox control are displayed in the same order as they were retrieved from the original table. In a "real" table with thousands of products, you wouldn't want to read the entire table into the DataSet. You should allow the user to specify the subset of the products they're interested in and upload only the matching rows to the client.

Building and Using Custom DataSets

In this section, we'll build a DataSet that's not connected to a data store. We'll create a new DataSet by specifying its schema with the XML Schema tools of the Toolbox. Then we'll make this DataSet the data source of a DataGrid control, and we'll be able to add data directly on the grid. With a few statements, we'll be able save the contents of the DataSet to a disk file and load it back from the disk file into the application.

Start a new project (it's the XMLGrid project on the CD) and add an XMLSchema component to the project. Right-click the project's name and, from the context menu, select Add New Item. Select the XML Schema template, specify a name for the new component (or accept the default name), and click OK to close the dialog box. An XMLSchema component will be added to the project; its default name is `XMLSchema1.xsd`. Double-click its icon to open it on the design surface.

Open the Toolbox, which now contains the XML Schema tools, and double-click the Element tool to add a new element to the XMLSchema. An XML element is equivalent to the table of a regular DataSet. The new XML element will be depicted on the design surface by an empty box. The default element's name is *element1*; change it to *GridData*. Each XML element has one or more attributes, so let's add a few. Open the Toolbox and drag the icon of the Attribute tool on the existing element. By default, new attributes are named attribute1, attribute2, and so on, and their default type is "string." Figure 22.5 shows an XML element with four attributes and the XML Toolbox.

FIGURE 22.5

Designing an XML schema

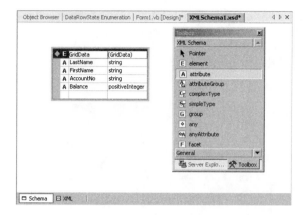

The box with the attribute's type is a drop-down list of all the data types you can assign to an attribute. The schema shown in Figure 22.5 contains an element with three string attributes and one positive Integer attribute. It's like a table with four columns—three string columns and one numeric column. As you will see shortly, if you attempt to assign a value of the incorrect type to an attribute, the attribute's current value won't change.

So far you've created the schema of the DataSet—the information that came from the database in the previous examples. Now we must use the XMLSchema component to create a DataSet object. Right-click somewhere on the XMLSchema design surface and, from the context menu, select Generate Dataset. Switch to the form and add a DataSet object. The Add Dataset dialog box pops up, prompting you for the dataset's schema information, as shown in Figure 22.6. Click OK and a new typed DataSet will be added to the project.

FIGURE 22.6

Adding a typed DataSet to a project

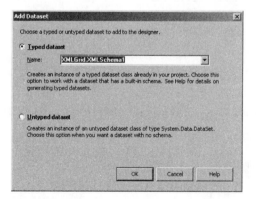

At this point, you're ready to use the custom DataSet. Place a DataGrid control on the form, set the control's DataSource property to `xmlschema11.GridData` (you'll select this item from a list), and run the project. You can optionally set some of the DataGrid control's attributes. You have a Data-Grid control that you can put any type of information on or use as a data-entry tool.

You can also add multiple elements to the XMLSchema and relate them to one another. Create each element separately and then add the appropriate relationships with the Relation tool.

Figure 22.7 shows the form of a simple application that allows you to populate a DataGrid control and persists the data to a file. It can also read the data from the disk file.

FIGURE 22.7

The main form of the XMLGrid project

To persist the data on the grid to a disk file, insert the code of Listing 22.15 in the Persist Data button's Click event handler. The Read Data button reads the data from the same file and populates the DataGrid control, and the code behind it is shown in Listing 22.16.

LISTING 22.15: PERSISTING DATASETS AS XML FILES

```
Private Sub Button1_Click(ByVal sender As System.Object, _
            ByVal e As System.EventArgs) Handles Button1.Click
    Dim FS As Stream
    FS = New FileStream("C:\GRID.XML", FileMode.OpenOrCreate)
    XmlSchema11.WriteXml(FS)
    FS.Close()
End Sub
```

LISTING 22.16: POPULATING A DATAGRID CONTROL WITH XML DATA

```
Private Sub Button2_Click(ByVal sender As System.Object, _
            ByVal e As System.EventArgs) Handles Button2.Click
    Dim FS As Stream
    FS = New FileStream("C:\GRID.XML", FileMode.Open)
    XmlSchema11.Clear()
    XmlSchema11.ReadXml(FS)
    FS.Close()
End Sub
```

You should also import the `System.IO` namespace, so that you won't have to fully qualify the FileStream objects. The XMLGrid project demonstrates how to design schemas for your DataSets. You can also create generic DataSets and use them as data-entry tools for many operations.

If you open the `GRID.XML` file created by this application, you'll see that it contains XML code. Figure 22.8 shows the XML generated by the data shown in Figure 22.7, opened with Internet Explorer.

FIGURE 22.8

Viewing an XML file with Internet Explorer

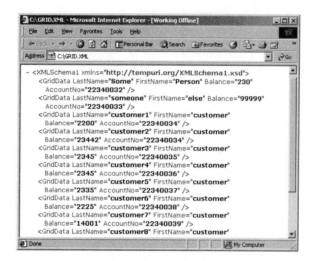

You may wish to explore XML in depth, as it's one of the hottest topics in the industry today. ADO.NET uses XML to format the data as well as describe the structure of its DataSets, and you can take advantage of this to move DataSets between computers or between applications. You're actually taking advantage of XML without having to write a single line of XML code.

Summary

You've learned a lot about ADO.NET in Chapters 21 and 22, but there's even more to learn. ADO.NET is one of the most elaborate and complex components of .NET, and it couldn't be exhausted in two chapters. These chapters were meant to help you familiarize yourself with the visual database tools, understand the structure of a DataSet, learn how to navigate the related tables of the DataSet and the rows of the individual DataTables, and know how to execute commands against the database. You should also be able to improve the code generated by the DataForm wizard and generate more robust and user-friendly applications.

Part VI

VB.NET on the Web

In this section:

Chapter 23

Introduction to Web Programming

IF THERE IS ONE technology that caught on overnight and has affected more computer users than any other, it is the World Wide Web—the set of all public Web sites and the documents they can provide to clients. The computers that host Web sites are called *servers*; their service is to provide the documents to the clients that request them. *Clients* are the millions of personal computers connected to the Internet. To exploit the Web, all you need is a browser, such as Internet Explorer, that can request documents and render them on your computer.

This chapter is a compendium of information on how to apply the knowledge you acquired in previous chapters to the Web—or, to use a popular term, how to *leverage* your knowledge of Visual Basic by applying it to the Web. To do so, you need a basic understanding of *Hypertext Markup Language (HTML)*, the language used to build Web documents, and a good understanding of how the clients interact with the servers on the Internet. Building a Web application with Visual Studio is very similar to building a Windows application, but there are many differences you should be aware of.

The Internet is a global, distributed network of computers that use a common protocol to communicate: *Transmission Control Protocol/Internet Protocol (TCP/IP)*. TCP/IP is a simple protocol because it had to be implemented consistently on all computers and operating systems. Indeed, TCP/IP is a truly universal protocol, but you needn't know much about it. It's there when you need it and allows your computer to connect to any other computer on the Internet.

If TCP/IP enables any two computers on the Internet to talk to each other, why do we need any other protocol? *Hypertext Transfer Protocol (HTTP)* is the protocol of the Web. Whereas TCP/IP allows two computers to connect on the hardware level, HTTP is the language servers and clients use to exchange information. HTTP is optimized for requesting and supplying HTML documents. The Internet is more than the Web (although it seems the Web is taking over). To exchange files through the Internet, for example, computers use File Transfer Protocol (FTP). The protocol that is used depends on the type of information to be exchanged. All other protocols, however, run on top of TCP/IP.

TIP   I need to begin with some basic concepts, such as the components of the Web and the evolution from static Web pages to Web applications. If you're already familiar with HTML or the Web, bear with us and pick up the discussion when we get to material that's new to you. If you have a good command of HTML and ASP, you can skip ahead to the section "Building a Web Application."

An HTML Primer

Hypertext Markup Language (HTML) is the language used to prepare most documents for online publication. HTML documents are also called *Web pages*; a page is what you see in your browser at any time. Each *Web site*, whether on the Internet or on an intranet, is composed of multiple related pages on a particular server, and you can switch among pages by following *hyperlinks*. The collection of public HTML pages out there makes up the *World Wide Web*.

A Web page is basically a text file that contains the text to be displayed and references to other elements such as images, sounds, and of course, other documents. You can create HTML pages with a text editor such as Notepad or with a "what you see is what you get" (WYSIWYG) application such as Microsoft FrontPage. In either case, the result is a plain text file that computers can easily exchange. The browser displays this text file on the client computer by interpreting part of the text as instructions and presenting the rest as content.

Web pages are stored on computers that act as *servers*: they provide a page to any computer that requests it. Each server computer has an address, or *Uniform Resource Locator (URL)*, that is something like the following:

```
http://www.example.com
```

The first portion, `http`, is the protocol used in accessing the server, and `www.example.com` is the name of the server on the Internet. All computers on the Internet have a unique, four-octet numeric address, such as 193.22.103.18. This numeric address is known as the Internet Protocol (IP) address, which is more difficult for us humans to remember than names. The server looks up the mnemonic names in tables and translates them into IP addresses.

To post an HTML document on a computer so that users can access and display it with their browsers, the computer that hosts the document must run a special application called the *Web server*. The Web server acknowledges requests made by other computers—the client computers—and supplies the requested document. The browser, which is the application running on the client computer, gets the document and displays it on the screen.

HTML Code Elements

The simplest component of the Web is HTML, which is a basic language for formatting documents that are displayed in a Web browser. The primary task of the browser is to render documents according to the HTML instructions they contain and display them on the monitor.

HTML is made up of text-formatting *tags* that are placed in a pair of angle brackets; they usually appear in pairs. The first, or *opening*, tag turns on a formatting feature, and the matching *closing* tag turns it off. To format a few words in bold, for example, enclose them with the <B> and </B> tags, as shown here:

```
Some <B>words</B> in the sentence are formatted in <B>bold</B>.
```

Of course, not all tags are as simple. The <TABLE> tag, for example, which is used to format tables, requires additional tags, like the <TR> tag, which delimits a new row in the table, and the <TD> tag, which delimits a new cell in a row.

Tags are also assisted by *attributes*, which are keywords with special meanings within a specific tag. The <A> or "anchor" tag, which is used to insert a hyperlink in the document, recognizes the HREF attribute. The syntax of a hyperlink to Microsoft's home page on the Web would be something like:

```
This <A HREF="http://www.microsoft.com">link</A> leads to Microsoft's home page.
```

The text between the <A> and </A> tags is marked as a hyperlink (displayed in a different color and underlined). The HREF attribute in the <A> tag tells the browser which URL, or address, to jump to when a user clicks this hyperlink. (For more on attributes, see the section "Attributes" later in this chapter.)

HTML Syntax and XHTML

HTML 4, the last version of the language, was released in 1997. In January 2000, the World Wide Web Consortium (W3C) released XHTML 1 (for Extensible HTML). This standard is a reformulation of HTML to comply with XML syntax rules; it uses almost the same set of tags, but with several restrictions:

◆ HTML 4 code was not case-sensitive; for example, you could enter the opening table tag as <table> or <TABLE>. Lowercase items will work with old or new browsers; but uppercase ones won't work with future versions, because XML (and therefore XHTML) won't read them. Note: In this book, I use uppercase for HTML tags, only so that they stand out. The projects on the CD use lowercase for tags.

◆ In HTML 4, attribute values only needed to be quoted in certain circumstances. In XHTML, all attribute values must be in quotation marks.

◆ In HTML 4, some tags didn't need to be closed; you could enter a <P> paragraph tag, type some text, and start the next paragraph with another <P>, without ever using a closing </P> tag. Browsers just figured it out; they'd "know" that when the new paragraph began, that meant the old one had to end:

```
<P>This is a paragraph.
<P>This is a new paragraph.
```

In XHTML, every element must be closed. This means that any element that includes content must have paired opening and closing tags.

```
<p>This is a paragraph.</p>
<p>This is a new paragraph.</p>
```

There are other differences, but these are the important ones during this transition phase from HTML to XHTML. You can learn more about XHTML from books such as *Mastering XHTML* by Tittel et al. (Sybex, 2001) or from the W3C Web site:

```
http://www.w3.org/MarkUp/
```

In addition to the formatting commands (HTML is basically a document-formatting language), HTML can handle a few controls, which are known as *HTML controls*. These controls include text boxes, radio buttons, check boxes, buttons (specifically, a Submit and a Reset button), and a few more simple controls. The user can enter data or make selections on these controls and submit them to the server by clicking the Submit button. The Submit button may have any caption, but its function is to submit the data on the various controls on the page to the server by appending them to the server's URL. The server reads these values, processes them, and prepares a new page, which is downloaded to the client. You'll find out more about the HTML controls and how they're submitted to the server later in this chapter.

You're more than familiar with this interaction model, and it's no different with ASP.NET. No matter what you do on the server side, it's the client's capabilities that determine the structure of the application running on the server. ASP.NET uses this model to interact with the browser. It does a fine job of hiding most of the mundane details and gives you the illusion that you're writing code for a client that can execute VB applications. But in reality, ASP accepts the values submitted by the client and creates a new HTML file to download to the client.

As a VB programmer, you'll have no problem picking up the syntax of HTML. It's a very simple language, and you can pick up the basics as you go along. The visual tools of VB.NET allow you to create HTML documents with point-and-click operations, so a thorough knowledge of HTML is not really required for developing Web applications. However, you need to understand how clients interact with Web servers.

Server-Client Interaction

A Web site consisting of HTML pages is interactive only in the sense that it allows the user to jump from page to page through hyperlinks. The client requests documents from the server, and the server supplies them. In this simple interaction model, which dominates the Web today, Web pages reside on the disks of the servers waiting to be requested by a client. Obviously, updating the information entails editing the HTML documents; no wonder most sites can't provide up-to-date information.

The disadvantage of this model is that the client can't engage in a conversation with the server so that information can flow in both directions. The development of gateway interfaces such as the *Common Gateway Interface (CGI)* has enabled Web authors to add dynamic content to the Web. The client can send specific requests to the server (e.g., "show me the invoices issued last month" or "show me the customers in North America"). The server doesn't return a static page (a page that exists on the disk and can be called by its name). Instead, it executes a script, or application, that extracts "live" data from a database, formats the data as an HTML document, and sends the document to the client. The client sees up-to-date, accurate information.

The disadvantage of gateway programs is that they are difficult to implement and maintain. To simplify CGI programming, Microsoft introduced several technologies, the most recent and popular being *Active Server Pages (ASP)*. An Active Server Page is a program (or script), usually written in VBScript, which interacts with the client. ASP scripts can also interact with other components on the server. The clients can't access a database directly, for example, but an ASP script can. By passing the proper parameters to the ASP script, an HTML page can request data from the database. The latest version of ASP, ASP.NET, is a greatly improved version of ASP and allows you to write scripts that run on the server in VB.NET. The first advantage of using VB.NET on the server is that the application running on the server is compiled and runs much faster that a script written in VBScript. Actually, you can use any language that runs in the environment of Visual Studio to write an ASP application—you can write Web applications in COBOL, if you wish. There are many more advantages, such as exploiting the features of the IDE.

ASP was limited to the HTML controls. ASP.NET uses a new family of controls, the Web controls. The Web controls exist on the server, and you can program against them, just as you program Windows controls. Your code resides on the server and manipulates Web controls. When it's time to send a response to the client, ASP.NET translates the Web controls into HTML controls and HTML code, and sends to the client a page that can be rendered by the browser. As you will realize after reading this and the following chapter, ASP.NET abstracts much of the mundane tasks of client/server interaction and makes the process look like programming a Windows application.

I should clarify this point for the benefit of readers who are already familiar with ASP. If you're new to Web programming, please bear with me. Before you reach the end of this chapter, everything will make perfect sense. With ASP, the browser submits the contents of the controls on the current page to the server when a special button is clicked, the Submit button. This button may be *named* anything: Go, Show Results, Place Order, whatever. The HTML code of the page uses a Submit button to send the data on the current page to the server (or post the page back to the server, as this process is known).

The ASP script on the server knows the names of the controls on the page and must extract their values from the QueryString property of the Request object. If the page being submitted contains two Text controls, named ProdID and Quantity, it must use the following statements to extract the values on these two controls:

```
ProductID = Request.QueryString("ProdID")
Quantity = Request.QueryString("Quantity")
```

Then, it must process them (retrieve the price of the specified product from a database, multiply it by the quantity ordered, and apply some discount) and create a page to send to the client. The page is created by sending HTML code to the client through the Write method of the Response object:

```
Response.Write "Thank you for ordering"
Response.Write "Your total is " & price * Quantity
```

where *price* is a variable that holds the product's price (I'm not showing the code that retrieves this value from the database).

With ASP.NET, you can use the TextBox Web control, which is very similar to the Windows TextBox control. Let's say that the names of the two TextBoxes are ProdID and Quantity, and that the form also contains a Label control. To program the application, you double-click the Submit button and insert the following statements in its Click event handler:

```
Label1.Text = "Thank you for ordering" & vbCrLf
Label1.Text = Label1.Text & "Your total is " & price * Quantity.Text
```

This is VB.NET code, which will be compiled and executed on the server. You don't have to use the Request object to retrieve the values of the TextBox controls, and you don't have to use the Response object to create a new page. The results of the processing are placed on a Label control on the current form, which is then sent to the client. Obviously, ASP.NET parses the data submitted by the client through the QueryString object and makes them available to your code as control properties.

In short, ASP.NET is a vastly improved version of ASP, abstracting many of the tasks in client/server interaction. It makes the whole process look like a Windows application to the developer, but behind the scenes it generates the HTML that will produce the desired page on the client. This page contains straight HTML code.

The Structure of HTML Documents

HTML files are text files that contain text and formatting commands. The commands are strings with a consistent syntax, so that the browser can distinguish them from the text. Every HTML tag appears in a pair of angle brackets (<>). The tag <I> turns on the italic attribute, and the following text is displayed in italics until the </I> tag is found. The statement

```
HTML is <I>the</I> language of the Web.
```

will render the following sentence on the browser, without the tags and with the word *the* in italics:

```
HTML is the language of the Web.
```

As I said earlier in the chapter, most tags act upon a portion of the text and appear in pairs. One tag turns on a specific feature, and the other turns it off. The <I> tag is an example, and so are the <B> and <U> tags, which turn on the bold and underline attributes. The tag that turns off an attribute is always preceded by a slash character. To display a segment of text in bold, enclose it with the tags <B> and </B>.

The structure of an HTML document is shown next. If you store the following lines in a text file with the extension HTM and then open it with Internet Explorer, you will see the traditional greeting. Here's the HTML document:

```
<HTML>
   <HEAD>
      <TITLE>Your Title Goes Here</TITLE>
   </HEAD>
   <BODY>
      Hello, World!
   </BODY>
</HTML>
```

To create the most fundamental HTML document, you must start with the <HTML> tag and end with the </HTML> tag. Within these tags should be a HEAD section and a BODY section. The BODY of the document is the portion that is presented within the browser window. The document's HEAD, marked with the <HEAD> and </HEAD> tags, is where you normally place the following elements:

- The document's title

- Information about the document, such as the META and BASE tags

- Scripts

The title is the text that appears in the title bar of the browser's window and is specified with the <TITLE> and </TITLE> tags. META tags don't display anywhere on the screen but contain useful information regarding the content of the document, such as a description and keywords used by search engines. For example:

```
<HTML>
   <HEAD>
      <TITLE>Your Title Goes Here</TITLE>
```

```
    <META NAME="Keywords"
          CONTENT="health, nutrition, weight control, chronic illness">
  </HEAD>
  <BODY>
     Hello, World!
  </BODY>
</HTML>
```

ATTRIBUTES

Many HTML tags understand special keywords, which are called *attributes*. The <BODY> tag, which marks the beginning of the document's body, for instance, recognizes the BACKGROUND attribute, which lets you specify an image to appear in the document's background. You can also specify the document's text color and its background color (if there's no background image) with the TEXT and BGCOLOR attributes, respectively:

```
<HTML>
  <HEAD>
    <TITLE>Your Title Goes Here</TITLE>
  </HEAD>
  <BODY BACKGROUND="paper.jpg" BGCOLOR="yellow" TEXT="black">
  <H1>Tiled Background</H1>
     <P>The background of this page was created with a small image, which is tiled
  vertically and horizontally by the browser. If the image can't display, the page
  will have a solid yellow background. Either way, the text will be black.</P>
  </BODY>
</HTML>
```

Background images start tiling at the top-left corner and work their way across and then down the screen. Many HTML tags accept attribute parameters that position them precisely on the page. Unfortunately, not all browsers understand these elements, so the same page may look perfect in Internet Explorer or Netscape and totally misaligned in another browser. The good news is that you don't have to learn all these attributes; if you're working with the Visual Studio IDE, the designer will insert them for you.

URLs and Hyperlinks

The key element in a Web page is the *hyperlink*, a special instruction embedded in the text that causes the browser to load another page. A hyperlink is a string that appears in different formatting from the rest of the text (usually in a different color and underlined); when the mouse pointer is over a hyperlink, the cursor changes, typically into a finger. When you click the mouse button over a hyperlink, the browser requests and displays another document, which could be on the same or another server.

To connect to another computer and request a document, the hyperlink must contain the name of the computer that hosts the document and the name of the document. Just as each computer on the Internet has a unique name, each document on a computer also has a unique name. Thus, each document on the World Wide Web has a unique address, which is called a Uniform Resource Locator (URL). The URL for a document is something like the following:

```
http://www.someserver.com/docName.htm
```

NOTE *You will notice that some HTML URLs end in* htm *and some end in* html. *They are identical; some older operating systems don't support long extensions, that's all.*

Every piece of information on the World Wide Web has a unique address and can be accessed via its URL. What the browser does depends on the nature of the item. If it's a Web page (file extension .html or .htm) or an image (such as a .gif file), the browser displays it. If it's a sound file (such as a .wav file), the browser plays it back. Today's browsers can process many types of documents; older versions can't. When a browser runs into a document it can't handle, it asks whether the user wants to download and save the file on disk or open it with an application that the user specifies.

The tag that makes HTML documents come alive is the <A> tag, or *anchor* tag, which inserts hyperlinks in a document. The <A> and </A> tags enclose one or more words that will be highlighted as hyperlinks. In addition, you must specify the URL of the hyperlink's destination. For example, the URL of the Sybex home page is:

```
http://www.sybex.com
```

The URL to jump to is indicated with the HREF attribute of the <A> tag. To display the string "Visit the SYBEX home page" and to use the word *SYBEX* as the hyperlink, you enter the following in your document:

```
Visit the <A HREF="http://www.sybex.com">SYBEX</A> home page
```

This inserts a hyperlink in the document, and each time the user clicks the SYBEX hyperlink, the browser displays the main page at the specified URL.

NOTE *You often need not specify a document name in the hyperlink. Servers are commonly configured to supply the default page, which is known as the* home page. *The home page is usually the entry to a specific site and contains hyperlinks to other pages making up the site.*

To jump directly to a specific page on a Web site, use a hyperlink such as the following:

```
View a document on <A HREF="http://www.example.com/HTMLTutorial.htm">HTML
programming</A> on this site.
```

Most hyperlinks on a typical page jump to other documents that reside on the same server. These hyperlinks usually contain a *relative reference* to another document on that server. For example, to specify a hyperlink to the document Images.htm that resides in the same folder as the current page, use the following tag:

```
Click <A HREF=".\Images.htm">here</A> to view the images.
```

The Basic HTML Tags

HTML is certainly easy for a Visual Basic programmer to learn and use. The small part of HTML presented here is all you need to build functional Web pages.

Although you can use the visual tools of the IDE, many times it's actually simpler to open the HTML file and edit it. The following are the really necessary tags for creating no-frills HTML documents, grouped by category.

HEADERS

Headers separate sections of a document. Like documents prepared with a word processor, HTML documents can have headers, which are inserted with the <H*n*> tag. There are six levels of headers, starting with <H1> (the largest) and ending with <H6> (the smallest). To place a level 1 header in the document, use the tag <H1>:

```
<H1>Welcome to Our Fabulous Site</H1>
```

A related tag is the <HR> tag, which displays a horizontal rule and is frequently used to separate sections of a document. The document in Figure 23.1, which demonstrates the HTML tags discussed so far, was produced with the following HTML file:

```
<HTML>
    <HEAD>
        <TITLE>
            Document title
        </TITLE>
    </HEAD>
    <BODY>
        <H1>Sample HTML Document</H1>
        <HR>
        <H3>The document's body may contain:</H3>
        <H4>Text, images, sounds and HTML commands</H4>
    </BODY>
</HTML>
```

FIGURE 23.1

A simple HTML document with headers and a rule

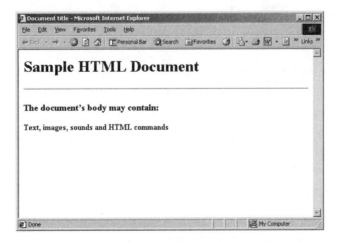

PARAGRAPH FORMATTING

HTML won't break lines into paragraphs whenever you insert a carriage return in the text file. The formatting of the paragraphs is determined by the font(s) used in the document and the size of the browser's window. To force a new paragraph, you must explicitly tell the browser to insert a carriage return with the <P> tag. The <P> tag also causes the browser to insert additional vertical space. To insert a line break without the additional vertical space, use the <BR> tag.

CHARACTER FORMATTING

HTML provides tags for formatting words and characters. Table 23.1 shows the basic character-formatting tags. The tags listed in pairs can be used alternately for the same effect; <B>...</B> produces the same look as <STRONG>...</STRONG> in most browsers.

TABLE 23.1: THE BASIC HTML CHARACTER-FORMATTING TAGS

TAG	WHAT IT DOES
<B> or <STRONG>	Specifies bold text
<FONT>	Specifies text characteristics such as typeface, size, and color
<I> or <EM>	Specifies italic text (for emphasis)
<TT> or <CODE>	Specifies the "typewriter" attribute, so text is displayed in a monospaced font; used frequently to display computer listings

The <FONT> tag specifies the name, size, and color of the font to be used. The <FONT> tag takes one or more of the following attributes:

SIZE   Specifies the size of the text in a relative manner. The value of the SIZE argument is not expressed in points, pixels, or any other absolute unit. Instead, it's a number in the range 1 (the smallest) through 7 (the largest). The following tag displays the text in the smallest possible size:

```
<FONT SIZE="1">tiny type</FONT>
```

The following tag displays text in the largest possible size:

```
<FONT SIZE="7">HUGE TYPE</FONT>
```

FACE   Specifies the font family. If the specified font does not exist on the client computer, the browser substitutes a similar font. The following tag displays the text between FONT and its matching tag in the Comic Sans MS typeface:

```
<FONT FACE="Comic Sans MS">Some text</FONT>
```

COLOR   Specifies the color of the text.

TIP   The XHTML specification recommends, but doesn't yet require, using external cascading style sheets instead of most formatting tags. (In technical language, tags such as <FONT> are deprecated.) At some point, browsers might not recognize formatting within your HTML document, but you can keep using it during this transition period.

Inserting Graphics

Graphics play an important role in Web page design. Almost every page on the World Wide Web uses graphics, and some pages contain hardly any text. Graphics are not inserted in the HTML document directly. The document itself contains special tags that reference the image to be inserted by the browser when the page is opened. Because of this, graphics files are downloaded separately and placed on the page by the browser.

On the Web, where every byte counts and downloads must be fast, images must contain as much information in as few bytes as possible. Despite the large number of graphics formats available today, two formats have dominated the Web:

◆ JPEG (Joint Photographic Experts Group)

◆ GIF (Graphics Interchange Format)

These formats are used because they compress graphics files to a manageable size. JPEG files can be compressed a good deal (albeit with some loss of detail), but they maintain a good image quality overall. The problems become evident when the compressed image is enlarged, but the graphics on Web pages are meant to be viewed in the context of the Web page to which they belong. The GIF file format is an old one, and it supports only 256-color images, but it has a few really handy features. It's the only format that supports transparency, and its compression ratio is even better than JPEG without losing detail.

To insert an image at the current location in the document, use the <IMG> tag with the SRC attribute, which specifies the image to be displayed. Figure 23.2 shows a page with a simple graphic, centered across the page.

FIGURE 23.2

Inserting a simple graphic file

Here is the HTML source code that produced the page in Figure 23.2:

```
<HTML>
   <HEAD>
      <TITLE>Graphics on Web pages</TITLE>
   </HEAD>
```

```
<BODY>
    <CENTER>
        <H1>Placing an Image on a Web page</H1>
        <IMG SRC="earth1.jpg" ALT="Earth photo"><BR>
        Our small planet, centered on the page
    </CENTER>
</BODY>
</HTML>
```

The <IMG> tag has the following syntax:

```
<IMG SRC="picture.jpg" ALT="alt text">
```

The <IMG> tag recognizes additional attributes, but you must include the SRC attribute, which is the location of an image file on the server or any URL on the Web. When you use the following attributes with the <IMG> tag, the browser can manipulate the image in several ways:

ALIGN aligns the image to the left, right, center, top, bottom, or middle of the screen.

WIDTH and **HEIGHT** specify the width and height of the image.

BORDER adds a border to the image, which is visible only if the image is a hyperlink.

VSPACE and **HSPACE** clear space around the image vertically or horizontally. The empty space is specified in pixels.

ALT includes a text message to be displayed if the user has turned off graphics.

If you want to change the size of an image, you can specify the size with the WIDTH and HEIGHT attributes, and the browser will size the existing file to the new values. For instance, to create a straight vertical line two pixels wide, simply use a square image two pixels on each side, and set the <IMG> tag's WIDTH and HEIGHT properties:

```
<IMG WIDTH="2" HEIGHT="200" SRC="picture.jpg">
```

Your image will stretch 200 pixels high. You can also distort bitmaps with the WIDTH and HEIGHT attributes.

The BORDER attribute specifies the width of the border to appear around an image. Borders two pixels wide automatically surround any image used as a hyperlink. You may want to eliminate this automatic border with the BORDER="none" attribute.

One aspect affecting the appearance of images, especially when they are surrounded by text, is the amount of space between the image and surrounding text. Space can be cleared horizontally and vertically with the HSPACE and VSPACE attributes. Simply specify the amount of space in pixels, for example, HSPACE="10" or VSPACE="20".

The *ALT* attribute displays alternative text for users whose browsers don't display images (to speed up the loading of the page or perhaps to use special software to accommodate a disability). The attribute ALT="Company Logo" tells the user that the image is not displayed in the browser. In addition, if the image takes a long time to download, the message "Company Logo" is displayed in the image's space on the page. If for some reason your images are not transmitted or don't show up, the user can still navigate your Web site and get the picture, so to speak.

Tables

Tables are invaluable tools for organizing and presenting data in a grid or matrix. Tables are used in an HTML document for the same reasons they are used in any other document. There is, however, one more reason for using tables with an HTML document: to align the elements on a page. A table's cell may contain text, hyperlinks, or images, and you can use the cell to align these elements on the page in ways that are simply impossible with straight HTML or even other tables. You can even use tables without borders, so your audience doesn't see how you accomplished your amazing (for HTML) feats of graphic design.

THE BASIC TABLE TAGS

Every table begins with the <TABLE> tag and ends with the </TABLE> tag. The attributes of the <TABLE> tag allow you to specify whether the table has borders, the width of borders, the distance between cells, and the proximity of cell contents to the edge of the cell. You can specify the width and height of the table either in pixels or as a percentage of total screen size.

Within the <TABLE> tags, each table row is marked by the <TR> tag. Each row's cells are marked by the <TD> tag. Here's the structure of a simple table. If you create an HTML file with the following lines and open it with your browser, you will see the items arranged as a table without any lines around them.

```
<HTML>
    <TABLE>
        <TR>
            <TD> Row 1, Column 1 </TD>
            <TD> Row 1, Column 2 </TD>
            <TD> Row 1, Column 3 </TD>
        </TR>
        <TR>
            <TD> Row 2, Column 1 </TD>
            <TD> Row 2, Column 2 </TD>
            <TD> Row 2, Column 3 </TD>
        </TR>
        <TR>
            <TD> Row 3, Column 1 </TD>
            <TD> Row 3, Column 2 </TD>
            <TD> Row 3, Column 3 </TD>
        </TR>
    </TABLE>
</HTML>
```

ALIGNING CELL CONTENTS

The ALIGN and VALIGN attributes specify the alignment of the cell's contents. The ALIGN attribute is used for horizontal alignment and can have the value LEFT, CENTER, or RIGHT. The VALIGN attribute specifies the vertical alignment of the text, and it can have the value TOP, MIDDLE, or BOTTOM. The default alignment is LEFT (horizontal alignment) and MIDDLE (vertical alignment).

A great deal of control over the alignment, spacing, and placement of cell contents within tables translates directly into excellent formatting capability for documents that would not ordinarily be built as tables. In fact, in HTML there are some effects you just can't get (in a practical way) without the effective use of tables.

TABLE WIDTH AND ALIGNMENT

All the examples we have looked at so far use the default table width, which is determined by the entries of the individual cells. If a column contains a very long entry, the browser will wrap its contents to make sure that all columns are visible. However, it is possible to specify the width of the entire table with the WIDTH attribute of the <TABLE> tag.

The WIDTH attribute can be a value that specifies the table's width in pixels or as a percentage of the window's width. The table defined as <TABLE WIDTH="50%"> occupies one-half of the window's width.

The table defined as <TABLE WIDTH="200"> will be 200 pixels wide, regardless of its contents and/or the window's size. If the window is less than 200 pixels wide, part of the table will be invisible. To display the part of the table that's outside the window, you'll have to use the horizontal scroll bar.

The <TABLE> tag can also take the ALIGN attribute, but instead of aligning the table contents, this aligns the table itself. If you don't include an ALIGN attribute, the table will be left-aligned in the browser's window.

TIP This is true of most elements; paragraphs (<P>) and images (<IMG>) can also use ALIGN, and if it's not present they default to aligning left.

MULTIPLE ROW AND MULTIPLE COLUMN CELLS

Quite often, tables don't contain identically sized rows and columns. Some rows may contain fewer and wider cells than the others, and some columns may span multiple rows. The figures in this section contain tables with peculiar formatting.

Figure 23.3 shows a table with cells that span multiple columns and rows. These cells use the ROWSPAN and COLSPAN attributes, which let you create really elaborate tables. Either or both can appear in a <TD> tag, and they merge the current cell with one or more of its adjacent cells on the same row (in the case of the COLSPAN attribute) or column (in the case of the ROWSPAN attribute). The number of adjacent cells to be merged is the value of the COLSPAN and ROWSPAN attributes; COLSPAN="2" means that the current cell covers two columns.

The table in Figure 23.3 was created with the HTML lines shown in Listing 23.1. The only thing I've done differently here is add the COLSPAN attribute in the appropriate <TD> tags to force some cells of the first row to span two columns, and I've added the ROWSPAN attribute to force some cells in the first column to span multiple rows. (The <TH> tag is simply a special table cell that indicates a table heading.) Other than that, the new table is as simple as those in the previous examples.

FIGURE 23.3

This table contains cells that span multiple rows and columns.

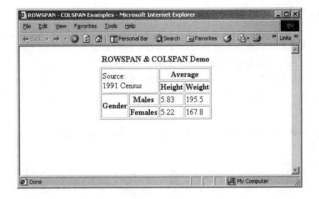

LISTING 23.1: THE ROWSPAN AND COLSPAN ATTRIBUTES

```
<HTML>
<HEAD>
   <TITLE>ROWSPAN - COLSPAN Examples</TITLE>
</HEAD>
<BODY>
   <TABLE BORDER="1" ALIGN="CENTER">
      <CAPTION><B>ROWSPAN & COLSPAN Demo</B></CAPTION>
      <TR>
         <TD COLSPAN="2" ROWSPAN="2">Source:<BR>1991 Census</TD>
         <TH COLSPAN="2">Average</TH>
      </TR>
      <TR>
         <TH>Height</TH>
         <TH>Weight</TH>
      </TR>
      <TR>
         <TH ROWSPAN="2">Gender</TH>
         <TH>Males</TH>
         <TD>5.83</TD>
         <TD>195.5</TD>
      </TR>
      <TR>
         <TH>Females</TH>
         <TD>5.22</TD>
         <TD>167.8</TD>
      </TR>
   </TABLE>
</BODY>
</HTML>
```

Forms and Controls

As you know already, HTML pages contain controls that let the user enter information, similar to the usual Windows controls: text boxes, option buttons, and so on. The areas on the HTML page where these controls appear are called *forms* (or Web forms), and the controls themselves are called *intrinsic controls*. HTML provides special tags for placing intrinsic controls on a form.

Before placing a control on the page, you must create a form with the <FORM> tag. Its syntax is:

```
<FORM NAME="name" ACTION="action" METHOD="method">
</FORM>
```

All the controls must appear between these two tags. The NAME attribute is the name of the form and is used when a page contains multiple forms. The ACTION attribute is the name of an application on the server that will be called to process the information. The METHOD attribute specifies how the controls' values will be transmitted to the server. All the information needed by the browser to contact an application in the server is contained in the <FORM> tag. But more on this later, in the section "Passing Parameters to the Server."

HTML provides support for the following intrinsic controls. Figure 23.4 shows a Web page with a form that contains most of HTML's intrinsic controls. You are going to see the HTML code that produced the page seen in the figure in the section "Processing Requests on the Server," later in this chapter.

THE TEXT CONTROL

The Text control is a box in which visitors can enter a single line of text (such as name, address, and so on). To insert a Text control on a form, use the following tag:

```
<INPUT TYPE="text" NAME="Publisher" VALUE="Sybex">
```

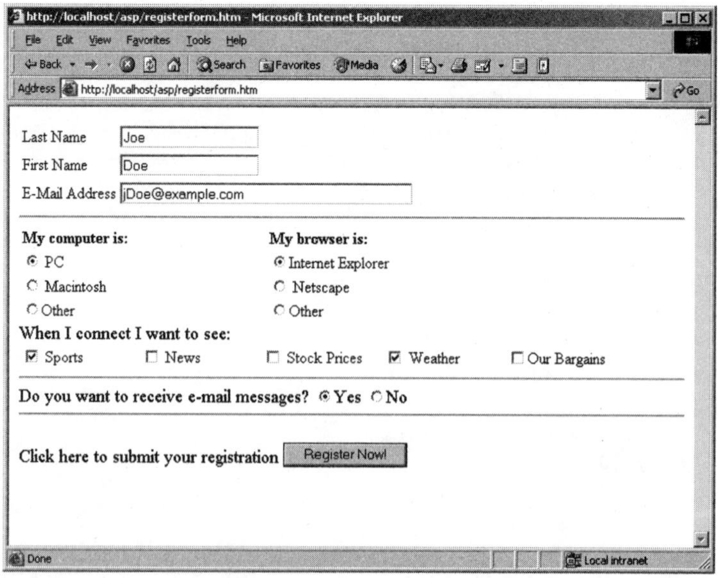

FIGURE 23.4

This form contains the intrinsic HTML controls.

The VALUE attribute specifies the initial value. After the visitor changes this entry, VALUE holds the new string. To edit the contents of a Text control, the visitor can use the common editing keys (Home, Del, Insert, and so on), but the text can't be formatted.

To control the size and contents of the control, use the SIZE and MAXLENGTH attributes. The SIZE attribute specifies the size of the control on the form, in number of characters, and the MAXLENGTH attribute specifies the maximum number of characters the user can type in the control. A variation of the Text control is the Password control, which looks identical but doesn't display the characters as they are typed. Instead, it displays asterisks, and it is used to enter passwords.

THE TEXTAREA CONTROL

The TextArea control is similar to the Text control, but it allows the entry of multiple lines of text. All the usual navigation and editing keys work with the TextArea control. To place a TextArea control on a form, use the <TEXTAREA> tag:

```
<TEXTAREA NAME="Comments" ROWS="10" COLS="30">The best editor I've ever
used!</TEXTAREA>
```

Because the TextArea control allows you to specify multiple lines of initial text, it's not inserted with the usual <INPUT> tag, but with a pair of <TEXTAREA> tags. The ROWS and COLS attributes specify the dimensions of the control on the page, in number of characters. Unlike the rest of an HTML document, white space in the content between the two <TEXTAREA> tags is preserved when the text is displayed on the control; line breaks you insert, for instance, will appear in the browser. Even if you include HTML tags in the initial text, they will appear as text on the control.

THE CHECKBOX CONTROL

The CheckBox control is a little square with an optional checkmark, which acts as a toggle. Every time the visitor clicks it, it changes state. It is used to present a list of options, from which the user can select one or more. To insert a CheckBox control on a form, use the <INPUT> tag:

```
<INPUT TYPE="checkbox" NAME="Check1">
```

To initially check a CheckBox control, specify the CHECKED attribute in the corresponding <INPUT> tag. The control's value can be ON and OFF (or 1 and 0), indicating whether it's checked or cleared, respectively.

THE RADIOBUTTON CONTROL

The RadioButton control is round and contains a dot in the center. RadioButton controls are used to present lists of options, similar to the CheckBox controls, but only one of a set can be selected at a time. Each time a new option is checked by the visitor, the previously selected one is cleared. To insert a RadioButton control on a form use the following:

```
<INPUT TYPE="radio" NAME="Radio1">
```

Whereas each CheckBox control has a different name, a group of RadioButtons all have the same name. This is how the browser knows which RadioButton controls belong to the same group and that only one of them can be checked at a time. To specify the control that will be initially checked in the group, use the CHECKED attribute. The following lines insert a group of four RadioButton controls on a form:

```
<INPUT TYPE="radio" NAME="Level">Beginner<BR>
<INPUT TYPE="radio" NAME="Level">Intermediate<BR>
<INPUT TYPE="radio" NAME="Level" CHECKED="checked">Advanced<BR>
<INPUT TYPE="radio" NAME="Level">Expert<BR>
```

THE MULTIPLE SELECTION CONTROL

The Multiple Selection control is basically a list of options. The visitor can select none, one, or multiple items in the list. The list is delimited with a pair of <SELECT> tags. Each item in the list is inserted with a separate <OPTION>. To place a Multiple Selection List on the form, add the following lines:

```
<SELECT NAME="MemoryOptions" SIZE="3" MULTIPLE="multiple">
   <OPTION VALUE="16">16 MB</OPTION>
   <OPTION VALUE="32">32 MB</OPTION>
   <OPTION VALUE="64">64 MB</OPTION>
   <OPTION VALUE="128">128 MB</OPTION>
   <OPTION VALUE="256">256 MB</OPTION>
</SELECT>
```

The SIZE attribute specifies how many lines will be visible. If you omit it, the list will be reduced to a single line, and the visitor must use the up and down arrow keys to scroll through the available options. If the list contains more lines, a vertical scroll bar is automatically attached to help the visitor locate the desired item. The MULTIPLE attribute specifies that the visitor can select multiple items in the list by clicking their names while holding down the Shift or Ctrl key. If you omit the MULTIPLE attribute, each time an item is selected, the previously selected one is cleared.

The <OPTION> tag has a VALUE attribute that represents the value of the selected item. If the user selects the 64 MB option in the earlier list, the value 64 is transmitted to the server. Finally, to initially select one or more options, specify the SELECTED attribute:

```
<OPTION SELECTED="selected" VALUE="128"> 128 MB</OPTION>
```

THE COMMAND BUTTON CONTROL

Clicking a Command button triggers certain actions. Without VBScript, Command buttons can trigger only two actions:

- Submit the data entered on the controls to the server.

- Reset all control values on the form to their original values.

With VBScript, Command buttons can trigger any actions you can program in your pages. You can place three types of buttons on a form: Submit, Reset, and General.

The most important button is Submit. It transmits the contents of all the controls on the form to the server (the values will be processed by an application whose URL is specified in the ACTION attribute of the <FORM> tag). The Reset button resets the values of the other controls on the form to their initial values. The Reset button doesn't submit any values to the server. Most forms contain Submit and Reset buttons, which are inserted like this:

```
<INPUT TYPE="submit" VALUE="Send Data">
<INPUT TYPE="reset" VALUE="Reset Values">
```

The VALUE attribute specifies the string that will appear on the button—its caption. The Submit button reads the name of the application that must be contacted on the server (the <FORM> tag's ACTION attribute), appends the values of the controls to this URL, and transmits it to the server.

Processing Requests on the Server

The RegisterForm.htm page, previously shown in Figure 23.4, contains several of the controls you can place on a Web page to request information from the user. The FORM section of the page is defined with the following tag:

```
<FORM ACTION="ASP/Register.asp" METHOD="GET">
```

The data collected on this page will be transmitted to the application Register.asp on the same server, and they will be processed there. Chapter 24 will show how to write a program to process the data submitted by the client. What you must keep in mind for now is that the browser will automatically submit the controls' values to the server. All you have to do is specify the URL of the program to intercept them on the server in the <FORM> tag. The URL used in this example begins with the ASP folder. With no protocol, domain, or other parent folder specified, the ASP folder has to be in the same location as the current document, and the browser remembers where that is. The URL of this example is equivalent to http://www.example.com/ASP/Register.asp (where the first part of the address is the location of the HTML page with the form). The data will be transmitted to the server when the Submit button (Register Now) at the bottom of the form is clicked.

The rest of the code is trivial. It uses the <INPUT> tag to display the various controls and most of the controls are grouped into tables for alignment purposes. You can open the RegisterForm.htm file, from this chapter's folder on the CD, to see the statements for creating the page shown in Figure 23.4. Listing 23.2 shows how the various inputs are constructed; I've listed the tags for the intrinsic controls only, omitting the table and text-formatting tags in the interest of conserving space.

LISTING 23.2: KEY ELEMENTS FROM THE REGISTERFORM.HTM PAGE

```
<FORM ACTION="ASP/Register.asp" METHOD="GET">
Last Name
   <INPUT TYPE="text" SIZE="20" MAXLENGTH="20" NAME="LName">
First Name
   <INPUT TYPE="text" SIZE="20" MAXLENGTH="20" NAME="FName">
E-Mail Address
   <INPUT TYPE="text" SIZE="46" MAXLENGTH="256" NAME="EMail">
My computer is:
   <INPUT TYPE="radio" CHECKED="checked" NAME="Hardware" VALUE="PC">PC<BR>
   <INPUT TYPE="radio" NAME="Hardware" VALUE="Mac">Macintosh<BR>
   <INPUT TYPE="radio" NAME="Hardware" VALUE="OtherHardware">Other<BR>
```

```
My browser is:
   <INPUT TYPE="radio" CHECKED="checked" NAME="Browser" VALUE="IE">Internet
Explorer
   <INPUT TYPE="radio" NAME="Browser" VALUE="Netscape">Netscape
   <INPUT TYPE="radio" NAME="Browser" VALUE="OtherBrowser">Other
When I connect I want to see:
   <INPUT TYPE="checkbox" NAME="Sports" VALUE="ON">Sports
   <INPUT TYPE="checkbox" NAME="News" VALUE="ON">News
   <INPUT TYPE="checkbox" NAME="Stock" VALUE="ON">Stock Prices
   <INPUT TYPE="checkbox" NAME="Weather" VALUE="ON">Weather
   <INPUT TYPE="checkbox" NAME="Bargains" VALUE="ON">Our Bargains
Do you want to receive e-mail messages?
   <INPUT TYPE="radio" CHECKED="checked" NAME="Mail" VALUE="YES">Yes
   <INPUT TYPE="radio" NAME="Mail" value="NO">No
Click here to submit your registration
   <INPUT TYPE="submit" NAME="Register" VALUE="Register Now!">
</FORM>
```

If you click the Register Now button, the browser displays a warning, indicating that it couldn't find the `Register.asp` application. This page can't be tested without a Web server running that program (otherwise, you'd get a result similar to that shown in Figure 23.5). You can view its contents like any other page, but it can't contact the server unless it's opened on a Web server.

To see how this form works with the Register application, copy the `RegisterForm.htm` file from the CD to the root folder of your Web server. The default root folder is `C:\InetPub\wwwroot`. Even better, create a subfolder under the root folder of the Web server and store the file there. For the example of this section, I have used the `ASP` folder. Then create a new file with the statements of Listing 23.3, name it `Register.asp`, and copy it into the same folder as the HTML file (or copy the `Register.asp` file from the CD to the ASP folder).

FIGURE 23.5

The output of the `RegisterForm` `.htm` page

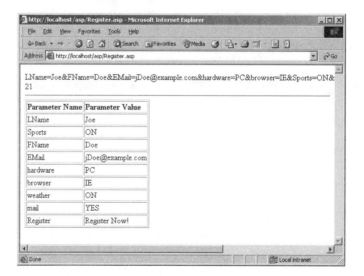

LISTING 23.3: READING THE PARAMETER VALUES PASSED TO THE SERVER

```
<HTML>
<BODY>
<%
Response.Write Request.QueryString
Response.Write "<HR>"
Response.Write "<TABLE BORDER='1' RULES='ALL'>"
Response.Write "<TR><TD><B>Parameter Name</B></TD><TD><B>Parameter
Value</B></TD></TD>"
Set Params = Request.QueryString
For Each PValue in Params
Response.Write "<TR><TD>" & PValue & "</TD><TD>" & Params(PValue) & "</TD></TR>"
Next
Response.Write "</TABLE>"
%>
</BODY>
</HTML>
```

Let me go through this script quickly. The tags <% and %> delimit the script, which is executed on the server. Anything that appears outside these two tags must be straight HTML code, which is sent to the client as is. The first two lines, as well as the last two, are sent to the client without any further processing. The lines between the <% and %> tags are considered statements and are executed on the server. The output they produce replaces them in the output. For example, the following code is a script that can be embedded anywhere on a page:

```
The date on the server is <% = Date %>.
```

When executed, this statement will send a string like "The date on the server is 3/21/2001."

The ASP script must prepare a new page to send to the client. Therefore, it must emit HTML code. The Response object represents the information you want to send to the client and you use the Write method of the Response object to send HTML code to the client. The Request object represents the request made by the client, and the QueryString property of the Request object holds the data passed to the server along with the request.

Now start Internet Explorer and open the `RegisterForm.htm` file by entering the following URL in the browser's Address bar:

```
http://127.0.0.1/ASP/RegisterForm.htm
```

Enter some values on the controls and click the Register Now button. The browser will request another page with a URL like the following:

```
http://127.0.0.1/ASP/Register.asp?LName=Doe&FName=Joe&EMail=JoeDoe@example.com&
Hardware=PC&Browser=Netscape&Sports=ON&Stock=ON&Mail=YES&Register=Register+Now%21
```

This is a long URL, but notice that it starts with the address of the ASP file that will process this page on the server. Following the question mark is a long string with the values you have entered on the controls. Each value is submitted to the server as a pair of a name and a value, and each name/value pair is delimited with the & symbol. This long string will be stored in the Request.QueryString property, and you can access this property from within the script's code. The expression Request.QueryString will return the string with the parameters following the name of the script. You can also access individual parameters by name. The value of the LName TextBox is returned by the expression Request.QueryString("LName").

The RegisterForm.htm page passes the parameters with the GET method. An alternative method of passing the parameters is the POST method (this is specified in the FORM tag). If you use the POST method, the parameter values are not displayed on the address bar and you can retrieve their values on the server through the Form property of the Request object. Change the <FORM> tag in the HTML page from

```
<FORM ACTION="ASP/Register.asp" METHOD="GET">
```

to

```
<FORM ACTION="ASP/Register.asp" METHOD="POST">
```

and then change the script as follows:

```
<%
Response.Write Request.Form
Response.Write "<HR>"
Response.Write "<BODY>"
Response.Write "<TABLE BORDER='1' RULES='ALL'>"
Response.Write "<TR><TD><B>Parameter Name</B></TD>"
Response.Write "<TD><B>Parameter Value</B></TD></TR>"
Set Params = Request.Form
For Each PValue in Params
    Response.Write "<TR><TD>" & PValue & "</TD><TD>" & Params(PValue) & "</TR></TR>"
Next
Response.Write "</TABLE>"
%>
```

The changes are trivial: just replace all instances of the QueryString property with the Form property. The two methods of passing parameter values to the server are equivalent, but the POST method allows you to pass longer strings and doesn't append the parameter values to the URL.

This is how ASP processes the requests. It's also how ASP.NET processes the requests, but ASP.NET makes it look as if you're working with a Windows form. As you will see shortly, it pretends that the LName control is a TextBox that exposes the Text property, and it allows you to access the contents of the LName control with the expression LName.Text. It generates a lot of code behind the scenes, but fortunately you don't have to see it. You work as if you're writing code for a Windows application, but what you get is an application that works with the browser.

The IDE may hide many of the low-level details of ASP.NET from you, but this doesn't mean you can ignore the structure of ASP applications and pretend it's almost like building Windows applications. As you will see, you will have to use ASP.NET objects, like the Request and Response object, from within your VB code.

You're halfway through this chapter, and you haven't seen any of the new tools for designing Web pages yet. That's what we're going to do in the second half of the chapter. This overview was meant for people who are new to ASP programming, and it should help you understand how clients interact with servers. The interaction model is totally different from the one used in Windows applications, and it's essential to understand it before you start using the visual tools of Visual Studio to build ASP.NET applications.

Building a Web Application

In this section, you'll build a Web application similar to the RegisterForm application of the preceding section. The first difference you will note between the two applications is that the new one displays the results on the same page. Typical Web applications don't let you display new information on the same page that submitted the data to the server (the reason being that it's much easier to create a new page, rather than reconstruct the page that submitted the request). ASP.NET makes it very easy to display the results of the processing on the same page that invoked the script. The control on which the results are displayed is a Label control, which is initially empty.

Start a new ASP.NET Web Application and name it Register. The project will be created in the `Register` folder under the Web server's root folder, which is `c:\Inetpub\wwwroot` by default. A Web project isn't compiled to an EXE file that can be executed by double-clicking its icon. You must start Internet Explorer, connect to the Web server where the Web application resides, and open its startup page, which is a file with extension ASPX.

Several items will be added to the Solution Explorer automatically, one of them being the Web-Form1 item. This is the equivalent of a Windows form, and it's the page users will see on their browser. The main pane of the IDE shows the `WebForm1.aspx` form in design view. You can open the Toolbox and select controls to place on the form. The Toolbox contains two tabs with controls you can use on a Web page: the Web Controls tab and the HTML Controls tab. The Web controls are a superset of the HTML controls, and you'll hardly ever use the plain HTML controls. You can actually turn any HTML control into a Web control by right-clicking the instance of the control on the form and selecting the Run At Server option.

Designing a WebForm is no different than designing a Windows form: just place controls on the form, size and align them, and set their properties, and you have built the Web application's user interface. The Web controls don't have as many properties as their Windows counterparts, but they have many more properties than the HTML controls. One property that's common to all Web controls is the EnableViewState property, which is True by default. This property determines whether the control's state is automatically saved during round trips to the server. Leave this property to True so that each time the page is returned to the client, the controls will retain their values. For example, if the user forgets to supply a value to a required field, don't make them retype everything. The controls will maintain their values, and the user can edit the one that's in error.

When you work with Web forms, the Toolbox displays the controls of the Web Controls tab. These are the controls you can use on a Web form. In addition to the Web controls, you can also place HTML controls on the form, but there's no good reason to do so. Web controls provide more properties and are easier to program. Add the appropriate controls to create the page of Figure 23.6. At the bottom of the page is a Label control, where we'll display the data entered by the user on the form. The Label control is invisible the first time the page is opened, because it has the same background color as the page. You can also set its Visible property to False and turn it back on when you want to display something on the control.

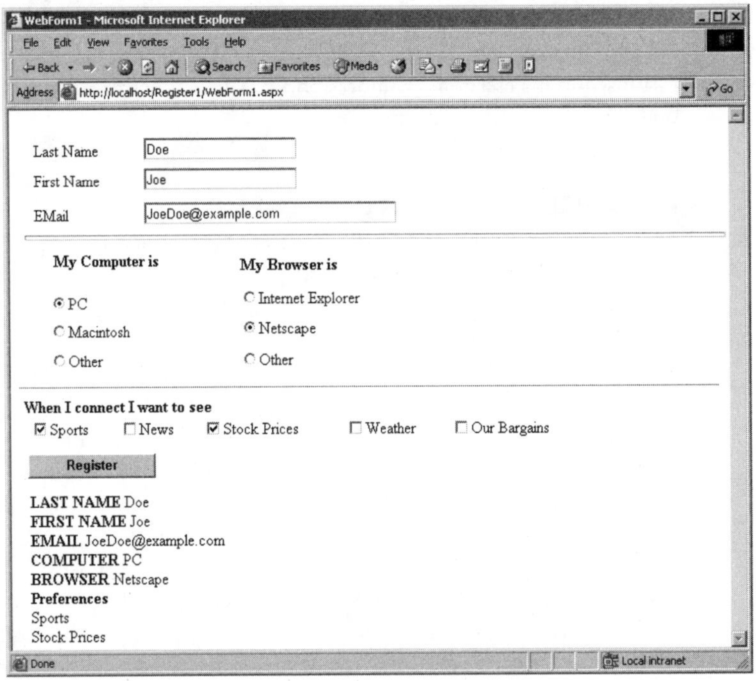

FIGURE 23.6

This page is similar
to the one shown in
Figure 23.4, only it
was designed with
Visual Studio.

When you design a page visually in the IDE, you see a grid and you can align the controls to the grid. The page has a property called pageLayout, which has two settings: GridLayout and FlowLayout. The default setting allows you to position controls anywhere on the form and use the alignment tools of the Format menu. The FlowLayout setting takes you back to plain HTML, where controls are placed next to one another. If you switch to the FlowLayout mode, you won't be able to precisely position your controls on the form.

Now we must add some code behind the Register button. When this button is clicked, the values entered by the user on the form are submitted to the server. All you have to do is read these values and display them on the Label control at the bottom of the form (the Values label). Our application won't process the values, but once you know how to read them, you can store them in a database, prepare a new page with the specified settings, and so on. Double-click the button on the form and you will see the declaration of the Click event:

```
Private Sub Button1_Click(ByVal sender As System.Object, _
            ByVal e As System.EventArgs) Handles Button1.Click

End Sub
```

This is clearly VB code. With ASP.NET, the code running on the server is no longer VBScript; you can write VB code, which will be compiled and executed as needed. The Click event of the Button1 control isn't fired when the user clicks the button on his browser. It will be fired when a request from this page arrives to the server. ASP.NET simply lets you program the Click event of the Button Web control as if it were a Windows Button control. Insert the statements of Listing 23.4 in the Click event handler, which will display the parameter values on a Label control. The Label control is another Web control that can render HTML code.

LISTING 23.4: DISPLAYING THE PARAMETERS PASSED TO THE WEBFORM

```
Private Sub Button1_Click(ByVal sender As System.Object, _
                ByVal e As System.EventArgs) Handles Button1.Click
    Values.Text = "LAST NAME " & txtLName.Text
    Values.Text = Values.Text & "<BR>" & "FIRST NAME " & txtFName.Text
    Values.Text = Values.Text & "<BR>" & "EMAIL " & txtEMail.Text
    Values.Text = Values.Text & "<BR>" & "COMPUTER " & _
                radioHardware.SelectedItem.ToString
    Values.Text = Values.Text & "<BR>" & "BROWSER " & _
                radioBrowser.SelectedItem.ToString
    Dim i As Integer
    Values.Text = Values.Text & "<BR><B>Preferences</B>"
    For i = 0 To chkView.Items.Count - 1
        If chkView.Items(i).Selected Then
            Values.Text = Values.Text & "<BR>" & chkView.Items(i).Value.ToString
        End If
    Next
End Sub
```

As you can see, this is straight Visual Basic (and it could have been any other language running in the Visual Studio environment, from C# to COBOL and FORTRAN). You're programming Web pages as if they were Windows forms. Of course, this is an illusion. Let's see what's sent down to the client. Press F5 to run the application, and Internet Explorer will pop up showing the page you designed. Before filling out the form, open the View menu and select Source. The page's source code will be displayed on Notepad. I will not repeat the code here, but it's plain HTML code that describes the contents of the page. The first TextBox control is inserted on the page with the following tag:

```
<INPUT NAME="txtLast" TYPE="text" ID="txtLast" TABINDEX="1"
    STYLE="z-index: 102; left: 120px; position: absolute; top: 12px" />
```

The TABINDEX attribute determines the position of the control in the Tab order (some browsers may not interpret this attribute) and the STYLE attribute determines the dimensions and position of the control.

Enter values on the controls and click the Register button. The form will be submitted to the server, where the VB code will prepare the new page. The new page isn't created from scratch. The code will send out the same page, but this time the Label control at the bottom of the form will contain the values submitted to the server.

If you view the new page's source code, the tag of the first TextBox has become:

```
<INPUT NAME="txtLast" TYPE="text" VALUE="Doe" ID="txtLast" TABINDEX="1"
    STYLE="z-index: 102; left: 120px; position: absolute; top: 12px" />
```

The only difference is that the VALUE attribute was added. This is what the EnableViewState property does: it causes the various controls to retain their values when a page is updated. If you refresh the page by pressing F5, the controls will be reset to their initial values.

Interacting with a Web Application

Here's what goes on when a Web application is executed. The first time a user connects to the server and requests the application's startup Web page, the VB code is compiled—that's why it takes several seconds for the page to be displayed. The compilation won't take place in subsequent requests. VB generates a new class that handles the interaction with the browser. This class reads the parameter values sent by the browser along with the request, processes them, and emits HTML code, which is sent to the client. You can create a new page and send it to the client, or you can change the values of the controls on the same page. This model of client/server interaction is closer to a Windows application. With ASP, it was easier to generate a new page with the results, rather than add a few more elements on the same page. The reason was that programmers had to generate all the elements of the current page from within their script and then add the new elements—and of course, it was simpler to create a new page with the new elements only. If this were a Windows application, you wouldn't display the results on a different form. Why do it with Web applications? It's a subtle departure from the traditional Web model, and it doesn't cost you anything. It's all done by the class that handles the request, and this class is generated and compiled on-the-fly; it doesn't even appear in the Solution Explorer.

Building a Web application is, in many ways, similar to building a Windows application. Of course, you should be aware of the limitations of the Web and not expect that a Web application will have the same capabilities and responsiveness as a Windows application. You should also keep in mind that the Web application's code runs on the server and "sees" the values of the controls only when the client submits them (that is, when the user clicks a button that submits the form to the server). While the form is open on the client's browser, the application doesn't even execute on the server. This is probably the most important difference between Web and Windows applications: the Web application isn't running at all times on the server. It starts every time the client submits a request to the server. It runs for a second (or many seconds), generates a new page, and then terminates. It doesn't remain inactive; it simply dies when it's done. And this raises the following question: what if we want to maintain the values of some variables between consecutive invocations of the server application?

This is a good point at which to overview the structure of Web applications. A Web application consists of a Web form (or multiple Web forms, as you will soon see). Each Web form consists of HTML tags and VB statements. The HTML part of the page is transmitted as is to the client, where it's rendered by the browser. In the context of this book, the HTML part is the form on which users enter data—I'm assuming another member of the team is responsible for generating a pretty page.

Another way to look at a Web application is to think of it as a Windows application written in VB, which is executing in the browser. The application's code is executed on the server, of course, but the application's interface is displayed on the browser. This is the very essence of a Web application: a visually rich application that appears to be executing in the browser.

Why execute an application in the environment of the browser? First, it's the simplest type of application to install—you don't install it. To use it, you just enter a URL in the browser's Address box. Because the application is not installed on your computer, you don't have to worry about patches or updates. Every time you connect to the server that hosts the application, you're executing the latest version of it. It doesn't take up any space on the disk, and you don't have to spend hundreds of dollars to buy it. You pay a small subscription, or you're charged for the time you use it. There are already sites that charge you to use resources like encyclopedias, news services, and so on. In the future, we'll see more online services, especially if Web services catch on as Microsoft hopes they will.

The VB code resides on the server and will be executed automatically when certain events are "fired." In reality, no event is fired. When the user clicks a button on the form, the client submits the data entered by the user on the form to the client. This action is called *postback:* the client sends the data on the current form to the server, and the server executes the appropriate event handler. Your VB code in the event handler reads the values entered by the user on the form by reading the properties of the various Web controls, processes them, and updates the values of certain controls on the same page or prepares a new page to download to the client. The Web controls are replaced by the plain HTML controls and, in some cases, one or more scripts in JavaScript.

There's a point I should stress here: the values of the various controls are not read directly off the controls. The controls reside on a page at the client. When a page is submitted to the server, the values of all the controls on the page are also uploaded to the server. Once the code on the server has prepared a new page (or updated the existing page) and sent it to the client, it forgets all about the interaction. That's why the client submits all the data to the server with every postback.

This observation raises naturally the following question: how can we maintain some variables through a session? How do we know that we're talking to the same client, for example, and how can we retrieve the customer's basket and add new products to it? There many ways to maintain state among multiple pages of a Web application, or multiple invocations of the same page, and we'll examine them in the following section.

Maintaining State

The second major difference between ASP applications and Windows applications is that HTML pages (and, therefore, Web forms) are totally independent from one another. If you want to persist some information between successive invocations of the same page, or multiple pages of the same application, you must do some extra work. The information you want to maintain is known as the application's *state.*

There are several methods to maintain state across the pages of a Web application. The simplest method is to create a few variables through the Session object. The Session object represents a specific session; it's created when a new user connects to the server and released when the user leaves the site. The Session object is discussed later in this chapter, but here's how you can add two variables named *Items* and *UID* to the Session object, and set their value to a number and a string respectively:

```
Session("Items") = 3
Session("UID") = "anonymous"
```

If a variable of the same name exists already, its value is overwritten. Session variables should be used to store relatively small pieces of information that apply to all the pages of the application, such as the user's name, ID, or preferences.

Another method of maintaining state is to use an ID that uniquely identifies a session. This ID is generated by the SessionID property of the Session object. Once you obtain an ID for the current session, you can store it in a Session variable and use it in your code to identify the session. This ID is passed back and forth between the client and the server and maintains its value for the duration of the session. You can use this value as a key to a table in a database that contains information such as the items ordered by a user—or any other data you want to access from within multiple pages or multiple invocations of the same page.

In the past, Web developers used to pass cookies and store them on the client computer. Many users are disabling cookies on their computers, so you can't rely on this technique for all clients. If the client computer doesn't accept cookies, your application should be prepared to maintain its state with a different method. If the client accepts cookies, use them to store information you want to maintain between sessions, like the basket's contents. The clients that accept cookies can place items in their basket and terminate the application without placing an order. The next time they will connect to your site, the items will still be in their basket. Cookies are discussed in detail later in this chapter.

A last, and very reliable, method of maintaining state among multiple pages and requests is to embed hidden fields in your pages and read them when the pages are submitted back to the client. This technique is equivalent to maintaining global variables, only the variables don't reside on the server. They travel back and forth and are always available when you want to process a page. This technique is used heavily by ASP.NET applications. If you open the source file of any page on the client, you will find statements like the following:

```
<INPUT TYPE="hidden" NAME="__VIEWSTATE" VALUE="dDwtMTMzNTkzMTE2Mjs7Pg==" />
```

This is a hidden field. Its *name* attribute is the name of the variable, and its *value* attribute is the variable's value. This variable is used on the server to maintain the state of the controls on the form throughout the session. The Hidden field is an HTML control, and there's no equivalent Web control. Normally, you need not add your own Hidden fields, but you can do so by adding one or more instances of the Hidden HTML control on a page.

The Web Controls

As you saw in the previous section, when you design a Web form, the Toolbox displays by default the tab with the Web controls. Many of these controls—the *simple* Web controls—have equivalent HTML controls. The Web controls provide more properties, and you have more control over their appearance. Of course, they're not real controls; when the page is sent to the client, they're rendered as HTML controls.

You're probably wondering when and how the Web controls are converted to HTML controls. When the page is executed (that is, when the client requests the page for the first time), the Common Language Runtime (CLR) creates a class behind the scenes and compiles it. You never see this class, but a DLL is created in the Debug or Bin folder of the application. This DLL, which is named after the application, handles the request and emits the proper HTML code to the client. Using the simple Web controls, like the TextBox and CheckBox controls, is straightforward—it's like using the equivalent Windows controls, only they don't have as many members. I will not discuss the trivial controls in this chapter; you already know how to use them.

In addition to the simple Web controls, the Web Controls tab of the Toolbox contains some advanced controls, which are known as *rich* Web controls. Among these are the validation controls (a group of controls for various types of data validation), the Calendar control, and the TreeView control. In the following sections, you'll find an overview of the most useful rich Web controls.

THE VALIDATION CONTROLS

If there's a universal task in programming Web applications, it's the validation of the values of the various controls. Most sites validate the controls on the server, and if there's a problem with the user-supplied data, they display the same page along with a message describing the error. Many programmers will also deploy client-side scripts to save the trip to the server. To simplify the validation of the data submitted to the server, ASP.NET provides five controls, collectively known as validation controls, and another control that displays the errors detected by the five validation controls:

RequiredFieldValidator   This validator ensures that all required fields have a value.

CompareValidator   This validator compares a control's value to a constant value, a property of another control, or even a database field. If the comparison fails, the control is in error and the user must supply a different value.

RangeValidator   This validator ensures that the value entered by the user in a control falls within a lower and upper bound. If not, the control is in error.

RegularExpressionValidator   This validator compares the value of a control against a regular expression. If the comparison fails, the control is in error.

CustomValidator   This control allows you to supply your own validation logic, and it's the most flexible validator. However, you must supply your own code.

ValidationSummary   This control can automatically display all the errors caught by the other validation controls on the form. Normally, we prefer to display the messages next to the control in error.

A *regular expression* is a string that determines the structure of the user-supplied value. The string ...\d\d means three characters followed by two digits. A string like ABC99 will pass the test, while a string like 9AA99 will fail the test. The period (.) stands for a character, the asterisk stands for any number of characters, and \d stands for a digit. The expression [A-Z] means any uppercase character between *A* and *Z*, and the expression [a-e] means any lowercase character between *a* and *e*. If a specific pattern is repeated a number of times, specify a numeric value in braces. The expression [0-9]{5} means five digits (use this regular expression to validate ZIP codes).

Each of the validation controls performs a specific type of validation on a specific control, which is specified with the validation control's ControlToValidate property. You can set this property in the Properties window, where all the names of the controls on the form will be displayed in a drop-down list and you can select the control to be validated. If a control must undergo multiple validations, you can have multiple validation controls for the same control (that is, multiple validation controls with their ControlToValidate property set to the same control ID). Each of the validation controls will perform a single validation.

Each validation control has a Text property, which is displayed on the validation control when a control on the form fails the validation test. To make sure that a TextBox control isn't left blank, place a RequiredFieldValidator control next to it and set its Text property to a string "This is a required field" or "You cannot submit a page without a user ID." Normally, the validation control remains blank. If the user attempts to submit the form without entering something in this field, the string will appear on the validation control (and the Submit button will not send anything to the server). Each validation control also has an ErrorMessage property, which you can read from within your code. The ErrorMessage property is displayed on the ValidationSummary control, if the form contains one.

Some of the validation controls have additional properties. The RangeValidator control, for example, has MinimumValue and MaximumValue properties, which are the valid minimum and maximum for the validated control. The CompareValidator control has ControlToCompare and ValueToCompare properties. If you want to compare a control's value to a constant, set the Value-ToCompare property to this constant. If you want to compare the control to value of another control, set the CompareValidator control's ControlToCompare property to the ID of another control on the form. To specify the type of comparison, set the CompareValidator control's Operator property to a comparison operator (Equal, Greater Than, Less Than, and so on). The valid settings of this property appear in a drop-down list in the Properties window. The CompareValidator control will compare the value of the control specified by the CompareTo property to the setting of the ValueToCompare or ControlToCompare property using the specified operator. If the comparison fails, an error message will appear on the validator control.

The last control in this family doesn't perform any validation. Instead, it displays all the errors on the form. In effect, it's a Label control on which the ErrorMessage properties of all validation controls is displayed. The validation control's Text property is displayed on the validation control, which is usually placed next to the control to be validated. The ErrorMessage property is the string that appears in the ValidationSummary control. You can set both the Text and ErrorMessage properties to the same string. Let's see some of the validation controls in action.

In Chapter 2, you developed a Web application that calculates the monthly payment of a loan. Let's add the appropriate validation controls to the WebLoanCalculator application. First, make a copy of the existing application. The new application is called WebLoanCalculator1, and you will find it on the CD. I've chosen this name because both applications must reside in the Web server's root folder—you can copy them to different subfolders of the root folder and name the project WebLoanCalculator. Or, instead of copying the original project application, you can open the WebLoanCalculator1 project on the CD and edit it.

Add three RequiredFieldValidator controls on the form, and place them next to each TextBox control, as shown in Figure 23.7. Set each validation control's ControlToValidate property to the ID of the Textbox next to it. Then place three RangeValidator controls on the form, place them on top of the three RequiredFieldValidator controls, so that their messages will also appear next to the control in error. Placing one control on top of another with the mouse can be tricky; use the commands of the Format menu instead.

FIGURE 23.7

The WebForm-Calculator page validates the form before submitting it to the server.

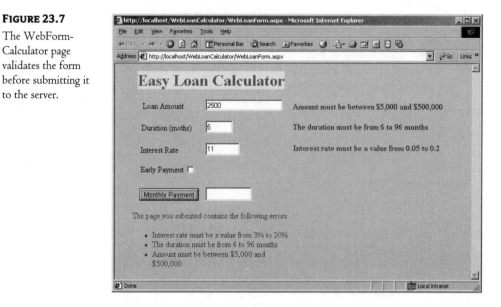

Property	Setting
RangeValidator1	
ControlToValidate	txtAmount
MinimumValue	5000
MaximumValue	500000
Text	"Amount must be between $5,000 and $500,000"
ErrorMessage	"Amount must be between $5,000 and $500,000"
RangeValidator2	
ControlToValidate	txtDuration
MinimumValue	6
MaximumValue	96
Text	"Duration must be from 6 to 96 months"
ErrorMessage	"Duration must be from 6 to 96 months"
RangeValidator3	
ControlToValidate	txtInterest
MinimumValue	0.05
MaximumValue	0.2
Text	"Interest rate must be a value from 0.05 to 0.2"
ErrorMessage	"Interest rate must be a value from 0.05 to 0.2"

If you run the application now and experiment with invalid values, you'll realize that the RangeValidator controls on the form will be ignored, if the controls are empty. The RequiredField-Validator controls take precedence over the RangeValidator controls, for obvious reasons, so the overlapping controls aren't going to interfere with one another—in other words, you'll never see two error messages one on top of the other.

You can open the WebLoanCalculator1 project and examine the settings of the various controls. No code is required to make the validation controls work. Just set some properties, and they'll validate the form.

You probably want to know where the validation code is running, right? Open the WebForm-Calculator with Internet Explorer and examine its source code. Toward the end of the document, you'll find the following script:

```
<SCRIPT LANGUAGE="javascript">
<!--
var Page_ValidationActive = false;
if (typeof(clientInformation) != "undefined" &&
clientInformation.appName.indexOf("Explorer") != -1) {
    if (typeof(Page_ValidationVer) == "undefined")
        alert("Unable to find script library
'/aspnet_client/system_web/1_0_2914_16/WebUIValidation.js'. Try placing this file
manually, or reinstall by running 'aspnet_regiis -c'.");
    else if (Page_ValidationVer != "121")
        alert("This page uses an incorrect version of WebUIValidation.js. The page
expects version 121. The script library is " + Page_ValidationVer + ".");
    else
        ValidatorOnLoad();
}
function ValidatorOnSubmit() {
    if (Page_ValidationActive) {
        ValidatorCommonOnSubmit();
    }
}
}
// -->
</SCRIPT>
```

This is JavaScript, and I will not explain how it works, because most readers aren't familiar with JavaScript. If you examine each line, you'll realize that it is very similar to VBScript, except for the semicolons and curly brackets. The ASP application on the server emits code that will validate the controls on the client. Of course, the code examines the type of browser running on the client, and if it's Internet Explorer, it will perform the validation on the client. In Microsoft's terminology, Internet Explorer is a so-called "up-level" browser. All other browsers are "down-level" browsers, and they won't perform the validation on the client. This will probably change in the near future, but there will always be browsers that will not be able to validate the form on the client. With down-level browsers, the form must be submitted to the server as usual, where the controls will be validated and the page with the error messages (if any) will be sent back to the client. No matter where the validation takes place, you don't have to do anything special. Just place the validation controls on the Web form, set their properties, and let ASP.NET handle the validation.

THE CALENDAR CONTROL

The Calendar control (Figure 23.8) provides similar functionality to the MonthCalendar Windows control. It displays the current month's calendar, and the user can select one or more days or weeks with the mouse. Your code on the server can detect the selected date(s) and act accordingly: display meetings, events, set reminders, and so on. While the Calendar you see on your Web form at design time looks like a separate control, at runtime it's rendered on the browser as a table.

FIGURE 23.8

Using the Calendar Web control on your Web pages

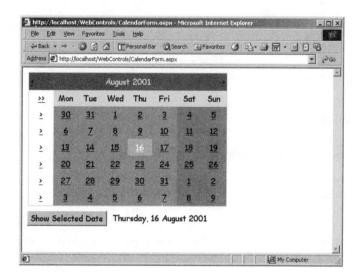

The Calendar control's SelectionMode property determines whether users can select a single day or a range of days, and it can be set to one of the following values: None, Day, DayWeek, DayWeekMonth.

When a new date is selected on the controls, the SelectionChanged event is fired. You can program this event to respond to a date selection, and the event's definition is shown next:

```
Public Sub Calendar1_SelectionChanged(ByVal sender As Object, _
        ByVal e As System.EventArgs) Handles Calendar1.SelectionChanged
```

The SelectionChanged event is fired when the user selects another date (or range of dates), but not when the selected date is changed from within your code. To retrieve information about the selected dates, use the following properties:

SelectedDate This property is a date value that represents the date selected by the user on the control. If multiple dates were selected on the control, this property contains the first date in the range.

SelectedDates   This property is a collection containing all the dates selected on the control. The dates in this collection are sequential, as the control doesn't allow the selection of multiple individual dates. The number of selected dates is given by the following expression `Calendar1 .SelectedDates.Count`. To iterate through the selected dates, set up a control like the following:

```
Dim dt As Date
For Each dt In Calendar1.SelectedDates
    Response.Write(dt.ToShortDateString)
    Response.Write("<BR>")
Next
```

You can also access the selected dates by index, with the Item property of the SelectedDates collection:

```
firstDate = Calendar1.SelectedDates.Item(0).Date
lastDate = Calendar1.SelectedDates.Item(Count - 1).Date
```

To control the appearance of the calendar, you can set the properties of the control shown in Table 23.2, all of which are TableItemStyle objects.

TABLE 23.2: STYLE PROPERTIES OF THE CALENDAR CONTROL

PROPERTY	REPRESENTS
DayStyle	The days of the current month
DayHeaderStyle	The row with the names of the days
NextPrevStyle	The links to the previous and next months on the upper section of the control
OtherMonthDayStyle	The days from the previous and next months that happen to appear on the current month's calendar
SelectedDayStyle	The day selected by the user
SelectorStyle	The left column that contains the links for selecting an entire week or month
TitleStyle	The calendar's title bar
TodayDayStyle	The style of the current date
WeekendDayStyle	The style of the weekend dates

All of the previous properties expose in turn their own properties, which are listed in Table 23.3. All the items of the previous table are cells of a table (because this is what the calendar is), and you can customize them by setting any of these properties in Table 23.3.

TABLE 23.3: APPEARANCE PROPERTIES OF THE TABLEITEMSTYLE OBJECTS

PROPERTY	REPRESENTS
BackColor	The background color
BorderColor	The border color
BorderStyle	The border
BorderWidth	The border's width
Font	The text's font
ForeColor	The foreground color
Height	The cell's height
HorizontalAlign	The cell's horizontal alignment
VerticalAlign	The cell's vertical alignment
Width	The cell's width
Wrap	A True/False value that indicates whether the text wraps within the cell

THE TREEVIEW CONTROL

This is one of the more advanced Web controls, and I'm sure many of you would like to include the functionality of this control to your pages. As you realize, the Web TreeView control (Figure 23.9) isn't comparable to the equivalent Windows control, but it's as close to a TreeView as you can get on a Web page. The first thing you must learn about this control is that, by default, every time its state changes (you expand or collapse a branch of the tree, or make a selection), the change is posted back to the server. The application running on the server raises the SelectedIndexChanged event. This may introduce a substantial delay. To change the default behavior of the control, you must set the AutoPostBack property to False (and you must then provide a button that will submit the data to the server).

FIGURE 23.9

Using the
TreeView control
on a Web page

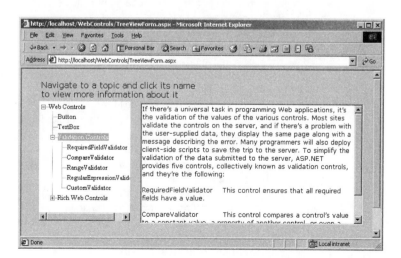

To populate a TreeView control, locate its Nodes property in the Properties window and click the button with the ellipsis next to it. The TreeNodeEditor dialog box will appear, where you can add nodes to the control, just as you add nodes to the TreeView Windows control. Each node has a Text property, which is the string displayed on the control for that node; an ID property, which uniquely identifies a node; and a NodeData property, where you can store additional data. The NavigateUrl property of each node allows you to specify a URL, which will be activated when the user clicks a node.

On the server, you can intercept the SelectedIndexChanged event to monitor the changes on the client. Every time the user selects another item on the control, the SelectedIndexChanged event is fired. You can also place a button on the form and ignore the action of selecting individual controls.

There are several properties you can use to retrieve the selected item. The SelectedNodeIndex returns a unique index value, which takes into consideration the hierarchy of the items on the control. The first root item's index is 0, the index of the first child node under the root is 0.0, the next child node's index is 0.1, and so on. You can use this indexing scheme to retrieve all the nodes in the path of the selected node.

There is no property that returns the text of the selected node. Instead, you can use the GetNodeFromIndex method to retrieve a Node object by index. Since the selected node's index is SelectedNodeIndex, you can retrieve the selected node's text with the following expression:

```
TreeView1.GetNodeFromIndex(TreeView1.SelectedNodeIndex).Text
```

The GetNodeFromIndex method returns a Node object, and you can use this access all the properties of the selected node. It's fairly easy to program the Web TreeView control. Keep in mind that it's not quite equivalent to the Windows TreeView control.

On up-level browsers (that is, Internet Explorer), the following script is executed to handle the expansion and collapsing of nodes. This script saves the client a trip to the server every time a node is expanded or collapsed. On down-level browsers, every time you change the status of the TreeView control, the form is submitted to the server, where the application generates the code that will render the new state of the control on the browser.

```
<tvns:treeview id="TreeView1" selectedNodeIndex="0"
    HelperID="__TreeView1_State__"
    systemImagesPath="/aspnet_client/webctrl/0_6/treeimages/"
    onexpand="javascript:
        if (this.clickedNodeIndex != null)
            this.queueEvent('onexpand', this.clickedNodeIndex)"
    oncollapse="javascript:
        if (this.clickedNodeIndex != null)
            this.queueEvent('oncollapse', this.clickedNodeIndex)"
    oncheck="javascript:
        if (this.clickedNodeIndex != null)
            this.queueEvent('oncheck', this.clickedNodeIndex)"
    onselectedindexchanged="javascript:
        if (event.oldnodeIndex != event.newnodeIndex)
            this.queueEvent('onselectedindexchanged', _
                event.oldnodeIndex + ',' + event.newnodeIndex)"
    style="height:236px; width:187px; z-index: 101; left: 8px;
            position: absolute; top: 8px">
```

The typical use of the TreeView control on a Web page is to act as an expandable table of contents. Every time the user selects an end node on the tree (a node that doesn't lead to another branch), a different document is displayed on a TextBox or Label control. You can use the control's SelectedNodeIndex property to find out which node was clicked and then update the page accordingly.

THE FILE HTML CONTROL

The control we'll explore in this section is a plain HTML control, but it can be converted to a server control by setting its runat property to Server. Actually, every HTML control can be turned into a server control, but it's simpler to start with a Web control, which is by definition a server control. The File control allows you to upload files to the server from within your browser. Using this control, you can prompt the users of your site to select one or more files to upload to the server and then click a Submit button to send the selected files to the server.

Once uploaded, you can access these files from within your Web application's code through the control's FilePosted property. Each instance of the File control on the form can upload a single file, and you can place as many of them on a form as you need.

The File control consists of a TextBox and a Button. Yet, it's a single control; the button appears next to the TextBox and you can't move it to another location. You can't even change the caption of the button, which is always "Browse," as shown in the WebFileControl sample program, illustrated in Figure 23.10. When the Browse button is clicked, the user is prompted to select a file on the client computer's file system through the Open dialog box. The selected file's path appears in the TextBox control, and no further action is taken. To upload the select file, the user must click a Submit button on the form. This event must be processed on the server, and it's the responsibility of the program that runs on the server to save the file to a disk file.

FIGURE 23.10

The WebFile-Control application lets you upload files to a Web server from your browser.

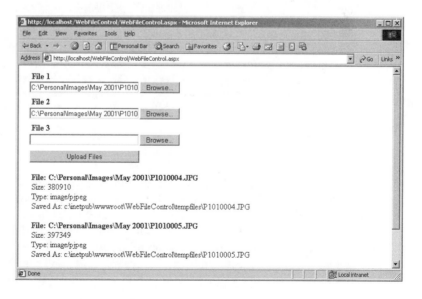

VB.NET at Work: The WebFileControl Project

To successfully upload data to the server, you must add the following attribute to the <FORM> tag:

```
ENCTYPE="multipart/form-data"
```

This attribute tells the form that it should upload all types of files, and you must insert it in the <FORM> tag manually. This is what the <FORM> tag of the WebFileControl project looks like:

```
<FORM ID="Form1" ENCTYPE="multipart/form-data" RUNAT="server">
```

 This attribute will not be inserted automatically to the <FORM> tag when you place a File control on the page; you must switch to the HTML view of the ASPX page and edit the <FORM> tag manually. Then place an instance of the File control on the form. Notice that this is an HTML control, and you'll find it in the HTML Controls tab of the Toolbox. Place two more File controls on the form as shown in Figure 23.10, an Upload Files button below the controls and a Label control at the bottom of the page. Double-click the button at the bottom of the form and enter the code from Listing 23.5 in its Click event handler. The WebFileControl project contains more code, but I'm only showing the code that handles the first file. The code for handling the other two files is almost identical.

LISTING 23.5: PROCESSING THE UPLOADED FILES ON THE SERVER

```
Private Sub UploadFiles_ServerClick(ByVal sender As System.Object, _
            ByVal e As System.EventArgs) Handles UploadFiles.ServerClick
   Dim fileName As String
   Dim filePath As String
   Dim UploadFolder As String = Server.MapPath("tempfiles")
   If File1.PostedFile.FileName <> "" Then
      fileName = System.IO.Path.GetFileName(File1.PostedFile.FileName)
      filePath = UploadFolder & "\" & fileName
      File1.PostedFile.SaveAs(filePath)
      Label4.Text = "<B>File: " & File1.PostedFile.FileName & "</B>"
      Label4.Text = Label4.Text & "<BR>Size: " & File1.PostedFile.ContentLength
      Label4.Text = Label4.Text & "<BR>Type: " & File1.PostedFile.ContentType
      Label4.Text = Label4.Text & "<BR>Saved As: " & filePath
   End If
End Sub
```

The Server object's MapPath method returns the path name of the specified folder—in the case of the example, the `tempfiles` folder. This is where the uploaded files will be stored. Later, you can copy them, or open them and process their data. `tempfiles` is a folder name under the application's folder, and the MapPath method will return a string like the ones shown at the bottom of Figure 23.10. Each instance of the File control exposes a PostedFile property. This property contains information about the posted file, such as its name, size, and content type. The files are uploaded to the server when you click the Upload Files button. They're automatically saved to temporary files, and you can't access them directly. You must call the PostedFile object's Save method to save the file to a disk file, and this must take place from within your Web application. After saving the uploaded files to the server file system, you can open and process them just like any other file.

By now, you have a good idea of how Web applications work. The user interface of a Web application is an HTML file that can be rendered on the browser. Since browsers haven't changed drastically in the last couple of years, nothing really exceptional takes place at the client. All the work is done on the server, by the code you place behind the controls of the application. The form you send to the client consists of HTML and Web controls. Web controls are just an illusion: they look like Windows controls, and you can program their events (which aren't many anyway), but the client sees HTML controls (and in some cases a few scripts).

To program a control, usually a button, enter the appropriate code in its Click event handler. You can access the various controls on the form as if you were programming a VB application. Is that all there is to Web applications? Hardly. This is what the IDE can hide from you, but there's a lot that can't be hidden. In the following section, I will go quickly through the basic ASP.NET objects and list their basic properties and methods. These are the objects ASP developers have had to work with, and ASP.NET is no exception.

The ASP.NET Objects

The following objects represent the basic entities of an ASP application. To make the most of ASP.NET, you must learn when and how to use these objects.

The Page Object

The Page object represents the page requested by the client. The requested page is an ASPX file, but the Page object is totally independent from this file. Unlike the other ASP.NET objects, the Page object exposes two events, the Load and Unload events, which are fired when the page is loaded and unloaded respectively. The most important method of the Page event is the IsPostBack property, which is True if the page is posted back. This property is False the first time the page is loaded and True when the Submit button on the page is clicked. Nearly every ASP.NET application uses the Load event and the IsPostBack property to determine whether it should initialize the page. If the page is posted back, we don't want to initialize its controls again. The following event handler is included in most ASPX pages:

```
Private Sub Page_Load(ByVal sender As System.Object, _
              ByVal e As System.EventArgs) Handles MyBase.Load
    If Not Page.IsPostBack Then
        { put user code to initialize the page here }
    End If
End Sub
```

The Page object exposes another very interesting method, the DataBind method, which causes all the data-bound controls on the page to be bound to their corresponding fields. You'll find more about binding Web controls to fields in the following chapter.

The Response Object

The Response object is derived from the HttpResponse object, which exposes the properties and methods you need to manipulate the output sent to the client computer from within your Web application's code. The properties and methods used commonly in ASP.NET programming are the following:

PROPERTIES

Buffer   When the Buffer property is True, the server buffers its output and sends it to the client after it has finished processing the request. When False, the output is sent to the client in pieces, as it becomes available.

ContentType   This property sets (or gets) the HTTP MIME type of the output. Its value for an HTML page is text/html.

Cookies   This property is a collection that contains the cookies placed on the client computer by the Web application. The Cookies collection is discussed in more detail later in this chapter.

Expires   This property gets or sets a period (in minutes) during which the current page in the client's cache will expire. Cached pages are not fetched from the server—they appear instantly because they've been cached to the client.

ExpiresAbsolute   This property is similar to the Expires property, but it specifies the absolute date and time at which the page will expire.

IsClientConnected   This is a read-only property that determines whether the client is still connected to the server. Use this property in a program that takes long to execute to find out whether the user has disconnected and, if so, interrupt the execution of the program, because the user will never see the results.

METHODS

ClearContent   Clears all content output from the buffer stream.

ClearHeaders   Clears all headers from the buffer stream.

Close   Closes the connection to a client.

End   Terminates the execution of the current request and sends all currently buffered output to the client.

Flush   Sends all currently buffered output to the client. If your application takes a long time to execute, call this method from time to time so that the user knows that the application is still running on the server.

Redirect   The Redirect method accepts a URL as argument and redirects the client to the specified URL. If the Web application consists of more than a single page (which is usually the case), use the Redirect method to invoke another page. For more information on using the Redirect method, see the section "Handling Multiple Forms in Web Applications," later in this chapter.

Write   Call this method to add information to the output stream. The simplest form of the Write method accepts a string as argument, but you can also send characters or even an object to the client.

WriteFile   This method sends the contents of a file on the server's file system directly to the client.

The Request Object

The Request object is derived from the HttpRequest object, which exposes the properties and methods you need to manipulate the requests made by the client computer from within your Web application's code. The properties of the Request object used commonly in ASP.NET programming are the following. The methods are fairly advanced and not as common in ASP.NET programming, so I've omitted them.

PROPERTIES

ApplicationPath   Returns the application's virtual root path on the server.

Browser   An object that returns information about the capabilities of the browser running on the client. Some of the properties exposed by the Browser object are the following:

Property of the Browser Object	Description
AOL	True if the client is an America Online (AOL) browser
BackgroundSounds	True if the browser supports background sounds
Beta	True if this is a beta release of the browser
Browser	The string (if any) transmitted in the User-Agent header
CDF	True if client supports Channel Definition Format (CDF) for webcasting
Cookies	True if client supports cookies. If the user has turned off the cookies, this property will still return True.
Crawler	True if the browser is a Web crawler search engine
Frames	True if client supports HTML frames
JavaApplets	True if browser supports Java applets
JavaScript	True if browser supports JavaScript
MajorVersion, MinorVersion	The major and minor version numbers of the browser
Platform	The name of the platform used by the client
Tables	True if browser supports HTML tables
VBScript	True if browser supports VBScript

ContentLength   The length (in bytes) of the content sent by the client. As you will see shortly, it is possible for a client to upload files to the server.

ContentType   Returns the MIME content type of the incoming request. The ContentType property of an HTML page is text/html.

Cookies   Returns a collection with the cookies sent by the client.

FilePath   Returns the virtual path of the current request.

IsSecureConnection   True if the connection uses secure sockets (that is, HTTPS).

PhysicalPath   Gets the physical file system path corresponding to the requested URL.

QueryString   Gets the collection of HTTP query string variables.

RawUrl   Gets the raw URL of the current request.

RequestType   Gets or sets the HTTP data transfer method (GET or POST) used by the client.

ServerVariables   Gets a collection of Web server variables.

TotalBytes   Gets the number of bytes in the current input stream.

Url   Gets information about the URL of the current request.

UrlReferrer   Gets information about the URL of the client's previous request that linked to the current URL.

UserHostAddress   Gets the IP host address of the remote client.

UserHostName   Gets the DNS name of the remote client.

UserLanguages   Gets a sorted string array of client language preferences.

The Server Object

This object exposes mostly methods, which are used as helper functions in processing Web requests.

PROPERTIES

MachineName   The server machine name.

ScriptTimeout   The request's time-out in seconds.

METHODS

Execute   Requests another page, whose URL is passed to the Execute method as argument. Optionally, you can retrieve the output generated by the second page and include it in the current page. See the section "Handling Multiple Forms in Web Applications" later in this chapter for more information on using this method.

GetLastError   Returns the last exception.

HtmlDecode   Accepts as argument a string that has been encoded to eliminate illegal HTML characters and decodes it. If you pass the following string to the HtmlDecode method,

```
HTML tags are delimited by the &lt; and &gt; symbols
```

it will return the string

```
HTML tags are delimited by the < and > symbols
```

HtmlEncode   Encodes a string so that it can be displayed on the browser. If you pass the following string to the HtmlEncode method,

```
HTML tags are delimited by the < and > symbols
```

it will return the string

```
HTML tags are delimited by the &lt; and &gt; symbols
```

You can then pass this string to the HtmlDecode method to reconstruct the original string.

MapPath   Returns the physical file path of a virtual path passed as argument. Notice that the virtual path need not exist. The MapPath method will prefix it with the path of the virtual folder in which the application resides. If you pass to the MapPath method the name of a folder, the method will assume that it's relative to the application's path.

Transfer   Aborts execution of the current page and transfers control to a new page. The new page is executed as if it were called directly by the client application. This method differs from the Execute method in that the control is not returned to the original page.

The Transfer method accepts a second optional argument, which is a True/False value that indicates whether the parameters passed to the original page (either through the QueryString or through the Form property) will be passed to the second page. The default value is False (the parameters are not passed to the second page).

UrlDecode   Decodes an HTTP-encoded string (such as the URL submitted to the server by the client).

UrlEncode   Encodes a string for HTTP transmission. The expression

```
Server.UrlEncode("who am I?")
```

will return the following string:

```
who+am+I%3f
```

UrlPathEncode   Encodes the path portion of a URL in a format suitable for transmission to the client. The statement

```
Response.Write(Server.UrlPathEncode("http://www.server.com/myfile.htm"))
```

will print this string on the page:

```
http%3a%2f%2fwww.server.com%2fmyfile.htm
```

Using Cookies

To access and manipulate cookies, use the Cookies collection. This collection is a property of the Response and Request objects and contains all the cookies currently on the client. To send a new cookie to the client, add it to the Cookies collection of the Response object.

Figure 23.11 shows the Cookies Web project, which adds three cookies to the client and then reads them back. Click the Add button to add the corresponding cookie and the Delete button to delete it. Click the Read All Cookies button to read the cookies currently on the client. The values of all cookies (not necessarily three) will appear on a Label control at the bottom of the form.

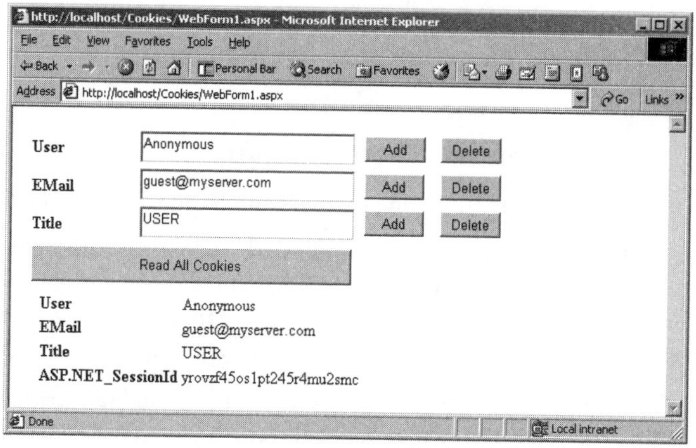

FIGURE 23.11

The Cookies Web application demonstrates how to use the Cookies collection.

To add a cookie, you must first create it; the simplest method of doing so is to call the Http-Cookie object's constructor passing the name of the cookie as argument:

```
Dim cookie As New HttpCookie("User")
```

Then you can access the properties of the *cookie* object. The Value property is the cookie's value, and the Expires property is a date/time value that determines when the cookie will expire. If you don't set this property explicitly from within your code, the cookie will expire at the end of the session. You can also create a cookie with multiple names and values (an array type of cookie). To set up this cookie, use the Values property, which is a collection of names and keys, all stored in a single cookie. The code in Listing 23.6 creates a new cookie and adds it to the Response object's Cookies collection.

LISTING 23.6: ADDING A COOKIE

```
Private Sub AddCookie1_Click(ByVal sender As System.Object, _
            ByVal e As System.EventArgs) Handles AddCookie1.Click
    Dim cookie As New HttpCookie("User")
    cookie.Value = txtCookie1.Text
    Response.Cookies.Add(cookie)
End Sub
```

NOTE   *It's possible to add new cookies to the Request object's Cookies collection. The Request object, however, doesn't affect the information sent out to the client. It represents the incoming information, and any cookies you add to the* `Request.Cookies` *collection will never be sent to the client. Use the* `Response.Cookies` *collection to send cookies out to the client and the* `Request.Cookies` *collection to read the cookies from the client.*

To delete a cookie, call the Remove method of the Cookies collection passing the name of the cookie to be deleted. Listing 23.7 demonstrates the method that removes the "User" cookie from the client computer.

LISTING 23.7: DELETING A COOKIE

```
Private Sub DelCookie1_Click(ByVal sender As System.Object, _
             ByVal e As System.EventArgs) Handles DelCookie1.Click
    Request.Cookies.Remove("User")
End Sub
```

The Read All Cookies button (Listing 23.8) goes through each item of the `Request.Cookies` collection and prints its Name and Value properties on a table. As you can see, in addition to the cookies you're adding to the client, there is one more cookie, the ASPSession_ID cookie. This is a string that uniquely identifies the current session.

LISTING 23.8: READING ALL COOKIES

```
Private Sub GetCookies_Click(ByVal sender As System.Object, _
             ByVal e As System.EventArgs) Handles GetCookies.Click
    Dim i As Integer
    Dim cookie As HttpCookie
    Label1.Text = "<TABLE>"
    For i = 0 To Request.Cookies.Count - 1
       cookie = Request.Cookies.Item(i)
       Label1.Text = Label1.Text & "<TR><TD><B>" & cookie.Name.ToString & _
                 "</B></TD><TD>" & cookie.Value.ToString & "</TD></TR>"
    Next
    Label1.Text = Label1.Text & "</TABLE>"
End Sub
```

Handling Multiple Forms in Web Applications

The last topic in this chapter is the handling of multiple pages. Any nontrivial Web application consists of multiple pages; you should be able to invoke a Web page from within another, and even share parameters between two pages (in VB terms, pass arguments to the page you're calling). The simplest method of invoking one page from within another is through a hyperlink. Just place a Hyperlink control on the form and set its NavigateUrl property to the ID of the form you want to invoke. If you locate this property in the Properties window, you will see a button with an ellipsis next to its setting. Click this button, and the Select URL dialog box appears (Figure 23.12). All the WebForms of the current project will be displayed, and you can select one by clicking its name. Or you can click the Browse button to locate any other WebForm on your server. This technique will work fine, as long as you don't need to pass any arguments to the page you're invoking. The new page will be sent down to the client, and it can retrieve status information through cookies or through session variables.

FIGURE 23.12

Use the Select URL dialog box to specify the destination of a Hyperlink control.

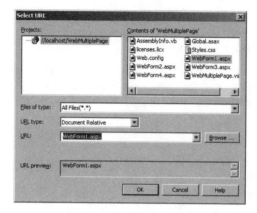

If you want to pass a few values to the new page, so that it can populate some of its controls or perform some other tasks before it's sent to the client, you can use either the `Response.Redirect` or the `Response.Execute` method. Let's look at the Redirect method first. This method accepts as argument the ID of the page to which you're redirecting the user. As you recall from our earlier discussion, the URL may contain parameter values. You can easily pass parameter values to the new page by appending them to its URL. You must separate the parameters from the URL with a question mark and delimit each pair or parameter name/value with the ampersand symbol (&). In addition, you must URL encode the string with the parameters by calling the `Server.UrlEncode` method.

Let's say the current page contains three TextBox controls (among other controls), and you want to pass the values of these parameters to the second page. The following statements prepare the URL of the page `WebForm3.aspx`, attach the three parameters, and then pass this string to the Redirect method:

```
Dim params As String
params = "Var1=" & Server.UrlEncode(TextBox1.Text) & " & "
params = params & "Var2=" & Server.UrlEncode(TextBox2.Text) & " & "
params = params & "Var3=" & Server.UrlEncode(TextBox3.Text)
Response.Redirect("WebForm3.aspx?" & params)
```

You can then read the values of the parameters from within the WebForm3 page's code and use them to initialize the page. The following statements in the page's Load event handler display the names and values of the parameters with the `Response.Write` method:

```
Private Sub Page_Load(ByVal sender As System.Object, _
            ByVal e As System.EventArgs) Handles MyBase.Load
```

```
' Put user code to initialize the page here
    Response.Write(Request.QueryString("Var1"))
    Response.Write(Request.QueryString("Var2"))
    Response.Write(Request.QueryString("Var3"))
End Sub
```

In an actual application, you'll use these variables in slightly more complicated calculations. This example demonstrates how to access the values of the parameters, and then you can do anything you want with them.

The Execute method is different in the sense that it doesn't actually display the new page. It accepts the URL of a page, executes it, and appends the HTML code generated by the page to the current page. The safest use of the Execute method is to read the output it generates into a StringWriter object and place it on a Label or TextBox control on the current page. The following statements call the page ShowBasket.aspx and append the output generated by this page to the current page:

```
Dim pageOut As New System.IO.StringWriter()
Server.Execute("ShowBasket.aspx", pageOut)
Response.Write("<H2>Your basket contains the following items:</H2>")
Response.Write("<BR>")
Response.Write(pageOut.ToString)
```

The *pageOut* variable receives the output of the ShowBasket.aspx page and sends it to the client. The Response.Write method doesn't clear the current page; it simply appends its output so the contents of the *pageOut* variable will appear at the bottom of the current page.

To access the controls of the current WebForm from within the page that's called with the Execute method, use a loop like the following:

```
Private Sub Page_Load(ByVal sender As System.Object, _
                ByVal e As System.EventArgs) Handles MyBase.Load
' Put user code to initialize the page here
    Dim key, value As String
    Response.Write(Request.QueryString)
    For Each key In Request.Form.Keys
        Response.Write(key & " = " & Request.Form.Item(key))
        Response.Write("<BR>")
    Next
End Sub
```

Compared to VB, this method of passing variables between pages is awkward. It's true that ASP hides many of the mundane operations you would normally have to code yourself, but this aspect of ASP.NET isn't as polished as it could be. Keep in mind, however, that Web pages don't communicate directly with one another. The WebMultiplePage project on the CD demonstrates how to call a WebForm from within another form and pass parameters to it.

Summary

This chapter was an introduction to Web applications. As you saw, developing Web applications requires some knowledge of HTML and the ASP.NET objects and a good understanding of the interaction model between servers and clients. The two major obstacles in programming Web applications are the lack of state and the fact the client doesn't support the rich controls of the Windows interface.

To maintain state during a session, you must move data between the server and the client, such as the session's ID. ASP.NET can deal with this problem as long as you set the AutoPostBack property to True. As for the interfaces of Web applications, you can only use the controls supported by the browser, which are the HTML controls. The Web controls of ASP.NET allow you to make the most of the HTML controls.

Finally, the code that drives the Web application resides on the server and is activated every time the client submits a page to the server. The Web application reads the data on the form, processes them, and responds to the client's request by submitting another page. This is how all Web applications work, and not just ASP.NET Web applications. Now that you know how to build functional Web applications, we can look into adding data-access capabilities in a Web application.

Chapter 24

Accessing Data on the Web

CHAPTER 23 WAS AN introduction to ASP.NET, a brand new technology for developing applications for the Web. At the very least, you've learned that ASP.NET does a lot behind the scenes to make developing Web applications look surprisingly similar to developing Windows applications. You have also learned the basic differences between a Web and a Windows application and how to access the native ASP.NET objects when you need them. You have also learned the differences between Windows applications and Web applications and how these differences affect the way you code Web applications.

Currently, the single most common type of applications running on the Web is simple applications that interact with databases. It seems as though everybody is publishing their databases on the Web, and most companies do so to sell on the Internet. In this chapter, we'll build a Web application that demonstrates the basic operations of a typical Web app: search a database, display the results of a search operation, add items to a basket, and finally place an order. We'll record the order to the database, and we'll do so in a transaction. It's not a trivial example, but it's not very complicated either. We'll go through all the steps, examine the code line by line, and when you're done, you'll have a better understanding of the structure of a Web application, as well as how to access databases through ASP.NET. Of course, I can't exhaust the topic of accessing data with ASP.NET, but the information in this chapter will help you feel comfortable with the new technology and explore it on your own.

The Data-Bound Web Controls

Like Windows controls, any Web control can be bound to a data source. The interesting data-bound controls, however, and the ones that are used most often, are the controls that can display multiple items:

DropDownList   Similar to a ListBox control that's dropped to select an item and retracts automatically.

DataList   Displays multiple items, each one in its own cell.

DataGrid   A grid control that displays one item per row.

Repeater   Displays items as templates; you can have different templates for different types of items.

We'll look at the first three controls in detail in this chapter. The Repeater control is the most elaborate, and its main advantage is that you can completely customize its appearance through your code. However, you have to design the templates yourself, and the Repeater control doesn't provide as much built-in functionality.

There are other types of data-bound controls as well, but either they're simple controls (like the TextBox or CheckBox control) or they're similar to the DropDownList control. The ListBox, CheckBoxList, and RadioButtonList are very similar to the DropDownList and expose similar properties, so we won't discuss them here. The DataGrid, DataList, and Repeater controls are the only ones that can display multiple fields, and they're the most flexible controls. The DropDownList control (and the other ones similar to it) can only display a single column.

To bind a Web control to a DataSet, you must set its DataSource property to the name of the DataSet to which the control will be bound, then call the DataBind method from within the page's Load event handler, and do that only if the request for the page isn't a postback. The DataBind method applies to specific controls and also to the current page. When you apply the DataBind method to the page (`Me.DataBind`), all data-bound controls are populated from their respective DataSets.

The DropDownList control has two more properties, the DataTextField and DataValueField properties. DataTextField is the name of a DataSet column that will populate the control. The DataValueField is the name of a DataSet column that identifies each row (usually the table's key field). When the user selects an item in the list, we retrieve the value of the DataValueField property and look up the selected row in the database. To display a list of customers on a DropDownList control, you must set the DataTextField property to the column of the DataSet that holds the customer names and the DataValueField to the column with the customer IDs.

You already know how to create the DataSet objects you need to populate your controls. You can use the visual tools (drop the tables on the design surface, configure the DataAdapter, create the DataSet) or create them from within your code. Since the process of creating DataSet (necessary for binding the various Web controls to) is the same as with Windows applications, I will assume you already know how to retrieve data from a database (or use the Query Builder to design your queries visually) and how to store the qualifying rows to a DataSet object. The process is described in detail in Chapter 21.

We'll start our exploration of data-binding techniques on the Web with a simple example that doesn't even use a database.

Simple Data Binding

Data-binding Web controls is similar to binding Windows controls and, in some ways, simpler. To begin with, Web controls can be bound to many different data sources, like arrays and ArrayLists. It's possible to populate an array (or an ArrayList object) in your code and bind a ListBox control to it. The list control will be populated with the elements of the list, and it will report the selected item—an ideal mechanism for lookup tables like product categories or states.

The current implementation of ASP.NET allows the binding of one-dimensional arrays only. Since arrays are no longer the preferred data type for storing sets of data, this isn't much of a problem. Use an ArrayList and you'll be able to store any number of fields, other than the one displayed on the control. To bind an array, or an ArrayList object, to a list control, populate the array, then set the control's DataSource property to the name of the array or the ArrayList, and finally call the

DataBind method. To demonstrate how to bind an ArrayList to a data-bound control, we'll build the DataBinding application, whose page is shown in Figure 24.1. The DropDownList control on the left is expanded and contains a few names. When a name is selected in the list, more information about the selected person is shown in the TextBox and RadioButton controls on the same form.

FIGURE 24.1

The DataBinding
Web application

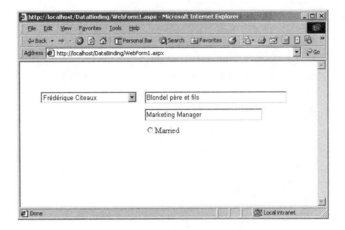

As you have guessed by now, we're going to populate an ArrayList object with the data we want to display on the form. Each element of the ArrayList object is a Contact person, based on the class detailed in Listing 24.1.

LISTING 24.1: THE CONTACT CLASS

```
Class Contact
    Dim _ID As Integer
    Dim _name As String
    Dim _title As String
    Dim _company As String
    Dim _married As Boolean
    Property ID() As Integer
        Get
            ID = _ID
        End Get
        Set(ByVal Value As Integer)
            _ID = Value
        End Set
    End Property
    Property Name() As String
        Get
            Name = _name
        End Get
        Set(ByVal Value As String)
            _name = Value
```

```
                    End Set
                End Property
                Property Title() As String
                    Get
                        Title = _title
                    End Get
                    Set(ByVal Value As String)
                        _title = Value
                    End Set
                End Property
                Property Company() As String
                    Get
                        Company = _company
                    End Get
                    Set(ByVal Value As String)
                        _company = Value
                    End Set
                End Property
                Property Married() As Boolean
                    Get
                        Married = _married
                    End Get
                    Set(ByVal Value As Boolean)
                        _married = Value
                    End Set
                End Property
                Public Overrides Function ToString() As String
                    Return (_name)
                End Function
            End Class
```

It's a lengthy listing, but you should be quite familiar with classes that expose simple properties. The next step is to declare an ArrayList and populate it with data. Here are the declaration of the ArrayList and the statements that add the first item:

```
Dim Contacts As New ArrayList()
Dim c As New Contact()
c.ID = 0
c.Name = "Maria Anders"
c.Company = "Alfreds Futterkiste"
c.Title = "Sales Representative"
c.Married = False
Contacts.Add(c)
```

 OK, we're ready to build the page. Start a new ASP.NET Web application, name it DataBinding, and insert the Contact class's code from Listing 24.1 and the code that populates the DropDown-List control in the form's Load event (you can open the project on the CD and copy the statements).

Then place the controls you see in Figure 24.1 on the page. The last step is to bind the DropDownList control to the ArrayList. Enter the following statements in the page's Load event handler:

```
If Not Me.IsPostBack Then
    DDListName.DataSource = Contacts
    DDListName.DataTextField = "Name"
    DDListName.DataValueField = "ID"
    DDListName.DataBind()
End If
```

The control is bound to its data source only the first time the page is loaded, not with every postback. If you bind the control every time the page is posted back, the DropDownList control will be populated from scratch and the first element will be selected automatically. Instead, we want the control to maintain its state. You must set the control's AutoPostBack property to True (so that it will report the SelectedIndexChanged event to the application) and bind it to its data source the first time it's loaded. After that, every time the user selects an item on the control, the SelectedIndexChanged event will be fired, which will be processed by the application. The processing consists of retrieving the ID of the selected contact and displaying the values of additional fields on the other controls on the Web form.

The Contacts ArrayList, however, is populated with every postback (the statements that populate it are outside the If statement). You're probably wondering about the efficiency of this approach. Can't we do something better than having to populate the ArrayList every time the page is posted back? The answer is no (short of storing the entire ArrayList to the Session object). This is the Web, and the client is totally disconnected from the server. An ASP application must retrieve the current status of the session when a client connects and re-create its data source. The only alternative is to store the data in a Session variable, but this object shouldn't be used for storing tables or excessive amounts of information. A Web application must service a request and then "die." If you keep it alive (that is, if you maintain a set of local variables for each session), your server will become unresponsive very quickly. A Web application shouldn't maintain a lot of data between sessions—and an ArrayList is a lot of information. We'll do the same with DataSets later in this chapter. We'll grab the data from the database, populate our page, and then close the connection to the database and discard the DataSet.

When the user selects a name on the DropDownList control, the SelectedIndexChanged event is fired. This is event isn't reported to the server by default; that's why you had to set the control's AutoPostBack property to True. In this event's handler, you must retrieve the index of the selected contact and use it to retrieve the selected item from the ArrayList and display its fields on the other controls. The code of the SelectedIndexChanged event handler is shown in Listing 24.2.

LISTING 24.2: DISPLAYING THE FIELDS OF THE SELECTED CONTACT

```
Private Sub DDListName_SelectedIndexChanged(ByVal sender As System.Object, _
            ByVal e As System.EventArgs) Handles DDListName.SelectedIndexChanged
    Response.Write(DDListName.SelectedItem.Value)
    Dim selIndex As Integer
    selIndex = DDListName.SelectedIndex
    txtCompany.Text = CType(Contacts(DDListName.SelectedIndex), Contact).Company
```

```
        txtTitle.Text = CType(Contacts(DDListName.SelectedIndex), Contact).Title
        radioMarried.Checked = _
                CType(Contacts(DDListName.SelectedIndex), Contact).Married
    End Sub
```

The first statement isn't really required, but I've inserted it to show you how to access the selected string on the control. The TextBox and RadioButton controls on the form aren't bound; we update them from within our code.

The DataBinding project is a simple example, but it demonstrates how to bind a list that resides on the server to a control on a Web form. To better understand how ASP.NET handles data binding, take a look at the code that was transmitted to the client. Press F5 to run the project and, when Internet Explorer appears on your monitor, open the View menu and select Source. In the page's source code, locate the SELECT control's tag. This is a plain HTML control that was placed on the page with the following statements:

```
<SELECT NAME="DDListName" ID="DDListName" ONCHANGE="__doPostBack('DDListName','')"
LANGUAGE="javascript" STYLE="height: 22px; width: 196px; z-index: 101; left: 42px;
position: absolute; top: 60px">
    <OPTION VALUE="0">Maria Anders</OPTION>
    <OPTION VALUE="1">Ana Trujillo</OPTION>
    <OPTION VALUE="2">Thomas Hardy</OPTION>
    <OPTION VALUE="3">Fr&#233;d&#233;rique Citeaux</OPTION>
    <OPTION VALUE="4">Elizabeth Brown</OPTION>...
```

Nothing unusual gets transmitted to the client. ASP.NET created a plain, vanilla HTML control and populated it with the names of the contacts. For those who haven't read the previous chapter, I'll repeat once again the recurring theme in designing Web applications. On the server's side, you write an application that's no different than regular Windows applications. When you execute the application, the compiler gets to work and generates HTML code that will render the Web form you designed as an HTML page, and it connects the events in the browser to event handlers in your application.

Have you noticed another difference between DataBinding and the equivalent Windows application? Don't you find all the code for updating the TextBox controls on the form a little heavy? In a Windows application, we'd retrieve the SelectedItem, which is an object, cast it to the proper type (the Contact type, in our example), and then call its properties. A statement like the following would be adequate:

```
    txtCompany.Text = CType(DDListName.SelectedItem).Company
```

That's because a Windows ListBox (or ComboBox) control can store objects. Once you get a reference to the selected object, you can access all its members directly. But HTML wasn't designed to handle objects. (Actually, HTML wasn't even designed to handle applications, and a replacement for HTML is overdue.) That's why we have to populate the ArrayList at every postback and use the index of the selected item to locate the corresponding element in the ArrayList. These are the differences you must bear in mind as you develop ASP.NET applications. The design process looks and feels like the design process of a Windows application, but it's not quite the same, because there are fundamental differences in the two environments.

Binding to DataSets

Real Web applications use databases, and it's time to look at the process of binding Web controls to DataSets. The control you'll be using most often in building data-bound Web applications is the DataGrid control. In Chapter 23, I expressed some concerns about the use of the DataGrid control for editing data, but most applications on the Web don't involve editing data. They simply present data to the users, and the DataGrid control is a fine tool for this task. Actually, the DataGrid control is rendered on the client as an elaborate HTML table.

VB.NET AT WORK: THE WEBPRODUCTS PROJECT

Let's start by building a simple application (Figure 24.2), similar to the ones we've designed in Chapter 21 and 22. We'll use a ListBox control to display product names (our navigational tool) and TextBox controls to display the fields of the selected product. The new Web application is called WebProducts, and you will find it in this chapter's folder on the CD.

FIGURE 24.2

The WebProducts Web page uses a data-bound ListBox control as a navigational aid.

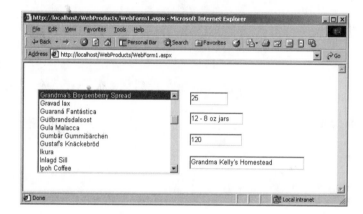

First, we'll build this WebProducts application using the visual tools, and then you'll see how to embed all the necessary code to retrieve and display the data in the page's Load event handler. Existing ASP programmers will actually find it easier to manually code the application.

Start a new ASP.NET Web Application project and name it WebProducts. When the Web-Form of the project appears in the designer's surface, place a ListBox control and four TextBox controls on it. The names of the TextBox controls are *txtPrice, txtPackage, txtStock,* and *txtSupplier.* The name of the ListBox control is *lstProducts.*

To create the DataSet with the product information, open the Server Explorer and drop the Products table on the form. Then rename the DataAdapter object to DAProducts and configure it. We want to retrieve the ProductID and ProductName columns of the Products table. This is all the information we need in order to use the ListBox control as a navigational tool. We'll display the product names and keep track of the ID of the selected product. Every time the user selects an item on the list, we'll make a trip to the database and retrieve the relevant fields of the selected product. The SQL statement you'll use for the SELECT command of the DAProducts DataAdapter is the following:

```
SELECT    ProductID, ProductName
FROM      dbo.Products
```

In the Generate SQL Statements window of the configuration wizard, click the Advanced button and clear the option Generate Insert, Update And Delete Statements. We only want to display data to the users, not edit them. Create the DSProducts DataSet by clicking the Generate DataSet link on the Properties window.

You must also create another DataAdapter that retrieves a product by its ID. This time we want to retrieve the supplier's name along with the product info. Building the appropriate SQL statement shouldn't be difficult. Drop the Products table on the design surface again, rename the new DataAdapter object to DASelectedProduct, and configure it. If you're using the Query Builder to build the SQL statement, its window should look like the one shown in Figure 24.3.

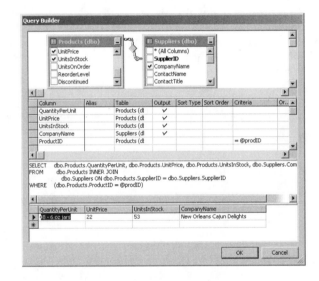

FIGURE 24.3

Building a query to retrieve the selected product along with its supplier's name

The equivalent SQL statement is:

```
SELECT    dbo.Products.QuantityPerUnit, dbo.Products.UnitPrice,
          dbo.Products.UnitsInStock, dbo.Suppliers.CompanyName
FROM      dbo.Products INNER JOIN
          dbo.Suppliers ON dbo.Products.SupplierID = dbo.Suppliers.SupplierID
WHERE     (dbo.Products.ProductID = @prodID)
```

Figure 24.3 shows the query executed for the product with ProductID = 4. The query's parameter must be set from within the page's code to the ID of the selected product. Then generate the DSSelectedProduct DataSet by clicking the Generate DataSet link on the Properties window.

OK, we've generated all the basic objects we'll use in our code, let's write some code. But first, we should bind the ListBox control to the DSProducts1 DataSet by setting the following properties to the values shown below:

Property	Setting
DataSource	DSProducts1
DataMember	Products

Property	Setting
DataTextField	ProductName
DataValueField	ProductID

Then enter the following statements in the page's Load event handler and run the project:

```
If Not Me.IsPostBack Then
    DAProducts.Fill (DSProducts1, "Products")
    lstProducts.DataBind()
End If
```

The first statement populates the DataSet object, as usual, and the second statement binds the ListBox control to the Products table. The details of the binding were set at design time through the Properties window. When the Web page appears in the browser, you will see the names of all products on the control, but nothing on the TextBoxes. We must write some code to update the remaining controls.

The TextBoxes will be bound to the second DataSet, which contains the row of the selected product. Select the *txtPrice* TextBox on the form, where the UnitPrice field will be displayed. Then locate the DataBindings property in the Properties window (it's the first property) and click the button with the ellipsis. You will see the DataBindings dialog box for the *txtPrice* control, which is shown in Figure 24.4. Expand the DSSelectedProduct1 item, then the Products item under it, then the DefaultView (twice), and you will see the fields of the DataSet, as shown in the figure. Click the column UnitPrice (not shown in the figure), then close the dialog box by clicking the OK button. Bind the other TextBox controls on the form to the appropriate columns by repeating the same process for each control.

FIGURE 24.4

Binding a TextBox control to a column

To update the TextBox controls on the form, we must program the SelectedIndexChanged event. To intercept this event in your code, you must set the ListBox control's AutoPostBack property to True. Then you must read the Value member of the SelectedItem object and use it as argument to the second DataAdapter object, which retrieves the details of the selected product. Enter the statements from Listing 24.3 in the ListBox control's SelectedIndexChanged event handler and run the project.

LISTING 24.3: BINDING THE TEXTBOX CONTROL TO A SINGLE-ROW DATASET

```
Private Sub lstProducts_SelectedIndexChanged(ByVal sender As System.Object, _
          ByVal e As System.EventArgs) Handles lstProducts.SelectedIndexChanged
   DASelectedProduct.SelectCommand.Parameters("@prodID").Value = _
          lstProducts.SelectedItem.Value
   DASelectedProduct.Fill(DSSelectedProducts1, "Products")
   txtPrice.DataBind()
   txtPackage.DataBind()
   txtStock.DataBind()
   txtSupplier.DataBind()
End Sub
```

You will see Internet Explorer displaying a form with a ListBox control that contains all the product names. Click a name to see the product's details, including its supplier's name.

The values on text boxes are reset each time we revisit a row. You can edit a field, move to another one, and then return to the edited row to find out that your edits were discarded. Do you see why? The DataSet is created every time you connect to the application. The server is not aware that the same page has been visited before. Every time, it will create the page from scratch, including its DataSet. If you find this behavior odd, consider what it would take to maintain a DataSet in memory for every user that connects to the server that hosts the application. Users might connect to your application and then switch to another application and keep the DataSet alive on the server for hours. Multiply this by hundreds or thousands, and you'll appreciate the disconnected nature of ADO.NET. You can always read the values on the controls and update the table in the database with a SQL statement or a stored procedure.

VB.NET AT WORK: THE CMDPRODUCTS PROJECT

In this section, we'll build the WebProducts project again, only this time without the visual tools. You've seen quite a bit of these tools, so it's a good time to refresh your skills on programming the ADO object. Start a new ASP.NET Web Application project and name it CMDProducts. You won't have to add any Connection or DataAdapter objects to the project; we'll create everything from within our code. Listing 24.4 shows the code that's executed when the page is loaded. The code sets up a new Command object, uses it to populate a new DataSet, and then assigns the DataSet to the ListBox control's DataSource property. It's the same thing we did visually in the previous section, only in code.

LISTING 24.4: POPULATING A DATASET WITH CODE

```
Private Sub Page_Load(ByVal sender As System.Object, _
            ByVal e As System.EventArgs) Handles MyBase.Load
' Put user code to initialize the page here
```

```
    If Not Me.IsPostBack Then
        Dim cmd As New SqlClient.SqlCommand()
        cmd.CommandText = "SELECT ProductID, ProductName FROM Products"
        cmd.CommandType = CommandType.Text
        cmd.Connection = SqlConnection1
        SqlConnection1.Open()
        Dim DS As New DataSet()
        Dim DA As New SqlClient.SqlDataAdapter()
        DA.SelectCommand = cmd
        DA.Fill(DS, "Products")
        ListBox1.DataSource = DS
        ListBox1.DataMember = "Products"
        ListBox1.DataTextField = "ProductName"
        ListBox1.DataValueField = "ProductID"
        ListBox1.DataBind()
        SqlConnection1.Close()
    End If
End Sub
```

How do we bind the TextBox controls? The TextBox control doesn't expose members for binding its text to a column. If you recall from the previous example, we had to bind the TextBox control through its DataBindings dialog box. If you take a good look at Figure 24.4, while you specified the column to which the TextBox control is to be bound, a lengthy expression appeared in the Custom Binding Expression field. This is the expression we must use in our code. The DataBinder object is equivalent to the DataBinding object we encountered in building Windows data driven applications. Its Eval method returns the value of a field in one of the tables.

The listing of the ListBox control's SelectedIndexChanged event handler is shown in Listing 24.5.

LISTING 24.5: RETRIEVING THE DETAILS OF THE SELECTED PRODUCT

```
Private Sub ListBox1_SelectedIndexChanged(ByVal sender As System.Object, _
                ByVal e As System.EventArgs) Handles ListBox1.SelectedIndexChanged
    Dim prodID As Integer
    prodID = ListBox1.SelectedIndex
    Dim cmd As New SqlClient.SqlCommand()
    cmd.CommandText = _
        "SELECT QuantityPerUnit, UnitPrice, UnitsInStock, CompanyName " & _
        "FROM Products INNER JOIN Suppliers " & _
        "ON Products.SupplierID = Suppliers.SupplierID " & _
        "WHERE ProductID = " & prodID
    cmd.CommandType = CommandType.Text
    cmd.Connection = SqlConnection1
    SqlConnection1.Open()
    Dim DS As New DataSet()
    Dim DA As New SqlClient.SqlDataAdapter()
    DA.SelectCommand = cmd
```

```
        DA.Fill(DS, "Products")
        txtPrice.Text = DataBinder.Eval(DS, _
                        "Tables[Products].DefaultView.[0].UnitPrice")
        txtPrice.DataBind()
        txtPackage.Text = DataBinder.Eval(DS, _
                        "Tables[Products].DefaultView.[0].QuantityPerUnit")
        txtPackage.DataBind()
        txtStock.Text = DataBinder.Eval(DS, _
                        "Tables[Products].DefaultView.[0].UnitsInStock")
        txtStock.DataBind()
        txtSupplier.Text = DataBinder.Eval(DS, _
                        "Tables[Products].DefaultView.[0].CompanyName")
        txtSupplier.DataBind()
        SqlConnection1.Close()
    End Sub
```

VB.NET AT WORK: THE PRODUCTSPERCATEGORY PROJECT

In this section, we'll develop a Web application that allows the user to select a category and then displays the products in the selected category. We'll implement two forms with same functionality, one using the DataList control and another using the DataGrid control. Displaying the data on these two controls is adequate for many types of applications, but for an application of this type to be really useful, you must be able to detect when the user selects an item on the control.

The ProductsPerCategory project has two forms, and you must change the project's startup page to set the other one. The form with the DataGrid control is shown in Figure 24.5, and the form with the DataList control is shown in Figure 24.6.

FIGURE 24.5

The DataGridForm of the Products-PerCategory project

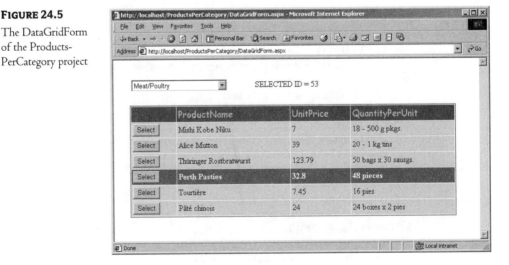

FIGURE 24.6

The DataListForm
of the Products-
PerCategory project

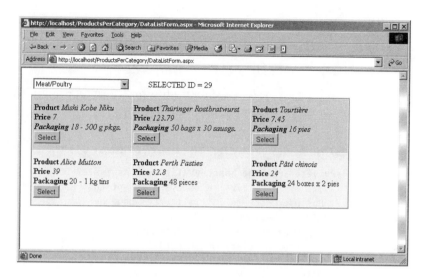

The DataGrid control on the form displays the products in the selected category. The Select buttons in the first column allow you to select a row, which is displayed with a different background color and in bold. The ID of the selected product is also displayed on a Label control at the top of the form. Once you can extract the key of the selected row, you can access the matching row in the database and manipulate it directly.

To build the application, you must create the appropriate objects to access the database. Drop the Categories and Products tables from the Server Explorer onto the form. Then configure the two DataAdapters and create two DataSets, one with all the rows of the Categories table and another with the products of a specific category. The process of creating DataSets has been described in detail in previous chapters, so I will only show you the SELECT statements for each DataAdapter. None of the DataAdapters support the update of the underlying tables.

The SELECT statement for DACategories is:

```
SELECT  CategoryID, CategoryName, Description, Picture
FROM    dbo.Categories
```

The SELECT statement for DAProductsInCategory is:

```
SELECT  ProductID, ProductName, QuantityPerUnit, UnitPrice
FROM    dbo.Products
WHERE   (CategoryID = @CatID)
```

Both forms have a DropDownList control, where the names of all categories are displayed. Here are the properties of the DropDownList control on both forms.

Property	Setting
DataSource	DSCategories1
DataMember	Categories

Property	Setting
DataTextField	CategoryName
DataValueField	CategoryID

When the page is loaded for the first time, we must populate the DropDownList control with the category names, using the code in Listing 24.6.

LISTING 24.6: POPULATING THE DROPDOWNLIST CONTROL

```
Private Sub Page_Load(ByVal sender As System.Object, _
                ByVal e As System.EventArgs) Handles MyBase.Load
' Put user code to initialize the page here
   If Not Me.IsPostBack Then
      DACategories.Fill(DSCategories1)
      DropDownList1.DataBind()
   End If
End Sub
```

In our code, we want to detect when an item was selected on the control. This action is signaled to the Web application through the control's SelectedIndexChanged, and we must insert the appropriate code in this event's handler to populate the DataGrid (or DataList) control with the products of the selected category. This event won't be fired unless you set the control's AutoPostBack property to True. Listing 24.7 presents the SelectedIndexChanged event handler of the DropDownList control.

LISTING 24.7: DISPLAYING THE PRODUCTS IN THE SELECTED CATEGORY

```
Private Sub DropDownList1_SelectedIndexChanged(ByVal sender As System.Object, _
                ByVal e As System.EventArgs) _
                Handles DropDownList1.SelectedIndexChanged
   DAProductsInCategory.SelectCommand.Parameters("@catID").Value = _
                DropDownList1.SelectedItem.Value
   DAProductsInCategory.Fill(DSProducts1)
   DataGrid1.DataBind()
End Sub
```

The code retrieves the ID of the selected category and passes it as argument to the DataAdapter's SelectCommand. This command is executed when the Fill method is called, and it populates the DSProducts1 DataSet with the matching rows. The last statement binds the DataGrid control to the newly created DataSet. The DataBind method instructs the compiler to use the data in the DataSet to create a grid-like structure with HTML statements to send to the client. After that, the DataSet is discarded.

The code of the Load event handler in the DataListForm is identical to Listing 24.6.

And so is the code—almost—of the SelectedIndexChanged event handler of the DropDown-List control. It differs in that it calls the DataBind method to bind a different control to the DataSet:

```
Private Sub DropDownList1_SelectedIndexChanged(ByVal sender As System.Object, _
            ByVal e As System.EventArgs) _
            Handles DropDownList1.SelectedIndexChanged
    DAProductsInCategory.SelectCommand.Parameters("@catID").Value = _
            DropDownList1.SelectedItem.Value
    DAProductsInCategory.Fill(DSProducts1)
    DataGrid1.DataBind()
End Sub
```

Let's switch our attention to the design of the DataList control. Unlike the DataGrid control, the DataList control doesn't autogenerate its items based on the columns of its data source. You'll have to step in and actually add a few lines of HTML code. What's really needed is a designer similar to the Web page designer for the cells of the control. Right-click the control and select Edit Templates ➢ Item Templates. You're ready to customize the template for each item.

In the gray area under the ItemTemplate heading, enter any strings you want to appear in the item's area. Enter the names of the fields as shown in Figure 24.7, and then format them. To specify the data-bound values that will appear next to the heading string, click the HTML tab at the bottom of the design surface, and you will see something like the HTML code shown in Figure 24.8. This is the HTML behind your page. As you can see, everything you do on the design surface with visual tools is translated into HTML, which can be sent to the client.

FIGURE 24.7

Customizing the appearance of a DataList control

Locate the captions you entered on the ItemTemplate box and modify them to look like Listing 24.8 (I'm showing the entire ItemTemplate and AlternatingItemTemplate here). After each title, insert the appropriate DataBinder expression to display each field next to its caption. You will also see many <P> and </P> tags (paragraphs), which insert vertical space. Remove most of them to conserve space on the cell, and use the <BR> tag to move to the next line. (The <BR> tag inserts a newline character but no additional vertical space.)

LISTING 24.8: CUSTOMIZING THE ITEMTEMPLATE AND ALTERNATINGITEMTEMPLATE OBJECTS

```
<ItemTemplate>
    <STRONG>Product</STRONG>
    <I><%# DataBinder.Eval(Container.DataItem, "ProductName") %></I>
    <BR><STRONG>Price</STRONG>
    <BR><STRONG>Packaging</STRONG>
    <I><%# DataBinder.Eval(Container.DataItem, "QuantityPerUnit") %></I>
    <BR><asp:Button id="bttnSeect" runat="server" width="53px" height="24px"
                    text="Select"></asp:Button>
</ItemTemplate>
<HeaderStyle Font-Bold="True" ForeColor="#E7E7FF" BackColor="#4A3C8C">
</HeaderStyle>
<AlternatingItemTemplate>
    <STRONG>Product</STRONG>
    <I><%# DataBinder.Eval(Container.DataItem, "ProductName") %></I>
    <BR><STRONG>Price</STRONG>
    <I><%# DataBinder.Eval(Container.DataItem, "UnitPrice") %></I>
    <BR><STRONG>Packaging</STRONG>
    <I><%# DataBinder.Eval(Container.DataItem, "QuantityPerUnit") %></I>
    <BR><asp:Button id="bttnSelect" runat="server" width="53px" height="24px"
                    text="Select"></asp:Button>
</AlternatingItemTemplate>
```

This code will retrieve the proper values from the DataSet and place them on the Item box at runtime. Designing the cells of the DataList control will turn out to be a trial-and-error process, because you must understand the code generated by the wizard and then insert your own HTML tags in it. My suggestion is to edit the cell visually, insert placeholders (like ID, Name, Price, and so on), format the strings as if they were the actual field values, and then replace the strings in the HTML code with the proper DataBinder expressions.

So far you've seen how the two controls are populated. How do we handle the selection of another row in the DataGrid control? If you run the application now, you will see two forms similar to the ones of Figures 24.5 and 24.6. We have not yet added the buttons on each product's row (for the DataGrid control) or each product's cell (for the DataList control). You will see one form at a time—whichever one is the project's Startup Page. Change the project's Startup Page to view the other.

Adding the Selection Buttons

Now we'll add the selection button in the first column of the grid (and in each item of the list). The buttons won't do anything special; they will simply print the ID of the selected item in a Label control. As you can understand, once you extract the key of the selected item, you can retrieve any related information from the database and display it on the Web form, or process it from within your code. In the section "A Master/Detail Form," later in this chapter, you'll see how you can program the Select buttons to update another control.

Right-click the DataGrid control and select Property Builder. In the DataGrid1 Properties dialog box (Figure 24.9), select the Columns tab. Clear the box Create Columns Automatically At Runtime, then add the Button Column item from the Available Columns list to the Selected Columns list. Set the new item's Text property to "Select" and its CommandName property to "Select" also. When a Select button is clicked, the ItemCommand event is raised in the application. In the Item-Command event's handler, insert the statements of Listing 24.9.

FIGURE 24.9

Setting the properties of the DataGrid

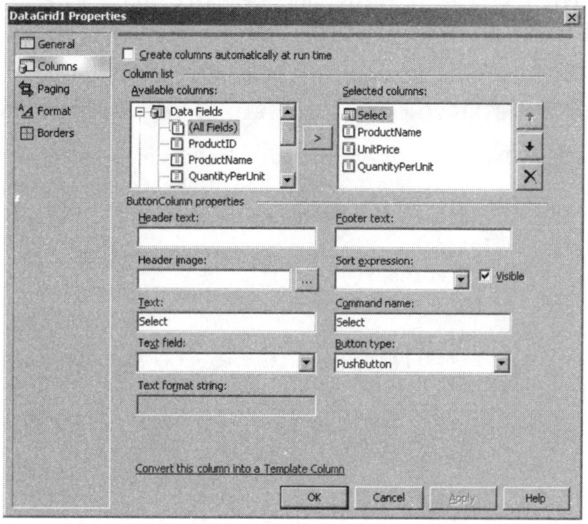

LISTING 24.9: HANDLING THE SELECTION OF A ROW ON THE DATAGRID CONTROL

```
Private Sub DataGrid1_ItemCommand(ByVal source As Object, _
            ByVal e As System.Web.UI.WebControls.DataGridCommandEventArgs) _
            Handles DataGrid1.ItemCommand
    Dim itm As Integer
    itm = e.Item.ItemIndex()
    Dim keys As DataKeyCollection
    keys = DataGrid1.DataKeys()
    Label1.Text = "SELECTED ID = " & keys(itm).ToString
End Sub
```

The `e.Item` object represents the selected item on the control. The ItemIndex property returns the item's index on the control. The DataKeys property of the DataGrid object is a collection of all the keys on the control. We retrieve the key of the selected item and display it on a Label control. Later in this chapter, you will see how to add the selected item to a basket. As long as you can retrieve the key of the selected item, you can access its row in the corresponding table of the database.

To add a button to the DataList control, switch to the Item Edit mode (Edit Templates ➤ Item Template from the context menu) and drop a Button control on the Item area and another one on the AlternatingItem area. Then open the HTML tab of the editor and edit the code to position the button just right on the cell. Again, this is the type of operation we should be able to perform visually, but the designer inserts far too many <P> tags in such a small area. After you're done editing the DataList control's template, select End Template Editing from the context menu.

When the button is clicked at runtime, the ItemCommand event is raised. In this event, we want to retrieve the ID of the selected product and use it in our code. The ProductsPerCategory application doesn't do anything with this ID except for displaying it on a Label control. The code that retrieves the ID of the product displayed on the selected cell of the control is shown in Listing 24.10.

LISTING 24.10: RETRIEVING THE KEY FIELD OF THE SELECTED PRODUCT

```
Private Sub DataList1_ItemCommand(ByVal source As Object, _
            ByVal e As System.Web.UI.WebControls.DataListCommandEventArgs) _
            Handles DataList1.ItemCommand
    Dim itm As Integer
    itm = e.Item.ItemIndex()
    Dim keys As DataKeyCollection
    keys = DataList1.DataKeys()
    Label1.Text = "SELECTED ID = " & keys(itm).ToString
End Sub
```

Is It a Grid, or a Table?

If you look at the source code of either page you created in the last section, you'll realize that it's plain HTML. There's no DataGrid or DataList control in the page sent down to the client—just a long HTML table. The Web controls are design-time tools. You see them on the designer's surface; you know what they will look like when rendered on the client; you can set their properties visually; but they don't make it past the compiler. When the compiler sees a DataGrid control, it knows that there's no HTML equivalent and tries to build something that looks like a grid on the client, but it's really a table.

ASP.NET is nothing more than a way to program the Web with VB and a visual designer. It allows you to design your pages visually and write VB code behind them. The controls you place on your Web forms are translated into HTML. The VB code stays at the server, and it's executed there in response to events that originate at the client but are transmitted to the server. However, the magic grows thin real quick, because you must understand how the Web works and learn to program in a disconnected environment. Is ASP.NET a revolutionary new technology? In my view, it's a better way of living with HTML. A technology that would allow us to design forms that can be used in both Windows and Web application—yes, that would be revolutionary. ASP.NET will buy us another couple of years, until we figure out a way to get rid of HTML.

Getting Orders on the Web

This is a rather ambitious project for this book, but it demonstrates a lot of interesting topics. It also shows you how to build a very practical Web application, and you can use the information presented in this chapter as your starting point for similar projects. Let me start with a short description of the ProductSearch project you'll build.

Our application starts with a page that lets users select products and place them in their virtual shopping basket. A real application that's driven by a real database might have to display thousands of products, and we simply can't afford to download all the products to the client. We prompt users to specify the products they're interested in, and then the program downloads only a small segment of the database. There are many ways to search the database, from very simple SELECT statements to complicated ones. The one used here is as simple as it gets (users must supply the name of the product, or a word that appears in the product's name). You can design an interface that displays all categories and downloads the products of the selected category, use price ranges, and so on. Search operations are implemented with SELECT statements that accept one or more parameters, and you know how to build those. Figure 24.10 shows the first form on the application.

The last column contains hyperlinks that place the corresponding products in the user's basket. Every time a link is clicked, another item of the product is added to the basket. If the item exists in the basket already, its quantity is increased by one.

At any point, users can view their basket's contents by clicking the My Basket button. This button opens the form shown in Figure 24.11, which displays the basket (the products, their prices, subtotals, and the order total). The basket's contents are displayed on a table, which is constructed from within the page's code. You could have used a DataGrid to display the items ordered, or any other control.

FIGURE 24.10

Adding selected products to one's basket

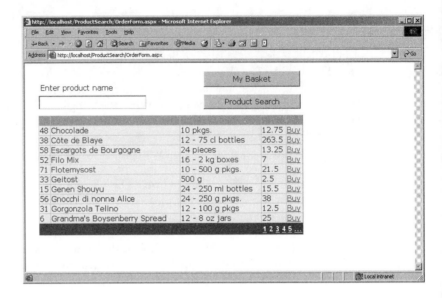

FIGURE 24.11

Reviewing the basket's contents

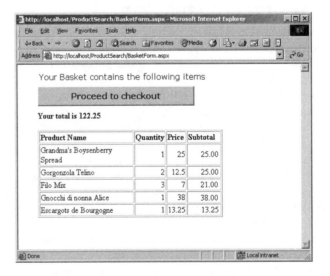

Once the user reviews the basket's contents, they can click the Proceed To Checkout button to actually place the order. On the last form of the application they must provide shipping information, as shown in Figure 24.12. The user is required to log into the database by supplying a UserID, which is the CustomerID field of the Customers table. You can use any authentication technique you deem appropriate, but this is a very simple one that doesn't require additional code. The ID is in the database, and you can easily identify the user.

FIGURE 24.12

Finalizing an
online order

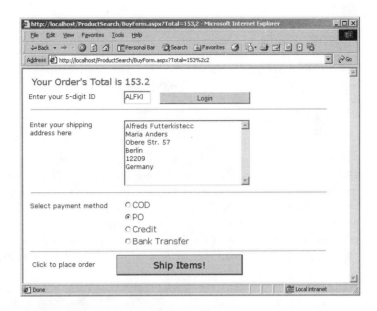

The Forms of the ProductSearch Application

Now we'll discuss the design process and the code behind the pages of the application. Start a new ASP.NET Web application project and add two more Web forms to it. The ProductSearch application's Web forms are called OrderForm, BasketForm, and BuyForm.

THE ORDERFORM WEB FORM

This is the application's startup page (shown in Figure 24.10), and it contains a TextBox (where users enter the search criteria), two buttons, and a DataGrid control, where the selected products are displayed. This form must retrieve data from the Products table, so we must create a DataSet where the selected products will reside. Drop the Products table onto the design surface, configure the DataAdapter object, and then create a DataSet object as usual. The SELECT statement of the DataAdapter object is shown next:

```
SELECT TOP 100 ProductID, ProductName, QuantityPerUnit, UnitPrice
FROM dbo.Products
WHERE (ProductName LIKE '%' + @name + '%')
```

In effect, we search for product names that contain the string enter by the user on the TextBox. The clause TOP 100 limits the size of the DataSet, because if the TextBox is blank, then the query will return all rows in the table. We don't want this to happen in a real application that could download 100,000 rows to the client.

With the DataSet object in place, you can configure the DataGrid control. Start by setting the following properties to these values:

Property	Setting
DataSource	DSPrducts1
DataMember	Products
DataKeyField	ProductID

The DataKeyField is the primary key (a value that's unique among all the rows of the control). The DataGrid will automatically generate one grid column for each column in the table. We want to create the structure of the DataGrid ourselves, so set the control's AutoGenerateColumns property to False.

Then right-click the DataGrid control on the form and select Property Builder. You will see the control's Properties dialog box, where you can specify the appearance of the control. On the General tab of the dialog box, you set the data-binding properties. We've already specified the setting of these properties in the Properties window, so the dialog box should look like Figure 24.13.

FIGURE 24.13

The General tab of the DataGrid control's Properties dialog box

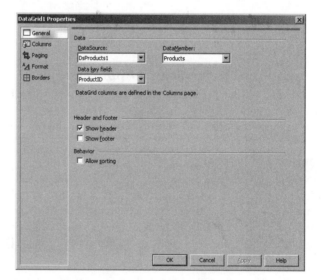

Switch to the Columns tab, where you specify the columns to be displayed on the control, as shown in Figure 24.14. The option Create Columns Automatically At Runtime must be cleared. Select the table columns you want to display on your control from the Available Columns list, and move them to the Selected Columns list by clicking the arrow button. As you add each table column, set the header of the equivalent grid column to the string you want to display at runtime.

Add all the fields and then locate the item Hyperlink Column in the list of available columns. The new column will contain a hyperlink for each row in the table, and you'll be able to program this hyperlink. Set the hyperlink's Text property to "Buy." You could also place a button in the column by adding the Select button item from the Available Columns list to the Selected Columns list.

FIGURE 24.14

The Columns tab of
the DataGrid con-
trol's Properties dia-
log box

FIGURE 24.14

The Columns tab of
the DataGrid con-
trol's Properties dia-
log box

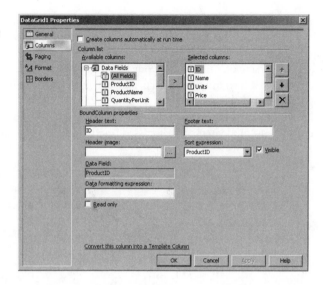

On the next tab of the dialog box, Paging (Figure 24.15), you can specify how the DataGrid will
handle multiple pages of data (instead of displaying too many rows at once). You can enable paging
and can set the page's size (number of rows per page), the navigational buttons, and the navigational
mode (whether there will be only Next and Previous buttons or a list of page numbers). You can
also customize the appearance of the paging by supplying your own code. We'll discuss the topic of
paging briefly in the following section.

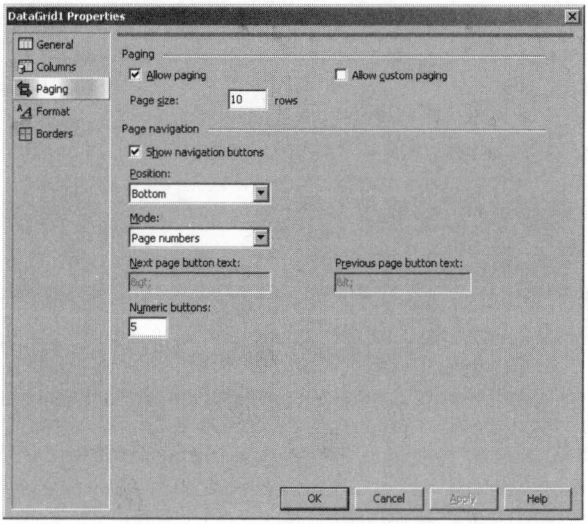

FIGURE 24.15

The Paging tab of
the DataGrid con-
trol's Properties
dialog box

On the other two tabs of the Properties dialog box, the Format and Borders tabs, you can customize the appearance of the control by setting its font, colors, borders, and so on. There are many options here, but it's relatively easy to figure out what they do. Experiment with the settings on these two tabs to get the hang of customizing your DataGrid controls.

The Format tab, shown in Figure 24.16, allows you to set the appearance of normal items and alternating items. Normal items are the odd-numbered rows and alternating items are the even-numbered rows. We usually set the background color of the two types of items to different values. The selected and edit mode items are discussed briefly in the following section.

FIGURE 24.16

Setting the appearance of a column's cells on the Data-Grid control

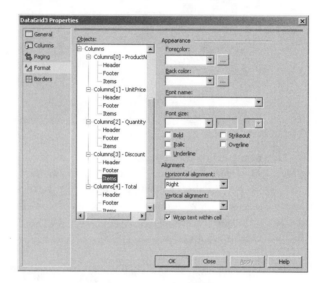

Now we must add some code behind the Product Search button. When this button is clicked, we pick the user-supplied search argument from the TextBox control and use it with the DAProducts DataAdapter's SelectCommand. We must execute the SELECT statement that retrieves the qualifying rows and then bind the DataGrid control to the DataSet. Listing 24.9 shows the code behind the Product Search button.

LISTING 24.11: DISPLAYING THE QUALIFYING ROWS FROM THE PRODUCTS TABLE ON A DATAGRID

```
Private Sub ProductSearch(ByVal sender As System.Object, _
            ByVal e As System.EventArgs) Handles bttnSearch.Click
    DAProducts.SelectCommand.Parameters("@name").Value = TextBox1.Text
    DAProducts.Fill(DSProducts1, "Products")
    DataGrid1.DataSource = DSProducts1.Products
    DataGrid1.DataBind()
    DataGrid1.Visible = True
End Sub
```

Every time the user clicks one of the Buy hyperlinks, we must extract the ID of the selected product and add it to the basket. The basket in this application is stored in the Session object. We create a new Session variable for each item added to the basket, set the name of the variable to the ID of the product, and set its value to the number of items ordered. If the user clicks multiple times on the same link, the quantity of the specific product in the basket increases.

How do we intercept the clicking of the Buy link in our code? Every time a link is clicked on the page, the ItemCommand event is raised in the application. Open the ItemCommand event handler for the DataGrid1 object and enter the code shown in Listing 24.12.

LISTING 24.12: HANDLING THE CLICK OF THE BUY LINKS

```
Private Sub DataGrid1_ItemCommand(ByVal source As Object, _
                ByVal e As System.Web.UI.WebControls.DataGridCommandEventArgs) _
                Handles DataGrid1.ItemCommand
    Dim ItemID As Integer
    If e.Item.ItemType = ListItemType.Pager Then Exit Sub
    ItemID = e.Item.Cells(0).Text
    Dim sItemID As String = ItemID
    If Session(sItemID) Is Nothing Then
        Session(sItemID) = 1
    Else
        Session(sItemID) = Session(sItemID) + 1
    End If
End Sub
```

Notice that the second argument carries information about the link that was clicked. Because the page numbers displayed at the bottom of the page also raise the same event, we examine the type of the item that raised the event. If the item was a pager item, we exit the subroutine.

If not, we add another item to the basket (or increase the quantity of the items ordered if the product exists in the basket). This application uses the Session object to store the IDs and quantities of the ordered products. You'll see how this information is used in the subsequent page. I suggest you modify the application so that it uses cookies instead (use the `Request.Cookies` collection to read the cookies and the `Response.Cookies` collection to add a new cookie or change the value of an existing cookie).

The other button on the form redirects the user to the BasketForm page, where the ordered items are displayed, and its code is shown next:

```
Private Sub bttnBasket_Click(ByVal sender As System.Object, _
            ByVal e As System.EventArgs) Handles bttnBasket.Click
    Response.Redirect("BasketForm.aspx")
End Sub
```

Run the project and check out how the OrderForm page works. Add items to the basket, bring in a different DataSet, and keep adding to the basket.

THE BASKETFORM WEB FORM

The BasketForm page doesn't interact with the user; it simply displays the basket's contents on a table. The user can click the Back button to jump back to the OrderForm page, or click the Proceed To Checkout button to place the order. All the action on the page takes place in its Load event handler. Before you can write any code, you must add the appropriate objects for accessing the database. When this page is invoked, all the information we have at hand are the IDs of the products in the basket and their matching quantities. We must retrieve all the product prices from the Products table, multiply them with the corresponding quantities, calculate each line's subtotal as well as the order's total, and create the table.

We're going to build a SELECT statement to retrieve the products ordered from the Products table in our code. Open the Server Explorer and drop the Products table onto the design surface. You need not configure the DataAdapter object; just clear its `SelectCommand.CommandText` property in the Properties window. Then enter the code of Listing 24.13 in the page's Load event handler.

LISTING 24.13: DISPLAYING THE BASKET'S CONTENTS

```
Private Sub Page_Load(ByVal sender As System.Object, _
                ByVal e As System.EventArgs) Handles MyBase.Load
' Put user code to initialize the page here
    Dim ck As Object, cmd As String
    cmd = "SELECT ProductID, ProductName, UnitPrice " & _
          "FROM Products WHERE ProductID IN ("
    For Each ck In Session
        cmd = cmd & ck.ToString & ", "
    Next
    cmd = cmd.Substring(0, cmd.Length - 2) & ")"
    SqlConnection1.Open()
    DASelectedProducts.SelectCommand.CommandText = cmd
    DASelectedProducts.SelectCommand.CommandType = CommandType.Text
    Dim Reader As Data.SqlClient.SqlDataReader = _
                DASelectedProducts.SelectCommand.ExecuteReader
    Dim prodName As String, prodID As Integer, prodPrice As Decimal
    Dim subTotal As Decimal, table As String
    table = "<TABLE BORDER='1'><TR>"
    table = table & "<TD><B>Product Name</B></TD><TD><B>Quantity</B></TD>"
    table = table & "<TD><B>Price</B></TD><TD><B>Subtotal</B></TD></TR>"
    While Reader.Read
        table = table & "<TR><TD>"
        prodName = Reader.Item("ProductName")
        prodID = Reader.Item("ProductID")
        prodPrice = Reader.Item("UnitPrice")
        table = table & prodName & "</TD>"
        table = table & "<TD ALIGN='right'>" & Session(CStr(prodID)) & "</TD>"
        table = table & "<TD ALIGN='right'>" & prodPrice & "</TD>"
        subTotal = prodPrice * Session(CStr(prodID))
```

```
      table = table & "<TD ALIGN='right'>" & subtotal & "</TD></TR>"
      total = total + subTotal
   End While
   table = table & "</TABLE>"
   table = table & "<P><B>Your total is " & total.ToString & "</B></P>"
   lblBasket.Text = table
   SqlConnection1.Close()
End Sub
```

The code builds a SELECT statement with the IN keyword, by reading the IDs of the selected products from the Session object, one at a time. If the basket contains three IDs, the corresponding SQL statement will be something like:

```
SELECT ProductID, ProductName, UnitPrice
FROM   Products
WHERE  ProductID IN (32, 40, 8)
```

When this statement is executed against the database, it will retrieve the IDs, names, and prices of the products in the user's basket. These rows aren't stored in a DataSet. In this page, I've used a DataReader object to go through the rows returned by the query and create the table with the basket's items on-the-fly. The products are returned in the same order as their IDs appear in the Session object. The first product's quantity is given by the expression: `Session(CStr(prodID))`. The *prodID* variable is numeric, so we must convert it to a string before using it as Session variable name. If the ID of the first selected product is 14, its quantity is `Session("14")`. The code shown here will work with nonnumeric product keys as well.

The table is built one row at time, as we go through the rows of the DataReader object. The three fields of the current row are stored in the variables *prodID*, *prodName*, and *prodPrice*, and these variables are used to build the table displayed on a Label control.

The Proceed To Checkout button redirects the user to the third page of the application, where he's asked to supply shipping and billing information to finalize the order. How do we redirect the user to the last page of the application? The Redirect method will work, but this time we want to pass some additional information to the page, which is the order's total. The last page displays the order's total on a Label control at the top, and there's no reason to recalculate the total—it's already been calculated on the current page. To pass the total as argument to the last page, we must append it to the URL of the destination. Instead of specifying the URL of the form, we can build a destination URL that includes a parameter, like the following:

```
BuyForm.aspx?Total=193.4
```

This is what takes place in the Click event handler of the Proceed to Checkout button, which is shown next:

```
Private Sub Button1_Click(ByVal sender As System.Object, _
            ByVal e As System.EventArgs) Handles Button1.Click
   Response.Redirect("BuyForm.aspx?Total=" & Server.UrlEncode(total))
End Sub
```

The code reads the value of the *total* variable (which is declared outside any procedure) and passes it to the BuyForm.aspx page. The UrlEncode method converts the value of the *total* variable to a URL-compliant format. On the last form of the application, we'll use the UrlDecode method to convert the argument back to its original format.

THE BUYFORM WEB FORM

When the Login button is clicked on the BuyForm Web form, the code shown in Listing 24.14 is executed. This event handler attempts to read the row with the specified ID from the Customers table. If it succeeds, it displays the customer's shipping address on a TextBox control and waits for the user to set the remaining fields and accept the order. If the specified ID doesn't match one of the IDs in the database, a warning appears next to the Login button in red and no further action is taken. The user must either supply a valid ID or click the Back button to return the previous page of the application.

LISTING 24.14: VERIFYING A USER'S ID

```
Private Sub Button1_Click(ByVal sender As System.Object, _
               ByVal e As System.EventArgs) Handles Button1.Click
    DACustomers.SelectCommand.Parameters("@CustID").Value = TextBox1.Text
    DACustomers.Fill(DSCustomers1, "Customers")
    If DSCustomers1.Customers.Rows.Count <> 1 Then
       lblError.Visible = True
    Else
       lblError.Visible = False
       Dim Address As String
       Address = DSCustomers1.Customers.Item(0).CompanyName & vbCrLf & _
                 DSCustomers1.Customers.Item(0).ContactName & vbCrLf & _
                 DSCustomers1.Customers.Item(0).Address & vbCrLf & _
                 DSCustomers1.Customers.Item(0).City & vbCrLf & _
                 DSCustomers1.Customers.Item(0).PostalCode & vbCrLf & _
                 DSCustomers1.Customers.Item(0).Country
       txtAddress.Text = Address
       bttnShip.Visible =true
    End If
End Sub
```

This example doesn't authenticate the user; it simply allows users to log in using an ID, which presumably isn't given to other users. In a real application, you should prompt for the user's e-mail or ID and a password.

The last piece of code in the form displays the order's total on a Label control with the following statement, which is executed in the page's Load event handler:

```
Private Sub Page_Load(ByVal sender As System.Object, _
               ByVal e As System.EventArgs) Handles MyBase.Load
' Put user code to initialize the page here
    lblTotal.Text = "Your Order's Total is " & Request.QueryString("Total")
End Sub
```

One drawback of the ProductSearch application is that it doesn't allow the user to remove an item from the basket. You can add a second column with hyperlinks or buttons to the DataGrid of the first page and, every time the user clicks it, remove the corresponding product from the basket. To add a column with Remove buttons, open the Property Builder of the DataGrid control on the form. Add a new Button column and set its Text property to Remove and its CommandName property to RemoveItem.

When any of the buttons in this column are clicked, the ItemCommand event will be raised. You must add some code in this event's handler to figure out what button was clicked (the Buy or Remove link) and act accordingly. Here's the code you must insert in the ItemCommand event handler:

```
If e.CommandName = "RemoveItem" Then
    If Not Session(sItemID) Is Nothing Then
        Session.Remove(sItemID)
    End If
    Exit Sub
End If
```

The ProductSearch project on the CD contains the code for saving the new order to the database. It requires that the NewOrder and NewOrderLine stored procedures (from Chapter 22) be attached to the database.

Paging Large DataSets

Large DataSets have always been a problem in presenting data on Web pages. Displaying hundreds of rows on a single page isn't very practical, and designers have come up with a technique for breaking the DataSet into pages. A *page* is a group of rows that are displayed on the same form. At the bottom of the form, there are usually links for the next and previous page, or links to all the pages that make up the DataSet. The user can click a link and jump to any other page of the DataSet. Paged DataSets are useful when they contain a relatively small number of pages. A DataSet with 300 pages isn't very practical, even though you're not displaying all the rows at once. How's the user supposed to figure out which page contains the row he's interested in? Very large DataSets aren't appropriate for typical Web applications. If a search returns more than 100 rows, you should probably ask users to be more specific.

Among its many other features, the DataGrid control supports paging. It provides properties and recognizes events that simplify displaying the page numbers at the bottom of the control and moving to the appropriate page when a page hyperlink is clicked. To enable paging, you must set the control's AllowPaging property to True and the PageSize property to the number of rows per page. The PagerStyle property determines the layout of the paging section of the control. This property is an object that exposes properties for setting the background/foreground color of the pager, the font, and so on. One of the properties is exposes is the Mode property, which can have one of the two values: NextPrev and NumericPages. These are the two pager modes that are supported automatically. You can also turn on AllowCustomPaging, in which case you must provide your own mechanism for paging through the DataSet (we will not discuss custom paging techniques in this book).

Once you've enabled paging, the control will receive the PageIndexChanged event every time one of the paging links is clicked. These links may be the previous/next arrows or page numbers. In this event's handler, you must set the page to jump to, and refill the DataSet. Listing 24.15 is a typical PageIndexChanged event handler.

LISTING 24.15: HANDLING PAGING EVENTS

```
Private Sub DataGrid1_PageIndexChanged(ByVal source As Object, _
            ByVal e As System.Web.UI.WebControls.DataGridPageChangedEventArgs) _
            Handles DataGrid1.PageIndexChanged
    DataGrid1.CurrentPageIndex = e.NewPageIndex
    DACustomers.Fill(DSCustomerNames1, "Customers")
    DataGrid1.DataBind()
End Sub
```

The property e.NewPageIndex is the page number selected by the user on the control. The transition to the new page isn't automatic; you must explicitly set the CurrentPageIndex property. You can also set this property to −1 to effectively cancel the paging action.

Then you must refill the DataSet and bind the control to it again to force its contents to change. The DataSet doesn't reside anywhere in the server's memory, so you must recreate it.

There's one last implication in programming DataSet paging events. Every time an item is clicked on the control, the ItemCommand event is also fired. We use this event to retrieve the selected item's ID, in order to retrieve additional information from the database and update another control on the form. This event will also take place even when a paging link is clicked; you must ignore this type of event in the ItemCommand event by inserting the following line at the beginning of the Item-Command event handler:

```
If e.Item.ItemType = ListItemType.Pager Then Exit Sub
```

WHEN TO USE PAGED DATASETS

A word of caution on using the paging capabilities of the DataGrid control. The control doesn't know how to retrieve the rows of the current page from the database. Instead, it retrieves all the qualifying rows and then displays the appropriate subset, taking into consideration the current paging settings. Every time you click the Next button, for example, you read all the qualifying rows from the database, display a small subset of the rows, and discard the rest. This isn't the most efficient method of handling paging. If you want to add paging capabilities to your application, you must customize the default pager and provide your own code. However, we have already limited the number of qualifying rows to 100. We can use the default pager to create 10 pages of 10 rows each (at most) without placing a real burden on the database server. I have seen paging schemes on the Web with lists of page numbers that take up a dozen lines on the page. Use the DataGrid's built-in paging features carefully, and make sure your pages will look good even if users select an enormous DataSet, like all history books. There's nothing wrong with limiting the selection to 100 or 200 rows. Users will have to be more specific about the rows they're searching for. Besides, what's the average user going to do with 2,500 rows that meet their criteria?

Paging has always been a sore point in designing Web applications, and programmers have tried all kinds of paging schemes. The problem is that the rows in a table are not numbered, and there's no SQL statement that can retrieve the N rows following a specific row. Even if the existing rows were numbered, how would you handle insertions and deletions? Paging is a technique for guiding the user close to the desired row. To use paging techniques efficiently, limit the number of rows returned by a query with the TOP keyword, so that you won't have to display 300 pages of 20 rows each.

A Master/Detail Web Page

This is one of the most common types of Web applications. Figure 24.17 shows a page with customers, orders, and order details. The top DataGrid control displays 10 customers at a time in paged mode. As explained already, paging doesn't save you from downloading the entire Customers table every time the user switches to another page. If your Customers table contains thousands of customers, you should combine this application with the techniques discussed in the WebProducts or ProductSearch applications to limit the number of customers in the DataSet (you can force users to select customers by country or state, company, and so on).

FIGURE 24.17

A master/detail Web form with two nested tables

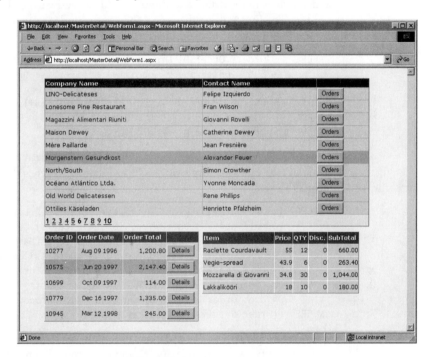

When the Orders button on a customer row is clicked, the selected customer's orders are displayed on the DataGrid below. This DataGrid control isn't paged (you can limit the orders to the current year, or even month, to make sure that the page doesn't grow too long or you can add paging to this control as well). When the Details button on an order row is clicked, the order's details are displayed on the third DataGrid control. MasterDetail is an interesting application that demonstrates data binding in a Web app, how to customize the DataGrid, and how to program the events of the DataGrid control.

Building the MasterDetail application is a lengthy process, but it's also an overview of the material covered in Chapter 21 (how to populate DataSets with the visual tools). Start a new ASP.NET Web application and name it MasterDetail. Then drop the Customers, Orders, and Order Details tables from the Server Explorer onto the design surface. Rename the three DataAdapter object that will be created to DACustomers, DAOrders, and DADetails. Configure them as follows.

DACustomers This DataAdapter retrieves all the customers of the Northwind database with the following SELECT statement:

```
SELECT CustomerID, CompanyName, ContactName FROM dbo.Customers
```

DAOrders This DataAdapter retrieves the orders of a selected customer. In Figure 24.17, you'll see that it includes a calculated field, the Order Total field. The total of an order isn't stored anywhere in the database and must be calculated by the SELECT statement that retrieves the orders. The DAOrders object's SELECT command is shown next (I've removed the table qualifiers to fit it nicely on the printed page):

```
SELECT    Orders.OrderID, Orders.OrderDate,
          SUM ((UnitPrice * Quantity) * (1 - Discount)) AS Total
FROM      dbo.Orders INNER JOIN Order Details
          ON dbo.Orders.OrderID = dbo.[Order Details].OrderID
WHERE     (Orders.CustomerID = @CustID)
GROUP BY  Orders.OrderID, OrderDate
```

DADetails This DataAdapter retrieves the details of a selected order and also calculates the subtotal of each line (quantity × price × (1 − discount)). Here's the SELECT statement of the DataAdapter:

```
SELECT [Order Details].OrderID, [Order Details].ProductID,
       [Order Details].UnitPrice, [Order Details].Quantity,
       [Order Details].Discount, Products.ProductName,
       [Order Details].UnitPrice * [Order Details].Quantity) *
          (1 - dbo.[Order Details].Discount) AS Total
FROM   dbo.[Order Details] INNER JOIN dbo.Products
       ON dbo.[Order Details].ProductID = dbo.Products.ProductID
WHERE  ([Order Details].OrderID = @orderID)
```

After configuring the three DataAdapters, create the corresponding DataSets. Create a separate DataSet for each DataAdapter, and name them DSCustomerNames, DSOrders, and DSDetails. Three instances of the DataSet class will appear on the Component tray, and they'll be named after the corresponding DataSet suffixed by the digit 1.

Your next step is to bind the DataGrid controls to the corresponding DataSets. The data-binding properties of the three controls are shown next:

Property	Setting
DataGrid1 Control	
DataSource	DSCustomerNames1
DataMember	Customers
DataKeyField	CustomerID

Property	Setting
DataGrid2 Control	
DataSource	DSOrders1
DataMember	Orders
DataKeyField	OrderID
DataGrid3 Control	
DataSource	DSDetails1
DataMember	Order Details

Customizing the Appearance of the DataGrid Control

At this point comes the most challenging part of the project, and it isn't its code. We must customize the DataGrid controls, and there are quite a few items you can customize: the pager section at the bottom of the top DataGrid control, the formatting of the date and numeric fields, and the alignment of the numeric fields (they must be aligned to the right).

All the formatting options are clustered together in the Properties dialog box of the DataGrid control. Right-click the DataGrid control you want to customize and select Property Builder. On the dialog box that appears, select Format, and you will see a list of items you can format separately (shown previously in Figure 24.16):

DataGrid Here you can specify the overall appearance of the DataGrid (its font, its foreground and background colors, and so on).

Header Here you can specify the appearance of the control's header.

Footer Here you can specify the appearance of the control's footer.

Pager Here you can specify the appearance of the pager.

Items An item is a row of the control, and there are several groups of rows. All rows in a group have common formatting. Here you can specify the appearance of the normal and alternating items, the appearance of the selected item, as well as the appearance of the row in edit mode.

Columns Here you can specify the contents of each column (you can also leave it to the control to automatically generate a column for each field in the DataSet).

Expand the Columns item in the Objects list, then expand one of the Columns. You will see the names of the columns, and under each column are three categories of items you can customize: the column's Header, Footer, and Items. Each cell in the specific column is formatted according to the settings of the Items object. You can set the foreground/background colors of the cell's text, the font and the alignment of the cell.

Besides the appearance of the cells, you will also have to specify how dates and numeric values will be formatted. In the Columns tab of the control's Properties dialog box, select a numeric or date field and enter the appropriate formatting expression in the Data Formatting Expression box. This expression is the same one you would use with the ToString method. The formatting expression {0: #,###.00} signifies that the amount (represented by the argument 0) must be formatted with a thousands separator and two decimal digits (the second argument is the format specification). A value like 14302.5785 will be formatted as 14,302.58, and a value like 14.496 will be formatted as 14.50. The same is true for dates. The specification {0:dd MMMM yyyy} will format the date 9/7/2001 as "07 September 2001."

On the Columns tab, clear the option Create Columns Automatically At Runtime and add the columns you want to display on the control (CompanyName and ContactName) from the Available Columns list to the Selected Columns list. (Figure 24.14 shows the same tab for another DataGrid control). Select each field in the Selected Columns list and set its text. Then add a Button column to the control, set the button's Text property to Orders, and set its ButtonType property to PushButton. This is the column with the buttons, and each one of them will populate the second DataGrid control with the selected customer's orders.

Do the same for the second DataGrid control with the Orders. Additionally, you must set the Data Formatting Expression for the OrderDate and OrderTotal columns. The formatting string for the OrderDate field is {0:dd MMM yyyy}, and for the OrderTotal field it's {0: #,###.00}. Finally, add the Details button.

Customize the third DataGrid control as discussed earlier, and set the formatting string for the SubTotal column to {0: #,###.00}.

Programming the Select Button

As for the code of the application, this is the simplest part. When the form is loaded for the first time, the DSCustomerNames DataSet is loaded and is used to populate the DataGrid control:

```
Private Sub Page_Load(ByVal sender As System.Object, _
              ByVal e As System.EventArgs) Handles MyBase.Load
    If Not Me.IsPostBack Then
        DACustomers.Fill(DSCustomerNames1, "Customers")
        DataGrid1.DataBind()
    End If
End Sub
```

The following code populates the second DataGrid control with the orders of the selected customer. This code must reside in the event handler that's raised when one of the buttons in the last column of the top DataGrid is clicked. This is the control's ItemCommand event:

```
Private Sub DataGrid1_ItemCommand(ByVal source As Object, _
              ByVal e As System.Web.UI.WebControls.DataGridCommandEventArgs)
              Handles DataGrid1.ItemCommand
    If e.Item.ItemType = ListItemType.Pager Then Exit Sub
    Dim custID As String = DataGrid1.DataKeys(e.Item.ItemIndex)
    DAOrders.SelectCommand.Parameters("@CustID").Value = custID
    DAOrders.Fill(DSOrders1, "Orders")
    DataGrid2.DataBind()
End Sub
```

The ItemCommand event is raised when any button or hyperlink on the control is clicked; that's why the code examines whether the event was fired by a pager item. In this case, the event handler is terminated. If the event was fired by a button, the code executes the DAOrders object's SelectCommand passing the selected customer's ID as argument and then fills the DSOrders1 DataSet. The last step is to refresh the DataGrid control with the orders by calling its DataBind method.

With similar statements, the third DataGrid control on the form is populated with the selected order's detail lines:

```
Private Sub DataGrid2_ItemCommand(ByVal source As Object, _
              ByVal e As System.Web.UI.WebControls.DataGridCommandEventArgs) _
              Handles DataGrid2.ItemCommand
    Dim orderID As Integer = DataGrid2.DataKeys(e.Item.ItemIndex)
    DADetails.SelectCommand.Parameters("@OrderID").Value = orderID
    DADetails.Fill(DSDetails1, "Order Details")
    DataGrid3.DataBind()
End Sub
```

For the sake of completeness, I'm including the listing of the control's PageIndexChanged event handler, which enables the user to navigate to another page of the DSCustomers DataSet by clicking one of the page links at the bottom of the control:

```
Private Sub DataGrid1_PageIndexChanged(ByVal source As Object, _
              ByVal e As System.Web.UI.WebControls.DataGridPageChangedEventArgs) _
              Handles DataGrid1.PageIndexChanged
    DataGrid1.CurrentPageIndex = e.NewPageIndex
    DACustomers.Fill(DSCustomerNames1, "Customers")
    DataGrid1.DataBind()
End Sub
```

The MasterDetail Web application is quite functional and is typical of the type of application you'll be called to develop, along with order-processing applications. The code is minimal, and all the functionality required to build the application resides in the control itself. It will take you longer to set the properties of the DataGrid control than to actually write the code.

Summary

This chapter was about ADO.NET on the Web. We focused on data-binding techniques and the visual tools, because this is how you're supposed to make the most of a rapid application development (RAD) environment like VB. Just about everything we did with point-and-click operations in this chapter can be done with code. As you familiarize yourself with both ASP.NET and ADO.NET, you'll be able to switch between the visual tools and the code at will.

If you were asked to compare the ease of use of ADO.NET with Windows applications and Web applications, wouldn't you agree that ADO.NET is better suited for Web applications? ADO.NET was designed for disconnected applications, and the only true disconnected applications are the ones that run on the Web. In Chapter 25, the last chapter of the book, you'll learn yet another way to use ADO.NET on the Web, through Web services. Web services are the hottest topic in the industry (along with XML, of course).

Chapter 25

XML Web Services

THE LAST TOPIC DISCUSSED in this book is one of the hottest new features of Visual Studio
.NET, XML Web services, or simply Web services. A Web service is a Class that resides on a
Web server and services requests, just like an ASP application. The difference is that the Web
service doesn't furnish HTML pages to the client. Instead, it behaves like a function: clients call
the function by name, pass arguments (if needed), and get back a result. The result can be number, a string, an object like a DataSet, or an image. In the examples of this chapter, you'll see how
you can write Web services that return DataSets and how these DataSets can be used to populate
DataGrids or other data-bound controls on the client. You can also save the DataSet's rows to a
local file in XML format and use it in other applications. This is actually a very efficient method
of making data like price lists available to a large number of recipients.

This is literally a how-to chapter that shows you how to build Web services. No special programming background is required to build Web services; if you can write a function in VB, you can
write a Web service. Of course, if your VB function must be executed in the environment of Internet Information Services (IIS), it must encode its result in a form suitable for transmission over the
HTTP protocol so that it can respond to requests made over the Web. Theoretically, you can write
an ASP application that does the same, but it's not an easy task. Visual Studio makes building and
using Web services as easy as writing and using VB functions in a Windows application. Visual Studio does a lot for you behind the scenes, so that you can think of Web services as regular classes that
expose methods—except these methods are available on the Web.

How to Serve the Web

A Web service is a Class that exposes methods, which are in effect functions. To contact the services of a Web service, you must create an object variable that references the specific Web service,
just as you can access the members of any class through a variable. Programmers and managers at
Microsoft think that Web services will take the Web by storm and that they'll change the way we
program on the Web. It just might happen. You may remember the Web Classes (a tool for
abstracting ASP applications that came with VB6). No real developer ever used this tool to build
ASP pages; they would much rather build ASP pages with VBScript.

Web services are not clumsy, like Web Classes were. It's a nicely implemented feature, and we should see many sites offering their services on the Web in the form of Web services. If you're wondering what type of services you might offer on the Web, I'll give a few examples momentarily. But first, I would like to make clear that Web services are nothing more than glorified classes or functions. If we pretend for a moment that we know nothing (or don't care) about the complexity of the Web or the problems with firewalls and security, we should be asking ourselves: If we can write a VB function and use in multiple Windows applications, why not be able to do the same with the Web? If this question sounds reasonable to you, then Web services are just classes that make their functionality available on the Web.

To better understand the need for Web services, I'll discuss a couple of examples. Let's say you're working for a publisher and you get requests from online stores for information about the books your company publishes. Webmasters need book descriptions, cover photos, anything that will help them better present your books on their site. You can create new documents and send them out on a daily basis, or come up a centralized mechanism for distributing the same information to multiple destinations. As you can guess, different sites may request this information in drastically different formats, from text or Excel files to XML documents.

The centralized mechanism is a business-to-business site that people can connect to and request information from. If they don't have the cover photo for a specific book, they should be able to connect to this site and make a request like "send me the cover image of the book with ISBN=xxx." This request should be implemented with a function like GetCoverByISBN(*isbnNumber*). The Get-CoverByISBN() function will return an image, which the other site can either store on its server and reuse or embed directly in its output for a specific client. You can do something similar by opening the HTML page of the book and downloading the file with the cover photo. This means that you must write a bit of code to parse the page, locate the name of the file, and then download it from the server. If the layout of the page changes, you must also change the code that parses the page.

If you could provide a function that could be called over the Web and return a single GIF file, then every online store could use this function. Programmers could even insert the name of the function in the place where the image would normally appear on the page. This way, every time a visitor hits the page, the image will be requested from your server and embedded in their page.

Another example is a function that returns the current price of a product. Any online store that sells your products will offer up-to-date prices and specials without any special arrangements. Or you can post a list of special offers and know that other sites can grab this information and use it immediately.

Other more advanced examples include integrated financial services. A highly secure site could collect information from banks, brokers, and credit organizations and present a unified picture of your finances. We expect to see this type of application in the very near future. Whether the information will flow from Web service to Web service remains to be seen, but this is one of Microsoft's contributions to an interconnected world of dissimilar computers.

But will other operating systems and Web servers be able to interact with Web services? The secret ingredients that make it all work are XML and SOAP (Simple Object Access Protocol). They're both open standards and are not very difficult to implement. You can actually write an ASP page that returns one or more values in XML or SOAP format and send it to the client instead of an HTML page. These two formats allow you to send any type of information over the HTTP protocol and through firewalls, so if the other end is capable of handling the XML tag, it will be able to use the Web service. As of now, all major players are promising to support XML, and this makes Web services a very promising technology, because they're based on standards.

Building a Web Service

In all previous chapters, I've used the visual tools for just about anything. Here I'll make an exception to show you how easy it really is to build a Web service. You'll build your first Web service with Notepad. The following listing is a simple class that exposes two simple members. The same class could appear in any VB project. Its two methods are way too simple, but they contain straight VB code and you can make them as complicated as you wish.

```
Public Class MasteringServices
    Public Function Add(ByVal a As Decimal, ByVal b As Decimal) As Decimal
        Return(a + b)
    End Function
    Public Function Multiply(ByVal a As Decimal, ByVal b As Decimal) As Decimal
        Return(a * b)
    End Function
End Class
```

To turn this class into a Web service, insert the following statements at the beginning of the file:

```
<%@ webservice class="MasteringServices" language="vb" %>
Imports System.Web.Services
```

The first statement is a directive that tells the compiler that the rest of the file is a Web service, written in Visual Basic. The name of the class is MasteringServices, but it will normally be a name made up from your company's (or department's) name and a name that reflects the functionality of the class. The second statement imports the `System.Web.Services` class, necessary for all Web services. Then prefix each method's definition with the following tag:

```
<WebMethod()>
```

The `<WebMethod()>` tag tells the compiler that the specific method is to be exposed to HTTP requests; the class may also contain private members. The WebMethod tag may also contain attributes, similar to the attributes of the members exposed by the controls. One of them is the Description attribute, whose syntax is shown next:

```
<WebMethod("Description", "This method adds two numbers")>
```

Listing 25.1 shows the code of your first Web service. Create a text file with these statements, and save it under the filename `Mastering.asmx` (the extension must be ASMX) in the Web server's root folder. You're actually ready to test your Web service.

LISTING 25.1: THE STRUCTURE OF A WEB SERVICE

```
<%@ webservice class="MasteringServices" language="vb" %>
Imports System.Web.Services
Public Class MasteringServices
    <WebMethod()> _
    Public Function Add(ByVal a As Decimal, ByVal b As Decimal) As Decimal
        Return(a + b)
```

```
      End Function
      <WebMethod()> _
      Public Function Multiply(ByVal a As Decimal, ByVal b As Decimal) As Decimal
          Return(a * b)
      End Function
End Class
```

To test the new service, start Internet Explorer and connect to the following URL:

`http://localhost/Mastering.asmx`

If you're using a Web server on another machine, replace the `localhost` specification with the appropriate server address or name. A few seconds later, you will see the page shown in Figure 25.1.

FIGURE 25.1

Testing the MasteringServices Web service

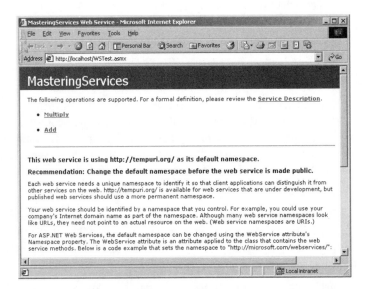

The page shown in Figure 25.1 isn't your page. Obviously, it was created on the fly and contains information about the MasteringServices Web service. Actually, you won't find this page anywhere on your server. When you contact the Web service for the first time, it's compiled and the compiler generates code to display the test pages as well.

Below the title of the Web service is a list of the members it exposes, the Add and Multiply methods. There's also a warning to the effect that it uses the default namespace, which is `http://tempuri.org/`. That's a placeholder domain name owned by Microsoft and stands for "temporary URI." When you post a Web service on the Web so that others can connect to it, you'll add the following attribute to the WebService tag:

`namespace="http://your.server.com/yourservices"`

as suggested at the bottom of the page.

The two methods are hyperlinks. Click the Add hyperlink and you'll see the arguments of the method on a new page, which is shown in Figure 25.2. On this page, you can enter two numeric values to be added and then click the Invoke button. A new page will appear, with the result returned by the Add method. The result returned by the method is:

```
<?xml version="1.0" encoding="utf-8" ?>
<decimal xmlns="http://tempuri.org/">18</decimal>
```

FIGURE 25.2

Connecting to a Web service with your browser

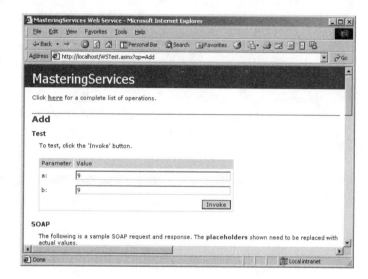

This is the XML description of a decimal value. Had you entered the values –0.91 and 1.92, the Add method would have returned the following value:

```
<?xml version="1.0" encoding="utf-8" ?>
<decimal xmlns="http://tempuri.org/">1.01</decimal>
```

Test the Multiply function as well; nothing will differ. You can also add more members to the test class; you can use any VB statement or function, as well as any of the Framework's classes, because the method's code is executed on a machine that has access to the .NET Framework.

A Web service is a Class that resides on a Web server and makes its members (usually methods) available to any client. In addition, it displays information about itself on a page that's built automatically when you attempt to contact one of the members of the Web service. This information includes the service's name and the members it exposes. As you saw, you can even test these members from within Internet Explorer. Of course, the format of the output is a little unusual, but this is the only way to get information to the client through the HTTP protocol. Besides, only text will go through firewalls. Web services use XML to format their return value and pass it to the client. In effect, the Web service and its *consumer* (the application that makes use of the Web service) pretend they're exchanging requests and HTML pages, all in textual format. As you can see, no special component needs to be installed on the client or the server.

Web services aren't necessarily text files created with Notepad. You will see in the following section how to create Web services in the environment of Visual Studio, but I wanted to demonstrate how easy it is to build a Web service.

Consuming the Web Service

The Web service is in place, and you have tested it with your browser. The ultimate goal is for an application to consume this Web service, so let's build one. Actually, we'll build two applications that consume the same Web service, a Windows app and an ASP Web app.

Start a new Windows Application project and place a Button control on its form. Since VB calculates sums too quickly to notice, let's use the Add method of the MasteringServices Web service. To access the members of a Web service, you must add a reference to it through the Project ➤ Add Web Reference command. When the Add Web Reference dialog box appears, enter the URL of the ASMX file in its Address bar and press Enter. You will see the description of the MasteringServices Web service on the dialog box, as shown in Figure 25.3. At this point, you can click the Add Reference button at the bottom of the window to add the Web service to the current project. This is similar to adding a reference to a regular class.

FIGURE 25.3

Referencing a Web service in a project

When you first open the Add Web Reference dialog box and before you select a Web service, you'll see a link that displays the Web services on the localhost (the Web References On Local Web Server link). In addition, you will see two links for the Microsoft's UDDI directory and Microsoft's UDDI test directory. Click the link to display the Web references on your local Web server. You will see the names of the Web services you may have already built, but the Mastering service won't be listed.

As you can see, each Web service is represented by a `.vsdico` file. This is called a *discovery* file and contains information about your service, and this is how clients that connect to your server can find out what services it provides. This file is created automatically by Visual Studio when you create a Web Service project, but we haven't created this project in VS—we simply creates an ASMX file to the Web server's root folder. We'll do so shortly, but in the meantime you can add a reference to the new Web service explicitly. Enter the URL of the `Mastering.asmx` file in the Address box of the Add Web Reference dialog box. This URL is the following:

```
http://localhost/mastering.asmx
```

You will see the names of the two methods in the left pane of the dialog box. Click the Add Reference button to close the dialog box and return to the project.

Then insert the following code in the button's Click event handler:

```
Private Sub Button1_Click(ByVal sender As System.Object,_
                ByVal e As System.EventArgs) Handles Button1.Click
    Dim WS As New localhost.MasteringServices()
    MsgBox(WS.Add(43.32, 22.1))
End Sub
```

You don't really need an elaborate interface to test the members of the simple Web service. Run the project, click the button, wait, and the sum of the two values should appear on a message box. The delay, which is more than noticeable, is due to the fact that the ASMX file must be compiled and contacted through the HTTP protocol. There's a lot of overhead, but then again Web services are not usual Classes. If you insert another call to the Add method (or a call to the Multiply method) in the Click event handler, the second call will be serviced immediately, because the class has been compiled and is ready to be used by any client.

ASP.NET Web Service Projects

In this section, we'll build a slightly more complicated Web service that exposes a single method to calculate monthly payments on a loan. We'll add some error handling to the method, to make it more robust than the first one. We'll also use the tools of the IDE to build the new service.

Start a new project and select the ASP.NET Web Service template. Call the new project WSLoan. Notice that, by default, all Web service projects are stored in the `localhost` virtual folder (this is the root folder of the Web server). Initially, the Designer will add to the project an ASMX file called Service1, a configuration file, and a discovery file. The configuration file contains configuration information for the Web server, and the discovery file (the one with extension `.vsdisco`) contains information that allows other applications that connect to your server to locate the specific service and see its "contract" (the names and the syntax of its members). The initial configuration of the IDE for an ASP.NET Web service project is shown in Figure 25.4.

The project we'll build in this section is within this chapter's folder on the CD. Copy the entire Loan folder in the Web server's root folder, and then open it with VB.

Ready to build another loan calculator? This example isn't going to be quite as trivial as you think. You'll see how you can raise exceptions from within a Web service and catch them in your VB code. Listing 25.2 shows the Loan class's source code. Right-click the design surface of Service1, select View Code from the context menu, and then enter the listing's statements in the editor.

FIGURE 25.4

Starting a new Web service project

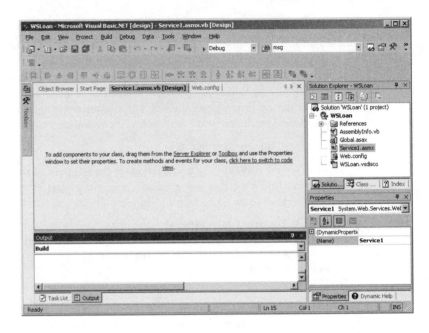

LISTING 25.2: THE LOAN WEB SERVICE

```
Imports System.Web.Services
Public Class Service1
   Inherits System.Web.Services.WebService
   <WebMethod()> _
   Public Function Loan(ByVal Amount As Decimal, ByVal Duration As Integer, _
                 ByVal Rate As Decimal, ByVal PayEarly As Boolean) As Decimal
      If Rate < 0 Then
         Throw New Exception("Interest rate can't be negative!")
      End If
      If Rate < 1 Then
         Rate = Rate / 12
      Else
         Rate = Rate / (12 * 100)
      End If
      Return Pmt(Rate, Duration, Amount, 0, PayEarly)
   End Function
End Class
```

The actual project on the CD contains one more method, which will be discussed shortly.

The Web service is ready to be tested. Press F5 and Internet Explorer will come up with the description of the new Web service. Click the Loan hyperlink to test the Loan method. On the page that appears (Figure 25.5), enter the parameters of the loan and click the Invoke button as before. The result for the loan shown in Figure 25.5 is:

```
<?xml version="1.0" encoding="utf-8" ?>
<decimal xmlns="http://tempuri.org/">-740.680595446082</decimal>
```

FIGURE 25.5

Testing the Loan method of the Service1 Web service

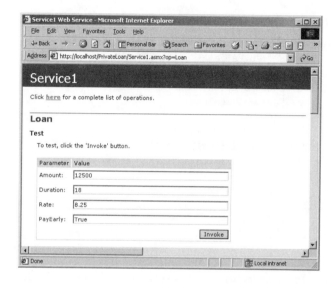

The Web service works; let's copy it to the Web server so that other applications can use it. Stop the project, and select the Copy Project command in the Project menu. In the subsequent dialog box (see Figure 25.6), specify the **Loan** folder under the Web server's root folder and click OK. All the files needed for the discovery and use of the Loan Web service will be copied in the specified folder.

FIGURE 25.6

Copying a project's files to the Web server

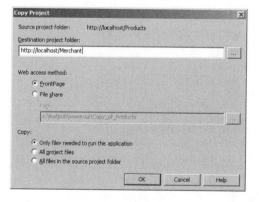

 Now start a new Windows application that will contact the Loan service. The test project on the CD is called TestLoan (unlike the Web Service project, the test project may appear anywhere on your hard disk). Make sure that you change the project type in the New Project dialog box, because the IDE remembers the type of the last project and will create another Web Service project. The test application's form is shown in Figure 25.7. To make use of the Web service, add a reference to it as explained in the previous example and enter the code of Listing 25.3 behind the Monthly Payment button.

LISTING 25.3: CONSUMING A WEB SERVICE FROM WITHIN A WINDOWS APPLICATION

```
Private Sub Button1_Click(ByVal sender As System.Object,_
              ByVal e As System.EventArgs) Handles Button1.Click
    Dim ws As New localhost.Service1()
    Dim amount, duration, rate As Decimal
    Dim payEarly As Boolean
    Try
        amount = CDec(txtAmount.Text)
        duration = CInt(txtDuration.Text)
        rate = CSng(txtRate.Text)
        payEarly = False
        If chkPayEarly.Checked Then payEarly = True
    Catch DataException As SystemException
        MsgBox(DataException.ToString)
        Exit Sub
    End Try
    Try
        txtPayment.Text = -Math.Round(ws.Loan(amount, duration, rate, payEarly), 2)
    Catch calcException As Exception
        MsgBox(calcException.Message)
    End Try
End Sub
```

FIGURE 25.7

The TestLoan application's form

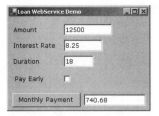

Run the application and see that it calculates the monthly payments of properly defined loans. Set the interest rate to a negative value, and the exception raised in the Web service's class will be caught in your VB application. But of course you should improve the exception-handling code; the exception's message is too lengthy and too technical for the average user (it's meant to help the developer, not the user). Figure 25.8 shows the error message cause by a negative interest rate. The original error message is embedded in the `Exception.Message` property, but it's a rather scary message for the end user.

FIGURE 25.8

This exception was raised by the Web service's class.

Maintaining State in Web Services

Like ASP.NET applications, Web services can also maintain state with the Application and Session objects. By default, a Web service doesn't maintain its state, but you can change the default behavior by setting the EnableSession attribute of the WebMethod tag to True. Listing 25.4 shows the Get-MyID method, which returns the ID of the current client. The program sets the ID when requested, but this is for demonstration purposes only. You should probably set this variable when the client goes through the authentication process.

LISTING 25.4: MAINTAINING STATE WITH A WEB SERVICE

```
<WebMethod(EnableSession:=True)> Public Function GetMyID() As Guid
    If Session("MyID") Is Nothing Then
        Session("MyID") = Guid.NewGuid
    End If
    Return Session("MyID")
End Function
```

The variable *MyID* maintains its value through the duration of the session. You can also maintain application-level variables with the Application object.

A Data-Driven Web Service

I'm sure you had enough with trivial examples; let's move on to something more practical. In this section, we'll build a Web service that moves DataSets to the client. This is the most practical thing you can do with Web services, and we'll consume this service from within an ASP application, as well as a VB application. Our Web service will expose two methods, the GetCategories and Get-Products methods. The first DataSet contains the product categories of the Northwind database. This is a very simple DataSet. The GetProducts method returns a DataSet with the Categories and Products tables. As you will see, we'll be able to bind a DataGrid control to this DataSet and display it hierarchically on the browser.

Start a new Web service project, name it Products, and drop the Categories and Products tables from the Server Explorer on the `Service1.asmx` file's designer surface. Two DataAdapter objects will be created automatically, one for each table. Rename them to DACategories and DAProducts. Then generate two DataSets, the DSCategories and DSProducts DataSets. I need not repeat the entire process here (it's described in detail in Chapters 21 and 22), so I'll only show you the SELECT statements for the two DataAdapters. The statement for the DACategories Data-Adapter is

```
SELECT CategoryID, CategoryName, Description
FROM dbo.Categories
```

Here's the statement for the DAProducts DataAdapter:

```
SELECT ProductID, ProductName, SupplierID,
       CategoryID, QuantityPerUnit, UnitPrice,
       UnitsInStock, UnitsOnOrder, ReorderLevel,
       Discontinued
FROM dbo.Products
```

Once the two DataAdapters are in place, create two DataSets, the DSCategories and DSProducts DataSets. Don't forget to check the option Add This DataSet To The Designer on the Generate DataSet dialog box. There should be five items on the service's design surface: the SqlConnection1 object, the two DataAdapter objects, and one instance of each DataSet object (DSCategories1 and DSProducts1), as shown in Figure 25.9.

FIGURE 25.9

Adding DataSets to a Web service

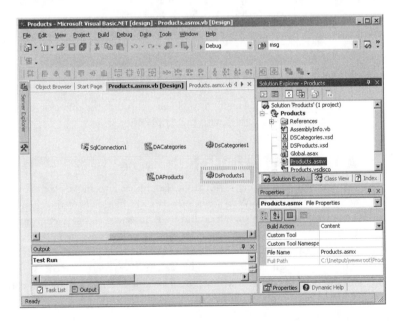

This is a good point to change the default name of the Web service from `Service1.asmx` to `Products.asmx`. Changing the name of the component on the Solution Explorer isn't adequate; for some reason, the IDE doesn't change the name of the class that implements the Web service. Right-click the design surface of the service and select View Code. The second line in this class is:

```
Public Class Service1
```

and you must change it to

```
Public Class Products
```

Now add the two methods to the class, using the code from Listing 25.5.

LISTING 25.5: THE GETCATEGORIES AND GETPRODUCTS METHODS

```
<WebMethod()> Public Function GetCategories() As DataSet
    DACategories.Fill(DSCategories1, "Categories")
    Return DSCategories1
End Function
<WebMethod()> Public Function GetProducts() As DataSet
    DAProducts.Fill(DSProducts1, "Products")
    DACategories.Fill(DSProducts1, "Categories")
    Return DSProducts1
End Function
```

Each method fills the appropriate DataSet and returns it to the calling application. In our case, the calling application is an application running remotely, but Visual Studio hides all the details from us. We write code as if the Web service's methods were local functions.

We have built our Web service, so let's test it. Press F5 and, a few seconds later, you'll see Internet Explorer displaying the summary of the Products Web service. Click the GetCategories link, and on the following page click the Invoke button (there are no arguments to specify here). You will see the page of Figure 25.10, which shows the rows of the Categories table in XML format. Close this window and then follow the Products hyperlink. This time you'll see all the categories and all products. The Categories DataSet contains the rows of the Categories table, but the Products table contains the rows of both the Categories and Products tables. The tables of the Products DataSet are not related. You can add a relationship between the two tables in the DataSet designer, but I'll show you later how to add a relation in the consumer application's code.

The Web service works. You can stop it and start building a consumer application for this service. Testing a Web service as a stand-alone application is straightforward and helps you make sure the Web service returns the correct result. If you want to call its method from within another application (probably a remote application), you must deploy it on your Web server.

Select Project ➤ Copy Project, and on the dialog box that appears (shown in Figure 25.6), specify the name of the Web service's root folder. Let's put our Web service in the folder `Merchant` under the server's root folder.

FIGURE 25.10

Viewing a DataSet on the browser

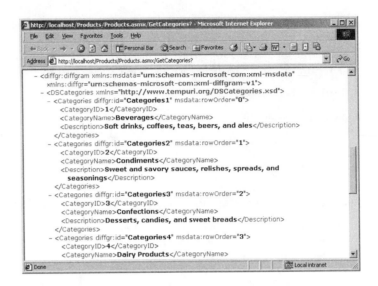

Now we're ready to build the test applications. Let's start with an ASP.NET Web application that will display a single page with a DataGrid control bound to the Categories DataSet. Create a new ASP application project to test the new Web service. The new project is called NWTest, and it's a single page with a DataGrid control and a Button control on it. The DataGrid's DataSource property will be set to the GetCategories method at runtime, every time the button is clicked. The application will go out to the Service1 Web service, request the GetCategories method, and then bind the DataSet returned by the method to the `DataGrid1.DataSet` property. Figure 25.11 shows the NWTest page with the DataGrid populated with the categories. The appearance of the DataGrid control leaves a lot to be desired, but you saw how to customize the control in the previous chapter.

As before, you must add a reference to the Web service through the Project ➤ Add Web Reference command. Place a DataGrid control and a Button control on the Web form, and then enter the following code in the button's Click event handler:

```
Private Sub Button1_Click(ByVal sender As System.Object, _
            ByVal e As System.EventArgs) Handles Button1.Click
   Dim WS As New localhost.Service1()
   DataGrid1.DataSource = WS.GetCategories
   DataGrid1.DataBind()
End Sub
```

Consuming the Products Web Service in VB

Now we'll build a Windows application to consume the Products Web service. The .NET version of the DataGrid control can display related tables, and we'll take advantage of this feature of the control. As you recall, the GetProducts method returns a DataSet that contains two tables, but no relationship between them. The test project is called WSDataSet, and you will find it on the CD. The main form of the application is shown in Figure 25.12.

FIGURE 25.11

Binding a DataGrid Web control to a method of a Web service

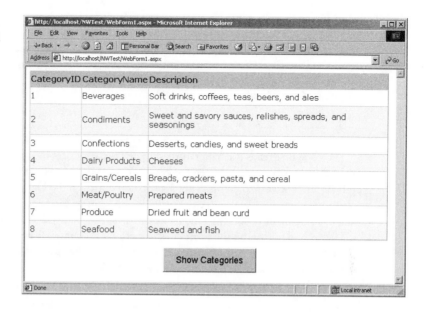

FIGURE 25.12

The WSDataSet project consumes the Products Web service.

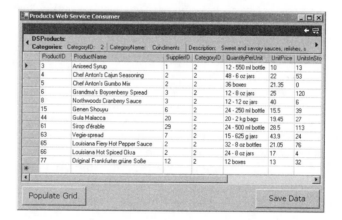

As usual, add a reference to the Web service, then enter the code shown in Listing 25.6 behind the Populate Grid button.

LISTING 25.6: BINDING A WINDOWS DATAGRID CONTROL TO A MEMBER OF A WEB SERVICE

```
Private Sub Button1_Click(ByVal sender As System.Object,_
            ByVal e As System.EventArgs) Handles Button1.Click
    Dim WS As New localhost.Service1()
    Dim localDS As DataSet
    localDS = WS.GetProducts
```

```
    Dim Prods As DataTable = localDS.Tables("Products")
    Dim Cats As DataTable = localDS.Tables("Categories")
    Dim CatProds As New DataRelation("CategoriesProducts", _
                    Cats.Columns("CategoryID"), Prods.Columns("CategoryID"))
    localDS.Relations.Add(CatProds)
    DataGrid1.DataSource = localDS
End Sub
```

The code first reads the data returned by the GetProducts method into a local DataSet. Then it establishes a relationship between the two tables based on the field CategoryID, which is common to both tables. The code then binds the DataGrid control to the DataSet by assigning the *localDS* variable to the control's DataSource property. If you want to bind the grid to a single table, set the control's DataMember property to the name of the appropriate table.

The second button on the form does something even more useful: it persists the data to a local file in XML format. The XML file can be used in another project, or move the data to a different database. Just add the file to the project (with the Add Existing Item command of the project's context menu). To persist the data to a file, the Save Data button calls the WriteXML method of the DataSet object:

```
Private Sub Button2_Click_1(ByVal sender As System.Object, _
            ByVal e As System.EventArgs) Handles Button2.Click
    localDS.WriteXML("c:\Products.xml")
End Sub
```

Summary

Visual Studio .NET allows you to build Web services with the same tools as for regular classes that expose methods. You've seen how easy it is to build Web services and how to consume them from within Web and Windows apps. The client applications contact a URL, which consists of the name of the server where the Web service is running, followed by the name of the service and the name of a method. The method returns its result in XML format, and you can use it in your code as if it were the result of a function call.

You're already seeing the value of XML. Throughout the book, I've tried not to shift the focus from VB and the visual tools to XML. Ideally, XML should be made transparent to the developer, and as you have seen, you don't need to know XML to create DataSets or XML Web services. It's good to know that there's a format that makes it all possible, but why should we have to get down to the details of that protocol? There are tools to manipulate XML files, but I've decided that the language, the visual tools, and the framework are plenty to keep you busy for a long time. Once you develop a solid understanding of .NET, you can move into XML and enjoy it.

Index

Note to the Reader: Throughout this index **boldfaced** page numbers indicate primary discussions of a topic. *Italicized* page numbers indicate illustrations. Page numbers prefixed with *chF* refer to the Bonus Reference VB.NET Functions, and page numbers prefixed with *chT* refer to the Bonus Reference Transact SQL. Both Bonus References are found on the accompanying CD-ROM.

A

<A> tag, 1001, 1006
Abort value, 213
Abs function, 155–156, **chF29**
abstract base classes, 382
abstraction, **367–368**
accent-sensitivity, 883
Accept buttons, 187
Accept or Reject Changes dialog box, *211*
AcceptButton property, **187**
AcceptChanges method, 987, 990, 992
AcceptsReturn property, **244**
AcceptsTab property, **244–245**
Access 2000, 870
access keys, **225**
access modes, 583
access modifiers, 84
access time of files, 581, 586
accessing
    files, **578–587**, **594–610**, *608*
    folders, **570–578**, **584–587**
ACTION attribute, 1014
Action property, 760
action queries, **904–906**
Activate events, **203**
Activate method, 65, 437
Activation property, **769–770**
active child forms, **849**, **854–855**
active documents, 437–438
active forms, 65
Active Server Pages (ASP), 1002–1003
Active state for controls, 423
ActiveDocument objects, 437–438, 440
ActiveDocument property, 435
ActiveMdiChild property, 848
ActiveX controls, **429–431**, *430–431*
Add Child button, 749
Add command, 73
Add Connection command, 878
Add Dataset dialog box, 993, *993*
Add Existing Project dialog box, 67
Add File Type command, 74

Add Folder command, 73
Add function, 163
Add Item command, 24
Add menu
    Add Class command, 331
    Add Existing Item command, 346
    Add Item command, 840
    File command, 73
Add method
    ArrayList collection, 490
    Columns collection, **770–771**
    Controls collection, 232
    DateTime class, 555
    Documents collection, 435, 437, 439
    HashTable collection, 498
    Images collection, 747
    Items collection, 169, 773
    ListBox controls, 264, **267–268**
    Matrix class, 388–389
    MenuItems, 228
    Nodes collection, **751–752**
    SortedList collection, 504
    TimeSpan class, **566**
    Web services, 1086–1088
    Worksheets collection, 454
Add New Project dialog box, 395
Add Reference dialog box, 346, 395, *396*, 434
Add/Remove Programs utility, 77–78, *78*
Add Root button, 749
Add Table dialog box, 908–909, 921
Add value, 845
Add Watch command, 805
Add Web Reference dialog box, 21, *1088*
AddACustomer stored procedure, chT37
AddCategories_Click subroutine, 755
AddColors_Click subroutine, 755
AddCookie1_Click subroutine, 1042
AddCustomer.SQL stored procedure, chT36
AddDays method, 381, 556
Added state, 986
AddElement subroutine, 278
AddExtension property, 298

TELL US WHAT YOU THINK!

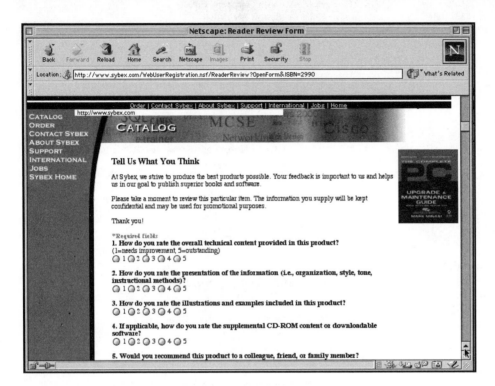

Your feedback is critical to our efforts to provide you with the best books and software on the market. Tell us what you think about the products you've purchased. It's simple:

1. Visit the Sybex website
2. Go to the product page
3. Click on **Submit a Review**
4. Fill out the questionnaire and comments
5. Click **Submit**

With your feedback, we can continue to publish the highest quality computer books and software products that today's busy IT professionals deserve.

www.sybex.com

SYBEX Inc. • 1151 Marina Village Parkway, Alameda, CA 94501 • 510-523-8233